"Anthony Thiselton is one of our leading theologians, equally at home in both New Testament studies and in philosophical and theological hermeneutics, and a collection of his major articles will be widely and warmly welcomed. He works across an astonishing range of topics, bringing profound reflection to bear on disputed issues and often moving the discussion to a higher level at which disputes turn out to be resolvable."

JOHN BARTON
*Oriel and Lang Professor of the Interpretation of
Holy Scripture, University of Oxford, UK*

"Thiselton's contribution to the intersection of hermeneutical theory and the practice of biblical interpretation is unmatched in recent time. This collection of his writings will prove an invaluable tool for those with an interest in either or both of the two foci of his work."

MEROLD WESTPHAL
Distinguished Professor of Philosophy, Fordham University, USA

"One of our most distinguished and trusted voices in the arena of biblical studies and hermeneutics, Tony Thiselton has drawn together work spanning a long, fruitful and impressive career. Because these contributions have appeared in such diverse and far-flung places, this collected work is especially welcome."

JOEL B. GREEN
Dean of the School of Theology, Asbury Theological Seminary, USA

"Anthony C. Thiselton combines analytical craftsmanship, a profound knowledge of contemporary (also Continental) hermeneutics and outstanding New Testament scholarship. His constructive work in systematic theology and theological hermeneutics is among the most exciting in contemporary theology."

MARCEL SAROT
Faculteit Godgeleerdheid, Utrecht

"Professor Thiselton has a grasp of the philosophical and hermeneutical debate as it bears upon the biblical texts which few if any can rival. His *Two Horizons* and *New Horizons* are a mine of valuable description and critique which anyone hoping to engage seriously with contemporary issues in interpretation simply cannot ignore. Many of his essays and book chapters have provided incisive and influential contributions to specific debates. Eerdmans and Ashgate are to be congratulated in providing this collection, in effect the best of AT, which will be eagerly sought out by his many admirers."

JAMES D. G. DUNN
Lightfoot Professor of Divinity, Durham University, UK

"Of a consistently high scholarly standard, these essays by Tony Thiselton traverse a broad range of themes in philosophical theology, doctrine and biblical interpretation. The gathering of these materials into a single collection should ensure that they continue to be studied and appropriated by others working in these fields."

DAVID A. FERGUSSON
Professor of Divinity, University of Edinburgh, UK

Hermeneutics is an interdisciplinary study of how we interpret texts, especially biblical texts, in the light of theories of understanding in philosophy, meaning in literary theory, and theology. This volume brings together the seminal thought of a leading contemporary pioneer in this field. Thiselton's *The Two Horizons* was a classic on how horizons of biblical texts engage creatively with the horizons of the modern world. The author's later *New Horizons in Hermeneutics* explored still more deeply the transforming capacities of biblical texts, while his massive commentary on 1 Corinthians interpreted an epistle.

This volume collects many of Anthony Thiselton's more notable writings from some seven books and seventy articles, to which he adds his own reappraisals of earlier work. It uniquely expounds the thought of a major contemporary British theologian through his own words, and includes his own critical assessments.

THISELTON ON HERMENEUTICS

Collected Works with New Essays

Anthony C. Thiselton

WILLIAM B. EERDMANS PUBLISHING COMPANY

GRAND RAPIDS, MICHIGAN / CAMBRIDGE, U.K.

Compilation © 2006 Anthony C. Thiselton
All rights reserved
Copyright of individual articles is listed
in the Acknowledgments, pp. xi-xiv

Published 2006
in Great Britain by
Ashgate Publishing Limited
Gower House, Croft Road, Aldershot, Hampshire, GU11 3HR
www.ashgate.com
and in the United States of America by
Wm. B. Eerdmans Publishing Co.
2140 Oak Industrial Drive N.E., Grand Rapids, Michigan 49505 /
P.O. Box 163, Cambridge CB3 9PU U.K.
www.eerdmans.com

Printed in the United States of America

11 10 09 08 07 06   7 6 5 4 3 2 1

Library of Congress Cataloging-in-Publication Data

Thiselton, Anthony C.
[Selections. 2006]
Thiselton on hermeneutics : the collected works and new essays
of Anthony Thiselton / Anthony C. Thiselton.
p.   cm.
Includes index.
ISBN-10: 0-8028-3236-9 / ISBN-13: 978-0-8028-3236-8 (cloth: alk. paper)
1. Hermeneutics. 2. Bible — Hermeneutics.
I. Title. II. Series.
BD241.T4652   2006
121'.686 — dc22
2005006308

Contents

Acknowledgements

The essays in this volume (with the exception of new and reappraisal essays at the end of each Part in this volume) are reproduced from the sources as listed below. Grateful acknowledgement is made to the copyright holders of these essays for their permission to reproduce them here.

PART I SITUATING THE SUBJECT

1. "Thirty Years of Hermeneutics" (1996), from J. Krasovec (ed.) *International Symposium on the Interpretation of the Bible* (Ljubljana: Slovenian Academy of Sciences and Arts, and Sheffield: Sheffield Academic Press), pp.1559–74.

2. "Biblical Studies and Theoretical Hermeneutics" (1998), from John Barton (ed.) *The Cambridge Companion to Biblical Interpretation* (Cambridge: Cambridge University Press), pp.95–113.

PART II HERMENEUTICS AND SPEECH-ACT THEORY

4. "The Supposed Power of Words in the Biblical Writings" (1974), from *Journal of Theological Studies* 25, pp.282–99 (Oxford University Press).

5. "Transforming Texts" (1992), from *New Horizons in Hermeneutics* (Carlisle: Paternoster Press, and Grand Rapids, MI: Zondervan), pp.31–35.

6. "Christological Texts in Paul" (1992), from *New Horizons in Hermeneutics* (Carlisle: Paternoster Press, and Grand Rapids, MI: Zondervan), pp.283–303.

7. "Christology in Luke, Speech-Act Theory, and the Problem of Dualism in Christology" (1994), from Joel B. Green and Max Turner (eds) *Jesus of Nazareth: Lord and Christ* (Grand Rapids, MI: Eerdmans, and Carlisle: Paternoster Press), pp.453–72.

8. "The Paradigm of Biblical Promise as Trustworthy, Temporal, Transformative Speech-Acts" (1999), from *The Promise of Hermeneutics* (Grand Rapids, MI: Eerdmans, and Carlisle: Paternoster Press), pp.223–39.

PART III HERMENEUTICS, SEMANTICS AND CONCEPTUAL GRAMMAR

10. "Language-Games and 'Seeing As': A Fresh Approach to Justification by Faith in Paul and James" (1980), from *The Two Horizons: New Testament Hermeneutics and Philosophical Description* (Exeter: Paternoster Press and Grand Rapids, MI: Eerdmans), pp.415–27.

PART V PARABLES, NARRATIVE-WORLDS AND READER-RESPONSE THEORIES

23. "The Varied Hermeneutical Dynamics of Parables and Reader-Response Theory" (1985), from Roger Lundin, Anthony C. Thiselton and Clarence Walhout, *The Responsibility of Hermeneutics* (Grand Rapids, MI: Eerdmans, and Carlisle: Paternoster Press), pp.83–106.

24. "The Parables as Language-Event: Some Comments on Fuchs's Hermeneutics in the Light of Linguistic Philosophy" (1970), from *Scottish Journal of Theology* 23, pp.437–68.

25. "The Two Horizons" and "Pre-Understanding" (1980), from *The Two Horizons: New Testament Hermeneutics and Philosophical Description* (Exeter: Paternoster Press, and Grand Rapids, MI: Eerdmans), pp.10–23 and 103–14.

26. "The New Hermeneutic" (1977), from I.H. Marshall (ed.) *New Testament Interpretation* (Exeter: Paternoster Press), pp.308–33.

27. "Types of Reader-Response Theory" (1992), from *New Horizons in Hermeneutics* (Carlisle: Paternoster Press, and Grand Rapids, MI: Zondervan), pp.515–46.

PART VI PHILOSOPHY, LANGUAGE, THEOLOGY AND POSTMODERNITY

29. "Language and Meaning in Religion" (1978), from Colin Brown (ed.) *New International Dictionary of New Testament Theology* (Grand Rapids, MI: Zondervan, and Carlisle: Paternoster Press, vol. 3), extracts from pp.1123–43.

30. "God as Self-Affirming Illusion? Manipulation, Truth and Language" (1995), from *Interpreting God and the Postmodern Self: On Meaning, Manipulation and Promise* (Edinburgh: T. & T. Clark, and Grand Rapids, MI: Eerdmans [*Scottish Journal of Theology* Lectures, University of Aberdeen]), pp.3–26.

31. "The Postmodern Self and Society: Loss of Hope and the Possibility of Refocused Hope" (1995), from *Interpreting God and the Postmodern Self: On Meaning, Manipulation and Promise* (Edinburgh: T. & T. Clark, and Grand Rapids, MI: Eerdmans [*Scottish Journal of Theology* Lectures, University of Aberdeen]), extracts from pp.121–63.

32. "Signs of the Times: Towards a Theology for the Year 2000 as a Grammar of Grace, Truth and Eschatology in Contexts of So-Called Postmodernity" (2000), from David Fergusson and Marcel Sarot (eds) *The Future as God's Gift: Explorations in Christian Eschatology* (Edinburgh: T. & T. Clark [Presidential Paper of the Society for the Study of Theology]), pp.9–39.

33. "'Behind' and 'in Front' of the Text – Language, Reference and Indeterminacy" (2001), from Craig Bartholomew, C. Green and K. Möller (eds) *After Pentecost: Language and*

Preface

The forty-two studies that make up this collection cohere together far more closely and clearly than I had imagined when the idea of this *Collected Works* was first considered. Together with their individual introductions and seven retrospective reappraisals they offer a structured and consistent account of hermeneutics as a developing and multi-disciplinary subject area, and of my attempts to contribute to it.

Ten of these articles or essays, almost a quarter of the collection, have not been published before, or were written in 2004. In addition to the seven retrospective reappraisals at the end of each Part, two others (Essays 20 and 34) have not been published elsewhere before now, while the tenth (Essay 18) appeared no earlier than in late November 2004.

I have arranged the essays under themes or topics rather than chronologically. Part I differs in style and level from Parts II–VII. As I explain in their respective introductions, the first two essays are not strictly research essays in the full sense of the term, but they offer distinctive introductions to the collection by outlining the history and motivations of my work on hermeneutics since about 1964, and introduce the shape of the subject. The third essay, which is a retrospective reappraisal of these, brings them up to date by suggesting extensions and supplementary additions that retrospective reflection today seems to suggest.

Parts II through to VII consider in turn six broad areas within hermeneutics: speech-act theory; semantics and conceptual grammar; lexicography, exegesis and reception theory; parables, narrative-worlds and reader-response theories; hermeneutics and postmodernity, and hermeneutics and Christian theology. Some of the retrospective reappraisals are more substantial than others. Thus perhaps one of the more significant is Essay 36, which offers further up-to-date reflections on postmodernity.

I have edited material here and there to improve clarity, or to avoid overlapping or undue length. I provide every essay with clear headings and/or subheadings at short intervals, with a phrase to indicate what issues, or what stage of the argument, each section addresses. I also introduce each essay with an explanation about its origin, purpose and arguments. These introductions may serve to inform any who wish to read only certain essays which most closely accords with their interests. (NB: Please note that footnotes citing 'loc. cit.' or 'op. cit.' may indicate references that have appeared in earlier essays in their respective volumes and are not repeated in this present volume.)

This collection arose from two occurrences. First, Union University, Jackson, Tennessee, set up a Faculty Forum when I was Visiting Scholar there to ask me questions of their choice. One asked whether I regretted anything about the story of my work. I replied that I regretted the higher ratio of research articles to books over the years: seventy research articles, but, at that time, no more than seven books. Second, when I recounted this episode to Ms Sarah Lloyd in the course of a conversation at the Society of Biblical Literature, she kindly raised the possibility that Ashgate Publishing might redress this imbalance. The thirty-five essays included here, together with their seven reappraisals, do not exhaust what we might have included, but I have selected those that best serve the coherence and distinctive multi-disciplinary themes of the present contribution.

To aim at this goal has given me great satisfaction, for which I thank Sarah Lloyd. On the other hand, editing and checking the MS laboriously at my computer has proved more burdensome and time-consuming than I had ever envisaged. Here, however, I have been assisted and supported by those who retyped the original articles onto disc, and facilitated this work in numerous ways. Once again, as with all my previous books, my wife Rosemary has spent long hours typing and checking the manuscripts, and I give her warmest thanks. Among others who have typed multiple articles I express my thanks in particular to Mrs Sheila Rees and to my daughter-in-law Jackie. I am grateful also for some funding assistance from the University of Chester. I thank all who have encouraged me in this endeavour amidst teaching commitments in Nottingham and Chester, as well as wider duties in and for the Church of England.

Anthony C. Thiselton
Department of Theology, University of Nottingham,
and Department of Theology and Religious Studies, University of Chester
22nd December 2004

PART I

SITUATING THE SUBJECT

CHAPTER ONE

Situating the Explorations:
"Thirty Years of Hermeneutics" (1996)

This essay was written for the International Symposium on the Interpretation of the Bible in Ljubljana, Slovenia, 17–20 September 1996, and published by The Slovenian Academy of Sciences and Arts, and Sheffield Academic Press, in 1998. I have edited the text a little here and there to take account of any observation that has been overtaken by events since 1996, or which otherwise might have been unclear.

The style and content of these first two essays differ in character from the other contributions included in this collection. All of the other essays are primarily research publications. By contrast this first article is an autobiographical account of my developing concerns from 1964 to 1996. I considered omitting it from this volume, but it provides an easily readable introduction to an agenda that has motivated much of my research and writing since 1964. I have indicated in particular the contexts and motivations that have influenced my work at each stage.

Professor José Krašovec has granted me a rare privilege, namely to offer "at least a short summary of your hermeneutical works". One could hardly volunteer such an enterprise, without undue self-advertisement. However, in response to this gracious invitation, I propose to trace how a series of issues emerged from a developing context of ideas in teaching and research in hermeneutics in four universities of the United Kingdom over some thirty years.

I shall also offer some tentative comments about prospects for the discipline. Here the issue of the challenge of postmodern perspectives looms large, and readers may note parallels, although not necessarily full agreements, with the contentions of Professor David J.A. Clines who writes elsewhere in this volume [that is, that published by the Slovenian Academy], and with whom I worked as a close colleague in the University of Sheffield from 1970 to 1985.[1]

I
Work on Fuchs, Wittgenstein and Austin (Bristol, 1964–70)

I was teaching in the University of Bristol when a student asked my advice about English-language books on hermeneutics. This seemingly innocent question initiated me into an almost fruitless literature search. Richard E. Palmer's *Hermeneutics* (1969) had not

---

[1] David J.A. Clines, "The Postmodern Adventure in Biblical Studies", in J. Krašovec (ed.), *Interpretation of the Bible* (Ljubljana: Slovenian Academy, and Sheffield: Sheffield Academic Press, 1998), pp.1603–18.

yet appeared, and Hans-Georg Gadamer's *Wahrheit und Methode* awaited translation successively in 1975 and again freshly in 1989. I had already worked both on NT interpretation and on the philosophy of language, especially on Wittgenstein, and these interacted to make me discontented with the more traditional textbooks on "biblical interpretation". Alongside these unimaginative text-books on biblical interpretation, there seemed to be only Robert W. Funk's *Language, Hermeneutic and Word of God* (New York: Harper & Row, 1966) and the volume edited by James Robinson and J. Cobb Jr, *New Frontiers in Theology: II, The New Hermeneutic* (New York: Harper & Row, 1964).

I was also invited to deliver a paper at Oxford on "The New Hermeneutic". I had already written a review on Ebeling's *Word and Faith* (1963), but now set myself to draft an outline of Ernst Fuchs's major writings, together with my own critical survey of Gadamer's *Truth and Method*. I was impressed by the notion of projected "worlds" into which the reader was drawn, especially where these "narrative worlds" constituted pre-cognitive value-systems into which the reader was seduced or enticed, only to find the world and the reader's expectations subverted and reversed. Fuchs undertook an excellent piece of work on the "reversal" of expectations of (mere) "justice" alone in the Parable of the Labourers in the Vineyard in Matthew 20:1–16.[2] I pressed on to explore "worldhood" in Heidegger's *Being and Time*, since Fuchs openly expressed his indebtedness to this work.

However, I came to believe that not all was well on the level of the philosophy of language. Funk had described the view of Fuchs on language-event (*Sprachereignis*) as "performative".[3] But from 1963 I had become increasingly familiar with the work of Wittgenstein and J.L. Austin. Austin's "performatives" presupposed *institutional states of affairs* and specific contextual *conventions*, whereas Heidegger and Fuchs regarded assertions, propositions and conventions as at best derivative and secondary to a kind of force that was different from Austin's illocutionary acts. I expressed this combination of appreciation and unease in "The Parables as Language-Event: Some Comments on Fuchs's Hermeneutics in the Light of Linguistic Philosophy" in 1970.[4]

I had been further alerted to the problems left by the "devaluing" of assertions in Heidegger and Gadamer by reading Wolfhart Pannenberg on hermeneutics. In 1969 my wife and I had the great privilege of entertaining Professor and Frau Pannenberg in our Bristol home for a few days, and his incisive oral comments on this issue convinced me further of this point. Pannenberg has always remained a major influence on my thinking. I attempted to present a balanced critique of the New Hermeneutic of Fuchs and Ebeling in the volume *New Testament Interpretation*. I wrote my essay in 1973–74, although it did not appear until 1977.[5] Meanwhile I remained concerned to draw equally on the Anglo-American tradition of philosophical analysis and on Continental European traditions. I viewed Wittgenstein as a key figure, who combined the incisiveness and rigour which

---

[2] E. Fuchs, *Zur Frage nach historischen Jesus* (Tübingen: Mohr, 1960, Eng. [part] in *Studies of the Historical Jesus*, London: SCM, 1964, 33–7); cf. *Marburger Hermeneutik* (Tübingen: Mohr, 1968), 171–81.

[3] R.W. Funk, *Language, Hermeneutic and Word of God* (New York: Harper & Row, 1966), 26–8.

[4] Anthony C. Thiselton, "The Parables as Language-Event", *Scottish Journal of Theology* 23 (1970), 437–68.

[5] Anthony C. Thiselton, "The New Hermeneutic" in I.H. Marshall (ed.) *New Testament Interpretation* (Exeter: Paternoster and Grand Rapids, MI: Eerdmans, 1977), 308–33.

largely characterized British analytical philosophy with the Continental suspicion of exclusively rationalist method and with a deeper concern about human subjectivity and life-worlds.[6] In Wittgenstein this was formulated in terms of "forms-of-life" and "language-games". Wittgenstein's observations on Frazer's *The Golden Bough* offers a seminal hermeneutic.[7]

II
Teaching Hermeneutics as an Interdisciplinary Course (Sheffield, 1970–85)

A decisive turning-point occurred for me when I moved to the University of Sheffield in 1970. Our Head of Department at Sheffield, Professor James Atkinson, gave his younger colleagues every encouragement to explore new avenues of enquiry and to design fresh courses for students. He encouraged me to design what I believe to be the first final-year Honours degree course in hermeneutics for students in Biblical Studies, Biblical Studies and English, or Philosophy and Theology. It was thus inter-disciplinary from the first, combining biblical studies, theology, philosophy and literary theory. I was warmly welcomed into the Department of Philosophy, where I offered public lectures on Wittgenstein in 1971–72, and into the Department of Linguistics where I shared some teaching on semantics and (later) shared doctoral supervision. The stage was set for teaching a full critical survey of hermeneutical theory, in the context of research in biblical studies, the philosophy of language, and literary theory.

My work on semantics and on persuasive definition led to "The Meaning of *Sarx* in 1 Cor. 5:5: A Fresh Approach in the Light of Logical and Semantic Factors".[8] What Paul perceived as "to be destroyed", I urged, was the incestuous man's disposition of complacent self-sufficiency, not his physical body. Paul had redefined *sarx* in the way that conveyed his theological point, and exclusion from the church was to lead to the man's salvation by striking at the root of his self-confidence. This more philosophical work on "persuasive definition" is nowadays seen more clearly in semiotic terms. An excellent example is John Moore's appeal to the notion of "code-switching" in Eco.[9] However, I felt that my most creative use of J.L. Austin appeared in "The Supposed Power of Words in the Biblical Writings".[10] O. Grether, W. Zimmerli, L. Dürr and even Gerhard von Rad had ascribed the "power" of words in the OT to their being *Kraftgeladen* in some *causal* sense, as "an objective reality endowed with mysterious power".[11] Zimmerli spoke of a world of curse or of blessing as "a missile with a time-fuse".[12] But Austin clearly drew a contrast between the *causal* force of *perlocutionary* speech-acts and the *institutional* force of

---

[6]   Anthony C. Thiselton, "The Use of Philosophical Categories in NT Hermeneutics", *The Churchman* 87 (1973), 87–100.

[7]   L. Wittgenstein, "Bemerkungen über Frazers *The Golden Bough*", *Synthese* 17 (1967), 233–53.

[8]   A.C. Thiselton, "The Meaning of *Sarx* ...", *Scottish Journal of Theology* 26 (1973), 204–28.

[9]   J.D. Moores, *Wrestling with Rationality in Paul* (Cambridge: Cambridge University Press, 1995 [SNTS Mon Ser 82]), 1–32 and 132–60.

[10]   Anthony C. Thiselton, *Journal of Theological Studies* 25 (1974), 283–99.

[11]   G. von Rad, *Old Testament Theology*, vol. 2 (Edinburgh: Oliver & Boyd, 1965), 85.

[12]   W. Zimmerli, "Wortes Gottes", *RGG* VI (1962), col. 1810.

illocutionary acts. A curse or a blessing could not be recalled not because it carries a mysterious *Kraftgeladen* word-magic, but because while the Hebrew-Christian tradition carries *institutional procedures* for, for example, "I bless", "I baptize", "I commit this body to the ground", it has no such procedure for "I un-bless", "I un-baptize", "I un-commit this body out of the ground again".

During my Sheffield period from 1970 to 1985 my lectures on hermeneutics developed in several directions. Initially I set Palmer's book *Hermeneutics* and several others, especially on Bultmann and myth.[13] The course included the origins and development of hermeneutics; the foundation of the modern discipline with Schleiermacher and Dilthey; Bultmann and demythologizing; Heidegger, Gadamer and the New Hermeneutic; functions of language with reference to Wittgenstein and to speech-acts in Austin; issues concerning theological context and the status of the Bible as Scripture; an evaluation of narrative theory, and the relation between hermeneutics and semantics. My concern for the multi-functional multi-level operation of language emerged in a short study on language in liturgy.[14]

Continuing work on semantics found expression in "Semantics and NT Interpretation" and another related paper.[15] There I took up, for example, the theme of Wittgenstein and Ramsey that everyday vocabulary is used with a particular contextual logic. I drew on Austin to illustrate that such speech-acts as "I repent" or "I believe" are *acts* of repentance or of commitment or confession, not attempts to inform God of a context of which he is aware. This also found expression in my formulating the *stance expressed in acts* (not in mental calculation) which constituted "expecting" the *Parousia*.[16] As Wittgenstein observes, we "expect" a guest when we tidy the house, check whether we have laid the table, and so forth, not when some abstract mental event of calculation occurs.[17] Paul Ricoeur's most brilliant works, *Time and Narrative* (Eng., 3 vols 1984–88) and *Oneself as Another* (Eng., 1992) were not accessible to English-speaking students until after my Sheffield period.[18]

In the late 1970s I began to see that Ricoeur and Habermas should be part of my hermeneutics course, together with an understanding of Emilio Betti. Ricoeur's *Freud and Philosophy* remained part of the constant central core, alongside Gadamer's *Truth and Method*[19] and Bultmann's works. In the mid-1970s I added a fresh topic on Latin American Liberation hermeneutics, and by 1980 a further unit on Reader-Response Theory.

---

[13] R.E. Palmer, *Hermeneutics: Interpretation Theory in Schleiermacher, Dilthey, Heidegger and Gadamer* (Evanston, IL: Northwestern University Press, 1969).

[14] Anthony C. Thiselton, *Language, Liturgy and Meaning* (Nottingham, Grove Liturgical Studies 2, 1975, 2nd edn 1986).

[15] Anthony C. Thiselton, "Semantics and NT Interpretation" in I.H. Marshall (ed.), *New Testament Interpretation* (Exeter: Paternoster, 1977), 75–104, and "The Semantics of Biblical Language as an Aspect of Hermeneutics", *Faith and Thought* 103 (1976), 108–20.

[16] A.C. Thiselton, "The *Parousia* in Modern Theology: Some Questions and Comments", *Tyndale Bulletin* 27 (1976), 108–20.

[17] L. Wittgenstein, *Philosophical Investigations* (Eng. and Ger., Oxford: Blackwell, 2nd edn, 1967) sects 72–86; and *Zettel* (Oxford: Blackwell, 1967), sects 58–68; cf. Thiselton, *The Two Horizons. NT Hermeneutics and Philosophical Description* (Carlisle: Paternoster and Grand Rapids, MI: Eerdmans, 1980), 383–84.

[18] Paul Ricoeur, *Time and Narrative* (3 vols, Eng., Chicago: Chicago University Press, 1984–88); and *Oneself as Another* (Eng., Chicago: Chicago University Press, 1992).

[19] Paul Ricoeur, *Freud and Philosophy. An Essay on Interpretation* (Eng., New Haven, CT and London: Yale University Press, 1970, and H.-G. Gadamer, *Truth and Method* (Eng., London: Sheed & Ward, 1975 and

III
The Two Horizons (Sheffield, 1980)

During the 1970s I wrote my most substantial work to date, namely *The Two Horizons* (1980) which ran to some 500 pages. It has since that time gone through many reprints and been translated into Korean (1990). How do the two horizons of the ancient text and of modern readers actively *engage with each other creatively without merely bland, passive, domesticating assimilation*? I began with Wink's illustration about the effects of the intervention of a long tradition that separated the two horizons historically, with effects that call for a creative hermeneutic of what Ricoeur would call suspicion and retrieval. I then surveyed the respective resources of the Continental philosophical traditions especially those of Heidegger and Gadamer, and the more incisive, suggestive, work of Wittgenstein. I sought as a preliminary to explore the issues of historical relativism, which in the UK had been emphasized especially by Denis Nineham. I also addressed issues in theology including "pre-understanding", the relation between hermeneutics and theories of language. These preliminaries covered the first 140 pages.

I turned next to Heidegger. I explored the usefulness of Heidegger's notion of "situatedness" (*Dasein*, being-there), and "horizon", which provisionally bounded possibilities of understanding. Much was of value, although I continued to query his equation of the cognitive with the secondary and derivative *in all cases*. Wittgenstein could have said that this might often reflect the case, but not necessarily always, and certainly not *a priori*, before *observing examples*. The most valuable resource to be derived from the earlier Heidegger is his notion of pre-cognitive "worlds", which Ricoeur would later develop as narrative-worlds of *possibility*.

I paid special attention next to those factors which decisively contributed to Bultmann's hermeneutics, and assisted in the due understanding and assessment of his work. I did not intend to imply that Bultmann was merely a conglomeration of "influences". But I identified at least nine or ten factors that drew Bultmann along certain lines of thought, not least his coupling of a Neo-Kantian theory of knowledge with a nineteenth-century version of Lutheranism. "Description" became linked with "law" and "works", while "address" related to grace and *kerygma*. Given further links with Jonas, Collingwood, Dilthey and others, an entirely coherent picture emerged, which even explained why Bultmann seemed unconsciously to operate with an ambivalent and ultimately self-contradictory notion of "myth".

In the Church of England Doctrine Commission Report *Believing in the Church* (1981) I argued that the ambivalent word "myth" should be banned from theological discourse since it carried too many conflicting meanings.[20] Only if we can go back to Hegel and Strauss, and then distinguish their universe of discourse from distinct issues about

---

revised 2nd Eng. edn from 6th Ger. edn 1989 and 1993). Joel Weinsheimer's fresh translation of Gadamer's *Truth and Method* contains numerous refinements over the earlier 1975 translation, which is scarcely surprising in view of Weinsheimer's excellent work *Gadamer's Hermeneutics* (New Haven, CT: Yale University Press, 1985).

[20] A.C. Thiselton, "Knowledge, Myth and Corporate Memory" in *Believing in the Church* (Doctrine Commission of the Church of England, London: SPCK, 1981), 45–78.

"objectification" in the distinct tradition of Kant can even a provisional understanding of "myth" begin.

In Gadamer I perceived the fundamental stance of respect for the *otherness* of the horizon of the other. He demonstrated the need *to listen and to question*, rather than to seek to "master" the other on one's own terms. This "mastery on one's own terms" characterizes what Gadamer and the later Wittgenstein view as the tendency to imperialize, associated with the "general method" of science.[21] Schleiermacher had perceived this in the context of nineteenth-century Romanticism, when he urged that the "strangeness" of the other eludes "system". Even in the *Speeches* of 1799 Schleiermacher attacks "miserable love of system" on the ground that one's own rationalist system leaves no room for "otherness", because what is other may not fit into one's own pre-formed expectations (cf. *On Religion: Speeches to its Cultured Despisers*, Eng., London: Kegan Paul, 1893, 55). But Gadamer tends to underrate Schleiermacher as too "psychological", and as not yet sufficiently "historical", in the sense in which Gadamer uses and approves the term with reference to an increasing emphasis upon "historicality" found in Hegel, Dilthey and especially Heidegger.

In my earlier evaluation of Gadamer in *The Two Horizons*, as against a more mature reflection in *New Horizons in Hermeneutics* of 1992, I had called attention especially to the contrast between Gadamer's more positive view of tradition and effective-history, or history of effects (*Wirkungsgeschichte*), and the later Heidegger's more negative assessment of Western tradition since Plato.[22] I did not at that stage note explicitly that what Gadamer calls "the primacy of the play over the player" and his description of "consciousness" (*Bewusstsein*) as a mere "flickering in the closed circuits of historical life" might arguably begin to make room for a "postmodern" view of human selfhood. Rather, I stressed the hermeneutical importance of "pre-judgements" (*Vorurteile*), or "prejudices" within pre-given horizons. These horizons, I pointed out, are not fixed, but are *on the move*.[23]

Yet in contrast to postmodern perspectives, I observed that Gadamer's acknowledges a degree of stability in the role of communal judgements, and in the corporate transmission of traditions. Even if a "classic" yields a plurality of actualizations, it belongs to cumulative traditions of acknowledged wisdom (*phronēsis*). These aspects laid the groundwork, first, for respect for the horizon of the other as *other*, and then in for a disciplined movement and progress towards a fusion between the two horizons (*Horizontverschmelzung*) of past (or text), and present (or readers).[24] This could be achieved not by a universal scientific method at the level of rational reflection alone, but by *hermeneutically trained judgement*.[25]

---

[21] Part I of *Truth and Method* therefore sets in contrast the rationalist, individualist "method" of Descartes, which imposes its own universal grid onto "objects" of scientific knowledge as against the Roman *sensus communis*, the work of Vico, and later traditions through Shaftesbury and Reid, and in Germany after Hegel.

[22] A.C. Thiselton, *The Two Horizons. New Testament Hermeneutics and Philosophical Description with Special Reference to Heidegger, Bultmann, Gadamer and Wittgenstein* (Grand Rapids, MI: Eerdmans and Exeter/Carlisle: Paternoster, 1980), 330–42.

[23] *The Two Horizons*, 295–300 and 304–10 (Korean 454–62 and 469–76) (Korean, Seoul: Chungshin Publishing, 1990, 507–26).

[24] *The Two Horizons*, 305–08 (Korean 470–75).

[25] *The Two Horizons*, 304–05 (Korean 454–56).

In my later discussion of Gadamer (1992) I came to appreciate more clearly the dialectic between tradition at the level of ontology, and the variable, finite, contextually conditioned contingencies of plural actualizations of the past in the present. Gadamer ultimately derives a measure of this dialectic in modified form from Hegel. In secondary literature on Gadamer, Georgia Warnke admirably expounds the former aspect of continuity and rational coherence, while Joel Weinsheimer no less admirably expounds the latter aspect of contingency and plural actualizations. In *The Two Horizons* I paid more attention to the potential value of Gadamer's for New Testament interpretation than to its more subtle and seminal significance as a philosophical contribution in its own right. It is part of the philosophical tradition that sought, in effect, and like Ricoeur, to wrestle with aspects of the contextually conditioned in features so prominently in postmodernity, without thereby having to surrender every anchorage in a relatively stable ontology of history, language and selfhood.

In the fourth main part of *The Two Horizons* I traced similarities between "hermeneutically trained judgement" in Gadamer and patterns of regularity in the public domain of inter-subjective life in the later thought of Wittgenstein. This inter-subjective, shared world, yields public criteria of meaning, by means of which regularities of language-uses may *count as* performing this or that intelligible action or function, within given traditions or forms of life. The later Wittgenstein, it seemed to me, presented an account of the *particularities of context-variable meanings* that simultaneously presupposed *stable anchorages within this inter-subjective public world*. Indeed the whole study that culminated in the published version began in origin as a study of the later Wittgenstein. As I worked, his contribution to the hermeneutical debate became clearer.

Like Gadamer, Wittgenstein rejected "the contemptuous attitude towards the particular case" and a "craving for generality which is the method of science" as an over-blunt instrument for the exploration of meaning and understanding.[26] We cannot ask, "What *is* meaning?" *outside* a particular context-in-life or language-game, for the criteria for assessing what *counts as* an answer do not remain uniform in every particular case. In this discussion of the later Wittgenstein, I make the claim that in every sense his thought is *profoundly hermeneutical. Communicative activity* or *action* takes place in ways that are conditioned by a given *Lebensform*, form of life, or "surroundings".[27]

In addition to exploring philosophy of language in the later Wittgenstein, I also undertook a *hermeneutical* exploration of some specific cases where to explicate conceptual grammar within the New Testament would influence and clarify interpretations of the text. In particular an understanding of "faith", "flesh" and "truth" as *polymorphous concepts*, of "expecting" as an issue of *stance or action rather than mental states*, and of the conceptual conditions for "*counting x as y*" in the context of justification by grace, all presented examples of hermeneutics of the Pauline epistles. In the interests of space, however, I discarded a mass of other notes on Wittgenstein and

---

[26] L. Wittgenstein, *The Blue and Brown Books: Preliminary Studies for the 'Philosophical Investigations'* (Oxford: Blackwell [1958] 2nd edn 1969), 18; cf. *The Two Horizons*, 370–79 (Korean 566–80).

[27] L Wittgenstein, *Philosophical Investigations* (Oxford: Blackwell, 2nd edn Ger. and Eng., 1967), 19; cf. *Zettel* (Oxford: Blackwell, 1967), sect. 173; and "Bemerkungen über Frazers *The Golden Bough*", *Synthese* 17 (1967), 233–53.

the New Testament that may perhaps one day be developed sufficiently well to see the light of day.

IV
Further Collaborative Research (Sheffield and Calvin College, 1982–85)

In retrospect, the article of 1982 on "The Morality of Christian Scholarship" owed more to hermeneutics than I perceived at the time.[28] The essay was commissioned by the Archbishop of Canterbury and edited by the Bishop of Birmingham for presentation to the Pope on the occasion of his visit to the United Kingdom. I argued that the two sets of constraints of intellectual integrity and loyalty to the Christian tradition to which a Christian scholar belonged reflected the sheer givenness of his or her commitment in life and thought to a plurality of communities and contexts. That this could be painful I conceded. In principle one might reach a point when one would need to rank a priority, but although I had experienced specific tensions and constructive conflicts, I had never experienced a conflict of principle. The attempt to hold together the social conditional of criteria of knowledge with respect for rationality in the public world would remain, in my view, a prerequisite for constructive hermeneutics.

During 1982–83 I spent a year at Calvin College, Grand Rapids, Michigan, where I worked on *The Responsibility of Hermeneutics* (1985) with two literary theorists, Roger Lundin and Clarence Walhout. Roger Lundin considered the relation between the aesthetic and the rational in the history of ideas, offering a critique of a shallow Cartesian approach for hermeneutics and literature. Clarence Walhout explored textual "worlds", partly in the light of Wolterstorff's philosophy, and the contribution of an "action" model. I tried to assess the value of action models, "worlds", and a trans-rational approach for interpreting the parables of Jesus, especially in terms of reader-response theory.[29]

I saw much of value in reader-response theory, especially for interpreting certain genres, but I also came to see how one-sided reader-response theory might be. I therefore attempted to offer a critique that may partly have fallen between two stools. In fact, all three of us felt some concern that a deadline at the end of the year made the research more rushed than we might have wished, and are currently [that is, as I was writing this in 1996] collaborating to rewrite virtually a new book which incorporates the better of the earlier ideas, but with much solid additional research, probably under the title *The Promise of Hermeneutics*. [This duly appeared under this title in 1999.] Reception theory and speech-act theory remain, to my mind, far more effective tools than reader-response theory, even if their purposes are different.

The period between 1985 and 1992 yielded only minor articles. This was because I assumed the principalship, first of St John's College, Nottingham, and then of St John's College, University of Durham, where the workload of administration, alongside

---

[28] A.C. Thiselton, "The Morality of Christian Scholarship", in Mark Santer (ed.), *Their Lord and Ours* (London: SPCK, 1982), 20–42.

[29] R. Lundin, C. Walhout, and A.C. Thiselton, *The Responsibility of Hermeneutics* (Grand Rapids, MI: Eerdmans and Exeter/Carlisle: Paternoster, 1985), 79–114.

teaching, was enormous. However, I began to write *New Horizons in Hermeneutics* during a four-month period of research leave at Durham.

V

New Horizons in Hermeneutics (Durham, 1992)

In County Durham, in addition to living in College premises in Durham City centre, I enjoyed the seclusion of a small house that overlooked the sea at Marsden Bay, and during research leave worked round the clock on *New Horizons*, apart from walks with my dog along the shore reflecting on the material. Although most reviews of *The Two Horizons* were very generous, one widespread response was also, in effect, to invite me to write a systematic volume setting out my own theory and practice of hermeneutics. *New Horizons in Hermeneutics* attempts to respond to this. It covers some 700 pages, commencing with the principle that biblical texts can transform readers, but readers also transform texts. Whereas my earlier major volume concerned *engagement* between two horizons, the theme of this still larger volume was that of *transformation*. Its subtitle is *The Theory and Practice of Transforming Biblical Reading*. This subtitle appears on the dust jacket but not the title page of the first hardback editions; however, is helpfully included on the cover of the American paperback reprint of 1997.[30] How does biblical material interact with readers in such a way as to effect a transformation of stance, without itself undergoing change and distortion in the very process?

Inevitably the study had to begin with comparing the different entailments of "reading", "interpreting" and "understanding" as aspects of the more value-neutral term "hermeneutics". Each of the other three terms carries with it a specific "grammar" to do with literary theory or with theories of truth or understanding. The nature of texts and textuality also demanded attention. Logically I placed a discussion of semiotics and deconstruction next, but in terms of ready communication this "difficult" area should perhaps have been postponed until later. Chapter I had begun with a simple model of speech-act theory. A covenant or a legal will can change a person's life when it becomes operative.

Some reviewers stated that I traced various models of hermeneutics in historical sequence. This is only partly true. I wished to clarify some popular misunderstandings of the hermeneutics of Origen, Gnosticism, Luther, Calvin and Tyndale and included these under "Pre-Modern Interpretation" and "The Hermeneutics of Enquiry". Luther's notion of *claritas scripturae*, I argue, must be viewed in three specific contexts, including his pleas for action in the face of controversy about scepticism and Erasmus's tendency to urge suspense of judgement in the face of uncertainty. Luther urges that the interpreter has enough to go on, to take one step at a time.

The heart of the argument is to assess the role of ten different models of hermeneutics. Schleiermacher's "Hermeneutics of Understanding", for example, is generally

---

[30] A.C. Thiselton, *New Horizons in Hermeneutics* (London: HarperCollins, 1992, rp Carlisle: Paternoster, 1995 and Grand Rapids, MI: Zondervan, 1992, rp paperback, 1997, [currently being translated into Romanian]).

undervalued because few appreciate its complexity and its explicit recognition that where emphasis falls in hermeneutics often reflects a decision of strategy. Ahead of his time, he anticipates Saussure's distinction between language-as-a-system (*la langue*) and language as an interpersonal event (*la parole*). Ahead of his time, Schleiermacher discusses not only what gives rise to utterances or to texts, but also their content and their effects.[31] I turned to Pauline material for a test case in relation to Schleiermacher, Dilthey and Betti.[32]

I remain convinced that "the hermeneutics of self-involvement", including speech-act theory, sheds a flood of light on the subject. In particular I drew on John Searle's philosophy of language to explain the transforming effects of the biblical writings (or relevant examples from them) as *promise*. By contrast, while brilliantly perceiving that the biblical writings were not primarily value-neutral description, Bultmann drew on models in Neo-Kantian thought and from Heidegger that proposed *a false either/or* concerning description and address. Searle, following Austin, perceives that the logic of illocutionary speech-acts, including acts of promise, direction and commission, *presuppose states of affairs* rather than either eliminating or describing them. I argued that this insight is essential for a hermeneutic of the Christology of the Synoptic Gospels. The status of Jesus as Christ is *presupposed but not declared* in such effective illocutionary acts as forgiving, liberating, promising, commissioning and commanding.

It would be tedious to map out the second half of the book over the next three or four hundred pages. I attempt a reappraisal of Gadamer, Ricoeur, Habermas and Rorty, as well as Latin-American, Black and feminist hermeneutics. I examine the impact of social pragmatism, narrative theory, reader-response theory and contextual relativism. However, this is to lay foundations for proposals about the respective validity and relevance of ten specific hermeneutical models for different aspects of the biblical writings in relation to different aspects of human life today. I draw on life-worlds and "directedness" which may embody historical reconstruction; existential disruptions that initiate active reading; narrative worlds and subversion; symbols and "productive", multi-level reading; reader-response and deconstruction; socio-critical, ideological reading; criteria of "relevance" in social science, and the relation between "believing" reading and pluralism.[33]

VI

On Speech-Acts, and *Interpreting God and the Postmodern Self* (Nottingham, 1992–96)

Some further work since 1992 has tended to major on the role of speech-act theory for hermeneutics. In addition to broadening my lectures to include more modern Christian theology, I resumed teaching philosophy of religion, and read widely and more deeply in speech-act theory. Two articles in 1994 attempt to develop this resource for questions

---

[31] A.C. Thiselton, *New Horizons*, 204–36.
[32] Ibid., 237–60.
[33] Ibid., 558–620.

about, respectively, Christology and biblical authority.[34] However, my main published work in the mid-1990s concerned the hermeneutics of selfhood and the problem of manipulation in a post-modern climate. The book *Interpreting God and the Postmodern Self* (1995) represents the first of the *Scottish Journal of Theology* series of lectures, delivered in 1994 in the University of Aberdeen. In these I accepted the strictures of Nietzsche and his postmodern successors that too often in religion and in hermeneutics appeals are made to "truth" when all that occurs is a rhetorical strategy of persuasion and power. However, I do not accept that this applies to *all* religion or to *all* interpretation. To argue this is to move from a valid hermeneutic of suspicion and ideological critique to a universal scepticism and indeed cynicism.

Much of the book concerns the self-defeating, self-contradictory nature of claims to transpose all truth-questions into power-questions. If this approach is valid, what is being put forward is *not an argument but yet another power-bid*. This also radically impinges on the hermeneutics of selfhood. The human self is more than a mere construct, in Hume's sense of the term, composed of postmodern forces of gender, race, social class and vested interest. These do indeed play a strong part, as Marx, Freud, Foucault and others urge. But, with Ricoeur, I argue that suspicion and social constructivism do not provide the whole picture. I added to my title the subtitle *On Meaning, Manipulation and Promise*, and attempted to offer a theology of promise that may perhaps, in an appropriate context, contribute to re-centring an unduly fragmented and de-centred self.[35]

VII
Some Possible Prospects and Agendas after 1996

These issues led to a tentative reflection on possible prospects for hermeneutical enquiry. I had argued in 1995 that two major paradigm-shifts have occurred in the history of biblical interpretation, each of which has served to break the spell of a previous controlling model. First, the quest for freedom from the dominance of ecclesial and dogmatic concerns is often associated with the era of J.S. Semler and a background of Enlightenment rationalism. However, this new-found freedom soon hardened into a second paradigm in which a specific type of reconstructionist historical hermeneutic once again tended to imperialize all other interpretative enquiries into its own mould: "The quest for freedom ends in constraint: the historical method becomes institutionalised into a universal paradigm."[36]

---

[34] For example, A.C. Thiselton, "Christology in Luke, Speech-Act Theory, and the Problem of Dualism after Kant", in Joel B. Green and M. Turner (eds), *Jesus of Nazareth: Lord and Christ* (Grand Rapids, MI: Eerdmans and Carlisle: Paternoster, 1994), 453–72. Cf. further "Authority and Hermeneutics", in P.E. Satterthwaite and D.F. Wright (eds), *A Pathway into the Holy Scripture* (Grand Rapids, MI: Eerdmans, 1994), 107–42.

[35] A.C. Thiselton, *Interpreting God and the Postmodern Self: On Meaning, Manipulation and Promise* (Edinburgh: T. & T. Clark and Grand Rapids, MI: Eerdmans, 1995).

[36] A.C. Thiselton, "NT Interpretation in Historical Perceptive", in J.B. Green (ed.), *Hearing the NT. Strategies for Interpretation* (Carlisle: Paternoster and Grand Rapids, MI: Eerdmans, 1995), 13; cf. 10–36.

This, in turn, has led to a more recent paradigm-shift. This is "the reactive quest for freedom" which recognizes that, in R. Morgan's words, "Interpreters choose their aims."[37] However, whereas the earlier historical paradigm at least had the merit of establishing *rapport* with a text's author and an insight of the factors which led up to the text and characterized its first communication processes to its own generation of readers, now, under a regime of hermeneutical pluralism, some define "success" in terms of defending some specific modern or postmodern ideology (for example, sometimes feminist or Black hermeneutics), others seek success in terms of textual effects (for example, reader-response theory, or pietism), others in terms of stages of undefined "edification" (perhaps the social pragmatism of Richard Rorty).

How does this avoid hermeneutical anarchy? How does it avoid the very processes of manipulation that hermeneutical enquiry first arose to avoid? One widespread strategy is to make everything depend on "ethics" in some form or another. D. Patte's work offers one example among many others.[38] However, Patte tends to give the game away when he urges "In order to be ethically responsible, we must assume responsibility for our choice of one reading as the one that *is most significant for us*" (my italics).[39] In practice, this tends to be, *for him*, "multidimensional and andro-critical". Whereas Dilthey, Gadamer, Apel, Jauss and other major theorists perceive the scope of history as a guiding perspective for hermeneutical enquiry, Patte seems to privilege what may appear to verge almost on a late twentieth-century fashion, namely what its most severe critics often dub "political correctness". Although it includes important values and correctives, this approach does not seem to wrestle with ethical problems in sufficient philosophical, theological and historical depth to meet the most profound problems of life, or issues of truth and criteria in hermeneutics. Certainly an ethic that goes more deeply may well carry us further forward. If we wish to pursue an agenda that encourages interaction between the interpretation of the Bible and political ethics, a more profound resource that takes full account of historical dimensions might be Oliver O'Donovan's *The Desire of Nations;*[40] while the ethical approach to hermeneutics represented by William O'Neill's *The Ethics of our Climate: Hermeneutics and Ethical Theory*, to which we refer below, engages with even closer relevance with the nature of hermeneutics.

My former colleague David Clines rightly perceives the shift from a simpler modernity to the multi-faceted power-interests of postmodern perspectives as of critical importance for prospects in hermeneutics. Questions remain, however, about the nature of such pluralism and its consequences. Can "hermeneutics" settle for the kind of pluralism that cannot arbitrate, or, more accurately, cannot explain what is at stake in each competing interest, in any way between competing goals and interests? The dilemma of postmodernism is that no single value-system can be privileged without ceasing to be "postmodern", including any dogmatic version of postmodernism. These complex issues

---

[37] "New Testament Interpretation", 17 and 18; R. Morgan, *Biblical Interpretation* (Oxford: Oxford University Press), 287; cf. 7, 8 and 171.

[38] D. Patte, *Ethics of Biblical Interpretation: A Re-evaluation* (Louisville, KY: Westminster and Knox, 1995).

[39] Ibid.

[40] Oliver O'Donovan, *The Desire of Nations: Rediscovering the Roots of Political Theology* (Cambridge: Cambridge University Press, 1996).

cannot be settled in a few sentences, but will form part of a necessary, if divisive, continuing agenda in the humanities as well as in biblical studies and theology.

The Presidential paper for the Society of Biblical Literature delivered by Phyllis Trible in 1994 illustrates how rational criteria, conceptual differentiation and theological truth-claims readily become "deconstructed" and "erased" in the semiotic play of postmodern hermeneutics.[41] There is no firm or *stable* "difference", it appears, between Elijah and Jezebel, other than transitory differences generated by the specificities of surface-theological contexts, but unmasked by the *political* or ethical processes of de-ideologizing and deconstruction. But here a fourth paradigm threatens to fall into the same trap as the second and third. Whereas the second threw off dogmatic theology only to sell itself into bondage to history, and the third threw off the bondage of history to become dominated by "literature", the fourth appears to throw off the rational canons embedded in history, theology and language anchored in the empirical or extra-linguistic world, only to find itself captive to *politics*: to the politics of gender, race, class, which are standard features in deconstructionist philosophies, and perhaps at a deeper, hidden level, to aspirations that relate as the only "quasi-absolutes" to political or commercial funding.

A more creative and authentic prospect for hermeneutics, in my view, is to engage once again more seriously with the problem of *manipulation*. In this specific sense authentic ethics and authentic theology speak with one voice. William O'Neill's study *The Ethics of Our Climate: Hermeneutics and Ethical Theory* (1994) relates hermeneutics to ethics in ways that look beyond mere contextual pragmatism.[42] For O'Neill, ethical enquiry, as in Gadamer, is *rooted in ontology and the wisdom of history (phronēsis)*. This approach draws on the more profound, less pragmatic insights of Habermas, Gadamer, MacIntyre, and especially Rahner, and to consider issues of self-transcendence.[43] Here Gadamer's former pupil Hans Robert Jauss leads the way to paths that acknowledge major paradigm-shifts and the dilemmas of hermeneutical pluralism, but place the present era in the broader context of the history of traditions and of the reception of texts.

Open and creative hermeneutics that follows Schleiermacher, Betti, Gadamer and Ricoeur in respecting the other as genuinely *"other"*, and is not to be assimilated into one's own historical, moral, or political interests, will share Jauss's concern about continuities, disjunctions and "provocations" in the history of the reception of texts, and will locate the present within that broader ongoing history.[44] *"Differences"* then appear *not as mere illusions* to be deconstructed or erased, nor as options between which no criteria for decision and ranking can be found, but as different responses to different questions within a different agenda.

Jauss draws on the logic of question and answer found in R.G. Collingwood and in Gadamer. He affirms "the coherence of literature as an event ... mediated in the horizon of expectations of literary experience of contemporary and later readers, critics and authors".[45] His acceptance of radical paradigm-shifts in hermeneutics avoids naïve

---

[41] P. Trible, "Exegesis for Storytellers and Other Strangers", *Journal of Biblical Literature* 114 (1995), 3–19.
[42] W. O'Neill, SJ, *The Ethics of Our Climate: Hermeneutics and Ethical Theory* (Washington, DC: Georgetown University Press, 1994), 81–148.
[43] Ibid., 107–45.
[44] H.R. Jauss, *Toward an Aesthetic of Reception* (Eng., Minneapolis: University of Minnesota Press, 1982).
[45] Ibid., 22.

objectivism, and gives due recognition to the opening-up of new perspectives and new horizons.[46] But these differences "raise to consciousness the history of ... reception ..." which relates in turn to changing horizons of expectation and transformation. In this sense, like Richard Bernstein he seeks a path "beyond objectivism and relativism".[47] Further, as we noted in Wittgenstein's exploration of the logical grammar of "expectation", this does indeed relate to a *stance* or to *action*.

In this respect the prospects for hermeneutics may indeed entail ethical action and ethical responsibility. But this is an ethic of non-manipulative respect for "the other"; for other persons, other communities, other value-systems and other religions and cultures. It allows for intellectual and theological integrity. I have tried to explore the transposition of truth-questions into power-questions and the replacement of rational argument by manipulative rhetoric in *Interpreting God and the Postmodern Self* (1995),[48] but these are questions that deserve more extensive examination and discussion, and they are likely to remain with us for some considerable time.

---

[46] Ibid., 25–8.

[47] R.J. Bernstein, *Beyond Objectivism and Relativism: Science, Hermeneutics and Praxis* (Oxford: Blackwell, 1983).

[48] Cited above, at the end of section VI.

CHAPTER TWO

Situating a Theoretical Framework: "Biblical Studies and Theoretical Hermeneutics" (1998)

I have pointed out that these first two essays are not research essays. The first introduced readers to concerns that motivated my writing, and the second, here, offers an introduction to the subject of hermeneutics. Hence they were written at a different level from that of the other thirty-nine research essays in this volume. As in the case of the previous essay, I pondered on whether to omit this from what is primarily a collection of research essays. Nevertheless it serves as an introduction and embodies some distinctive claims. I have also minimally edited the original text to improve the clarity of the earlier one, since the danger of seeking to cover such a broad area in relatively few words is that one or two minor qualifications may be needed to render broader descriptions and assessments more accurate.

Hermeneutics entails critical reflection on the basis, nature and goals of reading, interpreting and understanding communicative acts and processes. This characteristically concerns the understanding of texts, especially biblical or literary texts or those of another era or culture. However, it also includes reflection on the nature of understanding human actions, sign systems, visual data, institutions, artefacts or other aspects of life. In biblical studies it applies traditionally to the interpretation of texts, but also the interweaving of language and life both within the horizon of the text and within the horizons of traditions and the modern reader.

It remains helpful to distinguish hermeneutics as critical and theoretical reflection on these processes from the actual work of interpreting and understanding as a first-order activity. Often writers speak loosely of someone's "hermeneutic" when they refer only to how they go about the task rather then their reasons for doing so and their reflection on what is at issue in the process. The decisive foundation of theoretical hermeneutics as a modern discipline occurred with the work of Friedrich Schleiermacher over the first thirty years of the nineteenth century. All the same, scattered building-blocks for modern theory emerge at regular intervals from the ancient world to the post-Reformation period up to Schleiermacher. These might be regarded as constituting the prehistory of theoretical hermeneutics, in the modern sense of the term.

I

The Pre-history of Hermeneutics before the Work of Schleiermacher

I.1 The Ancient World

Plato and the Stoics debated the status of allegorical interpretations of Homer and Hesiod. However, these debates for the most part belonged to an agenda that concerned issues other than the specific nature of interpretation. Thus Plato's discussion of artistic productions as "copies of copies of Ideas" (in *Ion* and the *Republic* x) constituted part of his theory of Forms.

Aristotle, by contrast, considers the nature of "emplotment" and the communicative processes that it generates as an aspect of hermeneutical theory in his *Poetics*. As Paul Ricoeur points out, we are indebted to Aristotle for the notion that narrative plot draws together otherwise apparently isolated actions into an action-orientated purposive 'whole' (*teleios ... holēs*), which lends it coherence and intelligibility for the audience.[1] Equally, he is perhaps the first to formulate a theory of audience or reader effects, examining the goals and consequences of tragic plot for readers or audience. His work *On Interpretation* remains less useful for hermeneutics, since his main concern is about the logic and rhetoric of propositions. In biblical studies the significance of Aristotle's work regained recognition only with the advent of narrative theory and reader-response criticism in biblical hermeneutics around the later 1970s.

The biblical writings themselves offer many examples of interpretative processes, but few, if any, theoretical aspects. The nearest is perhaps the two-way principle in Luke 24 that texts illuminate the present while present circumstances may also illuminate texts (Luke 24:27, 32), and also Paul's insistence on Christology as a hermeneutic principle or key (2 Corinthians 3:15, 16). In rabbinic traditions, the so-called seven rules of Hillel offer rough guidelines about the extensions of texts to new situations. These hardly constitute hermeneutical theory, but offer a building-block that places especially "re-contextualization" and inter-textuality on an agenda awaiting further explication.

Among the earlier Church Fathers, perhaps only Origen (c.185–254) consciously formulated a theory of hermeneutics, examining interactions between levels of meaning, and purposes of interpretation in relation to different methods and tasks.[2] For the most part, even the significant work of Irenaeus and others tended to reflect polemical situations which in part substantiate Schleiermacher's valid diagnosis that most writers before him usually drew in "hermeneutics" simply as a court of appeal to try to validate some prior understanding of their own, or some prior tradition of understanding, rather than to *initiate* understanding. Hermeneutics arose when problems of "misunderstanding" occurred, rather than in order to explore what it might be *to understand*.[3] In this respect the discussion

---

[1] Aristotle, *Poetics* (Oxford: Oxford University Press, 1968), 50b, pp.23–4. See further Paul Ricoeur, *Time and Narrative*, 3 vols (Chicago, IL and London: University of Chicago Press, 1984–88), vol. 1, pp.31–51.

[2] Origen, *de Principiis* 4:1.

[3] Friedrich Schleiermacher, *Hermeneutics: The Handwritten Manuscripts* (ed. H. Kimmerle, Missoula, MT: Scholars Press and American Academy of Religion, 1977), p.49 (Aphorism 49), and more especially pp.110–13.

about tradition and interpretation in Irenaeus arises because texts, as he saw it, became distorted and "garbled" within the frame of reference brought by his gnostic opponents.[4] However, here he places an important theoretical and practical issue on the agenda.

I.2 Mediaeval and Reformation Traditions

The mediaeval tradition expanded questions about levels of meaning and theories of signs. Semiotic theory in Augustine and in Gregory the Great carried with it considerable theological importance.[5] But the discussion took a new turn with the polemical context of the Reformation. In the face of Erasmus's hesitancy about whether biblical interpretation remained too problematic and complex to allow any basis for action, in 1525 Martin Luther asserted its "clarity". But this is in no way to cut across his appreciation of problems of interpretation. Their debate partially anticipated the postmodern question of contextual relativism: can 'interpretation' ever yield firm enough ground for ethics or action outside some predetermined tradition of reading?[6] In his *Institutes* (1536–39) John Calvin endorsed the widespread Patristic understanding of the Bible as the word of God, but insisted that, "like a nurse", God accommodated revelation to the specificities of time, place and given human capacities, as God had also done in the incarnation.[7] He also called into question Melanchthon's method of interpreting the Bible by first identifying its *loci* or 'leading themes', on the ground that a running historical and contextual reading should determine first what counted as leading themes.[8] That this implies "theory" can be seen from Heinrich Bullinger's insistence in the same period (1538) that while contextual details (*causa, locus, occasio, tempus, instrumentum, modus*) shape our understanding of the text, our judgements about these depend equally on how we understand where the whole argument leads. Thus he offers a proto-version of the hermeneutical circle, which would be formulated by Friedrich Ast, and refined by Schleiermacher.

William Tyndale and J.M. Chladenius provide two further examples of approaches which only later attain a theoretical role. Tyndale's treatise *Pathway into the Holy Scriptures* might count today as an exposition of speech-act theory in biblical studies before its time. Scripture, he declares, *performs actions*: it wounds, heals, drives to despair, liberates, commands and above all promises.[9] He is clear that this focus on action stands at the heart of the matter. In 1742 Chladenius argued that all interpretations of the Bible depend

---

⁴ Irenaeus, *Adversus Haereses* 1:8:1; cf. 8:1–5 and 2:28:1–3.

⁵ See Robert A. Markus, *Signs and Meanings: World and Text in Ancient Christianity* (Liverpool: Liverpool University Press, 1996); [in 2004 we add: Telford Work, *Living and Active: Scripture in the Economy of Salvation* (Grand Rapids, MI: Eerdmans, 2002) pp.50–66, esp. p.52].

⁶ Martin Luther, *On the Bondage of the Will* (Edinburgh: T. & T. Clark, 1957), pp.66–7, 71, 125–9; and Desiderius Erasmus, *In Praise of Folly* (Chicago, IL: Pickard 1946), p.84; cf. the discussions in Richard H. Popkin, *The History of Scepticism from Erasmus to Spinoza* (Berkeley: University of California Press, 1979), pp.1–17; F. Beisser, *Claritas Scripturae bei Martin Luther* (Göttingen: Vandenhoeck & Ruprecht, 1966); and Anthony C. Thiselton, *New Horizons in Hermeneutics: the Theory and Practice of Transforming Biblical Reading* (London: HarperCollins and Grand Rapids, MI: Zondervan, 1992), pp.179–90.

⁷ John Calvin, *Institutes of the Christian Religion*, 2 vols (Edinburgh: T. & T. Clark, 1957), Bk 1: 13:1.

⁸ Ibid., III: 17:14 and IV: 16:13; cf. especially T.H.L. Parker, *Calvin's New Testament Commentaries* (London: SCM Press, 1971), pp.32–4; and on H. Bullinger, pp.38–40.

⁹ William Tyndale, 'Pathway into the Holy Scriptures', in *Doctrinal Treatises and Introductions to Different Portions of the Holy Scriptures* (Cambridge: Parker Society edn, 1848), esp. pp.3–13.

on "viewpoint" (*Sehe-Punkt*), which leaves the interpreter to construe what cannot immediately be seen from a limited historical vantage point.[10] In modern theory Wolfgang Iser's work rests on Roman Ingarden's theory of perception, in accordance with which the reader "fills in the gaps" that are presupposed as part of an active response to the text.[11] This heralds ahead of its time the entry of reader-response theory into biblical studies, especially for reading the parables of Jesus.

II
The Founding of Modern Hermeneutics: Schleiermacher and Dilthey

II.1 Schleiermacher

Friedrich Schleiermacher (1768–1834) established hermeneutics as a modern discipline in its own right. He combined a theory of language as a system with a theory of interpersonal communication to arrive at a particular process of understanding. The sophistication of his work is widely underrated. His drive towards theoretical reflection owed little or nothing to rationalism, but stemmed from his deep appreciation of the revolution brought about by Immanuel Kant's transcendental method of philosophy. Where Kant's predecessors had asked how we know or how we reason, Kant asked *on what basis* we know or reason, and explored the nature and boundaries of knowledge and reason. Similarly Schleiermacher considered that questions about whether this or that interpretation has validity were premature until we had examined the basis, nature and limits of human understanding, whether of a text or of another person. In 1805 and 1809–10 he sketched out a series of *Aphorisms* in hermeneutics, and produced his *Compendium* on hermeneutics in 1819. He added further notes in 1828 and 1832–33, and delivered his *Academy Addresses* on hermeneutics in 1829.

Schleiermacher criticized previous approaches for being "entirely mechanical", as if merely to observe "rules" guaranteed understanding.[12] This concern may represent a necessary condition as part of linguistic or "grammatical" hermeneutics, but never a sufficient condition. Interpretation is an "art".[13] Those who had appealed to hermeneutics as a "regional" discipline to validate some understanding supposedly reached already on some other ground failed to see that "in interpretation it is essential that one be able to step out of one's own frame of mind into that of the author".[14] This constitutes the interpersonal dimension, in contrast to the "grammatical" or "technical" axis, which Schleiermacher unfortunately termed "the psychological", giving rise to misunderstandings

---

[10] J.M. Chladenius, *Einleitung zur richtigen Auslegung vernünftiger Reden und Schriften* (reprinted Düsseldorf: Stern, 1969 [1742]), section 194.

[11] Wolfgang Iser, *The Act of Reading: A Theory of Aesthetic Response* (Baltimore, MD and London: Johns Hopkins University Press, 1978 and 1980).

[12] Schleiermacher, *Hermeneutics*, p.175; cf. p.49 (Aphorism 49), and pp.176–95, on F. Wolf.

[13] Ibid., p.176.

[14] Ibid., p.42 (Aphorism 8). On the lack of 'general hermeneutics' cf. p.95.

which stemmed from Wilhelm Dilthey's exposition of his work.[15] Strikingly anticipating Ferdinand de Saussure a century before the latter's work, Schleiermacher argued that understanding entails a dialectical appreciation both of "the communality of thought ... totality of language" (cf. Saussure's *la langue* or language-system) and "every act of speaking ... the speaker's thoughts" (cf. Saussure's *la parole*, as the act of speech).[16]

Very loosely, the comparative, more mechanical, more "masculine" quality of criticism addresses issues of language and genre concerning which some so-called "rules" may apply; but a more creative, more intuitive or supra-rational "feminine" capacity of perception is needed to recover the unique and holistic in interpersonal understanding. Neither task is "higher"; both are essential.[17] If either appears "higher" this arises from issues of strategy alone in how we approach a text, and the sequence of questions asked. But the process of understanding is lengthy and always subject to correction or expansion. For only "a complete knowledge of the language" coupled with "complete knowledge of the person" could bring the process to completion; meanwhile "it is necessary to move back and forth between the grammatical and psychological sides".[18]

It has often been mistakenly assumed that Schleiermacher collapses the task into exploring mental processes of intention, or commits the so-called generic fallacy of equating meaning with origins. But, as I have argued elsewhere, like Dilthey and the later Ludwig Wittgenstein and John Searle, he sees the currency of meaning as grounded in public life. Hence he insists on the importance of "New Testament authors in their time and place":[19] "Each text was addressed to specific people."[20] But the task does not end with identifying historical specificity. The task is "to understand the text at first as well as, and then even better then, its author ... The task is infinite."[21] Here Schleiermacher takes up his well-known notion of "the hermeneutical circle": "Each part can be understood only out of the whole to which it belongs, and vice versa ... Only in the case of insignificant texts are we satisfied with what we understand on first reading."[22] For subsequent readings correct and refine the prior agenda of questions, or "pre-understanding" (*Vorverständnis*) which we bring to the text in order to acquire a deeper understanding of it. The interpreter may even come "to transform himself".[23] The text in this respect produces "effects".[24]

---

[15] Ibid., pp.99 and 103. The misunderstanding is corrected by H. Kimmerle both in his 'Foreword' (pp.19–40) and in his 'Hermeneutical Theory or Ontological Hermeneutics', *Journal for Theology and the Church: 4, History and Hermeneutic* (Tübingen: Mohr and New York: Harper & Row, 1967), pp.107–21; and also in Thiselton, *New Horizons in Hermeneutics*, pp.223–5 and 558–61; cf. also pp.104–35.

[16] Schleiermacher, *Hermeneutics*, p.97.

[17] Ibid., p.99.

[18] Ibid., p.100.

[19] Ibid., p.104; cf. Thiselton, *New Horizons in Hermeneutics*, pp.223–5 and pp.558–61.

[20] Schleiermacher, *Hermeneutics*, p.107.

[21] Ibid., p.112.

[22] Ibid., p.113; cf. also p.148 and especially pp.195–6 in the *Second Academy Address*.

[23] Ibid., p.150.

[24] Ibid., p.151.

II.2 Dilthey

Schleiermacher's intellectual successor in hermeneutics was Wilhelm Dilthey (1833–1911). In Dilthey the theoretical aspect becomes still more clearly pronounced. He aimed to formulate a universal theory of human understanding, based on a critique of historical reason as profound and influential as Kant's critiques of pure reason and of practical reason. In the light of the debates that followed Hegel's formulations concerning historical reason, Dilthey placed "life" (*Leben*) and "lived experience" (*Erlebnis*) at the centre, where Locke, Hume and Kant had spoken of sensations, ideas, or concepts. Hermeneutics, as against rationalist, empiricist, or critical theories of knowledge, Dilthey urged, restored blood to the veins of the human subject.[25] Interactive historical understanding becomes objectified in institutions, and invites the enquirers to pay attention equally to the general and the particular, to the universal and the unique. Here "understanding" (*Verstehen*) differs decisively from "knowledge" and especially from "explanation". In his *Einleitung in die Geisteswissenschaften* (1883) Dilthey made this contrast foundational for the different methods of the natural sciences (*Naturwissenschaften*) and 'human' sciences (*Geisteswissenschaften*).

In his incisive work *Understanding and Explanation*, Karl-Otto Apel traces this "E–V" controversy, as he terms it (that is, *Erklärung*, explanation, vs. *Verstehen*, understanding) from Dilthey and Max Weber through Wittgenstein, Peter Winch and G.H. von Wright, to Hans-Georg Gadamer and Jürgen Habermas.[26] The contrast remains fundamental for Emilio Betti, is developed and modified by Habermas and Ricoeur, and is anathema to Gadamer. I have suggested elsewhere that it bears some relation to the use of Dilthey in Rudolf Bultmann's hermeneutics of the New Testament, where it encourages his dualism between history, law, myth and descriptive report (*Erklärung*), and faith, gospel, kerygma and personal address (*Verstehen*), although Martin Heidegger and neo-Kantian philosophy also widen this dualism.[27] Dilthey argued that the *Verstehen* of interpersonal relations between an I and a thou can become objectified through social institutions and historical habituation. On this basis a "science" of human studies may be founded on the hermeneutical category of understanding. In his essay on hermeneutics of 1900 Dilthey writes, "Our actions always presuppose understanding of other people ... empathy with the mental life of others. Indeed philology and history rest on the assumption that the understanding (*Verstehen*) of the unique can be made objective ... Only by comparing

---

[25] Wilhelm Dilthey, *Gesammelte Schriften*, 12 vols (Leipzig and Berlin: Teubner, 1962), vol. V, p.4; cf. vol. I, pp.xvii and 217. Dilthey's key essay of 1900, 'The Development of Hermeneutics' is available in English in H.P. Rickman (ed.), *Dilthey: Selected Writings* (Cambridge: Cambridge University Press, 1976), pp.246–63, and also in David Klemm (ed.), *Hermeneutical Inquiry*, vol. I, *The Interpretation of Texts* (Atlanta, GA: Scholars Press, 1986), pp.93–106.

[26] Karl Otto-Apel, *Understanding and Explanation: A Transcendental-Pragmatic Perspective* (Cambridge, MA, and London: MIT Press, 1984) esp. pp.1–82 and 243–50, but throughout.

[27] Bultmann's dualisms and their relation to Dilthey find some discussion in Anthony C. Thiselton, *The Two Horizons: New Testament Hermeneutics and Philosophical Description with Special Reference to Heidegger, Bultmann, Gadamer and Wittgenstein* (Exeter and Carlisle: Paternoster Press and Grand Rapids, MI: Eerdmans, 1980), pp.205–92, esp. pp.212–18, 234–40 and 245–51.

myself with others and becoming conscious of how I differ from them can I experience my own individuality."[28]

Dilthey's hermeneutics contain weaknesses as well as certain strengths, as indeed remains the case also with Schleiermacher. These will begin to emerge in the next section.

III
Hermeneutics as a Theoretical Discipline? Betti, Bultmann and Gadamer

III.1 Gadamer and Betti: the Question of "Method"

Hans-Georg Gadamer (1900–2002), for many years Professor of Philosophy at Heidelberg and a former pupil of Heidegger, has received wide recognition as perhaps the most influential hermeneutical theorist of the twentieth century. His *magnum opus*, *Truth and Method*, first appeared in German in 1960, and ran through at least five editions (revised English translation based on fifth German edition, 1989).[29] But Gadamer *opposes* "method" to truth. The whole notion of "method", he believes, stems from following the rationalism of Descartes, rather than the older, more historical, more communal, tradition of Vico and others, and reached its climax in the Enlightenment glorification of the sciences as methods of "mastering" truth.[30] This merely transposed "truth" into a passive object, shaped and construed, as Kant perceived, in terms of prior categorizations that the human subject imposed upon it. Thereby it reductively distorted truth.

To substitute *technē* for the cumulative wisdom of communities and traditions on which truth had made some irreversible impact was to turn the project of understanding upside down.[31] Following his former teacher, Heidegger, he urged that the subject matter of truth must address the human subject on its own terms, not on terms laid down in advance by the enquirer. Hence hermeneutics has in its goal not the formulation of methodological theory, in Dilthey's sense, but the "coming-to-speech" of the subject matter of truth (*das Zur-Sprache-Kommen der Sache selbst*).[32]

Does this mean that, after all, Gadamer does not expound a *theory* of hermeneutics, or even that he is hostile to theory as such? He does indeed attack theory if by "theory" we mean the kind of methodological foundation that Dilthey attempted to construct, and which many see as represented in the twentieth century more rigorously by Emilio Betti. At the same time, he expresses profound respect for Betti's work. He agrees with Betti that, as he expressed it as recently as 1991, hermeneutics concerns "an Other ... to whom we are bound in the reciprocation of language and life".[33]

---

[28] Wilhelm Dilthey, 'The Development of Hermeneutics' in Rickman, *Dilthey*, p.246 and Klemm, *Hermeneutical Inquiry*, p.93.

[29] Hans-Georg Gadamer, *Truth and Method* (2nd rev. edn from 5th Ger. edn, London: Sheed & Ward, 1989). (An earlier 1975 English translation is from the 2nd Ger. edn of 1965.)

[30] Ibid., pp.xxi–xxxviii, 3–34 and 277–307 (1975 edn pp.xi–xxvi, 5–33, and 245–74).

[31] Ibid., pp.307–41 (1975 edn pp.274–305).

[32] Ibid., p.379 (1975 edn p.341); German *Wahrheit und Methode* (2nd edn, Mohr: Tübingen, 1965), p.360; cf. p.379, and see whole section pp.362–79 and 389–405 (1975 edn pp.325–41 and 357–66).

[33] Hans-Georg Gadamer, 'Foreword' to Jean Grondin, *Introduction to Philosophical Hermeneutics* (New Haven, CT and London: Yale University Press, 1994) (Ger., 1991).

Emilio Betti (1890–1968) founded an Institute of Hermeneutics in Rome in 1955, and in the same year produced his massive *Teoria generale della interpretazione*, of which a German version, *Allgemeine Auslegungslehre der Geisteswissenschaften*, appeared in 1967.[34] His thesis that hermeneutics provides the theoretical methodology for *all* of the humanities and social sciences finds expression in the title of his work *Die Hermeneutik als allgemeine Methodik der Geisteswissenschaften* (1962).[35] Since Betti's major work pre-dated that of Gadamer, his main target is Heidegger, but in subsequent dialogue Betti accuses Gadamer of collapsing hermeneutics into a phenomenology that can offer no objective criteria for "valid" interpretation while Gadamer replies that he describes "what is" rather than some prior notion of what ought to be or should be.[36]

In the United States E.D. Hirsch presses Betti's case against Gadamer.[37] But Betti remains more careful and rigorous than Hirsch in avoiding reducing hermeneutics to *technē*. Betti sees hermeneutics more broadly and deeply as the general or universal foundation for all human studies, not least because, since he shares with Schleiermacher the view that processes of understanding are virtually infinite and always corrigible, hermeneutics calls for patience, tolerance, reciprocity and "listening" to the Other. Betti and Gadamer are at one in questioning the centrality of the self as that which "knows" other selves only on its own terms, rather than on the terms of the claims of "the Other".

III.2 Bultmann

Rudolf Bultmann (1884–1976) has achieved an enormous influence in biblical studies, and, like Betti, has engaged in dialogue with Dilthey and with Heidegger. But his hermeneutical theory betrays a supreme paradox. Too heavily influenced by radical nineteenth-century Lutheranism, by Kierkegaard's emphasis on the will, and by Wilhelm Herrmann's antipathy to doctrine, Bultmann's exposition of the impact of the Christian kerygma is voluntarist, existentialist and profoundly anti-theoretical, even anti-intellectual if not anti-rational. Yet he employs a complex network of theory drawn from Neo-Kantianism, from Dilthey and R.G. Collingwood, and from Hans Jonas and Heidegger, his colleagues at Marburg, to serve as a basis for his anti-theoretical interpretation of the New Testament.[38]

Faith is sheer venture. Hence on one side Bultmann engages in the work of historical reconstruction, notably in his early work *The History of Synoptic Tradition*. Yet faith does not depend on the reliability of historical reports: "I calmly let the fires burn ... 'Christ after the flesh' is no concern of ours. How things looked in the heart of Jesus I do not know and do not want to know."[39] Strictly, for Bultmann historical reconstruction offers

---

[34] Emilio Betti, *Teoria generale della interpretazione*, 2 vols (Milan: Giuffrè, 1955; new edn with additional MS notes, 1990); Ger. edn, *Allgemeine Auslegungslehre der Geisteswissenschaften* (Tübingen: Mohr, 1967).

[35] Emilio Betti, *Die Hermeneutik als allgemeine Methodik der Geisteswissenschaften* (Tübingen: Mohr, 1962).

[36] Gadamer's response appears in 'Supplement 1' to the 2nd–5th edns of *Truth and Method* (esp. pp.510–17; 2nd Ger. edn, pp.482–8) and the 'After-word' of the 1989 edn, pp.554–9.

[37] E.D. Hirsch Jr, *Validity in Interpretation* (New Haven and London: Yale University Press, 1967) and *The Aims of Interpretation* (Chicago, IL: University of Chicago Press, 1976), esp. pp.1–13 and 17–49.

[38] Expounded in detail in Thiselton, *The Two Horizons*, pp.205–92.

[39] Rudolf Bultmann, *Faith and Understanding*, vol. 1 (London: SCM Press 1969), p.132.

only a phenomenology of the faith-responses of early communities (apart from the bare "fact" of Jesus). But this is not kerygma; it is not the goal of "understanding" in the sense of hermeneutical engagement with the New Testament texts.

Bultmann agrees with Schleiermacher and Dilthey that "Exegesis is a work of personal art (*der persönlichen Kunst*) ... intensified by a thorough-going communion with the author".[40] Hence "the 'most subjective' [*subjectiviste*] interpretation is the 'most objective' [*objectiviste*], that is, only those who are stirred by the question of their own existence [*Existenz*] can hear the claim which the text makes".[41] But the "claim" and the "address" of the kerygma are wrapped up in "mythological" clothing: texts appear to describe or to report supernatural occurrences when their intended function is not descriptive but existential. He writes, "Myth should be interpreted not cosmologically but anthropologically, or better still existentially."[42] In a further essay he explains:

> The restatement of mythology is a requirement of faith itself. For faith needs to be emancipated from its association with every world-view expressed in objective terms ... Our radical attempt to demythologise the New Testament is in fact a perfect parallel to St Paul's and Luther's doctrine of justification by faith alone ... It destroys every false security ... security can be found only by abandoning all security.[43]

Bultmann's theory of hermeneutics does often assist the interpreter in coming to terms with "the point" of descriptive language that may serve some further purpose. For example, language about creation and the last judgement functions not primarily to satisfy curiosity by describing past or future events as such, but to call readers to responsibility as creaturely stewards of the earth who are accountable for their attitudes and actions. But such language cannot be *translated solely* into existential address comprehensively and without remainder, as if the descriptive dimensions were merely a linguistic cipher or strategy without content. Indeed Bultmann operates with a remarkably simplistic philosophy of language, as if all communication were *either* descriptive *or* expressive *or* voluntarist-existential. The tradition of speech-act theory from J.L. Austin to John Searle suggests that directive, self-involving language often presupposes that certain states of affairs are the case; while work from the later Wittgenstein to Barthes and Derrida underlines that language operates at various levels often simultaneously.

III.3 Gadamer Again: "A Reality that Surpasses" Individual Conscious Reflection

Gadamer offers a much more profound and influential account of hermeneutics. But can it be called a theory? We have noted that he replies to Betti, "Fundamentally I am *not proposing a method*; I am describing *what is the case*."[44] But is phenomenology (for example,

---

[40] Rudolf Bultmann, *Essays Philosophical and Theological* (London: SCM Press, 1955) p.238; German *Glauben und Verstehen*, 4 vols (Tübingen: Mohr, 1964–65), vol. II, p.215.

[41] Ibid., pp.210–11.

[42] Rudolf Bultmann's programmatic essay in Hans-Werner Bartsch (ed.), *Kerygma and Myth*, 2 vols (London: SPCK, 1964 and 1962), vol. 1, p.10.

[43] Bultmann, *Essays*, pp.210–11.

[44] Gadamer, *Truth and Method*, p.512 (his italics); (1975 edn, p.465; Ger. edn, p.183).

in Edmund Husserl) not a theory of description (as we may find in the later Wittgenstein) rather than only a method of approach? Gadamer's major point, like that of Wittgenstein, is that *only as part of the very process of understanding can we tell in each case, and not in advance*, what counts as an act or process of understanding.

Gadamer stands in the tradition of Hegel and of Heidegger, and traces what he regards as the limited and mixed success of Romanticist hermeneutics from Schleiermacher through Dilthey in rightly disestablishing the relentless drive of Enlightenment rationalism to "master" truth by "method". Enlightenment rationalism also failed to subject the consciousness of the individual interpreter to a sufficiently radical critique. Tracing the most positive aspects of hermeneutics from Johann Gustav Droysen and W. Dilthey through Graf Yorck and Martin Heidegger to his own work, he comments as recently as in 1991: "Subjectivity and self-consciousness ... lost their primacy. Now instead, there is an Other."[45]

The models of play, art and celebration clarify what is central for Gadamer. He writes, "Play does not have its being in the player's consciousness or attitude, but on the contrary, play draws him into its dominion ... The player experiences the game as a reality that surpasses him."[46] A game would not be a game if every player followed the same "correct" routine of identical moves, with a predictable and identical outcome on each occasion.[47] What counts as "*a correct presentation*" (*Darstellung*) of a theatrical play or recreational game is "highly flexible and relative".[48] Hence in a festival "its *celebration* [is] *sui generis* ... A festival exists only in being celebrated", and what is appropriate depends on its time and place within an expanding tradition.[49] One of his most reliable commentators, Joel C. Weinsheimer, succinctly comments: "There is such freedom that no game is ever played twice identically, and for all this variety it is still the one game."[50]

In biblical studies Gadamer's work has at the very least shaken to its foundations "the hermeneutics of innocence" of traditional Enlightenment thought. It provides the theoretical and philosophical groundwork for the view expressed by Robert Morgan and John Barton that what counts as criteria in interpretation depends, among other things, on the goal proposed for this or that process of interpretation.[51] It has also succeeded in showing the importance of the history of text-reception as worked out, for example, by Gadamer's pupil Hans Jauss.[52] In the New Testament hermeneutics of Ernst Fuchs, Gadamer's work provides a theoretical basis for his notion of a "projected world" in

---

[45] Gadamer, 'Foreword' to J. Grondin, *Introduction to Philosophical Hermeneutics*, p.x, in comparison with *Truth and Method*, pp.212–18 (Droysen), pp.218–42 (Dilthey), pp.242–54 (Yorck), pp.254–64 (Heidegger) and pp.265–379 (the central part of his work).

[46] Gadamer, *Truth and Method*, p.109.

[47] Ibid., p.118.

[48] Ibid., p.119.

[49] Ibid., pp.123–4.

[50] Joel C. Weinsheimer, *Gadamer's Hermeneutics* (New Haven, CT and London: Yale University Press, 1985), p.104.

[51] Robert Morgan (with John Barton), *Biblical Interpretation* (Oxford: Oxford University Press, 1988), pp.5–15 (esp. p.8), pp.167–200 (esp. pp.184–9) and 267–96 (esp. p.287).

[52] Hans R. Jauss, *Towards an Aesthetic of Reception* (Minneapolis: University of Minnesota Press 1982). Cf. also Robert C. Holub, *Reception Theory. A Critical Introduction* (London and New York: Methuen, 1984).

parable and narrative.[53] Within the "world", as in Heidegger's "worldhood" and in Gadamer's "game" or art, eventful actualizations may operate at a pre-conscious level in such a way as to lead to transformations of attitude that run deeper than "didactic" concepts. In the United States, Robert Funk has explored this perspective found in Fuchs and Gadamer for New Testament studies.[54]

IV
The Climax of Multidisciplinary Theory: Ricoeur on Deception and Creative Understanding

In an interview in the *Frankfurter Allgemeine* in October 1989, Gadamer insisted that his early work on dialectic in Plato held even more importance for him than his *Truth and Method*.[55] The open-ended nature of questions and conversation, he explained, alone avoided the possibility of manipulation, which assertions, by contrast, encouraged. Political propaganda and deceptive, manipulative ways of "imposing one's beliefs" upon another, or "the Other", represent another dimension of the "mastery" imposed by "method" in science. Robert Sullivan shows how this antipathy to propaganda was bound up, even if only in part, with Gadamer's suspicion of the Nazi regime, but especially with his work on Plato and dialectic.[56] All the same, does Gadamer offer any resources for a critique of manipulative texts or discourse?

IV.1 "Doing Away with Idols": Self-Deception, Double Meaning and Suspicion

Paul Ricoeur (b. 1913) has formulated a sophisticated theory of hermeneutics which addresses, on one side, the need for suspicion and the problem of deception and manipulation, and on the other side a programme for the creative retrieval of understanding, especially on the basis of projected narrative-worlds and the creative opening of new "possibility". His work remains directly relevant to biblical studies, although he writes as a multi-disciplinary philosopher for whom the Bible is a source of faith but not a major part of his professional concerns.

Ricoeur presses numerous disciplines into the service of hermeneutical theory: theories of the will and action; phenomenology, psychoanalysis, structuralism and semiotics; and linguistics and theories of metaphor, symbol and narrative. His greatest genius, however, is that while sharing with Gadamer the task of dethroning the self as the centre of the stage, where it came to stand from Descartes to later modernity, he also

---

[53] Ernst Fuchs, *Hermeneutik* (4th edn, Tübingen: Mohr, 1970); *Studies of the Historical Jesus* (London: SCM Press, 1964); 'The New Testament and the Hermeneutical Problem' in J.M. Robinson and J.B. Cobb Jr (eds), *New Frontiers in Theology: II, The New Hermeneutic* (New York: Harper & Row, 1964), pp.111–45.

[54] Robert W. Funk, *Language, Hermeneutic and Word of God* (New York: Harper & Row, 1966).

[55] Gadamer's interview is translated as 'Gadamer on Gadamer', in Hugh J. Silverman (ed.), *Gadamer and Hermeneutics* (New York and London: Routledge, 1991), pp.13–19. See also Hans-Georg Gadamer, *Dialogue and Dialectic: Eight Studies on Plato* (New Haven, CT: Yale University Press, 1980).

[56] Robert R. Sullivan, *Political Hermeneutics: The Early Thinking of Hans-Georg Gadamer* (University Park: Pennsylvania State University Press, 1989), esp. pp.171–81.

resists the postmodern reduction of so de-centring the self that it becomes a mere amalgam of imposed role-performances rather than an active, responsible, accountable agent whose life has purpose, continuity and destiny. This emerges in his splendid climactic work *Oneself as Another* (French edition, 1990; English edition, 1992).[57]

Ricoeur's interest in a hermeneutic of the self began with work under his teacher Gabriel Marcel, for whom selves were never mere statistics or case-numbers, but named persons with existential identity. During the war years Ricoeur became a prisoner in Germany, and there engaged closely with the work of Karl Jaspers, Husserl and Heidegger. In his earliest phase of writing, his work on the human will and experiences of alienation found expression in his writings *Fallible Man* and *The Symbolism of Evil* (French edition, 1960; English edition, 1967). Ricoeur notes that this work constantly brought to his attention "double-meaning" expressions, in which evil or guilt might be expressed as stain, blot, burden, bondage, or estrangement. He writes, "To interpret is to understand a double meaning."[58] Hence, "I had to introduce a hermeneutical dimension into reflective thought."[59]

Since persons are fallible and are capable of self-deception as well as of deceiving others, *suspicion* is demanded to understand double meaning. Here Ricoeur appeals positively to the "three great masters of suspicion", namely Karl Marx, Friedrich Nietzsche and Sigmund Freud. Nietzsche, for example "interpreted" the text "the salvation of the soul" as disguised code for "the world revolves round me".[60] The truth-claim "God forgiveth him that repenteth" is for Nietzsche a disguised power-claim: "forgiveth him that submitteth himself to the priest".[61] Ricoeur, however, finds the most constructive model of suspicion in Freud's interpretation of dreams. Freud believed that in the dream-as-dreamed ("dream-content" or "dream-account") the self disguises wishes that may be too painful for the conscious mind to accept and face. Hence when one level of meaning is repressed, what is recounted to the psychoanalyst is a distorted, "scrambled" version, involving the displacement, condensation and other protective strategies.[62] Psychoanalytical hermeneutics comes into play because "the subject is never the subject one thinks it is".[63]

Ricoeur does not accept Freud's mechanistic, causal world-view, which, he shows, goes hand in hand with Freud's use of causal or economic metaphors. Nevertheless, like Dilthey and Apel and contrary to Gadamer, he recognizes the place of "explanation" alongside "understanding". The former provides "a hermeneutic of suspicion"; the latter, "a hermeneutic of retrieval". Hence in a very important succinct summary of this central concern, he observes: "*Hermeneutics seem to me to be animated by this double motivation:*

---

[57] Paul Ricoeur, *Oneself as Another* (Eng., Chicago: University of Chicago Press, 1992).

[58] Paul Ricoeur, *Freud and Philosophy. An Essay in Interpretation* (New Haven, CT and London: Yale University Press, 1970), p.8.

[59] Paul Ricoeur, *The Rule of Metaphor: Multidisciplinary Studies of the Creation of Meaning in Language* (London: Routledge & Kegan Paul, 1978), p.317.

[60] Friedrich Nietzsche, *Complete Works*, 18 vols (London: Allen & Unwin, 1909–13), vol. XVI, *The Antichrist*, p.186, Aphorism 43.

[61] Ibid., p.161, Aphorism 26.

[62] Ricoeur, *Freud and Philosophy*, p.93.

[63] Ibid., p.420.

willingness of suspect, willingness to listen."[64] Ricoeur speaks of faith in this context. Idols must be destroyed, but this may generate "faith that has undergone criticism, post-critical faith ... a second naïveté".[65]

This has direct relevance to issues in biblical studies. The axis of suspicion encourages *Ideologiekritik* of the text, and suspicion concerning the vested interests of the interpreter and the interpreter's community-traditions. What subtexts operate beneath even the biblical text and certainly the interpreter's goals, methods and conclusions? We begin to travel the road of social and ideological critique of "interest" explored further by Habermas, as well as issues of manipulation and power exposed by Michel Foucault and others.

IV.2 "Post-Critical Naïveté": Narrative, Time and the Wisdom Literature

Nevertheless Ricoeur's most brilliant work stands on the side of retrieval and creative understanding. In particular, he sees symbol as giving rise to thought, especially at the level of word; metaphor interactively creates understanding at the level of sentence or statement; narrative projects a "world" which belongs to a stable frame of temporal continuity in which disparate elements acquire coherence and intelligibility through "plot". His superb exposition of narrative plot comes especially in his three-volume *Time and Narrative*. The self discovers temporal continuity and coherence in the emplotment of narrative, where, as in Aristotle, isolated or seemingly random actions achieve coherence as part of a single, larger action, and the discontinuities of time, to which Augustine drew attention, assume a medium of "human" time in which memory (past), attention (present) and hope (future) offer not the abstract intelligibility of logic, but the temporal logic of purposive life:[66] "The dynamic of emplotment is to me the key to the relation between time and narrative."[67]

Ricoeur has a special interest in Job. In Job 42:1–6 divine transcendence and hiddenness cannot be transcribed by speech; nevertheless the Book of Job also yields the wonder that God does *speak*, speaking not *about* Job, but *to* Job.[68] Alongside the narrative and wisdom modes, which Ricoeur especially considers as worthy of wider hermeneutical attention, the prophetic address from God to humankind (whether or not in indirect terms) operates with the hymnic mode of human address to God (especially in the Psalms) and the familiar prescriptive mode of texts of law or spiritual direction. No single revelatory mode and no single model of hermeneutics can be allowed to eclipse the resources of the others.

Ricoeur's hermeneutics have to this extent encouraged the hermeneutical pluralism of goals and models that characterize the post-Gadamerian period. But it remains clear from *Time and Narrative* and *Oneself as Another* that Ricoeur does not wish hermeneutics to

---

[64] Ibid., p.27 (my italics).
[65] Ibid., p.28.
[66] Ricoeur, *Time and Narrative*, vol. 1, pp.5–51.
[67] Ibid., p.53.
[68] Paul Ricoeur, *The Conflict of Interpretation* (Evanston, IL: Northwestern University Press, 1974), p.461, and *Essays on Biblical Interpretation* (London: SPCK, 1981), pp.86–9.

collapse into a diversity that loses its overall coherence and sense of direction. He resists the unqualified postmodern turn that might be said to characterize Roland Barthes and Jacques Derrida, even if he appreciates their concerns in the context of intellectual life in the Paris of the later 1960s and 1970s, and he shares some of them. The greatness of Gadamer and especially Ricoeur lies in their capacity to address with sympathy the distrust and suspicions of postmodern contextualism, while insisting that life and truth also entail more.

V
Four Further Observations by Way of Conclusion

(1) Our discussion has underlined, first, the need for a multi-disciplinary approach to hermeneutics, as exemplified, even if not exemplified exhaustively, in Ricoeur. Schleiermacher rightly saw that hermeneutics could not perform a creative and genuinely critical function if it remained a service discipline for particular traditions of theology. But his bold and valid attempt to establish the subject as the "art of thinking" based on a transcendental critique nevertheless lacked adequate resources for sufficient self-criticism.

Schleiermacher also still fell prey to Kantian notions concerning the centrality of the human subject, and arguably he shared too many Romanticist assumptions about the priority of experience over texts, and the status of doctrines as only derivative residues left by creative experience. Gadamer exposes these weaknesses, although it is also arguable that he underestimates the complexity and subtlety of Schleiermacher not least in his recognition of the extent to which decisions of interpretative strategy shape where we place the emphasis in our hermeneutical agenda. I have tried to redress this imbalance in *New Horizons in Hermeneutics*.[69]

By contrast, Ricoeur draws on so many diverse critical disciplines as to remain aware of the limitations and biases of each. Most especially his appreciation of several distinct traditions of philosophy, including the analytical and inter-subjective, gives rise to a deep and rich philosophy of language and an account of human responsibility, agency, stable selfhood and interpersonal relations that offer the most constructive frame of reference for hermeneutical theory to date.

(2) As against Gadamer and postmodern approaches, the work of Paul Ricoeur shows how it may be possible to appreciate a wide plurality of hermeneutical approaches without subscribing to a radical pluralism of world-views. Thus his use of Freud's psychoanalytic of suspicion in no way carries with it an endorsement of Freud's mechanistic world-view. Ricoeur points out that Freud's very drawing of metaphors from economics and the physical sciences predisposes him towards such a world-view, which Ricoeur rejects as inadequate and ill-founded.

Recently Francis Watson has rightly warned us that the strenuous efforts of hermeneutical theorists to expose the inadequacy of merely causal explanations of life

---

[69] Thiselton, *New Horizons in Hermeneutics*, pp.216–36 and especially pp.558–64.

and texts has failed to shift the prejudices of those biblical scholars who regard secular pluralism as value-free and Christian theology as value-laden.[70] Theology, Watson rightly insists, cannot be excluded from biblical interpretation. His appreciation of a number of aspects of postmodernity makes his warnings and appeals all the more convincing.[71] To destroy idols and to learn to listen does not mean to disengage from theology. In another work I have argued that the very opposite is the case.[72]

(3) We have not had space to explore in this discussion the potential of speech-act theory for biblical interpretation. Some expositions remain shallow and disappointing, but others hold out the promise of new advances. J.G. du Plessis explores speech-act theory with reference to G.N. Leech's pragmatics; Dietmar Neufeld approaches 1 John on this basis; I have attempted to show some implications of speech-act theory for New Testament Christology.[73] More remains to be explored in this area. It brings a needed approach to language, and coheres closely, as Tyndale urged, with the functions, effects and presuppositions of biblical texts. All the same, this approach does not provide a comprehensive theory of language. Like other linguistic theories, its insights complement other dimensions, and it does not stand alone in its service to hermeneutics.

(4) Lack of space [that is, in the original guidelines for the article as it was published in 1998] necessitated our omitting a full discussion of Jürgen Habermas (b. 1929), as we might have wished. In his early work Habermas explored the role of "interests", broadly in the sense of vested interests, as one determining factor for what is deemed to *count as* knowledge or understanding in given social contexts.[74] In dialogue with Gadamer and Ricoeur in the 1970s he rejects a positivist or supposedly value-neutral view of social science.[75]

The struggle against manipulative interpretation has become probably the most urgent project of hermeneutics, as the mood of postmodernity, even if not its more technically presented themes and content, invades cultures, institutions, politics, society, religions and churches. We note how in religious traditions, smaller groups break off from mainline churches initially to experience new freedom and a greater sense of corporate self-identity, but too often the new freedoms become routinized into new institutional constraints and power-structures. Domination and authoritarianism on the part of a new leadership may become self-sustaining because most stable criteria for biblical

---

[70] Francis Watson, *Text, Church and World. Biblical Interpretation in Theological Perspective* (Edinburgh: T. & T. Clark, 1994), pp.1–14.

[71] Ibid., pp.79–154.

[72] Anthony C. Thiselton, *Interpreting God and the Postmodern Self: On Meaning, Manipulation and Promise* (Edinburgh: T. & T. Clark and Grand Rapids, MI: Eerdmans, 1995).

[73] J.G. du Plessis, 'Speech-Act Theory: Speech-Act Theory and New Testament Interpretation with Special Reference to G.N. Leech's Pragmatic Principles', in P.J. Hartin and J.H. Petzer (eds), *Text and Interpretation. New Approaches in the Criticism of the New Testament* (Leiden: Brill, 1991), pp.129–42; Dietmar Neufeld, *Re-conceiving Texts as Speech Acts. An Analysis of 1 John* (Biblical Interpretation series, 7 Leiden: Brill, 1994); and Thiselton, *New Horizons in Hermeneutics*, pp.283–307, and 'Luke's Christology, Speech-Act Theory, and the Problem of Dualism in Christology after Kant', in Joel B. Green and M. Turner (eds), *Jesus of Nazareth, Lord and Christ* (Carlisle: Paternoster Press and Grand Rapids, MI: Eerdmans, 1994), pp.453–72.

[74] J. Habermas, *Knowledge and Human Interests* (Boston, MA: Beacon Press, 1971; 2nd edn, London: Heinemann, 1978).

[75] J. Habermas, *Zur Logik der Sozialwissenschaften* (5th edn, Frankfurt: Suhrkamp, 1982); and *Legitimation Crisis* (Boston, MA: Beacon Press, 1975).

interpretation and for appropriate life-styles have become internalized to the instantaneous corporate moods of the group. The biblical writings come to be used manipulatively to validate the new power structures.

The same phenomenon occurs in other parts of society. If, with Ricoeur, we have to turn to "masters of suspicion", the work, but not the world-views, of Nietzsche, Freud, Foucault and Derrida may play a part in the struggle *against* manipulative interpretation.[76] Habermas rightly places these issues on the agenda, even if we should find it difficult to subscribe to all of his proposals as a whole. The issue of manipulation becomes even more central for hermeneutics with the rise of liberation theologies, feminist hermeneutics and postmodern approaches to texts.

---

[76] Cf. Thiselton, *Interpreting God and the Postmodern Self*, pp.3–45 and 121–64.

CHAPTER THREE

Resituating Hermeneutics in the Twenty-First Century: A Programmatic Reappraisal (New essay)

A self-critical retrospective review of the first two essays with the hindsight of 2004 is hardly likely to offer as many distinctive suggestions or modifications of ideas as those other six reappraisals that address more creative research in Parts II–VII. I begin by tracing whether or how the works produced after their publication in 1997 (including my commentary on 1 Corinthians) might suggest anything further about the shape of hermeneutical enquiry. Next, I suggest what further issues I ought to have included in these first two essays with the hindsight of five more recent years. I should have included a critical consideration of at very least three other areas of the subject, namely: (1) the problem of how to formulate theological hermeneutics without compromising the distinctive claims of either discipline; (2) an exposition of the tasks and value of reception history, including its relation to a coherent theological tradition in the light of polyphonic biblical texts; and (3) a fuller exposition of the capacity of hermeneutics to nurture "listening" and respect for "the other" as other, rather than on readers' or interpreters' own terms.

Since I explore reception-history also in essays 18 and 40, I have ensured that each essay adopts an approach from a particular angle to avoid overlap. Thus this Essay 3 explores especially horizons of expectation, successive textual readings, responses to Räisänen's critical claims, and openness to texts; Essay 18 explores the different intellectual pedigrees of different versions of reception history or Wirkungsgeschichte; while Essay 40 focuses on poetics, the work of Tracy, extra-linguistic traditions, and defamiliarization.

I

The Range and Scope of Hermeneutics Illustrated from the Five Works Produced Before and After 1996

In the first essay of Part I, "Thirty Years of Hermeneutics" I traced how three of my works up to 1996 reflected understandings of the modern discipline of hermeneutics. *The Two Horizons* (1980) addressed the issue of *active engagement* between biblical material and today's readers, alongside the need for due recognition of differences between these two respective horizons. *New Horizons in Hermeneutics* (1992) concerned the *transformative* impact of the Bible upon readers, as well as challenging its readers, where necessary, to transform their modes of reading. *Interpreting God and the Postmodern Self* (1995) considered, we noted, strategies of *disguise and manipulation* deployed by readers and interpreters that had the effect of emasculating the biblical text as a vehicle of revelatory encounter and reducing it merely to an instrument for self-affirmation, control, or oppressive power.

Two more volumes in this series of hermeneutical investigations postdate the essays above of 1996 and 1998, and now also invite brief comment. *The Promise of Hermeneutics* (1999) includes a discussion of the contribution of speech-act theory to hermeneutics, and draws on narrative theory to explore issues of narrative-time and of "polyphonic" voices in narrative material. These contributions receive comment and some critical appraisal in specific essays included in other sections of this present volume.

A fifth work, *The First Epistle to the Corinthians: A Commentary on the Greek Text* (2000), also postdates the two essays above. This reflects more broadly traditional, multiform, research that involves especially historical, linguistic and theological enquiry. However, it constitutes, no less, a contribution to hermeneutics for all that.

It is deeply ironic, from the standpoint of biblical studies, that today it is this fifth area or dimension that often suffers most critical questioning, almost as if other more recent and supposedly more glamorous methods and models of interpretation had overtaken it. Some claim, for example, that it constitutes an antiquarian approach in which the text becomes locked up in the past. Others also claim that this approach entails the so-called genetic fallacy according to which "meaning" is mistakenly identified with originating motivations or forces behind a text. Such criticisms are wide of the mark.

It is too easy for some to forget that probably the most sophisticated and innovative nineteenth-century hermeneutical theorist, Friedrich Schleiermacher, urged the importance of the newly conceived and newly formulated area of "Introduction to the New Testament" on the ground that it is essential for making the texts of the New Testament come alive in the present not least *for Christian preaching*. During his years as Professor of Theology in the newly founded University of Berlin, Schleiermacher preached Sunday by Sunday in Trinity Church. His thirty-volume corpus of writings includes ten volumes on theology, ten volumes on philosophy and a further ten of sermons. It should not detract from its role in hermeneutical reflection that in many universities and colleges today as well as in the twentieth century, the subject of New Testament Introduction was and is often taught badly as the province of "scientific" technicians, historians of the ancient world and mere antiquarians.

Schleiermacher writes, "Only historical interpretation can do justice to the rootedness of the New Testament authors in their time and place."[1] He adds, "Each text was addressed to specific people, and their writings could not be properly understood in the future unless these first readers could understand them. But these first readers would have looked for what was specifically related to their own situations."[2] Yet Schleiermacher is no mere nineteenth-century romanticist concerned only with origins. He declares that understanding entails "consideration of two factors: the content of the text and *its range of effects*".[3] I have argued elsewhere that the so-called genetic fallacy, which is repeatedly attributed to Schleiermacher, cannot apply to his hermeneutical theory and strategies of reading.[4] Schleiermacher writes that without historical discipline

---

[1]   F.D.E. Schleiermacher, *Hermeneutics: The Handwritten Manuscripts* (edited by H. Kimmerle, Missoula, MT: Scholars Press, 1977), p.104.

[2]   Schleiermacher, *Hermeneutics*, p.107.

[3]   Ibid., p.151 (my italics).

[4]   Anthony C. Thiselton, *New Horizons in Hermeneutics* (London: HarperCollins, 1992), pp.559–60. For a definition of the fallacy see p.59.

the interpreter becomes a "nebulist"; if historical enquiry becomes a dominating end in itself, the interpreter is guilty of "pedantry".[5]

Part of the problem that gives rise to these misguided attacks on what many call "the historical-critical method" (as if there were only one!) too often springs from an inadequate awareness of what is actually involved in this kind of approach. It is worth making a very brief excursus, therefore, into the work that lay behind the commentary on 1 Corinthians to elucidate this, before we return to the main themes of this paper. It so happens that at a conference held in 2001 mainly for classicists I was requested to describe these processes.[6] I reported as follows.

(a) I engaged at every point with issues of Greek lexicography, syntax and grammar, and sought to establish a sound text on the basis of careful textual criticism. (b) I produced a fresh English translation, although I added the proviso that every proposed translation results from interactive judgments about lexicography, semantics, semiotics, exegesis, textual criticism, hermeneutics, historical reconstruction and theology. (c) I evaluated, and not merely replicated, the flood of research literature on the culture, social life and theology of the church in Paul's Corinth, together with research monographs and papers on particular passages or Greek words. (d) I sought to address "the varied range of serious and *responsible questions* that *readers of today* will bring to the text". This accords with the most basic and elementary principles of hermeneutics.

(e) Perhaps more distinctively I also offered a selective account of the *history of effects* (*Wirkungsgeschichte*) of a number of passages in accordance with the methods proposed by H.-R. Jauss.[7] However, in view of concerns about undue length I was requested to select only those examples in which the continuities and discontinuities of the history of reception were arguably the most significant or striking.[8] (f) Again more distinctively, in my Introduction I sought to identify resonances between Corinthian attitudes and what I have called "the postmodern mood" or "ethos" found in various quarters today. Social constructionism and the perceived "recognition" of a self-generated "virtual reality" promoted by a consumerist-orientated rhetoric are hallmarks of a postmodern mood, and tend in these quarters to be privileged over against given traditions and critical rationality.[9]

The interrelationship between these specific tasks entirely reflects what is known in hermeneutics as the hermeneutical circle. It is out of the question to settle upon a proposed English translation of the Greek until every other possible aspect of the total comprehensive enquiry has been completed. Yet the interpreter or commentator must begin with provisional, corrigible, working judgements about proposed translations and a proposed text before any further step can be taken. In none of this work was I conscious

---

[5] Schleiermacher, *Hermeneutics*, p.205.

[6] Paper delivered in The International Centre for the History of Slavery, University of Nottingham, 17 January 2001.

[7] Cf. H.-R. Jauss, *Literaturgeschichte als Provokation* (Frankfurt: Suhrkamp, 1970) and *Toward an Aesthetic of Reception* (Eng., Minneapolis: University of Minnesota Press, 1982).

[8] Anthony C. Thiselton, The *First Epistle to the Corinthians: A Commentary on the Greek Text* (Grand Rapids, MI: Eerdmans and Carlisle: Paternoster, 2000), pp.196–204, 276–86, 330–44, 479–82, 531–40, 658–61, 998–1026, 1306–14.

[9] Thiselton, *First Epistle*, pp.12–17, 40–43, 50–51, 75, 314, 548, 1002, 1054–9, 1259.

of restricting my attention to a "historical paradigm", and certainly not as *an alternative* to a different paradigm of "literature", theology, reader-response theory, rhetorical criticism, or philosophical hermeneutics. Although I endorse much of his argument in his book *Biblical Interpretation* (1988), I took gentle issue with Robert Morgan about his over-readiness to see these "paradigms" (his term in this context) as in effect competing rather than complementary ones.[10]

Several reviewers of my commentary offer observations that appear to confirm these perceptions. One speaks of "Thiselton's ability to *integrate* exegetical scholarship with current hermeneutical work … a major achievement in integrative work".[11] Another writes, "Thiselton's scholarship and hermeneutic expertise is evident throughout ... [and] brings the first century within the horizon of the 21st century".[12] A third sees the work's greatest innovation in "its combination of linguistic theory with philosophically informed and theologically directed exegesis".[13] Grant R. Osborne places his reputation on the line by writing for the publishers a commendation of truly over-generous proportions: "Thiselton is, I believe, the leading hermeneutical thinker of his generation. Now he has used his deep hermeneutical knowledge to produce what is one of the finest commentaries on any biblical book, let alone 1 Corinthians."

I include these comments not for their praise, but for their recognition of the *integrative nature of multi-disciplinary* interpretation and hermeneutics *in action*. I readily concede that the relative weight of "historical" and "literary" emphases will depend not on *a priori* abstract theory, but upon *a posteriori* judgements in the light of such particularities as genre and other contingent, textual, factors. All the same, hermeneutics embraces all of the questions addressed in my series of attempted contributions: questions about *active engagement* between readers and texts; questions about the *transformative* capacity of biblical texts; questions about the need to expose and to correct *manipulative* readings of biblical texts; and questions about *historical, literary,* and *theological* factors not least in the light of the resources bequeathed by modern specialist biblical research.

II
Three Further Questions Including How to Formulate a "Theological Hermeneutics"

I turn now to consider issues that in retrospect I wish that I had included in the proposed agenda formulated in the first two essays written six or more years ago. I should now place at least three further questions on the agenda in both the first and the second article. (1) Is it possible to formulate a more explicitly *theological hermeneutics* than I have done in my work without this ceasing thereby to remain *"hermeneutics"*? (2) What role and importance should we assign to the *history of reception of texts*? Might reception-history

---

10   Anthony C. Thiselton, "On Models and Methods: A Conversation with Robert Morgan", in D.J.A. Clines, S.E. Fowl, and S.E. Porter (eds), *The Bible in Three Dimensions* (Sheffield: JSOT Supplement Series, 87, 1990), pp.337–56. Cf. Robert Morgan with John Barton, *Biblical Interpretation* (Oxford: OUP, 1988).

11   Ruth Anne Reese, Review in *The Asbury Theological Journal*, Fall 2002/Spring 2003.

12   Barbara Stafford, Review in *Scripture Bulletin* 31, July 2001 [first page of review].

13   Alexandra Brown, Review, in *Interpretation*, January 2002 [first page of review].

also offer constructive resonances with my work on "polyphonic voices" while retaining a concern for coherence?[14] (3) How may we best identify and promote the habit of *respect for the "other"*, and of *listening* to the other *as "other"* as the heart of hermeneutical endeavour? Further, under this third heading, how may we best expose and resist *manipulative* interpretation and rhetoric?

The very question about theological hermeneutics poses a dilemma. If hermeneutics is genuinely theological, might not this hermeneutical approach became merely subsumed within, and subservient to, some prior system of theology? Yet, conversely, if hermeneutics is permitted to remain an authentic free-standing, transcendental, independent discipline, in what sense does it still give serious priority to its status as explicitly *theological* hermeneutics?

I have often wished that both *The Two Horizons* (1980) and *New Horizons in Hermeneutics* (1992) had embodied a more *explicit*, rather than *implicit*, Christian theology. Yet how could I have achieved this in the face of Schleiermacher's contention, with which I fully agree, that the kind of hermeneutics that *would best serve* theology for the good of theology itself would be a transcendental, independent, critical, discipline? It must successfully resist reduction and domestication into a merely "instrumental" hermeneutics that would merely be servant to the system of theology that it came about to affirm as "right".

Schleiermacher rightly argued that "regional" hermeneutics (as he sometimes terms instrumental hermeneutics) usually operates only *in retrospect* to eliminate "*mis*understandings that might conflict with the prior system of thought into which it has become, in effect, assimilated".[15] This kind of hermeneutics provides mere corporate or individual self-affirmation, rather than offering challenge and capacity for change. It fails to initiate, and provide tests for, meaning and truth *in* (rather than *after*) the actualization of biblical texts in processes of reading and communication. It concerns only retrospective reflection. If it serves only self-affirmation, it is little better than Richard Rorty's neo-pragmatic hermeneutics of "winners" in a postmodern key, presented in theological dress.

Nevertheless this articulates only one side of the dilemma. For might it not be argued, on the other side, that "understanding" should accord with the nature of that which it seeks to understand, and that in the case of theology and theological texts this must be an explicitly theological understanding? Notably Karl Barth and T.F. Torrance, among others, have set out a classic case for this view.[16] Further, Francis Watson, Kevin

---

[14] I have used the term "polyphonic voices" in my discussions of the plurality of "voices" in the Book of Job, in George Eliot's *Adam Bede*, and especially in Fyodor Dostoevsky's *The Brothers Karamazov*. This material appears below as Essay 40, and first appeared in R. Lundin, C. Walhout and A.C. Thiselton, *The Promise of Hermeneutics* (Grand Rapids, MI: Eerdmans, and Carlisle: Paternoster, 1999), pp.172–82. The importance of this dimension as a plural literary device in Dostoevsky found expression in Mikhail M. Bakhtin, especially *Problems of Dostoevsky's Poetics* (Ann Arbor, MI: Ardis, 1973); cf. also Malcolm V. Jones, "The Brothers Karamazov: the Whisper of God" in his *Dostoevsky after Bakhtin* (Cambridge: CUP, 1990).

[15] F. Schleiermacher, *Hermeneutics: The Handwritten Manuscripts* (ed. H. Kimmerle), (Missoula, MT: Scholars Press, 1977) "MS 1", pp.41–49 (1805, 1809) and "the Compendium", pp.108–12 (1819).

[16] Karl Barth, *Church Dogmatics*, especially II:1 (Eng., Edinburgh: T. & T. Clark, 1957), sect. 26 "The Knowability of God", and sect. 27 "The Limits of the Knowledge of God", pp.63–254; e.g. "God is known by God and by God alone", sect. 27, p.179. Cf. T.F. Torrance, *Theological Science* (London: OUP, 1969),

Vanhoozer, Christopher Seitz and Walter Moberly, also among others, have convincingly demonstrated that there is nothing whatever value-neutral about approaches to biblical hermeneutics that deliberately retreat from making theological judgements, or from embodying beliefs drawn from Christian theology.[17]

I shall argue that any attempt to formulate a distinctively theological hermeneutic cannot avoid engaging with the following four issues, among various others.

(1) What role is played by theological claims about the effect of human fallenness on the capacities of human reason, judgement, wisdom and understanding, in undertaking hermeneutical explorations or proposing hermeneutical advances? In New Testament studies the work of G. Bornkamm and especially Stanley Stowers on Paul's evaluation of human reason suggests more positive attitudes towards reason than some theologians concede, but the question must be assessed responsibly, with due regard also to the wider dimensions of transcendental reason and wisdom in human understanding.[18]

(2) The second issue concerns the role of *dialectic*. I shall argue that Gadamer's careful distinction between "problems" and *dialectic* offers another important key to a way forward that may do justice to both sides of the dilemma formulated above. "Problems" inhabit a more abstract, general and systematic domain than dialectic. They easily become reified. Gadamer comments, "The concept of the problem is clearly an abstraction"; it has become detached and abstracted "from the questions that in fact first reveal it".[19] He continues, "Such a 'problem' has fallen out of *the motivated context of questioning, from which it receives the clarity of its sense. Hence it is insoluble ...* 'Problems' have lost their original character as 'real questions'" (my italics).[20] However, dialectic is dynamic, and is rooted in the contingent dialogue of hermeneutical understanding, without yielding to mere fragmentation or incoherence. It offers a primary resource for theological hermeneutics that may avoid collapsing each side of the dilemma outlined above into the other. We shall explore the implications of this approach in due course.

(3) I shall argue that the phenomenon of *actualization* in hermeneutics resonates closely with a dispositional account of *belief* in theology, and the two offer complementary

---

pp.1–54, 75-85, 131-40 and 173-202; also *God and Rationality* (London: OUP, 1971), pp.3–28 and 137–92; and less directly *Divine Meaning: Studies in Patristic Hermeneutics* (Edinburgh: T. & T. Clark 1995), pp.10–74.

[17] Francis Watson, *Text, Church, and World: Biblical Interpretation in Theological Perspective* (Edinburgh: T. & T. Clark, 1994) and *Text and Truth* (Grand Rapids, MI: Eerdmans 1997); Kevin J. Vanhoozer, *Is there a Meaning in this Text?* (Grand Rapids, MI: Zondervan, 1998); Christopher R. Seitz, *Figured Out: Typology and Providence in Christian Scripture* (Louisville, KY: Westminster John Knox, 2001), esp. pp.13–68; R.W.L. Moberly, *The Bible, Theology and Faith* (Cambridge: CUP, 2000). More broadly, Bernard Lonergan, *Insight: A Study of Human Understanding* (New York: Harper & Row, 1978) and *Method in Theology* (London: DLT, 1972) offer further major resources on these issues.

[18] G. Bornkamm, "Faith and Reason in Paul", in *Early Christian Experience* (London: SCM, 1969), pp.29–46; and S.K. Stowers, "Paul on the Use and Abuse of Reason in Paul" in D.L. Balch, E. Fergusson and Wayne Meeks (eds), *Greeks, Romans, and Christians: Essays in Honor of A.J. Malherbe* (Minneapolis, MN: Fortress, 1990), pp.253–86.

[19] Hans-Georg Gadamer, *Truth and Method* (2nd Eng. edn, London: Sheed & Ward, 1989), p.376.

[20] Ibid., p.376.

resources for theological hermeneutics. In a dispositional analysis what a given belief or network of beliefs *amounts to* may be seen in terms of the believer's disposition to respond in ways that manifest this belief in attitudes, action, or life, when contingent situations evoke such responses. It deals in the cash-currency of belief, and its relation to life.[21] Wittgenstein writes, "Look and see what are the consequences of this belief, where it takes us."[22] One criterion of understanding, he observes, is that (for example, in mathematics) a person who "understands" can exclaim, "Now I can go on!"[23] Theological hermeneutics can be *neither a closed nor an abstract system* that remains unrelated to human life.

In the Pauline epistles this approach relates closely to the issue of "bodily" obedience. Ernst Käsemann rightly defines the use of the Greek word σῶμα (*sôma*), *body* in Paul as denoting "that piece of the world that we are". He writes, "In the bodily obedience of the Christian, carried out as the service of God in the world of every day, the Lordship of Christ finds visible expression, and only when this visible expression takes personal shape does the whole thing become credible as Gospel message."[24] Explorations that co-jointly take full account of hermeneutical actualization and a dispositional account of belief yield not an abstract, closed, belief-system, but regular patterns of *contingent* linguistic and extra-linguistic action that motivate both critical *reflection* and *self-involving* language, stance and action within the public world of everyday human life.[25]

(4) The fourth resource relates to the *reception history* of texts that shape theology, and which are shaped by theology. This approach involves tracing how the readings and interpretations of specific biblical texts in "motivating situations" are *influenced by* diverse understandings of the texts, and how in turn they *exercise influence upon* divergent traditions of understanding. The second of these tasks is necessary both for hermeneutics as such and all the more for theological hermeneutics. Some prefer to rename reception history (or more especially *Wirkungsgeschichte*) "the History of the Influences of Texts", although this influence is both influence *by*, and influence *upon*, their reading and use. This double dimension has given rise to a dual translation of *Wirkungsgeschichte* as both "effec*tive* history" and "effec*ted* history".

To try to expound each of these four resources would take us beyond the limits of this reappraisal of our two introductory essays. We shall return to these issues in the final essay of this volume when I seek to offer a retrospective reappraisal of Part VII. Meanwhile, with the judgement of hindsight, I should now have wished to include a section on reception history in each of these first two essays. Hence I offer a brief exploration of this area now.

---

[21] For one of many such approaches see Dallas M. High, *Language, Persons and Belief* (New York: OUP, 1967).

[22] L. Wittgenstein, *Philosophical Investigations* (Oxford: Blackwell, Ger. and Eng., 2nd edn, 1967), sect. 578.

[23] Ibid., sect. 151; cf. also sects 183 and 321-3.

[24] E. Käsemann, *New Testament Questions of Today* (Eng., London: SCM, 1969), p.135; cf. pp.132-7.

[25] On dispositional accounts of belief, see H.H. Price, *Belief* (London: Allen & Unwin, 1969), pp.29-91, 241-301, and throughout.

III
The Reception History of Texts

The history of reception concerns the impact of texts and *of successive readings* and interpretations of texts on subsequent generations of readers after a first reading. This is more than a history of exegesis, although it may include this. It concerns the impact of texts upon ecclesial and non-ecclesial communities, and also continuities and contrasts between manipulative and less consciously manipulative or less manipulative readings of texts. Hans Robert Jauss traces a history of the reception of literary texts that displays a thread of both continuities and discontinuities, often with a discernable, stable core, but sometimes revealing a disruptive pluralism. This sets the stage for a discussion of criteria of meaning and plural interpretations.

This may serve an additional goal of exploring how the biblical writings may serve as a foundation for Christian theology, not least because (not in spite of the fact that) they often speak with plural or "polyphonic" voices. To expect otherwise is to forget that at the very heart of hermeneutics stands a dialectical relation between particularity and universality, between contingency and coherence, and between a plurality of interpretations and a stable core of tradition. In this respect Hegel and Dilthey began to identify some seminal aspects of the subject, although neither of them adequately avoided what Wittgenstein called "our craving for generality".[26]

III.1 *Gadamer, Jauss and Plurality: Performance and Provocation*

Interpreters often perceive Gadamer's emphasis on multiple, contingent actualizations or "performances" of games, festivals, or plays in the theatre as a radically pluralist hermeneutics. No two actualizations of understanding and meaning are *replications*, just as play in successive games is never exactly "the same", without their ceasing to be games, and becoming contrived stylizations. However, Georgia Warnke redresses the balance in her essay "Prejudice and Tradition" by showing that for Gadamer "historical situatedness" and radical historical finitude constitute *only a part*, albeit an important part, of a wider picture.[27] Many of Gadamer's interpreters and critics seek to emphasize the *discontinuities and disruptions* of traditions and history more strongly than Gadamer, arguably perhaps, has done.

Hans Robert Jauss, Gadamer's former student, finds a place among these interpreters and sympathetic critics. Jauss draws much from Gadamer, which he utilizes for his pioneering work on reception history (*Rezeptionsgeschichte*). His explorations relate closely to the concept of "effective history" (*Wirkungsgeschichte*), to "the history of effects", or to "effected history", in Gadamer. (We noted above reasons for these multiple terms.) Central to Jauss's work stands the notion of a *horizon of expectation*. He derives this in part from Gadamer, but also from Husserl's phenomenology of perception, together with Karl Mannheim's utilization of the

---

[26] L. Wittgenstein, *The Blue and Brown Books* (Oxford: Blackwell, 1969), pp.17 and 18.
[27] G. Warnke, *Gadamer, Hermeneutics, Tradition and Reason* (Cambridge: Polity Press, 1987), pp.73–106.

concept in the social sciences.[28] Successive actualizations of reading texts *shape and reshape subsequent horizons of expectation.*[29] The expectations shaped within these horizons may be *fulfilled* or *disappointed, frustrated* or *subverted* by surprise, *affirmed* or *refuted.*[30] This plurality of effects suggests to Jauss that Gadamer may have overestimated the degree of continuity in this process. Disruption and even *"provocation"* may often characterize these successive actualizations of meaning and understanding.[31]

We discuss and compare the varied influences that shape the two respective emphases first on *Wirkungsgeschichte* (history of effects) in Gadamer, and second on *Rezeptionsgeschichte* (history of reception) in Jauss, in Essay 18 of this collection ("The Holy Spirit in 1 Corinthians: Exegesis and Reception-History in the Patristic Era"). We need not replicate this comparison here, since I attempt to avoid overlap between these essays as far as possible. We also explore reception history from other angles in Essay 40, "Dialogue, Dialectic and Temporal Horizons". But in this present essay I focus mainly on horizons of expectation, successive readings of texts and differences between them (illustrated from parable-interpretation), and their significance as a response to Räisänen, and "open" listening to the text; in Essay 40 I focus especially upon poetics, the relation to Tracy's approach, extra-linguistic tradition, sociology of literature, and defamiliarization.

III.2 Jauss and Successive Readings of Biblical Texts: Changed Horizons of Expectation

How does Jauss's theory of aesthetic reception or reception history address issues of biblical hermeneutics and less directly of theological formation?

Jauss distinguishes between horizons of expectation brought to texts during *first reading*, and the reshaped horizons of expectations generated by such readings and that engage in turn with the same texts on *second, third, or subsequent, readings.* This changing plurality of expectations, which makes further impacts and wields further influences, on understanding and subsequent action regularly confronts every biblical expositor, biblical specialist, or biblical preacher, as a matter of concern and reflection for hermeneutical and interpretative strategies.

How, for example, can we read the Parable of the Pharisee and the Tax Collector (Luke 18:9–14), or the Parable of the Labourers in the Vineyard (Matthew 20:1–16), or the Parable of the Good Samaritan (Luke 10:29–37), with *the same "effect" on a second or third reading,* or twenty centuries after they were spoken, as the effect made by their first reading, or by their first oral utterance? I utilized these examples in *The Two Horizons,* with reference to modes of parable-interpretation in Walter Wink, Ernst Fuchs, and John

---

[28] H.R. Jauss, *Toward an Aesthetic of Reception* (Minneapolis: University of Minnesota Press, 1982), p.xii (from Introduction by Paul de Man), especially "Thesis 3" in "Literary History as Challenge to Literary Theory" in *Reception*, pp.25–8, "Thesis 4", pp.28–32, and on Mannheim, under Thesis 7, p.40.

[29] "Rereading" a text can reflect, and bring about, reshapings of horizons of expectation; see Jauss on Michael Riffaterre, in *Reception*, pp.143–6.

[30] Jauss, "Literary History as Challenge" in *Reception*, p.25.

[31] A.C. Thiselton, *The Two Horizons: New Testament Hermeneutics and Philosophical Description* (Grand Rapids, MI: Eerdmans, 1980), pp.12–15, 335–45 and 352.

Dominic Crossan. We now "know", after repeated readings, that the Pharisee has come to be typified as the "bad" character; but on the occasion of a first hearing or reading, the verdict on the "good" Pharisee would have caused surprise, consternation and shock. Even so, the work of these three scholars, as well as mine, tended to focus only on a "first" reading.

It is important for biblical hermeneutics, therefore, that *Jauss distinguishes between the effects and dynamics of successive readings.* He calls a "first" horizon of expectation, that is, the horizon projected by the first reading, the horizon of *aesthetic* experience, or sometimes the horizon of *literary* expectation. He calls subsequent horizons, horizons of "lived experience". This recalls the notions of "life-worlds" in Husserl, and "life" (*Leben*) and "lived experience" (*Erlebnis;* cf. *Erleben* and *Nacherleben*) in Dilthey. The aesthetic or literary level of reading raises questions about genre, about literary conventions of the day, and about style and form. But literary conventions change over the generations. Hence the horizon of the text may become *alien* to a later generation of readers; it may even appear *"provocative"*. Horizons of expectation that earlier engaged *positively* with the text may now, through aesthetic distance, either stand *in tension* with the text or, alternatively, may become renewed and revitalized through, for example, surprise or shock. The power of a text to survive, and to retain its power, through multiple changes of horizons of expectation and still "speak" creatively is the mark of a "classic".

When texts continue to tell creative stories or communicate creative values anew over the generations, second and subsequent readings move beyond the literary or aesthetic level to challenge, or to interact with, the life-worlds of readers, and the cultural and social worlds of their communities. In Gadamer's terms something "more" may "arise" when two sharply differing horizons of expectations engage with the text. Jauss looks in the direction of a more than a passive "fusion" of horizons, projecting ways more active and perhaps less comfortable and more pluralist than those that Gadamer expounds.

III.3 Luz and Räisänen on History of Influences: Polyphonic Voices?

Some view this very disruption and pluralism, however, as suggesting a negative assessment of the relation between readings of the biblical material and Christian theology. Heikki Räisänen expounds such negative and sceptical conclusions. However, he begins with three entirely valid observations. First, he argues that the "effective history", or "history of effects", of biblical texts have been largely neglected in biblical interpretation with unfortunate results.[32] Second, he rightly distinguishes between the mere "history of exegesis", which falls short of reception-history, and the "effective history" of biblical texts as *"influences"*. He alludes in particular to Ulrich Luz's work on "history of influences" in his commentary on Matthew.[33] Luz views "the reception and actualization" of biblical texts as *"influences"*, most especially and notably "in sermons, in canon law, in psalms, in art, in the actions and sufferings of the church".[34] (I note this with

---

[32] H. Räisänen, "The 'Effective History' of the Bible: A Challenge to Biblical Scholarship", in his *Challenge to Biblical Interpretation, Essays 1991–2001* (Leiden: Brill, 2001), pp.263–82.
[33] Ibid., p.264 n.5.
[34] Ibid., p.269.

further comment in Essay 18 below on this subject.) Third, Räisänen also insists that a study of the influences of biblical texts should not be restricted to those within the church.[35] This third point is also valid. Nietzsche's reading of Paul, for example, is part of the deeper, wider picture of the history of influences, and should be assigned an important place especially in assessing and comparing divergent interpretations of Paul.

All the same, Räisänen moves onto more controversial ground. He first rejects the view found in Peter Stuhlmacher and others that "the effective history of the Bible is practically identical with the formation of the great confessional traditions in the churches".[36] In as far as the history of influences includes, and ought to include, such interpreters as Nietzsche and Marx, this view is strictly valid as it stands. However, in the context in which Stuhlmacher and Räisänen debate it, this idea becomes transposed into the related but distinct issue of whether we regard exegetical and interpretative traditions of the understandings of biblical texts, as well as the biblical texts themselves, as legitimate foundations for Christian theology.

The view that "Church History" may be viewed as the history of biblical interpretation has impressive advocates. Gerhard Ebeling, for example, entitled his Inaugural Lecture at Tübingen in 1947, "Church History as the History of the Exposition of Holy Scripture".[37] Karlfried Froelich defended this approach in his Inaugural Lecture as Professor of Church History in Princeton Theological Seminary.[38] Froelich writes:

> "Understanding" a biblical text cannot stop with the elucidation of its prehistory and of its historical *Sitz im Leben*, with its focus on the intention of the author. Understanding must take into account the text's post-history as the paradigm of the text's own historicity, i.e. as the way the text itself can function as a source of self-interpretation in a variety of contexts, and thus through its historical interpretations is participating in the shaping of life.[39]

Räisänen expounds a negative view with some force in his essay "The New Testament in Theology".[40] Christian doctrine, he asserts, cannot be based upon the New Testament because "the New Testament has turned out to be filled with theological contradictions ... [for example] different expectations of the future and different notions of salvation".[41] Attempts to identify a unifying factor fail. He includes among what he views as *unsuccessful* attempts to seek a "unity", especially James Dunn's *Unity and Diversity in the New Testament* (1990), which he dismisses as offering no more than "a thin and elusive bond". He concludes, "There is no direct path from historical study to present-day application."[42]

---

[35] Ibid., pp.271–2, 81.

[36] Ibid., p.265.

[37] Reprinted in G. Ebeling, *The Word of God as Tradition* (Eng., Philadelphia, PA: Fortress, 1968), pp.11–38.

[38] K. Froelich, "Church History and the Bible" in M.S. Burrows and P. Rorem (eds), *Biblical Hermeneutics in Historical Perspective* (Grand Rapids, MI: Eerdmans, 1991), pp.1–15.

[39] Froelich, "Church History and the Bible", p.9.

[40] Räisänen, "The New Testament in Theology" in *Challenge*, pp.227–49.

[41] Ibid., p.229.

[42] Ibid., p.230. For a part-reply to these claims see Peter Balla, *Challenges to New Testament Theology* (Peabody, MA: Hendrickson, 1998).

The work of Jauss, on the other hand, contrary to Räisänen's interpretation, seems to me to demonstrate the possibility of the reverse, namely how a necessary plurality of actualizations can be perceived not as "theological contradictions", but as the multiple voices required for a polyphonic harmony built from complementary viewpoints. These may be needed to provide a more complex and wide-ranging vision of a series of related questions and responses than a single writer could readily grasp and communicate within a single perspective. In 1742, as I have noted in the second essay above, J.M. Chladenius made the role of "viewpoint" (*Sehe-Punkt*) a major explanatory category in his treatise on hermeneutics.[43]

In literary theory Robert Alter has presented this argument about several biblical narratives, notably concerning the supposed "doublets" of different accounts of the call of David to kingship (1 Samuel 16 and 17).[44] In 1 Samuel 16, especially vv.12–13 the narrative tradition focuses upon the role of divine election and providence; in 1 Samuel 17 through to 2 Samuel 5:5 the narrative traces the ups and downs of the process of the call in human history, seen in "human" terms and viewpoints as taking place in "the brawling chaos" of everyday life.[45] Walter Moberly makes similar claims about complementary "points of view" especially in Genesis and Exodus.[46]

Long before engaging with Räisänen, I argued that the kind of analysis of "polyphonic voices" pioneered by Mikhail Bakhtin in his interpretation of Dostoevsky offered a frame of reference that facilitated our appreciation of such encounters with multiple or "polyphonic" voices. Multiple voices can communicate theological insights that spill over the limits of what any single writer or "school" can convey. I devote part of Essay 40 to a more detailed examination of these texts, so we need not explore them further in this essay.

Many of the Church Fathers took this basic dialectic of unity and plurality in their stride. They know well that (to borrow the terminology of Jauss) in the to-and-fro of biblical interpretation, as different individuals or traditions read the same passages sometimes in different generations or eras, and against the backgrounds of different situations, *horizons of expectation* are not uniform: some expectations become subject to frustration, or to being thwarted, surprised, or renewed. Yet these variations of expectation promote an "openness to tradition" that enhances engagement with texts, and enlarges and extends the horizons of the self *to listen to "the other"*.

Gadamer observes that this may serve as *a correction to self-deception*. He writes, "Every experience worthy of the name thwarts an expectation [that is, it never replicates exactly what we imagine or expect], but such expectation, thereby, may turn out in the process to have been 'something that deceived us and held us captive'."[47] This "*openness* to tradition" entails "openness to the other ... recognizing that I myself must accept some things that are against me, even though no one else forces me to do so".[48] This is precisely

---

43 J.M. Chladenius, *Einleitung zur richtigen Auslegung vernünftiger Reden und Schriften* (1742, reprinted Düsseldorf: Stern, 1969) sect. 194.

44 Robert Alter, *The Art of Biblical Narrative* (New York: Basic Books, 1981), pp.147–54.

45 Ibid., p.154.

46 R.W.L. Moberly, *At the Mountain of God* (Sheffield: JSOT Suppl. 22, 1983), pp.29–34.

47 Gadamer, *Truth and Method*, p.356.

48 Ibid., p.361.

not to be "captivated by dogma", but open to hear and to be challenged and changed:[49] "Anyone who listens is fundamentally open."[50]

This principle constitutes a key hermeneutical insight. It finds critically important expression also as a principle of Christian theology in the thought of Luther, Calvin, Barth, Ebeling and Bonhoeffer. Luther insists that it is when the Word of God encounters us as "our adversary" (*adversarius noster*) that the effect of the Bible as Scripture is at its most transformative. Dietrich Bonhoeffer expresses this axiom robustly. He writes, "If it is I who say where God will be, I will always find there a [false] God who in some way corresponds to me, is agreeable to me, fits in with my nature. But if it is God who says where he will be … that place is the cross of Christ."[51]

Pluralities of interpretation that emerge in the history of reception, then, do not simply cancel each other out, or invite dismissal as mere contradictions. They are usually born out of different contexts, situations, pre-understandings, and horizons. Far from "freezing" the biblical texts by embedding them within some fixed system of theology or world-view, the ongoing dynamic of the history of reception promotes a frame within which perspectives are deepened and comparative assessments emerge. Ormund Rush contributes a distinctive study of the relation between Jauss on reception theory and the "reception" of Christian doctrine and concepts of tradition in A. Grillmeier, G.H. Tavard, Y. Congar and others. Rush writes, "There is no one way of understanding, but only ways of understanding. Indeed one's own way of understanding must necessarily be a changing perspective and a broadening of one's horizon if understanding continues to occur."[52]

IV
Listening to, and Respect for, the Other as "Other": The Quest for Non-Manipulative Interpretation

With hindsight, once again, from the twenty-first century, I should now have placed a stronger and more explicit emphasis in these first two essays upon the cultivation of habits of respect for *the otherness of "the other"* as the heart of all hermeneutical endeavours. I would have linked this further with what is a strict entailment, namely the struggle to avoid consciously or unconsciously manipulative readings and interpretations of texts, especially when these are texts of the Bible.

IV.1 Gadamer and Betti on "the Other"

This is part of the driving force of Gadamer's work. Instead of rushing in to force the voice of the other to fit the prior categories shaped by "science" or by some prior grid of

---

49   Ibid., p.362.
50   Ibid., p.361.
51   Dietrich Bonhoeffer, *Meditating on the Word*, (Eng., Cambridge, MA: Cowley Publications, 1986), p.45.
52   Ormond Rush, *The Reception of Doctrine: An Appropriation of Hans Robert Jauss' Reception Aesthetics and Literary Hermeneutics* (Rome: Pontificia Università Gregoriana, 1997), p.290.

expectations and pre-formed concepts, hermeneutics (especially for Gadamer) aims to nurture habits of first *listening*, before assuming that "my" ready-made or pre-prepared concepts will exactly match what will be said. If we listen before we speak, we may perhaps *make space* for ways of perceiving the world that are more appropriate for those who seek "*to understand*" (*Verstehen*). A "scientific" method of "mastery" and "analysis" is different from a quiet readiness to listen and to meet "the other" on the terms that belong to "the other".

Gadamer also seeks to distance himself from any mode of discourse that smacks of propaganda.[53] This is one reason why he tends to react against the role of assertions or propositions. Unlike questions, they may more readily present some propagandist view. Nevertheless, even questions can be used to manipulate "the other" in the interests of the self. Hence Gadamer places all his weight on "*listening*" and "*openness*". This may help to explain why many of his critics argue that he hesitates to formulate any clear *content*, or adequate *criteria* of meaning and truth.

Each in his own way, Schleiermacher, Betti, Gadamer and Ricoeur, aim to offer a transformation of the traditional models of knowledge commonly associated with the rationalism of the secular Enlightenment. Some view this as an implicitly "theological" hermeneutics, since it replaces a concern to analyse and to "master" with a more humble and loving concern to place the "other" before the self, even if only to "understand" before making judgements. Yet the notion of aiming to facilitate a close *rapport* between the self and another, even if it embraces loving concern (*agapē*) for the neighbour-as-other is not the same as an explicitly "theological hermeneutics" of the kind with which we struggled to articulate in the first of our three questions. Perhaps it simply begins the journey, and perhaps it is ethical rather than fully theological.

From Schleiermacher onwards the goal of hermeneutics has been that of *listening* to "the other", rather than seeking mastery of "objects" to know "on my terms". Schleiermacher wrote in his early aphorisms, "In interpretation it is essential that one be able to step out of one's own frame of mind into that of the author."[54] The interpreter must "transform himself" into the author, or into another.[55] Gadamer looks back over a lifetime of hermeneutics, and observes: "Hermeneutics is above all ... the art of understanding ... In it *what one has to exercise above all is the ear*, the sensitivity for perceiving prior determinations, anticipations ... that reside in concepts".[56] He writes later in the same "Reflections": "It is the *other* who breaks into my ego-centredness and gives me something to understand. This ... motif guided me from the beginning ...".[57]

On this central question, however, Emilio Betti and Paul Ricoeur are even more explicit. Like Gadamer, Betti calls for "openness" or open-mindedness (*Aufgeschlossenheit*), with a view to, and for the cultivation of, sensitivity or "receptivity" (*Empfänglichkeit*).[58] Betti argues, "Nothing is of greater importance to humankind than living in mutual

53   See Robert R. Sullivan, *Political Hermeneutics: the Early Thinking of Hans-Georg Gadamer* (University Park: Pennsylvania State University Press, 1989).
54   Schleiermacher, *Hermeneutics*, p.42, Aphorism 8.
55   Schleiermacher, *Hermeneutics*, p.150.
56   H.-G. Gadamer, "Reflections on My Philosophical Journey", in Lewis E. Hahn (ed.), *The Philosophy of Hans-Georg Gadamer* (Chicago, IL: Open Court, 1997), p. 17 (my italics); see also pp.3–63.
57   Gadamer, "Reflections", in Hahn, p.46.
58   E. Betti, *Allgemeine Auslegungslehre als Methodik der Geisteswissenschaften* (Tübingen: Mohr, 1967), p.21.

understanding with one's fellow human beings".[59] However, this calls for the ethical virtues of "patience, tolerance, openness, and respect for the other".[60] He does not shrink from specifying explicitly ethical qualities that constitute requirements for understanding the other *as "other"*, for example, attentiveness, self-effacement, desire or will to understand, and humility.

Betti does indeed attack the self-centredness of an epistemological tradition that takes the self as its starting-point and its centre. Popularly this is often associated with Descartes, but more strictly it reflects the Cartesian tradition. However, Betti is also critical of the "existential" hermeneutics that he associates with Bultmann and even Dilthey. For by making "life-experience" and "pre-understanding" the key to hermeneutical understanding, they simply replace a *conceptual idea-centred self-centredness by an experiential or "life-experience" self-centredness.* Just as traditional rationalist epistemology imposes its own prior grid of *concepts* onto the "other", thereby assimilating the other into the pre-formed conceptual world of the self, so existential hermeneutics imposes onto the other its own prior hermeneutical categories, grid, or pre-shaped horizons, *thereby assimilating the other into the pre-formed life-world of the self*, no less than "scientific" or rationalist models of knowledge.

Yet can we avoid this? Betti offers several specific "canons" that in part address and, in his judgement, mitigate the problem. First, to recognize one's own prejudices and shortcomings, and to become critically aware of the narrowness of one's prior horizons, may serve to cultivate a humility that verges on "self-negation". This is not to set aside pre-understanding in favour of the objectivist illusion that Bernard Lonergan also attacks as "the principle of the empty head".[61] It calls for a self-critical humility. Second, Betti explicitly lays down a warning against self-righteousness, and against an undue readiness to view everything in terms of over-sharp black-and-white boundaries, rather than in terms of more nuanced shadings. Third, with Habermas, he recognizes the need for discernment to avoid any uncritical conformity with prevailing social or political interests, or with dominant, ascendant ideas. He shares with Gadamer an intense distrust of political propaganda and manipulative rhetoric.

To call attention to these positive ethical concerns is not necessarily to suggest that Betti's hermeneutics lack difficulties or unresolved problems. In part, like Dilthey, Betti defines "the other" arguably too much in terms of typified "objectifications" that represent outer or inter-subjective manifestations of inner intentions or "inner spirit". "Objective" interpretation involves the appeal to "typifications" in the context of historical reconstruction, alongside the more "subjective" process of sharing the other's "form of life" by entering into it.[62] Like Dilthey's notions of rapport or empathy and the rediscovery of the "I" in the "Thou", Betti calls for attention, sympathy, receptivity and humility, although against Dilthey he accepts the possibility of a more radical difference between the "I" and "the other" than Dilthey allows for. In positive terms, he reflects Schleiermacher's maxim that "In interpretation ... one must be able to step out of one's

59   E. Betti, *Die Hermeneutik als Methodik der Geisteswissenchaften* (2nd edn, Tübingen: Mohr, 1972), p.7.
60   E. Betti, *Allgemeine Auslegungslehre*, p.21; cf. also pp.211–13.
61   Bernard Lonergan, *Method in Theology* (London: DLT, 1971), pp.156–8.
62   Betti, *Allgemeine Auslegungslehre*, p.98; cf. also p.115.

own frame of mind", and also Ricoeur's appeal "to destroy the idols, to *listen* to symbols" (my italics).[63] Interpreters must not reshape "the other" in their own image.

IV.2 *Selfhood and "Otherness" in Ricoeur*

Paul Ricoeur expresses the importance of respect for the otherness of the other in less problematic contexts of thought. In his earlier work he begins with explanations of the fallibility of the human will, emphasizing the role of self-deception.[64] This invites inter-disciplinary dialogue with Freud's psychoanalytical work on disguise and double meaning within the human mind. I included comments on much of this aspect of Ricoeur's thought in the second essay of this volume, so it is unnecessary to replicate this here. Yet we repeat that it gives rise to an axiom for hermeneutics that we can hardly stress too often: "Hermeneutics seem to me to be animated by this double motivation: willingness to suspect, willingness to listen; vow of rigor, vow of obedience."[65] The former entails the fullest use of critical faculties; the latter leads to a post-critical "second naiveté", which serves as a means of *"hearing"* (my italics).[66] Freud, Nietzsche and Marx serve the "critical" pole by their "reductive" hermeneutics of suspicion, but in order to clear the ground for "listening" and for retrieval of "the other".[67]

Some claim that a view of meaning as multivalent allows the self to dominate the other. Ricoeur sees the matter the other way round: a cocksure limitation of meaning to "my" way of reading and understanding, or to that of "my" community, imposes constraints upon the otherness of the text, which I have captured as "mine". "The other" addresses the self in ways that are not exhausted by a single "first" reading. Indeed the "surplus" of meaning over a once-for-all reading gives rise to a "conflict" of interpretations, as Ricoeur suggests by the title that he assigns to one of his collections of essays. There may be "an ontological structure" capable of "re-assembling the discordant interpretations on the linguistic level", but only within a "dialectic of interpretations" that beckon toward "the promised land". The reflecting "subject" can only "glimpse" this from afar, like Moses "before dying".[68] The Promised Land is still "other", and its exploration remains "open".[69]

---

[63] F. Schleiermacher, *Hermeneutics*, p.42, Aphorism 8; Paul Ricoeur, *Freud and Philosophy. An Essay on Interpretation* (New Haven, CT: Yale University Press, 1970), p.54 (also cf. p.27); cf. Betti, *Allgemeine Auslegungslehre*, p.271 on symbols.

[64] Paul Ricoeur, *Fallible Man* (Eng., Chicago, IL: Regency, 1967); cf. also *Freedom and Nature: the Voluntary and the Involuntary* (Eng., Evanston, IL: Northwestern University Press, 1966; French, 1949).

[65] Ricoeur, *Freud and Philosophy*, p.27 and (in effect repeated) 54; on the role of suspicion, see pp.32–6; on allusion, cf. pp.230–60.

[66] Ibid., p.28.

[67] Paul Ricoeur, *The Role of Metaphor. Multi-Disciplinary Studies of the Creation of Meaning in Language* (Eng., London: Routledge & Kegan Paul, 1978), p.318.

[68] Paul Ricoeur, *The Conflict of Interpretations. Essays in Hermeneutics* (Evanston, IL: Northwestern University Press, 1974), pp.23–24. See also, Paul Ricoeur, *Interpretation Theory: Discourse and the Surplus of Meaning* (Fort Worth: Texas Christian University Press, 1976), esp. pp.45–95.

[69] Ricoeur, *Conflict*, p.223; cf. 223–35 in contrast to Heidegger's more self-centred hermeneutics of the "I am".

This explains why "the symbol gives rise to thought", rather than the other way round.[70] Symbol allows for "an horizon that may be enlarged".[71] This dialectic between concordance and discordance finds temporal and narrative expression in the key concept of "emplotment" in Ricoeur's masterpiece *Time and Narrative*. Temporal narrative exhibits distance and difference; emplotment exhibits a logic of coherence: interpretation respects "difference" in a dialectic that also embodies stability and "orderedness".[72]

In his crowning and no less magisterial *Oneself as Another* Ricoeur draws a contrast between the simplistic self-centredness of the "*cogito*" (of the Cartesian tradition) and "a hermeneutics of the self" in which the self as *agent* and as narrative *character* responds to the voice of "another" *in becoming aware of its identity as self*. A stable self ("*ipse*-identity" in "constancy") is not merely a bundle of properties (as a "*what*") but one *who relates to* "*another*" in such modes as testimony, promise and accountable responsibility (as a "*who*").[73] Ricoeur explains, "Facing the *speaker* in the first person is a *listener* in the second person."[74]

Ricoeur draws on P.F. Strawson's notion of "person" as a "primitive" concept, and also upon speech-act theory in J.L. Austin and F. Recanati. Within these frames he explores the stability of selfhood in terms of a reciprocal interactive encounter in language. Stability emerges, for example, in "keeping one's word in faithfulness to the word that has been given [in] self-consistency".[75] "Promising" also features as a dimension of the stable self. For promising presupposes acknowledging a continuity of constraint, derived from respect for the claims of "another".

Ricoeur engages with reductive views of the self, including those of David Hume and Derek Parfit. The self exhibits *both* "sameness-identity" *and* "variability, discontinuity" in a dialectic that is profoundly hermeneutical.[76] "*Otherness*" is not "*added on*" *from outside the self*. "Otherness" derives from "the tenor of meaning and ... the *ontological constitution* of selfhood" (my italics).[77]

Those who accuse Ricoeur of a kind of agnosticism in his philosophical journey often cite his conclusion that "the Other" may include either God, or another human face, or even an empty place. The first may reflect his theistic belief; the second, perhaps Levinas on the relational self; the third, possibly Derrida. Nevertheless Ricoeur makes it clear that this multivalent openness remains a strictly *philosophical* conclusion, not one drawn from theology. Further, he insists that "the polysemic character of otherness" shows that our encounter with "the Other" is not to be limited to psychological or interpersonal relations alone: "the Other is not reduced to the otherness of another Person".[78] This otherness includes both "the *foreign*" (looking to Heidegger), the inter subjective, and "conscience",

---

70 Ricoeur, *Conflict*, p.288, cf. 287–334; and *Freud and Philosophy*, p.543.
71 Paul Ricoeur, *Hermeneutics and the Human Sciences* (Eng., Cambridge: CUP, 1981), pp.61–62.
72 Paul Ricoeur, *Time and Narrative* (3 vols, Chicago, IL: Chicago University Press, 1984–88), vol. 1, pp.70–87, vol. 3, pp.244–74, and throughout.
73 Paul Ricoeur, *Oneself as Another* (Chicago, IL: University of Chicago, 1992; French, 1980), pp.16–55, 113–202 and throughout.
74 Ibid., p.43.
75 Ibid., p.123.
76 Ibid., p.140.
77 Ibid., p.317.
78 Ibid.

as well as the transformative vision within the self that beckons from "beyond" and especially "ahead".[79] It entails teleology, ethics and, implicitly, eschatology. Ricoeur speaks of the "structural, irreducible ... modality of otherness".[80]

It is scarcely surprising that a positivist or even rationalist system of thought would hardly be capable of providing even a starting-point for an understanding of this rich mode of perceiving selfhood in relation to the other as "who" rather than as "what". This requires the resources of hermeneutics. Yet conversely this also serves to identify what lies at the *heart of hermeneutical endeavour*. Whether with Gadamer, we emphasize the place of "the ear" rather than the mouth, or with Betti, the place of patience, humility, tolerance, restraint and respect for the other, or with Ricoeur, the ontological structure of selfhood as relational and implicitly inter-subjective, hermeneutics is not the way of self-assertion, self-affirmation and a "mastery" that understands the other in terms of self and self-interest.

This suggests, in turn, that it seeks to renounce manipulative ways of understanding and communicating. This yields huge problems for postmodern and neo-pragmatic systems of hermeneutics. Such types of thought often claim to represent the climax of hermeneutical thought as "radical" hermeneutics. In this volume I argue that far from constituting a climax, they actually undermine the very goals that hermeneutics came about to serve. This theme emerges in our discussions of postmodern approaches in various essays in this volume, and so it is unnecessary to embark on a full discussion at this point.

We pursue these themes in Part VI, on postmodernity and hermeneutics. In this context another major theme emerges, namely that of manipulative interpretation. Nietzsche pointed the way to a sharpened critical awareness of this problem in religions, including especially Christian traditions. We have also provided a reappraisal of greater length, detail and significance than at the conclusion of most of the other six Parts.

---

79 Ibid., p.318; cf. pp.329–41, and "Conscience", pp.341–55.
80 Ibid., pp.352–5.

PART II

HERMENEUTICS AND SPEECH-ACT THEORY

An Initial Application and a Caveat: "The Supposed Power of Words in the Biblical Writings" (1974)

This essay was first published in the Journal of Theological Studies, *volume 25, 1974, pp.283–99. It seeks to offer a more credible and convincing explanation about "the power of words" in Hebrew thought or in Old Testament texts than widespread assumptions among Old Testament scholars about their quasi-mechanical force, or, worse, appeals to primitive notions of word-magic. The proposed alternative explanation emerges in the context of speech-act theory as involving examples of performative and illocutionary linguistic acts. Although it was written more than thirty years ago, I continue to view this article as one of my more lasting contributions to varied issues of biblical interpretation, and as one of the earliest uses of speech-act theory on the part of a biblical specialist. The argument also draws on semantics. I have limited editing here only to the task of adding explanatory headings to numbered sections, and to reducing the length of some over-long paragraphs.*

I

Questionable Assumptions about the Nature and Functions of Language in a Dominant Tradition in Biblical Scholarship

According to a number of biblical scholars the spoken word in ancient Israel 'is never an empty sound but an operative reality whose action cannot be hindered once it has been pronounced'.[1] Several modern writers betray a fascination for analogies drawn from military weaponry. Zimmerli, following Grether, compares the word in Old Testament thought to a missile with a time-fuse.[2] Eichrodt insists that words, once spoken, remain effective or even dangerous 'for a long time, like a long-forgotten mine in the sea, or a grenade buried in a ploughed field'.[3] Edmond Jacob speaks of 'a projectile shot into the enemy camp whose explosion must sometimes be awaited but which is always inevitable'.[4]

Other writers speak explicitly of bullets, torpedoes and charges of high explosive. It is alleged, in the words of Procksch, that in Hebrew thought 'the word appears as a material force which is always present and at work'.[5] As Dürr repeatedly expresses it, the word is

---

[1] E. Jacob, *Theology of the Old Testament* (London, 1958), p.127.
[2] W. Zimmerli, 'Wort Gottes' in *R.G.G.* vi (Tübingen, 1962), col. 1810; cf. O. Grether, *Name und Wort Gottes im Alten Testament* (B.Z.A.W. lxiv; Giessen, 1934), especially pp.103–7.
[3] W. Eichrodt, *Theology of the Old Testament*, ii (London, 1967), p.69.
[4] E. Jacob, op. cit., p.131.
[5] O. Procksch, 'The Word of God in the Old Testament', under λέγω in G. Kittel, *Theological Dictionary of the New Testament*, iv (Grand Rapids, MI, 1967), p.93.

kraftgeladen; it operates as a power-laden force which irresistibly achieves its end.[6] Gerhard von Rad sees it as 'an objective reality endowed with mysterious power'.[7]

Almost all modern writings on this subject go back to the two classic studies by Grether in 1934 and by Dürr in 1938, sometimes with additional reference to a study by Hamp, also in 1938.[8] Ringgren, for example, follows these authors closely in his *Word and Wisdom*, and similar conclusions are either repeated or taken for granted by Eichrodt, Procksch, Knight, Jacob, Zimmerli, von Rad and (with one modification) by Boman.[9] This in turn has influenced certain writers on the New Testament. Bultmann, for example, takes as a starting point the assumption that the word in the Old Testament '*possesses power*', and goes on to say that 'for the New Testament, the use of the "word" which prevails in the Old Testament ... is definitive'.[10] Similarly Stauffer alludes explicitly to the work of Dürr for illumination of the New Testament statement that 'the word of God is living and active, sharper than any two-edged sword' (Heb. 4:12).[11] In the new hermeneutic Fuchs and Ebeling distinguish between words which merely convey *ideas* about reality, and words which supposedly have the power to convey reality itself; and this in turn receives some kind of support from Heidegger's approach to language.[12]

The Old Testament seems at first sight to contain abundant evidence for this kind of attitude towards language, and the relevant passages are too well known to require detailed or complete enumeration here. The most frequent cited examples include the following. The spoken word of the prophets has power 'to pluck up and to break down, to destroy and to overthrow ...' (Jer. 1:9–10).[13] The effectiveness of the word is like that of fire, or like that of a hammer which breaks the rocks in pieces (Jer. 5:14; 23:29). The word of God is as efficacious as the snow and rain which nourishes the earth: 'it shall not return to me empty' (Isa. 55:10, 11). Ringgren observes that this passage is a 'good instance' of the idea that 'the word of God is conceived as a concrete substance charged with divine power ... acting so to speak mechanically'.[14] Dürr believes that its language is more than poetic personification.[15]

---

[6] L. Dürr, *Die Wertung des göttlichen Wortes im Alten Testament und im antiken Orient* (Leipzig, 1938), pp.52, 61, and 71.

[7] G. von Rad, *Old Testament Theology*, ii (Edinburgh, 1965), p.85.

[8] O. Grether, op. cit., pp.59–158; L. Dürr, op. cit., especially pp.22–77 and 92–114; and V. Hamp, *Der Begriff 'Wort' in den aramäischen Bibelübersetzungen* (Munich, 1938).

[9] H. Ringgren, *Word and Wisdom* (Lund, 1947), especially pp.157–64; cf. W. Eichrodt, op. cit., pp.69–78; O. Procksch, loc. cit., pp.91–100 (cf. pp.69–137); G.A.F. Knight, *A Biblical Approach to the Doctrine of the Trinity* (Edinburgh, 1953), pp.14–16, and *A Christian Theology of the Old Testament* (London, 1959), pp.59–61; E. Jacob, op cit., pp.127–34; W. Zimmerli, loc. cit., cols 1809–11; G. von Rad, op. cit., ii, pp.80–98; and T. Boman, *Hebrew Thought Compared with Greek* (London, 1960), pp.58–69.

[10] R. Bultmann, 'The Concept of the Word of God in the New Testament' in *Faith and Understanding*, i (London, 1969), pp.287 and 297 (his italics).

[11] E. Stauffer, *New Testament Theology* (London, 1955), p.56; cf. further L. Alonso Schökel, *The Inspired Word: Scripture in the Light of Language and Literature* (London, 1967), pp.348–67.

[12] E. Fuchs, 'Das Wirkliche und das Wort' in *Marburger Hermeneutik* (Tübingen, 1968), pp.228–32 (cf. pp.236–45), and 'Das Wort Gottes' in *Zum hermeneutischen Problem in der Theologie* (Gesammelte Aufsätze, i; Tübingen, 1959), pp.323–33; and G. Ebeling, *The Nature of Faith* (London, 1961), pp.182–91.

[13] Cf. G. von Rad, op. cit., p.91, and also Jer. 20:9 and 47:6.

[14] H. Ringgren, op. cit., p.158. Cf. O. Grether, op. cit., pp.133–4; V. Hamp, op. cit., p.130; and L. Dürr, op. cit., pp.66–7, 123–4, 127 and 133.

[15] L. Dürr, op. cit., pp.123–4. Cf. also Isa. 44:26, 27 and 50:2.

This emphasis is by no means restricted to the prophets. In the Psalms God's word is said to bring about creation: 'he spoke and it came to be' (Ps. 23:9, cf. v. 6). At his rebuke the waters flee (104:7; cf. 106:9); his word melts ice and controls the elements (147:18). Indeed, as Albrektson has shown, God's word is active in nature as well as in history in Old Testament thought, just as the word of a deity is active in history as well as in nature among Israel's neighbours.[16] Taking up one of the psalms, the wisdom literature also expresses the idea that God's word heals sickness (Ps. 107:20; Wisd. 16:12). His 'all-powerful word' (ὁ παντοδύναμός σου λόγος) leaps from heaven like a stern warrior to bring destruction, effecting his commandment like a sharp sword (Wisd. 18:15, 16). In particular it is suggested that blessings and curse possess 'virtually a life of their own', and function, as it were, by 'innate power'.[17] Thus, even though his words are addressed to the wrong son, Isaac cannot revoke his blessing: '... I have made him your lord' (Gen. 27:33, 37). Similarly, Balaam tells Balak, 'I received a command to bless; he has blessed, and I cannot revoke it' (Num. 23:20).[18]

II
Illusory Support for these Mistaken Assumptions

On the basis of certain selected passages, some scholars have argued that the New Testament also reflects this same 'dynamic' view of words. We have already noted the statement in Hebrews that the word of God is 'living and active, sharper than any two-edged sword' (4:12). In the gospels Jesus speaks 'the word only', and the centurion's servant is thereby healed (Matt. 8:8). His word of forgiveness, followed by his word of command, brings cleansing and healing to the paralytic (Matt. 9:2, 5; Mark 2:5, 9; Luke 5:20, 23). In the Johannine writings his words are spirit and life (John 6:63). In the epistles the word of the cross is δύναμις θεοῦ for believers (1 Cor. 1:18; cf. Rom. 1:16); the word of God is the sword of the Spirit (Eph. 6:17); and words of Scripture have power (δυνάμενα) to impart a saving wisdom (2 Tim. 3:15). In apocalyptic passages Christ will slay the antichrist 'with the breath of his mouth' (2 Thess. 2:8); and from the mouth of the Son of Man proceeds a sharp two-edged sword (Rev. 1:16, cf. 19:21).

We have noted that Bultmann, Stauffer, and Alonso Schökel find a theological connection between these kinds of passages and the Old Testament attitude towards the power of words as Grether and Dürr outline it, followed by von Rad. But the point which is made by Dürr and others is precisely *not* a theological one, even though at one point, strangely in contrast to everything else that he has been saying, von Rad suggests that Israel's 'ideas of the power of God's word were entirely her own ... a quite unique theological achievement'.[19] The two points which are emphasized again and again are,

---

[16]   B. Albrektson, 'The Divine Word and the Course of Events' in *History and the Gods* (Lund, 1967), pp.53–67, where he criticizes the generalizations implied by Grether and by Dürr.

[17]   W. Eichrodt, op. cit., p.77, n. 5 and p.69; cf. O. Grether, op. cit., pp.70 and 130, n. I.

[18]   Cf. J. Hempel, 'Die Israelitischen Anschauungen von Segen und Fluch im Lichte altorientalischer Parallelen' in *Z.D.M.G.*, N.F. iv (1925), pp.20–110; J. Pedersen, *Israel: Its Life and Culture*, i–ii (Oxford, 1926), pp.167–8 and 182–212; and H. Ringgren, op. cit., p.191; together with the works (cited below) by Scharbert, and Wehmeier.

[19]   G. von Rad, op. cit., p.87.

first, that what is at issue is primarily *a particular view of language*, a view about how words relate to things; and second, that in this respect Israel's outlook was shared with others of her neighbours in the ancient Near East.

In terms of Israel's view of words, much has been made, at least prior to the work of James Barr, of the fact that *dābār* means both 'word' and 'thing'.[20] Thus Jacob makes the astonishing assertion, 'No term throws into clearer relief the fact that the Hebrew mind did not distinguish between thought and action.'[21] It is perhaps not entirely surprising to find the same kind of statement in Pedersen. He asserts, 'No distinction is made between the word and the matter described ... For the Israelites there is on the whole no difference whatever between the idea, the name, and the matter itself.'[22] But even von Rad makes a similar assessment about the relation between words and the reality which they signify. In contrast to the more modern notion that language merely conveys ideas, the Hebrew and his neighbours were 'unable properly to differentiate between word and object, idea and actuality'.[23]

This is what lies behind 'the word of power', and 'is in no way something peculiar to Israel'.[24] We are not simply concerned here with ideas about the power of *God's* word: 'even in everyday life ... certain words were thought of as having power inherent in them, as for example people's names'.[25] Language in general is 'a phenomenon composed of sounds which almost possesses a creative power of its own to conjure things up'.[26] It is as if 'objects in all their material solidity have been taken up into the word'.[27] In this sense, 'Israel took as her starting-point her conviction that the word possessed creative power.'[28]

III
"Primitive Word-magic"? – Or Another Explanation?

What are we to say about such an attitude towards language and words? Von Rad implies that this primitive outlook offers a positively richer view of language than that found in modern Western culture. He comments, 'One could ask whether language has not become impoverished because it has lost functions which at an earlier cultural level had once belonged to it.'[29] Similarly Alonso Schökel claims, 'The fault lies with us and with our ... impoverished experience of word in a culture which regards it as nothing more than a conventional ... "sign"'.[30] But the verdict forced upon us by modern general linguistics since the work of Saussure is that far from being 'richer', such a view of words

---

20 Cf. J. Barr, *The Semantics of Biblical Language* (Oxford, 1961), pp.107–60, especially 129–40.

21 E. Jacob, op. cit., p.128.

22 J. Pedersen, op. cit., pp.167–8.

23 G. von Rad, op. cit., p.81.

24 Ibid., p.82.

25 Ibid., p.83.

26 Ibid., pp.84–5.

27 Ibid., p.85.

28 Ibid., p.86. Cf. further Jacob Z. Lauterbach, 'The Belief in the Power of the Word', in *H.U.C.A.* xiv (1939), pp.287–8.

29 G. von Rad, op. cit., p.82.

30 L. Alonso Schökel, op. cit., p.357.

is simply wrong.[31] The relation between words and things is certainly not 'by nature' (φύσει), but rests on use, social tradition, rules of convention; on what Saussure himself called the first principle of language, namely *'l'arbitraire du signe'*.[32]

Far from being merely 'modern' and Western, this account of language is absolutely demanded by such phenomena as hyponymy and polysemy, opaqueness in vocabulary and arbitrariness in grammar, diachronic change in language, and the use of different words for the same object in different languages.[33] On the one hand it is simply not true, as we shall see, that a dianoetic or ideational view of words is the only alternative to the supposedly primitive one. On the other hand, a supposedly primitive view leads to a disastrously mistaken reification of abstractions.[34] S. Ullmann warns his readers against such reification, adding, 'It is this uncritical acceptance of ... "phantoms due to the refractive power of the linguistic medium" that philosophers and other critics of language never tire of denouncing'.[35] Among such philosophers Wittgenstein and Ryle immediately come to mind.[36]

Must we then reluctantly conclude that assessments of the power of words found in the biblical writings simply rest on a mistake? In answering this question, we shall allow two sets of commonly held assumptions to go unchallenged, since the arguments which will be put forward are not affected by their acceptance. First, it is not necessary to challenge the assumption that 'primitive' attitudes towards language existed, or to dispute the possible relevance of the kind of material collected and described by such writers as Malinowski and Cassirer. Malinowski writes concerning primitive attitudes, for example, 'The word ... has a power of its own, it is a means of bringing things about; it is a handle to acts and objects, and not a definition of them'.[37]

Cassirer asserts that in the phenomenon of 'word magic' men believe in 'the essential identity between the word and what it denotes'.[38] The same point is made with reference both to primitive cultures and to young children by writers as varied in their skills as Karl Bühler, Emile Durkheim, Jean Piaget, Stuart Chase, David Crystal and Sir James Frazer.[39] Even if it could be shown that such an assessment rested on an outdated anthropology, this would be beyond the scope of the present study.

---

[31] Ferdinand de Saussure, *Cours de linguistique générale* (Wiesbaden, 1967), pp.146–57; John Lyons, *Introduction to Theoretical Linguistics* (Cambridge, 1968), pp.4–8, 38, 59–70, 74–5, 272 and 403; and Stephen Ullmann, *Semantics: An Introduction to the Science of Meaning* (Oxford, 1962), pp.80–115.

[32] F. de Saussure, loc. cit.

[33] J. Lyons, op. cit., pp.35–6, 42–51, 90–91, 134–5, 403–7, 410–12 and 446–53; and S. Ullmann, *The Principles of Semantics* (Oxford, 1957), pp.106–38.

[34] Cf. especially S.I. Hayakawa, *Language in Thought and Action*[2] (London, 1965), pp.23–37 and 177–90.

[35] S. Ullmann, *Semantics*, p.39; cf. C.K. Ogden and I.A. Richards, *The meaning of Meaning*[1] (London, 1946), p.96.

[36] Cf. Ludwig Wittgenstein, *The Blue and Brown Books*[2] (Oxford, 1969), pp.26–31 and 107–9; and Gilbert Ryle, 'Systematically Misleading Expressions', in *Proc. of the Aristot. Soc.* xxxii (1931–32), pp.139–70.

[37] B. Malinowski, 'The Problem of Meaning in Primitive Languages', in Ogden and Richards, op. cit., pp.489–90; cf. 451–510.

[38] E. Cassirer, *Language and Myth* (New York, 1946), pp.49–50 and 58.

[39] Cf. J.G. Frazer, *The Golden Bough*[3], iii (London, 1938), pp.318–418 (especially pp.318–20 with reference to E.B. Tylor); the collection of writings under the heading 'Verbal Fascination' in I.J. Lee (ed.), *The Language of Wisdom and Folly: Background Readings in Semantics* (New York, 1949), pp.205–44; and D. Crystal, *Linguistics* (London, 1971), pp.41–4.

The second set of assumptions that will not be challenged is that many of the standard passages which are used to exemplify Israel's attitude towards words find parallels in the literature of her ancient Near Eastern neighbours. Thus Marduk speaks words of power in the Babylonian *enuma elish* epic; for example, he proves his kingship in heaven by speaking a word of power that annihilates a robe, and then re-creates it: 'At the word of his mouth the cloth vanished. He spoke again, and the cloth was restored.'[40] In a hymn to the moon-god Sin, it is said, 'When thy word settles down on the earth, green vegetation is produced ... Thy word makes fat the sheepfold ... Thy word causes truth and justice to be.'[41] An Egyptian hymn speaks of 'Amon Re-Atum-Har-ashti, who spoke with his mouth and there came into existence all men, gods ... cattle'.[42] The word is the instrument by which Thoth creates the world.[43] An attribute of the rule of Amon is *Hu*, his authoritative utterance: when *Hu* speaks, it is done.[44] It is unnecessary to labour the point by citing further examples, since these have been conveniently collected together by Dürr, and further discussions of some of the material occurs in such writers as Heinisch, Ringgren and Albrektson.[45]

If we accept these two sets of assumptions, however, must we also assume, with von Rad and others, that the primitive view of language which he outlines is demanded by the specific passages from the Old Testament which are usually cited as evidence for it? Do these passages genuinely suggest that 'objects ... have been taken up into the word', or that 'every דבר is filled with power ... as a material force'? I shall now call attention to four particular weaknesses, misunderstandings, or mistakes, on which I believe the traditional view to depend. I shall explore these four sets of issues in varying degrees of detail, and finally, I shall draw attention to counter-examples that suggest a different view of language.

IV
First Criticism: *Dābār* as Word and Thing

I begin with the only argument of the four that has already aroused certain suspicions, namely that which makes use of accidents in the semantics of word-history of *dābār*. The most controversial aspect of this argument concerns etymology. Grether, Jacob, Boman and Procksch all see significance in the hypothesis that etymologically *dābār* is connected with 'back', 'background', 'projection of what lies behind'.[46] Hence Procksch insists, 'In דבר one is thus to seek the "back" or "background" of a matter ... It is easy to see that in

---

40   *Enuma elish*, iv. 22–6.
41   J.B. Pritchard (ed.), *A.N.E.T.*² (Princeton, 1955), p.386 ('Hymn to the Moon-God').
42   Ibid., p.371, col. ii ('Hymns to the Gods as a Single God').
43   L. Dürr, op. cit., pp.23–31.
44   L. Dürr, op. cit., p.137; cf. J.B. Pritchard, op. cit., p.369, n. 17.
45   L. Dürr, op. cit., pp.3–21, 23–32 (Egypt), 32–7 (Babylonia-Assyria), 65–6, 92–9 (Egypt), 99–105 (Babylonia), *et passim*. Cf. further P. Heinisch, *Das 'Wort' im Alten Testament und im alten Orient* (Münster, 1922).
46   O. Grether, op. cit., pp.59–62; E. Jacob, op. cit., p.128; O. Procksch, loc. cit., p.92; and T. Boman, op. cit., p.65.

speech the meaning or concept stands for the thing, so that the thing ... has in its דבר its historical element, and history is thus enclosed in the דברים as the background of things'.[47] But the attempts of scholars to make undue capital out of this accident of word-history have been convincingly criticized in some detail by James Barr.[48]

More common is the attempt to make capital out of the fact that *dābār* can mean both 'word' and 'thing'. Pedersen, Jacob and Knight make much of this, for example. Knight urges, on this basis, 'Once a word, *dabhar*, is uttered with intent ... it becomes a thing'. A good analogy, he suggests, is that of the words in a children's comic: 'there the words ... are ringed around and connected by a line to the speaker's mouth. Their words ... have become an object, a thing, and are now separate from the person who uttered them. ... It has now become impossible to push the words back into the speaker's mouth. They are ... potent in themselves'.[49] Such an argument, however, as Barr rightly suggests, simply rests on a misunderstanding of the nature of polysemy in language.[50] Barr concludes, 'The senses "word" and "matter" are alternative ... We cannot therefore agree that the ancient speaker meant both.'[51]

We do not argue, for example, that because 'taste' in English, *goût* in French, *Geschmack* in German, and *gusto* in Italian, all mean either 'taste' in tasting food, or else 'taste' in aesthetic appreciation, Englishmen, Frenchmen, Germans and Italians all believe that good taste in society is connected with taste in the dining room, and are perhaps less able than other nations to distinguish the one from the other.[52] In practice, the phenomenon of polysemy, which is very frequent in most languages, may arise from any one of several sources which, as has been pointed out in modern semantics, often depend on historical accidents.[53]

One writer unintentionally provides what amounts to a *reductio ad absurdum* of arguments based on semantic accidents. In addition to insisting that the word is '*a unit of energy charged with power*' which 'flies like a bullet to its billet', John Paterson declares that the Hebrew was 'economical of words'; for 'Hebrew speech has less than 10,000 words, while Greek has 200,000. Thus a word to the Hebrew was something ... to be expended carefully ... The Hebrew knew there was power in words and that such power must not be used indiscriminately.'[54] Just *how* fallacious such an argument as this actually is fully emerges only in the light of what is universally said in general linguistics, first about the supposed 'richness' of one nation's vocabulary-stock as over against another's, and second about taking the 'word' to be an autonomous linguistic unit.[55]

---

[47] O. Procksch, loc. cit.
[48] James Barr, op. cit., pp.129–40, and more broadly 107–60. Cf. also J.F.A. Sawyer, *Semantics in Biblical Research* (London, 1972), pp.62 and 89.
[49] G.A.F. Knight, *A Christian Theology of the Old Testament*, p.59; also in *A Biblical Approach to the Doctrine of the Trinity*, pp.14–16. Cf. J. Pedersen, op. cit., p.167.
[50] J. Barr, op. cit., pp.133–8.
[51] Ibid., p.133.
[52] Cf. S. Ullmann, *Semantics*, p.167.
[53] Ibid., pp.159–75, and *Principles of Semantics*, pp. 114–25 and 174–80.
[54] J. Paterson, *The Book that is Alive* (New York, 1954), p.3 (his italics).
[55] Cf. J. Lyons, op. cit., pp.44–5, in which Lyons asserts 'No language can be said to be intrinsically "richer" than another'; cf. pp.54–70 and D. Crystal, op. cit., pp.49 and 188–92.

V
Second Criticism: Who Speaks these Words?

The nature of the second problem has not, it seems, been clearly recognized. Arguments are put forward about the nature of *words in general* on the basis of passages which speak not about words as such but about words which have been uttered usually *by a god*, or sometimes by a king or a prophet. But such arguments break down if words that have been spoken by Yahweh, or by Marduk, or by Atum or Khnum, are in practice regarded as 'power-laden' not because of the supposed nature of words in general, but precisely because *these* words proceed from the mouth of a god. We suggest that a generalizing argument has misleadingly been put forward on the basis of selected paradigms of a very special nature.

At least one writer has already expressed some suspicion about the standard passages cited in ancient Near Eastern texts. P. van Imschoot remarks, 'In Egypt and even Babylon one does not always see clearly whether the word acts by itself or by the power of a god.'[56] Certainly very many of the examples cited by Dürr simply could not be applied merely to *any* word, even a word spoken with solemn intent, but contain descriptions of the power of words which are necessarily words spoken by a god, or at very least by a king endowed by kingly authority. Thus 'the word which destroys the heavens above, the word which shakes the earth beneath ... a rushing torrent against which there is no resistance ... a storm bringing everything to destruction' can only be 'the word of Marduk'.[57] Indeed most of the chapters in Dürr concerns not human words at all, but exclusively 'the powers of the divine word in ancient near-Eastern hymns and prayers', 'the word of God as cosmic power', 'the word of God as hypostasis', and so on. The title of his book is explicitly *Die Wertung des göttlichen Wortes*.

Quite apart from questions about ancient Near Eastern texts, however, the standard passages cited from the Old Testament itself seem to underline the same point. In Isa. 55:10, 11, for example, is it that the word does not return empty because of Hebrew beliefs about the power of words in general, or because this particular word in question is spoken by Yahweh? If words in general could not return empty, the writer is saying little or nothing which is remarkable or even informative about God. Yet the whole emphasis of verses 6–11 is on Yahweh himself.

Dissenting from the usual understanding of 'word' in this passage, T. Boman comments 'It is not hypostasis or remnant of a hypostasis that stands in the foreground but it is Jahveh personally ... The word that proceeds from Jahveh's mouth is no ... substance, but is an effective and spoken word'.[58] This interpretation is entirely in accord both with the main point in 55:6–11, and with the theology of God in chapters 40–55. The admonition in 55:6 is to seek Yahweh himself, whose ways are entirely *different* from those men (v. 8). Whereas all flesh is grass, and the grass withers and passes away, Yahweh's

---

[56] P. van Imschoot, *Theology of the Old Testament*, i (Paris and New York, 1965), p.189.
[57] L. Dürr, op. cit., pp.8–9 (nos 1–3 of the texts edited by G. Reisner (Berlin, 1896); and in S. Langdon, *Sumerian and Babylonian Psalms* (Paris, 1900), pp.36–55; cf further Dürr's examples on pp.10–11, 24–38, 51–8, 66 and 92–105.
[58] T. Boman, op. cit., pp.61–2.

word will stand for ever (40:6–8, cf. 44:26). From the mouth of God goes forth 'a word that shall not return' because 'there is none besides me ... I am God and there is no other' (45:21–23).

The same principle applies to the vast majority of other passages that are regularly cited in support of a primitive view of the power of words. In Jer. 23:29 the word which is like a hammer in its effectiveness is explicitly the word of Yahweh. In Ps. 33:6, 9, it is Yahweh who speaks the word which brings things into existence. In Wisd. 18:15, 16, it is the word of God which leaps from heaven like a warrior. In Heb. 4:12 it is the word of God which is alive and active, and sharper than a sword. To explain such passages in the light of a particular view of language is to direct attention to the wrong thing.

Admittedly we have yet to note the significance of words spoken by men in blessing and cursing, or by prophets or kings. But these provide a relatively small segment of the passages which are usually cited, and we shall consider them under the next heading. We may conclude this point by making two further observations. First, it does not substantially affect the force of our argument whether or not 'word' is viewed as a hypostasis in parts of the Old Testament and in Judaism. For once again, the word in question is usually the word *of God*. W.D. Davies maintains, for example, that in Judaism 'the Torah was personified and endowed with a mystical life of its own which emanates from God, yet is partly detached from him'.[59] But this has no more relationship to a particular view of words or language than parallel ideas about the face of God or the wisdom of God have to notions about faces or wisdom.[60]

Second, even a writer as emphatic as Pedersen in his belief that 'no distinction is made between the word and the matter described' also gives tacit recognition to a quite different explanation of the power of words in certain passages, although he does not seem to realize the implications of offering what amounts to an alternative account. Pedersen writes, 'Behind the word stands the whole of the soul which created it. If he who utters the word is a strong soul, then the word expresses *more reality* (my italics) than a weak soul can put into it.'[61] In other words, even Pedersen sees that questions about the power of words depend at least partly on the authority and status of the speaker who utters them. Presumably it is his attempt to take account of these two very different approaches that leads von Rad to claim in one and the same breath that Israel's view of the power of the word was both shared with her Near Eastern neighbours and also 'entirely her own'.[62]

VI
Third Criticism: Blessing and Cursing as Illocutionary Speech-Acts

If we cannot reach general conclusions about words-in-general on the basis of selected paradigms concerning words spoken by God or gods, the same must be said about the

---

[59] W.D. Davies, *Paul and Rabbinic Judaism*[2] (London, 1955), p.170.
[60] G.A.F. Knight, *A Biblical Approach to the Doctrine of the Trinity*, pp.12–40.
[61] J. Pedersen, op. cit., p.167.
[62] G. von Rad, op. cit., p.87.

very special examples of blessing and cursing, and also of kingly and prophetic pronouncement. Blessing and cursing are prime examples of what J.L. Austin called performative language, namely, a language-use in which 'the issuing of the utterance is the performing of an action'.[63] It is 'an "illocutionary" act, i.e. performance of an act *in* saying something as opposed to performance of an act *of* saying something'.[64] Common examples of performatives in our own society include the following: 'I name this ship the *Queen Elizabeth*' (uttered by the appropriate person when smashing the bottle against the side); 'I give and bequeath my watch to my brother' (as occurring in a will); or 'I bet you ...' when a bet is being *made* rather than merely described.[65] When a bachelor in appropriate circumstances answers the question ' Wilt thou ... take this woman ...' with the words 'I do', he is not giving anyone information, he is actually marrying a bride. Similarly Austin includes blessing and cursing in a subclass of performatives that he calls 'behabitives'.[66] A man who pronounces a blessing is not primarily describing his own feelings; his words have 'power' in as far as they constitute an *act* of blessing: 'The performative should be doing something as opposed to just saying something.'[67]

At this point, however, several provisos must be made. First, the power of words in performative utterances has little or nothing to do with natural physical cause and effect. Austin comments, '*There must exist an accepted conventional procedure having a certain conventional effect.*'[68] 'The conventional procedure ... must exist and be accepted'.[69] Whether or not the utterance 'my seconds will call on you' functions effectively as a performative depends on whether the conventions relating to duelling are accepted. The words 'I hereby divorce you' can operate as an *act* of divorce only in a society where the mere utterance of this formula is enough to constitute a divorce.[70]

Second, Austin adds, '*the particular persons and circumstances in a given case must be appropriate*'.[71] If a private individual, rather than a queen or the shipping magnate's wife, says 'I name this ship the *Queen Elizabeth*', his words will not function performatively, unless he was appointed to do the job. These are examples of misapplications: '"I appoint you", said when you have already been appointed, or when I am not entitled to appoint ...; "I do", said when you are in the prohibited degrees of relationship ...; "I give", said when it is not mine to give ...; saying "I baptize this infant 2704" ...; or appointing a horse as consul'.[72]

Two points emerge from these considerations. First, in performative utterances we have an example of the power of words in which word and event are indeed one, but *not* on the basis of some supposedly primitive confusion between names and objects. Neither ancient nor modern society depends on mistaken ideas about word-magic in order to support the belief that words *do* things. Second, blessing and cursing constitute special

---

[63] J.L. Austin, *How to do Things with Words* (Oxford, 1962 and 1965), p.6.
[64] Ibid. p. 99; cf. also 'Performative Utterances' in *Philosophical Papers* (Oxford, 1961), pp.220–39.
[65] Cf. J.L. Austin, *How to do Things with Words*, p.5.
[66] Ibid., p.159.
[67] Ibid., p.132.
[68] Ibid., p.26 (Austin's italics); cf. p.14.
[69] J.L. Austin, 'Performative Utterances', loc. cit., p.224.
[70] J.L. Austin, *How to do Things with Words*, p.27; cf. pp.28–34.
[71] Ibid., p.34 (Austin's italics).
[72] Ibid., pp.34–5.

examples of this principle. Acts of blessing in the Old Testament rest on accepted *conventions*; on procedures or institutions accepted within Israelite society, and usually involving conventionally accepted formulae. They are effective, in most cases, only when performed by the appropriate person in the appropriate situation. Thus, when Isaac cannot revoke Jacob's blessing, this is not necessarily because his words are believed to be like a grenade whose explosion can only be awaited; but because, in Austin's terms, to give the same blessing to Esau would be like saying 'I do' to a second bride, or like saying 'I appoint you' when someone else has already been appointed. A convention for withdrawing the performative utterance did not exist; hence the original performative utterance remains effectively in force.

The history of research on blessings and cursing over the last twenty or thirty years tends to support our suggestion that it is unnecessary to resort to speculations about word-magic in order to explain the 'potency' of the blessing or curse.[73] Admittedly some writers have been slow to discard the older view. Thus Sheldon Blank wrote in 1950, '*The curse was automatic or self-fulfilling*, having the nature of "a spell", the very words of which were thought to possess reality and the power to effect the desired results.'[74] They represent 'words once spoken that have an enduring potency'.[75] Even S. Mowinckel believes, in language reminiscent of Pedersen, that 'man's blessing ... is the mysterious "potency" and power and strength, immanent in life itself', and corresponding 'in many ways' to the power of 'mana' in primitive religions.[76]

All this must be qualified, however, by two further observations. First, most writers stress that the effectiveness of blessing and cursing depends in a large measure both on the strength and status of the speaker who pronounces the blessing, and also on the receptivity of the person who is being blessed.[77] In other words, the 'power' of the pronouncement is by no means automatic. Indeed, Murtonen believes that the reason why Isaac did not try to recall his blessing from Jacob was not because of word-magic, but because, on the one hand, he believed that Jacob rather than Esau had 'ability to hold what was promised to him', and on the other hand, already 'God himself was called upon as the final authority.' Thus Murtonen convincingly argues that a supposition about word-magic 'does not seem necessary'.[78]

---

[73] In addition to the work cited above, cf. especially Josef Scharbert, *Solidarität in Segen und Fluch im Alten Testament und in seiner Umwelt* (Bonn, 1958); ' "Fluchen" und "Segnen" im Alten Testament', in *Biblica*, xxxix (1958), pp.1–26; and ברך ברכה in G.J. Botterweck and H. Ringgren, *Theologisches Wörterbuch zum Alten Testament*, i (Lieferung 6/7; Stuttgart, 1972), cols 808–41; S. Mowinckel, 'Psalms of Blessing and Cursing', in *The Psalms in Israel's Worship* (Oxford, 1962), ii, pp.44–52; S.H. Blank, 'The Curse, Blasphemy, the Spell and the Oath', in *H.U.C.A.* xxiii. 1 (1950–51), pp.73–95; A. Murtonen, 'The Use and Meaning of the Words lᵉbārēk and bᵉrākah in the Old Testament', in *Vetus Testamentum*, ix (1959), pp.158–77; H.C. Brichto, *The Problem of Curse in the Hebrew Bible* (SBL Monograph 13; Philadelphia, PA, 1963); H. Mowvley, 'The Concept and Content of "Blessing" in the Old Testament', in *The Bible Translator*, xvi (1965), pp.74–80; and especially Gerhard Wehmeier, *Der Segen im Alten Testament: Eine Semasiologische Untersuchung der Wurzel brk* (Basel, 1970).

[74] S.H. Blank, loc. cit., p.78 (his italics).

[75] Ibid., p.79.

[76] S. Mowinkel, op. cit., ii, pp.44–51; cf. J. Pedersen, op. cit., pp.209–12.

[77] E.g. J. Pedersen, op. cit., pp.183–90; S. Mowinckel, op. cit., p.45; and J. Scharbert, ברך, ברכה, loc. cit., cols 815–17.

[78] A. Murtonen, loc. cit., p.161.

Second, writers have given increasing prominence to the fact that, in blessing or in cursing, a man is in practice invoking *God*. Admittedly in the past some writers have resisted seeing the phenomena in this way. Blank insists, 'It is not addressed to God. Neither God nor any other agent is involved in the curse formula ... It is certainly a power other than God and is apparently a power inherent in ... the words themselves.'[79] But most writers follow Mowinckel's verdict that 'in Israel the word of blessing more and more took the form of a wish or prayer for Yahweh to bless'.[80] Thus Scharbert believes that the godly in Israel have 'for the most part left magical conceptions behind'.[81] And finally Wehmeier maintains that blessing is primarily *the gift of God*.[82] Even when blessing is pronounced by man, it involves blessing from God. But this is true only in later strata of the Old Testament. In spite of Blank's assumption to the contrary, H. Mowvley rightly comments on the ancient story of Balaam and Balak, 'Num. 22.6 indicates that in pre-Israelite days blessing was thought of as a magical formula or power. *Balak* regarded Balaam as possessing this power. As the story unfolds, however, it reveals the fact that the blessing is the prerogative of God. Balaam does not possess it as a magical power to be used irrespective of God. So, when God has blessed the Israelites, Balaam cannot curse them ... The Old Testament does not think of it as a magical power ... It is something which is dependent on God who himself alone can give or withhold it.'[83]

All this is in accord with what we have said about basing general arguments on special cases under the heading of our second criticism. Seen from one viewpoint, a blessing is supposedly power-laden if and when it is the blessing *of God*. But even if we leave theological beliefs in Israel out of account, we are still left with the concept of blessings and cursings as performative utterances which *do* things on the basis of conventional procedures in which the appropriate persons take part. Pronouncements by prophets or by kings may now be seen in this double light. They are effective because they are spoken by someone in authority, and may often take the form of a performative utterance.

Such pronouncements would belong to the two sub-categories which J.L. Austin has termed 'exercitives' and 'commissives'.[84] Exercitives, he suggests, include such examples as 'proclaim', 'announce', 'warn' (which are relevant to prophets), and 'enact', 'grant', 'repeal', 'pardon' and 'choose' (which are relevant to kings). Commissives include 'promise', 'swear', 'undertake', 'covenant' and 'champion'. Donald Evans makes the comment that *simply by uttering the appropriate words* 'the speaker, *exercising* authority, brings about a conventional or institutional state of affairs'.[85] The words themselves *effect* an award, a sentence, or a commitment. But they no more depend on primitive notions of word-magic than a modern judge and jury do when their words actually consign a man to prison or to freedom.

---

79 S.H. Blank, loc. cit., p.77 and 86.
80 S. Mowinckel, op. cit., p.46.
81 J. Scharbert, *Solidarität*, p.253.
82 G. Wehmeier, *Der Segen*, pp.75–97; cf. more broadly 97–188.
83 H. Mowvley, loc. cit., p.75 (my italics).
84 J.L. Austin, *How to do Things with Words*, pp.154–8.
85 D.D. Evans, *The Logic of Self-Involvement* (London, 1963), p.33 (his italics).

VII
Fourth Criticism: Dianoetic *'versus'* Dynamic?

The fourth issue need be set out only briefly. I suggest that Procksch and von Rad have artificially loaded the argument in favour of a 'dynamic' view of words by wrongly polarizing the discussion around two views of language which are portrayed as alternatives. The two views in question are called 'dianoetic' and 'dynamic', and it is assumed that if the dianoetic view cannot do justice to Hebrew-Christian attitudes towards language, this hereby demonstrates that these attitudes reflect a dynamic view of words. In practice, however these are not basic alternative accounts of language as a whole, but merely two of *many* possible ways of accounting for different uses of words.

The dianoetic view, as described by Procksch and Gerhard von Rad, is very like Locke's ideational view of language. Procksch writes:

> We must distinguish between the dianoetic and the dynamic element. Dianoetically דבר always contains a דבר, a thought ... But along with the dianoetic element is the dynamic ... Every דבר is filled with power ... By nature, the Greek word has a mainly dianoetic value; it receives the dynamic element only from the Hebrew דבר ... The word appears as a material force.[86]

Setting up the same contrast, von Rad writes, 'In modern languages ... the almost exclusive function of the word ... is to convey meaning. It is a phonetic entity ... a vehicle used for purposes of intellectual self-expression. The noetic function of the word ... conveying an intellectual idea, is far from covering the meaning which language had for ancient peoples'.[87]

Gerhard von Rad, however, has set up a false antithesis. For the dianoetic view of words is also far from covering the meaning which language has even for modern people. The whole phenomenon of performative language which we have discussed above is alone sufficient to show that many uses of language fall into *neither* of the categories outlined by von Rad. In terms of the modern study of philosophy of language, we need only point to the fact that virtually no specialist today would accept an ideational theory of language and meaning as an adequate, or even perhaps correct, account of it all.[88] The ideational theory is simply, as D.M. High has pointed out, a crudely referential theory of meaning, made even more problematic by bringing in further questions about private mental states and inner psychological experiences.[89] Wittgenstein, Black, Alston and many others insist that language is not merely an instrument to convey inner thought.[90] We must make, Wittgenstein urges, 'a radical break with the idea that language always functions in one way, always serves the same purpose; to convey thought'.[91] The functions of words are as diverse as the different functions of a row of tools. No single

---

[86] O. Procksch, loc. cit., pp.92 and 93.
[87] G. von Rad, op. cit., p.80.
[88] Cf. especially W.P. Alston, *The Philosophy of Language*, pp.22–5, and D.M. High, *Language, Persons and Belief* (Oxford and New York, 1967), pp.36–8.
[89] D.M. High, loc. cit., pp.28–44.
[90] L. Wittgenstein, *Philosophical Investigations*[3] (Oxford, 1967), especially sects 11–37; M. Black, *The Labyrinth of Language* (London, 1968), pp.9–19; and W.P. Alston, op. cit., pp.10–49.
[91] L. Wittgenstein, *Philosophical Investigations*, sect. 304.

theory of language, whether in terms of 'reference', 'use', or any other simplified slogan, is adequate. The question 'what is language?' needs to be answered in *many* ways.[92] The claim, therefore, that if and when a dianoetic account of language becomes inadequate, this implies the need for a 'dynamic' account, rests on a mistake. We are not obliged to choose one of only two alternatives; namely that a word is *either* 'a vehicle used for purposes of intellectual self-expression ... conveying an intellectual idea', *or* 'an objective reality endowed with mysterious power', 'a material force'.[93]

A careful consideration of these four major issues then compels a reassessment of the traditional view about the supposed power of words in the biblical writings. It remains only to point out the existence of one or two counter-examples which provide yet further embarrassment for the traditional approach.

In a short section entitled 'The weakness of words', Derek Kidner shows how a recognition of the limitation of words clearly exists in Proverbs.[94] Words are no substitute for deeds; for example, they cannot replace honest work (Prov. 14:23). Second, they cannot alter facts: 'like the glaze covering an earthen vessel are smooth lips with an evil heart' (26:23; cf. v. 26). Third, words alone cannot compel response: 'by mere words a servant is not disciplined; for though he understands, he will not give heed' (29:19). The effectiveness of a verbal rebuke is by no means automatic, but depends on the wisdom of him who receives it (17:10).

All the same we are not obliged to depend only on more sophisticated parts of the Old Testament for such counter-examples. Even in very early literature in the case of examples of blessings and cursing it is simply not true to say that a blessing or curse is always irrevocable. It is unnecessary and unconvincing to try to disguise the significance of this fact by describing it in terms of grossly materialistic metaphors. For example, Blank declares that in addition to rending one's garments 'a more effective means to neutralize a curse is to administer a blessing as an antidote'.[95] Even in the Gilgamesh epic Shamash persuades Enkidu to relent of his curse on the harlot, and Enkidu changes it into a blessing.[96] In Judg. 17:2, similarly, the mother of Micah does not regard the utterance of a curse as setting in motion a power-laden force that cannot be stopped; just as in 1 Kings 2:44, 45 Solomon does not attribute automatic power to the curse of Shimei. When God himself turns a curse into a blessing, it is simply 'because Yahweh your God loved you' (Deut. 23:5).

The well-known warning about πᾶν ῥῆμα ἀργόν (Matt. 12:36) presupposes the possibility of spoken words which are not grounded in appropriate attitudes, actions, or conduct, and has nothing to do with necessary small-talk. Similarly for Paul, it is not enough to proclaim the gospel only ἐν πειθοῖς λόγοις (1 Cor. 2:4; cf. v. 1). Far from being 'power-laden', λόγος actually stands in contrast to δύναμις. Thus Paul writes, 'I will find out not the talk of these arrogant people but their power. For the kingdom of God does not consist in talk but in power' (1 Cor. 4:19, 20). 'Our gospel came to you not only in word, but also in power' (1 Thess. 1:5).

---

[92] Ibid., sects 1–37, 43, 49, 65–7, 92, 97 and 108.
[93] G. von Rad, op. cit., p.80; and O. Procksch, op. cit., p.93.
[94] D. Kidner, *Proverbs: An Introduction and Commentary* (London, 1964), p.47.
[95] S.H. Blank, loc. cit., p.94.
[96] *Epic of Gilgamesh*, VII.iii–iv.

Concluding Summary

The permanent value of the classic work by Grether and Dürr is that they have collected examples of what words were thought to effect when behind them stood the authority of a god, or when special kinds of utterance were spoken by specially appointed speakers on the basis of conventionally accepted procedures. But it is misleading to draw inferences about words in general on this relatively narrow basis.

Analogies about grenades, missiles, torpedoes and mines may represent ways of making a point about a particular type of language-use, but without careful qualification they become more misleading than useful. More light can perhaps be shed on such phenomena as blessing and cursing by examining the principles involved in performative utterances. Certainly we are not obliged to accept the conclusion implied by the work of Gerhard von Rad and many other scholars to the effect that ideas about the power of the word in the biblical writings are somehow bound up with a mistaken view of the nature of language.

CHAPTER FIVE

Speech-Act Theory as One Tool Among Many: "Transforming Texts" (1992)

This is a very short extract from the first chapter of New Horizons in Hermeneutics (*London: HarperCollins and Grand Rapids, MI: Zondervan, 1992, subsequently reprinted in the UK by Paternoster Press, Carlisle), pp.31–6. I have included it only to show that while I call upon speech-act theory as one major explanatory tool for transformative texts, other strategies and functions take their place alongside speech-acts, thereby demonstrating that speech-act theory is only one tool among many others.*

Texts can actively shape and transform the perceptions, understanding, and actions of readers and of reading communities. Legal texts, medical texts and biblical texts provide examples. However, texts can also suffer transformation at the hands of readers and reading communities. Readers may misunderstand and thereby misuse them; they may blunt their edge and domesticate them; or they may consciously or unconsciously transform them into devices for maintaining and confirming prejudices or beliefs which are imposed on others in the name of the text. Readers and interpreters may also endow texts with new life in the context of new situations.

I
Speech-Acts as Potentially Transformative: A Legal Model

Hermeneutics entails a study of the processes and operative conditions of transforming texts, in both senses of the phrase. It also raises a large network of related questions about goals and models of interpretation, and what each may be thought to presuppose and to effect. The transforming effects of a text remain no more than *potential* ones all the while its writing, printing, or electronic display (or more debatably, sound) constitute nothing more than physical-spatial objects of visual (or tactile or aural) perception. Their potential begins to become *actualized* when a reader or reading community perceives that the signs constitute an intelligible sub-system of some larger linguistic or semiotic code, and processes of interpretation begin. When the necessary conditions for interpretation become operational, an event of communication takes place *within the temporal flow of the reader's life and experience.* The example of musical texts illustrates the relevance of this temporal axis well. The potential of the physical-spatial shapes of crotchets and quavers in a musical score become actualized only in the temporal flow of the performance, or when a skilled musician "reads" the score in his or her head.

In what way this temporal actualization of the text will be creative or transforming depends partly on the nature of the text in question. Hermeneutics has suffered grievously from the attempts of theorists to use one particular hermeneutical paradigm as an explanatory model for a large variety of texts. Briefly in *The Two Horizons* (1980) and in *The Responsibility of Hermeneutics* (1985) I tried to argue that the notion of speech-acts, alongside that of projected narrative-worlds, offered at least two explanatory models of how texts make a creative impact on readers.[1] Speech-act theory, as we have noted [in the Introduction to this work], is associated especially with the work of J.L. Austin and J.R. Searle, although its prehistory began with the later Wittgenstein. It has been further developed and modified by F. Recanati (French 1981, Eng. 1987), by Geoffrey Leech (1983) and by others.[2] More recently a number of biblical specialists have reopened questions about the relevance of speech-act theory for biblical interpretation in a volume of *Semeia* (41) edited by Hugh C. White under the title, *Speech Act Theory and Biblical Criticism* (1988).

Some legal texts of a certain kind offer an excellent example of the operational significance of texts that constitute speech acts. Parallels with biblical texts will soon become clear. *A text that constitutes a valid will,* duly signed and witnessed, *bequeaths an estate or a legacy to a named beneficiary.* Even if a will lies forgotten, unnoticed, or misplaced for a period, *it becomes operative as soon as it has been proven, and the text becomes an effective act of transferring property.* An operational text thereby changes the life of a beneficiary, perhaps giving rise to new hopes, new attitudes and new actions. In the case of the biblical writings, the persistence of the terms Old and New "Testament" serve to remind us of *a covenantal context in which pledge and promise feature* prominently.

The biblical writings abound in promises, invitations, verdicts, confessions, pronouncements of blessings, commands, naming and declarations of love. In his book *Conversation with the Bible* Markus Barth writes, "The unique power of the Bible flows from the fact that the biblical words are words of love ... between God and man. The reading of the Bible therefore should be compared to reading love-letters rather than the study and use of a law book."[3] The recipient of a love letter does not normally respond by acknowledging receipt of *information*. Reading here often (but not always) becomes *transactional*. It entails acts of acceptance, sometimes commitment, and probably deeper bonding.

---

[1] Anthony C. Thiselton: *The Two Horizons*, pp.335–51 (on narrative-world) and pp.133, 374–7, 384–5 and 436–7 (on speech-acts); with Clare Walhout and Roger Lundin, *The Responsibility of Hermeneutics* (Grand Rapids, MI: Eerdmans, and Exeter: Paternoster, 1985), especially pp.107–13; cf. also 42–57.

[2] F. Recanati, *Meaning and Force: The Pragmatics of Performative Utterances* (Eng., Cambridge: Cambridge University Press, 1967); cf. Geoffrey Leech, *Principles of Pragmatics* (London and New York: Longman, 1983). The two most relevant works by J.R. Searle are his *Speech Acts: An Essay in the Philosophy of Language* (Cambridge: Cambridge University Press, 1969); and *Expression and Meaning: Studies in the Theory of Speech Acts* (Cambridge: Cambridge University Press, 1979). But cf. also J.R. Searle, F. Kiefer and M. Bierwisch (eds), *Speech Act Theory and Pragmatics* (Dordrecht: Reidel, 1980); and Stephen C. Levinson, *Pragmatics* (Cambridge: Cambridge University Press, 1983). On speech-act theory in biblical studies, see Hugh C. White (ed.), *Speech Act Theory and Biblical Criticism, Semeia* 41 (1988).

[3] Markus Barth, *Conversation with the Bible* (New York: Holt, Rinehart and Winston, 1964), p.9.

II
Other Differently Functioning Transformative Models

Nevertheless speech-act theory does not offer a comprehensive paradigm for all biblical texts, let alone all non-biblical texts. *Texts shape and transform readers in many different ways.* For example, a narrative may draw the hearer into a projected narrative-world in which a flow of events and feelings are imaginatively experienced at a pre-reflective level. In this case, the "transaction" lies in the reader's willingness to step into this world, and to let his or her feelings and imagination be directed by the world of the text. The Book of Jonah, for example, invites us to travel in imagination with this self-important prophet. We hear him give his orthodox testimony to the sailors; we witness his prayers for death and his formalized thanksgiving for deliverance from death, carefully modelled like one of the psalms. We eventually follow him to Nineveh, and finally, to our horror, experience the shock of observing and feeling Jonah's intense concern about the welfare of a castor-oil plant which forms part of his immediate "world" against the background of his persistent unconcern about the welfare of Nineveh which never seriously becomes part of his own world of concerns (Jonah 1:2, 9; 2:2–9; 4:1–11).[4] Spending time with Jonah in the narrative-world projected by the text transforms feelings and attitudes about the wider world at a level that might not be reached by a theological sermon or treatise on mission or evangelism as a principle of life.

A quite different approach to the transforming potential of texts is suggested by the tradition of hermeneutical theory from Dilthey to Betti. The goal of interpretation according to Dilthey and Betti is to come to understand the mind, life-processes and life-world of a text's author. The reader must learn what it is to stand in the shoes of the author. This produces what Emilio Betti views as a cast of mind essential for the modern world, with its trends towards political confrontations and polarization. He writes, "For humankind, nothing lies so close to the heart as understanding one's fellow human beings."[5] The process entails recognition of the limits of my own understanding, and learning to listen, with patience and respect, not only to what the other person says, but also to why the other person says it.

In Christian spirituality or in pastoral theology we should probably describe this orientation initially as one of *openness*. To be open is to let oneself be sufficiently vulnerable to be influenced by the other towards self-change. According to Dilthey and Betti it would be false to set up a clear-cut contrast between "pastoral skills of listening" and reading ancient or modern texts with hermeneutical training and awareness. An openness to be willing to listen, to see the other person's point of view, and to be changed, characterizes any hermeneutically sensitive reading of texts, no less than in encounters between persons in everyday life.

These three models of textual activity, that of the speech-act, that of the narrative-world and that of interpersonal understanding, do not exhaust the variety of ways in which

---

[4] Cf. Edwin M. Good, *Irony in the Old Testament* (London: SPCK, 1965), pp.39–55; and Kornelis H. Miskotte, *When the Gods are Silent* (Eng., London: Collins, 1967), pp.422–38.

[5] Emilio Betti, *Die Hermeneutik als allgemeine Methodik des Geisteswissenschaften*, 2nd edn (Tübingen: Mohr, 1972), p.7.

texts, and especially biblical texts, can have transforming effects. As a fourth example in this chapter, we consider a model that is suggested by a hermeneutical category used by Hans Robert Jauss. Jauss was a former pupil of Gadamer, and is regarded as a leading exponent of reception theory. He follows Husserl, Heidegger, Gadamer and others in using the notion of "horizon", and in particular regards the central category of "horizon of expectation" as his "methodological centrepiece".[6] Every reader brings a horizon of expectation to the text. This is a mind-set, or system of references, which characterizes the reader's finite viewpoint amidst his or her situatedness in time and history. Patterns of habituation in the reader's attitudes, experiences, reading-practices and life define and strengthen his or her horizon of expectation.

A text, however, can surprise, contradict, or even reverse such a horizon of expectation. In earlier literary theory, the Russian formalist writer Viktor Shklovski had already explored this kind of phenomenon. He argued that the effective actualization of a work of creative literary art lay in its power to "de-habituate" the perceptions of readers.

In the case of the material of New Testament texts, Jesus, Paul and the apostolic community regarded the message of the cross as bringing to sharpest possible focus a clash with, and potential reversal of, very widespread horizons of expectation. Paul writes, "For the word of the cross is folly to those who are perishing, but to us who are being saved it is the power of God ... We preach a Christ crucified, a stumbling block to Jews and folly to Gentiles, but to those who are called, both Jews and Gentiles, Christ the power of God and the wisdom of God" (1 Cor. 1:18, 23, 24). The message of the cross brings about a reversal of evaluations, and a change in the mind-set and system of references that had previously constituted a horizon of expectation.

III
Reversals of Horizons of Expectation in Theology and in Reception History

The hermeneutical operation of this principle in some of the parables of Jesus had been explored (as is now well known) by Ernst Fuchs and other exponents of the so-called new hermeneutic. For example, in the Parable of the Labourers in the Vineyard (Matt. 20:1–15), the labourers and the readers share a horizon of expectation that is shaped and determined by the demands of justice. But this horizon is shattered, eclipsed and transformed by a verdict that communicates the generosity of grace. I have considered other examples elsewhere (for example, Luke 18:9–14; Luke 10:29–37).[7] The teaching of

---

6   Hans Robert Jauss, *Towards an Aesthetic of Reception* (Eng., Minneapolis: University of Minnesota Press, 1982), especially "Literary History as a Challenge to Literary Theory", pp.3–45; and *Aesthetic Experience and Literary Hermeneutics* (Eng., Minneapolis: University of Minnesota Press, 1982). On reception theory in general cf. Robert C. Holub, *Reception Theory. A Critical Introduction* (London: Methuen, 1984); and D.W. Fokkema and Elrud Kunne-Ibsch, *Theories of Literature in the Twentieth Century* (London: Hurst & Co, 1978), pp.136–64.

7   Anthony C. Thiselton, "The New Hermeneutic" in I.H. Marshall (ed.), *New Testament Interpretation* (Grand Rapids, MI: Eerdmans, and Exeter: Paternoster, 1977), pp.308–33; and *The Two Horizons*, pp.12–17 (Luke 18:9–14) and 344–52 (Luke 15:11–32; Luke 10:29–37).

Jesus constantly clashes with horizons of expectation: "Many that are first will be last, and the last shall be first" (Mark 10:31); "Whoever would be great among you must be your servant" (10:44). Even more sharply: "Whoever would save his life will lose it; and whoever loses his life for my sake and the gospel's will save it" (Mark 8:35: par. Matt. 10:39; Luke 17:33; John 12:25).

As Dietrich Bonhoeffer and others point out, such a reversal of expectations finds expression in the beatitudes: "Blessed are the *poor* ... Blessed are those who *mourn* ... Blessed are those who *hunger* ..." (Matt. 5:3–6, and especially Luke 6:20–22). Bonhoeffer comments on the principle that is involved, not as part of a hermeneutical theory at such, but as a comment on the significance of the biblical texts from the viewpoint of Christian theology, and in particular, a theology of the cross. In his book *Meditating on the Word* he writes:

> Either I determine the place in which I will find God, or I allow God to determine the place where he will be found. If it is I who say where God will be, I will always find there a God who in some way corresponds to me, is agreeable to me, and fits in with my nature. But if it is God who says where He will be, then that will truly be a place which at first is not agreeable to me at all, which does not fit so well with me. That place is the cross of Christ. And whoever will find God there must draw near to the cross in the manner that the Sermon on the Mount requires. This does not correspond to our nature at all.[8]

In hermeneutical terms, horizons of expectation need to be open to change and to transformation.

The history of the effects of texts bears witness to many experiences of this principle of transformation and reversal in the lives of a variety of people and communities. Perhaps the most widely celebrated example in Protestant Christendom is that of Martin Luther, who recounted the impact made on him by Paul's words: "He who by faith is righteous shall live" (Rom. 1:17). Luther recalls the sense of anger and fear with which he had hitherto reflected on biblical texts and on the gospels. But, he continues, when he came "to understand" both the text of Rom. 1:17 and its larger context, he felt that he was altogether "born again" and "entered paradise". A totally other face of the entire Scripture showed itself to him. In place of anger and fear, there came a love "as great as the hatred with which I had hated the word 'righteousness of God'".[9] The text in its proper context had transformed Luther's earlier horizon of expectation into another.

IV
Resisting Transformation: The Capacity of Readers to Transform Texts

All the same, if texts have the capacity to transform readers, readers (and texts) can and do transform texts. Hermeneutics traces paths by which this process occurs. Sometimes readers transform texts through ignorance, blindness, or misunderstanding. Sometimes

---

[8] Dietrich Bonhoeffer, *Meditating on the Word* (Cambridge, MA: Cowley Publications, 1986), pp.44–5.

[9] *Luther's Works* (eds J.J. Pelikan and H.T. Lehmann) (St. Louis, MO and Philadelphia, PA: Concordia Publishing House, 1955–), pp.336–7.

readers either consciously or through processes of self-deception find ways of rendering harmless texts that would otherwise prove to be disturbing and call for change. It is customarily acknowledged that understanding may be difficult in cases where the subject-matter of a text or its genre or code may be distant from the reader's assumptions and expectations and entirely unfamiliar. But texts may be transformed, no less, by habituated patterns of individual or corporate familiarity. These may rob the text of its power to speak to the reader *as "other"*. If, for example, biblical and other religious texts are to deliver us from self-centredness and to convey messages of judgement or of love, encounters with texts involve, as David Klemm insists, encounters with "otherness".[10]

In Paul Ricoeur's view, an authentic encounter with texts occurs when the reader both "conquer[s] a remoteness" and meets with *the other*: "It is thus the growth of his own understanding of himself that he pursues through his understanding of the other. Every hermeneutics is thus, explicitly or implicitly, self-understanding by means of understanding others."[11] This represents an entirely different starting-point from that of the isolated individualism of Descartes' *cogito*. If the reader's expectations and assumptions, especially those that have been ingrained by individual or corporate habit, transform the text into a reflection of the reader's own local and domestic concerns, the text's capacity to speak from within a horizon of *otherness* has evaporated.

---

[10]   David E. Klemm, *Hermeneutical Inquiry: I, The Interpretation of Texts* (Atlanta, GA: Scholars Press, 1986), p.3.
[11]   Paul Ricoeur, *The Conflict of Interpretations: Essays in Hermeneutics* (Evanston, IL: Northwestern University Press, 1974), p.17.

CHAPTER SIX

Changing the World – Illocutions, Christology and "Directions of Fit": "Christological Texts in Paul" (1992)

This extract from New Horizons in Hermeneutics *(pp.283–312) embodies more substantial research than the previous essay, which merely introduced part of the argument as a whole. One important aspect is the utilization of Searle's concept of "directions of fit" in speech-acts; another concerns implications for Paul's approach to a theology of the atonement. However, further implications for Christology are developed more fully and with more originality in the next essay on Christology in Luke, speech-acts, and two-level or dualist Christology after Kant.*

I
Christological Texts in the New Testament in the Light of Speech-Act Theory

In the case of the Christological texts that we find in Paul, we may begin either with the aspect of self-involvement or with more objective and descriptive aspects of Paul's Christology. It may be helpful to follow Johannes Weiss in exploring first the practical, operative, or self-involving aspects of the earliest Christian pre-Pauline confession "Jesus is Lord" (1 Cor. 12:3). Weiss begins by observing "What it means in a practical, religious sense will best be made clear through the correlative concept of 'servant' or 'slave' of Christ" (Rom. 1:1; 1 Cor. 7:22, 23; Gal. 1:10; Phil. 1:1).[1]

A person who sees himself or herself as Christ's servant or slave is wholly at the disposal of his or her "Lord". But he or she can also look to this Lord, as the one to whom they are solely and wholly responsible, not only in obedience, but also in trust. For in the first-century world, the "Lord" provided what his slave needed; this was not the concern of the slave. As Bultmann rightly observes, spelling out the self-involving aspect: for Paul the believer "no longer bears the care for himself, for his own life, but lets this care go, yielding himself entirely ... 'If we live, we live to the Lord; and if we die, we die to the Lord; so whether we live or whether we die; we are the Lord's' (Rom. 14:7, 8) ... He knows only one care: 'how he may please the Lord' (1 Cor. 7:32), and only one ambition: 'to please the Lord' (2 Cor. 5:9)."[2]

Werner Kramer retains this emphasis on self-involvement in this context, but he rightly expands the horizons of interpretation to include the community and also the future. He writes, "Because the Church (and the individual Christian, too) belongs wholly to the *Lord*, there is no place for fear, but only for confidence and for joy ... there

---

[1] J. Weiss, *Earliest Christianity*, 2 vols (New York: Harper, 1959), vol. 2, 458.
[2] R. Bultmann, *Theology of the New Testament* (London: SCM, 1952 & 1955), vol. I, 331 & 351.

is no limit, even in the future, to the power of the *Lord*, nor will the Church cease to belong to Him. What is true of the Lord now must continue to be true."[3]

All the same, this aspect of self-involvement logically depends on the truth of certain *assertions about* Christ. It is doubtful whether Bultmann is correct when he suggests that the Christological language of the gospels and of Paul tells us nothing "about the nature of Jesus".[4] J.L. Austin and D.D. Evans carefully examine the performative and illocutionary force of a number of verbs that we shall regard as characterizing the interpersonal involvement between *lord and servant* or slave.[5] Austin is concerned about the preconditions which must be operative when these verbs are effective as part of "the total speech-act". Austin and Evans expound the significance of the sub-category that they term *"exercitives"*, as a way of describing the effectiveness of the words spoken by a person in authority.

It is not of great moment at *this* stage of the argument that where Austin and Evans used the term "exercitive", John Searle, followed by François Recanati, Stephen Levinson and Geoffrey Leech, prefer the near-equivalent term "directive".[6] Thus, if "the word of the Lord" has power to *direct*, to *appoint*, to *authorize*, or to *order*, *directive authority is actually exercised in the exercitive or directive utterance*. Evans includes among his examples of exercitives: "I appoint ... I approve ... I authorize ... I give ... I order ...".[7] Austin includes "the exercising of powers ... appointing... urging, advising, warning, ordering, choosing, enacting, claiming, directing".[8] Clearly for these functions to be "performed" under *valid* and *effective* operative conditions, *more is at issue than the practical attitude of the servant or slave*. To ascribe "lordship" to someone who cannot rightfully exercise lordship is from the linguistic viewpoint *empty* or logically arbitrary and from the theological viewpoint *idolatrous*. The words "Jesus is Lord" express *both* factual or institutional truth *and* self-involvement.

The Pauline texts confirm this supposition decisively. In Pauline language, *God* designated Christ "Lord" in the resurrection; Christ's exaltation, and his receiving the name "Lord", is effected by the ontological and institutional action of *God* (Rom. 1:4; 10:9; Phil. 2:11). In Rom. 10:9, Dunn comments, Paul brings together the two central emphases of the gospel: "God raised Him from the dead" and "Jesus is Lord."[9]

This aspect of the logic of self-involvement receives further clarification when we examine two further relevant sub-categories of performatives expounded by Austin and by Evans. Searle and Recanati reclassify as "declaratives" the sub-category designated "verdictives" by Austin and Evans. This sub-category of *verdictives* includes "reckoning,

---

3   Werner Kramer, *Christ, Lord, Son of God* (Eng., London: SCM, 1966), 181 & 182.

4   R. Bultmann, *Essays Philosophical and Theological* (London: SCM, 1955), 280, cf. 273–90; Ger. *Glauben und Verstehen. Gesammelte Aufsätze*, 4 vols (Tübingen: Mohr, 1964–65), II, 252, cf. 246–61.

5   D.D. Evans, op. cit., 30–36, 46–78, 170–73; J.L. Austin, op. cit., 43–52, 78–90, 110–19, 150–61.

6   John R. Searle, *Expression and Meaning. Studies in the Theory of Speech Acts* (Cambridge: Cambridge University Press, 1979), 13–23; cf. 1–29; François Recanati, *Meaning and Force: The Pragmatics of Performative Utterances* (Eng., Cambridge: Cambridge University Press, 1987), 154–63; Stephen C. Levinson, *Pragmatics* (Cambridge: Cambridge University Press, 1983), 240–42; and Geoffrey Leech, *The Principles of Pragmatics* (London and New York: Longman, 1983), 205–12.

7   D.D. Evans, op. cit., 33.

8   J.L. Austin, op. cit., 150 & 154–5.

9   James D.G. Dunn, *Romans 9–16*, 616.

requiting, ruling, assessing".[10] Thus Paul declares, "I am not aware of anything against myself, but I am not thereby acquitted; it is the *Lord* who *judges* me" (1 Cor. 4:4). In addition to this sub-category that relates to *verdicts* (Austin) or to *declarations* (Searle), Austin and Evans identify another, which relates to contexts of *behaviour*. Under Austin's "behabitives" (which are like Searle's "expressives") Austin and Evans include "commending, accusing, reprimanding, applauding".[11] Paul writes: "It is not the man who commends himself that is accepted, but the man whom the *Lord commends*" (2 Cor. 10.18).

Although there are other reasons for the choice of the word *kyrios* in the Pauline texts and in other parts of the New Testament (also in the LXX, of God), Whiteley and Cullmann are probably still correct in seeing some element of the notion of "rightful" lord in the use of the term of Jesus, as against the more "arbitrary" lordship or mastership implied more readily in *despotes*.[12] Cerfaux underlines the ontological or objective basis of the application of the term *kyrios* in its close association with the *parousia* of Christ. He argues on the basis of the analogy of the lord or ruler whose coming to his city occasions a festive reception: "we shall be caught up together in the clouds to meet the Lord" (1 Thess. 4:17).[13]

Even when he is examining the cultic or liturgical contexts of *kyrios* texts, Bultmann stresses the aspect of existential experience. Thus he sees a close parallel between early Christian experience of Christ's lordship and that of being at the disposal of the cult-deities from whom they were converted, in the terms described in W. Bousset's *Kyrios Christos* (1913 and 1921). However, both aspects, the existential or self-involving, and the ontological or "institutional", belong to the logical function of *kyrios* texts. At the existential and self-involving level, they *invite trust, obedience, surrender and devotion*. They are not simply flat descriptions of abstract doctrinal truths or heavenly transactions. But at the level of their truth-claim about what is the case, the texts also speak of *God's instituting, appointing, or exalting Christ as Lord*. This aspect would remain *true* whether human consciousness wished to acknowledge it or not; but its operative *effects* and *hermeneutical currency* would be seen most clearly when such acknowledgement is made.

Questions about the *identity* of Jesus as Lord bring together not only these two distinct but related logical functions, but also provide a link between the Pauline texts and material in the Synoptic Gospels. The basis on which Jesus invites trust and obedience arises *both* from God's exaltation and vindication of his work in the event of his resurrection *and* from his identity and character, disclosed in the words and deeds of his earthly ministry. James Dunn rightly sees this identity as a unifying focus within a variety of New Testament texts. Together they offer "the affirmation of the identity of the man Jesus with the risen Lord".[14]

---

[10] J.L. Austin, op. cit., 152; J.R. Searle, op. cit., 16–20; and F. Recanati, op. cit., 138–54.

[11] D.D. Evans, op. cit., 36; cf. J.L. Austin, op. cit., 159–60.

[12] D.E.H. Whiteley, op. cit., 103; cf. Oscar Cullmann, *The Christology of the New Testament* (Eng., London: SCM, 1959), 200–13.

[13] L. Cerfaux, *Christ in the Theology of St Paul* (Eng., Freiburg: Herder, 1959), 469.

[14] James D.G. Dunn, *Unity and Diversity in the New Testament. An Inquiry into the Character of Earliest Christianity* (London: SCM, 1977), 227.

In the Synoptic Gospels and especially in Mark there is a reticence, the reasons for which we shall shortly note, in stating truths explicitly about the Christological status of Jesus. Nevertheless, the self-involving aspects of Jesus' pronouncements imply Christological *presuppositions*. Bultmann observes that Jesus' call "is the *call to decision*: Something greater than Solomon ... greater than Jonah, is here" (Luke 11:31, 32) ..."Follow me, and leave the dead to bury their own dead" (Matt. 8:22). Bultmann concedes that for the very earliest Christians "Jesus' call to decision implies a christology."[15] The words of Jesus perform a more than intra-linguistic function: they call for, and effect, total renunciation and obedient discipleship (Luke 14:27); they reinterpret traditions of the Old Testament which shaped the pattern of first-century Jewish life (Matt. 5:21–37); they proclaim the arrival of God's reign which characterizes and inaugurates the new age. Within the presuppositions of Jewish eschatology, this arrival of the Kingdom in the coming of Jesus constitutes not simply a national but also a *cosmic* turning-point (Mark 1:15).

In the triple tradition common to Mark, Matthew and Luke, a sequence of utterances emerges especially in the early chapters, which, from the viewpoint of Austinian logical analysis may be viewed as *exercitive* language-functions within a broader category of *performative utterances*. Jesus says to the paralytic: "My son, your sins are [hereby] forgiven" (Mark 2:5; par. Matt. 9:2; Luke 5:20). Mark and Matthew use the present, which is typical of, though not decisive for, performative utterances (*aphientai*). As we note in the next essay below, Luke uses the perfect (*apheontai*) perhaps to express "the abiding *force*" of the forgiveness.[16] Jesus' effective words of exorcism (Mark 1:25, "be silent, come out of him") are interpreted in the triple tradition not primarily as miracle as such, but as Messianic verbal-deeds which *in the speaking* constitute the binding of the "strong man" and the *act of plundering* his goods (Mark 3:23–27; par. Matt. 12:22–30; Luke 11:14, 15, 17–23). They meet Austin's criterion for *illocutionary speech-acts*: "the performance of an act *in* saying something".[17] The sovereign, authoritative, *exercitive* utterance "Peace! Be still" subjugates the winds and waves, *in* the act of being uttered (Mark 4:35–41; Matt. 8:23–27; Luke 8:22–25). Matthew, Mark and Luke all make room for the reader to reflect on the presuppositions that allow the exercitive to function effectively: "Who, then, is this ... (Matt. 8:27, what sort of person is this?) that even the wind and sea obey him?"

Interpreters and commentators, especially on the Matthean text, see at once existential parallels in the invitation to trust on the part of the storm-tossed church. Matthew's readers are invited to trust in their Lord. G. Bornkamm expounds this theme, in his essay on the Stilling of the Storm.[18] Matthew portrays Jesus, David Hill comments, as having "divine authority over creation, a man in whom absolute confidence may be placed because He is able to protect disciples in times of stress and danger".[19] The implications go even further. R.T. France adds, "In the Old Testament it was a mark of the sovereignty

---

15 Rudolf Bultmann, *Theology of the New Testament*, vol. II, 9 & 43.

16 I. Howard Marshall, *The Gospel of Luke. A Commentary on the Greek Text* (Exeter: Paternoster and Grand Rapids, MI: Eerdmans, 1978), 213.

17 J.L. Austin, op. cit., 99; cf. 94–119.

18 G. Bornkamm, "The Stilling of the Storm", in G. Bornkamm, G. Barth and H.J. Held, *Tradition and Interpretation in Matthew* (Eng., London: SCM, 1963), 52–7.

19 David Hill, *The Gospel of Matthew* (London: Oliphants & Marshall (New Century), 1972), 167.

of God Himself that the sea obeyed His orders (Job. 38:8–11; Psalm 65:5–8; 89:8, 9); a passage like Psalm 107:23–32 must have been in Matthew's mind as he narrated the story."[20]

If we move from the triple tradition to material which also reflects the theology of individual evangelists, we may identify a number of other examples of exercitive, verdictive and behabitive categories (or in Searle's terminology, directive, declarative and expressive speech-acts), each of which carries an existential resonance for the present reader which does not exhaust its further truth-claims. A number of writers, including Otto Michel, A. Vogtle and B.J. Hubbard have examined the *act of authorization* in post-resurrection commissioning of the disciples (Matt. 28:18–20). This, in Michel's view represents a key to Matthew's Christology: "All authority in heaven and on earth has been given me. Go, therefore, and make disciples of all nations ...".[21] Here the logic on which the *exercitive speech-act of authorization depends* is made clear and fully explicit: "All authority in heaven and on earth has been given me." Graham Stanton approves of Bornkamm's comment that the text functions as an endorsement by the exalted Lord of the authority of the commands of the earthly Jesus for his church, and as a pledge of his presence.[22]

Three sub-categories of performative or illocutionary force come into play: "Go therefore and make disciples" (Matt. 28:19) constitutes an *exercitive* which appoints, commands and *assigns* an "institutional" *role.* "Teaching them to observe all that I have commanded you" (Matt. 28:20) combines the *exercitive* and *behabitive* dimensions of *authorization.* "Lo, I am with you always, to the close of the age." (Matt. 28:20) represents a classic example of the sub-category identified by Austin, Evans, Searle and Recanati as *"commissives".* Bornkamm observes that the words embody the self-commitment of a *pledge* or promise. If a present-day reader feels any sense of identification with the addressees, the effect of the language transcends information, or narrative report. A commission *assigns* a task and a role; an authorization *confers* a status; a pledge or a promise *invites* trust, and also action that takes the promise for its basis.

We have not yet answered the question, however, which arises about a relative reticence found in the words of Jesus, and often in the evangelists to make explicit statements about the basis on which his own illocutionary utterances and the disciples' existential commitments were valid. One part of the answer is that Christology remained incomplete before the resurrection awaiting divine corroboration. As James Dunn urges, Christology concerns not only the life and consciousness of the pre-resurrection Jesus, but "the whole Christ-event", including "reflection on, and elaboration of, Jesus' own sense of sonship and eschatological mission".[23] But a further consideration also arises from Jesus' *uniqueness.* It was important that *an understanding of Jesus,* seen in his words and in

---

[20]   R.T. France, *The Gospel according to Matthew: An Introduction and Commentary* (Leicester: IVP and Grand Rapids, MI: Eerdmans, 1985), 162.

[21]   Otto Michel, "The Conclusion of Matthew's Gospel. A Contribution to the History of the Easter Message", in Graham N. Stanton (ed.), *The Interpretation of Matthew* (Philadelphia: Fortress and London: SPCK, 1983), 30–41.

[22]   Graham N. Stanton, ibid., 4; cf. G. Bornkamm, loc. cit., 228.

[23]   James D.G. Dunn, *Christology in the Making: A New Testament Inquiry into the Origins of the Doctrine of the Incarnation* (London: SCM and Philadelphia, PA: Westminster, 1980), 254.

his *completed work,* should *govern interpretations of conventional "messianic" language, rather than that ready-made assumptions about the meaning of such language should govern an understanding of Jesus.*

In this respect Perrin is right to note a certain open-ended quality, for example, in Jesus' language about the Kingdom of God.[24] It cannot become wholly clear what is the nature of God's active reign until Jesus has demonstrated its context paradigmatically in his life and work, including the cross and resurrection. Similarly language about the Son of Man remains open to a variety of interpretations.[25] Whether we seek to use contemporary Aramaic, Dan. 7:13, 14, or Psalm 8:4 as a key to its interpretation, it allows no packaged pre-judgements about Jesus, but invites understanding of Jesus only on the grounds of an identity revealed in his authoritative and saving words and deeds. Language about the Kingdom of God, however, does include the dual dimensions of the ontological and the existential. The Kingdom of God in the apocalyptic tradition represents God's cosmic reign; "taking upon oneself the yoke of the Kingdom" in rabbinic traditions entails human obedience and response.

The evangelists themselves also include material that reflects a more explicit Christology. There is general agreement that Mark embodies a central concern about Christology, which he unfolds in a distinctively narrative form. Robert Fowler (1981), Rhoads and Michie (1982), Ernest Best (1983) and Eugene Boring (1985) all stress the Markan use of narrative devices to involve the reader in reaching judgements about Christology, and we shall return to consider their arguments when we examine reader-response theory.[26] Graham Stanton distinguishes between Christological assumptions that operate *within* the narrative world of Mark, and what Mark addresses to the reader. Mark tells us in his opening line that Jesus is "Christ, the Son of God" (Mark 1:1): "As the story unfolds the true identity of Jesus is either kept secret from the participants in the story or misunderstood by them, but for the reader there is no secret."[27] In a recent number of *Semeia* on speech-act theory, Hugh White and Michael Hancher relate speech-act theory to narrative hermeneutics.[28] But their main concern is the broader one of locating speech-act theory in relation to Ricoeur, Ebeling, Barthes and Derrida rather than applying the theory more concretely to specific texts. Hancher rightly regards Derrida's interest in the theory as a paradoxical "betrayal" of it, since it is undermined if we eliminate the author.

Meanwhile Matthew's Christology demonstrates a relation to speech-act theory perhaps more clearly than Mark's, not least because Matthew's interest lies in the

---

[24] Norman Perrin, *Jesus and the Language of the Kingdom* (London: SCM, 1976).

[25] P. Maurice Casey, *Son of Man: The Interpretation and Influence of Daniel 7* (London: SPCK, 1979); Morna D. Hooker, *The Son of Man in Mark* (London: SPCK, 1967); and Barnabas Lindars, *Jesus Son of Man: A Fresh Examination of the Son of Man Sayings in the Gospels in the Light of Recent Research* (London: SPCK, 1983).

[26] Robert Fowler, *Loaves and Fishes. The Function of the Feeding Stories in the Gospel of Mark* (Chico: Scholars Press, 1981); Ernest Best, op. cit.; M. Eugene Boring, "The Christology of Mark: Hermeneutical Issues for Systematic Theology", in *Christology and Exegesis: New Approaches: Semeia* 30, 1985, 125–54.

[27] Graham N. Stanton, *The Gospels and Jesus* (Oxford: Oxford University Press, 1989), 28.

[28] Hugh C. White (ed.), *Speech-Act Theory and Biblical Criticism: Semeia* 41, 1988; Michael Hancher, "Performative Utterances, the Word of God, and the Death of the Author", 27–40, and Hugh C. White, "The Value of Speech-Act Theory for Old Testament Hermeneutics", 41–63. (See especially 27.)

authority of Jesus' *words and teaching*. Although he leaves his most explicit Christological declaration to the post-resurrection commissioning in Matt. 28:18–20, throughout his gospel Matthew interweaves inextricably his account of Jesus' teaching and commands with an emphasis on the uniqueness of his person. John P. Meier admirably captures the Matthean perspective. Meier writes, "What Jesus teaches depends on his own person for its truth, validity, and permanence. Teacher and teaching become inextricably tied together. You do not fully understand what the teaching is unless you understand who the teacher is. You cannot accept the teaching as true unless you accept the teacher as your Lord ...".[29] But why should this be the case, and why should the reader be involved? The answer concerns the Christological presuppositions on the basis of which the series of illocutionary acts depicted by Matthew operate: language which brings forgiveness; language which stills the storm, and language which authorizes and assigns a role. If the implicit Christology is false, the entire performative and exercitive dimension collapses and falls to the ground as nothing more than a construct of pious human imagination.

II

A Comparison with Other Speech-Act Approaches in this Area

Johannes G. du Plessis in his Stellenbosch study *Clarity and Obscurity* (1985) very generously comments about the origins of his research:

> The present study is conceived as an extension of the line of research initiated by Thiselton (1970), Aurelio (1977) and Arens (1982). Thiselton introduced the speech-act theory (which was developed by Austin, 1962) into parable research ... This was taken up by Aurelio ... Arens distinguishes his study from Thiselton's and Aurelio's by pointing out that they attempted to analyse the parables as individual speech-acts. Thus Arens turns his attention to a broader model of understanding within which the nature of the language of Jesus becomes evident as communicative action.[30]

E. Arens rightly recognizes that if he wishes to construct a speech-act theory of parables that could become the basis for a broader theological theory of action, he must look "behind" the New Testament parable-texts to take account of the entire speech-acts that are performed. Johannes du Plessis accepts this, but argues (with W.S. Vorster) that the context of speech-acts also embraces the wider textual embedding of the parables. The conclusion of du Plessis' detailed argument entirely coheres with the argument of the present chapter, with specific reference to the parables of Jesus. He writes:

---

[29] John P. Meier, *The Vision of Matthew: Christ, Church, and Morality in the First Gospel* (New York: Paulist Press, 1979), 43; cf. 42–51.

[30] Johannes G. du Plessis, *Clarity and Obscurity. A Study in Textual Communication of the Relation between Sender, Parable, and Receiver in the Synoptic Gospels* (Stellenbosch: University of Stellenbosch D.Theol. Dissertation, 1985), 2 and 3; cf. E. Arens, *Kommunikative Handlungen: die paradigmatische Bedeutung der Gleichnisse Jesu fur eine Handlungstheorie* (Dusseldorf: Patmos, 1982), 355; T. Aurelio, *Disclosures in den Gleichnissen Jesu: Eine Anwendung der disclosure-Theorie von I.T. Ramsey* (Frankfurt a/M: Lang, 1977); and Anthony C. Thiselton, "The Parables as Language-Event: Some Comments on Fuchs' Hermeneutics in the Light of Linguistic Philosophy", *Scottish Journal of Theology* 23, 1970, 437–68 [included in the present volume].

The thesis of this study is that the primary function of the parables in the narrative world of the gospels is *to establish Jesus*, as the narrator of the parables, *in an authoritative position towards his addressees.* The clarity and/or obscurity of the parables are intrinsic aspects of the parables as symbolic discourse. Both these aspects are manipulated to support Jesus' authoritative position. The gospels report [*sic*] the relationship between Jesus and his addressees in order that the recipients of the gospels may enter into the same dependent *relationship with Jesus* ... The obscurity and the perplexity are outshone by the focus on the power and authority of Jesus ... The parables' main aim is to let the recipients *recognize Jesus' authority* as the sole source of a salvific relationship with God.[31]

J.G. du Plessis' arguments throughout his study, however, draw not on theology, but on a view of the parables as part of a process of communicative action, examined in the light of the work of Austin, Grice, Searle, T. Aurelio, E. Arens (1982) and Geoffrey N. Leech (1983). He discusses Grice's principle of cooperative goals in his maxims of conversational implicature, to which we allude in more detail later in this book in our discussion of Ricoeur's narrative theory. In the context of the parables du Plessis takes up Wolfgang Iser's work (1980) on the interaction between what is explicit and what is implicit, between revelation and concealment, in texts. He distinguishes between "fictionality", which is a possible attribute not of texts but of the process of communication between author and audience, and "fictiveness", which can characterize texts, textual content, or textual devices. "Fictive" denotes a product of the imagination; "fictional" denotes a certain mode or category of speech-act. Although he cautiously accepts the operational value of Ricoeur's notion of narrative as "re-description" (which we examine in Chapter X of *New Horizons*), du Plessis calls attention to referential and contextual frames that constrain its limits.

In Chapters X and XV of *New Horizons* we develop these points with reference to John Searle's essay on the logic of fiction and to the important work of Nicholas Wolterstorff in his valuable and closely argued philosophical study *Works and Worlds of Art* (1980). With meticulous detail Wolterstorff demonstrates the role of human agency in performing actions which *"count as"* performances of other actions. His contrast between "cause-generation" and "count-generation" runs closely parallel to the contrast in Austin and Evans between causal and performative force, and he explicitly utilizes Searle's notion of "institutional facts" in which "X counts as Y in context C". On this basis we arrive at a philosophy of language in which the projection of "worlds" by human agents may include both a given propositional content *and variety of possible illocutionary effects.*

It is important to note that Wolterstorff, Searle and du Plessis all underline the fundamental *role of human agents within an extra-linguistic world for determining the operative nature and effect of certain speech-acts.* Differences between fiction, falsehood, historical report, or history-like narrative depend on what *status, stance, commitments and responsibilities* have been presupposed and accepted by authorial agents. They do not depend simply on judgements by communities of readers about systems of literary effects detached from the world of cause and count-generation. In Chapters X and XV, we underline the capacities of a single speech-act to perform a *variety* of illocutionary

---

31   Johannes G. du Plessis, op. cit., 5 and 269 (my italics).

functions, develop the issues further and also relate them to the problematic aspects of *"author's intention"*.

Du Plessis also notes, in common with Aurelio (and also my own earlier work) that parables may enact *various illocutionary acts at the same time*. Thus the Parable of the Lost Son (Luke 15:11–32) *both directs and invites* a potentially hostile audience of critics to a relationship of unconditional sharing and receiving, on the basis of Jesus' own "commitment" to sinners. Du Plessis agrees with Robert Funk that the audience has freedom to opt either for grace or for justice. But he dissents from Funk that the message cannot be specified further. Its "implicatures" also reveal the estrangement of "elder sons" and the experience of "coming home" as the security of the father's creative and sharing love.

In contrast to the more open-ended and pluri-valent interpretations of parables suggested by Funk, Crossan, Dan Otto Via, Susan Wittig and Mary Ann Tolbert, J.G. du Plessis argues their status and function as total speech-acts includes *both* their immediate conversational contexts in the gospel texts *and* their speech-relations to the speaker and to the audience. He insists that the parables are used in numerous instances as initiatory *gambits in a broader conversational pattern*. They belong to the strategy of the parables as a *macro speech-act* to be used in this way. The concluding authoritative remarks are an integral part of the parables. Du Plessis applies this approach to specific passages in a series of studies, in which he emphasizes extra-linguistic reality (1984), conversational implicature (1985, 1988, 1991) and the dimension of pragmatics (1987).[32]

The upshot of all this is that the research of Johannes du Plessis on speech-act theory, which he generously traces as arising from my 1970 essay, explores parallel paths, drawing mainly on Aurelio, Arens and Leech, with those which I have explored in my own work on speech-act theory, drawing more particularly on Searle, Recanati and Levinson, as well as Austin and Leech. In particular, we both draw similar implications for Christological texts, although we arrive at them in independent and different ways. Christological truth constitutes the basis on which, to borrow Recanati's phrase, there is more than a merely textual or intra-linguistic *claim* to perform acts in speech-utterances like those of actors on a stage; *the acts are effectively performed. They bring about a transformation in the extra-linguistic relationship between the speaker and the audience, and invite the reader to participate in that extra-linguistic transformation and relationship.*

III

Speech Acts in Searle and Recanati: Directions of Fit between Words and the World

John R. Searle explicitly acknowledges his indebtedness to two of his former teachers, J.L. Austin and P.F. Strawson. Following Austin, and less directly the later Wittgenstein,

---

[32] J.G. du Plessis, "Speech Act Theory and New Testament Interpretation with Special Reference to G.N. Leech's Pragmatic Principles", in P.J. Hartin and J.H. Petzer (eds), *Text and Interpretation: New Approaches in the Criticism of the New Testament* (Leiden: Brill, 1991), 129–42. Cf. also his "Pragmatic Meaning in Matthew 13: 1–23", *Neotestamentica* 21, 1987, 42–56; and "Did Peter Ask his Questions and How did Jesus Answer Him? Or Implicature in Luke 12:35–48", *Neotestamentica* 22, 1988, 311–24. See further Nicholas Wolterstorff, *Works and Worlds of Art* (Oxford: Clarendon Press, 1980).

Searle declares, "The unit of linguistic communication is not, as has generally been supposed, the symbol, word or sentence, or even the token of the word, symbol or sentence, but rather the production or issuance of the symbol or word or sentence in the performance of the speech-act."[33] Searle now elaborates a complex theoretical framework on the basis of which utterances perform a variety of specific acts, which in turn also entail a given propositional content. He draws attention to the nature of "speaking" as part of a rule-governed form of behaviour. But he also stresses that in Saussurian terms this does not imply that he is restricting his attention to Saussure's *parole*; Searle is also raising deeper questions about the presuppositions that constitute *langue*.[34]

This concern to construct a wider and deeper theoretical model represents a distinctive advance on Austin's work. Searle views his work as contributing to the philosophy of language, while Austin had adopted the so-called "ordinary language" approach of Oxford linguistic philosophy. Although he raises philosophically serious questions about moral responsibility and truth in such essays as "A Plea for Excuses" and "Truth", and although the volume edited by K.T. Fann examines the philosophical issues that Austin raises, nevertheless his work on illocutionary acts and performative language tended to operate at the level of everyday examples.[35] Yet it is worth pausing briefly to comment further on the background of speech-act theory in Austin's work, before introducing the specific methodological or theoretical devices with which we are most immediately concerned mainly from Searle but also from Recanati.

Austin does speak of the general contextual *presupposition* on the basis of which illocutionary acts operate, but he is more rigorous in his scrutiny of everyday examples than in a construction of a theoretical frame. His examples remain inimitable. He asks, how effective is the action of a team-captain in saying, "I pick George", if George grunts, "Not playing"?[36] If a conventional procedure has to be *accepted* for an utterance to constitute an act, what happens if someone concludes a quarrel with the words "My seconds will call on you", but we simply shrug it off?[37] How operative, if at all, are the words "I baptize thee", if the local minister is holding the wrong baby, or if he continues, "I baptize thee infant no. 2704"?[38] What happens if the Vice Chancellor or the Archbishop says, "I open this library", and the key snaps in the lock?[39]

Austin's examples serve to make clear the difference between *causal* power and what is *institutionally* operative. This provided the basis for Evans' work on biblical texts. Thus within a year after his work appeared, Donald Evans published his constructive book. In 1974 I attempted to draw on Austin's work a second time (the first was the comparison between Austin and Fuchs in context of parable study in 1970) to challenge prevailing assumptions about the language of "power" and more specifically blessing and cursing,

---

[33] John R. Searle, *Speech Acts. An Essay in the Philosophy of Language* (Cambridge: Cambridge University Press, 1969), 16; cf. also vii.

[34] Ibid., 17.

[35] J.L. Austin, *Philosophical Papers* (Oxford: Clarendon Press, 1961), 85–101 and 123–54; and K.T. Fann (ed.), *Symposium on J.L. Austin* (London: Routledge & Kegan Paul, 1969).

[36] J.L. Austin, *How to Do Things with Words*, 28.

[37] Ibid., 27.

[38] Ibid., 35.

[39] Ibid., 37.

in the Old Testament. It is unnecessary to rehearse these arguments again in this essay, since we have included this work in the present volume (Essay 4, above).[40] A very large number of Old Testament specialists had appealed to a supposedly "Hebraic" belief in the "innate power of words" to explain, for example, why Isaac, having been deceived into blessing the wrong son, could not revoke his words of blessing (Gen. 27:33–37). The same explanation was offered to account for the fact that apparently Balaam could not revoke his blessing of Israel, in the face of pressure from Balak (Num. 23:20). Gerhard von Rad and many others claimed that Hebrews held a view of language akin to word-magic, which saw it as "an objective reality endowed with mysterious power".[41] Grether and Zimmerli ascribed to "Hebraic" thought a view of words as like "a missile with a time-fuse"; while E. Jacob saw the Hebrew view of words as like "a projectile shot into the enemy camp whose explosion must sometimes be awaited but which is always inevitable".[42]

In Austin's terms, however, none of this line of reasoning was necessary. Isaac and Balaam were aware of operative conventional procedures for *blessings*. But *no procedure existed or was generally accepted* for *revoking* them. It would be like the bride or bridegroom saying solemnly "I do", and then expecting that the utterance "Sorry, I have changed my mind" could function with equal *performative* force as part of a supplementary appendix to the marriage service. In Austinian terms, it would be like requesting a service of "un-baptism". But "I un-baptize this infant ..." would not be a *performative* utterance, because such a procedure neither exists nor is accepted. "Power", I concluded in the 1974 study, does not function *causally* on the basis of a "Hebraic" view of language; but as an operational force resting on procedures and presuppositions in a *context of promise* relating to the *covenantal* God. It related to *institutional* features in Israel's life that set the stage for *effective speech-acts*.

John Searle moved well beyond Austin in developing a wider, more rigorous and more systematic framework of language-theory that addresses a broader range of issues. He published work in this area successively in 1969, 1979, 1980, 1983 and 1985.[43] Austin had worked with the three-fold categories of locutionary, illocutionary and perlocutionary acts. He defined these, respectively, as (i) a *locutionary* act *of* speaking which is "roughly equivalent to uttering a certain sentence with a certain sense and reference"; (ii) *illocutionary acts* such as "informing, ordering, warning, undertaking, i.e. utterances which have a certain (conventional) force", and (iii) *perlocutionary acts*, namely, "what we

---

[40]   Anthony C. Thiselton, "The Supposed Power of Words in the Biblical Writings", *Journal of Theological Studies*, 25, 1974, 283–99.

[41]   Gerhard von Rad, *Old Testament Theology*, vol. 2 (Eng., Edinburgh: Oliver & Boyd, 1965), 85.

[42]   W. Zimmerli, "Wort Gottes", *Religion in Geschichte und Gegenwart*, vol. 6 (Tübingen: 1962), col. 1810; O. Grether, *Name und Wort Gottes im Alten Testament* (Giessen: 1934), 103–7; Edmund Jacob, *Theology of the Old Testament* (Eng., London: Hodder and Stoughton, 1958), 131; Compare also L. Dürr, *Der Wertung des göttlichen Wortes im Alten Testament und im antiken Orient* (Leipzig, 1938), 52, 61 and 71.

[43]   John R. Searle, *Speech Acts* (as cited); *Expression and Meaning: Studies in the Theory of Speech Acts* (Cambridge: Cambridge University Press, 1979); John R. Searle, Ferenc Kiefer and Manfred Bierwisch (eds), *Speech-Act Theory and Pragmatics* (Dordrecht, London, and Boston: Reidel, 1980), esp. 221–32 (by Searle); John R. Searle, *Intentionality. An Essay in the Philosophy of Mind* (Cambridge: Cambridge University Press, 1983); and John R. Searle and Daniel Vanderveken, *Foundations of Illocutionary Logic* (Cambridge: Cambridge University Press, 1985).

bring about or achieve *by* saying something, such as convincing, persuading, deterring".[44] The fundamental difference between the second and third categories is that the second involves broadly *institutional* procedures, whereas the third may involve only *causal* power.

Searle accepts, although with some reservation, Austin's term "illocutionary acts", which typically involve the use of such verbs as "warn", "order", "approve", "promise" and "request". But he supplements them with three additional cross-categories of language-function which partly overlap, but also draw attention to other aspects of wider issues: (i) *performing utterance acts*, in which words or sentences are uttered; (ii) *performing propositional acts*, in which referring and predicating take place, and (iii) *performing illocutionary acts*, in which statements, questions, promises, or commands become operative. Searle declares, "In performing an illocutionary act one characteristically performs propositional acts and utterance acts."[45]

This gives rise to a fundamental distinction that remains operative in Searle's entire body of writings, including his work on intentionality. He distinguishes between *"illocutionary force indicators"* (usually denoted by a variable F) and *"proposition indicators"* (denoted by p).[46] The variable theoretical illocution "$F(p)$" may more specifically take the form of a warning "$W(p)$", or a promise "$Pr.(p)$". The negation of a propositional *content* can thus be kept distinct from the negation of illocutionary *force*. "I promise not to come" would be denoted by "$Pr.(-p)$"; whereas "I do not promise to come" would take the form "$-Pr(p)$".

This distinction is constructive for understanding the central issue discussed in the present chapter about hermeneutical theory and biblical texts. Two separate points need to be noted. First, Searle's distinction sheds light on the logical fallacy reflected in the overworn dualism of Kierkegaard, Heidegger and Bultmann between on the one hand, description, objectification, report and proposition, and on the other hand, address, promise, understanding and self-involvement. Biblical texts frequently *address the reader as warnings, commands, invitations, judgements, promises, or pledges of love.* But often these speech-acts also embody a propositional content. Thus, typically, the pattern of the earliest kerygma takes the form "$F(p)$", that is, "We preach (F) a Christ crucified (p)" (1 Cor. 1:23). Sometimes the dual function, as Searle has pointed out, may simply be implied, each by the other in the same utterance. Thus in the previous section on Pauline Christology we argued that the confession "Jesus is Lord" (1 Cor. 12:3) is neither simply p nor simply F but $F(p)$, or more specifically a commissive which entails the assertion of a state of affairs: "$Com(p)$".

The second point is even more fundamental. In his book *Expression and Meaning*, Searle introduces an illuminating and *far-reaching difference between the logic of promise* (and related language-functions) and *the logic of assertion*. He described the difference as *"differences in the direction of fit between words and the world"*. Some illocutions have part of their purpose or "point", "*to get the words* (more strictly, their propositional content) *to*

---

44   J.L. Austin, *How to Do Things with Words*, 108.
45   J.R. Searle, *Speech Acts*, 24.
46   Ibid., 31; cf. *Expression and Meaning*, 1; and *Intentionality*, 5–7.

match the world". This is the case with *assertions*. But others have the inverse function: *"to get the world to match the words"*.[47] This is the case with *promises* and *commands*.

By way of illustration from everyday life, Searle borrows an analogy from Elizabeth Anscombe's work on intention. We are asked to envisage a person who goes shopping, and is followed by a detective. The shopper has a list of words written on a slip of paper: "butter, eggs, bread, bacon ...". His or her aim is to transact the task as *to make the world of reality match the words* of the list. The transference of goods *changes the extra-linguistic world in accordance with the words* that embody *instructions, promises, or intentions*. The detective, on the other hand, does the converse. He carefully observes and notes down what takes place, that is, describes the world as it is. The purpose of his list is to provide a *descriptive report in words that match the reality of the world*. The propositional *content* (*p*) of the two lists will be identical: butter, eggs, bread and bacon. Their *force* (*F*) will be quite different, and will reflect a *different direction of fit between language and the world*. A final point in this analogy brings home sharply the limitations and weakness of hermeneutics which concern only intra-linguistic worlds in handling biblical texts. If, on reaching home, the *detective* realizes that he or she has made a mistake in a word of his or her *report*, there is need only to erase "margarine" and substitute "butter". But if the *shopper* has made a parallel mistake in his or her *performing* of instructions, his or her spouse may well send the shopper back to the store to rectify the problem. It is not a merely "intra-linguistic" affair.

Recanati takes up the same analogy to illustrate differences in the "'direction of correspondence' between words and the world".[48] As we have seen, Searle, Austin and Recanati diverge in their specific identifications of sub-categories of illocutionary acts, although Searle regards Austin's work as an "excellent basis" for development. More fundamentally, whereas Searle questions the sharpness of Austin's distinction between "meaning" and "force", Recanati defends it. Specifically, Recanati argues:

> If in virtue of the meaning it expresses, an utterance presents itself as having a particular illocutionary force, there is no certainty that it really does have the force that it has ... attributed to itself. Taken in Austin's sense, the force of an utterance must always go beyond its meaning; the latter includes a "projection" of the utterance's illocutionary force, not *the force itself*, which must be inferred by the hearer on the basis of the supposed intentions of *the speaker*.[49]

This entails a study of contextual inference.

For the purposes of this chapter, however, Austin, Searle and Recanati offer very broadly similar sub-categories of illocutionary acts, and Searle and Recanati agree on the suggestive importance of the model of "direction of fit" or "direction of correspondence" between words and the world. These represent our two working sets of methodological tools for the remainder of this chapter. Searle revises Austin's sub-categories partly because he claims that Austin has confused illocutionary *acts* with illocutionary *verbs*. Searle proposes to substitute: *assertives, directives, commissives* (Austin's sub-category is

---

[47] J.R. Searle, *Expression and Meaning*, 3 (Searle's italics).
[48] F. Recanati, op. cit., 150; cf. 150–63.
[49] Ibid., 27.

accepted), *expressives* and *declaratives*. These replace Austin's list of expositives, exercitives, behabitives, verdictives, and (commonly to Searle, Recanati and Austin) commissives. To place "assertives" among sub-categories of force may seem surprising, but it brings some advantages. It enables us to take account of different degrees of force with which an assertion states a propositional content: putting something forward as a tentative hypothesis stands at one end of the spectrum; insisting on the truth of something with total conviction stands at the other end. (This view has the further advantage of discouraging the disastrous Bultmannian antithesis between "faith", on the one hand, and positive response to the force of rational argument and evidence on the other. For affirmations of belief or faith combine *the two overlapping forces of assertions and commissives.*)

It is not entirely clear, however, that Searle's scheme improves on Austin's at every point. Dieter Wunderlich argues, "There is no clear classification of speech acts. Neither Austin's nor Searle's nor anybody else's attempts are really convincing."[50] But the value of the categories is operational and pragmatic in relation to given arguments and purposes. Issues of interpretative strategy will determine which system better matches specific questions and purposes in view. The major advantage of Searle's system is the possibility of tracing his own clear correlation between this classification of illocutions and his *directional* analysis of a word-to-world or world-to-word fit. *Assertives* fit reality (as we have seen) in a *words-to-world* direction. *Directives* and *commissives* (which include commands and promises) fit reality in the opposite direction of *world-to-words*. *What is spoken shapes what will be. Expressives* may presuppose either direction of fit. *Declaratives* in their very utterance *bring about* a particular direction of fit. Recanati's definition of declaratives is broader than Searle's. He argues that declarative sentences are "force-neutral", but also have illocutionary *potential*. All genuinely *performative* utterances "aim to *bring about*, not simply describe, the state of affairs they represent and that constitutes their propositional content".[51]

Searle retains these classifications and their corresponding directional relations in his subsequent book *Intentionality*.[52] From his work as a whole we may note two further points before we turn to the biblical texts. First, Searle underlines the importance of the institutional and extra-linguistic factors that were noted and expounded by Austin and Evans, but with special reference to *directives* (cf. Austin's *exercitives*). He declares, "It is *only given such institutions as the church, the law, private property, the state, and the special position of the speaker and hearer within these institutions* that we can excommunicate, appoint, give and bequeath ...".[53]

Searle exempts from this principle only certain utterances of God: "let there be light" (Gen. 1:3), and such intra-linguistic performances as "naming". But even here, many divine utterances perform actions because they operate commissively and directively as part of the covenant promise of God, and such intra-linguistic activities as "naming"

---

[50] Dieter Wunderlich, "Methodological Remarks on Speech-Act Theory", in J.R. Searle, F. Kiefer and M. Bierwisch (eds), *Speech-Act Theory and Pragmatics*, 297; cf. 291–312.

[51] F. Recanati, op. cit., 164 and 169 (his italics); and J.R. Searle, *Expression and Meaning*, 18.

[52] J.R. Searle, *Intentionality*, 165–7.

[53] J.R. Searle, *Expression and Meaning*, 18.

often depend on institutional factors. For example, if Joe Bloggs, the ship's engineer, "names" the ship, this naming is of a different order from when the shipping magnate's wife names it *performatively* at the appropriate ceremony. The act of naming a child on the birth certificate by parents is also *performative* in a way that is not the case if a "name" is suggested by a passing school enemy.

Second, Searle underlines the extra-linguistic factors involved in the logic of promise. Promise is typical of the force of many biblical texts. We cannot ignore the wishes and purposes of the speaker and the hearer in the promised commissive-transaction. In his book *Intentionality* this becomes part of Searle's wider and masterly discussion in which he insists, convincingly, that, provided that we do not view it primarily as a "mental act", the notion of the *purposive directedness of the author's intention against a background network of behavioural and contextual factors* is not only logically viable, but also logically *essential* for accounts of meaning that are balanced and comprehensive.[54] Whether we are speaking of intention or of promise, the logic of the concept and its practical operation in life presuppose some reference to the *wishes* of the speaker, and in the case of promise, both the speaker and the hearer.

If it were otherwise, we could not logically distinguish promise from threat. Searle observes, "A promise is a pledge to do something for you, not to you; but a threat is a pledge to do something to you, not for you. A promise is defective if the thing promised is something the promisee does *not want done* ... Furthermore, a *promise*, unlike an *invitation*, normally requires some sort of *occasion or situation that calls for the promise*."[55] The essential feature of the logic of promising is the attitude of commitment on the part of the speaker: "It is the undertaking of an obligation to perform a certain act."[56]

Searle's work thus seems to embody several theoretical developments beyond Austin, which we shall now examine in relation to specific biblical texts. First, he has modified Austin's sub-categories of illocutionary acts. Second, he has classified and set in a broader theoretical frame the interpersonal and institutional backgrounds against which illocutions become operative. Third, he has defended the role of purpose, directedness, or intentionality on the part of the speaker. Fourth, he has paid special attention to the logic of promise and other commissives. Most important of all he has drawn a very important distinction between language which operates in the direction of word-to-world, and language which operates in the direction of world-to-word.

Recanati parts company from Searle at several major points, including the issue of whether utterance interpretation can be reduced to sentence interpretation. But from the point of view of the present argument, Recanati's emphasis on the role of speaker or writer and addressee in an extra-linguistic context strengthens the significance of his work. It is possible for an explicit performative to be self-referential, as Austin and Benveniste have urged. Sometimes this is marked by some such phrase as "hereby". But the intra-linguistic markers of performative force are no guarantee of its effective extra-linguistic operation. Hence, Recanati rightly concludes, if we want to assess performative

---

[54] J.R. Searle, *Intentionality*, 1–36, 160–79 *et passim*.
[55] J.R. Searle, *Speech Acts*, 58 (my italics).
[56] Ibid., 60.

force not, as it were, like the activities of actors on a stage but as real-life acts, we need to look "behind the scenes" at the extra-linguistic context.

IV
The "World-to-Word Fit" of a Hermeneutic of Promise, with Some Implications for Interpreting the Atonement

We have spoken regularly of "transforming texts". When texts transform readers, situations, or reality, this force and function, as John Searle has pointed out, is characteristically that of *promise or pledge*, or sometimes that of *authorization or command*. The speaking of the words constitutes *an act that shapes a state of affairs, provided that* certain interpersonal or institutional states of affairs also hold. For example, as we saw in our discussion of Christological texts, whether the utterance "your sins are forgiven you" (Matt. 9:2) actually changes anything depends on the authority and institutional status of the speaker outside language, among other things. On the other hand, the declaration that a particular state of affairs is true ("Christ was buried, and was raised on the third day", 1 Cor. 15:4) has an *assertive* force, in which the *state of affairs* to be reported *determines the word* that is spoken. Characteristically, *promise shapes world-to-word; assertion shapes word-to-world.*

Some biblical texts perform both functions simultaneously. Sometimes the two components remain distinct: "We preach a Christ crucified" F (*p*), 1 Cor. 1:23. Sometimes the same form operates with dual force: "Jesus is Lord", F (*p*), that is, *commissive*, "We are Christ's bondslaves", (*world-to-word*); and *assertive* "God made Christ Lord" (*word-to-world*).

Although we note Searle's point that Austin sometimes confused illocutionary *acts* with a list of verbs in a given language which was used typically to perform such acts, the lists of such verbs drawn up under respective subheadings by Austin, Evans, Recanati and Searle himself help the interpreter to identify potential instances of illocutionary acts. A survey of a concordance to the biblical texts suggests that at least seventy verbs invite sub-classification as particular types of potential illocutionary acts. We may accept Dieter Wunderlich's assessment (noted above) that neither Austin's categories nor Searle's modifications of Austin, nor Recanati's modifications of Searle, may be regarded as definitive. The following verbs therefore are for the most part identified in terms of more than one system, and sometimes occur unavoidably in more than one sub-category. Wunderlich's call for a "workable" scheme is not invalidated by theoretical controversies between Searle, Recanati, and his own work.

Exercitives or *directives* include: appoint, adopt, bless, charge, choose, command, commission, confer, consecrate, convict, correct, curse, decree, direct, forbid, forgive, guarantee, hallow, invite, justify, name, ordain, pardon, preach, rebuke and send. *Commissives* include: acknowledge, adopt (also directive) bless (also directive), give, love (also expressive), magnify, obey, pledge, promised, repent (also expressive), swear, testify, trust and witness. *Declaratives* or *verdictives* include: acquit, correct, declare, deny, excuse, judge, justify (also directive) love (also commissive and expressive), pardon, preach (also directive), proclaim, reckon and reproach (also expressive). *Expressives* or *behabitives* include: appeal, confess, cry, complain, comfort, encourage, entrust, exhort, intercede, love (also commissive), magnify, mourn, praise, rejoice, repent, salute, thank, urge and worship. This list does not claim to be comprehensive.

The biblical texts abound in examples of occurrences of these verbs in institutional, situational and interpersonal contexts that render them performative speech-acts. One such context is that of *liturgy or worship*, of which the Psalms contain many instances. Thus the utterance "*I give thanks* to Thee, O Lord, with my whole heart" (Psalm 138:1) does not function to inform God about a state of mind, but has the force of an *act* of thanksgiving. Similarly, "*We give thanks* to Thee, O God, *We give thanks* to Thee" (Psalm 75:1) is followed by an *act* of invocation and by an *act* of praise: "*We call on Thy name*, and recount Thy wondrous deeds." Liturgy typically involves what Searle terms expressive illocutions, and Austin, behabitive performatives.

Institutional roles also provide a setting for illocutions and performatives. As an *apostle*, Paul writes: "*I urge you*, then be imitators of me" (1 Cor. 4:18). In his role as *king* and *intercessor* for the nation, Hezekiah declares, "*the good Lord pardon* every one who sets his heart to seek God" (2 Chron. 30:18, 19). As bearer of the authority of God, Jesus declares, "My son, your sins are *forgiven*" (Matt. 9:2; cf. John 20:23). The apostles combine exercitive authority and commissive promise in the utterance, "*Peace be to* this house" (Luke 10:5). Similarly, Jesus declares, "*Peace I leave with you*" (John 14:27), which constitutes the making of a promise and the giving of a gift, not simply a statement about a situation.

Some illocutions presuppose only a situation of interpersonal transaction, rather than more complex institutional factors. Thus the language of love can be spoken as an *act* of love: "*I love thee* O Lord, my strength ... my rock, my fortress, my deliverer" (Psalm 18:1, 2). The testimony of a witness may rest either on a formal or situational context: "*We testify* that the Father has sent the Son" (1 John 4:14); "*I affirm and testify* in the Lord ..." (Eph. 4:17). But other kinds of illocutions demand more formal relationships of status. In Zechariah an accusation is pre-empted by invoking the authority of God: "The Lord said, '*The Lord rebuke you* ... the Lord, who has chosen Jerusalem rebuke you'" (Zech. 3:2).

What is important about all these uses of language, however, is that they leave neither the speaker nor the hearer uninvolved and unchanged. In Evans' terminology they are self-involving; in Searle's terminology, all of the above examples operate in a *word-to-world* direction. Before we examine the effect of this principle for some major issues in biblical interpretation, we may note in passing that prior to Austin's work, the later Wittgenstein had noted this principle. He compares the respective logical force of "I am in pain" and "I love you." He comments, "One does not say: 'That was not true pain, or it would not have gone off so quickly.'" But one *could* say this of *love*: "Love is not a feeling."[57] Love, if it has operative meaning, has *commissive* consequences, so that the person who says, "I love you" *behaves* in the way indicated by the words, or they become empty. One could not say, "For a second I felt deep grief."[58] In contexts where we say, "I believe", "I love", "I grieve", "I mourn", or "I give", Wittgenstein urges, "My own relation to my words is wholly different from other people."[59]

---

[57]   L. Wittgenstein, *Zettel*, sect. 504.
[58]   L. Wittgenstein, *Philosophical Investigations*, II i, 174.
[59]   Ibid., II x, 192.

This constitutes, in effect, a further commentary on the logic and hermeneutic of promise. When God declares, "I have loved you with an everlasting love" (Jer. 31:3), the utterance entails a *world-to-word fit* in which the word guarantees that compatible patterns of action and states of affairs will come about, and incompatible ones be excluded. We shall argue shortly that the "world-to-word fit" aspect of biblical texts arises from the prominence of the category of *promise* in the biblical writings. Divine promise bridges the gap between what "is" and what "ought to be", and is interwoven with the themes of covenant and of eschatology. Nevertheless the contextual and institutional frame within which promises become effective also concerns *states of affairs*. Side by side with *promissory word-to-world language*, therefore, we also find *world-to-word language of assertion*.

With this principle in mind, we turn to Pauline language about the power of the cross. We address in particular to E.P. Sanders' claims about Paul. First, Sanders follows Stendahl in arguing against the traditional Lutheran interpretation that Paul first begins with the problem of human sin and then expounds the cross as its "solution". Second, Sanders draws a sharp distinction between "atonement" language and "participatory" language as ways of understanding Paul's theology of the cross. We shall argue that Sanders is wrong to give *priority* to the participatory model. Speech-act theory suggests that the *atonement language* constitutes *assertions about states of affairs* in which the *language reflects an accomplished reality*. But *participatory language* operates with the reverse direction of fit: it is *eschatological* and *promissory* language that *shapes actualities to the word*. It is part of the language of *transformation* but it depends for its operative effectiveness on the extra-linguistic state of affairs that the *atonement* language *asserts*.

In relation to current issues in Pauline interpretation, this seems partly to confirm (although also to modify) one recent emphasis and seriously to question another. First, it largely coheres with, but also sets in a new light, the emphasis since the 1970s (following initially some of Stendahl's questions in 1963) that Rom. 9:1–11:36 constitutes no mere appendix to Romans 1–8, but, rather, represents the theological crown, or at least continuation of the argument. Up until the 1970s, the common denominator between the reader and Paul was identified, as Stendahl expressed it, in the common human experience of bondage to sin which Paul articulates in Rom. 7:7–25. This approach matches both a Lutheran and an existential hermeneutic. But Stendahl, Sanders, and more recently others including Francis Watson and A.J.M. Wedderburn, have argued for a different emphasis.[60]

Sanders writes: "It seems likely ... that Paul's thought did not run from plight to solution, but rather from solution to plight. The attempts to argue that Romans 7 shows the frustration which Paul felt during his life as a practising Jew have now mostly been given up."[61] The "I" of these verses is not necessarily autobiographical. The major concern turns on how God determines to fulfil his covenant promises to his disobedient people.[62] What happens when God accepts the commissive force of a pledge, but his people effectively do not?

---

[60] A.J.M. Wedderburn, *The Reasons for Romans* (Edinburgh: T. & T. Clark, 1988); and Francis Watson, *Paul, Judaism and the Gentiles. A Sociological Approach* (Cambridge: Cambridge University Press (S.N.T.S.M. 56), 1986), 88–91 *et passim*.

[61] E.P. Sanders, *Paul and Palestinian Judaism*, 443.

[62] K. Stendahl, *Paul among Jews and Gentiles*, 23–40; and 78–96.

The key passages in Romans, including Romans 8, reaffirm the *world-to-word* effectiveness of the divine promise, but the realities of the human situation are also described in *word-to-world* assertions about the human plight. Nevertheless, this is not only a contextually relevant state of affairs; it is also to be *asserted that God has acted decisively in Christ*. Two sets of assertions (word-to-world) provide the context for questions about the effective power of promise (world-to-word). Neither dimension is addressed without reference to the other. Stendahl is correct when he tartly observes that whether we try to interpret everything in existential terms depends on whether "we happen to be more interested in ourselves than in God or the fate of his creation".[63] In Markus Barth's judgement, the issue centres on the faithfulness of God and on the church's acknowledgement of her "sisterly co-existence with Israel".[64]

Here, however, a second and more complex issue arises. In what way is the believer's situation affected by the coming of Christ? Is the key concept, for Paul, the "participatory" one of being-in-Christ, or does the possibility of salvation depend on the work of Christ understood as atonement? Sanders argues that the former is more important and forward-looking to the future. Atonement language merely relates to the past. But how are these two "logics" in Paul related?

First, even the "participatory" logic of being-in-Christ is complex. Schweitzer was correct to argue that being-in-Christ is an *eschatological* concept. In our terms, it has a promissory dimension. Schweitzer argued that the term applied to the new creation, to those who were "capable of assuming the resurrection mode of existence before the general resurrection of the dead takes place".[65] He rightly declares, "Being-in-Christ is not a subjective experience."[66] It refers to the "one new entity" (Gal. 3:28) that shares in Christ's death and resurrection (Rom. 6:4, 5, 13). Sharing in the "mystical Body of Christ" stands in contrast to being "in Adam" (1 Cor. 15:22–27, 45; Rom. 5:12–21).[67] Deissmann's approach in terms of experience neglects eschatology.[68]

Alfred Wikenhauser develops Schweitzer's view further. He comments, "This union with Christ has an objective character."[69] It is "not merely a subjective feeling of Christ's nearness".[70] But it is *not* the language of *bare assertion*. For, first, Christ's resurrection constitutes a *pledge* (Rom. 6:8) of that of believers, who will be caught up in God's eschatological promise (1 Cor. 15:20; Rom. 8:29). Second, it carries with it the self-involving dimension of Christ's "living in" believers (Gal. 2:20). Hence Wikenhauser concludes, rightly, that while the term "in Christ" is objective, the progressive dimension remains "incomplete". It is *"not something final"* but is *founded on promise*.[71]

---

[63] Ibid., 24.
[64] Marcus Barth, *The People of God* (Sheffield: J.S.N.T.S. 5, 1983), 26.
[65] A. Schweitzer, *The Mysticism of Paul the Apostle*, 101.
[66] Ibid., 117.
[67] Ibid., 123.
[68] A. Deissmann, *Paul*, 161.
[69] Alfred Wikenhauser, *Pauline Mysticism. Christ in the Mystical Teaching of St Paul* (Eng., Freiburg: Herder, and London: Nelson, 1960), 94.
[70] Ibid., 104.
[71] Ibid., 199; cf. 184 and 185.

Robert Tannehill's interpretation of Paul's language about dying and rising with Christ, and A.T. Hanson's more recent work on the paradox of the cross, make a parallel point.[72] Some references to sharing the death and resurrection of Christ include the *word-to-world* force of *assertion*. They assert the uniqueness of God's saving deed in Christ. Other Pauline texts have *directive*, *promissory* or *commissive* force, and concern present transformation of *world-to-word* (2 Cor. 4:10; Rom. 6:11). If we follow Recanati rather than Searle at this particular point, while all these references may be illocutionary, only some are performative *within* this category.

In this light we may now review E.P. Sanders' claims about the work of Christ in Paul. Sanders draws a sharp contrast between texts which stress the *participatory* significance of the cross and those which speak of its *atoning* significance. To the former category belongs the key verse: "One has died for all, therefore all have died ... that those who live might live no longer for themselves but for Him who for their sake died and was raised" (2 Cor. 5:13, 15). The thrust of Sanders' argument is that in Paul "the emphasis unquestionably falls ... not *backwards* towards the expiation of past transgressions, but *forwards* towards the assurance of life with Christ ... This, says Paul, is the *purpose* of Christ's death."[73]

Sanders is probably correct to trace two different kinds of "logic" to the "participation" texts and "atonement" texts respectively, although N.T. Wright expresses reservations about too sharp a contrast. J.K.S. Reid noted the point a number of years ago when he observed that the Pauline texts embody both "a principle of correspondence" ("because He lives, we shall live also"), *and* "a principle of contrariety": "Christ wins these benefits for us, who Himself has no need of them."[74] But the ground on which Sanders singles out the participatory category as where Paul's "emphasis unquestionably falls" is very uncertain. For it is not merely a matter of *past versus future* orientation. In Searle's terminology, the language of *atonement* makes *assertions* about the finished work of Christ, in which the direction of fit is from *world-to-word*: the word of the cross, in this context, communicates and asserts the reality of what God *has done*. That it is *past* is part of the logic of its description as a *completed* work to which humankind can contribute nothing. But the language of *participation* is bound up with *promise, commitment, declaration and directive*: it is *word-to-world* in that it *shapes the identity* of the Christian and *creates the reality of the new creation*.

This also helps us to see more clearly the issues discussed by Schweitzer and Wikenhauser about being in Christ. The phrase embodies a multi-layered logic. Its basis is objective, but in its eschatological frame it also operates with the logic of promise. Wikenhauser rightly stresses both its objectivity and its forward-looking self-involvement, inviting progressive transformation into the image of Christ. Robert Tannehill's work on death and resurrection with Christ and A.T. Hanson's book on the cross imply a similar conclusion. Some Pauline texts are *word-to-world directives*: "Reckon

---

[72] Robert Tannehill, *Dying and Rising with Christ. A Study in Pauline Theology* (Berlin: Topelmann, 1962), 1–47 and 75–129, and Anthony T. Hanson, *The Paradox of the Cross in the Thought of Paul* (Sheffield: J.S.N.T.S. 17, 1987), 24–78.

[73] E.P. Sanders, *Paul and Palestinian Judaism*, 465 (first italics mine; second his).

[74] J.K.S. Reid, *Our Life in Christ* (London: SCM, 1963), 90–91.

yourselves to be dead to sin" (Rom. 6:11). But other Pauline texts simultaneously assert a *world-to-word* deed of God in Christ and also create and shape reality, as promise in a *word-to-world* direction. God's "eschatological deed" constitutes "an act by which the old world is invaded and a new life in a new world is created".[75]

The proclamation of this deed is the word of the cross, and its power lies in its *operative effectiveness to transform*. From the point of view of hermeneutical theory, the upshot of all this is that a hermeneutic of self-involvement rests, in turn, on a hermeneutic of understanding, in which historical reconstruction constitutes part of a more complex and more comprehensive process. Our account of assertions or of "propositional content" follows Searle more closely than Recanati. Recanati differs from Searle on several major points, including the nature and scope of the distinction between locutionary and illocutionary acts. He criticizes Searle for, in effect, equating locutions with the propositional contents of illocutionary acts. But both Searle and Recanati, together with Austin, Daniel Vanderveken and others, agree together that factors in the speaker's (and audience's) context of utterance contribute to the conditions that affect the *actual performance* (as opposed to mere *semantic indications* of performance) of the illocutionary act.[76] Although he finds borderline counter-examples that raise some difficulties, Levinson cautiously confirms this principle.[77]

The fundamental place of *promise* in the biblical texts is confirmed with reference to a substantial area of the Old Testament in the work of my former colleague David Clines on the theme of the Pentateuch. Clines argues that the Pentateuch as a whole "receives its impetus" from "the promise to the patriarchs, with its various elements and in the various formulations".[78] The patriarchal promise is declared in Gen. 12:1–3: "Now the Lord said to Abram, 'Go from your country ... to the land which I will show you, and I will make of you a great nation, and I will bless you, and make your name great, so that you will be a blessing. I will bless those who bless you' ...". Clines traces seven elements of the promise, which fall into three main groups: the promise of posterity, the promise of a relationship with God, and the promise of land. The Pentateuch sets forth a partial fulfilment and partial non-fulfilment of these promises. The posterity element is dominant in Gen. 12–50; the relationship element, in Exodus and Leviticus, and the land element, in Numbers and Deuteronomy.

Clines traces what amounts to a number of promissory-commissive illocutions in the text under each heading. The promise concerning posterity is "to your seed" (Gen. 12:7); "Count the stars ... so shall your seed be" (Gen. 15:4, 5); "I will multiply your seed" (Gen. 16:10); "Sarah shall bear you a son ... I will establish my covenant with him..."(Gen. 17:19, 20); "By myself have I sworn ... that I will indeed bless you, and I will multiply your seed as the stars of heaven" (Gen. 22:16–18). He includes some twenty examples under this

---

[75]   Robert Tannehill, op. cit., 70.

[76]   See also J.R. Searle and Daniel Vanderveken, *Foundations of Illocutionary Logic*, 74–86; Daniel Vanderveken, "Illocutionary Logic and Self-Defeating Speech Acts", in J.R. Searle, F. Kiefer and M. Bierwisch (eds), *Speech Act Theory and Pragmatics* (Dordrecht and Boston, MA: Reidel, 1980), 247–72; and F. Recanati, op. cit., 265–6.

[77]   Stephen C. Levinson, *Pragmatics*, 226–83, esp. 276–8.

[78]   David J.A. Clines, *The Theme of the Pentateuch* (Sheffield: J.S.O.T.S. Press, 11, 1978), 26 and 27.

heading. Under the promise of relationships, Clines includes several passages that allude to covenantal promises: "Behold, my covenant is with you" (Gen. 17:1–11); "I will establish my covenant with him [Isaac] for an everlasting covenant" (Gen. 17:17, 18). The promise of relationship is formulated in different ways. Sometimes, for example, it takes the form of a pledge "to be with [you]" (Gen. 26:3, 24; 28:15). Clines comments, "The assurance that the God who speaks is the God who has pledged Himself to one's father and his descendants is a re-assurance of the hearer's own relationship to God."[79]

Clines compiles a list of nearly two hundred promises and allusions to the patriarchal promise in the Pentateuch.[80] Many constitute instances of *world-to-word commissives*. Clearly spoken acts of commitment ("I will be your God", Exod. 6:7; "This is my God", Exod. 15:2) bring about changes in situations or patterns of expectation and behaviour that would not otherwise take place. Associated with the promise, *directive* or *exercitive* world-to-word forces of utterance also operate. For example, Moses is addressed in language which begins as a *commissive* act of promise and becomes, in turn, an *exercitive* act of appointment or a *directive* act of commission: "I am the God of your father ... I will send you ..." (Exod. 3:6, 10). The divine revelation constitutes an act of disclosure (Exod. 6:3, 6). But some of these many instances have an assertive force. Exodus 6:1–9 combines promise, commission, declaration and disclosure with propositional content. Thus "I will bring you to the land which I swore to give to Abraham, to Isaac, and to Jacob" (6:8) takes the form $F(p)$ or $Pr(p)$. These assertions operate in the direction of a *word-to-world* fit.

The language of divine promise belongs to the context of covenant (Exod. 34:10). The commissives "You shall be my own possession" and "All that Yahweh has spoken we will do" (Exod. 19:5, 8) frame the so-called covenant code. Similarly, the Book of Leviticus, Clines argues, presupposes that response to the divine promise will take the form of *acts of worship*, which are seen as institutional "statutes and ordinances" (Lev. 26:46).[81] The sabbath (Lev. 26:43), the jubilee year (Lev. 27:23), confession of sin (Lev. 26:40) and tithes (Lev. 27:30) form part of an institutional context. On the other hand, the Book of Numbers gives the framework of promise a concrete form in terms of the physical *movement* towards the promised land. The "cloud" represents a *pledge*, which moves with Israel towards entry into the land, which God has promised (Num. 10:11, 12, 29).

We need not depend on some particular interpretation or dating of the idea of covenant in the Old Testament texts in order to draw attention to the role of promise. A recent study of the covenant by Ernest Nicholson vindicates the view that the covenant in Israel did *not* represent a merely "word-to-world" legitimization of an existing social order.[82] Nicholson discusses and evaluates the influence of Weber's sociological theory on A. Alt, M. Noth, and others, and assesses the more recent work of L. Perlitt and Kusch. He concludes that the Hebrew prophets, especially Hosea (Hos. 6:7; 8:1) developed a theology of covenant precisely to *de*-legitimize existing social structures by stressing Israel's unique relationship to the sovereign God, who had initiated the relationship.

---

[79] Ibid., 35.
[80] Ibid., 32–43.
[81] Ibid., 50–53.
[82] Ernest W. Nicholson, *God and His People: Covenant and Theology in the Old Testament* (Oxford: Clarendon Press, 1986).

Thus Nicholson's study of the covenant confirms the *world-to-word* dimension of covenantal promise, which we have been examining. Provided that we place sufficient emphasis on divine initiative and transcendence, there is still force in W. Eichrodt's early comment on the commissive nature of the covenant, to the effect that on the basis of the covenant a relationship is established in which human persons know where they stand.[83] The world-to-word fit of promise (F) is a promise that can be defined also in terms of a content (p).

We add a brief postscript on the Johannine writings in order to make a parallel comment. The aim of the Fourth Gospel is explicit: "These things have been written that you may believe that Jesus is the Christ, the Son of God, and that believing, you might have life by His name" (John 20:31). It is a well-known issue of interpretation that this refers either to a deepening of Christian belief that is in view (present tense) or to an evangelistic purpose of bringing the reader to faith (aorist). Throughout the Gospel a number of indicators of self-involving and commissive speech-acts occur. John stresses, for example, the commissive and declarative role of *witness* or *testimony*. John the Baptist performs the role of witness (John 1:7, 8, 15, 32, 34; 3:26; 5:33). The woman of Samaria testifies to Jesus before her neighbours (John 4:39); the disciples and the writer perform the role of witnesses (John 15:27; 21:24); Jesus bears witness to the Father (John 3:32, 33), and the Father bears testimony to Jesus (John 5:32, 37; 8:18).

In the Johannine epistles "we testify" constitutes an illocution (1 John 1:2; 4:14; cf. 5:6, 9; 3 John 3). In the vast majority of cases, however, *that to which* witnesses testify can be expressed in terms of a given propositional content: "They believed because of the woman's testimony (F), 'He told me all that I ever did' (p)" (John 4:39). The same principle applies to many instances of self-involving belief-utterances. The succession of Christological confessions, on the one hand, deeply affect and re-orientate the persons who utter or make them; on the other hand, they also embody a belief-content. The low-key beginnings in the earlier chapters: "He told me all that I ever did" (4:39) reach a grand climax in Thomas's Christological confession "My Lord and my God" (John 20:28).

The world-to-word direction of fit of belief-utterances in John is demonstrated by the connection between faith in Christ and *life*. It is no accident that the gift of life to Lazarus constitutes the climax of the section of the Gospel known as the Book of Signs (John 11:1–44). In this context Jesus declares, "He who believes in me, though he die, yet shall he live" (11:25). Once again, this has the force of a *promise* that has a *world-to-word* direction of fit. The transforming effects on the world of the words of Jesus are seen not only in the role of promise and self-involving confession, but also in the division, conflict and verdictive force which they inevitably bring: "Many of the disciples drew back ... Simon Peter said, 'Lord, to whom shall we go? You have the words of eternal life'" (John 6:66); "So there was a division among the people" (7:43); "Jesus said 'for judgement I came'" (9:39; cf. 16:8). But the call to faith, to decision and to confession rests on the truth of certain states of affairs.

Raymond Brown argues that Bultmann's "existential interpretation" of the Fourth Gospel "has not done Johannine studies a disservice" because of John's emphasis on

---

[83]   Walther Eichrodt, *Theology of the Old Testament*, vol. I (Eng., London: SCM, 1961), 38.

urgency and decision.[84] But Searle has reminded us that whenever promises, pledges, or other world-to-word utterances are effective and fully operative, a context and a background are presupposed concerning which word-to-world assertions can be made. In the enfleshment of the divine word of promise in the world in the incarnation of Jesus Christ (John 1:14) *these two "directions of fit" come together as one single transforming personal reality.* Jesus comes and addresses the reader in the Johannine writings as the word who, on the one hand, articulates a pre-existing ultimate reality (John 1:1–18), but who, on the other hand, promises world-to-word transformation (John 20:31). In the post-resurrection era the word of Jesus, who is the truth (14:6), will be mediated through the Spirit of truth (16:13). The Paraclete will speak *truth* "in Christ's name" (14:26); but will speak on this basis in ways that will bring about *world-to-word transformation.*

---

[84] Raymond E. Brown, *The Gospel according to John* (London: Chapman, 1971), lxxviii–lxxix.

CHAPTER SEVEN

More on Christology: "Christology in Luke, Speech-Act Theory, and the Problem of Dualism in Christology" (1994)

This essay was first published in Jesus of Nazareth: Lord and Christ, *edited by Joel B. Green and Max Turner (Grand Rapids, MI: Eerdmans and Carlisle: Paternoster, 1994), pp.453–72. These essays were in honour of I. Howard Marshall. By 1994 I came to see increasing points of relevance between biblical studies and speech-act theory, but this approach also points to connections between Luke's Christology and certain conceptual problems that have dogged modern theology since the time of Lessing and Kant. I should like to regard this work as a significant and original contribution to a long-standing debate. It also combines my four key inter-disciplinary interests of biblical studies, philosophy, language-functions and Christian theology.*

I
Christology after Kant: the Main Argument

The above title, with its three diverse points of reference, may appear to be so far-ranging as to necessitate an explanatory defence at the beginning of the argument. First, I have chosen to focus a good part of this essay on Luke partly because I. Howard Marshall, whom this volume duly honours and congratulates, has made Luke, as well as Christology, one of his own special areas of interest and expertise. Within his work on Luke, he has also refused to accept an artificial dualism between theology and history; to attack the supposed inevitability of such a dualism thus constitutes part of the agenda of this essay as well.

But at a still more important level in terms of the present argument, I propose that what has traditionally been termed "Luke's interest in history" should more constructively be termed, from the standpoint of hermeneutics and contemporary philosophical theology, Luke's concern about the importance of *the public domain*. The public domain constitutes a necessary context for Luke's Christology. In this respect it is arguable that Luke stands in contrast, at least in terms of emphasis, to Mark's concern to call attention to more enigmatic features which signal transcendence, and to Matthew's concerns about particular communities, particular traditions, and eschatology.

Second, speech-act theory sharpens the importance of the extra-linguistic features that lie in the stream of life out of which language operates, but may not always be "said". Speech-act theory in the tradition of J.L. Austin and J.R. Searle draws a careful distinction between what is "said" as a propositional *content* and the illocutionary *force* of an utterance in which an *act* is performed *in* the saying of the utterance or *in* the writing of a text. An appraisal of the force may "show" (if not "say") that certain presuppositions or implications must hold if this illocutionary force is to be successfully operative. This gives us the clue to what Marshall in *The Origins of New Testament Christology* (1976) has termed "the indirect approach to Christology".[1] As Marshall suggests, here we may distinguish between the question: "Did Jesus *say that* he was the Messiah?" (a question of propositional content) and the different question "Did Jesus *act* and speak as Messiah?" This latter question concerns performative force and implies a presupposition about an institutional status and role. This might, in turn, be translated into a theological proposition, but now one of a different order, about Christology.

In a recent essay, "The Son of Man and the Incarnation" (1991), Marshall distinguishes, by way of analogy, between the proposition "George was King", and the *implicature* that may be derived from a proposition that asserts a different matter of content: "King George died in 1952." He comments, "The use of the term 'King' carries a whole set of implications regarding the status and functions of the person thus described, and this aspect of the statement is distinguishable from the statement made about the subject, namely that he died."[2] On this basis, for example, Marshall disentangles issues about the messianic self-consciousness of Jesus from the question of whether he explicitly made assertions about his own messianic status and role. To confuse these two distinct issues, he points out, is quite simply "illogical".[3]

I propose to pursue this approach further, developing particular aspects of my work on speech-act theory in *New Horizons in Hermeneutics*.[4] In these pages I have argued, for example, that in the triple tradition of the Synoptic Gospels, the utterance of Jesus, "My son, your sins are [hereby] forgiven you" (Mark 2:5; par. Matt. 9:2; Luke 5:20), depends for its operative effectiveness on the presupposition that outside language Jesus possesses a particular institutional role and status.[5] Matthew and Mark use the present tense which normally (but not always) characterizes performative utterance (for example, "I give and bequeath ..."), but on Luke's use of the perfect Marshall rightly observes that ἀφέωνται expresses "the abiding force" (*sic*) of the forgiveness.[6]

Marshall notes in his commentary on this passage in Luke that the question posed in the minds of the witnesses, "Who can forgive sins except God?" (Luke 9:21), consciously raises the issue of "whether Jesus has any authorization to speak in this fashion".[7] In *New Horizons in Hermeneutics* I have urged that there is a crucial difference, developed in speech-act theory by Austin, Evans, Searle and Recanati, between *institutional* authority of an extra-linguistic nature and mere *causal* authority which may rest on little more than the force of self-assertion. Christology in the New Testament represents an affirmation of the former and a denial of the latter, and it is this which gives rise to reticence if or when Jesus *asserts* propositions *about* himself, ratter than *acts* and speaks as himself.

---

[1] I.H. Marshall, *The Origins of New Testament Christology* (London: Inter-Varsity, 1976).
[2] Marshall, "The Son of Man and the Incarnation", *Ex Auditu* 7 (1991), 30; cf. 29–43.
[3] Marshall, *Origins*, 55.
[4] A.C. Thiselton, *New Horizons in Hermeneutics: The Theory and Practice of Transforming Biblical Reading* (London: HarperCollins, 1992), 16–19, 274–75, 282–312, 361–67, 389–90, 559–60, 597–604.
[5] Thiselton, *New Horizons*, 286.
[6] Marshall, *The Gospel of Luke: A Commentary on the Greek Text* (Exeter: Paternoster, 1978), 212.
[7] Marshall, *The Gospel of Luke*, 214.

Two years after the publication of *The Two Horizons* (1980), in which I attempted (among other tasks) to explore the significance of Wittgenstein for hermeneutics, R.G. Gruenler published his book *New Approaches to Jesus and the Gospels: A Phenomenological and Exegetical Study of Synoptic Christology*.[8] Gruenler affirms both Marshall's exploration of "the indirect approach to Christology" and my own exploration of Wittgenstein's philosophy of language, although he also notes a certain difference of emphasis and area between his work and mine.[9] He does not explore in depth the philosophical issues which lie behind Wittgenstein's broadly Kantian concerns about the limits of language, nor does he appeal to a theory of speech-acts of the kind developed by Austin, Searle, or other post-Wittgensteinian writers. Nevertheless we share a common starting-point concerning the interweaving of language and life, especially in first-person utterances. We both allude to D.M. High's interpretation of Wittgenstein.[10]

The third point of reference in the title is to the problem of dualism in Christology after Kant. It is, to my mind, important to understand the dilemma posed by Kantian philosophy in order to see why, from Kant and Strauss to Bultmann and Robinson, a certain kind of dualism has bedevilled so many attempts to interpret the New Testament in such a way as to articulate a coherent Christology in the modern world. We may readily allow that the two-natures Christology of the patristic era and the Chalcedonian creeds had to steer a careful path to avoid its own kind of dualism. But the problem has taken on a new urgency since Kant. Hans Frei makes the point with acute perceptiveness in his carefully argued essay on D.F. Strauss. He writes:

> The dilemma is at least as old as the fourth- and fifth-century endeavour to describe the indivisible unity of the person of Christ and the presence of two unabridged natures, divine and human, in him. The modern shift in categories from those of substantialist personhood to self-conscious, inward, and at the same time historical personality, gave the problem new urgency and changed its expression.[11]

If rational inquiry, as Kant claimed, cannot move beyond that which the activity of the mind shapes and conditions in terms of the categories and structures of space, time, and causality through which it apprehends the phenomenological world of objects, persons and events within the historical continuum, how can Jesus Christ simultaneously constitute a full *manifestation of the divine and eternal*, while also remaining a full participant *in the nexus of the historical life within the world?*

This form of epistemological dualism poses sharper and more complex problems than the simpler pre-Kantian dualism imposed between contingent history and universal reason by Lessing's "ugly ditch". It constitutes a far more fundamental challenge to the attempt, sustained by Marshall and others, to hold together theology and history in the interpretation of christological data than more empirical fine-tuning concerning, for

---

[8] R.G. Gruenler, *New Approaches to Jesus and the Gospels: A Phenomenological and Exegetical Study of Synoptic Christology* (Grand Rapids, MI: Baker, 1982).

[9] Gruenler, *New Approaches*, 11, 109.

[10] Gruenler, *New Approaches*, 20; A.C. Thiselton, *The Two Horizons: New Testament Hermeneutics and Philosophical Description* (Exeter: Paternoster; Grand Rapids, MI: Wm. B. Eerdmans, 1980), 425; idem, *New Horizons*, 617.

[11] H. Frei, "David Friedrich Strauss", in *Nineteenth-Century Religious Thought in the West*, eds N. Smart et al., 3 vols (Cambridge: Cambridge University Press, 1988 [1985]), 1:254.

example, the accuracy of Luke's work as a historian. It is noteworthy that Marshall writes in his book aptly entitled *Luke: Historian and Theologian* (1970) that Luke's "view of theology led him to write history".[12] In the tradition of rationalism, from I. Newton's *Mathematical Principles* (1687) through Locke's *Reasonableness of Christianity* (1695) to Lessing's *Wolfenbüttel Fragments* (1777–78) and *The Education of the Human Race* (1780), "*history*" might seem to add nothing which might not also be apprehended by universal reason, even if the paradigm of mathematics seemed to some to assign to "*reason*" a purity and universality to which the accidental might-or-might-nots of history could never aspire. But in principle natural theology and special revelation might in the event cohere together. With the publication a year later of Kant's *Critique of Pure Reason* (1781, 2nd edn, 1787), a watershed was reached, and the nature of the problem of a dualism between history and reason passed a nodal point of transition.

In a clear essay on Kant, E. Fackenheim draws attention to some sentences from Kant which most sharply focus the problem:

> Even if God really spoke to man, the latter could never know it was God who had been speaking. It is radically impossible for man to grasp the Infinite through his senses ... If such an immediate intuition happened to me ... I should still have to use a concept of God as a standard by which to decide whether the phenomenon in question agreed with the necessary characteristics of a Deity.[13]

It is no answer to appeal to religious mysticism, for there is no way to know whether what is experienced or found "are the products of its own imagination mistaken for the divine".[14]

It would be a mistake, however, to relegate this problem to the peculiarities of a Kantian critical philosophy which could readily be discarded, or at least disregarded. It is quite clear that in the work of Strauss and many Hegelians, a dualism persisted between the raw data of the causal nexus of *Historie*, or "objective history" as it lay open to the scrutiny of reconstructive historical research, and "myth" or "idea" or "spirit" (depending on the writer) which might express a "value" dimension for the kind of Christology which might serve theology. The story is too well known to need to be retold. F.C. Baur resolved the dualism by giving priority to the social forces of the causal nexus of history. Strauss, when pressed, despaired of what history could offer, and saw the choice as lying between a mythological idea and the recognition of fiction for what it was. Kähler opted for the side of other dualism, which exalted the preached Christ at the expense of the so-called historical Jesus. Bultmann insisted that *Historie* possessed a certain importance, but so closely identified the appeal to history with an anti-Lutheran appeal to justification by the "works" of historical inquiry that the "history" side of the dualism was effectively minimized.

If it is thought that recent British scholarship fails to be touched by this legacy of philosophical theology, we may recall some sentences from J.A.T. Robinson in the well-known volume *Christ, Faith, and History* (1972). He seizes at once on the alleged dualism

---

12 Marshall, *Luke: Historian and Theologian* (Exeter: Paternoster, 1970), 52; see 21–52 *et passim*.

13 E.L. Fackenheim, "Immanuel Kant", in *Nineteenth-Century Religious Thought*, 31–2, cited from *Conflict of Faculties* in the Prussian Academy edition of Kant, *Werke: Akademie Textausgabe* (Berlin: de Gruyter, 1968), 7:63 and 8:142.

14 Fackenheim, "Kant", 32; *Werke*, 6:83.

of the Chalcedonian formulas as giving the impression that "Jesus was a hybrid ... a sort of bat-man or centaur, an unnatural conjunction of two strange species".[15] But the transposition into a different kind of linguistic dualism, which he suggests, simply reflects the tradition of D.F. Strauss. Following M. Wiles, Robinson declares: "What we are talking about are not two storeys [sic] but two stories. The one is natural, scientific, and descriptive. The other is supernatural, mythological, and interpretative."[16]

There remains, no doubt, an element of truth in what Robinson is seeking to convey. In the context of his firmly stated title *I Believe in the Historical Jesus* (1977) Marshall himself readily concedes, "The historical facts of the earthly ministry of Jesus were not by themselves sufficient to lead to Christian faith."[17] But his solution does not rest on the retelling of a supposedly mythological layer of events, as if to suggest that a story of empirical cause and effect and of social agency takes care of historical research and the philosophical criterion of falsification, while a story of mythological theology transcends the empirical world, but leaves points of contact with it problematic. Such a conceptual scheme hardly leaves room for a theology of "incarnation" and renders the notion more conceptually embarrassing than it was even in earlier times.

II
"Showing" and "Saying", and Illocutionary Speech-Acts

We may begin perhaps to clarify the issue and to make some tentative advance if we transpose Kant's critique of the limits of *thought* into parallel terms representing a critique of the limits of *language*. Although Mauthner had earlier formulated a critique of language, the classic formulation in terms reminiscent of Kant can be found in the early Wittgenstein. In his early *Tractatus* he writes, "The sense of the world must lie outside the world ... *In* it no value exists [his italics] ... If there is any value that does have value, it must lie outside the whole sphere of what happens and is the case. For all that happens and is the case is accidental."[18] He continues, "God does not reveal himself *in* the world ... There are indeed things that cannot be put into words. They *make themselves manifest* ... What we cannot speak about we must pass over in silence" (Wittgenstein's italics).[19]

A clue is given, however, about whether or how the Kantian fact-value disjunction can be bridged: what transcends the phenomenal world of spatio-temporal states of affairs (for example, that Jesus lived at Nazareth and was crucified) may make itself "manifest" (for example, that Jesus speaks as the word and presence of God). Wittgenstein earlier observed, "A proposition is a description of a state of affairs", and "What *can* be shown, *cannot* be said."[20]

---

[15] J.A.T. Robinson, "Need Jesus Have been Perfect?" in *Christ, Faith, and History: Cambridge Studies in Christology*, eds S.W. Sykes and J.P. Clayton (Cambridge: Cambridge University Press, 1972), 39.

[16] Robinson, "Need Jesus Have been Perfect?", 40. Cf. M.F. Wiles, "Does Christology Rest on a Mistake?", in *Christ, Faith, and History*, 3–12.

[17] Marshall, *I Believe in the Historical Jesus* (London: Hodder & Stoughton, 1977), 239.

[18] L. Wittgenstein, *Tractatus Logico-Philosophicus* (London: Routledge & Kegan Paul, 1961), 6.41 (p.145).

[19] Wittgenstein, *Tractatus*, 6.432, 6.4321, 6.522 and 7 (pp.150–51).

[20] Wittgenstien, *Tractatus*, 4.023 and 4.1212 (pp.41, 51).

The contrast between "saying" and "showing" takes us a little way forward in our understanding of how Christology finds expression in the Synoptic Gospels. Almost everyone, including Marshall, notes that even for Bultmann "Jesus' call to decision implies a christology."[21] The *authority* of Jesus to call is implicitly analytic, or grammatically internal, to the speech-act of calling in this context. Many of the parables of Jesus similarly "show" what cannot, with precisely the same effect, be "said". In the case of certain parables (though certainly not all parables) an "explanation" by its very nature undermines the suggestive and transcendent function of what is being "made manifest" with the same kind of clumsy inappropriateness as the uncomfortable experience of being asked to "explain" a joke. If the hearer does not "see" it, it is better left aside.

Literary theorists have drawn attention repeatedly to this feature in Mark, although some utterly misconstrue Mark's theological and christological purpose. The most notorious example is F. Kermode's tragically unfortunate reading in *The Genesis of Secrecy*, which fully appreciates Mark's reluctance to "say" certain propositions, but misconstrues this as a device for turning readers into "insiders" who can supposedly "see" what the manipulative Evangelist wishes them to "see", and "outsiders" who cannot or will not play the ecclesial game. Thus Kermode believes that Mark is "polyvalent" as a matter of strategy and principle, that he offers only "riddling parables", that he "banishes interpreters from the secret places", and that just as the reader begins to glimpse a vision Mark closes "the door of disappointment":[22] "Interpretation ... is bound to fail".[23] Graham Shaw attributes to Mark the same manipulatory ecclesial motives, driving a wedge, once again, between Jesus and the work of the Evangelists or redactors.[24]

A far more sensitive and perceptive account of the contrast between saying and showing in Mark is offered by P. Grant in his excellent study *Reading the New Testament* (1989). In Mark, he observes, "on the one hand we are summoned by the signs and promises to affirm a transcendent, beneficent reality, even as, on the other hand, we are warned against naïve interpretations of signs ... The cross is the sign which stands for the failure of signs to provide solace or certainty."[25] The reason for reticence about how much can be "said" depends on the nature of Christology in Mark, and on a dialectic between revelation and hiddenness of the transcendence of Jesus prior to the resurrection.

Although Luke does not hesitate to retain elements of Mark's tradition which witness to this emphasis. Luke's "showing" of a Christology which Jesus seldom seems to "say" takes the form of a more explicit portrayal of action and speech-acts based on institutional roles visible in the public domain. Before we examine Luke's material, however, more needs to be said about the development and conceptual tools of speech-act theory. We may trace the following stages or aspects of development.

21 R. Bultmann, *Theology of the New Testament* (London: SCM, 1952), 1:42; and Marshall, *Origins*, 29.

22 F. Kermode, *The Genesis of Secrecy: On the Interpretation of Narrative* (Cambridge, MA: Harvard University Press, 1979), 34, 141, 145.

23 Kermode, *Genesis of Secrecy*, 27.

24 G. Shaw, *The Cost of Authority: Manipulation and Freedom in the New Testament* (London: SCM, 1983), 190–268, esp. 255–7.

25 P. Grant, *Reading the New Testament* (London: Macmillan, 1989), 19, 21.

(1) Wittgenstein himself became dissatisfied with the unresolved dualism which had marked his earlier work in the *Tractatus*, although it is important to note that his vast accumulation of material and in particular the *Philosophical Investigations* "could be seen in the right light only by contrast with and against the background of my old way of thinking".[26] Wittgenstein in his later work saw proposition not as part of a logical calculus, but as embedded in a variety of concrete situations in the stream of life from which they derived particular currency. The notion of a "language-game" calls attention to a "whole, consisting of language and the actions into which it is woven".[27] Language about "love", "belief", "promise", or "expectation" draws its currency from actions and attitudes that precede and follow such language. To say "I love you" is to perform a speech-act of implied attitude or even commitment that would be undermined if my conduct before and after the utterance betrayed hostility or indifference. Similarly, Wittgenstein observes, "If there were a verb meaning 'to believe falsely,' it would not have any significant first person present indicative ... My own relation to my words is wholly different from other people's."[28] My attitude and actions "show" whether my words function as an operative and authentic speech-act.

(2) We have already earlier introduced the distinction between propositional *content* and illocutionary *force*. Such a distinction is fundamental to the work of J.L. Austin, J. Searle and F. Recanati. Propositions describe states of affairs, and may be true or false. But, Austin argues, it is logically odd to use "true" or "false" of performative speech-acts: "We do not speak of a false bet or a false christening."[29] An illocutionary act, in contrast to a bare locutionary act, is in Austin's terms the performing of an act *in* the saying of an utterance. Typically it entails a lack of logical symmetry between first-person and third-person utterances. If I say, "I hereby promise to ... ", and my subsequent actions stand behind my speech act, it becomes operative. But, as Austin observes, the anxious mother's assurance to an aggrieved neighbour, "He promises, don't you, Willie?" does not have the same *performative* force at all (at least not as *Willie's promise*, as against a veiled threat to Willie by the speaker).

Searle allows readily that "in performing an illocutionary act one characteristically performs propositional acts and utterance acts", but this does not invalidate the key distinction between "force indicators" and "proposition indicators".[30] Force indicators may need to be explicated logically – for example, "I promise" (Force, "F") that "I shall be there" (Proposition, "p") – when, as Austin and Recanati observe, everyday language may use an abbreviated form which may conceal the force indicator: "I'll be there" still assumes the same *logical* form, "F (p)".

---

[26] L. Wittgenstein, *Philosophical Investigations*, 2nd edn (Oxford: Blackwell, 1967), xe.

[27] Wittgenstein, *Philosophical Investigations*, sect. 7.

[28] Wittgenstein, *Philosophical Investigations*, II.x.190e, 192e.

[29] J.L. Austin, *How to Do Things with Words* (Oxford: Clarendon, 1962), 11.

[30] J.R. Searle, *Speech Acts: An Essay in the Philosophy of Language* (Cambridge: Cambridge University Press, 1969), 24, 31.

(3) Normally, speech-acts presuppose roles and carry consequences in the *extra-linguistic world*. That is to say, if I declare to my class, "I promise to assess your essays by next week", for this speech-act to function operatively, the act of promising presupposes that I have the right, status and capacity to make the assessment, and it further constrains me from using my time entirely for other purposes during the period of time in question. My status as assessor is presupposed but need not be stated; how I spend the next week conditions the level of trust which will be placed in future promises as operative speech-acts. I have given this matter some considerable attention with reference to biblical material in *New Horizons in Hermeneutics*, drawing in particular on Searle's illuminating essay, "The Logical Status of Fictional Discourse", on N. Wolterstorff's consideration of "the fictive stance" in his *Works and Worlds of Art*, and on some comments from F. Recanati.[31]

In christological terms, the *operative effectiveness* of "My son, your sins are forgiven" (Mark 2:5; Luke 5:20; cf. Matt. 9:2) depends on *a state of affairs about the identity, role and authority of Jesus*. The same principle applies to a speech-act of exorcism: "Be silent; come out of him" (Mark 1:25). In the triple tradition the "point" lies less in the miraculous or supernatural nature of the act than in the issue of *who* could be in a position to "plunder the goods" of the "strong man" (Mark 3:23–27; par. Matt. 12:22–30; Luke 11:14, 15, 17–23). Similarly the command of Jesus in the triple tradition "Peace! Be still!" to the wind and waves (Mark 4:35–41; par. Matt. 8:23; Luke 8:22–25) constitutes what Austin termed an "exercitive" speech-act, giving rise to the question (which is "the point"): "Who, then, is this that even the wind and sea obey him?" (cf. Matt. 8:27, "What sort of person is this ... ?").

(4) We come now to a crucial issue in speech-act theory. Austin's disciple D.D. Evans rightly draws a very careful distinction between *institutional authority* and *causal force*. In *New Horizons in Hermeneutics* I have followed the respective sub-classifications of Austin and Searle with reference to biblical material in parallel with what Searle grandly calls "taxonomy of speech-acts".[32] J.L. Austin and D.D. Evans used the term "exercitive" to denote a sub-category of performative utterances in which the uttering of a speech-act by an appropriately authorized person in an appropriate language situation served to constitute an act of (for example) appointing, commanding, commissioning, authorizing, and so forth. In Austin's terminology, exercitives identify "the exercising of powers ... warning, ordering, choosing, enacting, claiming, directing".[33] For technical linguistic and philosophical reasons which need not detain us here, Searle prefers to use the term

---

[31] Thiselton, *New Horizons*, 26–7, 128–30, 289–90, 352–54, 355–72, 388, 485, 527, 566, 570–75, 598–99, 615–16. More broadly in relation to textuality in Barthes and in Derrida, 92–141. The work of Searle and Wolterstorff is fundamental for parts of this argument as a whole. Cf. N. Wolterstorff, *Works and Worlds of Art* (Oxford: Clarendon, 1980), 198–239, esp. 231–4; J.R. Searle, "The Logical Status of Fictional Discourse", in *Expression and Meaning: Studies in the Theory of Speech Acts* (Cambridge: Cambridge University Press, 1979), 58–75. Cf. further F. Recanati, *Meaning and Force: The Pragmatics of Performative Utterances* (Cambridge: Cambridge University Press, 1987), esp. 260–66. It would constitute a digression from the present argument to consider the status of speech-acts in plays and fiction.

[32] Thiselton, *New Horizons*, esp. 298–300.

[33] Austin, *Things with Words*, 150, 154–5.

"directive" in place of Austin's "exercitive". The term functions with greater precision and symmetry within the system that Searle proposes and has generally superseded Austin's terminology in such writers as Recanati, Levinson and Leech.[34]

Searle's "directives" include such characteristic speech-acts as "appointing", "choosing", "commanding", "commissioning", "forgiving", "guaranteeing", "inviting", "naming", "ordaining" and "sending". (This is not an exhaustive list.) But to *appoint* with operative effectiveness I need to be *the holder of some appropriate institutional office*, such as dean, principal, captain, manager, committee chairperson, or even professional client. The notion of "guaranteeing" provides a powerful example in the commercial world: who stands behind the guarantee, and what is its official or legal status? Has someone the right to "send" me where I may not wish to go?

The same claim that an authoritative or *authorized status or role* must be *presupposed* if the speech-act is to operate effectively *as* a speech-act (that is, not merely by the *causal* force of persuasion) applies equally to the sub-category defined as that of "verdictives" by Austin, and as "declaratives" by Searle. The *verdict* of a judge, jury, referee, or umpire *determines* whether the player is *counted as* "out" or "offside", or whether an accused person *is* guilty. Thus Austin includes "reckoning, requiting, ruling, assessing" as "verdictives", while Searle includes the same examples under this sub-category of "declaratives".[35]

The *force* of *these* utterances as *acts* depends entirely on there being an *institutional* state of affairs in which the judge, jury, referee, or umpire is recognized as having a duly *authorized status and role*. In this case the performative force is identified by Austin and Searle as *illocutionary* force. This is distinct from that of the barrister, advocate, counsellor, or spectator who tries to persuade someone *causally* by *rhetoric* concerning the verdict. The rhetoric, if it were sufficiently persuasive, would constitute an example of *perlocutionary* force. In this case, the referee or judge would pronounce *legally* or *constitutionally* what is the case, even if the relatively recent and regrettable phenomenon of "disagreeing with the referee" represents an attempt to override *illocutionary* force by *perlocutionary* force.

The distinction is crucial for our interpretation of the Christology of the Synoptic Gospels on the basis of the words and deeds of Jesus and how Luke and other Evangelists perceived these. Explicit rhetoric urging christological claims risks subordinating illocutionary to perlocutionary force. On the other hand, operative illocutions raise the christological question (which may result in the inquirer's reaching a christological confession): Who has the right, status, and institutionally validated role to "acquit", to "judge", to "justify", or to "reckon as"? Is there not a veiled or "implicit" Christology in the verdict of the parable in Luke concerning the tax collector and the Pharisee that "this man ... was justified rather than the other" (Luke 18:14)?

---

[34] Searle, *Expression and Meaning*, 13–23; Recanati, *Meaning and Force*, 154–63; S.C. Levinson, *Pragmatics*, CTL (Cambridge: Cambridge University Press, 1983), 240–42; G. Leech, *The Principles of Pragmatics* (London: Longmans, 1983), 205–12.

[35] Austin, *Things with Words*, 152; Searle, *Expression and Meaning*, 16–20; Recanati, *Meaning and Force*, 138–54.

Clearly such language can be found in the utterances of Jesus. The climax of Matthew portrays an act of authorization and commission: "All authority in heaven and on earth has been given me. Go, therefore, and make disciples ..." (Matt. 28:18–20). The classic instance of the conversation between Jesus and the centurion whose servant was in need of healing (Luke 7:1–10) turns on notions of institutional authority. The centurion tells Jesus that he himself understands what is entailed in standing in a derivative chain of command: "I also am *under* authority", that is, "*derive* authority from my institutional status and role"; hence, "only *say the word* and my servant will be *healed*" (Luke 7:7–8).

On the basis of examples such as these it can readily be seen that the relation between perlocutionary language, on the one hand, and illocutionary speech-acts on the other, is radically different for Christology. The language not only of verdict ("your sins are hereby forgiven") but also of *promise* and *gift* depends for its operative effectiveness on the self-commitments, authority and status of the speaker. (Is the gift his to give? Will he stand behind, and execute, the promise?) Indeed we must go further. *Their respective significance for Christology is one of almost complete opposition and contrast.* For the performing of acts on the basis of *causal force* constitutes in essence an *act of power through self-assertion.* On the other hand, illocutionary acts which rest on institutional roles serve their purpose as *acts that point by implication away from the self to some source of authority which lies beyond the self alone.* In Kantian terms, they presuppose a transcendent dimension of Christology that seems all-too-readily to elude neat rational or conceptual packaging.

Kierkegaard was one of the few nineteenth-century thinkers to appreciate the logically contradictory character of Jesus' "saying" his own role and status, and thus risk the possibility of a self-assertive stance that would stand *in contradiction to the cross.* Kierkegaard's Christology rested on the "paradoxical" notion of Christ as "the God-Man", in which we may behold "the divine and the human together in Christ". But this "togetherness" could be revealed only through indirect communication.[36] Kierkegaard amplifies this by commenting that, if a witness of Jesus is not *present*, the communication for a later generation must be indirect.

Presumably disclosure occurs *either* through such forms as parable, irony and paradox, *or* in some sense in which that which lies "hidden" in terms of *description* may be "*shown*" in *action.*[37] In this sense, Christ remains for later generations of believers "just as contemporary with His presence on earth as were those [first] contemporaries. This contemporaneousness is a condition of faith." For Christ is "the inviter", who says, "come", but "from the seat of His glory he has not spoken one word. Therefore it is Jesus Christ in his humiliation, in the state of humiliation, who spoke these words."[38] The hiddenness of what cannot be "said" directly arises from the transvaluation of authority and power as determined by the nature of the cross. Hence, Kierkegaard writes, "Christ

---

[36] S. Kierkegaard, *Philosophical Fragments* (Princeton, NJ: Princeton University Press, 1936), 44; idem, *Training in Christianity* (Princeton, NJ: Princeton University Press, 1941), 28.

[37] Kierkegaard, *Training in Christianity*, 96; on this passage see also John Macquarrie, *Jesus Christ in Modern Thought* (London: SCM, 1990), 243.

[38] Kierkegaard, *Training in Christianity* (= *A Kierkegaard Anthology*, ed. R. Bretall [London: Oxford University Press, 1947] 375, 377, 387).

never desired to conquer in the world; He came to the world to suffer, *that* is what He called conquering."[39]

It is not surprising, therefore, if the primary data for Christology which may genuinely reflect the period before the resurrection arises not in the main from what Jesus "says" about his own power or identity, but from what has to be *presupposed* about his identity and authority on the basis of those speech-acts which rest on a more than earthly transcendent role and status, and point both to God and to the relation between God and Jesus. Admittedly, the relation of the presupposition entails more than strictly formal logical inference, since the institutional status and role in question is a more than "natural" one. In terms of speech-act theory, this may be described analogically as an institutional role and status, in as far as Christ is duly appointed and authorized by God. Indeed, it also reflects a certain *sharing* of a divine role and function, even if, in direct terms, this remains hidden. The role of theological propositions in such a Christology is not, in such a case, simply to describe the faith and experience of the earliest communities (Bultmann), or even the unconditioned religious experience of the ecclesial community (Schleiermacher). It is to describe those institutional features that the non-propositional force of the speech-acts of Jesus presupposes. In language that Marshall sometimes uses, such propositions serve to explicate an "implicit" Christology.

A theological counterpart to this kind of endeavour can be seen in certain areas of Barth's *Church Dogmatics*. Especially in Volume II, Part 2, Barth begins with the "institutional" concepts of divine *election* and *covenant* as the basis of the authorization under which Christ enacts the work of redemption and reconciliation. Barth asserts: "Election ... is the first ... and decisive thing. ... It is God's choice that under the name of Jesus Christ He wills to give life to the substance of his people's history ... constituting Himself its Lord and Shepherd".[40] For Bultmann, as for Kant, what is beyond time and space is effectively unspeakable, except through the distorted and misleading language of anthropomorphic myth. But for Barth, it is a presupposition and implicate of the active work of Jesus that "before time and space as we know them", Christ is the "Elected of His Father ... elected in his oneness with man", elected "in His pre-temporal eternity ... election which is absolutely unique, but which in this very uniqueness is universally meaningful and efficacious".[41]

Like Kierkegaard, Barth rightly urges the importance of the principle that "the *crucified* Jesus is the image of the invisible God" (Barth's italics).[42] Both the humiliation and humble self-emptying of Jesus and his authority to forgive, to invite and to reconcile are caught up, through divine election and appointment, into "the eternal will of God", in such a way that the two sides of the dualism of the eternal and finite, the transcendent and the this-worldly, "together acquire one name and the name of the one person ... the christological centre".[43] In his brief *Dogmatics in Outline*, Barth adds, "The work of the Son of God includes the work of the Father as its presupposition."[44]

39 Kierkegaard, *Training in Christianity*, 218.
40 Barth, *Church Dogmatics*, vol. II, pt 2 (Edinburgh: T. & T. Clark, 1957), 54.
41 Barth, *Church Dogmatics*, vol. II, pt 2, 101, 103, 104, 117.
42 Barth, *Church Dogmatics*, vol. II, pt 2, 123.
43 Barth, *Church Dogmatics*, vol. II, pt 2, 146, 147, 149.
44 Barth, *Dogmatics in Outline* (London: SCM, 1949), 71.

If we penetrate so deeply into the realm of Christian theology, however, is it still appropriate to distinguish between "institutional" authority (borrowed from social history or from sociology) and "causal" force? The work of Austin, Evans and Searle amply demonstrates the validity of the contrast. Someone whose work is unsatisfactory may respond to the warning of a friend by dint of causal force (persuasion); but this is different in official terms from a formal warning by the manager, which carries with it certain potential consequences in British employment law. An institutional status carries with it rights, obligations and a delegated authority, as well as a representational character; institutional roles generate patterns of action that may operate with legal and social effect in accordance with the status in question. Whether the performative utterances "You are fired" or "I acquit you of blame" have extra-linguistic consequences is bound up with the institutional status and role of the speaker. In this light, we may be hesitant to drive too sharp or large a wedge between so-called "functional" and "titular" Christologies. Perhaps, after all, Cullmann's comments about the titular status of the "rightful lord" acquire fresh point in this context.

(5) The aspect of Searle's speech-act theory that I have explored with most profit in *New Horizons in Hermeneutics* is his careful distinction between *two "directions of fit" between words and the world*.[45] In the case of what Searle and Recanati term *"the logic of assertion"* the "direction of fit" which is entailed is that of *words reflecting the world*. The "control" is the world, and the words that depict or report states of affairs perform their required function in so far as they "fit" the world which they describe. The reverse is the case in *"the logic of promise"*. Here the world, or states of affairs, must be changed in order to "fit" the *word of promise*. The language of biblical texts and of Christian theology operates in both directions. The important direction of fit in terms of *cash value for the process of salvation* is that *the promissory language of Jesus can transform states of affairs to fit the messianic word of promise*. Here the promissory *word* is primary and life changing. But this can be so, as we noted in our discussion of illocutions, only because certain *truths about the status, authority and the role* of Jesus can in principle be asserted – that is, that the word fits the state of affairs which it portrays.

Existential approaches to Christology may well be helpful in pinpointing the self-involving dimension of confession: human persons who make christological confessions from the heart are not left unchanged. Nevertheless the capacity for change is not self-generated; it rests on the possibility of accounting, even if retrospectively, for the basis beyond human persons which makes promissory language effective. On the other hand, it is equally only half of the story to reduce Christology to mere description alone. Christology has to do with an interplay between assertions which "fit" states of affairs and changes in states of affairs to make the "fit" a promissory word. The Fourth Gospel, partly because of its more explicit retrospective and cosmic perspective, allows equal prominence to be given to both directions of fit. The Synoptic Gospels make promissory language explicit, leaving the possibility of christological assertion to lie hidden *implicitly* behind the overt speech-acts of Jesus as that which gives them currency.

---

[45] Thiselton, *New Horizons*, 294–307.

In one case, the world shapes the words. Here descriptive report constitutes the primary model. In the other case, *directives*, or *directive speech-acts*, may function like a shopping list which I may carry with me around the stores: the words on the list ("peaches", "milk", "bread") determine how I shape the world in terms of what I remove from the shelves; whereas a store detective rehearsing a report when I forgot to pay uses words which describe a state of affairs in the world as he or she observed it to be.[46] Here a key paradigm suggested and developed by Searle and in *New Horizons* is that of *promise*.

What could be more central to an account of Christology that the notion of a *status and role appropriate to a mission to "change the world to match the work of promise"*? The many utterances, therefore, of what Jesus came to do carry presuppositions about his authorization and authority to put verbal promises, especially the promises of God, into *operative effect*, where prophets, wise people and others had failed to do so. It is at this point that Luke's concern for the world as a public domain of action and transformation comes into play as a contribution to christological understanding which characterizes his Gospel.

III
The Theology of Luke: Authorized Action in the Public World

In his detailed and thorough commentary on the Greek text of Luke, Marshall comments concerning Luke's choice of style for his preface (Luke 1:1-4): "... Luke was claiming a place for Christianity on the stage of world history. How far his predecessors had made such claims we do not know."[47] The often discussed triple dating of Luke 3:1, 2, with its six historical allusions, likewise, Marshall notes, serves "to give the Christian gospel its setting in imperial and local history".[48] In contrast to supposed or actual elements of secrecy in Mark, S. Brown urges in his essay on Luke's prologues (1978) that "Luke is telling his readers *all* there is to tell" (his italics).[49] While in certain parts of his argument he may well overstate a case, U. Wilckens rightly sees a contrast between Luke's concern for the public domain of history and tradition, and an existentialist emphasis among Bultmann and other interpreters on the individual, on personal decision, and on the transitory present moment.[50]

Many features that have traditionally been regarded as evidences of Luke's "universalism" may perhaps more strictly reflect his concern to present the Gospel and his Christology as truth in the public domain. The tracing of the genealogy of Jesus back to Adam rather than forward from Abraham may reflect not so much some particular attitude about Jews and Gentiles, but Luke's concern to disengage the Gospel from any supposedly sectarian ghetto-like tradition (Luke 3:38). The same comment might be

---

[46]   Searle, *Expression and Meaning*, 3–4.

[47]   Marshall, *Gospel of Luke*, 40.

[48]   Marshall, *Gospel of Luke*, 132.

[49]   S. Brown, "The Role of the Prologues in Determining the Purpose of Luke-Acts", in *Perspectives on Luke-Acts*, ed. C.H. Talbert (Edinburgh: T. & T. Clark, 1978), 105; cf. 99–111.

[50]   U. Wilckens, "Interpreting Luke-Acts in a Period of Existentialist Theology", in *Studies in Luke-Acts*, eds L.E. Keck and J.L. Martyn (London: SPCK, 1968), 60–83.

offered concerning Luke's extension of the quotation from Isaiah: "and all flesh shall see the salvation of God" (Luke 3:6), and perhaps the small touch in Luke which adds "from north and south" to Matthew's "from east and west" (Luke 13:29; par. Matt. 8:11).

Conzelmann's uneven work, with its idiosyncratic blend of the perceptive and the speculative, well underlines Luke's interest in public or "secular" history. As Conzelmann observes, "the State is here to stay", and Luke, far from seeing the world as a realm out of which the believer is to be taken, understands it as a public stage on which witness can be viewed, and as a socio-political reality which invites structure and order both inside and outside the Christian community.[51] It is perhaps less central an issue whether it is Jewish or Roman authorities who find Jesus innocent of any crime than a distinctive concern of Luke to place on public record that the duly appointed socio-political authorities who oversee law and order "find no crime in this person" (distinctive to Luke 23:4, of Pilate) or are simply frustrated in their misguided attempts to do so (distinctive to Luke 23:9–11, of Herod and "Herod's jurisdiction", v. 7). Three times the representative of Imperial government, as Conzelmann and others note, confirms the legal and political innocence of Jesus.[52]

What has often traditionally been regarded as Luke's "social concern" should also be seen in the light of its significance for the public domain. First, the universally recognized concerns about women, the poor and the outcasts, serve to de-privilege any suggestion that the Gospel is addressed primarily to the "inner" religious elite. The non-religious and the outsider are involved. Second, Luke's interest in the stewardship of riches, land and property calls attention to the public face of otherwise "inner" response. Hence Luke alone includes what one writer over-grandly called the "sociological" teaching of John the Baptist (Luke 3:10–14): repentance is to make an observable difference in the public world for tax collectors and for soldiers as well as for "the multitudes" (Luke 3:10, 12, 14). Kodell's comment that "Luke is not soft and easy-going" reflects not a character judgement, for Luke is an outstandingly warm and generous writer; but Luke's theological recognition that unless the Christian community can "show" where the transcendent dimension makes a difference in the public world, the credibility of the gospel becomes undercut.[53]

This does not lead Luke to underplay eschatological concerns, as H.W. Bartsch, S.G. Wilson, and others have pointed out.[54] Wilson is surely right to see a double pastoral concern on Luke's part in this respect (cf. Luke 12:38–48). But it may help to account for a perplexing ambivalence of emphasis on what many describe as Luke's preoccupation with "evidential" activities of the Holy Spirit in relation to Jesus as well as to the church.

Peculiar to Luke is Jesus' application of his synagogue reading of Isaiah 61:1–2: "The Spirit of the Lord is upon me, because he has anointed me to preach good news to the poor. He has sent me to proclaim release to the captives and recovering of sight to the

---

[51] H. Conzelmann, *The Theology of Luke* (London: Faber, 1960), 138.

[52] Conzelmann, *Theology of Luke*, 140.

[53] J. Kodell, "The Theology of Luke in Recent Study", *BTB* 1 (1971), 119.

[54] H.W. Bartsch, *Wachet aber zu jeder Zeit! Entwurf einer Auslegung des Lukasevangeliums* (Hamburg-Bergstedt, 1963); S.G. Wilson, *The Gentiles and the Gentile Mission in Luke-Acts* (Cambridge: Cambridge University Press, 1973), 59–87.

blind, to set at liberty those who are oppressed, to proclaim the acceptable year of the Lord" (Luke 4:18–19). James Dunn describes this as "almost certainly a Lukan construction on the basis of Mark" in which Luke brings forward in anticipation an earlier reference of messiahship than is historically probable, on the basis of Isaiah 61.[55] Dunn sees the reference to "the poor" in the Beatitudes as a further allusion to Isaiah 61 (Matt. 5:3; Luke 6:20), and more especially a third allusion in Jesus' reply to John the Baptist in Luke 7:18–23, par. Matt. 11:2–6. On the basis of the second and third examples Dunn concludes that "Isa. 61:1 played an important role in Jesus' own thinking", after a rigorous examination of theories about the original authenticity of 7:18–23.[56]

At first sight it may seem difficult to reconcile Dunn's comment that Jesus' "own experience of God, of divine power and inspiration" make him aware of the applicability of Isaiah 61:1–2 to himself, with C.K. Barrett's earlier penetrating conclusion that "Jesus acted under the necessity of divine constraint. Lack of glory and a cup of suffering were his Messianic vocations, and part of his poverty was the absence of all the signs of the Spirit of God. They would have been inconsistent with the office of a humiliated Messiah."[57] Indeed, can these two comments be reconciled, or does Dunn capture Luke's emphasis while Barrett communicates Mark's?

As both Barrett and Dunn confirm, the "anointing" of Jesus for his messianic office took place on his baptism. The spirit "descends" onto Jesus in all three traditions; although while the allusion to the dove in Matt. 3:16 and Mark 1:10 may suggest a parallel with divine creativity in Genesis, Luke's addition of "in bodily form" (σωματικῇ εἴδει, Luke 3:22) may perhaps hint at the notion of "visible appearance", which Marshall sees as potentially a possible interpretation of Mark 1:10, here "heightened by Luke".[58] At all events, three points are clear. First, as Dunn urges, in this experience Jesus recognized an awareness of the Spirit, which he understood as also a consciousness of sonship. Second, Marshall stresses this constituted an act in which "Jesus is commissioned and equipped for his task".[59] Third, as Barrett emphasizes, part of the total act is the initiation of Jesus into the temptation experience from which "Jesus returns from victory with the conviction that the way of God's Chosen is the way of humility and weakness, and from that time references to the Spirit are very few indeed."[60] It may be a different matter, Barrett adds, after the vindication and exaltation of Jesus.

Although it may be strictly justified, Dunn's language concerning Jesus as a "charismatic figure" may perhaps risk the possibility of confusions between *institutional authorization* to act as Spirit-anointed divine presence in the name of God and *causal power* to perform supernatural feats. This would once again open the door to the problems of a dualistic approach to Christology that we have been trying to avoid. It is considerably more helpful when in his *Christology in the Making* Dunn focuses on "Jesus' sense of sonship" with reference to issues about his messianic consciousness and of his sense "of

---

55 J.D.G. Dunn, *Jesus and the Spirit* (London: SCM, 1975), 54.
56 Dunn, *Jesus*, 55–60.
57 C.K. Barrett, *The Holy Spirit and the Gospel Tradition* (London: SPCK, 1958), 158; Dunn, *Jesus*, 61.
58 Marshall, *Gospel of Luke*, 153.
59 Marshall, *Gospel of Luke*, 154.
60 Barrett, *Holy Spirit*, 159.

eschatological significance, unique in the degree and finality of the revelation and authority accorded to him".[61]

So we return to specific examples of speech-acts in Luke which may "show" but not necessarily "say" christological dimensions of authorization, status and institutional role in the purposes of God for the world, even if as presupposition or implicates they may, in turn, give rise to christological propositions or even indirectly seem to presuppose the propriety of certain "titles". As we earlier conceded, such presupposition may entail more than a formal logical relation of implication, because a judgement about the transcendent nature of the authorization has still to be made. Further, whether Jesus explicitly "claimed" such titles transforms the agenda into something different from whether his speech-acts might presuppose their candidature for consideration. Some central examples in the triple tradition have already been mentioned: "My son, your sins are forgiven" (Mark 2:5; Matt. 9:2; Luke 5:20); "Peace! Be still!" (Mark 4:35–41; Matt. 8:23–27; Luke 8:22–25); "Be silent, come out of him" (Mark 1:25; cf. Mark 3:23–27; Matt. 12:22–30; Luke 11:14–23).

Some substantial further examples, however, remain peculiar to Luke. One of the most important is the raising of the widow's son at Nain: "Jesus came and touched the bier, and the bearers stood still. And he said, 'Young man, I say to you, arise.' And the dead man sat up, and began to speak" (Luke 7:14–15). Howard Marshall rightly calls attention to the sequel in which the witnesses reflect on what this might imply about the identity and role of Jesus. Jesus himself does not "say" what this is; but the bystanders speculate on the themes of "a great prophet" and "a divine visitation", and at very least conclude from what they see that "God has acted in the mighty work done by Jesus".[62]

The act of healing a crippled woman in the speaking of an utterance (Luke 13:10–17) also remains peculiar to Luke: "She was bent over and could not fully straighten herself. And when Jesus saw her, he called her and said to her, 'Woman, you are [hereby] freed from your infirmity', and immediately she was made straight, and she praised God" (13:12–13). Marshall rightly comments that both the immediate response of the woman (v. 13) and the second climax of the episode (v. 17, "rejoiced at the glorious things ...") stress "that the deeds of Jesus are the work of God".[63] They therefore reflect the institutional authority, status and role defined by what Barth (we saw) called the divine election of Jesus, rather than Jesus' reliance on unmediated causal power as such. Thereby his status as humiliated Messiah who points to God is not transposed into premature exaltation before the resurrection, but remains a cruciform mediation of divine presence and power. Jesus' christological status is sufficiently hidden to shift the focus of God; but sufficiently presupposed to give rise to themes of glory through his speech-acts.

It would be possible to multiply further instances from the triple tradition or from Luke. It is worth noting, for example, that in the triple tradition Jesus performs the act of giving sight to Bartimaeus, but only in Luke does this take the explicit form of a speech-act – "Receive [hereby] your sight" (Luke 18:42) – rather than a report of a healing (Matt.

---

[61]   J.D.G. Dunn, *Christology in the Making: An Inquiry into the Origins of the Doctrine of the Incarnation* (London: SCM, 1980); cf. 22–28.

[62]   Marshall, *Gospel of Luke*, 287.

[63]   Marshall, *Gospel of Luke*, 559.

20:34) or a reference to the man's faith with a different utterance (Mark 10:52, although "go your way" might equally be said to constitute a speech-act). Without doubt, the most explicit example of a speech-act that becomes operative *on the basis of institutional authority rather than causal power* occurs in the material peculiar to Luke in the healing of the centurion's servant (Luke 7:1–10). The whole basis of the centurion's grasp of the situation is, as Marshall suggests, that Jesus "can use his delegated authority to give orders that others must obey".[64] This expresses the heart of the matter.

Some might be tempted to associate this approach with an "adoptionist" Christology. But such a categorization would be crude and inaccurate, since what is at issue is a feature of language which allows the unity of the divine and human to be "shown", in terms of implicature, without risking a separation of the Jesus of history from the eternal Word or the Christ of faith. However, such a separation might be said to have characterized so-called "adoptionist" Christologies in the early church.

By contrast, I hope that the above arguments have signposted a possible approach that allows New Testament texts to engage with those horizons of our own day that are inevitably coloured by the problems bequeathed by Kant, without inviting the difficulties of Kantian dualism. John Macquarrie's magisterial book *Jesus Christ in Modern Thought* (1990) confirms, if any confirmation is needed, the pervasive difficulty posed by this Kantian legacy throughout most major strands in modern Christology. Kant himself, Macquarrie demonstrates, gave priority to the notion of Christ as "archetype" rather than as a historical figure in terms that were "fundamentally docetic".[65] Schleiermacher's hope to expound the incarnation "as a natural fact" was so heavily qualified as to frustrate his own intentions.[66] Hegel's privileging of speculative thought in the dialectical process led him to give priority to the "speculative Good Friday" over "the historical Good Friday".[67] Strauss, as we have noted, presided over a "collapse of the historical record", but whether entirely seriously or not also argued that "faith can survive unscathed".[68]

In our own century some, like Tillich, have entertained the hypothesis that a Christ without reference to history could still sustain faith. For the most part, however, writers have stressed the other side of the dualism, and J.A.T. Robinson's book *The Human Face of God* (1973) represents one of the most powerful and moving statements of the reality of the humanness of Jesus of Nazareth. But the sense of unease and discomfort about a dualistic chasm that can scarcely be bridged generates various symptoms, including the contemporary difficulty that too often, biblical specialists and systematic or philosophical theologians tend simply to "talk past" each other on the basis of a different agenda.

The approach outlined in this essay does not claim to resolve this problem. Indeed, it would be foolish to attempt to view this approach as a comprehensive or fully rounded model for Christology. The Fourth Gospel approaches matters from a different angle, even though we should not underplay the significance of *delegated* (and in this sense

---

64   Marshall, *Gospel of Luke*, 282.
65   J. Macquarrie, *Jesus Christ in Modern Thought* (London: SCM, 1990), 185.
66   Macquarrie, *Jesus Christ*, 208.
67   Macquarrie, *Jesus Christ*, 220.
68   Macquarrie, *Jesus Christ*, 229. On Hegel and on the period from Ritschl to Troeltsch, cf. also A. McGrath, The *Making of Modern German Christology* (Oxford: Blackwell, 1986), 322–93.

"institutional") authority focused in a Christ whose glory is seen in terms of humiliation, suffering, and self-giving service: "As the Father has sent me, even so I send you" (John 20:21).

In Luke, however, Searle's notion of a certain category of speech-act which operates with a "world-to-word" direction of fit touches a central nerve of Christology and perhaps allows some progress toward softening the problem of dualism in modern Christology. By virtue of an institutional status and role that is seldom "said" but often presupposed, the humiliated Messiah on his way to the cross begins decisively to transform the world in accordance with divine promise. His acts, and especially his speech-acts, "show" themselves in the public domain on the stage of historical life. What could be nearer to the heart of Christology than that Jesus begins to change the world in accordance with the divine word of promise, and that his speech and his acts "make themselves manifest" as the speech and acts of God?

CHAPTER EIGHT

More on Promising: "The Paradigm of Biblical Promise as Trustworthy, Temporal, Transformative Speech-Acts" (1999)

The title comes from the penultimate section of The Promise of Hermeneutics (*Grand Rapids, MI: Eerdmans and Carlisle: Paternoster, 1999), pp.223–39, and this extract includes the last section also. This work carries several ideas and themes further than in other essays up to 1999, and my one hundred or more pages in that volume complement, and draw together as a coherent argument, what my two American literary collaborators, Roger Lundin and Clare Walhout, wrote on hermeneutics in the Cartesian tradition, and on narrative hermeneutics, respectively. "Promising" constitutes a classic example of speech-action in many contexts, and it invites theological reflection on the covenant as a theological counterpart to "institutional facts" that provide conditions for the operative currency of illocutions or of other speech-acts.*

I
Promising as an Illocutionary Speech-Action

The understanding of the proclamation of the grace of God in Christ occurs frequently under the mode of promise of divine action. This theme receives special prominence in Paul, in the author of Hebrews, in Luther, in Tyndale and, in modern theology, among many others, in Barth, Rahner, Moltmann and Pannenberg. In the philosophy of language speech-act theorists have identified promise as one of the clearest models of illocutionary action. It meets so many criteria for illocutions that it becomes virtually a paradigm case of illocutionary speech-acts.

We should note at the outset that a variety of genres and locutionary acts of utterance in biblical texts and elsewhere do not necessarily correspond with the illocutions which these forms of language may be used to perform. This constitutes a widely recognized principle in speech-act theory from J.L. Austin and John Searle to Steven Davis and others.[1] Although elsewhere in my own work I have cited biblical Hebrew or Greek verbs which frequently signal the occurrence of illocutionary acts in the biblical writings, these provide no more than rough-and-ready indicators: the occurrence of the *word "promise"* does not necessarily signal or constitute an illocutionary *act of promising*, while the use of

---

[1] J.L. Austin, *How to Do Things with Words* (Oxford: Clarendon, 1962), 4–7, 58–78; J.R. Searle, *Expression and Meaning: Studies in the Theory of Speech Acts* (Cambridge: CUP, 1979), 8–29; D. Vanderveken, "A Complete Formulation of a Simple Logic of Elementary Illocutionary Acts", in S.L. Tsohatzidis, *Foundations of Speech-Act Theory. Philosophical and Linguistic Perspectives* (New York: Routledge, 1994), 99–131; and S. Davis, "Anti-Individualism and Speech Act Theory", in Tsohatzidis (ed.), *Foundations*, 208–19.

the future tense of another verb in an appropriate context of utterance (of situation, speaker and addressee) may in fact constitute a promissory act. Austin observes that "I'll be there" may constitute an illocutionary act of promise in appropriate circumstances, whereas an embarrassed mother's attempt to reassure an injured neighbour by insisting "He promises; don't you, Willie?" is not an illocutionary act at all.[2] Austin observes that we reach "an impasse over any *single, simple* criterion of grammar or vocabulary" (his italics).[3] Unless *the speaker has taken responsibility for his or her own speech and actions*, the utterance does not *count as an act* of making a promise. Searle adds: "Many of the verbs we call illocutionary verbs" are not always, or not necessarily, "markers" of completed illocutionary acts.[4]

Hence, while it remains undeniably true that the biblical writings perform multiple speech *acts* (for example, acts of praise, evaluation, acquittal, appointment, call, invitation, proclamation, declaration, thanksgiving, warning, promise) these do not correspond in one-to-one ways with the multiple speech-*forms* which writers such as A.N. Wilder identify as the "New Utterance" of the gospel with multiple "modes and genres".[5] Hymns, stories, reports, parables, letters, greetings, poems, allegories, sermons, dialogues, polemics, doxologies and other modes of utterance abound. Nevertheless a hymn of praise may also enact or embody a promise in the context of worship; a sermon may embody acts of acclamation in the course of teaching or warning; parables may project worlds, which both entice and promise, or both seduce and warn. I have argued elsewhere (n. 5) that Heb. 1:1–4 offers an outstanding example of multiple speech-acts as a dynamic model for the opening of a forceful and effective sermon.

Steven Davis insists that all illocutionary acts presuppose an inter-subjective public world. Expressed negatively, he argues explicitly that Cartesian individualism predisposes us to fail to notice illocutions. Yet if the biblical writings witness above all to a relationship or relationships, between God and Israel, or between God and Christian believers, or between believers and believers, or between the church and the world, language, which presupposes inter-subjectivity, may be expected. Moreover, given the biblical concern with the ethics of speech as faithful and true speech, it causes no surprise if the lynchpin of "institutional facts" which underlie such illocutions as promise or appointment rest on relations of *covenant*. While Paul and especially the Epistle to the Hebrews base promissory speech-acts on covenant, including divine covenant faithfulness, the Epistle of James pays attention to the ethics of speech both in terms of the causal perlocutionary effects of the tongue and the need for trustworthy, responsible speech which can provide a condition for illocutionary acts.[6] If a performative is to constitute an illocution rather than merely a perlocutionary act of persuasion, it is

---

[2] Austin, op. cit., 63 and 69.

[3] Ibid., 59.

[4] Searle, op. cit., 27.

[5] A.N. Wilder, *Early Christian Rhetoric* (London: SCM, 1964; American edn *The Language of the Gospel*, New York: Harper & Row, 1964), 9–47; cf. also Anthony C. Thiselton, "Hebrews", in J.W. Rogerson and J.D.G. Dunn (eds), *Eerdmans Commentary on the Bible* (Grand Rapids, MI and Cambridge: Eerdmans, 2003), pp.1454–7, on Hebrews 1.

[6] The most recent extended study is W.R. Baker, *Personal Speech-Ethics in the Epistle of James* (Tübingen: Mohr [Wissenschaftliche Untersuchungen zum NT ii 68], 1995).

fundamental that the agent or speaker of the utterance makes a self-involving commitment, or at least takes an appropriate expressive stance, in relation to the utterance. The ethics of speech provides a pivotal criterion for differences between illocutionary and perlocutionary acts. We shall return to speech-ethics in James when we have clarified this point.

Alexandra Brown's recent study *The Cross and Human Transformation* rightly understands 1 Corinthians 1:18–2:16 as "real world speech-act" in which Paul serves as "*'speech-act'ivist'*".[7] Paul's initial proclamatory acts led to the "founding of the church", but because the church at Corinth subsequently misinterprets what it is to live under the verdictive act of the cross, in effect (here Brown reflects Austin's terminology) "a prior speech act ... has misfired".[8] Brown perceives the word of the gospel as transformative and trustworthy, and as temporally contingent on the circumstances of Paul's utterances, oral or written.[9] Nevertheless, with Pogoloff, Clarke, Witherington and many others, she also perceives that Paul rejects the merely instrumental rhetoric of perlocution since for Paul the "power" of the cross does not lie in rhetorical or psychological persuasion: Greek, *ouk en sophiā logou* (1:17). This *empties* the cross of its power (1:17; 2:1; 2:5).[10]

Pogoloff convincingly shows that the combination of Greek *sophia* and *logos* in 1:17–2:5 signifies "far more than just technical skill in language. Rather, they imply a whole world of social status related to speech."[11] "Clever speech" and "high-sounding language" are the tools of the professional, competitive, rhetorician. As we have already observed, this stands in contrast to Paul's chosen status as menial leather-worker in the commercial agora, whose status as speaker derives from his apostolic life-commitment to the verdict of the cross and the transformative power of the resurrection of Christ. Pointing to this, and living it out, is the vocation of apostleship. To write *as apostle* is to point away from the self and to disengage from the *causal* power of rhetoric in order to allow the *kerygma* of the gospel of the cross to perform the *illocutionary* of act of transformation and promise in which both divine agent and apostolic agent had pledged themselves to constraints which made possible its operative performance. Graeco-Roman rhetoricians, by contrast, usually committed themselves to nothing. To try to convince an audience of an unjust case or untrue claim was a regular training routine in rhetorical competitions in performing *perlocutions*. Front-rank Roman rhetoricans such as Quintilian and reflective writers such as Plutarch disapproved of this scramble to be "greeted with a storm of ready-made applause", at the price of twisting truth: "the result is variety and empty self-sufficiency ... intoxicated by the wild enthusiasm of their fellow pupils".[12]

---

7   A. Brown, *The Cross and Human Transformation: Paul's Apocalyptic Word in 1 Corinthians* (Minneapolis, MN: Fortress, 1995), 19.

8   Brown, *The Cross*, 30; cf. Austin, op. cit., 16. Austin comments in a "misfire" the performative act "goes through the motions" but becomes "void" or is "botched". Clearly Austin's term only appropriates to Brown's point, since Paul does not doubt the genuineness of his converts' faith.

9   Brown, *The Cross*, 13–35, 65–169.

10   Ibid., 73.

11   S.M. Pogoloff, *Logos and Sophia: The Rhetorical Situation of 1 Corinthians* (Atlanta: Scholars Press [SBL Diss. Ser 134], 1992), 113.

12   Quintilian II: 2:9–12; cf. Pogoloff, op. cit., 173–8 and throughout, and Plutarch, *Moralia*, 801E and 802E. Cf. especially D.L. Clark, *Rhetoric in Greco-Roman Education* (New York: Columbia University Press, 1957), 67–262, for numerous examples and the reservations of Quintilian and Cicero about Provincial Schools and their techniques.

In this light, the promissory proclamation of the cross becomes perceived and (mis)understood as "folly" (Greek, *mōria*), even if to those who allow themselves to be transformed by the proclamation of Christ discover its operative effect (Greek, *dynamis tou Theou*, 1 Cor. 1:18). Brown rightly notes the ambivalence of Jewish "wisdom" traditions: Jewish "wisdom" is used both of divine wisdom and of that which nourishes a sense of "achievement".[13] The "wisdom" of the cross, however, "turns things upside down": those without influence, status, or learning (1:26) receive God's power, God's righteousness, God's wisdom through Christ and the subverting action of the cross (1:30, 31). Hence Paul adopts a style and mode of performing the declarative, proclamatory, promissory act of the *kerygma* "in weakness ... in trepidation ... that your faith might be built not on human wisdom but on the power of God" (1 Cor. 2:2–5), that is, on illocutionary promise, not on perlocutionary persuasion.

This does not preclude the use of rhetoric and persuasive power in other contexts. The Pauline epistles and the Epistle to the Hebrews abound in rhetorical devices where persuasion by argument constitutes the goal at hand, which it often does. Once an addressee has accepted and understood the verdictive and promissory frame of the cross and resurrection of Christ, Paul does not hesitate to use every kind of speech-act, including rhetoric and assertion. Even in 1 Corinthians he uses the rhetoric of irony, and the well-known device of the "rhetoric of affliction" (1 Cor. 4:7–13).[14] However, in such examples the illocutionary act whereby identification with the suffering and promissory power of Christ has been set in motion provide the larger frame of reference, which is presupposed.[15] Brown comments: "The God of the cross ... made weakness into power ... folly into wisdom".[16] Yet this also carries entailments about "knowing", with the proviso that "knowing" is grounded in the cruciform life. Luther makes this clear in his Pauline *theologia crucis*. Against the Corinthian *theologia gloriae* "he deserves to be called a theologian ... who comprehends ... the things of God seen through suffering and the cross".[17]

The nature of declaration or proclamation more explicitly as promise occurs where proclamation is enacted in the context of covenant, as happens in the act of "solemnly proclaiming (Greek, *kataggellete*) the Lord's death" (1 Cor. 11:26) by sharing in "the cup" as "the new covenant [ratified] in my blood" (Greek *to potērion hē kainē diathēkē ... en tō emō haimati*, v. 25). This pre-Pauline tradition goes back to the earliest time as an apostolic tradition traced back to Jesus, while the link between promise (Greek noun, *epaggelia*,

---

[13] Brown, op. cit., 33–63 and 77–89. The strongest case can be found in a re-written Nottingham PhD thesis, J.A. Davis, *Wisdom and Spirit. An Investigation of 1 Corinthians 1:18–3:20. Against the Background of Jewish Sapiential Traditions in the Greco-Roman Period* (Lanham, MD: University Press of America, 1984). The stress on eloquence could lead to elitism (143).

[14] K.A. Plank, *Paul and the Irony of Affliction* (Atlanta, GA: Scholars Press, 1987), esp. 33–70; S.M. Ferrari, *Die Sprache des Leids in den paulinischen Peristasenkatalogen* (Stuttgart: Katholisches Bibelwerk, 1991). More broadly, see D.F. Watson and A.J. Hauser, *Rhetorical Criticism of the Bible: A Comprehensive Bibliography with Notes on History and Method* (Leiden: Brill [Bib Interpretation 4], 1994).

[15] Cf. K.T. Kleinknecht, *Der Leidende Gerechtfertigte* (Tübingen: Mohr [Wissenschaftliche Untersuchungen zum NT ii 13], 1984), 208–304; and W Schrage, *Der erste Brief*, I, 330–50.

[16] Brown, op. cit., 147.

[17] Luther, *Luther's Works* vol. xxxi (American edn, Philadelphia, PA: Fortress, 1957), 40; also J. Atkinson (ed.), *Luther. Early Theological Works. The Heidelberg Disputation*, 291–4.

verb *epaggellomai*) and covenant (*diathēkē*) abounds in the Epistle to the Hebrews. Even God is understood as binding his future choices not only by a promise but by a promise endorsed (logically, redundantly) by an oath (Heb. 6:13, 16; 7:21; also 4:3, citing Psalm 95:11; 110:4). The first-century Jewish writer Philo expresses puzzlement over how the Psalms could speak of an oath on the part of One who already stands by his Word, and assumes that this is mere anthropomorphic accommodation to human doubt.[18] However, Hebrews has a *temporal* view of divine action which Philo's Hellenistic-Jewish thought lacks, and is concerned to make the point that in the series of pledges which God makes to Melchizedek, to Abraham, to Moses, to Israel in the old covenant and finally through Christ in the inauguration of the new covenant (Jer. 31:31–4; Heb. 8:10–13) and Christ's priesthood and sacrifice, the latter remains irrevocable and unsurpassable. This sworn promise opens "the new living way" through the mediation of Jesus Christ's own body and sacrificial death (10:20), but if this is rejected there is no further fall-back on some further divine commitment (10:26–31).

Heb. 9:15–18 shows in the clearest terms that the basis of this promissory act lies in the covenant (*diathēkē*) ratified by the blood of Christ, and (through conscious word-play) that this promissory covenant has the active force of a promissory testament or will (also Greek, *diathēkē*). Both *covenant* (*diathēkē*) and legal will or *testament* (also *diathēkē*) commit the covenant-partner and the testator: "Where there is a testament it is necessary for the death of the testator to be established; for a testament takes effect (*bebaia*, becomes valid) only when a death has occurred; it has no force (*mēpote ischuei*) while the testator is still alive" (Heb. 9:16, 17, REB). Both Greek words have precisely the force which denote operative speech-acts.[19] *Diathēkē, bebaios, epaggelia* and *ischuei* denote aspects or attributes of "institutional facts" in the first-century Graeco-Roman world. Contexts of "legally guaranteed security" relating to leases on property, terms of trade or employment, free-hold sales, political transactions and compacts, decrees of magistrates, or valid action, abound in non-literary sources in the papyri of the Graeco-Roman world of the first and second centuries.[20]

Hebrews looks both back to the promissory divine acts of the Hebrew scriptures (for example, "You are a priest for ever after the order of Melchizedek", Psalm 110:4 [cf. Gen. 14:18]; Heb. 5:6; 6:20; 7:17; or "I will make a new covenant ...", Jer. 31:31; Heb. 8:8; 10:16), and also to promised divine action yet to be performed (4:1; 11:13, 39). The *word* (noun and verb) *promise* occurs at least eighteen times in Hebrews, where the emphasis which we discussed above on *temporality* assumes many of its nuances: entry into God's promises is possible only at the opportune *kairos* of "today" (Heb. 3:7; 4:7), "while the promise of entering is still open" (Heb. 4:1). However, *tempo* plays its part. Jesus bears "patiently" with difficulty (5:2); the addressees were disillusioned that everything had

---

[18] Philo, *Legum alleg III*: 203–07; *de sacrif Abelis et Caini* 91:4.

[19] In legal contexts documents as a will become *bebaios*, "valid", "proven", "in force" when the necessary conditions are operative; cf. W. Bauer, W.F. Arndt, F.W. Gingrich and F.W. Danker, *Greek-English Lexicon of the NT* (2nd edn, Eng., Chicago: University of Chicago Press, 1979), 138; in other interpersonal context a reliable, dependable [word] that takes hold and has force (e.g. prophetic word in 2 Pet. 1:19. Similarly *ischuō* denotes "having valid force", "holding its power"; ibid., 383–4.

[20] See J.H. Moulton and G. Milligan, *The Vocabulary of the Greek Testament Illustrated from the Papyri and Other Non-Literary Sources* (London: Hodder, 1930), 107–8, 148–9; 226–7, 308.

not come right quickly, and "need patience" (10:36); "let us run with patience" (12:1), for *allotted* time defines "the race set before us" (12:1). Faith embraces what is "not seen" because it has not yet occurred (11:1). Nevertheless the history of Israel presents many examples of those who acted in the present on the basis of future promise, even if Noah's building a floating ark on dry land under a blue sky, or Joshua solemnly leading a procession round Jericho seven times, appeared foolish and groundless before the world (Heb. 11:7, 30). The givenness of *allotted time* and *periodicy* not only defines the eras of the old and new covenants, but means that even Jesus, who alone represents being human as God intended humans to be (Heb. 2:6–9; drawing on Psalm 8) experiences the need to trust in God (2:13; cf. v. 18), and in costly obedience and trust remains faithful (3:2). Temporality means that in assuming genuine humanness, Jesus as pioneer of the new humanity accepts the constraints of time and even weakness, rather than seeking the short cuts presented in the Messianic temptations which would supposedly offer an "easier" and less painful way to achieve the work.

Yet Austin, Searle and more recent writers remind us that vocabulary and grammar are not in themselves reliable criteria to identify speech acts. The vocabulary of promise, covenant, testament, valid force, and their related temporal correlates, do indeed signify a promissory context. Nevertheless even where such vocabulary is absent such language of address and invitation as "let us boldly approach the throne of grace that we may receive mercy" (Heb. 4:16) receives its dynamic by embodying an implicit promissory dimension, as we shall note in more detail. The address to Christ "You are a priest for ever" (5:6) is an act of appointment, which in turn rests in promise. Acts of promise may lie embedded in statement: "We have that hope as an anchor for our lives, safe and secure" (6:19); "the blood of Jesus makes us free to enter the sanctuary" (10:19). Some promises, however, are explicit without using the word *promise*: "I shall pardon ... Their sins I shall remember no more" (8:12; 10:17); "He who is to come will come" (10:32); "I will never leave you or desert you" (13:5).

Other New Testament writings share these characteristics, but lack of space prevents our exploring them. The earliest Christian preaching, according to Luke, represented "the promise to you and to your children" (Acts 2:39). The gospel fulfils promises made to Israel (Acts 13:23, 32; Rom. 9:9; 18:8). Justification by grace entails appropriating in the present a promise that in strict logic is eschatological (cf. Rom. 4:13–20; Gal. 3:14–29). For Karl Barth the promissory and covenantal dimensions arise because every act of divine speech is both an *act* and an act of *self-giving* in which *God in sovereign freedom chooses to be constrained* by covenant promise. Since Jesus Christ, rather than the scripture that witnesses to Christ, stands pre-eminently as the word of God, Jesus Christ constitutes the supreme model or paradigm case of "the Word of God in the humiliation of its majesty" in power, freedom, faithfulness and action.[21] This Word is temporal, eventful, promissory and active. God exercises his sovereignty by "choosing to love humanity", which entails constraint and "cost" to guarantee the fulfilment of "promise": God refuses to deal with the ungodly as the ungodly deserve, because this would countermand his promise to be gracious.[22]

---

[21] Barth, *Church Dogmatics* I: 2, sect. 21, 675.
[22] Barth, *Church Dogmatics* II: 2, sect. 34, 318 and 319.

Moltmann similarly urges that *promise* assumes a primary mode of divine speech when a description of the present stands in tension with that which should be and will be.[23] To assert the future as if it were present is presumption; to deny it is despair; to proclaim the gospel is promise and hope:[24] "Christian eschatology as the language of promise will then be an essential key to the unlocking of Christian truth."[25] Moltmann explicitly alludes to the enlargement of horizons in Gadamer and to temporal actualizations of traditions of expectation.[26] Like Jauss, Moltmann perceives that the process of hope and fulfilment throughout the biblical traditions and beyond into the history of the church leads to the reshaping of ever-new horizons of expectation as God both fulfils his promise, yet also does so often in surprising ways which creatively transcend human expectations.[27] The resurrection of Jesus Christ provides an example of faithful fulfilment side by side with the radically new which, within the established tradition of hope, opens far-reaching new horizons.[28] As Dietrich Bonhoeffer urges (in parallel with Jauss on hermeneutics), the cross exhibits disruption and discontinuity as well as making possible the continuity of promise.[29] Thus, against Nietzsche, God's Spirit, for Moltmann, signals an "unreserved 'yes' to life".[30]

We do not have space to trace these themes further in modern Christian theology. We should note, however, that Wolfhart Pannenberg also develops the importance of promise, holding together continuity of action by the faithful God with the possibility of novelty and surprise in the context of the reactualization of traditions. He also observes: "Perhaps the most important service Luther rendered as a biblical exegete was to discover in the biblical texts the temporal structure of faith and therefore its nature as an act of trust, corresponding to God's Word of promise".[31] "The truth of God must prove itself anew."[32] "The promises put the human present, with all the pain of its incompleteness and failure, in the light of God that comes to us as our salvation ... The concept of promise links our present ... to God's future".[33] Hence for Pannenberg while the history of tradition and its effects is constituted by promise to Abraham, promise to David, promises of post-exilic prophecy, and then to apocalyptic, acts of promise alone cannot be isolated from complex relations to truth and to states of affairs.[34]

---

[23] J. Moltmann, *Theology of Hope* (Eng., London: SCM 1967), 95–154.

[24] Ibid., 23; cf. 16–36.

[25] Ibid., 41.

[26] Ibid., 106–12.

[27] Ibid. Moltmann draws on Gerhard von Rad and W. Zimmerli as well as Gadamer.

[28] Ibid., 165–229.

[29] Moltmann cites Bonhoeffer, ibid. 198–9, and develops this theme in *The Crucified God* (Eng., London: SCM, 1974).

[30] J. Moltmann, *The Spirit of Life* (Eng., London: SCM, 1992), 97.

[31] W. Pannenberg, *Systematic Theology* vol. 3 (Eng., Grand Rapids, MI: Eerdman and Edinburgh: T. & T. Clark, 1998), 138.

[32] W. Pannenberg, *Basic Questions in Theology* (3 vols, Eng., London: SCM, 1970–73), vol. 2, 8.

[33] Pannenberg, *Systematic Theology* 3, 545.

[34] Ibid., 540–45.

II

Promising as a Paradigm for Understanding the Logic of Illocutions

We are now in a position to see why *promise* comes to constitute a paradigmatic workshop for an examination of the nature and currency of speech-acts in the biblical writings and in Christian theology. We may lay out the following proposals.

(1) The nature of promise in the biblical writings *presuppose institutional facts,* such as *covenant,* ratification by the blood of Christ, embodiments in such promissory signs of covenant as baptism and the Lord's Supper. *Yet these institutional facts cannot simply be absorbed into the intra-linguistic world*; not even into Frei's "history-like" linguistic world.[35] Two recent powerful advocates of this emphasis are Francis Watson in his work of 1997 and the forthcoming work of Vanhoozer, as well as Searle's "General Theory of Institutional Facts" which we have discussed above.[36] Searle concedes that "perceiving as" or "Background" plays a part in mediating, conditioning and construing extra-linguistic states of affairs *as* institutional facts.[37] Nevertheless, just as there could be no "institutional" facts of dollars or pounds sterling in the bank without paper or electronic signals, so there could be, I argue, no covenant without the history of events surrounding Moses, Israel, David, or the Patriarchs; no Lord's Supper without the crucifixion and the last supper; no ratification by blood without a sacrificial system and the violent death of Jesus. *Promise* presupposes *institutional facts*; but institutional facts can count as what they come to be only if at the end of the line certain *"brute facts"* (Searle) or states of affairs have occurred or occur in the extra-linguistic world. We may also note that the "historical" (*wirkungsgeschitlich*) perspective of Gadamer, Jauss and Pannenberg places "counting ... as ..." in a frame more closely related to inter-subjective (re)cognition than to individual non-cognitive perception. In a robust tradition that crosses contextual boundaries *"counts as"* is too weak; *"constitutes"* becomes a more adequate term.

(2) *Promising* provides useful examples of the variability *between explicit and implicit speech-acts*: between instances when *vocabulary* may seem to signal an illocution and when an illocutionary act of promise occurs *without* the use of expected or hoped-for vocabulary. Probably most acts of promise in the biblical writings *do not use the word "promise"*, for example, "I will be with you always" (Matt. 28:20); "Whoever believes in me, as scripture says, 'Streams of living water shall flow from within him'" (John 7:38); "Whoever has faith in me shall live, even though he dies" (John 11:25); "everyone who calls on the name of the Lord shall be saved" (Acts 2:21). Furthermore, the word *promise* may occur without initiating an illocution, as when Paul discusses the respective roles of law and promise in relation to Abraham (Rom. 4:13–22). Yet sometimes the use of the

---

[35] Cf. D.E. Demson, *Hans Frei and Karl Barth. Different Ways of Reading Scripture* (1997 cited above) especially in Barth's recognition (neglected by Frei) of "appointment, calling, commissioning" as extra-linguistic acts (107).

[36] F. Watson, *Text and Truth* (Edinburgh: T. & T. Clark, 1997), esp. 95–178; K. Vanhoozer, *Is There a Meaning in This Text?* (Grand Rapids, MI: Zondervan, 1998/9), to hand in pre-publication form after completion of this work; and J.R. Searle, *The Construction of Social Reality*, 113–26, cf. 127–76.

[37] Ibid., 131–4, for some examples from Searle.

word signals the illocutionary act, "Now he has promised, 'Once again I will shake not only the earth but the heavens also'" (Heb. 12:26); or elsewhere "I will fulfil the promise ... I will cause a righteous branch to spring forth from David, and he shall execute justice" (Jer. 33:14, 15).

This helps us to address a long-standing problem in speech-act theory that has persisted from Austin to the present. Austin rejected any criterion of vocabulary or grammar to isolate or identify illocutionary acts.[38] Yet he lists sixteen "behabitives", twenty-seven "verdictives", forty-six "exercitives", thirty-three "commissives", and more than fifty "expositives" in terms of English verbs.[39] Searle takes Austin to task for confusing "illocutionary verbs" with "illocutionary acts".[40] Yet his own revised "taxonomy of illocutionary acts" includes "such sentences as ..." with a utilization of similar lists, if under modified headings.[41] In Tsohatzidis's 1994 volume, Daniel Vanderveken contributes a characterization of illocutionary acts in the form of highly complex logical system in formally operational terms deemed to constitute non-basic productions of the five basic forces of "assert", "commit", "direct", "declare" and "express". His work here is logical, rigorous, and draws heavily on formal symbolic logical operators.[42] Nevertheless Vanderveken's 1990 volume includes a massive and detailed list (no doubt the largest and most comprehensive available) of (i) seventy English *verbs* are classified under "English assertives"; (ii) thirty-two English *verbs* under "English commissives"; (iii) fifty-six English *verbs* under "English directives; (iv) eighty-five English *verbs* under "English declaratives"; and (v) twenty-eight English *verbs* under "English expressives".[43] He lists nearly three hundred "performative" *verbs*. Yet Vanderveken recognizes the shape of the problem. He notes: "I will only be concerned here with the paradigmatic central illocutionary meanings of speech-act verbs, and I will have to idealize even these meanings somewhat in my semantic analysis";[44] "Many speech-act verbs have *several* uses" (his italics).[45] My work reflects the ambiguity found here when I listed twenty-seven "directives" or "exercitives" in the biblical texts; fourteen biblical "commissives"; fourteen biblical "declaratives", and some twenty "expressives" drawn from biblical texts.[46] Yet I also recognized that more was at issue than specific uses of specific vocabulary.[47]

The paradigm case of acts of promise serves to show that while the use of concordances may alert us to passages in the biblical writings which *prima facie* invite attention for the study of speech-acts, Hebrew or Greek verbs provide no more than *possible* indicators of illocutionary acts, which provide useful starting-points, but may

---

[38]   Austin, op. cit., 4–7, 58–78.
[39]   Ibid., respectively (i) 79 and 83; (ii) 152; (iii) 154–5; (iv) 156–7; (v) 161–2.
[40]   Searle, *Expression and Meaning*, 9–11.
[41]   Ibid., 21–9.
[42]   D. Vanderveken, "A Simple Logic of Elementary Illocutionary Acts", in S.L. Tsohatzidis (ed.), *Foundations of Speech Act Theory*, 99–131.
[43]   D. Vanderveken, *Meaning and Speech Acts: vol. I, Principles of Language Use* (Cambridge: CUP, 1990), 169–217.
[44]   Ibid., 169.
[45]   Ibid., 168.
[46]   Thiselton, *New Horizons in Hermeneutics*, 299.
[47]   Ibid., 283–307.

also signal dead-ends which fail to lead to illocutions. Literature on curses, vows, blessing, promise and confession assists our enquiry, but takes us only part of the way.[48]

(3) Acts of *promise* bring to light most clearly *the commitments and responsibilities of agents of promise within an inter-subjective public, extra-linguistic world of ethical undertaking and address.* Steven Davis makes clear in the first place that Cartesian individualism has no place in the speech-situation of promise. He writes, "the criterion of individuation of illocutionary acts like promising ... is not individualistic".[49] "An act of promising depends on the linguistic practice of a speaker's linguistic community ... an utterance of 'I promise to do A' will place him under an obligation to do A'", as Searle also affirms.[50] This provides a second consideration. Searle makes clear the inter-subjective aspects in his section subtitled "How to Promise".[51] He observes, "'I promise' and 'I hereby promise' are among the strongest illocutionary force indicating devices for *commitment* in the English language ... The essential feature of a promise is that it is the undertaking of an obligation to perform a certain act ... This condition distinguishes promises ... from other kinds of speech-acts" (his italics).[52]

This has exceptional importance both for biblical theology and for the hermeneutical significance of illocutions that are also commissives. First, Walhout's emphasis on *action and agency* is further vindicated, as is Lundin's critique of *individualism and autonomy*. Responsibilities and commitments radically condition "autonomy". This also strengthens Walhout's concern with *ethics and teleology.* We have already noted Pannenberg's comment that *temporal duration and separation* enhances what is at stake in living out the disposition or character of *being faithful* as part of one's stable identity.[53] The biblical writings place an emphasis on the ethical demand for faithfulness and speech-ethics that is difficult to exaggerate. "A lying tongue ... a lying witness" stand among what counts as "abominations" to the Lord (Prov. 6:17, 19). Deceitful speech does not go unpunished (Psalm 120:3, 4). Speakers will be held to account for speech that is "empty", unfulfilled or "inoperative" in life (Greek *argos*, Matt. 12:36). William Baker traces the biblical background to speech-ethics in his work on speech-ethics in James. Rash, unperformed promises are worse than no promises. Hence "set a guard over my mouth, O Lord ..." (Psalm 141:3, cf. Eccles. 6:11). "Controlled speech" is vital, in the Old Testament, Apocrypha and Pseudepigrapha, Qumran, rabbinic literature, the Graeco-Roman world and the New Testament.[54] The Epistle of James calls for "personal integrity in speech ...

---

48 Cf. H.C. Brichto, *The Problem of "Curse" in the Hebrew Bible* (Philadelphia, PA: SBL, 1963); T.W. Cartledge, *Vows in the Hebrew Bible and the Ancient Near East* (Sheffield: Sheffield Academic Press [JSOT Suppl 147], 1992); O. Cullmann, *The Earliest Christian Confessions* (Eng., London: Lutterworth, 1949); V.H. Neufeld, *The Earliest Christian Confessions* (Leiden: Brill, 1963); C. Rose "Verheissung und Erfühlung ...", *Bib Zeit* 73 (1989), 178–91; D.R. Worley, *"God's Faithfulness to Promise: The Hortatory Use of Commissive Language in Hebrews"* (PhD Diss, Yale, 1981).

49 S. Davis, "Anti-Individualism and Speech Act Theory", in S.L. Tsohatzidis (ed.), op. cit., 215; cf. 208–19.

50 Ibid., 216; also Searle, *Speech Acts* (Cambridge: CUP, 1969), 60.

51 "How to Promise", ibid., 57–61.

52 Ibid., 58 and 60.

53 Pannenberg, *Systematic Theology*, vol. 2, 202.

54 W.R. Baker, *Personal Speech-Ethics in the Epistle of James*, 27–33, 43–6, 49–52, 55–8, 75–9.

Uncontrolled speech is detrimental to society ... One's words should be consistent with one's deeds."[55] Elsewhere (see Essay 14) I have argued this point with reference to the logical paradox about "Cretan liars" in Titus 1:12, 13 where the coherence between first-person utterances and life-style is the unnoticed issue.[56]

This achieves its highest theological climax in the biblical understanding of God as one who chooses in sovereign freedom to constrain that freedom by graciously entering into the constraints imposed upon action by undertaking covenantal promise. On this basis believers can know where they stand with God and receive assurance: his promissory illocutions are liberative. This also has implications for the status of prophets or apostles who proclaim promise on behalf of God or in his name. Wolterstorff has shown the factors which make such a notion philosophically intelligible. In terms of speech-act theory it introduces a third point under the present consideration: in addition to the inter-subjective world of the speaker and addressee, and the responsibilities and ethical obligations of the agent of promise, attention needs to be paid to the *status* of the speaker. Does the speaker speak in his or her own name, or in the name of another? Has the speaker the right and the power, as well as the moral integrity, to make and to perform the promise? In biblical studies, discussions of apostleship are extensive and often (but not always) helpful.[57]

(4) *Promising* constitutes a *very strong illocutionary act*, in contrast to much wider definitions or understandings of speech-acts which at the opposite end of a spectrum taper into the *weak or trivial*. Wolterstorff seems to suggest that *any* utterance or "locution" can be used to *count as* an illocution *in* its utterance. In a "weak" sense this is true. Nevertheless, in 1973 Geoffrey Warnock proposed a very helpful distinction between *strong* and *weak* speech-acts, which lie at either end of a spectrum.[58] As we have observed Bultmann's entire programme of demythologizing depends on *counting* most "objective" descriptions in the New Testament *as* volitional, existential challenges. Here the problem derives not simply (as we argued above and elsewhere more extensively) from Bultmann's devaluing of description and his inability to explain how self-involving utterances relate to extra-linguistic states of affairs, but also because far from all of his transpositions constitute "strong" or "serious" speech-acts which are grounded in "institutional" facts. We argued above the precise nature of "institutional facts" permits *"counts as"* to become *"constitutes"*, especially, we may add, if the status of the speakers or agents is also affirmed in multiple traditions and contexts.

An increasing number of writers are now viewing *all* texts, including all texts of the New Testament, as speech-acts. This offers certain advantages. It ensures that agents

---

[55] Ibid., 281 and 284.

[56] A.C. Thiselton, "The Logical Role of the Liar Paradox in Titus 1:12, 13: a Dissent from the Commentaries in the Light of Philosophical and Logical Analysis", *Biblical Interpretation* 2 (1994), 207–23.

[57] One of the more suggestive studies which combines sociological and theological issues is J.H. Schütz, *Paul and the Anatomy of Apostolic Authority* (Cambridge: CUP [SNTS Mon 26], 1975), but most constructive in its emphasis on apostleship as pointing away from the self to the Christ-event in J.A. Crafton, *The Agency of the Apostle* (Sheffield: Sheffield Academic Press [JSNT Suppl 51], 1991).

[58] G.J. Warnock, "Some Types of Performative Utterance", in Isaiah Berlin (ed.), *Essays on J.L. Austin* (Oxford: Clarendon, 1973), 69–89.

"mean" what they wish or will purposively to declare, state, express, promise, convey, or whatever, as a temporally conditioned eventful action. It directs attention to speech as a communicative act between a "sender" and a "receiver", or between agents and audiences, and it avoids two assumptions which Wittgenstein identified as generating confusion. It avoids the assumption that language always serves to "convey thoughts"; and it avoids the mistaking of confusing the "physical properties" or *forms* of speech from speech-*functions* or constitutive use.[59] Early in my work I took several linguistic forms, for example "What about the points?" and "This is poison" to show these forms could perform utterly diverse functions (in the latter case, for example, a request to fetch a doctor, a warning not to drink from the same bottle, a cry for vengeance or a rebuke about an overstrong beverage).[60]

All the same, this "weak" understanding of speech-acts threatens to degenerate into the subjective (anything can "count as" anything); worse they may become so diffused that those important illocutionary acts which (i) *entail serious obligations on the part of the speaker*; (ii) *presuppose serious institutional facts* (which in the sense identified by Searle [1995] rest on extra-linguistic "brute" facts); and (iii) *achieve transformative effects not by causal perlocution but through institutional illocution*, come to *drop from view as paradigmatic or "strong" illocutions*. Savas Tsohatzidis therefore is right to commence his 500-page volume *Foundations of Speech Act Theory* (1994) with the declaration that "Illocutionary acts ... constitute the primary subject matter of speech act theory".[61] All illocutions are speech-acts. Whether or not all speech-acts are also illocutions, they are not all illocutions in the "strong" or *serious* sense characteristic of *promise*.

In our earlier book *The Responsibility of Hermeneutics* I conceded by way of analogy, that in extreme emergency a chisel *could* be used as (could count as) a screwdriver, or a priceless Beckstein *could* be counted as fuel for a fire. Newspapers *can* be used for wrapping paper (some deservedly so). Nevertheless in normal circumstances such counting ... as ... would be deemed *irresponsible*, even reckless.[62] When a tradition of the kind discussed by Gadamer and Jauss has become established and Jauss's "public intersubjective world" lies open to view, the promissory speech acts of, for example, the biblical covenants do not merely *count as* promises; they *constitute* promises. To "count" these "as" anything less is *ethically to violate* their textual action.

Here the importance of agency and action emerges once again. Indeed return to Walhout's territory, namely the relation between ethics and teleology or eschatology. The author of the Epistle to the Hebrews would never accept that Christian faith is action based *subjectively alone* on what believers *count as* promise, for his detailed exposition of the *institutional facts* of the sacrificial system, priesthood, Christology, the blood of Christ and above all the new covenant explain that all this *constitutes* guaranteed promise which is irrevocable. However, Walhout also explored the transformative effect of entering the

---

59 Wittgenstein, *Philosophical Investigations*, sect. 304, "a radical break with the idea that language always functions in one way ... to convey thoughts ..."; and sect. 108 "... stating the rules of the game not describing their [chess pieces'] physical properties".

60 Thiselton, *Language, Liturgy and Meaning* (Nottingham: Grove, 1975, 2nd edn 1986), 3 and 10.

61 S.L. Tsohatzidis, "Ways of Doing Things with Words", loc. cit., 1.

62 Lundin, Thiselton and Walhout, *The Responsibility of Hermeneutics*, 107–8.

"possible worlds" of fiction. In this context another of my doctoral candidates, Richard Briggs, is currently exploring the relation between imagination and "counting as" in speech-act theory. For without doubt, as we observed from reader-response approaches to the parables of Jesus, the first steps of faith may well begin with entry into a *"possible world"* where *counting as* begins to shape new understanding. The "weak" end of the spectrum may play an important role also.

(5) Finally, *promise* provides a paradigm case of *how language can transform the world of reality*. There is no need to recapitulate ground already covered here in *New Horizons in Hermeneutics*. There I endorsed Searle's contrast between a "direction of fit" in which (1) sometimes (for example, in assertions) language can reflect the world (that is, the world or reality remains the controlling test of the truth of speech); while (2) at other times (for example, in effective promises) language can bring the world of reality into a closer match with what has been written or spoken (that is, the words remain the controlling test of whether the promise has been performed or fulfilled).[63] Recanati similarly discusses the "direction of correspondence" between words and world.[64] *Directives*, it goes without saying, also seek to change extra-linguistic states of affairs by the utterance of appropriate words in appropriate situations by duly appointed persons, or by speaking agents with appropriate status.

What has been said about the context of *serious* responsibilities and *serious* institutional states of affairs applies here. We are not considering simply or primarily the causal rhetoric of psychological persuasion which results in perlocutions independently of illocutionary acts. In the context of biblical theology, the relation between illocutionary acts of *promise* and illocutionary *directives* sums up the heart of the gospel, including more strictly, the Pauline contrast between gospel and law. The world-order is characterized by a failure, evil, suffering and fallenness, which does not accord with God's will for its future. Hence *transformation* and *change* constitutes the purposive goal of God's word; of the word as Christ, the word as Scripture, and the word to which the church bears witness through its life and preaching. Two kinds of speech-act may bring the world into conformity with the purposes of God. *Directives* play a role, for faith entails obedience. Nevertheless a regime of *directives* corresponds to the dispensation of *law of change by human endeavour*. *Promise* provides the covenantal ground on which transformation by the gracious action of God ultimately depends. The covenant of *promise* is a dispensation of *grace: of change by divine agency, giving and given*. Only thus can the seer of the Apocalypse of John utter the declarative pronouncement: "I saw a new heaven and a new earth" and add the promissory utterance: "and God himself will be with them; he will wipe every tear from their eyes. Death will be no more ... It is *done*" (Rev. 21:3–6).

---

[63] Thiselton, *New Horizons*, 31–5 and 294–307; Searle, *Expression and Meaning*, 3–8.
[64] F. Recanati, *Meaning and Force. The Pragmatics of Performative Utterances* (Eng., Cambridge: CUP, 1987), 150–63.

CHAPTER NINE

A Retrospective Reappraisal of Work on Speech-Act Theory (New essay)

In this retrospective reappraisal I attempt to place my earlier arguments within the wider frame of multi-disciplinary reference that gives them greater point than they might otherwise seem to have as isolated studies. To cite one example, the 1994 essay on speech-acts and Christology might seem to go a long way round to achieve its goal unless or until we place it in clearer relationship to debates in modern Christology after Lessing and Kant. This reveals how much is at stake in seeking a reformulation of Christology in Luke and in other parts of the New Testament, which may in turn assist new formulations or understandings in systematic theology. The other main task of this paper is to trace developments both in my own thought about speech-acts (from 1974 through thirty years to 2004), and in speech-act theory itself. Do these more sophisticated developments invalidate or confirm my early work on the subject? I conclude that my 1974 essay stands as useful a study as ever it did. In the last section I take a tentative glance at politeness theory as a related approach that has not yet received adequate exploration as a tool for biblical interpretation. I suggest reasons why it may prove fruitful, but concede that as yet these remain only speculative.

I remain fully convinced of the value of speech-act theory for a variety of issues in the philosophy of language and in hermeneutics. On the other hand, in response to those who are sceptical about its achievement I readily concede that it provides only one approach among others. This is why I included what is probably the least original of the five research contributions in Part II, namely an extract from the Introductory Chapter 1 of *New Horizons and Hermeneutics*. My thought on speech-act theory has developed from simpler beginnings in the 1960s and 1970s to various advances in 1992, 1994 and again in 1999 with *The Promise of Hermeneutics*. All of my published work on this subject (except *Language, Liturgy and Meaning*, 1975) relates speech-act theory closely to biblical exegesis and interpretation. The debate about "institutional facts" also divides Searle from Derrida's postmodern approach to language.

I
Two Very Basic Foci in the Earliest Work: "Institutionally" Generated Speech-Acts and Multiple Self-Involving Illocutions

I.1 "Institutional" Force or Causal Power?

The difference between institutionally generated illocutions and causal power featured strongly in the various arguments presented in "The Supposed Power of Words in the

Biblical Writings", published thirty years ago (Essay 4, above). If an illocutionary speech-act is to be operative as such, Austin argued, "There must exist an accepted conventional procedure having a certain conventional effect ... and further the particular persons and circumstances in a given case must be appropriate for the invocation of the particular procedure invoked".[1]

This condition places certain illocutionary acts in Old Testament texts in a different world from the *causal power* of "a grenade buried in a ploughed field" (W. Eichrodt), "a missile with a time-fuse" (W. Zimmerli), or "an objective readily endorsed with mysterious power" (Gerhard von Rad).[2] "Performative" force or conditions has nothing to do with "primitive word-magic". This becomes particularly clear when we ask why Isaac cannot revoke the blessing manipulated by Jacob under false pretences. There does not exist (or in more theological terms, God has neither decreed nor established) a procedure for illocutionary acts of *un-blessing*, any more than in the Christian era there is any given procedure for un-baptism.

Those who appreciate dry humour will relish Austin's idiosyncratic and whimsical examples of inoperative or invaluable proclamation: "I baptize this infant 2704", or (as spoken perhaps by Caligula), "I hereby appoint my horse Consul."[3] Other memorable examples are readily at hand. What is the net effect if I smash a milk-bottle against the side of a rowing-boat in Durham's River Weir or in Nottingham's University Lake, while declaring, "I name this boat the *Lady Margaret Thatcher*?" The "institutional" states of affairs and procedures must be operative. Not only Austin, but, among others, D.D. Evans, John Searle, Terence Tilley and Nicholas Wolterstorff call attention to the importance of this dimension.

In the first essay "Thirty Years of Hermeneutics" I might well have included a comment on the significant influence that Professor George B. Caird of Oxford had upon my thinking on speech-act theory and the logic of self-involvement in the mid-1960s. I attended his lectures on "The Language of the Bible", and benefited from oral discussions with him. Caird insisted that New Testament studies at that time were unnecessarily sterile, not least because very few New Testament specialists seemed willing to engage with methods and approaches used in other academic disciplines. For his part, he drew on the work of his colleague and fellow Congregationalist churchman, Stephen Ullmann, who held the Chair of Semantics at Oxford. With Ullmann, Caird reassessed the role of metaphor and imagery in biblical texts. This led him to reject the "official" view among New Testament scholars that Jesus was mistaken about the Parousia and the end of the world. Jesus used "end-of-the-world" metaphors to communicate "end-of-the-world" events to those whose "world" was about to end, particularly that of Jewish leaders as leaders of a Jewish state.

However, in relation to speech-act theory, George Caird pointed me to Donald D. Evans, *The Logic of Self-Involvement*. He regarded this as a book of seminal insights for biblical studies, which biblical scholars unduly ignored to their detriment.[4]

---

1   J.L. Austin, *How to Do Things with Words* (Oxford: Clarendon, 1962 (also 2nd edn, 1980)), pp.14–15.
2   Sources all cited in Essay 4, first two pages.
3   Austin, *How to Do Things with Words*, p.35.
4   D.D. Evans, *The Logic of Self-Involvement: A Philosophical Study of Everyday Language with Special Reference to the Christian Use of Language about God as Creator* (London: SCM, 1963).

The two "basic foci" that I identify in the heading above feature at the very heart of Evans's work. He distinguishes fundamentally between *causal power* and language that effects new situations through *institutionally dependent "performative" force*. But second and further, he makes much of the capacity of performative speech-acts to perform *more than one kind of act at the same time*. Third, he perceives that performatives or illocutions often rest upon presuppositions and entailments that we may communicate as cognitive statements or propositions, and that embody truth-claims. Evans shows that this emerges, for example, in speech-acts of *acknowledgement*.

To illustrate each further (although in reverse order): "*I acknowledge* that Jones saved my life" performs an *act of acknowledgement* while *referring* "to the *fact* that Jones saved my life".[5] Further, Evans also pressed home the difference between "brute" efficient cause and "institutional" performative force in more explicit detail than Austin. Indeed he writes, "The performative force is usually *independent of* the causal power."[6] Thus in such a sentence as "the royal decree *took effect* in 1641", the performative force operated when it became a *binding law*, but the date of this occurrence may be different from that of its causal effect, namely when people *began to act upon it.*[7]

In terms of interpreting biblical texts, Evans argues that to believe that God is *Maker* of the universe is to assent to a proposition about divine *causal power*. On the other hand to appropriate biblical traditions that perceive God as *Creator* of the world and of Israel *ascribe a status, role* and *value* to Israel and to the world by virtue of the word-in-action. Creatures of God receive the status and role of responsible stewards and as recipients of divine love. Evans observes, "In the biblical context to believe in God was to acknowledge Him as Lord, Appointer and Evaluator, accepting His supreme authority. This is different from belief that God is Maker ...".[8] "God's creative word has a *twofold* efficiency: it has *causal power*, bringing about the sheer existence of the creature; and as a command it has *exercitive force*, involving a subordinate *status* of the creature so that the creature's very existence is 'obedience'."[9] Everything is created *with a role*: for example, sun, moon and stars allow an awareness of time as well as giving light; the creation of humankind entails their role as steward of the earth. Creation itself has a *value*: "it was very good" (Gen. 1:31; cf. also "Everything created by God is good, and nothing to be rejected if is received with thanksgiving ... " (1 Tim. 4:4–5)).[10]

D.D. Evans constituted a primary point of reference for my article of 1974. But other writers over these thirty years have remade and developed these points with increasing sophistication and cumulative force. In 1969 John Searle produced his foundational study *Speech Acts*. He asserts as a more general axiom, "Meaning is more than a matter of intention, it is also at least sometimes a matter of convention."[11] He includes a section under the subheading "The distinction between brute and institutional facts", in which

---

5   Evans, *The Logic of Self-Involvement*, p.43 (my italics).
6   Evans, *Logic*, p.70 (my italics).
7   Evans, *Logic*, p.72.
8   Evans, *Logic*, p.150.
9   Evans, *Logic*, p.152 (my italics).
10   Evans, *Logic*, pp.153–5.
11   John R. Searle, *Speech Acts: An Essay in the Philosophy of Language* (Cambridge: CUP, 1969), p.45.

institutions (for example, getting married, a trial in law, a baseball game, or a legislative action) are essential for linguistic action; in these cases the physical events alone "count" only "against a background of certain kinds of institutions".[12] Promises and pledges, for example, entail the condition that the speaker takes on certain *responsibilities*.[13] More specifically, performative force depends on a situation in which one linguistic act "counts as" what sets the illocution in force.[14]

The concept of *counting as* in the context both of art and language and of speech-acts becomes a major resource and a key tool in the arguments of Nicholas Wolterstorff. I had the privilege of conversing with him at regular intervals during my appointment as Visiting Fellow in Calvin College, Grand Rapids, Michigan, where he taught before moving to Yale. Wolterstorff's work has provided yet another significant influence, although not before 1980, with the appearance of his *Art in Action* and *Works and Worlds of Art* (1980).[15] He expounded "count-generation" for operative speech-acts first in these earlier works and then in relation to the biblical writings and to language about God in *Divine Discourse* (1995).[16] Actions may *count as* whatever the relevant "institutional facts" invite and permit them to count as, whether this might be signalling an intention in driving on the road, or "hearing" God speak through the medium of a biblical text.[17]

In the article of 1974, I relied almost entirely on the work of Austin and Evans. Since that time ever more sophisticated work on these issues has come from a series of writings from John Searle, Nicholas Wolterstorff, Terrence Tilley and many others. However, none undermines, but rather, underlines and endorses the basic earlier work in the 1974 article. Searle discusses related issues more deeply in *Expression and Meaning* (1979) and in *The Construction of Social Reality* (1995). In the latter he rejects Derrida's argument that (in Searle's words) "this is nothing outside texts".[18] In his "After-word" to *Limited Inc.* Derrida attempts partly to backtrack, at least from what is widely attributed to him about "free play" in language and non-referential or non-representational language, but Searle and Wolterstorff doubt how much would intelligibly (Searle) or logically (Wolterstorff) remain of any ground for his earlier assertions if this modification is regarded as a substantial one.[19] We reserve discussion of this, however, to the reappraisal of Part VI on postmodernism.

Terrence Tilley utilizes speech-act theory in his excellent book *The Evils of Theodicy* (1991). Here he reinterprets approaches to the problem of evil in Job, Augustine, Boethius and Hume in terms of an analysis of speech-acts. The first third of this book prepares the

---

12 Searle, *Speech Acts*, p.51.
13 Searle, *Speech Acts*, p.62.
14 Searle, *Speech Acts*, p.65.
15 On "count-generation", see N. Wolterstorff, *Works and Worlds of Art* (Oxford: Clarendon, 1980), especially pp.3–8 and 202–15; and on "The Action of World Projection", see *Art in Action* (Grand Rapids, MI: Eerdmans, 1980), pp.122–55. In addition to his recent and illuminating work on John Locke and "entitlement" to reasonable belief, see also among more recent works especially N. Wolterstorff, *Divine Discourse: Philosophical Reflections on the Claim that God Speaks* (Cambridge: CUP, 1995).
16 Wolterstorff, *Divine Discourse*, especially pp.75–94.
17 Wolterstorff, *Divine Discourse*, p.81.
18 John R. Searle, *The Construction of Social Reality* (London: Allen Lane, 1985), p.159.
19 J. Derrida, *Limited Inc.* (Eng., edited by G. Graff, Evanston, IL: Northwestern University Press, 1988 (French, Paris: Editions Galilée, 1990)).

ground for a fresh reading of these classic texts by exploring "Institutionally Bound Speech Acts" and "Institutionally Free Speech Acts" in religions.[20] He rightly rejects the simplistic division of language in religion into either "cognitive" or "non-cognitive": "Many institutionally bound speech acts are hybrids."[21] A speech-act is "institutionally free" if or when the conditions for its operative currency "do not require that the speaker have a specific role or status".[22] Praying, he argues, is not institutionally bound, but acts of absolving, appointing and marrying are bound to institutional facts. (A theologian rather than a philosopher might argue with validity that prayer is operative on the basis of divine covenantal promise; but Tilley is considering as "bound" those that depend on human institutions in the public world.) Tilley rightly concludes, "speech-act theory generally shows that we perform a *variety of acts* when we speak" (my italics).[23] He argues that "moralists" rarely consider this, while philosophical theologians tend to assume that hybrid speech-acts in Augustine and others have the status only of argumentative propositions.

It would carry us beyond the scope of this reappraisal to trace Tilley's arguments further. Our main point here is that those writers who (1) attribute "Hebrew" views of language to primitive word-magic, and (2) see such language as setting in motion a "power-laden force" like a grenade waiting to explode, and (3) draw huge inferences from the contingent fact that the Hebrew word *dabar* can mean *word* or *thing*, and (4) divide all language into two self-contained compartments called respectively "dianoetic" and "dynamic", seem to belong to a foreign, fantasy world that has little or nothing in common with the more rigorous and sophisticated worlds of Austin, Searle, Wolterstorff and Tilley. The necessity for inter-disciplinary interaction and dialogue is laid upon us if biblical scholarship and biblical interpretation is to retain credibility, let alone respect.

I.2 Multiple, Overlapping Speech-Acts

Donald Evans, we have just noted, argues for the simultaneous performance of varied and multiform speech-acts. His point is not only that God is more than "Maker" with causal power. In creating Israel and the world, God assigns *multiple roles* and a *status* to Israel and to humankind, and evaluates creation as "very good", but these multiple roles and evaluations entail *more than one type of illocutionary act*. When God creates a world that he evaluates as "very good", this act of evaluation functions as a *verdictive* or *declarative* act; when God appoints humankind as stewards of the earth, this constitutes an *exercitive* act; when God's creating through the divine Word counts as an expression of his outgoing, self-giving love, this also constitutes a *behabitive* or *expressive* performative illocution. Conversely, from the standpoint of humankind, God's creatures receive God's gifts with performative acts of thanksgiving (they count as *behabitive* or *expressive* acts), and they accept obligations that their correlative roles entail (these would count as *commissive* acts).

---

[20] Terrence W. Tilley, *The Evils of Theodicy* (Washington, DC: Georgetown University Press, 1991), pp.7–81.
[21] Tilley, *Evils*, p.34.
[22] Tilley, *Evils*, p.55.
[23] Tilley, *Evils*, p.76.

It is arguable that Evans may over-interpret *implicit* performatives as if they were explicit speech acts too readily, but he does pave the way for this by explicating Austin's distinction between "primitive" or "implicit" performatives and more formal speech-acts. In the same year as the appearance of *The Logic of Self-Involvement*, a New Testament specialist, Vernon Neufeld, published *The Earliest Christian Confessions*.[24] Neufeld's work strengthens the argument about multiple, overlapping speech-acts, but now from the standpoint of biblical and historical research. Confessions emerged historically as a way of nailing one's colours to the mast. They constitute expressive and commissive (or declarative) speech-acts. Very soon, however, they came to function no less as succinct summaries of Christian doctrine. In Neufeld's words, what were originally "a *perceived declaration* of faith" soon became also "the succinct expression of Christian faith ... a basis for developing creeds of the church ... expanded into more formal, articulate and complete *statements* concerning his [Christ's] person and work".[25] The multiplication of increasing diverse settings in the life of the church led to a corresponding diversity of the functions of multiform speech-acts. Oscar Cullmann has identified a number of these settings.[26]

Meanwhile philosophical corroboration of these arguments appeared four years later in D.M. High's study and exposition of the later Wittgenstein on the logic of first-person utterances, especially belief-utterances.[27] Wittgenstein, as I have observed elsewhere, identified what Austin called "performatives" before Austin. Thus he writes "for a funeral oration, 'We mourn our ... ' is supposed to be an expression of mourning; not to tell anything to those who are present".[28] He observes, "My own relation to my words is wholly different from other people's";[29] "If there were a verb meaning 'to believe falsely', it would not have any significant first person present indicative."[30] High rightly interprets Wittgenstein as observing that belief-utterances are not reports or descriptions of inner psychological states; rather, they offer "an explicit personal accreditation – my personal backing or signature – which I give to *p* [the proposition *p*] i.e. that it is 'true'";[31] "'Believing' is not describing something ... it is doing something ... close to what J.L. Austin has called ... 'performative' functions and 'illocutionary force'".[32]

High then develops an exploration of the relation between the "active" dimensions of belief-utterances and their "statement" dimension. To believe, he declares, "is an amphibious verb, sharing both in the assertive intensity of 'state' and in the performative intensity of 'promise'".[33] While "to believe" may move in the direction of

---

24   V.H. Neufeld, *The Earliest Christian Confessions* (Leiden: Brill and Grand Rapids, MI: Eerdmans, 1963).

25   Neufeld, *Earliest Christian Confessions*, pp.144 and 145 (my italics).

26   O. Cullmann, *The Earliest Christian Confessions* (London: SCM, 1949).

27   Dallas M. High, *Language, Persons and Belief: Study in Wittgenstein's Philosophical Investigations and Religious Uses of Language* (New York: Oxford University Press, 1967).

28   L. Wittgenstein, *Philosophical Investigations* (Eng. and Ger., Oxford: Blackwell, 2nd edn, 1967), Part II, p.189.

29   Wittgenstein, *Investigations*, Part II, p.192.

30   Wittgenstein, *Investigations*, Part II, p.190.

31   High, *Language*, p.142.

32   High, *Language*, p.150.

33   High, *Language*, p.151.

"an act of tentative assertion", "to believe in" is "chiefly characterized as an act of self-involvement".[34] In contrast to the view of speech-acts later explicated by Derrida, High draws from Wittgenstein the conclusion that speech-acts of believing "depend upon an extra-linguistic life".[35] This coheres with the biblical research of Cullmann and Neufeld.

II
The Next Stage of Development: "Directions of Fit" between Language and the World (1992)

Over the next fifteen or twenty years I reflected further on the complex relation between the performative dimension of *action*, especially of promising, and the dimension of *statement*, which often remained inseparable but distinct from the action-dimensions. In *New Horizons in Hermeneutics* (1992) I sought to come to terms with the advances achieved by John Searle in *Speech Acts* (1969), *Expression and Meaning* (1979), *Intentionality* (1983) and (with Daniel Vanderbeken) *Foundations of Illocutionary Logic* (1985), together with other related proposals from H.P. Grice (1971, 1975), Geoffrey M. Leech (1983) and François Recanati (1987).[36]

It is simply not the case (as Bultmann and a number of other biblical scholars imply) that statements are *alternative* ways of using language to those uses that are self-involving, existential, evaluative, directive, or "action"-related. It remains a source of puzzlement how so many biblical specialists became beguiled into accepting and promoting a grossly over-simple bi-partite view of language. It is little better, to follow Karl Bühler in promoting a tri-partite view of language as *either* cognitive, *or* expressive, *or* volitional. I had criticized this view at length as vitiating Bultmann's hermeneutics and his theology in *The Two Horizons* (1980). In *New Horizons in Hermeneutics* (1992) I extended my critique of Bultmann by comparing the one-sidedness of existential interpretation with the richer, fuller and more balanced resources of speech-act theory as able to account for *both* the transformative, active, self-involving dimensions of biblical texts *and* the states of affairs or ontological truth-claims on the basis of which such language could operate at all in transformative ways with more than psychological, and authentic, force. I turned to the issue of *actions and presuppositions* especially in relation to the Christology of the New Testament.[37] Since I developed these Christological issues further in a

---

34 High, *Language*, p.167.

35 High, *Language*, p.144.

36 The first two works are cited above; J.R. Searle, *Intentionality* (Cambridge: CUP, 1983); J.R. Searle and D. Vanderbeken, *Foundations of Illocutionary Logic* (Cambridge: CUP, 1985); H.P. Grice, "Meaning", in P.F. Strawson (ed.), *Philosophical Logic* (Oxford: OUP, 1971), pp.39–48, and "Logic and Conversation", in P. Cole and J.L. Morgan (eds), *Syntax and Semantics vol. 3, Speech Acts* (New York: Academic Press, 1975), pp.41–58; Geoffrey Leech, *Principles of Pragmatics* (London: Longmann, 1983) and F. Recanati, *Meaning and Force. The Pragmatics of Performative Utterances* (Eng., Cambridge: CUP, 1982).

37 Thiselton, *New Horizons*, pp.279–82 on Bultmann (a longer critique had already been provided in *The Two Horizons*, pp.205–92); pp.283–91 on Christological texts; these are part of the whole chapter, pp.272–312.

subsequent article of 1994, we shall return to these Christological texts after we have considered the argument about speech-acts in *New Horizons*.

The work explicitly on speech-acts took as its starting-point Searle's work on "direction of fit" between Words and the World. In summary, genuine illocutionary performatives, such as authentic actions of *promising*, serve to shape "the world" in accordance with "the word" as spoken or written linguistic action. Promises and commands, serve, in Searle's words, "to get the world to match the words".[38] By contrast, straightforward assertions seek to find descriptive words that "match the world". Searle borrows to good effect Elizabeth Anscombe's illustration of a shopping list that may be used either *to go shopping* or *to check the shopping*. In the act of shopping the list "shapes" the "world" of the shopper. If the list is used on return home to check how well the task has been done, the issue is reversed: does the "world" of the shopping-basket correspond with the word? Recanati also utilizes and develops a version of this "difference in the direction of fit".

In the section of *New Horizons* that follows this theoretical framework, I explore the application of this distinction to exegetical and theological problems about Christology, the Atonement in Paul, and promise in the Old Testament.[39] I have included this material in Essay 6, above, so it need not be replicated. It provides a solid foundation, I still believe, for further explorations. Indeed, I am encouraged that at least two writers, both of whom I greatly respect, have explicitly utilized this approach in and for their own work.

In his chapter "Literature, Story, and Worldviews", N.T. Wright alludes to my work in *New Horizons* on speech-act theory and Wittgenstein, and especially on "the 'fit' between what is said and events in the extra-linguistic world".[40] This comes in the context of his discussion of critical realism, in which he recognizes the importance of literary approaches to texts and of "story", but rightly concludes that this recognition in no way detracts from reference or from presuppositions that relate to the extra-linguistic world. Michael Gilbertson describes my approach to speech-acts as "a promising way forward" for understanding and formulating a theology of promise in his work on Pannenberg, Moltmann and the Book of Revelation.[41] Citing relevant work from *New Horizons*, Gilbertson comments, "The intertwining of 'directions of fit' is abundantly clear in the Book of Revelation. The seer makes assertions about the ultimate nature of reality (word-to-world fit), on the basis of which it is possible to articulate promises of transformation (world-to-word fit)."[42] He shows how this principle is worked out in subsequent chapters of his volume.

One possible fault in this chapter may be acknowledged. In 1992 I still tended to correlate, perhaps over-readily, a specific type of *speech-act* with specific examples of *vocabulary* as rule-of-thumb indicators of possible speech-actions. My former doctoral

---

[38] Searle, *Expression and Meaning*, p.3.

[39] Thiselton, *New Horizons*, pp.298–312.

[40] N.T. Wright, *The New Testament and the People of God* (Minneapolis, MN: Fortress and London: SPCK, 1992), p.68.

[41] Michael Gilbertson, *God and History on the Book of Revelation: New Testament Studies in Dialogue with Pannenberg and Moltmann* (Cambridge: CUP [SNTS Monograph 124], 2003), p.39.

[42] Gilbertson, *God and History*, p.40.

student, Richard Briggs, later picked me up over what he perceived as an over-readiness to assimilate speech-acts into the uses of a given vocabulary.[43] I seek to clarify this in my work of 1999, *The Promise of Hermeneutics*. Since I collected material in my files from discussions of this issue in the volume edited by S.L. Tsohatzides as well as notes in Wolterstorff's *Divine Discourse* and collaboration with Roger Lundin and Clare Walhout from earlier years, I was somewhat surprised to read Briggs's comment that in 1999 I simply "follow" his (Briggs's) argument, but he is correct in offering later the more neutral comment that my work embodies "several points of contact" with his.[44] Inevitably these issues were discussed in doctoral supervisions. As Gadamer points out, in genuine dialogical conversation new content may "arise" that may go further than the prior thought of either individual participant alone, and this is how it should be in good doctoral supervision. Be that as it may, whatever we conclude about directions of influence or sequence, there is common agreement between us that on one side vocabulary markers offer good, rough, preliminary guidance as starting-points for identifying given examples of illocutionary acts, while on the other side there is no guarantee that the use of the vocabulary will be *necessarily* symptomatic of the occurrence of speech-acts. Indeed, even for readers of *New Horizons* my regular warnings in publications since 1975 about the need to distrust vocabulary and grammar (as Fritz Mauthner, Wittgenstein, and Austin all urge) should serve to offer some protection against such possible misunderstanding.[45]

If there is a "fault", this may well relate more to a matter of presentation than to substance. The last chapter of *New Horizons* sets out *conditions* for operative speech-acts that cannot depend simply on the occurrence of a given vocabulary.[46] I observe, for example, that among other factors "something is at stake in the extra-linguistic attitudes and commitments of the *speaker or writer*" in the case of *promises or authorizations*. Conversely, "something is at stake in the extra-linguistic attitudes or commitments of those *readers* who participate in the speech-act character of the text as a speech act" in the case of *prayers and confessions*.[47]

I also try to explore whether biblical and theological notions of *covenant* may serve as an equivalent to what Searle calls "institutional facts" in the everyday world. The founding of covenant gives rise to habituated actions that become embedded in traditions and enacted in ritual or liturgy, and become a kind of authorized convention within the covenanted community. This substantiates further claims made earlier about

---

[43]   Richard S. Briggs, *Words in Action: Speech Act Theory and Biblical Interpretation* (Edinburgh: T. & T. Clark, 2001), pp.98–102; cf. 20–24.

[44]   Briggs, *Words in Action*, p.24.

[45]   For example, in A.C. Thiselton, *Language, Liturgy and Meaning* (Nottingham: Grove Liturgical Studies 2, 1st edn, 1975), pp.3–21. Chapter 1 includes the title "Vocabulary Versus Setting", pp.3–9.

[46]   Thiselton, *New Horizons*, pp.597–602.

[47]   Thiselton, *New Horizons*, p.598. I might have argued that Briggs' work on "confession" might be said to have "followed" some of my earlier work (Briggs, *Words in Action*, pp.183–216), but I had not noticed his comments about sources and sequences of ideas in the original PhD thesis of which the book is a revision, and I take for granted such building on ideas that have currency in a community of scholarship.

the difference between causal power and performative force. Again, I seek to develop this theme further in *The Promise of Hermeneutics*.

III

Speech-Act Theory in a Multi-Disciplinary Context: Biblical Studies, Modern Theology and Christology (1994)

III.1 The Emergence of a Dualist Framework in Modern Christology

The essay of 1994 ("Christology in Luke, Speech-Act Theory, and the Problem of Dualism in Christology", included above as Essay 7) is fully multi-disciplinary, drawing on New Testament studies and speech-act theory to address long-standing problems that have emerged in modern theology in attempts to provide a valid conceptual formulation for Christology. It addresses the dualism that has vitiated Christology since Lessing and Kant in terms of splitting apart the so-called "Christ of faith" from the Jesus of history. There is even some truth in the maxim that too often systematic theologians and New Testament exegetes simply "talk past" each other on this subject. At the very least, they inhabit different universes of discourse, in which, often, what seems self-evident within one appears problematic within the other. This dualism is often expressed in terms of spatial metaphors: Christology "from above" (often but not always in Christian theology), and Christology "from below" (often but not always in New Testament studies).

The divorce between two sides of this dualism came to be exacerbated in German Christology by Lessing's formulation about the "ugly ditch" that separated history from faith, and by Kant's disjunction between "fact" (associated with "history"), and "value" (often associated with "faith"). G.E. Lessing declared, "The accidental truths of history (*zufällige Geschichtswahrheiten*) can never become the proof of necessary truths of reason (*notwendige Vernunftwahrheiten*)."[48] Between the contingent probabilities or possibilities of history and the (logically) necessary truths of reason there lay "an ugly broad ditch" (*garstige breite Graben*). Most standard works in German Christology underline the importance of Lessing and Kant for this problematic approach to Christology.[49]

This approach set much of the agenda for nineteenth-century and earlier twentieth Christology from Schleiermacher, Hegel, Strauss, Kähler and Ritschl to Schweitzer, Harnack and Bultmann. David F. Strauss produced various editions of a *Life of Jesus* in which anything that might sustain a "Christian" Christology was "myth"; Martin Kähler argued that the only real or true Christ was "the preached Christ" in his work *The So-Called Historical Jesus as the Real, Biblical, Christ* (*Der sogenannte historische Jesus und der geschichtliche, biblische, Christus*). Karl-Josef Kuschel observes: "This is the problem of *all* modern theology"; but then adds the valid comment that this agenda that stems from

[48] G.E. Lessing, *Theological Writings* (London: Black, 1956), p.53.
[49] For example, A.E. McGrath, *The Making of Modern German Christology* (Oxford: Blackwell, 1986), esp. pp.11–18; John Macquarrie, *Jesus Christ in Modern Thought* (London: SCM, 1990), pp.175–303, esp. 176–9.

Lessing and heavily influences Bultmann may well be described as "Failed Conversations of Yesterday".[50]

Modern British Christology, in contrast to German debates, reflects a milder, less radical, dualism without such huge influence from Kant and neo-Kantian philosophy. However, the tendency remains to transpose "classical" formulations of "divine" and "human" into a *narrative* dualism of "two stories". One story tells of the earthly Jesus; the other of the heavenly Christ. Maurice Wiles writes, "We need to tell two stories", which come broadly to represent respectively history and myth, thereby recalling Strauss.[51] J.A.T. Robinson makes a similar point in the same volume, regarding the classical model as portraying Jesus like "Bat-man or a centaur".[52]

I have outlined these problems at length because from the vantage point of 2004 few formulations of Christology have successfully readdressed these problems. Perhaps only Pannenberg's Christology, and to some degree Moltmann's, has fully addressed these conceptual problems to date. The roots of the difficulty arise not only from Kantian dualism and from conceptual debates about necessity and contingency, they also stem from the tendency to construe biblical material in terms of an implicit dualism of "inner" and "outer", or in terms of such *spatially-grounded metaphors* as "above" and "below". Pannenberg and Moltmann rightly appeal to *eschatology and temporality* to reformulate these problems in more "biblical" terms. My essay of 1994 also seeks to bring into play not only eschatology, but also further *linguistic* factors that utilize speech-act theory to distinguish between *explicit action in the public domain* and *implicit presuppositions* that are *hidden in the eschatological interim* of the present but are potentially capable of communicating a conceptual content.

III.2 The Background in Lukan Studies

For a number of years I taught a course on New Testament literature in the University of Sheffield, and this included a substantial number of lectures on Luke's distinctive theology mainly in the light of redaction criticism. The reflections that this material provoked bore directly on the issues of Christology and speech-act theory, and in due time these became developed into the argument set out in the 1994 essay under discussion. Traditional textbooks on "New Testament Introduction" and many major commentaries regularly identified the same replicated list of Luke's distinctive interests, as follows. Luke was especially interested in *"history"*; in the socially underprivileged and in outsiders (particularly women, the poor, and Gentiles); in the *Roman* world; in *geographical* significance and "place"; and in a *"universal" perspective* (for example, his genealogy of Jesus relates to Adam rather than Abraham (as in Matthew), and he presents Jesus Christ as Saviour of the world, rather than as Messianic King of Israel).[53]

---

[50] Karl-Josef Kuschel, *Born Before All Time? The Dispute over Christ's Origin* (London: SCM, 1992), pp.30 and 35–60.

[51] Maurice Wiles, "Does Christology Rest on a Mistake?", in S.W. Sykes and J.P. Clayton (eds), *Christ, Faith, and History: Cambridge Studies in Christology* (Cambridge: CUP, 1972), p.9; cf. 1–12.

[52] J.A.T. Robinson, "Need Jesus Have been Perfect?", in Sykes and Clayton (eds), *Christ*, p.39.

[53] The evidence is presented in various ways. Cf. J.A. Fitzmyer, *The Gospel according to Luke* (New York: Doubleday [Luke I–IX], 1981), pp.3–34 and 107–270; Joel B. Green, *The Theology of the Gospel of Luke*

These themes are more than mere textbook conventions. A number of specialist studies explore individual themes convincingly.[54] However, we may go further. In my judgement, a *unifying factor that generates these multiple concerns* arises from Luke's perception of the importance of *the public world* as the public domain *of public action*, both for the outworking of divine purpose and for transparent Christian witness and discipleship. We shall consider this claim for a few paragraphs because it has a close bearing on our appeal to speech-act theory in this context. It is not a digression.

This claim was partly misconstrued by those scholars who sought to oppose Luke's "objective" history, or a focus on the historically past, together with his "institutional" concerns over against Paul's "present" and "existential" concerns. Supposedly Paul's eschatological perspective sat light to the world, while Luke-Acts "digs in", with the Church becoming an institution here to stay, even possessing past traditions from an idealized or bygone age. Vielhauer, Wilckens, Conzelmann and Haenchen, among others, tended to promote, or at least to encourage, this view, although mainly in the early 1960s.[55] A number of writers also argued to the contrary at the time that they had overdrawn this contrast.[56] By the late 1970s and early 1980s many had rejected Conzelmann's approach as untenable, and attention began to move once again to parallels with Graeco-Roman literature and socio-historical situations in the Graeco-Roman world of Luke's day.[57]

The more levelheaded and less speculative of these approaches underpins to some degree our comment about Luke's concern for the world as a *public domain* of *public action*. Thus Joel Green, in the same volume as the essay of 1994 under discussion, observes, "The current emphasis in Lukan studies on the material, *this-worldly* focus of Jesus' message in the Third Gospel represents a helpful advance on the spiritualized and end-time-orientated interpretations of previous decades" (my italics).[58] The poor, Green concludes, include the economically destitute, but Luke's term also relates to the human condition and social dynamics of the first-century Roman world. Writers on the Third Gospel return again to the polished Prologue of Luke 1:1–4, and to the careful triple dating (technically the six-fold dating) of Luke 3:1–2, which locates the beginning of the ministry of Jesus in public time in relation to the year of the Roman Emperor (Tiberius),

---

(Cambridge: CUP, 1995); Luke T. Johnson, *The Writings of the New Testament* (London, SCM, 1986), pp.200–23; Robert Maddox, *The Purpose of Luke-Acts* (Edinburgh: T. & T. Clark, 1982), pp.1–30 and 100–187; A. Wikenhauser, *N.T. Introduction* (Dublin: Herder, 1988), pp.212–21.

[54] The list is too long to enumerate. Cf. F. Bovon, *Luke the Theologian* (Alison Park, PA: Princeton Theological Monograph series 12, 1987); H. Moxnes, *The Economy of the Kingdom* (Philadelphia, PA: Fortress, 1988); S.G. Wilson, *The Gentiles and the Gentile Message in Luke-Acts* (Missoula, MT: Scholars Press, 1977); and to a large degree James L. Resseguie, *Spiritual Landscape: Images of the Spiritual Life in the Gospel of Luke* (Peabody, MA: Hendrickson, 2004).

[55] Several essays are collected in L.E. Keele and J.L. Martyn (eds), *Studies in Luke-Acts* (London: SPCK, 1968), including P. Vielhauer (pp.33–50); U. Wilckens (pp.60–83); E. Haenchen (pp.258–78); and H. Conzelmann (pp.298–316), for example.

[56] I.H. Marshall, *Luke Historian and Theologian* (Exeter: Paternoster, 1970) pp.13–102. Cf. H. Flinder, *St. Luke Theologian of Redemptive History* (London: SPCK, 1967); and Fitzmyer, *The Gospel of Luke* (cited above).

[57] Cf. for example, C.H. Talbert (ed.), *Perspectives on Luke-Acts* (Edinburgh: T. & T. Clark, 1978); Talbert (ed.), *Luke-Acts: New Perspectives from the Society of Biblical Literature Seminars* (New York: Crossroad, 1984).

[58] Joel B. Green, "Good News to Whom? Jesus and the 'Poor' in the Gospel of Luke", in J.B. Green and M. Turner (eds), *Jesus of Nazareth*, p.74; cf. 59–74.

of the civil authorities in Judea (Pontius Pilate), in Galilee (Herod), and in Iturea (Philip), and to the religious or high priestly authorities (Annas and Caiaphas).[59]

L.T. Johnson correctly observes that "Luke-Acts has a positive view of the world", but it places the emphasis in the wrong place to explicate this as "world affirmation".[60] Luke sees *public agents, public action, and the public domain* as the sphere in which God's purpose and divine action were "not done in a corner" (Acts 26:26, NRSV, Greek ἐν γωνίᾳ, *en gōnia*). These are "witnesses" to the acts of Jesus in his ministry and to his death on a cross, and if there were hidden dimensions before the resurrection, "God raised him on the third day *visibly*" (Greek, ἐμφανῆ, *emphanē*).[61] What a person does with their financial or other material resources provides a good index or criterion concerning the seriousness of their discipleship. This is why, while Jesus (and Luke) retain a special concern for the poor, it remains also true that "Jesus is found repeatedly frequenting the homes of the wealthy" (e.g. 5:29; 7:36, 14:1, 19:5).[62] The triple or six-fold dating shows the importance of the imperial, civil and religious dimensions of public life. Even Luke's "ordering" of events ("orderly account", 1:3) reflects his respect for "world-order".

In the earliest "reception" and expositions of this Third Gospel, it is no accident that Tertullian finds here his most powerful weapon against the false teaching of Marcion. Tertullian writes that Marcion adulterates the gospel by separating the Old Testament from the New "so that his own Christ may be separate from *the Creator*" (my italics).[63] Luke's Gospel presents the "Christ of the Creator ... the *Creator's* Christ".[64] Tertullian attempts to expound Luke's text chapter by chapter to substantiate this point.[65] At the end of his exposition he concludes, "We have set forth Jesus Christ as none other than the Christ of the Creator."[66] This rests partly on the continuity between the Old Testament and the New, but also partly on the "public" setting of the actions of Jesus in the everyday world. At the same time we cannot draw firm inferences from the respective uses of Luke by Marcion and Tertullian. Andrew Gregory has shown recently how fragile is the basis for theories about the reception of Luke in Justin, Marcion, Irenaeus and Tertullian.[67]

III.3 Public Speech-Action and Implicit Presuppositions

Against this background I have argued that in Luke Jesus performs *public speech-acts* that carry with them otherwise *hidden Christological presuppositions. To pronounce the declarative* (or verdictive) *act*: "My son, your sins are [hereby] forgiven you" (Luke 5:20; par. Mark

---

[59]   Cf. John Nolland *Luke 1–9:20* (Dallas, TX: Word, 1989), pp.139–41.

[60]   L.T. Johnson, "Luke-Acts", in *The Anchor Bible Dictionary* vol. 4 (New York: Doubleday, 1992), p.417, col. ii.

[61]   F.W. Danker and W. Bauer, *Greek-English Lexicon of the New Testament* (Chicago, IL: University of Chicago Press, third rev. edn [*BDAG*], 2000), p.325, col. ii.

[62]   Joel B. Green, "Good News to Whom?", *Jesus of Nazareth* (cited above), p.59. Green shows the complexity of this subject, citing a huge mass of research literature on the issues (pp.60–61, n. 7).

[63]   Tertullian, *Against Marcion*, IV: 6.

[64]   *Against Marcion*, IV: 7.

[65]   *Against Marcion* IV: 8–43.

[66]   *Against Marcion* IV: 43.

[67]   Andrew Gregory, *The Reception of Luke and Acts in the Period before Irenaeus* (Tübingen: Mohr, 2004), esp. pp.173–298.

2:5; Matt. 9:2) would not be operative or effective (except in a purely psychological sense) unless we are to presuppose that behind the scenes Jesus has been authorized to speak in God's name as an act of God. Indeed the question of Luke 9:21, "Who can forgive sins except God?" is entirely valid. If the utterance *is* indeed as an illocutionary act, it *entails a presupposition* that Jesus has the *institutional authority* to perform a speech-act of this kind.

It is unnecessary to trace this argument further, since this aspect is set out in the essay of 1994. Our task in this retrospective assessment has been to review and to expand its basis and its implications in relation to the multi-disciplinary explorations that underpin it from the respective areas of New Testament studies, modern Christological debates and speech-act theory. I argued in the 1994 that the *dimension of public acts* relates to *"showing"* openly, whereas Luke shares the perspective of the other Synoptic Gospels concerning a *reticence in "saying"* prior to the resurrection. After the resurrection Christology may also be "said". But the view that Christology in the Synoptic Gospels *either* rests on the "claims" of Jesus *or* is absent from view altogether, or is diminished, rests on a misunderstanding. It overlooks what has been presented in this paper.

If these arguments are valid, this approach coheres to some extent with the broad emphasis in Pannenberg and other writers when they argue that much has to await the event of the resurrection of Christ to become fully *explicated*. But Luke's eschatology is complex, combining an aspect of fulfilment with an aspect of futurity. Hence the pre-resurrection era is not, for Luke, one of total hiddenness. The acts of God occur upon an open stage. Nevertheless the Christological truth on which they rest for their actualization and action, *that which enables us to perceive them AS acts of God* remains at least partly hidden as presuppositions *yet to be explicated* in descriptive or ontological language.

One final footnote may be added. Jacques Derrida questions the relevance or possibility of an appeal to extra-linguistic presuppositions or states of affairs, largely on the ground that all speech-acts are *radically* context-variable. In technical terms, because any speech-act is "iterable", or may be repeated in any number of different contexts, a speech-act cannot retain any stable or univocal meaning. In accordance with Derrida's philosophical world-view, no single context can be privileged over others as normative. Theoretically each repetition of an utterance that may take the same linguistic form is therefore irreducibly different in meaning. Might this not invalidate our approach? Derrida famously asserts in his early work, "There is nothing outside the text."[68]

Three responses may be suggested, although very briefly in view of the confines of space. (1) Nicholas Wolterstorff offers a trenchant critique of Derrida's arguments. He sets out part of his response in his *Divine Discourse* (1995).[69] Here he argues that Derrida's approach is self-contradictory, not least because his anti-metaphysical stance presupposes a Derridean metaphysic. Wolterstorff attacks "the incoherence, for example, of conceding that truth and falsehood are metaphysical concepts that have to go, while arguing that metaphysics has to go because it is false".[70] Wolterstorff also contributes a

---

[68] J. Derrida, *Of Grammatology* (Eng., Baltimore, MD: Johns Hopkins University Press, 1976), p.158.
[69] N. Wolterstorff, *Divine Discourse* (cited above), pp.153–70.
[70] Wolterstorff, *Divine Discourse*, p.164.

more recent essay that explicitly concerns speech-act theory, and there he develops his critique of Derrida (2001).[71] Here he argues that Derrida's critique of textual-sense interpretation is "both misguided and ungrounded ... Never (to the best of my knowledge) does Derrida do anything more than announce that Fregean-Husserlian ontology is false; nowhere does he mount a substantive argument against it."[72]

Derrida's own claims do appear to be seriously ambivalent. He appears to argue for the absence of extra-textual or extra-linguistic references in *Disseminations, Of Grammatology*, and elsewhere. But in his *Afterword* to *Limited Inc.* he claims that "deconstruction should not lead to relativism or to any sort of indeterminacy".[73] It is unclear how radically arguments about iteration and irreducibly variable contexts are to be pressed; or perhaps more strictly, whether they apply to *every* kind of discourse.

Still further, from the standpoint of New Testament Christology, there are certain stable markers that resist and *prohibit and constrain the application of the relevant speech-acts of Jesus so that these cannot apply to an infinity of variable contexts*. The context (in terms of *speaking*) is *bound* to Jesus' institutional authorization as the One elected by God to speak God's word in God's Name. The context (in terms of *the hearer or "receiver"*) is bound and limited to those who know (in the case of acts of forgiveness) their need of forgiveness and who offer a potential or actual act of *acknowledgement* or *confession*. In contexts of commission or appointment, recipients of such speech-actions cannot be everyone or anyone. These issues clearly relate even more fundamentally to the conditions for operative *promise*. To this subject we now turn.

IV
Promising as a Paradigmatic Speech Act (1999)

There is little of substance that I should wish to change in the hundred pages of *The Promise of Hermeneutics* that are my own work. Although I am responsible for this section, over several years Roger Lundin and Clare Walhout travelled from the United States to confer with me in Nottingham, and I travelled to confer with them in Grand Rapids through the hospitality of Calvin College. During the period of writing I was simultaneously writing my substantial commentary on the Greek text of Paul's First Epistle to the Corinthians, and I have explored points of contact between these two projects.[74] Among other relevant literature, I noted Alexandra Brown's exploration of performative utterances in relation to Paul's proclamation in Corinth.[75] Performative

---

[71] N. Wolterstorff, "The Promise of Speech-Act Theory for Biblical Interpretation", in C. Bartholomew, C. Greene and K. Möller (eds), *After Pentecost: Language and Biblical Interpretation* (Carlisle: Paternoster and Grand Rapids, MI: Zondervan, 2001), pp.73–90.

[72] Wolterstorff, "Promise", p.80.

[73] J. Derrida, "Afterword: Toward an Ethic of Discussion", in *Limited Inc.* (Evanston, IL: Northwestern University Press, 1988), p.148; cf. pp.111–54.

[74] Anthony C. Thiselton, *The First Epistle to the Corinthians: A Commentary on the Greek Text* (Grand Rapids, MI: Eerdmans and Carlisle: Paternoster [NICGT], 2000).

[75] A.R. Brown, *The Cross and Human Transformation: Paul's Apocalyptic Word in 1 Corinthians* (Minneapolis, MN: Fortress, 1995).

speech is to be distinguished emphatically from the manipulative rhetoric used in Corinth.[76] The latter draws, in effect, on *causal power*; the former constitutes illocutionary performative actions.

I had also just completed at the time an exegetical contribution on the Epistle to the Hebrews to a large one-volume commentary, and found that several points of resonance between the two projects emerged. First, many agree that Hebrews 1–12 takes the form of a homily, and I noted the impressively multi-functional language of this epistle, especially in chapter 1. In my Introduction to the epistle I wrote that it "begins as a sermon ... with a marvellously crafted theological declaration, which serves as a multiple communicative act of creed, teaching, hymn, doxology, confession, exposition of scripture and acclamation".[77] Second, Hebrews contains probably more explicit theological reflection on the nature of the covenant than any other New Testament book. Work on this material confirmed my belief that, in the context of the New Testament and of Christian theology, *covenant* provides a specific paradigm of the broader role of "institutional facts" that provide foundations for valid illocutionary acts. Among these, *promise* claims special status as a speech-act in the context of covenant. The Epistle to the Hebrews expounds covenant and mediation as "guarantees" of promissory commitment and appropriate consequences in life.

This resonates, in turn with an approach in Christian theology that I have long respected and admired. From the 1960s to the present both Wolfhart Pannenberg and Jürgen Moltmann have produced an impressive series of constructive works in which promise features as a major theme or category. Pannenberg addresses numerous aspects of promise with logical and conceptual rigour. How can the sovereign God who is also "free" fulfil promises that entail a *commitment or pledge*, but also permit a *degree of openness* for the genuinely new, surprising and unexpected?[78] Moltmann distinguishes between genuine faith based on the appropriation of *promise* and misdirected, self-generated attitudes of *presumption* (an inappropriate, prematurely-timed, self-generated anticipation of a divine "yes"), or of *despair* (an inappropriate, prematurely-timed, self-generated anticipation of a divine "no").[79]

In the previous section I raised the issue of using vocabulary-markers as a means of offering an alert to the possible occurrence of speech-acts. In *The Promise of Hermeneutics* I draw on Daniel Vanderveken's work on illocutionary acts, although I have been aware of the problem over the years. I cite his comment to the effect that even when we identify "speech-act verbs", these verbs may have "many uses". As the first essay in Part II shows,

[76] I discuss this at length in my commentary. Cf. also S.M. Pogoloff, *Logos and Sophia: The Rhetorical Situation of 1 Corinthians* (Atlanta, GA: Scholars Press, 1992).

[77] Anthony C. Thiselton, "Hebrews", in James D.G. Dunn and John W. Rogerson (eds), *Eerdmans Commentary on the Bible* (Grand Rapids, MI and Cambridge: Eerdmans, 2003), p.1451; cf. pp.1451–82.

[78] Among his earlier writings, W. Pannenberg, *Basic Questions in Theology* (3 vols, Eng., London: SCM, 1969, 1971, 1973), vol. 2, pp.1–28 and esp. 234–49; and much of vol. 3, esp. 1–79, 144–77 and 192–210; among his more recent writings *Systematic Theology* vol. 3 (Eng., Grand Rapids, MI: Eerdmans and Edinburgh: T. & T. Clark, 1998), esp. pp.532–54, 603–7 and 642–6.

[79] Among his earlier works Jürgen Moltmann, *Theology of Hope* (Eng., London: SCM, 1967), pp.15–36, 197–227 and 272–338; among his more recent writings, *Experiences in Theology* (Eng., London: SCM, 2000), esp. pp.87–113. See also his two essays in Richard Bauckham (ed.), *God Will Be All in All: The Eschatology of Jürgen Moltmann* (Edinburgh: T. & T. Clark, 1979), pp.77–85 and 265–89.

I had undertaken research on such themes as cursing, making vows, confessing, blessing, and promising since before 1974.[80] Further, few of these are context-free. Pannenberg points out, for example, that the very concept of being faithful to a promise presupposes the reality of a lapse of time between the making of the promise and opportunities for its outcome or its betrayal.

V
"Politeness" Theory?

I hope and plan to develop these broad multi-disciplinary perspectives further. One of the doctoral research candidates whom I advise, William Olhausen, is currently working on "politeness" theory, as developed initially by Penelope Brown and Stephen C. Levinson. This approach also stems from earlier insights from H.P. Grice's theory of conversational implicature, to which I refer in essays included above.[81] Olhausen had already discussed "politeness" theory with me before I became involved in his doctoral research, and in 1992–94 I had also supervised a PhD by David Hilborn in Nottingham, "The Pragmatics of Liturgical Discourse".[82] In response to my paper "'Behind' and 'In Front of' the Text – Language, Reference, and Indeterminacy", Olhausen proposed "supplementing Thiselton's linguistic approach with insights drawn from recent developments in linguistic pragmatics", citing Brown and Levinson's work.[83] I share his view that politeness theory offers a promising tool for biblical interpretation. It resonates with the central concern of my 1994 essay about the importance of "public space" and of the interpersonal and inter-subjective character of communicative acts.[84] In principle it reflects Schleiermacher's fundamental conviction, too often neglected, that in hermeneutics *both* an originating setting on the part of "senders" or authors *and* what the text "sets going" in terms of its effects on "receivers" or readers remain valid foci of attention.[85]

In the New Testament, especially in Luke-Acts and in Paul's theology, as we have noted above, the public domain, or, for Paul, *the body* is perceived as part of "world" of interpersonal, inter-subjective discourse and human identity as relationally constituted.

---

[80]   Some of the relevant literature is cited in n. 48 of the 1999 essay, and been used in "The Supposed Power of Words".

[81]   Penelope Brown and S.C. Levinson, *Politeness: Some Universals in Language Usage* (Cambridge: CUP, 1978 and 1987).

[82]   William Olhausen, "A 'Polite' Response to Anthony Thiselton", in Bartholomew, Greene and Möller (eds), *After Pentecost*, pp.121–30; and David Hilborn, "The Pragmatics of Liturgical Discourse" (Nottingham University PhD, 1994). This was jointly supervised with a specialist in pragmatics, Vilama Herman. A revised version of the thesis is forthcoming from Paternoster Press under the title *Worship, Speech, and Action*. See also David Hilborn, "From Performativity to Pedagogy: Jean Ladrière and the Pragmatics of Reformed Works on Discourse", in Stanley Porter (ed.), *The Nature of Religious Language* (Sheffield: Sheffield Academic Press, 1995), pp.120–200.

[83]   Olhausen, in *After Pentecost*, p.122.

[84]   Olhausen borrows this phrase from C. Taylor, "Theories of Meaning", in Taylor, *Human Agency and Language: Philosophical Papers* (Cambridge: CUP, 1985), p.259; cf. 248–92.

[85]   F. Schleiermacher, *Hermeneutics: The Handwritten Manuscripts* (Missoula, MT: Scholars Press, 1977), pp.97–9, 101–4, 107, especially 150–51, and 205–8.

Politeness theory, first of all, takes this public, inter-subjective dimension seriously. Second, it also coheres with the later Wittgenstein's valid observations about *public criteria of meaning* and *"private" language* (that is, in his own special, technical sense of this term, which is too often misunderstood). Further, it accords, in the third place, with the importance that Gadamer attaches to "conversation" as having the capacity to draw upon pre-conscious commonalities and differences that transcend each individual speaker's conscious "ideas" at particular moments. "Conversation" can take us further than the sum of the individual participants' "lone" ideas.

In linguistic terms, politeness theory takes account of two factors that I emphasize in my writings: semantic or semiotic "competency" and human rationality, as well as public behaviour.[86] A key concept here in politeness theory is "face". "Positive Face" reflects the desire that our goals, possessions and achievements should elicit understanding, approval and acceptance on the part of others, especially our addressees. "Negative Face" reflects defensive strategies against threats to our face through disapproval and rejection on the part of others, especially our addressees.[87] "Politeness" expresses a speaker's intentions to mitigate "threats", or more strictly to mitigate "Face-Threatening Acts" (known by the acronym F.T.A.), as well as efforts "to save Face". The application of all this yields a communicative strategy: speakers perform communicative acts that seek to avoid damage to their "Face", in which they balance interests of accuracy and the desire to communicate against norms and conventions within their shared situation or culture that offer protections.

In turn, this involves both a "universal" and a "local" polarity, or dialectic. The common reference point arises from the inter-subjective norms of society and desires that spring from "being human". On the other hand, effective strategies for achieving face-saving "politeness" vary from culture to culture and have a strongly "local" dimension. In this respect William Olhausen is exploring how the respective cultures and contexts of Paul and the first-century culture of Corinth serve to condition their respective strategies of communication. Brown and Levinson readily acknowledge, "The very range of the material we have received might give rise to the suspicion that politeness, construed in this broad way, subsumes just about every facet of the social world."[88] But this sets a task of "fundamental reconceptualization from cross-cultural perspective".[89] This, of course, is part of the central task of hermeneutics, in which, as Schleiermacher urges, the comparative operates along side the divinatory, and, as Dilthey contends, dialectic operates between the universal and the particular or contingent.

The extensions of H.P. Grice's theory of conversational implicature often in the context of relevance theory might also be said to relate not only to hermeneutics but also to the explication of conceptual grammar as discussed in these essays. *Explication* constitutes an important interpretative resource, which often provides a conceptual grammar or depth-

---

[86]   I discuss "competency" in *New Horizons in Hermeneutics*, pp.497–508. If communication is to be a communicative events, a certain "competency" and "recourse" to readers has to be assumed.

[87]   See Brown and Levinson, *Politeness*, pp.13–15, on positive and negative Face, and on "cultural notions of 'Face'".

[88]   Brown and Levinson, *Politeness*, p.47.

[89]   Brown and Levinson, *Politeness*, p.48.

grammar that surface-grammar and syntax alone merely imply. Brown and Levinson suggest a number of conversational examples. Thus the surface-assertion "It's cold in here", or "This soup is a bit bland", or "What a boring film!" may be explicated as "logical" imperatives: "shut the window", or "pass the salt" or "let's leave".[90] Prior to the formulation of these theories in politeness theory, I formulated precisely this kind of example in my earlier work on functions of language and meaning in liturgy. I suggested that "this is poison" might serve to communicate a plea for help "Quick! Fetch the doctor!", or a proposal for action, "Avenge me of this criminal act"; or a reproach, "You have put sugar in my tea."[91]

As a *supplement* to other approaches, politeness theory may facilitate a balance with those approaches that move too readily towards exclusively *intra*-linguistic concerns, as well as those that focus too narrowly either upon *authors alone* or upon *readers alone*. As Wittgenstein observes, "The speaking of language is part of an activity, or of a form of life".[92] "What determines ... our concepts ... or the whole hurly-burly of human actions, the background against which we see any action";[93] "The common behaviour of mankind is the system of reference by means of which we interpret our unknown language."[94] However, what specific advances may ensue for biblical interpretation has yet to be demonstrated. At present this remains a hope rather than a reality.

---

[90] Brown and Levinson, *Politeness*, p.215.
[91] A.C. Thiselton, *Language, Liturgy and Meaning* (Nottingham: Grove Liturgical Studies 2, 1975), pp.10–12.
[92] Wittgenstein, *Philosophical Investigations* (Ger. and Eng., Oxford: Blackwell, 1967), sect. 23.
[93] Wittgenstein, *Zettel* (Ger. and Eng., Oxford: Blackwell, 1967), sect. 567.
[94] Wittgenstein, *Philosophical Investigations*, sect. 206.

PART III

HERMENEUTICS, SEMANTICS AND CONCEPTUAL GRAMMAR

Justification by Grace as Legal Fiction? "Language-Games and 'Seeing As': A Fresh Approach to Justification by Faith in Paul and James" (1980)

Many of the traditional difficulties that beset Paul's understanding of justification by grace through faith may be perceived differently when we formulate the issues in terms of a more adequate conceptual grammar. A clarification and reformulation of "logical" grammar softens or dissolves at least five sets of supposed contradictions, tensions, or perceptions of an impasse. Several types of conceptual clarification are needed, but here I draw especially on Wittgenstein's notion of "seeing as" within a system, and on D.D. Evans's notion of "onlooks". An appreciation of the different logical grammars of "faith" in different contexts also sheds further light on these problems. Paul and James offer coherent and compatible approaches. This extract comes from The Two Horizons *(Grand Rapids, MI: Eerdmans and Exeter: Paternoster, 1980), pp.415–27; also in Korean (Seoul: Chongshin, 1990), pp.636–53.*

I
Some Persistent Problems about Justification in Paul

The history of Pauline research over the last hundred years has raised at least five related problems about the nature of justification by faith. (1) Are the terms for "to justify" (δικαιόω) and "justified" or "righteous" (δίκαιος) primarily declaratory (to count righteous) or behavioural (to make righteous)? Whichever view is taken, does this mean that the believer is no longer in status or in actuality a sinner? *How do we hold together the so-called paradox of his or her being both righteous and a sinner?* (2) *How* central is justification in Pauline thought? This question tends to mean, in effect: to what conceptual scheme does it belong? (3) Is justification a present experience, or does it belong, more strictly, to the future, as an anticipated verdict of the last judgement? (4) What kind of faith is justifying faith? How do we avoid making "faith" a special kind of substitute for "works" which is somehow a more acceptable sort of human activity? (5) If we can arrive at a concept of faith that escapes this problem, how does it relate to the concept of faith in the Epistle of James?

Various attempts at solutions to these problems have been offered. However, the fact that scholars repeatedly return to them suggests that none of the proposed solutions is entirely satisfactory. We shall try to use some of Wittgenstein's own concepts and categories in order to approach these questions from a fresh angle. Our approach is by no means an alternative to traditional or more recent approaches, and it is not intended to undermine them. However, we do suggest that a new perspective is needed in the light of which certain conceptual clarifications may become possible.

The first problem concerns the declaratory or behavioural meaning of the δικαιόω terms. Some of the arguments on this question are primarily or at least partly linguistic. Thus in his recent study J.A. Ziesler argues that the traditional Protestant interpretation, in terms of status, rests primarily on the evidence of the verbal form δικαιόω, while the traditional Roman Catholic interpretation, in terms of behavioural or ethical righteousness, rests mainly on the use of the noun δικαιοσύνη and the adjective δίκαιος.[1] Both aspects, he argues, can be found in the Hebrew form צדק, although in the Hebrew the forensic is probably primary. Yet even Ziesler, whose study is largely linguistic, finds the logical and theological factors the decisive ones. He writes, "If God looks on believers only as they are found in Christ, he may properly declare them righteous, for in him ... they are righteous ... There is nothing fictional here."[2]

We need not delay on the question of whether Ziesler overpresses the contrast between the noun and the verb. We are more concerned with his theological arguments. Can we actually *ask* whether the believer is "really" righteous in Paul's view? We shall argue shortly that the believer becomes righteous *within the context of one language-game*, but that *in another context*, or language-game, even the Christian believer still remains a sinner. Ziesler, like most Pauline interpreters, tends to ask the question about righteousness *outside* a given language-game. There is no escaping the Lutheran formulation that, according to Paul, the believer is *simul iustus et peccator*, or *"semper peccator, semper penitens, semper iustus"*.[3] However firmly a behavioural interpretation is pressed, Paul would not have been willing to accept the assertion that *Christians are no longer sinners*. This possibility must be rejected in the light of such passages as 1 Corinthians 3:3; 4:4; 11:17, 28–32; 2 Corinthians 12:20b, and Philippians 3:12, 13.[4] This theological point lies behind many of the approaches which defend the forensic view. Thus J. Weiss writes that justification "does not say what a man is in himself, but it states what he is considered to be in the eyes of God".[5] Similarly H. Ridderbos asserts, "It is a matter of man as a sinner, and not yet of his future inner renewal."[6]

This, however, does not solve our problem, as advocates of the behavioural view are quick to note. Fernand Prat, for one, regards what he calls the "official" Protestant doctrine as flatly self-contradictory. He writes, *"How can the false be true, or how can God declare true what he knows to be false?"*[7] Similarly F. Amiot and L. Cerfaux consider that

---

[1] J.A. Ziesler, *The Meaning of Righteousness in Paul. A Linguistic and Theological Enquiry* (Cambridge: Cambridge University Press, 1972), pp.128–210 *et passim*.

[2] Ziesler, *Righteousness*, p.169.

[3] On Luther's language, cf. G. Rupp, *The Righteousness of God: Luther Studies* (London: Hodder & Stoughton, 1953), e.g. pp.225 and 255; and P. Stuhlmacher, *Gerechtigkeit Gottes bei Paulus* (Göttingen: Vandenhoeck & Ruprecht, 1965), pp.19–23.

[4] Cf. further R. Bultmann, "Das Problem der Ethik bei Paulus", in Z.N.W. XXIII (1924), 123–40.

[5] J. Weiss, *Earliest Christianity* (Eng., 2 vols, New York: Harper, 1959), II, 499.

[6] H. Ridderbos, *Paul. An Outline of his Theology* (Grand Rapids, MI: Eerdmans and London: SPCK, 1977), p.175.

[7] F. Prat, *The Theology of St. Paul* (Eng., 2 vols, London: Burns, Oates & Washbourne, 1945, vol. 2, p.247 (my italics).

this difficulty is a fatal objection to the traditional Protestant view.[8] E. Käsemann speaks of the "tensions" of Paul's language, and the "logical embarrassment" in which he places the modern reader.[9] Even Bultmann's "relational" concept of righteousness does not fully answer this particular problem.[10] For if man's relationship to God is right, is he still a sinner or not? Ziesler comments, "The resulting position is ... very similar to the usual Protestant one".[11] We seem, then, to have come up against a brick wall. The behavioural interpretation makes it difficult to see how man can still be regarded as a sinner from *a logical* viewpoint. For behavioural righteousness seems logically to exclude his still being a sinner, although this is patently at variance with other Pauline statements. On the other hand, the forensic interpretation makes it difficult to see how man can still be regarded as a sinner from a theological viewpoint. For forensic righteousness seems logically to exclude his being even considered a sinner.

II
A Fresh Approach: Wittgenstein on "Seeing ... As ..."

At this point we may turn to examine Wittgenstein's remarks about the phenomenon of "seeing ... as ...", or seeing x as y.[12] In his *Zettel* Wittgenstein writes, "Let us imagine a kind of puzzle picture ... At first glance it appears to us as a jumble of meaningless lines, and only after some effort do we see it as, say, a picture of a landscape. – What makes the difference ... ?"[13] What makes the difference, Wittgenstein asks, between seeing a diagram as a chaotic jumble of lines, and seeing it as representing the inside of a radio receiver?[14] How does someone who is unfamiliar with the conventions of how a clock signifies the time, suddenly come to see the hands as pointers which tell the time? Wittgenstein declares: "It all depends on the *system* to which the sign belongs."[15] We see a puzzle picture at first as a jumble of lines. Then suddenly *we provide a certain context*, and the lines portray a landscape. Only the person who knows the *system* of representation in radio circuitry can see the diagram as that of a radio receiver.

But Wittgenstein also asks: What is it about a special situation that allows me to see 'something *either as this, or as that*? He writes, "When I ... interpret, I step from one level of thought to another. If I see the thought symbol 'from outside', I become conscious that it *could* be interpreted thus or thus."[16] Wittgenstein's most famous example of this phenomenon comes not in the *Zettel* but in the *Investigations*, where he speaks about "the

---

8 F. Amiot, *The Key Concepts of St. Paul* (Eng., Freiburg: Herder, 1962), pp.120–25; and L. Cerfaux, *The Christian in the Theology of St. Paul* (Eng., London: Chapman, 1967), pp.391–400.

9 E. Käsemann, *New Testament Questions of Today* (Eng., London: SCM, 1969), p.171.

10 R. Bultmann, *Theology of the New Testament* (London: SCM, 1952), I, 270–85.

11 J.A. Ziesler, *The Meaning of Righteousness in Paul*, p.3.

12 L. Wittgenstein, *Philosophical Investigations* (PI) (Ger. and Eng., Oxford: Blackwell, 1967), sects 74, and II.xi, pp.193–214; *The Blue and Brown Books* (Oxford: Blackwell, 2nd edn., 1969), pp.163–74; and *Zettel* (Ger. and Eng., Oxford: Blackwell, 1967), sects 195–235.

13 L. Wittgenstein, *Zettel*, sect. 195.

14 *Zettel*, sect. 201.

15 *Zettel*, sect. 228 (Wittgenstein's italics).

16 *Zettel*, sects 234–3.

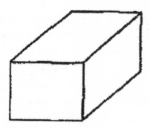
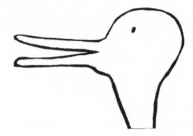

'dawning' of an aspect".[17] He cites the example of the "duck-rabbit" suggested in Jastrow's *Fact and Fable in Psychology*. The same figure can be seen either as a duck facing to the left, or as a rabbit facing upwards and a little to the right. The same lines that represent the beak in the duck-system also represent the ears in the rabbit-system. *What is seen* remains the same; *how* it is seen depends on the significance or function of the phenomenon within a given system, frame of reference, or setting in life. Wittgenstein also suggests the example of a two-dimensional drawing of a cube. It may be seen now as a glass cube, now as three boards forming a solid angle, now as a wire frame, now as an open box. Our interpretation depends on the context from life what system of reference we choose.[18] Another common experience is that of seeing a face in a crowd that we think we recognize. We slot it into a given context, and we think it is our friend, and then suddenly we realize that we are mistaken and the context is irrelevant.

This principle is of course highly suggestive for hermeneutics. Interpretation depends, as Schleiermacher saw, on relating what we see to aspects of our own experience. But this is not the primary point that concerns us here. Nor am I unaware that other interpreters of Wittgenstein have sometimes stressed other aspects of Wittgenstein's work on "seeing ... as ...".[19] Our concern here is with the relationship between "seeing ... as ..." and a system or context. In a valuable discussion Donald Evans makes the same point under the heading of what he calls "onlooks".[20] He writes, "'Looking on *x* as *y*' involves placing *x* within a structure, organization, or scheme. This often involves the description of a status ... to *x*". He adds, "Sometimes *x* is placed in a futural structural context rather than a present one."[21]

We return now to Pauline thought. The believer is "seen as" righteous, we shall argue, specifically within the context of eschatology, or at least in the context of the new age. Yet in the context, or frame of reference, of history and law, he or she remains a sinner. In order to elucidate this point, however, we must first move on to two other aspects of these persistent problems about the subject.

One of the key questions raised by this subject is whether justification in Paul is present or future. Some passages suggest that it is a present experience for the believer:

---

[17]   *PI*, p.194.

[18]   *PI*, p.193.

[19]   Cf. V.C. Aldrich, "Pictorial Meaning, Picture Thinking, and Wittgenstein's Theory of Aspects", in *Mind*, vol. LXVII, 1958, pp.70–79.

[20]   D.D. Evans, *The Logic of Self-Involvement. A Philosophical Study of Everyday Language with Special Reference to the Christian Use of Language about God as Creator* (London: SCM, 1963), pp.124–41.

[21]   Ibid., p.127.

δικαιωθέντες οὖν ἐκ πίστεως ἐιρήνην ἔχομεν πρὸς τὸν Θεόν (Rom. 5:1; cf. 5:9; 9:30; 1 Cor. 6:11). But Paul also declares unambiguously ἐκ πίστεως ἐλπιδα δικαιοσύνης ἀπεκδεχόμεθα (Gal. 5:5). Many interpreters of Paul, following J. Weiss and A. Schweitzer, urge that righteousness "belongs strictly speaking" to the future, even though it is effective in the present.[22] Both Bultmann and Barrett speak of the "paradoxical" nature of the situation when an eschatological verdict is pronounced in the present.[23] The importance of this eschatological frame is further underlined by recent attempts to ground justification in the context of apocalyptic. E. Käsemann has stressed the significance of such passages as Testament of Daniel 6:10 and *The Manual of Discipline* (from the Qumran Scrolls – 1QS 11.12), while C. Müller argues that Paul's thought on this subject is decisively influenced by apocalyptic-Jewish conceptions of the cosmic juridical trial in which God judges Israel and the nations.[24] The apocalyptic context of the concept is also emphasized by P. Stuhlmacher and K. Kertelge.[25] Kertelge shows how the forensic and eschatological aspects are brought together in the expectation of God's "rightwising" verdict at the end of time.

The fact that we have to do with the logic of evaluation or *verdict*, especially in an eschatological context, explains an important point. If we are confronted with two *statements*, one of which asserts *p* and the other of which denies *p*, we are faced with *a contradiction*. If one man claims "*x* is black" and another claims "*x* is white", one of them must be wrong. But the situation is different when we are faced with the logic of *evaluation* or *verdict*. If one man claims, "*x* is satisfactory", or "*x* is fast", and the other claims, "*x* is unsatisfactory", or "*x* is slow", each may be a valid assessment *in relation to a different frame of reference*. In the same way, if justification is a verdict, for God to declare the believer righteous in the context of eschatology does not contradict his declaring him or her a sinner in the context of history, or in terms of what he or she is in the natural world. In the context of the new age, the eschatological verdict of "righteous" which belongs to the last judgement is brought forward and appropriated by faith. In this sense, justification, although strictly future, is operative in the present "apart from the law" (Rom. 3:21; cf. Gal. 2:16; Phil. 3:9). In as far as the believer is accorded an eschatological status, viewed in that context he or she is justified. In as far as he still lives in the everyday world, he or she remains a sinner who awaits future justification. History and eschatology each provide a frame of reference in which a different verdict on the believer is valid and appropriate. This is neither contradiction nor even "paradox". In Wittgenstein's sense of the "home" setting of a language-game, eschatology is the home setting in which the logic of justification by faith properly functions.

We are now in a position to respond to the first three of our five questions. First of all, there is no contradiction involved in the verdict *simul iustus et peccator*, because there is room for a difference of verdict, "seeing ... as ...", or "onlook", when each operates within

---

22   A. Schweitzer, *The Mysticism of Paul the Apostle*, p.205; cf. J. Weiss, *Earliest Christianity*, vol. 2, p.502.

23   R. Bultmann, *Theology of the NT*, vol. 1, p.276; C.K. Barrett, *Romans*, p.75.

24   C. Müller, *Gottes Gerechtigkeit und Gottes Volk* (FRLANT 86, Göttingen: Vandenhoeck & Ruprecht, 1964).

25   P. Stuhlmacher, *Gerechtigkeit Gottes bei Paulus*; and K. Kertelge, *"Rechtfertigung" bei Paulus*, pp.112–60.

a different system or frame of reference. Thus the declarative view of justification is not involved in legal fiction or paradox. But it is a mistake to try to arbitrate between the declarative and behavioural views of righteousness by asking whether the believer is "really" righteous, as if this question could be asked *outside* a given language-game. The behavioural interpretation too often obscures this point, although it derives a measure of plausibility when, as in the work of Kertelge, a writer concentrates almost exclusively on the eschatological or apocalyptic context, since in *that* context "righteous" is indeed the only possible verdict.

Second, claims about the centrality of justification by faith in Paul have been bound up with the question, since the work of L. Usteri (1824) and H.E.G. Paulus (1831), of the relationship between a juridical conceptual scheme and that which centres on new creation and participation. As Schweitzer showed in his survey *Paul and his Interpreters*, this was a major issue for R.A. Lipsius (1853), H. Lüdemann (1872), and Richard Kabisch (1893);[26] and when Schweitzer himself discusses the place of justification in Pauline thought, it is not only the concept itself that is in question, but also the conceptual scheme to which it belongs.[27] What now emerges from our discussion is that from a conceptual or logical point of view, justification has a role within *both* schemes of thought. The juridical scheme underlines, in the best or perhaps the only way available to Paul, that we have to do with *verdictive* logic, not with the logic of assertion or statement. The "new creation" or "participation" scheme of thought underlines the point that this verdict is *eschatological*. The point of the "participational" conceptual scheme, as writers from Schweitzer to E.P. Sanders have emphasized, is that in union with Christ the believer is lifted out of the frame of law and history, even though in another sense he or she still lives in the world.[28] If this is correct, many of the standard attempts to devalue the importance of justification for Paul must fail. At least this is the case with those arguments which view justification only as a concept within the juridical scheme.[29] Even Schweitzer's criticisms were directed more against the importance of the juridical scheme as such, than against the concept of justification in itself.[30]

Third, we have seen why the problem arises about whether justification in Paul is present or future, and why there is truth in both claims. Since the frame of reference of eschatology, rather than of history, is the decisive one, the eschatological verdict can be anticipated even in the present by faith. But it is still a verdict which is appropriated in *faith*. As one who lives in the everyday world and as the product of his own historical decisions, the believer cannot deny that he or she is also a sinner. He or she has not yet been delivered out of the world. The notion that justification by faith is a legal fiction rests

---

[26] A. Schweitzer, *Paul and his Interpreters. A Critical History* (Eng., London: Black, 1912), pp.9–11, 19, 28–31 and 58–65.

[27] A. Schweitzer, *The Mysticism of Paul the Apostle*, pp.220–21 and 225.

[28] E.P. Sanders, *Paul and Palestinian Judaism* (London: SCM, 1977), pp.453–72.

[29] This is not to deny the importance of critiques of the traditional approach made from a different angle; cf. K. Stendahl, *Paul among Jews and Gentiles* (London: SCM, 1977). I am convinced that room must be found to hold together what is correct in Stendahl's analysis with the valid insights of Käsemann and the Reformers.

[30] I have argued this point in A.C. Thiselton, "Schweitzer's Interpretation of Paul", in *Expository Times* XC (1979), pp.132–7.

on viewing the problem *only* from the historical frame of reference, from which it appears that the believer is "counted" righteous, but is "really" a sinner. However, from the eschatological perspective the situation is seen differently. Thus from the historical viewpoint justification is still future, but by appropriation of the eschatological verdict it is possible to live by faith in the present experience of being justified. Thus J. Weiss speaks of a "pre-dating of what is really an eschatological act".[31]

This at once, however, leads us on to our fourth question. How is "faith" capable of doing this? How is it possible to speak of faith in such a way that it does not become a special kind of work? We shall now examine this question, together with the fifth issue, of the relationship between faith in Paul and faith in James.

III
Grammatical Relations and Dispositions: The Contrasting Conceptual Grammars of Faith and Believing in Paul and James

In the light of our discussions in the previous section we can now see that in Paul faith is related to justification *internally* or *grammatically*. This is why Paul can set the concept in contrast to works (Rom. 3:27–28; 4:2–6; 9:30–32). D.E.H. Whiteley correctly observes, "Faith is not 'another kind of work' which is a species of the same genus and operates in the same way: faith and works do not belong to the same genus at all."[32] G. Bornkamm makes a similar point.[33]

This is not to deny our earlier conclusions about faith as a polymorphous concept, for we are speaking about faith only as it is used in this present context or language game. In this context it means the acceptance of this future-orientated outlook as being effectively relevant in the present. The verdict that will be openly valid at the judgement day *is valid for faith now*. From a purely external or historical viewpoint, justification remains future; but faith involves stepping out of a purely historical frame of reference into that of eschatology. Thus Paul may not be as far as is sometimes assumed from the definition of faith in Hebrews 11:1 as ἐλπιζομένον ὑπόστασις. As Cullmann insists, the temporal contrast is no less important than the spatial one in primitive Christianity.[34] If this is correct, however, it shows that faith is not merely an external *instrument* which somehow "procures" justification; it is an indispensable feature of justification itself. *To have this faith is part of what justification is and entails*. It is part of the experience of it.

In Wittgenstein's language, to say that justification requires faith is to make a grammatical or analytical statement comparable to "every rod has a length", "green is a colour", or "water boils at 100° C". Faith is part of the *concept* of justification "just as works" are part of the *concept* of law. Certainly faith is not a special kind of work. The two categories stand in contrast to each other only because each is internally or analytically related to the system of concepts to which it belongs. Perhaps, strictly, the kind of

---

31   J. Weiss, *Earliest Christianity*, II, p.502.
32   D.E.H. Whiteley, *The Theology of St. Paul* (Oxford: Blackwell, 1964, and revised edn, 1971), p.164.
33   G. Bornkamm, *Paul*, pp.141–6.
34   O. Cullmann, *Christ and Time* (Eng., London: SCM, 1951), p.37.

grammar in question is more like that of class-two grammatical utterances than straightforward topic-neutral grammatical utterances. Those outside the New Testament or Pauline tradition might view the grammar of the concepts differently. But for Paul himself the grammar of the concepts in question is part of "the scaffolding of his thought"; "the hinges on which other propositions turn".

The conclusion that faith means, for Paul, the appropriation of an eschatological verdict as being effective in the present depends on the arguments put forward in the previous section. Given the validity of those arguments, faith assumes this role within the language-game. But this does not exclude us from viewing faith in a closely parallel but slightly different way as well. For Paul, the believer can anticipate by faith the verdict "not guilty" only because he has become part of the new creation and has entered the new age in union with Christ. Our argument, then, in no way denies the fact that faith is also closely related to the concept of Christ-union. Once again, it is internally or grammatically related to "Being-in-Christ", for faith is the appropriation of Christ-union rather than some external instrument that makes it possible. Once again, faith is not a special kind of work, but part of what is *entailed* in being united with Christ as part of the new creation. Faith does not *make* a man a Christian; but he or she cannot be a Christian without faith, for faith in Christ is part of the definition of what it means to be a Christian.

When we turn to the Epistle of James we enter a different world. We are especially concerned with the argument of James in 2:14–26: "What does it profit, my brethren, if a man says he has faith but has not works? Can his faith save him ... ? Faith by itself, if it has no works, is dead. But, some one will say, 'You have faith and I have works'. Show me your faith apart from your works, and I by my works will show you my faith ... Faith apart from works is barren (ἀργή)" (2:14, 17, 18, 20). Both Paul and James appeal to the verse, "Abraham believed God and it was reckoned to him as righteousness" (Gen. 15:6; Rom. 4:3, 9; Jas. 2:21). But whereas Paul understands this verse to refer to faith *in contrast to* works (Rom. 4:2–25), James declares that faith needs to be evidenced *by* works (Jas. 2:22–26). As J. Jeremias points out, the problem comes to a head most sharply when we compare Romans 3:28 with James 2:24.[35] Paul asserts, λογιζόμεθα γὰρ δικαιοῦσθαι πίστει ἄνθρωπον χωρὶς ἔργων νόμου (Rom. 3:28). James declares, ὁρᾶτε ὅτι ἐξ ἔργων δικαιοῦται ἄνθρωπος καὶ οὐκ ἐκ πίστεως μόνον (Jas. 2:24).

Jeremias is correct in his claim that this apparent contradiction is to be explained not in terms of a head-on clash between Paul and James, but partly in terms of their difference of concerns, and partly in terms of the radically different ways in which they use the same terminology. Jeremias argues that the concept of faith which James attacks is merely "the intellectual acceptance of monotheism", whereas the concept of faith which Paul defends is "the confidence that Christ died for my sins".[36] In broad terms, this is true. But it tends to suggest that James is merely the negative corollary of Paul, as if James merely accepted his opponent's inadequate concept of faith, and then argued that such faith (intellectual assent) must be supplemented by works. Thus in his commentary on James, Martin Dibelius asserts, "James ... cannot possibly be concerned about a

[35] J. Jeremias, "Paul and James", in *Expository Times* LXVI (1955), pp.368–71.
[36] Ibid., p.370.

theologically refined concept of faith. There is no special doctrine presupposed here, but rather the common meaning of the word 'faith'."[37] What some commentators have missed, however, is that especially in 2:18–26 James is not merely attacking an inadequate view of faith, but is also giving what amounts to a fairly sophisticated and positive account of the logical grammar of his own concept of faith. James is neither merely attacking someone else's view of faith; nor merely saying that faith must be supplemented by works. He is saying that his *concept* of faith would *exclude* instances of supposed belief that have no observable backing or consequences in life. In other words, whereas in Paul we see an *internal* or grammatical relation between faith and justification (because faith is entailed in the very concept of justification for Paul), in James we see an *internal* or grammatical relation between faith and works, because the very concept of faith entails *acting in* a certain way.

This principle receives clarification and illumination when we turn to Wittgenstein's remarks about belief-utterances. Wittgenstein argues that belief "is a kind of *disposition of* the believing person. This is shown in the case of someone else by his *behaviour;* and by his works."[38] It is of course possible, Wittgenstein allows, to think of belief as a state of mind. But this does not get to the heart of the matter, and even gives rise to conceptual confusions. For example, does a believer stop believing when he falls asleep? Wittgenstein writes in the *Zettel:* "Really one hardly ever says that one has believed ... 'uninterruptedly' since yesterday. An interruption of belief would be a period of unbelief, not e.g. the withdrawal of attention from what one believes – e.g. sleep."[39] "I can attend to the course of my pains, but not in the same way to that of my belief."[40] What *counts* as belief, then, is not simply what is going on in my head. Otherwise I become an unbeliever at some point every night.

The other way of approaching the grammar of the concept is to understand belief in terms of a disposition to respond to certain circumstances in certain situations. If I hold the belief "p", I shall act in certain ways, given the appropriate situation. Wittgenstein points out that belief, if it is genuine belief, carries certain *consequences* with it, or else it is not, after all, genuine. For example, I may say: "He believes it, but it is false"; but it would be nonsense to say: "I believe it, but it is false." Wittgenstein writes, "If there were a verb meaning 'to believe falsely', it would not have any significant first person present indicative."[41] What would it *mean* if a man said that he *believed* the gospel or the New Testament, but was an atheist or an agnostic? If I say that I believe, "my own relation to my words is wholly different from other people's".[42]

The importance and validity of Wittgenstein's analysis of belief have been defended by D.M. High. In a valuable chapter High refers to certain points of similarity between Wittgenstein's view of belief and that of M. Polanyi. Both writers, he urges, "view belief

---

[37]   M. Dibelius and H. Greeven, *James. A Commentary on the Epistle of James* (Hermeneia series; Eng., Philadelphia, PA: Fortress Press, 1976), pp.151–2.

[38]   *PI*, II. x, pp.191–2 (my italics).

[39]   L. Wittgenstein, *Zettel*, sect. 85.

[40]   Ibid., sect. 75.

[41]   *PI*, pp.190, 170.

[42]   *PI*, p.192.

not primarily in terms of mental states, but as a matter of personal accreditation ... personal backing, or signature".[43] This aspect of belief emerges not only in the *Investigations* and the *Zettel*, but also in Wittgenstein's *Lectures and Conversations*. Here, religious belief is seen as something which by definition cannot be isolated from given *attitudes*. As Wittgenstein says elsewhere, "The surroundings give it its importance... (A smiling mouth *smiles* only in a human face)."[44] D.M. High points out that Wittgenstein's work on the grammar of belief is part and parcel of his all-out attack on various kinds of dualism; between fact and value, between mind and body, between faith and reason, and between knowledge and belief.[45] Belief is not simply a mental state. It is no more possible to abstract believing from attitudes and actions than it is to extract the utterance "I promise" from questions about one's future conduct.

This is not of course to deny that in certain circumstances a man may act inconsistently with his beliefs, or be hypocritical or insincere when he affirms what he believes. But if his conduct were *consistently* unrelated to his belief, in what would his belief consist? What would it amount to? This question receives detailed discussion from H.H. Price.[46] In very broad terms we may say that, with some of the qualifications which Price formulates, "When we say of someone 'he believes ...' it is held that we are making a dispositional statement about him, and that this is equivalent to a series of conditional statements describing what he *would* be likely to say or do or feel if such and such circumstances were to arise."[47] For example, he might be likely to assert his belief if he heard someone else denying it or expressing doubt about it; or if circumstances arose in which it made a practical difference whether he held the belief in question, he would act as if it were true.

As we have said, this action need not always be consistent. Price discusses the phenomenon of "half-belief" when a man acts in accordance with his belief on some occasions, but on other occasions he acts in the same way as someone who did not hold this belief.[48] The Book of Jonah, for example, could be described as a satire on half-belief. Jonah believes that God "made the sea and the dry land", yet he flees to Tarshish "from the presence of the Lord" (Jon. 1:3, 9). He cries to the Lord in his distress, yet seems ready to throw away his life (1:12; 2:1–9; 4:3). He feels deep concern for the plant that shields him from the sun, but cannot understand why God should feel concern for the people of Nineveh (4:10, 11). The book is addressed to those who "believe in" missionary activity, but whose belief is belied by the fact that they fail to take it seriously in practice: "This is a satire ... We are supposed to laugh at the ludicrous picture."[49]

What, then, does faith without action *amount to*? This is precisely James's question. The opponents whom James criticizes may well have been thinking of faith as, in effect, "a mental state" to be set in contrast to outward "acts". If so, James is not simply saying that the outward act must *match* the inward faith, but that faith which has no backing in

---

[43] D.M. High, *Language, Persons and Belief*, p.142.
[44] *PI*, sect. 583. The metaphor refers primarily here to "hope".
[45] D.M. High, *Language, Persons and Belief*, pp.137–39.
[46] H.H. Price, *Belief* (London: Allen & Unwin, 1969), pp.27–8 and 290–314.
[47] Ibid., p.20.
[48] Ibid., pp.305–7.
[49] E.M. Good, *Irony in the Old Testament* (London: SPCK, 1965), pp.49–50; cf. pp.39–55.

attitude and action is not true *faith* at all. This explains the point behind James's statement about Abraham, and why he introduces into the discussion the question of how a believer responds to the brother or sister who is in need. Thus C.L. Mitton declares, "If a Christian claims to have faith, but is, for instance, dishonest, or harsh and callous to others in their need, it shows that his so-called faith is not true faith."[50] We cannot enter here into a detailed discussion of the Johannine epistles, but there is some kind of parallel between this dispositional perspective and the series of contrasts between word and deed in 1 John: "if we say we have fellowship with him while we walk in darkness, we lie ..." (1:6); "He who says he is in the light and hates his brother is in the darkness still" (2:9; cf. 2:4; 2:6; 3:9, 10, 17, 18, 24; 4:20; 5:18). That John is not teaching "sinless perfection", or that faith is *the same as* works, is clear from his recognition in 1:8–10 that even the believer sins.

An elucidation of the grammar of the concept of faith has helped us to see at least part of what is at issue in the apparent contradiction between Paul and James. We have seen that, as most writers urge, they do not contradict each other. But more than this, each has a rich and positive view of the grammar of faith, which emerges in the context of a given language-game or language-situation. It would be a mistake, as we argued in our section on polymorphous concepts, to ask what faith is in the New Testament, or even in Paul or in James, *in the abstract.*

This is one of many reasons why systematic theology must always return to the text of the New Testament. But this does not mean that, on the other side, what Paul or James says about faith is relevant only to the situation for which they were writing. For the situations that they address have parallels today, and their words still speak to those who find themselves in these parallel circumstances. The use of categories and perspectives drawn from Wittgenstein has not imposed something alien onto the text of the New Testament. It has simply helped us to see more clearly the logical grammar of what the New Testament writers are actually saying, and has provided tools which contribute towards a progressive interrelation between the horizon of the text and the horizon of the modern interpreter.

[50] C.L. Mitton, *The Epistle of James* (London: Marshall, Morgan & Scott, 1966), p.109.

CHAPTER ELEVEN

Descriptive, Evaluative, and Persuasive Meanings: "The Meaning of Σάρξ in 1 Corinthians 5.5: A Fresh Approach in the Light of Logical and Semantic Factors" (1973)

Traditional exegesis of 1 Corinthians 5:5 seems to suggest puzzling conclusions. Many assume that "the destruction of the flesh" denotes death, and that the agency of Satan in this process seems to confirm this. But in this case, how is the offender "saved" even eschatologically, unless repentance is either unnecessary or takes place as a post-mortal event? A reappraisal of the logical and conceptual grammar of the Greek term "sarx" (usually translated "flesh"), as well as semantic distinctions between descriptive and evaluative terms and between denotation and connotation, suggests a different way forward. This essay was first published in the Scottish Journal of Theology, *volume 26 (1973), pp. 204–28. I retain this approach, argued in less detail, in Thiselton,* The First Epistle to the Corinthians: A Commentary on the Greek Text *(Grand Rapids, MI: Eerdmans and Carlisle: Paternoster Press, 2000), pp. 392–400, with updated literature.*

I
Death – Or to Destroy Self-Sufficient Complacency? The Conceptual Grammar of σάρξ (*Sarx*)

Some writers express extreme confidence about the meaning of 1 Cor. 5:5: παραδοῦναι τὸν τοιοῦτον τῷ Σαρανᾷ εἰς ὄλεθρον τῆς σαρκός, ἵνα τὸ πνεῦμα σωθῇ ἐν ἡμέρᾳ τοῦ κυρίου. Ernst Käsemann, for example, asserts that it 'obviously entails the death of the guilty', and he is not alone in using such words as 'obviously' or 'only' in putting forward this interpretation.[1] Probably the majority of modern writers, with a little more caution, regard an allusion to death as the most likely explanation of a notoriously difficult verse.[2] Almost all the remainder believe that Paul is referring, if not to death, then to suffering which is necessarily physical.[3]

---

[1] E. Käsemann, *New Testament Questions of Today* (Eng., London: SCM, 1969), p.71. Similarly, J. Schneider (under ὄλεθρος) in G. Kittel (ed.), *Theological Dictionary of the New Testament*, V (Grands Rapids, MI: Eerdmans, 1968), p.169; and C.T. Craig in *The Interpreter's Bible*, vol. X (New York: Abingdon, 1951), p.62.

[2] Cf. C.K. Barrett, *The First Epistle to the Corinthians* (London: Black, 1968), pp.126–7; H. Lietzmann, *An die Korinther*) Tübingen: Mohr, ⁴1949), pp.29 and 173–4; E. Osty, *Les Épîtres de S. Paul aux Corinthiens* (Paris: Les Éditions du Cerf, ¹1964), p.34; H.D. Wendland, *Die Briefe an die Korinther* (Göttingen: Vandenhoeck & Ruprecht, ¹²1968), p.43; R. Bultmann, *Theology of the New Testament*, I (Eng., London: SCM, 1952), p.137.

[3] Cf. further, E. Schweizer, *Theologisches Wörterbuch zum Neuen Testament*, VII (Stuttgart: Kohlhammer, 1964), p.125; W. Bauer (W.F. Arndt and F.W. Gingrich), *A Greek-English Lexicon of the New Testament*

But is Paul using σάρξ in this verse specifically to denote the physical part of a man? In the course of an impressive study devoted primarily to Paul's uses of σάρξ in the major epistles Alexander Sand has recently applied to 1 Cor. 5:5 an observation about the functions of σάρξ and πνεῦμα which in connection with other passages is widely recognized.[4] The two terms, he comments, do not denote 'two different "parts" of the man'.[5] Either term can denote 'the whole man', although admittedly in terms of some particular aspect under which he is viewed. Thus 'the destruction of the flesh' does not necessarily specify death. It is envisaged that the offender reaches a state of penitence from which a fresh start can be made again.

This view goes part of the way towards the interpretation that will be put forward here. But in relation to certain fundamental questions it remains relatively close still to the traditional view, especially in the light of what it leaves unsaid. On the other hand, a recent article on the subject by J. Cambier has decisively reopened the whole question. Cambier categorically concludes, 'Nôtre passage n'a pas la valeur d'un rite exsécratoire infligeant la mort ou une maladie au pécheur de Corinthe; il ne le menace pas de la mort corporelle pour assurer le salut de son âme.'[6] The exegetical and theological arguments put forward by Cambier carry considerable weight. But if they are to receive the respect which they deserve, some further considerations may need to be taken into account. In particular, an adequate interpretation of this complex passage, I should like to argue, require a closer examination of semantic considerations.

At least three groups of issues deserve special attention. (1) Is Paul using σάρξ here only for description or denotation, or does he also wish to convey a value-judgement at the same time? If an evaluation is somehow involved, two further points arise: (a) what *kind* of evaluation is implied in Paul's words; and (b) how does the logic of description relate to the logic of evaluation if the same set of words are put to both uses? (2) How much light can be shed on this passage by maintaining a working distinction between more than one type or level of context? These include at least: (a) the extra-linguistic context of situation; (b) the broader and narrower linguistic contexts, and (c) the *working* frame of reference shared by Paul and his readers, and the logic which this dictates, for which we may very provisionally borrow Wittgenstein's term 'language-game'.[7] (3) What degree of specificity does Paul wish to achieve in this verse? Does he wish to leave certain aspects of the matter open-ended; or did he prefer to specify with logical determinacy and exclusiveness a reference either to sickness or to death, irrespective of the offender's reaction to the church's pronouncement?[8]

(Chicago and Cambridge, 1957), p.751; J. Héring, *The First Epistle of St. Paul to the Corinthians* (Eng., London: Epworth, 1962), p.35; and M.E. Thrall, *I & II Corinthians* (Cambridge, 1965), p.40.

[4] A. Sand, *Der Begriff 'Fleisch' in den Paulinischen Hauptbriefen* (Biblische Untersuchungen herausgregeben von Otto Kuss, Band 2, Regensburg: F. Pustet, 1967), pp.143–5.

[5] 'Fleisch' und 'Geist' sind dann nicht zwei verschiedene 'Teile' am Menschen ... ibid., p.144.

[6] J. Cambier, 'La Chair et l'esprit en 1 Cor. 5.5', in *New Testament Studies*, 15 (1968–69), pp.221–32; p.232.

[7] L. Wittgenstein, *Philosophical Investigations* (Ger. and Eng., Oxford: Blackwell, [3]1967), sects 7, 23, 24, 47, 50, 53, 65–9 *et passim*. In terms of a different philosophical tradition, it might be possible to speak of the horizons that bound the common 'world' of communication. Cf. H.-G. Gadamer, *Wahrheit und Methode; Grundzüge einer philosophischen Hermeneutik* (Tübingen: Mohr, [2]1965), especially pp.286–90.

[8] Any idea that specificity and precision is necessarily always a virtue is wide of the mark. Cf. W.P. Alston, *Philosophy of Language* (Engelwood Cliffs, NJ: Prentice-Hall, 1964), pp.84ff; and esp. L. Wittgenstein op. cit., sects 68–108.

In 5:2 Paul reapplies both to the community and perhaps also to the offender his earlier censure against self-satisfaction and complacency: καὶ ὑμεῖς πεφυσιωμένοι ἐστέ, καὶ οὐχὶ μᾶλλον ἐπενθήσατε … . It is to be noted that in 3:1ff he has already used the adjectival forms σαρκικός, σάρκινος and πνευματικός precisely to call attention to this attitude: ὅπου γὰρ ἐν ὑμῖν ζῆλος καὶ ἔρις, οὐχὶ σαρκικοί ἐστε (3:3).[9] Evidence will be considered for the now-widespread view that the so-called 'spirituals' or 'strong' at Corinth were pressing for a more radical and supposedly consistent expression of their status. They were, after all, 'free men', who had already been emancipated from the 'flesh'. Might not the offender of 5:5 have been an extremist among these extremists? Might not some of the 'strong' have regarded with something like awe a man who unashamedly paraded his freedom beyond the 'ordinary' man's wildest dreams? But if this were the situation hardly anything could shatter his ego more decisively than the experience of finding himself an outcast from the whole community. The event would be salutary for the church as well as for the man. This is not to say that the offender might not conceivably have remained intransigent, and thereby invited on himself the further punishment of physical suffering. But in advance of the outcome, Paul does not seem unduly concerned to predict hypothetical events. His emphasis falls on the *judgement* that the 'flesh' has yet to be destroyed. If the strong had claimed to be delivered from the flesh already, Paul had redefined both the term and the situation in 3:1ff.

These suggestions will inevitably meet with extreme scepticism if it is assumed that the traditional view of the verse encounters no serious difficulty. In sections V and VI, however, I shall try to show in some detail that arguments for the usual interpretation are very far from being conclusive. If this lengthens an already over-long study, this is partly because the discussion raises principles of method.

II
Description or Evaluation? Denotation or Connotation?

Descriptive uses of language concern the state of affairs that is being described, rather than, in theory, attitudes or outlooks on the part of the speaker or writer. By contrast, evaluative uses of language express verdicts or attitudes; characteristically, for example, of praise or blame, or of commendation or disapproval. In practice, language is seldom used exclusively for pure description or pure evaluation, although this does occur. Usually two or more functions overlap. This overlapping, however, in no way detracts from the importance of making the basic distinction. To take an example from everyday language, description and evaluation remain distinct but usually inseparable in ordinary uses of the word 'murder'. Since the term carries with it a judgement of blame and disapproval, only a pacifist could say that a soldier 'murdered' his country's enemies on the battlefield. But since it also implies a descriptive content, it is used ordinarily (aside from metaphor) only in relation to the taking of life.

---

[9] The connections between 'flesh' and 'self-glorying' are examined below with special reference to R. Bultmann and to J.A.T. Robinson.

In terms of various classifications and interests, many writers call attention to an inbuilt preoccupation in traditional language-study with denotation, or with reference, with description, at the expense of other language-use. These supposedly 'primitive' functions are selected as basic models for language-in-general.[10] Wittgenstein illustrates this with characteristic colour in the course of discussing our uses of the words 'exact' and 'inexact'. We assume all too readily that 'exact' has a stable descriptive content. But how does 'exact' in the context of the laboratory compare with 'exact' in the context of keeping an appointment or fixing a date in prehistory? The continuity depends primarily on its evaluative uses: '"Inexact" is really a reproach, and "exact" is praise ... Am I inexact when I do not give our distance from the sun to the nearest foot ...?'[11]

Paul, it has long been recognized, uses σάρξ both descriptively and evaluatively. Sometimes σαρκικός or σάρκινος more characteristically expresses evaluation, and the NEB sometimes signposts this use by employing 'unspiritual' as a translation. Since this kind of use essentially reflects a *judgement*, one logical consequence follows: its application may constitute a focal point of controversy between the speaker and his audience. Thus in 1 Cor. 3:1ff, we may doubt whether the self-styled 'spirituals' at Corinth would have accepted any too readily Paul's application of σαρκικός mainly on the basis of their strifes and divisions. Nor in Rom. 7:14 would Paul's rhetorical opponent agree without any question that the pious Jew who delighted in God's law should be called σάρκινος. This evaluative use is not an innovation in Paul, for parallels can be cited in the Septuagint.[12]

Does this use occur, however, in 1 Cor. 5:5? Some of the older commentators perhaps tended to call attention to the wrong thing by thinking in terms of a *kind* of evaluation that is almost certainly not in this verse. Some spoke of an 'ethical' meaning, according to which σάρξ referred to the offender's 'sinful lust' or 'lower nature'.[13] Other writers, in turn, regarded this quasi-evaluative 'ethical' use, as the only possible alternative to that of the denotative use for 'physical body'; understandably most of them preferred the latter. More recently, however, Rudolf Bultmann and J.A.T. Robinson have drawn attention to a different kind of evaluation that can be conveyed by uses of σάρξ, and this is acutely relevant to our verse. Admittedly, to be fair, neither Bultmann nor Robinson interprets the verse in these terms. Bultmann is thinking primarily of Pauline themes that belong more characteristically to Romans and Galatians. He notes, 'The attitude which

---

[10]   Cf. L. Wittgenstein, op. cit., sects 1–11, 114–15, 304 *et passim*; M. Black, *The Labyrinth of Language* (London: Pall Mall Press, 1968), pp.9ff; J. Wilson, *Language and the Pursuit of Truth* (CUP, 1956), pp.18ff and 56ff; S. Ullmann, *Semantics; An Introduction to the Science of Meaning* (Oxford: Blackwell, 1962), pp.128ff and R.H. Robins, *General Linguistics: An Introductory Survey* (London: Longmans, 1964), pp.25ff.

[11]   L. Wittgenstein, op. cit., sect. 88.

[12]   Cf. Ezek. 36:26 and the much-cited classic Isa. 31:3, where the LXX both softens and yet makes more explicit the functions of evaluation by rendering בשׂר לא רוח as ... ἵππων σαρκός, καὶ οὐκ ἔστι βοήθεια. The judgement concerns their strength or weakness, their effectiveness or ineffectiveness, against the situation. Evaluative uses in Paul occur clearly in Rom. 7:25; 8:7; 1 Cor. 3:4; 2 Cor. 1:12; 10:4, and Gal. 5:16–19; and more debatably perhaps in Rom. 7:15, 18; 8:4, 5, 8, 13; 2 Cor. 5:16; 10:2; Phil. 3:3, 4; and Col. 2:18. Cf. A. Sand, op. cit., pp.183–217.

[13]   Among nineteenth-century writers T.C. Edwards, *A Commentary on the First Epistle to the Corinthians* (London: Hodder & Stoughton, ²1885), p.127, attributes to 'flesh' 'an ethical meaning'; among more recent writers cf. F.W. Grosheide, *Commentary on the First Epistle to the Corinthians* (London: Marshall, Morgan and Scott, ²1954), p.123.

orients itself by "flesh" ... is the self-reliant attitude of the man who puts his trust in his own strength and in that which is controllable by him ... The attitude of self-reliance finds its extreme expression in man's "boasting" (καυχᾶσθαι).'[14] Robinson adds, further, 'The flesh ... represents human self-sufficiency', of the kind which is instanced in 1 Cor. 3:21, 'glorying in men' or 2 Cor. 19, 'trusting in ourselves'.[15]

The force of the argument for a connection between these comments and 1 Cor. 5:5 will emerge only when we take full account of its context at more than one level. But we have still to focus more sharply our questions about the effects of an overlapping between the logic of evaluation and that of description. The structure of the language, if nothing else, demands that σάρξ cannot be purely evaluative. It is not an evaluation that is to be destroyed, for it is *Paul's* evaluation which is being expressed in this use of the term. Different questions can be formulated in terms of criss-crossing categories. Does the term possess a denotative function? Does it perhaps denote the individual offender in so far as he also stands under a given evaluation? Or, since the offender has already been denoted by τὸν τοιοῦτον, does it serve rather to *connote* the general characteristics of a 'fleshly' outlook?[16] Further, how great or how prominent is the degree of description which is involved in any case in Paul's evaluation? The same evaluative word may vary greatly in its descriptive implications. 'Good', for example, as applied to a holiday may imply anything from sunny weather to jellied eels. 'Good' as applied to a doctor ordinarily implies some record of moderate competence or luck. Ultimately the descriptive implications of 'fleshly', like 'good' depend on the context of the situation. A comparison between the application of the term in Rom. 7:14ff and 1 Cor. 3:1ff seems to substantiate the point.

There is nothing odd about the suggestion that when overlappings of language-uses occur a logic of some complexity may lie hidden under a single word. A term may conceal highly compressed shorthand, which is intelligible only in the light of the situation for which it was used. What might it have meant, for instance, for Dr Jekyll to contemplate 'the destruction of Mr Hyde'? A full answer cannot be given without reference to the setting that lies behind the language.

III
Self-Congratulation and Triumphalism in Corinth

Wittgenstein's insistence that 'only in the stream of thought and life do words have meaning' is matched by an almost equal insistence on 'context of situation' in general and structural linguistics.[17] What is the context of situation behind the language of 1 Cor. 5:5?

---

14   R. Bultmann, *Theology of the New Testament*, I, pp.240 and 242. Cf. pp.239–46.

15   J.A.T. Robinson, *The Body: A Study in Pauline Theology* (London: SCM, 1952), pp.25–6.

16   It is unnecessary to allude at this point to the relatively unstable uses of 'denotation' and 'connotation' found even among some logicians, for they are used here only broadly. Cf. J. Hospers, *An Introduction to Philosophical Analysis* (London: Routledge & Kegan Paul, ²1967), pp.40–54.

17   L. Wittgenstein, *Zettel* (Ger. and Eng., Oxford: Blackwell, 1967), sect. 173. Cf. *Philosophical Investigations*, sect. 7; F. Waismann, *The Principles of Linguistic Philosophy* (London: Macmillan, 1965), p.193; F. de Saussure, *Course in General Linguistics* (Eng., London: Owen, 1960), pp.77–8; Z.S. Harris, *Structural*

In the light of much recent research, nowadays it may surely be taken for granted *either* that the Corinthians had overrealized their eschatology; *or* that they had fallen prey to ideas which very roughly might be called 'gnostic'; *or* (most probably) that their problems were aggravated by a combination of both factors.[18] This basic thesis is certainly not invalidated if we accept that W. Schmithals overstated his claims about gnosticism, or that the interpretation of U. Wilckens cannot be endorsed in its entirety.[19] Long before more recent phases of research on 1 Corinthians, A.D. Nock admirably captured the mood in question without any specific discussion of gnosticism and also little references to eschatology. He comments, 'Many of the converts, convinced that they were on a new plane of life, felt that they could do anything; they were kings (4:8), they were in the Spirit, they were dead to the flesh and emancipated – so that their physical conduct might seem to them a matter of indifference; thus we were altogether superior to the unchanged men around them.'[20]

This kind of reconstruction is all the more convincing because it discloses a logical connection between the various themes in this diverse epistle. With regard to 1:10–4:21, if Paul's readers were sufficiently 'spiritual' to discern wisdom for themselves, they need hardly feel dependent on any or every ministry, let alone those that they perhaps regarded as prosaically sub-spiritual. With reference to the next two main sections, the slogan πάντα μοι ἔξεστιν lay equally behind (a) a revision of conservative attitudes towards straightforward moral issues (5:1–6:20); and (b) a bold settlement of the more delicate questions about voluntary restraints (7:1–11:1).[21] Parallel to the stirrings in the Empire for greater female emancipation, claims were put forward on theological grounds for a consistent implementation of a new status shared by all believers (11:2–16). The Lord's Supper was marked by a revelry befitting victors at an apocalyptic banquet who

---

Linguistics (Chicago, IL: University of Chicago Press, 1951; Phoenix Books 1960), p.187; R.H. Robbins, op. cit., pp.2 and 26–8; J. Lyons, *Introduction to Theoretical Linguistics* (CUP, 1968), pp.410–20.

[18] See E. Käsemann, op. cit., pp.125ff; J.C. Hurd, op. cit., pp.152ff, 198, and 284ff; E. Haenchen in *Religion in Geschichte und Gegenwart*, II (Tübingen: Mohr, ³1958), p.1652; J. Munck, *Paul and the Salvation of Mankind* (Eng., London: SCM, 1959), p.165; W.G. Kümmel, *Introduction to the New Testament* (Eng., London: SCM, 1966), p.202; R.M. Grant, *A Historical Introduction to the New Testament* (London: Collins, 1963), pp.204ff; R. Bultmann in Kittel (ed.), *Theological Dictionary of the New Testament*, I, pp.703–11; J. Cambier, 'La Liberté chrétienne selon saint Paul', in F.L. Cross (ed.), *Studia Evangelica*, II, Part I (Berlin: Akademie Verlag, 1964), pp.315–53; J. Héring, 'Saint Paul a-t-il enseign deux résurections', in *Revue d'Histoire et de Philosophie religieuse*, XII (1932), pp.300–20; J. Dupont, *Gnosis: La Connaissance religieuse dans les épîtres de S. Paul* (Louvain²: Nauwelaerts, 1960); and U. Wilckens, *Weisheit und Torheit: eine exegetisch-religionsgeschichtliche Untersuchung zu L Kor. I und 2* (Tübingen: Mohr, 1959), esp. pp.10ff, 20 and 64ff.

[19] W. Schmithals, *Die Gnosis in Korinth: eine Untersuchung zu den Korintherbriefen* (Göttingen: Vandenhoeck & Ruprecht, ²1965), especially pp.146ff and 206ff on σάρξ and ἐλευθερία. Cf. the critique in C. Colpé, *Die religionsgeschichtliche Schule*, I (Göttingen: Vandenhoeck & Ruprecht, 1961). Significant points in U. Wilckens' *Weisheit und Torheit* are criticized by R. Scroggs, '"Paul" ΣΟΦΟΣ and ΠΝΕΥΜΑΤΙΚΟΣ', *New Testament Studies*, 14 (1967–68), pp.33–55; and by R.W. Funk, *Language, Hermeneutic and the Word of God* (New York: Harper & Row, 1966), pp.277ff.

[20] A.D. Nock, *St Paul* (London: Thornton Butterworth, 1938), p.174. Cf. his further comments in *Conversion: The Old and the New in Religion from Alexander the Great to Constantine* (OUP, 1938), especially pp.118ff.

[21] This argument is not necessarily weakened by R. Kempthorne's recent article 'Incest and the Body of Christ', in *New Testament Studies*, 14 (1967–68), pp.568–74; nor, as Kempthorne seems to imagine, by J.C. Hurd, op. cit., p.165. Moreover his article serves to show more clearly a developing sequence of thought for the inclusion at this point of 6.1–11 (ibid. p.569).

had left struggle and pilgrimage behind them (11:17–34). The more spectacular *charismata* that clearly marked out the 'spiritual' were much in evidence (12:1–14:40). Finally, there were certain embarrassments about the idea of a resurrection that had still to take place (15:1–58).

This, then, seems to constitute the extra-linguistic background which conditions the use of such terms as 'wisdom' and 'folly', 'lawful' and 'free', 'strong' and 'weak', 'spiritual', 'fleshly' and 'flesh'.

IV
The Greek Terms καυχάομαι (*Kauchaomai*), φυσιόω (*Physioō*) and πνεῦμα (*Pneuma*)

The wider linguistic context of 1 Cor. 5:5 points in the same direction. Bultmann, we noted, associated σάρξ in the sense of self-glorying primarily with themes in Romans and Galatians. But even a lexical study of 1 Corinthians could serve to question this. The centre of gravity in Paul's censure of 5:1ff, we observed, found expression in his indignant remonstration καὶ ὑμεῖς πεφυσοιωμένοι ἐστέ ... (v. 2). But it is striking to examine other occurrences of φυσιόω in Paul. Out of a total of seven uses, no less than six occur in 1 Corinthians.[22] One comes in connection with gnosis (8:1) and another occurs in the hymn about love, which, as one writer convincingly argues, reflects exactly, by means of its contrasts, the blemishes of the Corinthian church.[23] The remainder all appear as part of a refrain in the fourth chapter, which leads naturally towards the thrust of Paul's censure in 5:1ff.[24]

This perspective is retained when we further compare Paul's uses of καυχάομαι, καύχημα and καύχησις.[25] Even if Karl Barth's comment was perhaps predictable, he is surely no less right when he concludes that 'Let no man glory in men' (3:21) and 'He who glories, let him glory in the Lord' (1:31) represent the negative and positive thrust of the first four chapters and probably of the whole epistle.[26] What is it that goads Paul into his most ironic or satirical attack in the whole epistle? He parodies the attitude of the 'spirituals': ἤδη κεκορεσμένοι ἐστέ; ἤδη ἐπλουτήσατε; χωρὶς ἡμῶν ἐβασιλεύσατε; only adding καὶ ὄφελόν γε ἐβασιλεύσατέ, Ἵνα καὶ ἡμεῖς ὑμῖν συνβασιλεύσωμεν (4:8). This, he tells them, is exactly why they *cannot* claim the title 'spiritual', but must accept the verdict expressed in σαρκικός. The words φυσιόω and καύχημα respectively introduce and conclude the rebuke of 5:2–6.[27]

---

[22] 1 Cor. 4:6, 18, 19; 5:2; 8:1; 13:4; and Col. 2:18.

[23] Cf. J. Moffatt, *Love in the New Testament* (London, 1929), p.182. Even if it is argued that its style and rhythm make the hymn unPauline in origin, Paul's inclusion of the hymn at this juncture speaks for itself.

[24] The change of mood at 4:14 signifies not a change of subject but Paul's concern that the purpose behind his use of such biting irony should not be misunderstood.

[25] Cf. 1 Cor. 1:29, 31; 3:21; 4:7; and 5:6; as against Rom. 2:17, 23; 3:27; and 4:2. On the parallel between Romans and 1 Corinthians, see especially Hans Conzelmann's comments on 'The Word as the Crisis of Self-Assertion' and 'The Word as Folly' in *An Outline of the Theology of the New Testament* (Eng., London: SCM, 1969), pp.236–8 and 241–7.

[26] K. Barth, *The Resurrection of the Dead* (Eng., London: Hodder & Stoughton, 1933), p.17.

[27] Admittedly apart from the context φυσιωμένοι ἐστέ *could* mean 'you are still complacent' in the sense advocated by A. Robertson and A. Plummer: 'He does not mean that they were puffed up *because* of

An examination of the narrower linguistic context of σάρξ would to some extent anticipate the critique of the traditional interpretation. In section V the function of the ἵνα clause is discussed in detail; and it will be argued that 'delivery to Satan' has no more *necessary* reference to physical suffering than to the more general idea of being vulnerable to woes of various unspecified kinds. In so far as any degree of specificity is intended, the phrase is no less likely to call to mind Satan's equally established role as accuser. It may be useful, however, to outline in advance some considerations about the semantic relationship between σάρξ and πνεῦμα.

In modern Pauline scholarship the pendulum has swung to and fro in relation to supposedly 'Hebraic' and 'Greek' understandings of πνεῦμα. Rudolf Bultmann boldly asserts concerning the 'concept' of spirit in Paul: '*Pneuma* does not mean "spirit" in the Greek-Platonic and idealist sense; i.e. it does not mean mind in contrast to body.'[28] On the other hand S. Laeuchli makes a vigorous protest against any exaggeration of Paul's supposed monism.[29] Paul, he argues, still thinks in Greek because he speaks and writes in Greek.[30] It is virtually impossible to speak of a Pauline 'concept' of πνεῦμα because his uses of the term leave unresolved tensions in his writings.[31]

There is a sense in which both of these sets of comments are justified. Laeuchli rightly insists that we cannot, with a sweep of the hand, reduce Paul's various uses of πνεῦμα to a supposedly single Pauline concept. Sometimes Paul does wish to draw a contrast between mind and body, and occasionally he uses πνεῦμα to make this distinction.[32] Nevertheless a considerable amount of painstaking research has shown that Bultmann's generalization retains its validity, provided that it is treated as a *working* generalization.[33] In so far as Paul uses πνεῦμα to refer to man at all, often 'your spirit' means no more than 'you'; whilst such phrases as ἐν τῷ πνεύματί μου regularly have the effect of an adverbial force conveying the intensity, or the extent of involvement, with which a person is affected by an action.[34] Thus, in relation to 1 Cor. 5:5, E. Schweizer declares, 'Certainly it (πνεῦμα) is not just the human soul, for Paul never reckons with the salvation of a mere soul ...'.[35] Similarly, D. Hill observes, 'Here πνεῦμα refers to the real self, the real person.'[36] One cannot help recalling the warnings of Käsemann and Bornkamm against

---

this outrage ... but in *spite of it*', *The First Epistle of St. Paul to the Corinthians* (Edinburgh: ICC, T. & T. Clark, [2]1914), p.96 (their italics). But the other occurrences of the same verb, as well as more recent research on the background of the epistle, seem to suggest otherwise.

[28] R. Bultmann, *Theology of the New Testament*, I, p.153.

[29] S. Laeuchli, 'Monism and Dualism in the Pauline Anthropology', in *Biblical Research*, 3 (1958), pp.15–27.

[30] Ibid., p. 24.

[31] Ibid., p. 27.

[32] E.g. 1 Cor. 5:3, Col. 2:5. For a sustained criticism of generalizations about 'concepts' on the basis of word-usage cf. J. Barr, *The Semantics of Biblical Language* (OUP, 1961), *passim*.

[33] Cf. E. Schweizer, *Theological Dictionary of the NT*, VI, pp.415ff; David Hill, *Greek Words and Hebrew Meanings* (Cambridge, 1967), pp.265–85; W.E.D. Stacey, *The Pauline View of Man* (London: Macmillan, 1965), pp.174–80; D.E.H. Whitely, *The Theology of St. Paul* (Oxford: Blackwell, 1964), pp.31–44; and W.D. Davies, *Paul and Rabbinic Judaism* (London: SPCK, 1948), pp.17ff and 177ff.

[34] Gal. 6:18; Phil. 4:23 and Philemon 25: 'the grace of the Lord Jesus Christ be with your spirit'; and Rom. 1:9; 2 Cor. 2:13; 7:13, 20; on which see especially D. Hill, op. cit., pp.283–5.

[35] E. Schweizer, loc. cit., p.435, n. 691.

[36] D. Hill, op. cit., p.285.

misconstruing Paul on the model of a later pietism, in which 'the inner life' of a private individual is marked off too sharply from the overt realm of public behaviour.[37]

These arguments become all the more impressive when we consider uses of πνεῦμα, not in isolation from other terms, but specifically when they occur in explicit opposition to σάρξ. Even if σάρξ, on its own, sometimes means physical body, and even if πνεῦμα, on its own, occasionally designates the non-physical, when the two terms stand *together* in opposition the contrast which results is almost always a different one.[38] We are not concerned at this point with occurences of σάρξ and πνεῦμα where their relationship is other than one of opposition.[39] Nor does this concern passages where, as in 1 Cor. 5:3, πνεῦμα as a negation of the purely physical opposes not σάρξ but σῶμα.[40] In the overwhelming majority of instances in which σάρξ and πνεῦμα oppose each other, they set up a polarity between what accords with the working of the Spirit of God and human characteristics which, to all intents and purposes, have been arrived at independently.[41]

Further considerations about σάρξ and πνεῦμα must be postponed. For even these very brief comments may serve to question whether their explicit opposition in Paul can be interpreted in terms of soul and body unless the *context* points clearly in this direction.[42] In 1 Cor. 5:5, in fact, the reverse seems to be the case. Both the context of situation and the broader linguistic context of the earlier chapters suggest that 'flesh' and 'fleshly', together with 'spirit' and 'spiritual' had already acquired a highly evaluative and even *emotive* significance.

V
The "World" of the Addressees and Persuasive Definition

In 1 Corinthians, perhaps more conspicuously than in any other epistle, Paul strives to share and to speak the language of his readers. Sometimes he may wish to state clearly some maxim or slogan that he then criticizes partly to avoid further misunderstandings.[43] Sometimes he may wish to expose their view in the course of a *reductio ad absurdum*. But neither of these explanations can account for Paul's repeated use of their language.

---

[37]   E. Käsemann, 'Worship and Everyday Life', op. cit., especially pp.191 and 194; and G. Bornkamm, *Early Christian Experience* (Eng., London: SCM, 1969), p.25.

[38]   Cf., for example, Rom. 8:4–10; Gal. 3:3; 4:29; 5:17–19; 6:8; and possibly such references as Rom. 13:4; as against Col. 2:5, which seems to constitute the only important exception.

[39]   E.g. 1 Cor. 7:34 and 2 Cor. 7:1.

[40]   Even in the Synoptic Gospels the 'dualist' contrast of Matt. 10:28 opposes only τὸ σῶμα and ἡ ψυχή.

[41]   Cf. the fifth category under πνεῦμα in W.F. Moulton and A.S. Geden, *A Concordance to the Greek Testament* (Edinburgh: T. & T. Clark, ²1899), pp.821–3; the second category under σάρξ, pp.887–8; and cognates on pp.824 and 886–7. Cf., further, A. Sand, op. cit., pp.165–217. On semantic complementarity, see John Lyons, *Introduction to Theoretical Linguistics*, pp.360ff; and *Structural Semantics: An Analysis of Part of the Vocabulary of Plato* (Oxford: Blackwell, 1963), pp.59ff. On 'opposition by cut' cf. C.K. Ogden, *Opposition: A Linguistic and Psychological Analysis* (Bloomington: Indiana University Press, ²1967), pp.19–20, 58–60 *et passim*.

[42]   On the decisive importance of context when words may have more than one meaning, see S. Ullmann, op. cit., pp.167ff, and *The Principles of Semantics* (Oxford: Blackwell, ²1957), pp.60–65; and the repeated warnings in James Barr, loc. cit.

[43]   Cf. 1 Cor. 5:9–11 for the classic example of such a misunderstanding.

Robert Funk rightly points out that Paul's initial concern is to establish a common 'world' of understanding so that genuine communication becomes possible.[44] From time to time he positions himself within *their* horizons; he participates in their language-games. For, once the uses of particular terms have become firmly embedded in a given logic, to abstract them without warning from their 'home' setting in the community is simply to invite misunderstanding and conceptual confusion. Wittgenstein reminds us, 'One must always ask oneself: is the word ever actually used in this way in the language-game which is its original home?'[45]

But in terms of Wittgenstein's question, what is the *original* home of terms such as 'flesh' and 'spirit', 'wisdom' and 'folly', or 'free' and 'in the power of'? Paul enters the horizons of the Corinthians only in order to transform them. Their own language-games are placed, once again, within the wider framework of the message of the cross. And this, in turn, conditions once again the logic of their terms. Paul takes up their use of σοφία as that which is reserved only for the mature (2.6). But 'wisdom' and 'mature' are also redefined in the light of the cross (1:18ff). He shares their conviction that 'the spiritual man judges all things, but is himself to be judged by no one' (2:15). But does 'spiritual' apply to the readers in their present frame of minds? (3:1ff). If he accepts that 'an idol has no real existence', or even that 'all things are lawful', neither statement retains the force which it had in its setting at Corinth (6:12ff; 8:1ff; 10:23ff).

It does not affect the arguments decisively if it can be shown that some of these instances do not in fact represent direct quotations from the Corinthians.[46] Further instances can be cited, although these will be more controversial: 4:8 (a); 6:18 (a); 7:1 (b); 8:1 (b) and several fragments from 8:4–8, 9:1 (a); 10:26, 29 (b); and perhaps 11:2 (b) and 13:11[47] The deeper point at issue is Paul's whole manner of dialogue. According to Exler, dialogue that is based on a community of interests constitutes the fundamental form of the ancient Greek letter.[48] And Bultmann's invaluable comparison between Paul's style and that of the diatribe abounds in concrete examples of the moods and form of the dialogue.[49]

---

[44]   R.W. Funk, op. cit., pp.275–305, especially p.284. Funk, of course, owes little or nothing to the Wittgenstein approach to language, and he perhaps weakens rather than strengthens his important insights by an undue preoccupation with Heidegger's perspective. Cf. my arguments in 'The Parables as Language-Event: Some Comments on Fuchs's Hermeneutics in the Light of Linguistic Philosophy', *Scottish Journal of Theology*, 23 (1970), pp.437–680.

[45]   L. Wittgenstein, *Philosophical Investigations*, sect. 116. See also sects 47, 90, 96, and 115–17.

[46]   Cf. for example, Robin Scroggs' critique of Ulrich Wilckens, *Weisheit und Torheit*, loc. cit.

[47]   See J.C. Hurd, op. cit., pp.66–9 *et passim*. On 6.18 (a) cf. C.D.F. Moule, *An Idiom-Book of New Testament Greek* (CUP, ²1959), p.197.

[48]   F.X.J. Exler, *The Form of the Ancient Greek Letter: A Study in Greek Epistolography* (Washington, DC: Catholic University of America Dissertation, 1923), pp.15–16; cf. the style of the treatise, pp.17–20.

[49]   R. Bultmann, *Der Stil der paulinischen Predigt und die kynisch-stoiche Diatribe* (Göttingen: Vandenhoeck & Ruprecht, 1910), especially pp.64–74. Cf. also pp.10–46 and 74–96. Often Paul's style follows that of oral dialogue; cf. οὐκ οἶδας; and similar expressions, in Rom. 6:16; 1 Cor. 9:24; direct address introduced by such terms as ἄνθρωπε, Rom. 2:1, 3; 9:20; or ἄφρων, 1 Cor. 15:36; replies and counter-replies, Rom. 3:1–9, 27–31; 1 Cor. 10:29; 15:35; Gal. 3:19; references to situations characteristic of the readers, 1 Cor. 7:18–19, 27; Rom. 14:6; and familiar catalogues of terms, Rom. 1:18ff. All these find parallels in other writers. Cf. Epictetus, *Diss*. I. 2.22; 4.16; 28.21; 29.2; II. 2.26; 16.27–8; III. 5.7; 22.21–2, 27–30; Seneca, *de prov*. 5.5; 6.7; *de vit. beat*. 9.1; 10.1–2; 16.112; Plutarch, *de tranq. an*. 467 D–F, 469E; etc. cf. also Rom. 4:1–3, 9, 10; 6:1–3, 15, 16, 21; 7:1, 7, 13; 9:14–24, 30; 11:1–4, 11, 13–16; 14:4, 10; 1 Cor. 1:13; 3:1–5, 16; 4:7, 8, 21; 5:2, 6, 12; 6:1–9, 15–16, 19; 7:18, 21; 8:10; 9:1, 4–12; 10:16–22, 29, 30; 11:13–15, 22; 14:6–9, 16, 36; 2 Cor. 1:17; 11:17–33; 12:17–19; 13:5; Gal. 3:1–5, 21; 4:21.

Inevitably, however, in this situation there arises a phenomenon that is sometimes called, technically, 'persuasive definition'. From various parts of the epistle it may be inferred that 'spiritual' had acquired a favourable but highly *emotive* meaning at Corinth. It had virtually ceased to retain its original cognitive content, to which Paul recalls his readers in 12:1–3 and elsewhere. On the general phenomenon of persuasive definition John Hospers comments, 'When a word or phrase has already acquired a favourable emotive meaning, people often want to use the word or phrase to carry a cognitive meaning different from its ordinary one, so as to take advantage of the favourable emotive meaning that the word already has ... The same thing can happen ... with *un*favourable emotive meaning'.[50]

From the evidence of the earlier chapters it seems likely that 'flesh' and 'fleshly' had also slipped their original cognitive anchorage. To implement one's new-found 'freedom' to the extent of demonstrating one's own superiority to the law was supposedly a mark of deliverance from 'the flesh'! To cultivate only like-minded believers and teachers was supposedly 'spiritual'. Since the terms had evaporated into little more than value-judgements of *approval or disapproval*, they could be used for almost any purpose, whilst beguiling probably *both the speaker and the hearer* into thinking that he had put forward a genuine criterion of assessment. But Paul shatters all this preoccupation with countless evaluation. Any evaluation at all remains provisional before that day of the Lord (3:13–15; 4:3–5). But certainly in the case of the offender, this much can be said: the 'flesh' has yet to be destroyed.

VI
Vagueness and Specificity: Six Arguments and Counter-Arguments

Questions about the relative degree of vagueness or specificity in Paul's use of 'flesh' cannot be isolated easily from a consideration of arguments for the traditional view of the verse. These, therefore, we now examine. Six points, it may be urged, combine to make the customary interpretation seem likely.

(1) 1 Cor. 5:5 does not stand alone in the New Testament as the only verse in which the death of an individual is instigated by an apostolic pronouncement. In Acts 5:5, 10, the deaths of Ananias and Sapphira follow dramatically on Peter's rebuke. In Acts 13:11, Paul pronounces a sentence of blindness, although not of death, on Elymas the magician. 1 Tim. 1:20 records the punishment of Hymenaeus and Alexander, which, if no less obscure than 1 Cor. 5:5, is generally interpreted in similar terms. Furthermore, allusion is often made to the effects of wrongful participation in the Lord's Supper in 1 Cor. 11:29–32.

(2) It is generally accepted that the punishment of 1 Cor. 5:5 involves exclusion from the Christian community. To be excluded from the church is in a sense to be more vulnerable to the one whom Paul elsewhere describes as ὁ θεὸς τοῦ αἰῶνος τούτου (2 Cor. 4:4). The parting shot of 1 Cor. 5:13 seems to confirm this impression.

---

50 J. Hospers, *An Introduction to Philosophical Analysis* (London: Routledge & Kegan Paul, [2]1967), pp.53–4. Hospers cites the examples of 'cultured' giving rise to '*true* culture is ...'; or the unfavourable use of 'bastard'.

(3) As a special extension of this argument, it is further suggested that Satan represents the legal and social sanctions of society outside the church, and that in this case the Roman law would administer death or some other severe penalty.[51]

(4) In answer to difficulties about the precise force of the Ἵνα clause, reference can be made to the doctrine, which was familiar in Judaism, that the godly are punished in this life in order that they may enjoy uninterrupted blessing in the life to come.[52] The idea, it is argued, persists in the New Testament.

(5) The agency of Satan is connected specifically with sickness and death in various strands of Judaism.[53] Traces of this connection remain in the New Testament.[54]

(6) Paul often uses σάρξ to denote the physical part of man, and πνεῦμα can denote simply 'spirit' in its modern sense. It is urged that we must guard against an unduly 'Hebraic' interpretation of Paul.

Do these arguments contain the force that is claimed for them? The first three require only brief comments. The fourth and fifth will be considered in some details; but the sixth point has to some extent already been anticipated.

(1) and (2): To begin with, neither of the first two observations points decisively to any *one* interpretation. The first provides a *prima facie* case for the *possibility* of the traditional view. But I should not be rash enough to argue that this view is impossible; only that it does not seem to me to constitute the only possibility. With regard to the second point, it serves as a basis for more than one interpretation, including the one suggested here.

(3): The third argument belongs to a different category altogether. Even if we grant some kind of connection between Satan and society, it is impossible to find conclusive evidence that the sanctions of Roman law would have operated in the way that is claimed. There are many variable factors. Even if relevant laws had once existed, for example, were they still enforced in AD 56? The *lex Iulia de adulteriis* seems relatively soon to have become a dead letter. To what extent did the Roman administration allow a measure of autonomy in a city such as Corinth? Perhaps more to the point, even if laws were meant to be enforced, were they in practice enforceable? However serious the offence, in the view of 6:1ff it is inconceivable that Paul expected the Corinthians themselves to instigate proceedings. Yet the consensus of opinion seems to be that by the beginning of the reign of Nero neither the authorities nor private citizens would be especially likely to take action.[55] Isolated instances in which the Jews appear to 'execute'

---

51   On the connection between Satan and society, cf. T. Ling, *The Significance of Satan* (London: SPCK, 1961), especially pp.81–92.

52   Sources in Judaism are too numerous to cite. Cf. G.F. Moore's comment in *Judaism* (3 vols, Harvard, 1927–30), vol. II, pp.253–4: 'That sufferings, borne as chastisements, are an atonement for sins is the common belief.' Cf. also Luke 16:25, and J. Klausner's comments on suffering in *The Messianic Idea in Israel* (Eng., London: Allen & Unwin, 1956), pp.441ff.

53   Cf., among other possibilities, Job 2:5, 6; Jub. 11:11, 12; 48:2, 3; 49; Test. Benj. 3:3; I QS. 4:14; C.D. 2.6; 4.13; and Rabbinic sources cited in H.L. Strack and P. Billerbeck, *Kommentar zum Neuen Testament aus Talmud und Midrasch* (Munich: Beck), I (1922), pp.144–9 and IV (1928), pp.501–35. Cf. also J. Weiss, loc. cit., and H. St. John Thackeray, *The Relation of St. Paul to Contemporary Jewish Thought* (London: Macmillan, 1900), p.171.

54   E.g. Luke 13:11, 16; 2 Cor. 12:7; and just possibly 1 Thess. 2:18.

55   See A. Berger, *An Encyclopedic Dictionary of Roman Law* (Philadelphia, PA: American Philosophical Society, 1953), pp.352, 402, and 407; H.J. Greenidge, *The Legal Procedure of Cicero's Time* (Oxford: Clarendon

offenders by stoning them to death represent, in the judgement of A.N. Sherwin-White, unauthorized acts of mob violence.[56] Gentiles in easy-going Corinth would be unlikely to take such hot-blooded action; and if Jews (for the sake of argument) were going to take it at all, they would hardly have waited in defence for the man's formal departure from the church.

(4): With regard to the Ἵνα clause, Paul explicitly states that a purpose of salvation lies behind the guilty man's punishment. But C.K. Barrett voices the problem: 'It is not clear how the destruction of the physical side of man's nature can effect the salvation of the immaterial side. Suffering may indeed be remedial, but nothing in the context suggests this thought.'[57] If ὄλεθρον τῆς σαρκός is taken to refer to death, it is hard to believe that Paul has specifically in view a post-mortal repentance. Yet it would be even harder to construe this solemn verdict as little more than sheer bluff, offering only the *threat* of death.

We are forced, then, to reconsider the doctrine 'that sufferings, borne as chastisements, are an atonement for sin'.[58] Certainly dying with Christ and accepting his στίγματα are as much a part of Christ-union as being raised with Christ. But this is utterly different from any idea that believers who fall beneath a certain standard of conduct pass a nodal point in the scale of suffering which is never reached by those who remain above it. Almost the reverse seems to be the case. Especially in 2 Corinthians, sharing the sufferings of Christ is seen as an authentic mark of discipleship.[59] Apart from this, it can only be said that dying with Christ, like the death of Christ, concerns the *whole* company of believers.[60]

There are supposedly two other alternatives that are compatible with the traditional view of 1 Cor. 5:5. C.K. Barrett comments with some hesitancy, 'The thought may be that the devil must be given his due, but can claim no more; if he has the flesh, he has no right to the spirit, even of the sinner.'[61] This would reflect a contrast of the kind made in Matt. 10:28, and might be connected with Paul's allusion to chastening in 1 Cor. 11:32. But this solves one problem at the expense of another. For in relation to 1 Cor 5:5 this now reduces the purposive force of ἵνα to such an extent as to undermine the question which the

---

Press, 1901), pp.376–80; B. Cohen, *Jewish and Roman Law: A Comparative Study* (2 vols, New York: Jewish Theological Seminary of America, 1966), pp.374 and 742; J. Carcopino, *Daily Life in Ancient Rome* (London: Routledge, 1941), pp.94ff; W.S. Davies, *The Influence of Wealth in Imperial Rome* (London: Macmillan, 1910), pp.303–4; R.H. Barrow, *Slavery in the Roman Empire* (London: Methuen, 1928), pp.151–6; and A.N. Sherwin-White, *Roman Society and Roman Law in the New Testament* (Oxford: Clarendon Press, 1963), pp.41–2 and 100–101. (Cf. also pp.71–98.)

[56] A.N. Sherwin-White, loc. cit., and in 'The Trial of Christ' in *Historicity and Chronology in the NT* (Theological Collections 6, London: SPCK, 1965), pp.106–10, especially p.109. Cf. John 8:1–11 (the woman taken in adultery) and Acts 7:54–8 (the stoning of Stephen).

[57] C.K. Barrett, op. cit., p.126.

[58] See above, note 52.

[59] Cf. 2 Cor. 1:3–9; 4:7–14; 7:3; 12:9; and 13:4; and especially the discussions of these verses in R.C. Tannehill, *Dying and Rising with Christ* (Berlin: Töpelmann, 1967), pp.84–100.

[60] See especially E. Schweizer, 'Dying and Rising with Christ', in *New Testament Studies*, 14 (1967–68), pp.1–14; M. Bouttier, *Christianity according to Paul* (Eng., London: SCM, 1966); and R.C. Tannehill, op. cit. This applies equally if Col. 1:24 is interpreted in terms of a 'quota' of suffering for the Messianic community; cf. C.F.D. Moule, *The Epistles to the Colossians and to Philemon* (Cambridge, 1957), pp.75–80.

[61] C.K. Barrett, loc. cit.

explanation was to answer. Admittedly the force of ἵνα is strikingly variable in the New Testament.[62] But many writers, including C.K. Barrett, draw attention to its purposive function in this verse.

The same difficulty faces the other expedient of assuming that in Paul's view 'baptism in and of itself produces salvation'.[63] Even if ἵνα is said to have no purposive thrust, it remains to be explained why as a corollary of baptism a believer undergoes death specifically when he falls below some predetermined level of conduct. Further, if there is no question whatever that the offender will be saved irrespective of any response to the church's censure, the logical emphasis now falls entirely on τὸ πνεῦμα, as the only novel element of the clause. But unless σάρξ and πνεῦμα are being used evaluatively, this flatly contradicts the comment which we noted from Schweizer to the effect that 'Paul never reckons with the salvation of a mere soul.'[64]

A slightly different way of meeting the difficulty is offered by Ernst Käsemann in his illuminating study of Holy Law in the New Testament.[65] Käsemann gives the clause its greatest possible force. In the first place, he calls attention to four main examples of judgement-utterances in the Pauline writings. The word, he claims, 'is lifted out of the sphere of mere information ... to hear this Word is to be thereby condemned or pardoned'.[66] Paul's language in these examples does indeed function performatively. In J.L. Austin's terms, they represent illocutions that function more specifically as verdictives, and in some cases also as exercitives.[67] In the second place, Käsemann continues, these utterances reflect an eschatological orientation: 'Cursing and blessing ... anticipate the eschatological judgement'.[68] This verdict may reach the believer as a pronouncement of grace, although it may also reflect 'the perspective of eschatological law'.[69]

Up to this point the whole argument may seem convincing. Other writers have already shed light on Paul's view of justification and of baptism by reassessing their significance in this perspective. An act of judgement that we might expect to result only in penalty turns out to be, after all, an act of grace and salvation.[70]

But does this principle genuinely apply to what is at issue in 1 Cor. 5:5? In the context of justification a so-called paradox arises because the eschatological verdict is brought forward, whilst the believer's empirical life as a sinner has not yet caught up with the

---

[62]   In addition to Blass-Debrunner and Moulton-Howard-Turner, cf. C.F.D. Moule, *An Idiom-Book of NT Greek*, pp.142–3.

[63]   J.C. Hurd, op. cit., p.137. Cf. H. Conzelmann, op. cit., p.270.

[64]   See the arguments of section III and IV and especially n. 35.

[65]   E. Käsemann, op. cit., pp.66–81.

[66]   Ibid., p.73. 1 Cor. 3:17; 5:5; 14:38; and 16:22.

[67]   J.L. Austin, *How to Do Things with Words* (Oxford: Clarendon Press, 1962), pp.4ff, 88–90; 98–101; and 150–56.

[68]   E. Käsemann, loc. cit., pp.70 and 73.

[69]   Ibid., p.74.

[70]   Cf. C.F.D. Moule, 'The Judgement Theme in the Sacraments', in W.D. Davies and D. Daube (eds), *The Background of the New Testament and its Eschatology* (Cambridge, 1956), pp.464ff; J. Weiss, *Earliest Christianity*, II (New York: Harper, 1959), especially p.502; R. Bultmann, op. cit., pp.274ff; and J. Jeremias, *The Central Message of the New Testament* (London: SCM, 1965), pp.64ff. Cf., not least, E. Käsemann, op. cit., pp.15, 108ff, and 168ff.

final reality of his situation before God. But in 5:5 the situation, or the point at issue, is different. Here the act of judgement involves exclusion from the Christian community, and it is difficult to see in what sense *this* represents an anticipation of the believer's final destiny.

Furthermore, the number of so-called 'paradoxes' which are now involved becomes suspiciously large, even granted the eschatological complexities pointed out in the first place by Albert Schweitzer.[71] On the one hand, it is argued, the guilty man experiences actual death; on the other hand 'he is thereby brought to repentance'.[72] Excommunication 'cannot annul the event of baptism', yet 'delivery over to Satan as being "severed from Christ" ... is the antithesis of baptism'.[73] Characteristically: 'In being handed over to Satan he is only falling in another mode than hitherto into the hands of his Lord, i.e. into the realm of the ὀργὴ Θεοῦ, and this, very paradoxically, to the end that thus he may yet be saved.'[74] In general, Käsemann's study of Holy Law is convincing and illuminating. But in the interpretation of 1 Cor. 5:5, the paradoxes which emerge seem perhaps to owe more to the author than to Paul.

VII
An 'Illegitimate Totality Transfer'?

(5): We have noted that Satan is connected with sickness or death in the Old Testament, in the Pseudepigrapha, in rabbinic sources and in Qumram.[75] But this must not be taken to imply that this is a *necessary* connection in the general 'concept' of Satan and his activities. Sickness and death constitute *examples* taken from Satan's less specific role as destroyer. A careful survey of references in inter-Testamental Jewish writings reveals that Satan is thought to pursue his destructive role primarily by seeking to disrupt man's relationship with God; sometimes by tempting him to sin, sometimes by accusing him before God, and sometimes by bringing various unspecified woes or pressures to bear on him. In Foerster's words, 'The destruction which he brings embraces harmful processes of every kind.'[76]

The traditional view of 1 Cor. 5:5 derives some of its plausibility from what James Barr has called 'illegitimate totality transfer'.[77] Interpreters note that *in many instances* Satan is said to bring about a man's destruction by bringing sickness and finally death. But these instances are then conglomerated together until destruction by sickness and death

---

[71] See A. Schweitzer, *The Mysticism of Paul the Apostle* (Eng., London: Black, 1931), especially chapters IV–VII. Cf. also M. Bouttier, op. cit., pp.19ff.

[72] E. Käsemann, op. cit., pp.71–2.

[73] Ibid.

[74] Ibid.

[75] See note 53.

[76] W. Foerster in G. Kittel (ed.), *Theological Dictionary of the New Testament*, II, p.80; cf. pp.73–81. In addition to the sources alluded to in n. 53 above, cf. especially Zech. 3:1ff; Eth. Enoch 40:7; Jub. 1:20; 48:15, 18; I QS. 3.21ff and 4.9–14. Even in Job, Satan makes his appearance in the first place as accuser, and inflicts physical suffering only within this framework.

[77] J. Barr, op. cit., p.218. Cf. also pp.36ff, 70ff, and 217–19.

becomes a necessary part of some total 'concept' which lies behind Paul's words. This ignores, however, two basic principles that are firmly established in semantics. First, it ignores the now hallowed distinction, which goes back to Saussure, between a historical (diachronic) orientation to language-study and the use of descriptive (synchronic) methods.[78] Second, it ignores the fact that some words or phrases perform distinctive functions in language on account of their very *lack* of specificity.

The variety of methods by which Satan seeks to destroy men is equally in evidence in the New Testament. He seeks this end as tempter, as deceiver, and as accuser.[79] D.E.H. Whiteley interprets both 1 Cor. 5:5 and 2 Cor. 12:7 in the traditional way, but he also adds the warning: 'We must resist the temptation to see Satan whenever the Apostle speaks of disease *or vice versa* ... When St. Paul tells us in 1 Thess. 2:18 that Satan thwarted his intention of going to Thessalonica, we cannot be sure that an attack of illness prevented him, although this is perfectly possible; it may have been the travelling arrangements which broke down.'[80] In so far as allusions to Satan in the New Testament possess any common characteristic at all, this might also be said to lie in the open-endedness or vagueness that marks his many guises, methods and aims.

If we insist, however, on specifying some particular characteristic to which allusion is made or implied in 1 Cor. 5:5, then the interpretation which is proposed in this study calls to mind Satan's role as accuser, which has firm roots in the Old Testament in the prologue to Job and in Zech. 3:1ff. For we have already considered the effects of the offender's exclusion from the community. The more he had hitherto overestimated his status as a 'spiritual' man, the more desperate, in his own eyes, would be his fall. Thus exclusion from the community provides, most of all, an opportunity for accusation before God.

The objection may be put forward: why should Satan be said to instigate a process that could lead to the offender's salvation? But if it is a difficulty, this applies not to any given interpretation, but to the presence of the ἵνα clause in the text itself. In any case, the idea that Satan's evil designs can nevertheless be turned to good account occurs regularly in the New Testament.[81] The classic example of the ἄγγελος Σατανα in 2 Cor. 12:7 has the salutary effect ἵνα μὴ ὑπεραίρωμαι. Further, here again arguments that τῇ σαρκί can *only* be physical are not perhaps quite conclusive.[82] But even if they are, this is more than offset by the fact that the whole context of this verse is one of glorying or boasting (καυχάομαι, 12:5, 6; and ὑπεραίρομαι, 12:7 (a) and (b). The activity of Satan has the end-effect of taking away any ground for self-glorying.

In as far as it is present in 1 Cor. 5:5, however, the idea of accusation remains contingent on the more primary context of exclusion from the community. The offender re-enters the realm of ὁ θεὸς τοῦ αἰῶνος τούτου as a lone individual who is utterly

---

[78] F. de Saussure, op. cit., pp.79–100. Cf. J. Lyons, *Introduction to Theoretical Linguistics*, pp.45ff; S. Ullmann, *The Principles of Semantics*, pp.36–9; and J. Barr, op. cit., pp.36ff.

[79] Matt. 4:10; John 8:44; 2 Cor. 2:11; 11:14; 2 Thess. 2:9; 1 John 3:8 and especially Rev. 12:9 and 10 (κατήγωρ). Cf. J.Y. Lee, 'Interpreting the Demonic Powers in Pauline Thought', in *Novum Testamentum*, XII (1970), pp.54–69.

[80] D.E.H. Whiteley, op. cit., p.22 (my italics).

[81] E.g. John 13:27ff and probably 1 Cor. 2:8.

[82] See P.H. Menoud, 'L'Écharde et l'Ange satanique', in *Studia Paulina: in Honorem J. de Zwaan* (Haarlem: Bohn, 1953), pp.163–71.

vulnerable to forces of destruction. It is not surprising that Paul should use ὄλεθρος in this context of thought. He has just referred to the one who is the destroyer; in his passionate indignation about the whole affair he insists the 'flesh', far from belonging only to the past, has yet to be destroyed; and the term functions in quasi-opposition to σωθῇ; following the series of contrasts marked by ἀπολλυμένοις and σωζομένοις in 1:18ff. In 3:15–17 a similar polarity is expressed by a parallel vocabulary. If it could be shown, as Schneider claims, that the term has special eschatological significance, it functions all the more naturally as a corollary to salvation in the setting of ἐν τῇ ἡμέρᾳ τοῦ κυρίου.[83] Whether or not, however, Héring is right to connect 3:17 directly with 5:1ff, we are not obliged to follow Robertson and Plummer in inferring a specific kind of suffering from the strength of the term ὄλεθρος.[84] It just as easily reflects the intensity of Paul's own feeling of indignation, conditioned further by the context of thought that he has in mind. The whole phrase τῷ Σατανᾷ εἰς ὄλεθρον τῆς σαρκός remains open-ended and in some directions unspecific.

(6) We have already examined some of the problems which attach to interpreting σάρξ and πνεῦμα respectively as 'the physical part of man's nature' and 'the immaterial side'.[85] All that remains is to qualify what has been said in sections IV and V in two ways. First, when two terms function together in semantic opposition they share the same type or range of logical functions. To say, for example, that Africa was hot but the welcome was cold, or that the tide is rising but hopes are falling, is not to oppose two sets of things, but at best 'to be making a poor joke'.[86] If, therefore, σάρξ means only the physical part of man, Paul's use of πνεῦμα can *only* refer to his immaterial soul. Conversely if, as has been suggested, σάρξ conveys both description and evaluation (and indeed implicitly places two different evaluations side by side), the same can be said about πνεῦμα. When the whole man experiences his final salvation at the day of the Lord, his orientation will be the very opposite of self-glorying or self-satisfaction.

In the second place, we must underline our earlier contention that the punishment of the offender *may or may not* have included physical suffering in its outworking. To suggest this is quite different from claiming that it was non-physical, since this imposes on the verse precisely the degree of specificity that we are rejecting. Käsemann rightly warns us that a specifically non-physical interpretation imposes a mind–body dualism on Paul's thought although he does not seem to be troubled by the fact that his own interpretation assumes that Paul's thought is already running along the lines of these two categories.[87]

---

[83] Cf. J. Schneider in G. Kittel (ed.), *Theological Dictionary of the New Testament*, V, pp.168–9.

[84] J. Héring, op. cit., p.24; A. Robertson and A. Plummer, loc. cit.

[85] C.K. Barrett, op. cit., p.126. See above, especially the second part of section III.

[86] See especially Gilbert Ryle, *The Concept of Mind* (Hutchinson, 1949, Peregrine Books edn, 1963), p.24. Cf. pp.20–24.

[87] E. Käsemann, op. cit., p.71. Cf. also K. Grobel, 'Σῶμα as "Self", "Person", in the Septuagint', in *Neutestamentliche Studien für Rudolf Bultmann* (Berlin: Töpelmann, 1954), pp.52–9.

VIII

The Value of Non-specificity for Certain Uses of Language

It will now seem that much of this essay calls for a recognition of vagueness or open-endedness in Paul's language, although it raises questions about overlappings between description and evaluation. Philosophers of language seem to have accepted more readily than many Biblical interpreters the fact that we often *choose* to use language vaguely for very good reasons.[88] Terms such as 'middle-aged', 'warm', or 'urban' are not inferior substitutes for the use of statistics or precise quantification.

Biblical interpreters have been inclined to give expression to this principle more recently than in earlier years. Might Ernst Sellin, for example, have been spared the agony of successively pinpointing the Suffering Servant as Zerrubbabel (in 1898), as Jehoiachin (in 1901), as Moses (in 1922), and as the author of the Songs (in 1930)?[89] Does 'the horrifying abomination' of Mark 13:14 necessarily refer *specifically* to a statue of Titus or Hadrian; or to an attempted profanation by Caligula; or to the violence of the zealots; or to the heathen insignia of the Roman troops? Similar questions might be asked about huge terms such as 'Son of Man', or inconspicuous phrases such as ἔτι μικρόν in the Farewell Discourses (John 14:19; 16:16, 19).

To force a pre-determined degree of specificity onto the meaning of 1 Cor. 5:5 may well be to go beyond Paul's own intention. It is no more difficult, although it may be easier, to interpret σάρξ as self-satisfaction (as in 3:1ff and elsewhere) than it is to insist that Paul is specifying the physical part of a man in contrast to his soul. It remains as easy to envisage Satan in the role of accuser, as it is to insist that his role is exclusively specified as the bringer of sickness and death. Indeed it becomes easier still to imagine that his role is open-ended. On the other hand, to assert that Paul alludes *necessarily* to sickness or, even more, to death, encounters the series of difficulties that we have outlined.

---

[88] W.P. Alston, op. cit., pp.84–96; M. Black, op. cit., pp.134ff; J. Hospers, op. cit., pp.67–76; F. Waisemann, op. cit., pp.69ff and 176–90; L. Wittgenstein, *Philosophical Investigations*, sects 68–71, 79, 83, 88, 168, 173–4; S. Ullmann, *The Principles of Semantics* pp.92–6 and 117–25; and W.V.O. Quine, *Word and Object* (MIT Press, ²1960), pp.125–56.

[89] See the comments on Sellin by C.R. North, *The Suffering Servant in Deutero-Isaiah* (OUP, 1948), pp.49–55 and 79–82; Sellin wrote 'always in a tone of complete finality' (p.81).

CHAPTER TWELVE

"Faith", "Flesh" and "Truth" as Context-Dependent Concepts: "Language-Games and Polymorphous Concepts" (1980)

Some New Testament exegetes and theologians have been too readily seduced into asking what faith or truth "is" in Pauline thought. But "polymorphous" concepts may mean different things in different contexts, and philosophers of language and linguistic philosophers provide multiple examples of this conceptual phenomenon. This short extract from The Two Horizons *(Grand Rapids, MI: Eerdmans and Exeter: Paternoster, 1980), pp.407–15, argues that this applies to such concepts as "faith", "flesh", and "truth" in the Pauline writings. Since a more detailed account of "truth" in the biblical writings occurs in another essay of this present volume (no. 17), the consideration of truth in this short extract has been abbreviated to avoid overlap.*

I
Polymorphous Concepts

We have noted how Wittgenstein rejected what he called "the craving for generality" and "the contemptuous attitude towards the particular case".[1] For him language itself is not just "one thing". What language *is* depends on the setting or language-game in which the term "language" is used. He writes, "We ask: *'What is* language?', *'What is* a proposition?' – And the answer to these questions is to be given once for all, and independently of any future experience." But this rests on the illusion that words like "language", "experience", and so on are "super-concepts" *(Über-Begriffen)*: "The language-game in which they are to be applied is missing."[2]

Most of Wittgenstein's considerations of particular concepts illustrate this principle, for it is a theme that dominates all his later work. We have already seen how it operates in the case of the words "exact" and "expect". What "exactness" *is* varies from situation to situation. If I am measuring the distance from the earth to the sun, it is quantitatively different from what it is when I am giving a joiner instructions about mending a piece of furniture. "Expecting" when someone is due to come to tea is not exactly the same as it is when I am expecting an explosion.[3]

In the same way Wittgenstein shows how misleading it is simply to ask, "What *is* thinking?" In the sections that follow this question he distinguishes between a diversity of concrete situations in which to ask, "What was 'thinking?'" would invite different

---

[1] L. Wittgenstein, *The Blue and Brown Books* (Oxford: Blackwell, 2nd edn, 1969), p.18.
[2] L. Wittgenstein, *Philosophical Investigations (PI)* (Oxford: Blackwell, 1967), sects 92, 96, and 97.
[3] L. Wittgenstein, *Zettel* (Oxford: Blackwell, 1969), sects 58–68 and 71–2, and *PI*, sects 572–86.

answers.[4] For example: "Thinking is not an incorporeal process ... which it would be possible to detach from speaking ... One might say 'Thinking is an incorporeal process', however, if one were using this to distinguish the grammar of the word 'think' from that of, say, the word, 'eat'."[5] This, of course, was Wittgenstein's point about the word "game": "Don't say 'there *must* be something common, or they would not be called 'games' – but *look and see* whether there is anything common to all." Wittgenstein's own term for the similarities between particular examples of games was "family resemblances".[6]

Wittgenstein's observations came to have the status of a standard methodological device in linguistic philosophy. F. Waismann, for example, argues that "to try" is something different in "trying to lift a weight", "trying to do a calculation", and "trying to go to sleep".[7] Gilbert Ryle applies the principle to a whole range of mental activities such as thinking or attending, while G.E.M. Anscombe pays special attention to "intention", and A.R. White specially considers "attention".[8] In some circles the term "polymorphous concepts" is used to indicate the kind of concepts that have this kind of logical grammar.

II
Examples from Pauline Thought: Faith

I suggest that the theological vocabulary of the New Testament contains some polymorphous concepts. The clearest examples include perhaps "faith" (πίστις), "flesh" (σάρξ) or "fleshly" (σαρκίκός), and "truth" (αλήθεια). What does it mean to "have faith"? It is well known that Rudolf Bultmann declares, "*Paul understands faith primarily as obedience;* he understands the act of faith as an act of obedience." He adds, "This is shown by the parallelism of two passages in Romans: 'because your faith is proclaimed in all the world' (16:19). Thus he can combine the two in the expression ὑπακοὴ πίστεως ('the obedience which faith is', Rom. 1:5) to designate that which it is the purpose of his apostleship to bring about."[9] We have seen in our three chapters on Bultmann [*The Two Horizons*, pp.205–92] that there are important reasons why he wishes to view faith as obedience rather than, for example, as intellectual assent. What Bultmann is doing, however, in arguing that this meaning is "primary", is viewing the concept of faith "outside *a particular language-game*": "The language-game in which (it) is to be applied is missing."

It does violence to the situational character of the New Testament writings to insist on isolating the "essence" of faith. For the New Testament writers, including Paul, can say

---

[4] L. Wittgenstein, *PI* sects 327–49.
[5] Ibid., sect. 339.
[6] Ibid., sect. 66–7.
[7] F. Waismann, *Ludwig Wittgenstein und der Wiener Kreis*, pp.183–4.
[8] G. Ryle, *The Concept of Mind* (London: Hutchinson, 1949; Penguin Books, 1963); G.E.M. Anscombe, *Intention* (Blackwell, Oxford, ²1963); and A.R. White, *Attention* (Oxford: Blackwell, 1964).
[9] R. Bultmann, *T.N.T.* I, 314 (his italics).

what faith *is* only in relation to *the issue at stake in a given context*. In Romans 4:5, "faith", especially in relation to the faith of Abraham, is the activity or disposition of "one who does not work but trusts him who justifies the ungodly". As J. Weiss comments, "Faith is not 'a work' to be substituted for other works ... It is nothing but a giving up of one's own activity."[10] J. Jeremias makes the same point with reference to Romans 3:28: "a man is justified by faith apart from works of the law". Here faith means, Jeremias urges, a renunciation of one's own achievement, and an attitude that attends solely to God.[11] On the other hand, in 2 Corinthians 5:7 the issue is a different one: "we walk by faith, not by sight". Here faith has a future orientation, as it does in Hebrews 11:1. Yet again, in Romans 10:9, faith entails an intellectual conviction, even if it is also belief in the truth of a self-involving confession: "if you confess with your lips that Jesus is Lord and believe in your heart that God raised him from the dead, you will be saved". In Galatians 1:23 "the faith" means simple "Christianity"; while in 1 Corinthians 13:2 faith that can move mountains seems to be a gift that is given only to certain Christians and not to all. We must agree with A. Schweitzer that when Paul speaks of faith, he does not speak of it "in the abstract".[12] G. Bornkamm provides a point of departure when he says, "The nature of faith is given in the object to which faith is directed."[13] But this must be taken much further. Faith in the New Testament is a polymorphous concept, and therefore questions about faith must not be answered "outside a particular language-game".

III
A Further Example: "Flesh" σάρξ – (*Sarx*) and "Fleshly" σαρκίκός – (*Sarkikos*)

The same principle applies to Paul's language about "flesh" and "fleshly". Sometimes Paul uses the term to denote physical substance, as in 1 Corinthians 15:39 and 2 Corinthians 3:2, 3. The phrase "a thorn in the flesh" (2 Cor. 12:7) is rendered by the NEB "a sharp physical pain". In Romans 1:3 "seed of David according to the flesh" may either refer to physical descent, or else to the parentage of Jesus "from an ordinary point of view". At all events, this second alternative is the meaning of σοφοί κατὰ σάρκα in 1 Corinthians 1:26. In 2 Corinthians 11:18 "glorying after the flesh" means glorying in such ordinary human phenomena as pedigree, rhetoric, recommendation and "success". In numerous passages Paul borrows the Old Testament emphasis on "flesh" as that which is creaturely, weak and fallible. As J.A.T. Robinson puts it, "Flesh represents mere man, man in contrast with God – hence man in his weakness and mortality."[14] Fleshly wisdom (2 Cor. 1:12) is merely human wisdom. "Walking according to the flesh" (2 Cor. 10:2) is not sensuality but ineffectiveness. In Galatians 5:19, 20, "the works of the flesh" include attitudes which are not restricted to the physical or sensual, but simply receive an adverse ethical evaluation. Finally in Romans 8:7, 13 and elsewhere, Bultmann rightly

---

10   J. Weiss, *Earliest Christianity* II, 508.
11   J. Jeremias, *The Central Message of the New Testament* (London: SCM, 1965), pp.65 and 68.
12   A. Schweitzer, *The Mysticism of Paul the Apostle* (Eng., London: Black, 1931), p.206.
13   G. Bornkamm, *Paul* (Eng., London: Hodder & Stoughton, 1972), p.141.
14   J.A.T. Robinson, *The Body. A Study in Pauline Theology* (London: SCM, 1952), p.19.

defines "flesh" as "trust in oneself as being able to procure life by the use of the earthly, and through one's own strength". It is "the self-reliant attitude of the man who puts his trust in his own strength".[15]

In Chapter 10 [*The Two Horizons*, pp.252–92, esp. 279–80] we argued that the recent study by Robert Jewett serves to confirm the value of Bultmann's work on the concept of "flesh", which was illuminated in turn by Heidegger. However, this point must now be qualified. Both Bultmann and even Jewett aim to suggest a unifying category that somehow binds together these varied uses of "flesh" into a single whole. Bultmann does this by applying *Sachkritik* in order to distinguish characteristic from uncharacteristic meanings; Jewett does it by postulating a particular theory about the origins of Paul's own concept of "flesh" in relation to the Galatians debate about circumcision. Thus Jewett attacks and criticizes the careful account of seven different categories that would account for Paul's varied uses.[16]

Admittedly Jewett is usually aware of the need to pay attention to a wide range of settings behind Paul's uses of anthropological terms. But in the case of "flesh" he seems reluctant to give adequate emphasis to the variety of language games in which "flesh" actually occurs, and which determine the meaning in particular passages. Thus he argues that the legalist error of "shifting one's boasting from the cross of Christ (Gal. 6:14) to the circumcised flesh (Gal. 6:13)" is really the same error as the libertine one of seeking satisfaction in sensuality, since both aim at securing "life" in one's own strength. This provides "the key to the interpretation as well as *the* source of the *sarx* concept in Paul's theology".[17] But it is no more necessary to seek for a common "essence" of the fleshly attitude than it is to find the essence of "exact", "expecting", "thinking", "trying", or "game". Paul does not wish to say that being "fleshly" is one *thing*. The "fleshliness" of the Corinthians was evident in a *variety* of ways; the "fleshliness" of the two groups in Galatians was perhaps exactly identical with none of them. Indeed what Paul attacks in 1 Corinthians is a generalization and hence undiscriminating application of the correlative term "spiritual". What it is to be "fleshly" depends on the nature of the *issue, which is in turn determined by the situation or language-game.* Questions of interpretation cannot be asked "outside" given language-games.

IV

A Final Example: Some Initial Comments on "Truth"

As a third example of a polymorphous concept in the New Testament we may consider the varied uses of the word "truth". Is it possible to say what the "essence" of truth is in the biblical writings, apart from the meaning that it has in given language-games? Or does the meaning of the word, in the sense of what *constitutes* truth, vary from context to context?

---

15 R. Bultmann, *T.N.T.* I, 239 and 240.
16 R. Jewett, *Paul's Anthropological Terms*, pp.59–60.
17 Ibid., p.95 (my italics); cf. pp.103–14.

Certainly in the case of the history of philosophical thought and even in ordinary language no *single* uniform concept of truth exists. In the context of considering a descriptive report, truth is a matter of correspondence with the facts. But when Kierkegaard declares that subjectivity is truth, what is at issue is something different from correspondence with facts. What may be said to constitute truth varies again in the context of Heidegger's thought, as we have already seen. Similarly the truth of a poem is not the same kind of thing as the truth of a proposition in the *Tractatus*. Do we not meet the same multiform phenomena in the New Testament? I discuss the use of the various words for truth in the biblical writings in greater detail elsewhere in this volume [Essay 17], drawing on an essay of 1978.[18] In this present short summary I have distinguished between the following uses of the word.

(1) In Greek literature and in the Old and New Testaments there are abundant examples of uses of the word "truth" in which the point at issue is correspondence with the facts of the matter. In Homer Achilles sets an umpire to tell the truth of a race, that is, to report the state of affairs as it really was (*Iliad* 23.361). Plato uses "truth" to mean simply "the facts of the matter" (*Epistles* 7.330). More explicitly Aristotle declares, "We call propositions only those sentences which have truth or falsity in them" (*On Interpretation* IV.17a.4); "The truth of a proposition consists in corresponding with facts" (ibid., IX.19a.33). Many scholars expect to find this usage in Aristotle, but tend to play down examples of the same use in the Old Testament.

However, the Old Testament offers many examples of this "factual" use. In Genesis 42:16 Joseph wishes to establish whether his brothers have told the truth. In Exodus 18:21 the men of truth who have a bribe are not only "reliable"; they also take account of all the facts and hide nothing. As a champion of truth, the king in the Psalms is to expose whatever is shady, underhanded, or false (45:4). In Tobit 7:10, "truth" is used of giving a true report; "Putting away falsehood, let every one speak the truth with his neighbour" (Eph. 4:25). Paul declares that everything he said was true (2 Cor. 7:14). The woman of Samaria speaks factual truth about her marital status (John 4:18). Everything that John the Baptist says about Jesus is true (John 10:41). It is clear that very often in the biblical writings "truth" draws its meaning from its function within the language-game of factual report.

(2) In other passages, however, a different language-game determines a different meaning for the same word. It is well known that the Hebrew word ᵉ*met* can mean either truth or faithfulness. This does not of course mean that it bears *both* of these meanings in the *same* set of contexts. There is no doubt, however, that in *certain* contexts "truth" is used in the sense of faithfulness, honesty, or reliability. The collectors in Josiah's reformation deal "honestly" (2 Kings 22:7). Most notably, when it is said that God is true, the writer means that God proves his faithfulness to men afresh.

This connection between faithfulness and truth depends, however, not on any semantic factors which are peculiar to the Hebrew language, but on the fact that when

───────────────

[18] A.C. Thiselton, "Truth (*Alētheia*)", in C. Brown (ed.), *The New International Dictionary of New Testament Theology* III (Exeter: Paternoster, 1978), pp.874–902.

God or man is said to act faithfully the issue at stake is a correspondence between his word and deed. We are now in a different language-game from that of factual report. When the Psalmist exclaims that "all the paths of the Lord are mercy and truth" (Ps. 25:10), he is testifying that God's dealing with his people are utterly trustworthy, because they are characterized by loyalty to the covenant. In the context of this kind of language-game, Pannenberg is correct when he says that in the Old Testament "the truth of God must prove itself anew".[19] This is because of the nature of the language-game, not because of some supposedly "Hebraic" peculiarity of thought. What is "Hebraic" is simply the frequency with which this particular language-game is used, as against others.

(3) There are other contexts in which "truth" means neither correspondence with the facts, nor faithfulness and integrity, but the gospel of Christ in contrast to some other gospel or view of the world. As J. Murphy-O'Connor convincingly argues, "truth" occurs in the writings of Qumran with the meaning of "revealed doctrine" (1 QS 6:15; cf. 1:15; 3:24), and this meaning is retained in parts of the New Testament.[20] Thus "truth" cleanses a man from sin (1 QS 4:20, 21). What is at issue between Paul and the Judaizers is "the truth" (Gal. 2:5). Truth, for Paul, stands in contrast to "another gospel" (2 Cor. 11:4). This is almost certainly the meaning of "knowledge of the truth" in the Pastorals (1 Tim. 2:4; 2 Tim. 3:7), where the word cannot simply mean knowledge of true facts. Men will turn away from hearing "the truth" in order to listen to more myths (2 Tim. 4:3, 4).

(4) Philo describes God as the God who is true, in the sense that he is "real", like a coin that is genuine rather than counterfeit, or an article that is what it seems, and not merely veneer (*The Preliminary Studies*, 157). In the Fourth Gospel, Jesus says that his flesh is "real" food and his blood is "real" drink (John 6:55). Those who worship God must worship him in Spirit and reality (John 4:23, 24). The context of this passage makes it plain that what is at issue is not "sincerity" but worshipping God on the basis of the reality disclosed through divine revelation, rather than on the speculations of human religious aspiration. If we extend our investigation of ἀληθής and ἀλήθεια in order to include ἀληθινός, there are a number of further examples in John. Jesus is the real bread, in contrast to the manna (6:32). He is the real vine, in contrast to Israel (15:1). This remains a conceptual rather than a lexicographical point, however, for in a different context ἀληθινός may also denote a saying which corresponds with the facts (John 4:37).

(5) Sometimes truth is used in contrast to that which is hidden. Whereas the devil has no truth in him because he is a deceiver (John 8:44, 45), the Spirit of truth "exposes" what is the case; he "brings things to the light of day" and "shows a thing in its true colours" (John 14:17; 15:26; 16:13; cf. 1 John 4:6; 5:6).[21]

(6) It is possible to distinguish other nuances of meaning, such as that of "valid" witness (John 5:31, 32). Yet we must also allow for the use of the word "truth" in an overarching way that holds together several of these other uses. We find this overarching meaning, for example, when Jesus in the Fourth Gospel says that he *is* the truth (John

---

[19] W. Pannenberg, "What is truth?", in *Basic Questions in Theology*, vol. II (London: SCM, 1971), p.8; cf. pp.1–27.

[20] J. Murphy-O'Connor, "Truth: Paul and Qumran", in *Paul and Qumran* (London: Chapman, 1968), pp.179–230.

[21] C.K. Barrett, *The Gospel according to St. John* (London: SPCK, 1955), p.76.

14:6). John has already introduced his readers to the idea that the testimony of Jesus is valid; that he reveals the truth of the gospel; that his words correspond with his deeds, and that his statements correspond with the facts. Hence none of these concepts of truth can be excluded. Nevertheless, this in no way invalidates our argument that truth in the New Testament is a polymorphous concept. For in the first place, even this overarching use occurs only in a given type of context, for example, in the context of Christology. In the second place, even then it is hardly possible to define the "essence" of truth in a single uniform way. We cannot ask questions about "the New Testament concept of truth", or even "John's concept of truth", *outside* a given context or language-game.

We have only to look at the history of research into the subject to see how some scholars have been led astray by failing to understand this point. The basic procedure in the nineteenth century was first of all to draw a clear-cut contrast between the "theoretical" concepts of truth in Greek thought and the "practical" concept in Hebraic thinking. The theoretical view was based on the correspondence theory of truth, while the practical view was connected first of all with the semantic accident that ᵉmet could mean either truth or faithfulness, and partly with the interest of the Old Testament writers in the reliability of God. Research on Paul is still today dominated by the question raised by H.H. Wendt in 1883 about which of the New Testament writers was most influenced by this supposedly "Hebraic" concept of truth.[22] In a study of 1928, Bultmann argued what Wendt's thesis of Hebraic influences applied to Paul, but not to John.[23] The same clear-cut contrast is the basis for D.J. Theron's study of truth in Paul, published in 1954, and L.J. Kuyper's article of 1964 on truth in John.[24]

The failure to notice the polymorphous character of this concept led many scholars into a blind alley. They looked for what Paul saw as the *essence* of the concept, or what the Hebrews or John saw as its essence. But what truth *is* or *consists in* varies from language-game to language-game. The question "What is truth?" cannot be asked *outside* a given language-game. It is unnecessary to offer further examples here, for we have included another essay, Essay 17 in this present volume, on this particular subject.

---

[22] H.H. Wendt, "Der Gebrauch der Worter alētheia, alēthēs, and alēthinos im N. T. auf Grund der alttestamentlichen Sprachgebrauches", in *Theologische Studien und Krtiken, eine Zeitschrift für das gesamt der Theologie* LXV (1883), 511–47.

[23] R. Bultmann, "Untersuchungen zum Johannesevangelium", in *Z.N.W.* XXVII (1928), 113–63; cf. Bultmann's article in *Theological Dictionary of the New Testament* I, pp.242–50.

[24] D.J. Theron, "Alētheia in the Pauline Corpus", in *E.Q.* XXVI (1954), 3–18; and L.J. Kuyper, "Grace and Truth", in *Reformed Review* XVI (1962), 1–16, and "Grace and Truth. An Old Testament Description of God and its Use in the Johannine Gospel", in *Int.* XVIII (1964), 3–19.

CHAPTER THIRTEEN

Semantics Serving Hermeneutics: "Semantics and New Testament Interpretation" (1977)

This article was a revision and expansion of an oral presentation delivered at Tyndale House, Cambridge, at a conference of New Testament scholars in 1973. It eventually appeared with the other conference papers in the volume entitled New Testament Interpretation, *edited by I. Howard Marshall (Exeter: Paternoster Press, 1977), pp.75–104. Four or five pages of the original essay have been omitted, in one case to avoid overlap with another essay included in this volume, and in another case to avoid taking space with didactic, rather than research, material. Even so, some material that was the fruit of genuine interdisciplinary research in 1973 and in 1977 may appear now, for some, to represent more mundane didactic material. However, the semantic principles discussed in this article remain of fundamental methodological importance for biblical interpretation and for hermeneutical theory, and even if some principles are regarded nowadays as axiomatic for some, their application to specific case studies and examples in biblical interpretation remains the fruit of inter-disciplinary research, and retains a continuing hermeneutical significance. The discussions of field semantics, synonymy, opposition, vagueness, translation and metaphor constitute cases in point.*

I
Introduction

Semantics is the study of meanings; but not simply the meanings of words. What is at issue is the varied meanings and kinds of meanings which belong both to words and to sentences as they occur within a context that is both linguistic and extra-linguistic. John Lyons comments in his *Structural Semantics*, "Any meaningful linguistic unit, up to and including the complete utterance, has meaning in context. The context of the utterance is the situation in which it occurs ... The concept of 'situation' is fundamental for semantic statement ... Situation must be given equal weight with linguistic form in semantic theory."[1]

It will be seen that this is not very far from the traditional concerns of New Testament exegesis, in which the aim is to discover and interpret the meaning of an utterance in relation to its historical and literary context. Semantics, however, also raises explicit questions about such issues as synonymy, multiple meaning, types of semantic opposition, kinds and degrees of vagueness and ambiguity, change of meaning, cognitive and emotive factors in meaning and so on.

---

[1] John Lyons, *Structural Semantics. An Analysis of Part of the Vocabulary of Plato* (Oxford, 1963), pp.23–4. Cf. C.K. Ogden and I.A. Richards, *The Meaning of Meaning* (London, 1923), pp.306–7; cf. pp.308–36 and also Stephen R. Schiffer, *Meaning* (Oxford, 1972), pp.1–5.

The relevance of semantics to biblical interpretation was demonstrated for the first time, but demonstrated decisively, with the publication in 1961 of James Barr's epoch-making book *The Semantics of Biblical Language*. Since that time there have been other attempts to apply principles of semantics, or at least of linguistics, to biblical interpretation, including most recently the very different approaches of Erhardt Güttgemanns, René Kieffer, John Sawyer and K.L. Burres.[2] Although the study of semantics can be approached from the side of philosophy as well as linguistics, James Barr and in practice all these writers draw their insights exclusively from linguistics. Indeed the claim that will be put forward here is that in spite of his obvious knowledge of more recent writers, the fundamental inspiration behind Barr's contribution is the figure of Ferdinand de Saussure whose famous *Cours de linguistique générale* was published posthumously in 1915. Apart from some brief attempts by the present writer, perhaps the only studies to date to draw on more philosophical work in the service of biblical interpretation are those of D.D. Evans and, less directly, O.R. Jones.[3]

If semantics is so important to New Testament interpretation, why have we had to wait until after 1961 for its insights and potentialities to become apparent? It seems that either the exegete can manage very well with only his or her traditional questions about vocabulary and grammar; or else some convincing explanation is needed of why biblical scholars have been slow to avail themselves of its insights.

II
The Inhibiting Effects of Traditional Assumptions about Language

Part of the answer to this question is suggested by Stephen Ullmann's description of semantics as "the youngest branch of modern linguistics".[4] The earliest hints of a fully modern semantics came towards the end of the nineteenth century with the work of Arsène Darmesteter and more especially Michel Bréal.[5] Semantic study at this period,

---

[2] J. Barr, *The Semantics of Biblical Language* (Oxford, 1961); E. Güttgemanns, *Studia Linguistica Neotestamentica. Gesammelte Aufsätze zur linguistischen Grundlage einer Neutestamentlichen Theologie* (Beiträge zur evangelischen Theologie Bd. 60; Münich, 1971); R. Kieffer, *Essais de méthodologie néotestamentaire* (Lund, 1972); J.F.A. Sawyer, *Semantics in Biblical Research, New Methods of Defining Hebrew Words for Salvation* (London, 1972) and Kenneth L. Burres, *Structural Semantics in the Study of the Pauline Understanding of Revelation* (unpublished PhD Dissertation, Northwestern University, Evanston, IL, 1970; University Microfilms Xerox, Ann Arbor, MI, 71–1810). Cf. also the journal edited by Güttgemanns, entitled *Linguistica Biblica: Interdisziplinäre Zeitschrift für Theologie und Linguistik*, and published in Bonn: see also the discussions of Barr's work in: G. Friedrich "Semasiologie und Lexicologie", in *TLZ* 94 (1969) cols 801–16, especially cols 803–7; cf. also T. Boman, ibid. 87 (1962), cols 262–5; D. Hill, *Greek Words and Hebrew Meanings. Studies in the Semantics of Soteriological Terms* (Cambridge, 1967); J. Barr "Common Sense and Biblical Language", in *Biblica* 49 (1968), pp.377–87; and especially K. Arvid Tangberg, "Linguistics and Theology: an Attempt to Analyse and Evaluate James Barr's Argumentation ...", in *The Bible Translator* 24 (1973), pp.301–10. For other articles involving semantics see G.B. Caird, "Towards a Lexicon of the Septuagint", in *JTS* 19 (1968), pp.453–75.

[3] For my articles see notes 9, 48, 73, 76, 86. For D.D. Evans see n. 91 and for O.R. Jones see n. 93.

[4] S. Ullmann, *The Principles of Semantics* (Oxford 1957[2]), p.1.

[5] A. Darmesteter, *La vie des mots étudiée dans leur significations* (Paris, 1895[5]) especially in pp.138–48 on synonymy; and M. Bréal, *Semantics, Studies in the Science of Meaning* (London, 1900), especially chapters 14 and 15 on polysemy.

however, was seriously hampered by a number of mistaken assumptions, some of which still find their way into the outlook of some interpreters of the New Testament even today.

These false assumptions include the following:

1 That the *word, rather than the sentence or speech-act,* constitutes the basic unit of meaning to be investigated;[6]
2 That questions about *etymology* somehow relate to the real or "basic" meaning of a word;
3 That language has a relation to the world which is *other than conventional,* and that its "rules" may therefore be prescriptive rather than merely descriptive;
4 That *logical and grammatical structure* are basically similar or even isomorphic;
5 That meaning always turns on the relation between a word and the object to which it *refers;*
6 That the basic kind of language-use to be investigated (other than words themselves) is the *declarative proposition* or statement; and
7 That language is an *externalization,* sometimes a merely imitative and approximate externalization, of inner concepts or ideas.

Commenting only on three of these assumptions, Max Black writes, "Until comparatively recently the prevailing conception of the nature of language was straightforward and simple. It stressed communication of thought to the neglect of feeling and attitude, emphasized words rather than speech-acts in context, and assumed a sharp contrast between thought and its symbolic expression."[7] While such assumptions held sway, semantic enquiries could not advance beyond an elementary point.

An especially disastrous assumption for semantics was logico-grammatical parallelism.[8] When interest grew in eighteenth and nineteenth-century linguistics in the relation between language-structure and national character, the effects of this error were particularly unfortunate. Supposed differences of conceptual thought were based on arbitrary differences of grammar.

II.1 Surface Grammar versus Logical Function

The influence of such a view persists in biblical studies in a work such as T. Boman's *Hebrew Thought Compared with Greek,* and we shall trace some of the ways in which James Barr rightly criticizes it. On the other hand, once we recognize that logical function, or meaning, is not wholly determined by grammar, huge questions in New Testament

---

[6] "Probably all mediaeval philosophers, all the 16th and 17th century authors, and later Johnson and Mill, and still later Frege ... Meinong, Russell ... and Wittgenstein (in their earlier work) – all of them *de facto* constructed theories of meaning of *names,* and tried, with varying success, to extend them to all linguistic expressions, above all to sentences. In doing so they were motivated by the belief that the meaning of a sentence ... is a function of the meaning of its components." J. Pelc, *Studies in Functional Logical Semiotics of Natural Language* (The Hague, 1971), p.58.

[7] M. Black, *The Labyrinth of Language* (London, 1968), p.9.

[8] S. Ullmann, *The Principles of Semantics,* p.16.

interpretation are opened up. Is Bultmann correct in claiming, for example, that what looks like an objective declarative statement, "God will judge men at the last day", really *means* an imperative: "act responsibly in the present ..."? Certainly in everyday speech I may use an indicative to function as an imperative. If I exclaim, "This is poison", I *may* be making a declarative descriptive statement. But I may also be uttering an urgent imperative, "Quick! Fetch a doctor"; or giving a warning, "Look out! Don't drink this"; or even uttering a reproach, "You forgot to put sugar into my coffee."[9] The meaning of the words depends on their setting or non-linguistic situation, even more than upon grammar. Yet on the basis of the traditional view, "this is poison" is simply a statement, for "is" is a third-person singular present indicative form in grammar.

The traditional view received two deathblows, one from linguistics and one from philosophy. From the direction of linguistics, Saussure pointed out the arbitrary character of grammatical forms.[10] More sharply and decisively still, in his philosophical discussion of logic Russell showed in his theory of descriptions that "the apparent logical form of a proposition need not be the real one".[11] Denoting phrases such as "the present king of France" or "the author of *Waverley*" cannot be reduced to simple referring expressions: "Denoting phrases never have any meaning in themselves."[12] The linguistic form "a round square does not exist" does not logically make an assertion about some non-existent entity called a round square; it is a *negation* of the statement, "an *x* exists which is such that 'round' and 'square' can be predicated of it simultaneously". The linguistic form of the expression conceals its logical function. But once this principle is accepted, the New Testament interpreter should be extremely cautious about making too much of such maxims as "this word is in the indicative, therefore it is a statement"; or "this verb is an imperative, therefore it expresses a command". Whether it *is* a command depends on the whole context and situation in which it is uttered. Thus, we shall be cautious about reading too much into the fact that, for example, an imperative or an indicative features in a particular verse. In Philippians 3:1 and 4:4, for instance, "rejoice in the Lord" (χαίρετε ἐν κυρίῳ) is admittedly a second person plural present imperative. On this basis Karl Barth writes that rejoicing "must" take place, because it is "expressed as an imperative", and W. Hendriksen insists that we are bidden "to rejoice *in obedience to a command*".[13] But, first, it is possible that χαίρετε is a form of greeting, which is no more a command than "how do you do?" is a question. On the basis of grammar, one can imagine an exegete interpreting "how do you do?" as a call to self-examination! When Judas greets Jesus with a betraying kiss in Matt. 26:49, χαῖρε means simply "hello", and

---

9 I have used this example in A.C. Thiselton, "The use of Philosophical Categories in New Testament Hermeneutics", in *The Churchman* 87 (1973), p.96.

10 Ferdinand de Saussure, *Cours de linguistique générale* (édition critique par R. Engler; Wiesbaden 1967, 3 fascicles), fasc. 2, pp.147–73 and 303–16; cf. E.T. *Course in General Linguistics* (London, 1960, ed. by C. Bally et al.), pp.67–78 and 134–9.

11 Cf. L. Wittgenstein, *Tractatus Logico-Philosophicus* (London, 1961), 4.0031; and B. Russell, "On Denoting", in *Mind* 14 (1905), pp.479–93.

12 B. Russell, loc. cit., p.480.

13 K. Barth, *The Epistle to the Philippians* (London, 1962), p.121; and W. Hendriksen, *Philippians* (London, 1962, rp. 1973), p.192 (his italics). Similarly cf. J.J. Muller, *The Epistles of Paul to the Philippians and to Philemon* (Grand Rapids, MI, 1955), p.140.

certainly not "rejoice". In Phil. 3:1 and 4:4 F.W. Beare translates the word "Farewell".[14] Secondly, even if we insist, after examining the historical and literary setting (which Barth and Hendriksen fail to do), that χαίρετε still means "rejoice", the fact that it occurs in the imperative is no guarantee that it must be understood as a "command". If I cry "Help!" in the imperative, or "Lord, save me", this is a plea; if someone tells me, "enjoy yourself", but in the end I spend a miserable afternoon, this need not be "disobedience to a command".

The task of Bible translation also reveals the utter impossibility of remaining wedded to the idea of logico-grammatical parallelism. In 1 John 2:26, for example, the writer states, "I have written this to you (ταῦτα ἔγραψα ὑμῖν) concerning those who would mislead you." But ἔγραψα, although it is an "indicative" (I have written) does not serve primarily to *describe* the action of writing here; it in fact signals the end of a topic. So the *New English Bible* sensibly renders it, "*So much for* those who would mislead you."

In Bible translation, the rejection of logico-grammatical parallelism stems not only from structural linguistics (discussed in section III.2), and from a recognition of the conventionality of grammatical form (discussed in section III.3), but also from the influence of Noam Chomsky's type of "transformational" generative grammar (discussed in section IV). Eugene A. Nida and William L. Wonderly accept the principle of transformation in terms of *"kernel"* sentences as an *axiom* of Bible translation.[15] Thus the complex RSV sentence in Ephesians 1:7 " ... we have redemption through his blood, the forgiveness of our trespasses" is analysed into four "kernel" sentences: (1) (God) redeems us; (2) (Christ) died (or shed his blood); (3) (God) forgives (us), and (4) we sinned. The "quasi-kernel" structure is now: "we sinned. But Christ died; therefore God redeems us and he forgives us." *Today's English Version* then renders this: "by the death of Christ we are set free, and our sins are forgiven"; whilst the *New English Bible* has: "in Christ our release is secured and our sins are forgiven through the shedding of his blood". Neither *grammatical* structure follows the Greek at all closely. Whether such a handling of the text is justified cannot be determined without carefully examining the issues which are discussed in the remainder of this essay.

II.2 An Atomistic Approach to "The Meaning of a Word"

Genuine advances in semantics were decisively inhibited all the while the *word* was viewed as the basic unit of meaning. But in some types of exegesis the assumption still lurks in the background that words are the basic carriers of meaning, whilst sentences convey the exact sum of the semantic values of their verbal components. A virtue is made out of the method of moving over a text "word by word". Side by side with this is often the assumption that exhaustive interpretation must proceed by way of *analysis*, atomizing language into ever-smaller and smaller units.

---

[14] F.W. Beare, *The Epistle to the Philippians* (London, 1959), pp.100 and 145–6. Cf. W.F. Arndt and F.W. Gingrich (W. Bauer), *A Greek-English Lexicon of the New Testament and Other Early Christian Literature* (Chicago, IL, 1957), p.882.

[15] E.A. Nida, *Towards a Science of Translating* (Leiden, 1964), especially pp.9–10 and 60–63 and chapters 8–10; and W.L. Wonderly, *Bible Translations for Popular use* (London, 1968), pp.50–55 and 149–72.

Such an approach may seem to be connected with a theory of "verbal" inspiration, but is in reality based, rather, on ignorance about the nature of language. As Saussure has shown decisively in one way, and Wittgenstein decisively in another, the meaning of a word depends not on what it is in itself, but on its relation to other words and to other sentences that form its context. Dictionary-entries about words are rule-of-thumb generalizations based on assumptions about characteristic contexts. Admittedly these comments will be qualified in due course; for words do indeed possess a stable core of meaning without which lexicography would be impossible, and there is also a legitimate place for word-study. Nevertheless, the most urgent priority is to point out the fallacy of an atomizing exegesis that pays insufficient attention to context.

This should heighten our appreciation of the value of all technical work in biblical studies that seeks to shed light on the historical and literary contexts of utterances. In a valuable article John F.A. Sawyer compares the emphasis placed on "context of situation" in linguistics with the account taken of situation, setting, or *Sitz im Leben* in form criticism.[16] Indeed he goes as far as to claim, "The relation between *Gattung* and *Sitz im Leben* in Old Testament literary theory is potentially more important for *semantic* theory [my italics] than a number of situational theories put forward by the professional linguistician from Bloomfield to Firth."[17]

Thus the necessity and value of standard techniques in New Testament studies is not simply a question that can be decided on theological grounds alone. Because biblical language *as language* can only be understood with reference to its context and extra-linguistic situation, attention to the kind of question raised in critical study of the text is seen to be necessary on purely *linguistic* grounds. To try to cut loose "propositions" in the New Testament from the specific situation in which they were uttered and to try thereby to treat them "timelessly" is not only bad theology; it is also bad linguistics. For it distorts what the text *means*. This point will emerge with fuller force when we look at the structural approach of Ferdinand de Saussure (below, section III.2).

There are also other inbuilt limitations in the traditional approach to language. For example, a persistent preoccupation with descriptive assertions or "propositions" tends to flatten out the distinctive contributions of biblical poetry, metaphor, parable and apocalyptic, reducing it all to the level of discursive "units of information". A consideration of the issues discussed in the remainder of this essay, however, will show that a "mechanical" emphasis on verbal and propositional forms is not only precritical in terms of Biblical studies, it is also obsolete in terms of *semantics*, violating virtually every modern insight into the nature of meanings.

---

[16]   J.F.A. Sawyer, "Context of Situation and *Sitz im Leben*. Some Questions Concerning Meaning in Classical Hebrew", in *Proceedings of the Newcastle on Tyne Philosophical Society* 1 (1967), pp.137–47. Similarly, cf. the important work of Erhardt Güttgemanns, *Offene Fragen zur Formgeschichte des Evangeliums* (Beiträge zur evangelischen Theologie, 54; Munich, 1971²), pp.44–68; 174–7; *et passim*.

[17]   J.F.A. Sawyer, loc. cit., p.140.

III
Some Fundamental Principles in Saussure and in Modern Linguistics and Their Place in the Work of James Barr

Ferdinand de Saussure (1857–1913) is rightly regarded as the founder of modern linguistics. He viewed language as a social and structured system, thereby preparing the way for a structural semantics. We may trace the outlines of his thought under four headings: (1) the contrast between synchronic and diachronic methods of language-study; (2) the structural approach to language; (3) the connection between structuralism and conventionality, with its implications about the relation between language and thought, and (4) the basic contrast between *langue*, the language system, and *parole*, actual speech. All four principles are fundamental for semantics, and three, at least, feature prominently in the work of James Barr.

III.1 Synchronic and Diachronic Approaches to Language

By "diachronic" linguistics Saussure means the study of language from the point of view of its *historical evolution* over a period of time. By "synchronic" linguistics he means, "the relations of co-existing things ... from which the intervention of time is excluded ... the science of *language-states (états de langue)* ... *Synchrony* and *diachrony* designate respectively a language-state and an evolutionary phase."[18] Saussure's point is not, as is occasionally thought, that one of these methods is right and the other wrong, but that the two methods are fundamentally *different*, and perform different tasks. Certainly of the two, synchronic linguistics has priority both in importance and in sequence of application. But as long as the two methods are kept distinct, each has its own role to play.

During the nineteenth century comparative philology had become the centre of interest in linguistics, and much energy went to the formulation of *laws of development*, such as Grimm's law and Verner's law, which could account for the phenomena of language-change in terms of general scientific principles.

It is against this background that Ferdinand de Saussure voiced his protest: "The linguist who wishes to understand a state (*état de langue*) must discard all knowledge of everything that produced it and ignore diachrony. He can enter the mind of the speakers only by completely suppressing the past."[19] Saussure illustrates the principle from chess. To understand the *state* of a game it is unnecessary and irrelevant to know how the players arrived at it. A chess problem is simply set out by describing the state of the board.

During the years between Saussure and Barr, the priority of synchronic description became a fundamental and universally accepted principle in semantics; the distinction between synchronic and diachronic perspectives has become an axiom in linguistics.[20] In

---

[18] Ferdinand de Saussure, *Course in General Linguistics*, pp.80–81; cf. *Cours de linguistique générale*, pp.177–8.

[19] Saussure, *Course in General Linguistics*, p.81 (édition critique, pp.181–2).

[20] E.g. J. Lyons, *Introduction to Theoretical Linguistics*, pp.45–50; S. Ullmann, *The Principles of Semantics*, pp.144–52; A. Martinet, *Elements of General Linguistics* (London, 1964), pp.37f; David Crystal, *Linguistics, Language and Religion* (London, 1965), pp.57–9; and K.L. Burres, *Structural Semantics in the Study of the Pauline Understanding of Revelation*, pp.36–40.

particular this principle strikes at etymologizing in semantics. Many writers, including a number of biblical scholars, believe that the etymological meaning of a word is somehow its "basic" or "proper" meaning. As James Barr comments, "We hear from time to time that 'history' 'properly' means 'investigation' (Greek ἰστορία) or that 'person' 'basically' means 'mask' (Latin *persona*)."[21]

But can an etymological meaning based on diachronic investigation, or even inference, concerning the long-distant past be the "real" meaning of a word from the point of view of synchronic enquiry? The English word "nice" is said to be derived from the Latin *nescius*, ignorant. Is "ignorant" the "basic" meaning of "nice"? When Englishmen say "Good-bye" do they "properly" mean "God be with you"? "Hussy" is etymologically a doublet of "housewife", but can it be said on this basis that if I were to call someone a hussy I "properly" meant only "housewife"?[22] As James Barr rightly asserts, "The main point is that the etymology of a word is *not a statement about its meaning but about its history*."[23] Hundreds of words diverge from or even (like "nice") oppose their etymology.

We may admit that in lexicography, etymological considerations may occasionally be of value, as, for example, in cases of homonymy, when two distinct words of different meanings have the same lexical form. But biblical scholars have not been content to restrict their study of etymology to such cases. As a general principle Edmond Jacob declares, "The first task of the Hebraist in the presence of a word is to recover the original meaning from which others were derived."[24] The very arrangement of the Hebrew lexicon of Brown, Driver and Briggs may seem to encourage such a procedure. Some writers, says J. Barr, have even interpreted the word "holy" in terms of an *English* etymology. Contrary to actual usage in Hebrew and Greek, they take its "basic" meaning to be that of "healthy" or "sound". But in practice, Barr insists, this is only "a kind of opportunist homiletic trick" whereby "holy" may be thought to lose some of its less attractive and more challenging features.[25] Norman Snaith certainly goes to the Hebrew, rather than to the English, for the meaning of "Blessed is the man ..." in Psalm 1:1. But he claims that "happiness of" or "blessed" is related by etymology to the idea of "footstep", or "going straight ahead". Hence, supposedly, "this shows how apt is the use of the first word ... The happy man is the man who goes straight ahead." Barr observes, "There is not the slightest evidence that these associations were in the mind of the poet, and indeed some of them were almost certainly unknown and unknowable to him."[26]

When we come specifically to the New Testament, it will be seen that it can be seriously misleading to base the meanings of words on their use in Plato or in Homer, let alone on their etymologies. For example, it is sometimes suggested, as Barr points out, that λειτουργία "means" a work (ἔργον) performed by the people (λαός) perhaps through a priestly or kingly representative. But at least by the time of Aristotle the word

---

[21]   J. Barr, op. cit., p.108.

[22]   Some of these examples, and many more, are suggested by S. Ullmann, *Semantics*, pp.97–9, and *Principles of Semantics*, pp.171–257.

[23]   J. Barr, op. cit., p.109 (my italics).

[24]   E. Jacob, *Theology of the Old Testament* (London, 1958), p.159.

[25]   Ibid., p.113.

[26]   Ibid., p.116; cf. N. Snaith, "The Language of the Old Testament", in the *Interpreter's Bible* (Nashville, 1952), vol. 1, p.224.

had simply become a generalized one for any kind of "service" or "function".[27] Sometimes interpreters seek to read too much into a dead metaphor. Thus "to show compassion" (σπλαγχνίζομαι) is said to be a matter of one's innermost being, since σπλάγχνα means "internal organs". But the metaphor is no longer any more a live force than when we speak of "losing heart". Similarly, it is sometimes claimed that ὑπηρέτης in 1 Cor. 4:1 "literally" means the under-rower (ὑπό + ἐρέσσω) of a ship.[28] But the word has become a dead metaphor meaning simply "servant" or "assistant"; no more than "dandelion" "literally" means *dent de lion* or "lion's tooth". Occasionally someone even uses diachronic investigation in a way that leads to sheer anachronism, as when we are told that "witness" (μαρτύριον) means "martyrdom"; or, worse still, that δύναμις in the New Testament "properly" means "dynamite"!

Neither Saussure nor Barr rules out diachronic linguistics as illegitimate. Indeed it may be helpful to use diachronic study to demonstrate that the meaning of a Greek word has *changed* in between Plato and the New Testament. It is proper to trace the historical evolution of a term and its changing semantic value, provided that two factors are borne in mind; first, that synchronic description is the prerequisite of diachronic study at every separate stage; secondly, that adequate attention is paid to the phenomenon of semantic change. David Crystal sums up the point made by Saussure: "Both are subjects in themselves, with different procedures of study and largely different aims. Neither excludes the other ... But ... a synchronic description is pre-requisite for a proper diachronic study".[29]

III.2 *The Structural Approach to Language*

In his introduction to the English edition of Saussure's work, W. Baskin, his translator, comments, "Saussure was among the first to see that language is a self-contained system whose interdependent parts function and acquire value through their relationship to the whole."[30] In Saussure's own words, "Language is a system of interdependent terms (*les termes sont solidaires*) in which the value (*la valeur*) of each term results solely from the simultaneous presence of the others."[31] He adds, "Within the same language, all words used to express related ideas limit each other reciprocally ... The value (*la valeur*) of just any term is accordingly determined by its environment."[32] Words or other linguistic signs have no "force", validity, or meaning, independently of the relations of equivalence and contrast which holds between them.

Once again Saussure illustrates the point with reference to chess. The "value" of a given piece depends on its place within the whole system. Depending on the state of the whole board when one piece is moved, resulting changes of value will be either nil, very serious, or of average importance. A certain move can revolutionize the whole game, that

---

[27] J. Barr, op. cit., pp.149–51.

[28] As in C. Hodge, *The First Epistle to the Corinthians* (London, 1958), p.64.

[29] D. Crystal, op. cit., p.58.

[30] Saussure, *Course in General Linguistics*, p.xii.

[31] Ibid., p.114, and *Cours de linguistique générale* (édition critique) fasc. 2, p.259 col. i (Baskin's translation has not been without criticism).

[32] Saussure, *Course in General Linguistics*, p.166 (édition critique, pp.261–2).

is, radically affect the value of all the other pieces: "Exactly the same holds for language."[33]

This brings us to a major part of categories which are fundamental and central in modern linguistics, namely to *syntagmatic and paradigmatic relations*. A linguistic unit, Saussure pointed out, is related to the rest of the system within which it functions in two distinct ways. First, it has a *linear* relationship with other words or units with which it is chained together: "Combinations supported by linearity are *syntagms*."[34] In the phrase "a crown of thorns", the word "crown" stands in syntagmatic relationship to "a" and "of thorns"; just as in the phrase "God is righteous", "righteous" has a syntagmatic relation to "God is". From a semantic viewpoint, if "eat" stands in syntagmatic relationship to "bread", "meat" and "cheese" but not to "water", "tea", or "beer", this contributes to establishing its *meaning*, as the ingestion of solid food.

The *paradigmatic* relation was called by Saussure an *associative* relation, although writers in linguistics prefer the former term. This is the relation between a word or linguistic unit and another such unit which is *not* present in the actual utterance, but which might have been chosen *in its place*. In the phrase "a crown of thorns" the words "laurel" or "gold" could have been slotted in, in place of "thorns". Thus "thorns" stands in a paradigmatic relation to "laurel", "gold", "silver", and so on. In "God is righteous", the word "righteous" stands in paradigmatic relation to "good", or "merciful". This principle is so important that John Lyons states that one of the two "defining characteristics" of modern structural linguistics is the axiom that "linguistic units have no validity independently of their paradigmatic and syntagmatic relations with other units".[35]

The relevance of this principle to New Testament interpretation has been conclusively demonstrated by Erhardt Güttgemanns and by Kenneth L. Burres.[36] Güttgemanns, for example, shows how the meaning of "righteousness" in Romans turns partly on its syntagmatic relations to "of God" (Θεοῦ) and "on the basis of faith" (ἐκ πίστεως). Burres discusses the meaning of "reveal" (ἀποκαλύπτω) partly in terms of its syntagmatic or "syntactic" relations to "righteousness of God", "wrath of God", and other phrases; partly in terms of its paradigmatic or "paratactic" relations to φανερόω and its two-way relations (for example, in 1 Cor. 14:6) to γνῶσις and προφητεία. The aim in the case of Burres' work is to build up a semantic field of terms relevant to the semantic value of "reveal" in Paul.

The notion of paradigmatic relations is connected with the semantic axiom that meaning implies *choice*. For example, "pound" (weight) draws part of its meaning from the fact that it functions to *exclude* ton, stone, ounce, or dram. It also draws part of its meaning from its syntactic relation to butter, cheese, or apples. On the other hand, "pound" (money) draws part of its meaning from its paradigmatic relation to 50p, 100p

---

[33] Ibid., p.89; cf. p.110.

[34] Ibid., p.123.

[35] J. Lyons, *Introduction to Theoretical Linguistics*, p.75. Similarly, cf. R.H. Robins, *General Linguistics. An Introductory Survey* (London, 1964), pp.47–50; David Crystal, *Linguistics* (London, 1971), pp.163–6; and Herbert E. Breckle, *Semantik. Ein Einführung in die sprachwissenschaftlich Bedeutungslehre* (Munich, 1972), pp.81–8.

[36] E. Güttgemanns, *Studia Linguistica Neotestamentica*, especially pp.75–93; and K.L. Burres, op. cit., pp.59–123.

or £5, and part of its meaning from its syntagmatic relation to "pay me a" or "change for a". Thus Güttgemanns examines the paradigmatic relations of "righteousness of God" to "power of God" and "wrath of God", as well as its syntagmatic relations to "on the basis of faith" and "on the basis of law". Similarly the meaning of κατὰ σάρκα depends not only on its syntagmatic relation to Ἰσραήλ ("earthly" Israel) or σοφοί (wise according to "human standards"), but also on its paradigmatic relation to κατὰ πνεῦμα (spirit).

Sausure's notion of "associative fields", which depends largely on paradigmatic relations, thus provides a way into the task of mapping out a semantic field. K.L. Burres uses both syntagmatic and paradigmatic relations to map the semantic field surrounding Paul's uses of words that mean "to reveal".[37]

In view of the importance of the field, Barr and Burres each supports Trier's point that a word has meaning not autonomously or independently but "only as part of the whole" (*nur als Teil des Ganzen*), that is, only within a field (*im Feld*).[38] All the same, criticisms about words as units of meaning should not be taken too far. No less an authority than G. Stern has written: "There is no getting away from the fact that single words have more or less permanent meanings, that they actually do refer to certain referents, and not to others, and that this characteristic is the indispensable basis of all communication."[39] Or as Stephen Ullmann puts it, more moderately, "There is usually in each word a hard core of meaning which is relatively stable and can only be modified by the context within certain limits."[40] Word-studies, then, are not to be dismissed as valueless.

When James Barr ruthlessly criticizes many of the articles in G. Kittel's multi-volume *Theological Dictionary of the New Testament*, it might be tempting to imagine that he is mainly attacking the method of word-study. But word-study *as such* is not his main target of criticism. His real complaint is against what he calls "*illegitimate totality transfer*".[41] This occurs when the semantic value of a word as it occurs in *one context* is *added* to its semantic value in *another context*; and the process is continued until the *sum* of these semantic values is then *read into a particular case*.

Barr illustrates this fallacy with reference to the meaning of ἐκκλησία, church, in the New Testament: "If we ask 'What is the meaning of ἐκκλησία in the New Testament?' the answer may be an adding or compounding of different statements about the ἐκκλησία in various passages. Thus we might say (a) 'the Church is the Body of Christ' (b) 'the Church is the first instalment of the Kingdom of God' (c) 'the Church is the Bride of Christ', and other such statements."[42] In *one* sense Barr concedes, this is the "meaning" of "church". But it is certainly *not* "the meaning of 'church' *in Matt. 16.18*", yet preachers and expositors often lump together the meanings of words drawn from various different contexts, and "expound" them as the meaning of the word in a given verse. Barr quite successfully shows, for example, that Grundmann commits this error in his article on ἀγαθός, "good", in Kittel's *Dictionary*.

---

[37] K.L. Burres, op. cit., pp.107–23 and 222–307; cf. especially charts 5–7 on pp.282–3, 291 and 294–7.

[38] Trier, *Der Deutsche Wortschatz im Sinnbezirk des Verstandes* (Heidelberg, 1931), p.6.

[39] G. Stern, *Meaning and Change of Meaning: With Special Reference to the English Language* (Göteborgs Högskolas Arsskrift, 38, Gothenburg, 1931), p.85.

[40] S. Ullmann, *Semantics*, p.49.

[41] Ibid. p.218.

[42] Ibid.

This error stands in complete contrast to the principles elucidated in modern linguistics after Saussure by Eugene A. Nida and by Martin Joos in particular. Nida asserts, "The correct meaning of any term is that which contributes least to the total context."[43] For example we might define the semantic values of "green" in several ways: as a colour, as meaning inexperienced, as meaning unripe, and so on. Similarly, we might define "house" as a dwelling, lineage, and a business establishment. But as soon as we place "green" and "house" in syntagmatic relation to each other, we minimize the semantic values of each, so that "green" can only be a colour, and "house" only a dwelling. In the case of "greenhouse" the contribution of "green" almost disappears. Yet if "green house" were a phrase in the New Testament, we could imagine an expositor exploring the supposed "richness" of each term separately, and then adding together the components into one great theological compound.

On the other hand Martin Joos calls it "semantic axiom number one" that in defining a word it must be made to "contribute least to the total message desirable from the passage where it is at home, rather than e.g. defining it according to some presumed etymology or semantic history".[44] Nida concludes, "Words do not carry with them all the meanings which they may have in other sets of co-occurrences."[45] Thus, in a balanced comment on the whole question of word-meaning, R.H. Robins adds that words may be convenient units about which to state meanings *provided that* it is borne in mind that words have meaning by virtue of their employment in sentences ... and that the meaning of a sentence is not to be thought of as a sort of summation of the meaning of its component words taken individually".[46]

III.3 Conventionality in Language and its Connection with Structuralism

Saussure was certainly not the first to show what he called "the arbitrary nature of the sign" in language. "No-one", he writes, "disputes the principles of the arbitrary nature of the sign, but it is often easier to discover a truth than to assign to it its proper place." What was distinctive about Saussure's assessment was, first, that he described it as the very first principle in language-study, which "dominates all the linguistics of language; its consequences are numberless".[47] Secondly, the far-reaching effects of this principle on the relationship between language and thought, or between words and concepts, emerge clearly only against the background of structuralism. Saussure's structural approach, we have seen, calls in question a semantics that is based entirely on the word as a unit of meaning. This now enables us to expose what Barr has called the one-word/one concept fallacy, and also to challenge the drawing of inferences about national "thought" made on the basis of linguistic distinctions which turn out to be arbitrary.

---

[43] E.A. Nida, "The Implications of Contemporary Linguistics for Biblical Scholarship", in *JBL* 91 (1972), p.86 (cf. pp.73–89).

[44] M. Joos, "Semantic Axiom Number One", in *Language* 48 (1972), p.257 (cf. pp.258–65, in which Joos acknowledges his indebtedness for this approach to Stern).

[45] E.A. Nida, loc. cit., p.86.

[46] R.H. Robins, *General Linguistics*, p.22.

[47] F. de Saussure, op. cit., p.68 (cf. édition critique, pp.152–3).

There are everyday phenomena in language that make it clear that the relations between language and the world depend in many respects on arbitrary or conventional factors rather than on "nature" or even logic. These include *homonymy* (when two words of different meanings have the same form, for example, "he *left* me", as against "turn *left*"); *polysemy* (when one word has multiple meanings, for example, "*board* and lodging", "*board* of directors", "*board* from the floor"); *opaqueness* in vocabulary (for example, in contrast to the transparent meaning of onomatopoeia), and diachronic *change* in language.[48] Saussure, however, points simply to the very basic fact of differences both in vocabulary and in grammar between different languages, when logically the same semantic value is involved. The relation between the French word *soeur* and a sister is no more "natural", "inner", or "logical" than it is in the case of the German *Schwester* or the English *sister*. Similarly, in terms of grammar, in the sentence *ces gants sont bon marché*, "these gloves are cheap", *bon marché* functions logically or semantically as an adjective, but is not an adjective from the arbitrary viewpoint of grammar.[49] (We have already referred, in philosophy, to the parallel observations of Russell about such phrases as "the present King of France", or "a round square".) Further, in terms of morphology, *bon marché* is composed of two words that correspond to the one word "cheap". Even the limits of the word as a unit have an arbitrary element. In Latin and in Greek *amo* and φιλῶ or ἀγαπῶ must be translated by two words in English and in German, "I love," and "*ich liebe*". Saussure concludes, "The division of words into substantives, verbs, adjectives, etc., is not an undeniable linguistic reality."[50]

We have already noted some of the fallacies involved in logico-grammatical parallelism. The other side of the coin is the equally misguided attempt to draw inferences about the distinctive thought of a people, for example, about "Hebrew thought" or "Greek thought", on the basis of its grammatical categories. Eugene A. Nida writes:

> The idea that the Hebrew people had a completely different view of time because they had a different verbal system does not stand up under investigation. It would be just as unfounded to claim that people of the English-speaking world have lost interest in sex because the gender distinctions in nouns and adjectives have been largely eliminated, or that Indo-Europeans are very time conscious because in many languages there are tense-distinctions in the verbs. But no people seem more time-orientated than the Japanese, and their verbal system is not too different from the aspectual structures of Hebrew. Furthermore, few people are so little interested in time as some of the tribes in Africa, many of whose languages have far more time distinctions than any Indo-European language has.[51]

J. Pedersen, T. Boman and G.A.F. Knight are among the many biblical scholars who have made pronouncements about "Hebrew thought" on the basis of grammatical categories.

---

[48] Cf. A.C. Thiselton, "The Supposed Power of Words in the Biblical Writings", *JTS* 25 (1974), pp.283–99; J. Lyons, *Introduction to Theoretical Linguistics*, pp.4–8, 59–75, 272 and 403; S. Ullmann, *Semantics*, pp.80–115; L.R. Palmer, op. cit., pp.175–8; E.A. Nida, *Towards a Science of Translating* (Leiden, 1964), pp.46–51; P. Naert, "Arbitraire et nécessaire en linguistique", in *Studia Linguistica* (1947), pp.5–10.

[49] Saussure, op. cit., p.109.

[50] Ibid., p.100.

[51] E.A. Nida, "The Implications of Contemporary Linguistics for Biblical Scholarship", loc. cit., p.83.

Knight, for example, asserts, "The Hebrew almost invariably thought in terms of the concrete. There are few abstract nouns in the Hebrew language."[52] T. Boman argues, again mainly on the basis of a grammatical and morphological investigation of linguistic categories, that Israelite thinking is "dynamic, vigorous, passionate" while "Greek thinking is static, peaceful, moderate, and harmonious."[53] For example, he claims that even stative verbs in Hebrew express an activity rather than portray a static state of affairs. Some of his most extreme arguments occur in connection with quantity and number. The so-called "concept of number" is arrived at in Greek and in modern thinking in terms of visual representation. But the distinctive "concept" in Hebrew is evident from the "meaning" of the word "*two*": "*Shenayim* comes from the verb *shanah* – double, repeat, do for the second time. Thus the Hebrews form the concept of number not, as we do, through visual perception, but through frequent repetition of the same motion."[54] Similarly, the two words for "small" come from verbal forms meaning "to diminish", "to become less"; the word *min* which expresses "more than" in comparative degree really means "away from". Boman actually concludes "Number or quantitive variety is thus not something spatial and quantitive."[55] When Saul is said to be "taller than" all the people, he dynamically towers over and "away from" the others!

However, not only is this to argue on the basis of a supposed logico-grammatical parallelism, it is also to compound this particular error with further arguments of a diachronic or even etymological nature, and to ignore the role of context in semantics. If, for example, *min* means "away from" in *many* contexts, its context *in a comparison* restricts its semantic value to "more than". On the one hand, Boman's method flies in the face of structuralism; on the other hand, as Barr concludes, "Boman's kind of interpretation of language ... depends to a great extent on the logico-grammatical unclarities of the older grammar, and evaporates with the stricter method of modern linguistics".[56] This is not to say that all of Boman's conclusions are wrong. For sometimes, as Barr admits, he expresses an insight that may have independent value as an *exegetical* observation.[57] Barr does not dispute that Hebrew uses of language may *sometimes* be more "dynamic" than Greek or English near-equivalents. The error, however, is to attempt to base such conclusions on dubious linguistic arguments which ignore structuralism and conventionality in language, and Barr has performed a valuable service in subjecting this approach to systematic criticism.

This brings us to a fundamental principle in semantics, about the relationship between language and "concepts". Commenting on claims made about the Hebrew or Greek "mind" or "way of thinking", David Crystal makes a crucial observation. He writes:

> One often hears statements of the form "Language X has a word for it, but Y has not, therefore X can say something Y cannot", or "X is a better language than Y". This fallacy stems from the misconception ... that the unit of translation-equivalence

---

52 G.A.F. Knight, *A Biblical Approach to the Doctrine of the Trinity* (Edinburgh, 1953), p.8.
53 T. Boman, *Hebrew Thought compared with Greek* (London, 1960), p.27.
54 Ibid., p.165.
55 Ibid.
56 J. Barr, op. cit., p.67; cf. pp.46–88.
57 E.g. Boman's remarks about practical atheism in Psalm 14:1, op. cit., pp.48–9.

between languages is the word ... *The fact that Y has no word for an object does not mean that it cannot talk about that object; it cannot use the same mechanical means to do so, but it can utilize alternative forms of expression in its own structure for the same end.*[58]

The implication that is made by the vast majority of writers in linguistics is that, in John Lyons' words, "No language can be said to be intrinsically 'richer' than another – each is adapted to the characteristic pursuits of its users."[59] The number of classifications under which "life" or "the world" could be described is virtually infinite. The distinctions that already exist within a given language, then, reflect only those that have hitherto in the past been of importance for that particular culture. But they do not absolutely *determine* the limits of what can be said in the future, for example by a creative thinker within that culture, or by a translator. This is not entirely to deny that there may be *some* element of truth in the well-known hypothesis of B.L. Whorf, based on the outlook of Wilhelm von Humboldt, that the structure of a language may influence a culture in terms of its thought. For, first, the translation or expression of certain ideas may be made *easier or more difficult* by the presence of this or that distinction, or lack of distinction, already to hand in a language. Second, *habits* of language-*use* make certain ways of thinking easier or more difficult in the sense shown by Wittgenstein. But difficulty does not mean impossibility. Max Black has demonstrated the weaknesses of the Whorf hypothesis, among others in several discussions.[60] Even so-called primitive languages are, as Edward Sapir admits (in the words of David Crystal) "not better or worse; only different".[61]

Biblical scholars, however, have been quick to draw far-reaching conclusions about Hebrew or Greek "thought" on the basis of vocabulary-stock. John Paterson, for example, makes the far-fetched statement that the ancient Israelite was "economical of words", because "Hebrew speech has less than 10,000 words while Greek has 200,000. Thus a word to the Hebrew was something ... to be expended carefully". He was a man of few words, for "He knew there was power in words and that such power must not be used indiscriminately."[62] I have tried to expose the fallaciousness of this whole approach in the study to which I have referred on the supposed power of words in the biblical writings.

James Barr has little difficulty in citing and criticizing what he calls "arguments of the 'the Greeks had a word for it' type which so proliferate in Biblical theology".[63] For example, J.A.T. Robinson writes, "If we ask why it was that the Jews here (i.e. in language about "flesh" and "body") made do with one word (*basar*) where the Greeks required two (σάρξ and σῶμα) we come up against some of the most fundamental assumptions of Hebraic thinking about man." The difference in vocabulary-stock shows, according to Robinson, "that the Hebrews never posed, like the Greeks, certain questions the answer

---

[58] D. Crystal, *Language, Linguistics and Religion*, p.144 (my italics).

[59] J. Lyons, *Introduction to Theoretical Linguistics*, p.45.

[60] Cf. M. Black, *The Labyrinth of Language*, pp.63–90; and "Linguistic Relativity. The Views of Benjamin Lee Whorf", in *Philosophical Review* 68 (1959), pp.228–38; cf. also S. Ullmann, "Words and Concepts", in *Language and Style* (Oxford, 1964), pp.212–28.

[61] D. Crystal, *Linguistics*, p.72; cf. p.49.

[62] J. Paterson, *The Book that is Alive, Studies in Old Testament Life and Thought as Set Forth by Hebrew Sages* (New York, 1954), p.3.

[63] J. Barr, op. cit., p.35; cf. pp.21–45.

to which would have forced them to differentiate the 'body' from the 'flesh'".[64] Barr comments, "This statement could not have been written except in a total neglect of linguistic semantics."[65] It may be that this criticism should be softened in the light of the half-truth represented by the Whorf hypothesis. But the main force of Barr's criticism is undoubtedly correct.

Barr also criticizes the methodological procedure of Kittel's *Theological Dictionary of the New Testament* according to which in effect, "the *lexical*-stock of N.T. Greek can be closely correlated with the *concept*-stock of the early Christians".[66] The *Dictionary* is a dictionary, in practice, of *words*; but it purports to be a "*concept*-history" (*Begriffsgeschichte*). Thus a contributor writes not about "the Greek word – but "the Greek concept". The temptation to which this leads is to commit the "illegitimate totality transfer" (which we described and discussed in section III.1). Since words and concepts do not necessarily correspond with each other isomorphically, such ambiguity of terms can only be misleading, and the confusion becomes still worse when some German scholars use *Begriff* to mean both "concept" and "word".

III.4 Langue *and* Parole

The distinction between *langue* and *parole*, so important for Saussure, has been taken up in connection with the form criticism of the gospels by Erhardt Güttgemanns. According to Saussure, language (either *langue* or, in a different sense *langage*, cf. *Sprache*) must not be confused with speech or actual speaking (*parole*, cf. *sprechen*). *Langue* "is both a social product of the faculty of speech and a collection of necessary conventions that have been adopted by a social body to permit individuals to exercise that faculty". It is inherited within the community; and is "the sum of word-images stored in the minds of all individuals ... a *storehouse* filled by the members of *a given community* ... Language is not complete in any (individual) speaker, it exists perfectly only within a collectivity." *Langue* is thus the language-system which, as it were, waits in readiness for acts of speech. By contrast, *parole* is "the executive side of speaking ... an individual act".[67]

Parole, the actual concrete act of speaking on the part of an individual, is the only object directly available for study by the linguist, although from its study he draws inferences about the structure of a *langue*. In his work on form criticism E. Güttgemanns stresses the sociological and communal character of a *langue*, in contrast to the individual origin of *paroles*.[68] The *paroles* of the individual are objectified in written forms, for only an individual can do the actual writing. On the other hand the written *paroles* reflect the *oral* tradition of the *langue* of the community. One of Güttgemanns's points is that just as *langue* should not be confused with *parole*, so the "laws" which apply to the growth of oral traditions should not be made to apply to forms which already have been committed to writing by individuals. He believes that traditional form criticism in Germany has not

---

[64]   J.A.T. Robinson, *The Body, A Study in Pauline Theology* (London, 1952), pp.12 and 13.
[65]   J. Barr, op. cit., p.35.
[66]   Ibid., p.207; cf. pp.206–19.
[67]   Saussure, op. cit., pp.9 and 13–14 (my italics); cf. H.E. Brekle, *Semantik*, pp.50–54.
[68]   E. Güttgemanns, *Offene Fragen zur Formgeschichte*, pp.50–54.

been careful enough in keeping apart (1) written forms, individual speech, *parole*, and (2) oral forms, the language of the social community, *langue*.

One consequence of Saussure's distinction between *langue* and *parole* is of interest to the New Testament interpreter. We have already stressed in connection with paradigmatic relations (in section III.2) that "meaning is choice". The interpreter cannot know how much significance to attach to an author's use of word *x* until he also knows *what alternatives were available* to him at the same time. It is often said, for example, that the choice of ἀγαπῶ and ἀγάπη to mean "love" in the New Testament is especially significant because Christian writers chose them in preference to ἐρῶ and ἔρως and also to φιλῶ and φιλία. Supposedly *agapē* is a discerning and creative love; *erōs* is a passionate love which seeks self-gratification; whilst *philia* is a more general word for solicitous love or kindly inclination. But before we can say with certainty that a New Testament writer "chooses" to use ἀγάπη we must first establish whether the other two words for love were genuinely live options in the contexts concerned. It is not enough to ask whether different words for "love" might be available in first-century Greek in general. In this respect a lexicon may even be misleading. We must also ask: what words for love were available for use in the linguistic repertoire of the New Testament writer in question? Words may perhaps exist in Greek of which he is unaware, or for which he has a personal dislike for any of a variety of reasons. It would then be thoroughly misleading to argue that he has chosen word *x* as against *these*.

IV

Other Basic Tools in Field Semantics, Linguistics and Philosophy

IV.1 Tools in Field Semantics, Types of Opposition and Synonymy

We have already seen the principle laid down by J. Trier that a word has meaning "only as part of the whole ... it yields a meaning only within a field" (*nur im Feld gibt es Bedeutung*). Following the implications suggested by Saussure's structuralism, the task of the semanticist, as Trier saw it, was to set up lexical systems or sub-systems (*Wortfelder*) in terms of semantic relations of sameness or *similarity* of meaning (synonymy); of opposition or *incompatibility* of meaning (antonymy or complementarity), and of a special kind of *inclusiveness* of meaning (hyponymy) as where one word expresses a class ("furniture") to which the items belong ("chair", "table"). In broad outline this describes the programme of field semantics.[69]

E.A. Nida has suggested that more use should be made of the methods of field semantics in Biblical lexicology. He writes, "Quite new approaches to lexicology must be introduced ... Critical studies of meaning must be based primarily upon the analysis of *related meanings of different words*, not upon the *different meanings of single words*."[70]

---

[69] Cf. J. Trier, op. cit., pp.6ff. I am not concerned to draw too careful a distinction between the "linguistic field" (*sprachliches Feld*) of Trier and the "semantic field" (*Bedeutungsfeld*) of Ipsen or Porzig. For the distinction see S. Ullmann, *The Principles of Semantics*, pp.156–69; cf. also J. Lyons, *Structural Semantics*, pp.44–50.

[70] E.A. Nida, "The Implications of Contemporary Linguistics for Biblical Scholarship", loc. cit., p.85 (my italics), cf. also E. Güttgemanns, *Offene Fragen zur Formgeschichte des Evangeliums*, pp.54–7.

According to the traditional method, the lexicographer would take a word such as "run", for example, and distinguish in terms of its syntagmatic relations, that is, (1) running along the road, (2) running a business, (3) a run on the bank, and so on. But the method in field semantics would be to compare "run" in the first sense with words to which it stood in paradigmatic relation, such as "walk", "skip", "crawl"; and to compare "run" in the second sense with "control", "operate" and "direct". In this way a "field" very much like Saussure's "associative field", or system of paradigmatic relations, may be constructed.

The traditional attention to syntagmatic relations in lexicology is in fact *complementary* to newer methods. In New Testament Greek, a traditional lexicon-entry under πνεῦμα for example, would distinguish between (1) wind or breath, (2) men's spirit, (3) the Spirit of God, and (4) spirit-beings. The "field" approach would examine the first category in relation to ἄνεμος, πνέω and λαῖλαψ; the second category in relation to σάρξ, ψυχή σῶμα, and so on. The diagram below illustrates how the two approaches can be complementary.

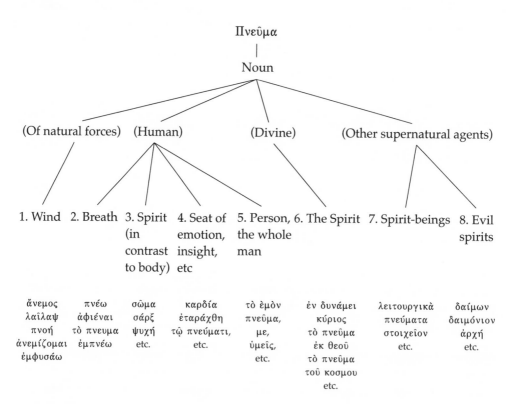

Katz and Foder put forward a comparable system of lexicology, in which they call the first explanatory term (noun) a *grammatical* marker; the second set of terms (for example, human, divine) *semantic* markers; and the third set of subdivisions within the semantic markers (for example, mind, breath) semantic *distinguishers*. I have then added Greek words that *commence* the construction of a semantic field.

We must now look more closely at different type of *opposition*. In a whole book devoted to the subject C.K. Ogden lists some twenty or so examples, much of which involve a distinctive type of semantic opposition.[71] The basic distinction, however, is between what he calls opposition by cut and opposition by scale. The sharpest type of opposition by cut is the relation of two-way exclusion known as *complementarity*. The denial of the one involves the assertion of the other, and vice versa. Paul sets the word χάριτι "by grace", in opposition to ἐξ ἔργων "by works" in this way in Romans 11:6 – "grace" and "works" derive their *semantic* value from their very relation of complementarity. Thus Paul writes, "if it is by grace, it is no longer on the basis of works; otherwise grace would no longer be *grace*". Similarly E. Güttgemanns attempts to shed light on δικαιοσύνη θεοῦ, righteousness of God, in Romans 1 by showing that in that chapter it stands in a relation of opposition to ὀργὴ θεοῦ, wrath of God.[72]

Not every kind of opposition functions in this way, however. What is strictly termed a relation of *antonymy* is a one-way relation of opposition that is relative and gradable by scale. Romans 5:6–8 illustrates this kind of opposition. To say that a man is "good" (ἀγαθός) is to deny that he is positively bad. On the other hand, to say that he is "not good" does not entail "he is bad". For "good" may stand in contrast to "law-abiding" (δίκαιος) and a man may be law-abiding but neither good nor bad. Similarly in the Gospels a "great" crowd or a "large" crowd stands in opposition to a "small" crowd; but a crowd that is "not large" need not be small. The type of opposition involved in grading-words like "good" and "great" is different from that entailed by such terms as "grace" and "works". In an article published elsewhere I have tried to unravel the complex semantic relationship between πνεῦμα, spirit, and σάρξ, flesh.[73] In certain contexts, to live according to the Spirit stands in a relation of complementarity to living according to the flesh (cf. Rom. 8:9, 12). On the other hand, whilst the Corinthian believers are in some sense men of the Spirit (1 Cor. 2:6–16, 12–14) in another sense Paul refuses to accept their inference that therefore they are "not fleshly" (3:1–4).

One more type of opposition deserves attention, namely that of *converseness*. "Buy" and "sell" stand normally in a relation of converseness, for if *a* buys *x* from *b*, it can be said that *b* sells *x* to *a*. But when Paul says in 1 Cor. 6:19 that Christians are "bought" (ἀγοράζω) with a price, we cannot transform this into a converse sentence using "sell". The semantic application here is the warning that theological uses of ἀγοράζω entail a slightly different *meaning* from "buy" in ordinary commercial contexts.

---

[71] C.K. Ogden, *Opposition: A Linguistic and Psychological Analysis*, (Bloomington 1967[2]), especially pp.65–90. On the three most basic types of opposition, however, see J. Lyons, *Introduction to Theoretical Linguistics*, pp.460–70.

[72] E. Güttgemanns, *Studia Linguistica Neotestamentica*, pp.87–93. On antithesis in Paul see especially Norbert Schneider, *Die rhetorische Eigenart der paulinischen Antithese* (Tübingen, 1970); J. Nélis, "Les Antitheses litteraires dans les épîtres de S. Paul", in *Nouvells Revue Théologique* 70 (1948), pp.360–87; J. Weiss, "Beiträge zur Paulinischen Rhetorik" in *Theologische Studien Bernhard Weiss* (Göttingen, 1897), pp.165–247; and Willard H. Taylor, "The Antithetic Method in Pauline Theology" (unpublished doctoral dissertation for Northwestern University, Evanston, IL, 1959).

[73] A.C. Thiselton, "The Meaning of Σάρξ in 1 Corinthians 5:5: A Fresh Approach in the Light of Logical and Semantic Factors", in *SJT* 26 (1973), pp.204–28; Essay 11 in this volume.

There are also different types and degrees of *synonymy*, or sameness or likeness of meaning. Absolute, total and complete synonymy is extremely rare in ordinary language. Absolute synonyms, if they do exist, are usually technical terms from areas such as medicine; perhaps "semantics" and "semasiology" are absolute synonyms. The major test of synonymy is *interchangeability*. S. Ullmann writes, "Only those words can be described as synonymous which can replace each other in any given context, without the slightest alteration either in cognitive or emotive import."[74]

A moment's reflection will disclose two principles. First, most so-called synonyms are *context-dependent*. In many contexts "jump" is synonymous with "leap"; but we do not say "that noise made me leap". "Sick" often means the same as "ill"; but we do not talk about a bird of sick omen, nor say that we are ill of repeating the same thing. Similarly in New Testament Greek καινός and νέος are clearly synonymous when both mean "new" as applied to the "covenant" (διαθήκη, for example, cf. Heb. 8:8 with Heb. 12:24); but a writer would not presumably speak of καινὸν φύραμα (dough) or of a young man as καινός. It could be misleading, then, to answer "yes" or "no" to the simple question: are καινός and νέος synonyms? The semanticist will ask, rather: in what kinds of context, if any, are they synonymous?

Second, many words are synonymous with others at a cognitive level, but not in emotive terms or in terms of register. We might write to "decline" an invitation, but hardly to "reject" it; yet it is difficult to see any great difference between them in cognitive scope. "Decease" is more formal and professional than "death"; whilst "passed on", "popped off", "was called to higher service" and "kicked the bucket" all have their own special overtones. Similarly in certain contexts Mark's κράβαττος, mattress, may be cognitively synonymous with Matthew and Luke's κλίνη, bed; but the colloquial overtones of Mark's word are deemed inappropriate by Matthew and Luke. Sometimes similar actions or attitudes can be described by terms suggesting overtones of moral approval or blame. Thus Bertrand Russell begins his well-known "emotive conjugations" as follows: "I am firm, you are obstinate, he is pig-headed ... I have reconsidered, you have changed your mind, he has gone back on his word." "Reasoning" in the New Testament can be alluded to with overtones of disapproval (διαλογισμός) or either neutrally or with approval (cf. νόημα, νοῦς).

Three further comments may be made about synonymy. First, another test of context-dependent synonymy can be provided by antonymy. "Wide" is a synonym of "broad", for example, in contexts in which "narrow" would be applicable: a narrow plank or a narrow road. But we do not talk about a narrow accent; only of a broad one. "Deep" and "profound" thought stand in opposition to "shallow" thought; but the opposite to a deep voice is a high one.

Second, synonymy may be explored in diachronic linguistics. Sometimes over a period of many years two words may move more closely together in meaning, and if they

---

[74] S. Ullmann, *The Principles of Semantics*, pp.108–9; cf. pp.110–14, and *Semantics*, pp.141–55 and J. Lyons, *Introduction to Theoretical Linguistics*, pp.446–53. From the philosophical side cf. W.P. Alston, op. cit., pp.44–7; J. Searle, op. cit., pp.5–12, N. Goodman, "A Note on Likeness of Meaning", in *Analysis* 10 (1950), pp.115–8; and other contributions in *Analysis* by Rollins and Thomson, in 11 (1951), pp.18–19, 38–45 and 12 (1952), pp.73–6.

become total synonyms one may eventually disappear. David Clines has shown in an unpublished study that this happens to ἀγαθός and καλός. In classical Greek they are distinct, ἀγαθός being reserved mainly for moral goodness; in New Testament Greek they are usually synonymous; in modern Greek ἀγαθός has disappeared. Sometimes, however, the procedure may be reversed, and what were once synonyms may develop in different directions.

Third, synonymy raises questions of style. Many writers call on similar terms, for example, simply to avoid repetition of the same word.[75] In such contexts similar terms may become more clearly synonymous. It is likely that this is the case, for example, with ἀγαπῶ and φιλῶ in John 21:15–17.

IV.2 Types of Vagueness and Metaphor

Certain kinds of vagueness are useful and desirable. Language would be impoverished if we could never talk about "furniture", but only about chairs and tables; or never talk about something's being "red", without specifying whether we mean crimson or scarlet; or never talk about "flowers" without explicating whether we mean tulips, roses, or a mixture of both. When the New Testament interpreter comes across a superordinate term like κακία, badness, *it is a mistake to insist on a greater degree of precision than that suggested by the text.* I have argued this point in two articles, one with reference to the applications of the parables, the other with reference to the meaning of σάρξ in 1 Cor. 5:5.[76]

One type of vagueness is due to lack of *specificity*, of which superordinate terms supply some, but not all, examples. A skilful politician may retain universal support, for example, if he promises to "take steps" to meet a crisis; he loses some votes if he is forced to specify *what* steps. Another type of vagueness is due to lack of clear *cut-off* point on a scale. Words like "urban", "warm" and "middle-aged" are very useful, not least because they are *not* quantified precisely like "above 60°F" or "between 39 and 61 years old."

A third type of vagueness is that of *polymorphous* concepts, which are of special interest in philosophy. [We devote a brief essay to this in the present volume (Essay 12); hence we abbreviate the paragraphs of this essay in its original form.] The meaning of a word of this type cannot be given in generalizing terms, but only as different meanings apply by way of example in different contexts. Ludwig Wittgenstein, Gilbert Ryle and others insist that we cannot say in general what "thinking" *is*; only give examples of the application of the term in specific situations. G.E.M. Anscombe examines the logic of "intention" in this way, and A.R. White underlines the polymorphous character of "attention". What attending *is* depends on what we are attending *to*. It seems likely, to my mind, that πίστις, faith, has this polymorphous character, especially in Paul. Depending on the situation or context it may involve intellectual assent, or practical obedience; it may stand eschatologically in contrast to sight; or mean a Christ-centred appropriation of God's gift. (See Essay 12.)

---

[75] See S. Ullmann, *Semantics*, pp.152–3.

[76] A.C. Thiselton, "The Parables as Language-Event. Some Comments on Fuchs's Hermeneutics in the Light of Linguistic Philosophy", in *SJT* 23 (1970), especially pp.450–58 and 461–7 [included in this present volume, Essay 24, especially Section VI]; and "The Meaning of Σάρξ in 1 Cor. 5:5", op. cit., especially pp.207–8, 217–18 and 227–8 .

However, other types of vagueness may play a positive role. Too often in biblical interpretation exegetes have looked for exactness where the author chose vagueness. *Must* the "horrifying abomination" in Mark 13:14 refer specifically to the violence of the zealots, or to a statue of Titus, or to Caligula or Hadrian? Must "Son of man" be robbed of an ambiguity that may have commended the term to Jesus? Might not the New Testament writers have wished to keep some ideas open-ended no less often than we do?

We must also glance briefly at *metaphor*, which is not unrelated to questions about vagueness. A live metaphor presupposes a well-established use of language (often popularly called the "literal" meaning) and then extends this use in a way that is novel or logically odd. The aim of this extension is twofold. First, it sets up a tension that is intended to provoke the hearer into some reaction; second, it provides a model, or picture, or frame of reference, according to which the hearer now "sees" the point in question in a new way. It should be stressed, however, that this happens only when a metaphor is genuinely "live". Most metaphors very soon become dead metaphors. This is one crucial difficulty confronting the New Testament interpreter about biblical metaphors. The well-known metaphor of the Christian's armour in Ephesians 6:14–17 has become a dead metaphor, or even a mere analogy or simile, because a term like "sword of the spirit" has itself become an established use of language. Sometimes a new translation will recapture some force by replacing an old metaphor by a new but closely related one. Thus "gird up the loins of your mind" in 1 Peter 1:13 becomes "stripped for action" in the NEB. On the other hand "anchor of the soul" (Heb. 6:19), "fed you with milk" (1 Cor. 3:2) and "living stones" (1 Pet. 2:5) still retain an element of their original tension without alteration.

The interpreter must steer a very careful path between evaporating the *force* of a metaphor by total explication, and leaving its meaning open to doubt. If a metaphor is already dead even in the New Testament, no harm is done by erring on the side of clarity. Thus "hand of the Lord" (Acts 11:21) becomes "the Lord's power" in *Today's English Version;* and "pass from me this cup" (Luke 22:42) becomes "free me from having to suffer this trial" in the Spanish *Version Popular.* But it is a different matter when the metaphor is a live one. It is difficult to justify, for example, the rendering of Paul's "put on Christ" (Gal. 3:27) by "take upon themselves the qualities of Christ himself" (*Today's English Version*). A metaphor is to make the hearer think for himself, often by means of some deliberate ambiguity. It gives us something as a model for something else without making explicit in exactly what way it is supposed to be a model.[77] We could say of metaphor what F. Waismann says of poetry: "Its mission is to break through the wall of conventional values that encloses us, to startle us into seeing the world through fresh eyes."[78] If metaphor is eliminated or turned into simile, as W. L. Wonderly recommends as a "basic technique" of popular Bible translation, this entire dimension is lost.[79]

---

[77] W.P. Alston, *Philosophy of Language* (Englewood Cliffs, NJ, 1964), op. cit., p.102.

[78] F. Waismann, "The Resources of Language", in M. Black (ed.), *The Importance of Language* (Englewood Cliffs, NJ, 1962), p.116.

[79] W. Wonderly, op. cit., pp.121–8.

The literature on metaphor is extensive.[80] It should warn us against ever talking about biblical metaphors as "mere" metaphors, as if to imply that metaphorical language is somehow inferior to non-metaphorical discourse. But it is also evident from this range of literature that there are different types of metaphors with different purposes; and that the line between metaphor and non-metaphor is not in fact a line but a continuous scale, passing through "dead" metaphor and merely figurative language such as metonymy or synecdoche. Robert Funk and Sallie TeSelle have argued that the parables of Jesus function as a metaphor; and in theology, especially with reference to Bultmann, it is crucial to distinguish between metaphor and myth.

IV.3 Some Effects of Recent Approaches in Linguistics

Ideally a comprehensive discussion of the present subject would include an examination of transformational grammar with special reference to the work of Noam Chomsky. However, in practice this area is far too complex and technical to allow for a brief summary in a few paragraphs. Our aim in this section, therefore, must be more modest. We shall attempt to describe and evaluate only the uses to which this approach has been put at the hands of those engaged in Bible translation. This concerns especially the work of Eugene A. Nida, who speaks enthusiastically of the insights of transformational grammar, and in particular draws on the technique of reducing the surface structure of stretches of language to its underlying kernels.

Nida and Taber write, "One of the most important insights coming from 'transformational grammar' is the fact that in all languages there are half a dozen to a dozen basic structures out of which all the more elaborate formations are constructed by means of so-called 'transformations'. In contrast, back-transformation, then, is the analytic process of reducing the surface structure to its underlying kernels."[81] We have already illustrated this principle by noting certain kernel forms behind Ephesians 1:7. Nida and Taber further cite the example of Ephesians 2:8, 9: "For by grace you have been saved through faith; and this is not your own doing, it is the gift of God – not because of works lest any man should boast." This can be reduced to seven kernel sentences: (1) God showed you grace; (2) God saved you; (3) you believed; (4) you did not save yourselves; (5) God gave it; (6) you did not work for it; (7) no man should boast.[82] The kernel sentences may in principle undergo further transformation in terms of what Chomsky calls "deep structure", but whilst this is of interest in theological linguistics Nida and

---

[80] The following selection is of special value: W.P. Alston, *Philosophy of Language*, pp.96–106; Mary A. McCloskey, "Metaphor", in *Mind* 73 (1964), pp.215–33; C.S. Lewis, "Bluspels and Flalansferes", and O. Barfield, "Poetic Diction and Legal Fiction", both in M. Black (ed.), *The Importance of Language*, pp.46–50, and 51–71; J. Pelc, *Studies in Functional Logical Semiotics of Natural Language*, pp.142–94; C.M. Turbayne, *The Myth of Metaphor* (New Haven, CT, 1962); Marcus B. Hester, *The Meaning of Poetic Metaphor. An Analysis in the Light of Wittgenstein's Claim that Meaning is Use* (The Hague, 1967), especially pp.114–92; M. Black, *Models and Metaphors* (New York, 1962), pp.25–47; and J. de Waard, "Biblical Metaphors and their Translation", in *the Bible Translaltor* 25 (1974), pp.107–16; cf. also V. Heylem, "Les Métaphores et les métonymies dans les Epîtres Pauliniennes", in *ETL* 8 (1935), pp.253–90.

[81] E.A. Nida and C.R. Taber, *The Theory and Practice of Translation* (Leiden, 1969), p.39. Cf. also E.A. Nida, *Towards a Science of Translating*.

[82] E.A. Nida and C.R. Taber, op. cit., pp.53–4.

Taber question its principal value for the Bible translator. The translator's task, they suggest, is first to reduce utterances to kernel sentences by "back-transformation" (if necessary making explicit any elements that are still ambiguous), and then at the end of the process to reformulate the kernels into a linguistic structure which best accords with a native speaker's understanding in the receptor language.

One merit of this approach is to demonstrate, once again, the arbitrariness of surface grammar and the fallacy of assumption about logico-grammatical parallelism. The surface grammar of the final translation may not necessarily correspond to the surface grammar of the original Greek. In this respect, translation is a creative task and not merely a mechanical one.

We must also note, however, that the contrast between surface grammar and deep grammar is used as a means of eliminating certain types of *ambiguity*. As long ago as 1924, Otto Jespersen noted the fundamental difference in structure between two such superficially parallel phrases as "the doctor's arrival" and "the doctor's house". The reason for the difference is that, in Chomsky's terms, "the doctor's arrival" derives from the transform "the doctor's arrived", which has the form NP/Vi (noun phrase/intransitive verb); whilst "the doctor's house" derives from the transform "the doctor has a house", which has the form NP/Vt//N^a (noun phrase/transitive verb//noun in the accusative).[83]

This example of transformational techniques is already employed, by implication, in New Testament exegesis and in traditional grammar. The traditional contrast between "objective genitive" and "subjective genitive" is usually explained in what amounts to transformational terms. In 1 Cor. 1:6, for example, the phrase "the testimony of Christ" (τὸ μαρτύριον τοῦ χριστοῦ) is, as it stands, ambiguous. If it is subjective genitive it derives from the transform "Christ testified", in which "Christ" is subject; if it is objective genitive it derives from the transform "Paul testifies to Christ", in which "Christ" is the (indirect) object. Similarly, as the phrase stands, "love of God" (ἡ ἀγάπη τοῦ Θεοῦ) in 1 John is ambiguous, and must be interpreted as deriving either from the transform "God loves ..." (subjective genitive), or from "... loves God" (objective genitive), it is a regular manoeuvre in *Today's English Version* to remove ambiguity of this kind by clearly reflecting one particular transform. Thus "light of the world" (Matt. 5:14) becomes "light for the world" (objective genitive, from "lights the world"), and "the promise of the Holy Spirit" (Acts 2:33) becomes "the Holy Spirit, as his Father had promised" (objective genitive, from the transform "the Father promised the Holy Spirit", excluding the alternative transform "the Holy Spirit promised").

Transformational grammar often seeks to make explicit elements of meaning that are implied, but not expressed, in a sentence. Chomsky comments, "Surface similarities may hide distinctions of a fundamental nature ... It may be necessary to guide and draw out the speaker's intuition in perhaps fairly subtle ways before we can determine what is the actual character of his knowledge."[84] This principle is of positive value in Bible translation, provided it is recognized that, once again, translation inevitably becomes *interpretation*. Sometimes it is possible that this technique of making linguistic elements

---

[83] N. Chomsky, *Aspects of the Theory of Syntax* (Cambridge, MA, 1965, rp. 1970), p.21. Cf. also J. Lyons, *Chomsky* (London, 1970), pp.47–82 and pp.247–69.

[84] N. Chomsky, op. cit., p. 24. Cf. pp.179–82, on "deletion".

explicit goes further than the text allows. Thus it is questionable whether *Today's English Version* is justified in translating καὶ Ἰδὼν ὁ Ἰησοῦς πίστιν αὐτῶν as "Jesus saw *how much* faith they had" (Mark 2.5). The RSV simply has "when Jesus saw their faith". But presumably the translators of *Today's English Version* would claim to be making explicit what *they judged* was implicit in the text.

One further point that *statistical* statements about word-occurrences may often be superficial or even misleading guides to the occurrence of actual concepts. K.L. Burres makes this point about "boasting" in Romans 3:27.[85] The text reads: "Then what becomes of our *boasting*? It is excluded. On what principle? On the principle of works? No, but on the principle of faith." In this form of the text "boasting" occurs once only. But if we allow a transformational analysis to unpack occurrences that are implicit but functionally operative, Burres suggests that we now have: "Then what becomes of our *boasting? Our boasting* is excluded. On what principle is our *boasting* excluded? Is our *boasting* excluded on the principle of works? No. Our *boasting* is excluded on the principle of faith". "*Boasting*" now occurs five times.

Although Nida succeeds in demonstrating points of value in transformational approaches for Bible translation, however, I still have hesitations about certain uses of these techniques. First, in spite of Nida's obvious awareness of the problem, the translator must be on guard against thinking of semantic equivalence in cognitive terms. If "decease", "departure from this life", and so on, could all be transformed into the kernel sentence "he dies", it would be easy to overlook the emotive, cultural, or religious overtones of meaning which may have been important in the original utterance. Nida would no doubt agree that every effort must be made not to lose sight of this problem. Indeed he and Taber stress this very point in a chapter entitled "Connotative Meaning". Second, the notion of kernel sentences comes too near for comfort to Wittgenstein's earlier notions in the *Tractatus* about elementary propositions. We cannot attempt to evaluate the theories of the *Tractatus* in this essay, but it is not irrelevant to point out that in his later writings Wittgenstein expressed his own deep dissatisfaction with theories of meaning that are arrived at in this way. Theories about a "universal" grammar of objects, events, abstracts and relations are too reminiscent of the theory of language that Wittgenstein first propounded and then rejected. These criticisms do not invalidate this whole approach, but they perhaps call for caution over the ways in which it is used.

[In its original form this article concluded with a final section of several pages on the logical grammar of justification by grace in Paul in the light of Wittgenstein's observations concerning "seeing as", and the concept of "onlooks" in D.D. Evans. However, I developed these ideas first in article for *Studia Evangelica* published by the Berlin Academy, and then in *The Two Horizons*. I have included this *Two Horizons* version among the essays of this present volume ("Justification by Grace as Legal Fiction?", Essay 10). Hence I have deleted the original formulation from this essay in order to avoid overlap in this volume. The penalty for this is that an otherwise rounded conclusion appears to end abruptly at this point.]

---

[85] K.L. Burres, op. cit., p.105.

CHAPTER FOURTEEN

Does the Bible Call All Cretans Liars? "The Logical Role of the Liar Paradox in Titus 1:12, 13: A Dissent from the Commentaries in the Light of Philosophical and Logical Analysis" (1994)

The extent to which too many biblical exegetes remain isolated from an awareness of problems of philosophy and logic becomes apparent in the wooden and humourless exegesis of Titus 1:12–13 that biblical commentaries offer. These appear to presuppose that the writer accuses the people of Crete of always being liars, and many also compound this mistake by seeking to find ways of excusing the writer from racial or national stereotypification and prejudice. Many also solemnly regard the additional comment "this statement is true" in the mouth of a Cretan as no more than an inept self-contradiction, and, again, seek to find excuses for this supposed fundamental logical blunder. I argue that all this misses the entirely different point that the writer is making, but also offer reasons why this mistaken exegetical tradition may have arisen. My new suggestion fits the context in Titus exactly, and also draws on ancient and modern philosophical logic as well as on biblical exegesis. The article below first appeared in Biblical Interpretation, *vol. 2 (1994), pp.207–23.*

I
The Argument

Appeals to paradoxes often perform specific roles in exploration and argument. This can be demonstrated from the ancient logical paradoxes formulated by Zeno of Elea to modern critical discussions in Bertrand Russell and Gilbert Ryle. I shall argue that the writer of Titus 1:12, 13 is well aware that placing the proposition "Cretans are always liars" in the mouth of a Cretan transforms the status of the proposition into one which does *not assert a contingent state of affairs about Cretans*. It functions, in effect, as *meta-language*, asserting a proposition that *prima facie* entails its own denial by *logical necessity*. The additional comment "This testimony is true" is not a sign that the writer (or an editor) is oblivious to the nature of paradox; it is more likely to have been intended as a light touch underlining the absurdity of a regress *ad infinitum*.

The more that commentators seek to excuse the writer from the tactlessness or thoughtlessness of making what appears to be a prejudicial stereotypification about a minority community, namely Cretans within the Graeco-Roman world, the more conspicuously they fall into the trap of misconstruing the purpose and logical status of the proposition in question. Eubulides of Miletus had long since formulated the liar paradox in the fourth century BCE. The reason why the writer of this epistle appeals to this well-known paradox is not to assassinate the character of all Cretans in general, but *to demonstrate a logical asymmetry between first-person and third-person utterances.* First-person utterances often presuppose a *personal backing in life,* which third-person utterances may not presuppose, and the writer is concerned with this "life" dimension. To paraphrase Wittgenstein and Strawson, the logical status of the proposition "I am a liar" is quite different from that of the proposition "He/she/they are liars."

The context of Titus 1:12, 13, I shall argue, confirms the argument that where purely theoretical debate has degenerated into a fruitless, self-defeating, circular, even mutually recriminating process, the only way forward is to look beyond the words to the style of life which gives each claim or counter-claim its currency as operative language. The connection between a proposition about the nature of Christian communication and the life-style of the bishops and elders who articulate the message of the Christian tradition is not accidental. If there is no substantial difference between this match of word and deed among Christians and the rest of the Cretan community at large, the danger emerges of generating a merely formal level of argument in which empty debate escalates into impatient, immoderate and self-defeating confrontation.

I detect no evidence whatever that the commentaries have grasped the special role of 1:12, 13 in the wider argument, with the tragic result that the author of the verses is credited in popular folklore with crass anti-Cretan prejudice. In practice, it may well be that the phrase "this testimony is true" is intended to bring out the ironic humour which might be suggested by the unstoppable infinite regress of meta-language set in motion by trying to accord truth-value to a self-defeating logical paradox.

Every commentary which I have consulted up to the present assumes that the propositions of Titus 1:12 serve, in the end, to describe a state of affairs about the character of Cretans. That this is the case is confirmed by the curious evaluation of v. 13a as allegedly evidential corroboration of the previous empirical proposition either by its reflecting and representing an endorsement from personal experience, or corroboration on the basis of public consensus. None of these solemn discussions even ask whether the writer realizes that to assert "this testimony is true" (1:13a) as a truth-claim accorded to the proposition asserted by a self-confessed habitual liar can have any truth-function. Yet logically it becomes self-contradictory because it may function to endorse *either the truth or the falsity* of the liar's assertion, and thus endorses *neither.*

II
The Commentaries and the Context

To avoid making a merely generalizing and unsupported claim about commentators and commentaries, following an initial glance at Calvin as the generally-acknowledged first modern commentator, I shall cite twenty-four specific examples of writers from 1900 to the present who unanimously interpret Titus 1:12, 13a as embodying contingent or empirical prepositional truth-claims about Cretans rather than logically necessary prepositional truth-claims about language. Calvin (1549) follows Patristic interpreters in understanding the proposition about Cretan lies to rest originally on a tradition about Cretan claims to possess the tomb of the immortal Jupiter. He comments on v. 13a: "Paul accepts the truth that he has spoken, for there is no doubt that the Cretans ... were very wicked men. The apostle ... would not have spoken so harshly of the Cretans without the best reasons."[1] This sets the tone for subsequent commentators.[2]

The majority of commentators simply misconstrue the logic of an utterance spoken by a Cretan whose speech has already been deemed by him and others to be false. Only in a consciously ironic sense (which is absent from the observation) could the most recent comment offered by George W. Knight III (1992) apply: "Paul quotes an evaluation of the Cretans by their own fellow countryman and their own prophet. This gives a perspective that nothing else could. Paul affirms the truthfulness of the evaluation in v. 13a with 'this testimony is true.'"[3] In logical terms this is tantamount to interpreting him as saying "the proposition '*p* implies *not-p*' implies *not-p* and *not-p* implies *p*." It is perhaps not surprising that some commentators, notably J.L. Houlden, content themselves with a masterly silence over this issue.[4]

The labour which many commentators bestow in attempting to excuse the writer's pastoral tactlessness or to explain away an embarrassingly judgmental and prejudicial stereotypification while understanding the passage to assert precisely such a generalizing judgement about Cretans leaves us in no doubt about their determination to read the passage in the traditional way, whatever the logical consequences. Thus, for example, Guthrie observes: "Because a well-known Cretan condemns his own people the apostle cannot be charged with censoriousness for his exposures."[5] Rendle Harris claimed in

---

[1]   John Calvin, *Second Epistle to the Corinthians and the Epistles to Timothy, Titus and Philemon* (Eng. Trans., Edinburgh: St Andrew Press, 1963), pp.363–64.

[2]   R.F. Horton, *The Pastoral Epistles* (Edinburgh: Jack, 1901), p.179; Rendle Harris, *Expositor 7* (1906), pp.305–11; J.H. Bernard, *The Pastoral Epistles* (Cambridge: Cambridge University Press, 1906), p.161; E.F. Brown, *The Pastoral Epistles* (London: Methuen, 1917), pp.98–9; R. St John Parry, *The Pastoral Epistles* (Cambridge: Cambridge University Press, 1920), p.76; W. Lock, *A Critical and Exegetical Commentary on the Pastoral Epistles* (Edinburgh: T. & T. Clark, 1924), pp.134–5; A.T. Robertson, *The Epistles of Paul* (Word Pictures of the N.T. IV; New York: Smith, 1931), pp.600–01; E.F. Scott, *The Pastoral Epistles* (Moffatt Commentaries; London: Hodder & Stoughton, 1936), pp.159–60; C. Spicq, *Les Épîtres pastorales* (Paris: Gabalda, 1947), pp.242–5; B.S. Easton, *The Pastoral Epistles* (London: SCM, 1948), pp.86–7; E.K. Simpson, *The Pastoral Epistles: Greek Text with Introduction and Commentary* (London: Tyndale Press, 1954), pp.99–100; F.D. Gealy, "1 Timothy, 11 Timothy, Titus: Exegesis", in *The Interpreter's Bible*, vol. 11 (Nashville, TN: Abingdon, 1955), pp.530–31; D.Guthrie, *The Pastoral Epistles* (London: Tyndale Press, 1957), pp.187–8; C.K. Barrett, *The Pastoral Epistles* (Oxford: Clarendon Press, 1963), pp.131–2; J.N.D. Kelly, *The Pastoral Epistles* (London: Black, 1963), pp.235–6; Martin Dibelius and Hans Conzelmann, *Die Pastoralbriefe* (Tübingen: Mohr, 4th edn, 1966), pp.101–03 (Eng. Trans. by H. Koester, Philadelphia, PA: Fortress, 1972), pp.135–7; A.T. Hanson, *The Pastoral Letters* (Cambridge: Cambridge University Press, 1966), pp.110–11; E.G. Hinson, "1-2 Timothy and Titus", in *The Broadman Bible Commentary*, vol. 11 (London: Marshall, Morgan, Scott, 1972; Broadman, 1971), p.365; G.D. Fee, *1 and 2 Timothy and Titus* (San Francisco, CA: Harper & Row, 1984), pp.133–4; Philip H. Towner, *The Goal to Our Instruction: The Structure of Theology and Ethics in the Pastoral Epistles* (JSNT Suppl. 74; Sheffield: Sheffield Academic Press, 1989), pp.155–6; J.D. Quinn, *The Letter to Titus* (AB, 35; New York: Doubleday, 1990), p.278 and Excursus "Truth", pp.276–82; and George W. Knight III, *The Pastoral Epistles: A Commentary on the Greek Text* (New International Greek Testament Commentary; Grand Rapids, MI: Eerdmans and Carlisle: Paternoster Press, 1992), pp.298–300.

[3]   George W. Knight III, p.298.

[4]   J.L. Houlden, *The Pastoral Epistles* (London: Penguin, 1976 and London: SCM, 1989), pp.144–5.

[5]   D. Guthrie, p.188.

1906 that the accusation concerned only the religious falsehood of the affirmation that Zeus was buried in Crete.[6] Ernest Brown identifies the point of the proposition as "his low estimate of the Cretan character".[7]

E.G. Hinson clearly experiences embarrassment about the need to defend the writer from "a charge of nationalist bigotry".[8] But he does so not by re-assessing the logic of the central proposition, but by seeking support for such stereotyping from other ancient Greek writers. Such a ploy would make the author's condoning of such stereotyping of a minority group all the worse, however, for our own contemporary notions of what is socio-politically "correct". J.N.D. Kelly excuses the author on the ground of a crime of passion under severe provocation: "The Apostle is alarmed and angry at the sectaries' conduct, and in such a mood people do not always mince their words. In any case he would scarcely have expected the true Christians in the Cretan communities to suffer from nationalist touchiness."[9]

Dibelius and Conzelmann slightly soften the issue by attempting to reproduce the quotation in its hexameter style: "Cretans are mostly liars/brutes and loitering gluttons," but by rendering the Greek ἀεί, "always," as "mostly" (a use which according to most lexicographers is possible but uncharacteristic except for the woodenly over-literal), these commentators prove beyond doubt that they have entirely missed the logical status of the utterance as a deliberate use of paradox.[10] C.K. Barrett makes surprisingly heavy weather of it. He comments, "The introduction of *Cretans* is not easy to understand after the reference in v. 10 to Jewish converts. Either the author has not fully thought through his material (cp. Jewish myths in v. 14) or the Jews are to be thought of as in great measure assimilated to Cretan life."[11] Spicq had earlier noted the same problem about Jews and Crete, but believes that the solution lies in "Paul's appealing to their own terminology, that of their own race, and indeed well recognised by their own contemporaries".[12] Thus like Dibelius, Conzelmann and Kelly, Spicq effectively confirms the *contingent* or socio-historical status of the proposition by looking beyond it for *further empirical grounds* which may seem to serve to validate it.

The commentaries of A.T. Hanson, E.F. Scott, and E.K. Simpson invite further comment. Each partially notes, at least initially, the distinctive logic of the liar paradox, but after coming so near to offering a new interpretation, simply falls back into the wholly traditional understanding of the passage as offering an empirical assertion about Cretans, not a logical proposition about language. Thus A.T. Hanson argues that the writer's rhetorical purpose is "in order to impale the false teachers on the horns of a dilemma: either they accept the truth of the quotation and stand self-condemned; or else they deny it and condemn their own prophet. It is very difficult to believe that Paul would use so childish a device for refuting opponents."[13] It is entirely valid to argue that

---

[6] Rendle Harris, pp.305–11.
[7] Ernest F. Brown, p.99.
[8] E.G. Hinson, p.365.
[9] J.N.D. Kelly, p.233.
[10] M. Dibelius and H. Conzelmann (Eng. Trans.), p.135.
[11] C.K. Barrett, p.131.
[12] C. Spicq, p.242.
[13] A.T. Hanson, pp.110–11, loc. cit.

such rhetoric would be weak. To condemn their own prophet would *not*, as Hanson seems to imagine, actually entail *rejecting* the prophet's statement, since the liar paradox that the Cretan "prophet" utters fully allows for the utterance *to be false by logical necessity as a first-person utterance of a Cretan who tells lies.*

In purely *logical* terms it would therefore no less encourage the Cretans to *lie* than to speak *truth*. Further, it is precisely *not the addressees* who are impaled on the horns of a dilemma, but *the speaker or writer* who has damaged his case, in this interpretation. It is he, not the reader, who has uttered "*p*" and "*not-p*" in the same breath. Hanson seems to realize that his explanation verges on confusion for he hastily adds: "The author, however, may have an ulterior object in mind: perhaps ... to discredit all things Cretan". But this is to leap out of the frying pan into the fire. The interpretation now suggests the very stereotyping of a national character which many commentators seem anxious to soften, to excuse, or to disown.

E.F. Scott's earlier commentary in the Moffatt series more explicitly recognizes that the liar paradox constitutes a "puzzle in Greek logic".[14] But on the verge of a constructive insight, like Hanson, he retreats back into the exegete's preoccupation with socio-historical data and contingent states of affairs. He sees "Epimenides" *not as a logician concerned to make a logical point* but as a historical or legendary figure who perceives himself "badly used" by his fellow countrymen. This explains why there is an *empirical basis* for the logically contingent accusation. The quotation therefore allegedly occurs in Titus 1:12, 13 to make the charge "generally acceptable". Scott confirms that by now he has entirely lost sight of the logical status of the paradox as an assertion *about logic and language (not* about *Cretans),* by interpreting "this testimony is true" (v. 13a), not as an ironic comment on logical regress *ad infinitum*, but as an appeal to the *empirical evidence* either of "popular opinion" or of "personal experiences". Thus by now, he has travelled close to Gealy's view that "This verse savagely attacks the Cretan heretics with a singularly indiscreet quotation which over-reaches itself to defame all Cretans. Out of their mouths they stand condemned."[15] But this is logical nonsense. If a Cretan has warned his audience that whatever he says is likely to be false, to deduce that Cretans are always liars is to suggest a *false* claim, or more strictly, a *self-defeating* truth-claim. Again, as in the case of Hanson's interpretation, the liar paradox leaves egg on the face of the *writer*, not the reader. If such an interpretation were valid, the writer has simply made a fool of himself (as some do not hesitate to deny) and the reader would be likely to perceive this.

Finally, the only commentator who seems to see that the use of paradox here is light, rather than heavy, is E.K. Simpson (1954). Like Hanson, he argues that the writer placed the reader on the horns of a dilemma, but he rightly adds, "with a twinkle in his eye".[16] Yet even Simpson fails to appreciate what this suggests. He spoils his own initial insight by discussing how the truth of the empirical assertion *that Cretans are liars* could be *verified*. His only exegetical achievement is to note that, if the writer offers what appears to be a vulnerable argument, a little *mutual* self-mockery might be in order to soften the crassness of the harsh generalization about Cretans. But this operates as little more than

---

14 E.F. Scott, p.159.
15 F.D. Gealy, p.530.
16 E.K. Simpson, pp.99–100.

a stylistic or rhetorical device, without bringing about a radical change in understanding the fundamental function of the passage. In the end, it takes its place firmly among all the traditional interpretations.

This survey, especially the last three examples from Hanson, Scott and Simpson, demonstrates that a formal recognition of the embodiment of the liar paradox in Titus 1:12, 13a offers no more than a first step towards its necessary re-evaluation. All of the cited twenty-four comments transpose the short section about self-defeating truth-claims (1:10–15) into a digression concerning "false teachers" rather than as an integral part of the main argument of the whole Epistle, that elders and churchpeople should lead a blameless life that avoids "stupid controversies" (3:9): "A bishop ... must be blameless. He must not be arrogant or quick-tempered" (1:7); he must be "holy and self-controlled" so that he may give suitable instruction and credibly "confute those who contradict it" (1:9). Mere verbal contradiction alone leads nowhere; indeed verbal conflict can escalate into abuse and recrimination that smacks of loss of self-control and blameless lack of verbal aggression.

What is needed is that style of integrity in life which exposes the troublemakers as "empty talkers" (1:10) who "profess to know God but deny him *by their deeds*" (1:16). Thus elders, by contrast, must be "temperate, serious, sensible, sound in faith, in love" (2:2). The whole emphasis on "self-control" serves "sound doctrine" by giving it credibility. Hence a life-style of obedience and honest work coheres with the exhortation "to speak evil of no-one, to avoid quarrelling, to be gentle, and to show perfect courtesy toward all" (3:1, 2). There is a limit to what can be achieved by verbal conflict alone (3:10).

The thrust of 1:12, 13a offers two possibilities. *Either* the writer throws to the winds the courtesy, gentleness and self-control which he urges throughout the entire epistle *or* he employs the liar paradox quite specifically to demonstrate the self-defeating ineffectiveness of making truth-claims which are given the lie by conduct which fails to match them. Indeed, the currency of language depends for its force on how it is embedded in life. Nothing makes this clearer than the lack of logical symmetry between first-person and third-person utterances, since the former demand a performative dimension by logical entailment. To unpack this point more clearly we must step back and review the functions of logical paradox.

III
Functions of Logical Paradox

The earliest well-known exploration of logical paradox seems to have been that of Zeno of Elea who flourished in the fifth century BCE. Zeno, we need to note, was a pupil of Parmenides, and his appeal to paradox is part of a serious polemic in the context of the very different theories of reality formulated respectively by Parmenides and by Heraclitus of Ephesus, and also by Pythagoras of Samos in the sixth century.[17] Heraclitus

---

[17] Herman Fränkel, "Zeno of Elea's Attacks on Plurality", *American Journal of Philosophy* 63 (1942), pp.1–25 and pp.193–206; H.N. Lee, "Are Zeno's Arguments Based on a Mistake?" *Mind* 74 (1965), pp.563–90; G.E.L. Owen, "Zeno and the Mathematicians", *Proceedings of the Aristotelian Society* 58 (1957–58), pp.199–222; and H.D.P. Lee, *Zeno of Elea* (Cambridge: Cambridge University Press, 1936).

characterized reality as ever-changing flux. Pythagoras viewed reality as a pluralism of change constituted by the shifting dimensions of numbers and space. By contrast, Parmenides had argued primarily on the basis of *logic* that reality was stable and a single unity. In logical terms, in principle only three alternative characterizations of reality remain possible: either (i) Being is; or (ii) Being is not; or (iii) It both is and is not. Of these options the third excludes itself as self-contradictory. The second is problematic in logical terms. Hence only the first proposition, Parmenides argued, remains, and asserts the existence of one, unchanging, reality.

The Pythagoreans, however, put forward counter-arguments. These stressed the plurality of points in space and of instants in time. But Zeno, in turn, attempted to address these counter-arguments. He argued that such sub-divisions of continuity into points, or into instants or processes within motion, entailed self-defeating logical paradoxes. The best-known paradoxes that Zeno formulated are paradoxes of motion. They include the Dichotomy, Achilles and the Tortoise, and the Arrow, all of which offer variants on the same theme.[18]

Zeno argued that before a moving object can travel a given distance, it must first travel half that distance, then half the remainder, and so on without limit. But *to reach the goal, the number of sub-divisions must logically be infinite*. On the other hand, *how could this occur within a finite time-span?* When this paradox is applied to the example of a race between Achilles and the Tortoise, if the Tortoise is given a head-start, it is logically arguable, Zeno claimed, that since by the time Achilles has reached the starting-point of the Tortoise, the Tortoise will have reached a new point *ad infinitum, Achilles will never overtake the Tortoise*. We need not suppose that Zeno wished to deny the actuality of motion itself. Rather, he intended to deny the logical coherence of the pluralistic view of reality that the Heraclitan and Pythagorean traditions advocated.

The importance of Zeno's paradoxes lay in philosophical agendas to which they gave rise. In one direction, in the tradition of Aristotle and of Thomas Aquinas, they initiated Aristotelian reflection on the nature of change. But for our present purposes, and in the tradition of logical theory that takes us through Russell to Gilbert Ryle, one principle which begins to emerge is an *asymmetrical relation between formal logic as an abstract system, and the point of view of a speaker or observer in the actualization of the system in a specific utterance.*

Ryle devotes an essay to "Achilles and the Tortoise" in his book *Dilemmas* (1954).[19] Zeno, Ryle argues, "seems to prove one thing, namely that the chase cannot end, but really proves, perfectly validly, a different and undisturbing conclusion".[20] Achilles' whole course is "not the sum of all its parts but one; it is the sum of *all* those flagged parts *plus* the outstanding *unflagged* one".[21] But why was the final stage "unflagged"? "A flag-planting procedure each stage of which was, by rule, non-ultimate" in the sense that "we are induced to look at the race through Achilles' own eyes".[22] This is what gives

---

18 In addition to the above sources, on "Achilles and the Tortoise" see the definitive essay by Gilbert Ryle in *Dilemmas* (Cambridge: Cambridge University Press, 1966 [1954]), pp.36–53.

19 G. Ryle, pp.36–53.

20 G. Ryle, p.37.

21 G. Ryle, p.61 (my italics).

22 G. Ryle, pp.43–4.

plausibility to the paradox. From one viewpoint (that of Achilles) the logical agenda addresses the question: "How many portions have you *cut off* the object?"; from the other viewpoint (that of the logician's overview) it addresses the issue: "How many portions have you *cut it into?*"[23] Ryle rightly concludes that *logically necessary propositions* that may seem to express "a logician's platitude" are distinct from *historico-contingent propositions,* which gave us "news about what happens".[24] Only if we fuse (like a zeugma) the "nursemaid's truisms" to the "logician's truisms" we appear to face a logical paradox. Or to put it the other way round, paradox signals a difference in approach between the *practical* concerns of the nursemaid and the logician's love of *abstract* theory. The two angles of approach are not symmetrical, not speaker-neutral, not context-neutral.

In philosophical theology this same principle gives rise to an unnecessary debate about time. Some see a conflict or paradox between the claim that believers who die enter *instantaneously* into the condition of being "with Christ" (Phil. 1:23) and the claim that believers who die remain "asleep" *awaiting* the Last Day (1 Cor. 15: 51). But this is because neither truth-claim is context-free. One can be made only from the *participant* standpoint. The participant in the process experiences instantaneous transformation. The second proposition is not that of a practical post-mortal nursemaid, but that of a cosmic logician. Under the *cosmic* standpoint, the believer "waits" for the final consummation of all things, when the resurrection becomes a public, corporate, event.

The liar-paradox is most clearly associated with Eubulides. Like Zeno, his Megarian School opposed the theory of reality represented by Heraclitus or by the Pythagoreans. Cicero later reformulates the liar-paradox, but perhaps with less logical accuracy.[25] Interest in the liar-paradox then declined, apart from a brief revival in the mediaeval period. However, the development of mathematical logic at the end of the nineteenth century brought about a renewal of inquiry into paradox, especially in terms of relations between numbers, sets and sub-sets.

The most widely known example is that of "Cantor's paradox", formulated in 1899. But this was partially anticipated by the Burali-Forti paradox, which posed the question: if a class or set cannot contain a component or sub-set greater than itself, what is the "greatest" ordinal, or class of a cardinal number? Georg Cantor developed and refined the discussion in terms of the "set of all ordinals" in 1895 and 1896. In particular, what is the relation between the greatest cardinal number and the "set of all sets" (1899)? The key point, for the purposes of our present discussion, is that formal mathematical logic found itself having to move out of its single internal system to posit some such trans-finite notion as, in Cantor's phrase, "the power of the continuum".[26]

---

[23] G. Ryle, p.46 (Ryle's italics).

[24] G. Ryle, p.52.

[25] Cicero, *De Divinatione* II: 11.

[26] In Cantor's theory "aleph null" denotes the trans-finite sets of all things that can be placed in isomorphic correspondence with the totality of natural numbers. But the *set* of all natural numbers is infinite, while, paradoxically, the cardinal number of the set of real numbers is *larger* than aleph. But how can anything *in practice* be "larger" than "infinite", yet *logically* be required to be so? Cantor appealed to "the power of the continuum" in an attempt to formulate some basis for the paradox. Like meta-language, this is not itself algebraic or denumerable (i.e., *within* the system) but transcendental. Cantor's major writings include *Groundwork for a Theory of Sets* (1883) and *Contributions to the Founding of a Theory of Transfinite Numbers* (1895–97).

Throughout the history of modern philosophy the positing of a logical reflexive *aporia* or paradox has led to what may be termed "a shift of frame" involving something beyond and outside the original system. Thus Kant's critique of reason led to transcendental questions about the trans-rational basis of reason. The early Wittgenstein's realization that a system of language could not depict the means of projection by which it served to depict the world led eventually to questions about life outside the formal system of logic. Hence he reaches the conclusion in his later work that "my own relation to my words is wholly different from other people's".[27]

In his earlier writing Wittgenstein appealed to the contrast between "saying" and "showing" as a possible means of reaching outside the single logical system. Thus he observes in the *Tractatus*: "Propositions can represent the whole of reality, but they cannot represent what they must have in common with reality in order to be able to represent it – logical form ... Propositions *show* the logical form of reality."[28] In his later work he appeals from time to time to the distinctive grounding in life entailed in first-person utterances. Thus it makes sense to assert: "He believes it, but it is false" but it would be nonsense to declare, "I believe it, but it is false." Wittgenstein thus observes in the *Investigations*: "If there were a verb meaning 'to believe falsely', it would not have any significant first-person present indicative."[29]

This logical asymmetry between first-person and third-person utterances was developed further in the philosophy of J.L. Austin, P.F. Strawson and John Searle. Austin and Searle explore the distinctive logic of performative or illocutionary speech-acts, while Strawson defended a performative account of truth-claims offered by a speaker or writer. To say "it is true that *p*", Strawson argues, is to say more than "*p*": it is to stand behind, and to endorse, *p*.[30] In theory, this seems to throw doubt upon a meta-linguistic approach to the liar-paradox. In more traditional terms, the statement "What I am saying now is false" is, if it is true, a false proposition: if it is false, it is a true proposition. Here is unresolved paradox. However, a performative approach suggests that the "paradox" becomes self-defeating in assertive force rather than contradictory in prepositional content.

This appropriately concludes our survey of uses of paradox from Zeno and Eubulides to Cantor and Ryle. For it sums up the thrust of this work on paradox for our understanding of Titus 1:12, 13a. The writer cites the liar-paradox by placing the proposition "Cretans always tell lies" in the mouth of a Cretan speaker, almost without doubt Epimenides of Crete who is explicitly associated with the liar paradox. The aim is to demonstrate that, *anchored to an inappropriate behaviour context, first person* utterances can become *self-defeating*. They can be reversed and re-minted into operative currency not by verbal conflict and reassertion ("this is true", v. 13a), which merely exposes the invitation to infinite regress and circularity, but by a renewed and reoriented life-style

[27] L. Wittgenstein, *Philosophical Investigations* (Oxford: Blackwell, 2nd edn, Ger. and Eng., 1967), II.x, p.192e.

[28] L. Wittgenstein, *Tractatus Logico-Philosophicus* (London: Routledge, Ger. and Eng., 1961), 4.12 and 4.121; cf. 6.24.

[29] L. Wittgenstein, *Philosophical Investigations* II.x, p.190e.

[30] P.F. Strawson, "Truth", *Analysis* 9 (1949), especially pp.93–5.

which gives credibility and currency not by arrogant self-assertion (1:7), not by being "empty talkers" (1:10), not by upsetting people (1:11), not by "professions of knowledge of God denied by deeds" (1:16), not by verbal style (3:2), but by being "upright, holy and self-controlled" (1:8), by being a "model of good deeds" (2:7), and thereby to offer "health-giving speech that cannot be censured, so that an opponent may be put to shame, having nothing evil to say of us" (2:8).

IV
How a Misleading Exegetical Tradition Emerged

Why, then, did the "empirical" understanding of 1:12, 13a as contingent propositions about Cretans ever arise? If the liar paradox represented a familiar puzzle in the ancient Greek world, why have so many commentators failed to see its logic?

From the Patristic era onwards, commentators and philosophers have suggested that this verse in Titus alludes to a quotation from the Cretan Epimenides. Clement of Alexandria, Chrysostom and Jerome ascribe the quotation to him, as Dibelius, Spicq, Conzelmann and Knight, among others, point out.[31] Clement declares that Epimenides of Crete is said to be one of the seven wise men "whom the apostle Paul cites in his letter to Titus when he says 'Cretans are always liars'".[32] But was Epimenides a wise man in the sense of being a propounder of logical puzzles and axioms, or a prophet in the sense of attacking false superstition? Jerome was aware that Epimenides was said to be the originator of the axiom "*Cretenses semper mendaces*". But in the Patristic era what originated as an instantiation of a principle of logic became confused with a particular tradition about a *false truth-claim asserted by Cretans about the tomb of Zeus*. The intensity of debate that surrounded this claim probably owed its origin to the debate between Origen and Celsus. In *Contra Celsum* III:43, Origen addresses the accusation of Celsus that Christians allegedly

> ... ridicule those who worship Jupiter because his tomb is pointed out in the island of Crete; and yet we worship him who rose from the tomb, although ignorant of the grounds on which the Cretans observe such a custom. Observe now [Origen continues] that he [Celsus] thus undertakes the defence of the Cretans, and of Jupiter, and of his tomb ... But ... we reply that Callimachus the Cyrenian ... accuses the Cretans in his hymn addressed to Jupiter in the words: "The Cretans are always liars for thou dost not die ...".[33]

Understandably enough, the accusation that "Cretans always tell lies" became part of a polemical debate in the Patristic era about the empty tomb of Christ's resurrection and claims that might be taken to undermine its uniqueness. In other words, the empirical or

---

[31] Clement of Alexandria, *Stromata* 1:59:2; M. Dibelius and H. Conzelmann, *Die Pastoralbriefe*, pp.101–03 (Eng., pp.135–7); C. Spicq, *Les Épîtres pastorals*, pp.242–5; G.W. Knight III, pp.298–9; similarly, cf. C.K. Barrett, pp.131–2; J.N.D. Kelly, pp.235–6; and D. Guthrie, pp.187–9. Cf. also this view in Bertrand Russell, *History of Western Philosophy* (London: Allan & Unwin, 1946), p.346.

[32] Clement, *Stromata*, loc. cit.

[33] Origen, *Contra Celsum* III: 43; cf. Callimachus, *Hymnus in Iovem*, i.

contingent application of the original proposition became recontextualized so that in Christian apologetics its significance as a device of logic became lost from view. This was compounded by confusions of tradition about Epimenides. An Epimenides of Crete who flourished in the sixth and fifth centuries BCE was probably a philosophical logician who receives mention in ancient writings in connection with the liar paradox. But is this the Epimenides of Crete to whom Aristotle alludes as a "diviner"?[34] By the time of Cicero, Epimenides has come to be perceived as a prophet who could predict the future when mental control was released.[35] Does Titus 1:12 employ the word "prophet" because falsehood or self-defeating truth-claims are associated, with a hint of double-meaning, with lack of self-control (Titus 1:8; 2:6; cf. 2:12; 3:2, 3, 10)? Or has the tradition of a philosopher Epimenides already become confused with the tradition of a prophetic Epimenides who denounced false claims about the divine mortality of Zeus?

It is impossible to pinpoint at what stage in the development of tradition the notion of "Cretan liar" came to be dominated by the issue concerning the tomb of Zeus, and the significance of the example as a logical puzzle more readily lost from view. Indeed it is quite possible that the logician's example was borrowed from an existing tradition to add colour and potential humour to the issue. At all events, it is easy to see why early commentators became distracted. The bane and blessing of writing commentaries, however, is that each commentator all too often attempts to stand on the shoulders of his or her predecessor. Thus the whole array of modern commentators comes to direct their attention to the traditional issues and agenda: did the writer quote from Epimenides or from Callimachus (Hanson, Knight)?[36] Does the notion that a pagan prophet can speak "truth" have implications for theology, or is it to be categorized alongside the prophecy of Caiaphas or even Balaam's ass (Spicq)? How do "Cretans" relate to "Jewish" converts and to "Jewish" myths (Barrett)? Once Theodore of Mopsuestia had suggested that the quotation might come from Callimachus rather than from Epimenides, the die had been cast. For the interest of Callimachus in Cretan lies had nothing to do with logic, but only with empirical truth-claims about the tomb of Zeus.

V
"Empty Talkers": Heightened Paradox for a Pastoral Context

The appeal to logical paradox exposes precisely the logical asymmetry between first-person and third-person utterances, which calls for self-involvement in life on the part of the bishops and elders. There remains perhaps only one loose end that we must address if the argument put forward here is not to be dismissed as vulnerable. Why does the writer add to the paradox that a Cretan says "Cretans are always liars" the further proposition "evil beasts, lazy gluttons", if the proposition is to be construed as a logical rather than contingent or descriptive one?

---

[34] Aristotle, *Rhetoric*, 3:17.
[35] Cicero, *De divinatione* I, 18:34.
[36] G.W. Knight III, p.299.

Three points may be suggested by way of possible reply. First, we cannot be certain whether the continuation of the version of the liar paradox used here had already acquired this extension in popular first-century tradition. The continuation of probable hexameter suggests so. This may have owed something to the very early confusion, prior to the first century, between the tradition of the liar paradox associated with Epimenides the philosopher and speculation about Cretan claims concerning the tomb of Zeus and Epimenides the prophet, whether or not these allude to the same Epimenides. Second, the addition of the words "evil beasts, lazy gluttons" in no way undermines, but on the contrary emphasizes, the logical asymmetry between first-person and third-person utterances. The notion of a Cretan's saying, "We are always evil beasts" is as logically implausible as Wittgenstein's aphorism that if there were a verb "to believe falsely" it would have no *first*-person indicative active. The addition merely extends the scope of the liar paradox to other first-person utterances of a parallel order, though not of the same purely *formal* level of contradiction. Third, the paradox "Everything that I say is a lie: is this true?" invites a further proposition to exemplify the formal principle of the paradox. If the speaker is a liar, the proposition "I am now (or always) lying" constitutes a paradox of formal logic, while the further proposition "I am now lying" ("p") and "We are evil beasts" ("q") invites the further dilemma: if (p implies not-p) implies not-p, while not-p implies p, what are we to make not only of p, but of q asserted in the same format?

The addition of "evil beasts, lazy gluttons", then, by no means sinks the argument. At very least its inclusion is capable of explanation, or a combination of explanations, and does not undermine the thrust of the argument as a whole.

Reflection on the operative nature of Christian communication in a hostile context is part of the duties of bishops and elders. Stepping back from a frame of discourse that has come to be unproductive or self-defeating is analogous to seeing the limits of what can be said *about* a set or system from *within* the set or system. Hence attention must be shifted to the conduct in life that gives the language of communication and argument its operative currency.

The argument put forward here does not overlook the technical inadequacies of the so-called performative view of truth often associated with Strawson and others as a supposedly comprehensive theory of truth. But it appeals to its specific agenda of the relation between truth-claims and personal signature, or in Searle's language, between propositional content and propositional force. Yet all the standard commentaries, it seems, construe Titus 1:12, 13 as a contingent proposition about Cretans, sustaining the popular mistake that the writer is guilty of prejudicial and tactless racial stereotypification. Such an expression of bigotry would be all the worse (not more excusable) if it merely reflected a general cultural consensus in criticism of a minority group in the Graeco-Roman world, as many commentators suggest. The writer, however, is articulating a logical proposition which concerns not Cretans but the method of approach to be adopted by bishops and elders in the pastoral context which the letter as a whole addresses. This radically changes the role and function of Titus 1:12, 13 within the wider argument of the epistle.

CHAPTER FIFTEEN

A Retrospective Reappraisal: Conceptual Grammar and Inter-Disciplinary Research (New essay)

Part III contains four essays that explore conceptual grammar, and one on semantics. Those that utilise conceptual or logical explorations tend to do so in terms of a specific agenda. The essay on justification by grace through faith, for example, focuses on "internal grammar" and aspective onlooks; that on truth and faith, on polymorphous concepts; and that on Cretan liars, on the functions of logical paradoxes and first-person utterances. In this reappraisal, I return to Wittgenstein's understandings of conceptual or logical grammar to reappraise its potential for further explorations, with a less circumscribed agenda than those of the articles above. I recognize that the era of trying to "solve" every philosophical problem by means of the tools of "linguistic philosophy" is largely in the past, but I argue that the resources bequeathed by Wittgenstein and exemplified in such approaches as H.H. Price's work on dispositional accounts of belief still offer ways forward for biblical interpretation. The approach has to stand on its own feet as a viable or proven resource, and I stand by my belief that such accounts as my distinctive interpretation of Titus 1:12–13 would not carry full weight without appealing to the resources of conceptual grammar.

I
Conceptual Grammar with Particular Reference to Wittgenstein

From the first I have firmly argued the importance of exploring conceptual grammar for biblical interpretation, and have also argued that Wittgenstein stands alongside Schleiermacher, Dilthey and Gadamer as a profound exponent of hermeneutical thinking. I argued this in *The Two Horizons*, and now should add only that Paul Ricoeur stands beside Gadamer as the most seminal and creative thinker in philosophical hermeneutics in the last quarter of the twentieth century and up until the first four years of the twenty-first century.[1]

"Conceptual grammar", generated initially through the acute observations and aphorisms of the later Wittgenstein, became almost an over-routinized and over-replicated "tool" in many Faculties or Departments of Philosophy in the middle decades of the twentieth century. Nevertheless Wittgenstein offered productive observations with an unrivalled intensity and originality. Hence I have taken his later writings as our starting-point in this brief attempt to vindicate explorations of conceptual grammar in research articles from 1970 to the present. I also offer renewed arguments for the view that Wittgenstein provides a genuine hermeneutic of understanding, and make a plea for

---

[1] Anthony C. Thiselton, *The Two Horizons: New Testament Hermeneutics and Philosophical Description* (Grand Rapids, MI: Eerdmans and Carlisle: Paternoster 1980), pp.370–85.

inter-disciplinary or multi-disciplinary research among biblical interpreters. The discipline suffers too readily from an artificial division between biblical hermeneutics and philosophical hermeneutics, as well as between philosophical hermeneutics and literary and linguistic explorations.

"Conceptual grammar" stands at the heart of Wittgenstein's later explorations. In his *Philosophical Investigations* he observes, "In the use of words one might distinguish 'surface grammar' from 'depth grammar'. What immediately impresses itself upon us about the use of a word is the way it is used in the construction of a sentence, the point of its use – one might say – that can be taken in by the ear. – And now compare the depth grammar, say of the word 'to mean', with what its surface grammar would lead us to suggest."[2]

Wittgenstein approaches a number of specific concepts, particularly those used in philosophy or in philosophy of language with this distinction in mind. Surface grammar may direct our attention to the wrong thing in relation to the questions that we bring. It would not help to respond to the question "Why has butter risen in price?" to examine the composition of butter rather than the dynamics of economic trends. This humdrum example captures the principle, but does not operate at the level of complexity found in Wittgenstein's more characteristic philosophical wrestling. These typically explore such concepts as: *thinking, meaning, understanding, knowing, believing, expecting, loving, picturing, dreaming, intending, hoping, laughing, repenting,* or *giving.*

In Wittgenstein's view, the "surroundings" in human life shape and condition the possibilities of conceptual grammar, or the *logical* grammar of concepts. John Searle's exposition of what he calls "Background" (as a technical term) is akin to this, shaping the potential for linguistic competency and communicative action.[3] The respective conceptual grammars of pain-language (in the context of pain-behaviour) and love-language (in the context of love-behaviour) provide a well-known example in Wittgenstein's writings. In the *Zettel* he writes, "Love is not a feeling ... [But] one does not say 'That was not true pain, or it would not have gone off so quickly.'"[4] In the *Philosophical Investigations* he remarks "Could someone have a feeling of ardent love or hope for the space of one second – no matter what preceded or followed the second? ... The surroundings give it its importance."[5] Surface grammar may suggest that if we can say, "I feel intense pain. – Oh, it's gone off now!" – we could equally construct a syntax: "I feel intense love. – Oh, it's gone off now."

An examination of the *concept,* or the *uses* of the word in speech (that is, as *parole,* not as *langue*) reveals that love does not operate with the same conceptual grammar as pain. We may be pardoned for asking, however, how far most lexicographical analyses of words for love in the biblical writings even begin this kind of exploration. If they did, we might encounter more about the *attitudes* and *stance* that love-language often presupposes, and less about *feelings* and *isolated actions* in this universe of discourse. It is not enough, and indeed it may mislead us, to speak of love, pain, belief, expectation and

---

[2] Ludwig Wittgenstein, *Philosophical Investigations* (Oxford: Blackwell, Ger. and Eng., 2nd edn, 1967), sect. 664.

[3] J.R. Searle, *Intentionality* (Cambridge: CUP, 1983), pp.19–20 and 144–59.

[4] L. Wittgenstein, *Zettel* (Oxford: Blackwell, Ger. and Eng., 1967), sect. 504.

[5] Wittgenstein, *Investigations,* sect. 583.

understanding as "inner mental states". Yet the "surroundings" in human life shape conceptual grammar at every level. Wittgenstein observes, "Only someone who can reflect on the past can repent":[6] "Why can't a dog simulate pain? Is he too honest?"[7]

My article on Titus 1:12–13, included above as Essay 14, captures "the point" of these verses, I believe, in ways that eluded the ingenuity of commentators. They widely express embarrassment at the supposed "description" of Cretans as liars, especially from the lips of a Cretan! Is this racial prejudice, or a gauche logical blunder? My different approach takes its starting-point from Wittgenstein's observations about the conceptual grammar of *first-person* utterances: "If there were a verb meaning 'to believe falsely', it would not have any significant first person present indicative."[8] He adds, "My own relation to my words is wholly different from other people's."[9] The philosophical context of these observations is an exploration of "Moore's paradox" and of belief-utterances.[10] Yet for most biblical exegetes and interpreters this has remained a largely strange, unexplored, territory. Most, or perhaps even all, of the main commentaries leave out of account (1) the distinctive conceptual grammar of first-person utterances; and (2) the varied constructive functions of logical paradoxes in ancient and modern philosophical logic. But these illuminate the meaning of the verses in a way that fully coheres with their linguistic and situational context in this chapter and in Titus as a whole.

Wittgenstein implicitly states that a "grammatical" investigation is a hermeneutical one: "Our investigation is therefore a grammatical one. Such an investigation sheds light on our problems by *clearing misunderstandings away* ... caused, among other things, by certain analogies between forms of expressions in different regions of language".[11] This requires close attention not only to varied settings, "worlds", and "surroundings" of language, but also to a *particularity* that cannot be assimilated into the mere general or abstract. The later Wittgenstein is no less aware of the conceptual limitations of "the generalizing method of science" than Gadamer is.[12] "Super-concepts" easily mislead us.[13]

If the work of using *surface* grammar is like describing the *physical shapes* of chess pieces to try to explain the game, in exploring *conceptual* grammar "we talk about it as we do about pieces in chess when we are stating *the rules* of the game, not describing their physical properties".[14] Sometimes to explore "rules" is simply to become aware that "a language-game ... rests on a tacit presupposition" that shapes its conceptual grammar distinctively.[15] When he formulates the aphorism "Theology as grammar", Wittgenstein is exploring distinctions between *kinds* of objects or utterances, and what may be their "point".[16] This is close to the ultimate *aim* of Bultmann (even if we may doubt whether he

---

6 Wittgenstein, *Zettel*, sect. 519.
7 Wittgenstein, *Investigations*, sect. 250.
8 *Investigations*, Part II, p.190.
9 *Investigations*, Part II, p.192.
10 *Investigations*, Part II, x.
11 *Investigations*, sect. 90 (my italics).
12 L. Wittgenstein, *The Blue and Brown Books* (Oxford: Blackwell, 2nd edn, 1969), p.18; and H.G. Gadamer, *Philosophical Hermeneutics* (Berkeley, CA: University of California Press, 1976), pp.3–17.
13 Wittgenstein, *Investigations*, sect. 97.
14 *Investigations*, sect. 108.
15 *Investigations*, Part II, p.179e.
16 *Investigations*, sect. 373.

fully achieves it) of seeking to uncover *"the point"* of New Testament material that may have been misconstrued and obscured by "surface-grammar".[17] Wittgenstein declares, "What I am looking for is the grammatical difference."[18]

II
Wittgenstein, Grammar and Hermeneutics

We shall return in due course to multi-disciplinary research as a requirement for fruitful hermeneutical enquiry, as the essays above (10–14) seem to indicate. Meanwhile we may first develop further some of the many ways in which the thinking of the later Wittgenstein, especially on conceptual grammar, deserves to be regarded as profoundly hermeneutical. We select six modes of approach by way of example.

(1) As Schleiermacher and Gadamer, among others, insist, hermeneutics does not permit "the particular case" to become subsumed under the merely general. Wittgenstein deplores "the contemptuous attitude towards *the particular case"* and the seductive "craving for generality" found too often even among philosophers:[19] "Philosophers constantly see the method of science before their eyes ... This tendency ... leads the philosopher into complete darkness".[20] The same kind of remark readily occurs in Gadamer's "Reflections on My Philosophical Journey" and in his *Philosophical Hermeneutics*.[21] Hermeneutics *begins* with particularity, even it also leads to broader horizons. Richard Bauckham also makes a broadly similar point. Hermeneutical enquiry, like the Bible itself, concerns "the relationship between the particular and the universal".[22]

(2) Wittgenstein observes, and does full justice to, the *historical, developing, expanding* nature of language and its uses within *the horizon of time* (as Heidegger called it). Language "can be seen as an ancient city, a maze of little streets and squares, of old and new houses, and of ... additions from various periods ... new boroughs with straight, regular, streets and uniform houses".[23] Hence "to imagine a language is to imagine a form of life" (*Lebensform*).[24] This clearly resonates with W. Dilthey's appeal to hermeneutics. Social and historical "life" (*Leben*) and "living through" an experience (*Erlebnis*) are fundamental for Dilthey's hermeneutics.[25] In Wittgenstein this conditions *meaning*: "Only

---

[17]   L. Wittgenstein, *Remarks on the Foundations of Mathematics* (Oxford: Blackwell, Ger. and Eng., 1956), sect. 16, p.8. On Bultmann, see Thiselton, *The Two Horizons*, pp.252–92.
[18]   Wittgenstein, *Investigations*, Part II, p.185.
[19]   Wittgenstein, *The Blue and Brown Books*, p.18.
[20]   *Blue and Brown Books*, loc. cit.
[21]   As cited above, *Philosophical Hermeneutics*, pp.3–17; also from earliest years in Gadamer, "Reflections on My Philosophical Journey", in Lewis E. Hahn (ed.), *The Philosophy of Hans-Georg Gadamer* (La Salle & Chicago, IL: Open Court, 1997), pp.3–18.
[22]   Richard Bauckham, *The Bible and Mission: Christian Witness in a Postmodern World* (Carlisle: Paternoster, 2003), pp.1, 11, 24, 84–5 and 92–3.
[23]   Wittgenstein, *Investigations*, sect. 18.
[24]   *Investigations*, sect. 19.
[25]   W. Dilthey, *Gesammelte Schriften* vol. VII (Leipzig and Berlin: Teubner, 1927), pp.203–16.

in the stream of thought and life do words have *meaning*."[26] No less, it shapes *concepts* and conceptual grammar: "What determines our concepts ... is the whole hurly-burly of human actions, the background against which we see any action".[27]

This recalls Dilthey's profoundly hermeneutical comment: "Not through introspection but through history do we come to know ourselves."[28] In Locke, Hume and Kant, "in the veins of the knowing subject *no real blood flows*".[29] Hermeneutics does not rest upon "logical abstraction" but on "life (*Leben*) as the interweaving of ... humankind".[30] Dilthey rigorously speaks of the "inter-connections (*Zusammenhung*) of human life as well as its particularity. Linking grammar with life-surroundings, Wittgenstein observes (as we have noted), "The kinds of use [that is, of language] we feel to be '*the point*' are connected with the role that such-and-such has in our whole life."[31] Both Dilthey and Wittgenstein perceive the role of particularity in understanding, but (against the pluralist interpretations of Richard Rorty and others) also recognize that "the common behaviour of humankind (*die gemeinsame menschliche Handlungsweise*) is the system of reference by means of which we interpret an unknown language".[32] "Why can a dog feel fear but not remorse? ... Only someone who can reflect on the past can repent."[33] Yet within human life as a whole, particular traditions of life may seem "to exempt certain propositions from doubt".[34]

(3) This brings us to Wittgenstein's third hermeneutical theme or axiom: the major role of traditions, customs, or training: "The child learns by believing the adult. Doubt comes after belief."[35] "Understanding is effected by exploration (*Erklärung*); but also by training (*Abrichtung*)."[36] "Traditions" provide backgrounds that range from linguistic competence to a grounding of regularities in human behaviour ("rules" in a descriptive, not prescriptive, sense) that make new kinds of communicative acts intelligible. Strawson writes, "The efficacy of those procedures [of understanding] depends on the existence of a prepared framework of linguistic training."[37] Like Schleiermacher, Wittgenstein finds a model for interpreting language in how a child learns to use language, and this involves "training" rather than simply "exploration".[38]

(4) Further, how a person or a community stands within a given tradition or culture shapes what we might regard as *"rational"* or *intelligible* understandings of utterance and

---

26 Wittgenstein, *Zettel*, sect. 173.
27 Wittgenstein, *Investigations*, sect. 23.
28 W. Dilthey, *Gesammelte Schriften* vol. VII, p.279.
29 W. Dilthey, *Gesammelte Schriften* vol. V (Leipzig and Berlin, 1927), p.4 (my italics).
30 *Gesammelte Schriften* vol. VII, p.131.
31 Wittgenstein, *Remarks on the Foundations of Mathematics* sect. 16, p.8 (as cited above, my italics).
32 Wittgenstein, *Zettel*, sect. 206.
33 *Zettel*, sect. 519.
34 L. Wittgenstein, *On Certainty* (Oxford: Blackwell, Ger. and Eng., 1969), sect. 88.
35 *On Certainty*, sect. 160.
36 Wittgenstein, *Zettel*, sect. 186.
37 P.F. Strawson, "Critical Notice", in H. Morick (ed.), *Wittgenstein and the Problem of Other Minds* (New York: McGraw-Hill, 1967), p.5.
38 Wittgenstein, *Blue and Brown Books*, p.80; *Investigations*, sect. 5.

actions *within a cultural frame of reference*. Wittgenstein offers an incisive critique of James Frazier's once highly influential *The Golden Bough*.[39] Frazer's "explanations" of meanings in other cultures and eras presuppose that they relate to persons "who think in a similar way to himself".[40] Hence he presents some of their practices, in effect, "as *stupidities* [Wittgenstein's italics] ... What narrowness of spiritual life we find in Frazer! ... How impossible for him to conceive of a different way of life from the English one of his time. Frazer cannot imagine a priest who is not basically an English parson ...".[41]

The publication of Wittgenstein's *Culture and Value* brought to light many parallel hermeneutical observations mainly from the period 1945–51. For example, "One age misunderstands another; and a *petty* age misunderstands all the others."[42] "The *words* you utter ... are not what matters so much as the difference they make at various points in your life. How do I know that two people mean the same when each says he believes in God? ... *Practice* gives the words their sense."[43] "Humour is not a mood, but a way of looking at the world."[44] "There are remarks that sow, and remarks that reap."[45]

(5) Wittgenstein's observations on *"private language" and public criteria of meaning* raise his work on *traditions and training* to new levels. "Private", here, is a technical term that is widely misunderstood; David Pears proposes "unteachable" as a close synonym.[46] What makes language "teachable" is its anchorage in observable regularities of use in the public domain. Wittgenstein's most memorable example of "private language" is his critical hypothesis about the "beetle in the box": "Suppose everyone had a box with something in it: we call it a 'beetle'. No one can look into anyone else's box, and everyone says he knows what a beetle is only by looking at *his* beetle – Here it would be quite possible for everyone to have something different in his box."[47] Could they "know" that they had a "beetle" in their box? Elsewhere Wittgenstein comments, it is "as if someone were to buy several copies of the morning paper to assure himself that what it said was true".[48] Or more strictly: "Imagine someone saying 'But I know how tall I am', and keeping his hand on his head to prove it."[49] Intelligibility and conceptual formation presuppose a *background of regularities within a public tradition*.

I have argued in various publications that this hermeneutical axiom provides initial communicative access to the conceptual grammar of "God" in the Hebrew-Christian tradition of the biblical writings. A "regularity" or *continuity of tradition* comes to be built when "God" is identified as "the God of Abraham, the God of Isaac, and the God of

---

[39] L. Wittgenstein, "Bemerkungen über Frazers, The Golden Bough", *Synthese* 17 (1967), pp.233–53.
[40] "Bemerkungen", p.235.
[41] "Bemerkungen", pp.235–6, and 237–8.
[42] L. Wittgenstein, *Culture and Value* (Oxford: Blackwell, Ger. and Eng., 1980), p.86 (1950).
[43] *Culture and Value*, p.85 (1950).
[44] *Culture and Value*, p.78 (1948).
[45] Ibid.
[46] David Pears, *Wittgenstein* (London: Collins, 1971), p.147.
[47] Wittgenstein, *Investigations*, sect. 293.
[48] *Investigations*, sect. 265.
[49] *Investigations*, sect. 279. For an exposition of the private language argument see O.R. Jones *The Private Language Argument* (London: Macmillan, 1971), especially p.14.

Jacob" (Exodus 3:16).[50] Similarly the starting-point for a conceptual grammar or understanding of *redeem* (Hebrew גָּאַל *gā'al*, and פָּדָה *pādah*) and *redemption* emerges from recurrent events that provide a *pattern of regularity* in Exodus-Judges. The further celebrations and "recitals" of God's saving acts in the Psalms and Isaiah solidify this conceptual grammar, and begin to place certain defining boundaries around it, although *not* in such a way as to exclude future twists and turns and substantial surprises. This is the kind of "open" yet identifiable logical grammar that Wittgenstein illustrates with his simile of language being like an ancient city with modern developments.

This acknowledgement of the necessary and critical role of continuity of tradition, even an "open" tradition with turnings and surprises, finds a central place in philosophical hermeneutics of Gadamer and the theological hermeneutics of Wolfhart Pannenberg's earlier writings.[51] Gadamer entitles his section on tradition "The rehabilitation of authority and tradition", and I appeal to his work in Essay 34 of this volume. By contrast, this emphasis exposes a cardinal weakness in Bultmann's hermeneutics, which remains largely focused on the lone individual in the tradition of Descartes, Kant, Kierkegaard and Neo-Kantian philosophy, over against the communally focused traditions of Vico, Schleiermacher, Dilthey, Gadamer, Apel, Habermas and Ricoeur. With a double-edged allusion of theology, Wittgenstein observes, "how words are understood is not told by words alone (Theology)".[52] Pannenberg comments, "The significance of individual moments in life shifts for us in the process of our history, for we see the place of individual experiences in the whole from perspectives that are always new."[53] The "backing" lies in a trans-individual tradition rooted in history and in life, but this is always on the move, incorporating novelty and surprise alongside continuities.

(6) Gadamer places *"the hermeneutic priority of the question"* at the heart of hermeneutical endeavour, citing the model of Plato's dialectics and "the logic of question and answer".[54] He writes, "Openness to the other, then, involves recognizing that I myself must accept some things that are against me, even though no one else forces me to do so";[55] "Discourse that is intended to reveal something requires that that thing be broken open by the question."[56] Questions often need to be indirect and subtle. Hence Gadamer

---

[50]   A.C. Thiselton, *Language, Liturgy and Meaning* (Nottingham: Grove Liturgical Studies, 1975, 2nd edn, 1986), pp.10–16, and *The Two Horizons*, pp.383–5.

[51]   Hans-Georg Gadamer, *Truth and Method* (Eng., London: Sheed & Ward, 2nd Eng. edn, 1989), pp.277–307 and indirectly throughout. W. Pannenberg is more explicit on this subject in his earlier than in his later works. See "Hermeneutics and Universal History" and "On Historical and Theological Hermeneutics", in *Basic Questions in Theology* (Eng., London: SCM, 3 vols, 1970–72), vol. 1, respectively pp.96–137 and 137ff; on tradition, "The Revelation of God in Jesus of Nazareth", in James M. Robinson and J.B. Cobb (eds), *New Frontiers in Theology vol. 3, Theology as History* (New York: Harper, 1967), pp.101–33; and *Philosophy of Science and Theology* (London: DLT, 1976), where Pannenberg seeks to complement hermeneutics with a more "scientific" or coherent resistance to retreat from "general accepted criteria" (p.13). For a more recent comment see his *Systematic Theology*, vol. 3 (Eng., Edinburgh: T. & T. Clark, 1998), pp.168–72, esp. 212.

[52]   Wittgenstein, *Zettel*, sect. 144.

[53]   Pannenberg, *Systematic Theology*, vol. 3, p.170, where he also discusses Dilthey.

[54]   Gadamer, *Truth and Method*, pp.362–79.

[55]   *Truth and Method*, p.361.

[56]   *Truth and Method*, p.363.

appeals to the example of R.G. Collingwood and his logic of questions.[57] If we go *"behind* what is said"*, we come to ask "questions *beyond* what is said".[58]

Wittgenstein, no less than Gadamer, recognizes the importance and role of questions that lead on to understanding. Surface grammar may encourage superficial questions that merely give us "mental cramp", such as "where does the past go to?" or "Where does the flame of the candle go to when it's blown out?"[59] Problems confront us when "the question is wrongly formed".[60] In accord with Gadamer's comment about accepting "some things that are against me", Wittgenstein observes, "You can't think decently if you don't want to hurt yourself."[61] A question, he declares, is "a commission ... a challenge ... It spurs us on to some activity."[62] This is why the *Philosophical Investigations* asks 784 questions, of which only 110 are answered, and of these "answers", some 70, Anthony Kenny judges, are meant to be "wrong".[63] Wittgenstein aims not to produce "results", but "a way of investigating".[64] Moreover "answers", such as they are, are never "once for all", or given "independently of any future experience".[65] They remain corrigible.

III

A Reappraisal of the Need for Multi-Disciplinary Hermeneutics: The Pontifical Biblical Commission and the Example of Paul Ricoeur

From the vantage point of 2004 the importance of inter-disciplinary and multi-disciplinary research in the service of hermeneutics appears more important and more urgent than ever before. In support of this claim I shall argue that a number of the suggestions put forward in the previous five essays of this Part III would have escaped the notice of biblical exegetes and biblical interpreters if such inter-disciplinary research had not been undertaken, and this also applies, I believe, to numerous examples in other Parts of this volume, including Parts II and V.

In more general terms, I first appeal to the remarkable document prepared by the Pontifical Biblical Commission, *The Interpretation of the Bible in the Church*.[66] This stresses the need for multi-disciplinary hermeneutics, including philosophical hermeneutics, for biblical interpretation. Pope John Paul II wrote that he "joyfully accept[s] this document" as the fruit of collegial work undertaken on the initiative of Cardinal Joseph Ratzinger.[67] The disciplines include historical-critical method, literary analysis (narrative, rhetorical

---

57 *Truth and Method*, pp.370–73.
58 *Truth and Method*, p.370.
59 Wittgenstein, *The Blue and Brown Books*, p.108.
60 Wittgenstein, *Zettel*, sect. 142.
61 Norman Malcolm (with G.H. von Wright), *Ludwig Wittgenstein: A Memoir* (Oxford: OUP, 1958), p.40.
62 Wittgenstein, *Zettel*, sects 695–6.
63 A. Kenny, "Aquinas and Wittgenstein", *The Downside Review* 77 (1979), p.235, provides these figures.
64 Rush Rhees, *Discussions of Wittgenstein* (London: Routledge, 1970), pp.42–3.
65 Wittgenstein, *Investigations*, sect. 92.
66 The Pontifical Biblical Commission, *The Interpretation of the Bible in the Church: Address of His Holiness Pope John Paul II and Document* (Quebec: Editions Paulines, 1964). Cf. also J.L. Houlden (ed.), *The Interpretation of the Bible in the Church* (London: SCM, 1995), with individual responses.

and semiotic analysis), canonical criticism and history of influence (*Wirkungsgeschichte*), sociological, psychological and cultural-anthropology approaches, together with liberation and feminist approaches.[68]

A second example of the fruitfulness of multi-disciplinary practice is that of Paul Ricoeur.[69] A philosophical career that began with profound questions about human selfhood and finitude then explored symbols and "double-meaning" expressions, including Freud's claims about dreams, self-deception and disguise, proceeded through explorations of semantics, semiotics, metaphor and narrative, to return eventually once again to responsibility, identity, inter-subjectivity and selfhood, all within the framework of hermeneutical enquiry.

We shall consider Ricoeur's example in more detail shortly. Yet one question remains in the background. Do investigations of conceptual grammar in the tradition of the later Wittgenstein earn a place within what is strictly necessary for fruitful multi-disciplinary hermeneutics? The idea that many philosophical problems can be resolved in terms of some sort of "grammatical" solution reached a high-point in the late 1950s and 1960s with the publication of works by Wittgenstein, Gilbert Ryle and other linguistic philosophers of the so-called analytical or "Oxford" philosophical tradition. Over the last quarter of the twentieth century such confidence has faded, although some, including perhaps Peter Hacker, continue to sustain this kind of tradition in broader terms.[70] Yet what emerged in the middle decades of the twentieth century remains as a resource in the repertoire of most university faculties or departments of philosophy, even if it has lost its spell as a focus of fashion. We shall address this more specific question of whether explorations of conceptual grammar provide a needed resource for hermeneutics in the next section. Meanwhile we return to Paul Ricoeur.

Ricoeur traces his intellectual pilgrimage through a variety of disciplines up to 1971 in the lecture to which we have already referred.[71] Born in 1913, in the 1930s he studied in Paris under Gabriel Marcel, who, although popularly described as an existentialist philosopher, focused on the nature of interpersonal understanding in contrast to the more technological language of the applied sciences. This personal dimension involves participation. Marcel also explored issues of human finitude, fallibility and will, which featured in Ricoeur's earliest major publications *Freedom and Nature: The Voluntary and Involuntary* (English, 1966; French, 1949); and *Finitude and Guilt* (French, 1960), translated into English-speaking editions as *Fallible Man* and *The Symbolism of Evil* (1967). If the human will is finite and fallible, Ricoeur distinguishes between the philosophical notion of limitation or finitude, and the theological notion of guilt. However, this at once raises questions of hermeneutics. For fallible human will frequently deploys not only ambiguous language, but often "double-meaning" expressions that serve to protect the self from accusations or self-accusations of fortune and guilt.

---

[67] Pontifical Biblical Commission, *Interpretation*, p.7.

[68] Pontifical Biblical Commission, *Interpretation*, pp.34–69.

[69] See especially Ricoeur, *The Rule of Metaphor: Multi-Disciplinary Studies of the Creation of Meaning in Language* (London: Routledge, 1978), especially on his own career up to that date, pp.315–22.

[70] Cf., for example, Peter Hacker, *The Great Philosophers: Wittgenstein* (London: Wiedenfeld & Nicolson, 1997).

[71] Ricoeur, *Rule of Metaphor*, pp.315–22.

During the period of the war (1939–45) Ricoeur became a prisoner in Germany, and used the opportunity to undertake a closer study of German philosophy, especially that of Jaspers, Husserl and Heidegger. In due course the psychological insights of Jaspers, the phenomenology of Husserl, and Heidegger's notion of "worlds", "time" and "possibility", would feature as contributions to Ricoeur's greatest works, not least to his magisterial *Time and Narrative* (English, 3 vols, 1984–88). Some of these concepts and themes find their way into his comparably great *Oneself as Another* (French, 1990; English, 1992).

Ricoeur observes, "I had to introduce a *hermeneutical dimension* into reflective thought", for what he perceived as "double-meaning" expressions invite interpretation at more than one level.[72] They involve layers on meaning, and *transcend the merely empirical, reflective, or "explanatory"*. Indeed, on the path towards his next major milestone publication he wrote of the need to explore *indirect* language, including a diagnostic approach to "dreams and symptoms".[73]

This next major work was Ricoeur's *Freud and Philosophy: An Essay on Interpretation* (English, 1970; French, *De l'interpretation: Essai sur Freud*, 1965).[74] He did not share Freud's non-theistic or anti-theistic belief-system, and regarded his methods as reductionist and too mechanistic. Nevertheless recognition of the roles played *both* by the level of quasi-causal explanation *and* that of interpersonal understanding led him to retain the hermeneutical resources of Schleiermacher and Dilthey (*Erklärung* and *Verstehen* in Dilthey; the comparative and the "divinatory" in Schleiermacher) in contrast to Gadamer's assimilation of "explanation" into hermeneutical understanding. I have expounded Ricoeur's use of Freud elsewhere, and Karl-Otto Apel offers a classic treatment of what he calls the "E-V" controversy on explanation (*Erklärung*) and understanding (*Verstehen*).[75]

Ricoeur's appeal to "explanation" as a critical and comparative tool to constrain sheer credulity, mere *self-affirmation*, and ultimately *idolatry* remains *fundamental for hermeneutics*. Freud, as well as Ricoeur in his earlier works *Fallible Man* and *The Symbolism of Evil* underlines the capacity of the human heart for self-deception and manipulation. Their accounts of dreams invite both "understanding" of an interpersonal nature and "explanation". The latter exposes the role of Freudian "condensation", "displacement" and "overdetermination". Displacement may scramble and rearrange sequences and images that the censor represses for self-protection, while overdetermination presents multiple interpretations or "readings" of the same phenomena. Hence in a key comment Ricoeur brings together the dual function of the *critical* and the *listening*: "Hermeneutics seems to me to be animated by this double motivation: willingness to suspect, willingness to listen; vow of rigor, vow of obedience. In our time we have not finished doing away with *idols*, and we have barely begun to listen to symbols."[76] Freud's most

---

[72] *Rule of Metaphor*, p.316.
[73] *Rule of Metaphor*, p.317.
[74] Paul Ricoeur, *Freud and Philosophy: An Essay on Interpretation* (New Haven, CT: Yale, 1970).
[75] Karl-Otto Apel, *Understanding and Explanation* (Cambridge, MA: MIT Press, 1984), cf. Thiselton, *New Horizons in Hermeneutics*, pp.346–51.
[76] Ricoeur, *Freud and Philosophy*, p.27.

distinctive contribution, Ricoeur suggests, is to make clear that "the subject is never the subject one thinks it is".[77] In hermeneutics "the idols must die – so that symbols may live".[78]

Ricoeur continues his philosophical explorations, but now more broadly with reference to a variety of philosophical traditions. His epistemology goes beyond that of Descartes, Kant and Hegel, and interacts with the work of Husserl and Heidegger. Subjectivity is not mere introspection, but emerges in the context of inter-subjectivity. In common with much in French intellectual life in the late 1960s, Ricoeur moves beyond existentialism and opposes any "totalitarian" interpretations of the world. Alongside critical differences, this is his closest point of affinity with Lyotard and Derrida, for whom Freud, Husserl and Heidegger are suggestive resources. Hence, for Ricoeur, the "openness" of texts and the phenomenon of "double-meaning" suggest varied ways of interpreting texts and human life. This plurality emerges in *The Conflict of Interpretations*.[79] Ricoeur seeks to hold together some critical axis with a legitimate plurality of interpretation by turning to structuralism, semantics and semiotics, in his work on texts in his early-middle period. This emerges especially in his *Interpretation Theory* (1976).[80]

Ricoeur's inter-disciplinary research into language and literature enhances his insight into the creative power of symbol by extending this to metaphor and narrative emplotment. *Symbol* relates to the creativity of *words* and concepts as *metaphor* relates to the creativity of *sentences* and propositions, and as *emplotment* yields creativity in *story and narrative*. Combining Max Black's notion of metaphor as *interactive* with Heidegger's notion of "possibility" as entailing projected "worlds", Ricoeur is *en route* to produce his masterpiece *Time and Narrative*. Yet prior to this, in 1975 he contributed to the biblical studies journal *Semeia* on "Biblical Hermeneutics", while his *Essays on Biblical Interpretation* appeared in 1981.[81] This involvement with biblical studies continues to the end of his life.[82]

Time and Narrative brings together Ricoeur's research and thinking over the years on the philosophy of the self, unity and plurality, hermeneutics, literary theories of narrative, ancient philosophical and Christian thought, and virtually all that we have outlined above. The dynamics of "emplotment" take place within a dialectical relation of "concordance" and "discordance". Ricoeur focuses the first in the light of Aristotle's conception of the unity of a temporal logic of plot, and the second in the light of

---

[77] *Freud and Philosophy*, p.420.

[78] *Freud and Philosophy*, p.531.

[79] Paul Ricoeur, *The Conflict of Interpretations: Essays in Hermeneutics* (Evanston, IL: Northwestern University Press, 1974).

[80] Paul Ricoeur, *Interpretation Theory: Discourse and the Surplus of Meaning* (Fort Worth, TX: Christian University Press, 1976).

[81] Paul Ricoeur, "Biblical Hermeneutics", *Semeia* 4 (1975), 29–148; and *Essays on Biblical Interpretation* (London: SPCK, 1981). Cf. also his "The Bible and the Imaginations", in H.D. Betz (ed.), *The Bible as a Document of the University* (Chico, CA: Scholars Press, 1981), pp.49–55.

[82] Paul Ricoeur, *Forgiving the Sacred* (Minneapolis, MN: Fortress, 1995), especially Part III, "The Bible and Genre: The Polyphony of Biblical Discourses", pp.129–202, and its Parts IV and V, pp.236–61 and 303–14; and also *Thinking Biblically: Exegetical and Hermeneutical Studies* with André La Cocque (Chicago, IL: University of Chicago Press, 1998).

Augustine's conception of the stretching-apart of time in human experience.[83] We resist the temptation to expound the detailed argument of these rich three volumes here. We discuss Ricoeur here *solely for the purpose of demonstrating concretely the need and value of multi-disciplinary enquiry in hermeneutics.*

This dialectic of unity and plurality is profoundly hermeneutical, and it gives rise to Ricoeur's no less magisterial book *Oneself as Another*. The self emerges as a stable "Who?" in contrast to a mere "what?".[84] Human selfhood reflects a parallel dialectic to that of hermeneutics: that between *continuity* (self) and *variability* (the other), in which personal identity achieves its stability and creativity in relation to the inter-subjective world. In these pages Ricoeur calls not only upon the resources mentioned above, but *also upon the conceptual grammar of "person"*, the *transcendental* conditions of communication and philosophy of language, and *"the conceptual of scheme of action and the question 'who?'"*.[85] Ricoeur explicitly appeals to Wittgenstein. He writes that his *"conceptual analysis of the notion of intention ... is responsible for producing the sort of nuanced and many-levelled analysis inherited from the Wittgenstein of the 'Philosophical Investigations'"*.[86] The subtlety of Wittgenstein's approach serves to avoid exaggerated "symmetrical polarities", and is supplemented by Elizabeth Anscombe's intention (in the same tradition).[87] Wittgenstein's incisive observations about the conceptual grammar of "the same" and "identity" feature at various points.[88]

IV

Multi-disciplinary Research – But Conceptual Grammar?

These observations from Ricoeur suggest that explorations of conceptual grammar are not as irrelevant to philosophical hermeneutics today as some believe. Further, the hermeneutics of Karl-Otto Apel rest upon a sustained engagement with the later Wittgenstein and "analytical philosophy" not only in his earlier work, but also in his mature hermeneutical writings, while Gadamer and Habermas also find resonances between Wittgenstein and their own work.[89] To argue that conceptual grammar should feature within the inter-disciplinary concerns of exponents of biblical hermeneutics initially goes no further than these writers.

---

[83] Paul Ricoeur, *Time and Narrative* (Eng., Chicago, IL: University of Chicago Press, 3 vols, 1984–88), vol. 1, pp.3–90.

[84] Paul Ricoeur, *Oneself as Another* (Eng., Chicago, IL: University of Chicago Press, 1992), pp.1–25, 40–55, 240–356, and throughout.

[85] *Oneself as Another*, pp.35–44, 44–55 and 52–73 (my italics).

[86] *Oneself as Another*, p.67 (my italics).

[87] Ibid.

[88] *Oneself as Another*, pp.51–4, 64–8, 283 and 325.

[89] See Karl-Otto Apel, *Analytic Philosophy of Language and the Geisteswissenschaften* (Dordrecht: Reidel, 1967); and *Towards a Transformation of Philosophy* (Eng., London: Routledge, 1980), especially "Wittgenstein and the Problems of Hermeneutic Understanding", pp.1–45. Cf. H.-G. Gadamer, *Philosophical Hermeneutics* (Berkley, CA: University of California Press, 1976), pp.xxxiii–xxxiv (by the ed. D.E. Linge), 126–7 and 175–7.

In more pragmatic terms my approach to the interpretation of Titus 1:12–13 (Essay 14, above) offers, I believe, a more convincing exegesis of this passage within its context in Titus and in the Pastoral Epistles than any proposal found in the biblical commentaries to date. Yet this approach rests not only on traditional historical and contextual exegesis, but also on perceiving such logical and conceptual features as the logical asymmetry between first-person and third-person utterances, appreciating the diverse functions of appeals to logical paradoxes from Zeno in the ancient world to Gilbert Ryle in the twentieth century, and contextualizing the tradition of logical paradox and first-person utterances in terms of traditions in Crete and the history of the reception of early exegetical traditions that led to a false start. All this might be called inter-disciplinary research.

My account of the logical grammar of Paul's language about justification by grace, I believe, in terms of Wittgenstein's aspective "seeing as" and D.D. Evans "onlooks within a system" delivers exegetes from asking fruitless questions about which aspect (put right or sinful) is "really true". Further it saves us from making unduly heavy weather out of a supposed contradiction between Paul and James. Furthermore, to explicate "faith" in terms of (1) "internal" grammar, and (2) dispositional belief, seems to yield a remarkable logical coherence and transparency between the various foci of the theme, which I do not readily find elsewhere in these studies that remain wedded to the single discipline of biblical studies alone.

The contribution on semantics would not be widely contested. As I have observed elsewhere in this volume, I received strong encouragement to explore this inter-disciplinary resource in oral conversations with George B. Caird of Oxford in the mid-1960s. He himself believed that his collaboration with his fellow-professor in Oxford, Stephen Ullmann, on semantics, shed a flood of light in the use of metaphorical "end-of-the-world" language in the Synoptic Gospels. James Barr generously expressed strong approval of such articles as "The Supposed Power of Words in the Biblical Writings", although in the 1980s he still expressed to me privately some reservation about the value of philosophical hermeneutics and explorations of conceptual grammar for biblical interpretation. In the end, perhaps the value of research in conceptual grammar will either stand on its own feet or will continue to meet with a degree of scepticism. Appreciation of its potential may come through either or both of two routes. One is a deeper awareness of the implicit use of conceptual grammar in Ricoeur's hermeneutics, especially in *Oneself as Another*, and perhaps, even if less strikingly, in Apel and Habermas. The other is by patient trial and error in the case of biblical passages and texts where confusion or stalemate appears to remain in spite of exegetical endeavour.

I conclude by suggesting one further example of specific biblical material where prevailing interpretations may perhaps receive some illumination from directions that emerge from outside the discipline. The conceptual grammar of *"expecting"* may repay exploration, not least in the context of expecting the Coming of Christ or the final *Parousia*. In my essay above on Luke's Christology (Essay 7) I have argued that a dispositional account of *belief* coheres with Luke's emphasis upon the public domain as the arena or sphere of practical discipleship. Wittgenstein observes concerning both belief and expectation: "An expectation is embedded in a situation from which it arises ... If someone whispers 'It'll go off now', instead of saying 'I expect the explosion at any moment', still his words do not describe a feeling, although they ... may be a manifestation of his feeling".[90] Wittgenstein insists again and again that in their proper context such expressions as "I hope", or "I expect" are "not giving myself a *report*. It may be a sigh, but it need not."[91] Certainly if someone asks "How do you know you believe?" (or "How do you know you expect?"), it would be odd to reply "I know it by introspection."[92] "I expect" is not primarily a description or assertion about an inner state. But if it is not an assertion, can it be a true-or-false proposition?

A wish, a suspicion, an expectation, is "something unsatisfied".[93] Wittgenstein writes, "To say that someone perceives an expectation *makes no sense*."[94] All that would make sense is to say that one perceives the expression of an expectation.[95] It is quite possible, even usual, to say, "I am expecting him", though "his coming does not occupy our thoughts".[96] It may be tantamount to saying, "I shall be surprised if he did not come", and "that will not be called a state of mind".[97] The "grammar" of *expect* and *believe* can be seen by asking "what consequences [follow], where it takes us".[98]

To say "I expect him for tea" does not refer "to one state of mind going on throughout that interval" [that is, until his arrival]. What "expecting" consists in is the *disposition* to respond with *actions* such as the following: "I prepare tea for two; I think for a moment, 'Does B. smoke?' and put out cigarettes; towards 4.30 I begin to feel impatient ...".[99] Sometimes, that is, in other "surroundings" or contexts, "we might use the word 'longing' (where 'longing' is used intransitively) and don't know what we are longing for".[100] The logical tensions increase if we insist on interpreting an expectation as an inner mental state tied to the language of assertion or description. Wittgenstein presses the disanalogy: "How can we expect a fact which does not exist? ... What we expect is not the fact ...".[101]

Arguably, then, New Testament language about "expecting" the *parousia* concerns *the actions that manifest an attitude or stance of expectancy, not a mental state of which the content can be described as true-or-false*. This accords with New Testament eschatology: to expect the coming of God or the coming of Christ is to sit light to earthly possessions and to place a question-mark against earthly securities. *It is not that which can have a truth-value or be "a mistake" if it is not a description proposition*. However, it may indeed function as a *presupposition*. Hence Paul could hardly have said in 1 Thess. 4:15, "*Those* who are alive and remain ..." without disengaging himself from the *stance*

---

90   Wittgenstein, *Investigations*, sect. 582.
91   *Investigations*, sect. 585 (my italics).
92   *Investigations*, sect. 587.
93   *Investigations*, sect. 438.
94   *Investigations*, sect. 453.
95   *Investigations*, loc. cit.
96   *Investigations*, sect. 577.
97   *Investigations*, loc cit.
98   *Investigations*, sect. 578.
99   Wittgenstein, *Blue and Brown Books*, p.20.
100 *Blue and Brown Books*, p.29.
101 *Blue and Brown Books*, p.36.

of expectation which the construction "*we* who are alive and remain" would suggest. This is not the place to expand this argument in detail. My aim is simply to indicate the productive lines of thought that explorations of conceptual grammar may unlock, without suggesting that these necessarily "solve" every problem. However, this reappraisal of the vexed question of "eschatological imminence" coheres well with G.B. Caird's re-examination of "end-of-the-world" language in the New Testament in the light of semantic analysis.[102]

---

[102] G.B. Caird, *The Language and Image of the Bible* (London: Duckworth, 1980).

PART IV

LEXICOGRAPHY, EXEGESIS AND RECEPTION HISTORY

Greek Lexicography and the Context of Argument: "The 'Interpretation' of Tongues? A New Suggestion in the Light of Greek Usage in Philo and Josephus" (1979)

In Essay 3 I pointed out that interpretation was not a separate task from translation and lexicographical research. Before 1979 I had come to experience serious doubts about both the traditional translations of 1 Corinthians 14:13, and its being understood in terms of an "interpreter" of tongues whose identity was different from that of the one who spoke in tongues. These doubts were simultaneously lexicographical (does the Greek word διερμηνεύω *(diermēneuō) necessarily or even probably mean "to interpret" rather than "to articulate in words"?), exegetical and interpretative (does not Paul more usually conceive of glossolalia as utterance of some kind to God, rather than to persons?), and syntactical (where is the missing word for "someone" in the Greek?). This article, accepted for publication in* Journal of Theological Studies, *vol. 30, 1979, pp.15–36, brings all these dimensions together as a hermeneutical whole. By the time when I wrote my commentary on First Corinthians, I found support for my understanding of glossolalia especially in Gerd Theissen,* Psychological Aspects of Pauline Theology *(Eng., Edinburgh: T. & T. Clark, 1987), pp.59–114 and 292–341. I discuss this further in* The First Epistle to the Corinthians: A Commentary on the Greek Text *(Grand Rapids, MI: Eerdmans and Carlisle: Paternoster, 2000), pp.1074–1146.*

In the passages which relate to speaking in tongues in 1 Corinthians 12–14, there are four occurrences of the verb διερμηνεύω (12:30; 14:5, 13, 27), two uses of the noun ἑρμηνεία (12:10 and 14:26), and one occurrence of διερμηνευτής (14:28).[1] In all the major English versions, including the NRJV, NJB, NIV, REB and NEB, each of these seven occurrences is taken to refer to the 'interpretation' of tongues. Liddell and Scott place the passages in 1 Corinthians under the heading of 'interpret, expound' (διερμηνεύω), and 'interpreter' (διερμηνευτής). Whilst they include a wider range of meanings under ἑρμηνεία they do not refer to 1 Corinthians in this connection.[2] The entries in Bauer-Arndt-Gingrich [at the time of writing, the 1957 edition was the only English edition published] also relate διερμηνεύω in these chapters to the 'interpretation' of ecstatic speech, and ἑρμηνεία is placed under the heading 'translation, interpretation'.[3]

---

[1]   B and D* read the variant ἑρμηνευτής.
[2]   H.H. Liddell, R. Scott, H.S. Jones and R. McKenzie, *A Greek-English Lexicon* (Oxford, 1940), pp.425 and 690.
[3]   W.F. Arndt and F.W. Gingrich (W. Bauer), *A Greek-English Lexicon of the New Testament and Other Early Christian Literature* (Cambridge, 1957), pp.193 and 310.

None of the twenty-five commentaries that I consulted on these verses suggests the possibility of any alternative understanding of the words, except that some commentators, including Conzelmann, leave open the alternatives of 'interpretation' or 'translation'.[4] The purpose of this article is tentatively to suggest the possibility of a third alternative. I shall offer lexicographical evidence from Philo and Josephus that shows that these words often mean not to translate or to interpret, but simply 'to put into words'. This has considerable consequences for our understanding of parts of 1 Corinthians 12–14.

In the first half of this study I shall examine the lexicographical evidence, and then turn in the second half to exegetical considerations that the six passages in question in 1 Cor. 12–14 raise. However, before we begin to look in detail at the writings of Philo and Josephus, a preliminary indication may be given of how this suggestion might affect our understanding of Paul's argument.

I

Some Critical Markers that Shape the Discussion

In 1 Cor. 14:13 Paul writes ὁ λαλῶν γλώσσῃ προσευχέσθω ἵνα διερμηνεύῃ. Traditionally this has been taken to mean: 'He who speaks in a tongue should pray for the power to interpret' (RSV). But on the basis of the lexicographical evidence presented below, the sentence might equally well be taken to mean: 'He who speaks in a tongue should pray for the power to produce articulate speech.' The question which we shall ask towards the end of this study is whether this does not in fact do better justice to Paul's argument at this precise point than to understand him to refer to the more obscure notion of 'interpreting' tongues. By way of anticipating our later discussion, we may observe three points.

First, the general thrust of the argument relates to the contrast between speaking in tongues and *prophecy*. We shall argue that this is precisely Paul's point in this particular verse. The man who speaks in tongues must pray for the power to put his experience into words, so that he can thereby minister to the whole community. Second, Paul's argument calls for the use of *the mind*. But again (as we shall see especially from some of the examples in Philo), this is precisely what is involved in expressing something in an articulate way; far more obviously, it may be added, than it has to do with 'interpreting' tongues. Third, this verse now becomes in effect Paul's most explicit statement in the chapter that ideally, speaking in tongues should not occur at all *in public*. Here, once again, the point exactly matches the context. Paul has just said that tongues are a private matter between the individual and God: 'one who speaks in a tongue speaks not to men but to God ... He who speaks in a tongue edifies himself, but he who prophesies edifies the church' (14:2, 4).

This brings us to a second example, which follows the verse just quoted. In the midst of Paul's argument the RSV, following tradition, introduces a reference to an *interpreter* of

---

4   H. Conzelmann, *1 Corinthians. A Commentary on the First Epistle to the Corinthians* (Eng., Philadelphia, PA, 1975), pp.209, 234–5, 237 and 244–5.

tongues: 'He who prophesies is greater than he who speaks in tongues, unless *someone* interprets, so that the church may be edified' (14:5, my italics). According to the traditional view, Paul urges a certain line of argument with all his might, but concedes, in passing, that the bottom is knocked out of this entire argument if an 'interpreter' happens to be present at the public worship and also is willing to play his part. When we turn to the Greek, however, we find no reference to 'someone' at all. Paul simply says: μείζων δὲ ὁ προφητεύων ἢ λαλῶν γλώσσαις, ἐκτὸς εἰ μὴ διερμηνεύῃ, ἵνα ἡ ἐκκλησία οἰκοδομὴν λάβῃ. He who prophesies is greater than he who speaks in tongues, unless he (the latter himself) can put it into words. The exception clause is now no longer a mysterious tailpiece to Paul's argument, but expresses the thrust of all that he says from 14:1 to 14:33, if not from chapters 12 to 14.

We shall postpone considerations of other passages, and indeed also of these in detail, until we have first tested our lexicographical claim. Before we turn to Philo, however, two other points may be briefly anticipated. First, at the end of our lexicographical sections we shall consider the force of arguments which have been put forward to the effect that speaking in tongues, in these chapters, means the gift of speaking foreign languages. For some time this view had been out of general favour, but more recently fresh arguments in support of it have been put forward by Davies and Gundry.[5] If these arguments were totally convincing we should have to return to the idea of a 'translation' of tongues. We shall endeavour to show, however, why in our own view they fail to do justice to the situation reflected in these chapters.

Second, we shall also try to show why it is that in the view of Paul *both* speaking in tongues *and* the gift of moving beyond this stage (ἑρμηνεία γλωσσῶν) can equally be thought of as genuine gifts of the Spirit. Stendahl describes speaking in tongues as relating to 'high voltage religion ... raw and fresh primary experience', especially on the part of 'those who are not professional in the shaping of words'.[6] For Christian believers in that situation, Paul expresses his gladness that an outlet has been found for their inarticulate sighs of longing or praise or worship. Whether such a gift should be exercised in public remains another matter. However, Stendahl also questions whether this particular 'high-voltage' experience is always appropriate to Christians as they mature in their religious experience.[7] The 'gift' that is then needed is that of being able to put their experience into intelligible speech, which can build up the community. How this gift relates to προφητεία and why the actual phrase used is ἑρμηνεία γλωσσῶν we shall discuss in due course. We shall also seek to draw support for our argument from two sociological analyses of the situation at Corinth recently put forward by Gerd Theissen and by W.J. Hollenweger.[8] The ability to articulate experience which hitherto found expression only in tongues appears all the more intelligibly as a genuine gift of the Spirit

---

[5] Cf. J.G. Davies, 'Pentecost and Glossolalia'; *J.T.S.* n.s. 3 (1952), pp.228–31; and especially R.H. Gundry, '"Ecstatic Utterance" (N.E.B.)?' *J.T.S.* n.s. 17 (1966), pp.299–307.

[6] K. Stendahl, 'Glossolalia – The New Testament Evidence', in *Paul among Jews and Gentiles* (London, 1977), p.122; pp.109–24 *passim*. Cf. also J. Behm, *T.D.N.T.* vol. 1, pp.721–6.

[7] K. Stendahl, op. cit., p.123.

[8] G. Theissen, 'Soziale Schichtung in der korinthischen Gemeinde. Ein Beiträg zur Soziologie des hellenistischen Urchristentums', *Z.N.W.* 65 (1974), pp.232–72, and W.J. Hollenweger, *Konflikt in Korinth und Memoiren eines alten Mannes. Zwei narrative Exegesen* (Munich, 1978).

when we consider the serious discrepancy in social background between the secretary-slave or property-owner, who already knew all about words, and the worker-slave who came from a non-literate background. The latter, at least initially, needed the gift of tongues more than anyone else. But no less precious to such a one was the gift, when it came, of being able to put it all into words.

II

Lexicographical Evidence from First-Century Hellenistic Greek: A First Set of Nine Examples from Philo

In Philo's writings the noun ἑρμηνεία occurs thirty times; ἑρμήνευμα once; and ἑρμηνεύς thirty-eight times. Philo uses the adjective ἑρμηνευτικός three times, whilst the verb ἑρμηνεύω occurs as often as 153 times. The compound verb διερμηνεύω is used eighteen times, and διερμηνευτέον and διερμήνευσις each occur twice. In the case of the compound forms with the διά prefix, no less than three-quarters of the uses refer to the articulation of thoughts or feelings in intelligible speech. Fifteen instances can have only this meaning. 'Interpret' or 'translate' would be almost impossible in these instances. In three cases the precise meaning is uncertain. Only the remaining four examples clearly refer to translation or interpretation.

At first sight statistics may seem to be considerably less impressive in the case of ἑρμηνεύω forms which do not have the διά prefix. Out of the overall total of 225 occurrences, 127 refer either to interpretation or translation. Sixty-four uses clearly relate to the production of articulate speech, whilst thirty-four instances cannot be classified with certainty. However, two points should perhaps be noted. First, when Paul has the choice of using the verbs ἑρμηνεύω or διερμηνεύω he seems to prefer the compound form, whereas the only alternative abstract noun to the simple form ἑρμηνεία would be the very rare word διερμήνευσις, used by Plato to mean 'parleying' (*Timaeus*, 19C).[9] Second, it is arguable that the contexts in Philo in which the forms mean 'to put into words' are closer to the issues at stake in 1 Cor. 14 than those in which they can only mean to 'interpret'.

Three of the fifteen διερμηνεύω occurrences appear in the same broad and significant context in *De migratione Abrahami*. God's promise to Abraham 'I will bless you' is interpreted by Philo to mean that God will give him 'excellent speech' (εὐ-λογήσω). The gift of *eu-logos* has two parts: the power of thought, and the power to articulate that thought in speech. Two illustrations of this principle are suggested. (1) First, Philo suggests a model in which the mind is seen as a spring (πηγή) and speech is seen as constituting its outflow (ἀπορρέω, *De mig. Abr.* 72). In this way, he asserts, speech 'gives articulate expression' (διερμηνεύοντος) to thought (73). (2) Second, the need for articulate speech over and above rational thought is illustrated by the role played by Aaron in relation to Moses

---

[9] The fact that διερμηνεία exists only as a variant in 1 Cor. 12:10 cuts both ways. If Paul did coin the word, it strengthens our argument considerably. But if he did not, it might be argued that it would have been open to him to do so.

(Exod. 4:10–16). Of Aaron it is said, 'He will put your message into articulate speech' (οἷον διερμηνεύσει, 81). The issue here does not turn on meaning, in the sense of translation, but on the intelligible articulation of νοήματα. (3) A third example occurs earlier in the same treatise (De mig. Abr. 12). Once again, the context concerns the contrast between inner activities of the mind and outward verbal expression (ἑρμηνεία). This verbal expression, Philo argues, is like a shadow (σκιά) or copy (μίμημα). But the actual content of 'the matters that have been articulated' (τῶν διερμηνευομέων ... πραγμάτων) resembles the substance and the archetype (σώμασι δὲ καὶ ἀρχετύποις). Here, once again, the context demands 'to put into words', rather than 'to interpret', and certainly not 'translate'.

We may consider next (4) a straightforward example in which Philo speaks of 'what our senses perceive, or our speech articulates, or our emotion causes us to feel' (ἡ αἴσθησις ᾔσθετο ἢ ὁ λόγος διηρμήνευσεν ἢ τὸ πάθος διέθηκεν, De conf. Ling. 53). (5) In his treatise on Joseph, Philo recounts how the brothers tried to persuade Jacob to let Benjamin go to Egypt, putting forward the fourth in age who was a competent speaker (δυνατὸν εἰπεῖν) to act as spokesman to put into words what they all thought (διερμηνεύειν ἔπεισαν τὰ δοκοῦντα πᾶσιν, De Iosepho, 189). (6) In his discussion of the contemplative life Philo describes how on the Sabbath the Therapeutics deliver and hear a wise discourse which is not mere rhetoric or sophistry, but which embodies 'careful expression' of the exact meaning of the preacher's thoughts (De vit. cont. 31). (7) In the Embassy to Gaius, Philo recounts how the emperor sneered at them with an invocatory address 'which it is a sin to listen to, let alone articulate in actual words' (οὐχ ὅτι διερμηνεύειν αὐτολεξεί, Leg. ad Gaium 353). (8) The noun διερμήνευσις occurs in the passage about Aaron which we have already noted. The point here is that Aaron articulates the message in a way which is vivid and fluent (ἀπτείστῳ καὶ εὐτρόχῳ διερμηνεύσει ..., De mig. Abr. 79).

It is perhaps unnecessary to set out in full the remaining seven passages in which διερμηνεύω means to produce articulate speech.[10] It will readily be seen that the context of all passages relates to questions about language and communications, but not to translation. We may recall Paul's concern, as he expresses it in 1 Cor. 14:9, 'If you in a tongue utter speech that is not intelligible, how will anyone know what is said?' (cf. 14:2, 4, 6). By contrast, the passages in Philo in which διερμηνεύω means 'to translate', do so in a thoroughly obvious and straightforward way. Thus, for example, Isaac 'means' laughter (Leg. all. 3.87); the law is 'translated' into Greek (De vit. Mos. 2.31), and Edom is 'interpreted' as meaning earthly one (Quod deus sit immut. 144).

III
A Further Seventeen Examples from Philo

We now turn to the ἑρμηνεύω forms in Philo which do not retain the διά prefix. (9) As our first example of these we may select a passage in which Philo's argument cannot fail

---

10   De opif. mund. 31; De sobr. 33; De vit. Mos. i. 286; ii. 34; De spec. leg. ii. 256; iv. 132; and Quis rer. div. her. 63.

to remind us of that of Paul in 1 Cor. 14:6–12. Paul proposes an analogy between speaking in tongues and the unskilled use of a musical instrument: 'If even lifeless instruments, such as the flute or harp, do not give distinct notes, how will anyone know what is played? ... So with yourselves, if you in a tongue utter speech that is not intelligible, how will any one know what is said?' (14:7, 9). Philo has a broadly similar analogy, in that, like Paul, he makes a comparison between the differentiation of notes by the skilled musician and the use of the mind to produce articulate speech (ἑρμηνεὺς πραγμάτων γινόμενος). In *De post. Caini* 100–11, he turns his attention to Jubal, the father of music. The name Jubal, he argues, is a figure for the uttered word (ὁ κατὰ προφορὰν λόγος, 100). This is because, according to Philo, it means 'inclining now this way, now that', and this is said to point to the differentiations of tone or tongue that are presupposed in music or, equally, in speech. Music produced by ordinary (cf. Paul's ἄψυχα) instruments does indeed charm the ear and deserve praise. But the music of the human voice, Philo argues, ranks still more highly. For the human voice has the pre-eminent gift of articulation (τὴν ἔναρθρον σαφήνειαν, 105). Man has been endowed with articulate utterance (ἀρθρωθείς) both in speech and in song. Melody, Philo continues, is analogous to the articulate expression of thought in speech, since musical skill achieves in the one case what the active mind achieves in the other: 'An instrument put into the hands of an unmusical person is tuneless ... In exactly the same way speech set in motion by a worthless mind is without tune ... Speech, if not struck (i.e. like an instrument) by the ruling faculty of necessity maintains silence.' But speech can be, as it were 'tuned' by the active mind. Then 'speech proves itself an harmonious instrument, articulating in language the matters in question' (ὁ λόγος συνῳδός τις ἑρμηνεὺς πραγμάτων γινόμενος ἀμυθήτους λαμβάνει μεταβολάς, 108).

The similarities of thought between Philo and Paul are too close to ignore. In Philo the ἑρμηνεύω form can refer only to the production of articulate speech. Must we not say the same about Paul's use of these words? Both writers are concerned here not only with the analogy between melody and intelligible speech, but also with the use of the mind: 'If I pray in a tongue ... my mind is unfruitful' (1 Cor. 14:14). It is noteworthy that Paul's analogy and this sentence come immediately after one of the main verses under discussion in this study. Moreover, if there should still be any lingering doubt about the meaning of ἑρμηνεύς in this passage in Philo, we may also note that he uses ἑρμηνεύω again with this meaning only a few lines later. (10) Philo moves on to the subject of rhetoric. We shall see in example (14) that he follows the practice of using ἑρμηνεία to denote articulation, as one of the three main areas of rhetoric. Thus in *De post. Caini* 110 Philo points out that a speaker does not articulate (ἑρμηνεῦσαι) the content of his thought in a consistently uniform way when his audience and actual subject-matter may vary.

(11) In *Leg. alleg.* 1.10 Philo argues that by the age of seven years, a human being has become a fully reasoning creature. The evidence for this, he asserts, is that by this time a person can use nouns and verbs in an articulate way (ἤδη ἱκανός ἐστιν ἑρνηνεὺς εἶναι). There can be no question here of the word meaning 'interpreter' or 'translator'. (12) Later in the same treatise Philo uses the phrase δεινὸν ἑρμηνεῦσαι τὸ νοηθέν to mean 'clever at expressing his ideas' (*Leg. all.* 1.74). He is referring to the ability to

articulate an utterance that results in action, and the word cannot mean interpretation in this passage. (13) In *Leg. all.* 3.121 Philo states that an oracle should be not only true, but also clear. Hence he uses the phrase τρανὴν μὲν καὶ σαφῆ τὴν ἑρμηνείαν ποιεῖσθαι to denote clear and distinct expression. (14) In *De cher.* 105 Philo follows the practice of distinguishing between three areas of rhetoric: first, invention (εὕρεσις); second, expression, articulation, or style (ἑρμηνεία), and third, practicalities concerning the delivery itself (ὑπόκρισις). Thus rhetoric 'seeks out and weighs the materials for shrewd treatment ... and welds them to the linguistic expression that is appropriate' (τὴν πρέπονσαν ἑρμηνείαν).

The treatise *Quod deterius potiori insidiari soleat* provides a number of memorable examples of the 'articulate' meaning. (15) We find occurrences of the ἑρμηνεύω words in connection, once again, with the contrast between Moses as man of God and Aaron as his spokesman. Moses is ἄλογος, not in the sense that he is said to be without reason, but in the sense that, without Aaron, he lacks something of the power to articulate God's message. By the election of Aaron 'God ... perfected all the qualities which are essential to the articulation of thought' (πρὸς ἑρμηνείαν, *Quod det. pot. insid.* 39). In the very same section, in two parallel sentences, Moses calls Aaron his 'mouth' (στόμα), and his 'mouthpiece' (ἑρμηνέα 39). (16) In the next section, mind is again described as the spring or fountain of words, and speech as its outflow. Speech is that which puts into words (ἑρμηνεύς) plans that would otherwise remain secret (40). (17) A little later in the same treatise Philo returns to the terminology of rhetoric. Life itself is not inarticulate, but has a voice. Utterance is an operation of the organ of speech (τῆς ἑρμηνείας, 68). The broad context shows that it is beyond doubt that the issue turns on production or articulate speech, not on 'interpretation'. Abel, according to Philo, was insufficiently articulate to withstand the arguments of Cain; but Moses succeeds where Abel failed, because Aaron speaks for him. Yet even so, Abel's blood is in a sense, 'articulate'. For the life is in the blood, and where there is life there is articulate speech. (18) Still in this same treatise Philo condemns those who can 'articulate' philosophical concepts yet indulge in wicked practices (74). (19) Similarly, Philo speaks about 'beauty of expression' (ἑρμηνείας) when he refers not to 'interpretation', but (as in the next sentence) to 'lofty phrasing' (79). (20) The role of speech in 'articulating' (ἑρμηνεύς) thought is evidenced by the fact that speech has no other proper function: ἴδιον δὲ λόγου τὸ λέγειν (129).

We have already noted in connection with the διερμηνεύω forms that certain passages about thought and language in *De migratione Abrahami* are of special interest. This remains true in the case of the forms without the διά compound. (21) Philo recounts his own experiences of what it is to be inspired for the work of writing. There are times when he cannot give birth to a single idea. But there are other times when 'ideas fall in a shower from above'. Then he becomes so absorbed in his work that he forgets the people around him and the place where he is. For he has come into the possession of the power to put it all into words: ἔσχον γὰρ ἑρμηνείαν (*De Migr. Abr.* 35).[11] (22) Later in the same treatise Philo turns his attention to those who seem to have excellent powers of thought, but who are betrayed by their inability to articulate clearly what is in their mind (ὑπὸ δὲ

---

[11] The variant readings in some editions do not significantly affect the point.

ἑρμηνέως κακοῦ προὐδόθησαν, 72). This is once again elaborated in terms of thought as a spring (πηγή) and language as its outflow (ἀπορρέω), thereby demonstrating that ἑρμηνεύς can have only this meaning here.

It is one of Philo's themes, as we have already noted, that part of Abraham's 'blessing' (εὐ-λογέω) is excellence of speech. (23) Several times he describes how Abraham receives 'all the virtues of linguistic expression (τὰς πρὸς ἑρμηνείαν ἁπάσας ἀρετάς, *Quis rer. her.* 110). (24) In his treatise on the use of preliminary studies, Philo argues that Sarah and Leah needed 'handmaids', which represent the Encyclia. Thus Leah has for her handmaid 'the power to put things into words' (ἑρμηνευτικὴ δύναμις) in the sense of having at least some skill in rhetoric (*De congr. erud. causa* 29). The word ἑρμηνεία is used twice more in this way in this early part of the treatise. (25) Even when ἑρμηνεία is used in connection with expounding or giving the law of God, certain contexts demand that the meaning is 'expression' rather than 'interpretation' (although we are not claiming this for every possible occurrence of this phrase). For example, in *De mut. nom.* 126, the word must refer to the putting into words of the divine laws in human speech, since what is described here is not how Moses interpreted the laws, but how he communicated them.

We need comment perhaps on only one further example in Philo. We suggested that example (9) provided a close parallel to Paul's concerns in 1 Corinthians 14. But this is not the only example in Philo that reminds us of this chapter. (26) In his first (that is, first extant) treatise on dreams Philo discusses the verses in Genesis which lead up to the episode of Jacob's dream. He is especially interested in 'the well of the oath'. Isaac did not find water here. This is taken by Philo to indicate that some knowledge lies beyond us. The first three wells are represented by body, senses and speech, of which we can have clear knowledge. But the hidden depths of the fourth denote mind. Sense and speech both related to knowledge, since both are involved in the principle of differentiation or articulation. Sound can be communicated and appreciated because one note differs from another, and melodies have distinct shape. In other words such sound is articulate (τῆς ἐνάρθρου φωνῆς, *De somn.* 1.29).

Similarly and significantly, when the tongue differentiates between sounds (ἡ γλῶσσα πλήττουσα τῇ τῆς φωνῆς τάσει τὸ ἔναρθρον ἐνσφραγίζεται καὶ λόγον) it does not merely produce 'empty sound and unshapen noise' (φωνὴν ἀργὴν καὶ ἀδιατύπωτον ἦχον), but responds to the *mind* (νοῦν) *of the one who produces articulate speech* (ἑρμηνέως, 29). Philo argues, once again, as Paul does in 1 Corinthians 14, that, as in the case of music, *on one side stands* νοῦς, τάξις *(29), and* ἑρμηνεία; *on the other side stands* φωνὴ ἀργός.

These twenty-six examples by no means exhaust the evidence in Philo concerning passages in which the probable meaning of ἑρμηνεύω or διερμηνεύω is that of putting something into words, or producing articulate speech. A selection of some further examples is given below.[12] Before we leave Philo, however, a possible objection to our argument must be anticipated. Philo, it may be argued, presupposes a sharp dualism

---

[12] *Leg. all.* iii. 207; *De cher.* 53; *De sacr. Abr.* 30, 35; *Quod det. pot. insid.* 43, 44, 127, 133; *De mig. Abr.* 78, 81, 84, 219; *Quis rer. div. her.* 108; *De cong erud.* 17, 33; *De mut. nom.* 56, 193, 208; *De somn.* i. 33; 2. 262, 274; *De vit. Mos.* I. 84, 277; 2. 129; *De spec. leg.* i. 65; 4. 49; *De vit. cont.* 76.

between thought and language, which is not present in Paul. We are claiming that διερμηνεύω in Paul describes putting a mood or experience into words which has not yet been conceptualized, whereas in Philo it might be urged, the contrast is a different one, since language for him is usually viewed in the outward expression of rational ideas or concepts. In other words, in Philo the contrast seems to be between cognition and expression, whereas in Paul, on the basis of our argument it is between pre-cognitive experience and linguistic articulation.

There seems to be little doubt that Plato's writings are characterized by this kind of dualism.[13] However, in his detailed study *Das Sprachverständnis bei Philo von Alexandrien* Klaus Otte argues that in Philo language is not simply the expression of thought, but is grounded in Being.[14] For Philo, Being (or God) comes-to-speech in language. We may readily admit that Otte himself may at times overstate his case, particularly with reference to supposed affinities between Philo and Heidegger. However, his warning on this general point remains valid, and in any case we are not obliged to depend on Otte alone. Émile Bréhier also urges that, especially in the context of divine revelation, language in Philo is not so much an external expression of inner thought, as that which is virtually synonymous with thought itself.[15] Both Otte and Bréhier support their claims with reference to a number of specific passages in Philo. This objection, then, would be misplaced. Further, this short discussion has also enabled us to see why 'articulation' or simply 'putting something into words' is a more satisfactory rendering for the ἑρμηνεύω forms than 'expression'. For *'expression' tends to presuppose an idealist or Lockean view of language*, according to which what is articulated in language is a set of concepts or ideas which has *prior existence in the mind independently of language*. We should not impose this particular theory of language on to Paul, especially in 1 Cor. 14; and in the light of Otte's warnings we should also be cautious about identifying it too closely with Philo. By contrast, 'articulation' retains the open-endedness that we require.

IV
Corroborative Lexicographical Evidence from Josephus – Five Selected Examples

As we might expect from a comparison of the subject-matter of their respective writings, Josephus uses the ἑρμηνεύω forms only about a tenth as often as Philo. The total of occurrences amounts only to twenty-four. Two other factors also warn us not to expect too much from this part of the enquiry. First, Josephus does not employ the verb διερμηνεύω at all, leaving us to draw what conclusions we can from the forms without the διά prefix. Second, since Josephus has a special interest in the Greek translation of the Jewish Scriptures, we should naturally expect that very many of his uses of the ἑρμηνεύω forms would occur in this context, and would necessarily mean 'translation'.

---

[13]   H. Steinthal, *Geschichte der Sprachwissenschaft bei den Greichen und Römern* (2 vols, Berlin, 1890, rpt. Hildesheim, 1961), vol. 1, pp.146–7; H.-G. Gadamer, *Truth and Method* (Eng., London, 1975), pp.366–78.

[14]   K. Otte, *Das Sprachverständnis bei Philo von Alexandrien: Sprache als Mittel der Hermeneutik* (Tübingen, 1968).

[15]   Émile Bréhier, *Les idées philosophiques et religieuses de Philon d'Alexandrie* (Études de philosophie médiévale, VIII; 3rd edn, Paris, 1950), esp. pp.103–7.

At least sixteen of the twenty-four occurrences of all the forms do mean 'translation'. However, no less than twelve (half of the total occurrences) appear in Book 12 of the *Antiquities*, which concerns the ordering and execution of the Greek translation of the Scriptures. One of the main concerns of Josephus is to insist that the chosen translators δυνήσονται τὴν ἑρμηνείαν αὐτῶν ἀκριβῆ ποιήσασθαι (*Ant.* 12.49; cf. 12.39, 104 and 108). Other occurrences of ἑρμηνεία and ἑρμηνεύς relate to the approval of the work both by Ptolemy Philadelphus and the people (12.197, 114).

Once again, however, what is important in the present enquiry is not simply word-statistics, but the contexts in which they occur. There are several examples of passages in Josephus in which ἑρμηνεύω can refer only to the production of articulate speech, where the context is of special interest. (1) A striking example can be found in *Bellum Judaicum* (*B.J.*) 5.182. Josephus faces the task of trying to describe the many wonders of Herod's palace. But in fact these wonders are 'beyond all words' (παντὸς λόγου κρείσσων, 5.176). After mentioning the walls, towers and banqueting-halls, he again exclaims that what was inside them defies description (ἀδιήγητος, 178). He tries to describe the precious stones, the lavish decorations, the cloisters and gardens, but once again the task is too much for him. He concludes, ἀλλὰ γὰρ οὔθ ἑρμηνεῦσαι δυνατὸν ἀξίως τὰ βασίλεια (182). *Josephus cannot find articulate speech to match the reality or experience that overwhelms him.* The word ἑρμηνεύω cannot refer here to the interpretation or translation of what has already been articulated in some other language.

(2) In *B.J.* 5.393, Josephus remonstrates with those who wish to prolong resistance against Rome, by reminding them of part of the history of Israel. Zedekiah resisted Babylon against the counsel of Jeremiah. Yet even Zedekiah and the people of that day were more moderate than those whom Josephus now addresses, 'for it would be beyond me *to put into words* (ἑρμηνεῦσαι ... ἀξίως) your enormities' (393). (3) In the *Antiquities* Josephus recounts how Jonathan swore an oath of friendship to David, invoking the God who already knows the heart πρὶν ἑρμηνεῦσαί με τοῖς λόγοις τὴν διάνοιαν (*Ant.* 6.230). (4) After the thunders of Sinai, Moses returns to the people and addresses them. He is about to speak words that come from God, but warns the people not to scorn them 'by reason of the fact that it is a human tongue that speaks' (*Ant.* 3.85). For 'it is not Moses ... but he who compelled the Nile to flow ...' who speaks (86): 'He it is who favours you with these commandments, through me his mouthpiece' (δι ἑρμηνέως ἐμοῦ, 87). It would be quite foreign to the context to introduce the idea of interpretation here. The ἑρμηνεύς in this passage, is he who articulates God's commandments for the people.

To these four quite certain examples of ἑρμηνεύω forms, we may perhaps also add a fifth, which is admittedly more open to question. (5) It is highly probable that in the very last sentence of the *Jewish War* Josephus wishes to contrast the actual content of his narrative with the particular form of words in which it was expressed (πῶς μὲν ἡρμήνευεται, 7.455). He insists on its truth, but leaves the reader to judge its style. It is just possible that Josephus is alluding to its translation from the Aramaic original into Greek. On the other hand, in his reference to this translation in *B.J.* 1.3, he uses not a ἑρμηνεύω form, but the phrase Ἑλλάδι γλώσσῃ μεταβαλών. Moreover, whilst he could hardly claim that the truth of the account (περ τῆς ἀληθείας δέ ...) is quite unrelated to how well it has been translated, Josephus may indeed claim that its truth remains independent of its style. We have already observed that Philo more than once takes over this use of ἑρμηνεία from the standard terminology of rhetoric.

The evidence from Josephus is admittedly less impressive than it is in the case of Philo. But it does at least serve to establish that the use of ἑρμηνεύω forms to refer to *putting something into words*, rather than to 'interpretation', is no mere idiosyncrasy of Philo's. Furthermore, as in the case of Philo, when these forms are used in the sense of 'translation', the context is always a thoroughly straightforward one that demands this meaning in a clear and obvious way. It is our contention that the thought of 1 Cor. 14 is far closer to the contexts in Josephus which concern communication as such, rather than those which related to routine matters about translation, or when Josephus discusses the translation of the Scriptures into Greek (*Ant.* 12.11–108).

We may conclude our lexicographical survey by noting that the ἑρνηνεύω forms may sometimes mean 'to put into words' or 'to produce articulate speech' in classical Greek literature. Thucydides talks about knowing the right measures to take, and how 'to put them into words' (ἑρμηνεύειν, ii. 60.5). Lucian declares that the historian needs two qualities: first, political insight, and second, power to put things into words (δύναμιν ἑρμηνευτικήν), that is, to be a *competent communicator* (*Hist. Conser.* 34). Xenophon similarly speaks of the power to communicate in articulate speech (ἑρμηνείαν, *Mem.* iv. 3.12). Strikingly, Aristotle uses the same word to refer to communication between different birds, where the word cannot conceivably mean interpretation or translation: χρῶνται τῇ γλώττῃ καὶ πρὸς ἑρμηνείαν ἀλλήλοις πάντες (*de Part. An.* 660a, 35). This is not an isolated example in Aristotle, and further instances can be found in Plato, Hippocrates and probably Sophocles.[16] There is less point, however, in spending time investigating the earlier history of these words long before Paul, than in looking closely at the Greek of Paul's own day. Liddell and Scott do record instances of these particular meanings in classical Greek authors. Nevertheless they indicate neither the frequency with which they occur in Philo, nor their existence in Josephus. Hence, as we already noted, in their only references to 1 Cor. 12–14 it is simply assumed that these verses come under the headings of 'interpreter', or 'interpret, expound'.[17]

V

Paul and Acts: Claims about "Translatable" Language

We may now return to 1 Corinthians, where two tasks await us. First, we must examine claims that Paul himself regarded tongues in these chapters as translatable languages. Second, we must look more closely at the exegesis of the six verses under discussion.

Many of the older commentators from Calvin to Hodge believed that speaking in tongues in 1 Cor. 12–14 was to be understood on the basis of the references to foreign languages in Acts 2:4–11.[18] For a number of reasons this view lost favour with the rise of

---

[16] E.g. Aristotle, *On the Soul*, 420b, 20; *On Breath*, 476a, 20; Plato, *Rep.* vii. 524b; *Laws*, 996b; Hippocrates, *Epid.*, v. 74; and probably Sophocles, *Oed. Col.*, 398.

[17] H.G. Liddell, R. Scott, H.S. Jones and R. McKenzie, *Lexicon*, pp.425 and 690.

[18] C. Hodge, *An Exposition of the First Epistle to the Corinthians* (rpt. London, 1958), p.248.

modern critical scholarship. Two points in particular were emphasized. First, it was argued that the interpretation of Acts 2 presented considerable difficulties, not least because the introduction of foreign languages was unnecessary for Hellenistic Jews in Palestine. Many argued that Luke's perspective was later than Paul's, and that his point was theological rather than historical. Second, it was urged that 1 Cor. 12–14 should be interpreted in the light of history-of-religions phenomena, especially that of Hellenistic ecstatic religion. Perhaps not surprisingly, however, more recently several scholars, including J.G. Davies and Robert H. Gundry, have advocated a return to the older view. We can no longer say that it is entirely out of favour.

What is the weight of the arguments put forward? In the first place, we sympathize with the endeavour of these writers not to drive any undue wedge between Acts and Paul. They are right to ask again whether a history-of-religions background helps us to understand Paul better than that of Acts. Further, Acts 2 should not be too easily dismissed, simply because of the place that it gives to the miraculous. Gundry stresses that this, rather than the question of communication as such, was the key point for Luke. Tongues are a miraculous gift from God. In the second place, we must also give due weight to the argument put forward by J.G. Davies and repeated by Gundry that the word γλῶσσα often means 'language', and that this use 'far exceeds its use for obscure speech, especially in biblical Greek'.[19] Third, Paul's description of the experience of appearing as a βάρβαρος to Greek-speaking Corinthians depends on the analogy of speaking a foreign language (1 Cor. 14:10, 11).

On the other hand Gundry's remaining two arguments are less impressive. Uses of ἑρμηνεύω in the Septuagint, where it very often quite naturally and obviously means 'to translate', must be weighed against the lexicographical considerations put forward in this study. Further, his argument that 'the association of Luke with Paul makes it very likely that Luke's presentation of glossolalia reflects Paul's own understanding of the phenomenon' must be carefully assessed in the light of the first of the points that we are about to present.[20] In spite of his five arguments, we do not believe that Gundry's account wholly matches the situation reflected in 1 Cor. 12–14. We offer six points by way of reply, although these are of varying weight.

(1) The events described in Acts 2:4–11 would remain unique to Pentecost, even if 1 Cor. xiv refers to 'translation'. Stendahl rightly comments, 'The situation is the opposite of that in Corinth: this glossolalia is not in need of interpreters.'[21] It is not that tongues are in order, as long as there is a translator (that is, on the basis of Gundry's reconstruction of 1 Cor. 14 rather than ours). The whole process of translation *back* is by-passed in Acts 2. In this respect, Stendahl concludes, 'The account of Pentecost is unique.'[22] We cannot even appeal to the other references to tongues in Acts, for neither 10:46 nor 19:6 refer to foreign languages. Simply from the viewpoint of Luke alone, speaking in tongues might not have been a single phenomenon of only one kind. Perhaps this, rather than a reference to

---

19 R.H. Gundry, '"Ecstatic Utterance" (N.E.B.)?', loc. cit., p.299.
20 Ibid., p.300; cf. p.303.
21 K. Stendahl, 'Glossolalia – The New Testament Evidence', op. cit., p.117.
22 Ibid., p.118.

different 'kinds' of foreign languages, is the point behind Paul's phrase γένη γλωσσῶν (1 Cor. 12:11).

(2) It is astonishing that if speaking in tongues regularly constituted the miraculous phenomenon of speaking unlearned foreign languages, the evidence in early Christian sources for this tradition should be virtually confined to Acts 2 and a very few scattered and debated references. Gundry cites early evidence for this view of tongues in Irenaeus, but S.D. Currie shows that in another reference Irenaeus thought of tongues as constituting a meaningless babble of sounds, a random vocalization, or 'lalling'.[23] Certainly, as Currie also shows, Celsus charges Christians with producing nonsense syllables: a charge which, one imagines, would have been quickly rejected with the obvious retort, had the early Christians understood speaking in tongues in the way advocated by Gundry. The most that can be offered is a dubious appeal to Irenaeus, Chrysostom, and perhaps the longer ending of Mark. On the whole, Currie concludes, the evidence outside the New Testament 'does not permit the formulation of a precise description of the phenomenon'.[24] If speaking in tongues means simply 'ecstatic speech', this fact is not surprising. Glossolalia may not have taken one single determinate and easily definable form. But for the early church to have forgotten, or to have failed to mention, that it possessed the miraculous gift of speaking unlearned languages seems very much more difficult to explain.

(3) One or two older writers, including Schmiedel and Grieve, argue that Paul deliberately avoids using the word γλῶσσα to denote foreign languages in 14:10, 11, unexpectedly choosing φωνή to mean language.[25] Certainly the word does seem to mean 'language' (RSV) in this context, although Héring argues that it means 'word' here.[26] Whilst this point is not a decisive one, it is nevertheless worth noting Conzelmann's comment: 'Paul would have chosen the word φωνή to designate language, because γλῶσσα has already another meaning in the context.'[27]

(4) Another argument which is admittedly not among the strongest but which nevertheless carries some weight, is that on the basis of the older view we have to do with a gift which is a theological curiosity. It cannot be argued that he who spoke with foreign tongues really knew what this foreign language meant, but simply failed to bother to translate it; since (on the basis of this view, not on the basis of ours) in 14:13 Paul tells him to *pray* for the power to translate it. But if he himself does not in fact know what he is saying whilst speaking a foreign language, we have a very curious kind of miracle indeed. We cannot even see in what sense it can be true that 'he who speaks in a tongue edifies himself' (14:4); nor in what sense tongues can be used for private devotion. On the other hand, if speaking in tongues

---

[23]   S.D. Currie, '"Speaking in Tongues": Early Evidence Outside the New Testament', *Interpretation* 19 (1965), p.290; cf. pp.274–94.

[24]   Ibid., p.294.

[25]   P.W. Schmiedel, 'Spiritual Gifts', *Encyclopaedia Biblica* (London, 1907), iv; col. 4763; and A.J. Grieve, 'Charismata', in J. Hastings, E.R. iii (Edinburgh, 1910), p.370.

[26]   J. Héring, *The First Epistle of St. Paul to the Corinthians* (Eng., London, 1962), p.148.

[27]   H. Conzelmann, op. cit., p.236.

denotes a kind of non-conceptual, pre-rational outlet for a powerful welling-up of emotions and experiences, it can readily be seen that this could benefit the inarticulate man who comes from a non-literate background, even if Paul also wants him to move beyond this relatively immature stage. On this basis, all of Paul's injunctions about the use of the mind, and ministry to the whole community, become readily intelligible.

(5) One of the strongest arguments against the 'translation' view is the difficulty of explaining why Paul seems to be so disparaging about tongues, if they involved a miracle of the kind described by Gundry. We should also expect to detect in these chapters traces of a more developed Corinthian defence of the phenomenon. Gundry suggests that what Paul attacks is only *untranslated* tongues. But the contrast in these chapters is not primarily (if at all) between translated and untranslated tongues, but between speaking in tongues and prophecy. This point is made strongly by J.C. Hurd. He writes:

> Clearly in this chapter Paul expresses his preference for prophecy ... The fact that in this chapter Paul never directly condemned the practice of glossolalia ... should not be allowed to conceal the fervour with which he sought to persuade the Corinthians to minimize or abandon the practice ... Paul here damned glossolalia with faint praise. He went on to give a long succession of arguments against the practice.[28]

As H. Chadwick has shown, and as I have also argued in two articles on aspects of this epistle, in 1 Corinthians Paul goes as far as he can in sharing common ground with opponents, and hence does not simply condemn speaking in tongues without qualification.[29] Chadwick rightly concludes, 'The entire drift of the argument of 1 Cor. xii–xiv is such as to pour a douche of ice-cold water over the whole practice.'[30] F.F. Bruce also quotes this verdict with approval.[31] We may sum up our point by citing the verdict of Ernest Best, that if glossolalia meant speaking foreign languages, 'Paul would hardly then have criticized it since it would have been so useful in evangelism, and certainly could not have been described as speech to God alone.'[32]

(6) This general point receives further elaboration with reference to Paul's language about 'giving up childish ways' (13:11) and being childish in the use of the mind (14:20; cf. 13–19). Both his references to childhood and to using the mind are significant for the present issue. Thus Hurd writes concerning 12:30, 13:1 and 11, and Chapter 14, 'It seems most probable that Paul meant to imply that the ecstatic bubblings (glossolalia) of the Corinthians were like those of babies ... Of himself Paul said, however, "When I became a man, I gave up childish ways."'[33] Similarly, with reference to Paul's language about the

---

[28]   J.C. Hurd, Jr., *The Origin of 1 Corinthians* (London, 1965), pp.188–9.

[29]   H. Chadwick, 'All Things to All Men', *N.T.S.* 1 (1954–55), pp.261–75; and A.C. Thiselton, 'The Meaning of Σάρξ in 1 Cor. 5.5: A Fresh Approach in the Light of Logical and Semantic Factors", *S.J.T.* 26 (1973), pp.204–28 [Essay 11 here], and 'Realized Eschatology at Corinth', in *N.T.S.* 24 (1978), pp.510–26.

[30]   H. Chadwick, loc. cit., p.268.

[31]   F.F. Bruce, *1 and 2 Corinthians* (London, 1971), p.130.

[32]   E. Best, 'The Interpretation of Tongues', *S.J.T.* 28 (1975), p.47; cf. pp.45–62.

[33]   J.C. Hurd, *Origin*, pp.113 and 189. Hurd is not alone in linking the reference to childhood with glossolalia; cf. D.M. Smith, 'Glossolalia and Other Spiritual Gifts in a New Testament Perspective', *Interpretation* 28 (1974), p.310; cf. pp.307–20.

use of the mind, Smithals insists, 'This speaking in tongues is portrayed by Paul as an ecstatic condition ... The natural functions of man are not involved.'[34]

The combined force of these six arguments do more than put a question-mark against the older view. Were it not for the hermeneutical problem of relating the Corinthians question to modern charismatic phenomena, we could also cite a seventh argument concerning the findings of modern linguists and anthropologists. Whilst their conclusions cannot be used as an argument for reconstructing the situation at Corinth, it is nevertheless worth noting in passing that writers such as W.J. Samarin, J.P. Kildahl and Felicitas D. Goodman reject the idea that speaking in tongues, as it is usually understood and practised in Pentecostal or revivalist circles today, has anything to do with what they term 'xenoglossia'.[35] Samarin declares that such phenomena reveal 'only a façade of language'; whilst Goodman concludes that glossolalia 'is not the surface structure of a linguistic, symbolic code, of a linguistic deep structure, but ... an artifact of hyperarousal dissociation'.[36] Such an observation is not entirely out of place for the present discussion, since the case for interpreting the New Testament phenomena sympathetically in the light of the modern charismatic movement has been recently very firmly defended by Ernest Best.[37]

Some of our six arguments may also apply to the question of whether the Corinthians might have thought of tongues as a 'heavenly' language, of the kind discussed by Lietzmann.[38] The suggestion is purely speculative, since with the possible exception of 13:1, there seem to be no traces in these chapters of any explicit claim by the Corinthians that they were actually speaking the language of heaven itself. Since appeal cannot now be made to Acts 2 for support of this view, it tends to fall between two stools, and although Ellis has recently urged that it remains a possibility, scholarly opinion does not in general favour it.[39] Moreover, some of the six arguments brought forward above still need an answer. For example, in what sense, if any, could the use of the language of heaven be described as childish? All the same, our argument does not necessarily depend on the rejection of this theory. Conzelmann, we may note, rejects this view on the ground that 'if the speaker with tongues speaks the language of heaven, then the angels speak "natural" languages'.[40] This objection may seem to require an undue degree of sophistication in linguistic theory from Paul and the Corinthians. However, in another respect it underlines the point that even if this improbable view of glossolalia were accepted, it is hardly the kind of 'speech' that can be 'translated'. It would still remain a matter of 'putting it into words'.

---

[34]   W. Schmithals, *Gnosticism in Corinth* (New York, 1971), p.173.
[35]   W.J. Samarin, *Tongues of Men and Angels. The Religious Language of Pentecostalism* (New York, 1972); J.P. Kildahl, *The Psychology of Speaking in Tongues* (New York, 1972); and F.D. Goodman, *Speaking in Tongues: A Cross-Cultural Study of Glossolalia* (Chicago, IL, 1972).
[36]   W.J. Samarin, op. cit., p.128; and F.D. Goodman, op. cit., p.152.
[37]   E. Best, 'The Interpretation of Tongues', loc. cit., esp. p.52.
[38]   H. Lietzmann, *An die Korinther I–II* (Tübingen, 1949), pp.68–71.
[39]   E.E. Ellis, 'Tongues, Gift of', *I.D.B. Supplement* (Nashville, TN, 1976), p.908.
[40]   H. Conzelmann, op. cit., p.209, n. 30.

VI
Paul's Argument in 1 Corinthians 12–14

We return, first, to the six passages in 1 Cor. 12–14 in which διερμηνεύω, διερμηνευτής and ἑρμηνεία occur. We shall consider these under three headings. First, there are two sets of passages (14:5 and 14:27, 28) in which our suggestion seems to do better justice to the Greek syntax than the traditional view. Second, the only passages that seem to cause difficulty are those that supposedly describe the 'interpretation' of tongues in the context of listing differing spiritual gifts in the community (12:10, 30; 14:26). Third, there is the explicit injunction that he who speaks in a tongue should pray for the power to translate, to interpret, or to produce articulate speech (14:13).

(1) We have already noted that in 14:5 the traditional English rendering 'unless *some one* interprets' (RSV) has no foundation in the Greek text. Several commentators, including very recently W.F. Orr and J.A. Walther, argue that whilst the Greek contains no reference to a separate interpreter, 'the list of gifts in 12.10, 30 ... seems to differentiate the person who speaks from the interpreter, and 14.26–28 suggests the same'.[41] In other words, 'some one' is read into the text on the basis of other passages. Héring argues that τις is to be understood by implication; in the same way as φησί can be used impersonally to mean 'they say'.[42] But this is only an assumption, on the basis of a given view of the whole phenomenon under description. Strictly on the basis of the Greek, there is no need to revise G.G. Findlay's early comment: '*To supply* τις *with* διερμηνεύῃ, *supposing another interpreter is meant, is ungrammatical; the identity of the speaker and interpreter is the essential point.*'[43] C.K. Barrett confirms this by explicitly translating the passage: 'He who prophesies is greater than he who speaks with tongues (unless the latter interprets what he says).'[44] Interpretation, Barrett adds, 'had the effect of turning tongues into prophecy'.[45] But this is precisely the point. Paul declares, 'He who prophesies is greater than he who speaks with tongues, unless he (the latter) can put it into words.' This understanding of the passage matches both the Greek and also the precise context of Paul's argument in 14:1–5.

There is a similar difficulty about the Greek of 14:27, 28 on the basis of the traditional view. Paul writes, εἴτε γλώσσῃ τις λαλεῖ, κατὰ δύο ἢ τὸ πλεῖστον τρεῖς, καὶ ἀνὰ μέρος, καὶ εἷς διερμηνευέτω. ἐὰν δὲ μὴ ᾖ διερμηνευτής, σιγάτω ἐν ἐκκλμσίᾳ, ἑαυτῷ δὲ λαλείτω καὶ τῷ θεῷ. Many versions and commentators assume that Paul simply uses εἷς in place of τις. Thus the NEB has: '*someone* must interpret. If there is no interpreter, the *speaker* had better not address the meeting at all.' The RSV has 'let one interpret. But if there is *no one* to interpret, let each of them keep silence in church.' Lietzmann similarly has 'if no interpreter is present'.[46] Barrett translates, 'Let one member interpret. If there is no one to interpret, let the man who would speak with tongues keep

---

41   W.F. Orr and J.A. Walther, *1 Corinthians* (New York, 1976), p.301.
42   J. Héring, op. cit., p.147 n. 2.
43   G.G. Findlay, *Expositor's Greek Testament* II (Grand Rapids, MI, n. d.), p.903 (my italics).
44   C.K. Barrett, *A Commentary on the First Epistle to the Corinthians* (London, 1968), p.316.
45   Ibid.
46   H. Lietzmann, op. cit., p.74.

silence.'[47] But why should we assume that the different verbs take different subjects? J. Weiss rightly points out that the very same subject is involved in διερμηνευέτω, ἢ διερμηνευτής, σιγάτω, and ἑαυτῷ λαλείτω (cf. ἑαυτὸν οἰκοδομεῖ,14:4).[48] This is the most natural way to understand the syntax, and adequately explains the use of εἷς rather than τις without introducing speculative theories about Paul's limiting the numbers of possible 'interpreters'.

Why, then, have so many commentators been persuaded otherwise? The answer is that this understanding of the passage appears awkward all the while it is assumed that διερμηνεύω can *only* mean 'to interpret'. The difficulty disappears, however, as soon as we consider the possibility that the word might simply mean 'to put into words'. Paul is now saying: 'Let one of them put it into words. But if he cannot put it into words, let him remain (altogether) silent in the assembly, and let him speak to himself and to God.' The syntax flows on smoothly, and the verses make excellent sense.

(2) The greatest difficulty involved in our suggestion is the understanding of ἑρμηνεία γλωσσῶν (12:10), of διερμηνεύω (12:30), and of ἑρμηνεία (14:26) in contexts which seem to differentiate this gift from προφητεία (12:10; cf. προφῆται, 12:29). In practice there are two difficulties. First, if speaking in tongues constitutes a gift of the Spirit how can ceasing to speak in tongues also constitute a gift of the Spirit? Second, how are the different items in the list of gifts related to one another?

We have alluded briefly to the sociological analyses of the situation at Corinth put forward by Theissen and Hollenweger. These analyses emphasize the considerable difference in social background between, on the one hand, the wealthy property-owner and even the educated slave-secretary, and on the other hand the non-literate slave who served as a manual worker.[49] The non-literate Christian convert, it is urged, would not, at least to begin with, be able to share in the more intellectual expressions of the community's life and worship. Especially for men and women from this background, speaking in tongues provided a very necessary outlet for the expression of their response to the new reality that overwhelmed them. We need not assume that in the very first days or weeks of response after Christian conversion this expression was confined only to the non-literate. But it is clear that it would have been easier for the more literate sections of the congregation to move beyond this stage than it would have been for others. For the non-literate section of the congregation, speaking in tongues was, at least at the beginning, a very special gift, since it allowed them to express their worship and praise in a non-intellectual way (14:14–19). Nevertheless, *for the very same people*, the ability to move on and join in fully articulate praise and worship of the assembly was, in its turn, no less wonderful a gift. We need not follow the suggestion that we might perhaps take to be implied by Hollenweger, namely that the sociological division *perpetuated* a parallel difference of emphasis in the worship. Paul wanted all Christians, regardless of their

---

[47] C.K. Barrett, op. cit., p.328.

[48] J. Weiss, *Der erste Korintherbrief* (Göttingen, 1910, rpt. 1977), p.340.

[49] G. Theissen, 'Soziale Schichtung in der korinthischen Gemeinde', loc. cit., esp. pp.264–72; and W.J. Hollenweger, *Konflikt in Korinth*. Cf. also E.A. Judge, *The Social Pattern of the Christian Groups in the First Century* (London, 1960), pp.58–60.

backgrounds, to enter fully into the use of their minds, and there is no evidence that this desire was consciously resisted after the reading of 1 Corinthians 12–14.

It is not difficult to see, therefore, how speaking in tongues and 'putting it into words' could *both* have been viewed as spiritual gifts, each of which ministered to a different stage of Christian growth (13:11; 14:20). But in this case, how does ἑρμηνεία differ, if at all, from προφητεία? It is perhaps a mistake to try to draw rigid distinctions between each of the gifts that are listed. For example, 'miracles' and 'healing' presumably overlap (12:29), the latter being a specific example under the heading of the former. Similarly, it is not easy to draw clear-cut lines between a word of wisdom, a word of knowledge, prophecy, and teaching. Barrett simply describes prophets as 'local ... Christians, inspired to address the word of God to the church, and, at least on occasion, to non-Christians also, who might be converted by their speech (14:24)'.[50] But he also describes a word of wisdom and a word of knowledge in very similar terms (14:8).[51] Once we grant that these gifts may overlap in content, we are free to look elsewhere for what might make each distinctive.

In the case of ἑρμηνεία and προφητεία, we suggest it is not so much the content of the gift that distinguishes them, as the circumstances in which they are given or used, or even perhaps the identity of the recipients of the gifts. The term προφητεία implies nothing about the identity of the prophet. (If 'prophet' did constitute a special office, this would solve our problem, but it seems to be precluded by 14:5, 6.) On the other hand, the man who has received the gift of ἑρμηνεία is one who either formerly or still in the present (privately) spoke or speaks in tongues, but who can now articulate his experience for the benefit of the community. ἑρμηνεία γλωσσῶν, then, is the gift of being able 'to put it into words', when the gift is received by one who would otherwise be speaking in tongues. The only remaining difficulty is that γλωσσῶν has to be understood as a shorthand term for the whole experience involved in speaking in tongues. But then, as advocates of the 'foreign languages' theory regularly points out, Paul uses γλῶσσα precisely in this way in the list in 14:26, as he does γένη γλωσσῶν in 12:10. On the basis of other uses of the term in these chapters, then, this is exactly what we should expect.

(3) We may now return to our original point of departure, which is the meaning of 14:13: ὁ λαλῶν γλώσσῃ προσευχέσθω ἵνα διερμηνεύῃ. This passage comes in the course of Paul's long and sustained argument that the man who speaks in a tongue should move beyond this stage for the benefit of the community, or else that at very least he should exercise this gift in private. It is possible, we have urged, that the allusions in chapter 13 to moving on from childhood form part of this argument: 'Love does not insist on its own way ... Tongues will cease' (13:4, 8). Whether or not this is so, in 14:1–5 Paul explicitly argues that whilst prophecy builds up the whole community, speaking in tongues edifies only the individual concerned (14:3, 4). Paul then amplifies this principle with reference to the analogy of hearing unintelligible foreign language (14:6–12). The whole thrust of the argument is now expressed in summary form in 14:13: 'Therefore, he who speaks in

---

50 C.K. Barrett, op. cit., p.295.
51 Ibid., pp.284–5.

a tongue should pray for the power to produce articulate speech.' This moves on, exactly as this rendering might lead us to expect, to an emphatic plea concerning the use of the mind (14:14–19). For this is precisely what is implied by our interpretation of 14:13. Immature ways are to be left behind (14:20). Tongues, Paul warns his readers, are a sign for unbelievers, in the sense that, as Allo suggests, the experience of being surrounded by unintelligible speech was precisely the situation that characterized God's unbelieving people under punishment for their sin (Isa. 28:11, 12).[52] Glossolalia erects a barrier within the believing community, making some feel like unbelievers, who do not understand what is being said. Paul finally sums up his conclusions in 14:26–33.

The lexicographical evidence from Philo and from Josephus has shown that ἑρμηνεύω and διερμηνεύω frequently bear the meaning of 'to put into words'. In the exegetical part of our discussion we have tried to show that in some passages in 1 Cor. 12–14 this meaning seems to do better justice to the syntax of Paul's Greek than the traditional view, and that in all the relevant passages in these chapters our suggestion makes very good sense. Certainly it seems to do full justice to the content and to the central thrust of Paul's main argument.

---

[52] E.-B. Allo, *Saint Paul. Première Épître aux Corinthiens* (Paris, 1934), pp.365–6.

CHAPTER SEVENTEEN

Does Lexicographical Research Yield "Hebrew" and "Greek" Concepts of Truth? (1978), and How Does This Research Relate to Notions of Truth Today? (New summary)

Although this was originally written as a dictionary article, this work is neither merely didactic nor merely a lexicographical survey. With the editor's agreement it entirely replaced the German-language article that it was first designed only to supplement. The article in the German edition had presupposed the dichotomy between "Hebrew" and "Greek" concepts of truth in ways that were open to question in the light of both semantic theory (not least in the work of James Barr), and actual lexicographical research, which invited fresh evaluation. The inclusion of the classical and Old Testament backgrounds makes the fallacies of the older approach clearer. This research remains in many ways a companion piece to "The Supposed Power of Words in the Biblical Writings" (Essay 4) although the latter draws on speech-act theory, which places it in Part II.

The article comes from Colin Brown (ed.), The New International Dictionary of New Testament Theology, *volume 3 (Exeter: Paternoster Press, 1978), pp.874–902, but has been abbreviated in order to omit material that may not bear directly on the argument. The breadth of lexicographical data might seem at times to verge on the tedious, but the argument depends on covering a fair range of specific cases and evidence. The original article concluded with a substantial discussion of modern philosophical theories of truth. This is too lengthy to retain here, but a brief summary has been rewritten for this volume (2004) to demonstrate the role of the argument for the "second horizon" of hermeneutics.*

I
Questionable Methodological Assumptions, and Clearly Varied Meanings of "Truth" in Classical Greek Literature

I.1 *Methodological Assumptions*

For many years there has been a tendency in biblical studies to over-generalize about the uses of ἀλήθεια (*alētheia*) and ἀληθής (*alēthēs*) in classical Greek. This has come about partly with a view to drawing a clear-cut contrast between Greek and Hebrew *concepts* of truth. It is then argued that whilst some New Testament writers preserve "the Hebrew" concept, other writers, especially John, achieve a fusion of these two conceptual views. Thus Rudolf Bultmann too readily speaks of "the Greek use" of *alētheia* as over against "the Semitic use".[1]

---

[1] R. Bultmann, ἀλήθεια, in G. Kittel (ed.), *Theological Dictionary of the New Testament*, vol. 1 (Grand Rapids, MI: Eerdmans, 1964), p.238; cf. pp.232–50.

According to this theory, *alētheia* in classical Greek denotes truth in contrast to mere appearance, whilst in Hebrew the parallel word denotes stability or faithfulness. It is also urged that truth in Greek writers is timeless, raised above the temporal and material world. It relates only to extra-historical being. Most scholars also insist that the basic meaning of *alētheia* in classical Greek is that of un-hiddenness or unveiling. These traditional claims of nineteenth- and twentieth-century biblical scholarship are valid up to a point, but can be misleading unless they are carefully qualified.

The traditional approach depends largely on three arguments. First, much is made of the *etymology* of ἀλήθεια (*alētheia*) in ancient Greek. The word is said to derive from *lēthō* or *lanthanō* (λανθάνω), meaning to escape notice or to cause to forget, together with *alpha* privative prefix, which negates the idea. The difficulty, however, is to show that the etymology of the word played a decisive part in determining its meaning in later Greek of the classical and Hellenistic periods. Indeed, even Homer shows little evidence that the word has this special nuance.

Second, *alētheia* does indeed mean truth in contrast to mere appearance in much Greek philosophy. But the vast majority of classical Greek writers and readers were not philosophers. J.B. Skemp observes, "There is one particular vice in the theological picture (or rather, caricature) of the Greeks. They are always represented as philosophical thinkers ... Such a description of the Greeks ignores the fact that many other Greeks at all the relevant times thought differently, and that a multitude of them did not think in this systematic way at all."[2]

Third, admittedly the notion that "truth" when it stands in contrast to mere appearance belongs only to the realm of timelessness and immateriality does find strong support in Parmenides and especially Plato. Nevertheless, even within Greek philosophy we find other views of truth besides Plato's. We may cite, for example, that of the Sophists, which Plato himself attacks, as well as that of Aristotle. In these writers truth has a positive relation to the contingent, temporal, and material world of states of affairs.

I.2 Classical and Hellenistic Greek Texts

In Homer *alētheia* most frequently occurs in contrast to telling a lie or to withholding information, for example, "Tell me all the truth (*pasan alētheian*) whether my son is by the ship" (*Iliad* 24, 407); "I will tell you all the truth" (*Odyssey* 11, 507). When Odysseus with cunning "spoke not the truth", he simply tells a lie (*Odyssey* 13, 254). Achilles set an umpire to tell the truth of a race, that is, the state of affairs as it really was (*Iliad* 23, 261). However, this is not the only meaning of *alētheia* or *alēthēs* in Homer. In *Iliad* 12, 433 *gynē chernētis alēthēs* means a woman who is careful, honest, accurate, or perhaps reliable.

Truth (*alētheia*) usually stands in opposition to falsehood in Herodotus, Thucydides and Xenophon. The cowherd in Herodotus "tells the truth" under threat of violence (1, 116). Thucydides speaks of "the actual truth" in contrast to mere empty boasts (2, 41, 2). An oracle provides true answers to enquiries (Herodotus, 1, 55).

---

[2] J.B. Skemp, *The Greeks and the Gospel* (London: Carey Kingsgate Press, 1964), pp.3–4.

These uses also persist in later Hellenistic writers. Epictetus draws a contrast telling the truth and using deceiving flatteries (*Discourse* IV, 1, 6, 7). Philo writes that Moses marvelled at the delusion (*pseudos*) that the multitude had bartered for the truth (*alētheia*) (*De vita Mosis* 2, 167). The evil spies sent out to view the land prefer deceit (*apatē*) to truth (*De vita Mosis* 1, 235). Josephus uses *alētheia* in several different senses. Truth is that which corresponds to the facts of the matter. Thus Jonathan did not question the truth (veracity) of David's words (*Antiquities* 6, 225). Truth is also proved to be such by historical events (*Antiquities* 2, 209; 6, 225; cf. also 8, 360).

I.3 Greek Philosophical Texts

The use of *alēthēs* in Greek philosophical texts emerges most clearly in Parmenides, the Sophists, Plato and Aristotle. Some of Plato's uses also appear in Philo. (1) Parmenides asks what is the nature of real being, and draws a contrast between the way of *truth* and the way of *seeming*. Change belongs only to the material world, which is the realm of mere appearance. There can be no change in what really exists (*Fragment* 8, 29). "What is not" is unthinkable and unknowable, but change would be the supposed movement of what is to what is not, or of what is not to what is. Hence truth, in contrast to appearance, belongs to the extra-historical realm of the changeless. That such a view occurs in Greek philosophical literature is therefore clear. What is less certain is the extent to which ordinary Greek writers shared the view of Parmenides.

(2) The Sophists clearly held a different view. In particular Protagoras refused to view the material world as mere illusion. In his famous dictum that "Humankind is the measure of all things" he did not intend merely to propound, as Plato implied, an extreme form of relativism. To underline the phenomenon of viewpoint, he cited the example of a wind that may seem warm to one person and cool to another. It is not necessary, he urged, to say that one view is true and the other false. Each may be true for the person concerned. In this way Protagoras comes near to the modern notion of existential truth, as well as to aspects of postmodernity.

(3) Plato rejects this view. He replied that if "true" and "false" are only relative to the individual thinker, then as soon as someone says that the philosophy of Protagoras is false for him, it is therefore false (*Theaetetus* 171a). Falsehood, for Plato, is a matter of deception. It conceals reality (*ta onta*). False words, he believed, are merely a copy (*mimēma*) of deception in the soul (*Republic*, 2, 21, 382a–383b). Falsehood is the presentation of what is only appearance (*phantasma*). By contrast "the divine and divinity are free from falsehood [*apseudes ... to theion*]". God is true in deed and word (*alēthēs en te ergō kai en logō*) and neither changes himself nor deceives others (382e). Plato thus returns to the view of Parmenides that truth stands in contrast to appearance and to change, although he goes further than Parmenides in locating it in the realm of ideas. At the same time Plato also uses *alētheia* and *alēthēs* in more ordinary and less metaphysical ways. Truth sometimes means simply "the facts of the matter" (*Epistles* 7, 330). *alētheia* stands in contrast to legend (*Timaeus* 22d). "Equal to equal ... because of truth" (*Leges* 3, 668a).

(4) Aristotle takes us closest to the view of truth found in modern propositional logic. First, Aristotle distinguishes between the genuine proposition, which is true-or-false,

and sentences such as pleas or commands: "We call propositions only those (sentences) which have truth or falsity in them" (*On Interpretation* 4, 17a, 4). Second, he considers the logical conditions under which the truth of a proposition entails the denial of its contrary. If it is true to say "Socrates is well", it is therefore false to assert, "Socrates is ill" (*Categories* 19, 13b, 14–35). Third, he argues, "the truth of a proposition consists in corresponding with facts" (*hoi logoi alētheis hōsper ta pragmata*, *On Interpretation* 9, 19a, 33). The principle is said to include statements about future states of affairs (18a–b). Often, however, the actual word *alētheia* is used in its ordinary everyday sense without philosophical content. The philosopher seeks to discover "the truth" that is in the universe (*De Mundo* 4, 391a).

(5) Philo uses *alētheia* in ordinary ways as we have seen. As a Jewish theologian he speaks of "true doctrine" (*alēthēs dogma*, *Legum Allegoriae* 3, 229). But as a speculative writer who has been influenced by Platonism he also contrasts truth with mere appearance: "Moses desired truth rather than appearance (*tou dokein*)" (*De vita Mosis* 1, 48). However, he also sees the truth of God manifested in historical events, as in a quick punishment for unbelief (*De vita Mosis* 2, 284).

II
Issues of Method and the Old Testament Material

II.1 The Status of Some Traditional Arguments

The Hebrew word which is the nearest equivalent to *alētheia* is אֱמֶת (*'emet*). Whilst the LXX regularly translates *'emet* (אֱמֶת) as *alētheia* (ἀλήθεια), the English versions sometimes render it as "truth", and sometimes as "faithfulness". Indeed the majority of Old Testament scholars claim that for the Hebrew writers "truth" is close to faithfulness in meaning, suggesting the idea of stability, firmness, or reliability. A. Jepsen writes, "By way of summary: *'emet* was used of things that had to be proved to be reliable ... 'Reliability' would be the best comprehensive word in English to convey the idea ... *'emet* is that on which others can rely". This applies, Jepsen concludes, to God's truth as well as to man's. As the God of truth, "Yahweh is ... the God in whose word and work one can place complete confidence".[3]

For many scholars, this argument is strengthened by a consideration arising from etymology. It is widely agreed that *'emet* is derived from the root *'mn*, which has the meaning "to be firm". On this basis it is often argued that truth in the Old Testament is not merely theoretical or abstract, but is grounded in the faithfulness of God. If this view is adopted we have all the ingredients for postulating a radical and clear-cut contrast between Hebraic and Greek conceptions of truth. We have already suggested, however, that whilst such a contrast has validity in certain respects, it can be misleading and simplistic to build arguments on this foundation.

---

[3]   A. Jepsen, אֱמֶת in G.J. Botterweck and H. Ringgren (eds), *Theological Dictionary of the Old Testament*, vol. 1 (Grand Rapids, MI: Eerdmans, 1974), p.313.

(1) Justice must be done, as James Barr insists, to the variety of different contexts in which *'emet* (אֱמֶת) is employed in the Old Testament.[4] Even the statistical distribution should make us hesitate to assume that it performs the same role for all biblical writers. In the Psalms, where the word often means faithfulness, אֱמֶת (*'emet*) occurs thirty-seven times. It is used twelve times in Isaiah, and eleven each in Proverbs and Jeremiah, but is entirely absent from a number of writers, including Job. This is not necessarily, however, because, as Jepsen suggests, the author of Job has nothing on which he can rely.[5]

(2) The Qal of *'āman* may admittedly mean to support or to sustain. In Numbers 11:12 it is used of a nurse carrying a child. In the *hiphil* of the Hebrew verb it has the sense of putting confidence in something, and is used of having confidence in God (Deut. 1:32). In the *niphal* of the verb-form it is used of a firmly fixed peg (Isa. 22:23, 25); whilst the noun *'omnâh* means a post or pillar on which a structure may lean (2 Kings 18:16). At first sight, therefore, through *'āman* the connection between *'emet* and the idea of firmness may seem to be well established. But the fact that the word is historically derived from a root of which other forms mean "firm" does not give us any precise information about its own distinctive uses in a subsequent period of linguistic history. Etymology provides only statements about the past history of a word; not about its use at some later stage. Hence arguments about the nature of truth which depend on the etymology of *'emet* are no more conclusive than those which we earlier considered and rejected concerning connections between *alētheia* and *lēthō* or *lanthanō*.

(3) It is much more significant that the LXX translates אֱמֶת (*'emet*) not only as ἀλήθεια (*alētheia*) truth, but also πίστις (*pistis*), faith, or faithfulness. We do not deny that *'emet* does frequently mean "faithfulness". However, it is possible to offer two quite different explanations for this. First, it is usually assumed that since *'emet* means both truth and faithfulness, each concept necessarily entails the other, with the result that faithfulness is a necessary part of the distinctively Hebrew concept of truth. But another explanation may also be offered. Second, we have here an example of polysemy, or multiple meaning. *The Hebrew word* אֱמֶת (*'emet*) *means "truth" in some contexts, and "faithfulness" in other contexts.* We may compare the parallel semantic phenomenon in the case of the word "taste" in English, French, German and Italian (*goût, Geschmack, gusto*). The word means taste by the tongue in eating in some contexts, and taste in aesthetics in other contexts.

The semantic phenomenon does not commit us to the conclusion that there is a distinctive Western European concept of taste, according to which aesthetic judgements have a close connection with enjoying food. The same principle can be applied to the Hebrew word דָּבָר (*dābār*), which can mean either word or thing.[6] All the same, so much is made of this polysemic vocabulary that we must examine it more closely.

First of all, it is the case that *'emet* means *faithfulness* in a number of instances in the Old Testament. We may compare the similar use of the noun אֱמוּנָה (*'emūnāh*), which is also

---

4   James Barr, *The Semantics of Biblical Language* (Oxford: OUP, 1961), pp.187–205.
5   Jepsen, אֱמֶת, in *Theological Dictionary of the O.T.*, vol. 1, p.310.
6   See James Barr, *Semantics of Biblical Language*, pp.129–40; and essays in this volume, namely 4, "The Supposed Power of Words in the Biblical Writings" (from *Journal of Theological Studies* 25, 1974, 282–99) and 13, "Semantics and New Testament Interpretation" (from I.H. Marshall, ed., *New Testament Interpretation*, 1977, pp.75–104).

derived from the same root *'mn*. *'emūnāh* and *'emet* are both often translated by *pistis* in the sense of fidelity or faithfulness in the LXX. But whereas *'emūnāh* hardly ever means "truth", as against faithfulness, *'emet* embraces both word-uses. Normally the nearest that *'emūnāh* comes towards meaning "truth" is in the sense of *reliability, trustworthiness*, or *honesty*. In 2 Kings 22:7 no accounting of money is made concerning the collectors under Hilkiah in Josiah's reformation "because they deal honestly", that is, they act with fidelity (*'emūnāh*). Further, *'emūnāh* at least on one occasion means *firm* or *steady*, and this may appear to support the usual theory about its etymological root *'mn*. In Exodus 17:12 Aaron and Hur hold up Moses' hands so that they remain "*steady*" (Heb. *'emūnāh*; LXX *estērigmenai*) until the sun goes down.

Sometimes, however, it is not entirely clear whether *'emūnāh* means *faithfulness*, or *honesty* or even *integrity*. In 1 Samuel 26:23 and in Isaiah 11:5 the word occurs in parallelism with "righteousness": "The LORD rewards every man for his righteousness and his faithfulness [honesty?]"; "Righteousness shall be the girdle of his waist, and faithfulness the girdle of his loins."

As we shall see, the connection between *faithfulness* and *truth* depends not on semantic considerations said to be peculiar to the Hebrew language, but on the fact that when God or man is said to act faithfully, *often this means that his word and his deed are one*. He has acted faithfully in accordance with his spoken word. Hence the believer may lean his whole weight confidently on God, and find him faithful. What is perhaps most distinctively "Hebraic" is the notion that even God binds himself to his word once spoken, especially in the covenant. [We explore this in Essay 8 on the hermeneutics of promise as an illocutionary speech-act.] Hence, the biblical writers speak repeatedly of the faithfulness of God, with whom word and deed are one.

Second, when it is used in the sense of faithfulness, *'emet* frequently occurs in parallelism with the word חֶסֶד (*hesed*), *steadfast love*. This conjunction of *hesed* and *'emet* is said by many writers to lie behind the phrase "grace and truth" in John's prologue, as we discuss below. However, we must still distinguish between contexts in which *'emet* (in syntagmatic relation to *hesed*) means *faithfulness*, and those in which it means *truth*. When Abraham's servant Eliezer asks Bethuel and Laban to show *hesed* and *'emet* to Abraham (Gen. 24:49) it is possible that both words mean loyalty and fidelity, but more likely that we should follow the RSV phrase "deal *loyally and truly*" [retained by the NRSV], in the sense of acting with honesty and *integrity*.

Characteristically the Psalms offer both praise and prayer repeatedly on the basis of God's *faithfulness*. Over half of the occurrences of *'emet* have this meaning. When he exclaims that "all the paths of the LORD are mercy and truth" (Psalm 25:10), the Psalmist testifies that God's dealings with his people are utterly trustworthy, because they are characterized by loyalty to the covenant.[7] "Faithfulness" is also the meaning of *'emet* when it occurs in conjunction with *hesed* in Psalms 57:3, 10; 61:7; 69:13; 85:10; 108:4; and 115:1. Even the phrase "word of truth" in Psalm 119:43 is interpreted by A.A. Anderson to mean the record of God's faithfulness to his people.[8]

---

[7] M. Dahood, *Psalms 1–50* (New York: Doubleday [Anchor Bible], 1966), vol. I, p.156.

[8] A.A. Anderson, *The Book of Psalms* (London: Oliphants [New Century], 1972), vol. II, p.821.

II.2 Polysemy and a Range of Counter-examples

It would be a mistake to infer from these examples that *'emet* always means reliability in a theological sense, rather than simply "truth" in contrast to deceit or falsehood. This is not to say that truth in the Old Testament is merely theoretical and abstract. Rather, we must first complete our survey of *different* uses of *'emet* before endeavouring to reach larger conclusions about the matter.

(a) *Truth* stands in *semantic contrast to deceit or falsehood* in a number of places. In Genesis 42:16 Joseph says that he wishes to establish whether the brothers have told the truth. Admittedly it may be claimed that he is testing their "reliability"; but this sense of the term would apply equally to statements about testing the truth in Homer or Herodotus. The issue is whether their statements accord with the facts, and are therefore correct. The same principle applies to Exodus 18:21, where Moses selects men of truth who hate a bribe, to help him with the burden of administration. To be sure, these men are to be reliable and trustworthy. But the reference to bribery implies that their trustworthiness rests on their honesty and integrity. They themselves are to reach decisions and to make judgements on the basis of truth, that is, by taking account of *all the facts* and hiding nothing. Similarly in Deuteronomy 13:14 the injunction is given to check whether or not *the report* that citizens have been seduced into idolatry is actually *true*. Whether the report is reliable depends on whether it accords with *fact* (cf. 17:4). In 1 Kings 17:24 the widow acknowledges the truth of Elijah's word when he restored her son to life. It may be said that his word is reliable, but equally that he has spoken the truth, and not deceived her.

(b) In the Wisdom literature, *'emet* is sometimes used in the sense of faithfulness (Proverbs 3:3; 16:6), but probably more often against the background of the contrast between *truth and falsehood* or *deception*. When Wisdom says, "My mouth will utter truth" (Proverbs 8:7), the point is that she will not deceive the one who embraces her. Indeed, she will bring the disclosure that comes through instruction and knowledge. In Proverbs 12:19 truthful lips are set in contrast to a lying tongue. The whole passage attacks lies, deceit and false witness (vv. 17–22). In 22:21 truth is disclosed in order that a true answer may be given, that is, that there be no lie or deception. Finally, the injunction to "buy" truth (23:23) *can hardly refer to stability or reliability*. What can be "acquired" is knowledge of the true *facts* of the matter, and *an end to deception* through false or partial information. The emphasis is on the value of good education.[9]

(c) In probably three passages in the Psalms, truth stands in contrast to concealment almost in a sense that many scholars claim to find exclusively in Greek literature. In Psalm 43:3 the psalmist prays, "Send out thy light and truth." This is not a prayer for God to remain faithful, but that God will show him the truth of the matter in the face of the enticing words of "deceitful persons" (v. 1). Hence he needs truth and *light*. Truth enables him to escape from the dark, and *to see things for what they are*. In the same way the king

---

[9] R.B.Y. Scott, *Proverbs, Ecclesiastes* (New York: Doubleday [Anchor Bible], 1965), p.143.

in Psalm 45:4 is to be a champion of truth. Here the thought is not so much his reliability as his readiness to expose whatever is shady, underhand, unfair, or false. He defends the afflicted by bringing their cause out into the open.

The well-known reference to "truth in the inward parts" in Psalm 51:6 is less clear. A.A. Anderson insists that here 'emet means faithfulness.[10] But the idea seems to be that the psalmist pleads not for loyalty but for liberation from *self-deception*. The theme of the psalm is confession, which is an acknowledgement of truth of the state of affairs as God sees it. This interpretation is even more likely to be correct, if we understand "inward parts" to denote "that which is covered over" in the context of the need for revelation.[11]

(d) The prophets also use 'emet not only in the sense of faithfulness, but also to denote truth in contrast to falsehood. In Isaiah 43:9 the nations are to come together as a judicial assembly to determine whether the claim of Yahweh or of the pagan gods is true. The claim is reliable only if it accords with the facts of the matter.[12] In Isaiah 59:14 the complaint that truth is lacking seems at first sight to be an allusion to Israel's unfaithfulness, since v. 13a refers to "turning away". But on closer inspection it is clear that the real cause of complaint is "lying words" (v. 13b). Jeremiah similarly complains that "every one deceives his neighbour, and no one speaks the truth; they have taught their tongue to speak lies" (9:5). Admittedly this had the consequence that no one can trust his brother (v. 4). But it is the lying itself that is the main issue here. Zechariah expresses the same concern: "Speak the truth to one another; render in your gates judgements that are true ... Love no false oath" (8:16, 17). In Daniel the truth of God is set in contrast with the deceptions of godless powers (8:12; 9:13).

Even when we take account of the varied ways in which 'emet is used, it is still clear that in the vast majority of contexts truth is not a merely abstract and theoretical concept. Certainly it is never located, as it is in Plato, in some timeless extra-historical realm. To this extent W. Pannenberg is correct when he asserts that in accordance with the Old Testament background "the truth of God must prove itself anew".[13] The God of Israel reveals truth not only in words but also in deeds, and this truth is proved in practice in the experience of God's people. Similarly, people express their respect for truth not in abstract theory, but in their daily witness to their neighbour and their verbal and commercial transactions. It is not surprising, then, to find at times what would nowadays be called an existential view of truth in the Old Testament. For example, when it is said in Ps. 119:142 that "the law is true", this acknowledgement has the existential ring of testimony on the part of one who delights in God's law (v. 143). However, it is not *only* existential truth. For in v. 105 the law of God is a lamp and a light that shows the believer the true state of affairs, although admittedly the true state of affairs as it relates in practice to his life.

---

[10] A.A. Anderson, *The Book of Psalms*, vol. 1, p.396.
[11] E.A. Leslie, *The Psalms* (Nashville, TN: Abingdon Press, 1949), p.400.
[12] C. Westermann, *Isaiah 40–66* (Philadelphia, PA: Westminster, 1969), pp.121–2.
[13] W. Pannenberg, *Basic Questions in Theology*, II (Eng., London: SCM, 1971), p.8.

Such truth can be relied on, and is firm. But this insight is not arrived at on an exclusively *theological* basis. Certainly the believer may confidently rely on God because of God's covenant faithfulness ('*emet, hesed, '*mūnāh*). But this particular use of '*emet* does not lie behind every occurrence of the word. The Hebrews recognized the *logical* truth that others also recognized, that a true word can be relied upon because it accords with reality, and that both for a God of truth and for a man of truth, word and deed are one. Those who call on God "in truth" (Ps. 146:18) do so honestly. God's decrees are enacted with '*emet* (Ps. 111:8), because there is agreement between the sayings and doings of God. This is the logical point that lies behind the connection between truth and faithfulness, and it is not to be confused with arguments about "faithfulness" found in most studies of this subject.

II.3 Post-Canonical Uses of the Term and Varieties of Uses in Qumran

In the post-canonical Jewish writings, *alētheia* is used mostly but not always to mean truth in contrast to falsehood. In Sirach [Ecclesiasticus] 7:20 the servant works reliably indeed, but the main point is that he is "true" in the sense of being honest. In Tobit 7:10 truth is used of giving a *true report*. Truth is especially prominent in the Dead Sea Scrolls, perhaps most of all in the Thanksgiving Hymns. God is the God of truth (1QH [*The Hymns*] 15:25), and the phrase "truth of God" also occurs (1QS [*The Rule of the Community*] 3:6; 11:4; 1QM [*The War Rule*] 4:6). J. Murphy-O'Connor points out that the word often occurs as a designation of revealed doctrine, which embodies both the law and its interpretation.[14] But no less strongly, truth is also emphasized as a quality of moral behaviour. Entrance into the Qumran community is conversion to truth (1QS 6:15), and the initiates bind themselves to the precepts of truth by oath (1QS 1:15). They are now within the sphere of influence of "the spirit of truth" (1QS 3:24). J. Murphy O'Connor observes, "This is the crucial point, for it is in proportion as a man is dominated by this spirit that he loves truth (1QS 4:17, 24)" ("Truth", p.184). Truth plays a part in cleansing him from sin; he grows in the knowledge of truth; and at the end of time all lies will be done away with (1QS 4:20–21; 9:17). Meanwhile, it is binding on the members of the community to practise truth (1QS 1:5; 5:4; 8:2). A person is not established in truth if he has a double heart. Only by responding to God in singleness of heart can a person embrace truth (1QH 4:14; 16:17). Finally the community are "witnesses of truth" (1QS 8:6). As against those fellow Jews whom they regarded as apostate, the Qumran community see themselves, in effect, as the "true" Israel. Truth, then, is used in a *variety of ways* in the Qumran writings. Their uses of the term have their basis in the Old Testament, but also offer a striking point of comparison with the New Testament writings. In particular the community's conception of God's revelation as "the truth" invites comparison with Paul, and the notion of "the spirit of truth" invites comparison with John.

---

14 J. Murphy-O'Connor, "Truth: Paul and Qumran", in *Revue Biblique* 72 (1965), 29–76, reprinted in *Paul and Qumran* (London: Geoffrey Chapman, 1968), pp.179–230.

III
The New Testament

III.1 The Synoptic Gospels

Although the words for "truth" and "true" become very important in Paul and John, *alētheia*, *alēthēs*, and *alēthinos* occur relatively seldom in the Synoptic Gospels and Acts, and even then they have little distinctive theological significance.

(1) On the lips of Jesus himself these terms occur only in Luke 4:25, 9:27, 12:44 and 21:3. In the first two instances the first two forms "I tell you in truth" (*ep' alētheias*) or "I tell you truly" (*alēthōs*) serve to introduce a solemn statement, and are presumably Luke's translation into Greek of the characteristic *amēn*-formula used elsewhere by Jesus. In spite of Berger's arguments, J. Jeremias has argued convincingly that the *amēn*-formula takes us back to the *ipsissima verba* of Jesus. Jesus uses it, Jeremias argues, to strengthen his words, to express his authority, and to underline the certainty of his message.[15]

(2) At the same time the isolated occurrences of *alētheia* and *alēthēs* in the Synoptics do not exhaust what we may infer about Jesus' attitude to truth. Negatively, many of his sayings attack hypocrisy, or, more generally, any discrepancy between word and deed, or between word and reality: "The Pharisees ... preach but do not practise ... You tithe mint and dill ... and have neglected the weightier matters of the law ... straining out a gnat and swallowing a camel" (Matt. 23:2, 3, 23, 24); "Woe to you lawyers, for you load men with burdens hard to bear, and you yourselves do not touch the burdens with one of your fingers" (Luke 11:46; cf. Matt. 23:4). Such an attitude is untruthful, for it is deceitful, and based on a contradiction between word and deed.

Positively, Jesus' own words always accord with his deeds and with actuality. He proclaims grace to the outcast; therefore he eats with tax collectors and sinners. He is Messiah in word, proclaiming the advent of the kingdom of God; therefore he is also Messiah in deed, demonstrating the advent of the kingdom by works of power. Jesus' life of integrity culminates in the cross. Thus *his life provides backing* that gives *the status of reliable currency to his words*. Whether or not this has any special connection with the notion of truth or reliability in the Old Testament, we have argued that this aspect of truth is bound to come into prominence whenever emphasis is laid upon a *correspondence between word and deed*. It is left to John to show how this correspondence exhibits the truth of Jesus' words especially in the context of his christological claims.

(3) Other occurrences of *alētheia* and *alēthēs* in the Synoptic Gospels and Acts either have the sense of truth in contrast to falsehood, concealment, or deception, or else refer to honesty or sincerity. In Matt. 22:15 (parallel Mark 12:14) the Pharisees and others seek to entrap Jesus with their questions and introduce this query with the words, "We know that you are true (*alēthēs*) and teach the way of God truthfully (*en alētheia*)." The point here is that Jesus will not conceal the truth through any fear of the consequences of stating it. He is known to be honest in stating his views. This can be called the Greek view of truth

---

[15] J. Jeremias, *New Testament Theology: I, The Proclamation of Jesus* (Eng., London: SCM, 1971), pp.35–6; and *Abba* (London: SCM, 1996), pp.148–51.

only on the unwarrantable assumption that the contrast between truth and concealment occurs only in Greek literature. This same meaning of *alētheia* occurs in Mark 5:33, when the woman with a flow of blood who touched Jesus in the crowd tells "the whole truth", that is, conceals nothing. However, in Mark 12:32, to speak *ep' alētheias* is simply to state *the facts* of the matter accurately or correctly. This accords with the statement in Acts 26:25: "I am not mad, most excellent Festus, but I am speaking the sober truth." The words are based not on fancy but on fact.

III.2 *The Pauline Literature*

(1) Research on the Pauline uses of *alētheia* is still dominated by the question that Wendt raised in 1883 about the extent to which New Testament writers are influenced by a distinctively Hebrew understanding or "concept" of truth.[16] In a study of 1928, prior to his article in *Theological Dictionary of the New Testament*, Rudolf Bultmann agreed that Wendt's thesis applied to Paul, but not to John.[17] An unduly clear-cut contrast between Greek and Hebrew views of truth also marks D.J. Theron's study of truth in Paul in 1954.[18] We have already seen that such an approach needs to be qualified in the light of concrete examinations of specific passages and word-uses.

(2) One of Paul's most distinctive uses of *alētheia* within the New Testament (especially if we include the Pastorals) is in his use of the phrase "the truth" (*hē alētheia*) to characterize the gospel itself. Although this is most prominent in the Pastorals, this meaning already occurs in Galatians and perhaps 2 Thessalonians. The actual situation in Galatians, rather than considerations about a Greek or Hebrew background, makes this correlation intelligible. In Gal. 2:5 Paul declares that what is at issue in his conflict with the Judaizers is quite literally "the truth of the gospel". In Paul's judgement, enticement to compromise the Gospel is an enticement to compromise the truth, and vice versa. To give way is to deny the truth, both in the sense of his personal integrity and in respect to the actual situation as it now is. Hence in Gal. 5:7 "the truth" has become synonymous with the gospel itself: "What hindered you from obeying the truth?" Murphy-O'Connor rightly comments "No single term could better mark the contrast between the reality of the Gospel and the ineffectiveness of the Law."[19] He also correctly notes the parallel between this use of *alētheia* in Paul, and the use of the term to mean revealed truth or correct doctrine in Qumran.

It is open to question whether *pistei alētheias* in 2 Thess. 2:13 also has this meaning. As E. Best argues, the phrase is already ambiguous, meaning either the truth which creates saving faith, or the faith which is placed in the truth.[20] Whichever interpretation is

---

[16] H. Wendt, "Der Gebrauch der Wörter *alētheia, alēthēs* und *alēthinos* im N.T. auf Grund der alttestamentlichen Sprachgebrauches", *Theologische Studien und Kritiken: eine Zeitschrift für das Gesamt der Theologie*, 65 (1883), 511–47.

[17] R. Bultmann, "Untersuchungen zum Johannesevangelium", *Zeitschrift für Neutestamentliche Wissenschaft* 27 (1928), 113–63; cf. *Theological Dictionary of the New Testament*, I, pp.242–50.

[18] D.J. Theron, "*Alētheia* in the Pauline Corpus", *Evangelical Quarterly* 26 (1954), 3–18.

[19] J. Murphy-O'Connor, *Paul and Qumran*, p.195.

[20] E. Best, *The First and Second Epistles to the Thessalonians* (London: Black, 1972), p.315.

accepted, *alētheia* here may mean either the Gospel, as the message of salvation, or else (more probably) that which is real, in contrast to mere human imaginings. Another ambiguous reference is 2 Cor. 13:8, which Bultmann places under this heading, in analogy to Dan. 8:12.[21] Truth here, he argues, means true doctrine, as opposed to "a different gospel" (11:4). Bultmann's suggestion about this verse is possibly correct, although open to question. However, his attempts to assimilate several other passages from 2 Corinthians (for example, 4:2) must be rejected, since the issue behind these allusions to truth concerns a correspondence between speech and conduct.

(3) Paul also uses *alētheia* in a similar but definitely broader sense, to mean God's revelation of his will or of his being either through the law or, at one point, through creation. This use is characteristic of the first two chapters of Romans. People by their wickedness "suppress the truth" (Rom. 1:18), and exchange the truth about God for a lie (*pseudei*) (1:25). The law itself, by contrast, is the embodiment of knowledge and truth (2:20, *tēn morphōsin tēs gnōseōs kai tēs alētheias* ...). The truth at issue here is not primarily the truth of the Gospel. People are without excuse not because (as in John) they lay claim to a knowledge which would allow them to recognize the messiah, but because they reject the truth about God as creator and judge. Paul does not say that the whole Gentile world has wilfully rejected gospel-truth, but that it has wilfully suppressed (*katechein*) what may be seen about God and his sovereign claims from creation: "the invisible attributes of God are plainly seen, namely, his eternal power and deity" (Rom. 1:20). That "the truth" here does not mean specifically the truth of the Gospel is clear when we remember that Paul is stating a central principle of Jewish synagogue preaching in Hellenistic cities. Even Karl Barth allows that nature and the order of creation at least disclose, to those who will see, "the insecurity of our whole existence, the vanity and utter questionableness of all that we are".[22] To say that the law is an embodiment of truth (2:20) does not narrow this concept of truth, but is to say only that this truth comes to a focus in the law of God as revealed in men's hearts. Admittedly, once again, Paul is taking up standard Jewish sermon-material, with a view to using it against the Jews themselves. But he does not deny its general validity.

(4) Truth in Paul often stands in contrast to lying or deception. Indeed, together with Wisdom 13 and 14, Paul inherits the traditional Hebrew prophetic view that divine truth stands in contrast to idolatry, precisely because idolatry is a deception and delusion (cf. Rom. 1:25). We have already said that there is nothing distinctively Greek about this contrast. Paul used the word in a thoroughly natural sense when he asserts, "I am speaking the truth in Christ; I am not lying" (Rom. 9:1); "Everything we said to you was true" (2 Cor. 7:14). Whereas some writers employ this contrast in a primarily intellectual way, others underline its ethical and practical significance for life. This is not, however, chiefly a contrast between Hebrew and Greek thought, but between those for whom practical integrity is important, and those whose main concerns are more strictly to do

---

[21] Bultmann, *Theological Dictionary of the N.T.*, I, p.244.
[22] Karl Barth, *The Epistle to the Romans* (Eng., Oxford: OUP, 1933), p.46.

with theoretical knowledge. Thus we find that for Paul, as for Jesus, truth becomes a matter of correspondence between word and deed.

(5) These two aspects of *alētheia* are brought together in a striking way in 2 Corinthians. On the one hand, Paul was accused of vacillation and change, and asserts his own concern for the truth in the sense of an honesty or integrity in which word and deed correspond. Indeed, he urges, it is the false apostles who need artificial commendation, rather than that of a costly and fruitful ministry that proves the worth of words. On the other hand, Paul is also accused of veiling his gospel. Once again, he urges it is not he but his opponents who tailor the Gospel message to conform to human expectations and demands. Hence he exclaims: "We have renounced disgraceful, underhanded ways: we refuse to practise cunning or to tamper with God's word (*mēde dolountes ton logon tou theou*), but by the open statement of the truth we would commend ourselves to every man's conscience in the sight of God" (4:2). But together with this emphasis on truth as un-concealment (the so-called Greek view), Paul stresses his unity of word and conduct: "We commend ourselves [cf. 4:2] ... through great endurance, in afflictions, hardships, calamities ... by truthful speech ..." (2 Cor. 6:4–7).

(6) Paul believes in the power of truth. Truth exposes lies (Rom. 3:4, where divine truth exposes human falsehood for what it is). Love of the truth can even lead to salvation (2 Thess. 2:10), although this means not mere theoretical admiration of intellectual truth, but commitment to the truth as this is expressed in the Gospel. To encounter the truth as it is in Jesus leads on to transformation of life, in which the believer turns away from old deceits (Eph. 4:21, 22). Thus in 2 Cor. 6:7 "truthful speech" occurs in parallel with the power of God and weapons of righteousness. Paul does not use the weapons of power politics or psychological pressure, but with honest integrity speaks and acts in truth and righteousness. Similarly in Eph. 6:14 truth is part of the Christian's armour, which provides protection in the face of attack. 2 Cor. 4:2 have the same flavour. Paul's statement in 13:8, "We cannot do anything against the truth, but only for the truth", may just possibly refer to truth as a synonym for the Gospel, as R. Bultmann maintains, but more probably conveys the idea that the power of truth is such that openness to truth, whatever its consequences, can only further the cause of Christ and the Gospel.

(7) Truth is demanded of the Christian as a corollary of his union with Christ and status as a new creation. In 1 Cor. 5:8 the Christian celebrates the festival of the new life with sincerity and truth, banishing all impurity and deception or dishonesty, just as the Jews banished the old leaven from their houses at Passover time. Truth and purity stand in contrast here to *kakia*, *ponēria* and *porneia*. The new life is to be untarnished; free from anything that spreads corrupting influences by virtue of its impurity or duplicity. The same idea occurs in Eph. 4:25, with more explicit reference to falsehood. Because the believer has put on the new nature (v. 24), Paul adds: "Putting away falsehood (*to pseudos*), let every one speak the truth with his neighbour, for we are members one of another." The word for "putting away" (*apothemenoi*) is the same as that which is used in v. 22 for "putting off" the old nature. [I discuss the sentences "love rejoices at the truth"

(1 Cor. 13:6), and "love bears all things" (*panta stegei*, v. 7) in Essay 19 on 1 Corinthians 13, included in this volume.]

(8) The Pastoral Epistles reflect a distinctive outlook, although they take up and develop a trend which we have already noted in Galatians and Romans. Truth is essentially the revealed truth of the Gospel message. This is because the problem of false doctrine looms as large as it did earlier in Galatians. To become a Christian is "to come to the knowledge of the truth" (1 Tim. 2:4; 2 Tim. 3:7). By contrast, the great danger which is under attack is that people will listen only to teachers who "suit their own likings, and will turn from listening to the truth and wander into myths" (2 Tim. 4:3, 4). Such men have a "morbid craving for controversy and for disputes about words ... wrangling among men who are ... bereft of the truth" (1 Tim. 6:5). [I examine the background further in Essay 14 on Titus 1:12–13, on the paradox on the Cretan liar, also included in this volume.]

[In the rest of the New Testament apart from the Johannine writing and Revelation *alētheia* is used only 8 times; *alēthēs* twice; and *alēthinos* three times. *alēthōs* and *alētheuō* do not occur at all. In the original article I examine these uses, but this section is omitted here.]

III.3 The Johannine Writings

(1) Considerations about word-frequency alone suggest the importance of truth in John and the Johannine Epistles. Nearly half of the 109 occurrences of *alētheia* appear in the Johannine writings (twenty-five times in the Gospel and twenty times in the Johannine Epistles). *alēthēs* is used seventeen times out of a total of twenty-six occurrences in the New Testament; whilst *alēthinos* appears twenty-three times (including ten times in Revelation) out of a total of only twenty-eight uses in the whole New Testament. In all, therefore, over half of the New Testament uses of all three words occur in the Johannine writings. Thus it is all the more unfortunate that many scholars allow their exegesis of passages about truth to be dominated by the questions of whether John holds *the* "Greek" or "Hebrew" view of truth. Rudolf Bultmann and C.H. Dodd argue that John sees truth primarily as reality in contrast to falsehood or appearance, but insist on seeing this as evidence of a Hellenistic view of truth in John. Other writers, including most emphatically L.J. Kuyper and more moderately C.K. Barrett, Leon Morris and R.E. Brown, underline instances in John where *alētheia* may possibly mean faithfulness, as evidence of affinities with the Old Testament and Judaism.[23]

This way of posing the question, however, is unsatisfactory for two main reasons. First, we have seen that an unduly clear-cut contrast between Hebrew and Greek views of truth stands in question. Second, it is misleading to tie exegetical conclusions about the meaning of *alētheia* to a theory about Johannine affinities of thought. The view adopted in this article is that John uses *alētheia* regularly to denote reality in contrast to falsehood or mere

---

[23] L.J. Kuyper, "Grace and Truth: An Old Testament Description of God and its Use in the Johannine Gospel", *Interpretation* 18 (1964), 3–19.

appearance, but that this does not provide evidence of Greek affinities of ideas, or of disregard for the Old Testament traditions.

(2) Special consideration may be given to the use of the phrase "full of grace and truth" (*plērēs charitos kai alētheias*) in the Prologue (1:14; cf. *hē charis kai hē alētheia*, 1:17). Numerous scholars find the background to these verses in Exod. 34:6: "The Lord, a God merciful and gracious, slow to anger, and abounding in steadfast love and faithfulness" (Hebrew נֶאֱמֶת חֶסֶד־רַב, *rab ḥesed weʾemet*; LXX, *polyeleos kai alēthinos*). The LXX use of *eleos* to translate *ḥesed* represents a standard procedure, but this need not be an obstacle to the argument that John takes up this phrase from Exodus 34. John does not always follow the LXX verbatim, and in any case in later Greek *charis*, grace, comes regularly to replace *eleos*, mercy, as the standard translation of *ḥesed*.[24] L.J. Kuyper urges that the Old Testament idea of covenant loyalty, expressed in *ḥesed*, completely determines the meaning of the whole phrase "grace and truth" in John. Anthony T. Hanson argues forcefully that Exodus 34 lies behind these verses.[25] Moses had made the bold request that he might see God's glory (Exod. 33:18). God replied that no one might see his face and live; but he promised, "You shall see my back." The phrase cited in John 1:14 describes this experience of "seeing" God. But John gives the phrase fresh point. He says that truly to "see" God is to see nothing other than his glory in *Christ*. This interpretation of John 1:14–18 is convincing.

However, does *alētheia* (vv. 14 and 17) therefore, on this ground, necessarily mean faithfulness (Kuyper), reliability (Morris), or constancy (Brown)? C.K. Barrett sees the idea of God's covenant faithfulness in the background.[26] But what John wishes to stress in these verses is that, in Christ the Logos, humankind can see God in genuine actuality and reality. If people can see God's *reality* anywhere, it is in Christ. Thus R. Schnackenburg rightly comments that whilst it is just possible to understand *alētheia* here as steadfastness, "the evangelist probably took it to mean 'divine reality' in a more strongly ontological sense (cf. v. 17) as he understands *alētheia* in 4:23; 8:44; 14:6; 17:17; 18:37d. The hymn sees in the bodily presence of the Logos among men the eschatological fulfilment of God's dwelling among his people."[27] This would accord entirely with the sense of v. 17. The law does indeed constitute a witness to God, as does Moses; but *the reality itself*, to which everything else witnesses, is encountered in Christ.

(3) There can be no doubt that sometimes in John *alētheia* and *alēthēs* mean simply *truth in contrast to falsehood*. In John 4:18 the woman of Samaria speaks the truth about her marital status. In 10:41 it is affirmed that everything that John the Baptist said about Jesus is true. The statement "I tell you the truth; it is to your advantage that I go away" (16:7) dispels any suspicion that the words may have been tailored to provide some illusory comfort. In 1 John a liar is one who does not speak the truth (2:4; cf. 2:21, 27). To err from the truth is to be deceived (1 John 1:8). The notion of witness is very prominent in the

---

[24] J.A. Montgomery, "Hebrew *Ḥesed* and Greek *Charis*", *Harvard Theological Review* 32 (1939), 97–102.
[25] A.T. Hanson, *Grace and Truth* (London: SPCK, 1975), pp.5–11.
[26] C.K. Barrett, *The Gospel according to St. John* (London: SPCK, 1958), p.139.
[27] R. Schnackenburg, *The Gospel according to St. John*, I (London: Burns & Oates, 1968), p.273.

Fourth Gospel, and much is made of the fact that the witness to Christ is true (John 5:31f). However, the notion of a witness who is true rather than false leads on to the question of the validity of that witness, and thereby to the use of *alētheia* in the sense of validity.

(4) The debate about truthful witness, which is touched on in John 5:31, is developed more fully in 8:13–58. Here it may seem that we come closest in John to the so-called Hebrew concept of truth as reliability. Witness to Jesus Christ is reliable because it comes from God, and from more than one witness (8:17, 18). But on closer inspection the issue turns on validity, rather than reliability as such. The witness to Jesus Christ is valid, because there is no higher court of appeal than God himself. The witness of those who judge "according to the flesh" (v. 15) is not necessarily dishonest (although there may be a hint of this in 9:41); but such testimony is untrue in the sense that it is invalid. Valid witness depends on revelation.

(5) One of the most important uses of *alētheia* and *alēthēs* in John is to convey the idea of reality, in contrast to whatever the situation may seem to look like on the surface. (i) The clearest example of this use is when the adjective *alēthēs* is used in the same sense as the more characteristic word *alēthinos* to mean "real". Thus in 6:55 Jesus says that his flesh is real food, and his blood is real drink. It is more genuinely food and drink than other things that go under these names. Real food gives more lasting satisfaction and nourishment than other things which men call "food". (ii) Those who worship God in Spirit and in truth (4:23, 24) are not those who worship in sincerity and inwardness. The Samaritans are not criticized for lacking sincerity. True worship is that *which accords with reality*, which people grasp on the basis of revelation.

(6) The phrase *"doing the truth"* in John and the Johannine Epistles deserves particular note. At first sight it may seem simply to reflect the Old Testament and Jewish usage according to which it need mean little more than practising fidelity. But C.H. Dodd and others are correct in rejecting this interpretation of the phrase in John. It combines an allusion to the way of Christian revelation with a further reference to the contrast between truth and falsehood. Thus in John 3:21 the statement "He who does what is true comes to the light that it may be clearly seen that his deeds have been wrought in God" cannot simply refer to persons who live up to their aspirations faithfully. This would undercut the thrust of the chapter, namely that even a good person needs to be born anew. C.K. Barrett, therefore, understands the phrase to mean: "he that practises the true (Christian) faith and life".[28]

However, the verse also means more than this. For there is the additional thought that such persons will in practice wish to hide nothing. Truth can only serve Christian faith and Christian life. 1 John 1:6 similarly combines the notion of truth as revelation with truth in contrast to falsehood. A sharp tension between profession of faith and actual practice is both inconsistent with Christian revelation and also in principle self-

---

[28]   Barrett, *John*, p.182.

contradictory. Hence if believers claim to have fellowship with God but walk in darkness they "do not live according to the truth".

(7) Several passages in John yield meanings of *alētheia* or *alēthēs* too broad to be equated with any one of these categories. One of the most important of these is John 14:6 where Jesus declares, "I am the way, the truth, and the life; no one comes to the Father, but by me." I. de la Potterie offers a survey of interpretations of this verse.[29] Dodd and Bultmann interpret it along the lines of a Hellenistic or gnostic dualism, to mean that through Christ the soul ascends to the heavenly realm of truth. We question Bultmann's assumptions about the relevance of the Gnostic background, but he is correct when he writes that Christ is "the way" in such a manner as to be at the same time the goal; "for he is also *hē alētheia* as the revealed reality of God ... The discovery of this *alētheia* is not something...at man's disposal ... Jesus *is* the truth; he does not simply *state* it. One does not come to him to ask about truth; one comes to him as the truth."[30]

Jesus Christ is both the way and also the goal of any search, for "he who has seen me has seen the Father" (v. 9). When he declares that he *is* the truth, therefore, at least three ideas are combined. First, truth is not abstract or suprahistorical, but revealed in the *actual, contingent, personal life* of the Word made flesh. This looks back to the point made with reference to the Synoptic Gospels about the correspondence between word and deed in the life of Jesus Christ. Second, Christ is also the truth because he is the *revelation of God*, and therefore his own witness is valid. Third, truth also stands *in opposition to deception or falsehood*. In the case of divine revelation, this means that Christ is both truth and reality.

It is probable that the same range of meaning applies to the assertion "Thy word is truth" in John 17:17. The context of thought is the distinctiveness of the community of believers as over against the world. The community is holy, for it belongs to God and is founded on God's word. However, the very word on which the community depends for its existence and its consecration is also a word of commission that sends it out into the world (v. 18). In both respects, this word from God is valid, effective, in no way false, and in accord with reality. It is all these things precisely because it is the revealing word of God himself. Thereby the sanctification of the community is assured, and its commission validated.

In John 8:44, 45, the truth spoken by Jesus is set in contrast to the lie spoken by the devil. The devil "has nothing to do with the truth, because there is not truth in him [*en tē alētheia ouch hestēken; hoti ouk estin alētheia en autō*]". Here truth is primarily but not exclusively contrasted with falsehood or deception. There is doubtless an allusion here to the deception by the serpent in Gen. 3:4, 5. The implication is that by opposing the truth of Jesus (here, also in the sense of the authentic divine revelation), the Jews are actually doing the devil's work. Bultmann argues that truth in this verse stands in opposition not only to falsehood, but also to reality and to authentic existence.[31] The devil seduces men away from reality and life.

---

[29] I. de la Potterie, "'Je suis la Voie, la Vérité et la Vie' (Jn. 14:6)", *Nouvelle Revue Théologique* 88 (1966), 907–42.

[30] R. Bultmann, *John*, pp.605–6.

[31] Bultmann, *John*, pp.320–22.

By contrast, the Spirit of God is the Spirit of truth (John 14:17; 15:26; 16:13; cf. 1 John 4:6; 5:6). It is striking that this phrase is repeated in no less than three of the five Paraclete sayings. This harmonizes well with C.K. Barrett's understanding of the work of the Paraclete as that of a prosecuting counsel who "exposes" (*elenchein*) the facts of the matter. He brings things "to the light of day" or "shows a thing in its true colours". It is "the activity of a judge and prosecuting counsel in one".[32] The Spirit places the Christian community in the light of judgement which belongs, strictly speaking, to the last day. Hence his verdict is unconditionally valid and needs in no way to be modified by fresh knowledge.

IV
Relation to Notions of Truth Today (2004)

The original 1978 article moved from considering the biblical lexicography to notions of truth in modern philosophical and theological thought. I have omitted this final extensive section because its length would be inappropriate here. It is also the case that these more philosophical debates have moved on. Nevertheless a brief comparison between our lexicographical conclusions and notions of truth in the twenty-first century has distinct and distinctive hermeneutical significance.

If we had accepted the force of the older arguments and methods associated with H. Wendt, A. Jepsen, Rudolf Bultmann and many others, we should have perpetuated a resultant dualism or dichotomy between a "Greek" concept of truth as one that broadly matches a correspondence and coherence theory of truth, and a "Hebrew" concept that broadly matches a contingent, performative and pragmatic theory of truth. The biblical writings, some might then suggest, reflect mainly the latter view, but with some accommodation to the former also. This dualistic view too readily collapses into a Kantian type of dualism between truths of fact and truths of value. In another form it relates to the dualism of Wittgenstein's early writings that he later rejected.

The debates surrounding G.E. Moore and Bertrand Russell, J.L. Austin and P.F. Strawson, and F.P. Ramsey and Alfred Tarski, reveal the complexity of modern explorations of truth. When we add the American pragmatic debates of William James and John Dewey, and the transposition of "truth" in postmodernity at the hands of Nietzsche, Derrida, and Lyotard in Europe, or of Rorty and Fish in America, the complexity becomes boundless. The old, over-worn, "Hebrew" versus "Greek" debate in this light makes biblical notions of truth appear naïve and irrelevant to our times.

Yet closer, more careful, attention to issues of method and to lexicographical research reveals a very wide range of understandings of truth (and of uses of the word "truth") in the biblical writings. The biblical writings are clearly not committed to a formal "correspondence theory" of truth as a *general* theory, but biblical writers regularly use "truth" in the non-technical everyday sense of *what corresponds with the facts of the case.* Such uses are indispensable to ensure a semantic exclusion of deception, lies and

---

[32] Barrett, *John*, p.76.

ignorance. On the other hand, the "performative" view of truth advocated by P.F. Strawson finds a ready place among the biblical writings. To add "it is true that" is neither empty not a mere semantic meta-language (as Tarski held), but an *act of accepting and endorsing* the claim to truth made in an utterance or statement in question. The Old Testament, the Synoptic Gospels, Paul and John, are fully aware of this view of truth, and they presuppose its relevance, as we have seen.

In all of these writings truth often points to a close match between word and deed. I discuss this in my essay on "first-person utterances" and the use of the liar paradox in Titus 1:12–13 (Essay 14). This approach receives strong emphasis in John, 2 Corinthians, and elsewhere in the New Testament. It resonates with a theology of the incarnation of the Word, and with the later Wittgenstein's observation that human life and action may serve as a kind of gold standard that "backs" and tests the truth-currencies claimed for words.

However, this is grounded more deeply than in merely pragmatic theories of truth or their postmodern counterparts. Although they were wrong in the methods that they borrowed to suggest that truth in the Old Testament denoted "reliability" or "faithfulness", Jepsen and Bultmann were right to perceive that biblical writers frequently associated truth with what is *sufficiently stable to invite trust and reliance*. Unlike pragmatism, truth in the biblical writings does not slip away and reappear in radically different forms with the changing criteria of passing history. Rather, as Pannenberg observes, history brings fresh moments to prove its reliability anew, as truth anchored *both* in contingency *and* in coherence, because in the end truth derives its ground from the self-consistent, faithful, God of promise.[33]

This certainly does not suggest some *generalizing* "concept of truth". As John Macquarrie urges, "Theological statements ... are on the way to truth; they do not freeze the question".[34] Truth, as I argue in Essay 12, remains a *polymorphous concept*, often context-dependent for its meaning. But because truth relates to revelation, to divine judgement, and to eschatology, a "final" truth awaits the world in the light of which it stands under judgement. Karl Rahner speaks of this when he writes concerning "reverence for truth". The revelation of truth makes "the need to hide" and the need for self-deceptive defensiveness unnecessary and indeed obsolete.[35] Yet in the interim truth remains complex and many-sided. Our lexicographical research has shown that biblical writers were not wholly unaware of these complexities. The biblical writings never reflected a naïve dualism between "Hebrew" and "Greek" *general concepts* of truth. They speak with more intelligence and critical awareness to our world than this.

---

[33] W. Pannenberg, "What is Truth?", in *Basic Questions in Theology*, vol. 2 (London: SCM, 1971), pp.1–27.

[34] J. Macquarrie, "Truth in Theology", in *Thinking about God* (London: SCM, 1975), p.25.

[35] K. Rahner, "On Truthfulness", in *Theological Investigations*, vol. VII (London: DLT, 1971), pp.229–39.

CHAPTER EIGHTEEN

Reception History or *Wirkungsgeschichte*? "The Holy Spirit in 1 Corinthians: Exegesis and Reception-History in the Patristic Era" (2004)

This essay was first prepared as a contribution to a Festschrift *for James D.G. Dunn, who has been a good friend over many years, and also at Durham a kind and wise colleague. It was published under the title* The Holy Spirit and Christian Origins: Essays in Honor of James D.G. Dunn *(eds Graham N. Stanton, Bruce W. Longenecker and Stephen C. Barton, Grand Rapids, MI and Cambridge: Eerdmans, 2004), pp.207–28, and presented to James Dunn on 21 November 2004. I find myself in close agreement with much of his work, and had to strive hard to suggest two differences of emphasis on the subject of the Holy Spirit in 1 Corinthians. One concerns reservations about the propriety of the terms "supernatural" and "spontaneous" in this context; the other invites a willingness to perceive a bolder notion of "Trinity" in Paul. Another distinctive contribution of this essay is to explore distinctions between different approaches to the history of the reception of New Testament texts, and to trace some points in the history of reception of passages in 1 Corinthians about the Holy Spirit that bear on the other arguments of this essay.*

I
"Spirit" and "Spiritual" in Pauline Texts and their Post-History

During a class in 1958 one of my fellow-students asked, "Dr Simon, what is a *'Festschrift'*?" Never one to lose a chance for a touch of irony, Ulrich Simon replied (best sub-vocalized with a mildly Germanic accent): "When you are old, and have lost all interest in your subject, they give you a book of essays about those things concerning which you no longer wish to know."

James Dunn has never lost his infectious zest and enthusiasm for Pauline theology and exegesis. Nevertheless, lest there could be even the smallest grain of truth in Ulrich Simon's ironic comment, this chapter is not only about the Holy Spirit in 1 Corinthians, but also about the post-history of Pauline texts in Patristic writings. A little seasoning may be added by seeking to identify two points of tentative reservation concerning James Dunn's claims about the Holy Spirit in 1 Corinthians, alongside my admiration for, and agreement with, his work on this subject in general.

My first reservation concerns the use of such terms as "supernatural", "miraculous" and "spontaneous" to describe of some of the gifts and work of the Holy Spirit in 1 Corinthians. Is it true, to cite one example, that prophetic speech in 1 Corinthians is necessarily "a spontaneous utterance"?[1] Second, can we not find in Paul the foundations

---

[1] James D.G. Dunn, *Jesus and the Spirit* (London: SCM Press, 1975), p.228.

of a Trinitarian *theology* or *ontology*, which a number of the later Church Fathers believe they find in 1 Corinthians? Dunn concedes "there is what might be called *a 'Trinitarian' element in the believer's experience* ... (Rom. 8:15f; 1 Cor. 12:3)"(his italics).[2] But later attempts to trace ontological or metaphysical dimensions on the basis of this Christian experience may do "more to retard the Gospel than to advance it".[3] The subject index to *Jesus and the Spirit* contains only a single reference to the Trinity (namely that just cited), while that of Dunn's *The Theology of Paul the Apostle* appears to contain none, even if half a page addresses the actualization by the Spirit of the *Kyrios* confession (1 Cor. 12:3) and the cry "Abba, Father" (Rom. 8:15).[4] Discussions of the theme "God is one" focus more especially upon possible christological ramifications apparently without reference to the Spirit.[5]

Like Dunn himself, however, many of the Church Fathers draw on 1 Corinthians to engage with issues of exegesis that have remained central for the Christian church over the centuries. First, many are well aware of the very varied semantic and lexicographical range of πνεῦμα and πνευματικός and of the need to identify instances where these terms distinctively denote the Holy Sprit or what characterizes the actions of the Holy Spirit. Dunn reflects a growing consensus when he rightly insists, "Πνευματικός ... expresses so clearly the sense of belonging to the Spirit, embodying Spirit, manifesting Spirit, of the essence or nature of Spirit".[6] Cyril of Jerusalem and Augustine provide striking examples here. Cyril writes, "For many things are called spirits. Thus an angel is called 'spirit'; our soul is called 'spirit'; the wind that blows is called 'spirit' ... Beware, therefore, such is not the Holy Spirit ... He comes to save and to heal ... to enlighten the mind".[7] Augustine distinguishes between the meaning of "spirit" in Rom. 12:2 (the spirit of your mind) and 1 Cor. 14:14 (my spirit prays) from that of "Spirit" as denoting "the Holy Spirit", and from spirit-as-soul, or from the breath of life in created beings of various orders.[8]

Similarly both Dunn and many Patristic writers address the difficulty of how to be clear about whether Paul's description of certain gifts of the Spirit actually corresponds with what later generations claim as "the same" gifts or experiences under the same name. Augustine, for example, is so convinced, at least in some later writings, that *"glossolalia"* does not necessarily entail a miraculous ability to speak some other "language", that he reserves the term *jubilatio* to describe the phenomenon to which Paul alludes in 1 Cor. 14:2–27, leaving others to use *glossolalia* to denote the popular understanding of what many then and now believe that it denotes. Augustine anticipates the view of "wordless praise", advocated by Stendahl, Theissen, Macchia and (since 1979) also regularly by the present writer, as a more adequate account of the phenomenon in 1 Corinthians.[9] Augustine writes:

---

2   Dunn, *Jesus and the Spirit*, p.326.
3   Dunn, loc. cit.
4   James D.G. Dunn, *The Theology of Paul the Apostle* (Edinburgh: T. & T. Clark, 1998), p.264.
5   Dunn, *Theology*, pp.31–50; 252–65; 272–93; and *Jesus and the Spirit*, pp.318–26.
6   Dunn, *Jesus and the Spirit*, pp.207–8. On the history of interpretation of πνεῦμα (mainly on "human spirit") see Robert Jewett, *Paul's Anthropological Terms* (Leiden: Brill, 1971), pp.167–200 and 451–3.
7   Cyril of Jerusalem, *Catechetical Lectures*, 16:12–16.
8   Augustine, *On the Trinity*, 14:22; see also *On the Soul and its Origin*, 4:36:22.
9   Anthony C. Thiselton, "The 'Interpretation' of Tongues in 1 Corinthians 14:13: A New Suggestion in the Light of Greek Usage in Philo and Josephus", in *Journal of Theological Studies* 30 (1979), pp.15–36: and

In jubilatione cane ... Quid est in jubilatione canere? ... Verbis explicare non posse quod canitur corde; ... in verbis canticorum exsultare laetitia, veluti impleti tanta laetitia, ut eam verbis explicare non possint, avertunt se a syllabis verborum, et eunt in sonum jubilationis ... Et quem decet ista jubilatio, nisi ineffabilem Deum? Ineffabilis enim est, quem fari non potes ... ut gaudeat cor sine verbis ... Bene cantate ei in jubilatione.[10]

That 1 Corinthians provokes these reflections more than any other Pauline epistle is not surprising. In practice the term πνεῦμα and its cognate adjective and adverb πνευματικός and πνευματικῶς, occur here more frequently than in any other epistle: some fifty-two times, as against thirty-five in Romans, less than half that number in 2 Corinthians and in Galatians, and less than half-a-dozen times each in Philippians, Colossians and 1 and 2 Thessalonians. Yet word-frequency alone is an unreliable guide. It is more significant that in 1 Corinthians Paul goes out of his way to correct and to redefine his readers' understanding of πνευματικός, "spiritual", for example, in 1 Cor. 3:1–3. More than this, Paul takes pains to underline the "otherness" and transcendence of the person and work of the Holy Spirit (1 Cor. 2:10–16) as well as the christological criticism of the Spirit's authentic action (also 12:1–8); he redefines their questions about spiritual gifts (or "spiritual" people, περὶ δὲ τῶν πνευματικῶν, 12:1) in different terms as a matter of διαιρέσεις δὲ χαρισμάτων (12:4) and χαρίσματα (12:9, 18, 30, 31); he insists on the holiness of the Holy Spirit (3:16–17; 6:19–20); and he prepares the way in earlier argument (2:10–16; 3:1–3; 12:1–3) for the definition of the σῶμα πνευματικόν in 15:44 on the resurrection as deriving its semantic and theological force by its contrast with ψυχικόν (v. 44, twice) and the christological association (15:44–49). All of these seminal thoughts and watersheds feature among Patristic writers, as we observe below.

In practice virtually all the main classic Patristic sources on an explicit theology of the Holy Spirit tend to select the same eleven passages from 1 Corinthians as a basis for their reflection on this subject. Among the classic sources, in addition to earlier scattered references from Irenaeus, Clement of Alexandria, and Tertullian, we include: Origen, *On First Principles*, 1:3; Cyril of Jerusalem, *Catechetical Lectures*, 4, 16 and 17; Hilary of Poitiers, *On the Trinity*, 2:29–35; Athanasius, *Letters to Serapion*, 1–3; Basil of Caesarea, *On the Holy Spirit*; Gregory of Nazianzus, *Theological Orations*, 5; Ambrose, *On the Holy Spirit*; Chrysostom, *Homilies on 1 Corinthians*, and scattered sections from Augustine, *On the*

---

in *The First Epistle to the Corinthians; A Commentary on the Greek Text* (Grand Rapids, MI: Eerdmans and Carlisle: Paternoster Press, 2000), pp.1094–1111; K. Stendahl, "Glossolalia" in *Paul among Jews and Gentiles* (London: SCM Press, 1977), pp.109–24; G. Theissen, *Psychological Aspects of Pauline Theology* (Edinburgh: T. & T. Clark, 1987), pp.59–114 and 292–341; and F.D. Macchia, "Sighs too Deep for Words: Toward a Theology of Glossolalia", in *Journal of Pentecostal Theology* 1 (1992), pp.47–73.

[10] Augustine, *Expositions on the Book of Psalms*, 32: *enarratio* ii, *sermo* 1; 8 [on v. 3], C.C. vol. 38, p.254. The Latin exposition on wordless praise is omitted from the English Post-Nicene Library Series 1, vol. 8, p.71, but can be found in J.-P. Migne (ed.), *P.L.* vol. 36 (1861), col. 283. An English translation might run: "Sing in jubilation ... What is it to sing in jubilation? ... It is to be unable to explain in words what is sung by the heart; ... to exult with joy in the words of a song, just as it is to be filled with so great a joy that they cannot set it forth with words, and turn away from the syllables of words to pass to the sound of 'jubilation' ... And to whom is this jubilation fitting, unless to the God who is ineffable? For he is ineffable whom you cannot grasp by word ... so that the heart rejoices without words ... 'Sing well and in jubilation.'" (Psalm 32:3).

Trinity, especially 2:5–7; 5:11–15 and 15:17–27. These writers repeatedly cite, discuss and develop the following eleven passages from 1 Corinthians as seminal texts: 1 Cor. 2:4;[11] 2:9–12;[12] 2:15–16;[13] 3:16–17;[14] (less directly but also of importance) 8:6;[15] 12:3;[16] 12:4–7;[17] 12:8–11;[18] 12:13;[19] 14:2, 14–25;[20] and 15:44–50.[21] Depending, then, on what we seek in considering the "post-history" or *Wirkungsgeschichte* of these texts in the Patristic church, a dialogue between their exegesis and their reception may perhaps be of value.

II
"Post-History", "Wirkungsgeschichte", or "Rezeptionsgeschichte"?

The ways in which Patristic writers "received" Pauline texts and allowed them to provoke fresh, creative reflection provide instances of what has widely come to be known as the *Wirkungsgeschichte* of the text. However, this is different from simply "a history of interpretation" of the text. Three terms are often used interchangeably, but in more technical uses they may not strictly denote the same agenda. In my commentary I used the most general term, "the post-history" of the text.[22] This carries perhaps the least explicit theoretical commitments. Wolfgang Schrage regularly uses the phrase

---

[11]   E.g. Athanasius, *Letters to Serapion*, 1:17; Greek, J.-P. Migne, *P.G.*, vol. 26, cols 569–71; critical English text, C.R.B. Shapland, *The Letters of Athanasius concerning the Holy Spirit* (London: Epworth Press, 1951), pp.103–6; Cyril of Jerusalem, *Catechetical Lectures*, 4:16, 17; Gregory Nazianzus, *Theological Orations* 5:32.

[12]   Irenaeus, *Against Heresies*, 1:9:1; 5:8:4; Clement, *Stromata*, 5:5; Tertullian, *Against Marcion*, 5:6; Origen, *On First Principles*, 1:3:4–5; Cyril, *Catechetical Lectures*, 4:16–17; Athanasius, *Letter to Serapion*, 16:38; 19:50; 24:56; Basil, *On the Holy Spirit*, 16:38, 40; 19:50; 24:56. See also Chrysostom, *Homilies on 1 Corinthians*, 7:6–9.

[13]   Clement, *Stromata*, 5:5; Origen, *On First Principles*, 4:1:11, and "Fragments on 1 Corinthians", sects 11 and 17, in *JTS* 9 (1908), pp.240–41; Cyril, *Catechetical Lectures*, 17:1; Athanasius, *Letter to Serapion*, 1:22, 25, 26; Ambrose, *On the Holy Spirit*, 2:9:99; 2:11:122; and 3:3:16; cf. Chrysostom, *Homilies on 1 Corinthians*, 7:8–12.

[14]   Irenaeus, *Against Heresies*, 5:6:2; Athanasius, *Letters to Serapion*, 1:19,20; 3:3; Ambrose, *On the Holy Spirit*, 3:12:90; Augustine, *On the Trinity*, 7:3:6.

[15]   Although 8:6 does not mention the Spirit, the monotheistic creedal form plays a vital role in the discussion, e.g. Ambrose, *On the Holy Spirit*, 1:3:32; 3:11:84; Athanasius, *Letters to Serapion*, 3:1 and *Against the Arians*, 3:16. A second "indirect" passage is 1 Cor. 10:2–4, where the phrase πνευματικὸν ἔπιον πόμα is related to the "procession" of the Spirit, e.g. Basil, *On the Holy Spirit*, 14:31–32.

[16]   Tertullian, *Against Marcion*, 5:8; Origen, *On First Principles*, 1:3:2; 3:7; Basil, *On the Holy Spirit*, 11:27; 16:38; 18:47; Ambrose, *On the Holy Spirit*, 1:4:56; 1:11:124; 3:11:20; Augustine, *On the Trinity*, 1:8:18; 5:14–16.

[17]   Tertullian, *Against Marcion*, 5:8; Cyril of Jerusalem, *Catechistical Lectures*, 16:1–4 and 16:12; Athanasius, *Letters to Serapion*, 1:31 and 3:5–6; Basil, *On the Holy Spirit*, 16:37; cf. Chrysostom, *Homilies on 1 Corinthians*, 29:1–6.

[18]   Clement, *Stromata*, 4:21:134; 5:13:89; Tertullian, *On the Soul*, 9:3–6: Origen, *On First Principles*, 1:3:7; Cyril, *Catechetical Lectures*, 16:12, 23 and 25 and 17:2; Basil, *On the Holy Spirit*, 16:37 and *Against Eunomius*, 3:4; Ambrose, *On the Holy Spirit*, 1:1:18; 2:12:139–41; 2:13:143, 152; 3:6:38; Augustine, *On the Trinity*, 15:19:34.

[19]   Athanasius, *Letter to Serapion*, 1:19–20; Basil, *On the Holy Spirit*, 10:26; Ambrose, *On the Holy Spirit*, 1:3:45; Augustine, *On the Trinity*, 15:19:33.

[20]   Basil, *On the Holy Spirit*, 16:37; Ambrose: *On the Holy Spirit*, 2:12:131; 3:11:70, Gregory Nazianzus, *Theological Orations*, 5:12.

[21]   Irenaeus, *Against Heresies*, 5:7:1–2; Tertullian, *Against Marcion*, 5:9–10; Chrysostom, *Homilies on 1 Corinthians*, 41:4–8.

[22]   Anthony C. Thiselton, *First Epistle to the Corinthians*, pp.196–204; 276–86; 330–44; 479–82; 531–40; 658–61; 908–1026; and 1306–14.

Auslegungs- und Wirkungs-geschichte.[23] Ulrich Luz uses *Wirkungsgeschichte* alone in his commentary on Matthew, which his translator, Wilhelm C. Linss consciously and deliberately translates "history of influence".[24] However, Luz comments in his Introduction that the term denotes "history, reception and actualising of a text *in media other than a commentary*, e.g. in sermons, canonical law, hymnody, art, and in the actions and sufferings of the church" (my italics).[25] Here "actualization" or "appropriation" plays a part, in life as well as in thought; and Luz implicitly alludes to "Reception Theory" or to reception-history (*Rezeptionsgeschichte*). These terms come out of a similar but nevertheless distinct intellectual matrix or background from that of *Wirkungsgeschichte*. Hence some clarification of these terms may be needed.

The term *"Wirkungsgeschichte"* derives most typically from within philosophical hermeneutics, especially from Hans-Georg Gadamer (1900–2002). In the first English edition of *Truth and Method* (1975 from German, 2nd edn 1965, 1st edn 1960), Garrett Barden and John Cumming translated the German as *"effective history"*.[26] In the improved second revised English edition (1989, and 1993) from the German fourth edition (and from *Gesammelte Werke*), Joel Weinsheimer and Donald G. Marshall translate the German as *"history of effects"*. More significantly the earlier translation of *wirkungsgeschichtliches Bewusstsein* as "effective historical consciousness" has been replaced in the revised edition (after careful discussion) by *"historically effected* consciousness" (my italics).[27]

This change from the active (effective) to the passive (effected) denotes "a consciousness that is doubly related to tradition, at once 'affected' by history (Paul Ricoeur translated this term as 'consciousness open to the effects of history') and also itself brought into being – 'effected' – by history and conscious that it is so".[28] We shall shortly note how closely this relates to a hermeneutic of question and answer, as dialectic.

The term *Rezeptionsgeschichte* primarily derives from Hans Robert Jauss and the literary theorists of the University of Constance. Wolfgang Iser and his reader-response theory contributed to the notion of a *potentiality* of textual effects. Drawing on Husserl and Roman Ingarden, Iser drew on the analogy of "filling in", or "completing", what perception did not directly apprehend but could be presupposed. Jauss's Inaugural Lecture in the University of Constance in 1967 was later published as *Literaturgeschichte als Provokation für die Literaturwissenschaft*.[29] Reception Theory then, emerged as a sub-genre of *reader-response theory*, while *Wirkungsgeschichte* emerged from *philosophical hermeneutics*.

---

[23] Wolfgang Schrage, *Der erste Brief an die Korinther* (4 vols, Zürich: Benziger and Neukirchen-Vluyn: Neukirchener Verlag, 1991, 1995, 1999 and 2002 [E.K.K.]) vol. 1, pp.163–5; 190–203; 218–22; 236–8, 269–78; 284–6; 317–18; 327–9; 350–51; 365–7 (simply up to 4:21 alone by way of example).

[24] Ulrich Luz, *Matthew 1–7: A Commentary* (Edinburgh: T. & T. Clark, 1989), p.11; cf. 95–9; and *Matthew 8–20* (Philadelphia, PA: Fortress, 2001); Translated from *Das Evangelium nach Matthäus* (Zürich: Benzinger and Neukirchen: Neukirchener Verlag [E.K.K.], 1990).

[25] Luz, *Matthew 1–7*, p.95.

[26] H.–G. Gadamer, *Truth and Method* (1st Eng. edn., London: Sheed & Ward, 1975), pp.267–74, 305–10 and 324–5.

[27] H.–G. Gadamer, *Truth and Method* (2nd revised Eng. edn., London: Sheed & Ward, 1989 and 1993), p.xv; cf. also pp.300–307; 341–6 and 377–8. Gadamer, *Gesammelte Werke* (10 vols, Tübingen: Mohr, 1985–95) contains the 5th edition of *Wahrheit und Methode* as vol. 1 and its supplementary essays in vol. 2 (both 1986).

[28] Gadamer, *Truth*, 2nd Eng. edn, p. xv.

[29] Hans Robert Jauss, *Toward an Aesthetic of Reception* (Minneapolis: University of Minnesota Press, 1982) pp.3–45.

Gadamer shows the limitations of abstract, reflective reason, which supposedly has no grounding or contingent situatedness within history and traditions.[30] Experience (*Erfahrung*) embodies a dialectic, which "leads on", enabling an appropriation of yet further experience. Yet "every experience worthy of the name thwarts an expectation ... [It] involves an escape from something that had deceived us and held us captive."[31] Genuinely "hermeneutical experience" entails "openness to tradition" and especially "*openness to the other* ... recognizing that I myself must accept some things that are against me ... This readiness is what distinguishes historically effected consciousness (*wirkungsgeschichtliches Bewusstsein*)" (my italics).[32]

Nevertheless we cannot have experiences, Gadamer claims, "without asking questions".[33] We must respect "the priority of the question".[34] He declares, "That a historical text is made the object of interpretation means that *it puts a question to the interpreter*" (my italics).[35] In Gadamer's view this "*logic of question and answer*" (exemplified in R.G. Collingwood) differs in kind from the notion of *solving "problems"* (exemplified in Kant): "The identity of the problem is an empty abstraction."[36] However, if this emptiness is recognized, a process of questioning may be begun which arises "out of the motivated context of questioning from which it receives ... its sense".[37] Gadamer invites us to provide a critique of the concept of *"problem"*, and thereby "to destroy the illusion that problems exist like stars in the sky. Reflection on hermeneutical experience *transforms problems back to questions that arise and derive their sense from their motivation*" (my italics).[38]

To trace the formulations, modifications and reformulations of ongoing *agendas* yields an appreciation of the distinctiveness of that of each generation. But it yields more, namely an appreciation of dialectic of continuities and discontinuities that form the ongoing agendas of history. Further, *to ask how the text questions each agenda that is brought before it* in turn tells us more about the Pauline text and its effects than defining a one-dimensional set of "problems" reconstructed as if from some supposed Archimedean point *outside* history. To recognize the priority of the question over de-historicized "problems" may provide a useful hermeneutical resource. It may also provide a constructive approach (which I am currently exploring) to a "hermeneutics of doctrine", designed to avoid the regrettable dichotomy between biblical interpretation and "systematic theology" as it is too often practised. "History" and the interpreter's own historical situation colour the agenda brought *to* the text; but the text itself also *shapes successive agendas by and through the effects that it produces.*

Thus, for Athanasius and for Basil of Caesarea, Paul's language about the Holy Spirit of God in 1 Cor. 2:6–16 *demands* that they "hear" how it shapes questions and answers

---

[30]   Gadamer, *Truth*, (2nd Eng. edn) pp.341–6.
[31]   Gadamer, *Truth*, p.356.
[32]   Gadamer, *Truth*, pp.361–2.
[33]   Gadamer, *Truth*, p.362.
[34]   Gadamer, *Truth*, p.363.
[35]   Gadamer, *Truth*, p.369.
[36]   Gadamer, *Truth*, p.375. On this aspect of Gadamer's thought, see also Brook W.R. Pearson, *Corresponding Sense: Paul, Dialectic and Gadamer* (Leiden, Boston, MA and Cologne, 2001), pp.93–7.
[37]   Gadamer, *Truth*, p.376.
[38]   Gadamer, *Truth*, p.377.

about the deity and personal agency of the Holy Spirit, as well as questions more explicitly asked by Paul about revelation, wisdom and divine transcendence.[39] 1 Cor. 12:3–7 *demands* that questions and answers relating to God as Trinity are addressed in the light of these verses. The successive readings of 1 Cor. 1:18–25 over generations establish a dialectic of continuity and contrast about *how* the proclamation of the cross involves what Gadamer calls "accepting some things that are against me". What "folly" and false "wisdom" amount to may not be exhaustively defined by a single generation.[40]

Jauss, no less than Gadamer, perceives texts of literature as "existing" in the process of their collective interpretation of successive generations of readers, and in the textual *effects*, or *actualizations*, of hitherto potential meaning by these successive generations. Each generation (or more strictly, each "audience") interacts with the text in terms of a different "horizon of expectations" (*Erwartungs-horizont*). Like Gadamer, Jauss regards the text as "potential" until it is "performed", like a script or score that finds its "reality" in the play or the concert that performs it interactively with an *audience* as an *event*. He declares, "The coherence of literature as an event is primarily mediated in the horizons of expectation of the ... experience of contemporary and later readers, critics and authors".[41] Further, "A literary event can continue to have an effect only if those who come after it still, or once again, respond to it."[42]

Jauss sets out seven "theses". Thesis 1 explicitly endorses Gadamer's rejection of "historical objectivism", and develops an emphasis on question and answer: "The dialogical character of the literary work ... establishes why ... understanding can exist only in a perpetual confrontation with the text".[43] It is not enough to establish past "facts" about the text once-and-for-all; it requires successive engagements with successive readers to bring out its potential meaning in interaction with a series of horizons. Like Iser and Eco, Jauss sees this eventfulness in terms of "productivity" and "completion" of meanings.

Theses 2 and 3 explicate this principle further. Only in interactions between texts and readers does a "directed perception come into play whereby the text may be comprehended according to its constitutive motivations and triggering signals ...".[44] A horizon of expectation, built up from earlier texts, may become "varied, corrected, altered", although it may also be "just reproduced".[45] Reception can result in a "change of horizons". Jauss expresses in *literary* terms a parallel with the observations of Luther, Calvin and Bonhoeffer about the word of God as "our adversary", which, in turn, recalls Paul's assertions in 1 Cor. 1:18–25, on the cross. When the text blandly accords with readers' prior assumptions, it is like what Jauss dismissively calls "culinary" (that is, like

[39] E.g. especially Athanasius, *Letters to Serapion*; and Basil, *On the Holy Spirit*, on which cf. Michael A.G. Haykin, *The Spirit of God: The Exegesis of 1 & 2 Corinthians in the Pneumatomachian Controversy of the Fourth Century* (Leiden, New York and Köln: Brill 1994), pp.59–169.

[40] Cf. Ulrich Wilckens, *Weisheit und Torheit. Eine exegetisch-religionsgeschichtliche Untersuchung zu 1 Kor. 1 und 2* (Tübingen: Mohr, 1959) pp.5–41 and 205–24.

[41] Jauss, *Towards an Aesthetic of Reception*, p.22.

[42] Jauss, *Reception*, p.22.

[43] Jauss, *Reception*, p.21.

[44] Jauss, *Reception*, p.23.

[45] Jauss, *Reception*, p.23.

a mere kitchen recipe) or "chat" texts (*Unterhaltungskunst*).[46] By contrast a capacity to satisfy, surpass, disappoint, or refute the expectations of its first audience provides a positive criterion of "its aesthetic value".

Theses 4–7 highlight the value of reception theory for offering "controls" in understanding the text, and for the *formation* of understanding. Texts are "socially formative".[47] Jauss not only addresses issues about the creative and formative potential of texts, but also seeks to offer constraints on the historical relativity of the "latest generation" of interpreters. He also explores the difference (so relevant to the reading of the Bible as Scripture) between an *initial* reception of a text and a "retrospectively interpretive reading".[48]

Jauss draws on Thomas S. Kuhn's well-known concept of "paradigms" in *The Structure of Scientific Revolutions*. As history and experience advance, the emergence of *more complex issues and agenda* call for fresh conceptual schemes. These may generate fresh paradigms. The "older" paradigm may still serve the earlier agenda that the text addressed, and which may still arise; but new paradigms also expand the ground beyond the capacities of earlier paradigms to address in full. This is precisely the conceptual and hermeneutical frame within which questions arise about a Trinitarian *ontology* when this has been placed on the agenda. Does this not "arise" from Pauline texts? Jauss here begins to explore "change in belief" and "liberation ... of mind" produced by shifts in norms.[49] However, the confines of space prohibit further discussion of Jauss.

III
Semantic Strategies for Maintaining Contrasts within Polysemic Meaning: πνεῦμα as the Transcendent Holy Spirit

Eugene Nida regularly argued that in modern lexicography we should begin not with polysemic meaning, that is, with the different meanings of single words as such, but with the paradigmatic relations between different words (very frequently in semantic opposition) that attach to each separate instance of meaning conveyed by the single word.[50] Thus, to take a familiar example, rather than comparing simply the different meanings of the English word "run" in such examples as "run a race", "run a business", and a "run on a bank", in the first instance "run" stands in opposition to "walk" or "crawl"; in the second instance it stands in contrast to "direct" or "participate in", and in the third instance it may stand in paradigmatic relation to "an acquisition of new securities". My collaboration with James Dunn (and one of the editors) began not less

---

46 Jauss, *Reception*, p.25.
47 Jauss, *Reception*, pp.32, 36 and 45; and pp.32–45 throughout.
48 H.R. Jauss, "The Poetic Text within the Change of Horizons of Reading" in *Reception*, pp.139–85, where he selects Baudelaire's "Spleen II" as a textual example.
49 H.R. Jauss, *Aesthetic Experience and Literary Hermeneutics* (Minneapolis: University of Minnesota Press, 1982), p.92. See further, *Question and Answer: Forms of Dialogue Understanding* (Minneapolis: University of Minnesota Press, 1989).
50 E.A. Nida, "The Implications of Contemporary Linguistics for Biblical Scholarship", *Journal of Biblical Literature* 91 (1972), 85; cf. 73–89.

than thirty years ago in 1973, when we produced a volume on New Testament interpretation, in which I included a semantic tree-diagram of uses of πνεῦμα in the New Testament.[51]

In 1 Corinthians Paul is careful to disengage his uses of πνεῦμα to denote the Holy Spirit from these other meanings conveyed by the same Greek word. In 1 Cor. 2:12 he uses the device familiar in modern semantics under the term "safeguards" in instances of polysemic meaning. One standard "safeguard" is clarification and explication by the addition of another word or phrase. Ullmann cites the example of the English word "fair".[52] This word may denote a measure of size or achievement that is not less than medium or average; or in other contexts, a judicious balance of assessment that is fair to all sides, or a colour which stands in semantic opposition to "dark". By adding a hyphenated word to form a compound we may, for example, differentiate between fair-sized, fair-minded, or fair-haired. Thus in 1 Cor. 2:12 Paul anticipates this *semantic* device by a "safeguard" which would develop into a feature of profound *theological* significance for later Christian doctrine. In place of the simple genitive used to qualify πνεῦμα in the first half of the verse, οὐ τὸ πνεῦμα τοῦ κόσμου, he adds the preposition ἐκ, *from* or *out of*, to form an adjectival phrase to indicate a distinctive nuance of this use of πνεῦμα, namely, ἀλλὰ τὸ πνεῦμα τὸ ἐκ τοῦ θεοῦ. H.B. Swete compares the parallel notion of the Spirit's "going forth from" ἐκπορεύεται ἐκ God in John 15:26–27.[53] This coheres with Johannes Weiss's point about "the essential difference between the Stoa and Paul. The former thinks of an innate and inborn divine nature; the latter, of the divine, supernatural equipment given [by God]."[54] This stands in contrast to the immanental perspective of Epictetus: "Our souls are joined together with God as parts and fragments of him."[55]

While several Patristic writers address the issue of semantic polysemy, many stress the transcendent character of the Holy Spirit as "Other" and distinctively "of God" on theological grounds. We have already drawn attention to the awareness of semantic polysemy shown by Cyril of Jerusalem. He adopts both approaches. Cyril opens *Lecture 16* by reminding his hearers of what is at stake in "blasphemy against the Holy Spirit", and asserts, "The Holy Spirit is a most mighty power, a Being divine."[56] The Spirit apportions grace and gifts as he wills (1 Cor. 12:11).[57] He then cites the range of *charismata* enumerated by Paul in 1 Cor. 12:7–11. In this context he introduces his warning against semantic confusion between different meanings of πνεῦμα.[58] In this context πνεῦμα emphatically does not denote the human spirit. Equally, πνεῦμα does not here denote simply that from which the physical or bodily is absent: "Such is not the Holy Spirit."[59] Cyril expounds

51   A.C. Thiselton, "Semantics and New Testament Interpretation", in I. Howard Marshall (ed.), *New Testament Interpretation* (Exeter: Paternoster, 1977), pp.75–104 [Essay 13 above]; tree diagram on p.91; cf. J.D.G. Dunn, "Demythologizing ...",pp.285–307; and G.N. Stanton, "Presuppositions ...", pp.60–74.

52   S. Ullmann, *Semantics* (Oxford: Blackwell, 1967), pp.158–80.

53   H.B. Swete, *The Holy Spirit in the New Testament* (London: Macmillan, 1909), p.155.

54   J. Weiss, *Earliest Christianity* (New York: Harper edn, vol. 2, 1959), p.512.

55   Epictetus, *Discourses*, 1:14:6.

56   Cyril, *Catechetical Lectures*, 16:1, 3.

57   Cyril, *Lectures*, 16:12.

58   Cyril, *Lectures*, 16:13.

59   Cyril, *Lectures*, 16:15, 16.

those activities of the Spirit (comfort, enlightenment, intercession for believers – Rom.8:26), which, he insists, underline his divine, rather than creaturely, agency. The climax of this part of the argument finds expression in an appeal to 1 Cor. 2:10, 11 and 12:11.[60]

The possibility of semantic confusion indeed found expression long before Cyril. Irenaeus discusses the differences between human spirit, the Spirit of God, and that which is "spiritual" on the ground that "they ['spiritual people'] partake of the Spirit, and not because their flesh has been stripped off and taken away ... To be 'spiritual' is the handiwork of God, the Spirit of God."[61] Later, Gregory of Nanzianzus urged the need to address "the task of examining carefully, and distinguishing, many senses of the word πνεῦμα ... in holy scripture ... The combination of the two words ... 'Holy Spirit' is used in a peculiar sense".[62] Gregory also calls attention to the transcendent divine agency which characterizes the Holy Spirit as Other. Commenting on prayer in the Spirit in 1 Cor. 14:15, he writes: "Therefore to adore or to pray to the Spirit seems to me to be simply Himself offering prayer or adoration to Himself [through us]. Who can disapprove of this because of the equality of honour and deity between the Three?"[63]

R.B. Hoyle traces the wide-ranging use of πνεῦμα in Hellenistic literature to convey the notion of a pervasive, animating, quasi-substance that permeates the world.[64] I discuss this background, together with 2:11, in my commentary, and conclude: "Paul's use of the phrase τὸ πνεῦμα τὸ ἐκ τοῦ θεοῦ, *the Spirit who issues from God*, thus stands in semantic opposition or contrast to *the spirit of the world* ... The divine Spirit comes from 'beyond' to impart a disclosure of God's own 'wisdom'."[65] On v. 11 I urged that only a superficial reading could suggest that Paul "argues on the basis of a natural correspondence between human spirit/human person and divine Spirit/God, as if *Spirit*, πνεῦμα, embodied a natural continuity between the two instantiation of the term".[66]

Some Patristic writers expound theologically the transcendence and "otherness" of the Spirit in 2:12 on the basis of the prepositional phrase, even if without semantic discussion. Athanasius rightly sees that v. 12 qualifies v. 11 and exclaims, "What kinship could there be, judging by the above [vv. 11 and 12] between the Spirit and the creatures? That which is from God (ἐκ τοῦ θεοῦ) could not be from that which is not (ἐκ τοῦ μὴ ὄντος).[67] We shall return to 2:12 in section V, below. Meanwhile, Dunn fully addresses the semantic range of πνεῦμα, and the transcendent power of the Holy Spirit.[68] The background of רוח in the Old Testament remains significant here. The adjectival πνευματικός also reflects this emphasis when it denotes that which is characterized by the Holy Spirit.[69]

---

[60] Cyril, *Lectures*, 16:25. See also 4:16–17.

[61] Irenaeus, *Against Heresies*, 5:6:1.

[62] Gregory, *Theological Orations*, 5:2.

[63] Gregory, *Orations*, 5:12.

[64] R.B. Hoyle, *The Holy Spirit in St Paul* (London: Hodder & Stoughton, 1927), p.219.

[65] Thiselton, *First Epistle to the Corinthians*, p.263; cf. pp.257–64.

[66] Thiselton, *First Epistle to the Corinthians*, p.257.

[67] Athanasius, *Letters to Serapion*, 1:22. Greek, Migne, *P.G.* 26, col. 58, and critical English text, C.R.B. Shapland, *The Letters of Saint Athanasius Concerning the Holy Spirit* (London: Epworth Press, 1951), p.121 (including n.1).

[68] Dunn, *Jesus and the Spirit*, pp.201–3.

[69] See Dunn, *Jesus and the Spirit*, pp.207–9, and further F.W. Danker and W. Bauer, *Greek-English Lexicon of the New Testament and Other Early Christian Literature* [*BDAG*] (Chicago, IL, University of

IV
The Holy Spirit and "Miracles"?

Dunn speaks of " those charismata which are most obviously a display of divine power, that is, miracles. So in [1 Cor.] 12:10 we read, "To another is given the operation of miracles (ἐνεργήματα δυνάμεων) ... *The charisma is the actual miracle, or the miracle-working power operating effectively in a particular instance*" (his italics).[70] To be sure, the NRSV, NJB, AV/KJV, C.K. Barrett and, in effect, R.F. Collins, translate the Greek phrase as "the working of miracles", while the REB, NIV and Moffatt translate it as "miraculous powers". Yet I see no ground for Dunn's assumption that this is likely to denote primarily "a non-rational power".[71] In my commentary I have translated ἐνεργήματα δυνάμεων as "actively effective deeds of power" on the basis of a carefully-argued case.[72] Calvin and Barth, it so happens, tend to view *power* (δύναμις) at least in this epistle as denoting what is *effective* (since its semantic opposites include *weakness* and *"mere" word*), rather than what is necessarily miraculous or spectacular.[73] What lacks "power" is not the ordinary, but what is ineffective, idle or empty. As *BDAG* (Danker-Bauer, 3rd edn), makes clear, "capability, ... ability to carry out something ... resource" denote the thrust of the term, even if "the power that works wonders" conveys a given nuance in specific contexts.[74] Do the contexts in 1 Corinthians demand this specific sense?

There are many levels of discussion at which this case may be pursued. One is that of lexicography and its contextual qualifiers. Another is that of Pauline theology, and whether Paul differentiates between a "natural" and "supernatural" level of divine operation. Does this impose onto Paul an anachronistic world-view of largely post-Enlightenment thought? A third level or area invites a re-evaluation of the probable semantic scope of each of the *charismata*. Dunn acknowledges, especially in his later *Theology of Paul* that these "included more humdrum tasks and organizational roles, as well as eye-catching prophecy, tongues and miracles".[75] But were *even* these last three necessarily "eye-catching", and was "prophecy" necessarily "not ... a previously prepared sermon ...", but "a spontaneous utterance ... (14:3)" in *all* cases?[76]

I leave aside discussion of the exegetical details to be assessed in part by comparing these claims with the different ones proposed in my commentary. There I translated κυβερνήσις as "ability to formulate strategies";[77] and χαρίσματα ἰαμάτων as "gifts of various kinds of healings", where I argue for the generic use of the plural. This does not

---

Chicago, 3rd edn, 2000), pp.832–7; and G.W.H. Lampe, *A Patristic Greek Lexicon* (Oxford: Clarendon, 1961), pp.1097–105 (some 18 columns of close print).

[70] Dunn, *Jesus and the Spirit*, p.210. Cf. further pp.206–65; and also cf. Dunn, *The Theology of Paul*, pp.554–9.

[71] Dunn, *Jesus and the Spirit*, p.210.

[72] Thiselton, *First Epistle to the Corinthians*, pp.952–6.

[73] J. Calvin, *First Epistle to the Corinthians* (Edinburgh: Oliver and Boyd, 1960), p.262; and Karl Barth, *The Resurrection of the Dead* (London: Hodder & Stoughton, 1933), pp.18, 24, 26, 49, 52, 75 and 79–82.

[74] *BDAG*, pp.262–3. Cf., more strikingly, Lampe, *Patristic Greek Lexicon*, pp.389–91 (6 cols).

[75] Dunn, *Theology of Paul*, p.556.

[76] Dunn, *Jesus and the Spirit*, p.228.

[77] Thiselton, *First Epistle to the Corinthians*, pp.1021–2.

exclude Bengel's *"per naturalia remedia"*.[78] I translate προφητεία as "prophecy", but this does not exclude the views of David Hill, Ulrich Müller and T.W Gillespie that this would include applied, pastoral preaching;[79] and γένη γλωσσῶν as "species of tongues", which leaves room for at least some types to correspond with the "wordless praise" mentioned above in connection with Augustine, Stendahl and Theissen. I render ἑρμηνεία γλωσσῶν as "intelligible articulation of what is spoken in tongues", which is what transposes otherwise wordless praise into public edification. There is no τις (someone) in 14:13 to denote an "interpreter" other than the speaker.[80]

I do not propose to repeat old arguments. I appeal, instead, to a fourth, fresh consideration that relates to Patristic sources. A seminal paper by M. Parmentier concedes that in the Patristic era "A distinction was often made between ordinary and extraordinary, inner and outer, normal and miraculous, gifts of the Spirit."[81] Everyday talents such as serving, teaching and being a leader (as Rom. 12:7–8) did not pose any problems, but "special", miraculous, powers (as in 1 Cor. 12:8–10) did. Parmentier continues, "However, Paul himself does not make such a distinction anywhere, and he would surely have rejected it."[82]

Parmentier concedes that many of the early Church Fathers did understand the *charismata* in this way. Irenaeus argues that Christians perform miracles in the name of Christ for the well-being of other people, and that this vindicates certain christological claims. He adds that such miracles include foreknowledge, prophecy, healing the sick and even raising the dead.[83] Tertullian also speaks of experiences of visions "in ecstasy, which means abeyance of mind, if there is added also an interpretation of the tongue".[84] He also describes a worship assembly in which *charismata* include experiences "in the Spirit" by ecstasy, converse with angels, and the hearing of mysterious things.[85] To be sure, matters seem to have changed by the fourth century, since Eusebius quotes Irenaeus as a witness to the possibility of the miraculous in the second century, but also implies that this is no longer actual in his own day.[86] A number of Patristic writers state or imply that certain "miraculous" gifts faded from view at an early date. Cyril of Alexandria and Chrysostom both appear to believe that *glossolalia*, as a gift of *languages*, existed in the early Church, but no longer now. This perspective finds clear expression in John Chrysostom. He writes, "For in truth the church was a heaven then, the Spirit governing all things ... But not so now: the present church is like a woman who has fallen from her

---

[78] Thiselton, *First Epistle to the Corinthians*, pp.946–51; cf. J.A. Bengel, *Gnomon Novi Testamenti* (Stuttgart: Steinkopt, [1773] 1866), p.652.

[79] Thiselton, *First Epistle to the Corinthians*, pp.956–65 and 1087–94 (two Notes); cf. U.B. Müller, *Prophetie und Predigt im NT* (Gütersloh: Mohn, 1975), and T.W. Gillespie, *The First Theologians: A Study in Early Christian Prophecy* (Grand Rapids, MI: Eerdmans, 1994), especially pp.97–164.

[80] Thiselton, "The 'Interpretation' of Tongues? ...", *Journal of Theological Studies* 30 (1979), pp.15–36.

[81] M. Parmentier, "The Gifts of the Spirit in Early Christianity", in J. den Boeft and M.L. van Poll-van de Lisdonk (eds), *The Impact of Scripture in Early Christianity* (Leiden, Boston and Köln: Brill, 1999), pp.58–78.

[82] Parmentier, "The Gifts of the Spirit", in *The Impact of Scripture*, p.58.

[83] Irenaeus, *Against Heresies*, 2:32:4–5.

[84] Tertullian, *Against Marcion*, 5:8:12.

[85] Tertullian, *On the Soul*, 9:3–4.

[86] Eusebius, *Ecclesiastical History*, 5:7.

former prosperous days and in many respects retains the symbols only of that ancient prosperity; displaying indeed the repositories and caskets of her golden ornaments, but bereft of her wealth."[87]

We have already noted above that Augustine distinguishes between "wordless jubilation" as "exceptionally suitable for the praise of God, who is ineffable", and as a permanent gift of the Spirit, and an earlier gift of "languages" for the initial Gospel era.[88] Parmentier now makes his main point. This gift of the Spirit "is *a continuous phenomenon in Christian tradition, from the first Pentecost until now*".[89] He insists that it would be an un-Pauline reception of the texts to read them in such a way as to predispose later readers to perceive *earlier* experiences of the Spirit as somehow *more intense, or more authentic* than later, current, ones. He then couples this with a closely related concern. Paul formulates a criterion for authentic activity of the Spirit not in terms of "miracle" or "power", but as a *christological criterion*. Thus in 1 Cor. 12:3 the confession Κύριος Ἰησοῦς is fundamental as a criterion of the Spirit's presence and activity, as well as of Corinthian claims to be a πνευματικός. Parmentier observes, "John Cassian, who ... knows powerful charismatic works from his own experience, shows clearly how miracles in themselves mean nothing, because Satan can work them also. What matters is love. The imitation of Christ does not consist in the imitation of his signs, but in the imitation of his patience and his humility."[90] This is why, I have argued, it is not only the case that chapter 13 on love illuminates everything about the gifts of the Spirit, but also that the chapters on these gifts form part of the long section on respect for the "other" in various contexts: that of food offered to idols (chapters 8 and 10); the principle of forbearance for the sake of others on the matter of patronage and apostolic stipend (chapter 9); mutuality between men and women (chapter 11:1–16); and love on the part of the "haves" for the "have-nots" at the Lord's Supper (11:17–end).

That an emphasis upon "miraculous" gifts might be pastorally unhelpful or distracting cannot of itself be determinative or even significant for exegesis. However, Parmentier's concerns suggest that our other arguments cohere sufficiently closely with Paul's pastoral and theological aims to be brought into play. At very least, they suggest that the burden of proof may belong to claims that certain *charismata necessarily* must be understood as "supernatural", "miraculous", "spontaneous", or "non-rational". This is not to limit divine sovereignty in any way at all. It is to affirm that the activity of the Spirit may be experienced in what theologians might describe as "incarnational" modes of ordinary human life, without prejudice to the precise "how" of divine agency.

V

Trinitarian Experience – and Ontology?

James Dunn helpfully reminds us that the Pauline churches approached issues about the role of the Holy Spirit in relation to God in terms of "experience", not of theological

---

[87] Chrysostom, *Homilies on 1 Corinthians*, 36:7.
[88] Augustine, *On the Psalms*, 32:ii:1; 8 (see above, n. 10 for sources and texts).
[89] Parmentier, "The Gift of the Spirit", in *The Impact of Scripture*, p.73 (my italics).
[90] Cassian, *Consolationes*, 15:1, and Parmentier, "Gifts of the Spirit", in *Impact*, p.78.

theory, let alone theological polemic.[91] As a contributor to successive Reports of the Church of England Doctrine Commission, I identify with this approach. In such a Report we wrote: "The attempt has been to indicate an experience of prayer from which pressure towards Trinitarian thinking might arise ... We start with the recognition of a vital, though mysterious, divine dialogue within us ... the flow of Trinitarian life".[92] Prayer prompted by the Spirit is typically prayer made *to* God as Father, offered *through* Christ, inspired *by* the Holy Spirit. The Report cites Pauline material, especially Rom. 8:15–16, 21–22, 26; 1 Cor. 2:9–16; 12:3; Gal. 4:6, but equally insists that Basil and other Fathers combine experiential considerations with theological formulations designed to guard against invalid inferences.

In our discussion of *Wirkungsgeschichte* above, we noted that, for Athanasius and for Basil, Paul's language in 1 Cor. 2:6–16 and 12:3–7 "demands" that they "hear" how these texts engage with questions and agendas of their day, as long as this does not obscure or distort Paul's immediate concerns. Michael Haykin observes, "Athanasius' argument for the divinity of the Holy Spirit ... is coupled with the exegesis of the Corinthian correspondence ... [especially] the concordance of ... 1 Cor. 2:11–12, 12:11, 13, 6:11 ...".[93] Citing these texts from 1 Corinthians, Athanasius writes: "Why then do they [the Pneumatomachi of Thmuis] say that the Holy Spirit is a creature (κτίσμα), who has the same oneness (τὴν αὐτὴν ἔχον ἑνότηα) with the Son (πρὸς τὸν Υἱόν) as the Son with the Father?"[94] If it were the case that the Spirit belonged to the created order, and was not God, "on this showing once again the Triad (δείκνυσι τὴν Τριάδα) is no longer one (ἕν) but is compounded of two differing natures (ἐκ δύο διαφόρων φύσεων)".[95] This would run entirely counter to 1 Cor. 2:10–15; 8:6; and 12:4–6.

On the basis especially of these texts in 1 Corinthians, Athanasius writes again, "The Spirit is not a creature (κτίσμα) ... For if he were a creature, he would not be ranked with the Triad (οὐ συνετάσσετο τῇ Τριάδι). For the whole Triad is one God (ὅλη γὰρ εἰς Θεός ἐστι)."[96] Again, this reflects 1 Cor. 12:4–6 as well as 8:6 and 2:12. The metaphors of "drinking", or being saturated by, the Spirit in 1 Cor. 12:13 (ἓν πνεῦμα ἐποτίσθημεν) resonate with τὸ πνεῦμα τὸ ἐκτοῦ Θεοῦ in 2:12, and allusively with πνευματικὸν ἔπιον πόμα in 10:4. Hence, not surprisingly, Athanasius uses the image of a flowing fountain (πηγή) to denote the relation of the Spirit to God as Father and Source, from whom he flows or proceeds, but not as a created being. In *Letters* 1:19, he explicitly quotes 1 Cor. 12:13, and then in 1:20 comments, "Who can separate either the Son from the Father, or the Spirit from the Son?"[97] Athanasius insists that this qualitative difference between the Holy Spirit and "creatures" is warranted wholly by the scriptures.[98]

---

[91] Dunn, *Jesus and the Spirit*, p.326 (cited above).
[92] Doctrine Commission of the Church of England, *We Believe in God* (London: Church House Publishing, 1987), p.111; cf. pp.104–21, "God as Trinity: an Approach through Prayer".
[93] Haykin, *The Spirit of God*, p.67.
[94] Athanasius, *Letters to Serapion*, 1:2, Greek, Migne, *P.G.* vol. 26, 533A; English, Shapland, *Letters*, p.62.
[95] Athanasius, *Letters to Serapion*, 1:2; Migne, *P.G.* 26, 533A; and Shapland, *Letters*, p.63.
[96] Athanasius, *Letters to Serapion*, 1:17; Migne, *P.G.* 26, 569C; and Shapland, *Letters*, p.103.
[97] Athanasius, *Letters to Serapion*, 1:20; Migne, *P.G.* 26, 577A; Shapland, *Letters*, p.113.
[98] Athanasius, *Letters to Serapion*, 1:21; Migne, *P.G.* 26, 581A; Shapland, *Letters*, p.120.

Many Patristic specialists would be reluctant to conclude that Athanasius fails to find "ontology" in the texts of 1 Corinthians to which he appeals, even if the allusion to "flowing" is one short step away from exegesis. T.C. Campbell, for example, points out that Athanasius uses ὕπαρξις and ὑπάρχειν to characterize the actuality of the "Triad".[99] As Haykin observes, *Letters to Serapion* 1:22 discusses 1 Cor. 2:12 (ἐκ τοῦ Θεοῦ) precisely to explicate an ontology of the nature of the Spirit.[100] In 1 Cor. 6:11, and also 3:16, 17, the Spirit is uniquely the Spirit of holiness, who has no need of a derived holiness, but in whom "all the creatures are sanctified".[101] To be sure, we cannot impose all this onto modern exegesis uncritically, but when the related evidence of 1 Corinthians is viewed as a whole, is this "ontology" more than a logical explication of Paul's thought?

In Basil's *On the Holy Spirit* (especially 10–27), the basis for Trinitarian theology again comes from 1 Cor. 2:9–16; 3:16–17; 8:6; and 12:3–7, 12–13. Basil cites 1 Cor. 2:10–11 to urge that God as Father cannot be known except by the Son and the Spirit.[102] The Holy Spirit is divine because he shares in all the action properly ascribable only to God:[103] "The Spirit knows 'the deep things of God' [1 Cor. 2:10, 11] ... The Spirit gives life ... raised Christ from the dead ... comes 'that we might know the things freely given by God' [1 Cor. 2:12)]".[104] Basil turns especially to 1 Cor. 12:4–6 and 11 when he insists that "the Holy Spirit is inseparable and wholly incapable of being parted from the Father and the Son... 'There are diversities of operations, but it is the same God who works ...'" (1 Cor. 12:4–6).[105] Basil pays particular attention to 1 Cor. 12:13, ἐν ἑνὶ πνεύματι ἡμεῖς πάντες ἐν σῶμα ἐβαπτίσθημεν, a passage on which Dunn has written most constructively.[106] Basil understands this verse to confirm the inseparability of Father, Son and Holy Spirit. Once again, we may concede that this is not Paul's first concern here, but since, in Dunn's words, "the baptism of the Spirit is what made the Corinthians members of the body of Christ", is it conceivable that Basil's point is not a Pauline presupposition?[107]

Gregory of Nazianzus, Ambrose and Augustine maintain and develop these themes, but they also believe, no less than Basil, that these are founded on Pauline (and Johannine) exegesis, perhaps most especially on 1 Cor. 2:10–15. In his *Theological Orations* Gregory insists that a "swarm" of biblical passages point to the divinity of the Holy Spirit.[108] Gregory insists that the Holy Spirit is "not a creature, in that he proceeds from the Father".[109] His use of the Greek verb πορεύω (proceed, come forth) and the cognate noun ἐκπόρευσις (procession) may reflect John 15:26, but, as Haykin observes, "The use

---

[99] T.C. Campbell, "The Doctrine of the Holy Spirit in the Theology of Athanasius", in *Scottish Journal of Theology* 27 (1974), pp.408–40, esp. pp.430–33.

[100] Haykin, *The Spirit of God*, pp.78–83.

[101] Athanasius, *Letters to Serapion*, 1:22–24, Migne, *P.G.* 26, 584A–C; Shapland, *Letters*, pp.122–3 and 126.

[102] Basil, *Against Eunomius*, 1:14; Migne, *P.G.* 29, 544B.

[103] Basil, *Against Eunomius*, 3:4; Migne, *P.G.* 29, 664C.

[104] Basil, *On the Holy Spirit*, 24:56; Migne, *P.G.* 32, 172C.

[105] Basil, *On the Holy Spirit*,16:37.

[106] J.D.G. Dunn, *Baptism in the Holy Spirit* (London: SCM, 1970), pp.127–31; cf. pp.103–38; and Basil, *On the Holy Spirit*, 12:28, Greek, Migne, *P.G.* 32, 117A.

[107] Dunn, *Baptism*, p.129.

[108] Gregory, *Orations*, 31:29.

[109] Gregory, *Orations*, 31:8.

of the preposition 'from within' (ἐκ) instead of the Johannine 'from' (παρά) probably reflects the influence of 1 Corinthians 2:12."[110] The "procession" of the Holy Spirit from God the Father is parallel with, but not exchangeable with, the "generation" (γέννησις) of the Son. Both terms signify that neither the Son or the Spirit share the status of a merely created being. Gregory's use of the term "proceeds" (about AD 380) finds its way into the formulations of Constantinople in 381. In Gregory's view not only does the term "proceeds" rest on sound exegesis; the belief that the Spirit is no mere "creature" rests on a multiplicity of biblical passages.

Gregory of Nyssa shares many of the assumptions of his brother, Basil, even if he writes less on the subject of the Holy Spirit. In some ways he may be even closer to Paul, since he believes that to call the Holy Spirit "God" relates primarily to divine activity. Gregory writes, " Being God, as says the apostle, he searches all things, even the deep things of God" (1 Cor. 2:10); but he is more hesitant than Basil or Gregory of Nazianzus to speak of the Holy Spirit as "one in being" or "essence" with God, on the basis of several Pauline texts, including 1 Cor. 2:11.[111] Nevertheless he believes that the divine character of the Spirit's activity demands that together with the Father and the Son, the Spirit receives divine honour and glory in Christian worship.

These interpretations of passages in 1 Corinthians are not confined to the Cappadocian Fathers. In the West, Ambrose and Augustine share this tradition. Ambrose's *On the Holy Spirit* probably also stems from 381. Citing 1 Cor. 8:6, Ambrose firmly asserts that God is one.[112] Nevertheless there are differentiations between divine agencies: the Holy Spirit reveals (1 Cor. 2:10), and gives such gifts as the word of wisdom (12:8); although "there is no distinction of the divine power that can arise ... No doubt all things are of him through whom all things are."[113] Ambrose draws a logical inference from an exegesis of 1 Cor. 2:11. He writes, "'No one knows the things of God except the Spirit of God'; not that he [the Spirit] knows by searching, but he knows by nature; not that the knowledge of divine things is an accident in him [the Spirit], but it is natural knowledge." Hence, Ambrose concludes, a oneness of nature and of knowledge holds between God and the Holy Spirit.[114]

Ambrose now goes further, but still in the belief that he does so on the basis of exegesis. He cites the diversity of the gifts of the Holy Spirit in 1 Cor. 12:4, 5, 6, and 8–10, and on the basis of 12:5, writes:

> If the Holy Spirit is of one will and operation with God the Father, he is also of one substance, since the Creator is known by his works. So, then, it is the same Spirit, he [Paul] says, the same Lord, the same God. If you say "Spirit", he is the same; and if you say "Lord", he is the same; and if you say "God", he is the same. Not the same, so that himself is Father, himself Son, himself Spirit, but because both the Father and the Son are the same power. He is then, the same in substance and in power.[115]

---

[110]   Michael Haykin, *The Spirit of God*, p. 217.
[111]   Gregory of Nyssa, *Against Eunomius*, VII:1.
[112]   Ambrose, *On the Holy Spirit*, II:9:85.
[113]   Ambrose, *On the Holy Spirit*, II:9:99–100; also 11:122–3.
[114]   Ambrose, *On the Holy Spirit*, II:11:127.
[115]   Ambrose, *On the Holy Spirit*, II:12:138–42.

We do not suggest that all this is explicit in Paul. Nevertheless the inferences that Ambrose draws firmly discourage too much hesitancy in ascribing divinity to the Holy Spirit. Such hesitation seems to miss some of the logical implications of texts in 1 Corinthians. Ambrose also includes arguments of a less metaphysical and more practical nature. For example he cites 1 Cor. 3:16, "You are the temple of God, and the Holy Spirit dwells in you", and comments, "Now ... a creature has no temple. But the Spirit, who dwells in us, has a temple."[116]

Augustine is more complex, and draws on a wider and more general range of biblical passages than Athanasius, Basil, the Cappadocians and Ambrose. However, in several places he appeals to the logic of 1 Cor. 2:11. Commenting on this verse in *City of God*, he notes the distinctive meaning "Spirit" as applied to the "*uncreated* Creator Spirit" (Latin, *non creatura, sed creator*). The Spirit to whom this verse alludes is "the Creator Spirit who in the Trinity is distinctively called the Holy Spirit", and "with whom is the Trinity, the Father and the Son and the Holy Spirit ... Creator (*cum quo est trinitas pater et filius et spiritus sanctus ... creator*)".[117] Appealing elsewhere to the same verse, together with 1 Cor. 12:4–7, Augustine observes, "The Spirit is sometimes spoken of as if he alone were entirely sufficient [that is, apart from the Son]."[118] In such cases, however, this cannot be taken to imply a "separation" within the one God: "For the Spirit of God is one: the Spirit of the Father and Son, the Holy Spirit, who works all in all" (1 Cor. 12:6; cf. vv. 4–7).[119] To be sure, Augustine also enters into metaphysical complexities that take us, arguably, far from Pauline exegesis; but we are *not* claiming that *all* material about the Holy Spirit in the Patristic era contributes to a post-history of the exegesis of 1 Corinthians.[120] Debates about οὐσία and ὑπόστασις take us well beyond Paul.

The varied agendas brought to our attention by *some* Patristic writings may serve *to explicate what is often presupposed* in Pauline texts. This need not lead to imposing Greek metaphysics onto Paul in the interests of a later theology, although this risk must be kept in mind. The claim to explicate what may lie beneath Paul's conscious thought as a presupposition recalls Schleiermacher's maxim that interpretation may go beyond the conscious awareness of an author.[121] As one who believes, like James Dunn, that Pauline exegesis is rooted in "Pauline theology", I share serious caution about going beyond the mind of Paul. Yet Theissen's work *Psychological Aspects of Pauline Theology* illustrates something of the point (as well as limits) of Schleiermacher's maxim.[122] Theissen penetrates beneath the surface of Pauline texts to explore concepts of which Paul himself might scarcely have been fully conscious as conceptual tools or categorizations. Yet if he were given a retrospective understanding of modern notions of the unconscious and of related mechanisms of self-deception, might not Paul have

---

[116] Ambrose, *On the Holy Spirit*, III:12:90.

[117] Augustine, *The City of God*, 13:24; cf. also 14:4.

[118] Augustine, *On the Holy Trinity*, I:(8):18.

[119] Augustine, *On the Holy Trinity*, IV:(20):29.

[120] One example would be Augustine, *On the Holy Trinity*, VII:(6):11, on "essences".

[121] F.D.E. Schleiermacher, *Hermeneutics: the Handwritten Manuscripts* (Missoula, MT: Scholars Press, 1977, edited by Heinz Kimmerle), p.246, n.12; and 112; and the more recent critical edition, *Hermeneutics and Criticism, and Other Writings* (Cambridge: CUP edited by A. Bowie, 1999).

[122] G. Theissen, *Psychological Aspects of Pauline Theology* (Edinburgh: T. & T. Clark, 1987).

said with reference to language about the human heart, "Yes, this is the kind of thing that I wish to convey."

Wrestling with *Wirkungsgeschichte* or reception history opens the door to exegesis as explication: an explication that permits us to see dimensions of meaning that *successive contexts of reading bring into sharper focus* for our attention. On the present subject I have suggested that in the light of Patristic exegesis, new contexts have sharpened many of the themes treated in James Dunn's exegesis of Pauline texts about the Spirit, in ways that fully cohere with Dunn's work. On two issues, however, I have also suggested that this post-history may invite greater caution about speaking of "supernatural" gifts of the Spirit in this epistle, and also a greater boldness to speak of an implied "Trinitarian" theology in these texts.

CHAPTER NINETEEN

Exegesis, Lexicography and Theology: "'Love, the Essential and Lasting Criterion', 1 Corinthians 13:1–7" (2000)

This extract comes from The First Epistle to the Corinthians: A Commentary on the Greek Text *(New International Greek Testament series, Grand Rapids, MI: Eerdmans and Carlisle: Paternoster Press, 2000), pp.1027–60. To avoid undue length the bibliography for Chapter 13 has been omitted, and a little editing has abbreviated the material here and there. Each section of the text began with a new English translation, which I explain and defend in the commentary, together with a short introduction to each section in addition to the general introduction to the epistle. Here the emphasis in the Introduction falls upon the unity of this chapter with 12–14, and indeed with Paul's argument throughout the epistle. Much of the research on the text of 13:1–7 concerns lexicography, and the meaning of Greek vocabulary relating to love remains of widespread interest. However, the research behind this extract relates no less to issues of exegesis, interpretation and theology. This extract demonstrates the need for various interactive levels of exegetical, theological and hermeneutical enquiry.*

English Translation of 1 Corinthians 13:1–7

(1) If I were to speak with human or angelic tongues, but if I had not love, I would have become only a resonating jar or a reverberating cymbal. (2) And if I should have the gift of prophecy, and if I penetrate all the depths too profound for mere human discovery and have all "knowledge", and if I possess the gifts of every kind of faith sufficient to remove mountains – but, after all, may lack love, I am nothing. (3) Even if I should divide up all my possessions to feed the needy, and if I hand over my body that I may glory, but have not love, it counts for nothing. (4) Love waits patiently; love shows kindness. Love does not burn with envy; does not brag – is not inflated with its own importance. (5) It does not behave with ill-mannered impropriety; is not pre-occupied with the interests of the self; does not become exasperated into pique; does not keep a reckoning up of evil. (6) Love does not take pleasure at wrongdoing, but joyfully celebrates truth. (7) It never tires of support, never loses faith, never exhausts hope, never gives up.

Introduction to Chapter 13

Spicq observes that this chapter "contains the word *agapē* ten times" and "is undoubtedly the most important in the entire NT concerning charity".[1] Spicq himself

---

[1] C. Spicq, *Agapē in the New Testament* (3 vols, Eng., London: Herder, 1963), II, p.139.

entertains no doubt that Paul himself is the author of this chapter, although he acknowledges that many argue to the contrary partly on the ground that it appears to constitute a literary rather than an epistolary style, and that supposedly it interrupts the flow of chapters 12–14 on gifts within the church. But he rightly urges that it precisely fits its context, and remarks tartly that anyone who has done any preaching will know full well that on occasion a preacher draws on a more lyric expression, perhaps to return again later to a more prosaic, conceptual, or cognitive communicative mode:[2] "He [Paul] varies his style constantly ... doctrinal, catechetical, moral, sapiential, and even juridical ... Chapter 13 ... is a necessary link in the argument putting charisms in their proper place".[3] It also takes its place among the themes that concern worship, from idol-foods (chs 8–10), dress in worship (11:2–16), and the eucharist (11:17–34), to the use of charisms during worship (12:1–14:40): "The whole presentation begins with a summons to *agapē* (8:1)".[4] We shall argue that this perception is entirely valid.

One of the most sustained attacks on the contextual integrity of the chapter comes from J. Weiss, who argues that the material is a polemic against gnostics and gnosticism, and that it belongs with 8:1–13, not with 12:1–14:40. The statement that love is not "puffed up" (οὐ φυσιοῦται, 13:4) belongs with 8:1, "Knowledge puffs up (ἡ γνῶσις φυσιοῖ) but love builds up (ἡ δὲ ἀγάπη οἰκοδομεῖ)."[5] Weiss further argues that ἀγάπη does not occur in 12:1–30 and 14:1–40, and that this is a further symptom of displacement. Héring, Senft, Schmithals, Titus and Conzelmann all take up and develop these arguments.[6] But among these writers, only Titus appears to exclude Pauline authorship; whereas even Schmithals, who proposes that Paul wrote nine letters to Corinth (of which thirteen or perhaps even fourteen fragments make up our present 1 Corinthians), opts for the view that a copyist simply made a mistake in inserting omitted material in the wrong place.[7]

Against this Margaret Mitchell argues convincingly that "the objection that 1 Cor. 14 does not fit with chap.13 because the word ἀγάπη is not used there is easily refuted because in the syllogism of 8:1 Paul had already explicitly equated ἀγάπη with the οἰκοδομή, which figures prominently in the argument in chap.14".[8] Further alongside his detailed attention to compositional questions, J.C. Hurd asserts that "1 Cor. 13, moreover, manifests the same interest as ch.14."[9] In practice, chapter 13 takes up the themes of γνῶσις, *knowledge* (13:2, 8, 9; cf.13:12), γλῶσσαι, *tongues* (13:1, 8), and προφητεῖαι,

[2] Ibid., pp.140–41.
[3] Ibid., p.140.
[4] Ibid.
[5] Weiss, *Der erste Korintherbrief* (Göttingen: Vandenhoeck & Ruprecht, 1910), pp.309–16; *Earliest Christianity* (New York: Harper edn, 1959, II, pp.569–71 and "Beiträge zur paulinischen Rhetorik", in *Theologische Studien* (Göttingen: Vandenhoeck & Ruprecht, 1897), pp.196–200; cf. 165–247.
[6] J. Héring, *First Epistle to the Corinthians* (Eng., London: Epworth, 1962), p.134; C. Senft, *La Première Épitre de S. Paul aux Corinthiens* (Geneva: Labor et Fides, 2nd edn, 1990), pp.165–6; W. Schmithals, *Gnosticism in Corinth* (Eng., Nashville, TN: Abingdon, 1971), pp.90–96, esp. 95–6, n. 23; E.L. Titus, "Did Paul Write 1 Cor. 13?", *Journal of Bible and Religion* 27 (1959), pp.299–302; and H. Conzelmann, *1 Corinthians* (Philadelphia, PA: Fortress Press, 1975), p.217.
[7] Schmithals, loc. cit. pp.95–6, n. 63; cf. his "Die Korintherbriefe als Briefsammlung", *ZNW* 64 (1973), pp.263–88.
[8] M.M. Mitchell, *Paul and the Rhetoric of Reconciliation* (Tübingen: Mohr, 1992), p.270.
[9] J.C. Hurd, *The Origin of 1 Corinthians* (London: SPCK, 1965; 2nd edn, 1983), p.189.

prophecies (13:2, 8, 9) which are central to chapters 12 and 14. This point is firmly made also by Allo, Bruce, Grosheide, Fee, Moffatt and Hays and conclusively answers the objection of the previous paragraph.[10] Grosheide comments, "Chapter 13 is not to be regarded as interrupting the discourse concerning the charismata. On the contrary, it is a necessary link in the argument which has as its purpose to assign the glossolalia its rightful place."[11] Schrage also sees chapter 13 as a "criterion" (cf. our heading) that explicates 12:31 and indeed 12:1–14:40.[12]

Grosheide's argument is correct, except that Paul's target concerns all kinds of self-centred "spirituality", *including* the public use of glossolalia *especially as a perceived status-indicator*. Just as Spicq's study *Agapē in the NT* constructively informs his exegesis, even so Moffatt's *Love in the NT* gives him an insight into the role of 1 Cor. 13, and (in accordance with the hermeneutical circle) vice versa: Moffatt produced both a commentary on 1 Cor. (1938) and a full-length study of love in the NT (1929). Both are full of good sense. Moffatt urges that even if Paul did not compose "the lyric on love" in the midst of his dictation, nevertheless "This 'Hymn of Love' was written out of a close and trying experience. *If it is a rhapsody, it is the rhapsody of a realist who has come safely through contact with the disenchanting life of the churches* ... wrung from long intercourse with *ordinary Christians, especially those at Corinth*" (my italics).[13]

Moffatt hits the centre of the target here. Indeed best of all is C.T. Craig's comment: "On closer examination it is seen that *almost every word in the chapter has been chosen with this particular situation at Corinth in mind* ... The mood is instructive fully as much as lyrical" (my italics).[14] The one hindrance to imagining its being dictated is the polished metrical nature of the phrases, vocabulary and rhythm, which Hitchcock, among others sees as the fruit of careful composition.[15] But F.F. Bruce and C.T. Craig paint exactly the right picture. Might not the composition have come to Paul as he churned over in his mind, before writing this part of the letter, the stances at Corinth which "**inflated** the self" (cf. 8:1); which claimed the thrones and **tongues of angels** (4:7–13; 6:3); which prized **knowledge** above concern for the weak (8:1–13; 12:8); which showed **jealousy** over high status (3:1–3; 13:4–7), and which held a *triumphalist over-realized eschatology* without a *theologia crucis* (1:18–25; 4:8–13; 13:8–13)? If Spicq can respond to Weiss about the experience of *preaching* in various styles, what of the experience of mulling over the next

---

[10]   E.-B. Allo, *Saint Paul. Première Épitre aux Corinthiens* (Paris: Gabalda, 2nd edn, 1956), pp.340–42; F.F. Bruce, *1 & 2 Corinthians*, NCBC (London: Oliphants, 1971), pp.124–6; F.W. Grosheide, *Commentary on the First Epistle to the Corinthians* (Grand Rapids, MI: Eerdmans and London: Marshall, Morgan and Scott, 1953, 2nd edn, 1954), p.303; Mitchell, *Rhetoric*, pp.270–71; G.D. Fee, *First Epistle to the Corinthians*, NICNT (Grand Rapids, MI: Eerdmans, 1987), pp.626–8, esp. 626, n. 5–n. 8; R.B. Hays, *First Corinthians*, Interpretation (Louisville, KY: Knox, 1997), pp.221–2; R.F. Collins, *First Corinthians*, SacPag 7 (Collegeville, MN: Glazier/Liturgical Press, 1999), p.471.

[11]   Grosheide, loc. cit.

[12]   W. Schrage, *Der erste Brief an die Korinther*, EKKNT 7 (Neukirchen-Vluyn: Neukirchener Verlag and Zürich and Düsseldorf: Benziger Verlag, 3 vols to date, 1991, 1995 and 1999), vol. III, pp.276–7.

[13]   J. Moffatt, *Love in the NT* (New York: Richard Smith, 1930), p.182; cf. also his *First Epistle*, p.191.

[14]   C.T. Craig, "The First Epistle to the Corinthians", in *Interpreter's Bible* (New York: Doubleday, 1953), vol. X, p.165.

[15]   F.R.M. Hitchcock, "St. Paul's Hymn of Love", *Theology* 26 (1933), pp.65–75; cf. also his "Structure of St. Paul's Hymn of Love", *Exp. T.* 34 (1922–23), pp.488–92.

day's sermon during a sleepless night? At all events, if the chapter was composed before the dictation, it must have been composed with the Corinthian situation bubbling in the mind.

The mass of "comparisons" and "parallels" collected by Conzelmann, Sigountos and others should not distract us from the force of these factors. If it is the case that this chapter is to be as a rhetorical *encomium* with a patterned rhetorical format or structure, Paul is using it for his own ends and for Corinth. It would not distract from the chapter if resonances of rhetorical images and devices from, for example, popular repetitions of part of Plato's *Symposium*, or 1 Esdras 3 informed Paul's conscious or subconscious mind.[16] Carson and Fee are among those who offer warnings about attaching too much importance to parallels of this kind.[17] But the issue, in a sense, is value-neutral. Neither too little nor too much should be inferred from the fact that, as Spicq observes, for Paul to be "inspired" to produce "the musical effect of pleasant-sounding words; the choice of images; the balance and parallelism of its propositions; the use of antithesis, chiasmus, hyperbole, and anaphora; and above all its lyric tone ... and elevated thought", is it any less "Paul's own" if he draws on imagery and rhetoric from Jewish wisdom literature or from Graeco-Roman philosophers or poets (whether conscious or unconscious)?[18] "There is no evidence of direct borrowing", however, even if it *might* occur.[19] We need not therefore enter into speculative debates about whether or not this chapter can be called a hymn, or epideictic rhetoric, or an encomium, or a "word of wisdom".[20] M.M. Mitchell's conclusion that it is "deliberative rhetoric" designed to persuade is sufficiently broad to remain acceptable, but no single language-function should obscure its multi-layered character.[21] Most writers on the structure perceive a chiasmic form, which clearly divides into three blocks: (a) vv. 1–3, (b) vv. 4–7, and (c) vv. 8–13. Some also argue for a three-fold movement within each of the main parts.[22]

Commentary on 13:1–13

We follow the widely accepted division into 13:1–3; vv. 4–7; and vv. 8–13 (or vv. 8–12, with v. 13 as a climax).[23] Our proposed headings approximate to those of Bornkamm, which

---

[16]   J.G. Sigountos, "The Genre of 1 Cor. 13", *NTS* 40 (1994), pp.246–60, argues for close parallels especially with Plato, *Symposium* 197 C–E, and with 1 Esdras 3:34–40. This need not imply Paul's *direct* knowledge of the *Symposium*, although we need not exclude the possibility either.

[17]   Fee, *First Epistle*, p.626; D. Carson, *Showing the Spirit* (Carlisle: Paternoster, 1995), p.52.

[18]   Spicq, *Agapē*, II, pp.141–2.

[19]   Ibid., p.142.

[20]   Astonishingly, such is the fashion of rhetorical theory in NT studies that some spill blood on the carpet to defend or to attack these categories.

[21]   Mitchell, *Rhetoric*, p.273.

[22]   Collins, *First Cor.*, p.472; cf. Mitchell, *Rhetoric of Reconciliation*, pp.165–7, 274; and O. Wischmeyer, *Der höchste Weg. Das 13 Kapitel des 1 Kor* (Gütersloh: Mohn, 1981), pp.205–8.

[23]   O. Wischmeyer, *Der höchste Weg*, pp.205–8, in fact distinguishes the common form of 13:1–3 and 8–13, in which the worth or *usefulness* of love is praised, with the different formal style of vv. 4–7 as a series of *confessions* (*Bekenntnisreihe*) of the general ethical character of love. Similarly Mitchell sees vv. 1–3 and 8–13 as "deliberative rhetoric", and vv. 4–7 as "a very brief encomium on love" with positive and negative epithets (*Rhetoric*, p.274; cf. pp.165–7).

are also broadly followed by Craig.[24] In Barth's words (a) "love ... alone decisively determines human life ... It is love alone that counts"; (b) "love alone ...triumphs"; (c) on the basis of "the promise which has eternal content ... it is ... love alone that endures".[25]

(a) The Fruitlessness of All "Gifts" without Love – 13:1–3

v. 1 If I were to speak with human or angelic tongues, but if I had not love, I would have become only a resonating jar or a reverberating cymbal.

Although λαλῶ and ἔχω could be either indicative (*if I speak ... if I do not have*), the use of μή rather than οὐ, coupled with ἐάν rather than εἰ establishes that Paul uses the subjunctive. The hypothesis is indefinite rather than contingent, and (especially since Dautzenberg and others draw inferences from ἀγγέλων) is perhaps best translated as *If I were to speak in human or in angelic tongues, but if I had not love, I would have become ... .* REB achieves the same result by recasting the syntax: *I may speak in tongues ... but if I have no love ...* (as against NRSV, RV and NIV, *if I speak ...*; AV / KJV, NJB, *though I ...*). Conzelmann is correct to observe, "It is ... a vitally important point that Paul begins with values that are significant in the community at Corinth: speaking with tongues, prophecy, etc.".[26] This makes the indefinite syntax all the more important pastorally. It is not an open attack: *if I speak with tongues, but do not have love ...* , but *at this point* the more deliberative category of rhetoric advocated by M.M. Mitchell: *suppose that this situation were to arise ... what would it amount to?* (that is, you tell me!). In hermeneutical language, it invites reader-response.

The dative is a straightforward instrumental use: **to speak with human or angelic tongues.** The distinction between **human** and **angelic** could either (i) reflect a difference of view at Corinth as to whether speaking in-or-with **tongues** signified inspired human utterances or a "language of heaven"; or (ii) it could refer to human gifts ἐν παντὶ λόγῳ (1:5 *speech*) and also (secondly) to speaking in-or-with **tongues** (12:10); or (iii) it may refer to **tongues** with an added hyperbole (following Sigountos): *yes, even if these tongues were to be* **angelic** *language itself* (as some seem to think!).[27] On the meaning of **tongues** and *speaking with* **tongues**, see above. Here in our view Paul begins with the notion of **tongues** as that which gives expression to the secret yearnings and praise of the depths of the **human** heart, and escalates to a hypothesis considered at Corinth but not necessarily endorsed by Paul that **tongues** is the **angelic** language of heaven. See above on 12:10 where these views relate to the work of Theissen and of Dautzenberg. A full discussion occurs above on 12:10, in an **Extended Note.**

Any translation must allow an emphasis to fall upon ἀγάπην (with δέ and μή): *but if I had not love.* In the index to his second volume of *Agapē in the NT*, which is almost

---

[24] G. Bornkamm suggests "vanity of all values without love ... the nature and reign of love ...; the immortality of love", "The More Excellent Way" in his *Early Christian Experience* (Eng., London: SCM, 1969), pp.180–93. Craig proposes: "the superiority of love ... the nature of love ... the permanence of love" ("1 Cor." in *IB* X, 167, 172 and 185). But an emphasis on the gifts in vv. 1–3, on the dynamic character of the verb in vv. 4–7, and on eschatological permanence in vv. 8–13 is also required.

[25] Barth, *Church Dogmatics* IV:2, sect. 68, p.825; cf. 727–840.

[26] Conzelmann, *1 Cor.*, p.221.

[27] J.G. Sigountos, "The Genre of 1 Cor. 13", *NTS* 40 (1994), p.252; cf. 246–60. See further, Senft, *La Première Épitre*, p.167.

entirely on the Pauline corpus (with Hebrews and 1 Peter) Spicq lists over a hundred "activities", qualities, or effects of ἀγάπη.[28] The vast majority of writers agree that the noun ἀγάπη "love" is relatively rare in Greek literature outside the NT and early Christian writings. But the verb ἀγαπᾶν is more frequent, and indeed very frequent in the LXX. These lexicographical observations may be confirmed not only from linguistic sources (for example, Liddell-Scott-Jones, Hatch-Redpath, *BAGD*) but also from specialist studies from Wischmeyer and Stauffer to Nygren, Moffatt and Spicq.[29] In particular R. Joly stresses the frequency of the verb ἀγαπᾶν outside the NT.[30] Paul is concerned to disengage "love" in his own theology, Nygren and Moffatt argue, from Greek and other pagan ideas of love as primarily emotional, sexual, or ecstatic. They write that "to speak of God's force of love is in itself a credo" (Moffatt), and "Agape comes to us as a quite new creation of Christianity ... Without it nothing that is Christian would be Christian" (Nygren).[31] Nevertheless uses of the *word* must not be confused with Paul's theological emphasis. The worst thing that could happen Nygren continues, is for Christian uses of ἀγάπη to become confused with non-Christian notions of love through which "the new idea can be drained away from within ... by the other ... Agapē entered into a world that had already received the impress of Eros."[32]

One problem about Nygren's identification of ἀγάπη as a distinctive "motif" is the possible confusion between *words* and *concepts*. As Barr reminds us, it is one thing to claim that *conceptual uses of* the word in Paul and the NT are distinctive; it is quite a different matter to suggest that the *word* ἀγάπη itself is distinctive.[33] This has flawed so many parallel claims in "biblical theology" that the temptation is to rebound away from Nygren's important account of Paul's *theological uses* of the word in certain contexts. As a *theological construct based on selected contexts* his claim remains *profoundly true* that when Paul uses ἀγάπη of God it is "unmotivated"; "indifferent to [prior] value" on the part of the loved one; "creative" of value; and characterized by a fellowship or relationality that reflects God's elective relation with the world, and also, we might add, God's Trinitarian nature.[34] But to read such qualities back into every occurrence of ἀγάπη, in Paul, would be to commit what Barr terms "illegitimate totality transfer", imposing an accumulation of meanings from various passages onto every specific use of the word.[35]

---

[28] Spicq, *Agapē*, II, pp.445–7.

[29] Hatch-Redpath, *Concordance to the Septuagint* (Athens: Beneficial Book Publishers, rp., 1977), I, pp.5–7; Liddle and Scott, *Greek-English Lexicon*, p.6; Bauer-Arndt-Gingrich-Danker, *Greek-English Lexicon of the NT*, pp.4–6; Wischmeyer, *Der höchste Weg*, pp.23–26; and her "Vorkommen und Bedeutung von Agape in der ausserchristlichen Antike", ZNW 69 (1978), pp.212–38; E. Stauffer, ἀγαπάω, *TDNT* I, pp.21–55; A. Nygren, *Agapē and Eros* (Eng., London: SPCK, 1957), pp.53–67; Moffatt, *Love in the NT*, pp.4–63; Spicq, *L'agape de 1 Cor XIII, Un example de contribution de la semantique à l'exégèse NT* (Paris: Gabalda, 1955); cf. further W. Harrison, "The Idea of Agapē", JR 31 (1951), pp.169–82; Louw-Nida, I, pp.293–6; W. Günther, "Love", *NIDNTT* II, pp.542–50.

[30] R. Joly, *Le vocabulaire chrétien de l'amour, est-il original?* (Brussels: Univ de Bruxelles, 1968).

[31] Moffatt, *Love*, p.5; Nygren, *Agapē and Eros*, p.48.

[32] Nygren, *Agapē and Eros*, p.53.

[33] J. Barr, *The Semantics of Biblical Language* (Oxford: OUP, 1961), pp.215–43; cf. 206–14. See more specifically J. Barr, "Words for Love in Biblical Greek", in N.T. Wright and L.D. Hurst (eds), *The Glory of Christ in the NT: [for G B Caird]* (Oxford: OUP, 1990), pp.3–18.

[34] Nygren, *Agapē and Eros*, pp.75–81.

[35] Barr, *Semantics*, p.218; cf. 70–71 and 216–19.

We have cleared the way, however, to appreciating why Paul wishes to disengage ἀγάπη from the sensual, emotive, erotic or even ecstatic nuances which the noun ἔρως, *passionate love* and less often the verb ἀγαπᾶν can convey in secular or non-Christian religious Greek texts. For Paul ἀγαπᾶν enters his thinking as the usual LXX translation for the Hebrew אהב (*'āhēb*) *to love*, of which Hatch-Redpath cite around 130 occurrences in the LXX, and the noun ἀγάπη translates אהבה (*'ahᵃbāh*) "love" sixteen times in the LXX.[36] In an interesting research article B. Gerhardsson sees ch.13, especially 13:8–13, as a rhetorical-didactic poem (not a hymn) drawing on wisdom traditions associated with אהב (*'āhēb*) mediated through rabbinic tradition associated with Hillel.[37] Even more ingeniously, M. Fishbane argues for midrashic word-plays in 13:12 reflecting Ezk. 43:3 and Num. 12:8, which we shall consider when we comment on that verse.[38] Together with the OT tradition, however M.M. Mitchell argues forcefully that while Paul may distance himself from Greek ἔρως, one strand in Greek uses of ἀγάπη or ἀγαπᾶν remains closely relevant to 1 Cor. 13:1–13. She provides instances where φιλία and other words for love denote the mutual respect or reconciliation which follows the restoration of concord after division and strife.[39] This may well contribute to Paul's use of the word, in which ch.13 belongs integrally to 12:1–14:40.

Nevertheless, whereas Nygren's otherwise excellent work risks our reading too much into every use of the word ἀγάπη, in our view Mitchell's correct attempt to contextualize the meaning of "love" in 1 Cor. 13 risks, equally, narrowing it too specifically. Clearly it is *much deeper and more fundamental in theology* for Paul than any *rhetorical* context about concord might suggest. At least two themes determine a distinctive theological emphasis which the word itself carries in 13:1–13. First, *love* represents "the power of the new age" breaking into the present, "the only vital force which has a future".[40] *Love* is that quality which distinctively stamps the life of heaven, where regard and respect for the other dominates the character of life with God as the communion of saints and heavenly hosts. The theologian may receive his or her redundancy notice; the prophet may have nothing to say which everyone else does not already know; but *love abides* as the character of heavenly, eschatological existence.

Second, as we have noted, *love* (ἀγάπη) denotes above all a *stance* or *attitude* which shows itself *in acts of will* as *regard, respect and concern for the welfare of the other*. It is therefore profoundly *christological*, for *the cross is the paradigm-case of the act of will and stance* which *places welfare of others above the interests of the self*. Here Moltmann and Jüngel rightly relate this to the *self-giving grace of the cruciform, christomorphic, God*. We cannot read the Johannine "God is love" onto Paul, but in fact it is already there in Paul, and the biblical exegete has no need to compromise the distinctive witness of each biblical source or tradition. It lies at the heart of Paul's theology of grace, and hence *by means of these*

[36] Hatch-Redpath, I, pp.6–7.
[37] B. Gerhardsson, "1 Kor 13. Om Paulus och hans rabbinska Bakgrund", *Svensk Exeg Ars* 39 (1974), pp.121–44 (also in German in *Donum Gentilicum* [1978], pp.185–209).
[38] M. Fishbane, "Through the Looking Glass: Reflections on Ezek 43:3, Num 12:8 and 1 Cor 13", *Heb. Ann. Rev.* 10 (1986), pp.63–75.
[39] Mitchell, *Reconciliation*, pp.165–71; cf. Aristotle, *Eth. Nic.* VIII:1:4 (of φιλία); IV Macc. 13:23–26 (φιλανθρωπία); cf. 1 Clem. 49, esp. 1 Clem. 49:5.
[40] E. Stauffer, ἀγαπᾶν, *TDNT* I, p.51.

considerations Nygren's points carry *indirect* weight for 13:1–13. Nygren's work has particular value for the emphasis of v. 5 (see below). This is confirmed by the specific and explicit contrasts in 13:1–3. Whereas *tongues* (v. 1) (in certain contexts) minister primarily to the self (14:4, ἑαυτὸν οἰκοδομεῖ); and *knowledge* (γνῶσις) may inflate the self rather than build the other (8:1b); and even good deeds without love can amount to *self-glorification* (13:3), *love does not seek its own personal good* (13:5), but the welfare of *the other*.[41]

Every word of the entire clause which makes up the apodosis of the conditional provides much interest: γέγονα χαλκὸς ἠχῶν ἢ κύμβαλον ἀλαλάζον. The general sense is clear enough: "No matter how exalted my gift of tongues, without love I am nothing more than a resounding gong or a clanging cymbal. This value judgement is meant to be shocking ... It is not the gift of tongues that is only a resounding gong ... but I, myself" (Carson).[42] But each word or phrase invites detailed comment.

χαλκὸς ἠχῶν is the subject of a research article by W. Harris under the title "'Sounding Brass' and Hellenistic Technology".[43] Harris discusses the phenomenon of acoustic resonance systems to which Vitruvius alludes in his work *On Architecture* (c.30 BC). Material of *bronze* (χαλκός) was constructed in such a way as to amplify sound by functioning as an *acoustic resonator* or *resonating acoustic jar*, rather than as some kind of musical instrument or *gong*. Hence ἠχῶν means *sounding* in the sense of *sound-producing*: not of *pitching* a sound. This matches uses of ἠχέω to mean *not to pitch* sound, but *to transmit and to resonate sound*, for example, the roar of the sea or thunder. Paul uses the continuous present participle (Himerius, *Or.* 40; Ps. 45:4, LXX; cf. the noun ἠχῶ, sound, in Wis. 17:18).[44] ἠχῶν therefore does not make ἀλαλάζον redundant, but conveys the notion of *endlessly continuing resonances which have no musical pitch*.

Vitruvius, Harris demonstrates, speaks of **resonating jars** or *bronze vases*, which were placed in niches around the periphery of an auditorium. Such a system seems to have operated at Corinth in the second century BC, although the Roman governor Lucius Mummius later had them removed and sold to raise public funds. Harris concludes that whether or not the Corinthians replaced "the acoustic amplifying system", Paul's readers would know of **resonating** *acoustic bronze* **jars** used to project the voices of actors on stage and music.[45]

William W. Klein supports and develops Harris's view, against virtually all the standard translations and commentaries.[46] **Noisy** *gong* occurs in NRSV, NASB, Goodspeed, and Moffatt, while *gong* with a different adjective (*resounding gong*) in NIV, and (*gong booming*) in NJB. Neither *clanging bronze* (Barrett) not *blaring brass* (Phillips) conveys the primary notion of resonance, although Knox's *echoing bronze* comes near, and AV/KJV *sounding brass* (followed by Collins) is not a bad translation. Klein notes that Lenski and Grosheide view it as an instrument, and Moffatt's suggestion that it was *a gong* used in pagan temples, especially in the cults of Dionysius and Cybele, has attracted

---

41 See P. Vielhauer, *Oikodomē: Das Bild vom Bau in der christlicher Literatur* (Karlsruhe: Harrassowitz, 1940), esp. pp.85–8, and his comments on 14:4 (see below).
42 D.A. Carson, *Showing the Spirit*, p.59.
43 W. Harris, in *Bib. Arch. Rev.* 8 (1982), pp.38–41.
44 Cf. *BAGD*, p.349.
45 In addition to *Bib. Arch. Rev.* 8; cf. *Journal of the Acoustical Society of America* 70 (Oct. 1981), pp.1184–5.
46 W.W. Klein, "Noisy Gong or Acoustic Vase? A Note on 1 Cor. 13:1", *NTS* 32 (1986), pp.286–9.

wide support.[47] C. Forbes, however, has vigorously and strenuously rejected this last suggestion, partly with reference to Klein's study.[48] Klein infers (a) that we must relinquish the supposed temple context of pagan religious ecstasy, and (b) that *tongues without love* are still, however, merely "a reverberation, an empty sound coming out of a hollow, lifeless vessel".[49]

Klein agrees with virtually all lexicographers and commentators that κύμβαλον ἀλαλάζον denotes "a musical instrument".[50] I can find no evidence for R.L. Laurin's assertion that it "referred to metal castagnettes" (our modern castànets); K.L. Schmidt includes an article on it in the *Theological Dictionary of the Old Testament* (*TDNT*) arguing for *cymbal*, but the word occurs only here in 13:1 within the whole of the NT.[51] It derives from κύμβη, a hollow vessel or hollow dish, and, denotes a shallow metallic rounded dish, which is struck against its partner to give out a resounding note. In the LXX it translates the Hebrew מצלתים (*mᵉtsilttaīm*) from the verb צלל (*tsālal*) *to clash, crash, clang*, which verges on the onomaptopaeic (mainly 1 and 2 Chron., Ezr., Neh., for example, 1 Chron. 13:8). Although the AV/KJV image of a *tinkling cymbal* is the subject of mirth, it is just arguable that in 1 Kings 18:6 the term untypically refers to a three-cornered instrument such as a *triangle*, while Zech.14: 20 might denote *bells*.[52] For the bells of a harness might include bosses, and cymbals also could have bosses. Modern musicologists distinguish between the *crotal*, which goes back thousands of years, which is a thicker metal plate than the modern *orchestral cymbal*, which is of Turkish origin. The *crotal* had "a definite pitch" and could be hit head-on (unlike the modern orchestral cymbal) or struck by a club or hammer.[53] This latter method may account for the singular **a cymbal**, here. (If so, *clash*, NJB is questionable).

Paul couples with κύμβαλον the adjective ἀλαλάζον. This also is onomatopoeic from the tradition of wailing loudly in lament. Like ἠχῶν it is technically a present participle of continuous action rather than an adjective. The verb ἀλαλάζω means *to wail loudly* in its only other occurrence in the NT (Mark 5:38). A lexicographical search reveals that, according to the occasion (and the agents?) *loud noise* and the action of continuous *reverberating* can be *either majestic and splendiferous* (Ps.145:4, 5, LXX brings together τύμπανον, probably *kettle drum* and κύμβαλον, *crotal* or (broadly) *cymbal* with ἀλαλαγμοῦ, *sonorous* or *intrusive, invasive and self-important*. (Both the second edition of

[47] Moffatt, *First Epistle*, p.192. Followed by J.P.M. Sweet, "A Sign for Unbelievers: Paul's Attitude to Glossolalia", *NTS* 13 (1966–67), pp.240–57.

[48] C. Forbes, *Prophecy and Inspired Speech in Early Christianity* (Tübingen: Mohr, 1995), pp.38–9, 135–6; cf. also 20.

[49] Klein, loc. cit., p.288.

[50] Ibid., p.287.

[51] Laurin, *First Corinthians*, p.228; Schmidt, "κύμβαλον", *TDNT*, III, pp.1037–9.

[52] Ibid., p.1037.

[53] S. Kruckenberg, *The Symphony Orchestra and its Instruments* (New York: Crescent and Gothenburg: AB Nordbook, 1993), pp.193–5. The modern orchestral cymbal must be struck quasi-horizontally because of the resistance of air pressure, with its larger size (14–22 inches). It would also be anachronistic to assume that even if (wrongly) χαλκός were to be translated *gong*, this was to be equated with the modern orchestral *tam-tam*. This has a diameter of up to five feet (150 cm), and even if Hollywood directors project these back into ancient Greece or into ancient Egypt, such overwhelming *fortissimo* seems to have emerged only in the Romantic period of the last 125 years (e.g. with Respighi or Wagner) although it may indeed use bronze.

Bauer-Arndt-Gingrich-Danker's *Greek Lexicon* (known as *BADG*, 1979) and the more recent third edition of Danker with Bauer (known as *BDAG*, 2000) interpret the verbal form τυμπανίζω to mean "to torture with the τύμπανον".)[54]

This issue becomes controversial in one further recent study by T.K. Sanders, which seeks to re-*valuate* all previous interpretations of this verse, on the basis of the meaning of ἀλαλάζον together with the work of Klein. Sanders argues that the Greek participle ἤ (translated above and elsewhere as *or*), means *rather than*. He proposes the meaning: *I have become* **only a resonating acoustic jar** *rather than a flourish of* **cymbals**.[55] Sanders accepts and defends the empty, noisy, negative character of **mere resonating acoustic jar**. But he rejects the view that ἀλαλάζω refers in most cases to *a loud wailing*: "the interpretation of κύμβαλον ἀλαλάζον as discordant cacophony is inconsistent with the discriminating tastes of antiquity".[56] He therefore turns his attention away from the two pairs of adjectives and nouns to explore ἤ as "a particle denoting comparison" which is "equivalent to the English 'than'".[57] He concedes that either *than* or *and* are in theory possible translations, but concludes that since κύμβαλον ἀλαλάζον is more likely to denote "a sound which was pleasant to Paul's readers", *than* is the obvious "solution" to speculations about χαλκός and ἀλαλάζον.[58] The cry ἀλαλαί, he urges, appears in the LXX as one of joy and enthusiasm (for example, when the walls of Jericho fall, Jos. 6:20; when David triumphs, 1 Kings 17:52; cf. Ps. 42:2; 65:1; 80:2; 97:4, 6). This accounts for the translation proposed by Collins: *I have become sounding brass rather than a resounding cymbal*; and views the latter as a metaphor "for harmonious sound".[59]

The argument of Todd Sanders is innovative and ingenious and deserves respect. He uses Hatch-Redpath, Josephus, other sources, and works on music in the ancient world.[60] But his thesis fails to take adequate account of three factors and a fourth consideration. First, the Graeco-Roman converts who prized "wisdom", "speech", "rhetoric" and social position, even though many spoke with tongues and all were exposed to the OT as the church's Scripture, would be unlikely to regard *the crash of cymbals* as the height of their ambition. To be sure, they are triumphalist (4:8), but to build the rhetorical focus of a carefully designed didactic poem on an introductory contrast between *acoustic bronze* and *reverberating cymbals*, even *celebratory, festal, "good"* **cymbals** hardly accords with the rhetorical and lyric weight of all of the other images and contrasts. Second, what is majestic and impressive in one context (especially, as we noted above, the louder cymbals and kettle-drums) become, as the lexicographers rightly have it, "torture" in another context. When the Queen opens the Church of England General Synod in Westminster Abbey, one's spirit may soar with the decibels of the organ's thunder, when the same

---

[54] The array of lexicographical entries speak for themselves. Cf. esp. *BAGD* (1957), pp.34 and 829; and *BDAG* (2000), pp.40 and 1019. The third edition of 2000 had not yet appeared in time for use in my commentary.

[55] Todd K. Sanders, "A New Approach to 1 Cor. 13:1", *NTS* 36 (1990), pp.614–18.

[56] Ibid., p.616.

[57] Ibid.

[58] Ibid., p.617.

[59] Collins, *First Cor.*, pp.471 and 475.

[60] Cf. his use of I.H. Jones, "Musical Instruments in the Bible, I", *BT* 37 (1986), pp.108, 109; A. Sendrey, *Music in the Social and Religious Life of Antiquity* (Rutherford-Madison, NJ: Fairleigh Dickinson University, 1974); and K. Rengstorf, *Complete Concordance to Josephus*.

level of decibels would for some be sheer torture from a local amateur music group. To identify "good" contexts does not mean that noise is always good. Third, to interpose a logical disjunction of a reflective nature in one line of this rhythmic stanza places too much cognitive weight on a supposed pause in the flow.

The alternative proposed by Harris and Klein leaves no difficulty. For the fourth factor is that to which D.A. Carson drew our attention (noted above).[61] Paul is not simply saying that if *love* is absent, *tongues* are hollow and mere noise. He is suggesting that in cases where even a tongues-speaker might be without love in his or her life-style, *the persons themselves* **would have become merely a resonating jar or a reverberating cymbal.**[62] The perfect tense γέγονεν in place of an expected future suggests: "look at what such a person *would have become*". Empty, noisy reverberations go on and on. In Yorkshire idiom in the north of England, they are "now't but wind and rattle".

v. 2 And if I should have the gift of prophecy, and if I penetrate all the depths too profound for mere human discovery, and have all "knowledge", and if I possess the gifts of every kind of faith sufficient to remove mountains – but, after all, may lack love, I am nothing.

Paul has considered the highest conceivable evaluations of the gift of **tongues** as either the expression of the yearnings of the human heart or even as part of the praise of heaven, but concluded that even a person so gifted is mere noise without love. Now he turns to communicative and "wisdom" gifts of **prophecy** and **knowledge**, and to the action gift of **faith** of a special kind that produces dramatic effects. We follow the syntactical subdivision of **prophecy, knowledge** and **faith** proposed by Heinrici and Spicq except that whereas Heinrici links the knowledge of "mysteries" or **the depths too profound for human discovery** with **prophecy**, we argue that this belongs, in terms of Corinthian aspirations, more readily with γνῶσις (**knowledge**).[63] Moreover "the verb εἰδῶ controls both nouns, 'all mysteries' and 'all knowledge'" (Fee).[64]

Our proposed translation endeavours to bring out the indefinite character of the conditional, the escalating protasis, and the contrastive apodosis which Paul introduces by ἀγάπην δέ ... to conclude not *I am no one*, but with the neuter singular οὐθέν, **I am nothing.** We have tried to convey the anticlimactic fall after the escalating protasis by adding **after all** to the Greek, which is not explicit (but remains implicit) in the text. The subjunctives invite the opening signal **And if I should ...**, but it would be heavy-handed to labour them further. We use **penetrate** (as NJB) for εἰδῶ, the perfect subjunctive of οἶδα used in a present sense. To translate *if I know* would not only be stylistically repetitive, but would fail to convey the perfect subjunctive *have come to know* (NRSV, *understand*; NIV, *fathom*; REB, *have knowledge of*). On the sensitive and major word μυστήριον, translated above as **the depths too profound for mere human discovery**, see above on 2:1 and more especially 2:7 (also used in 4:1; 14:2; 15:51; and Rom. 11:25; 16:25; 2 Thess. 2:7; six times in Eph., four times in Col., and twice in 1 Tim.). Under 2:7 we noted

---

[61] Carson, *Showing the Spirit*, p.59.
[62] In our **Note** on Pentecostal writings on Spirit-Baptism under 12:13, we observed that recent Pentecostal writers have also underlined this point.
[63] Heinrici, *Das erste Sendschreiben*, pp.416–17; Spicq, *Agapē*, II, pp.144–5.
[64] Fee, *First Epistle*, p.632 n. 34.

Marcus Bockmuehl's careful argument that at its heart the term denotes a contrast between **mere human discovery** and that which lies beyond unaided human powers and initiatives.[65] Almost any other translation tends to fall either into ambiguity or blandness, when we recall that what constitutes a μυστήριον may well have been at issue between Paul, some at Corinth, and their non-Christian religious environment which may have involved the mystery religions.[66] Our translation at least holds in common Corinthian perceptions and Pauline theology. Logically one use of πάντα relates to the other: Paul escalates the entailments of the gifts *wisdom, revelation* and **knowledge** to the utmost. **To penetrate** τὰ μυστήρια πάντα (**all the depths**) opens the door to all "knowledge" (γνῶσις).

We have placed the term **knowledge** in quotation marks to signal a Corinthian catchword: see above on 1:5 and 8:1 (also used in 8:7, 10, 11; 12:8; 13:8; 14:6). As we noted above, out of about twenty-six occurrences in the NT, twenty-two occur in Paul, and of these, fifteen occur in 1 and 2 Cor., that is, more than half of the entire collection of uses of γνῶσις in the NT are addressed to Corinth. Furthermore, even at Corinth and in Paul's mind **knowledge** is used in various ways. In one sense πάντες γνῶσιν ἔχομεν (8:1); in another sense, ἀλλα᾽ οὐκ ἐν πᾶσιν ἡ γνῶσις (8:7).[67] It would not be adequate if we failed to place an explicit marker against **knowledge** as a major semantic competitor to love. Nygren observes "In 1 Cor. xiii there is a definite opposition, a contrast, between two different 'ways', two different kinds of fellowship with God: on the one side, the Gnostic-mystical 'vision of God' typical of Hellenism; and, on the other, the primitive-Christian and Pauline way of Agapē ... 'Gnōsis puffs up, Agapē builds up'."[68] In what sense is one related to Christ and to the cross, while the other not? Nygren declares: "*Gnōsis is egocentric, Agapē theocentric*" (his italics).[69]

A pattern now begins to emerge. For Paul's major critique of the *way* in which **tongues** were used as a *public* gift is that **tongues** *build up (only) the self* (14:4); similarly γνῶσις, **knowledge**, unless it is controlled by love, also ministers *to the self* (cf. Nygren's "egocentric"). By contrast, just as Christ lived and died "for others" supremely in the cross, **the way** of the *cross* and **the way** of **love** equally serve *others*; they are *"for others"*, as Paul will unfold in 13:4–7.[70]

On **faith** (πίστις) see above on 12:9. We noted that there is virtually unanimous agreement among commentators and theologians of every era that this *gift of* **faith** in 12:9 must be distinguished from *saving faith* through which all Christians appropriate the saving work of Christ as "for them" or "for us". We argued that "miraculous faith"

---

[65] Bockmuehl, *Revelation and Mystery in Ancient Judaism and Pauline Christianity* (Tübingen: Mohr [WUNT 2nd ser. 36], 1990); also Wolff, *Der erste Brief*, p.315. See further Hays, *First Cor.*, p.224, on Corinth and apocalyptic "mysteries".

[66] Cf. the different approaches in e.g. R. Reitzenstein, *Hellenistic Mystery – Religions* (Eng., Pittsburgh, PA: Pickwick Press, 1978); H.A.A. Kennedy, *St. Paul and the Mystery-Religions* (London and New York: Hodder and Stoughton, 1913); and G. Wagner, *Pauline Baptism and the Pagan Mysteries* (Edinburgh: Oliver & Boyd, 1967).

[67] Cf. C.E. Glad, *Paul and Philodemus*, pp.283–5.

[68] A. Nygren, *Agapē and Eros*, p.134; cf. 134–45.

[69] Nygren, ibid., p.143.

[70] On the contrast, see P. Vielhauer, *Oikodomê* on self-edification in "tongues", and Strobel, *Der erste Brief an die Korinther* (Zürich: Theologischer Verlag, 1989), pp.199–200, on love for "the other".

betrays not only an over-dualistic world-view which belongs more to Kant and to the Enlightenment than to biblical traditions, but also an over-wooden understanding of **to remove mountains**. *An especially robust, infectious, bold, trustful faith may well be a special gift that performs a special task within a community faced with seemingly insuperable problems.*

To remove mountains is an echo of a tradition that appears in Mark 11:23, 24 and Matt. 17:20 (cf. Matt. 21:21) as a saying of Jesus.[71] In her commentary on Mark, Morna D. Hooker comments, "Moving a mountain appears to have been a proverbial saying for doing difficult tasks."[72] Similarly on the Matthew saying R.T. France describes it as "a proverbial expression for the most improbable occurrence".[73] This is how Paul uses the phrase. Just as **knowledge** transcends **mere human discovery**, so the kind of **faith** which is a gift here transcends mere human capacity and expectation. But there is no need either to defend or to attack world-views relating to "miracle". The verb μεθιστάνειν means **to remove** from one place and to transfer an object to another, here used as part of the proverbial imagery. Finally, πᾶσαν τὴν πίστιν is likely to be a generic use of **all: gifts of every kind of faith**. But it may signify either an *ideal* (Godet), that is, *all possible faith*, or an ultimate, that is, *absolute faith* (Moffatt, Héring).[74]

The anticlimactic οὐθεν brings the readers back from triumphalist fantasies of glory to the real world. If I can **penetrate all the depths too profound for human discovery ... have all "knowledge"** ... and be known by the congregation to have the kind of **faith** that can soar above anything and overcome all difficulties, if I still **lack love**, I myself as a person am simply **nothing**. *To all these imagined* pretension: "it falls like a chopper" (Senft).[75] If the charismatic has no charity, he is spiritually zero" (Spicq).[76]

v. 3 Even if I should divide up all my possessions to feed the needy, and if I hand over my body that I may glory, but have not love, it counts for nothing.

Textual Notes This constitutes one of the most widely known examples of a crux of textual criticism in the NT. The 4th revised edition of the UBS Greek text (1993) reads ἵνα καυχήσωμαι, **that I may glory**, but classifies it as "C", that is, "the Committee had

---

[71] The Greek vocabulary and syntax of Matt. 17:20 and Mark 11:23, 24 are different but the image is the same. On Paul's use of the sayings of Jesus, see esp. F. Neirynck, "Paul and the Sayings of Jesus" in A. Vanhoye (ed.), *Apôtre Paul: Personalité, style et conception du ministère* (Louvain: Leuven University, 1986), pp.265–321. Neirynck finds only two instances of "an explicit reference to a command of the Lord, in 1 Cor. 7:10–11 and 9:14, but there is no 'quotation'" (320). But Neirynck is prepared to accept that there are a number of "allusions". See further D. Wenham, "Paul's Use of the Jesus Tradition: Three Samples", in D. Wenham (ed.), *Gospel Perspectives, 5: The Jesus Tradition Outside the Gospels* (Sheffield: JSOT, 1985), pp.7–35; and S. Kim, "Jesus, Sayings of", in G. Hawthorne and R.P. Martin (eds), *Dictionary of Paul and his Letters* (Leicester and Downers Grove, IL: IVP, 1993), pp.474–92. D.L. Dungan appears not to address this verse in his *The Sayings of Jesus in the Churches of Paul* (Oxford: Blackwell, 1971). Barrett, *First Epistle*, p.301, doubts whether v. 2 alludes to the Jesus tradition, but clearly the matter cannot be proved.

[72] M.D. Hooker, *The Gospel according to St. Mark* (Peabody, MA: Hendrickson, and London: Black, 1991), p.269.

[73] R.T. France, *Matthew* (Grand Rapids, MI: Eerdmans and Leicester: IVP, 1985), p.266.

[74] F. Godet, *Commentary on St. Paul's First Epistle to the Corinthians* (Edinburgh: T. & T. Clark, 1915), II, p.239; Moffatt, *First Epistle*, p.192; Héring, *First Epistle*, p.135.

[75] Senft, *Première Épitre*, p.167, where the French *tombe comme un couperet* comes into its own for eloquence!

[76] Spicq, *Agapē*, II, p.147.

difficulty in deciding which variant to place in the text". The UBS 3rd edition (1975) also read καυχήσωμαι and ranked it "C", but the 1975 "C" denoted "a considerable degree of doubt whether the text ... contains the superior reading" (as against "D", which denoted "a very high degree of doubt" in the 3rd edition.[77] In general four readings are considered by most critical editions and textual critics: (i) p[46], ℵ, A, B, 6, 048, 33, Sahidic and Bohohairic Coptic, Clement, Origen and Jerome (Latin and Greek) read ἵνα καυχήσωμαι, **that I may glory**; (ii) ἵνα καυθήσομαι, *that I should be burned*, is found in C, D, F, G, L, Clem. Stromata IV:8, Basil, Chrysostom, Cyril and Theodoret; (iii) a closely-related grammatical variant of (ii) which carries in effect the same meaning, καυθήσωμαι (late fut subj., rare in first century) is found in K, Ψ, Old Syriac, fourth-century Gothic, fifth-century Armenian VSS, Ethiopic (Praetorius), Tertullian and Cyprian; (iv) καυθήσεται, the 3rd sing. fut. ind. passive of καίω, *to burn*, which has virtually no support (basically, 1877, fourteenth century; and 2492 (thirteenth century) and "nobody seems to take seriously".[78] But while he reads **that I may glory**, of the other three readings Héring asserts that *that it [my body] might be burned* is more likely than (ii) or (iii).[79]

Metzger lists "several very evenly balanced considerations".[80] The external evidence for **that I may glory** is "both early and weighty" (a) p[46] is usually dated c. AD 200, and its combination with ℵ, A, B seems exceedingly strong, even if D, F and C diverge. (b) It is also easy to understand how the escalation to martyrdom by fire might be read as the highest possible sacrifice over which even love takes priority. The UBS Committee gave weight to these two arguments together with the fact that (c) ἵνα καυθήσομαι becomes cumbersome, if not clumsy, after παραδῶ τὸ σῶμά μου, which already essentially makes the point. On the other hand, καυθήσομαι, **that I should be burned** has strong support especially in Patristic tradition. "If the motive for giving up life is pride and self-glory", the allusion to love becomes "superfluous".[81]

For these last reasons *to be burned* is favoured by Bachmann, Weiss, Lietzmann, Bruce, Barrett, Conzelmann and Collins and especially in research articles by Caragounis and by Elliott.[82] Elliott and others perceive the minor difference between καυθήσομαι (first. pass. ind.) and καυθήσωμαι (pass. subj.) to be of merely scribal significance and thus to represent a single combined group of witnesses. Collins argues that the sight and sound of the two main readings are so similar that scribal error could readily account for the variant, and the allusions to burning are "explicable" especially in the light of Caragounis's work.[83]

---

[77] UBS 3rd edn, xiii, 4th edn, "Introduction 3*".

[78] J.H. Petzer, "Contextual Evidence in Favour of καυχήσωμαι in 1 Cor. 13: 3", *NTS* 35 (1989), p.230; cf. 229–53.

[79] Héring, *First Epistle*, p.137.

[80] Metzger, *Textual Commentary* (2nd edn, 1994), p.497; cf. 497–8.

[81] Ibid., p.498.

[82] J.K. Elliott, "In Favour of καυθήσομαι at 1 Cor. 13:3", *ZNW* 62 (1971), pp.297–8; C.C. Caragounis, "'To Boast' or 'To be Burned'? The Crux of 1 Cor 13:3", *Svensk Ex Års* 60 (1995), pp.115–27; also Grosheide, *First Epistle*, p.305; Godet, *First Epistle*, II, pp.241–3; Morris, *First Epistle*, pp.180–83; Bachmann, *Der erste Brief*, pp.388–96; Weiss, *Der erste Kor*, pp.314–15; Robertson and Plummer, *First Epistle*, pp.290–91; Bruce, *1 & 2 Cor.*, p.124; Lietzmann, *An die Kor*, p.65; Conzelmann, *1 Cor.*, p.217 n. 1; Barrett, *First Epistle*, pp.302–3. Collins, *First Cor.*, p.476. Cf. A. Souter, *Novum Testamentum Graece*, 2nd edn, 1956; and also Zuntz, *Text*, pp.35–7.

[83] Collins, *First Cor.*, pp.476–7.

Arguments in favour of καυχήσωμαι, however, are in our view stronger. For one thing, as Héring notes, at this early date reference to martyrdom by fire is "improbable ... this punishment was unknown in the Graeco-Roman world [at this date]. It would seem rather strange, then, for Paul to select just this one case [that is, the tradition of Daniel 3:28 or 2 Macc. 7:37] as his example."[84] The most readily conceivable use of *burn* would be that of selling oneself into slavery to provide funds for the poor, and thus to be branded by a hot iron. But would Paul use such a specialized example in this genre for this purpose?

A more decisive study, however, comes from J.H. Petzer.[85] After considering the state of the discussion, Petzer bases his arguments on (a) the parallelism and climactic structure in vv. 1–3; and (b) the literary and semiotic phenomenon of defamiliarization. We have already established the issue of parallelism and climax: the familiar part of each protasis focuses on the respective gifts of **tongues** (v. 1), and on **prophecy, knowledge** and **faith** (v. 2). Now Paul uses the "shock-effect" of defamiliarization "to put even more emphasis on ἀγάπη".[86] *Defamiliarization* entails re-reading what had appeared *familiar or ordinary* in a context that transposes it into the *no-longer familiar* and *no-longer ordinary*, to produce *reappraisal by shock*.[87] To anticipate Petzer's arguments about defamiliarization would plunge us into exegesis; we therefore consider them under the section "**exegesis**" below.[88] It is enough to state here that they counter the only serious argument against this reading, namely the suggestion that glory represents "an impure motive" here. This would indeed make the punch line redundant and without force. But such an interpretation of **that I may glory** is unnecessary and misleading. In spite of such weighty support as that of those already cited, we believe that καυχήσωμαι is the more probable reading on both external and internal grounds.[89] Lang shares with Petzer the view that **may glory** is used in a positive sense (cf. Phil. 2:16). Schrage agrees with Wischmeyer that Paul takes up the theme of self-glorying as "nothing" which can profit.[90]

Exegesis The first word κἄν is *crasis* for καὶ ἐαν, **even if**. This signals the escalating rhetoric to which we have already given attention. The verb ψωμίσω (1st aor. subjunct. act. of ψωμίζω) functions again as an indefinite protasis, and a lexicographical comment on ψωμίζω is necessary. The noun ψωμίον means *a small piece of bread*, or *morsel of food*.

---

84 Héring, *First Epistle*, p.137. The tradition is discussed by Schrage, *Der erste Brief*, III, p.291, including the notion of branding as a slave.

85 J.H. Petzer, *NTS* 35 (1989), pp.229–53 (cited above already).

86 Ibid., p.238.

87 Although the concept or device was first explored in Russian formalism, its use in literary theory in the diagnosis of the dynamics of textual forces is now widespread. I have discussed elsewhere its origins in V. Shklovsky to its use by J.D. Crossan and others in interpreting the parables of Jesus: Thiselton, *New Horizons in Hermeneutics*, pp.117–20. When pressed further and coupled with a postmodern stance it leads to deconstruction (ibid., pp.120–32).

88 Petzer, loc. cit., p.244, points out that *giving over one's body to be burned* remains at the level of human action, whereas **angelic tongues, all knowledge, to remove mountains** and being accorded **glory** lie beyond the sphere of unaided human action in this context.

89 See further Fee, *First Epistle*, p.629, n.18, and also pp.634–5 rightly stresses the excellent quality of the Egyptian tradition; K.W. Clark, "Textual Criticism and Doctrine", in J.N. Sevenster (ed.), *Studia Paulina: in honorem J de Zwaan* (Haarlem: Bohn, 1953), pp.61–2; cf. 52–65; Orr and Walter, *1 Cor.*, p.291; Lang, *Die Briefe*, p.183.

90 Schrage, *Der erste Brief*, III, p.290, esp. n. 72; O. Wischmeyer, *Der höchste Weg*, p.84.

If the emphasis of the cognate verb lies on *breaking up* a piece of bread into small morsels, ψωμίζω means to *divide into small pieces* (especially to give away), or even *to fritter away*. If the emphasis lies on the *bread*, ψωμίζω primarily means *to give someone food, to feed* (as clearly in Rom. 12:20). *BAGD* and M.R. Vincent note the double meaning.[91] We attempt to capture both aspects of what may well be a conscious word play by proposing **Even if I should divide up all my possessions to feed the needy.**

παραδῶ (2nd aor. subj. act. of παραδίδωμι) means to **hand over. Handing over** one's **body** could in theory refer to selling oneself into slavery in order to provide the funds for the needy to which allusion has just been made. But especially in view of 7:17–24, even as a scenario this seems too specific. Paul means putting one's whole being, including the physical body, at the disposal of others. Presumably Paul imagines that this may be done out of a sense of duty rather than out of concern for others' welfare. Lang, Petzer, and Orr and Walter insist that this need not imply selfish motives. Orr and Walter assert "Paul's ambivalent attitude towards 'boasting' is plain in 9:15–16 ... cf. II Cor. 11:16–30", while Lang alludes to Phil. 2:16.[92] To appreciate fully Paul's logic and meaning, we need to recapitulate in summary the thrust of vv. 1 and 2, especially in the light of Petzer's comments on parallelism, ascending climactic structure and defamiliarization (see under "Textual Comment", above).

Quite independently of Petzer's arguments, which reach similar conclusions by a different route, we have argued that each parallel in vv. 1 and 2 takes up the "gifts of the Spirit" in the sequence: (i) gifts of worship and spiritual exultation, **tongues**; (ii) gifts of speech, wisdom and communication, **prophecy, knowledge**; (iii) unusual gifts resulting in visible consequences, **faith**. But each pursues a climactic escalation from gifts-as-they-are *to scenarios or imagined projections of the utmost that they could be*: (i) **tongues** are not only (a) expressions of the deepest yearnings and praise which constitute subconscious "secrets of the **human** heart" (Theissen); but also (b) imagined participation in **angelic** worship-speech of heaven (Dautzenberg), which Paul takes up from notions discussed at Corinth but does not necessarily agree with or endorse. (ii) **Prophecy** is not only (a) wise, reflective, inspired pastoral preaching which includes announcements of judgement and grace; but also (b) leads on to the next gift of: (iii) **knowledge**, which is not only (a) **knowledge** of God's self-revelation as the one God (8:1–13) and other gospel truths, but also (b) in the view of those who aspired to the greatest heights at Corinth ability **to penetrate everything too deep for merely human discovery**, thus embracing **all** (conceivable) **knowledge**; (iv) **faith** is not (a) a special, robust, infectious confidence in God which overcomes great difficulties and helps the congregation to do so, but also (b) *achieves the "impossible"*.

Now Paul moves to (iv) the relatively familiar (Petzer) phenomenon of (a) **dividing up all my possessions to feed the needy**, which escalates to (b) an imagined scenario of **handing over my body**, perhaps selling myself into slavery to gain funds for further provision of funds. If such a person no longer has control of any possessions, or even of their own body, is not that (c) real **glory**? It ranks with **angelic tongues, all knowledge,** and **removing** impossible **mountains**. The fourth group, Petzer argues, even begins the

---

[91] *BAGD*, p.894; M.R. Vincent, *Word Studies in the NT* (London: Scribner, 1887 and Grand Rapids, MI: Eerdmans, 1946), III, p.263; Meyer, *First Epistle*, I, pp.390–91.

[92] Orr and Walter, *1 Cor.*, pp.291–2; Lang, *Die Briefe*, p.183; Elliott, loc. cit.

sense of shock by proposing a costly action that seems to outrank the individual "gifts" explicated in 12:8–10 and 28. Yet the most comprehensive possession of gifts, even when these are extrapolated into triumphalist fantasy (Petzer uses the term *reductio ad absurdum*, but they are not [yet] "reductions") end up (i) as the noise of resonating acoustic jars (v. 1); (ii) as simply nothing (v. 2), "spiritually zero" (Spicq); and (iii) what counts as nothing (v. 3), if love does not provide the motivation, context, and goal.[93]

The phrase οὐδὲ ὠφελοῦμαι is difficult: the passive of ὀφείλω, *I owe, I ought*, with an accusative. The traditional rendering *it profiteth me nothing* (AV/KJV, RV) is reflected in the majority of translations *I gain nothing* (NRSV, REB, NIV, cf. Collins, *it is not to my advantage*). This does tend, however, to presuppose that the reading *that I may boast* (NRSV) is negative self-glory (REB and NIV presupposed *to be burned*, with NJB). Admittedly the notion of *financial debt* or *moral debt* lies at the heart of uses of ὀφείλω. But this word also has extended uses.[94] There is much to be said in favour of R. Knox's translation *it goes for nothing*. But a hint of the idea of financial or moral debt or evaluation may be conveyed by a compromise proposal, **it counts for nothing**. The 1st pers. subj. is now merely implicit, but the reference is clear enough from the context. The *logical* (as against *grammatical*) subject is the series of acts which build up from the familiar to a projected climax: *all this* **counts for nothing**. Petzer's analysis of defamiliarization applies. What seemed *ordinary* and obvious now appears in a new, *unfamiliar* light, which produces *shock*.[95] These wondrous gifts and triumphant victories all amount to **nothing,** unless **love** directs them, with its Christ-like concern and regard for "the other".

(b) The Nature and Action of Love – 13:4–7

One important grammatical point affects our understanding of these four verses. Most English translations render the Greek as if it used *adjectives* to describe the *nature* of love "timelessly", for example, *love is patient; love is kind; love is not envious or boastful or arrogant or rude* (NRSV). But "the nature of love is expressed by Paul in a *series of verbs, the active character of which may not be fully indicated by ... adjectives*" (Craig) (my italics).[96] Hence we have added the word *Action* to our sub-heading.

v. 4 Love waits patiently; love shows kindness. Love does not burn with envy: does not brag – is not inflated with its own importance.

Textual Note   The third occurrence of ἀγάπη is ranked "C", and UBS 4th edn places it in square brackets as incapable of a clear decision. It is omitted by p46, B and 33, but "the majority of the Committee was impressed by the weight of witnesses that include the words" (Metzger).[97]

---

93   Petzer, loc. cit., p.240; cf. esp. 237–45.
94   *BAGD*, pp.598–9; cf. G.G. Findlay in *Expositor's Greek Testament* (London: 1900; rp. Grand Rapids, MI: Eerdmans 1961), II, p.898.
95   Petzer, loc. cit., pp.233–4.
96   Craig, "1 Cor.", *IB*, X, p.172.
97   B.M. Metzger, *Textual Commentary on the Greek N.T.* (Stuttgart: UBS, 2nd edn, 1994), pp.498–9. Metzger may be right. The third ἀγάπη is supported e.g. by A, C, D, F, G, Ψ, 048, Origen, and other

Exegesis Our translation strives to preserve the verbal structure of the Greek, as against the adjectival structure of many English versions. The verb μακροθυμέω may mean *to be patient* or *to have patience*. The older English *suffereth long* (AV/KJV, RV) more strictly conveys the compound form made up of μακρός *long* (in time or in extended space) with θύμος, which may denote either *passionate longing* or *wrath*, to denote the compound *long-tempered* (curiously absent in English as opposed to its opposite *short-tempered*): colloquially "with a very long fuse", if θύμος means *wrath*; but **waits patiently** if θύμος means *passionate longing*.[98] In the LXX μακροθυμεῖν may translate אַף הֶאֱרִיךְ (*he'erīk aph*), *to be slow to anger* (Prov. 19:11) but also to take time patiently (Prov. 25:15; Eccl. 8:12, Heb. אָרַךְ (*'ārak*).[99] More notably, in Eccl. 7:8, *those who are patient in spirit*, or in disposition-to-act (LXX, μακρόθυμος ... μνεύματι, Heb. אָרֵךְ, *'ārēk*) are better than the proud in spirit (LXX, ὑψηλόν); hence, *do not be quick to anger* expresses the negative parallel (Eccl. 7:9). Similarly Paul enjoins believers to give their support to "the weak" and to act patiently (μακροθυμεῖν) toward all (1 Thess. 5:14). Elsewhere in the NT the word occurs only in Jas. 5:7, 8 (**wait patiently** *therefore brothers and sisters* ἕως τῆς παρουσίας τοῦ Κυρίου); Matt. 18:26, 29, **wait patiently** *for me and I will pay you everything*; Luke 18:7, Heb. 6:15, and 2 Pet. 3:9. In 2 Pet. 3:9 the *patience* of the Lord is exhibited in his *waiting for the time appropriate* for the readers themselves, not in mere delay in fulfilling a promise; while similarly in Heb. 6:15 the writer commends Abraham as a model of one who **waits patiently** for God's *timing*, leaving the timing to God. Traditions that attempt to stress "eschatological urgency" need to ensure that this quality is not undermined.

Love, Paul urges, **waits patiently** not only because it deals patiently with the loved one, but also because it recognizes that *the right timing* plays a huge part in securing the welfare of the other. Love does not blunder in. The Corinthians, by contrast, were all too ready to jump the gun both in their assumptions about Paul and other ministers (1 Cor. 4:5), and in anticipating their own triumphs (4:8). George Herbert (1593–1633) captures the notion of love as **waiting patiently** for the understanding of the beloved:

> Love bade me welcome, yet my soul drew back,
>   Guilty of dust and sin.
> But quick-ey'd Love, observing me grow slack
>   From my first entrance in,
> Drew nearer to me, secretly questioning,
>   If I lack'd any thing.
> "A guest", I answered, "worthy to be here".
>   Love said, "You shall be he".
> "I, the unkind, ungrateful? Ah my dear,
>   I cannot look on thee".
> Love took my hand, and smiling did reply,
>   "Who made the eyes but I?"
>
> (Herbert, *Love*, Stanzas 1 & 2)

---

witnesses. But nothing other than stylistic rhythm is at stake, and no degree of certainty is possible. Cf. G. Zuntz, *The Text of the Epistles* (London: Oxford University Press, 1953), p.68 who argues for "love is patient, is kind; love does not envy ...".

   98   *BAGD*, p.488; cf. also p.365.

   99   Hatch-Redpath, II, p.893. Strobel calls attention both to the OT background and to the Christ-like nature of this quality in contrast to apocalyptic notions of a warrior Messiah (*Der erste Brief*, p.203).

The verb χρηστεύεται, **shows kindness** occurs only here within the NT, and otherwise only in Christian literature in Clement of Rome (c. 96 AD) and in Eusebius. The use in 1 Clem. 14:3, ὡς χρηστεύεσθε, οὕτως χρηστευθήσεται ὑμῖν, *as you show kindness, so kindness will be shown to you* underlines the verb as dynamic action, **to show kindness**, as against the more static adjective *is kind.*[100] The adjectival form χρηστός, *kind, kindly, benevolent,* was used widely in the first century (for example, Philo, *Embassy to Gaius,* 67; Josephus, *Ant.* VI:92; IX:133; cf. P. Oxy. 642; Cass. Dio. 66:18), but not the verb. Findlay thinks that Paul may have coined the verb for his purpose.[101]

The cognate noun χρηστότης, *kindness, generosity, uprightness,* however also occurs along with the adjective regularly in Hellenistic literature. Hence (a) there is no doubt about the meaning of the verb; and (b) the choice of the dynamic verbal form is deliberate, even if only to play its part in a chain of active temporal processes. Spicq observes that the word "suggests the warm, generous welcome the Christian always gives his brothers ... does his utmost to be thoughtful, helpful and kind, always in a pleasant way ... and confirms the element of magnanimity in *agapē*".[102] In his commentary on this verse Origen expounds the verb as showing "sweetness to all persons" (γλυκὸς πρὸς πάντας τοὺς ἀνθρώπους).[103] Chrysostom perceives **love** here as that which breaks the spiral of passion, anger and resentment by **showing kindness**: "not only by enduring nobly, but also by soothing and comforting do they cure the sore and heal the wound of passion".[104]

On the meaning of ζηλόω, see above on 12:31, where we commented on ζηλοῦτε δὲ τὰ χαρίσματα τὰ μείζονα. There we observed in a footnote that in the LXX ζηλόω translates קָנָא (*qinnê*), and applies the notion of *burning* or *boiling* metaphorically to *burning* or *boiling emotions, stance, or will* either for *earnest striving,* or for *passionate zeal,* or for **burning envy**. Whether it is constructive *zeal* or destructive **envy** depends on the context. Again, Paul chooses the verb: **does not burn with envy**. *BAGD* translate the verb "to be filled with jealousy or envy", but *burning* conveys the intensity more precisely than the hydrodynamic metaphor of *filling.*[105] Only the translation by Charles B. Williams, *Love never boils with jealousy,* seems to retain this nuance explicitly. Clearly the word alludes to 3:3: ὅπου γὰρ ἐν ὑμῖν ζῆλος καὶ ἔρις ... The **envy** which is carried over from a status-seeking non-Christian Corinthian culture into the Christian church is not "of the Holy Spirit" (1 Cor. 3:1–3), and is deemed to be incompatible with **love**, which *does not begrudge the status and honour of another, but delights in it for the sake of the other.* How accurately, once again, the "didactic poem" addresses Corinth appears from the socio-rhetorical studies of Corinthian culture by Pogoloff, Witherington, Clarke and others (see above on passages relating to rhetoric and status).

Most English translations render οὐ περπερεύεται as [love is] not *boastful* (NRSV, REB, NJB; cf. AV / KJV, RV, *vaunteth not itself,* NIV, *does not boast;* Collins, *is not conceited*). Moffatt

---

[100] Schrage, *Der erste Brief,* III, pp.295–6 also stresses the active character of the word.
[101] Findlay, *Exp. Greek T.,* II, p.899. cf. *BAGD,* p.886.
[102] Spicq, *Agapē,* II, p.151.
[103] Origen, *1 Cor Frag,* LI: pp.6–7 (text in *JTS* 10 [1909], p.34, ed. Jenkins).
[104] Chrysostom, *Homily on 1 Corinthians,* Hom. XXXIII:1.
[105] *BAGD,* p.338; further Schrage, loc. cit., p.296.

has *makes no parade*. But lexicographical research, together with special attention to first-century literature including Stoic texts makes it certain that Barrett's translation (also in Spicq) **does not brag** precisely captures the semantic force and primary connotations of the verb.[106] Again, Moffatt, Barrett and NIV (against Collins) convey the dynamic force of the choice of a verb rather than an adjective. This is the earliest occurrence of the verb περπεπεύομαι, but it occurs in Epictetus *Diss.* II: 1:34, III: 2:14, and in Polybius XXXII: 2:5 and XXXIX: 1:2 and later in Marcus Antoninus V: 5, clearly to express the verbal action cognate with the form πέρπερος (cf Latin, *perperus*) *braggart*.[107] An even better translation might be that of Moulton-Milligan and with Robertson and Plummer: [Love] *does not play the braggart*. But this seems too heavy and convoluted for the rhythm and relatively crisp sequence of verbs. Again the verb underlines the issue of status seeking and triumphalism at Corinth. Even believers seemed to come to act the part of braggarts, which was at odds with cruciform, Christ-like, **love**.

In the context which has steadily been built up, οὐ φυσιοῦται is best rendered by combining the metaphor of **inflating** (cf. AV/KJV *is not puffed up*) with the implicit emphasis on **its own importance** (cf. Moffatt, and Goodspeed, *gives itself no airs*; NRSV, *arrogant*; REB, NJB, *conceited*; Collins, *inflated*). NIV, *proud*, is too wooden and loses the metaphor. For once, our proposal comes near to J.B. Phillips' extended paraphrase: *nor does it cherish* **inflated** *ideas of* **its own importance**. For a detailed comment on the verb φυσιόω see above on 4:6, 18, 19, 5:2, and 8:1: "The word φυσιόω is a key term of the letter" (Craig).[108] Of the seven uses of this verb in the entire NT, six occur in these references in the epistles. (The other is Col. 2:18.) Paul hammers home the incompatibility of **love** as respect and concern for the welfare of the other and obsessions about the status and attention accorded to the self. How much behaviour among believers and even ministers is actually "attention-seeking", is designed to impress others with one's own supposed importance? Some "spiritual songs" may appear to encourage, rather than discourage, this preoccupation with the self, rather than with others and with God. Here is Luther's antithesis between *theologia crucis* and *theologia gloriae*, and in part why Paul leaves ch. 15 to the end: "Ostentation is the chief idea" (that is, which Paul rejects).[109] Paul sets in contrast with **love** "the thoughtlessness" of "all things are permissible" (Spicq).[110]

v. 5 It does not behave with ill-mannered impropriety; is not preoccupied with the interests of the self; does not become exasperated into pique; does not keep a reckoning up of evil.

On οὐκ ἀσχημονεῖ, it does not behave with ill-mannered impropriety, see above on 7:36, which is the only other use of the verb in the NT. There we translated the verb as: *if anyone*

---

[106] C.K. Barrett, *A Commentary on the First Epistle to the Corinthians* (London: Black, 2nd edn, 1971), p.303; and Spicq, *Agapē in the NT*, II, p.153.

[107] Moulton-Milligan, *Vocabulary of the NT*, p.510 (in addition to the Epictetus sources cited by others, they also cite Basil, *Regulae* XLIX: 423A); LSJ 1204; A.T. Robertson, *Word Pictures of the New Testament* (New York: R Smith, 6 vols, 1931), IV, p.178; BAGD, p.653; A.T. Robertson and A. Plummer, *First Epistle of Paul to the Corinthians* (Edinburgh: T. & T. Clark, 2nd edn, 1914), p.293.

[108] Craig, "1 Cor." *IB*, X, p.175.

[109] Robertson and Plummer, loc. cit.

[110] Spicq, *Agapē*, II, p.153.

thinks that **he is not behaving in a proper way** *towards his betrothed.* The adjective
ἀσχήμων occurs in the NT only at 12:23 where Paul alludes to **unpresentable** parts of
the body, that is, those which good taste and public respect expect to be clothed. In all
three contexts the contrast defines the opposition between on one side *courtesy, good taste,
good public* **manners** and **propriety**, and on the other side thoughtless pursuit of the
immediate wishes of the self regardless of the conventions and courtesies of interpersonal life. Thus *"Agapē* is not **ill-mannered"** (Spicq).[111] Love does not act in ways
which are "contrary to the requirements of propriety and good order, committed by some
ill-mannered members" (Héring).[112]

This paves the way for the contrastive force of εὐσχημόνως, where Paul urges that
worship services should be conducted *with "propriety"*, that is, with order, good taste,
courtesy, and lack of an egocentric concern to draw attention to one's own gifts and
rhetoric at the expense of the decorum of the whole.[113] **Love** does not elbow its way into
conversations, worship-services, or public institutions in a disruptive, discourteous,
attention-seeking way. In so far as courtesy (vs. discourtesy) and politeness (vs.
impoliteness) relate to what is deemed publicly pleasing or displeasing, **love** does not
rush in to impose its idiosyncrasies on those for whom bad manners are offensive. 14:40
applies this to *worship*, as well as to life: "Jesus did not make a virtue out of non-
conformity ...".[114]

The background here may allude to the intrusion of tongues or prophecies at
inappropriate moments (cf. ch. 14). But today it may also include any kind of
monopolizing of a congregation's time and attention in the service of the self: in the tone,
style and vocabulary adopted in notices, sermons, or worst of all the minister as over-
familiar chat-show host or as "prophet" of ill-mannered rebuke. Paul asks, *what does
respect and* **love** *for the other* actually invite? As Bonhoeffer observed, a theological
doctrine of the church and of grace implies its own sociology of the church as a society.

The traditional AV / KJV [Love] *seeketh not her own* correctly conveys the structure of the
Greek οὐ ζητεῖ τὰ ἑαυτῆς. Yet most modern translations prefer a more explicit reference
to **the self**: hence, *is never selfish* (REB, Moffatt); *is never self-seeking* (Twentieth-century
NT); *does not pursue selfish aims* (O.M. Norlie); *is not self-seeking* (NIV); *does not insist on its
own way* (NRSV). To seek the affairs of one's own self (reflexive pronoun), however, also
conveys the idea of *seeks its own advantage* (NJB). Ever since the rise of the Frankfurt
School, Critical Theory, and J. Habermas, the term **interest** says it all within the setting of
a postmodern turn-of-the-century culture today. Hence **is not preoccupied with the
interests of the self** conveys to our culture what the Greek conveyed to first-century
readers, combining *self-centredness* with *self-interests* (neuter plural τά). Collins translates
does not seek its own interests, which captures the main idea.

---

[111] Spicq, *Agapē,* II, p.154.

[112] Héring, *First Epistle,* p.139.

[113] Spicq, loc. cit., R.B. Hays, *First Corinthians* (Louisville, KY: Knox, 1997), p.226 insists that *rude*
(NRSV, NIV) is weak; it is a "stronger term referring to shameful behaviour".

[114] G. Deluz, A *Companion to 1 Corinthians* (London: DLT, 1963), p.190. Deluz uses strong language
about Christians who excuse themselves from "rules of propriety and social conventions, the polite
behaviour customary in their own world" (loc. cit.). To do this on grounds of "freedom" or "knowledge"
is precisely to commit the error of Corinth with which Paul wrestles here.

The lexicography, however, brings us back to the profound point that Nygren and others underline for Paul's *theology*. Love as *Eros* does indeed seek its own satisfaction: *Eros* seeks to "possess" the object of love; in myth, *Eros* is the suitor, ever in need of the gratification of its own desires. By contrast, Nygren writes, *Agapē* in Paul stands in *"opposition to all that be called 'self-love'"* (his italics).[115] "It is thus the direct opposite of acquisitive love ... '*Agapē* seeketh not its own' (1 Cor. 13:5, but this is a self-evident consequence of the theocentric nature of his [Paul's] idea of love. Agapē spells judgment on the life that centres round the ego and its *interests* [my italics] ... For when God's *Agapē* is shed abroad in a man's heart through the Holy Spirit (Rom. 5:5) his life thereby gains a new centre. The emphasis is transferred from his own ego to Christ."[116] It is because Eros does "seek its own interest" that Eros-Cupid is depicted in Graeco-Roman myth not only as a suitor, but also as one with "cunning, seductive and winning ways. That is why Love is shown as armed with bows and arrows. He is a clever hunter."[117] Even the love of Eros-piety, Nygren and Deluz conclude, seeks to grasp the object of its own desire.[118]

Spicq makes the same point in a different way. If love is "disinterested" (that is, without personal interests for advantage), "there is no greater sign of a pure love than that".[119] He alludes to Matt. 5:38–42, where the giving up of "rights" corresponds with Paul's injunctions about "rights" to do anything (1 Cor. 6:12). "*Gnosis*", Spicq observes, also operates on a different level. "Knowledge" and Eros have to do with the *mastery* of an object: "Agapē is not looking for its own advantage, but for the good of others ... 'Christ did not please himself' (Rom. 15:3) ... 'No one should look after his own advantage, but after that of his neighbour' (1 Cor. 10:24)."[120] Spicq compares "the interests of the other" in Phil. 2:4 and 2:21. Existentialist philosophy of the kind expounded by G. Marcel and Martin Buber focuses the ways in which Eros-love can transpose a person, a Thou, into an object, an "it" of possession where love becomes possession, domination and lust. Hence Paul will speak in due course of the personal reciprocity of "knowing and being known".

The coupling of **behaving with ill-mannered impropriety** and **not preoccupied with the interests of the self** alludes to such conduct at Corinth as (i) insisting on one's way about idol-food (10:24, 33); (ii) rushing ahead with the Lord's Supper in a "better" room (the *triclinium*) while the latecomers are squeezed into the *atrium* (11:21, 22); (iii) interrupting speakers with supposed "instant revelations" during worship, or alternatively carrying on at an inordinate length when someone else has an important contribution to make (14:29–33); and imposing unintelligible tongues into a sequence of worship when the utterance cannot be communicated but remains a purely individual welling up of pre-cognitive expression (14:27, 28). Agapē-prompted worship and social relations become contaminated and distorted by Eros-piety, in which self-affirmation is

---

[115]   Nygren, *Agapē and Eros*, p.130.
[116]   Ibid., pp.130–31.
[117]   Deluz, *Companion*, pp.190–91.
[118]   Nygren, *Agapē*, pp.30–34, 41–58, 75–81, 115–33; Deluz, *Companion*, pp.130–32.
[119]   Spicq, *Agapē*, II, p.155.
[120]   Ibid., II, pp.155–6.

disguised as religion. Nietzsche offers an incisive analysis of this attitude, for example, his aphorism "The 'salvation of the soul' – in plain English [German] 'the world revolves around me'."[121] As Nygren, Spicq and others urge, these verses exclude such a notion from Paul.[122]

It is easier to express the force of παροξύνεται through a series of descriptive sentences than to propose a succinct translation. The heart of the word conveys the semantic force of **to exasperate**, *to irritate*, as metaphorical extensions of *to make sharp, to make pointed, to make acid*.[123] Moulton-Milligan cites examples in the papyri for the traditional translation *is not easily provoked* (AV/KJV). In one example a wife complains that her sister is provoking her husband into anger against her.[124] Some insist that especially here the issue is that of being provoked into "irritation rather than rage".[125] This distinction depends on context, since lexicography yields both meanings. In the LXX the verb can mean to provoke to anger (Prov. 6:3), and in the only other instance of παροξύνομαι to occur in the NT (besides 1 Cor. 13:5) Paul is *"provoked to anger* (REB, *outraged)* to see the city so full of idols" (Acts 17:16). However, "the kindred noun παροξυσμός, in Acts xv: 39, describes the *irritation* which arose between Paul and Barnabas" (Vincent's italics).[126] Barrett's succinct translation *is not touchy* does indeed convey readiness to over-react on one's own behalf. But it does not adequately portray the process of being on the receiving end (passive voice) of provocative or irritating behaviour which, where there is **love that shows patience** (13:4) a person cannot be *goaded into the sharp retort of irritation.*

Virtually every lexicon and primary source indicates the notion of reaching a level of **exasperation**. But how does this express itself? The English **pique** combines the same range of nuances as the Greek: something *between irritation and anger* which takes offence because one's *self-regard has been dented, wounded, or punctured by some sharp point.* **Love**, Paul urges, **does not become exasperated into pique**, partly because **patience** delays *exasperation*, and partly because lack of **self-interest** diverts a sense of self-importance away from reacting on the grounds of wounded pride: "it is not embittered by injuries, whether real or supposed."[127]

At Corinth, one group paraded their gifts and status with **ill-mannered impropriety** because they thoughtlessly ignored the well-being and feelings of others; the less-gifted or less status-endowed group allowed themselves to become **exasperated into pique** at the aggressive triumphalism and ostentation of the others because they were more wrapped up in their own feelings than in sharing the sense of joy or liberation of others.

[121] Friedrich Nietzsche, *Collected Works* (18 vols, London: Allen & Unwin, 1909-13), XVI, *The Antichrist* 186, aphorism 43.
[122] I have offered a detailed critique of Nietzsche's incisive critique in A.C. Thiselton, *Interpreting God and the Postmodern Self: On Meaning, Manipulation and Promise* (Edinburgh: T. & T. Clark and Grand Rapids, MI: Eerdmans, 1995), pp.3–45 and 121–64.
[123] Rightly, Spicq, *Agapē*, II, p.156; cf. *BAGD*, p.629; *LS*, p.1158; Moulton-Milligan, p.496; Edwards, *First Epistle*, p.345; Meyer, *First Epistle*, I, p.392; Fee, *First Epistle*, pp.638–9; Bittlinger, *Gifts*, p.86.
[124] Moulton-Milligan, loc. cit., PSI I:41:13; cf. BGU II:588:7.
[125] Craig, "1 Cor.", 1B, X, p.178.
[126] M.R. Vincent, *Word Studies in the NT*, III, p.265.
[127] Robertson and Plummer, *First Epistle*, p.294; cf. Schrage, *Der erste Brief*, III, pp.298–9, where he compares the LXX and Heb. background further.

Many local churches and many theological colleges contain *some who parade their "gifts" while others nurse their "hurts". Does either side, Paul asks, genuinely put the other before the self?*

The verb λογίζομαι means both **to reckon** in a theological sense (Rom. 2:26; 3:28; 4:3–11, of justification by grace through faith); to *count as* in an evaluative sense or the "count-generation" (as in Wolterstorff) which ascribes roles, status, or responsibilities (Rom. 6:11; 8:36; 1 Cor. 4:1; 2 Cor. 3:5); and (as here) **to reckon up** as in the context of accountancy. *BAGD* interpret the verb in this verse to mean *love does not take evil into account.*[128] They reach this conclusion largely on the ground that in the LXX λογίζομαι can mean *to count something against someone* (for example, Zech. 8:17). On the basis of the LXX, however, Spicq suggests that it might mean *love thinks no evil.* This might mean, in turn, either that love "does not suspect its neighbour of evil or that it does not think about committing evil itself".[129] Spicq further understands Zech. 8:17 in the sense of *plotting an evil scheme.* Love, by contrast, remains "innocent of any of the machinations or plots". Although he prefers *love takes no note of injury,* he declares, "once more it is hard to decide exactly what the verb means".[130]

There may be a link, however, between Spicq's interpretation and the notion of **reckoning up.** He observes: "Instead of nursing the memory of an injury … charity refuses to notice that anything has happened" (cf. 2 Cor. 3:5; Phil. 4:8).[131] Conzelmann favours the sense of **reckoning up** by translating *it keeps no score of wrongs* (as also REB; cf. NIV, *keeps no record of wrongs*; NJB, *does not … store up grievances*). The NRSV *resentful* presumably seeks to compromise between *thinketh no evil* (AV/KJV) or *taketh not account of evil* (RV) and a gesture towards *keeps no score.* But the NRSV lacks the dynamic pictorial imagery in which every verb depicts action or stance usually under the guise of a metaphor or pictorial image. Thus we have encountered, for example, images of *boiling* or *burning* (ζηλόω), *inflating* or *filling with air* (φυσιόω), behaving in *unpresentable, ill-mannered* ways (ἀσχημονέω), being *probed with a sharp spike* to provoke someone (παροξύνομαι), and now *an accountant* **reckoning up** *accounts* (λογίζομαι). Most English translations, including especially NRSV and often NIV, simply abstract the conceptual content of the metaphor from its forceful emotive imagery. F.F. Bruce agrees that **reckoning up** plays a part, but as a matter of "paying the offender back in his own coin".[132] Conzelmann argues for *keeps no score* on the ground that "λογίζεσθαι corresponds to חשב (*chāshabh*), 'to set to someone's account'".[133] He is not alone in this view.[134] Love does not have "the habit still widespread even among Christians of keeping a reckoning of the faults of others".[135] Wolff points out that "not keeping a score" which

---

[128] *BAGD,* pp.475–6. Similarly Collins, *First Cor.,* p.481, *nor does it calculate evil* (cf. Prov. 25:21–22) "makes use of a commercial term sometimes used in political discourse".

[129] Spicq, *Agapē,* II, p.156.

[130] Ibid.

[131] Ibid., p.157.

[132] Bruce, *1 and 2 Cor.,* p.127.

[133] Conzelmann, *1 Cor.,* p.224; hence Collins's observation (see above).

[134] Cf. H.W. Heidland, *TDNT* IV, pp.284–92; in part Robertson and Plummer, loc. cit., *stores up no resentment;* but esp. Allo, *Première Épitre,* p.346, "*elle ne tient compte du mal* (Loisy)".

[135] Héring, *First Epistle,* p.139.

is **reckoned up** coheres well with *counting* attitudes or actions *as* evil, and invites the *double* meaning.[136]

v. 6 Love does not take pleasure at wrongdoing, but joyfully celebrates truth.

We have supplied the English subject **Love** which serves as the subject of the verb implicitly rather than explicitly in the Greek, simply because modern English style increasingly demands shorter cues. The preposition ἐπί with the dative τῇ ἀδικίᾳ is best translated **at wrongdoing**. Apart from the force of ἐπί, *in wrongdoing* would miss the point and verge on tautology: someone else's **wrongdoing** is at issue. Several writers insist that ἀδικία in Paul has its full theological sense of *unrighteousness* rather than moral *injustice* (cf. Rom. 1:32).[137] But along with virtually every other declaration in these verses, Paul probably alludes to a situation of contrast at Corinth. This could either be (i) the sense of inflated self-importance and complacency (πεφυσιωμένοι) with which people at Corinth viewed the **wrongdoing** of the incestuous men in 5:1–5, especially if patronage, property, or social status was involved (see above on 5:1–5); or (ii) the tacit or overt approval of the **injustice** entailed in seeking to use the manipulative machinery of a local Gentile magistrate's court for the acquisition of property-rights (see above on 6:1–11); or (iii) more broadly, to the competitive status-seeking culture at Corinth which would encourage taking **pleasure at** the loss of esteem suffered by another if their complicity or involvement in some **wrongdoing** came to be exposed (see above, Introduction to the Epistle, and on 1:12–2:5).

Contextual factors suggest that **wrongdoing** embraces a wider range of possibilities than theological *unrighteousness* or moral *injustice*. Further, these factors suggest that F.F. Bruce's interpretation (with Moffatt) in terms of *Schadenfreude*, malicious joy or gloating, that is, over people's failures, cover much of the ground but probably not all of it.[138] Barrett considers in addition to the issue of "superiority", part of the matter concerns "being censorious".[139] If we genuinely love a person, we should **not take pleasure at** conduct that gives us the opportunity to lecture them or to rebuke them about their **wrongdoing**. Here, again, may be an allusion to over-ready pleasure in *prophetic rebuke* and *pronouncing judgement* on failures within the congregation. Does such a prophet or preacher genuinely **love** those whose welfare he or she claims to cherish if this gives **pleasure**?

Many commentators appear to miss Paul's point about **truth**. Fee considers that the term stands in opposition to evil in the sense of "the gospel and all that is opposed to it ... behaviour that reflects the gospel".[140] But this use of truth occurs mainly in the later writings of the NT and abruptly introduces a fresh idea without preparation.[141] Moffatt

---

[136] Wolff, *Der erste Brief*, pp.319–20.

[137] Notably A.T. Robertson, loc.cit., IV, p.178. For the semantic range of *BAGD*, pp.17–18, and Meyer's critique of Chrysostom, Theodoret and mediaeval and Reformation commentators, *First Epistle*, I, pp.392–3.

[138] Bruce, *1 & 2 Cor.*, p.127. Cf. Moffatt, *Love in the NT*, pp.180–81: "it does not discuss a scandal with gloating".

[139] Barrett, *First Epistle*, p.304.

[140] Fee, *First Epistle*, p.639.

[141] On *truth* in the NT and in modern thought see A.C. Thiselton, "Truth, ἀλήθεια", in C. Brown (ed.), *NIDNTT* III, pp.874–902. See also J. Murphy O'Connor, "Truth: Paul and Qumran", in *Paul and Qumran*, pp.179–230.

simply equates **truth** with *goodness*.[142] Would the addressees interpret this verse in either of these ways, and would Paul expect them to do so? Wolff alludes to the conjoining of ἀδικία and ἀλμθεια in 3 Ezra 4:33–39, which may shed some light on the relationship.[143] However, Spicq comes nearer to the heart of the matter when he explores the reason for the compound verb συγχαίρει translated above as **joyfully celebrates**. With Barrett and Fee, Spicq sees the συν- (συγ-) prefix as primarily intensive: "it shows the intensity and expressiveness of the joy in truth".[144] But rightly he goes beyond Barrett and Fee in understanding the *"with"* aspect of συν- to denote "active participation", with the classical meaning of "congratulate ... felicitate ... applaud ... Agapē's fundamental meaning 'to acclaim' is plain here."[145] What is it that love **joyfully celebrates** or *acclaims*? At one level Chrysostom convincingly contrasts *the truth* about someone's well-being with reports about their supposed failure. Love "feels pleasure with those who are well spoken of", as against enjoying someone's loss of standing.[146] But probably the disinterested character of ἀγάπη is even more clearly at issue. The proximity between postmodernity after Nietzsche and Derrida to the rhetorical stances applauded at Corinth places us in a better position to appreciate Paul's meaning than commentators from the mediaeval period to the 1980s. Postmodern philosophers and critical theorists perceive as clearly as Paul did that virtually every action and stance bears some relationship to the power-interests of the self, or to one's peer group. Genuine **love**, as I argue as my main thesis in *Interpreting God and the Postmodern Self*, alone *de-centres* the power-"interests" of the self and of its peer group, and in re-centring them in the Other (primarily in God, but also in the other person) disengages from self-interest.[147] Only now can **truth** emerge as disengaged from a power-agenda. True disinterested integrity is free to seek for **truth**, without anxiety about what it helps or hinders in one's personal agenda. **Love**, Paul says, has discovered *integrity*: as Nygren constantly declares, because it is disinterested and creative of value, it delights in **truth**.[148] The definite article with the abstract noun τῇ ἀληθείᾳ does not commit us to the translation *the* **truth**, although admittedly it cannot be excluded. If the article is translated, it probably denotes *the truth* in this or that situation rather than gospel truth *as such*.

The practical thrust of *love* **joyfully celebrates truth**, then, is that love does not use manipulative devices and subtexts to protect itself from **truth** or from *the* **truth**. It is honest and open, not defensive, for it has placed the good of the other above the good of the self. Theology enters the picture in a different way from that envisaged by most commentators. As Karl Rahner observes, the person who has placed everything in the hands of God has no need to fear, or to hide from, the truth. For God already knows it and has accepted the believer as he or she is.[149] The symmetry of v. 6a and v. 6b is now

---

142   Moffatt, *Love in the NT*, p.181.
143   C. Wolff, *Der erste Brief des Paulus an die Korinther* (Leipzig: Evangelische Verlagsanstalt, 1996), p.320. Schrage, *Der erste Brief*, III, n. 128 cites many more passages from the LXX and inter-Testamental literature.
144   Spicq, *Agapē*, II, p.158.
145   Ibid.
146   Chrysostom, *1 Cor Hom*, XXXIII:4.
147   Thiselton, *Interpreting God and the Postmodern Self*, loc. cit. (as cited above under v. 5).
148   Nygren, *Agapē and Eros*, pp.77–8.
149   K. Rahner, "On Truthfulness", in *Theological Investigations* VII (Eng., London: Darton, Longman & Todd, 1971), pp.229–59. Cf. W. Pannenberg, "What is Truth", in *Basic Questions in Theology* II (London: SCM, 1971), pp.1–27.

apparent. No taint of evil can enhance or give pleasure to love, where love is genuine. Love takes no pleasure in someone else's failure, and delights in integrity and reality. If the situation is bad, love wants to help; if the situation is good, love wants to celebrate. It wants no hidden interests that disguise truth as something that it is not. Deluz links this verse with the thought of v. 7 that love "does not exaggerate, but it ... tries to understand ... bears with it".[150]

v. 7 It never tires of support, never loses faith, never exhausts hope, never gives up.

Our translation restructures the Greek syntax for two reasons, both of which concern the distinction between a logic of inclusion and a logic of exclusion in conveying the force of Paul's four-fold repetition of πάντα, *all things*. First, this four-fold πάντα serves to convey "the absence of all limits" (Héring).[151] It thus *excludes* the *limits* of ἀγάπη rather than defining an *all-inclusive* content. The REB is the only major VS to appreciate that this is best rendered in modern English by negating a series of negations: *There is nothing love cannot face; there is no limit to its faith, its hope, its endurance.* Even Collins produces an all-inclusive translation: *"It bears everything, believes everything, hopes everything, endures everything* (loc. cit., p.478).

Second, the traditional translations invite the kind of misunderstandings of Paul and indeed of Christianity that fuel the critiques of Feuerbach, Marx, Nietzsche and Freud. The well-known AV/KJV and RV rendering *beareth all things, believeth all things, hopeth all things, endureth all things* appears to support Marx's notion of Christianity as opium for the people, or Nietzsche's concept of Christianity as "servile mediocrity". Paul's notion of the cross and of love, Nietzsche asserts, "has sided with everything weak, low and botched; it has made an ideal out of antagonism towards ... strong life ... the will to nothingness sanctified".[152] For Nietzsche, Paul was "full of superstition and cunning", for, by reinterpreting language about the law, he became "the destroyer of the Law" and thereby of criteria other than self-construed outlooks: "Morality itself was blown away, annihilated ... 'I am above the Law', thinks Paul."[153] If Paul enjoins his readers to bear, believe, hope and endure *everything*, Nietzsche can say "truth has been turned topsy-turvy ... transvaluation of all values!" while Michel Foucault can perceive it as the promotion of conformist "docility", Marx construes it as "opium", and Freud as a projection derived from inner conflicts resolved by wishful thinking which "believes all things", in order to "endure all things".[154]

None of this, however, accords with Paul. It is Corinth who coins the slogan "All things are lawful"; "We reign as kings." It is Paul who insists on discrimination and differentiation, especially in prophecy and worship. Moreover ἀγάπη is precisely *not*

---

[150] Deluz, *Companion*, p.193.
[151] Héring, *First Epistle*, p.141.
[152] F. Nietzsche, *Works – XVI: The Antichrist*, p.130 (Aphorisms 5 and 6), p.131 (Aphorism 7) and p.146 (Aphorism 18), cf. pp.142–50 (Aphorisms 16–21).
[153] Nietzsche, *Works, IX: The Dawn of Day*, pp.67–70 (Aphorism 68, cf. 66–71).
[154] Nietzsche, *Works, XVI: The Antichrist*, p.138 (Aphorism 12) and p.231 (Aphorism 62); cf. M. Foucault, *Discipline and Punish* (Eng., New York: Pantheon, 1977), e.g. in medicine, religion or the penal system, pp.190ff.

"docile" or conformist; it does not seek a quiet life by "servile mediocrity". Nygren's exposition of Paul's theology reveals the reverse: it is creative, innovative, transforming and indifferent to "returns" in the sense of lacking the very "interests" on which the analyses of Feuerbach, Marx, Nietzsche and Freud depend. Therefore we must use the semantic strategy of protecting Paul's meaning by using a logic of negation as the least ambiguous way to exclude the partial, as we shall also explore in 15:43, 44, where similar logical and linguistic problems await us. Paul declares: *Love* **never tires of support, never loses faith, never exhausts hope, never gives up**. The four-fold **never** with four negative actions provides rhetorical force of Paul's four-fold *all things* (πάντα) which clearly invites misunderstanding by readers in a post-Freudian, post-Nietzschean world. The REB offers a good precedent for the basic strategy. Yet again the precise semantic range of at least one of the verbs remains in question. The meaning of στέγει remains open to debate. Lexicographers and exegetes generally agree that the cognate noun στέγη, *roof* (as in Mark 2:4) offers a starting-point. But this may be connected with the verb στέγω in one of several ways. It may mean *to cover*, as a *roof covers* a house. In biblical Greek the verb occurs only (apart from here) in Ecclus. 8:17 (LXX) in 1 Cor. 9:4 and in 1 Thess. 3:1, 5. In Ecclus. 8:17 λόγον στέξαι means *to conceal the matter*. This would then accord with the maxim "*Charity shall cover* (καλύψει) *the multitude of sins*" (1 Pet. 4:8, AV/KJV).

Conzelmann uses *cover* in his translation and suggests in his exegesis that στέγει means either "(a) 'draw a veil of silence over'; [or] (b) 'bear'".[155] The latter receives some support from Paul's use of the verb in 1 Cor. 9:4, where it means *to bear* in the sense of *to put up with*. But it is generally agreed that this is not a frequent meaning of the verb. *BAGD* conclude that "perhaps" in 13:7 στέγει means "love throws a cloak of silence over what is displeasing in another person" (Harnack).[156] Peter Lombard and many mediaeval interpreters adopt this meaning in the belief that Paul offers a model of God's love to persons.

Several versions associate στέγει with *roof* in the sense *to protect* rather than *to cover*, that is, *bearing* in the sense of *carrying* or **supporting** rather than of *to put up with*. NIV renders *always protects*; NRSV plays a lexicographically safe but theologically dangerous game with *bears all things*; NJB expands the "covering" theme with *it is always ready to make allowances*, which embodies a notion of **support**. G.H. Whitaker attempted to preserve the roof imagery by suggesting, "Love springs no leak."[157] Godet, following Bengel, urges that *to bear*, in the sense of *to put up with* is tautologous in relation to ὑπομένει and hence means *to cover* in the sense of *to excuse*.[158] Spicq and more recently Lang have put forward exactly this argument, to conclude that it means *cover*.[159] Our understanding is closest to that of H.A.W. Meyer, Barrett and Schrage. Citing the Vulgate *suffert*, Meyer proposes a distinction between στέγει and ὑπομένει. The latter sustains its support in *putting up with everything* for a limitless *duration*; the former **supports** a

---

155   Conzelmann, *1 Cor.*, p.224; also p.224 n. 64 and p.225 n. 65.
156   *BAGD*, pp.765–6.
157   Whitaker, "Love springs no Leak", *Expositor* 21 [8th ser.] (1921), p.126.
158   Godet, *First Epistle* II, p.247.
159   F. Lang, *Die Briefe an die Korinther* (Göttingen & Zürich: Vandenhoeck & Ruprecht, 1994), p.185; and Spicq, *Agapē*, II, p.159. Also Senft, *Première Épitre*, p.169.

limitless *load*: "holds out under them (*suffert*) without ceasing to love, – all burdens, privation, trouble, hardship, toil occasioned by others"; Schrage links *suffert* with *sustinet*.[160] **Support** well conveys this, with a clearer hint at the structure which supports the roof than *bear*. Barrett adds yet further weight to **support** by appealing to the tradition of the Jewish Mishnah stemming from Simeon the Just (third century BC) that *service* is **support** of the world.[161] Kierkegaard's analogy of a mother's love which ceaselessly gives **support** to her child is helpfully noted by Schrage (see below).

Meyer's exegesis and our proposed translation lends weight to the assumption which lies behind the debate between Elizabeth Stuart and C.J. Walters that here "Love is ... Paul", that is, Paul perceives himself as so manifesting his love and concern for Corinth as the Other that this love **never tires of support, never loses faith, never exhausts hope, never gives up**.[162] Stuart finds a manipulative strategy in Paul: by defining "love" in terms that relate more closely to his own values than those of the "gifts" at Corinth, Paul effectively claims to be *the* paradigm through whom God's love is experienced. Walters attacks and rejects the argument about manipulation, mainly on the ground that Paul associates love with *truth* and disinterested concern *in principle* rather than in personal terms. But neither disputes that Paul himself seeks to live out what he ascribes to **love** in 1 Cor. 13.

Stuart's approach, it need hardly be said, brings us back to power-issues shared by A.C. Wire, E. Castelli and M. Foucault. Wire asserts, "Paul's sharp contrast of this love to the exercise of all spiritual gifts suggests that the Corinthian prophets' highest value may be seen by reversing these verbs. They no longer suffer but zealously pursue a new life, not orientating themselves kindly on others' needs, but rejoicing in what the spirit has done in them."[163] Thus Wire returns to reading Paul like Feuerbach and Nietzsche: Paul is the dull proponent of servile mediocrity, while the Corinthian women prophets "dare to exhibit the spirit's creativity":[164] "The woman prophets of Corinth [are] on another social trajectory than Paul, and with a different experience of Christ ... a different social practice and theological integrity".[165] Castelli does not directly address 1 Cor. 13, but if Wire, Stuart, and others are right (as we agree) in discerning a barely veiled description of Paul's own goals in 13:7, then all of Castelli's observation about the links between Pauline *mimêsis* and Foucault's notions of power and conformity come into play.[166] However, it must be emphasized that the traditional translations of 13:7, especially in AV/KJV, RV, RSV and NRSV, add fuel to the fire and give more hostages to their arguments than is necessary. We must hold to the demonstration primarily in Nygren but

---

[160]   H.A.W. Meyer, *Critical and Exegetical Handbook to the Epistles to the Corinthians* (Eng., 2 vols, Edinburgh: T. & T. Clark, 1892), I, p.393; Schrage, *Der erste Brief*, III, p.341. Schrage also compares the readings of Calvin and Kierkegaard, where the latter compares how a mother *supports* her child in limitless practical ways.

[161]   Barrett, *First Epistle*, p.304; Mishnah, *Aboth* I:2.

[162]   E. Stuart, "Love is ... Paul", *Exp. T.* 102 (1991), pp.264–6; and C.J. Walters, "' Love is ... Paul' – A Response", *Exp. T.* 103 (1991), p.75.

[163]   A.C. Wire, *The Corinthian Women Prophets* (Minneapolis, MN: Fortress, 1990), p.139.

[164]   Ibid.

[165]   Ibid.

[166]   E. Castelli, *Imitating Paul* (Louisville, KY: Westminster/Knox, 1991), pp.97–115 and throughout. She discusses Foucault on pp.35–58 and 119–24.

also in Spicq that for ἀγάπη to be manipulatory and concerned for its own interests would be a logical contradiction.

For further considerations about Paul's personal relation to this verse, we refer to the discussions of O. Wischmeyer, H.J. Blair and others.[167] To translate πάντα πιοτεύει as **never loses faith** meets Calvin's point (repeated by Lang): "not that a Christian ... strips himself of wisdom and discernment ... not that he has forgotten how to distinguish black from white!"[168] But in the absence of our explicating a logic of negated exclusion rather than universal inclusion even Calvin speaks of being rid of "ill-founded suspicion", and Spicq of "giving a favourable interpretation of everything".[169] Augustine, too, interprets this as "believing the best" of all people.[170] But Barrett writes: "Not 'always believes the best about people', but 'never loses faith'".[171] Whether we accept Heinrici's interpretation as belief in "the invincible power of good" depends on whether this implies human good (which would be *Eros*) or the transformative power of divine ἀγάπη which does provide grounds for **never loses faith** in Paul's thought.[172] The parallel phrase **never exhausts hope** scarcely requires further explanation. **Faith** and **hope** come to be associated with **love** in vv. 8–13. ὑπομένει refers to an *endurance* of setbacks and rebuffs which **never gives up** on people, whatever they do. This again bears the stamp of Paul's enduring concern for the people of Corinth. Deluz writes, "Like Christ on the cross, love endures scorn, failure, ingratitude ... At the end shines out the light of Easter. For *love never ends.*"[173]

---

[167] Wischmeyer, *Der höchste Weg*, and Blair, "First Corinthians 13 and the Disunity at Corinth", *Theol. Ed.* 14 (1983), pp.69–77.

[168] John Calvin, *The First Epistle of Paul to the Corinthians* (Edinburgh: Oliver & Boyd, 1960), p.278; cf. Lang, *Die Briefe*, p.185.

[169] Ibid., and Spicq, *Agapē*, II, p.159

[170] Augustine, *Confessions*, X:3. However, in *Freedom and Letter* 32, Augustine explains it as belief in the word of God.

[171] Barrett, *First Epistle*, p.305.

[172] C.F.G. Heinrici, *Das erste Sendschreiben des Apostels Paulus an die Korinther* (Berlin: Hertz, 1880, 2nd edn, 1896), p.421.

[173] Deluz, *Companion*, p.193.

CHAPTER TWENTY

"Meanings and Greek Translation Relating to 'Spiritual Gifts' in 1 Corinthians 12–14: Some Proposals in the Light of Philosophy of Language, Speech-Act Theory and Exegesis" (Paper delivered 2000, new essay)

This is a hitherto unpublished paper given at the Biblical Greek Language and Linguistics Section of the Society of Biblical Literature, at Nashville, Tennessee, on 20 November 2000. I argue that many modern translations and widespread understandings of a number of controversial terms and sentences in 1 Corinthians 12–14 deserve reconsideration, especially 12:3 and 12:8–10. Once again a narrow concern with lexicography alone, while essential, is not enough. The phenomena familiar in philosophy of language of persuasive definition, code switching, self-involving speech acts, count-generation, and value-laden translations in the target language more specific than in the source language, provide awareness and resources for a reappraisal of some influential verses in these chapters. Throughout, however, the context of situation in Paul's Corinth remains an indispensable key for which no amount of alternative resources could offer a substitute.

I
"Spiritual", Spirituality, or "What Comes from the Holy Spirit"? Persuasive Definitions of Πνευματικός and Code Switching

Many of the Christians at Corinth claimed "spirituality" or being "spiritual" as a "status indicator", although Paul denied the applicability of such language in their case ʼοὐκ ἠδυνήθην λαλῆσαι ὑμῖν ὡς πνευματικοῖς, 1 Cor. 3:1).[1] This coheres with the stream of research that convincingly portrays Corinthian culture in the period AD 51–55 as obsessed with "status" and "recognition". Further, this obsession related to "status" as defined by a diversity of quasi-independent value-systems. Wayne Meeks and Gerd Theissen speak convincingly of pluralist systems of "status inconsistency" and "social stratification". "Status" in first-century Corinth was a "multidimensional phenomenon", in accordance with which people measure[d] ... rank along *each* of [a series of] relevant dimensions".[2] Since, as Meeks agues, "the weight of each dimension depends on who is doing the weighing", *spirituality* may more readily lend itself to constituting a source of supposed

---

[1]   Cf. Dale B. Martin, *The Corinthian Body* (New Haven, CT: Yale, 1995), p.88.
[2]   W.A. Meeks, *First Urban Christians* (1983), p.54; cf. G. Theissen, *The Social Setting of Pauline Christianity: Essays on Corinth* (Eng., Philadelphia, PA: Fortress, 1982), pp.69–120; B. Witherington, *Conflict and Community in Corinth* (Carlisle: Paternoster, 1995), pp.5–19, 50–53.

status or "recognition" than the less easily constructed values of wealth, influence, high birth, or other inherited or hard-earned sources of recognition (cf. 1:26–31).

I have argued in my commentary that three distinct factors arising from the above served to promote in the Corinth of Paul's day a mood and ethos that nowadays we might readily describe as "postmodern".[3] Leaving aside for the moment the notion that "postmodernism" often denotes a reaction against high modernity and Enlightenment rationalism, David Harvey, David Lyons and many other writers perceive "postmodernity" as a social phenomenon in which social construction and virtual reality are accorded privilege over the "hard givens" of human life; consumerism and consumer profiles are accorded privilege over states of affairs; and mass advertising, media-spin and rhetoric are accorded privilege over truth and rational criteria of judgement.[4] In terms of the culture and mood or ethos in Corinth, these three themes readily relate to the following. (1) To define status or identity in terms of "recognition" in the eyes of others reflects a move towards a social constructionism or a step towards a kind of "virtual reality". (2) To place concerns about consumers and consumer profiles over given states of affairs reflects an audience-orientated way of shaping the Christian proclamation in contrast to the "affront" of the apostolic Gospel, and the preferences and criteria of a "local" peer group above a trans-contextually grounded message in apostolic and catholic tradition. (3) To place the effect of rhetoric and "spin" above truth emerges with close similarities in first-century Corinth and those features of the twenty-first-century West that reflect postmodernity. In several other publications I have defended the ascription of the term "postmodern mood" to a pre-modern culture, especially that of Corinth.[5]

All of this paves the way for a helpful rhetorical analysis of chapters 12–14 proposed by J Smit.[6] Smit argues that chapters 12–14 from a rhetorical unit introduced by an *exordium* designed to gain a sympathetic hearing. The beginning, which includes the notorious crux concerning the translation of τῶν πνευματικῶν (12:1) constitutes a rhetorical *insinuato*, in which the positive and coveted adjective πνευματικός serves to introduce under this positive term a more confrontational and critical antithesis between προφητεία and γλῶσσαι, or intelligible prophetic discourse and glossolalia. Smit notes that γλῶσσα [γλῶσσαι] occurs twenty-one times in chapters 12–14 but not elsewhere in this epistle, while προφητεία occurs twenty times but otherwise only at 11:4–5 (in the context of his approval of women leading in public worship).

We should add two major points to Smit's reconstruction. First, while for many at Corinth πνευματικός denoted a quality of *spirituality* capable of conferring status, admiration, recognition, or respect, for Paul the term primarily denotes *that which pertains to the Holy Spirit*. Hence his conscious redefinition of πνευματικός through code

---

[3]   Anthony C. Thiselton, *First Epistle to the Corinthians: a Commentary on the Greek Text* (Grand Rapids, MI: Eerdmans, and Carlisle: Paternoster, 2000), pp.12–17, 40–43, 50–51, 314, 548, 1002, 1054–9 and 1255.

[4]   David Harvey, *The Condition of Postmodernity* (Oxford: Blackwell, 1989), pp.3–9 and throughout, and David Lyon, *Postmodernity* (Buckingham: Open University, 1994), pp.6–7.

[5]   See especially A.C. Thiselton, "Can a Premodern Bible Address a Postmodern World?", in Paul Gifford et al. (eds), *2000 Years and Beyond* (London: Routledge, 2003) and included as Essay 35, below.

[6]   J. Smit, "Argument and Genre of 1 Cor. 12–14", in S.E. Porter and T.H. Olbricht (eds), *Rhetoric and the NT* (Sheffield: JSNT Supplement Series 90, 1993), pp.211–29.

switching and through the application of Christological and Christomorphic criteria mean that Paul cannot apply the term πνευματικός to them in this latter sense without strong qualification (3:1–3).[7] By contrast a raised entity capable of identifiable recognition in the intersubjective public domain (σῶμα) receives as a divine gift a mode of existence characterized by the uninterrupted fullness of the Holy Spirit (σῶμα πνευματικόν, 15:44; cf. v. 49 on being also characterized by the image of Christ).

Second, Paul does envisage the possibility of a "spirituality" which may be *self-induced*. This is arguably the point of the allusion in 12:2 to τὰ εἴδωλα τὰ ἄφωνα. In the absence of revelation from beyond, "spirituality" becomes self-generated from within. P. Vielhauer is persuasive in his suggestion that Paul's critique of ἑαυτὸν οἰκοδομεῖ (14:4) also conveys this nuance of self-induced "spirituality".[8] Schrage is not dismissive of such a suggestion.[9] If the heart of a Christomorphic Spirit-inspired experience and mind-set is Christ's concern for "the other" (as it is throughout this epistle), "building" the self denotes a different scale of priorities that does not fully cohere with what the Holy Spirit genuinely promotes.

This perspective now assists us with the long-standing division of opinion about whether we should translate περὶ δὲ τῶν πνευματικῶν as *Now about spiritual persons* (following, for example, Grotius, John Locke, Heinrici, Weiss, Hurd, Bruce, Wire and Blomberg); or as *Now about spiritual gifts* (AV / KJV, RSV, NRSV, JB, NIV) or *gifts of the Spirit* (NJB, REB).[10] The latter view is found in Tertullian, Novatian, Cyril of Jerusalem, Robertson and Plummer, Kistemaker, Conzelmann, Lang, Senft and Collins among others.[11] Allo, Barrett, and Harrisville despair of finding any criterion by which to reach a decision.[12] Schrage, however, is surely right to suggest that while the Corinthians viewed spirituality largely in terms of what it meant to be regarded as a *"spiritual"* person, Paul directs attention to God who is the source of all *freely bestowed gifts of grace*. Paul clearly prefers to use the term χαρίσματα (12:4–11). The code switching conveyed

---

[7] On code switching, Thiselton, *First Epistle*, pp.43, 123–75, 240, 325–6, 469, 499–500, 560–61, 627, 930, 996, 1024; and J. Moores, *Wrestling with Rationality in Paul* (Cambridge: CUP [SNTS Mon. Ser.], 1995), pp.26–8, 133–5. Not only πνεῦμα, but σοφία and several other terms offer examples.

[8] P. Vielhauer, *Oikodomê: Das Bild vom Bau in der christlichen Literatur vom NT bis Clemens Alexandrinus* (Karlsruhe: Harrassowitz, 1940), pp.91–8.

[9] W. Schrage, Der *erste Brief an die Korinther* (Neukirchen: Neukirchener Verlag, and Zürich: Benzinger, III, 1999), p.388.

[10] J. Locke, *Paraphrase and Notes on the Epistles of St Paul* [1707] (Oxford: Clarendon Press, 1987), p.446; C.F.G. Heinrici, *Das erste Sendschreiben des Apostels Paulus an die Korinther* (Berlin: Hertz, 1880), p.353; J. Weiss, *Der erste Korintherbrief* (Göttingen: Vandenhoeck & Ruprecht, 1910), p.294; J.C. Hurd, *Origin of 1 Corinthians* (London: SPCK, 1965), pp.192–5; A.C. Wire, *Corinthian Women Prophets* (Minneapolis, MN: Fortress, 1990), p.135; F.F. Bruce, *1 & 2 Corinthians* (London: Oliphants, 1971), pp.116–17; C.L. Blomberg, *1 Corinthians* (Grand Rapids, MI: Zondervan, 1994), p.243.

[11] E.g. Tertullian, *Against Marcion*, 5:8; Novatian, *On the Trinity*, 29; Cyril, *Lectures*, 16:1; Robertson and Plummer, *First Epistle to the Corinthians* (Edinburgh: T. & T. Clark, 1914), p.259; J. Kistemaker, *1 Corinthians* (Grand Rapids, MI: Baker, 1993), pp.412–13; F. Lang, *Die Briefe an die Korinther* (Göttingen: Vandenhoeck & Ruprecht, 1994), p.162; H. Conzelmann, *1 Corinthians* (Philadelphia, PA: Fortress, 1975), p.204; C. Senft, *La Première Épitre aux Corinthiens* (Geneva: Labor et Fides, 1990), p.155; R.F. Collins, *First Corinthians* (Collegeville, MN: Glazier, 1999), pp.446–7.

[12] E.-B. Allo, *Première Épitre aux Corinthiens* (Paris: Gabalda, 1956), p.320; C.K. Barrett, *First Epistle to the Corinthians* (London: Black, 1971), p.278; R.A. Harrisville, *1 Corinthians* (Minneapolis, MN: Augsburg, 1987), p.205.

initially in the rhetorical *insinuato* which Paul uses *both* as a favourable term in the eyes of the readers *and* as a lever for the issue of a Christomorphic criterion for what is "of the Holy Spirit" is therefore best conveyed *in this context* by translating: "Now about things that 'come from the Spirit'", that is, people *say* that this is the source of their status, but *how are we to know*? "Well, Paul replies, I do not want you to be *'not* knowing' (ἀγνοεῖν) i.e. to remain without knowledge."[13]

This coheres with Chrysostom's comment that Paul is considering criteria concerning what "are the works of the Spirit alone, human effort contributing nothing", and with H.A.W. Meyer's observation that Paul addresses "the forms of action which proceed from the Holy Spirit and make manifest his agency".[14] This proposal for translation brings together contextual considerations with rhetorical analysis and the phenomenon of redefinition and especially code switching in the philosophy of language.[15]

II
Self-Involving Speech Acts of Christological Confession as Criteria for Claims about being "Spiritual" or Gifted through the Holy Spirit: Count-Generation and Multiple Speech-Acts

The issue of criteria concerning things that "come from the Spirit" is explicated in terms of antithetical *speech-acts of self-involving confession*, which function multi-dimensionally as commissives, declaratives and verdictives (12:1, 3). I shall argue that Nicholas Wolterstorff's notions in his philosophy of language of "double agency discourse" (or "deputized discourse") and "count-generation" (counting one speech-act as another) shed light on the role of 12:3 as a criterion of the transparent action of the Holy Spirit (1) as part of an inter-Trinitarian "divine dialogue", and (2) as a criteriological confession embracing life, attitude and stance as well as words as such.[16]

Two preliminary points concern the contrast of the notoriously difficult expression Ἀνάθεμα Ἰησοῦς (12:3a), and the logical force of οὐδεὶς δύναται (v. 3b). Paul's use of antithesis has been thoroughly investigated by Schneider.[17] In my commentary I discuss the merits of twelve or more hypotheses concerning the meaning this part of the verse 3. The more serious include: (1) pressure under a setting of persecution (Cullmann); (2) a disparagement of the earthly Jesus by so-called proto-gnostic Christians (Schmithals) or (3) by "enthusiasts" in uncontrolled ecstasy (Weiss, Lietzmann); (4) mere lack of control of what was repressed, now released through ecstatic rapture (Allo, Barrett); (5) allusions to pre-conversion settings or to settings in a Jewish synagogue (Bassler, or in a novel version, Derrett); or (6) confession of the atonement in which the "curse" of the Deuteronomic law rested on Jesus, but without faith in his resurrection as Lord (van

[13] Thiselton, *First Epistle*, pp.910–11.
[14] Chrysostom, *Homilies on 1 Corinthians*, Hom. 29:2; H.A.W. Meyer, *Epistles to the Corinthians*, (Edinburgh: T. & T. Clark, 2 vols, 1892), I, p.354.
[15] See esp. Umberto Eco, *Semiotics and the Philosophy of Language* (1984); and Thiselton, *New Horizons in Hermeneutics* (1992), pp.526–9, and "The Meaning of *sarx* in 1 Cor 5.5 ...", *SJT* 26, 1973, pp.204–28.
[16] N. Wolterstorff, *Divine Discourse* (Cambridge: CUP, 1995), pp.37–54 and 75–94.
[17] N. Schneider, *Die rhetorische Eigenart der paulinischen Antithese* (Tübingen: Mohr, 1970).

Unnik). These remain merely speculative hypotheses, however, which may account for the sharpness and force of Pauline antithesis.[18] [*Editorial Comment*: from the hindsight of 2004, I include in the re-appraisal below the recent suggestion of Bruce Winter, which probably makes better and more convincing sense than any of the twelve listed or the six cited here.]

The main function of the antithesis is to emphasize that Christian confession prompted by the Holy Spirit is "more than a formula".[19] T. Holz, C. Wolff and W. Schrage rightly urge that in 12:3, as also in Rom. 10:9, confessions entail *both* a belief about the identity and status of Jesus *and* an orientation of heart which is self-involving, commissive and performative.[20] The importance of this dual dimension in early Christian confessions is well argued by Vernon Neufeld mainly on an exegetical basis.[21]

In terms of speech-act theory, this underlines the close relation between illocutionary force and propositions about states of affairs, which I have urged repeatedly in various works on this subject.[22] The allusion to the earthly Jesus of history also resonates closely with the study of speech-acts in 1 John by Dietmar Neufeld. He urges, "The cash value of Christological statements is seen in corresponding ethical conduct and proper confession."[23] The antithetical stances of respectively denying or believing that Jesus Christ came in the flesh do not turn on "passive recitation of orthodox Christological formulas", but on self-involving commissive, declarative and verdictive speech-acts engaged "in the re-constituting character of the word which is life ... Denying and believing make plain to which sphere they belong."[24] The utterances are "commissive and expressive" of stances, attitudes and practical life-styles.[25]

This underlines the *logical* rather than *contingent* or empirical force of δύναται. Indeed the parallel clause λαλῶν λέγει (3a) confirms this. To claim "spirituality" while living a life-style incompatible with that of a believer who serves Christ as Lord would be *logically self-contradictory*. Conversely, to claim, "Jesus is Lord" while experiencing a purely *self-induced* "spirituality" which does not "come from the Spirit", also entails logical contradiction and logical exclusion. Weiss expresses this confessional content of the *Kyrios* acclamation well: what this amounts to "in a practical sense will best be made clear through the correlative concept of servant or slave of Christ".[26] This coheres with 6:20, "You do not belong to yourself; you were bought with a price." Whereas Deissmann had

---

18 A comprehensive list of sources may be consulted in A.C. Thiselton, *First Epistle*, pp.918–25, where twelve distinct theories receive full documentation and discussion.

19 A. Bittlinger, *Gifts and Graces: A Commentary on 1 Corinthians 12–14* (London: Hodder, 1967), p.17.

20 T. Holz, "Das Kennzeichen des Geistes (1 Kor. 12:1–3)", NTS 18, 1972, pp.365–76; C. Wolff, *Der erste Brief* (1996), pp.286–7; W. Schrage, *Der erste Brief*, III, pp.123–4.

21 V. Neufeld, *The Earliest Christian Confessions* (Leiden: Brill, 1963), esp. pp.13–33, 42–68 and 140–46.

22 E.g. Thiselton, *New Horizons in Hermeneutics: The Theory and Practice of Transforming Biblical Reading* (London: HarperCollins, Grand Rapids, MI: Zondervan, and Carlisle: Paternoster, 1992), pp.283–307; *The Promise of Hermeneutics* (with Lundin and Walhout, Carlisle: Paternoster and Grand Rapids, MI: Eerdmans, 1999), pp.209–40; "The Supposed Power of Words ...", JTS 25, 1974, pp.283–99; "Christology in Luke, Speech-Act Theory ...", in Joel Green and Max Turner (eds), *Jesus of Nazareth* (Grand Rapids, MI: Eerdmans, 1994).

23 D. Neufeld, *Reconceiving Texts as Speech-Acts: An Analysis of 1 John* (Leiden: Brill, 1994), p.3.

24 Neufeld, loc. cit., pp.79 and 132.

25 Neufeld, loc. cit., p.134.

26 J. Weiss, *Earliest Christianity* (New York: Harper edition, 1959 [Eng. 1937]), vol. II, p.458.

appealed to inscriptions at Delphi and elsewhere concerning the sale and purchase of slaves by, or in the presence of, Apollo, Athene, or Asklepios to emphasize *freedom* after manumission, recent research by Scott Bartchy, Dale Martin and others expose the mistaken emphasis of Deissmann (followed by Conzelmann): purchase was *into* a new "slavery" of *belonging to the Lord Christ*. The nature of the condition of slavery rested entirely on a spectrum of circumstances depending ultimately on the decision, attitude, character and evaluation of a new *kyrios*.[27] To become the *responsibility of the Lord*, into whose *care* the slave enters, entails, for the Christian, trust, obedience and the freedom of the Lord's taking responsibility *for his life and actions*. Hence the self-involving commissive speech-act of confession Jesus is [my/our] Lord both draws on a currency of Spirit-led life and commits the self to an operative currency of Spirit-led life. We might well be shocked if, when authorities call to account a destructive badly-behaved child, the child points at us and screams "He's my Dad/She's my Mum!" Yet to confess Christ as Lord is effectively to refer others to Christ as the one who bears responsibility for us. This is the two-sided force of an illocutionary speech-act of this nature.

This falls under the category of Wolterstorff's "count-generation". Against the institutional background of divine promise and covenantal grace, the confession "Jesus is Lord" *counts as* performing *several simultaneous speech-acts*: it *declares* a state of affairs about God's vindication and enthronement of Christ as Lord; it *commits* the one who makes the confession to a life appropriate to, and coherent with, reflecting the Christomorphic pattern of the One who has taken the care of him or her and responsibility for them; it thereby *counts as a* two-sided criteriological verdictive, that is, a criterion of "what comes from the Spirit", since without the agency of the Holy Spirit Christomorphic formation is impossible, and a criterion of how the confessing believer regards Jesus Christ.

Still more profoundly, if the Holy Spirit is the agent who inspires and promotes the illocutionary utterance, the confession falls into Wolterstorff's "double-agency" or "deputized discourse" category. Wolterstorff offers a series of analogues: a secretary produces documents or directives on behalf of a president, chairperson, or officer who signs them.[28] Even if the executive signs the letter, the representative who acts on the executive's behalf communicates the actual text of the letter. It is no accident, however, that Paul inserts a "Trinitarian frame" between the *exordium* (12:1–3) and the specific list of *charismata* concerning which a Christological and Christomorphic criterion, alongside that of "building" the "other" and the whole community has been, and will further be, formulated (12:8–11; cf. 12:12–30, and chapters 13–14). In 12:4–7 "the same Spirit ... the same Lord ... the same God assume respective responsibility for different apportioning of gifts, varieties of ways of serving and what activates effects ... in everyone" (vv. 4–6). This becomes a publicly transparent manifestation of the Spirit for common advantage (v. 7).

---

[27] A. Deissmann, *Light from the Ancient East* (Eng., London: Hodder, 1927), pp.319–32; H. Conzelmann, *1 Cor.*, p.113; as against convincing evidence and criticism by D.B. Martin, *Slavery as Salvation* (New Haven, CT: Yale, 1990), pp.xiix and 63–5; Scott Bartchy, Μᾶλλον Χρῆσαι: *First Century Slavery and the Interpretation of 1 Cor. 7:21* (Missoula, MT: Scholars Press, 1973, rp. 1985), pp.121–5; cf. C. Wolff, *Der erste Brief*, pp.131–2; I.A.H. Combes, *The Metaphor of Slavery in the Writings of the Early Church* (Sheffield: Sheffield Academic Press, 1998), pp.77–94; and Thiselton, *First Epistle*, pp.475–9.

[28] N. Wolterstorff, *Divine Discourse*, pp.38–42.

Hence the very speaking of "given", "revealed", or "authentic" utterances (both the *kyrios* confession in 12:3 and gifts relating to speech in 12:8–10) constitute examples of "double-agency". Although a Christian believer utters the words in the public world, the utterances are counterparts to what the Holy Spirit utters and inspires. Thereby *the believer becomes taken up into a divine intra-Trinitarian discourse* (in accordance with Wolterstorff's title, *Divine Discourse*).

This is no mere speculative philosophy of language or exegesis. It coheres with Paul's analysis of the dynamics of divine and human speech in Romans 8:26: the Spirit *takes part with, comes to the aid of* (συναντιλαμβάνεται) believers at the point of their weakness, since how or what they ought to pray, τὸ γὰρ τί προσευξώμεθα καθὸ δεῖ they do not know, ἀλλὰ αὐτὸ τὸ πνεῦμα ὑπερεντυγχάνει ... , that is, the Spirit himself intercedes with sighs too deep for words (ἀλαλήτοις). Whatever the mistakes and inadequacies of his *Kyrios Christos* in terms of his theories about Hellenism, Bousset rightly relates 1 Cor. 12:3 to "outcries of prayer, sighs of the ... overflowing heart which in worship were addressed to Jesus ... yearning for the Lord".[29] This is not to disengage the criteriological dimension from the cognitive truth-claims of a shared pre-Pauline tradition, since multi-dimensional functions are frequently performed by a single speech-act utterance which "counts as" further linguistic actions of differing force and roles.[30]

This establishes fundamental logical and rhetorical links and presuppositions which are fundamental for our understanding of such spiritual gifts as prophetic discourse or discourse of wisdom, which still reflect this Lordship, and especially to glossolalia, which G. Theissen and the Pentecostalist writer F.D. Macchia relate to "sighs too deep for words".

III
Are Translations of "Gifts of the Spirit" in 12:8–10 Too Value-Laden?
How Open-Ended and Context-Dependent is the Greek?

We proceed next to proposals about the meaning and translations of the Greek words that denote what "God bestows through the Spirit" (v. 8a) in 12:8–10, and the differentiating gifts that within their unity, reciprocity and mutuality constitute features of the limbs or organs of Christ's body, the church in 12:28–30. Speech-act theory contributes to this, if only in a subsidiary fashion, not least in the case of prophetic discourse. For even if the appeal to the so-called *oracular* nature of prophecy carried necessary weight, the use of this argument to suggest that prophecy in the New Testament epistles is typically "spontaneous" rather than "given" by the Spirit through processes of wise habituated judgement and reflection is *to confuse "oracle" (with a supposed instantaneous temporality) with a declarative, directive, or verdictive illocutionary or sometimes perlocutionary speech-act*. Such speech-acts generally, although not invariably, operate within an institutional context, and often, although not always, presuppose some reflection or prepared readiness.

---

[29] W. Bousset, *Kyrios Christos* (Eng., Nashville, TN: Abingdon, 1970), p.133.

[30] On the relation to tradition and truth, cf. A. Eriksson, *Traditions as Rhetorical Proof. Pauline Argumentation in 1 Corinthians* (Stockholm: Almqvist & Wiksell, 1998), pp.111–14 and 217–22.

We translate 12:8–10 into modern English: "To one person, on his or her part, God bestows through the Spirit articulate utterance relating to 'wisdom'; to another, in accordance with the same Spirit, discourse relating to 'knowledge'. To a different person faith by the same Spirit; to another gifts for various kinds of healing by the one Spirit; to another, effective deeds of power; to another, prophecy; to another, discernment of what is 'of the Spirit'; to another, species of tongues; and to another, intelligible articulation of what is spoken in tongues."

In contrast to the understandings of "word of wisdom", "word of knowledge", in various popular church circles, it is inconceivable that Paul switches to a use of σοφία and γνῶσις that bears no relation at all to his earlier prolonged redefinition of these terms as Corinthian catchwords or slogans. σοφία was clearly a catchword at Corinth (cf. 1:17, 19, 20, 21, 22, 24, 30; 2:1, 4, 5, 6, 7, 13; 3:19 et al.) that is, sixteen uses in our epistle in contrast to only two further uses in the four major epistles of comparable date (Rom. 11:33; 2 Cor. 1:12).[31] Virtually all others occur in Colossians and Ephesians. Hence we place the English within quotation marks: "wisdom". Whereas the Corinthians tend to claim "wisdom" as "higher" esoteric insight, Paul *redefines* wisdom in terms of a Christocentric proclamation of the gospel centred on the cross. To assume that a "word of wisdom" transmits "horizontal" messages to specific individuals would presuppose a *more individualistic and less cross-centred* use than Paul has hitherto employed as his. The suggestion that it relates to "God's plan of salvation" and its careful, appropriate, effective communication coheres with the comments of Schatzmann, Kistemaker and Schrage: in 1 Cor. 1–3, "Paul identified the wisdom from God with God's saving deed in the crucified Christ, particularly in the proclamation of the saving event."[32]

It is axiomatic that λόγος has an infinitely wider and more varied semantic range than English *word*. The disastrous link with the colloquial idiom of "having a word with someone" distorts the received understanding. *Word* should be avoided as a translation. In its major use in 1 Cor. 1:18, ὁ λόγος ὁ τοῦ σταυροῦ denotes the [sustained and articulate] proclamation of the cross, that is, the gospel's proclaimed *kerygma*. However, a *corporate application* of a Christ-centred and cross-centred gospel that *builds up the Christian community as a whole* coheres equally with 2:6–16. This culminates in a reference to a Christ-like mind-set whether or not Paul is requoting Corinthian phrases here in a readjusted context which recognizes the transcendent Otherness of the Holy Spirit (2:10–14; cf. 12:7).

Not least because of limits of time for this paper, together with the availability of more detailed comments in my commentary, we cannot delay unduly on "discourse relating to knowledge". γνῶσις (8:1, 7, 10, 11; also 1:5; 13:2, 8; 14:6) is even more clearly a Corinthian catchphrase which firmly qualifies and redefines by limiting its constructive currency to its co-joint function with love and concern for "the other". It is reasonable to assume that discourse inspired by the Holy Spirit that draws upon "knowledge" will carry with it this

---

[31] See especially S.M. Pogoloff, *Logos and Sophia: The Rhetorical Situation of I Corinthians* (Atlanta, GA: Scholars Press, 1992); and J.A. Davies, *Wisdom and Spirit* [on 1:18–3:20] (Lanham, MD: University Press of America, 1984).

[32] S. Schatzmann, *A Pauline Theology of the Charismata* (Peabody, MA: Hendrickson, 1987), p.36; W. Schrage, *Der erste Brief*, III, p.149; and Kistemaker, *I Cor.*, p.421.

practical respect for the other, and will reflect Paul's earlier discussion of γνῶσις. A wealth of both Patristic and modern exegesis does not yield convincing criteria for differentiating the two gifts clearly, other than in terms of their contextual backgrounds. Augustine insists that both phrases "concern the believer's relationship to Christ, activated through the Spirit".[33]

Although the issue of "spontaneity" more widely relates to prophetic speech, many, including James Dunn, argue that the Spirit inspires such an utterance "only in the act and moment of uttering it".[34] However, Dunn's main concern is less with temporal fleetingness than with the false triumphalism that treats the charisma as "mine": "The charisma of God is no possession of man to be used at his will."[35] Dunn identifies one side of a danger. However, the *undervaluing of sustained reflection, pastoral or spiritual training, character formation and habituated judgement as no less a charisma of the Holy Spirit must be accorded no less emphasis. Some* of these gifts are *sometimes* "spontaneous", but it is simply false to assert that *all* are *always* spontaneous. Senft, for example, views the discourses relating to wisdom and knowledge as "gifts of *theological reflection*".[36] In the context of pastoral care we cannot exclude this *a priori*, while Banks' proposal that they denote the capacity to expound the Old Testament correctly invites respect and careful study.[37]

Prophetic discourse is fundamentally defined in terms of its function to build the community (14:3, 4, 5, 12, 17, 26; cf. 3:10, 12, 14). Kitzberger rightly explicates the key semantic opposition between *building* (οἰκοδομέω) and *self-inflation* or inflating others' self-esteem (φυσιόω).[38] Vielhauer, we noted, also argued that building up (only) the self amounted to self-induced spiritual inflation (see above). Further, however, prophetic speech encourages, exhorts and challenges (παρακαλέω, παράκλησις), an activity that the Fourth Gospel ascribes directly to the work of the Holy Spirit as Paraclete. David Aune is right to urge that we cannot identify prophecy in the NT in term of any specific "form", and that the role of the prophet in the OT and Judaism should be kept in mind.[39] Is prophetic discourse clearly different from applied pastoral preaching of the gospel message?

Dunn insists, "It is a spontaneous utterance ... (14:30)".[40] Turner declares, "For Paul, prophecy is the reception and subsequent communication of spontaneous, divinely given *apokalupsis*."[41] Forbes agrees that it is the "public declaration of spontaneous, (usually) verbal, revelation".[42] Forbes even claims that it is not *preaching*, for Paul "nowhere calls preaching a *charisma*".[43] This is an assertion of dubious significance if (as is generally

---

33 Augustine, *On the Trinity* 13:(19), 24; cf. para 22 and 25.
34 J.D.G. Dunn, *Jesus and the Spirit* (London: SCM, 1975), p.221.
35 Ibid.; see also Dunn, *Theology of Paul* (Edinburgh: T. & T. Clark, 1998), pp.555–61.
36 C. Senft, *Première Épitre*, p.158.
37 R. Banks, *Paul's Idea of Community* (Peabody, MA: Hendrickson, rev. edn, 1994), p.96.
38 I. Kitzberger, *Bau der Gemeinde: Das paulinische Wortfeld oikodomï* (Würzberg: Echter Verlag, 1986).
39 D. Aune, *Prophecy in Early Christianity* (Grand Rapids, MI: Eerdmans, 1983), p.195.
40 Dunn, *Jesus and the Spirit*, p.228 (although in part modified in his *Theology of Paul*, 1998).
41 M. Turner, "Spiritual Gifts Then and Now", *Vox Evangelica* 15, 1985, p.10; and further, *The Holy Spirit and Spiritual Gifts Then and Now* (Carlisle: Paternoster, 1996).
42 C. Forbes, *Prophecy and Inspired Speech in Early Christianity and its Hellenistic Environment* (Tübingen: Mohr, 1995), pp.229 and 236.
43 Ibid., p.229.

agreed) the listing of *charismata* in the NT is not exhaustive. In fact, Paul applies the word *charisma*, that which God has freely given "without strings", to activities and dispositions which cannot logically by definition be "spontaneous", unless our translation and exegesis where these occur are wildly wrong. In 7:7 Paul uses χάρισμα ἐκ θεοῦ to denote the *"given" sustained attitude which enables him to live the celibate unmarried life without frustration*. In 12:28 the *gift of teaching* (parallel in syntax with *prophecy*, and with χαρίσματα in v. 29) presupposes *habits* of sustained study and communication, and *processes* of growing understanding.

Since χαρίσματα ἰαμάτων presents a plural which is probably generic (γένη γλωσσῶν, 12:10), even such Pentecostal writers as Donald Gee acknowledge that these should "not preclude ... the merciful and manifold work of medical healing", which even in the pre-modern era of Galen and Luke presupposed a measure of training.[44] Bengel urged that to include the miraculous is not to exclude *naturalia remedia*.[45]

The charisma of κυβερνήσις may very broadly denote *forms of leadership* (NRSV; cf. AV/KJV, RV, *governments*), but for a maritime port such as Corinth the notion of *pilot* or *steersman* would most readily spring to mind, as Paul (who lived there for some eighteen months) would well know. In our view the appeal to ability to "steer the ship" denotes the gift of formulating church strategy; of *steering* the community forward in the right direction. Similarly in a culture of managerial enterprise, where ventures would soon require business infrastructure, ἀντιλήμψεις is likely to denote kinds of *administrative support*.[46] Administration cannot be done "spontaneously", but requires sustained reflection and attention to detail, planning, priorities, and consequences. Even if, however, we return to NRSV's *forms of leadership*, this gift is not received and used overnight, but presupposes a process of maturity of character, judgement and spiritual stature.

In the case of *prophetic speech*, an exegesis which urges "spontaneity" on the basis of 14:30 remains flawed.[47] It is not that the Spirit becomes wearied with agent A and "falls upon" agent B. This would be closer to the mood of the early pre-canonical prophets from whom the eighth and seventh-century OT prophets seek to disengage themselves. Such a view presupposes the individualism and *deus ex machina* view of modernity that, ironically, is often imposed upon Paul by the very pietist traditions that reject secular Enlightenment modernity and rationalism. But unlike Enlightenment modernity, Paul's interest is centred on *God's creative sovereign agency as such*, without categorizing it as "inside" or "outside" the causal nexus or cause-effect processes of "nature". Wayne Grudem is commendably cautious about the use of the term "supernatural", without losing or diminishing any emphasis upon sovereign divine agency and human reflection or self-control.[48]

---

[44]   D. Gee, *Spiritual Gifts in the Work of the Ministry Today* (Springfield, MO: Gospel, 1963); and P.S. Brewster (ed.), *Pentecostal Doctrine* (Cheltenham: Brewster, 1976), pp.47–62.

[45]   J.A. Bengel, *Gnomon Novi Testamenti* (Stuttgart: Steinkopf, 1866 [1773]), p.652.

[46]   In more detail, Thiselton, *First Epistle*, pp.1019–22, and "Introduction", pp.1–29.

[47]   Cf. U.B. Müller, *Prophetie und Predigt*, esp. p.14.

[48]   W. Grudem, *The Gift of Prophecy in I Corinthians* (Lanham, MD: University Press of America, 1982), pp.136–7 and 179; cf. also *The Gift of Prophecy in the New Testament and Today* (Westminster, IL: Crossway, 1988).

An unexpected and unlikely alliance of interest sometimes emerges between those who defend "spontaneity" here and those who supposedly perceive "oracular" prophetic pronouncements in the sayings of Jesus behind, or within, form-critical reconstructions of Jesus-traditions. To state that prophecy was stereotypically oracular speech may sometimes apply to a particular category of prophecy, but does it apply to all forms? This offers only one sub-category. David Hill argues that even if the Corinthians themselves identified "prophecy" with "a series of short-ejaculatory words of revelation", Paul seeks to correct this.[49] In my commentary in extended Notes I have explained why I follow David Hill, U.B. Müller, and T.W. Gillespie (in part also Grudem) in understanding *prophetic discourse as reflective and applied pastoral preaching*.[50]

Whether prophets sometimes spoke a few words, or whether at other times they gave a homily comparable in form (though not in content) with the synagogue homilies known to Paul and to a number of Christians at Corinth cannot be more than speculation. We do know that unlike most modern preaching it was clearly "tested". However, *prophetic* proclamation applies to practical living and conduct and is self-involving. Hence prophecy, in a Pauline sense, often functions as *declarative, verdictive, or directive speech-acts*. Such terminology would be far more accurate and constructive, and less misleading as a designation, than to speak of so-called "oracular" pronouncements, let alone always in unprepared, ejaculatory, "messages" to individuals. Argument, applicatory or hermeneutical understanding, and practical exposition of Scripture, would more typically reflect Paul's own communicative strategy.[51]

IV
Translation of γένη γλωσσῶν (12:10) and Some Related Issues

Some residual issues of meaning and translation remain to be addressed, albeit in brief summary. *Species of tongues* (12:10) may denote more than one single phenomenon. Surprisingly many simply ignore γένη. Unlike the modern practice of presupposing that these represent a coded message *from* God awaiting "interpretation", Paul explicitly states that ὁ λαλῶν γλώσσῃ οὐκ ἀνθρώποις λαλεῖ ἀλλὰ θεῷ (14:2). No amount of gloss that this denotes only "uninterpreted" tongues can avoid the double assertion, "*not to people, but to God*". All γένη seem to fall into this category, at least in the Corinthian epistles. Paul speaks primarily of prayer, praise, yearning, doxology, indeed of the "sighs too deep for words" inspired by the agency of the Holy Spirit in Rom. 8:26. This entirely accords with Bousset's observations about the confessional acclamation "Jesus is Lord", which now becomes transparent as a constitutive criteriological authentication concerning "what comes from the Spirit". Practical Christomorphic life-style and a heart which cries to Jesus as Lord from its deepest recesses of yearning in forms or modes yet

---

49 D. Hill, *New Testament Prophecy* (London: Marshall, 1979), p.123.
50 U.B. Müller, *Prophetie und Predigt im N.T.* (Gütersloh: Mohn, 1975); D. Hill, *New Testament Prophecy*; and T.W. Gillespie, *The First Theologians: A Study in Early Christian Prophecy* (Grand Rapids, MI: Eerdmans, 1994), esp. pp.23–32 and 97–164.
51 Cf. Anders Eriksson, *Traditions as Rhetorical Proof*, throughout.

pre-conceptual and barely conscious play a part in affirming the genuineness of what is from the Spirit, especially when many merely *say* that they have γνῶσις and are πνευματικός, a *spiritual person*.

I have argued in detail that other theories of glossolalia carry far less conviction in the light of sheer exegetical evidence. In particular I discuss in my commentary: (1) tongues as "angelic speech" (Ellis and Dautzenberg); (2) tongues as miraculous power to speak foreign languages (Gundry and Forbes); (3) tongues as rhythmic or archaic liturgical speech (Bleek and Heinrici); and (4) tongues as "ecstatic" speech (Kleinknecht and Currie, modified by Boring and Johnson).[52]

By contrast, the approach to Paul's understanding of *the heart* as the seat of hidden, unconscious yearnings, longings, drives and desires (including, under the Spirit, a desire for God as worthy of honour or praise) carries conviction. Theissen, most of all, shows how it resonates with the notion of a glorious release of inhibitions imposed by the conscious mind, but thereby it accounts for Paul's insistence that it belongs to the *private* sphere.[53] Theissen writes, "Glossolalia is language of the unconscious – language capable of consciousness."[54] Like laughter or tears, it expresses what transcends words, but is potentially anti-social and distracting in ordered public worship, especially if it makes fellow-believers feel like strangers in an exotic land to which they do not belong (14:1–4, 11–25, cf. Βάρβαρος (11), ἑτερογλώσσοις ... σημεῖον ... τοῖς ἀπίστοις (v. 22) since Paul cites the Isaiah passage concerning exile as aliens in a strange land because of unbelief). Are believers to be allowed to feel "not *at home*"?

Against this background it is easy to see why Paul requires those to whom God has given this gift of longings and sighing which bubble up from the depths of the heart and evade the censor should pray for the further *charisma* of being able to put into words (14:13) what has welled up in the glossolalia. The Greek here contains no τις: there is no second person who "interprets" some coded "message" which has bypassed the mind of the first.[55] Just as the Holy Spirit has bestowed a gift of release, so the Spirit can grant the further gift that these pre-cognitive yearnings be transformed into an articulate doxological paean of praise that celebrates Christ's Lordship and builds up of the whole church.

The phrases of chapter 13 echo this situation. Loud cries or sighs which are unintelligible are obtrusive; if the one who speaks in tongues imagines that they sound "angelic", they are more like resonating jars (Harris) or *acoustic resonators* designed to increase decibels but without pitch or melody (χαλκὸς ἠχῶν, 13:1).[56] They make a sound like a κύμβαλον ἀλαλάζον, a cymbal or crotal which resonates without specific pitch (13:1). Genuine love for "the other" will wait patiently (13:4) to see whether the Spirit will give the gift of articulation or of prophecy, or will defer to another's prophetic discourse

---

[52] Thiselton, *First Epistle*, pp.970–89; cf. 1094–130.

[53] G. Theissen, *Psychological Aspects of Pauline Theology* (Eng., Edinburgh: T. & T. Clark, 1987), pp.59–95 and 271–342.

[54] Theissen, *Psychological Aspects*, p.306; cf. 312–13.

[55] Thiselton, "The 'Interpretation' of Tongues? ...", *Journal of Theological Sudies* 30, 1979, 15–36, included in this volume as Essay 16.

[56] W. Harris, "Sounding Brass and Hellenistic Technology", in *Biblical Archaeologist Reader* 8 (1982), pp.38–41.

(μακροθυμέω, 13:4). Love will show kindness (χρηστεύεται) to the other (13:4); will not seek to brag or become inflated with self-importance when a χάρισμα is received, nor will it have burning envy for the gifts of others (οὐ ζηλοῖ ... οὐ περπερεύεται, οὐ φυσιοῦται, v. 4). It is not ill-mannered (οὐκ ἀσχημονεῖ, v. 5).

Finally, amidst all this material on criteria and self-knowledge we cannot translate ἀγάπη ... πάντα πιστεύει (v. 7) as Love ... believes all things (NRSV) or even as "love ... always trusts" (NIV), while always ready ... to trust (NJB) goes beyond the Greek to solve this genuine difficulty. As Eriksson and Moores show in other contexts, Paul's logic is capable of sophistication and rigour. His purpose is to negate a logic of exclusion, although he uses a shorthand, "sense" construction.[57] We translate: love never loses faith. Smit is right about the rhetorical unity of chapters 12–14. Paul goes on wrestling with the theological, pastoral and socio-ethical problems at Corinth because love never tires of support, never loses faith, never exhausts hope, never gives up (13:7).

---

[57] Thiselton, First Epistle, pp.1056–60.

CHAPTER TWENTY-ONE

The Hermeneutics of Pastoral Theology: Ten Strategies for Reading Texts in Relation to Varied Reading-Situations (Excerpts, 1992, with new material)

This essay is the longest in the collection because it illustrates in practice the wide plurality of hermeneutical models and strategies that fit specific reading situations. In other words it explores the match between types of texts, the goals of readers or interpreters, and appropriate hermeneutical resources. Some approach biblical texts as enquirers; others may exemplify a model of "believing" reading, in which they perceive a personal stake; others may remain immune to the impact or meaning of a text unless existential shock or the seduction of a transforming narrative "world" operates. Further, strategies for reading didactic texts, reading poetic or symbolic texts, reading parables, or reading different types of narrative can and do vary. "Hermeneutics" is no one single thing, but a vast variety of interpretative strategies, each of which depends for its value and effectiveness on the nature of the text and the varied goals and situations of readers. Each strategy has its strengths and each has its limitations.

This wide-ranging critical discussion also focuses upon the relation between biblical hermeneutics and pastoral theology. It includes constructive and critical observations about the latter. In particular it criticizes according undue privilege to "present relevance" where this is at the expense of due respect for the past, for texts, or for future promise. I present ten models of possible relations between interpretations of biblical texts and pastoral situations, of which the narrative model receives four further subdivisions.

This study broadly follows the text of chapters 15 and 16 of New Horizons in Hermeneutics *(London: HarperCollins also rp. Carlisle: Paternoster and Grand Rapids, MI: Zondervan, 1992), but I have abbreviated an original text of around 30,000 words to 19,000 words, with some inevitable editorial adjustments and minor revisions for easier reading. The last few paragraphs appear in Essay 42.*

Introduction: the Contingency and Particularity of Pastoral Theology and of Reading-Situations

Biblical interpretation and pastoral theology both address issues of *contingency and particularity* as well as questions about theological coherence. Both are concerned with *life-worlds, situations and horizons.* Paul Ballard observes, "Pastoral theology is reflection on the pastoral situation. The pastoral situation is by definition *particular in time and space.*"[1] Don

---

[1] Paul H. Ballard, "Pastoral Theology as Theology of Reconciliation", *Theology* 91 (1988), p.375 (my italics); cf. 375–80.

Browning notes that pastoral theology is informed by an ethical vision, but "mediated to individuals and groups in all their situational, existential, and developmental *particularity*".[2] Similar language could be found in David Tracy, Edward Farley and Thomas Groome.[3] Browning also observes that these contingent particularities become more diverse in the light of today's pluralism. Pastoral theology, he urges, addresses "the *diversity* found in the public world outside the church" as well as "*diverse* publics within specific churches".[4]

A *prima facie* case exists, then, for claiming that the task of hermeneutical understanding, in contrast to that of scientific, generalizable, quantifiable theoretical explanation, embraces pastoral theology as well as biblical studies. If the particularities of the "first" horizon of the biblical text provide a primary focus for biblical specialists, the particularities of the "second" horizon of present situations and readers offer a primary focus for pastoral specialists. But this raises a difficulty. As Edward Farley and others point out, such an assignment of professional sub-disciplines within theology splits apart and fragments a single hermeneutical task. The practical character of theology as "*habitus*", or as wisdom-based action, he argues, "appear(s) to be defeated from the start by the dispersion of theology into independent areas of scholarship".[5]

The criticism that is addressed to many biblical specialists on the basis of this artificial division of labour is predictable. Biblical scholars who concentrate on the historical aspects of their task are accused of becoming locked up into the past. In the first quarter of the twentieth century, Karl Barth and Rudolf Bultmann raised powerful voices of protest against the limitations of a merely historical "liberal" exegesis which left the task of biblical interpretation only half done. Robert Morgan, as we have noted, renews the protest against a slippage that moves from using *historical method as part of a larger hermeneutical task* to substituting a *historical aim as the goal of hermeneutics*. This reduces biblical texts to the status of instrumental "sources" for historical reconstruction.[6] This protest about using texts simply as "sources" reflects Bultmann's point in his *Theology of the New Testament*, except that Bultmann's interests are more narrowly kerygmatic, while Morgan addresses a wider pluralism.

By the same token, however, a less familiar but *by no means less important mirror-image argument can be put forward about pastoral theology*. Might it be that many pastoral theologians, by concentrating on the segment of the process that concerns the *present*, have fallen into *the very same trap of objectifying pastoral phenomena in ways that give privilege to the present as over against the biblical text?* Just as some biblical specialists ignore the meaning-*effects* of texts for present situations, might it not also be the case that some pastoral theologians tend to ignore historical factors that relativize present criteria of

---

[2] Don S. Browning, "Pastoral Theology in a Pluralist Age", in Don S. Browning (ed.), op. cit., p.187 (my italics); cf. 187–202.

[3] Edward Farley, "Theology and Practice Outside the Clerical Paradigm", in Don S. Browning (ed.), *Practical Theology* (San Francisco, CA: Harper & Row, 1983), pp.21–41; David Tracy, "The Foundations of Practical Theology", ibid., pp.61–82; and Thomas H. Groome, *Christian Religious Education. Sharing our Story and Vision* (San Francisco, CA: Harper & Row, 1980).

[4] Don S. Browning, *Religious Ethics and Pastoral Care* (Philadelphia, PA: Fortress, 1983), p.17.

[5] Edward Farley, "Theology and Practice Outside the Clerical Paradigm", loc. cit., pp. 23 and 30.

[6] Robert Morgan (with John Barton), *Biblical Interpretation* (Oxford: OUP, 1988), p.287.

relevance, as if these were not in process of *shifting and undergoing transformation through encounter with biblical texts and with Christian traditions?*

I am extremely cautious about George Lindbeck's tendency to locate the meaning of biblical texts in intralinguistic or "intratextual" categories to the exclusion of presuppositional and extra-linguistic contextual factors about states of affairs in the world. But on the issue of what he calls "the direction of interpretation" Lindbeck's work serves to question this tendency to give privilege to the present in a necessary way. He writes, "It is the religion instantiated in Scripture which defines being, truth, goodness, and beauty, and the non-scriptural exemplifications of these realities need to be transformed into figures (or types or antitypes) of the scriptural framework ... It is the text, so to speak, which absorbs the world, rather than the world the text."[7] Lindbeck cites the example of the relation between the cross and human suffering. It is inadequate, he argues, to objectify present suffering and then to see the cross as a figurative representation of it; rather, the cross addresses present suffering *in ways that transform it into cruciform suffering.*

Even Lindbeck, however, tends to do less than justice to the particularities of different biblical horizons and types of texts, speaking too often only about biblical texts-in-general. But the flow of interpretation between the horizons of biblical texts and the horizons of pastoral situations assumes different forms and different functions as the two sets of *particularities* change. One reason why so many books on hermeneutics remain unsatisfying is that generalization too often either restricts work to theory alone or becomes trivial because it articulates only what can be universally observed about general patterns. But didactic texts, narrative texts, poetic texts, boundary-situation texts, apocalyptic texts, promissory texts and so forth, perform *different, though often overlapping, hermeneutical functions, especially in relation to different reading-situations.*

In the review of models and resources set out below, an attempt is made for the equal benefit of biblical interpretation and of pastoral theology to outline the diversity of some of the models which we have already discussed, and *to propose paradigmatic or optimal reader-situations in relation to which their most distinctive hermeneutical functions most readily become apparent.* Our discussions of socio-pragmatic and metacritical hermeneutics signal our awareness of the complexity of speaking of "optimal" reader-situations: the discussion must first be allowed to stand on its own feet and to speak for itself before we refer back to this.

In the case of the first three models some further theoretical issues also need brief consideration. For certain residual theoretical issues which we have not yet fully explored come to a head in the present context of discussion. Misunderstandings still initiate appeals to the theoretical model of *reconstruction,* and especially to the role played by *"author's intention"* in related approaches. It is a mistake, however, either to construe "intention" as a matter of "having certain mental processes" which can usually be observed only by introspection, or of assigning the *same role* to intention in different kinds of texts. We begin, then, by drawing some *points of contrast* between *particular examples* of

---

7   G. Lindbeck, *The Nature of Doctrine. Religion and Doctrine in a Postliberal Age* (London: SPCK, 1984), p.118.

biblical texts and of reading situations which invite the use of a *reconstructionist* model as a resource, and a different type of biblical text and reading-situation which invites, by contrast, the use of an *existentialist* model.

I

Life-Worlds, Intentional Directedness, and Enquiring Reading in Reconstructionist Models: A Clarification of "Author's Intention"

The *hermeneutics of understanding*, developed by Schleiermacher, Dilthey and Betti, entail *much more than historical reconstruction*. In pastoral terms, the emphasis placed by Schleiermacher on what he called the "feminine" quality of creative immediacy of understanding, by Dilthey on imaginative empathy and rapport, and by Betti on openness, listening, patience and respect for "the other", describe qualities which relate as closely to pastoral sensitivity towards persons as to the understanding of biblical texts. For these theorists it would be wide of the mark to associate "listening skills" exclusively with pastoral theology and comparative, critical "objective" distance with historical biblical studies. Interpersonal understanding embraces understanding the processes that lie behind production of communicative language as a means of understanding persons. But understanding remains a single, complex, interactive process, in which the interpreter's own developing understanding undergoes constant revision, modification and correction.

The work of Schleiermacher and of Dilthey often suffers unfair criticism on the ground that it is impossible "to step into someone else's shoes" or "to think his or her thoughts"; still less, to reconstruct that person's *intentions*. Further, I have argued that Schleiermacher's close attention to language as both system (cf. Saussure's *langue*) and as temporal speech-act or event (cf. Saussure's *parole*), together with other careful qualifications which are very often overlooked, does not compel us to tie Schleiermacher's hermeneutics with "psychologizing" notions of intentionality, as if to imply that these represent mental processes to be observed by introspection.[8] It is possible to accept Bauman's antithetical polarity between "thinking the thoughts of others" and "sharing in a form of life" *only* if we interpret the former in a psychologistic rather than linguistic-interactive way.[9] Schleiermacher and Dilthey saw *flow-of-life* (cf. Wittgenstein's term "stream of life") as a hermeneutical key, and to "re-live" the life-experiences that led to the production of the text was for them to reconstruct its life-world and to seek to enter it by sharing in its form (cf. Wittgenstein's "form-of-life").

This angle of approach helps us to see *why in the case of many biblical texts* (not all) *it is necessary to include the work of historical reconstruction*. This has nothing *directly* to do with allegedly falling prey to the genetic fallacy: Schleiermacher does not imagine that enquiries about antiquarian *origins as such* provide answers to all hermeneutical questions. His *reason* for historical enquiry arises from the task of determining the *life-*

---

8   Thiselton, *New Horizons in Hermeneutics*, chapter 6.
9   Zygmunt Bauman, *Hermeneutics and Social Science* (London: Hutchinson, 1978), p.217.

world in relation to which the text draws its currency. It is closely parallel to Searle's technical notion of "Background", which, in Searle's terminology is "pre-intentional ... a set of pre-conditions of Intentionality ... the biological and cultural resources that I must bring to bear on this task".[10] Searle insists that situational Background has nothing directly to do with mental states; it concerns *pre-conditions* (cf. Schleiermacher's pre-understanding) for meaning. It is against the *Background*, Searle observes, that "I can intend to peel an orange, but I cannot in that way intend to peel a rock or a car."[11] As Wittgenstein observes in his *Zettel*, often the grammar of meaning is "embedded in a situation from which it takes its rise".[12] It operates "under particular circumstances ... Only in the stream of thought and life do words have meaning."[13]

Explicitly for Wittgenstein and for Searle, and implicitly for Schleiermacher, "to intend" a linguistic meaning is emphatically *not to perform some action or process separable from the linguistic act or process itself.* It is not, in this sense, an *"act"* at all. Wittgenstein points out that the imperative: "Intend to ..." would be as far-fetched as the imperative, "Laugh heartily at this joke."[14] *Intention is better understood adverbially: to write with an intention is to write in a way that is directed towards a goal.* Searle identifies a linguistic category within which the criterion of intention, far from involving psychological hypotheses, coincides precisely with the criterion used for effective performative force. In expressive illocutions, such as, "I apologize ...", "I congratulate ...", and "I thank ..." the *directedness* of the utterance is *internal to its meaning and force.*[15] No one could imagine that some second shadow-process called intention was involved; but nor could it be denied that as illocutions these embody intentions of writers or of speakers. But why should this understanding of intention be restricted to this paradigm only?

We may summarize a defence of the model used in the hermeneutics of understanding, then, and its traditional role in biblical studies, by calling attention to four theoretical features.

1   In many cases (not necessarily all) a *reconstruction of the stream of life, life-world, or extra-linguistic context which surrounds a text* is indispensable to understanding its meaning. *This is not a "genetic" fallacy.*

2   It is *inaccurate and misleading to associate historical reconstruction with a restriction of method to scientific positivism or rationalism.* Schleiermacher, Dilthey, and Betti disclaim the adequacy of purely rationalist enquiry. Dilthey's paradigm of *life* had little to do with Descartes' scientific model of mathematics. Indeed Dilthey argued that in Locke's subject "no real blood flowed".

3   *Many* (not all) *biblical texts address a directed goal* that may rightly be identified as its author's intention, provided that intention is understood only "adverbially". This is *not an example of the "intentional fallacy".* A mistakenly psychologistic dimension is

---

10   John R. Searle, *Intentionality*, p.143.
11   Ibid., p.144.
12   L. Wittgenstein, *Zettel*, sects 67 and 116.
13   Ibid., sect. 173.
14   Ibid., sect. 51.
15   John R. Searle, *Intentionality*, p.173; cf. 166–76.

avoided if we follow Leith and Myerson in seeing as a feature of the category of texts under discussion "some feeling of *address* towards another ...".[16]

4   It is a common mistake to claim that Schleiermacher gives priority to *authors over texts*. We quoted Schleiermacher's words from his *Compendium* of 1819, confirmed by his marginal notes of 1828, that "to understand what is said in the context of the language with its possibilities" [cf. the semiotic system] and the communicative act "in the thinking of the speaker" [cf. *parole* as communication of the author's thought] constitute "*two hermeneutical tasks* [which] *are completely equal*".[17] Well ahead of his time, Schleiermacher perceived that which of these two axes received primary emphasis remained a *matter of interpretative strategy*.

As a footnote for pastoral theology we may also note that Dilthey's struggle over the hermeneutical relation between the general and the particular lay behind his articulation of "re-discovering the 'you' in the 'me'", and of "putting myself in your place".[18] On the one hand it remains a principle of pastoral theology and indeed of Christian love that one should try to put oneself into someone else's place, whether one seeks simply to understand, or to "do to others what you would have them do to you" (Matt. 7:12). On the other hand, to measure others by our own feelings, experiences, norms and life-world may fail to take adequate account of *differences as well as similarities* between others and ourselves. For Emilio Betti these differences are what lead to a call for openness, patience, tolerance and respect for the other.

This model operates characteristically in cases in which biblical texts serve primarily as *transmissive and communicative vehicles to express the thought of an author towards a given directedness* (though Schleiermacher's Romanticist emphasis on imagination has relevance to "open" or to "productive" literary biblical texts). Paul's pastoral and didactic responses to issues about the Lord's Supper (1 Cor. 11:17–22), food offered to idols (1 Cor. 8:1–11:1), gifts of the Spirit (1 Cor. 12:1–14:40) provide classic examples of communicative texts, even if more "open" or "productive" texts (for example, 1 Cor. 13) form part of the extended discourse. Jerome Murphy O'Connor's use of archaeological research together with the kind of socio-historical reconstruction undertaken by Gerd Theissen and contributions such as those of J.C. Hurd, R.A. Horsley and Peter Marshall, shed light especially on the meaning of such texts.[19]

---

16   Dick Leith and George Myerson, op. cit., p.170.
17   F.D.E. Schleiermacher, *Hermeneutics: The Handwritten Manuscripts*, pp.98–9.
18   W. Dilthey, op. cit., pp.7, 191.
19   Mostly cited above; cf. especially J. Murphy-O'Connor, *St Paul's Corinth* (1983); and "Food and Spiritual Gifts in 1 Cor. 8:8", *Catholic Biblical Quarterly* 41 (1979), pp.292–8, and "Freedom or the Ghetto (1 Cor. VIII.1–13, X.23–XI.1)", *Revue Biblique* 85 (1978), pp.543–74; R.A. Horsley, "Consciousness and Freedom among the Corinthians: 1 Cor. 8–10", *Catholic Biblical Quarterly* 40 (1978), pp.574-89; and G. Theissen, *The Social Setting of Pauline Christianity: Essays on Corinth* (Eng., 1982).

II
Second Model: Disruptions of Passive Reading in Existentialist Interpretation

Our arguments concerning existential hermeneutics have often reflected our concern to demonstrate its *limitations*.[20] We alluded to the values and limits of the model with particular reference to early New Testament confessions of Christ as Lord (1 Cor. 12:3). The cash-currency of such confessions can be seen in existential attitudes of surrender, obedience, reverence and devotion. To confess Christ as Lord, as Bultmann rightly observes, is to let the care of oneself go, to place oneself entirely in the sovereign hands of the one who is "Lord": "If we live, we live to the Lord; and if we die, we die to the Lord ..." (Rom. 14:7). Yet, as speech-act models show so clearly, the self-involving dimensions of direction and commitment depend on a certain state of affairs, namely that God has appointed or declared Christ Lord in the resurrection (Rom. 1:3, 4). In this respect Christ is Lord, irrespective of our human response.

Nevertheless existentialist hermeneutics reflect far more than a dimension of practical human will and language-effect. If we go back to Kierkegaard, existential critique entails above all *a discontinuity and description of communal habituations of meanings* that depend on convention. *These models speak especially to those situations that Karl Jaspers identified as boundary situations.* In this respect, they do not share the social and communal perspectives of socio-pragmatic or even speech-act models. Understanding in the genuinely existentialist model is precisely *not* determined in terms of *the expectations of a reading community*. Equivocation and ambiguity characterizes a text, of a kind which can be resolved only by an *individual decision*. Biblical texts become *individuating* vehicles. This principle operates in the case of Bultmann's sermon on the text "Adam, where art thou?" (Gen. 3:9). Adam can no longer hide among the "trees" of anonymity and the crowd. In his sermon on Acts 17: 31, Bultmann translates universal judgement into individual existential responsibility: "Man stands before God alone ... in stark loneliness".[21]

In terms of *pastoral theology*, this existentialist model speaks not only to readers who, in situation or in personality-type, relate *more readily to doing than to reflection*, but also to those who perceive themselves *as loners or as outsiders*. On one side it is partly those for whom the *shared habits, practices and expectations of the reading-community somehow ring hollow*, for whom existential models may optimally offer a potential resource. Conversely, on the other side, if *these* readers find *affirmation* in such existentialist readings those who unthinkingly equate faith with mere *passive acceptance of the religious conventions of a particular sub-culture or group* may be roused to perceive the dimension of *individual obedient venture* in a transforming reading which gives birth to more authentic faith.

A well-known example of this model of reading biblical texts arises from Kierkegaard's struggle to come to terms with the meaning of Abraham's command to slay the son of promise (Gen. 22:1–19). Virtually the whole of his *Fear and Trembling* (1843) wrestles with this passage and *compares how it will be "understood" by different readerships*.

---

[20] See, for example, *New Horizons in Hermeneutics*, chapter VI, and *The Two Horizons* on Bultmann.
[21] Rudolf Bultmann, *This World and Beyond: Marburg Sermons* (London: Lutterworth Press, 1960), p.21.

The wider background to his approach lies in his belief that Hegel's notion of "the System" offers only an armchair spectator's approach to participatory faith and to decision. Such an approach cheapens faith, and encourages second-hand, and therefore illusory, understanding. From the viewpoint of *generality*, it remains perfectly possible to pour out speech *about* Abraham and *about* Abraham's faith; but to admire it and to praise it is not to *understand* it. In *Point of View for my Work as an Author*, Kierkegaard saw his own task as that of showing what it is to *live* the gospel, rather than to *think about* it.

Kierkegaard's narrower and more specific "pre-understanding" was shaped also by a sharpened awareness of different "levels" of interpretation, none of which can grasp the full meaning of a paradoxical phenomenon independently of other levels. His broken engagement with Regine Olsen, which Kierkegaard terminated two years before *Fear and Trembling*,brought this home to him. A merely *conventional* understanding of this broken engagement suggested that it constituted an unjustified violation of social norms, just as a *conventional* understanding of Abraham's potential act of slaying Isaac suggested the worst kind of murder. But even a trans-conventional "reading" which "suspended the ethical" in the light of the individual could still miss the heart of the paradox and thereby *hide* the truth. If Kierkegaard or if Abraham become "heroically resigned" to their sacrifice, the sharp edge of choice-in-the-face-of-paradox has been blunted. Such a reading-strategy may *conceal unworthy* motivations. Only where these various levels intersected in order to be transcended could the command to slay the son of promise be understood as inviting *an act of faith*.

Kierkegaard's model is different from Schleiermacher's. On the approach of different interpreters Kierkegaard writes with tongue-in-cheek that "if the interpreter had known Hebrew, then perhaps it might have been easy for him to understand the story of Abraham".[22] Even Isaac could not "understand" the demeanour and conduct of Abraham; while Abraham himself "left his worldly understanding behind and took with him only faith".[23] Abraham's agony lay in "disappointed expectation". Time had stretched out inordinately as he had waited for the fulfilment of the divine promise for Isaac's birth, and then abruptly he was called upon to negate the very hopes that had reversed years of hope that had been disappointed: "Now all the horrors of the struggle were to be concentrated in one moment ... 'Take now thy son, thine only son Isaac whom thou lovest ... Offer him there for a burnt offering' (Gen. 22:2) ... what *meaning* could there be in it if Isaac was to be sacrificed?"[24] Yet Abraham "believed the ridiculous ... He knew that no sacrifice was too hard when God demanded it – and he drew the knife."[25]

Understanding runs its head against the limits of the conventional community world. In terms of *pragmatic contingency*, the act of obedience destroys the possibility of blessing mediated through Abraham's line; in terms of "*universals*" it violates universal ethical principles through an act of murder. But Kierkegaard will not collapse the paradox into a "justification" or "understanding" of one side at the expense of the other: if he becomes

---

[22]   Søren Kierkegaard, *Fear and Trembling: Dialectical Lyric by Johannes de Silentio* (Eng., ed. A. Hannay, London: Penguin edn, 1985), p.44.

[23]   Ibid., pp.45 and 50.

[24]   Ibid., pp.52–3.

[25]   Ibid., pp.54, 55.

"resigned" to the death of Isaac, Abraham has thereby surrendered his faith in God's promise of blessing. So the paradox cannot be resolved in this way.

Thereby Abraham's dilemma exposes the illusion of Hegel's "system": some things refuse to be systematized. Moreover, as in the case of his own decision about Regine Olsen, some decisions can only be decided, apart from the expectations and conventions of the crowd. In his *Purity of Heart* Kierkegaard writes, "The most ruinous evasion of all is to be hidden in the crowd in an attempt to get away from hearing God's voice as an individual."[26] A paradox that transcends logic and community norms seems to reach into the absurd. But Abraham "acts on the strength of the absurd ... As a single individual he is higher than the universal. The paradox cannot be mediated. On the strength of the absurd he got Isaac back."[27]

In broad terms this does not presuppose an exegesis radically different from the kind of historical exegesis that we find among Old Testament specialists. Gerhard von Rad and Bruce Vawter also stresses the unwavering character of Abraham's faith in the divine promise (cf. also Rom. 4:19–22; Heb. 11:17–19), the inexorable demand for obedience, and the turmoil generated by the need for such a decision. Vawter adds that a textual prehistory may include a prohibition against human sacrifice, and that this may remain in the suggestion that "there were sacrifices that he (God) did not want at all".[28] Kierkegaard's own existential and anti-Hegelian pre-understanding, however, sharpens what it is at stake in the lonely subjectivity of creative decision, where packaged assumptions and passively accepted conventions of understanding run out in the face of some unpredicted event or demand.

In this respect existentialist hermeneutics shares with speech-act theory an emphasis on the self-involvement of readers. Genuine and creative understanding, as opposed to that of passive acquiescence to convention, Kierkegaard maintained, *never leaves the reader unchanged, uninvolved, or untransformed.* Existential hermeneutics reminds us of this with reference both to textual effects *on* readers, and also with reference to persons *within* texts. Thus Dan Otto Via brings out from Matt. 25:14–30 that the one-talent man who refused to take any risk wanted *to remain unchanged in an unchanged situation. He would not venture,* but insisted on *perceiving himself as the victim* of his employer's demand for action.[29] He did not want the risk of novel opportunities, and so the inbuilt "internal" judgement was that he would remain permanently without them, permanently inactive.

Geraint Vaughan Jones likewise shows how the Prodigal Son's remorse, nostalgia and longing for return *changes him into a different person* from the defiant young man who left home demanding his "rights" (Luke 15:11–32). In his experience of alienation the son lost the dignity of personhood by becoming anonymous and unwanted (when his money ran out) in a strange land. But on his return his father restored to him his dignity as a person by placing a ring on his finger and shoes on his feet, and by celebrating his return.[30]

---

[26] S. Kierkegaard, *Purity of Heart is to Will One Thing* (London: Collins (Fontana edn) 1961), p.163.

[27] S. Kierkegaard, *Fear and Trembling*, p.85; cf. Anthony C. Thiselton, "Kierkegaard and the Nature of Truth", *Churchman* 89 (1975), pp.85–107.

[28] Bruce Vawter, *On Genesis: A New Reading* (New York: Doubleday, 1977), pp.254, 255 and 258.

[29] Dan Otto Via, *The Parables: Their Literary and Existential Dimension*, pp.113–22.

[30] Geraint Vaughan Jones, *The Art and Truth of the Parables* (London: SPCK, 1964), pp.167–205.

D.D. Evans, we have noted, also underlines the role of self-involvement. He examines the creation accounts (Gen. 1:1–2:25, cf. Ps. 8:4–9). These are not simply flat descriptions of "objective" creative processes (though they are not less) but involve all human readers in recognizing their own creatureliness, responsibility and roles as created beings, including stewardship of ecological resources. In the broad sense, Gen. 22:1–19, Matt. 25:14–30, Luke 15:11–30 and Gen. 1:1–2:25 all *involve* readers; but in different ways, at different levels, and with different demands.

III
Drawing Readers into Biblical Narrative-Worlds: Four Theories of Narrative in Relation to Reading-Situations

Narratives that project "worlds" for readers to enter offer hermeneutical advantages not provided by most other categories of texts. Readers have become habituated to enter narrative-worlds almost every day, through television or through fiction. They often suspend their own belief-systems or even their customary moral defences for the sake of being carried along by the flow of the story. Resistances or prejudices become weaker, or even provisionally lifted, although in such contexts as ecclesial or propagandist settings non-verbal cues may reinstate them. Millions choose to become caught up in the temporal life-flow of plots and sub-plots on television or in popular literature even when the same regularities of narrative grammar are employed (discussed elsewhere in the context of the work of Propp, Greimas and others).[31] We also discussed the role played by flashbacks, by pre-views, by speeding up or slowing down narrative-time, by suspense, by surprise, and by point of view. Often, in Propp's language, a hero struggles with a villain: helpers assist the hero while opponents hinder the quest or struggle; closure brings victory, restoration of fortunes, return, or love and marriage. In terms of pastoral theology, the functions of narrative are manifold. We select four.

III.1 Narrative World as Seductive Invitation Leading to the Unexpected

In the classic parable-form, exemplified in Nathan's parable of the rich man who took his poor neighbour's lamb (2 Sam. 12:1–6) *narrative can catch readers off-guard*. Because the narrative entices them into its world and enthrals them, they become unconsciously exposed to viewpoints, judgements and reversals of assumptions which in other modes of discourse would have called explicitly for conscious willingness to be "open" and to "listen to the text". Narrative can *reverse expectations which initially would be hostile* to its viewpoint. In different reading-situations narrative may achieve a second function.

In Gadamer (partly following the later Heidegger), "worldhood" is grounded ontologically in the *pre-judgements* of language and effective-history. Ernst Fuchs draws on the notion of narrative-world to trace the hermeneutical function of the parable of the labourers in Matt. 20:1–16.[32] The audience is caught up in the good fortune of those who

---

31 See *New Horizons in Hermeneutics*, chapter 13.
32 Ernst Fuchs, *Studies of the Historical Jesus*, pp.32–8 and 154–6.

successively find employment in difficult times, and in the suspense of waiting to see what those who had worked longest will receive for their wages. The shared presuppositions on which the momentum of the plot is constructed encourage the audience to expect a *"just"* reward. But this preconception is shattered: the crowd is deeply shocked, and *feels* it, by the way in which grace supersedes justice. This narrative-dynamic, Fuchs urges, functions quite differently from any bald theological *statement*, from "the pallid requirement of belief in God's kindness".[33] The story-world engages with different people at a deeper-than-intellectual level. Moreover, Fuchs urges, in his *love* Jesus uses narrative to prepare a *place of meeting* which is not merely a confrontation of "viewpoints" or of "ideas"; grace is not simply a "doctrine" to be prematurely rejected. Like the world of Gadamer's "conversation", the hearer is led into sharing presuppositions that allow fresh understanding and avoid a premature dismissal of ideas.[34]

III.2 Narrative Identity and Inter-Subjective Personhood

In narrative theology that draws on categories used in literary theory, the notion of *narrative-coherence on the basis of narrative-time* assumes a special importance. Stephen Crites, David Kelsey and Stanley Hauerwas, stress the *primordial character of narrative as an expression of human experience and, still more fundamentally, of human personhood and of individual and corporate identity.*[35] For human experience is *temporal*; it is orientated towards, and organized in terms of, a temporal history. *Narrative provides an organizational coherence and structure that is operational in terms of temporal flow rather than in terms of abstract logic.*[36] Narrative in Crites's view is bound up with our understanding of *identity*. In the story we encounter a "tensed unity" of a temporal experience which is more than bare natural succession. On this basis George Stroup declares, "Christian narrative, therefore, assumes a literary form akin to that of confession or religious autobiography."[37] He writes, "Christian narrative emerges from the collision between an individual's identity narrative and the narratives of the Christian community."[38] He uses the term "collision" because encounter in faith with texts or with traditions may "transform" a person's identity. As we have seen, in the work of David Kelsey and Frances Young this transformation of personal identity is a function of reading biblical texts.

George Stroup spells out further implications of this approach. Reading narrative-texts "is not simply a matter of meditation and self-discovery"; understanding revelation entails "an activity ... in relation to an 'other' called 'God'". The narrative-history of the

---

[33] Ibid., pp.33–7.

[34] Discussed further in *The Two Horizons* and in "The New Hermeneutic" (Essay 26, below).

[35] Stephen Crites, "The Narrative Quality of Experience", *Journal of the American Academy of Religion* 39 (1971), pp.291–311; and Stanley Hauerwas, *A Community of Character* (Notre Dame, IN: University of Notre Dame Press, 1981); and David H. Kelsey, "Biblical Narrative and Theological Anthropology", in Garrett Green (ed.), *Scriptural Authority and Narrative Interpretation* (Philadelphia, PA: Fortress Press, 1987), pp.121–43.

[36] Paul Ricoeur provides a close study of this; see also *New Horizons*, chapters 10, pp.344–78, and 13 pp.479–99.

[37] George W. Stroup, *The Promise of Narrative Theology* (London: SCM, 1984 (John Knox, 1981)), p.91.

[38] Ibid.

Christian community provides the context in which the individual encounters God ...".[39] William Hordern pointed out in his work on Wittgenstein and religious language that stories identify the personhood of persons in ways impossible for abstract, generalizing thought or for scientific treatises or philosophical essays. He writes, "A young man does not fall in love with a specimen of the class of females, aged twenty, good-looking, likeable, socially adjusted, and so on. On the contrary, he falls in love with Mary Jones, and his love is directed precisely to those aspects of Mary that make her unique. Here is the distinction between love and lust."[40] To categorize a person in terms of qualities may help in identification (for example, in a police search) but they constitute categories of an *object*. We can best describe their *personhood* by telling stories about what they did on some particular occasions, what peculiarities of action they have performed, and so forth. This perspective is important for Ronald Thiemann and in the same way, Stroup insists, "the Markan Gospel constitutes a *narrative text*": it is "neither a treatise on christology nor a doctrinal discussion", because it provides *"a narrative in which his (Christ's) identity emerges from those events that make up his personal history"*.[41]

Narrative biblical texts, in this sense, witness to the personhood of God more effectively by proclaiming *a history of the acts of God* than abstract theological language which rehearses Aristotelian-like "divine attributes" of righteousness, holiness and love. Ronald F. Thiemann develops this point further than Stroup, characterizing biblical narrative-texts as conveying divine hiddenness and divine identity: "God's complex identity is presented through narrative accounts of his action which stress both his immanence and his transcendence, his presence and his hiddenness."[42] The narrative of Jesus portrays God's hidden but active power.

Many narratives, then, *found and create*, rather than subvert, *worlds*. The Exodus narratives of release from bondage to liberty (Exod. 12:31–15:21) are more than bare description, for they embody a plot and unfold through narrative time, with coherence and closure (Exod. 12:31–14:31). We observed these characteristics in Wesley Kort's discussion of the texts of Exodus. They also function *to celebrate* the events they tell, strengthening thereby the *community bonds* of those who share in "remembrance" and liturgical recital of these events (Exod. 15:1–27).

Ronald Thiemann selects the Gospel of Matthew as an example of narrative-texts which hold together the identification of Jesus Christ with a recognition of divine hiddenness (1985, 1987). Matthew's narrative presents "a uniquely identifying description of God". The Matthean goal is "to identify Jesus ... Emmanuel, the Son of God, the one who enacts God's intention to save his people".[43] In Matt. 1:1–4:16, Thiemann argues, Jesus' formal identity is specified as the Son of God who fulfils the divine mission and promise, while 4:18–20:34 specify the individual personal identity of Jesus, which is not without some degree of ambiguity. Finally Matt. 21:1–28:20 connects the formal and personal

---

[39]   Ibid., p.202.

[40]   William Hordern, *Speaking of God. The Nature and Purpose of Theological Language* (London: Epworth Press, 1965), p.147.

[41]   George W. Stroup, op. cit., p.163 (my italics).

[42]   Ronald F. Thiemann, *Revelation and Theology. The Gospel as Narrated Promise* (Notre Dame, IN: University of Notre Dame Press, 1987 (1985)), p.89.

[43]   Ronald Thiemann, *Revelation and Theology. The Gospel as Narrative Promise*, p.113.

identifications. Jesus receives divine authority (28:18), and through the unity of his person and mission with God (3:17; 17:5; 26:36–46) identifies God as his Father and as the God of promise who enacts his intentions in Jesus. The extension of the final promise (28:20) "functions to carry the world of the Gospel narrative into that of the reader ... Precisely as the narrative provides its definitive identification of God and Jesus, it also functions as a promise of direct address ... Thus the discourse functions ... as an invitation to enter the world of the text".[44]

Thiemann's approach to Matthew runs parallel with Stroup's observations on the text of Mark. Stroup urges, "Mark clearly demonstrates that one cannot know who Jesus is apart from the narrative of his personal history."[45] Stroup argues that the question of Jesus's identity is prompted by the authority which Jesus exercises in the narrative texts (Mark 1:24 – "Have you come to destroy us? I know who you are"): "The question of Jesus's identity is intensified by the issue of his authority ... 'Who can forgive sins but God alone?'" (Mark 2:7).[46]

The work of Stroup and of Thiemann looks back in part to the seminal work of Hans Frei in 1967, later republished with a new introduction under the new title *The Identity of Jesus Christ* (1975). There is hiddenness in the Gospel texts, because as the witness to God Jesus "points away from himself".[47] But for believing readers, whom Frei distinguishes from unbelievers and also from pilgrims, the identity of Jesus Christ is given in and through the narrative texts, together with the presence of Christ which is one with his identity.[48]

III.3 Narrative Imagination, Art and "Possible Worlds"

This kind of narrative theology, however, accounts for only one particular segment of a wider variety of functions ascribed to narrative in broader literary and semiotic theory. Stories can be told for one purpose, and retold for another. In folk literature one narrative becomes superimposed onto another, and inter-textual relations begin to form productive "texts" that can offer polyvalent readings. Robert Alter sees conscious artistic plurality and internal tension in the stories of David's rise to kingship, and David Clines sees layered texts in Job that undermine any dogmatic conclusion by deconstructing the narrative-texts which seem to lead to it.[49] Here the temporal logic carries readers with it in different ways and with different effects, although "narrative" only thinly and perhaps superficially frames the genre of wisdom discourse.

Ricoeur finds a significant hermeneutical resource in Heidegger's technical notion of *possibility* for his theory of narrative. This relates well with Heidegger's and Ricoeur's

---

[44] Ibid., pp.142 and 143.
[45] George W. Stroup, op. cit., p.161.
[46] Ibid., p.157.
[47] Hans Frei, *The Identity of Jesus Christ. The Hermeneutical Bases of Dogmatic Theology* (Philadelphia, PA: Fortress Press, 1975), pp.164–5.
[48] Ibid., pp.3–9.
[49] Robert Alter, *The Art of Biblical Narrative* (New York: Basic Books, 1981); and D.J.A. Clines, "Deconstructing the Book of Job", in M. Warner (ed.), *The Bible as Rhetoric* (London: Routledge, 1990), pp.65–80.

notions of "world". Narratives project *possible* worlds that engage the imagination by providing strategies of projection for *future* action. These possibilities may be fictive, that is, formational, and they may or may not also be fictional. In this model, narrative *stimulates the imagination*, and offers constructs which project possibilities for *future action*. They *activate* the eschatological call of Christian pilgrimage, in the sense of beckoning onwards towards new future action, or in some cases also warning readers of projected possibilities to be avoided. They provide a resource by which readers can transcend the present.

Even within this category functions of narratives may be diverse, even, also, in the case of the same biblical narrative. The Book of Esther offers an example. The following "readings" do not necessarily compete with one another. John Goldingay is sympathetic with G. Gerlemann's reading of the Book of Esther as a diaspora version of the new exodus.[50] It projects a narrative-world in which every Jew, in whatever situation, is invited to take responsibility, even at personal risk, to assist the Jewish people. David Gunn argues that one special strength of the narrative-worlds of Ruth and of Esther is that they merge much more readily with the worlds and horizons of most modern readers than "the grandiose world of parting seas and tumbling walls and floating axe-heads".[51] David Clines offers five or six distinct reading-strategies for Esther (1990) in addition to the exegesis of his earlier commentary on the book (1984).[52] Vashti's story offers a satire on the power of the Persian king, but also portrays the courage of a woman in the face of an oppressive power structure. In literary formalist terms it embodies a plot in which tension and struggle achieves resolution.

III.4 Narrative, Count-Generation and Self-Involvement

In literary theory, the distinction between narrative and flat description rests on contrasts between plot and natural sequence, or between narrative-time and natural-time. In the philosophy of language a more logically rigorous distinction performs the same function. In his meticulously argued and creatively important book *Works and Worlds of Art* (1980), Nicholas Wolterstorff develops conceptual tools found in speech-act theory. He distinguishes between a propositional content (p) which functions as *description*, and illocutions which convey a content with a certain force (F). We discussed the importance of this distinction for Searle and Recanati in Essay 8. But Wolterstorff designates this force axis more strictly in these examples as "*mood-actions*". Just as D.D. Evans distinguished between *causal* and *institutional* force in his Austinian "logic of self-involvement", so Wolterstorff distinguishes between the *causal* generation of the world of art through uses of its physical materials and the "*count-generation*" which transforms narrative-elements into the events and characterizations of the coherent "world" of a narrative-plot.[53] *Count-*

---

[50] John Goldingay, *Theological Diversity and the Authority of the Old Testament* (Grand Rapids, MI: Eerdmans, 1987), pp.51–2.

[51] David M. Gunn, "Reading Right: Reliable and Omniscient Narrator, Omniscient God, and Foolproof Composition in the Hebrew Bible", in David J.A. Clines, S.E. Fowl and S.E. Porter (eds), op. cit., p.63; cf. 53–64.

[52] David J.A. Clines, "Reading Esther from Left to Right", ibid., pp.31–52.

[53] Nicholas Wolterstorff, *Works and Worlds of Art* (Oxford: Clarendon Press, 1980), pp.3–8 and 202–15.

generation therefore includes *more than the linguistic or narrative conventions themselves*. Like Searle, Wolterstorff ascribes "rights and responsibilities" to authors as *agents* who exercize these to project the art-world.[54]

In his book *Art in Action* (1980) and more rigorously in *Works and Worlds of Art*, Wolterstorff follows Searle in drawing out the fundamental philosophical consequences which flow from the difference between *descriptive* language and the projection of a narrative-world in which a "*mood-stance*" generates assertions, questions, expressions, or promises.[55] In fiction, the fictive mood-stance "consists of *presenting*, of *offering for consideration* certain states of affairs" for reflection, exploration, edification, cathartic cleansing, or for sheer delight.[56] But whereas fiction neither affirms nor denies a propositional content (*p*), the liar and the historian both take up an assertive stance, even if the historian also projects a narrative-world.[57] This world presupposes assertive truth-claims, rather than simply providing bare "description".[58] For Wolterstorff, as for Searle, however, *the status of authors as human agents capable of assuming commitments and responsibilities remains fundamental.* We cannot speak here, as in the Gadamerian, semiotic, or Barthesian models, of the death of the author who simply falls from view in written narrative texts.

Wolterstorff's speech-act account of worlds of art invites questions about the status of illocutionary forces generated in or by narrative-worlds. In some cases the narration of a story *counts as* an act of description; in other cases it *counts as* an act of exploration, suggestion, or promise. In earlier times conservative interpreters tended to assume that *all* biblical narration *counted as* referential description. But a number of conservative writers feel free nowadays to allow such issues to be determined through enquiry about *genre* and *hermeneutical functions*. Thus Sidney Greidanus argues that in the case of Job and Jonah "the historical referent is *hermeneutically* inconsequential" (his italics), whereas "the historical referent of the Exodus narrative ... is indispensable".[59] In the Westminster Theological Seminary symposium *Inerrancy and Hermeneutic* (1988), Tremper Longman III argues not only that Job contains "literary artifice", but also that "the Scriptures are multi-functional", and that Alter is right to draw attention to "conventions of biblical storytelling".[60] Literary artifice can be "true".

In terms of the vocabulary used by Wolterstorff for broader philosophical questions, we may say that the creation-narratives in Gen. 1:1; 2:25 are more than "cause-generated" texts; their act of projecting a narrative of creation *counts as* an act of ascribing a status and role to humankind, as well as counting as an assertion about origins and existence.[61] The language does not simply represent, but represents *as*: it represents humankind *as*

---

[54] Ibid., p.205.
[55] Nicholas Wolterstorff, *Art in Action: Towards a Christian Aesthetic* (Grand Rapids, MI: Eerdmans, 1980), esp. pp.122–55, and *Works and Worlds of Art*, pp.222–31.
[56] N. Wolterstorff, *Works and Worlds of Art*, p.233.
[57] Ibid., p.231; cf. 232–4.
[58] Ibid., p.239.
[59] Sidney Greidanus, *The Modern Preacher and the Ancient Text. Interpreting and Preaching Biblical Literature* (Leicester: IVP, and Grand Rapids, MI: Eerdmans, 1988), pp.194 and 195.
[60] Harvie M. Conn (ed.), *Inerrancy and Hermeneutics. A Tradition, A Challenge, A Debate* (Grand Rapids, MI: Baker, 1988), pp.140, 148 and 149; cf. 137–49.
[61] On "count-generation" cf. Nicholas Wolterstorff, op. cit., pp.202–15.

creaturely beings, *as* stewards of created resources, *as* authorized to eat produce and to procreate. In D.D. Evans' language, the creation accounts assign institutional *roles* to humankind in relation to each other and to God. In Wolterstorff's terminology, these narrative-texts embody more than an *assertive* "mood-stance": they *authorize* certain patterns of action (1:29; 2:16); they *evaluate and celebrate* all creation as "good" (Gen. 1:12, 18, 21, 31); they *direct* (1:28; 2:17).[62] The performative illocutionary acts of giving and blessing (1:28, 29) take the form of address.

Literary theories and models of narratives demonstrate the multiformity of their possible functions for a multiformity of possible reading-situations. But here the narrative-world often (but not always) constitutes a *possible* world which projects *future possibilities for action and scenarios for imaginative exploration.* Speech-act approaches to "count-generated" narrative-worlds that embody stances that initiate a *more specific range of acts.* These may also perform multiform tasks for different readers, but within a different category: they may *offer pardon* to the guilty, may *liberate* the oppressed, may *comfort* the sorrowing, may *warn* the overconfident, or may *pledge promises* to those who are trustful.

IV
Fourth Model: Biblical Symbols: "Productive" Reading with Questions Partly from Freud and Jung for Pastoral Theology

The biblical texts abound in images. Northrop Frye observes in *The Great Code*: "City, mountain, river, garden, tree, oil, fountain, bread, wine, bride, sheep ... recur so often that they clearly indicate some kind of unifying principle".[63] But is image the same as symbol? In twentieth-century Christian theology two very influential writers on symbol in theology, Paul Tillich and Paul Ricoeur, contribute significantly to this area. Tillich expounds his view of symbol against the background of Jung's psychology and Jung's theory of archetypes; Ricoeur participates in a dialogue about the status of symbol with Freud and with the psychoanalytical tradition.

For Ricoeur, symbols constitute "double meaning" expressions.[64] To speak of evil as a "burden" or as "bondage" is to interpret these terms within a trans-empirical framework so that they operate at a higher or second level of meaning. Evil in this way can be symbolized as a blot or stain, and sin as deviation from a path. Two consequences follow from this for Ricoeur. First, symbols invite *critical* interpretation. For multi-signification allows room for self-deception and for the projection of human will to create values which might serve self-interest. Freudian psychoanalysis, we noted, offers one type of critical tool.[65] Second, symbols may *creatively* give rise to thought and to understanding in a "second naïvety". The critical dimension is explanatory; the creative dimension is

---

62   Ibid., pp.226–31, on mood-stance and stance-indicators.
63   Northrop Frye, *The Great Code*, p.xiii.
64   Paul Ricoeur, *Interpretation Theory*, pp.45 and 55–7; and cf. also *The Conflict of Interpretations*, pp.287–334.
65   Paul Ricoeur, *Freud and Philosophy*, pp.93–4, 420 and 543 *et passim*.

hermeneutical. Symbol thus represents components which, in sentence form, become metaphor, and in sequences of metaphor become narrative.

Where Ricoeur, in continuity with Freud, stresses the *"double meaning"* nature of symbol, with its capacity either to deceive the self or creatively to transcend it, Tillich, in continuity with Jung, stresses the *participatory and integrative* function of symbols. As Wayne Rollins observes, Jung noted in his earliest work the "emotion-laden" character of certain words for his psychiatric patients.[66] For Freud and for Jung equally, dreams constitute symbolic texts. In Freud's analysis, dream-symbols can *disguise the repressed wishes* or contents of the unconscious; in Jung's view, they *compensate for one-sided or absent features* in consciousness, and perform a constructive role in the movement towards maturity and integration.[67] Thus where Ricoeur focuses on the contrast between deceptive disguise and creative revelation, Tillich focuses on the contrast between the fragmenting character of conceptual subject–object language and the integrating power of the wholeness disclosed through symbol.[68]

As his research on dreams developed, Jung became convinced that certain recurring images and patterns reported in dreams reflected parallels and similarities found in a diversity of mythic and historical materials from cultures which differed widely in geographical and chronological origin. In 1919 Jung revived the term *archetype* from second-century Egyptian gnosticism to denote the "patterning tendency" which he attributed to the human psyche not simply as an unconscious reservoir of images for the individual, but on the basis of what he termed the "collective" or universal consciousness of humankind.[69] He also spoke of "primordial images". *Archetypal images*, in Jung's view, include the masculine figures of the father, the ominous giant or ogre, the hero or noble knight and the wise old man; the feminine figures include the mother, the princess, the wicked queen and the wise old woman. But Jung also worked on the development of individuation: the process of "becoming one's own self". In the earlier part of our lives, he believed, we promote those features which our orientations already emphasize as "established": as technical thinkers, as feelers, as sensors, or as intuitive thinkers. In the later part of our development, however, sides of the self hitherto undeveloped call for attention. Aspects that Jung calls "contra-sexual" ingredients and "shadow" aspects need to be integrated with those other elements to which earlier life has accorded prominence. The path to integration lies not in bare rational reflection and in the manipulation of concepts, but in the healing power of deeper forces, including especially the power of symbols.[70]

---

[66]   Wayne G. Rollins, *Jung and the Bible* (Atlanta, GA: John Knox Press, 1983), pp.18–20.

[67]   Ibid., pp.24–6, 37–40; and Paul Ricoeur, *Freud and Philosophy*, p.5; cf. *The Rule of Metaphor*, p.318.

[68]   Tillich's major discussions of symbol occur in addition to his *Systematic Theology* (Eng., London: Nisbet (3 vols) 1953, 1957 and 1964), in *Dynamics of Faith* (London: Allen & Unwin, 1957), esp. pp.42–7; *Theology of Culture* (New York: Oxford University Press, Galaxy edn, 1964), pp.53–67; and "The Meaning and Justification of Religious Symbols" and "The Religious Symbol", in Sidney Hook (ed.), *Religious Experience and Truth* (Edinburgh: Oliver & Boyd, 1961; New York, 1961), pp.3–11 and 301–21, also rp. in F.W. Dillistone (ed.), *Myth and Symbol* (London: SPCK, 1966), pp.15–34.

[69]   Wayne G. Rollins, op. cit., p.74; cf. 72–92.

[70]   Carl Gustav Jung, *Man and his Symbols* (New York: Doubleday, 1971); cf. Jolande Jacobi, *Complex, Archetype, Symbol in the Psychology of C.G. Jung* (Eng., Princeton, NJ: Princeton University Press, 1959); and Hans Schaer, *Religion and the Cure of Souls in Jung's Psychology* (Eng., New York: Pantheon, 1950).

In Jung's view, biblical texts offer such a resource when they are *more than vehicles for the conscious thought-processes of an argument*. Their integrative and healing power operates optimally when they evoke "the depths of God ... not taught by human wisdom" (1 Cor. 2:10, 13). Image, figure, parable, dark saying, poetry, or whatever presupposes the inadequacy of plain descriptive speech or rational argument functions, for Jung, with this kind of effect, especially if it evokes *feelings* at the deepest level. Jung finds some typical examples in the Book of Revelation: "But I saw a beast rising out of the sea, with ten horns and seven heads, with ten diadems upon its horns ... let him who has understanding reckon the number of the beast, for it is a human number, its number is six hundred and sixty-six" (Rev. 13:1, 18). Numerology in Revelation provides further examples of symbols. The "four corners of the earth" (Rev. 7:1) and "the four living creatures" (Rev. 6:1) denote wholeness or completeness; the number seven denotes perfection ("the seven spirits of God", Rev. 4:5, cf. 3:1; "the seven seals", Rev. 6:1; "the seven bowls", 15:1). "The tree" symbolizes physical and spiritual growth and well-being rooted in the divine (Ps. 1:3; Prov. 11:30) and becomes a source of life identified with the cross (1 Pet. 2:24; Rev. 22:2).

Paul Tillich takes up this Jungian approach and develops it not only for his systematic theology, but also for his exposition of the principle of correlation that shapes his hermeneutics and his pastoral theology. Tillich writes, "Religious symbols ... are a representation of that which is unconditionally beyond the conceptual sphere". They transcend the realm "that is split into subjectivity and objectivity".[71] Symbol "grasps our unconscious as well as our conscious being. It grasps the creative ground of our being."[72] The main function of the symbol, therefore, is "the opening up of levels of reality which otherwise are hidden".[73] Symbol thus provides a pre-conceptual bridge between the human psyche and what is symbolized. Tillich asserts, "Every symbol is two-edged. It opens up reality, and it opens the soul."[74] "It opens up hidden depths of our own being."[75] Following Jung, again, Tillich declares that symbols "grow out of the individual or collective unconscious and cannot function without being accepted by the unconscious dimension of our being".[76]

All this dwells on meaning-*effects* in biblical texts as sources of integration and healing power. Like Norman Holland's work on the formation and recognition of *identity* through reading, and David Bleich's emphasis on *feeling*, this approach demonstrates the *power* of symbols to achieve certain operative effects in terms of *reader-response*. Paul Ricoeur has firmly pointed out, however, that to determine whether symbols achieve any more than *pragmatic self-affirmation or wish-fulfilment* a critical hermeneutic of suspicion needs to operate interactively with *post*-critical attention to symbol. Indeed Tillich admits that in principle symbols can destroy as well as create. Symbols, as Wittgenstein constantly remarks about pictures, can be *variously interpreted*.

---

71 Paul Tillich, "The Religious Symbol", in Sidney Hook (ed.), op. cit., p.303.
72 Paul Tillich, *The Shaking of the Foundations* (London: SCM, 1962), p.86.
73 Paul Tillich, *Theology of Culture*, p.56.
74 Ibid.
75 Paul Tillich, *Dynamics of Faith*, p.43.
76 Ibid.; cf. *Theology of Culture*, pp.57–8.

For this reason the symbol in biblical texts may remain *primary as a vehicle of power*, but always context-dependent and in this sense *derivative as a vehicle of truth*. It functions on the basis of traditions of interpretation which have been established in the light of critical reflection, including the use of communicative and didactic texts, and narrative-texts which offer patterns of personal identification. In pastoral theology this suggests at least two particular functions. First, with a stable tradition of interpretation established on other grounds, symbols provide material *for healing and integrative meditation in the tradition of lectio divina or spiritual reading*. In Jung's language, they nourish the human soul. Second, they may also provide *exploratory resources for enquiring readers* outside given traditions, *provided that* it is recognized, as Ricoeur rightly insists, that without a hermeneutic of suspicion they *may* operate only as windows on the human unconscious, or on the social history of arbitrary conventions inherited and transmitted in given societies.

These two principles require some further brief elucidation, defence and exemplification. In meditative "spiritual reading" the power of the eschatological symbols in the Apocalypse may be perceived within the Christian tradition to convey truth. They function as both communicative and productive texts: "The river of the water of life" flows from God's throne (Rev. 22:1); "the leaves of the tree were for the healing of the nations" (22:2); "His name shall be on their foreheads" (22:14). Without some structure of interpretation provided by a tradition, however, "water" and other symbols can be variously understood. In primitive mythology water spawns life, but water may also destroy by drowning, or bring oblivion in the river Lethe, and in depth psychology may be associated with the feminine unconscious.[77] In the Book of Revelation, however, as Caird, Beasley-Murray and others point out, the river of the water of life reflects primarily the restoration at the End-time of the primal river of Eden (Gen. 2:9, 10) together with a further allusion to the river-symbolism of Ezekiel (Ezk. 47:1–12).[78]

If "spiritual reading", then, is undertaken with particular reference to the boundaries of the Christian canon or of a stable Christian tradition of interpretation we arrive at an example of the *lectio divina* of an earlier age. The non-cognitive feeling-related dimensions of symbol may operate productively and healingly because a community has already established an interpretative tradition which embodies cognitive hermeneutical judgements.

Nevertheless symbols engage more than intellect, emotion and imagination. In psychiatry, Rollo May urges, symbol "is given its power and character as a symbol by the *total situation of the patient's life at that moment*".[79] It is this investment of the self and of the total situation at a given time which makes symbol especially important for pastoral

---

[77] The huge variety of possible symbolic interpretation which is evident from ancient and modern sources can be seen in such works as J.E. Cirlot, *A Dictionary of Symbols* (Eng., London: Routledge & Kegan Paul, 2nd edn, 1971; New York: Vail-Ballou Press, 1983).

[78] G.R. Beasley-Murray, *The Book of Revelation* (London: Marshall, Morgan & Scott, 1974), pp.330–31; and G.B. Caird, *The Revelation of St John the Divine* (London: Black, 1966), pp.280–81.

[79] Rollo May, "The Significance of Symbols", in Rollo May (ed.), *Symbolism in Religion and Literature* (New York: Braziller, 1960), p.18 (my italics); cf. 11–49.

theology. Jung argued that engaging with the biblical texts and their symbols entailed asking questions both about the text and also "the meanings of the text *in the personal life of the reader*".[80]

This brings us explicitly to pastoral theology and to reading-situations. Jung insisted that symbols in biblical texts could perform healing and interpretive functions for varieties of readers. But this cannot apply in every case, unless, two principles are acknowledged: first, the interactive plurality of biblical symbols is recognized, and, second, their effect is acknowledged to be ambivalent, even if also very powerful. The symbol of "father" represents a classic case. Dominique Stein, for example, expresses "unease" about the symbol of God as father.[81] Freud, as we know, saw the father figure as representing both a plea for protection and a desire to kill and to displace, which at the infantile level gave rise to projecting a super-father figure beyond attack. But fatherhood of this kind is left behind in maturity. Hence Stein views the father symbol as one implying *psychological regression*. Yorick Spiegel, in the same volume as that in which Stein writes, addresses the problems of sociology, where language concerning authority-figures, whether father or king may be associated with so-called pre-egalitarian political romanticism.[82] In Spiegel's view this symbol is *sociologically regressive*. Elisabeth Moltmann-Wendel follows Mary Daly in calling for "a replacement of the Father ... His activities reflect predominantly male actions ... The God whom Jesus proclaimed is rooted in the matriarchal Sophia tradition."[83] Moltmann-Wendel rejects the implied *maleness* of the symbol. For Daphne Hampson the symbol is destructive and irretrievable, for this reason, and in the end untranslatable.[84]

If *all* symbols receive this treatment, the biblical texts would function with less immediacy and power, and all symbols would be transposed into concepts. The process of reducing symbolic polyvalence by a conceptual removal of ambiguity inevitably reduces symbolic power and the capacity of symbols for integrative shaping. Hence the more traditional and effective response in pastoral theology has been neither to eliminate symbols nor to qualify the varying effects of symbols by cerebralizing them. Unwanted or destructive resonances have been neutralized by embracing the reciprocal mutuality of a plurality of symbols within the biblical texts. Specific reading-situations call for an *avoidance of an obsessive preoccupation with single isolated symbols*. For example, for a reader who suffers from over-burdened problems of guilt, an obsessive focus on the symbol of judge and judgement could become a destructive and disintegrating force. Yet alongside conceptual discourse about release and forgiveness, speech-acts and symbols which express freedom from guilt would perform a decisive function. The power of the sin-bearing sacrificial substitute or the abrogation of the bill of debt offers a healing resource for such a situation (Col. 2:14; 2 Cor. 5:18–20; Heb. 9:12–14).

---

[80]   Wayne G. Rollins, *Jung and the Bible*, p.101 (my italics).

[81]   Dominique Stein, "The Murder of the Father and God the Father in the Work of Freud", in Johannes-Baptist Metz and Edward Schillibeeckx (eds), *God as Father? Concilium* (Edinburgh: T. & T. Clark; New York: Seabury Press, 1981), pp.11–18.

[82]   Yorick Spiegel, "God the Father in the Fatherless Society", ibid., pp.3–10.

[83]   Elisabeth Moltmann-Wendel, *A Land Flowing with Milk and Honey. Perspectives on Feminist Theology* (Eng., London: SCM, 1986), pp.91 and 101.

[84]   Daphne Hampson, *Theology and Feminism* (Oxford: Blackwell, 1990), pp.86–96.

Othmar Keel reviews the variety of symbolic resources offered by Old Testament texts, especially the Psalms, in the cultural settings of ancient Near-Eastern traditions.[85] God is a fortress and a rock, and a "height that offers refuge" (Ps. 31:2; 46:7, 11; 48:2, 3; 61:3). The symbol draws on images of an impregnable fortress built on a hill, to which people could withdraw from smaller towns in times of attack (1 Sam. 13:6; Jer. 4:29). God is a lamp (Ps. 18:29; 2 Sam. 22:29) whose presence and word is light (Ps. 36:9; 119:105), and from whom flow the fountains of life. He offers intimate shelter, like a bird, under his wings (Ps. 17:8; 36:7; 57:1; 61:4; 63:7; 91:4). God is a welcoming host who protects his guests and fills their cups (Ps. 23:5; 63:5). He is a trustworthy shield (Ps. 7:10; 18:2; 28:7; 33:20).[86] God provides a defence against destructive forces also portrayed in symbol: against the pit, against the desert, against the raging storm, against the night, and against collapse into dust (Ps. 16:10; 49:9; 63:1; 90:3; 104:29; 107:5, 29–30).

The power and potential multivalence of symbols also becomes evident in the Fourth Gospel. Johannine material is organized around certain structured themes which, before the discoveries of Dead Sea Scrolls at Qumran, were often prematurely ascribed to "hellenistic dualism": life, death (John 1:4; 10:10; 11:23) light, darkness (1:5; 3:19; 8:12; 9:5) truth, falsehood (8:32; 14:6); Spirit, creaturely humanity (3:6; 6:63). To these may be added such familiar symbolic imagery as that of the good shepherd (John 10:11), the bread of life (6:35), the door (10:7) and the true vine (15:1). Most readers have a deep personal investment in such symbols: from early childhood doors which are open or shut signal access and welcome or exclusion and loneliness; light removes fear of unknown nocturnal terrors or fear of losing one's way; the figure of the good shepherd is rooted in images of caring, tender, wisdom, usually idealized and thus immunized against "bad" experiences which may colour symbols such as father.

Nevertheless, in the Johannine texts, contextualizing settings and textual allusions also constrain meaning by situation-directedness in ways which may be perceived by some readers, but not by others. Light, for example, is *used* by John in a consciously double way to signify *both* "shedding light upon" persons and situations in judgement (a more likely meaning of *photizo* in 1:9 than the RSV "enlightens every man") and illuminating and enlightening them. Light, in John, chases away the fears and terror of darkness, but only by first exposing everything as what it is, that is, by act of judgement.

Symbols, models and events in John serve most characteristically to articulate Christology. The divine *logos* is enfleshed in Jesus and in identifiable patterns of word and deed. Traditions found in the Old Testament already provide a frame of reference for the understanding of such language as "bread", "vine" and "shepherd". This background provides a semiotic code which allows them to function communicatively as well as productively. On the one hand *the symbols remain sufficiently multivalent for readers to see their own lives and well-being at stake in them.* On the other hand they are also sufficiently situation-specific within a variety of patterns of traditions to function *communicatively as well as productively* in a text which has an explicitly *situation-directed goal*: "that you may believe that Jesus is the Christ ... and that you may have life in his name" (John 20:31).

---

85 Othmar Keel, *The Symbolism of the Biblical World. Ancient Near Eastern Iconography and the Book of Psalms* (Eng., New York: Seabury Press, 1978).

86 Ibid., pp.179–92, 222–5.

V

Model Five: Semiotic Productivity

The fifth of our ten models is that of semiotic productivity. The impact of semiotic theory on biblical interpretation has two quite different effects for pastoral theology. On one side, it is possible for the interpreter to stand *outside the semiotic system* of codes through which textual meaning is generated. In this case a socio-critical or political assessment of the semiotic system may be offered as a critique of the institutional structures in which it is embedded. "Materialist" readings by Michel Clevenot, socio-political readings by Norman Gottwald, and "demystifying" interpretations of texts by Roland Barthes offer examples. But on the other side, readers can stand *inside the semiotic system*. If a straight match of shared code between the author and the reader occurs, a clear-cut communicative or transmissive process of understanding may be set in motion. But self-conscious enquiries about semiotic codes generally arise when the codes are *mismatched*, or, more typically, when *two or more semiotic systems operate simultaneously in the texts*. Here the "first" reading can become a code or matrix for "second" and subsequent readings.

A semiotic approach shares with structuralism and with literary formalism the presupposition of a model in which meaning is generated by a language-*system* rather than by the conscious choices, judgements and goals of an author as an *agent* who determines how such a system *is put to operational use*. As structuralism gave way to a post-structuralist phase, such a perspective remained congenial to postmodernist, post-Freudian, and post-Marxist *suspicions of consciousness*. It also reflects postmodernist diagnoses of the arbitrary role of *social conventions* as devices which mask power-interests of those in control in communities. The status of semiotic systems remains a fundamental philosophical and theological issue; it is not simply one for literary theorists, social historians, or biblical interpreters. *Precisely the symbols which Jung and Tillich see as integrating personhood through interaction with the unconscious also betray the social conventions of organized codes relative to cultures. "Archetypal images", in Jung's terminology, of the king, and the son, or of the prince and the princess, constitute functions within a gender-system or a hierarchical power-system.* Hero and villain, trickster and wise counsellor, trial and restoration, represent semiotic components within a directed structure of quest.

What gains, if any, can be achieved for readers by drawing a boundary round the text which excludes its author and situation *for purposes of hermeneutical strategy?* John Barton reminds us that support for such an approach comes "from a most surprising source: an essay by C.S. Lewis". Lewis argues (1939) that a passage such as Isa. 13:19–22a cannot be attributed to any single human individual, and has nothing to do with the personality or intentions of the author. It is like a work of art which takes on new colours never foreseen or intended by the artist. We can have poetry without the poet. In his small book *An Experiment in Criticism* (1961) C.S. Lewis defends the older formalist theory of reading texts "in their own right" rather than as expressions of what the author wills to communicate or the reader wishes to "use".[87]

---

[87]   C.S. Lewis, *An Experiment in Criticism* (Cambridge: Cambridge University Press, 1961), pp.5–13, 16–39 *et passim*; see also John Barton, *Reading the Old Testament*, p.194.

Barton recognizes that this approach, for all its apparent dignifying of "the text alone" in practice transfers the onus for interpretation and understanding, and even in a sense co-authoring, onto the reader. Barton observes, "Lewis is saying, in effect, that the meaning (or at any rate *a* valid meaning) of the text is constituted by our conventions for reading it, by the expectations we bring to it."[88] Once semiotic systems are perceived not only to generate meaning on the basis of systems without agents (other than readers) or on the basis of interactions with other systems or matrix-generators, we move into the area of reader-response theories, as Susan Wittig's work on polyvalent meaning in the parables of Jesus demonstrates.

But here, from the point of view of philosophy of language as well as for pastoral theology, some complex issues arise. As Stephen Schiffer observes at the very beginning of his book *Meaning*, the logical grammar of "Seymour meant something" is different from that of "That mark means something."[89] In the former case, a human agent usually produces meaning by *doing* something, by *performing an act entailing choices and uses*, by drawing on the repertoire of some prior linguistic or semiotic system. *Simply within the system* an artefact such as a signal flag produces meaning not at this *systemic* level by virtue of some action but by virtue of its conventional status within some inherited semiotic code.[90] The flag "means" something *potentially*. But if it is selected from a box, and waved by a human agent, the human agent "means" something by this *use* of the flag at the *operational* level. The ambiguity of the active and derivative sense of "means" can be illustrated from traffic signs in the Highway Code. Signs for falling rocks or for pedestrians crossing "mean" potentially in a booklet only as *possibilities*: when a human agent selects them from others and places them by a cliff or a crossing their meaning becomes *operational by virtue of the agent's action*. Learning about the semiotic system is *learning about the possibilities which conventions can generate*. In Wittgenstein's simile there is all the difference between *watching* a board game and learning its rules and actually *moving* a piece in the game.[91] The latter is the analogue of *operational* meaning; the former, only of systemic or *potential* meaning.

What, then, does this suggest for pastoral theology or for varied reading-situations? One effect is to enhance readers' understandings of the contrast used by Lotman and Eco between productive and communicative texts. To use one semiotic system as a matrix to generate meaning within a further system produces complex and sometimes novel effects. The Book of Revelation utilizes the texts of Ezekiel, Daniel, Isaiah, Zechariah and other scriptures to generate productive, symbolic imagery. George Caird calls attention to its surrealist, kaleidoscopic, dream-like texture with the warning that we should not attempt *"to unweave the rainbow"*; these texts have "evocative and emotive power".[92] In apocalyptical imagery, *everything is at stake for the reader*. The Apocalypse uses Ezk. 1:5, 16–18 as a matrix for productive imagery about "four living creatures ... full of eyes inside and out" (Rev. 4:8). The voice that speaks "with the sound of many waters" (Rev. 1:13)

---

88   Ibid., p.196.
89   Stephen R. Schiffer, *Meaning* (Oxford: Clarendon Press, 1972), p.1.
90   Cf. ibid., pp.1–16, 118–55.
91   L. Wittgenstein, *Philosophical Investigations*, sects 30, 31 and 49.
92   George B. Caird, *The Revelation of St John the Divine*, p.25 (my italics).

evokes a sense of awe at God's unutterable transcendence on the basis of Ezk. 43:2. *To transpose these texts, as some popular translations tend to do, into mere communicative description of an omniscient intelligence or a superhuman voice has reductionist effects.*

Nevertheless Revelation remains *also* a communicative text which presupposes, in its directedness towards oppressed readers, some overlapping or even sharing of codes. As Beasley-Murray notes, many of the images represent recognizable stereotyped cartoons or caricatures, like John Bull or Uncle Sam, within traditions used in apocalyptic literature of the day.[93] Readers knew that "144,000" (Rev. 14:1) does not stand in a semiotic system of mathematics in which the adjacent semantic choice would be 143,999. In these texts a *productive* axis signals that *everything, including one's own life, is at stake,* while a *communicative* axis conveys a message concerning *God's sovereign purposes and modes of action in relation to reading-situations of oppression, suffering and marginalization. The text is multi-functional.*

VI
Sixth Model: Reader-Response Theories

Very significant differences exist between the various formulations of reader-response theory. Elsewhere I have identified such differences between Iser, Eco, Culler, Holland, Bleich and Fish.[94] We considered some specific examples of readings of biblical texts especially within the first two sub-categories. Susan Wittig's work on the parables (1977) drew on the theory of Wolfgang Iser, and included a reading of the parable of the Prodigal Son (Luke 15:11–32), Resseguie considers Mark 10:17–22 in relation to the responses of readers today; Robert Fowler and Jouette Bassler expound Mark 6:30–44; Mark 8:1–10; and Mark 14:22 within this context.[95] Alan Culpepper's work on the Johannine narrative-text places the activity of the reader within the frame of narrative theory in Genette, Chatman and others, as well as that of Iser's reader-response theory.

These approaches contribute to discussions in pastoral theology in as far as they serve to clarify issues about the nature of reading-processes *within the time-horizons of readers.* In common with the reception-theory of Hans Robert Jauss, Iser, Eco, Holland, Fish and others give attention to the role played by *expectation, construction, projection and surprise in processes of engagement between readers and texts.*[96] For pastoral theology it is constructive to identify what may be entailed in the *activity* of readers and reading. To repeat an analogy that may be in danger of being overworked, the musical score must be *played,*

---

[93] G.R. Beasley-Murray, *The Book of Revelation,* p.16.

[94] In *New Horizons in Hermeneutics,* chapter 14, pp.516–57.

[95] Sources are cited in *New Horizons,* loc. cit.; but cf. Susan Wittig, "A Theory of Multiple Meanings", *Semeia* 9 (1977), pp.75–105; J.L. Resseguie, "Reader Response Theory and the Synoptic Gospels", *JAAR* 52 (1984), pp.307–24; Robert Fowler, *Loaves and Fishes* (Chico, CA: Scholars, 1981); and R.A. Culpepper, *Anatomy of the Fourth Gospel* (Philadelphia, PA: Fortress, 1983).

[96] Sources are cited in *New Horizons,* loc. cit.; however cf. for example W. Iser, *The Act of Reading* (Baltimore, MD: Johns Hopkins University Press, 1978); Umberto Eco, *The Role of the Reader* (London: Hutchinson, 1980); N. Holland, *5 Readers Reading* (New Haven, CT: Yale University Press, 1975); and Stanley Fish, *Doing What Comes Naturally* (Oxford: Clarendon, 1989).

whether by a soloist or a chorus, or an orchestra as a temporal process and an *event*. No two performances will be identical, but it still makes sense to speak of a *good* performance as being one that includes both *faithfulness to the score* (pace *Fish*), *and a creativity* that transcends merely *wooden, mechanical, or repetitive routine*. Readers are invited to perform *active and creative* roles in reading-processes.

In *New Horizons in Hermeneutics* I have criticized Fish for seductive strategies used to attack Iser and others for allegedly half-hearted compromises in their moderate reader-response approaches. I stand by my critique. Yet even Fish's overstatement may have positive value for pastoral theology in at least one respect. Exponents of this approach focus attention on how readily goals of interpretation are often *uncritically presupposed* within given communities. They unmask what are often viewed as *"natural"* meanings or *"natural" norms when these are often community-relative constructions* of convention and habit. These are born out of *routinization*. A community of readers, it is urged, so repeatedly and consistently presupposes certain habits of reading that what in actuality represent no more than community-relative assumptions and practices become elevated to the supposed status of "natural" or universal principles.

Reader-response theory could in principle stop short of contextual pragmatism, and offer a positive critical tool for pastoral theology by inviting provisional and corrigible metacritical reflection on the status of the critical norms used within a community. This becomes an increasingly urgent task in relation to pluralistic cultures and theologies. But the literary theorists who see most clearly the problematic nature of this area seem also to be determined to transpose this model of reading into a narrative philosophy which, to recall the admirable comment of Christopher Norris cited above, makes "use of a liberal rhetoric to frame an authoritative message", pressing its claims "under cover of its liberal-pluralist credentials".[97] At this point reader-response theory, in effect, merges into another distinct model, namely that of neo-pragmatism.

VII
Seventh Model: Neo-Pragmatic Self-Affirmation

Neo-pragmatic theories seem on first acquaitance to explain so much, and may seem initially to liberate the exegesis of biblical texts from control by communities of realists or sectarians, or conversely from a narrow "objectivist" agenda fixed by the biblical guild of historical and lexicographical specialists. It universalizes Robert Morgan's observation that "some disagreements about what the Bible means stem not from obscurities in the texts, but from conflicting aims of the interpreters".[98] It seems to provide an intellectual and philosophical explanation for the gut-level feeling shared equally by many right-wing conservatives and left-wing radicals, that not only is the ideal of disinterested scholarship an outdated liberal illusion; but also that all biblical exegesis can be *predicted by socio-political typifications* of "conservative", "neo-liberal", "radical", "historical-

---

[97] Christopher Norris, *The Contest of Faculties* (London: Methuen, 1985), p.159.
[98] Robert Morgan (with John Barton), op. cit., p.8.

critical", "moderate", or "pleasing the Board and the Constituency" goals of interpretation.

There can be little doubt that *some* communities and *some* individuals do allow such interests to shape the agenda with which they come to biblical texts. A deeply ingrained habit of mind and fierce loyalty to a given tradition provides a sincere but illusory belief that what they perceive as meaning is *"natural"*, *"plain"*, and *"given"*. Honesty can hardly be at issue if a community's presuppositions make them blind to other options before their eyes. In the context of pastoral theology *either sustained scepticism and unbelief or blinkered loyalty to given pietist or doctrinaire theological traditions may have the same effect*. A corporate context-relative mind-set elevates "our church" or "the modern world" to the status of a trans-contextual universal.

Pastorally it is crucially important to provide an individual with the hermeneutical understanding to dislodge and to disentangle the claims of a given sub-cultural group to be sole custodians of the "natural" meanings of biblical texts, especially if in practice these claims are founded not on painstaking exegesis and hermeneutical reflection but on exegetical *fiats* arising from a need to defend community interests. But *it is precisely here that neo-pragmatic or socio-pragmatic hermeneutics reveals its pastoral inadequacy*. For if *all* claims to patient exegesis are merely internally generated by communities governed by interests, *no claim can be ranked in relation to any other claim* except among those who share the same "ethnocentric" or "local" interests.

Socio-pragmatic theory rests on the same kind of desire to cut the knot, or avoid "the slippery slope" as ultra-fundamentalism. It offers a false polarization between *either* formalism and old-fashioned liberal impartiality *or* the end of Fish's "anti-formalist road" in which socio-political conventions swallow up all pretensions to achieve a standpoint outside one's own reading community. But to say, rightly, that no one can fully *reach* the goal of impartiality does not logically entail the proposition that no one can begin to travel along the road toward more critical openness. He or she can enter into dialogue with other traditions with special reference to the points at which overlapping and criss-crossings between community boundaries occur. Fish is aware that we live with multiple roles: as parents, teachers, homeowners and so on.[99] But this ought to make him more sympathetic, rather than less sympathetic, to the human capacity to distinguish between what Alan Montefiore terms "neutrality" and "impartiality".[100] As members of a family or city, sports referees will hardly be "neutral" in their wishes for a team's success. But in applying the same rules to each side, they are trusted to be impartial. In a study entitled "The Morality of Christian Scholarship" (1982), I developed this distinction for Christian academic commitment and openness.[101] Some indication of the *possibility* of trans-contextual openness lies in the experience of *pain and distress* that we feel when respect for truth forces us to abandon a cherished

---

[99] Stanley Fish, *Doing What Comes Naturally*, pp.30–32.

[100] Alan Montefiore (ed.), *Neutrality and Impartiality. The University and Political Commitment* (Cambridge: Cambridge University Press, 1975), p.12.

[101] Anthony C. Thiselton, "The Morality of Christian Scholarship", in Mark Santer (ed.), *Their Lord and Ours: Approaches to Authority, Community, and the Unity of the Church* (London: SPCK, 1982), pp.20–45. Included here as Essay 37.

belief *even though colleagues and our ecclesial or social community may hold these beliefs, or may set some different agendas.*

When the *meaning* of biblical texts, especially Rom. 1:17, opened a new world for Luther, more was at stake than exchanging one set of community interests and expectations for another. The process of anguish, pain, disruption, discontinuity, emancipation, joy and freedom was more than a phenomenon of social history to be accounted for in social or ecclesial terms, even though no doubt social historians can offer purely causal explanatory hypotheses. It would be more accurate to say that a world of textual meanings *constructed the community* of the Reformation than that the Protestant communities of the Reformation *"constructed" the meanings of the texts.*

Nevertheless, two reading-situations, each the converse of the other, stand especially *to gain* from a consideration of the socio-pragmatic model. On the one hand, some, as we have observed, find themselves oppressed and under pressure because sometimes contrary to their own judgements or instincts, a community imposes upon them oppressively certain biblical textual "meanings" as the only *natural, obvious, or plain* meaning of the text. Rorty and Fish are right to insist that *what counts as "natural" is relative to assumptions, habits of reading, expectations and norms held within the community of readers.* We need simply recall the manipulative use of biblical texts to inspire or to validate conquest of land or support for such institutions as slavery. Joshua 1 has no doubt played a part in the former.

On the other side, neo-pragmatic or socio-pragmatic hermeneutics addresses those individuals *who underestimate the role of community contexts* in one direction for *shaping their own individual reading habits* and in another direction, for providing a *stable and affirming framework* within which as individuals, they may explore texts. Reading remains in principle a corporate rather than individual activity. On one side, sharing common readings of texts nourishes social bonding; on the other side, a sense of expectancy within a gathered or worshipping community heightens the actualizations of texts.

VIII
Eighth Model: Deconstruction

We do not have space to expound deconstructionist theory here. We have discussed this in detail elsewhere, with particular reference to Barthes and to Derrida.[102] One of the most illuminating examples of its application to biblical interpretation is that of David Clines' approach to the Book of Job with particular reference to Job 42:7–17. We may also compare J.D. Crossan's work on some of the parables of Jesus, as well as on the relation between the Ezra tradition and Ruth 1:16; 4:17–22; and on parts of Ecclesiastes (for example, Eccles. 2:16; 9:11). Although these examples from Crossan are not technically "deconstruction" in the fullest sense, they offer examples of iconoclasm broadly in this kind of tradition.

The *reader-situation* that deconstructionist models address emerges from what Clines calls the *craving of the heart for fixed dogma.* Within such a horizon everything is expected

---

[102] See *New Horizons in Hermeneutics*, chapter 3, pp.80–141.

to be fixed, sharply bounded and absolute. In this case it does not help, Clines urges, to try to "cure the problem of a dogma with another dogma. Whenever you have a case of dogma eat dogma, you always have one dogma surviving and snapping at your heels." Deconstruction "loosens our attachment to any one of them *as dogma*" (his italics).[103] In pastoral theology a very fine and delicate line needs to be drawn between the legitimate and necessary use of *coherent formulations in creeds* for the stable transmission of traditions which maintain some consistency of theological identity and a doctrinaire scholasticism in which an *obsession with doctrine* can become an end in itself that even displaces faith and restricts personal growth by placing sharp and brittle boundaries everywhere.

Nevertheless although deconstructionist theories have some value, by definition they remain primarily negative, iconoclastic and context-dependent. They function with a degree of prophetic protest where tradition has become *fossilized* and no longer serves the vision that it emerged to articulate. It comes into its own in biblical hermeneutics in reader-situations where understanding has become exclusively tied to some *single controlling paradigm* as a fixed centre.

All the same, "undoing" in Paul de Man, and "play" in Derrida, involve something more radical than correcting traditions. The most problematic factor lies in a preoccupation with the *sign system* at the expense of the *human life-world*. The major premise, shared by Barthes, Foucault and Derrida, is that the semiotic system is only conventional and arbitrary, and this need not be denied. But their minor premise that meaning this system generates meaning begs the question of *how* it generates it. The conclusion that meaning is arbitrary and pluriform rests on glossing over the role of human agents in constraining, judging and choosing, *from* the *possibilities* of the system. Amos Wilder, who receives praise from Crossan for bringing a high degree of literary sensitivity to biblical studies, expresses the greatest possible reserve towards any approach that forgets that in many biblical texts "the witness in the word was *inseparable from the witness in action and behaviour*": "The word was made flesh" (John 1:14).

In the case of language that reflects beliefs, neither belief nor the role of the human agent can be "de-centred" without self-contradiction. For, in terms of perspectives shared by Wittgenstein, Austin and others, in certain instances the expression "*p* is true" *includes* "an explicit personal accreditation – my personal backing or signature – which I give to *p*".[104] This "backing" needs to be evidenced in the public arena of life. In the New Testament it is *kerygma* and *confession*. Its nature and implications for language and for texts bring us to speech-act models in hermeneutical theory and in the practice of reading.

Clear affinities and parallels exist between the respective roles of system, tradition and contextually shifting life-worlds. In the dialogue between the "local" and radically contextual and the coherent and trans-contextual, the biblical writings *point beyond the fallible church and its own local context* to that which lies beyond it, especially to the divine

---

[103] David J.A. Clines, "Deconstructing the Book of Job", loc. cit., 79. David Clines has reprinted the essay in somewhat altered form in D.J.A. Clines, *What Does Eve Do to Help? And Other Readerly Questions to the Old Testament* (Sheffield: JSOT Suppl. 94, 1990), pp.103–26.

[104] Dallas M. High, *Language, Persons and Belief: Studies on Wittgenstein's Philosophical Investigations and Religious Uses of Language* (New York: Oxford University Press, 1967), p.142.

promise of the future, and the universals of the cross and the resurrection. In language reminiscent of Habermas and of Pannenberg, life-world interacts with open system to promote both stable identity and creative movement and surprise.

IX
Ninth Model: Speech-Actions and their Significance for "Believing Reading" as Reading with a Personal Stake in the Text as Address

In speech-act theory the determinant for the effects which an utterance or written communicative message produces is *the nature of the act which the agent performs*. It has a quality of *directedness* that in Searle and other post-Wittgensteinian theorists denotes the "adverbial" *intentionality* of the speech-act. The effects are usually performative or illocutionary within the extra-linguistic world. Normally their directedness implies either that they are addressed to a specific situation or that they apply types or patterns of situation. *Promises*, characteristically, are seldom indiscriminate (though they can be, for example, when declared by politicians in elections). They carry with them *commitments to action* on behalf of specific persons or on behalf of persons in given patterns of situations. *They may authorize* addresses, often in relation to certain institutional categories or extra-linguistic situations. Acts of *forgiveness and liberation* likewise presuppose appropriate *conditions*, for example, a situation of recognized guilt or bondage, or a desire to take advantage of freedom.

Contextual pragmatism and reader-response hermeneutics envisage processes and effects that differ both in their nature and in the conditions from which they derive their currency. In liturgical texts, for example in the Psalms, *readers* are invited to perform illocutionary acts that carry commitments and responsibilities additional to the saying of the words themselves. But these transcend social convention: they entail extra-linguistic *pledges or attitudes, or other "backing"*. In reader-response theory the effects are determined by the contingent social horizons. If any act of will is involved, this can be traced only to routinization, which originated in the community. Speech-acts proceed on a different basis.

In the case of *promises* or *authorizations* (and even non-fictional acts of assertion) something is *at stake* in the *extra-linguistic attitudes and commitments* of the *speaker* or *writer*. In the case of *prayers, confessions*, or utterances of repentance or of faith, something is *at stake* in the extra-linguistic attitudes or commitments of *those readers* who participate in the speech-act character of the text as a speech-act. It begins to emerge here that certain qualities characterize *"believing" reading*. It is not that believers understand some new propositional content unknown to unbelievers or to enquirers; it is that they participate in the *count-generated act*, to borrow Wolterstorff's term. They perceive themselves as *recipients or addressees* of directed acts of commitment, or of promise. They perceive the utterances in question as carrying with them illocutionary and extra-linguistic *consequences*.

In theological terms, readers may perceive themselves as liberated, empowered, authorized, forgiven and loved in and through the operation of the text. The theological basis for such illocutionary language lies to hand in the broad notion of covenant, which, whatever its sociological origins in the Old Testament, runs through the later Old Testament writings to become central in the New Testament. The shedding of blood focused in the pre-Pauline *paradosis* of the Lord's Supper is expressed in terms of "the new covenant in my blood" (1 Cor. 11:25; cf. Mark 14:24; Matt. 26:28). In the theology of the Epistle to the Hebrews there is a play on the performative effect of covenant and legal testament by means of the same dual-purpose Greek word *diathēkē* (Heb. 9:15; cf. 7:22; 8:8). Law and promise for Paul both reflect performative and self-involving dimensions of covenant (Gal. 3:17). The logical issue is not whether the propositional content of a promise is true or false in Galatians 3, but whether its force is "void" or operative (3:17).

This presupposes, however, a *directedness* on the part of texts, or a dimension of *interpersonal address*. If the word of God is perceived as an act of divine love, expressing divine purpose or evaluation, this word has the status of an expression of the divine *will*. To read this word only as religious phenomenology is very much like Austin's example of pseudo-promise and pseudo-response as in the example: "Willie promises, don't you Willie?" It describes a *third-person* assumption about the *possibility* of a first-person promise.

In pastoral theology, then, these linguistic and logical issues become crystallized into questions about what a reader *stakes* in the reading of biblical texts. Does the text "O God in thee I trust" (Ps. 25:2) come to be read as an affirmation or self-involving act of trust? Does it count-generate acts of renewed faith, or does it merely generate a portrayal of the Psalmist's trust? The logical direction of fit between language and reality is, to use Searle's and Recanati's terminology, opposite in each case. If the words express only the Psalmist's trust, they reflect a *word-to-world* direction of fit; if they commit the reader to an act of trust, they embody a *world-to-word* direction of fit. The latter is not force-neutral. It functions *as a self-involving illocutionary act, which carries practical consequences for the life and behaviour of the reader.*

The difference between a force-neutral reading and a self-involving illocutionary reading of "O God, in thee I trust" *does not* (as Searle and Wolterstorff rightly insist about intention and count-generated acts) consist in some supposed second shadow-action or mental process or vocal or emotional intensity; it lies in the capacity of the same linguistic act to *count* as a commissive and as an expressive act which also carries self-involving consequences in practical life. Wittgenstein observes that the locution "I am in pain" is compatible with saying "It's all right; it has gone off now"; but if I say "I love you" – "oh it has gone off now" the behaviour surrounding the speech-act would make it empty: "One does not say: 'That was not true pain, or it would not have gone off so quickly'."[105] To say "In thee I trust" as a self-involving illocution invites the test that the succession of attitudes and behaviour in which it is embedded will not consist predominantly in fear, doubt, or undue self-reliance. One *could* say, "That was not true trust, or it would not have gone off so quickly."

By the same logic, pledges of love ascribed to God or to Christ in biblical texts can be interpreted with the same propositional content either as force-neutral narrative projections in which God is *described as* making pledges by biblical writers (cf. Austin's

---

[105] L. Wittgenstein, *Zettel*, sect. 504.

"he promises, don't you, Willie?") or as *commissive-expressive illocutions in which a pattern of consequences are locked into its illocutionary force.* Dallas High regularly uses the term "personal backing" to describe the logical asymmetry between first-person and third-person utterances identified by Wittgenstein in such examples as "I love; he loves"; "we mourn; they mourn"; "I believe; she believes".[106] One can say "he believes it but it is false"; but not "I believe it but it is false", because "I believe", like "I love", carries *consequences which constrain possible future language and behaviour.* If it is possible to speak of divine love or divine promise as involving constraints, this may be expressed theologically as the voluntary constraints of covenant faithfulness.

Some critical theorists regard such an approach as over-simple. Derrida offers a critique of Austin's approach, and Stanley Fish, in turn, evaluates Derrida's assessments of Austin in his essay "With the Compliments of the Author: Reflections on Austin and Derrida".[107] Clearly, Austin's notion, shared by Searle, that an author's real-life public commitments "stand behind" the illocutionary force of speech-acts contradicts Derrida's axiom about "orphaned" or "distanced" speech in written texts, and differs from Barthes's principle about the "death of the author". Fish observes that in Austinian traditions of speech-act theory "distanced or orphaned speech" together with "fictional speech" are regarded "as deviations from the full presence and normative contextuality of face-to-face communication".[108]

Derrida's line of approach is to argue that what Austin views and discusses as a series of *contingent* explanations for *"infelicities"* (that is, for conditions that render illocutions "hollow", "void", or inoperative) are actually not contingent but systematic and constitutive for the structure on which they rest. Derrida quotes Austin against Austin himself on the "infelicities" of *all* speech-acts. Fish predictably subsumes everything under "distinctions between different kinds of interpretative practice". The key issue turns on *what we think that "context" means.* Fish asserts:

> It is the difference between thinking of a context as something *in* the world and thinking of a context as a construction *of* the world, a construction that is itself performed under contextualized conditions. Under the latter understanding one can no longer have any simple (that is non-interpretative) recourse to context in order to settle disputes or resolve doubts about meaning, *because contexts,* while they are productive of interpretation, are *also products of interpretation* [first italics, Fish's; second, mine].[109]

This largely represents a reformulation of the issues that we have discussed exhaustively. We need not rehearse here the arguments that we have deployed elsewhere, including in several essays in Part VI of this volume.[110] If "context *in* the world" can be reduced exhaustively and without remainder to a *"construction of* the world", we cannot speak of divine action or revelation *in history* in any way that systematically sustains a clear-cut contrast between revelation and idolatry. *Distinctions ultimately collapse between idolatry*

---

106 Dallas M. High, op. cit., p.124; cf. 146–63.
107 Stanley Fish, *Doing What Comes Naturally*, pp.37–67; cf. 488–92.
108 Ibid., p.40.
109 Ibid., p.52.
110 See, for example, Essay 36, this volume.

and faith; between trust in what is worthy of trust and credulity about what is empty but plausible; and between the worship of community-projections and worship in response to that which addresses us from beyond.

In Essay 7 we have argued that some of the performative utterances pronounced by Jesus presuppose a Christology. Many examples of promise presuppose states of affairs both on the part of a speaker or writer and the addressee. The invitation "Let him who is thirsty come, let him who desires take the water of life without price" (Rev. 22:17) operates as an *invitation* only if the power to relieve thirst can be exercised, and the addressee perceives himself or herself as being in need. Promise, acknowledgement and confession presuppose the states of affairs on the basis of which they operate.

X
Tenth Model: Critical Theory or "Socio-Critical" Theory

Socio-critical models also seek to disengage texts and their uses from wish-fulfilments or social constructs that serve only to affirm and to legitimate individual or social interests. In the context of feminist hermeneutics Janet Radcliffe Richards offers a comment that clearly marks the difference between neo-pragmatic or socio-pragmatic theory and critical or socio-critical theory. On one side she affirms the need for feminist hermeneutics. On the other side she asserts: "Feminism is not concerned with *a group of people it wants to benefit*, but with *a type of injustice it wants to eliminate*" (her italics).[111] On this basis, feminist hermeneutics would not seek to use texts *instrumentally to serve interests already predetermined*, but *transcendentally* to explore *trans-contextual criteria* that would define and evaluate in what justice for women and men would consist.

This exposes the heart of the *theological* problem implicit in the contemporary trend to welcome a wide plurality of interpretative purposes and interests *without the further task of metacritical ranking*. Many respected colleagues seem to adopt this pluralism. Thus John Barton writes that we are no longer entitled to speak of *"correct"* methods or *"successful"* procedures: "The basic flaw ... is the belief that the question 'How should we read the Old Testament?' can be answered".[112] It is a different matter when Robert Morgan writes: "Several *different* aims are *legitimate*. It is these, not the different *methods*, which provide the best guide through the contemporary maze, because they focus attention on the central problem of biblical interpretation in the West today: The tension between uses of the Bible as scripture in religious contexts and the frequently non-religious aims of modern biblical scholarship."[113] The "legitimacy" of *various* aims is not being called into question. But: *if interests wholly determine how we read the text, and if any interest represents as good a candidate as another, how can biblical texts do more than instrumentally serve interests rather than shape, determine and evaluate them? How can they unmask oppressive interests if the status of a socio-critical reading is ranked no higher than a socio-pragmatic reading that serves the interests of the oppressor?*

---

111 Janet Radcliffe Richards, *The Sceptical Feminist*, pp.17–18; cf. 11.
112 John Barton, *Reading the Old Testament*, p.207.
113 Robert Morgan (with John Barton), op. cit., p.271 (his italics).

The problem, in this case, is that pragmatic hermeneutics is *diametrically opposed in practice* to the deepest theoretical concerns which lie behind liberation hermeneutics: those whose readings of texts win the day can only be *the power groups*: the most militant, the most aggressive, the most manipulative.

By contrast, Rowland and Corner remind us that the challenge of liberation hermeneutics is that of how biblical texts may transform *the horizons and the situations of those who have been marginalized*. They refer, for example, to "the subversive memory" of the Apocalypse, "with its alternative horizon beckoning towards a different future". The forces which undergird oppression and injustice are "shown to be unstable and destined to defeat (Rev. 17:16) ... In contrast the apparent fragility of the witness of those who follow the way of Jesus is promised ultimate vindication (Rev. 7 and 14)."[114] But the Book of Revelation does more than offer dreams of the future. It encourages the faithful to create some ethical distance from the typical behaviour of an oppressive society (Rev. 2:14, 20) and resists compromise. Rowland and Corner, however, offer a further contribution when they attack the assumption that liberation "readings" address *only the reading-situations of the oppressed*. They write, "The First World is already intimately involved in the patterns of oppression in the Third World ... The issue of poverty is not a national one, but an international one."[115]

David Kelsey and Frances Young ascribe to biblical texts as Christian Scripture the capacity "*to shape persons' identities so decisively as to transform them*" (Kelsey's italics).[116] But in pastoral theology many writers and teachers tend to allow reflection to revolve round "the present situation". Don Browning observes, "It is the primary task of pastoral theology to bring together theological ethics and the social sciences to articulate a normative vision of the human life cycle"; while David Deeks writes in his book on pastoral theology (1987) "Pastoral theology begins with the search we all make for meaning in life."[117] We have reservations about a tendency to grant too great a privilege to the present situation, as if this provided the one fixed point around which theological reflections should revolve in pastoral theology. Without doubt, while the centre of gravity in neo-pragmatic hermeneutics lies predominantly in the present, critical or socio-critical hermeneutics offers resources to locate interpretation and meaning on a broader canvas that respects the importance of a foundational past, a promised future and the possibility of judgement and grace "from beyond" the local world.

The practical character of theological endeavour, Farley rightly complains, is "defeated from the start by the dispersion of theology into independent areas of scholarship".[118] Nicholas Lash criticizes a divided "relay-race" model of hermeneutics.[119] Biblical scholars of a certain kind assume that they can package "what the text meant", and pass it on to

---

[114] Christopher Rowland and Mark Corner, op. cit., pp.141, 142 and 147.

[115] Ibid., pp.157 and 163.

[116] George Lindbeck, op. cit., p.118; and David Kelsey, op. cit., p.91.

[117] Don Browning, "Pastoral Theology in a Pluralistic Age", loc. cit., p.187; and David Deeks, *Pastoral Theology: An Inquiry* (London: Epworth Press, 1987), p.67.

[118] Edward Farley, "Theology and Practice Outside the Clerical Paradigm", in Don S. Browning (ed.), op. cit., p.30.

[119] Nicholas Lash, "What Might Martyrdom Mean?", in N. Lash, *Theology on the Way to Emmaus* (London: SCM, 1986), p.77; cf. 75–92 (also in *Ex Auditu*, vol. 1).

the systematic and pastoral theologians for contemporary processing as if it were an entity that could be abstracted from the whole hermeneutical process itself. Thus a single hermeneutical process of understanding the interactive horizons of past and present is split apart and segmented into "stages" in which *biblical* specialists are tempted to regard the texts as "objects" of historical-past enquiry; *systematic theologians* are tempted to abstract doctrine from its double-sided historical contingency, and *pastoral* theologians are tempted to privilege the present as the key determinant of "relevancy" for assessing what sources and traditions of the past can meaningfully address the present.

If hermeneutical theorists are right to attack this seemingly innocent descriptivism, should not the same challenge be addressed to those pastoral theologians who begin with bare "description" of the present situation *in abstraction from its past and future context* of theological foundation and theological promise? Might we not justly conclude about some methods of pastoral psychology and the use of sociological data that this, equally, can come *"dangerously close to endorsing the positivist myth that it [social and pastoral analysis] is not yet interpretation"*?[120]

On the other hand, the relation between biblical material and the present situation cannot be regarded as fully symmetrical. One test question is this: would it be the same, in principle, to de-centre the present situation as a criterion of theological relevance and truth as to de-centre the biblical texts and their witness to Christ and to the cross as a criterion of relevance and truth? Pannenberg has convincingly argued that the *present* can be understood only in the light of the past *history* of traditions as these move towards the promised goal of the *future* revealed in a provisional and preliminary way in the resurrection of Christ.[121] For Moltmann, too, the future promise of God may itself bring transforming discontinuities, which transform the meaning of the present in the light of a new future.[122] *Divine promise shapes both the nature of reality and how the present is to be understood.* Promissory biblical texts, we argued in Part II, operate with illocutionary force in terms of a "world-to-word" direction of fit creatively and they *de-centre the present situation as a fixed or immutable point of reference in transformative action.*

We have edited out the concluding paragraphs of this chapter from *New Horizons* because these paragraphs will come more appropriately in the last essay of this volume. They can be found there if any reader wishes to trace the final argument that brings the last chapter of *New Horizons* to its completion.

Towards the end of his masterly survey, *Hermeneutics and Social Science*, Zygmunt Bauman argues that the task of hermeneutics for social science is that of *"constructing a form of life of a 'higher order' which will incorporate previous [ones] as ... sub-forms"* (his italics).[123] This can be achieved, he explains, "by spotting the general in the particular, by enlarging both the alien and one's own experience so as to construct a large system in which each 'makes sense' to the other".[124] It will be apparent that Bauman shares some of

[120] Nicholas Lash, loc. cit.
[121] W. Pannenberg, *Basic Questions in Theology*, 3 vols (Eng., London: SCM, 1970–73), vol. 1, p.15; and throughout his works, including *Basic Questions in Theology*, vol. 3, pp.192–210.
[122] J. Moltmann, *Theology of Hope* (Eng., London: SCM, 1967); and many subsequent works.
[123] Zygmunt Bauman, op. cit., p.217.
[124] Ibid., p.218.

the major operational hermeneutical tools which Wittgenstein, Habermas and Apel also share. Bauman follows Habermas and Apel in arguing that hermeneutical understanding rests ultimately on *"a broader basis of intersubjectivity which forms of life could share"* (his italics).[125] His main points are that: (a) understandings of "present situations" are always interactive understandings, *always on the move*; and (b) that *in principle* the present is to be understood as a sub-form of life to be contextualized within the *larger or "higher"* frame.

We understand the present by *incorporating it within some larger frame*; we do not "understand" simply by making "the present situation" equivalent to the horizon of understanding. It would be over-simple to transpose this into a well-worn polarization between "Bible-centred" and "experience-centred" orientations in theology; it arises from deeper and wider questions about the very nature of understanding, and the relativizations of the present within the larger frame of past, present, and future. Theology itself is co-extensive with the larger frame of biblical and eschatological horizons within which sources and interpretations of both past and present operate.

(3) At first sight the importance of *"relevancy"* seems to call strongly for decisive emphasis on the present situation and its particularities. But a careful examination of one of the most important sociological expositions of this concept seems to suggest a surprising conclusion, which brings us back to questions about *enlarged horizons* and eventually to universals. The work to which we refer is the important contribution of Alfred Schutz. His work on criteria of relevance appears in his *Collected Papers* (Eng. edn, 1962, 1964, 1966) and in his *Reflections on the Problem of Relevance* (Eng. edn, 1970).[126]

Alfred Schutz developed the category of *life-world*, found in Husserl, and, less directly, Dilthey. Like Husserl and Dilthey, Schutz was concerned about the status of "objective" understanding of the subjectivities of persons and of social actions and agencies. He parted company from Husserl, however, in refusing to "bracket out" the pre-reflexive life-world, but by beginning with it. The life-world yields routine patterns which we scarcely notice because we take them for granted. Retrospectively we assign meaning to *what is relevant to particular purposes at hand by processes of typification*. In his study of Schutz's theory of relevance, Ronald Cox urges that "systems of relevance" move on and undergo change "as we work toward our purposes and goals"; they apply "until further notice".[127] Even more important, because typifications gloss over unique particularities, the *group* becomes fundamental in *sharing* systems of relevance. Hence: the emerging of new purposes and new interests in the context of a new or wider social interaction and fresh information-inputs will produce new criteria of relevance and revise prior typifications.

A concrete illustration will illuminate the principle. We may envisage *the transformation of criteria of relevance brought about by the experience of loving another person.* Examples from everyday life abound on all sides. A young person may share with an "in-group" interests in rock music and motorbikes. He or she falls in love with someone whose peers from a different "in-group" reflect typifications and relevances drawn from an enthusiasm for

---

[125] Ibid., p.240.
[126] Alfred Schutz, *Collected Papers* (3 vols) (The Hague: Nijhoff, 1962, 1964 and 1966); and *Reflections on the Problem of Relevance* (ed. R.M. Zaner) (New Haven, CT: Yale University Press, 1970).
[127] Ronald R. Cox, *Schutz's Theory of Relevance: A Phenomenological Critique* (The Hague: Nijhoff, 1978), pp.3 and 5.

classical music and English cathedrals. If the two persons are really "in love", each of them will discover that his or her criteria of relevance rapidly expands and becomes transformed. Further, their *prior typifications of each other's relevances will be shattered and disengaged from stereotypes.*

In theological terms love represents the major transforming force of all systems and criteria of relevance. Interests which have hitherto gathered round the self as a system of self-centred relevance begin to be regrouped and reranked round the self of another, or even the Other. Ultimately, and in the sharpest theological terms, a person may share in the experience to which Paul alludes: "The love of God is poured into our hearts through the Holy Spirit, who has been given to us" (Rom. 5:5). In this case, the outgoing love from the heart of God to his creation will constitute a new motive-force that *redefines criteria of relevance for the Christian believer: the goal of transformation into the image of Christ is to see the world through the eyes and interests of God's purposes for the world.*

The example of the young couple whose criteria of relevance and interest become transformed when they fall in love, and when they interact with each other's "group", brings into focus one way of understanding the relation between meta-critique and pluralism. In one sense their experience affirms the reality and inevitability of pluralism: what, up to that moment, they had taken for granted as the *only* obvious way of understanding and evaluating the world has become relativized as no more than one option among others. But in another sense, their love-relationship has now *enlarged* their understanding, with the result that their former interests and stereotypifications appear from their new and transformed vantage point to be relatively *narrow, ill-informed* and *self-centred.* Whether or not they have ever encountered the term "meta-critical", their new attitudes will at very least imply fresh *judgements*, including *reassessments* of earlier *criteria* of relevance, that is,a *critical reranking* of their earlier *critical norms.*

In Christian theology every tradition in the New Testament about *the cross* challenges any context-relative or ethnocentric understanding of its status: the cross impinges equally on "Jew and Greek, slave and free, male and female" (Gal. 3:28). It reverses all contextual traditions of wisdom including scribal authorities, wisdom traditions, philosophical world-views and religious hunger for pragmatic criteria (1 Cor. 1:18–25). Christ cannot be parcelled out (1 Cor. 1:13). The single new creation embraces all in one new person (2 Cor. 5:17; Eph. 2:15); for all merely contextual criteria of relevance, especially criteria centred on the individual or corporate self, share a single all-embracing crucifixion (Rom. 6:3–11). Baptism constitutes the sign of oneness that transcends ethnocentric division in the one baptism (Mark 10:38; Eph. 4:4, 5). The cup that proclaims the cross (1 Cor. 11:26) is, like the bread, one (1 Cor. 10:16, 17). Whereas Paul underlines the *transcending of ethnic relativity* in the cross, the writer to the Hebrews stresses its *temporal finality*, as finished, entire, complete, and definitive, and wholly incapable of future revision (Heb. 1:3; 5:9; 6:19, 20; 7:11–28; 8:5, 6; 9:11–14, 26; 10:12, 14; 11:1).

Thus the hermeneutical point about the cross lies in its discontinuity with contextual or self-centred criteria of relevance. The cross establishes new criteria of relevance. Moltmann declares that the cross and the resurrection have a capacity to transcend and to surprise all prior human expectations which are projected forward simply on the basis of present states of affairs.

CHAPTER TWENTY-TWO

A Retrospective Reappraisal: Lexicography, Exegesis and Strategies of Interpretation (New essay)

This reappraisal, written in December 2004, takes account of some recent publications that post-date the composition of the essays that constitute Part IV. I argue that the magnificent third edition of the standard Greek lexicon of the New Testament revised by F.W. Danker (BDAG, 2000) appears to corroborate some of the lexicographical conclusions urged in the above essays. I also take note of Bruce Winter's recent arguments (2003) about the meaning of the notoriously difficult verse 1 Corinthians 12:3. I conclude after careful evaluation that I now favour his proposed exegesis of this verse. The final part of this essay argues for the importance of exploring varied hermeneutical strategies for relating two sets of variables: on one side varied biblical genres and texts, and on the other side the variable situations of readers, considered within the context of pastoral theology. The essay concludes with a brief comment on reception history, although Essay 40 also returns to this subject.

Four of the six essays above in this Part IV draw upon lexicographical research (especially 16, 17, 19 and 20); two are primarily exegetical (18 and 19); while the former of these also explores reception history. The longest and most substantial of the essays (21) sets out specific hermeneutical models and interpretative strategies for facilitating understanding, engagement and (where appropriate) transformation, in relating different types and genre of biblical texts to different situations among readers. This raises cognate questions about the nature of pastoral theology especially in relation to hermeneutics. I offer here some retrospective comments under three headings: lexicography, exegesis and hermeneutical strategies for differing reading situations.

I

Lexicography

I had completed and sent to the publishers my commentary on the Greek text of 1 Corinthians before the appearance of Frederick William Danker's magnificent third edition of Walter Bauer (with W.F. Arndt, F.W. Gingrich and F.W. Danker), *A Greek-English Lexicon of the New Testament* (1979). The third edition (2000) is now known as *BDAG* in distinction from *BAGD* (second edition of 1979; first edition, 1957).[1] Up to 2000 (and the

---

[1] Frederick W. Danker (ed.), *A Greek-English Lexicon of the New Testament and Other Early Christian Literature* (3rd edn (*BDAG*), Chicago, IL and London: University of Chicago Press, 2000); based on *BAGD* 2nd edn, and the German 6th edition of Walter Bauer, *Grieschisch-deutsches Wörterbuch* (ed. by K. Aland and B. Aland with V. Reichmann).

publication of my commentary) I had utilized for my lexicographical research only the second edition of 1979, alongside such other standard resources as Grimm-Thayer, Moulton-Milligan's *Vocabulary*, Louw-Nida, Liddell-Scott-Jones, G.W.H. Lampe's *Patristic Greek Lexicon* (where relevant), and other resources.[2]

Since the interpretation of the terminology for gifts of the Spirit in 1 Cor. 12–14 remains common to three of the essays (16, 18 and 20), a first question arises from the possible impact of the third edition of *BDAG* upon Paul's deployment of the Greek vocabulary on which he draws to refer to these phenomena. The three key terms here are χάρισμα, γλῶσσα and προφητεία although other terms also come into play.

On the first of these three terms, it is noteworthy that the third edition does not seek to over-specify the nature of χάρισμα in sensitive contexts in 1 Corinthians. *BDAG* makes the central point that χάρισμα denotes "that which is freely and graciously given", and this coheres very well indeed with the approach that I have adopted above.[3] In a broad sub-classification the third edition places under "gift" such straightforward passages as Rom. 11:29; 1 Cor. 1:7 and Rom. 6:23. With justified caution, *BDAG* places under "special gift" such passages as Rom. 12:6, 1 Cor. 7:7 and 1 Cor. 12:4, 9, 28, 30 and 31.[4] *Such valid caution avoids any over-translation that goes further than the text.* "Special gift" suggests, rightly, a gift given for some *specific purpose*, although this *may or may not* be given for some particular temporal event or occasion. This accords exactly with my argument that whether these "special gifts" are spontaneous or "supernatural" is *unspecified* in the text of the epistle. To claim that this is the case requires internal or external evidence beyond the meanings of the terms that Paul employs in these verses.

The grouping of Pauline uses of χάρισμα is also constructive, and consonant with the arguments of these essays. The "general" meaning of the first group underlines the point that the "gift" remains "freely and graciously given", without strings. In Rom. 6:23 χάρισμα stands in semantic opposition to a wage that is earned by achievement, and Rom. 11:29 corroborates this. Hence Paul's substitution of the Corinthian preferred term περὶ δὲ τῶν πνευματικῶν (1 Cor. 12:1) in favour of his preferred term χαρισμάτων (12:4) or χαρίσματα (12:9) underlines his rejection of any claim to regard "gifts" from the Holy Spirit as indicators of achievement or "high status".

In the period that postdates my arguments to this effect in these essays, David R. Hall's perceptive book *The Unity of the Corinthian Correspondence* (2003) adds yet further weight to this diagnosis of the major difference between Paul and many of the Christians in

---

2   C.L.W. Grimm and J.H. Thayer, *A Greek-English Lexicon of the New Testament* (4th edn, Edinburgh: T. & T. Clark, 1901, rp. 1953); J.P. Louw and E.A. Nida, *Greek-English Lexicon of the New Testament Based on Semantic Domains* (2nd edn, New York: United Bible Societies, 2 vols, 1988–89); J.H. Moulton and G. Milligan, *The Vocabulary of the Greek Testament Illustrated from the Papyri and Other Non-literary Sources* (London: Hodder & Stoughton, 1930, rp. 1952); H.G. Liddell and R. Scott, *A Greek-English Lexicon* (new edn, ed. H.S. Jones and R. McKenzie, Oxford: Clarendon Press, 1940); and G.W.H. Lampe (ed.), *A Patristic Greek Lexicon* (Oxford: Clarendon Press, 1961), which is an invaluable resource also for the history of the reception of texts. In addition broader approaches were consulted in G. Kittel and G. Friedrich, *Theological Dictionary of the New Testament* (10 vols, Grand Rapids, MI: Eerdmans, 1964–76); and H. Balz and G. Schneider (eds), *Exegetical Dictionary of the New Testament* (3 vols, Eng., Grand Rapids, MI: Eerdmans, 1978–80).

3   *BDAG*, p.1081.

4   Loc. cit.

Corinth.[5] Hall regards the point at issue between them as primarily "the clash between two different understandings of prophetic inspiration. Paul believes inspired prophets were still in control of themselves (14:32) ... Some argumentative people at Corinth (11:16) who described themselves as 'spiritual' (14:37) believed in an ecstatic type of inspiration that made self-control impossible."[6] "Their exercise of spiritual gifts was individualistic and competitive ..."[7]

BDAG's judicious grouping of "special" gifts is no less helpful to our arguments. Rom. 12: 6–8 includes among these "special gifts" not only προφητεία (v. 6), but also διακονία and διδασκαλία (v. 7), and παράκλησις (v. 8). The REB translates vv. 7–8: "the gift of administration to administer, the gift of teaching to teach, the gift of counselling to counsel". Neither administration nor teaching nor counselling can be "spontaneous"; *spontaneous administration is a contradiction in terms*. Even if we translate διακονία as "service", this remains a sustained activity. Moreover the parallel articular participles, ὁ διδάσκων ... ὁ παρακαλῶν suggest habituated capacities freely given, not *ad hoc*, intermittent, irregular phenomena. This is precisely the meaning and force of 1 Cor. 7:7, which BDAG includes in this group. It is a "special gift", but its mode and duration remains unspecified. In my commentary on the Greek Text I translated this verse, "But each person has his or her own gift freely bestowed from God: one person, this kind; and another, that kind." This reflects Paul's later emphasis in Romans on "different gifts" (διάφορα, Rom. 12:6), together with a parallel entailment of a *sustained, habituated, gift* in the case of a gift to be fully content with a celibate life (v. 7a, ὡς καὶ ἐμαυτόν). It is inconceivable that the freely given gift of contentment with the celibate state could be spontaneous or intermittent.

BDAG rightly place 1 Cor. 12:4, 9, 28, 30 and 31 within the same lexicographical sub-classification, for there is no clear explicit evidence in the text to suggest otherwise. None of this excludes the possibility that *some* "special gifts" may *sometimes* be "spontaneous" or intermittent, for Paul constantly stresses not only their variety but also in some cases their generic variety: they are of "various kinds" (cf. χαρίσματα ἰαμάτων, 12:9; and especially γένη γλωσσῶν, 12:10). To assume that they must be spontaneous is to read more into the Greek than the text will support. The gift of faith (πίστις) is admirably described as a "special" gift. Clearly it is given to some Christians and not to others, and is distinct from the "saving" faith of every Christian. It probably denotes a robust trust in God's purposes in difficult times.[8]

BDAG rightly observes the same degree of non-specificity in its entry under προφητεία.[9] Prophetic speech denotes: (1) an act of interpreting the divine will and purpose (as in Rom. 11:6); (2) a gift of interpreting the divine will and purpose (as in 1 Cor. 12:10; 13:2; 14:22; Rom. 12:6), including "various kinds and grades of prophetic gifts" (1 Cor. 13:8; 1 Thess. 5:20); and (3) utterances of one who interprets the divine will

---

[5]   David R. Hall, *The Unity of the Corinthian Correspondence* (London and New York: T. & T. Clark and Continuum, 2003), especially pp.51–79.

[6]   Hall, *Unity*, p.71.

[7]   Hall, *Unity*, p.74.

[8]   See Thiselton, *First Epistle to the Corinthians: A Commentary on the Greek Text* (Grand Rapids, MI: Eerdmans, 2000), pp.944–8, precisely headed "faith as a special gift" (p.944).

[9]   BDAG, p.889, col. ii–p.890, col. i.

and purpose, including "inspired statements in the form of a prophetic saying" (1 Cor. 14:6; 1 Thess. 5:20; Rev. 1:3).[10] The use of the Greek term to denote an act, a gift, or an utterance directed towards understanding and articulating the divine will and purpose fully accords with our arguments in the essays above.

These careful and judicious explications of meaning, once again, go no further than the text. They allow room for the views of David Hill, Ulrich Müller and T.W. Gillespie that prophetic speech, for Paul, includes Christian preaching with pastoral and practical application to life.[11]

In my commentary I consider the Hellenistic background (including the conflicting views of R. Reitzenstein on one side, and C. Forbes and M.E. Boring on the other); questions about an apocalyptic background (including the claims of G. Dautzenberg), and the shape of the debate as a whole. I conclude with Hill, Müller and Gillespie (and in part anticipating Hall) that the prevailing view in Corinth is different from Paul's, and that Paul's example of prophetic utterance is close to the model of the pastoral sermon. In particular prophetic preaching is likely to include themes of judgement and grace. The important arguments of K.O. Sandnes and P. Vielhauer confirm that prophetic speech, at least for Paul, has as its main aim the corporate building-up of the whole church.[12]

The late twentieth-century notion of ejaculating individuated "messages" to particular persons within a congregation hardly fits this corporate Pauline frame of thought very readily. Further, David Hall, as we noted, affirms the different standpoints on the part of Paul and many in Corinth with detailed cumulative argument and with additional reference to 2 Corinthians.[13] Hall urges that the differences between Paul and many in Corinth over their respective understandings of "inspiration" amount to belief in "another Spirit" and "another Gospel". The Corinthian view is at variance with the life-style of those "called to share the weakness and humiliation of their crucified Lord".[14] This radical difference manifests itself also in quite different uses of the terms "freedom", "wisdom", "foolishness" and "testing". This is "the clash of two different understandings of prophetic inspiration".[15]

Two extended Notes on prophetic speech in my commentary cohere closely with many of the comments offered by Gillespie and Hill. We conclude that many attempts to reconstruct the phenomenon of prophecy in the New Testament are simply too specific to follow from the strictly limited evidence. On what grounds can Cothenet, for example, assert that "free" exposition of scripture was "a defining characteristic" of New Testament prophecy?[16] Even Dunn's assertion, "it does not denote a previously prepared

---

[10] *BDAG*, loc. cit. The entries under προφήτης and προφητείω do not significantly change the emphasis.

[11] D. Hall, *New Testament Prophecy* (London: Marshall, 1979), esp. pp.110–40 and 193–213; U.B. Müller, *Prophetie und Predigt Im N.T.* (Güttersloh, Mohn, 1975); T.W. Gillespie, *The First Theologians: A Study in Early Christian Prophecy* (Grand Rapids, MI: Eerdmans 1994).

[12] K.O. Sandnes, *Paul – One of the Prophets?* (Tübingen: Mohr [WUNT 243], 1991), and P. Vielhauer, *Oikodome: Das Bild vom Bau in der christlichen Literatur vom Neuen Testament bis Clemen Alexandrinus* (Karlsruhe: Harrarowitz, 1940).

[13] David R. Hall, *Unity*, especially pp.77–9 and 149–70.

[14] Hall, *Unity*, pp.163 and 183.

[15] Hall, *Unity*, p.71.

[16] E. Cothenet, "Les prophètes chrétiens comme exégètes charismatiques de l'écriture", in J. Panagopoulos (ed.), ἡ ἐκκληΐα προφητῶν (Athens: Historical Publications, 1979), pp.77–107.

sermon ... It is a spontaneous utterance" (discussed in Essay 18), may be true of some prophetic utterances, but on what grounds can we regard it as true of *all* such speech?[17] In 1 Cor. 14:3 Paul explicitly states that the task of the prophet is to build, to encourage, to exhort, and to bring comfort (οἰκοδομή, παράκλησις, παραμυθία). It builds the church as a whole (ἐκκλησίαν οἰκοδομεῖ, v. 4b) in contrast to the more pejorative and individualistic flavour of v. 4a, which Vielhauer understands to denote *self-induced* "inspiration".[18]

A third lexicographical entry from *BDAG* also seems to strengthen the conclusions of the essays above, namely the entry on γλῶσσα.[19] Again the categorization and grouping is very helpful. Under (1) γλῶσσα denotes "organ of speech, tongue" as in Luke 16:24, Mark 7:33, 35; Rom. 3:13; 14:11; James 1:26; 3:5–6; and 1 Cor. 14: 9. (2) The third edition rightly distinguishes this first use from a second, namely: "a body of words and systems that makes up a distinctive language", as in Acts 2:6, 11. Other examples include Rom. 14:11; Phil. 2:11; and Rev. 5:9; 7:9. (3) The third category is "an utterance outside the normal pattern of intelligible speech and therefore requiring special interpretation, ecstatic speech" as in 1 Cor. 14:1–27, 39; and also 1 Cor. 12:10, 28, 30; 13:8; Acts 10:46; 19:6. "There is no doubt about the thing referred to, namely the strange speech of persons in religious ecstasy."[20]

This supports the view that I have advocated above, in common with Krister Stendahl and Gerd Theissen. The separation of uses (1) and (2) is important. It removes the force of a spurious counter-argument that some have addressed to my essays above (especially to Essay 16), namely the reply: "but γλῶσσα *means* 'a language'". Such an answer presupposes a conclusion to the very question that is open and at issue! When and whether γλῶσσα denotes "a language" depends entirely on contextual factors, as the separation of categories in *BDAG* helpfully indicates. The essays above appeared not only before *BDAG* but also before the long extended Notes and comments on "speaking in tongues" in my commentary.[21]

Once again Paul leaves the meaning open-ended by stating that there are "species" or "kinds" of tongues (γένη γλωσσῶν, 12:10). Theissen observes in his *Psychological Aspects of Pauline Theology* that the phenomenon may refer to a welling-up of pre-conscious or subconscious yearnings or intuitive intimations of wonder, and this makes it entirely credible that, like experiences of laughter or tears, a private release of praise may count as a genuine gift from the Spirit, even if Paul also expresses the hope that these pre-conscious experiences will become conscious and capable of being articulated publicly for the building up of the whole church.[22] In Essay 16 I argue that it is the person who speaks in a tongue from whom Paul hopes for articulate communication. There is no need to postulate a supposed third-party "interpreter", not least since τις (someone) does not occur in the Greek of 14:13.

---

[17] J.D.G. Dunn, *Jesus and the Spirit* (London: SCM, 1975), p.228.
[18] For a fuller discussion with documentation , see Thiselton, *First Corinthians*, pp.956–65 and 1087–95.
[19] *BDAG*, p.201, col. ii, and p.202, col. i.
[20] Loc. cit., p.201, col. ii.
[21] Thiselton, *First Epistle*, pp.1096–118.
[22] G. Theissen, *Psychological Aspects of Pauline Theology* (Eng., Edinburgh: T. & T. Clark, 1987), pp.59–114 and 292–341.

II

Exegesis

A striking publication caused me to have second thoughts about the exegesis of a notoriously difficult passage in 1 Corinthians. A new suggestion came from Bruce Winter in a study published in 2001, after I had completed both my commentary and all but one of the essays in Part IV.[23] The difficult verse is 1 Cor. 12:3a, which the NRSV renders, "Therefore I want you to understand that no one speaking by the Spirit of God ever says, 'Let Jesus be cursed'". Verse 3b is relatively unproblematic: "and no one can say 'Jesus is Lord' except by the Holy Spirit". This is usually understood as antithetical to v. 3a.

In my commentary on the Greek text I have listed and evaluated twelve interpretations of v. 3a as worthy of mention.[24] Of these, four command some support from respected groups of scholars:

(1) Oscar Cullmann calls attention to the possibility of a persecution setting, in which Ἀνάθεμα Ἰησοῦς would function as a way of renouncing the gospel.[25] This is conceivable, but two problems come to mind. (a) Is systematic persecution evident at this early date? (b) Further, why should anyone assume that the Holy Spirit could ever prompt such a renunciation?

(2) Margaret Thrall, W. Schmithals and J. Weiss suggest that self-styled "spiritual people might utter the 'curse' under a trance-like ecstatic state".[26] In favour of this: (a) "spiritual people" in Corinth may well have held an extremely radical affirmation of "freedom" to let "the Spirit" do or say anything; and (b) modern psychiatric research about the removal of the censor under certain conditions lends a prima facie plausibility to this possibility. But the situation does nevertheless seem to stretch credibility, although it remains entirely possible.

(3) A variant of this suggests that the "curse" relates to the earthly Jesus of Nazareth, in contrast to a "spiritual" focus on the raised, "spiritual" Christ.[27]

(4) W.C. van Unnik proposes that the "cursed" Jesus is the Jesus of the cross bearing the curse of God upon sin as sin-bearer and atonement (cf. Deut. 21:23 and Gal. 3:13). In this case v. 3a signifies the confession of those who believe in the efficacy of the cross as atonement but not in the resurrection of Christ.[28] This may have more to commend it than

---

[23] Bruce Winter, "Religious Curses and Christian Vindictiveness, I Cor. 12–14", in *After Paul left Corinth* (Grand Rapids, MI: Eerdmans, 2001), pp.164–83.

[24] Thiselton, *First Epistle*, pp.917–25.

[25] O. Cullmann, *The Christology of the New Testament* (Eng., London: SCM, 1959), pp.218–20; and *Les Première Confessions de Foi Chrétiennes* (Paris: Presses Universitaires de France, 2nd edn, 1948), p.13.

[26] M. Thrall, *1 and 2 Corinthians* (Cambridge: CUP, 1965), p.86; J. Weiss, *Der erste Korintherbriefe* (Göttingen: Vandenhoeck & Ruprecht, 1910), pp.295–7; W. Schmithals, *Gnosticism in Corinth* (Eng., Nashville, TN: Abingdon, 1971), pp.124–32.

[27] See Schmithals, loc. cit.

[28] W.C. van Unnik, "Jesus: Anathema or Kyrios (1 Cor. 12:3)", in B. Lindars and S.S. Smalley (eds), *Christ and the Spirit in the New Testament: Studies in Honour of C.F.D. Moule* (Cambridge: CUP, 1973), pp.113–26.

the other views (1)–(3), but seems to emerge without adequate context except for anticipating ch. 15.

Bruce Winter has recently put forward the following proposal. First, it is beyond dispute that in the context of hellenistic and oriental religions, many worshippers of cult deities sought to "use" prayers to the deity to gain some advantage for themselves over against some rival, notably in business or in capturing the affections of a lover. The so-called Magical Papyri contain abundant evidence of this. Paul states in 1 Cor. 3:1–3 that the attitude of jealousy and competitive strife shown by Christians in Corinth cannot be ascribed to the Holy Spirit, although those concerned still viewed themselves as "spiritual". In fact, Paul insists, such people are the opposite, namely σαρκικοί (v. 3).

Second, in recent years some twenty-seven ancient "curse" tablets, made of lead, have been discovered in or around Corinth, fourteen on the slopes of Acrocorinth within the precincts of pagan temples. These constitute clear evidence of requests from worshippers "to curse" the attempts of personal rivals to gain advantage in commerce, in love, or in other spheres. Worshippers explicitly request their cult deity to curse their rivals.

Third, although every major English VS translates "Jesus be (or is) cursed", the Greek of 12:3a is simply Ἀνάθεμα Ἰησοῦς, and Winter understands this to mean "May Jesus *grant* a curse", in the active sense.

The meaning of v. 3a now seems clearer and more likely to fit the situation. To try to "use" Jesus to gain advantage over others coheres with the competitive attitude of strife and manipulation that Paul finds in Corinth (cf. 3:1–3; 6:1–8). Further, some, according to 3:1–3, see as such a competitive, even malicious, attitude as compatible with claims to be "spiritual" or inspired by the Spirit. In 12:3 Paul rejects such a view, stating that the criterion for being led by the Spirit or open to the Spirit includes (1) ethical transformation, and (2) transparent allegiance in life and thought to the practical Lordship of Christ.

This suggestion is forceful. It may perhaps contain two possible weaknesses, although both can be answered. (1) Is v. 3a now antithetical in linguistic structure to the structure of v. 3b? Even if it does not, the ideas and concepts remain antithetical whether or not the syntax matches its opposite linguistic expression precisely. (2) A second query might concern the semantic and lexicographical scope of ἀνάθεμα. BDAG lists three main categories of meaning.[29] These are: (1) "that which is dedicated as a votive offering"; (2) "that which has been cursed, *cursed, accursed*", in accordance with the LXX's generally using the term in a *passive* sense to translate the Hebrew חרם, either *consecrated* or *accursed*; and (3) "the context that is expressed in a curse, a *curse*". The third edition BDAG placed 1 Cor. 12:3 under category 2, and this would militate against Winter's exegesis. But if we regard 12:3 as coming within category 3, we should not unduly stretch the Greek to assume a contextually implicit verb: Jesus [grant] a curse. Moreover there is a strong counter-argument. The lexicographical evidence for uses in the papyri and non-literary Greek seems to counter-balance BDAG. Moulton and Milligan find no problem in construing ἀνάθεμα to mean "Curse!" (as a plea or directive) in first- and second-century

---

[29]   BDAG, p.63.

curse tablets, including the lead tablets found at Knidos in 150 BC and up to later fourth-century Attic examples.[30] In the light of the detailed discussion on all sides, I have therefore changed my view from a tentative leaning towards the possibility of van Unnik's suggestion (with that of Weiss and Thrall as a possible alternative) to the careful conclusions of Bruce Winter.

This in no way diminishes my main argument about 1 Cor. 12:3 as a *self-involving speech-act*. This early Christian confession concerns daily life and practical attitudes as well as cognitive content. I have explicated this in Essay 20, above.

I have already alluded to another work that postdates the essays above, namely David R. Hall, *The Unity of the Corinthian Correspondence* (2003). In virtually all work on 1 Corinthians I have stressed not only my belief in the integrity of the epistle in contrast to partition theories, but also to a *very close unity and coherence of thought* throughout 1 Corinthians. I argue strongly for this, for example in Essay 41, below. I have urged in other writings that respect for "the other" permeates Paul's arguments from not later than ch. 7 through to the end of ch. 11, and then most emphatically in 12:1–14:40.

Margaret Mitchell and others have well argued the first point against partition theories.[31] However, I read with delight the forceful comments of David R. Hall concerning the unity of *thought and argument* as well as the literary unity that characterizes 1 Corinthians, and indeed also Paul's continuing dialogue into 2 Corinthians.[32] Although I wish that Hall had made more of my attempts to identify numerous links between chapters 7–11 and 12–14 in terms of respect and love for "the other", I regard his cumulative argument as adding force to mine, and thereby confirming the exegetical trends reflected in Essays 16, 18, 19 and 20.

If I have reservations about some of Hall's arguments, I remain to be more fully convinced about his conclusions on 1 Cor. 6:1–8, and I am less certain than he that Theissen's identification of "the strong" in social terms necessarily excludes the role that Hall rightly assigns to "spiritual persons" in Corinth. It is conceivable that each version of elitism added force to the other. Hall's reappraisal of the social situation behind 11:12–34 may be less clear-cut than he suggests. On the other hand I find his general approach convincing, and he provides incisive arguments and suggests pause for further thought on many major questions.

III

Ten Strategies for Interpretation in Relation to the Varied Situations of Readers, and the Value of Reception History

After the publication of *The Two Horizons* in 1980, reviews were usually more than generous, but one or two offered the comment that more on my own personal views concerning hermeneutical models and practical procedures would be welcome in a

---

30 Moulton-Milligan, *Vocabulary of the Greek Testament*, p.33.
31 M.M. Mitchell, *Paul and the Rhetoric of Reconciliation* (Tübingen: Mohr, 1992).
32 Hall, *Unity*, especially pp.30–50, but also throughout.

subsequent book. I tried to achieve this in *New Horizons in Hermeneutics* in 1992, and perhaps the climax of this aspect comes in Chapters 15 and 16. An edited and radically abbreviated version of these chapters appears as Essay 21, above. This has been edited more than has been the case for other essays to avoid undue length. It has puzzled me, however, that *New Horizons* has remained less widely known than the earlier work, in spite of my responding to this request.

Hermeneutics demands respect for contingency and particularity. Many textbooks on this subject are disappointing largely because they too readily generalize and remain in the realm of the abstract, unless of course, they descend to being only handbooks of exegesis. If wrestling with Wittgenstein and Gadamer achieves anything, this confirms that *what understanding amounts to* emerges in the very process of interaction between *particular* interpretative procedures, *particular* readers, and *particular* genres, and *particular* texts. Nevertheless, it also emerges that this does not achieve *a hermeneutic* if we merely descend into the *anarchy of radical contextual relativism*.

Hence the explication of ten distinct reading-strategies in Essay 21 fulfils three purposes in such a collection as this. First, it *steers a middle course* between the wooden generalizations of "rules" of interpretation on one side and contextual or neo-pragmatic anarchy on the other. Second, it demonstrates the *huge variety of resources and models* that emerge from multi-disciplinary hermeneutics. Third, it shows *how hermeneutical theory operates in practice with cash-currency in a variety of practical or pastoral situations*.

In some respects Essay 21 constitutes, therefore, the heart of this collection. Moreover I did not select the term "pastoral theology" lightly. This essay explores the impact of hermeneutics upon pastoral theology, and suggests implications for the nature of pastoral theology. Some readers have stated that they see this material as "the best" from *New Horizons* as a whole. Nevertheless a painstaking assessment of the value and significance of a variety of hermeneutical resources from speech-act theory, through Gadamer and Ricoeur, to feminist and liberation hermeneutics and narrative theory remain indispensable for this subject.

Reception history (Essay 18) has now become a growing interest in hermeneutics. Ideally, given more time and no limit to the length of the essay, I should not have limited it to the Patristic period. But the purpose of the volume also suggested engagement with the work of James Dunn. While Patristic writers read texts about the Holy Spirit in 1 Corinthians often with an eye to explicating questions of ontology and about the Trinity, the Reformers often preferred to explicate epistemological questions that related to revelation.

I agree with Ulrich Luz and those other writers who suggest it that the history of influence (*Wirkungsgeschichte*) transcends the history of interpretation as evidenced only in commentaries over the centuries. The impact of texts upon human life and conversely the shaping of interpretative agenda through events in human life draw upon many sources above and beyond commentaries.

One concern therefore is that those who pursue "reception history" have enough patient multi-disciplinary scholarship behind them to be at ease in drawing together a sensitive awareness of issues in hermeneutics and biblical interpretation with an additional sensitivity to the contours of historical theology, church history and the history of ideas as such. If this is not achieved, reception history runs the risk of ending as a shallow fashion that has not delivered what it seems to promise. In my judgement, it is one of the most important and critically creative aspects of hermeneutics, provided that its exponents have the background and the capacity to explore all the appropriate fields that it requires. One series of commentaries that promises work on reception history does not fully provide this in its early volumes, but there is some evidence that some volumes still in process of being written may succeed in seeking to rectify this. This is vital for the credibility of this area.

PART V

PARABLES, NARRATIVE-WORLDS AND READER-RESPONSE THEORIES

The Varied Hermeneutical Dynamics of Parables and Reader-Response Theory (Excerpts, 1985)

This is a relatively early evaluation of some twenty years ago of the hermeneutics of parables and of the application of reader-response theories to parable-interpretation. It comes from The Responsibility of Hermeneutics *(Grand Rapids, MI: Eerdmans and Carlisle: Paternoster, 1985), and was written in collaboration with Roger Lundin and Clare Walhout, two American literary theorists, in the Calvin Centre for Christian Scholarship, Grand Rapids, Michigan, USA.*

In this piece I urge first the importance of applying different hermeneutical models to the interpretation of different types of parables. The parables of Jesus embrace various sub-genres. In the second section I distinguish between different types of response theory both in terms of different disciplines and pedigrees, and in terms of the place of each on a spectrum from moderate or cautious to radical. The third and fourth sections consider respectively some of the values and limitations of these of approaches. However, this remains more text-related than the sharpened philosophical and theological criticisms of Stanley Fish that I put forward in New Horizons in Hermeneutics *in 1992 (included as Essay 27, below). There I argue that Fish holds an inadequate philosophy of language, especially when compared with the approach of the later Wittgenstein, and a hermeneutic that places communities including the church beyond critiques of biblical texts.*

Throughout the discussion I also try to address a dilemma that emerges between respecting the cognitive content of parables, which can be abstracted from them retrospectively as "teaching", and respecting the initial hermeneutical dynamic of parables as "projected worlds", as address, as seductive and transforming narratives, and in other ways. Twentieth-century biblical scholarship witnesses to both approaches, each with its respective contributions and pitfalls.

I
Examples of Major Differences of Hermeneutical Dynamic even within the Broad Category of Parable

The example of the parables of Jesus is instructive for hermeneutical theory, in the first place, because Jesus himself underlines the need for some interpretive act or process on the part of the hearer if the parables are to achieve their effect. If the meaning of every parable were immediately apparent, why then did the disciples inquire about their interpretation (Mark 4:10–20; parallel, Matt. 13:10–23, Luke 8:8–15)? Indeed Adolf Jülicher could insist on the supposed obviousness of their meaning only by regarding all evidence in the Gospels to the contrary as inauthentic and misconceived constructions of the evangelists read back on to the lips of Jesus or into the original situation.[1]

Jülicher's fundamental mistake, however, was to presuppose that all parables performed the *same* hermeneutical function, namely that of illustrating certain broad and general truths which the Jesus of nineteenth-century theological liberalism was thought to teach. The lesson for biblical hermeneutics is that it is unwise for interpreters to presuppose the so-called obviousness of any set of biblical texts or related methods *in advance of* considering their particular nature and function. In the case of the parables, we may distinguish various sub-categories within the form by examining degrees of open-endedness and levels of reader-involvement.

At least three sets of variables determine the differences between these sub-categories. They include differences of genre or hermeneutical function, differences of situation, and differences of audience. These differences naturally overlap. Jesus sometimes used example stories like that of the tower builder which do not entail the more complex transference of interpretive judgement to a second-level characteristic of the parable form. Eta Linnemann comments, "In the parable the evaluation that the narrative compels one to make has to be carried over to another level (from 'picture' to 'reality'). In the illustration it refers directly to the reality and only needs to be generalized."[2] Bultmann makes the same kind of distinction: "Exemplary stories have a striking formal relationship to parables ... [They] offer examples ... models of right behaviour".[3] In contrast to the sub-categories of metaphor, similitude and parable, Bultmann finds instances of such example stories in the Good Samaritan, the Rich Fool, the Rich Man and Lazarus, and the Pharisee and the Publican. Nevertheless on closer inspection some of these, most notably the parable of the Good Samaritan, reveal more subtle and complex hermeneutical functions. As J.D. Crossan rightly observes, if the purpose of this particular parable was to invite a Jewish audience to imitate the model of neighbourly concern represented in the leading figure in the story, "for such a purpose it would have been far better to have made the wounded man Samaritan and the helper a Jewish man outside clerical circles".[4] To interpret this parable, we need a more adequate hermeneutical insight than that suggested by the sub-category of "example story".

One radical difference between example story and parable proper is in the sense of shock, disclosure, revelation, or disorientation and reorientation that may occur in the case of the latter. Nathan's parable to David is a classic case. David becomes totally absorbed in Nathan's vivid portrayal of the rich man who took from the poor man the one thing that he had: "the poor man had ... one little ewe lamb ... He brought it up, and it grew up with him and with his children; it used to eat of his morsel, and drink from his cup, and lie in his bosom, and it was like a daughter to him" (2 Sam. 12:3). As he sits on the edge of his chair, David feels righteous indignation when the rich man takes away the ewe lamb, and anger that the rich man "was unwilling to take one of his own flock or

---

[1] Adolf Jülicher, *Die Gleichnisreden Jesu* (2nd edn, Freiburg: Mohr, 1899), pp.1–148.
[2] Eta Linnemann, *Parables of Jesus: Introduction and Exposition* (London: SPCK, 1966), p.5.
[3] Rudolf Bultmann, *History of the Synoptic Tradition* (Oxford: Basil Blackwell, 1963), pp.169–79.
[4] John Dominic Crossan, *In Parables: The Challenge of the Historical Jesus* (New York: Harper and Row, 1973), p.4.

herd to prepare for the wayfarer who had come to him, but he took the poor man's lamb". The hermeneutical dynamic of the parable is revealed in the close juxtaposition of two sentences. "David's anger was greatly kindled ... and he said to Nathan, 'As the Lord lives, the man who has done this deserves to die ... because he did this thing and because he had no pity.' Nathan said to David, 'You are the man'" (vv. 6, 7). Caught off guard by his involvement in the narrative world, David finds that the story is really about him before he has had the chance even to consider putting up moral defences.

The difference between this kind of parable and the allegory is even more striking and fundamental. The reader can never be absorbed or "lost" in the world of the allegory in a way that conceals his or her own involvement in it. The parallels, applications, or relevance of the parts of an allegory are not experienced as a final, coherent surprise or revelation. Rather, they are a series of quasi-independent and repetitive or diffused correlations between the image and what the image represents that must be understood as the story proceeds. In Bunyan's *Pilgrim's Progress*, the reader knows that Christian's burden is really sin; that Mr Worldly-Wiseman is a conceptual construct of worldly-wise people who impinge on Bunyan's and the reader's own lives; that the room in the house of the interpreter is really a human heart; that the oil poured on the fire is really the Holy Spirit, and so on. At each stage the reader is required to bring along an interpretive key. Interpretation of this sort is very different from what it is in the case of Nathan's parable. We do not ask whether the ewe lamb is a good symbol for Uriah's wife; we discover that the relevance of any element in the narrative consists not in its being one of a sequence of *independent referential correspondences* but in its role within the *totality* of the constructed narrative world of the parable. Hermeneutically, the parable and the allegory function with quite different dynamics.

Long ago Calvin described multipoint allegorical interpretations as idle fooleries. Certainly since Jülicher's work this pejorative assessment has become commonplace in most serious parable interpretation, although with exceptions. Even here we need to remain cautious about the peril of generalizing, for Jesus sometimes used allegory, sometimes used non-allegorical parable, and sometimes moved between the two. The Jewish and rabbinic term מָשָׁל (*māshāl*, Aramaic *mathlā*) only roughly approximates to the Greek word παραβολή (*parabolē*), and embraces parable, allegory, story, riddle, proverb, example, symbol and other related forms. In Matt. 22:1, for example, we are told that Jesus spoke in "parables", and we are drawn at first into a narrative about a king who gave a wedding banquet for his son and was dismayed when his guests declined their invitations. However, the story continues: "The king was angry, and he sent his troops and destroyed those murderers and burned their city" (22:7). It is difficult to see how this sentence could function as a coherent element within the single narrative perspective of the wedding parable, and it is pointless to try to ask whether declining the invitation could merit such severe military reprisals. The point is, rather, that the existence of a tradition of understanding the eschatological kingdom as a festal banquet to which disobedient Israel refused to come triggers a second-level interpretation, namely the destruction of Jerusalem, before the narrative comes to its close.

This reveals how closely questions about genre, sub-genre and mixed genre impinge upon an understanding of the situation common to the speaker and first readers. Without some understanding of the interpretive situation of the parable, the modern interpreter may be tempted simply to spend time fruitlessly puzzling over why the declining of an invitation leads to the burning of a whole city, or might suggest that the internal coherence of the narrative world of a parable is in general unimportant. In either case what we are to do when we interpret a parable depends on a number of specific questions about the particularities of the text, including (in many cases) its setting and its audience. It would be a mistake to argue that such questions needlessly complicate the process of interpretation. Abstract, context-free approaches do not solve these problems; they merely sweep them under the carpet. They seduce the unwary reader or the interpretive community to approach all parables or all texts with the same horizon of expectation. This leaves any that are at odds with the a priori model simply to take care of themselves as "problem" passages.

Similar difficulties have resulted in almost every historical period whenever interpreters have worked with generalizing hermeneutical models. As we shall see, many Patristic writers tended to adopt an interpretive procedure that made the parables primarily an instrumental support for church doctrine already derived largely from other biblical texts. Irenaeus may have been correct solely in theological terms when he preached on God's successive calls through creation, through the Abrahamic covenant, through the ministry of Christ, and through the present preaching of the church. But it is questionable whether that represents the "meaning" of the parable of the labourers in the vineyard with reference to their successive calls to employment. Irenaeus assumes that the meaning of the parable is generated by the sequence of referential correspondences between the two levels of what would then constitute an allegory. But this prematurely breaks up the internal coherence of the narrative world as a single narrative, and it no longer functions as a single whole.

One major reason for early Patristic concerns over an appropriate hermeneutical framework lay in gnostic uses of a rival theological framework. An instructive example may be found in the interpretation of the parable of the lost sheep in the Gospel of Truth. In Luke 15:4–7 the shepherd leaves the ninety-nine to seek the one lost sheep, and the emphasis falls on the joy of receiving the lost, in contrast to the grumbling of Jesus' pharisaic critics (15:1, 2; cf. v. 7). In the Gospel of Truth, by contrast, the restoration of the "one" that changes the ninety-nine to one hundred is related to the custom of reckoning the hundred figure on the right hand, while the ninety-nine figure represents the highest possible calculation which can be indicated by gestures of the left fingers. The completion of the hundred thus supposedly points to the truth of a major gnostic doctrine: that the God of perfection is the antithesis of finitude, imperfection, or lack (represented by the left hand). The ninety-nine reflect Sophia's falling into pre-cosmic error; the wandering sheep represent the wandering planets (Greek *planē*, error), while Jesus fills up the lack: "For the 'ninety-nine' is a sum [reckoned] on the left hand, which holds it. But at the time when the 'one' shall be found, the entire sum is wont to change over to the right. As that which lacks the one … takes it from the left side and transfers it to the right, so the sum makes one hundred, the sign of Him who is … the Father" (Gospel of Truth 32:1–17). Against this background it is understandable that several of the Church Fathers would wish to interpret parables within an orthodox, "closed" frame. But they pay the price of changing the dynamic of some of the parables.

We might expect that the rise of modern biblical scholarship would bring with it a more liberating pluriformity in handling of the parables. Adolf Jülicher did indeed observe that the Gospels contained different types of parabolic material. But such was Jülicher's liberal *theological* insistence on the uniform purpose of Jesus to teach "general truths" that he could not treat as authentic any material which seemed to reflect a more subtle, or simply different, purpose. All parables genuinely spoken by Jesus, he assumed, were similes, not metaphors; they were clear, not puzzling. In effect they all articulated general truths in a manner that made them self-explanatory. Admittedly Jülicher divided his broad category of *eigentliche Rede*,[5] or simile in contrast to metaphor, into at least three subcategories: the similitude (*Gleichnis*) compares sentences or thoughts; the parable proper (*Parabel*) unfolds an imagined story; while example stories (*Beispielerzählung*) draw points of comparison between characters in the story and the reader.[6] Nevertheless, the hermeneutical function remains broadly the same. It is largely didactic, cognitive, cerebral and direct.

Thus the parable of the dishonest manager (Luke 16:1–8) in Jülicher's approach is simply a tale with the general moral that wise use of the present is the condition of a happy future.[7] The parable of the talents tells the reader that a reward is earned only by performance.[8] Jülicher's hermeneutics reflects his own horizon of expectation concerning the method and message of Jesus, and in this respect it controls the text more decisively than the text controls the hermeneutics.

More recently a steady trend has emerged in the direction of allowing particularities of the text to shape hermeneutical theory. Even so, some approaches turn out to be less flexible than they appear. Some approaches that emphasize polyvalence of meaning often still carry with them some overarching theory about hermeneutical function. J.D. Crossan writes simply: "Myth establishes world ... satire attacks world. Parable subverts world."[9] But if parable always subverts world, does this mean that it subverts, on a second reading, the new world of Jesus' world for which it has already made space, or alternatively that the parable can say nothing to one whose world has already been subverted? Clearly this relates to questions about tradition, about so-called insiders and outsiders, and about audience criticism. The problem is not that the hermeneutical theorist should refrain from offering general hermeneutical models. Crossan's work at this point, at any rate, is fruitful and constructive. The problem is that such models are sometimes treated as overarching interpretive keys rather than as exploratory or functional working models. The search for pluriform models that relate to different texts and different genre remains a fundamental and indispensable part of hermeneutics.

Jesus' own words about the purpose of parabolic speech in Mark 4:10–12 and its parallel in Matthew explain why this is so, including the importance of difference of genre. P.S. Hawkins suggests that the difficult truth about some parable[s] is the fact that often "they are the *utterance but not the unveiling* of what has been hidden; a proclamation

---

5 Jülicher, *Die Gleichnisreden Jesu*, vol. 1, pp.25–118, esp. 52–8 and 92–111.
6 Ibid., pp.92–111.
7 Ibid.
8 Ibid. p.495.
9 John Dominic Crossan, *The Dark Interval: Towards a Theology of Story* (Niles, IL: Argus, 1975), p.59.

of mystery rather than an explanation of it".[10] This both illuminates and relativizes the distinction between parable and allegory. As Hans Josef Klauck insists, we do not do justice to the parables by using the kind of allegorical interpretation which presupposes some general key as a decoding device.[11] On the other hand parables may and do include allegory in the form of extended metaphors which demand perception, engagement and interpretation on the part of the audience. Madeleine Boucher rightly comments, "The charge ... that Mark distorted the parable as a verbal construct is simply unfounded. Mark has not taken clear, straightforward speech, the parable, and transformed it into obscure esoteric speech, the allegory. He has rather taken ... the double-meaning effect, and made it the starting-point of a theological theme concerning the audience's resistance to hearing the word." The parables, she continues, "convey not secret information, but the requirements made of the hearer ... Those who do not understand are those who will not allow its lesson to impinge on their own existence."[12]

II
Audience Criticism and Reader-Response Hermeneutics: Different Literary Categories and Different Traditions or Pedigrees

If the parables of Jesus demand from the reader a readiness to respond, naturally the biblical interpreter will want to explore the model of reader-response hermeneutics in literary theory. However, the place of the reader or audience in the interpretative process has been stressed in three quite distinct ways in three different movements of thought: in biblical studies, in literary and aesthetic theory, and in philosophical hermeneutics.

At the outset we should stress that the movement known in biblical studies as audience criticism is very different in both concern and perspective from reader-response theory in literary studies and aesthetics. But this very difference makes it even more necessary to compare the two movements for their respective strengths and weaknesses for biblical interpretation.

II.1 Audience Criticism

Audience criticism in biblical studies of the Gospels is notably represented in J. Arthur Baird's *Audience Criticism and the Historical Jesus*.[13] Baird begins by pointing out that Jesus was a selective teacher. Jesus spoke in parables "as they were able to hear it", but "privately to his disciples he explained everything" (Mark 4:33, 34); "not all men can receive the precept but only those to whom it is given" (Matt. 19:11). But the Evangelists

---

[10] P.S. Hawkins, "Parables as Metaphor", *Christian Scholar's Review* 12 (1983), p.226; cf. 226–36.

[11] Hans-Josef Klauck, *Allegorie und Allegorese in synoptischen Gleichnistexten* (Münster: Aschendorff, 1978), pp.29–31, 132–47 and 354–60. Cf. Hans Weder, *Die Gleichnisse Jesu als Metaphern* (Göttingen: Vandenhoeck und Ruprecht, 1978).

[12] Madeleine Boucher, *The Mysterious Parable: A Literary Study* (Washington, DC: Catholic Bible Association of America, 1977), pp.83–4.

[13] J. Arthur Baird, *Audience Criticism and the Historical Jesus* (Philadelphia, PA: Westminster Press, 1969).

were no less concerned than Jesus about the audience and audience identification. As Baird points out, of the 422 units of the Huck-Lietzmann synopsis of the first three Gospels, the audience is clearly designated in 395, or 94 per cent. Broad audience identifications differentiate the twelve disciples; the larger "crowd" of disciples, or "those who were with the Twelve"; the opponent crowd, and the opponents themselves.

Each group, however, includes further sub-categories: the opponents, for example, include Pharisees, scribes, lawyers, the high priests, elders and the sanhedrin. In this opponent group Baird examines seventeen sub-categories represented by corresponding Greek words or phrases.[14] Baird further considers the use of audience criticism as a tool of inquiry to investigate the relations between specific audience identifications and sources, forms and redactions. This last exercise entails meticulous statistical examinations that draw on computer data and a very close knowledge of the text. With respect to the parables this leads to such specific questions as that of the correlations between types of metaphorical imagery and types of audience.[15]

Three conclusions, among others, emerge from Baird's careful work. First, Baird shows by his uncovering of certain irregularities and patterned correlations in the text itself that many *logia* that have been attributed by a number of scholars to the early church or to redactional activity do go back to Jesus himself. Baird reaches a more positive verdict both about the historicity of the *logia* and about the genuineness of their audience settings than most of his predecessors.

Second, his work in effect reiterates the point that what constitutes explication, interpretation, or understanding of the parables depends partly on questions about audience. *What "making clear" consists of depends on the question "clear to whom?"* Because the parables entail at least four kinds of audience, there seem to be at least four ways of understanding the meaning of the parable. Baird terms these "semi-allegorical", "thematic", "contextual", and "internal".[16]

Third, and most important for this stage of the present discussion, Baird expounds audience criticism "as a hermeneutical tool". He declares, "The audience was of great importance to those who recorded the tradition because they believed the message of the *logia* itself was audience-centred." Jesus accommodated his message to his audience

> ... to such a degree that the nature of the audience became an important part of the message of the *logion* itself. This was then preserved with unique fidelity for ... the audience was needed for the correct and meaningful reproduction of his teaching. This means to us that the audience has become a hermeneutical factor of first importance. It means that we cannot really understand what the *logia* are saying until we understand the audience to which they are attributed.[17]

The originality and importance of Baird's work on the Gospels has received less attention than it deserves. Only K.L. Schmidt and T.W. Manson seem to have studied with adequate seriousness, before Baird, the role of audiences in the Gospels, even though in

---

[14]   Ibid. p.47.
[15]   Ibid. pp.97–101.
[16]   Ibid. pp.103–5.
[17]   Ibid. p.134.

the area of the New Testament Epistles the hermeneutical significance of the audience has long been recognized as being of primary importance. It has long been taken for granted that questions about Paul's readers and the Pauline churches shed important light on both the meaning and the relevance of his words.[18] A recent study by Robert Jewett applies audience criticism to the non-Pauline Epistle to the Hebrews.[19] However, Baird's work represents a turning-point for work on the Gospels, especially on the parables. The hermeneutical significance of the audience criticism movement can be seen not only in its concern about situational particularity but also in two equally important directions: first, the participatory dimension of reader-response, and second, the need for answering questions about application or relevance with at least some reference to whether there is any correspondence between the situation of the audience to whom the text was first directed and that of the reader to whom it is directed today.

II.2 Reader-Response Approaches in Literary Theory

The second movement to be considered is the application of reader-response hermeneutics that first emerged in the context of literary theory. In some respects it parallels audience criticism in biblical studies in so far as both movements pay attention to the reader's status and situation, but it is much more radical and much less controlled in its conclusions. Responsible interpretation in audience criticism depends on a rough correspondence between the situation of the original addressees of the text and that of a modern reader or interpretive community. By contrast, it is far more difficult to stipulate the limits of interpretive responsibility in the case of a radical version of reader-response theory.

Already within the last few years reader-response theory has entered New Testament studies as an interpretive tool. The work of Robert Fowler on the feeding miracles in Mark (1981) and that of R. Alan Culpepper on the literary design of the Fourth Gospel (1983) provide two examples.[20] Fowler builds partly upon the approach of Wayne Booth in his books *The Rhetoric of Fiction* and *A Rhetoric of Irony*. The Gospel of Mark, Fowler argues, is written in such a way as to take account of expectations on the part of the reader that the Markan text may subsequently confirm, fulfil, frustrate, or revise. This explains why Mark drops certain clues in otherwise surprising places which encourage certain attitudes concerning Jesus. In particular, Fowler sees this concern to utilize, even

---

[18] Cf. J.C. Hurd, Jr, *The Origins of I Corinthians* (London: SPCK, 1965), and Anthony C. Thiselton, "Realized Eschatology at Corinth", *New Testament Studies* 24 (1978), pp.510–26.

[19] Robert Jewett, *Letters to Pilgrims: A Commentary on the Epistle to the Hebrews* (New York: Pilgrim Press, 1981).

[20] Robert M. Fowler, *Loaves and Fishes: The Function of the Feeding Stories in the Gospel of Mark*, Society of Biblical Literature Dissertation Series 54 (Chico, CA: Scholars Press, 1981), and R. Alan Culpepper, *Anatomy of the Fourth Gospel: A Study in Literary Design* (Philadelphia, PA: Fortress Press, 1983). Since this manuscript was completed, James L. Resseguie has published a survey of reader-response approaches and their relevance to material in the Gospels ("Reader-Response Criticism and the Synoptic Gospels", *Journal of the American Academy of Religion* 52 [1984], pp.307–24). Resseguie considers a range of approaches in literary theory, rather than literature of New Testament scholarship or on the parables. But he usefully explores the differing textual and reading strategies discussed by such writers as Norman Holland and David Bleich, observing particularly the textual strategies of defamiliarization and entrapment, the role of expectation, and the building of self-identity in the active experience of the reader.

to manipulate, reader expectations as the key to the so-called doublet about two feedings of the multitudes in Mark 6:30–44 and in 8:1–10.[21] Mark, he believes, includes his own Markan account of the feeding of the five thousand before the traditional material about the feeding of the four thousand two chapters later in order to point up the unbelief of the disciples' question in 8:4: "How can one feed these men with bread here in the desert?" Mark is concerned not *simply to narrate* a miracle, but *to produce a particular active perception of its significance on the part of the reader.*

The prima-facie absurdity of the disciples asking how Jesus could feed four thousand people, when two chapters earlier he has already fed five thousand, provides the conditions for what Wayne Booth had called "intended irony". The intended or implied reader's expectation is consciously, and sharply, at variance with that of the disciples, and the disciples' view of Jesus now becomes consciously transcended by the reader. Fowler sees Mark's strategy as a subtle one, namely to invite the reader actively to come to see the inadequacy of the Christological faith of the disciples at this stage. Can they not see what is abundantly clear to the reader about Jesus?

Fowler's work thus utilizes in the service of Markan studies some of the standard tools of reader-response theory, in which attention is paid to the roles, expectations and attitudes of the implied reader envisioned by the author. Culpepper applies these working tools to the Gospel of John, drawing distinctions (borrowed from Iser and others) between (1) John's actual readers, (2) John's authorial audience, (3) a narrative audience who accepted the story on its own terms, and (4) his ideal narrative reader. This ideal reader accepts John's own judgements and appreciates his irony in such a way as to move toward fresh appreciations through the Gospel's story and symbolism. The Johannine narrative, he concludes, *operates retrospectively*, telling a story that is a blend of historical tradition and faith. The Gospel narrative, in sum, "draws together the reader and the author, readers and Jesus, this world and the world above".[22]

Culpepper's work builds largely on that of Wolfgang Iser no less explicitly than Fowler builds on that of Iser and Wayne Booth. But in literary theory the term "reader-response" denotes a wide range of perspectives and approaches. At one end of the spectrum there is a general emphasis on the reader, and this may be broader and less specific than the methods of Booth and of Iser. The other end of the spectrum is far more radical in its hermeneutical implications, most notably of all in the reader-response hermeneutics of Stanley Fish.[23]

It is also possible, though perhaps less helpful, to use the term "reader-response" in a looser sense to indicate a broad group of writers who share a general concern to move hermeneutic emphasis away from the authors of texts to their readers. Such a tendency is apparent in works as diverse as Foucault's essay "What Is an Author?", Roland Barthes' "From Work to Text", and some writings of Jacques Derrida.[24] Todorov's work

---

21   Fowler, *Loaves and Fishes*, especially pp.91–148; cf. 149–79.

22   Culpepper, *Anatomy of the Fourth Gospel*, p.233.

23   Cf. Stanley Fish, *Is There a Text in This Class? The Authority of Interpretive Communities* (Cambridge, MA: Harvard University Press, 1980) and *Doing What Comes Naturally* (Oxford: Clarendon, 1989).

24   Roland Barthes, "From Work to Text", and Michel Foucault, "What Is an Author?", in J.V. Harari (ed.), *Textual Strategies: Perspectives in Post-Structuralist Criticism* (Ithaca, NY: Cornell University Press, 1979), pp.73–81 and 141–60.

on reading as construction and Maranda on how readers use texts to come to terms with their own worlds also features within this broader category.[25]

Meaning, for most of these writers, is always *potential* in terms of the *text*, but *actual* in relation to the *reader*. No meaning is already "there" in a text, or at least "there" in some objectivist sense, apart from a horizon of expectations brought to a text by the reader. As a suggestive aphorism by Fish asserts, "the reader's response is not *to* the meaning; it *is* the meaning".[26] Fish traces the story of his own intellectual pilgrimage since 1970 by describing how his earlier doubts about the autonomy of the text gave way gradually to a much more radical appreciation of the decisive role played by the reader not only in the process of understanding and interpretation but even in the birth of meaning.

This process began, for Fish, with an appreciation of the *temporal dimension* in which the potential meanings made possible by the text are actualized only in a process of readings. The spatial form of the text provides a less important key to the nature of its meaning than its temporal appropriation in a series of concrete interactions with the expectations and projections of its readers. The question "What does this mean?" came to be replaced by a second "What does this do?" This led, secondly, to an investigation of the part played by interpretive communities: how their very expectations concerning what might *count* as meaning were inseparable from their assumptions or even conclusions about what kind of meaning *lay*, as it were, already in the text. Later still, Fish perceived that this position was, in a sense, self-defeating. He comments, "I did what critics always do: I 'saw' what my interpretive principles permitted or directed me to see, and then I turned around and attributed what I had 'seen' to a text and an intention. What my principles direct me to 'see' are readers performing acts."[27] Units of sense generated by the text "do not lie innocently in the world; rather, they are themselves constituted by an interpretive act. The facts one points to are still there (in a sense that would not be consoling to an objectivist) but only as a consequence of the interpretive (man-made) model that has called them into being."[28]

Fish's most recent conclusion, then, expressed negatively, is that a text does not generate determinate meaning "independently of social and institutional circumstances".[29] The reader and the reader's social-ethical-intellectual community contribute decisively to the final meaning of the text. However, many exponents of audience response do not go as far as Stanley Fish. Susan Suleiman significantly entitles one essay "Varieties of Audience-Oriented Criticism".[30]

II.3 *The Role of the Reader in Theological Hermeneutics*

The third parallel movement is the application of similar principles in systematic and philosophical theology combined to emphasize the interpreting subject and the

---

[25] Cf. Tzvetan Todorov, "Reading as Construction", and P. Maranda, "The Dialectic of Metaphor", in Susan R. Suleiman and Inge Crosman (eds), *The Reader in the Text. Essays on Audience and Interpretation* (Princeton, NJ: Princeton University Press, 1980), pp.67–82 and 183–204.

[26] Fish, *Is There a Text in This Class?*, p.3.

[27] Ibid., p.12.

[28] Ibid., p.13.

[29] Ibid., p.371.

[30] Susan Suileman in Suileman and Crosman (eds), *The Reader in the Text*, p.3.

importance of his or her pre-understanding in the act or process of communication. Although a major turn in hermeneutics took place with Schleiermacher, in theological hermeneutics the far-reaching effects of Karl Barth's commentary on Romans marked another turning-point. Barth's fundamental methodological claim was that the objectivism of liberal scholarship represented by Jülicher and by Harnack could not as a matter of principle do justice to the biblical text. James Robinson explicates the radical epistemological and hermeneutical effects of this.[31] This methodological claim shared some common ground with Rudolf Bultmann's emphasis on the kerygmatic nature of the New Testament. The New Testament, Bultmann urged, did not convey timeless information unrelated to situations and hearers, but addressed the hearer with a practical (or existential) message that demanded practical (or existential) response. But if this is so, he urged, the preliminary questions or expectations with which the reader approaches the text decisively shape what he or she will "find" there.

In the era following Barth and Bultmann, Ernst Fuchs, Gerhard Ebeling, and Robert Funk in America, developed distinctive perspectives that underlined these concerns with the role of the reader.[32] These approaches strengthened the notion that communication and interpretation were to be seen as *events* or *processes*, rather than merely the expression of ideas. Two very different philosophical traditions gave further impetus to this perspective: on the one hand, the philosophies of Heidegger and Gadamer; on the other hand, even if less directly, the work of Wittgenstein, Austin and speech-act theorists such as J.R. Searle. As my title *The Two Horizons* suggests, hermeneutics came to be seen as an operative engagement or interaction between the horizon of the text and the horizon of the reader.[33]

To sketch these three very different audience-oriented movements in hermeneutics is not necessarily to defend them. Whether these approaches result in gain or whether they risk loss will become apparent not when we theorize about them in the abstract, but when we test their adequacy in the light of case studies. This includes our specific inquiries about the parables of Jesus, which of all biblical genres lends itself most clearly to reader-response strategies of reading.

III
Reader-Response Approaches to the Parables: Some Values

By contrast with recent developments in parable interpretation during the last decade, the work of Jülicher tends to reduce the role of the reader to a bare minimum. But the reason for this can easily be mistaken. The problem is not primarily that Jülicher's "one-point" approach oversimplifies the parables, although this does occur. The difficulty is

---

[31] James M. Robinson, "Hermeneutic Since Barth", in James M. Robinson and J.D. Cobb (eds), *New Frontiers in Theology, 11: The New Hermeneutic* (New York: Harper and Row, 1964), pp.1–77.

[32] Ernst Fuchs, *Hermeneutik*, 4th edn (Tübingen: Mohr, 1970); Gerhard Ebeling, *Word and Faith* (London: SPCK, 1963), and *Introduction to a Theological Theory of Language* (London: Collins, 1973); and Robert W. Funk, *Language, Hermeneutic and Word of God* (New York: Harper and Row, 1966).

[33] Anthony C. Thiselton, *The Two Horizons. New Testament Hermeneutics and Philosophical Description* (Grand Rapids, MI: Eerdmans, 1980), pp.10–23 *et passim*.

rather that, as Robert Funk has more than once stated, "the parables were understood [by Jülicher] as example stories or as illustrations of a point that could have been made without essential loss, in discursive, non-figurative language".[34] The parables tend to function, in Jülicher's work, as broad, easily assimilated truths that can be too neatly packaged as a bundle of cognitive concepts.

In fairness to Jülicher, we ought not to accept without qualification the verdict of A.M. Hunter and others that his interpretations of the parables reduce them to nothing more than prudential platitudes. Jülicher certainly moves too far in this direction. For example, when he carefully examines in considerable detail the three seed parables in Mark 4 (the sower, 4:3–8; the seed growing of itself, 4:26–29; and the mustard seed, 4:30–32), Jülicher insists that these convey not a merely prudential lesson about uninterrupted growth but a prophetical assurance, in the face of anxious concern, that future fulfilment of the kingdom is certain.[35] Thus the sower parable teaches that the seed of the word finds a lasting place only among those who respond to the gospel and bear fruit. The seed growing "of itself" shows that the certainty of the kingdom's reaching its purpose does not depend on human capacities for good or evil. The mustard seed suggests that we cannot tell the nature of the end simply by looking at the apparent insignificance of the beginning.[36]

Certainly this is not, as is sometimes claimed, mere nineteenth-century liberal theology; Jülicher's attention to exegetical detail takes him beyond this. Nevertheless, there is neither the challenge nor the offence nor the transformation of values that makes heavy demands on the reader and which historically actually led Jesus to the cross. The telltale phrase Jülicher uses is that the interpreter can easily sum up the chief thoughts of these parables – and these "chief thoughts" prove in the end to be not very contestable.[37] They are essentially "teaching".

At one level Jülicher was not wholly wrong to stress the cognitive content of the parables. Later interpreters need to see in the parables a body of material that can be described conceptually in order *retrospectively* to abstract and retrospectively define their content. Biblical research has shown that while it is useful to draw a working distinction between preaching (*kerygma*) and teaching (*didachē*) this distinction is not absolute. Preaching *includes* information about states of affairs. But Jülicher's mistake lay in his preoccupation with this aspect, as if cognitive abstraction was the primary or even sole hermeneutical goal and as if meaning were reducible to conceptual content alone, in isolation from problems about function, pre-understanding, temporality and recontextualization. In any case, very many of Jülicher's interpretations are even broader, more general, and more abstract than those we have cited by way of example. For instance, after some twenty-five pages of discussion of the rich man and Lazarus (Luke 16:19–31), he interprets the story as passing on the lesson of "joy in a life of suffering and fear at a life of enjoyment".[38] There is an unmistakable flattening reduction in "thoughts" that simply invite fairly easy assent.

---

34   Robert W. Funk, *Parables and Presence* (Philadelphia, PA: Fortress Press, 1982) p.30; cf. pp.1–80.
35   Ibid., pp.88–9.
36   Ibid., pp.580–81.
37   Ibid.
38   Ibid., p.638.

C.H. Dodd moved further in the direction of reader-response theory when he insisted that the parable "arrests the hearer by its vividness or strangeness ... leaving the mind in sufficient doubt about its precise application to tease it into active thought".[39] Funk rightly comments, "The parable is not closed, so to speak, until the listener is drawn into it as participant. The application is not specified until the hearer, led by the 'logic' of the parable, specifies it for himself."[40] Dodd's exposition of the parable of the dishonest manager (Luke 16:1–13) as a parable of crisis illustrates this principle.[41] We miss the point if we debate the ethics of the rogue, who threatened with dismissal, set up questionable deals with the owner's creditors so that they would see that he would not suffer when he lost his job. Why does the master (Whether *ho kyrios* means the employer or Jesus) "commend" the manager who has just reduced the amounts owed by his employer's debtors? The reader wrestles with the message on two levels. First, it appears that at least the dishonest manager may be commended for being a shrewd fellow who knows how to serve his own interests when he is up against a crisis. Second, it becomes clear at the level of *kerygma* that the crisis provoked by the coming of Jesus also, and no less, demands the kind of urgent action which makes all other considerations subordinate ones.

The major problem left by Dodd's interpretation concerns the status of the so-called editorial conclusions. Do vv. 8b–12 actually undermine the hermeneutical function of this parable as Jesus told it? I have tried to come to terms with this difficult exegetical problem in an article that includes this issue.[42] The major point, however, remains that even when certain specific maxims are placed at the end of the parable, there remains an element of open-endedness or ambiguity that can be resolved only when the hearer or reader actively wrestles with the text. The reader has to put two and two together unassisted by a third party's key to interpretation; if someone else supplies the "answer", it is no longer the same discovery.

Even for Dodd, however, this process of interpretation remains primarily one of conscious cognitive operation. He stresses situation, *kerygma* and response, but praxis seems to be a second step that follows *after* cognitive reflection. Dodd's approach fits in with Hirsch's distinction between meaning and significance, but it does not quite do justice to the subtle relation between the two.

Joachim Jeremias builds on, develops and modifies Dodd's approach. Using form-critical tools, Jeremias sees the parables as *announcements*. He declares, "One thing above all becomes evident: it is that all the parables of Jesus compel his hearers to come to a decision about his person and mission."[43] Jeremias' work is rightly regarded as a major classic of modern biblical studies. The sixth German edition of 1962 also took account of the then-discovered Gospel of Thomas and its possible significance for parable interpretation. Yet hermeneutically Jeremias' work remains profoundly ambiguous.

---

39 C.H. Dodd, *Parables of the Kingdom* (London: Nisbet, 1935), p.16.

40 Robert W. Funk, *Language, Hermeneutic and Word of God*, p.133.

41 Dodd, *Parables of the Kingdom*, pp.29–32. Dodd offers two possible interpretations of this parable.

42 Anthony C. Thiselton, "The Parables as Language-Event", *Scottish Journal of Theology* 23 (1970), pp.437–68.

43 Joachim Jeremias, *The Parables of Jesus*, 2nd edn (New York: Scribner, 1963), p.230.

On the surface Jeremias repeatedly puts forward the claim that the hermeneutical function of the parables is to compel *decision*. Yet, as Norman Perrin points out, the major concern of Jeremias' book is to view the parables as "sources" for a reconstruction of the content of the *message* of Jesus of Nazareth.[44] Although *kerygma* and *didachē* are never equated with each other, the world "message" or "announcement" is sometimes replaced by "instruction". The message of the parables becomes an exposition of "themes" of instruction. For example, "Now is the day of salvation" becomes "a threat or cry of warning ... to illustrate his [Jesus'] instruction".[45] All of Jesus' parables can in Jeremias' view be classified under eight broad themes: the day of salvation; God's mercy for sinners – the great assurance; the imminence of catastrophe; it may be too late; the challenge of the hour; realized discipleship; the Via Dolorosa; and the consummation. This aspect of Jeremias' work has evoked the most criticism from more recent hermeneutical approaches.

Perrin calls these themes "rubrics" and comments:

> Whereas a summary of Jülicher's general moral principles looks very much like a manifesto of nineteenth-century theological liberalism, this list of rubrics [that is, Jeremias' themes] looks very much like a summary of a rather conservative Lutheran piety. But ... what is important is that the very nature of the parables of Jesus as texts forbids the reduction of his message to a series of general moral principles or to a set of rubrics. Parables as parables do not have a "message", they tease the mind into ever new perceptions of reality.[46]

With an implied allusion to Paul Ricoeur, Perrin adds, "They function like symbols in that they 'give rise to thought'."[47]

The accuracy or validity of Perrin's comments about the hermeneutical function of parables need not be decided at this point, although arguably they set up an unnecessary polarization between message and reader-orientation. The approach of Jeremias, however, admittedly focuses too narrowly on one aspect of interpretation because he allows his methodological goal of using the parables in the service of a historical reconstruction of the message of the Jesus of history to occupy too central a place as a hermeneutical model. Jeremias allows the ambiguity between an emphasis on thematic truths and reader-decision to arise because he fails to see the full consequences of the *action* model of parabolic language to which his constructive emphasis on language intention almost brings him. He is correct in seeing the parables of Jesus as, in effect, speech-acts; that is, they attack, they rebuke, they claim, they defend. They are acts of utterance produced in situations of conflict and tension. But by allowing a concern for historical reconstruction to dominate his hermeneutical work, Jeremias allows this functional perspective, this action model, to slip from view as he gives more and more emphasis to a process of retrospective abstraction that reduces the parables to components of an overall message.

This produces, in turn, a further problem, for now the cognitive content of the message of Jesus himself comes to be regarded as different in form and content from the subject

---

[44] Norman Perrin, *Jesus and The Language of the Kingdom* (London: SCM, 1976).

[45] Jeremias, *The Parables of Jesus*, p.120.

[46] N. Perrin, *Jesus and The Language of the Kingdom*, pp.105–6.

[47] Ibid., p.106.

matter which emerges when the post-Easter community recontextualizes the parables.[48] The "authentic" parables of Jesus are expanded, interpreted and recontextualized by the Evangelists and the early community through such processes as translocation, changes of audience, allegorization and the addition of hortatory and moralizing conclusions. A radical reader-response approach, such as we find in Stanley Fish, would claim that these acts of recontextualization on the part of successive layers of readers do in practice *constitute* the meaning of the parables. But since Jeremias' concern is to attempt "to recover the original significance of the parables", the status of their interpretation by the Evangelists remains unclear.[49]

Jeremias' work left a hermeneutical vacuum that a number of more recent writers have hastened to fill. The problem is that in their enthusiasm to explore the role of the reader many have assumed that the inadequacies of Jeremias' work arose from his having a historical rather than a literary concern, as if somehow an interpreter could not, or should not, combine both concerns. The model of speech act-in-situation has been effectively ignored, and a concern with history or situation increasingly neglected. The unspoken assumption seems to be that a historically serious hermeneutic cannot do full justice to the role of the modern reader. Thus the promise held out by Baird and audience criticism is ignored in the rush to cash in on "literary" approaches.

The most recent of those who have polarized the history-versus-literature perspectives is John Sider in his current article "Rediscovering the Parables: The Logic of the Jeremias Tradition".[50] In his first section, entitled "Literature vs History?", he exploits the notion that to heed the lessons offered by literary critics such as Helen Gardiner, C.S. Lewis, or Northrop Frye is thereby to reject the importance of historical inquiry. But there are at least two confusions that run through this article. First, some perfectly valid and forceful criticisms of Jeremias' specific historical judgements are treated as if they were grounds for dismissing historical inquiry even of a more careful and judicious kind. Second, Sider confuses the kind of historical inquiry that uses texts merely as tools for the reconstruction of ideas or events by the religious historian with the kind of historical inquiry which proceeds in order to do full justice to the texts themselves.[51]

In an attempt to move forward more constructively it is necessary to take at least the following five steps: (1) to appreciate the positive and indispensable nature of historical inquiry, (2) to become aware of its limitations, (3) to appreciate the positive and constructive gains of reader-response hermeneutics and literary theory, (4) to become aware of their one-sidedness and inadequacy as general hermeneutical theories, and (5) to explore what hermeneutical models might allow us to hold together all that has been learned from these first four steps.

While no single hermeneutical model holds the key to all problems, this present discussion urges the view that an action model moves the discussion forward more constructively than most other models. Action-theory models bring into focus the

---

48   Jeremias, *The Parables of Jesus*, pp.11–21.
49   Ibid., p.220.
50   John Sider, "Rediscovering the Parables: The Logic of the Jeremias Tradition", *Journal of Biblical Literature* 102 (1983), pp.61–83.
51   Cf. Barthes, "From Work to Text".

multilevel functions of speech-acts without committing us to the anarchy of radically polyvalent meaning. A speech-act, or series of speech-acts, may be able simultaneously to project narrative-worlds *and* assert states of affairs *and* transform the perceptions of readers.

At the same time, certain fundamental distinctions remain in force. In Wolterstorff's words, an action model allows us to "distinguish clearly between the action of fictionally *projecting* a world, on the one hand, and the action of *describing* the contents of an already projected world, on the other" (my italics).[52] Jeremias is too eager to move from a speech-act (for example, attacking pharisaic assumptions) to the content of a projected world (for example, the message of God's mercy for sinners). As his critics see, Jeremias overlooks other dimensions and effects of the speech-act. As Wolterstorff observes: "By performing one and another action ... the artist generates a variety of other, distinct, actions".[53] But this does not mean, as some of Jeremias' critics fail to see, that the situation of the speech-act surrenders its role as a control over what reader-acts might now be considered as *appropriate* or *responsible* acts.

IV
Problems of Some Reader-Response Approaches to the Parables

Crossan takes up the notion of a projected "world". This category finds its place in parable studies in the first place not so much from literary theory as from the thought of Martin Heidegger and mediated through Ernst Fuchs. A parable projects a world that is at first familiar to the hearer, in which the hearer is at home. Narrative, together with metaphor, draws the hearer in as participant rather than as spectator. Metaphor is neither a merely explanatory nor ornamental device, but that which draws the hearers into *"seeing" new possibilities.* But when metaphor is extended into a metaphorical narrative, the initial invitation to enter a familiar "world" may not be as innocent as it at first seems. As the reader is enthralled and drawn along, he or she arrives at the place where a further action occurs: an act which surprises, or reverses, the reader's prior expectations. The parable world diverges so drastically from the reader's own that it constitutes a challenge, and the reader must go along with it or reject it. However, perceptual and pragmatic dimensions are intertwined. The parable world projects a perspective which the reader otherwise might not have been able to grasp.

Crossan's interpretation of the parable of the Good Samaritan (Luke 10:30–37) provides a concrete example. He insists, "the point is not that one should help the neighbour in need".[54] If so, Jesus might better have made the wounded man a Samaritan and the helper a lay Jew representative of Jesus' audience. Since Jews "have no dealings with Samaritans" (John 4:9), the story challenges the hearer "to put together two impossible and contradictory words for the same person: 'Samaritan' (10:33) and 'neighbour' (10:36)".[55] The parable's *action* at the deepest level is to overthrow or to

---

[52] Nicholas Wolterstorff, *Art in Action* (Grand Rapids, MI: Eerdmans, 1980), p.125.
[53] Ibid., p.16. Cf. also Nicholas Wolterstorff, *Works and Worlds of Art* (Oxford: Clarendon Press, 1980).
[54] Crossan, *In Parables*, p.64.
[55] Ibid.

subject the hearer's preconceived notions about goodness and evil, to make room for an experience and understanding of divine grace. Such an interpretation does not conflict, however (as Crossan thinks it does), with the lawyer's question and reply in the Lukan frame. The question in v. 37b puts the lawyer's horizon of expectations in question not only by relativizing his prior notions of good and evil but also by placing him alongside the Samaritan. The action of the parable involves both the transformation of his perceptions and the transformation of his practical attitudes. What it is *not* is simply a moralizing tale; *nor* is it an allegory of the incarnation. What it *is* entails a reader-response perspective.

Crossan's positive emphasis on reader-response also has its drawbacks, and we shall consider these shortly. First, however, we examine Susan Wittig's use of semiotic theory to explore a reader-response approach. She begins her study by asking the question: how is it that a text can be plurisignificant, or polyvalent? She offers two answers. One source of polyvalence is the differences of purposes, goals, and methods that the interpreter brings to the text. A second source is the multiplicity of ways in which the reader may "complete" the meaning of the text. She defines a parable, from a semiotic viewpoint, as "a duplex connotative system in which the precise significance is left unstated".[56] At the level of the narrative world alone, a linguistic signifier (for example, "a certain man had two sons", Luke 15:11) denotes a referent such as an object or event, real or fictional (for example, the father and the two sons in the story world).

This entire unit of first-order signifier and signified, Wittig suggests, now functions as a second-order signifier to designate some unstated signified which can only be a psychological construct supplied by the hearer. Whereas the first-order signifier and signified are linked by linguistic convention, no social system of linguistic conventions forms the basis upon which the hearer constructs the signified at the second level: "The second-order signifier ... is linked iconically to its unstated, implicit signified".[57] The hearer must make the link; the purpose of the parable is to allow him or her to do this: "The final signified remains unstated, giving to the system a dynamic unstable indeterminacy which invites, even compels, the perceiver to complete the signification."[58]

Those familiar with reader-response theory in literary studies will recognize the influence of Wolfgang Iser. The strength of Wittig's approach is the role accorded to the hearer or the reader of a kind that Jülicher and Jeremias neglected. Difficulties, however, cluster around three distinct issues. First, work on polyvalent meaning may lead to the kind of radical pluralism that invites the reader not simply to construe meaning actively, but also to make whatever they like of the text. This would entail some of the problems that attach to the latest work of Stanley Fish. Second, at a more pragmatic level, are the specific interpretations of parables suggested by those who favour such pluralism actually plausible? How successful is Mary Tolbert, for example, in utilizing Wittig's approach while attempting to interpret parables in ways "congruent" with the text? How "congruent" are her psychoanalytical "meanings"? Finally, can any theory of

---

56 Wittig, "A Theory of Multiple Meanings", p.84.
57 Ibid., p.86.
58 Ibid., p.87.

hermeneutics claim to be adequate when it relies entirely on one hermeneutical model alone, namely that of reader-response?

Crossan explicitly poses the first problem, that of radical pluralism, when he traces the transition from existentialism through structuralism to the post-structuralism of Derrida. The "existential nausea", he writes, was "the ontological disappointment of one who, having been taught that there is some overarching logical meaning beyond our perception, has come at length to believe that there is no such fixed centre towards which our searchings strive. Existentialism is thus the dull receding roar of classicism and rationalism while structuralism is a new flood of the tide."[59] Crossan attempts to show that the increasingly conscious conviction from Nietzsche through Freud and Heidegger to Derrida reaches its climax in the metaphor of the hermeneutical labyrinth. *The labyrinth has no centre and is infinitely expansible* since we create it by our language and interpretive perceptions as we move through it ourselves.

The only appropriate response is that which takes its starting-point from Johann Huizinga's *Homo Ludens*, modified and developed by Jacques Ehrmann. It is a process of "free activity" in an orderly manner in the course of which "'All reality is caught up in the play of the concepts which designate it.' ... A megametaphor, ... the play of semiosis".[60] Polyvalence of meaning and interpretation is inevitable, for everything exists within signs and even the distinction between signifier and signified dissolves. If anything is "reality", it is what we experience in the play of semiosis.

Parables function in this semiotic context to break images, to challenge fixed assumptions and to carry us forward in the only way that can handle the ultimate paradox of hermeneutics: how can we think of anything as anything if we are still making up our minds what to think of it *as*? Parables subvert, relativize and re-relativize each and every reading:

> The game can be played repeatedly and continuously. So also with the play of interpretation on ludic allegory in parable. Since you cannot interpret absolutely, you interpret forever. This paradox ... precludes any final or canonical interpretation ... Positively, it turns the story outward as a metaphor for its own very process of interpretation. This is polyvalent narration or ludic allegory at its deepest level.[61]

Crossan comes close here to the philosophy of Richard Rorty. Rorty writes, "Hermeneutics is not 'another way of knowing' – 'understanding' as opposed to 'explanation.' It is better seen as another way of coping."[62] Radical hermeneutics is simply a way of responding to the acknowledged relativity of all interpretation by choosing practice rather than theory. The text is no more and no less than what the reader makes it. In literary theory this is close to the position of Stanley Fish. Fish spells out his position with delightful and disarming honesty in the giveaway title of the introduction to his recent book: "How I Stopped Worrying and Learned to Love Interpretation".[63] A

---

[59] John Dominic Crossan, "Finding Is the First Act: Trove Folk Tales and Jesus' Treasure Parable", *Semeia* 9 (1977), p.111.

[60] Ibid., pp.115, 117 and 121.

[61] Ibid., p.139.

[62] Richard Rorty, *Philosophy and The Mirror of Nature* (Princeton, NJ: Princeton University Press, 1980), p.356.

[63] Fish, *Is There a Text in This Class?*, p.1.

thinker can "stop worrying" only when either of two events occurs: (1) when he finds the solution to all the serious problems that face him, or (2) when he endures the tension of these problems no longer and is driven to the belief that one side of the tension rests on an illusion. Then he can without bad conscience simply cut the knots on the ground that the problem was never genuine in the first place.

Hermeneutics often cuts through interpretive knots by *either one* of two *opposite* claims: either (1) the claim that the text has some *inherent, internal, or "obvious"* meaning apart from the stance and expectations of the interpreter, or (2) the claim that the text has *no* meaning apart from the stance and expectations of the interpreter. The first view represents a kind of objectivism that is at odds with the whole discipline of hermeneutics; the second view reduces hermeneutics to radical relativism and scepticism. Fish throws all his weight behind the view that the meaning of a text *seems* "inescapable" only when the reader brings some prestructured understanding to the text.[64] The title *Is There a Text in This Class?* illustrates this claim. From within one horizon of expectation it means quite "obviously": "Does this class have a set text?" From within a different horizon of expectation it "obviously" means "Is this class conducted on the assumption that a text has a givenness and stability which is more than merely a reader's response?" Stanley Fish can "stop worrying" only by entirely subordinating the givenness of the horizon of the text to the horizon of the reader. But this is not a *solution*, it is merely a *decision* and, given the standpoint of Rorty, Crossan, Derrida and others, it cannot be defended by granting it any other status. In Derrida, truth has virtually become merely autobiography.

We come to the second difficulty. What, in practice, has been the outcome of applying this approach to the parables? We might easily cite irresponsible and unscholarly examples of this approach, but this would not constitute a fair assessment of the method. The work of Mary Ann Tolbert represents a careful and conscientious attempt to draw on the work of Crossan and Wittig while remaining faithful, as far as possible, to the text. From Fish's standpoint, though, hers is still the work of a worrier, and to my mind it is all the better for that. Tolbert repeatedly asserts, "The interpretation must 'fit' the parable story. Further, it must deal with the entire configuration of the story and not just one part of it."[65] At the same time, on the basis of Susan Wittig's reader-response approach, "There is no one correct interpretation of a parable, though there may be limits of congruency that invalidate some readings."[66]

Some actual examples of such interpretation, however, will dismay most biblical specialists, at least after the initial comments. The parable of the prodigal son, Tolbert urges, employs three characters, an adult and two "children".[67] The adult must mediate between the two children. One son has wasted himself on a dissipated life; the other son is judgmental and unforgiving: "These three elements are present in the psyche of every individual. The voice inside us that demands the fulfilling of every desire, the breaking of every taboo, is pitted against the often equally strong voice of harsh judgment on those

---

[64] Ibid., p.106.
[65] Tolbert, *Perspectives on the Parables*, p.71.
[66] Ibid., p.39.
[67] Ibid., p.101.

desires ... Mediating between these two voices is the one who attempts to bring unity and harmony ... the resolution of conflicts within the psyche of every individual".[68]

Tolbert appears to view it as a short step to represent the father, the elder son and the prodigal son as, respectively, the ego, the superego, and the id of Freudian psychology: "Just as the younger son of the story embodies some of the aspects of Freud's conception of the id, the elder son exhibits striking analogies with the ego ideal or 'conscience.' The superego ... is the seat of morality, religion, law, and judgment."[69] The father, however, is at pains to say that he needs both sons. Both sons are necessary and valued elements of the family. The father corresponds to the Freudian ego, for "the father is both the unifying center of the parable and its most vacillating figure".[70]

At the end of this account, Tolbert points out that once the reader is in the domain of psychoanalysis, there is no reason why this account should have *automatically* privileged status over others. So she suggests a "second reading" in which other psychological categories are employed. She recognizes that these are "contextual systems", that they must be open to evaluation, and that they must be faithful to the text. While she allows these other psychological approaches as valid interpretations, in the end she decides that her first reading is more appropriate when she examines "internally" the totality of the story again in relation to her interpretation.

In effect, though, the only working criterion for valid interpretation Tolbert applies is one of general "congruence" with a text which is virtually cut loose from its situation and left open to use by a reader who is free to utilize different aspects of his or her own "contextual system". Susan Wittig also relies on the criterion of "congruency", but her admission concerning its open-endedness is more radical and explicit. She concedes, "From the sender's point of view, the receiver who arrives at a signified other than the one which was intended is 'wrong' ... [But] from another more objective point of view what is demonstrated here is the ability to semantically alter a sign by embedding it within another belief-system, and validating the new significance by reference to those beliefs."[71]

At this point, however, an interpretive community that regards the words of Jesus of Nazareth as privileged or authoritative cannot but feel ill at ease. Christian interpreters may even begin to regret too hastily criticizing the attention paid by Jeremias and others to the Jesus of history and the situations out of which he spoke. But this brings us back to our earlier claim about undue polarization, and the need for multiple models. Reader-response theory may carry us forward constructively, especially in interpreting particular types of parables, but clearly a parable such as the Parable of the Prodigal Son does not invite the injunction, "Go and make whatever you like of this." This is not equivalent to "Let the person who has ears to hear, hear ...". We cannot accord to a *single* hermeneutical perspective the status of a comprehensive hermeneutical model. Neither the multidimensional character of speech-act theory nor the complexities of the process of recontextualization receives adequate attention in these approaches. Our next task [in further material in this piece] will be to examine these aspects more closely.

---

[68]   Ibid., pp.101–2.
[69]   Ibid., p.104.
[70]   Ibid., p.106.
[71]   Wittig, "A Theory of Multiple Meanings", p.92.

CHAPTER TWENTY-FOUR

Parables, "World" and Eventful Speech: "The Parables as Language-Event: Some Comments on Fuchs's Hermeneutics in the Light of Linguistic Philosophy" (1970)

This article first appeared in Scottish Journal of Theology *volume 23 (1970), pp.437–68. It is the earliest of the present collection, and witnesses to a consistent interest in the relation between hermeneutics, biblical studies, theology, European Continental philosophy, and philosophy of language in the traditions of Wittgenstein and also of Austin. Many agree that to try to understand the thought of Fuchs provides a tough challenge in itself, and part of the original aim was to offer an exposition of his complex approach. However, alongside his more incisive insights Fuchs leaves some significant difficulties. As in the case of Bultmann also, if due respect is paid to certain principles that emerge in the later Wittgenstein and other philosophers of language, it might be easier to identify and to avoid them. This article explores this possibility. It also has a second aim, namely to shed some fresh light on the parables of Jesus themselves with special reference to their linguistic forms and functions.*

I
Fuchs's Approach to Language

The first of the issues requires only brief mention, by way of introduction. Rightly or wrongly, the supposed obscurity of Fuchs's writings has become almost a legend.[1] But behind the legend lies a concrete problem which can be plainly stated; namely the difficulty of relating his arguments to recognisable landmarks in more general linguistic studies. Admittedly he insists that 'faith's "doctrine of language" ... is ... not meant in the sense of linguistics'.[2] New Testament hermeneutics remain 'the hermeneutic of faith'.[3] But his work cannot be isolated, as I shall try to show, from well-established linguistic principles. When we reach firm and charted linguistic ground, it becomes easier to see the value of Fuchs's approach, as well as some specific strengths and weaknesses in his hermeneutics.

---

[1] Cf. for example, F.G. Downing's frank admission in *The Church and Jesus* (London: SCM Press, 1968), p.93, n.2, and E. Käsemann's criticism in *New Testament Questions of Today* (E.T., London: SCM Press, 1969), p.121, n.16.

[2] E. Fuchs, 'Response to the American Discussion', in J.M. Robinson and J.B. Cobb Jr (eds), *New Frontiers in Theology II: The New Hermeneutic* (New York: Harper and Row, 1964), p.241.

[3] E. Fuchs, 'The New Testament and the Hermeneutical Problem', in J.M. Robinson and J.B. Cobb (eds), op. cit., p.141. Cf. also E. Fuchs, *Zur Frage nach dem historischen Jesus* (Tübingen: J.C.B. Mohr (Paul Siebeck), 1960), pp.399–400 (E.T., *Studies of the Historical Jesus*, London: SCM Press, 1964, p.186; and *Hermeneutik* (Tübingen: J.C.B. Mohr (Paul Siebeck), ⁴1970), pp.11, 111–26, *et passim*.

The second issue concerns Fuchs's emphatic contrast between functions of language-event (*Sprachereignis*) and the place of propositions or assertions.[4] Jesus does not use the language of parables to convey ideas or concepts (*Vorstellungen*).[5] In the very uttering of the parables, Jesus calls (*berufen*),[6] promises (*verheissen*),[7] demands (*fordern*),[8] or gives (*geben*).[9] Clearly this is very different from merely talking *about* actual or possible promises, or actual or possible gifts. The language of Jesus effects a change in the situation; it enacts an event.

In this connection, Robert Funk has made a brief but very useful suggestion, which I propose to develop in due course. He suggests that a parallel occurs between 'language-event' in Continental hermeneutics, and J.L. Austin's important work on performative utterances.[10] In each case, to use Austin's terms, 'the issuing of the utterance is the performing of an action'.[11] Funk leaves the discussion here. But it is precisely at this point that crucial difficulties begin to emerge, which, however, can subsequently be turned to good account. For unlike Fuchs, Austin does not cling at all costs to a clear-cut contrast between performative language and propositions which convey ideas. The two categories, he argues, often overlap. Indeed, 'for a certain performative utterance to be happy, certain statements have *to be true*'.[12] With typical gentle irony he observes, 'Perhaps indeed there is no great distinction between statements and performative utterances.'[13]

If Austin's comments are now applied to questions about the parables, significant consequences begin to emerge. At the most general and fundamental level, Fuchs's approach seems to be corroborated. The parables do far more than merely illustrate theological or ethical concepts. But is this the whole story? Are we obliged to conclude, with Fuchs, that when parables contain informative assertions or truth-claiming propositions, these undermine their hermeneutical function and force? Might they not rather, at least in certain cases, constitute a condition of effective performative force?

This, at any rate, is what I shall try to argue. But this is in no way simply a return to more traditional 'ideational' interpretations.[14] For the crux of the matter is that *assertions*

---

⁴ Cf., for example, *Zur Frage nach dem historischen Jesus*, pp.405-30 (E.T., pp.191–212), and E. Fuchs, *Zum hermeneutischen Problem in der Theologie: Die existentiale Interpretation* (Tübingen: J.C.B. Mohr (Paul Siebeck), 1959), pp.281–305.

⁵ *Zur Frage nach dem historischen Jesus*, pp.410–11 (E.T., pp.195–6), and *Zum hermeneutischen Problem in der Theologie*, pp.14–51. Cf. also *Hermeneutik*, pp.92, 97–8, 121 and 219–30.

⁶ *Zur Frage nach dem historischen Jesus*, pp.226, 291, 346 and 415 (E.T., pp.38, 94, 140 and 199).

⁷ Ibid., pp.288 and 291 (E.T., pp.91 and 93).

⁸ Ibid., pp.224 and 226 (E.T., pp.36 and 38).

⁹ Ibid., p.347 (E.T., p.141).

¹⁰ R.W. Funk, *Language, Hermeneutic, and Word of God* (New York: Harper and Row, 1966), pp.26–8. A parallel comment also occurs in J.M. Robinson, 'The Parables as God Happening', in F.T. Trotter (ed.), *Jesus and the Historian: Written in Honor of Ernest Cadman Colwell* (Philadelphia, PA: Westminster Press, 1968), p.142.

¹¹ J.L. Austin, *How to Do Things with Words* (Oxford, 1962), p.6.

¹² Ibid., p.45 (Austin's italics).

¹³ Ibid., p.52.

¹⁴ Cf. R.W. Funk, op. cit., pp.146–50. Funk asserts, 'like Jülicher, Dodd and Jeremias derive a set of ideas from the parables ... The ideational *point* of Jülicher remains ideational' (p.149, Funk's italics). On the other hand David Wenham has drawn my attention to passages in Jülicher which partly question Funk's generalization. Jülicher stresses, for example, that Jesus used pictorial imagery not simply for description but to win the mind, and thence to *capture the will* ('*gewinnen ... gefangen ... nehmen*'). Cf. A. Jülicher, *Die*

themselves may function in various ways and with various effects, as Wittgenstein and others have conclusively demonstrated.[15] In fact we might take a further cue from Wittgenstein, to ask a specific question: could it be that in certain parables which embody multiple assertions, this form does not spring merely from unimaginative editing, but functions, by *intention*, as part of a 'language-family'?[16] In this connection, Wittgenstein's notion of 'Now I can go on' bears a striking relation to some of Fuchs's concerns.[17] But before we examine these possibilities, we must first return to Fuchs's work, and to the tradition of hermeneutical philosophy which bears on it more directly. In terms of this broader background, he explicitly alludes to Heidegger and Gadamer, as well as to the theology of Ebeling and Jüngel.[18]

II

Language-Event and "World": The Way of Love

In Heidegger and Gadamer, as well as in Fuchs, 'language-event' stands in contrast to all modes of language which function primarily to convey concepts or ideas, as information.[19] Fuchs's cautious, if not negative, attitude to this latter type of language

---

Gleichnisreden Jesu (Freiburg: Mohr, 1899) vol. I, p.105. Similarly, in Nathan's *verdict* (*Urteil*) 'thou art the man', the purpose of the parable is 'to strike home'. Both words (*Urteil* and *treffen*) are used characteristically by Fuchs. Cf. A. Jülicher, loc. cit., p.103.

[15]   Cf. L. Wittgenstein, *Philosophical Investigations* (Oxford: Blackwell, ²1958, reprinted 1967), §§ 23, 24, 79 *et passim*. Four points may be made at this juncture about concrete examples in the Synoptic Gospels. (I) In most cases, truth-claiming assertions *also* function in other ways (e.g. as verdictives or implied imperatives). Cf. Matt. 18:33, 'So also my heavenly Father will do ...'; Luke 15:7 and 10, 'There will be more joy in heaven ...'; and Luke 14:11 and 18:14b, 'Every one who exalts himself ...'. In crude and provisional terms, we may admit that these are *more* than propositions, but deny that they are *less* than propositions. Similarly, to describe assertions about the *future* as 'propositions' is not to deny their *additional* feature of 'symmetry in the grammar of temporal expressions' (L. Wittgenstein, *The Blue and Brown Books* (Oxford: Blackwell, ³1969), p.109).

(2) It is impossible to draw up a list of propositions *on the basis of grammar*. For example, in Luke 11:13, what is grammatically a question functions logically as a statement inviting response: 'How much more will your heavenly Father give the Holy Spirit to those who ask him?' Wittgenstein cites examples of questions used as statements (e.g. 'Isn't the weather glorious today?'); of questions used as commands (e.g. 'Would you like to ...?'); and of statements used as commands (e.g. 'You will do this'). Cf. *Philosophical Investigations*, § 21.

(3) From the standpoint of New Testament criticism, the originality of assertions within given settings is not primarily at issue. The issue is whether *within* their existing settings they conflict with, or support, the hermeneutical function of parables. (Cf. above on Luke 14:11 and 18:14b.)

(4) Broadly it remains characteristic of propositions that they should stand in some kind of logical relationship to other propositions which are true-or-false. But this must not be equated with narrower notions such as we find in Wittgenstein's *Tractatus Logico-Philosophicus*. See below. First-century Jews were aware of logical relationships more subtle than that of direct deduction or entailment (see also below).

[16]   Ibid., §§ 66 and 67 (pp.31–2). Discussed further below.

[17]   Ibid., §§ 138–242 (pp.53–88), especially §§ 172–86 (pp.70–75).

[18]   Cf. E. Fuchs, 'Das hermeneutische Problem', in E. Dinkler (ed.), *Zeit und Geschichte: Dankesgabe an Rudolf Bultmann zum 80. Geburstag* (Tübingen: J.C.B. Mohr (Paul Siebeck), 1964), especially pp.357–60; and *Hermeneutik*, pp.8, 62–72, 125 and 269.

[19]   Cf. M. Heidegger, *Unterwegs zur Sprache* (Neske, Pfullingen, 1960), pp.241–68 (cf. also pp.83–153); and H.-G. Gadamer, *Wahrheit und Methode: Grundzüge einer philosophischen Hermeneutik* (2nd edn, Tübingen: J.C.B. Mohr (Paul Siebeck), 1965), pp.361–465.

might well have provided the best starting-point from which to elucidate his hermeneutics. But it would also have involved delay before viewing his account of the parables more directly. Hence questions about this contrast and its implications have been postponed until the next section. Central to all positive work in the hermeneutical tradition is the question: how does the subject matter or content of language 'come to speech' as event? (*das Zur-Sprache-kommen der Sache selbst*).[20]

In his approach to the parables, Fuchs begins with the point that the language of Jesus creates a 'world' (*Welt*) into which he draws his hearers.[21] The hearer does not merely observe this 'world' as a spectator; he enters it, and becomes a participant. He actively assumes one of the concrete roles that it offers him, and he finds himself carried forward by a kind of inner logic of consequences which his chosen role brings with it. He has now lost the capacity as human subject to interrogate the parable as an object of scrutiny which he can manipulate. Indeed, the hearer himself has now become the object of scrutiny. In Fuchs's words, 'The truth has ourselves as its object.'[22] He observes, 'The text is therefore not just the servant that transmits kerygmatic formulations, but rather a master that directs us into the language-context of our existence ... "before God" ... It is really the present that is interpreted with the help of the text.'[23]

Fuchs expounds this principle concretely in relation to a number of specific parables. Thus, in the parable of the Labourers in the Vineyard (Matt. 20:1–16), he calls attention to the drama of events as they unfold. The last are paid first, 'so that we, too, share the inevitable reaction of the first'.[24] The style of the whole parable, he argues, is significant: 'the circumstances surrounding the hire of the labourers; the minute attention to detail, almost from hour to hour; then the correspondingly quicker acceleration ... its relentless course, leading to the release of tension in the dialogue ... singles out the individual and grasps him deep down'.[25] The parable 'effects and demands a decision' as well as containing Jesus's pledge 'in a concrete way'.[26] Fuchs adds later concerning the same parable, that the hearer who is called 'is drawn over on to God's side, and learns to see everything with God's eyes. He then understands God, as a child understands his father.'[27] Similar comments are made on other parables, including that of 'the prodigal sons' (Luke 15:11–32);[28] the treasure in the field and the pearl of great price (Matt. 13:44–46);[29] and the mustard seed (Matt. 13:31–32).[30]

---

[20] H.-G. Gadamer, op. cit., p.360. Cf. also the translator's comments in *Studies of the Historical Jesus*, p.141n; M. Heidegger, *Unterwegs zur Sprache*, pp.159ff; and G. Ebeling, *The Nature of Faith* (E.T., London: Collins, 1961), p.16.

[21] Cf. Fuchs, *Zur Frage nach dem historischen Jesus*, pp.295–6 (E.T., pp.97–8), and *Zum hermeneutischen Problem in der Theologie*, pp.14ff; and H.-G. Gadamer, op. cit., pp.97ff and 415ff.

[22] E. Fuchs, 'The New Testament and the Hermeneutical Problem', loc. cit., p.143. Cf. also *Hermeneutik*, pp.64ff and 119ff.

[23] E. Fuchs, *Studies of the Historical Jesus*, pp.211–12 (German, pp.429–30; Fuchs's italics).

[24] Ibid., p.33 (German, p.220).

[25] Ibid., pp.34–5 (German, p.222).

[26] Ibid., pp.36–7 (German, pp.224–5).

[27] Ibid., p.155 (German, p.363).

[28] Ibid., pp.20ff and 160–62 (German, pp.153ff and 369–71).

[29] Ibid., pp.94–5 and 124–30 (German, pp.291–3 and 327–35).

[30] Ibid. pp.90–94 (German, pp.287–91).

Fuchs's analysis of the structure of parables acquires its greatest significance in this connection. He contrasts the 'image part' of the parable (*Bildhälfte*) with its 'material part' or 'content part' (*Sachhälfte*).[31] To begin with, the image part looks deceptively innocent and thoroughly familiar. It thus entices the hearer into entering the 'world' of the parable, and adopting a role within it that would correspond with his own regular scale of values and self-assessment. Nevertheless, events fail to take a predictable and familiar course. Suddenly the hearer finds himself exposed and put on trial in a *strange* world. Conventional values and conventional criteria are transcended and perhaps even reversed. Depending on what role he has adopted, the effects on the hearer may vary from that of outrage, to that of joyful acceptance. Fuchs observes, 'Jesus is in this way pointing out the *difference* [*Unterschied*] between the *image* [*Bild*] and the *truth* [*Wahrheit*].... Jesus draws the hearer over to his side by means of the artistic medium [*Kunstmittel*] so that the hearer may think together with Jesus.'[32] On the use of such a method, Fuchs adds, 'Is this not the way of true love? Love does not just blurt out. Instead it provides in advance the sphere in which meeting takes place.'[33]

III
Worlds and Horizons of Understanding in Heidegger and in Fuchs

The main outlines of Fuchs's interpretation seem both illuminating and convincing, especially in the light of Funk's contentions about the parable as metaphor.[34] But it would be a mistake to infer from this that Fuchs's orientation springs from *distinctively* theological insights. Indeed for the purposes of this present study it is important to see that this is not so, in several specific respects.

Gadamer[35] shows conclusively that roots of the hermeneutical tradition go back much further than Dilthey and even Schleiermacher. The 'conventional' notion that man seeks knowledge (*Erkenntnis*) through observation, generalization, and inductive and deductive reasoning, springs from the 'scientific' orientation of the Cartesian tradition. But as Vico and others before him had seen, man needs more than this to arrive at understanding (*Verstehen*) of 'life', especially from a historically conditioned viewpoint. Man reaches this broader and deeper understanding through 'modes of *experience* in which truth comes to light' (*Erfahrungsweisen*).[36] Such real-life experience (*Wirklichkeitserfahrung*) comes to a man, perhaps, when he stands within a 'world'

---

31 Ibid., pp.33ff, and especially pp.126–30 (German, pp.220ff and 329–35). Cf. E. Linnemann, *Parables of Jesus: Introduction and Exposition* (E.T., London: SPCK, 1966), pp.23–33 (here, 'picture part' and 'reality part'); and especially R.W. Funk, op. cit., pp.14–18 and 124–222, where the issue is expounded magnificently under roughly parallel categories, derived partly from Owen Barfield.

32 E. Fuchs, ibid., p.129 (German, p.333; Fuchs's italics).

33 Ibid. It should not be forgotten that the basic contrast between *Bild* and *Sache* goes back at least as far as Jülicher. Cf. A. Jülicher, op. cit., vol. 1, p.70, with E. Fuchs, *Hermeneutik*, pp.220ff. On the broader hermeneutical principle cf. *Hermeneutik*, pp.5, 12, 63–8, 126ff, and especially p.91.

34 R.W. Funk, op. cit., pp.133ff.

35 H.-G. Gadamer, op. cit., pp.1–39, especially pp.16ff.

36 Ibid., p.xxvi (my italics).

which is not simply his to manipulate, but in which language or creative art takes hold of him at the deepest level.[37] Those who stand, for example, outside the 'world' created by a work of art are never seized by its *reality*. They view it as something 'presented for the benefit of the spectator', as a mere object of scrutiny, or source of theoretical concepts.[38]

Gadamer elucidates the point by means of a striking simile. Partly like a work of art, he suggests, a game, too, creates a distinctive 'world' of experience. Even if the spectator knows all about its theory, 'the *reality* of a game is something shared by the players in the play itself'.[39] In entering its common world, a player does more than think certain thoughts; he adopts the presuppositions and attitudes that go with a given role within the game.

Some kind of parallel to Gadamer's approach can be found outside as well as inside hermeneutical philosophy. In his *Zettel*, Wittgenstein draws a contrast between 'interpreting ... "from outside"' ('*deuten* ... "*von aussen*"') and *entering into* something as a participant (*leben ... in ...*).[40] Comparing the two activities, he writes, 'It is as if ... we looked at a picture so as to enter into it and the objects in it surrounded us like real ones; and then we stepped back, and were now outside it; we saw the frame, and the picture was a painted surface'.[41] Similarly, we may imagine that 'we are sitting in a darkened cinema and entering into the film [*leben im Film*]. Now the lights are turned on, though the film continues on the screen. But suddenly we are outside it [*stehen wir ... ausserhalb*] and see it as movement of light and dark patches on screen.'[42] Wittgenstein now adds a crucial comment which continues the parallel with Fuchs and Gadamer. In the experience of participation, or of 'entering into ...', 'I do not interpret, because I feel at home ... When I interpret, I step from one level of thought to another. If I see the ... symbol "from outside", I become conscious that it *could* be interpreted thus or thus.'[43]

It is arguable that even earlier in the *Tractatus* Wittgenstein implied some notion of a 'world', or viewpoint, which is existentially 'mine', because it is bounded by 'my' horizons of thought, language and understanding. He writes, '*The limits of my language* mean the limits of my world ... The world is *my* world ...'.[44] But the context of discussion is different.[45]

It is hardly necessary to call attention to Heidegger's categories of 'world' and 'worldhood', since these feature prominently throughout the first half of *Being and Time*,

---

[37] Ibid., p.72, cf. pp.66–96.

[38] Ibid., p.104.

[39] Ibid. (my italics). Cf. pp.98–102. Gadamer draws on the work of Buytendijk and Huizinga, but not directly on Wittgenstein.

[40] L. Wittgenstein, *Zettel* (Oxford: Blackwell, 1967), §§ 231–5.

[41] Ibid., § 233.

[42] Ibid.

[43] Ibid. §§ 234–5 (Wittgenstein's italics). Cf. E. Fuchs, *Hermeneutik*, pp.92, 109 and 119–26.

[44] L. Wittgenstein, *Tractus Logico-Philosophicus* (E.T., London: Routledge and Kegan Paul, 1961), 5.6 and 5.62 (Wittgenstein's italics). Cf. also 5.63, 5.641, and 5.6431.

[45] Cf. G. Pitcher, *The Philosophy of Wittgenstein* (Englewood Cliffs, NJ: Prentice-Hall, 1964), pp.144–5; G.E.M. Anscombe, *An Introduction to Wittgenstein's Tractatus* (London: Hutchinson, ³1967), pp.166–73; N. Smart, *Philosophers and Religious Truth* (London: SCM Press, ²1969), pp.163ff; and W.H. Poteat in D.Z. Philips (ed.), *Religion and Understanding* (Oxford: Blackwell, 1967), pp.199ff.

and are presupposed by his later work.[46] But the part played by language in 'establishing' such worlds remains of crucial significance for an understanding and assessment of Fuchs's work.[47] Here, once again, it is Gadamer who provides the most lucid discussion, by means of his deservedly well-known simile of merging horizons (*Horizontsverschmelzung*).[48] The closest parallel in Fuchs and Heidegger can be found in the more obscure notion of language as 'gathering'. In Heidegger's words, 'The essence of language is found in the act of gathering.'[49] Fuchs declares, '*The language of faith brings into language the gathering* [die Versammlung] *of faith, and thereby Christ.*'[50]

Gadamer points out that when language brings a new 'world' into existence, the hearer who enters this world becomes aware of the new horizons of meaning. But these necessarily differ from the horizons of understanding that have hitherto marked the extent of his own world. Thus, to begin with, two different worlds stand over against each other, each with its own horizon. Yet the peculiarity of horizons is that their positions are variable, in accordance with the position from which they are viewed. Hence adjustments can be made in the hearer's own understanding until the two horizons come to merge into one. A new comprehensive horizon now appears, which serves as the boundary of an enlarged world of integrated understanding.[51]

Although Fuchs is not dependent on Gadamer's work, this sheds considerable light on factors in his approach to the parables which otherwise seem to remain more obscure. When a hearer enters the 'world' of the parable and of its language, new horizons of meaning come to view that may expose him to unexpected verdicts. If he *believes* the words of Jesus, he accepts his place in this 'world', and strives to readjust his own horizon until *his* world is also the world of Jesus. Thus Fuchs declares, 'To have faith in Jesus now means essentially to repeat Jesus' decision.'[52] For 'to believe in Jesus means to believe *like* Jesus'.[53]

This further clarifies two other elements in Fuchs's approach. First, if only the believer can stand with Jesus in a fused and enlarged world of understanding, this seems to explain the precise *sense* in which Fuchs's hermeneutics are particularly 'hermeneutics of faith'. Indeed the conclusion coincides exactly with A.N. Wilder's verdict: Fuchs's 'initial approach is not dictated by a dogmatic Christian standpoint. When, however, New Testament texts are dealt with, it is assumed ... that the unbeliever will either become believer and so understand the text, or remain unbeliever and not understand it'.[54] Second, this welding together concerns not only Jesus and the individual believer, but the

---

[46]   M. Heidegger, *Being and Time* (E.T., London: SCM Press, 1962), especially §§ 12–27. In particular cf. pp.93–5.

[47]   Cf. E.Fuchs, Hermeneutik, pp.126ff.

[48]   H.-G. Gadamer, op. cit., pp.286–90. Cf. also pp.356ff.

[49]   M. Heidegger, *An Introduction to Metaphysics* (E.T., Yale, 1959; Anchor edn 1961), p.145.

[50]   E. Fuchs, *Studies of the Historical Jesus*, p.209 (German, p.426; Fuchs's italics).

[51]   H.-G. Gadamer, op. cit., pp.232, 286 and 288–90. On the importance of this concept cf. W. Pannenberg, 'Hermeneutics and Universal History', in R.W. Funk (ed.), *Journal for Theology and the Church*, vol. 4: *History and Hermeneutic* (Tübingen: J.C.B. Mohr (Paul Siebeck), and New York: Harper and Row, 1967), especially pp.137–52.

[52]   E. Fuchs, *Studies of the Historical Jesus*, p.28 (German, p.164).

[53]   Ibid., p.63 (German, p.256; Fuchs's italics).

[54]   A.N. Wilder, 'New Testament Hermeneutics Today', in W. Klassen and G.F. Snyder (eds), *Current Issues in New Testament Interpretation* (London: SCM Press, 1962), pp.40–41.

whole believing community. Fuchs observes, 'In the proclamation of the word ... community [*Gemeinde*] is formed. This was the intention.'[55] Hence, similarly, 'This community has its being [*Sein*], its "togetherness" [*Beieinander*], in the possibility of its being able to speak the kind of language in which the event of its community [*das Ereignis ihrer Gemeinschaft*] is fulfilled.'[56] With these two statements it may be useful to compare Heidegger's comment, 'Language ... comes to its truth only when speaking and hearing are orientated towards logos as collectedness in the sense of being'.[57]

When a parable functions as language-event, therefore, it first of all creates a world in which distinctive values and verdicts confront the hearer at a deeper level than that which may be reached by theoretical discussion. The language of Jesus 'strikes home' (*treffen*) to the hearer, partly because it may force him to see horizons which he might otherwise not have chosen to see; and partly, also, because it grips him at every level of attitude, thought and emotion. In the parable of the Prodigal Son, for example, those who unselfconsciously think of themselves as 'good' are drawn into accepting the role of the 'good' son. The consequences of this role, however, emerge with inescapable clarity. The situation is transformed from hypothesis to imagined experience. Similarly, in Fuchs's discussion of the parable of the Unmerciful Servant, 'Matthew wanted to say to Israel ... God is harder than you are. And to the Church, he wanted to say: God insists upon his privilege of indulgence.'[58] But if the parable is turned into a theoretical generalization, it can only be described in self-contradictory terms, as 'a comforting warning'.

If the message of the parable is accepted, a second objective is achieved. According to Fuchs, the hearer discovers what it means to think and even to decide 'with' Jesus, so that he, in turn, now also *speaks* the language of faith. The point that he rightly makes is that a response concerns more than some invisible change of 'mental state'; it affects the hearer's disposition and 'language'. Perhaps pressing the issue further, however, than the pages of the Gospels can directly justify, he concludes, 'Certainty of faith is established in the hearer when he hears in such a way that he is no longer divided ... He recognizes this by his ability to describe to others what has struck home, in such a way that they can likewise find it striking them (Rom. 14:7–9). The fact of having heard provides the believer with a new *command of language*.'[59] In this way, it may become apparent that the

---

55 E. Fuchs, *Studies of the Historical Jesus*, p.203 (German, p.419).

56 Ibid., p.209 (German, p.426).

57 M. Heidegger, *An Introduction to Metaphysics*, p.145.

58 E. Fuchs, 'The Parable of the Unmerciful Servant', in *Studia Evangelica* (ed. by K. Aland, F.L. Cross, et al.; Berlin: Akademie Verlag, 1959), p.493 (cf. pp.487–94). See also *Hermeneutik*, pp.67ff; *Zum Hermeneutischen Problem in der Theologie*, pp.281ff; and *Studies of the Historical Jesus*, pp.196 and 202 (German, pp.411 and 418). Also relevant to these considerations is Fuchs's essay 'Must one believe in Jesus if he wants to believe in God?', in R.W. Funk (ed.), *Journal for Theology and the Church*, vol. 1: *The Bultmann School of Interpretation: New Directions?* (Tübingen: Mohr, and New York: Harper and Row, 1965), pp.147–68, especially p.152, on the contrast between 'attitudes' (*Einstellungen*) and 'conceptions' (*Vorstellung*). (Cf., further, J.M. Robinson, 'Jesus' Parables as God Happening', loc. cit., pp.134–50; and R.W. Funk, *Language, Hermeneutic and Word of God*, pp.163–98. On the parable of the Great Supper, Funk comments, 'Each hearer is drawn into the tale as he wills ... As the story unfolds, he must make up his mind whether he can unfold it', ibid., p.192.)

59 E. Fuchs, *Studies of the Historical Jesus*, p.198 (German, p.414; Fuchs's italics). On the notion of sharing Jesus's experience, cf. Fuchs's essay 'Bemerkungen zur Gleichnisauslegung', *Theologische Literaturzeitung* LXXIX (1954), reprinted in *Zur Frage nach dem Historischen Jesus*, pp.136–42.

language of Jesus has taken *full effect*. His promise or his gift has been fully appropriated; his claim of his pledge, fully accepted; or his demand, or his call, obeyed. His words have struck home as language-event.

IV
Language, Propositions and Truth

It is clear that much more is involved in the notion of language-event than any clear-cut contrast between performative language and the language which conveys information. The contrast remains relevant, as far as it goes. But a more important distinction has also come to light. On the one hand language may function at the purely cognitive level in the form of conscious and detached discursive reasoning; on the other hand, it may strike home at a deeper level, by exposing or reorienting attitudes and presuppositions, as well as conscious thoughts. But this now raises a further question: how far, if at all, do these two pairs of contrasts logically involve each other? Has anything so far been said which *directly* concerns the functions of assertions, and their place in the parable?

Heidegger's views have remained basically consistent on this question, and Gadamer shares them.[60] The problem is not to ascertain their views, but to disentangle some five contributory factors that support them.

(1) Both writers imply that the traditional view of language as an information-carrying medium depends on the kind of rationalism that flourished during the Enlightenment. A very different approach emerged with the work of J.G. Hamann, J.G. Herder, and especially Wilhelm von Humboldt, whom Gadamer calls 'the creator of modern philosophy of language'.[61] Locke and others had assumed that men first possessed rational ideas, and then sought to communicate them through language. But according to Humboldt and his predecessors, language first emerged, or emerges, at a *pre*-rational level. As R.L. Brown puts it, the unit of language is believed to precede the unit of thought, and indeed to determine its limits.[62] On such a basis, therefore, it may well seem that, in Hamann's words, 'poetry is the mother tongue of mankind'; whilst propositions appear to represent a secondary linguistic activity. In this sense Fuchs declares, 'Language is not the abbreviation of thought; thought is the abbreviation of language.'[63]

---

[60] Cf. M. Heidegger, *Being and Time*, § 33, pp.195–203. Cf. also *Vom Wesen der Wahrheit* (Frankfurt-am-Main: V. Klosterman, 1961), pp.5–12 (reprinted in *Wegmarken*, Frankfurt-am-Main: V. Klosterman, 1967, pp.73ff).

[61] H.-G. Gadamer, op. cit. p.415.

[62] R.L. Brown, *Wilhelm von Humboldt's Conception of Linguistic Relativity* (The Hague: Mouton, 1967), p.54. Brown's illuminating study traces the important connections between Hamann, Herder and Humboldt, and adds useful comments on the linguistic significance of this whole approach. Cf. especially pp.24–39 and 54–68.

[63] E. Fuchs, *Studies of the Historical Jesus*, p.210 (German, p.428). Cf. M. Heidegger, *Unterwegs zur Sprache*, pp.37–82 and 241–68.

(2) Heidegger and Gadamer trace the notion that propositions convey truth in the form of ideas or concepts to origins in Plato's dualism. Appearance, Heidegger argues, 'was declared to be mere appearance, and thus degraded. At the same time "being", as *idea*, was exalted to a supra-sensory realm. A chasm ... was created'.[64] Gadamer outlines the linguistic consequences. In Plato's *Cratylus* words are only imitations (μιμήματα) of immaterial concepts, and living language is thus reduced to the status of functional ciphers.[65] Words have become merely labels for concepts. But only because of their 'sheer immateriality' (*vollendeten Geistigkeit*) do they retain any semblance of supposed objectivity.[66] The circularity is hidden only by Plato's doctrine of Ideas.

(3) As soon as we abandon Plato's idealism, however, it becomes clear that such an approach relates to a 'correspondence' view of truth. Heidegger calls this 'the conventional view of truth'. Man is measuring his own thoughts and concepts by means of further thoughts and concepts which spring from the same source. Heidegger comments, 'He is always thrown back on the paths that he himself has laid out ... He turns round and round in his own circle.'[67] For this reason, he observes elsewhere, truth does not have its ground in the proposition (*im Satz*);[68] the practice of attributing it primarily to the statement (*die Aussage*) falls to the ground.[69]

Parallels with Fuchs now emerge much more clearly. On the basis just outlined, it is arguable that assertions reduce language to the functions of a tool at man's disposal, whereby he can manipulate theoretical concepts. But both Fuchs and Heidegger contrast this with the language-event. We may compare their comments. Heidegger declares, 'Language is not a tool at his disposal; rather it is that event which disposes the supreme possibility of human existence.'[70] Fuchs similarly observes, 'What does language do? ... It permits being to be present [*anwesen*] in time; it makes being into an event [*Ereignis*].' This stands in contrast to 'a being that is always *already objectified* [*ein immer* schon objektiviiertes *Sein*] ... which is at everyone's disposal'.[71]

(4) From this there logically follows a clear-cut contrast between functions of assertions and language as event. If the subject–object perspective fragments reality into manageable concepts, these can be manipulated, first, within the framework of propositions, and then, finally, within the framework of a comprehensive calculus of logic. It becomes possible, in principle, to set up a formal system of truth-functions and truth-arguments, reminiscent of the mathematical philosophy of Frege and his successors. Wittgenstein in his earlier period attempted to construct such a calculus in the *Tractatus*. But he admitted that it implied a radical division between what can be 'shown'

---

[64]   M. Heidegger, *An Introduction to Metaphysics*, p.89.
[65]   H.-G. Gadamer, op. cit., pp.383–91. Cf. pp.384 and 387.
[66]   Ibid., p.388. Cf. also Fuchs's comments in *Hermeneutik*, pp.71 and 129f.
[67]   M. Heidegger, *An Introduction to Metaphysics*, p.132.
[68]   M. Heidegger, *Vom Wesen der Wahrheit*, p.12 (*Wegmarken*, p.81).
[69]   Ibid. (*Wegmarken*, pp.80–81).
[70]   M. Heidegger, 'Hölderlin and the Essence of Poetry', in *Existence and Being* (London: Vision Press, 1968, ed. by W. Brock), p.300.
[71]   E. Fuchs, *Studies of the Historical Jesus*, p.207 (German, pp.424–5).

and what can be 'said'.[72] In contrast to such an approach to language (which Wittgenstein himself subsequently abandoned), the language-event *gathers together* the subject matter of speech into a unified reality which confronts and addresses the hearer. The event cannot be manipulated, or simply shrugged off.[73]

(5) Gadamer also makes a similar point about the isolating effect of assertions. Whilst language as a whole gathers up all past acts of understanding, assertions isolate what comes reflectively to individual consciousness.[74] But he also makes a further point. If truth is *experienced* rather than 'known', any act of understanding may be called in question by future experience.[75] There is an element of *incompleteness* about all hermeneutical experience. Hence, horizons of meaning must remain open-ended (*unabschliessbar*) and capable of subsequent enlargement.[76] Yet, according to Gadamer, assertions close these horizons and permanently fix their position. The statement abstracts a fixed content from a potentially fuller source. Thus the full meaning 'becomes hidden with methodical exactness. What is left is the "pure" meaning of the thing-as-stated.' But this is 'always a disfigured meaning [*immer ein entstellter Sinn*]'.[77]

This, too, has close parallels in Fuchs as well as in Heidegger. Thus Fuchs declares that in genuine faith, 'there is always something open (*offen*)'.[78] The content of faith cannot be tied down, for the language of Jesus is concerned with freedom.[79] By contrast, 'Propositions are self-contained statements [*geschlossene Aussagen*], language-constructions in the spirit of objectification.'[80]

V

A Second Look at Thought and Language and at Propositions, Especially in the Light of the Later Wittgenstein

Some useful results seem to emerge if we turn at this point to the later work of Ludwig Wittgenstein, and to one or two *roughly* like-minded philosophers in Britain. Wittgenstein does not adopt the *generalizing* attitude towards propositions or assertions that we found in Fuchs, or in Heidegger and Gadamer. Admittedly in the *Tractatus*, he did generalize about propositions, as if all served to depict the physical world in a uniform way. Indeed we have just noted that Fuchs and Gadamer might well have been justified in their appraisal of propositions if 'propositions' means only what it conveys in the *Tractatus*.

---

72 Cf. L. Wittgenstein, *Tractatus Logico-Philosophicus* (London: Routledge and Kegan Paul, 1961), 4.1212 ('What *can* be shown, *cannot* be said'). On the concept of a comprehensive logical calculus cf. 2.0201, 4.26, 5.101, 5.123 *et passim* (especially the whole of 5). On 'what we cannot speak', cf. 5.6, 5.61, 6.41. 6.42, 6.421 and from 6.432 to 7.

73 Cf. Fuchs, 'The New Testament and the Hermeneutical Problem', loc. cit., pp.132ff.

74 Cf. H.-G. Gadamer, op. cit., pp.361ff, 415ff, and especially pp.444–6.

75 Ibid., pp.338 and 339.

76 Ibid., p.255.

77 Ibid., p.444.

78 E. Fuchs, *Studies of the Historical Jesus*, p.29 (German, p.165).

79 Ibid., pp.74–82 (German pp.268ff).

80 Ibid., p.202 (German p.418). Cf. *Hermeneutik*, pp.132–3, 151, 182 and 184–5.

Wittgenstein later speaks of the *'preconceived idea* of crystalline purity' which had once dominated his view of language and logic.[81] In his later work he utterly repudiates all sweeping pronouncements about their functions and effects. On the other hand, however, whether or not surprisingly, he is fully aware of all that lies behind the five points that have just been outlined.

(1) Wittgenstein gives considerable attention to the relationship between language and thought, and he could hardly stand further away than he does from anything like the rationalism of the Enlightenment.[82] He declares, 'In order to *want* to say something one must also have mastered a language.'[83] He continues, 'Thinking is not an incorporeal process ... which it would be possible to detach from speaking'.[84] If we imagine that a thought is 'there' before its expression, perhaps this is because we are picturing some special situation, such as remembering, or translating. But such a picture misleads us if it is applied to every situation. For 'what did the thought consist in, as it existed before its expression?'[85] This particular problem, however, seems nowhere to affect Wittgenstein's assessment of assertive language.

(2) Nothing could be less compatible with Wittgenstein's view of language than that which Heidegger and Gadamer attack in Plato. Once again, the trouble comes from a misleading picture. As Waismann puts it, 'It really looks as if we compare the words with the thought, as a copy of the original', although this is 'decidedly misleading'.[86] The ideational theory is in any case merely a special offshoot of referential theories of meaning, and this can only apply, if at all, in a very limited number of language-uses. Words do not acquire meaning simply by 'referring' to 'ideas'.[87] But the caricature of propositions found in Heidegger and Gadamer seems to be based on the assumption that *propositional* language functions *only* in this way.

(3) One of the most striking features of Wittgenstein's work is his constant awareness of the possibility of *deception* in language. Language, he stressed, can be manipulated artificially, until it bewitches our intelligence. Some analogies make this clear with typical vividness and force. Imagine, Wittgenstein suggest, that 'someone were to buy several copies of the morning paper to assure himself that what it said was true'.[88] Or, 'Imagine someone saying "But I know how tall I am!" and laying his hand on top of his head to prove it.'[89] If language has an anchor anywhere, he admits, it is found in the life of the language-community.[90] But he does *not* argue from this that propositions are more prone to abuse than, say, questions.

---

[81] *Philosophical Investigations*, § 108 (Wittegenstein's italics). In this connection cf. Peter Winch's illuminating remarks in P. Winch (ed.), *Studies in the Philosophy of Wittgenstein* (London: Routledge and Kegan Paul, 1969), pp.1–19.

[82] L. Wittgenstein, *Philosophical Investigations*, especially §§ 316–94 and II.xi, pp.216–23. Cf. also *Zettel* (Oxford: Blackwell, 1967), §§ 88–137.

[83] L. Wittgenstein, *Philosophical Investigations*, § 338.

[84] Ibid., § 339. Cf. also §§ 32 and 257.

[85] Ibid., § 335.

[86] F. Waismann, *The Principles of Linguistic Philosophy* (London: Macmillan, 1965), p.269. Cf. pp.295–8.

[87] Cf. L. Wittgenstein, *Philosophical Investigations*, §§ 38–59 and 375–87.

[88] Ibid., § 265.

[89] Ibid., § 279. Cf. §§ 293–309.

[90] Ibid., § 241, and II.xi, p. 226e.

(4) Wittgenstein's work on 'understanding' and on belief represents one of his most profound achievements. He is no less aware than Fuchs or Gadamer that when a hearer responds, 'Now I understand ...' or, 'Now I know how to go on', more is involved between speaker and hearer than conscious reasoning or logical inference alone.[91] Teaching someone how to read for example, involves his 'going on ... *independently'*.[92] When understanding, or belief, takes place in the hearer, something far deeper has occurred than merely a change in his so-called mental states.[93] It affects his disposition.[94] The speaker has somehow 'changed his *way of looking at things'*.[95] Yet Wittgenstein never argues that, if the logical 'must' is not enough, then propositions perform a dubious function in hermeneutical endeavour.

(5) Wittgenstein argues brilliantly and convincingly that concepts and assertions *need* not be 'closed' by logically sharp boundaries. Thus he writes, 'I *can* give the concept "number" rigid limits ... but I can also use it so that the extension of the concept is *not* closed by a frontier [*nicht durch eine Grenze abgeschlossen ist*]. And this is how we do use the word "game". For how is the concept of game bounded? ... Can you give the boundary? No.'[96] In this sense, '"Game" is a concept with blurred edges.'[97] Similarly, how 'exact' are such statements as 'The ground was quite covered with plants', or 'The ground looked roughly like this'?[98] Probably Wittgenstein's most notable example in this connection concerns the statement 'Moses did not exist.' Depending on the situation in which it was spoken, he comments, "It may mean, the Israelites did not have a *single* leader when they withdrew from Egypt – or: their leader was not called Moses – or: there cannot have been anyone who accomplished all that the Bible relates of Moses – or: etc, etc.'[99] *Some* kind of assertion has certainly been made. But its horizon of meaning remains more or less open-ended, in accordance with its relationship to other assertions and its own linguistic setting.

Wittgenstein's main point about assertions, therefore, is that *we cannot legitimately generalize about their effect*. It is seriously misleading to talk about 'the general form of propositions', or about the functions of assertions.[100] We are tempted to do this, Wittgenstein maintains, only when a picture misleads us, 'as if the sense [*Bedeutung*] were an atmosphere accompanying the word'. In spite of the frequency of such questions in Fuchs and especially in Heidegger, to ask, in general, '*What is* language?' or '*What is* a proposition?' is entirely misconceived.[101] The whole approach springs from a 'craving for generality', and a determination 'to look for something in common to all the entities which we commonly subsume under a general term'.[102] We are deceived by uniform

---

[91] Ibid., especially §§ 138–242. Cf. *Zettel*, §§ 155–97.
[92] L. Wittgenstein, *Philosophical Investigations*, § 143 (my italics).
[93] Ibid., § 154.
[94] Ibid., § 149.
[95] Ibid., § 144 (Wittgenstein's italics).
[96] Ibid., § 68 (pp. 32e–33e).
[97] Ibid., § 71.
[98] Ibid., § 70.
[99] Ibid., § 79. Cf. also F. Waismann, op. cit., pp.69–71, for a similar example and comments.
[100] L. Wittgenstein, *Philosophical Investigations*, especially §§ 113–17.
[101] Ibid., § 92 (Wittgenstein's italics). Cf. also §§ 91–117 and 134–6.
[102] L. Wittgenstein, *The Blue and Brown Books* (Oxford: Blackwell, ²1969), p.17.

appearance of certain linguistic forms, and forget that language functions in various types of ways.[103] In view of the close connections between hermeneutical philosophy and the outlook of the *Geisteswissenschaften*, it is ironic that Wittgenstein declares, 'Our craving for generality has another main source: our preoccupation with the method of science', with its sometimes 'contemptuous attitude toward the particular case'.[104]

The question, then, is not *whether* assertions occur in parables, but *how* they occur in parables. It is noteworthy that Wolfhart Pannenberg arrives at a similar *kind* of conclusion from a very different angle. Reaching the heart of the matter he declares:

> Gadamer's accurate insight, namely that every spoken word has an infinite, unspoken, background of meaning, does not therefore demolish the significance of the statement ... because that background of meaning can be grasped only on the basis of the statement ... Gadamer's argumentation affects only an abstract treatment of statements that does not pay attention to their unspoken horizon of meaning.[105]

VI
Understanding and Appropriating Parables

The modern interpreter of the parables has to steer agonizingly between a Scylla and Charybdis. On one side, Adolf Jülicher set up a clear warning against any confusion between parable and allegory. He opposed both an atomizing tendency to draw separate lessons from each feature of a single parable and the arbitrary multiplicity of homiletical applications. The parable, he urged, presents one truth, by means of one comparison.[106] On the other side, Fuchs does not stand alone in issuing warning of a very different kind. A parable, C.H. Dodd insists, does more than merely propagate general truths.[107] It leaves the mind 'in sufficient doubt about its precise application to tease it into active thought'.[108] J. Jeremias impressively underlines Dodd's warning partly by developing the question of whether generalizing *logia* in the Gospels themselves, originally belonged to the settings of the parables in which they now occur.[109]

Dodd pointed to 'the volcanic energy of the meteoric career depicted in the Gospels'.[110] The language of Jesus, he urged, is creative. Nothing could be more mistaken than to view the parables as homely illustrations of already-familiar moral maxims. Thus we return to Fuchs. Creative language carried with it open-ended horizons of meaning. Whatever the content, the language of Jesus occurs as an event, above all to interpret *the*

[103] L. Wittgenstein, *Philosophical Investigations*, §§ 11, 12, 23–27, *et passim*.

[104] L. Wittgenstein, *The Blue and Brown Books*, p.17. On the whole question cf. G. Pitcher, *The Philosophy of Wittgenstein* (Englewood Cliffs, NJ: Prentice-Hall, 1964), pp.197–227.

[105] W. Pannenberg, 'Hermeneutics and Universal History', loc. cit., p.144.

[106] A. Jülicher, *Die Gleichnisreden Jesu*, vol. 1 (Freiburg, Leipzig and Tübingen: J.C.B. Mohr (Paul Siebeck), ²1899), p.105, 'Das ὅμοιον ist ihr Ziel, nicht ὅμοια.'

[107] C.H. Dodd, *The Parables of the Kingdom* (London: Nisbet, 1936), pp.24–6.

[108] Ibid., p.16.

[109] J. Jeremias, *The Parables of Jesus* (E.T., London: SCM Press, ²1963), especially pp.105–14. Cf. also R. Bultmann, *The History of the Synoptic Tradition* (E.T., Oxford: Blackwell, 1963), pp.179ff. Bultmann distinguishes carefully between the point of a parable and its application (p.182).

[110] C.H. Dodd, op. cit., p.25.

present.[111] But here is the Scylla and Charybdis: on one side, Jülicher's 'one point' threatens to melt and flatten into a generalizing assertion; on the other side, if the parable remains open-ended, with neither conceptual content nor recognizable semantic boundaries, it threatens to dissolve into something as vague and non-cognitive as a Zen Buddhist *koan.*[112]

Wittgenstein's work on language, however, suggests one possible method of meeting this difficulty. There was perhaps a bare hint of something like this kind of approach in S. Goebel's book on the parables as long ago as 1879.[113] Goebel noted two opposite dangers in interpreting parables: one might try to force every nuance of meaning into unison with its supposed central point, or one might try to draw separate lessons from each of its parts. But there is a third alternative to either generalizing or atomizing. One can inquire into the interrelations that together make up the whole. Wittgenstein's major conception of 'family resemblances' in language represents a full and technical development of this kind of inquiry.

Wittgenstein explains the principle by means of concrete examples, to which Waismann adds yet others.[114] 'Game', for example, seems to be one of those words that defies definition in terms of some supposed common essence. Its meaning accurately emerges only when we give paradigms of particular cases, and add some such words as 'and so on'. Wittgenstein writes, 'How should we explain to someone what a game is? I imagine that we should describe *games* to him, and we might add: This *and similar things* are called "*games*".'[115] He insists:

> If you look at them you will not see something common to *all*, but similarities, relationships, and a whole series of them at that ... look for example at board games ... Now pass to card-games ... In ball games there is winning and losing; but when a child throws his ball at the wall and catches it again, this feature has disappeared ... We see a complicated network of similarities overlapping and criss-crossing ... I can think of no better expression to characterize these similarities than 'family resemblances'.[116]

The point about this kind of family in language, as Waismann carefully notes, is that it allows two fundamental principles to operate simultaneously. First, it allows language to function *creatively*. It offers 'a flexibility and suppleness and adaptability of use' which allows horizons of meaning to expand without predetermined limit.[117] But, second,

---

[111]   In addition to the discussion above, cf. E. Fuchs, *Studies of the Historical Jesus*, p.212 (German, p.430); *Zum Hermeneutischen Problem in der Theologie*, pp.281ff; and *Hermeneutik*, pp.182ff and 219ff.

[112]   The *koan* is a question that defies answer at a logical, rational, or conceptual level, but which is intended to open one's understanding to the deeper truth of Zen. It 'unexpectedly opens up a hitherto unknown region of the mind'. Cf. D.T. Suzuki, 'The Koan', in N.W. Ross (ed.), *The World of Zen* (London: Collins, 1962), p.53. It is highly significant that Martin Heidegger is said to have remarked about one of Suzuki's books, 'This is what I have been trying to say in all my writings' (ibid., p.344, cited by William Barrett).

[113]   S. Goebel, *Die Parabeln Jesu* (Gotha, 1879). Cf. (E.T.) *The Parables of Jesus* (Edinburgh: T. & T. Clark, 1900), especially pp.24–6.

[114]   The clearest discussion in almost any writer occurs in F. Waismann, op. cit., pp.164–90.

[115]   L. Wittgenstein, *Philosophical Investigations*, § 69. On Wittgenstein's more complex uses of the term 'language-game' see R. Rhees, 'Wittgenstein's Builders', in *Proceedings of the Aristotelian Society* LX (1959–60).

[116]   Ibid., §§ 66–7.

[117]   F. Waismann, op. cit., p.182. Cf. pp.176–87.

meanings *cannot expand arbitrarily*. They cannot expand in any and every direction. For each contributory feature of the whole is 'connected by intermediate links with every other, so that two closely related members have common characteristics, while those less closely related need have nothing in common'.[118] A 'greater or lesser resemblance to certain paradigms' provides the needed degree of cohesion.[119]

All this relates closely to the notion of 'going on independently' which is both implied in the teaching of Jesus and explicitly examined by Wittgenstein. In contrast to the traditions of rabbinic Judaism, Jesus did not lay down legislation in advance for every possible contingency which life might bring. His teaching, like his deeds, presented challenging paradigms of the *kind* of attitude and conduct which was appropriate for believing disciples.[120] Most of the parables, therefore, are neither copybook examples designed for slavish imitation, nor homiletical illustrations designed to serve general propositions. Many constitute paradigms that belong to a varied family of cases. In this connection it may be useful to note a comment of Wittgenstein's:

> We shall be making an important distinction between creatures that can learn to do work, even complicated work, in a 'mechanical' way, and those that make trials and comparisons as they work. But what should be called 'making trials' and 'comparisons' can in turn be explained only by giving examples, and these examples will be taken from our life, or from a life that is like ours.[121]

For, in Fuchs's words, 'Jesus wants his hearers to gain freedom.'[122]

If some of the parables do indeed function in this way, a further consequence follows when we compare Fuchs's hermeneutics with the 'dispositional' view of belief adopted by many linguistic philosophers, *partly* following Wittgenstein. In H.H. Price's words, belief is regarded as 'a multiform disposition, which is manifested or actualized in many different ways'.[123] To say that someone believes is roughly equivalent to making 'a series of conditional statements describing what he *would* be likely to say or do or feel if such and such circumstances were to arise'.[124] Thus, if someone denies what we believe, our reaction to their denial would expose the nature of our belief. Would we, for example, if circumstances arose to demand it, stake everything on the supposition of its truth?

It is arguable that many of the parables function in this way. In the parable of the Good Samaritan, for example, the hearer 'must decide how to comport himself: is he willing to allow himself ... to be served by an enemy?'[125] The response, Funk continues, 'is decisive for him ... Every hearer has to hear it in *his* own way.'[126] But the parable is a paradigm suggesting a family of cases; it suffers loss if it is interpreted as a generalizing assertion

---

[118]   Ibid., p.183.

[119]   Ibid., p.180.

[120]   Cf. C.H. Dodd, *Gospel and Law* (Cambridge: Cambridge University Press, 1951), pp.64–83; and W. Manson, *Jesus and the Christian* (London: Clarke, 1967), pp.50–57.

[121]   L. Wittgenstein, *Zettel*, § 103.

[122]   E. Fuchs, *Studies of the Historical Jesus*, p.73. Cf. pp.73–83.

[123]   H.H. Price, *Belief* (London: Allen and Unwin, 1969), p.294.

[124]   Ibid., p.20.

[125]   R.W. Funk, *Language, Hermeneutic, and the Word of God*, p.214.

[126]   Ibid., (On the other hand, cf. J. Jeremias, op. cit., p.205. Questions about the *settings* of parables place some degree of limitation on this approach.)

about human relationships. E. Linnemann comments, 'For to know "what can be required of me" is like a shell inside which one can live peacefully, because everything inside it is familiar ... The ideal is to have everything cut and dried ... The law puts the world in our hands as something perfectly laid out and so basically controlled.'[127] But Jesus 'calls man forth' from this viewpoint.[128]

VII
A Tentative Proposal: Open-Ended Applications that Reflect Family Resemblances, rather than Closed Generalizations?

It is also arguable that this principle of 'family resemblances' operates significantly, and rather differently, in a particular class of parables, namely where the Evangelist himself includes a series of applications. The parable of the Unjust Steward, as Jeremias suggests, provides a typical example (Luke 16:1–8a, 8b–13).[129] It is virtually impossible to lay down a *generalizing* interpretation of the entire passage, which does full justice to each of the applications as they stand. Admittedly Jeremias insists that 'Jesus' command to be resolute and to make a new start embraces the generosity of v. 9, the faithfulness of vv. 10–12, and the rejection of mammon in v. 13.'[130] But the problem here is that from something as broad and indeterminate in content as 'being resolute', or 'beginning again', almost *any* application might be equally in order. Furthermore, Jeremias has earlier argued that the allusion to unrighteous mammon (v. 9) represents 'an entirely different application ... from that which is given in v. 8a'.[131]

In view of the resistance of the passage to a single general interpretation, many have resorted to various expedients. W.L. Knox regards it as 'quite inexplicable ... except on the hypothesis of a primitive corruption of the text'.[132] Dodd's interpretation is disappointingly atomistic.[133] Bultmann leaves a degree of open-endedness when he comments on vv. 1–9, 'The Parable ... is obviously meant to say that one can learn even from the slyness of a deceiver; but in what way?'[134] Another writer relates different aspects of the passage in terms of 'the primary purpose' and 'subsidiary teaching'.[135]

None of this, however, exhausts the various ways in which the applications included by Luke may be related. J.D.M. Derrett has suggested a new and brilliantly illuminating interpretation of the passage more recently.[136] Derrett does not seek to flatten the verses

---

127 E. Linnemann, op. cit., p.52.
128 Ibid., p.55. Cf. E. Fuchs, *Hermeneutik*, pp.5, 64, 113–14 and 182–91.
129 J. Jeremias, op. cit., p.108. Cf. also pp.45–48 and 181–2. On the indispensable character, from a logical point of view, of parabolic interpretations, see T.F. Torrance, *Theological Science* (Oxford: Oxford University Press, 1969), pp.273–7.
130 J. Jeremias, op. cit, p.48.
131 Ibid., p.46.
132 W.L. Knox, *The Sources of the Synoptic Gospels*, vol. 2 (Cambridge: Cambridge University Press, 1957), p.93. Cf. also A Jülicher, op. cit., vol. 2 (1899), pp.495–514.
133 Cf. C.H. Dodd, *The Parables of the Kingdom*, p.30.
134 R. Bultmann, op. cit., pp.199–200.
135 W.O.E. Oesterley, *The Gospel Parables in the Light of their Jewish Background* (London: SPCK, 1936, p.202).
136 J.D.M. Derrett, 'Fresh Light on St. Luke xvi: I The Parable of the Unjust Steward; II Dives and Lazarus and the Preceding Sayings', in *New Testament Studies* 7 (1961), pp.198–219 and 364–80.

into a single generalizing theme; but he speaks of 'a connected message', and of 'connecting thread' such as often occurs in midrashic discourse.[137] With this we may compare Wittgenstein's comment on 'family resemblances' that 'we extend our concept ... as in spinning a thread we twist fibre on fibre. And the strength of the thread does not reside in the fact that some one fibre runs through its whole length, but in the overlapping of many fibres.'[138] Thus if the four or so applications of the parable are represented by (a), (b), (c) and (d), it may be that whilst (a) has little or nothing *directly* in common with (d), nevertheless (a) genuinely relates to (b), and so on. In addition to this, logical connections of a secondary nature may exist between, say, (a) and (c), or between (b) and (d). This would then constitute a 'network of similarities overlapping and criss-crossing'.[139] One has only to recall the hermeneutical principles of Hillel and his successors to note that there was awareness in first-century Judaism of various logical relationships other than that of direct entailment.[140]

Derrett's arguments cannot be followed here in detail. They are put forward with meticulous care. But on the basis of his work, the following connections might be established. (a) The general public would thoroughly applaud the steward's action in cancelling debts based on usury from fellow-Jews.[141] Given the circumstances, the master, also, approved the cancellation, and was not wholly the loser for it.[142] The steward's fraudulence concerns only events which set the scene for the parable; everyone agreed that the steward subsequently acted prudently (φρονίμως, v. 8a). This, however, 'affords a necessary bridge' to: (b) the saying about men of the world, and their shrewd practicality (v. 8b).[143] Many of the Pharisees who called themselves Children of Light had used the 'tricks and devices' of casuistry to allow themselves to serve both the law of God and financial greed.[144] But thereby they had deprived themselves of the worldly man's capacity to 'deal with worldly property single-mindedly ... Inappropriate scruples are as much a hindrance to obedience to God as disingenuous or inaccurate juristic subtlety.'[145]

It is easy, now, to see the connection between (b) and (c), the saying about the use of 'unrighteous mammon' (v. 9). The saying explicates and repudiates Pharisaic scruples about using tainted money, whether or not for good; it reinforces, by citing a specific example, the earlier exhortation to all-out action towards a specific goal.[146] Similarly, (c) leads on directly to (d), the sayings about being faithful in little ... (vv. 10–12): 'One must, if one wishes to possess the promise (i.e. about eternal tabernacles) to be faithful in dealing with (i) unimportant, ill-esteemed, trifling wealth (that is, 'unrighteous

---

[137]   Ibid., pp.199 and 364.
[138]   L. Wittgenstein, *Philosophical Investigations*, § 67. Interestingly, according to B.T.D. Smith, the Rabbis spoke of '*mashal* added to *mashal* like cord joined to cord'; cf. his *The Parables of the Synoptic Gospels* (Cambridge: Cambridge University Press, 1937), p.14.
[139]   Ibid., § 66.
[140]   Cf. H.L. Strack, *Introduction to the Talmud and Midrash* (E.T., Philadelphia, PA: Jewish Publication Society, 1945), pp.93–8. Cf. also J.L. Austin, op. cit., pp.47ff.
[141]   J.D.M. Derrett, loc. cit., pp.204–16.
[142]   Ibid., pp.202–3, 210 and 216–17.
[143]   Ibid., p.217.
[144]   Ibid., pp.206–9.
[145]   Ibid., p.219.
[146]   Ibid., pp.217–18 and 366.

mammon'), and (ii) property (of both sorts) which are not your own.'[147] Finally, we come to (e) the assertion that serving God cannot be comprised by service of mammon (v. 13). This directly takes up (b) and (d). Since the steward, however, saw that 'on dismissal his duty towards his master faded before the practical necessity to recognize his duty towards God', (e) also relates, perhaps less directly, to (a).[148] On the other hand, it hardly follows from (c), except by the 'intermediate links' shared among family resemblances. The five points cannot be cashed into a single generalizing truth; but they offer a coherent network of overlapping and criss-crossing thrusts.

Even if Derrett's interpretation is rejected, however, the principle similarly applies to the kind of treatment offered by Dodd and by Jeremias. (a) The commendation of shrewd, resolute behaviour is not incompatible with (b) a qualifying caveat that the parable is not commending any and every kind of shrewd action. The logical connexions would be parallel to that of the qualifying *gemara* which W.D. Davies finds in Matt. 7:6, as a warning against pressing the previous saying too far.[149] (c) The concluding assertions of v. 13 overlap with both (a) and (b), but are hardly common to them.

To discuss further examples would take us too far away from the questions which gave rise to the present inquiry. The principle might apply, however, to the parable of the Prodigal Son and the Elder Brother (Luke 15:11–32), to the parable of the Sower and its interpretation (Mark 4:3–20, and parallels), and to the applications connected with the parable of the Burglar (Matt. 24:43–44, Luke 12:39–40; cf. 1 Thess. 5:2ff and Rev. 3:3, 16:15).[150] Certainly if Fuchs is correct about the significance of roles within the world of the parable, the father and his two sons, for example, inevitably confront hearers with more than one possible message. Yet to describe these as two or three different messages would be inaccurate and misleading.

VIII
Creative Language and Understanding: Further Dialogue with Linguistic Philosophy

We began by trying to clarify Fuchs's hermeneutics against the background of parallel considerations in Heidegger and in Gadamer. We then inquired specifically whether the use of assertive language necessarily closed horizons of meaning against possible expansion. We next asked whether Wittgenstein's notion of 'family resemblances' offered a clue to the kind of assertions that might meet the hermeneutical requirements of genuinely creative speech, such as we find in the parables. Finally, we have looked at two types of parables, to make tentative suggestions about two ways in which these principles may operate. An attempt will now be made to draw these various threads together, by suggesting some concrete conclusions.

---

[147] Ibid., p.366.
[148] Ibid., p.216. (See also below.)
[149] Cf. W.D. Davies, *The Setting of the Sermon on the Mount* (Cambridge: Cambridge University Press, 1964), p.392.
[150] Cf. E. Fuchs, *Studies of the Historical Jesus*, pp.141–2, and 160ff; and *Hermeneutik*, p.223; J.Jeremias, op. cit., pp.48–51, 77–81 and 149–51; and E. Linnemann, op. cit., pp.73–81 and 114–19.

(1) Fuchs is correct in claiming that the 'must' of certain parables is more than a purely logical one. When a hearer genuinely enters the 'world' created by Jesus, the language of the parables strikes home to him at the very deepest level. It affects not only his conscious state of mind, but also his attitudes and actions. In Fuchs's terms, it is 'language-event'. But all this has certain parallels in the more precise and developed terminology of linguistic philosophy.

(a) At very least, the logic of many parables is self-involving.[151] They function *partly* as performatives. As we have seen, Fuchs believes that the parables constitute linguistic acts of calling (*berufen*), promising (*verheissen*), giving (*geben*), or demanding (*fordern*).[152] He also believes that they effect an offer (*Angebot*), a proclamation (*verkündigen*), a pledge (*Zusage, Einsatz*), a naming (*nennen*), permission (*Erlaubnis*), admission (*Einlass*), claim (*Anspruch*), and especially verdict (*Urteil*).[153] Each of these twelve terms for various uses of language belongs firmly to the category of *illocutionary* acts.[154] Thus, giving, claiming and naming explicitly feature in Austin's list of exercitives; promising and pledging appear in his list of commissives, and a whole range of words is listed as verdictives.[155] If 'permit' is taken as 'grant', 'demand' as 'order', and so on, virtually all of Fuchs's terms are listed by Austin alone.[156] Their function, or part-function, as performatives seems thus to be adequately confirmed. And the importance of a *working* distinction between performatives and assertions has been sufficiently demonstrated by Austin and Evans. To talk about a promise is not necessarily to make one.

(b) Fuchs insists that the parable as language-event 'strikes home' to the hearer and 'grasps him deep down'.[157] It involves, primarily, his attitudes, and only secondarily his conscious states. Gadamer shares this kind of view.[158] But a further parallel emerges in the later Wittgenstein and his successors, namely the view of belief as relating primarily to *dispositions*, and only secondarily, if needed at all, to 'mental states'. The dispositional approach is not familiar but now virtually dominant in linguistic philosophy in Britain. H.H. Price, to whose work we alluded, provides a full and considered account of it.[159] In view of its ramifications, it seems surprising that few writers, other than Karl-Otto Apel, have noted or discussed the parallel.[160] Its immediate significance for the present study is at least twofold. First, it forestalls any suggestion that Fuchs's hermeneutics is somehow

---

[151] Cf. D.D. Evans, *The Logic of Self-Involvement* (London: SCM Press, 1963), in which the author provides a most useful discussion of J.L. Austin's work in relation to biblical language about creation.

[152] See above.

[153] E. Fuchs, *Studies of the Historical Jesus*, pp.91, 95, 196, and especially 35–43, 161 and 209 (German, pp.288, 293, 411, 223–32, 370 and 426–7). Cf. also 'The New Testament and the Hermeneutical Problem', loc. cit., pp.124–30, 136–45; and *Hermeneutik*, pp.68, 119, 133 and 190.

[154] On the distinction between illocutionary acts (performing an act *in* saying something) and perlocutionary acts (achieving effects *by* saying something) cf. J.L. Austin, op. cit., pp.99–131.

[155] Ibid., pp.150–63. Cf. also Fuchs's reference to judgement in *Hermeneutik*, p.189.

[156] For a slightly different list of illocutionary verbs, cf., for example, W.P. Alston, *Philosophy of Language* (Englewood Cliffs, NJ: Prentice-Hall, 1964), pp.35–6.

[157] E. Fuchs, *Studies of the Historical Jesus*, p.35.

[158] H.-G. Gadamer, op. cit., pp.261ff.

[159] See above.

[160] Cf. K.-O. Apel, *Analytic Philosophy of Language and the Geisteswisseschaften* (E.T., Dordrecht: Reidel, 1967), pp.35ff. and 51–7. Apel interprets the later Wittgenstein, however, in a way which too nearly assimilates him into Peter Winch.

too profound, or too theological, to receive light or correction at the hands of Wittgenstein. Second, it adds considerable weight to the otherwise tentative proposal that some parables represent paradigms of how given dispositions manifest themselves in given situations.

(2) Fuchs's attempts to generalize sweepingly about assertions encounter insuperable difficulties. Nor, it seems, are they more than partly relevant to the hermeneutical principles which he otherwise expounds more convincingly. Admittedly his approach yields dividends from time to time. It is right, for example, that the exclamatory pronouncements of the beatitudes (Matt. 5:3–12) should not be reduced to the status of informative propositions, let alone, as W. Manson saw, about 'antecedent states or qualities of character'.[161] But Fuchs's attempts at generalization break down on at least three related issues.

(*a*) This kind of generalization depends on the assumption that every assertion functions in the same way, to produce the same type of effect. As we have seen, however, one of Wittgenstein's most important achievements was to demonstrate that this is by no means the case.[162] The full significance of this emerged when it was shown, positively, that an assertion such as 'Moses did not exist' could retain the kind of open-endedness that Fuchs, Heidegger and Gadamer broadly associate with creative language.

(*b*) At the beginning of this study we noted Austin's extreme reluctance to draw any firm boundary between assertions and performatives. Austin explicitly declared that for a certain performative utterance to function effectively, 'certain statements have *to be true*'.[163] For example, the utterance 'I hereby give you ...' cannot be effective unless it could be asserted at the time of the utterance that the proposed gift rightfully belonged to the speaker, as his to give.[164] To take a second example, 'I name this ship the Queen Elizabeth' performs the said action only if several assertions are true, namely: (i) the assertion that the speaker is fully authorized to assume this role at the launching ceremony, (ii) that 'Queen Elizabeth' was the destined name, (iii) that the utterance was spoken on the day of the launching; and so on.[165]

Austin rightly points out that whilst it is only propositions that carry entailments, most or all performatives carry *presuppositions* and *implications*.[166] Mostly these are indispensable to their effective function (for example, 'I divorce you' presupposes 'he is married'), and usually they are most naturally expressed in the form of assertions.[167]

It is scarcely surprising, therefore, that the same principle operates in biblical language, and even in the parables. If assertions which come at the end of a parable, for

---

161 Cf. Fuchs, *Studies of the Historical Jesus*, pp.91–3, and W. Manson, *Jesus and the Christian*, p.53.

162 See above. Cf. also L. Wittgenstein op. cit., §§ 1–25 and 60–108.

163 J.L. Austin, op. cit., p.45 (Austin's italics).

164 N. Malcom describes Wittgenstein's typically unusual way of making this kind of point: 'On one walk he "gave" to me each tree that we passed, with the reservation that I was not to ... do anything to it, or prevent the previous owners from doing anything to it: with those reservations it was henceforth *mine*' (*Ludwig Wittgenstein: A Memoir* (Oxford: Oxford University Press, 1966), pp.31–2).

165 Cf. J.L. Austin, op. cit., pp.23–4.

166 Ibid., pp.47–52.

167 Ibid., pp.53–5. Cf. also the extended discussion in T.F. Torrance, op. cit., pp.247–80.

instance, are genuinely implied, or presupposed, by its performative logic, it would be misleading to claim that these are, automatically, *logia* which originally occurred in a different setting. Thus in the parable of the Unjust Steward, which we examined in some detail, it might be suggested that on Derrett's interpretation the saying about God and mammon (v. 13) represents a presupposition behind the parable, whilst the earlier statements of vv. 8–12 are implications. On the other hand, if we follow Dodd or Jeremias, it might be claimed that v. 8 (the saying about prudence) expressed the presupposition, whilst subsequent verses developed implications. At all events, a language without assertions, whether implied or explicit, is a featureless waste, in which every meaning may be swallowed up by another.

(*c*) Fuchs seems also to stand on weak ground in attempting to generalize about parables. Many writers have drawn attention to the very wide variety of forms which can broadly be included under the terms מָשָׁל, παραβολή and παροιμία.[168] Jeremias lists nearly twenty categories that the terms might cover, including, for instance, allegory, fable, proverb, riddle, example, argument and jest.[169] The most striking comment of all comes from A.N. Wilder. He declares, 'Jesus uses figures of speech in an immense number of ways. The variety of the parables is only one aspect of this variety ... Indeed we may say that the term "parable" is misleading, since it suggests a single pattern, and often distorts our understanding of this or that special case.'[170]

The implication of all this is that the word 'parable' itself, like such words as 'game', 'number', or 'try', embraces a network of family resemblances, rather than a single sharply bounded concept.[171] This is why, in the present study, suggestions have been made, not about *the* parables, but about certain parables, many parables, or given types of parables. Can it even be said that *all* parables function as language-event, let alone that assertions are *always* out of place in them? Yet the disease of easy generalization has struck deep. When Dibelius claims, for example, that '*all* the parables of Jesus are intended *rather* to arouse feelings *than* to give information', can we say more than that this is broadly on the right track, but could also be seriously misleading?[172]

(3) Wittgenstein and more explicitly Waismann confirm, in effect, the view of Fuchs, Heidegger and Gadamer, that creative language requires a flexibility of usage or meaning which cannot be provided by completely 'closed' concepts or completely 'closed' assertions. But at this point agreement ends. For Wittgenstein rightly assumes that there are virtually endless *degrees of variation* between completely closed and completely open horizons of meaning. On the other hand, Fuchs, Heidegger and Gadamer have either failed to notice this possibility, or else failed to see its full significance.

---

[168]   Cf. A.T. Cadoux, *The Parables of Jesus, their Art and Use* (London: Clarke, n.d.), pp.57–8; W.O.E. Oesterley, op. cit., pp.3ff; G.V. Jones op. cit., pp.20–21, 24–5 and 110ff; and R.W. Funk, *Language, Hermeneutic and Word of God*, pp.124ff. In complete contrast, cf. Jülicher's optimistic heading, '*Das Wesen der Gleichnisreden Jesu*', op. cit., vol. 1, p.25.

[169]   J. Jeremias, op. cit., p.20.

[170]   A.N. Wilder, *Early Christian Rhetoric* (London: SCM Press, 1964), p.81.

[171]   Cf. F. Waismann, op. cit., pp.183–7.

[172]   M. Dibelius, *A Fresh Approach to the New Testament and Early Christian Literature* (E.T., London: Ivor Nicholson and Watson, 1936), p.30 (my italics).

Behind this whole issue stands the figure of Gottlob Frege. Frege suggested a simile between a semantic area and an area of ground that was duly marked out. He argued that its boundaries should be clear, precise and complete. Wittgenstein, however, challenged this. He did not argue that boundaries should be abolished (which follows, in effect, from the views of Gadamer or Fuchs). But he insisted that it is often useful to regard boundaries as blurred and incomplete. He writes, 'Here one thinks perhaps: if I say "I have locked the man up fast in the room – there is only one door left open" – then I simply haven't locked him in at all ... an enclosure with a hole in it as a good as *none*. – But is it true?'[173] He asks, 'Is it ... always an advantage to replace an indistinct picture by a sharp one? Isn't the indistinct one often exactly what we need?'[174]

It would be a serious mistake to regard this suggestion as an eccentric quirk of the later Wittgenstein. It has now become an established principle in semantics that 'the vagueness of our words is a handicap in some situations and an advantage in others'.[175] Thus 'green' usually speaks more eloquently in poetry than the more precise colour-terminology that is needed in the paint-factory.[176] The same might be said about multiple meanings: 'Polysemy is an invaluable factor of economy and flexibility in language'; although the degree of ambiguity to which it may give rise depends on the type and number of linguistic 'safeguards' that accompany it.[177] Wittgenstein thus rightly saw that there are different *degrees* and *types* of open-endedness in meaning. From this, two consequences follow for interpretations of the parallels.

(a) In order to function creatively, the parable does not need to remain *entirely* open-ended. Indeed, if it were so, it would be impossible to identify its creation. Its status would have been reduced to that of a psychological stimulant which might propel the hearer in any or every direction. *The degree of open-endedness varies from parable to parable.* Since some writers have claimed that the message of parables is often clear and self-evident, at least some of the parables, and especially the shorter ones which approximate to similes, create horizons of meaning which are relatively sharp from the very first.[178]

(*b*) The principle of family resemblances, it has been suggested, represents one possible way in which an effective but limited degree of openness is achieved. But even this principle may operate in various ways. We selected for comment two types of parable, each of which is often regarded as problematic in its present form. (i) In some instances, it is possible that what appears to be simply a generalizing assertion or exhortation is in fact offered as a paradigm of the *kind* of attitude which characterizes Christian belief, or perhaps unbelief. (ii) In other cases, where a series of 'applications' occur together, they

---

173 L. Wittgenstein, *Philosophical Investigations*, § 99.

174 Ibid., § 71.

175 S. Ullmann, *Semantics: An introduction to the Science of Meaning* (Oxford: Blackwell, 1962), p.118. See pp.116–28, and W.P. Alston, op. cit., pp.84–106.

176 On the blurred boundaries of colour-words cf. J. Lyons, *Introduction to Theoretical Linguistics* (Cambridge: Cambridge University Press, 1968), pp.55–9.

177 S. Ullmann, op. cit., pp.168–9. Cf. also pp.156–92; M. Black, *The Labyrinth of Language* (London: Pall Mall Press, 1968), pp.97–113; and the comments of T.F. Torrance, op. cit., pp.15–16, and J. Macquarrie, *Principles of Christian Theology* (London: SCM Press, 1966), pp.405–6.

178 Cf. A. Jülicher, op. cit., vol. 1, pp.25ff and 103ff; R. Bultmann, op. cit., pp.166ff; and J. Jeremias, op. cit., p.12. In this connection, however, many writers rightly distinguish between simile and metaphor. Cf. R.W. Funk, *Language, Hermeneutic and Word of God*, pp.133–62.

are not necessarily in competition; nor do they necessarily function to close every possible gap in boundary of meaning. By pointing to more than one landmark in only roughly the same direction, they guide the hearer within certain limits, but allow him freedom to 'go on' for *himself*. Thus the language of Jesus does not become, as Fuchs may fear, a mere tool at his disposal. Rather, the parable repeatedly directs him, but freshly as he enters each new present.[179]

The work of Wittgenstein and Austin has confirmed that, in general outline, Fuchs's understanding of the parables as language-event stresses, or at least gropes after, several important points in biblical hermeneutics. However, it also suggests that, like many pioneers, he has pressed certain ideas too far. Further, this work also hints at some new ways of looking at the parables. Meanwhile, it remains to be seen what further light the resources and techniques of linguistic philosophy may shed both on the parables and on other forms of biblical literature.[180]

---

[179] Cf. Fuchs's comments in 'Jesus' Understanding of Time', in *Studies in the Historical Jesus*, pp.161–2 and 164–6.

[180] It is fruitful, for example, to compare the logical relationship between the *Bildhälfte* and the *Sachhälfte* in parables with I.T. Ramsey's important suggestions about models and qualifiers in *Religious Language: An Empirical Placing of Theological Phrases* (London: SCM Press, 1957).

CHAPTER TWENTY-FIVE

The Bible and Today's Readers: "The Two Horizons" and "Pre-Understanding" (1980)

This essay comes from The Two Horizons *(Grand Rapids, MI: Eerdmans and Carlisle: Paternoster Press, 1980), pp.11–23 [sections I and II], and 103–14 [sections III and IV]. In 1980 many biblical scholars were still in process of coming to recognize the two-sidedness of the hermeneutical problem, and therefore some uses of the word "new" here may appear obsolete today. Nevertheless some misunderstandings of "pre-understanding" and "the hermeneutical circle" persist, and this essay combines specific examples from the biblical text with philosophical formulations in Heidegger, and with theological approaches in Fuchs, Ebeling and liberation hermeneutics. Like most of these essays it is consciously multi-disciplinary in scope.*

I
The Two Horizons as the Underlying Problem of Hermeneutics

Traditionally hermeneutics entailed the formulation of rules for the understanding of an ancient text, especially in linguistic and historical terms. The interpreter was urged to begin with the language of the text, including its grammar, vocabulary and style. He or she examined its linguistic, literary and historical context. In other words, traditional hermeneutics began with recognition that a text was conditioned by a given historical context. However, hermeneutics in the more recent sense of the term begins with the recognition that historical conditioning is two-sided: *the modern interpreter, no less than the text, stands in a given historical context and tradition.*

Before we illustrate the point at issue with reference to a particular text, we should also note that a second contrast is bound up with the first. Traditionally it was often supposed, or implied, that the understanding of an ancient text could be achieved by the observance of hermeneutical rules. However, a modern reader might have access to all necessary linguistic and historical information, and even apply this information scientifically to the text, and yet lack the creative insight to understand it. Gerhard Ebeling underlines the importance of this point both negatively and positively when he asserts that hermeneutics must not be "reduced to a collection of rules, but on the contrary must serve the understanding".[1] He asks, "Can the event of the Word of God be served at all by scientific methods?"[2] By way of reply he does not question the role of critical historical methods as such, but he nevertheless stresses that biblical criticism can take us only part of the way towards understanding the ancient text.[3]

---

[1] G. Ebeling, *Word and Faith* (Eng., London: SCM, 1963), p.313.
[2] Ibid., p.314.
[3] Cf. also Ebeling's essay "The Significance of the Critical Historical Method for Church and Theology in Protestantism", in *Word and Faith*, pp.17–61.

James Robinson and John Cobb have tried to pinpoint this double contrast between older and newer understandings of the scope of hermeneutics by drawing a contrast between "hermeneutics" (plural), denoting the traditional approach, and "hermeneutic" (singular), denoting more recent perspectives. They discuss its linguistic justification on the basis of an analogy with the singular form *Hermeneutik*, and several other writers have taken up this suggestion as a new convention.[4] Carl Braaten, however, sharply criticizes the proposal in his article "How New is the New Hermeneutic?". He attacks the broadening of the term, and argues that the use of the singular noun is "too artificial to be taken seriously".[5] We agree with Braaten that it seems artificial to mark these basic contrasts by using the singular rather than the plural form, except in the actual phrase "new hermeneutic", since this has already become virtually a technical term. However, we agree with Robinson that the change in meaning is fundamental. The nature of the hermeneutical problem cannot be discussed today without reference to the two sets of contrasts that we have just described. Robinson himself in his essay "Hermeneutic Since Barth" comments on this change of perspective in a striking way, by going so far as to describe traditional hermeneutics as "superficial". He asserts, "One can say that the new hermeneutic began to emerge in a recognition of the superficiality of hermeneutics."[6]

Theologians who have been trained in the traditions of German philosophy find little problem in taking seriously the double-sided nature of historicality, or historical conditionedness, on the part of *both* the ancient text *and* the modern interpreter. However, a number of British and American scholars seem to view the problem as a merely theoretical one that is only of peripheral concern to the New Testament interpreter. It is perhaps necessary, therefore, to offer a concrete example of the problem, which will illustrate its importance at a commonsense level. Only then can we escape the suspicion that the problem before us is merely a product of complex Germanic minds, which would never have been formulated without the aid of Dilthey and Heidegger.

In Luke 18:9–14 Jesus tells the parable of the Pharisee and the tax collector. The historical particularities of the text are fruitfully discussed and expounded by such writers as Jülicher, Dodd, Jeremias and Linnemann. The following points shed light on the historical context of the parable and its linguistic features.

(1) Klostermann and Jeremias interpret σταθεὶς πρὸς ἑαυτὸν ταῦτα προσηύχετο (v. 11) to mean "he took up a prominent position and uttered this prayer". Πρὸς ἑαυτόν "renders an Aramaic reflexive (*leh*) which lays a definite emphasis on the action".[7] However, following the manuscript reading ταῦτα πρὸς ἑαυτὸν προσηύχετο, Jülicher interprets it to mean "prayed with himself". This might convey either the idea of "an inaudible prayer uttered in the heart", or of a prayer "spoken in an undertone, not intelligible to the bystanders, as the Jewish rule was (cf. *Berakoth* V.1.31a)".[8]

---

[4] J.M. Robinson and J.B. Cobb, Jr (eds), *New Frontiers in Theology: The New Hermeneutic* (New York: Harper, 1964), pp.ix–x.

[5] C.E. Braaten, "How New is the New Hermeneutic?", *Theology Today* XXII (1965), p.220; cf. also pp.218ff.

[6] J.M. Robinson, "Hermeneutic Since Barth", in *New Hermeneutic*, p.21.

[7] J. Jeremias, *The Parables of Jesus* (Eng., London: SCM, rev. edn, 1963), p.140.

[8] E. Linnemann, *The Parables of Jesus: Introduction and Exposition* (Eng., London: SPCK, 1966), p.143 n.2.

(2) The piety of the Pharisee is partly expressed in the words νηστεύω δὶς τοῦ σαββάτου, ἀποδεκατῶ πάντα ὅσα κτῶμαι (v. 12). These are voluntary deeds, involving personal sacrifice. The Law laid on every Jew one fast each year as a day of repentance, but the Pharisee fasted not only on the Day of Atonement but on Mondays and Thursdays. As Linnemann comments, "To do this he has to give up not only food but also drink completely from sunrise to sunset, which in the heat of the East is a great act of self denial."[9] The fasting was not simply a self-centred work of merit, but was regarded as an act of intercession or even vicarious atonement for the sins of his people. Strack and Billerbeck elucidate this background.[10] On the matter of tithing, the Pharisee made sure that he used nothing that had not been tithed, even though the producer should have already tithed corn, new wine and oil. This extra voluntary tithe would have involved considerable economic sacrifice.[11]

(3) Jesus' hearers would not have interpreted the Pharisee's prayer as one of arrogance or hypocrisy, but as a genuine prayer of thankfulness that God had given him the opportunity and inclination to carry out this practical piety. Prayers of this kind were not exceptional. A very similar one has been handed down in the Talmud, and another comes from the time of Qumran.[12]

(4) While state officials collected such taxes as poll tax and land-tax, the customs of a district could be farmed out for collection by a τελώνης who would bid for this right. Although tariffs were probably fixed by the state, these collectors had no lack of devices for defrauding the public: "In the general estimation they stood on a level with robbers; they possessed no civil rights; and were shunned by all respectable persons."[13] Or, as another writer expresses it, the tax-collector "not only collaborated with the Roman occupation powers, who oppressed the people of God, and continually hindered it in the fulfilment of its religious duties, but he belonged to a profession that as a whole was regarded as being no better or worse than swindlers".[14]

(5) The phrase ἔτυπτεν τὸ στῆθος αὐτοῦ (v. 13) admittedly expressed deep contrition according to the conventions of the day. Nevertheless, when the tax-collector stands "afar off", in the view of Jesus' audience this is the place where he naturally belongs.

(6) Jesus' verdict that the tax-collector went home δεδικαιωμένος παρ ἐκεῖνον (v. 14) is interpreted by Jeremias in an exclusive rather than comparative sense. He cites several examples of where the Hebrew comparative *min* is used to convey the idea of "one, not the other", rather than "more than the other" (for example, 2 Sam. 19:44 and Ps. 45:8).[15] It is the tax collector, not the Pharisee, whom God declares righteous.

These six points help to explain how the meaning of the parable is conditioned by various historical, sociological and linguistic factors which relate directly to its setting in

---

[9]   Ibid., p.59; cf. J. Jeremias, *The Parables of Jesus*, p.140.

[10]   H.L. Strack and P. Billerbeck, *Kommentar zum Neuen Testament aus Talmud und Midrasch* (6 vols, Munich: Beck, 1922 onward), II, pp.243–4.

[11]   J. Jeremias, *The Parables of Jesus*, pp.140–41; and E. Linnemann, *The Parables of Jesus*, p.59.

[12]   E.g. *b. Ber.* 28b; cf. J. Jeremias, ibid., E. Linnemann, ibid., and J.D. Crossan, *In Parables. The Challenge of the Historical Jesus* (New York: Harper and Row, 1973), p.69.

[13]   J. Jeremias, *The Parables of Jesus*, p.41.

[14]   E. Linnemann, *The Parables of Jesus*, p.60.

[15]   J. Jeremias, *The Parables of Jesus*, pp.141–2.

first-century Palestine. These are precisely the kind of questions that concern New Testament scholars like Jeremias.

However, with the dawn of discussions about hermeneutics in the sense of "understanding", John D. Crossan and Walter Wink have drawn attention to a further dimension of the problem of interpreting this parable. Because he expressed the point so strongly, it is worth quoting Wink's words in full. He begins, "The scholar, having finished his work lays down his pen, oblivious to the way in which he has *falsified the text* in accordance with unconscious tendencies; so much so that he has maimed its original intent until it has actually turned into its opposite."[16]

Wink explains:

> Any *modern* reader at all familiar with the text knows that (1) "Pharisees" are hypocrites, and (2) Jesus praises the publican. The unreflective tendency of every reader is to identify with the more positive figures in an account. Consequently, modern readers will almost invariably identify with the *publican*. By that inversion of identification the paradox of the justification of the *ungodly* is lost ... The story is then deformed into teaching cheap grace for rapacious toll collectors.[17]

Wink concludes, "All this because the exegete hid behind his descriptive task without examining the recoil of the parable upon contemporary self-understanding. I know of no more powerful way to underline the inadequacy of a simply descriptive or phenomenological approach which fails to enter into a phenomenology of the exegete."[18]

We may admit that in one or two respects Walter Wink probably overstates the case. It is not the biblical scholar who "falsifies" the text. Indeed a careful examination of how Pharisees and tax collectors were regarded in ancient Palestinian Judaism takes us a considerable way forward in the task of interpreting the parable for modern man. Simply as a piece of scholarly research into the historical context it is possible to see, as Wink admits, that the original hearer "would at first identify with the Pharisee as the bearer of religious and social status, and then suffer shock and consternation at the wholly unexpected justification of the publican".[19] However, Wink is correct to point out that in terms of the horizons of hearers who already stand at the end of a long Christian tradition, the impact of the parable is quite different from what it was in its original setting. Pharisaism is nowadays so nearly synonymous with self-righteousness and hypocrisy that, far from suffering a sense of shock at the verdict of Jesus, the modern audience expects it.

John D. Crossan underlines the importance of this point almost as emphatically as Walter Wink. Again, it is perhaps worth quoting several lines in full. He writes, "There is an immediate problem. Parables are supposed to overturn one's structure of expectation and therein and thereby to threaten the security of one's man-made world. Such terms as 'Pharisee' and 'Publican' (or toll collector) evoke no immediate visual reaction or expectation from a modern reader. In fact ... the former have become almost stereotyped

---

[16] W. Wink, *The Bible in Human Transformation: Toward a New Paradigm for Biblical Study* (Philadelphia, PA: Fortress Press, 1973), p.42 (Wink's italics).

[17] Ibid., pp.42–3 (Wink's italics).

[18] Ibid., p.43 (Wink's italics).

[19] Ibid., p.42.

villains rather than the revered moral leaders they were at the time of Jesus. So our structure of expectation is not that of the original hearer of the parable."[20] Hermeneutically, Crossan concludes, this raises a serious difficulty. In one sense the parable can be "explained"; but "a parable which has to be explained is, like a joke in similar circumstances, a parable which has been ruined *as parable*".[21]

The comments of Crossan and Wink illustrate exactly the two-sidedness of the hermeneutical problem. To pay attention to the historical particularities and historical conditionedness of the text remains of paramount importance, and the use of works such as Jeremias' remains indispensable for interpreting the ancient text. However, the modern reader is also conditioned by his own place in history and tradition. Hence the hermeneutical problem assumes new dimensions. No one today wishes to be cast in the role of a Pharisee. Hence in our example from Luke 18 the parable is usually "understood" as a reassuring moral tale that condemns the kind of Pharisaism that everyone already wishes to avoid. A parable that originally had the function of unsettling the hearer and overturning his values now serves to confirm him in the values that he already has. This situation illustrates one of the major aspects of the problem of hermeneutics.

Even if, for the moment, we leave out of account the modern reader's *historical* conditionedness, we are still faced with the undeniable fact that if a text is to be *understood* there must occur an engagement between two sets of horizons (to use Gadamer's phrase), namely those of the ancient text and those of the modern reader or hearer. The hearer must be able to relate his own horizons to those of the text. Gadamer compares the analogy of the "understanding" which occurs in a conversation: "In a conversation, when we have discovered the standpoint and horizon of the other person, his ideas become intelligible, without our necessarily having to agree with him."[22] Nevertheless, Gadamer goes on to argue that in hermeneutics the modern interpreter must also try to become aware of the distinctiveness of his own horizons, as against those of the text. On the one hand, "every encounter with tradition that takes place within historical consciousness involves the experience of the tensions between the text and the present. The hermeneutic task consists of not covering up this tension by attempting a naive assimilation but consciously bringing it out."[23] On the other hand, Gadamer adds, for understanding to take place there must also occur what he calls a "fusion of horizons" (*Horizontverschmelzung*).[24] We will try to make clear how these two apparently contradictory principles can be held together when we discuss Gadamer's philosophy. Meanwhile, we may note that his simile has been taken up by several writers, including Moltmann and Pannenberg.[25]

Richard Palmer also makes much of the concept of a fusion of horizons. Meaning, he argues, depends on "a relationship to the listener's own projects and intentions ... An

[20] J.D. Crossan, *The Dark Interval: Towards a Theology of Story* (Niles, IL: Argus Communications, 1975), pp.101–2.

[21] Ibid., p.102 (Crossan's italics); cf. *In Parables*, pp.68–9.

[22] H.-G. Gadamer, *Truth and Method* (Eng., London: Sheed & Ward, 1975), p.270.

[23] Ibid., p.273.

[24] Ibid. For the German term, cf. *Wahrheit und Methode*, pp.286–90.

[25] E.g. W. Pannenberg, *Basic Questions in Theology* (London: SCM, 3 vols, 1970–73), I, pp.117–28.

object does not have significance outside of a relationship to someone."[26] He continues, "To speak of an object apart from a perceiving subject is a conceptual error caused by an inadequate realistic concept of perception and the world."[27] Hence: "Explanatory interpretation makes us aware that explanation is contextual, is 'horizontal'. It must be made within a horizon of already granted meanings and intentions. In hermeneutics, this area of assumed understanding is called pre-understanding."[28] Understanding takes place when the interpreter's horizons engage with those of the text: "This merging of two horizons must be considered a basic element in all explanatory interpretation."[29]

Gadamer and Palmer formulate in more general terms the problem that Wink and Crossan illustrate with reference to particular texts. The nature of the hermeneutical problem is shaped by the fact that both the text and the interpreter are conditioned by their given place in history. For understanding to take place, two sets of variables must be brought into relation with each other. Gadamer's image of a fusion of horizons provides one possible way of describing the main problem and task of hermeneutics. So important for hermeneutics is the issue behind Gadamer's formulation that we have used the phrase "The Two Horizons" as the main title of the present study. A preliminary word of explanation about this title was given in the introduction.

II
Some Issues which Arise from the Hermeneutical Problem

It has sometimes been suggested that to formulate the hermeneutical problem as a two-sided one moves the centre of gravity entirely from the past to the present in the task of interpretation. Everything becomes dominated, it is argued, by the interpreter's own pre-understanding and the ancient text becomes merely a projection of his own ideas or preconceptions.

This issue can be illustrated with reference to two suggestions put forward by Palmer and by Smart. We have seen that Palmer follows Gadamer in viewing understanding in terms of a relation between two horizons. He claims to find a precedent for this view of hermeneutics in Luke 24:25–27, in which Christ interprets the Old Testament in terms of his own messiahship. Luke writes, "Beginning with Moses and all the prophets, he interpreted (διερμήνευσεν) to them in all the Scriptures the things concerning himself." This "interpretation", Palmer argues, does not entail a mere repetition of the ancient texts, nor even an examination of them in the context to which they already belong. It involves *placing* the Old Testament texts in the context of the *present* events of Jesus' messiahship, and at the same time expounding his own sufferings in the context of the Old Testament passages. Meaning depends on context. More specifically it involves establishing a relationship between *two* horizons. The disciples "understood" the texts when this subject matter could be viewed within their own fame of reference.

---

[26] R.E. Palmer, *Hermeneutics*, p.24.
[27] Ibid.
[28] Ibid.
[29] Ibid., p.25.

Such a perspective, however, at once raises the issue, to which we have alluded, of whether the present becomes a wholly dominating factor in understanding the past. Cannot the past somehow be understood on its own terms? Is it not a fatal flaw in Palmer's formulation of the hermeneutical problem that his approach seems to imply that Christian disciples were the first to "understand" the Old Testament passages in question?

James D. Smart also seems to come near to such a position in his discussion of the interpretation of certain parts of Isaiah. Second Isaiah, he urges, "seems fairly knocking on the door of the Christian gospel, and yet it was five hundred years and more before he was heard in such a way that the content of his words shaped the life of a people ... He had to wait centuries to be understood."[30] Smart himself believes that, in the fullest sense of the word "understanding", certain parts of the Bible including the Old Testament, can be understood only from within a Christian frame of reference. He asserts, "Something more was needed than philosophical, historical, and literary expertness combined with religious and ethical earnestness. A key to its meaning was missing."[31]

Bultmann, Fuchs and Ebeling would agree that a text cannot be understood without an appropriate pre-understanding; but all of them would deny that its pre-understanding need be distinctively Christian. Bultmann declares, "the interpretation of the biblical writings is not subject to conditions different from those applying to all other kinds of literature".[32] Fuchs puts the matter more theologically. How can we claim, he argues, that the biblical writings can *create* Christian faith, if we also insist that an understanding of them *presupposes* faith?[33]

Before we follow this debate further, we may also compare the approach of Palmer and Smart with the claims put forward by Prosper Grech in an article published in 1973 under the title "The 'Testimonia' and Modern Hermeneutics".[34] The New Testament writers, Grech argues, interpreted Old Testament texts "within the framework of a tradition and of contemporary events". The context of a work of Scripture was "*no longer the original context in which it was written but the context of their own Kerygma* based on the recent crucifixion and resurrection of Jesus of Nazareth".[35] They were "not interested", he declares, "in the objective scientific interpretation of scripture. No one even dreamt of interpreting Pss. ii and cx, for example, as coronation psalms addressed to the king by a court poet. The scriptures speak to the Church now."[36]

However, Grech considers that "this does not mean that their exegesis was arbitrary or out of context". It means simply that "Scripture was read with a pre-understanding (*Vorverständnis*)."[37] "The words of Scripture were interpreted within a double context: that of God's salvific action in the past and that of contemporary happenings."[38] Grech

---

[30]   J.D. Smart, *The Interpretation of Scripture* (London: SCM, 1961), p.14.

[31]   Ibid., p.16.

[32]   R. Bultmann, "The Problem of Hermeneutics", in *Essays Philosophical and Theological*, p.256.

[33]   E. Fuchs, *Zum hermeneutischen Problem in der Theologie* (Tübingen: Mohr, 1959; Gesammelte Aufsätze I), pp.9–10; and *Studies of the Historical Jesus* (Eng., London: SCM, 1960), p.30.

[34]   P. Grech, "The 'Testimonia' and Modern Hermeneutics", in *N.T.S.* XIX (1973), pp.318–24.

[35]   Ibid., p.319 (my italics).

[36]   Ibid.

[37]   Ibid., p.320.

[38]   Ibid.

concludes, "The New Testament authors make no attempt to give an objective, detached, explanation of the texts in question. Their vision is a subjective one, but it is not arbitrary, it is hermeneutical ... They begin with a pre-understanding."[39]

Although he also calls attention to the belief of the New Testament writers concerning a continuity in the work of the Holy Spirit in inspiring both the Old Testament and the saving events of the apostolic age, Grech believes that in terms of relating two sets of contexts the hermeneutic which is presupposed is similar to that expounded by Heidegger and especially Gadamer.[40] The New Testament authors, he declares, come to terms with the hermeneutic gap which otherwise existed between the Old Testament writers and their own day.

Questions about the primitive Christian interpretation and understanding of the Old Testament throw this issue into very sharp relief. However, it should not be assumed that the problem is entirely peculiar to primitive Christianity, or to those who follow Gadamer or Bultmann in their views about pre-understanding. Daniel Patte has shown how the same issue arises, even if admittedly in a less radical form, within Jewish hermeneutics.[41] In his recent work *Early Jewish Hermeneutic in Palestine* he carefully discusses the use of Scripture in classical and sectarian Judaism, and concludes that in all strands of Judaism there is a dialectical emphasis, now on the past, now on the present. One pole stresses the Torah, and the anchorage of Judaism in the "salient history" of the past. Here Scripture is used to preserve Jewish self-identity by maintaining continuity with the past. The other pole stresses "the history of the cultural changes" which invites reinterpretation of the ancient texts in the light of new experiences and situations.[42] Here Scripture is orientated towards the present. The degree of emphasis may vary, for example, between the Sadducees, the Pharisees, or the Qumran community. But the tension between the two poles was never entirely absent. Midrash, or "inquiring of God" was done "either by scrutinizing scripture in the light of the new cultural situation, or by scrutinizing Tradition in the light of scripture".[43] In either case, two horizons are brought together in the hermeneutical process.

The conclusions of Grech and Patte demonstrate that the two-sided nature of the underlying problem of hermeneutics is more than a novel creation of Bultmann, Gadamer and the exponents of the new hermeneutic. In this sense, they serve to confirm that the problem outlined is a genuine one. However, far from solving the problem about whether the centre of gravity lies in the past or the present, in certain respects they further aggravate it. For neither primitive Christian hermeneutics not Jewish hermeneutics entailed the use of critical historical inquiry. How does the use of historical criticism affect the questions we are asking?

No modern scholar denies that critical historical inquiry remains indispensable in the interpretation of ancient texts. Even James Smart, in spite of a theological position that

---

[39] Ibid., p.321.

[40] Ibid., pp.321–4.

[41] D. Patte, *Early Jewish Hermeneutic in Palestine* (S.B.L. Dissertation Series 22, Scholars Press, University of Montana, 1975).

[42] Ibid., pp.120–27 *et passim*.

[43] Ibid., p.124.

reflects affinities with Barth, fully endorses the need for such criticism. Although in some ways (as will become clear) his actual formulation of the principle begs a key question in hermeneutics, we may accept his principle provisionally when he states, "All interpretation must have as its first step the hearing of the text with exactly the shade of meaning that it had when it was first spoken or written."[44] To return to Smart's own example of Second Isaiah, we cannot short-circuit the painstaking inquiries of scholars such as C.R. North by appealing directly and uncritically to a Christological interpretation of the figure of the servant. To put the matter crudely, if an "understanding" of Isaiah depends entirely on the possession of a Christian frame of reference, Isaiah himself must have lacked an understanding of what he wrote, since he lived in pre-Christian times.

Some theologians would reply that a text may well transcend the conscious horizons of an author on the basis of a theological doctrine of *sensus plenior*. This question will be left over for the present, but we may note, further, that even from a purely philosophical viewpoint, Gadamer insists that in the case of any historical text we cannot simply restrict its meaning to what was in the mind of the original author. As a *philosophical* and *hermeneutical* principle Gadamer declares, "Every age has to understand a transmitted text in its own way ... The real meaning of a text, as it speaks to the interpreter, does not depend on the contingencies of the author and whom he originally wrote for."[45] Gadamer continues, "An author does not need to know the real meaning of what he has written, and hence the interpreter can, and must, often understand more than he. But this is of fundamental importance. *Not occasionally only, but always, the meaning of a text goes beyond its author.* That is why understanding is not merely a reproduction, but always a productive attitude as well."[46] In due course we shall attempt to assess whether Gadamer goes too far in making such assertions. However, our present purpose is to demonstrate that neither a theological hermeneutic such as Smart's, nor a philosophical hermeneutic such as Gadamer's, with all their emphasis on the present and on developing tradition, excludes the place of historical criticism as a starting-point. The issue is not *whether* historical criticism has a necessary place; but what that place should be. To invoke a doctrine of *sensus plenior* in order to exclude historical criticism would certainly be, as Grech remarks, to try to establish a hermeneutic based on an unjustifiable appeal to a theology of *deus ex machina*.[47]

Gerhard Ebeling considers the role of historical criticism in hermeneutics at great length. He stresses both its necessity and its limitations. Uncompromisingly he states, "Literal historical exegesis ... is the foundation of the church's exposition of scripture".[48] Only when he has firmly established this principle does he admit: "Nevertheless the possibilities of conflict between the literal meaning and the requirements arising from the application to the present are not entirely excluded."[49] Even Bultmann adopts a similar starting-point, although (like Ebeling) he stresses the importance of pre-understanding

---

[44] J.D. Smart, *The Interpretation of Scripture*, p.33.
[45] H.-G. Gadamer, *T.M.*, p.263.
[46] Ibid., p.264 (my italics).
[47] P. Grech, *N.T.S.* XIX, 324.
[48] G. Ebeling, "The Significance of the Critical Historical Method for Church and Theology in Protestantism", in *W.F.*, p.32.
[49] Ibid.

and indeed is criticized by Ebeling (as well as by other writers) for going too far in separating historical-critical inquiry from Christian faith.[50] Bultmann writes, "The old hermeneutic rules of grammatical interpretation, formal analysis, and explanation of the basis of the conditions of the historical period are indisputably valid."[51]

Ernst Fuchs and Walter Wink also acknowledge the necessity for historical criticism, but equally stress its limitations. Fuchs writes, "There is no objection to the historical method", for "the historical method may establish what things were once like".[52] Nevertheless, as "an important point" it must be said that "every *analysis* of the text *must* in the first instance 'strike the text dead'".[53] This constitutes a necessary stage in the hermeneutical process, even though it can hardly be said to represent the most creative moment in the whole enterprise. Once again, whether Fuchs may be overstating the case is left open for future discussion.

If Fuchs' simile is striking, Wink's comments are still more emphatic. He declares, "The historical critical method has reduced the Bible to a dead letter. Our obeisance to technique has left the Bible sterile and ourselves empty."[54] The biblical writers, he argues, addressed concrete situations in life; but the biblical scholar who adopts the methods of historical criticism suppresses the very questions that are most fruitful to ask in order to arrive at an understanding of the text. Wink states, "The outcome of biblical studies in the academy is a trained incapacity to deal with the real problems of actual living persons in their daily lives."[55] Critical inquiry, he concludes, too often asks questions that are acceptable only to "the guild of biblical scholars" rather than ones which the text itself demands.[56]

In spite of the manner of his approach, it would be a mistake to assume that Wink leaves no room for critical historical inquiry. Such inquiry performs, in his judgement, the key function of insuring a necessary measure of objectivity in hermeneutics. This is associated with the process that he describes as "distancing", which is probably inspired by closely parallel ideas in Gadamer. Wink observes, "Though objectivism has been exposed as a false consciousness, objectivity cannot be surrendered as a goal ... so the scholar distances the Bible from the church, from the history of theology, from creed and dogma, and seeks to hear it on its own terms".[57] Indeed in discussion of specific New Testament passages in which he illustrates his own hermeneutical procedure, Wink consistently begins with the kinds of questions which can only be answered with reference to critical historical research undertaken by biblical scholars.[58] "Critical procedure", he urges, is indispensable as a matter of principle.[59]

---

[50] G. Ebeling, *Theology and Proclamation. A Discussion with Rudolf Bultmann* (Eng., London: Collins, 1966), pp.32–81 *et passim*.
[51] R. Bultmann, "The Problem of Hermeneutics", in *E.P.T.*, p.256.
[52] E. Fuchs, "The Reflection which is Imposed in Theology by the Historical-Critical Method", in *S.H.J.*, pp. 42–3; cf. pp.32–47.
[53] E. Fuchs, *S.H.J.*, p.194 (his italics). Cf. also "Die historisch-kritische Methode", in *Herm.*, pp.159–66; and *Marburger Hermeneutik* (Tübingen: Mohr, 1968), pp.95–134.
[54] W. Wink, *The Bible in Human Transformation*, p.4.
[55] Ibid., p.6.
[56] Ibid., pp.2–15.
[57] Ibid., p.24 (Wink's italics).
[58] Ibid., pp.52–5, on Matt. 9:1–8 and parallels.
[59] Ibid., p.53.

Why, then, does Wink attack the use of standard methods and methodologies in biblical studies? His reservations about critical methods are twofold. First of all, they do not complete the whole hermeneutical process. They begin it, but they do not end it, and we must not mistake the part for the whole. Second, while the questions posed by critical historical research are admittedly necessary, they are not always the questions which best allow the text to "speak" to man today. The texts of the Bible, he insists, speak to more practical issues about life, especially life within communities. These are not always the same as the questions that win a hearing from the scholarly guild.

We must now try to draw together some of the threads of this section. We first identified the underlying problem of hermeneutics as a two-sided one, involving the historical conditionedness both of the ancient text and of the modern interpreter. We have now seen that at least four specific issues arise from this.

(i) The horizons of the modern interpreter, or any interpreter standing in a tradition subsequent to the ancient text, mark out the area of his pre-understanding. How is this category of pre-understanding to be described, and what are its implications for the tasks of hermeneutics?

(ii) Once we allow the importance of questions about pre-understanding and the interpreter's own horizons, need this mean that the centre of gravity now shifts from the past entirely to the present? We shall argue in the third chapter [of *The Two Horizons*] that while the problem should not be exaggerated, nevertheless the difficulty raised by the pastness of the past in hermeneutics cannot be sidestepped. Further in the course of our discussion of Bultmann and Wittgenstein, we shall argue that in neglecting to give adequate place to the Old Testament as a history of publicly accessible tradition, Bultmann has made the hermeneutical problem more difficult. For if we reduce the hermeneutical question to a wholly present question about meaning "for me", it becomes almost impossible to heed Wittgenstein's warnings about private language.

(iii) If the New Testament writers approached the Old Testament in the light of a pre-understanding that was theologically informed (for example, by Christology), does this not mean that in order to be true to the tradition of the New Testament itself the interpreter will consciously approach the text from a particular theological angle? This raises very far-reaching questions about the relationship between exegesis and systematic theology, and about historical and theological objectivity. We shall touch on these issues in the third and fourth chapters, but our main consideration of them will come in chapter eleven [of *The Two Horizons*], when we examine the hermeneutical implications of Gadamer's philosophy.

(iv) The question that is never far in the background is to what extent philosophical description can help us to find answers to these and to other similar questions. We shall try to show shortly why in particular we have selected Heidegger, Bultmann, Gadamer and Wittgenstein as our four major representatives of philosophical or hermeneutical thought and inquiry. We shall then examine three broader issues: hermeneutics and history, hermeneutics and theology, and hermeneutics and language [in subsequent chapters].

III
Understanding and Pre-understanding: Schleiermacher

Before we can try to evaluate the force of theological criticisms brought against the notion of pre-understanding, we must first outline what is often under attack. We have already argued that theological considerations do not short-circuit the relevance of hermeneutics as the problem of human understanding. Further, in the first chapter [that is, above] we argued that understanding takes place when two sets of horizons are brought into relation to each other, namely those of the text and those of the interpreter. On this basis understanding presupposes a shared area of common perspectives, concepts, or even judgements. Fuchs describes this as the phenomenon of "common understanding" (*Einverständnis*). But if understanding, as it were, presupposes understanding, how can it begin?

Friedrich Schleiermacher was one of the first major thinkers to wrestle with this problem. His early aphorisms on hermeneutics in 1805 and 1806 were sparked off by his critical dialogue with Friedrich Ast (1778–1841) and Friedrich August Wolf (1759–1824). Schleiermacher frequently alludes to these writers, especially in his comments on their approach written in August 1829.[60] Schleiermacher saw that what is to be understood must, in a sense, be already known. If this seems to involve a circularity or even a contradiction, it can only be said that this very account of understanding is true to the facts of everyday experience. Schleiermacher drew attention to this when he wrote. "Every child arrives at the meaning of a word only through hermeneutics (*Jedes Kind kommt nur durch Hermeneutik zur Wortbedeutung*)."[61] On the one side, the child attempts to relate a new word to what he already knows. If he cannot achieve this, the new word remains meaningless. On the other side (as Gadamer phrases it in his comment on Schleiermacher's aphorism), the child has to assimilate "something alien, universal, which always signifies a resistance for the original vitality. To that extent it is an accomplishment of hermeneutic."[62] Schleiermacher adds that since understanding new subject-matter still depends on a positive relation to the interpreter's own horizons, "lack of understanding is never wholly removed".[63] It constitutes a progressive experience or process, not simply an act that can be definitively completed.

Richard Palmer defends Schleiermacher's approach. He writes, "Is it not vain to speak of love to one who has not known love, or of the joys of learning to those who reject it? One must already have, in some measure, knowledge of the matter being discussed. This may be termed the minimal pre-knowledge necessary for understanding, without which one cannot leap into the hermeneutical circle."[64]

Although it has now become a fixed and unalterable technical term in hermeneutics, the phrase "hermeneutical circle" is in one respect an unfortunate one. For although the

---

[60] F.D.E. Schleiermacher, *Hermeneutik*, pp.123, 125–6, 128–9, 133 and 152–5.
[61] Ibid., p.40.
[62] H.-G. Gadamer, "The Problem of Language in Schleiermacher's Hermeneutic", *Journal for Theology and Church* VII (1970), p.72; cf. pp.68–95.
[63] F.D.E. Schleiermacher, *Hermeneutik*, p.141.
[64] R.E. Palmer, *Hermeneutics*, pp.87–8.

centre of gravity moves back and forth between the two poles of the interpreter and the text, there is also an ongoing movement and progressive understanding which might have been better conveyed by some such image as that of the spiral. There is also the additional problem that the phrase "hermeneutical circle" is used in two distinct ways. Often, as in other parts of this present study, it is used in connection with the process of putting questions to the text, which are in turn reshaped by the text itself. Here, however, we are concerned with the principle that understanding a whole stretch of language or literature depends on an understanding of its component parts, while an understanding of these smaller units depends, in turn, on an understanding of the total import of the whole. For example, in attempting to grapple with the meaning of a difficult philosophical text such Heidegger's *Being and Time*, we understand paragraphs and sentences only if we understand individual words within them. Yet the words cannot be understood by looking up their separate meanings in a dictionary. They depend for this meaning on their role within the sentence, paragraph, or chapter. Even the use of a technical glossary to explain individual terms depends on the understanding of the work as a whole arrived at in this case vicariously through the compiler of the glossary. In principle, the truth of the hermeneutical circle holds good. This is why a really difficult text which deals with new or seemingly strange subject-matter may require a second or even a third reading if satisfactory understanding is to be achieved. This way of describing the issue, of course, only scratches the surface of Schleiermacher's hermeneutics, and we shall return to his approach again.

Meanwhile, in effect we have been exploring the category of pre-understanding (*Vorverständnis*). John Macquarrie helpfully expounds this concept in a way that takes up the approach which we have been observing in the writings of Schleiermacher. He comments, "We could never enter any understanding of it [a text] unless there were at least some minimum of common ground between ourselves and the text."[65] "If it ... did not link up at any point with our experience, we could make nothing of it".[66] This link is a matter of the interpreter's pre-understanding: "He already has certain categories of understanding under which the meaning of the text can be grasped, and these constitute the pre-understanding which he brings to the text."[67]

We shall see in due course how both Bultmann and Heidegger take up this principle. Heidegger writes, "In every case this interpretation is grounded in *something we have in advance* – in a fore-having (*Vorhabe*)." Understanding depends always on having a particular "point of view"; it is grounded in a "fore-sight" (*Vorsicht*). It entails a given way of conceiving something; therefore "it is grounded in ... a *fore-conception (Vorgriff)*".[68] Heidegger continues, "An interpretation is never a presuppositionless apprehending of something presented to us."[69] Everything is understood in a given context and from a given point of view. Man's "world" and man's existence are bound up together. Hence, "In every understanding of the world, existence is understood with it and vice versa ...

---

[65] J. Macquarrie, *The Scope of Demythologizing. Bultmann and his Critics*, p.45.
[66] Ibid.
[67] Ibid., pp.45–6.
[68] M. Heidegger, *Being and Time*, p.191 (German, p.150; his italics).
[69] Ibid., pp.191–2.

any interpretation which is to contribute understanding must already have understood what is to be interpreted".[70] To be sure, the process seems to be circular: *"But if we see this circle as a vicious one and look out for ways of avoiding it ... then the act of understanding has been misunderstood from the ground up"*.[71]

Schleiermacher distinguished between the linguistic or "grammatical" aspects of hermeneutics and the "psychological" aspects of the subject. Heinz Kimmerle traces his shift in emphasis in his earlier and later writings in his introduction to Schleiermacher's *Hermeneutik*, and the volume is arranged in such a way that it is easy to note the chronological development of Schleiermacher's thought.[72] After twenty pages of aphorisms composed in the period between 1805 and 1809, the work is divided into five further sections covering the periods 1810–19 and 1820–29 as well as material from the actual years 1819 and 1829.[73] Grammatical hermeneutics, Schleiermacher writes, requires the use of objective linguistic resources. Psychological hermeneutics involves penetration into the *inner* connections of thought that characterize an author's own consciousness. The linguistic and psychological aspects, therefore, correspond to the two poles of outward and "inner" reality, as Schleiermacher saw them. The interpreter must strive to enter into the mind of the author of the text that is to be understood, in an act of imaginative and sympathetic understanding. Just as, on the grammatical level, an understanding of individual words demands an understanding of the whole, and vice versa, so on the psychological level each individual "thought" that lies behind single linguistic articulations must be understood in the whole context of the author's life. But the hermeneutical circle does not end even here. For an understanding of the author's life and consciousness depends on an understanding of human life and existence as a whole.

T.F. Torrance admirably expresses how this psychological aspect of hermeneutics relates to the pre-understanding of the interpreter himself in his article on Schleiermacher's hermeneutics.[74] The interpreter's understanding, he writes:

> ... depends upon his own ability or art to recreate in himself the basic determination of consciousness he finds in the author. This is the principal element in Schleiermacher's hermeneutics that was taken over and developed by Dilthey in his notion of hermeneutics as the rediscovery of the I in the Thou through a transposition by the interpreter of his own self into the other and a reliving of his experience in himself. From these views of Schleiermacher and Dilthey no extension is needed to the theory that *the key to the interpretation of a text*, whether of Plato or of St. Paul, *is self-understanding*.[75]

Three comments may be suggested at this point. First, Schleiermacher's attempt to relate hermeneutics to pre-understanding and to self-understanding rings true to the facts of everyday experience both in religious and secular life. We have only to compare our own

---

[70] Ibid., p.194 (German, p.152).

[71] Ibid. (German, p.153; Heidegger's italics).

[72] In addition to his introduction cf. H. Kimmerle, "Hermeneutical Theory or Ontological Hermeneutics", in *J.T.C.* IV, p.107.

[73] F.D.E. Schleiermacher, *Hermeneutik*, pp.31–50 (1805–09); 55–76 (1810–19); 79–109 (1819); 113–20 (1820–29); 123–56 (1829) and 159–66 (1832–33).

[74] T.F. Torrance, "Hermeneutics according to F.D.E. Schleiermacher", in *S.J.T.* XXI (1968), pp.257–67.

[75] Ibid., p.261 (my italics).

"understanding" of such literature as the Psalms or even Shakespeare in childhood, youth, early adulthood and later life, to see how this understanding is profoundly conditioned by our own experience. Can someone who has never suffered the pangs of guilt before God know what it is to appropriate the glad assurance of the Psalmist, "Though he fall, he shall not be utterly cast down" (Ps. 37:24)? Can someone who has never experienced the ups and downs of life enter into the hopes and fears of some of Shakespeare's more profound characters?

Second, however, Schleiermacher's emphasis on self-understanding also raises serious problems. James B. Torrance calls attention to these problems in his article "Interpretation and Understanding in Schleiermacher's Theology: Some Critical Questions".[76] Schleiermacher shares with romanticism the emphasis on feeling and subjective experience. But when he turns to questions about Christian faith, does he not go too near to translating Christian doctrine into descriptions of human states? Torrance allows that Schleiermacher does not reduce all theological content to human consciousness without qualification, but questions whether he pays adequate attention to "the 'objective' 'factual' reference of theological statements".[77] The weakness of this type of approach from the standpoint of Christian theology is that "it becomes so pre-occupied with the self-understanding of the human subject, that it fails to yield any positive affirmation about the Being of God as He is in Himself".[78] This is a recurring difficulty in the application of hermeneutics to theological texts. While as a hermeneutical starting-point Bultmann rightly begins with the problem of pre-understanding, many writers have argued that in the end he reduces theology to anthropology. Whether this criticism is justified with reference to Bultmann we must postpone until a later chapter. However, we may note that the problem itself begins to emerge with Schleiermacher, as soon as we have a sensitive awareness of the problem of pre-understanding.

Third, we may also note that Schleiermacher's recognition of the importance of understanding the whole as well as the parts, together with his emphasis on the role of sympathetic imagination, finds further expression in his notion of "divination". Divination entails a "leap" into fresh understanding. Schleiermacher writes, "The divinatory is that in which one transforms oneself into the other person in order to grasp his individuality directly."[79] Once again, this is connected with the hermeneutical circle. For Schleiermacher states that one must have an understanding of man himself in order to understand what he speaks, and yet one comes to know what man is from his speech.[80] Thus, understanding, once again, is not merely a matter of scientific "rules", but is a creative act.

---

[76] J.B. Torrance, "Interpretation and Understanding in Schleiermacher's Theology: Some Critical Questions", in *S.J.T.* XXI, pp.268–82.

[77] Ibid., p.272; cf. p.274.

[78] Ibid., p.278.

[79] F.D.E. Schleiermacher, *Hermeneutik*, p.109.

[80] Ibid., p.44.

IV

Pre-Understanding and Theology

We shall postpone until the middle of the three chapters on Bultmann's hermeneutics our fuller discussions of Bultmann's use of the category of pre-understanding. However, one or two preliminary comments may be made, since it is most frequently in the context of Bultmann's thought that the concept of pre-understanding is attacked. We shall see that Bultmann is heavily indebted to Dilthey for the belief that understanding of a text depends on a prior relation to "life". Thus Bultmann writes, "Can one understand economic history without having a concept of what economy and society in general mean? Can one understand the history of religion and philosophy without knowing what religion and philosophy are? ... One cannot understand the Communist Manifesto of 1848 without understanding the principles of capitalism and socialism."[81] Bultmann concludes, "A specific understanding of the subject-matter of the text, on the basis of a 'life-relation' to it, is always presupposed by exegesis."[82]

Two elements in Bultmann's hermeneutics are attacked on the basis of their alleged dependence on his view of pre-understanding. First of all, he is attacked for laying down the principle that, in his own words, "The interpretation of the biblical writings is not subject to conditions different from those applying to all other kinds of literature."[83] Second, Bultmann also insists that for the interpreter to begin with questions about his or her own existence (*Existenz*) is thereby to ask questions about God. In *Jesus Christ and Mythology*, for example, he asks: What is the "life-relation" which the interpreter already has in advance to the theological subject-matter of the New Testament? He is moved, he answers, "by the question about his personal existence". He then adds: "The question of God and the question of myself are identical."[84] Similarly, in his essay on hermeneutics Bultmann writes, "In human existence an *existentiell* knowledge about God is alive in the form of the inquiry about 'happiness', 'salvation', the meaning of the world, and ... the real nature of each person's particular 'being'".[85]

In our later discussion of Bultmann's hermeneutics we shall attempt to show how these two principles relate to his wider thought. For instance, it would be unwise to jump to conclusions about any supposed naturalism or immanentism implied by the second principle until we have first noted how strongly Bultmann is influenced by dialectical theology and by his recognition of the limitations of theological liberalism. His thought on this subject is complex, not least because he is attempting to do justice to a variety of theological perspectives, not all of which are clearly compatible with one another. However, our immediate purpose is simply to note that a number of writers, including Karl Barth, James Smart and Carl Braaten, among others, explain these principles on the

---

[81] R. Bultmann, "Is Exegesis Without Presuppositions Possible?", in *Existence and Faith*, p.347; cf. pp.342–51.

[82] Ibid.

[83] R. Bultmann, *E.P.T.*, p.257.

[84] R. Bultmann, *Jesus Christ and Mythology* (London: SCM, 1960), p.53; cf. pp.52–6.

[85] R. Bultmann, *E.P.T.*, p.257.

basis of Bultmann's view of pre-understanding.[86] Carl Braaten writes, "The Achilles heel of Bultmann's hermeneutical proposal is his narrow conception of the pre-understanding appropriate in Biblical interpretation."[87]

In practice, however, other theologians invoke the category of pre-understanding without accepting the two principles that are so often attacked in Bultmann's hermeneutics, and certainly without accepting an existentialist analysis of human existence. We shall illustrate this point by selecting for consideration the hermeneutics of some theologians who write from the standpoint of very different theological traditions. We shall refer briefly to some statements made by two Catholic theologians, Edward Schillebeeckx and Bernard Lonergan. We shall then compare the approach to New Testament hermeneutics represented by Latin-American theologians such as Gustavo Gutiérrez and José Porforio Miranda. After all this we shall turn, finally, to the work of the philosopher Paul Ricoeur, in order to show that the category of pre-understanding is fruitfully employed by a thinker who cannot be accused of having any particular theological axe to grind.

We begin with a brief reference to the hermeneutics of Edward Schillebeeckx and Bernard Lonergan. Both stress that the truth of the New Testament is communicated through ordinary human language and appropriated by the normal processes of human understanding. In his wide-ranging book, *The Understanding of Faith*, Schillebeeckx gives more than adequate weight to distinctively theological considerations about faith.[88] However, he also emphatically asserts, a relationship with "lived experience" is an indispensable criterion for the meaning of theological interpretation.[89] He writes, "Language only communicates meaning when it expresses an experience that is shared."[90] That is to say, he advocates what he calls "hermeneutics of experience".[91] He points out that he is not claiming that it is possible to deduce from ordinary human experiences the meaning of, say, the resurrection of Jesus Christ. He goes on: "What I am saying, however, is that the Christian meaning of the resurrection ... will be *a priori* unintelligible to us ... if the universally intelligible content of this concept does not include human experience".[92] The criterion of intelligibility is "the relationship with lived human experience".[93] In effect this is a defence of the category of pre-understanding as a necessary hermeneutical tool and as grounded in human life.

Bernard Lonergan also argues for the importance of pre-understanding, simply as a given fact of life by virtue of the nature of language and understanding. We cannot claim to find meaning in a biblical text, he argues, if we approach it on the basis of "the principle of the empty head".[94] This approach is merely "naive". We see that it is naive,

---

[86] K. Barth, "Rudolf Bultmann – An Attempt to Understand Him", in *Kerygma and Myth*, II, pp.83–132; J.D. Smart, *The Interpretation of Scripture*, p.48; and C.E. Braaten, *New Directions in Theology Today: 2, History and Hermeneutics*, p.135.

[87] C.E. Braaten, ibid.

[88] E. Schillebeeckx, *The Understanding of Faith, Interpretation and Criticism* (Eng., London: Sheed & Ward, 1974), e.g. pp.5–19 and 135–55.

[89] Ibid., pp.14–17.

[90] Ibid., p.15.

[91] Ibid., p.16.

[92] Ibid., p.17.

[93] Ibid.

[94] B.J.F. Lonergan, *Method in Theology* (London: Darton, Longman and Todd, 1972), p.157.

he argues, as soon as we pause to think what the "empty head" will in practice see: "There is just a series of signs. Anything over and above a re-issue of the same sign in the same order will be mediated by the experience, intelligence and judgment of the interpreter. The less that experience, the less cultivated that intelligence, the less formed that judgment, the greater will be the likelihood that the interpreter will impute to the author an opinion that the author never entertained."[95]

This conclusion, which Lonergan states in his book *Method in Theology*, also echoes his more general comments in his earlier work *Insight: A Study of Human Understanding*. In this earlier work he writes, "If a correct interpretation is possible, it has to be possible ... for interpreters to proceed from their own experience, understanding, and judgment, to the range of possible meanings of documents."[96] Lonergan does not seem to suggest in his later book on theology that when the subject matter to be understood is theological, more general theories of understanding become irrelevant.

Hermeneutics and especially theological questions about the significance of pre-understanding have been given a new turn in the last few years by the emergence of the theology of liberation in Latin America. In a survey-article about this movement, published in 1976, José Miguez Bonino of Buenos Aires writes that biblical studies constitute a challenge for the theology of liberation not least because "we have, in the first place, the question of hermeneutics: Is it legitimate to start Biblical interpretation from a contemporary historical interpretation? ... How can the freedom of the text be maintained?"[97] Bonino gives a wider description of the hermeneutics of the movement in his book *Revolutionary Theology Comes of Age*, and the hermeneutics can be seen in action in such works as José Porfirio Miranda's *Marx and the Bible*.[98] The hermeneutics of the movement is also critically discussed in a recent doctoral thesis by J. Andrew Kirk.[99]

These writers, together with others such as Gustavo Gutiérrez, Juan Luis Segundo and Hugo Assmann, stress that biblical hermeneutics turns on a pre-understanding that is shaped, in turn, by *praxis*. Theoretical knowledge, it is argued, especially the philosophical values associated with the Western bourgeoisie, distort the message of the Bible and obscure the rights of the text. There is no such thing as purely neutral knowledge. Bonino asserts, "The sociology of knowledge makes abundantly clear that we think out of a definite context ... *out of a given praxis*. What Bultmann has so convincingly argued concerning a *pre-understanding* which every man brings to his

---

[95]   Ibid. Cf. pp.153–266.

[96]   B.J.F. Lonergan, *Insight. A Study of Human Understanding* (London: Longmans, Green and Co., 2nd edn, 1958), p.578.

[97]   J. Miguez Bonino, "Theology and Theologians of the New World: II. Latin America", in *Exp.T.* LXXXVII (1976). 199; cf. pp.196–200.

[98]   J.P. Miranda, *Marx and the Bible. A Critique of the Philosophy of Oppression* (Eng., Maryknoll, NY: Orbis Books, 1974); G. Gutiérrez, *A Theology of Liberation* (Eng., Maryknoll, NY: Orbis Books, 1973); and other writers discussed in J. Miguez Bonino, *Revolutionary Theology Comes of Age* (Eng., London: SPCK, 1975), especially the selection "Hermeneutics, Truth, and Praxis", pp.86–105.

[99]   J.A. Kirk, *The Theology of Liberation in the Latin American Roman Catholic Church Since 1965: An Examination of its Biblical Basis* (unpublished PhD thesis, University of London, 1975). Part II concerns especially pre-understanding and hermeneutics. Cf. also J.A. Kirk, *Liberation Theology. An Evangelical View from the Third World* (London: Marshall, Morgan & Scott, 1979).

interpretation of the text *must be deepened and made more concrete.*"[100] Pre-understanding, Bonino continues, relates to such concrete considerations as a man's social class and nationhood. Freud and Marx, he argues, were correct in their suspicions about hidden factors which control conscious accounts of life and literature. The Latin-American theologians are especially suspicious of approaches to the Bible undertaken from bourgeois or non-Marxist perspectives: "Why is it, for instance, that the obvious political motifs and undertones in the life of Jesus have remained so hidden to liberal interpreters until very recently?"[101] Juan Luis Segundo argues that theologians have managed to draw from the Bible and Christian tradition the image of a timeless and impersonal God only because their interpretations were shaped by a prior view of life in which God was relegated to an "inner" or "private" zone: "Hermeneutics in this new context means also an identification of the ideological framework of interpretation implicit in a given religious praxis."[102]

Many of the Latin-American theologians themselves quite explicitly and consciously interpret the New Testament in terms of a pre-understanding oriented towards Marxist perspectives. Thus Bonino asks, "Is it altogether absurd to re-read the resurrection today as a death of the monopolies, the liberation from hunger, or a solitary form of ownership?"[103] José Porfirio Miranda's *Marx and the Bible* provides a more detailed example. Too often, he complains, the biblical interpreter has approached the text with a pre-understanding of man as an abstraction, "a Platonic essence valid *semper et pro semper*, not real flesh-and-blood humanity, a humanity of blood and tears and slavery and humiliations and jail and hunger and untold sufferings".[104] Miranda also stresses that pre-understanding must be oriented to *praxis*. Otherwise the interpreter becomes sidetracked into merely dealing in "concepts" *about* God. The God of the Bible, he declares, is the one "to objectify whom is to break off the imperative relationship".[105]

Yet Miranda and Bonino do not wish to open the door to subjectivism (as against subjectivity). Miranda asserts, "I am not reducing the Bible to Marx ... I only wish to understand what the Bible says ... We want to take the Bible seriously."[106] Indeed, he argues that his own approach is motivated by an attempt to read the Bible on its own terms. It is precisely *not* simply all "a matter of the mind of the interpreter". It is only the defeatist and cynical belief that "Scripture has various 'meanings'" that (in Miranda's view) allows conservative theologians of the West "to prevent the Bible from revealing *its* own subversive message. Without recourse to this belief, how could the West, a civilization of injustice, continue to say that the Bible is its sacred book? Once we have established the possibility of different 'meanings' each as acceptable as any other, then Scripture cannot challenge the West."[107] Bonino also insists that critical appraisal must

100 J. Miguez Bonino, *Revolutionary Theology Comes of Age*, p.90.
101 Ibid., p.91.
102 Ibid., p.94.
103 Ibid., p.101.
104 J.P. Miranda, *Marx and the Bible*, p.31.
105 Ibid., p.41.
106 Ibid., pp.35 and 36.
107 Ibid., p.36.

take place to insure that "reading" the New Testament does not become a matter of "only arbitrary inventions".[108]

Andrew Kirk sums up the perspective as follows: "The Marxist interpretation provides an ideological mechanism which is capable of exposing the intentions of any exegesis seeking, through the employment of pre-understanding tied to conservative philosophical systems, to use the Biblical text ... to defend the status-quo of a pre-revolutionary situation".[109]

The effect of this approach is first of all to stress the importance of questions about pre-understanding, and second to show that the use of this category in New Testament hermeneutics does not belong exclusively to those who start from the standpoint of Heidegger and existentialist philosophy, nor even from the philosophical tradition of Schleiermacher and Dilthey. But thereby they provide two warnings that we must heed when we look at Bultmann's thought more closely. First of all, the fact that Marxist interpreters do in fact tend to arrive at Marxist interpretations of the Bible even when they are aware of their own pre-understanding sharpens the problem of objectivity in biblical hermeneutics. A mere awareness of the problem of pre-understanding is not enough to solve the problems to which this phenomenon gives rise. We have arrived at the point where the problem is less "the pastness of the present" than that of evaporating past meaning in the horizons of the present. Second, if such different pre-understandings seem to lead on to such different ways of interpreting the New Testament, we must beware of the claim of any one New Testament interpreter to start from the "right" pre-understanding. This is sometimes urged as a criticism of Bultmann, and we shall see in due course that it is not entirely without some truth. On the one hand, Bultmann sets too high a value on the *one* starting-point of the earlier Heidegger's view of existence; but on the other hand he does also stress that any pre-understanding is provisional and open to later correction.

As a final comment on the subject of pre-understanding in general we may also note that the debate, in effect, is even more wide-ranging than we have yet seen. The philosopher Paul Ricoeur (as well as others, including, for example, Peter Homans) shows how hermeneutics is affected by considerations that emerge not only from Marx but also from Sigmund Freud.[110] One of the most startling features of Ricoeur's discussion from the point of view of the present study is that it serves in effect to demonstrate that conclusions about the importance of pre-understanding can be arrived at from *two radically opposing philosophical traditions*. We have seen that in the tradition of Schleiermacher hermeneutical principles are formulated from the point of view of an emphasis on human consciousness. Freud (together with Nietzsche and Marx) approaches the problem of meaning on the basis of a *rejection* of the category of human consciousness as the key starting-point. Because of the complexity of the human mind, Freud argues that meaning is not always synonymous with *consciousness of* meaning.

---

[108]   J. Miguez Bonino, *Revolutionary Theology Comes of Age*, p.100.

[109]   J.A. Kirk, *The Theology of Liberation*, Part II, sect. 2-1.

[110]   P. Ricoeur, *The Conflict of Interpretations*, pp.99–208, especially "The Place of Freudian Hermeneutics", pp.142–50. Cf. also P. Homans, "Psychology and Hermeneutics", *Journal of Religion* LV (1975), pp.327–47.

Ricoeur comments, "these three exegetes of modern man (Freud, Nietzsche and Marx) ... all attack the same illusion, that illusion which bears the hallowed name of self-consciousness ... These three masters of suspicion, however, are not three masters of skepticism ... Marx, Nietzsche and Freud triumph over their doubt about consciousness through an exegesis of meanings. For the first time comprehension is hermeneutics."[111]

However, in each individual case, these thinkers approach questions about meaning with pre-understandings that, in their view, unlock and disclose them. Freud believes that the key to meaning comes from the unconscious psyche. Hence he interprets consciousness from the standpoint of this pre-understanding. Nietzsche approaches the matter in terms of man's will to power. Marx interprets life and history with presuppositions about man as a social being. Their view of "meaning" is inseparable from their own pre-understanding. None of these three thinkers could achieve his goal by ignoring or suppressing his own pre-understanding. "Understanding" dawns in the interaction between pre-understanding and meaning.[112]

We cannot claim, then, that the importance of pre-understanding in New Testament hermeneutics depends either on special pleading in theology or on too narrow a philosophical base. The problems posed by this phenomenon cannot be avoided. In the words of the Church of England's Doctrine Communion Report *Christian Believing*, "No one expounds the Bible to himself or to anyone else without bringing to the task his own prior frame of reference, his own pattern of assumptions which derives from sources outside the Bible."[113]

---

[111] Ibid., pp.148–9.
[112] Ibid., p.150.
[113] "The Christian and the Bible", in *Christian Believing*, p.30.

CHAPTER TWENTY-SIX

Entering a Transforming World: "The New Hermeneutic" (1977)

Like its companion piece "Semantics and New Testament Interpretation", this essay first emerged as a conference paper in Tyndale House, Cambridge, in 1973, and appeared in I. Howard Marshall (ed.), New Testament Interpretation *(Exeter: Paternoster Press, 1977), pp.308–33. In order to preserve the flow of the argument some degree of overlap with one or two other essays in this volume has proved difficult to avoid. A number of insights into "worldhood" and "projected worlds" in biblical narrative and in the parables of Jesus have now become established hermeneutical resources, and some merely associate the new hermeneutic of Fuchs and Ebeling with a movement of the late 1950s and early 1960s that took its bearings from Heidegger. But this is to undervalue their contribution.*

Fuchs strongly influenced Robert Funk in America, but he also has distinctive perspectives of his own, not least in his concern for Christian preaching. He asks what the preacher has to do at his or her desk to make "the word" a living word in the pulpit. He is also deeply concerned with how texts create faith, rather than simply presupposing faith. Yet he does tie his theory of language too closely to Heidegger, and his hermeneutic and his theology invite serious critique as well as positive if cautious attention. When this essay was first published, Stephen Neil published a review in which he complained that having offered a positive exposition of Fuchs and Ebeling, I then retracted this more positive picture. However, it is this mixture of the constructive and the mistaken or injudicious that merits retaining these thinkers on the hermeneutical agenda today. They address questions that are still live and ongoing in the twenty-first century.

I
Aims and Concerns: How May the Text Speak Anew?

I.1 The Task of Exposition and Pastoral Responsibility

The approach to the New Testament that came to be known as the new hermeneutic is associated most closely with the work of Ernst Fuchs and Gerhard Ebeling.[1] Both of these writers insist on the practical relevance of this work to the world of today. How does language, especially the language of the Bible, strike home (*treffen*) to modern hearers?[2]

---

[1] For objections to the customary use of the term, see C.E. Braaten, "How New is the New Hermeneutic?", in *Theology Today* 22 (1965), pp.218–35; and J.D. Smart, *The Strange Silence of the Bible in the Church* (London: SCM, 1970), pp.37–8; as against James M. Robinson, "Braaten's Polemic. A Reply", in *Theology Today*, loc. cit., pp.277–82.

[2] E. Fuchs, "Zur Frage nach dem historischen Jesus", *Gesammelte Aufsätze* II (Tübingen: Mohr, 1960), pp.411–14 and 418; cf. *Studies of the Historical Jesus* (London: SCM, 1964), pp.196–8 and 202.

How may its words so reach through into their own understanding that when they repeat them they will be *their* words? How may the word of God become a living word, which is heard anew?

This emphasis on present application, rather than simply antiquarian biblical research, stems partly from connections between the new hermeneutic and the thought of Rudolf Bultmann.[3] However, it also springs from a pastor's deep and consistent concern on the part of Fuchs and Ebeling, both of whom served as pastors for some years, about the relevance and effectiveness of Christian preaching. Central to Fuchs's work is the question "What do we have to do at our desks, if we want later to set the text in front of us in the pulpit?"[4]

It would be a mistake to conclude that this interest in preaching, however, is narrowly ecclesiastical or merely homiletical. Both writers share an intense concern about the position of the unbeliever. If the word of God is capable of *creating* faith, its intelligibility cannot be said to *presuppose* faith. Thus Fuchs warns us, "The proclamation loses its character when it anticipates (i.e. presupposes) confession."[5] More clearly Ebeling asserts, "The criterion of the understandability of our preaching is not the believer but the non-believer. For the proclaimed word seeks to effect faith, but does not presuppose faith as a necessary preliminary."[6]

Nevertheless the problem goes even deeper than this. Modern hearers, or interpreters, stand at the end of a long tradition of biblical interpretation; a tradition which, in turn, moulds their own understanding of the biblical text and their own attitudes towards it. Their attitudes may be either positive or negative, and their controlling assumptions may well be unconscious ones.[7] The New Testament is thus interpreted today within a particular frame of reference which may differ radically from that within which the text first addressed its hearers. Hence simply to *repeat* the actual words of the New Testament today may well be, in effect, to say something different from what the text itself originally said. Even if it does not positively alter what was once said, it may be to utter "nothing more than just a tradition, a mere form of speech, a dead relic of the language of the past".[8] For never before, Ebeling believes, was there so great a gulf between the linguistic tradition of the Bible and language that is actually spoken today.[9]

Two undue criticisms must be forestalled at this point. First, some may believe that this problem is solved simply by an appeal to the work of the Holy Spirit. Fuchs and Ebeling are fully aware of the role of the Holy Spirit in communicating the word of God; but they rightly see that problems of understanding and intelligibility cannot be short-circuited by a premature appeal of this kind.[10] The New Testament requires hermeneutical translation

---

[3]   E. Fuchs, *Hermeneutik* (Tübingen: Mohr, 1970⁴), p.281; cf. R. Bultmann, *Essays Philosophical and Theological* (London: SCM, 1955), p.14. Cf. further, E. Fuchs, *Hermeneutik*, p.182, and R. Bultmann, *Faith and Understanding* (London: SCM, 1969), pp.286–312.

[4]   E. Fuchs, *Studies of the Historical Jesus*, p.8.

[5]   E. Fuchs, *Studies of the Historical Jesus*, p.30; cf. *Zum Hermeneutischen Problem in der Theologie*, (*Gesammelte Aufsätze* Bd. I, Tübingen: Mohr, 1959), pp.9–10.

[6]   G. Ebeling, "Non-religious Interpretation of Biblical Concepts", in *Word and Faith*, p.125.

[7]   G. Ebeling, *The Word of God and Tradition* (E.T., London: SCM, 1968), pp.11–31, especially 26, 28.

[8]   G. Ebeling, *God and Word* (Philadelphia, PA: Fortress, 1967), p.3; cf. pp.8–9.

[9]   Ibid., p.4.

[10]   E. Fuchs, "Proclamation and Speech-event", in *Theology Today* 19 (1962), p.354; and G. Ebeling, *Theology and Proclamation* (E.T., London: Collins, 1966), pp.42 and 100–102.

no less than it obviously requires linguistic translation. This point will become clearer as we proceed.

Second, Fuchs and Ebeling do not in any way underestimate the power of the New Testament to interpret itself, and to create room for its understanding. Ebeling insists that hermeneutics "only consist in removing hindrances in order *to let the word perform its own hermeneutic function*".[11] "Holy Scripture, as Luther puts it, is *sui ipsius interpres.*"[12] The "one bridge" to the present is "the Word alone".[13] Similarly Fuchs stresses the importance of Heb. 4:12–13 – "The word of God is living and active, sharper than any two-edged sword" – even in the present moment.[14] Indeed it is crucial to Fuchs's position, as we shall see, that the New Testament itself *effects changes* in situations, and changes in people's pre-conscious standpoints. The language of Jesus "singles out the individual and grasps him deep down".[15] "The text is itself meant to live."[16]

The key question in the new hermeneutic, then, is how the New Testament may speak to us *anew*. A literalistic repetition of the text cannot *guarantee* that it will "speak" to the modern hearer. He may understand all of its individual words, and yet fail to understand what is being said. In Wolfhart Pannenberg's words, "In a changed situation the traditional phrases, even when recited literally, do not mean what they did at the time of their original formulation."[17] Thus Ebeling asserts, "The *same word* can be said to another time only by being said differently."[18]

In assessing the validity of this point, we may well wish to make some proviso about the uniquely normative significance of the original formulation in *theology*. The problem is recognized by Fuchs and Ebeling perhaps more clearly than by Bultmann when parallel questions arise in his programme of demythologizing.[19] It is partly in connection with this problem that both writers insist on the necessity of historical-critical research on the New Testament.[20]

At the same time, at least two considerations re-enforce their contentions about the inadequacy of mere repetition of the text from the standpoint of *hermeneutics*. First, we already recognize the fact that in translation from one language to another, literalism can be the enemy of faithful communication: "To put it into another language means to think

---

11   G. Ebeling, *Word and Faith*, pp.318–19.

12   Ibid., p.306.

13   Ibid., p.36.

14   E. Fuchs, *Hermeneutik*, p.92.

15   E. Fuchs, *Studies of the Historical Jesus*, p.35.

16   Ibid., p.193.

17   W. Pannenberg, *Basic Questions in Theology* I (E.T., London: SCM, 1970), p.9.

18   G. Ebeling, "Time and Word", in J.M. Robinson (ed.), *The Future of our Religious Past: Essays in Honour of Rudolf Bultmann* (London: SCM, 1971), p.265 (translated from *Zeit und Geschichte*, 1964) (my italics). Cf. further, W.G. Doty, *Contemporary New Testament Interpretation* (Englewood Cliffs, NJ: Prentice-Hall, 1972), pp.34–7.

19   See Ian Henderson, *Myth in the New Testament* (London: SCM, 1952), p.31; A.C. Thiselton, *The Two Horizons* (Exeter: Paternoster and Grand Rapids, MI: Eerdmans, 1980), pp.205–93; and "Myth, Mythology", in *The Zondervan Pictorial Encyclopedia of the Bible* (Grand Rapids, MI: Zondervan, 1975), vol. 4, pp.333–43.

20   G. Ebeling, "The Significance of the Critical Historical method for Church and Theology in Protestantism", in *Word and Faith*, pp.17–61; and E. Fuchs, *Hermeneutik*, pp.159–66, and especially *Studies of the Historical Jesus*, pp.95–108.

it through afresh."[21] Second, we already have given tacit recognition to this principle whenever we stress the importance of preaching. The preacher "translates" the text, by placing it at the point of encounter with the hearer, from which it speaks anew into his own world in his own language.[22] But this hermeneutical procedure is demanded in *all* interpretation which is faithful to the New Testament. For "God's revelation consisted simply in God's letting men state God's own problems *in their language*, in grace and judgement."[23]

I.2 Making the Word of God More Transparent: More than Vocabulary or "Rules"

How, then, may the text of the New Testament speak anew? Four sets of considerations are relevant to a positive answer, each of which turns on a given point of contrast.

First, Fuchs and Ebeling draw *a contrast between problems about words (plural) and the problem of the word (singular)*. Ebeling laments the fact that too often preaching today sounds like a foreign language.[24] But he adds, "We need not emphasize that the problem lies too deep to be tackled by cheap borrowing of transient modern jargon for the preacher's stock of words. It is not a matter of understanding single words, but of understanding the word itself; not a matter of new means of speech, but of a new coming to speech."[25] Mere modern paraphrase of the New Testament does not answer the problem. The concern is, rather, that the word of God itself should "come to speech" (*das Zur-Sprache-Kommen der Sache selbst*), in the technical sense which this phrase has come to bear in the philosophical writings of Martin Heidegger and Hans-Georg Gadamer.[26]

Second, hermeneutics in the writings of Fuchs and Ebeling concerns "the theory of understanding", and *must not be reduced "to a collection of rules"*.[27] Indeed, because it concerns the whole question of how someone comes to *understand*, Ebeling asserts, "Hermeneutics now takes the place of the classical epistemological theory."[28] This is why hermeneutics cannot be separated from philosophy. Because it concerns "a general theory of understanding", hermeneutics is "becoming the place of meeting with philosophy".[29]

---

[21]   G. Ebeling, *The Nature of Faith* (E.T., London, 1961), p.188.

[22]   E. Fuchs, "Translation and Proclamation", in *Studies of the Historical Jesus*, pp.191–206; cf. *Hermeneutik*, pp.249–56, and *Marburger Hermeneutik* (Tübingen: Mohr, 1968), pp.2–4, Fuchs's approach is related to that of Manfred Mezger. See M. Mezger, "Preparation for Preaching: the Route from Exegesis to Proclamation", in R.W. Funk (ed.), *Journal for Theology and Church* 2, *Translating Theology into the Modern Age* (Tübingen: Mohr, 1965), pp.159–79, especially p.166.

[23]   E. Fuchs, "The New Testament and the Hermeneutical Problem", loc. cit., pp.135–6. (Fuchs writes almost the whole sentence in italics.)

[24]   G. Ebeling, *The Nature of Faith*, p.15, cf. *Introduction to a Theological Theory of Language* (London: Collins, 1973), pp.15–80.

[25]   G. Ebeling, *The Nature of Faith*, p.16; cf. *God and Word*, pp.2–3, and E. Fuchs, "The New Testament and the Hermeneutical Problem", loc. cit., p.125.

[26]   H.-G. Gadamer, *Wahrheit und Method. Grundzüge einer philosophischen Hermeneutik* (Tübingen: Mohr, 1965²), p.360; and E.T., *Truth and Method* (London: Sheed & Ward, 1975), p.350. [2nd Eng. edn, 1989, p.388 – Ed.]

[27]   G. Ebeling, "Word of God and Hermeneutics", in *Word and Faith*, p.313.

[28]   Ibid., p.317.

[29]   Ibid., cf. *The Word of God and Tradition*, p.9.

Similarly for Fuchs the central question of hermeneutics is, "how do I come to understand?"[30] Yet both writers are concerned not simply with the theory, but with the *practice* of setting understanding in motion. Fuchs suggests an analogy. It is possible, on the one hand, to theorize about an understanding of "cat" by cognitive reflection. On the other hand, a practical and pre-conceptual understanding of "cat" emerges when we actually place a mouse in front of a particular cat. The mouse is the "hermeneutical principle" that causes the cat to show itself for what it is.[31] In this sense biblical criticism and even the traditional hermeneutical "rules" do "not *produce* understanding, but only the preconditions for it".[32]

This distinction goes back in part to Schleiermacher. An illuminating comment comes from the philosopher Heinz Kimmerle, whose research on the earlier writings of Schleiermacher is important for the new hermeneutic. He writes:

> The work of Schleiermacher constitutes a turning point in the history of hermeneutics. Till then hermeneutics was supposed to support, secure, and clarify an *already accepted* understanding (of the Bible as theological hermeneutics; of classical antiquity as philological hermeneutics). In the thinking of Schleiermacher, hermeneutics achieves the qualitatively different function of first of all *making understanding possible*, and deliberately *initiating understanding* in each individual case.[33]

This in turn touches on yet another central and cardinal feature of the new hermeneutic. The concern is not simply to support and corroborate an *existing* understanding of the New Testament text, but to lead the hearer or the interpreter onwards *beyond* his own existing horizons, so that the text addresses and judges him *anew*. This fundamental principle emerges more clearly in Hans-Georg Gadamer.

I.3 Making the Word More Transparent: Einverständnis *and "World"*

Third, the problem of initiating understanding brings us to another concept which is also central in the thinking of Fuchs, namely that of *das Einverständnis*.[34] This is often translated as "common understanding", "mutual understanding" or "agreement", and in one essay as "empathy". Fuchs illustrates this category with reference to the language of the home. Members of a close-knit family who live together in one home share a common world of assumptions, attitudes and experiences, and therefore share a common language. A single word or gesture may set in motion a train of events because communication functions on the basis of a common understanding. Fuchs explains, "At home one does not speak so that people may understand, but because people understand."[35] The problem of understanding a language, in the sense of "appropriating"

---

30   E. Fuchs, "The New Testament and the Hermeneutical Problem", loc. cit., p.136.
31   E. Fuchs, *Hermeneutik*, pp.109–10 ("*die Maus das hermeneutische Prinzip für das Verständis der Katze zu sein ...*").
32   G. Ebeling, *The Word of God and Tradition*, p.17.
33   H. Kimmerle, "Hermeneutical Theory or Ontological Hermeneutics", in R.W. Funk (ed.), *J. Th. Ch.* 4, *History and Hermeneutic*, p.107 (my italics); cf. 107–21.
34   See E. Fuchs, *Marburger Hermeneutik*, pp.171–81 and 239–43.
35   E. Fuchs, "The New Testament and the Hermeneutical Problem", loc. cit., p.124; cf. *Marburger Hermeneutik*, p.176.

its subject matter, "does not consist in learning new words – languages are learned from mothers".[36]

So important is this category of *Einverständnis* for Fuchs that in the preface to the fourth edition of *Hermeneutik* he stresses that "all understanding is grounded in *Einverständnis*", and in a later essay he sums up the thrust of his *Hermeneutik* with the comment, "Ernst Fuchs, *Hermeneutik* (is) an attempt to bring the hermeneutical problem back into the dimension of language with the aid of the phenomenon of 'empathy' (*des Phänomens des Einverständnisses*) as the foundation of all understanding."[37]

Jesus, Fuchs maintains, established a common understanding with his hearers, especially in the language of the parables. Or more accurately, the parables communicated reality effectively because they operated on the basis of this common understanding, which they then extended and reshaped.[38] The hermeneutical task today is to re-create that common world of understanding which is the necessary basis of effective communication of language and appropriation of its truth. Such a task, however, stands in sharp contrast to a merely cognitive and conscious exchange of language. Like Heidegger's category of "world", it is pre-conceptual: "It is neither a subjective nor an objective phenomenon but both together, for world is prior to and encompasses both."[39] It is therefore, for Fuchs as for Gadamer, primarily a "linguistic" phenomenon, reflecting ways in which men have come to terms with themselves and with their world.[40]

I.4 Making the Word Transparent and Creative: Action, Effect, and Event

Fourth, both Fuchs and Ebeling view language as much more than being only a means of information. Ebeling writes, "We do not get at the nature of words by asking what they contain, but by asking what they effect, what they set going …".[41] In the terminology of J.L. Austin, Fuchs and Ebeling are most interested in the *performative* functions of language, in which "the issuing of the utterance is the performing of an action".[42] The word of God, Ebeling believes, enacts "an event in which God himself is communicated … With God word and deed are one: his speaking is the way of his acting."[43] Thus the

---

[36]   E. Fuchs, "The Hermeneutical Problem", in J.M. Robinson (ed.), *The Future of Our Religious Past*, pp.267–8 (translated from E. Dinkler, ed., *Zeit und Geschichte*, p.357).

[37]   Ibid., p.270; German from *Zeit und Geschichte*, p.360. Cf. *Hermeneutik*, p.136.

[38]   E. Fuchs, "The New Testament and the Hermeneutical Problem", loc. cit., p.126; "Proclamation and Speech-Event", loc. cit., pp.347–51; *Hermeneutik*, pp.219–30; *Studies of the Historical Jesus*, pp.97–9 and 130–66; and *Marburger Hermeneutik*, pp.231–2. The parables are discussed further below.

[39]   Richard E. Palmer, *Hermeneutics. Interpretation Theory in Schleiermacher, Dilthey, Heidegger, and Gadamer* (Evanston: Northwestern University Press, 1969), p.139.

[40]   This point is elucidated below, but for a simple introduction to this aspect of Fuchs's thought, see Paul J. Achtemeier, *An Introduction to the New Hermeneutic* (Philadelphia, PA: Fortress, 1969), pp.91–100.

[41]   G. Ebeling, *The Nature of Faith*, p.187.

[42]   J.L. Austin, *How to Do Things with Words* (Oxford: Clarendon Press, 1962), p.6; cf. *Philosophical Papers* (Oxford: Clarendon, 1961), pp.220–39. Cf. further A.C. Thiselton, "The Parables as Language-Event: Some Comments on Fuchs's Hermeneutics in the Light of Linguistic Philosophy", *Scottish Journal of Theology* 23 (1970), pp.437–68, especially 438–9; R.W. Funk, *Language, Hermeneutic and Word of God* (New York, 1966), pp.26–8; J.M. Robinson, "The Parables as God Happening", in F.T. Trotter (ed.), *Jesus and the Historian* (Philadelphia, PA: Fortress, 1968), p.142; and W.G. Doty, op. cit., pp.39–43.

[43]   G. Ebeling, *The Nature of Faith*, pp.87 and 90.

word of Jesus in the New Testament does not simply provide information about states of affairs. His language constitutes a call or a pledge.[44] He promises, demands or gives.[45] Actually to *make* a promise, or to *convey* a gift is very different from talking *about* promises or gifts. The one is action; the other is mere talk.

In the terminology used by Fuchs, language which actually conveys reality constitutes a "language-event" (*Sprachereignis*), whilst Ebeling uses the term "word-event" (*Wortgeschehen*) in much the same way.[46] Fuchs comments, "The true language-event, for example an offer, shows that, though it sets our thoughts in motion, it is not itself thought. The immediate harmony between what is said and what is grasped is not the result of a process of thought; it takes place at an earlier stage, as event ... The word 'gets home'."[47] For example, to name a man "brother" performatively is thereby to admit him into a brotherly relationship within the community.[48] In this sense, when the word of God addresses the hearers anew, it is no longer merely an object of investigation at the hands of the interpreter. Fuchs concludes, "The text is therefore not just the servant that transmits kerygmatic formulations, but rather a master that directs us into the language-context of our existence."[49] It has become a language-event.

II
Subject and Object in Epistemology: Understanding as Experience

Two further principles now emerge from all that has been said. The first concerns the interpreter's experience of life, or subjectivity. Ebeling writes, "Words produce understanding only by appealing to experience and leading to experience. Only where word has already taken place can word take place. Only where there is already previous understanding can understanding take place. Only a man who is already concerned with the matter in question can be claimed for it."[50] This is certainly true of a text which concerns history: "It is impossible to understand history without a stand-point and a perspective."[51] This provides explicit connections between the new hermeneutic and Bultmann's discussion about *pre-understanding*.

The second principle concerns the direction of the relation between the interpreter and the text. In traditional hermeneutics, the interpreter, as knowing subject, scrutinizes

---

[44] E. Fuchs, *Zur Frage nach dem historischen Jesus*, pp.291 and 293 (cf. *Studies of the Historical Jesus*, pp.94–5).

[45] E. Fuchs, loc. cit. (German) pp.288 and 291 (English, pp.91 and 93); 224 and 226 (English, pp.36 and 38); and 347 (English, p.141).

[46] Cf. E. Fuchs, *Zum hermeneutischen Problem in der Theologie*, pp.281–305; *Marburger Hermeneutik*, pp.243–5; and *Studies of the Historical Jesus*, pp.196–212; and G. Ebeling, *Word and Faith*, pp.325–32; and *Theology and Proclamation* pp.28–31. On the different terminology in Fuchs and Ebeling, James Robinson explains, "*Sprachereignis* and *Wortgeschehen* are synonyms ... The choice depends on which Bultmannian term serves as the point of departure, *Heilsereignis* or *Heilsgeschehen*" (*New Frontiers in Theology, 2: The New Hermeneutic*, p.57).

[47] E. Fuchs, *Studies of the Historical Jesus*, p.196 (German, p.411).

[48] Ibid.

[49] Ibid., p.211.

[50] G. Ebeling, *Word and Faith*, p.320.

[51] G. Ebeling, *The Word of God and Tradition*, p.18; cf. E. Fuchs, *Hermeneutik*, pp.103–26.

and investigates the text as the object of his knowledge. The interpreter is active subject; the text is passive object. This kind of approach is encouraged by a notion of theology as "queen of the sciences". But it rests upon, or presupposes, a particular model in epistemology, a model which is exemplified in the philosophy of Descartes. If understanding is viewed in terms of experience rather than knowledge, a different perspective may also be suggested. James Robinson offers an illuminating comment. In the new hermeneutic, he explains, "The flow of the traditional relation between subject and object, in which the subject interrogates the object ... has been significantly reversed. For it is now the object – which should henceforth be called the subject-matter – that puts the subject in question."[52] Thus Fuchs asserts, *"The truth has us ourselves as its object."*[53] Or even more strikingly, *"The texts must translate us before we can translate them"* (my italics).[54]

II.1 Language, Pre-Understanding, and the Hermeneutical Circle

It is well known that Rudolf Bultmann, among others, has repudiated the idea that an interpreter can "understand" the New Testament independently of his own prior questions. One cannot, for example, understand a text about economic history unless one already has some concept of what a society and an economy are.[55] In this sense Bultmann rightly insists, *"There cannot be any such thing as presuppositionless exegesis* ... Historical understanding always presupposes a relation of the interpreter to the subject-matter that is ... expressed in the texts".[56] "The demand that the interpreter must silence his subjectivity ... in order to attain an objective knowledge is therefore the most absurd one that can be imagined".[57] "Pre-understanding", or a prior life-relation to the subject matter of the text, implies "not a prejudice, but a way of raising questions".[58]

This principle must not be rejected merely because it has particular connections with other assumptions made by Bultmann in his programme of demythologizing. Other more moderate thinkers including, for example, Bernard Lonergan and James D. Smart, have made similar points.[59] Lonergan rightly asserts:

> The principle of the empty head rests on a naïve intuitionism ... The principle ... bids the interpreter forget his own views, look at what is out there, and let the author interpret himself. In fact, what is out there? There is just a series of signs. Anything over and above a re-issue of the same signs in the same order will be mediated by the experience, intelligence, and judgement of the interpreter. The less that experience, the

[52] J.M. Robinson, *New Frontiers in Theology 2: The New Hermeneutic*, pp.23–4.

[53] E. Fuchs, "The New Testament and the Hermeneutical Problem", ibid., p.143 (his italics).

[54] E. Fuchs, "The Hermeneutical Problem", loc. cit., p.277 (*"die Texte zuvor uns übersetzen müssen bevor wir sie übersetzen können"*, in E. Dinkler, ed., op. cit., p.365). Cf. G. Ebeling, *Word and Faith*, p.331.

[55] R. Bultmann, "Is Exegesis Without Presuppositions Possible?" in *Existence and Faith* (London: SCM, 1964), p.347; cf. pp.342–51. R. Bultmann, "The Problem of Hermeneutics", in *Essays Philosophical and Theological*, pp.242–3 (cf. pp.234–61).

[56] R. Bultmann, *Existence and Faith*, pp.343–4 (my italics) and 347.

[57] R. Bultmann, "The Problem of Hermeneutics", loc. cit., p.255.

[58] R. Bultmann, *Existence and Faith*, p.346.

[59] Cf. B.J.F. Lonergan, *Method in Theology* (London: Darton, Longman & Todd, 1972), pp.156–8 (cf. 153–266); and J.D. Smart, *The Interpretation of Scripture* (London: SCM, 1961), pp.37–64.

less cultivated that intelligence, the less formed that judgement, the greater will be the likelihood that the interpreter will impute to the author an opinion that the author never entertained.[60]

In this connection both Bultmann and the new hermeneutic look back to Wilhelm Dilthey, and beyond to Friedrich Schleiermacher.[61] Both the later thinking of Schleiermacher after 1819 and also the earlier thinking as rediscovered by Heinz Kimmerle relate in different ways to the new hermeneutic. At first sight, Fuchs's central concept of *Einverständnis* seems to resonate with the later Schleiermacher's insistence that the modern interpreter must make himself contemporary with the author of a text by attempting imaginatively to relive his experiences. Especially if we follow the translator who rendered *Einverständnis* as "empathy", this looks like Schleiermacher's procedure of entering into the hopes and fears, desires and aims of the author through artistic imagination and rapport.

We have seen, however, that "mutual understanding" in Fuchs operates at a pre-conscious level. It is not primarily, if at all, a matter of psychology, as it may have been in the later thought of Schleiermacher. With Manfred Mezger, Fuchs believes that this psychological approach founders on the existential individuality of the "I" who is each particular interpreter.[62] Thus Mezger asserts that we must find "the new place at which this text, without detriment to its historical individuality, meets us. The short cut by which I picture myself as listener in the skin of Moses or of Paul is certainly popular, but it is not satisfactory, for I am neither the one nor the other" (that is, neither Moses nor Paul).[63] Mezger adds that the way to overcome this problem is "not by treating the particular details with indifference, thus effacing the personal profile of the text, but by becoming aware of the involvement (*Betroffenheit*) which is the same for them as for me, but which is described in a particular way in each instance".[64] He then quotes Fuchs's redoubled warning that the modern listeners "are not the same men to whom the gospel was first proclaimed"; although their concrete situation can nevertheless be "appropriated" today, when the text is accurately translated.[65]

In the earlier writings of Schleiermacher, however, as Kimmerle has shown, hermeneutics are more language-centred, and less orientated towards psychology. Understanding is an *art*, for the particular utterance of a particular author must be understood "in the light of the larger, more universal, linguistic community in which the individual ... finds himself".[66] "Rules" perform only the negative function of preventing false interpretation. Even on a purely linguistic level the subjectivity of the interpreter has a positive role to play. What we understand forms itself into unities made up of parts. In understanding a stretch of language, we need to understand words in order to

---

[60]   B.J.F. Lonergan, op. cit., p.157. A.C. Thiselton, "The Use of Philosophical Categories in New Testament Hermeneutics", *The Churchman* 87 (1973), pp.87–100.

[61]   R.E. Palmer, op. cit., pp.94–6 (cf. F. Schleiermacher, *Hermeneutik und Kritik*, ed. by F. Lücke, p.29).

[62]   E. Fuchs, *Hermeneutik*, p.281 (my italics)

[63]   M. Mezger, "Preparation for Preaching: The Route from Exegesis to Proclamation", loc. cit., p.166 (cf. J.M. Robinson, op. cit., p.59).

[64]   Ibid.

[65]   Ibid., pp.166–7.

[66]   H. Kimmerle, "Hermeneutical Theory or Ontological Hermeneutics", loc. cit., p.109.

understand the sentence; nevertheless our understanding of the force of individual words depends on our understanding of the whole sentence. But this principle must be extended. Our understanding of the sentence contributes to our understanding of the paragraph, of the chapter, of the author as a whole; but this understanding of the whole work in turn qualifies and modifies our understanding of the sentence.

This principle prepares the way for hermeneutics in Heidegger and Gadamer, as well as in Fuchs and Ebeling, and is in fact tantamount to a preliminary formulation of the theory of the hermeneutical circle.[67] It shatters the illusion, as Dilthey later stressed, that understanding a text could be purely "scientific". As Richard Palmer puts it, "Somehow a kind of 'leap' into the hermeneutical circle occurs and we understand the whole and the parts together. Schleiermacher left room for such a factor when he saw understanding as partly a comparative and partly an intuitive and divinatory matter ...".[68]

Still commenting on Schleiermacher but with obvious relevance to Fuchs's notion of *Einverständnis*, Palmer adds, "The hermeneutical circle suggests an area of shared understanding. Since communication is a dialogical relation, there is assumed at the outset a community of meaning shared by the speaker and the hearer. This seems to involve another contradiction: what is to be understood must already be known. But is this not the case? Is it not vain to speak of love to one who has not known love ... ?"[69] Thus we return to Ebeling's comment, "Words produce understanding by appealing to experience and leading to experience. Only where word has already taken place can word take place. Only where there is already previous understanding can understanding take place."[70]

This helps to explain why new hermeneutic inevitably involves problems of philosophy.[71] But it also raises theological questions. In one direction, the New Testament cannot be understood without reference to the interpreter's own experiences of life. Thus Fuchs insists, "*In the interaction of the text with daily life we experience the truth of the New Testament.*"[72] In another direction, it raises questions about the relation between exegesis and systematic theology. For the *total* context of any theological utterance is hardly less than Scripture and the history of its interpretation through tradition. In Heinrich Ott's words on the subject, Scripture as a whole constitutes "the 'linguistic room', the universe of discourse, the linguistic net of co-ordinates in which the church has always resided ... Heidegger says, 'Every poet composed from only a single poem ... None of the individual poems, not even the total of them, says it all. Nevertheless each poem speaks from the whole of the one poem and each time speaks it.'"[73]

---

[67] Cf. M. Heidegger, *An Introduction to Metaphysics* (E.T., New Haven, CT: Yale University Press, 1959, and New York: Anchor edn, 1961), pp.123–38.

[68] R.E. Palmer, op. cit., p.87.

[69] Ibid.

[70] G. Ebeling, *Word and Faith*, p.320.

[71] Ibid., p.317.

[72] E. Fuchs, "The New Testament and the Hermeneutical Problem", p.142 (his italics).

[73] H. Ott, "Systematic Theology and Exegesis", in his essay "What is Systematic Theology?", in J.M. Robinson and J.B. Cobb Jr (eds), *New Frontiers in Theology: I, The Later Heidegger and Theology* (New York, 1963), pp.86 and 87; cf. M. Heidegger, *Unterwegs zur Sprache* (Pfullingen: Neske, 1959, 1960²), pp.37–8.

II.2 The Interpreter and the Text: Understanding and Application

All that has been said about the subjectivity of the interpreter, however, must now be radically qualified by the second of the two major principles at present under discussion. We have already noted Fuchs's assertions that the texts must translate us, before we can translate them, and that the truth has "ourselves" as its object. It is not simply the case that the interpreter, as active subject, scrutinizes the text as passive object. It is not simply that the present experience throws light on the text, but that the text illuminates present experience. Ebeling insists, "*The text ... becomes a hermeneutic aid in the understanding of present experience*".[74] In an important and often-quoted sentence in the same essay he declares (his italics) "*The primary phenomenon in the realm of understanding is not understanding OF language, but understanding THROUGH language.*"[75]

Both Ebeling and especially Gadamer call attention to the parallel between theological and juridical hermeneutics in this respect.[76] The interpretation of legal texts, Gadamer insists, is not simply a "special case" of general hermeneutics, but, rather, reveals the full dimensions of the general hermeneutical problem. In law the interpreter does not examine the text purely as an "object" of antiquarian investigation. The text "speaks" to the present situation in the courtroom, and the interpreter adjusts his own thinking to that of the text. Each of our two principles, in fact, remains equally relevant. On the one hand, the interpreter's own understanding of law and of life guides him in his understanding of the ancient legal texts; on the other hand, that preliminary understanding is modified and moulded, in turn, as the texts themselves deliver their verdicts on the present situation. Even outside the courtroom itself, Ebeling believes that "the man who has no interest in giving legal decisions will be a poor legal historian".[77] Similarly Gadamer asserts, "*Understanding the text is always already applying it*" (my italics).[78]

These two principles operate together in Gadamer's version of *the hermeneutical circle*. We have already noted the idea in Schleiermacher and in Heidegger that we can understand a whole only in the light of its parts, but also that we can understand the parts only in the light of the whole. But Heidegger and especially Gadamer take us a step further.[79] The "circle" of the hermeneutical process begins when the interpreter takes his own preliminary questions to the text. But because his questions may not be the best or most appropriate ones, his understanding of the subject matter of the text may at first remain limited, provisional and even liable to distortion. Nevertheless the text, in turn, speaks back to the hearer: it begins to interpret him; it sheds light on his own situation and on his own questions. His initial questions now undergo revision in the light of the

---

74 G. Ebeling, *Word and Faith*, p.33 (his italics).

75 Ibid., p.318.

76 H.-G. Gadamer, *Wahrheit und Methode*, pp.307–24, especially p.311 ; E.T., 1st edn, pp.289–305 [2nd edn, 1989, 324–41 – Ed.]; cf. G. Ebeling, *Word and Faith*, p.330.

77 G. Ebeling, loc. cit.

78 H.-G. Gadamer, *Wahrheit*, p.291; cf. pp.290–95; English, *Truth*, pp.274–8 [2nd Eng. edn, 1989, pp.307–11 – Ed.].

79 H.-G. Gadamer, *Wahrheit*, pp.250–90, especially 250–61 and 275–90; English, *Truth*, pp.235–74, 235–45, 258–74. Cf. M. Heidegger, *Being and Time* (E.T., Oxford: Blackwell, 1962), pp.188–95.

text itself, and in response to more adequate questioning the text itself now speaks more clearly and intelligibly. The process continues, while the interpreter achieves a progressively deeper understanding of the text.

Walter Wink develops his own particular version of this kind of approach.[80] He criticizes New Testament scholars for failing to interpret the New Testament in accordance with its own purpose, namely "so to interpret the scriptures that the past becomes alive and illumines our present with new possibilities for personal and social transformation".[81] Because of a deliberate suspension of participational involvement, "the outcome of biblical studies in the academy is a trained incapacity to deal with the real problems of actual living persons in their daily lives".[82] The kind of *questions* that New Testament scholars ask, he insists, are not those raised by the text, but those most likely to win a hearing from the professional guild of academics.[83] Scholars seek to silence their own subjectivity, striving for the kind of objective neutrality that is not only an illusion, but which also requires "a sacrifice of the very questions the Bible seeks to answer".[84]

Nevertheless, Wink is not advocating, any more than Fuchs, a suspension of critical studies. In order to hear the New Testament *speak for itself*, and not merely reflect back the interpreter's own ideas or the theology of the modern church, the interpreter must allow critical enquiry first to *distance* a reader from the way in which the text has become embedded in the church's tradition. The text must be heard as "that which stands over against us".[85] Only after this "distance" has first been achieved can there then occur "a communion of horizons" between the interpreter and the text.[86] Thus whilst Wink acknowledges the necessity for "rigorous use of biblical criticism", his primary concern, like that of Fuchs, is "for the rights of the text".[87]

Hans-Georg Gadamer makes some parallel points. Descartes' theory of knowledge, in which man as active subject looks out on the world as passive object, provides only *one* possible model for the apprehension of truth. This model is more appropriate to the "method" of the sciences than to the art of understanding in hermeneutics. There has always been a tradition in philosophy that stressed the connection between understanding and *experience*. For example, Vico, with his sensitivity for history, rejected the narrow intellectualism of Descartes' notion of truth, even in the latter's own lifetime. In ancient times the Greek idea of "wisdom" included practical understanding of life as well as intellectual theory.[88] Later Shaftesbury stressed the role of wit, Reid stressed that of common sense, and Bergson stressed the role of intuitive insight, all as valid ways through which truth could be revealed.[89] It is not simply a matter of discovering

---

80   W. Wink, *The Bible in Human Transformation: Towards a New Paradigm for Biblical Study* (Philadelphia, PA: Fortress, 1973).

81   *Bible*, p.2.

82   *Bible*, p.6.

83   *Bible*, p.10.

84   *Bible*, p.3.

85   *Bible*, p.32.

86   *Bible*, p.66.

87   *Bible*, p.62.

88   H.-G. Gadamer, *Wahrheit und Methode*, pp.17–18; English, *Truth*, 1st edn, pp.20–21 [2nd Eng. edn, pp.22–5 – Ed.].

89   *Wahrheit*, pp.21–4; English, *Truth*, 1st edn, pp.24–6 [Eng., 2nd edn, pp.25–7 – Ed.].

theoretical "methods" by which man can arrive at truth. In true understanding, man is grasped *by* truth through modes of experience.[90] A more adequate model than that provided by Descartes is the experience of truth in a work of art, in which something real and *creative* takes place. We shall refer to Gadamer's comments on this in our third section.

One reason why hermeneutics, according to Gadamer, must take account of something more than cognitive "knowledge" (*Erkenntnis*) is that every interpreter already stands within a historical tradition, which provides him with certain presuppositions or pre-judgements (*Vorurteile*).[91] Gadamer insists, "An individual's prejudgements, much more than his judgements, are the reality of his being (*die geschichtliche Wirklichkeit seines Seins*)."[92] To bring these pre-judgements to conscious awareness is a major goal of hermeneutics, and corresponds to what Walter Wink describes as "distancing". For Gadamer believes that the very existence of a temporal and cultural *distance* between the interpreter and the text can be used to jog him into an awareness of the differences between their respective horizons. The interpreter must cultivate a "hermeneutically trained" awareness, in which he allows the distinctive message of the text to reshape his own questions and concepts.[93]

Once this has been done, the interpreter is free to move beyond his own original horizons, or better, to *enlarge* his own horizons until they come to *merge* or *fuse* with those of the text. His goal is to reach the place at which a merging of horizons (*Horizontverschmelzung*), or fusion of "worlds", occurs.[94] This comes about only through sustained dialogue with the text, in which the interpreter allows his own subjectivity to be challenged and involved. Only in the to-and-fro of question and answer on both sides can the text come to speech (*zur-Sprache-kommen*).[95] Thus in Gadamer's notion of the merging of horizons we find a parallel to Wink's ideas about "fusion" and "communion", and to Fuchs's central category of *Einverständnis*. But this is achieved, as we have seen, only when, first, the interpreter's subjectivity is fully engaged at a more-than-cognitive level; and when, second, the text, and the truth of the text, *actively* grasps *him* as its object.

III
Establishing New "Worlds" in Language: Heidegger and the Parables

To achieve a merging of horizons, or an area of shared understanding amounting to *Einverständnis*, involves in effect the creation of a new "world". In common with Heidegger's philosophy in both the earlier and later periods, Fuchs believes that human persons stand within a linguistic world which is decisively shaped by their own place in history, that is, by their "historicality". But together with the later Heidegger, Fuchs also

---

90   *Wahrheit*, pp.xxvi and 77–105; English, *Truth*, 1st edn, pp.xxv–vi, 73–99 [Eng., 2nd edn, 1989, pp.xxxvi–viii and 81–110 – Ed.].
91   *Wahrheit*, pp.250–61;English, *Truth*, 1st edn, pp.235–45 [Eng., 2nd edn, 1989, pp.265–77 – Ed.].
92   *Wahrheit*, p.261; English, *Truth*, 1st edn, p.245 [2nd edn, 1989, p.277].
93   *Wahrheit*, pp.282–3; English, *Truth*, 1st edn, p.266 [2nd edn, 1989, p.299].
94   *Wahrheit*, pp.288–90; English, *Truth*, 1st edn, pp.270–74 [2nd edn, 1989, pp.286–90].
95   *Wahrheit*, p.345; English, *Truth*, 1st edn, pp.326–7 [2nd edn, 1989, pp.363–4].

looks for a *new* coming-to-speech in which the confines and conventions of the old everyday "world" will be set aside and broken through. The language-event, especially the language-event of the parables of Jesus, corresponds to the establishment of a new world through language.

III.1 Heidegger's Approach to "Worldhood" and Language, and its Appropriation in Fuchs and Ebeling

It is difficult to summarize Heidegger's view in a few paragraphs, but we may note the following major themes.

(1) Humankind is radically conditioned by its place within history, that is, by a radical "historicality". People view objects from the perspective of their own "world". They see things from the point of view of this relation to their own purposes, as if through a kind of grid of egocentric functionalism. A hammer, for example, is not merely a neutral "object" of wood and metal; but a tool which can be used for certain jobs. Thus a hammer is something very different from a broken hammer; although in "neutral" terms of their physical properties the difference would not be very great.[96] Human language reveals, creates and sustains this perspective. Thus in everyday language "time", for example, "has ceased to be anything other than velocity, instantaneousness ... Time as history has vanished from the lives of all peoples."[97]

(2) Humankind has lost touch with genuine reality still further by accepting in intellectual orientation the legacy of Plato's dualism. In Heidegger's words, Western philosophy since Plato has "fallen out of Being".[98] It embodies a split perspective, in which subject becomes separated from object: "Appearance was declared to be mere appearance and thus degraded. At the same time, Being as *idea* was exalted to a supra-sensory realm. A chasm ... was created."[99] Man thus looks out, in the fashion of Plato and Descartes, onto a merely *conceptualized* world, a reality of his own making. He himself, by seeing "reality" through the grid of his own split perspective, becomes the measure of his own knowledge.[100] An example of the evil consequences of this can be seen in the realm of art. Art is divided off into one of the two realms, so that it is *either* a merely "material" thing, in which case it cannot reveal truth; *or* it is conceptualized into "aesthetics" in which case it becomes tamed and emasculated and, once again, unable to reveal truth. By contrast "on the strength of a recaptured, pristine, relation to Being, we must provide the word 'art' with a new content".[101]

(3) The combined effect of these two factors is to lead to circularity and fragmentation in the use of *language*. The truth of language now depends on an artificial correspondence

---

[96] M. Heidegger, *Being and Time*, sect. 15, pp.95–102.

[97] M. Heidegger, *An Introduction to Metaphysics*, p.31.

[98] *Introduction*, p.30.

[99] Ibid., pp.89–90.

[100] Cf. M. Heidegger, *Nietzsche* (2 vols, Pfullingen: Neske, 1961), vol. 2, pp.148–89 (especially on Descartes).

[101] M. Heidegger, *Introduction to Metaphysics*, p.111; cf. *Unterwegs zur Sprache* (Pfullingen: Neske, 1959 and 1960), pp.83–155, especially 86–7; and *Holzwege* (Frankfurt: Klosterman, 1963⁴), pp.7–68. Heidegger's essay "The Origin of a Work of Art", is translated in A. Hofstadter and R. Kuhns (eds), *Philosophies of Art and Beauty* (New York, 1964).

between human concepts and what we suppose to be "reality", but which is in fact another set of our own concepts.[102] For everything which we think and see, we think and see through the medium of our own "linguisticality", or language-conditionedness. Thus, Heidegger concludes, "He [man] is always thrown back on the paths that he himself has laid out; he becomes mired in his paths, caught in the beaten track ... He turns round and round in his own circle."[103]

Fuchs and Ebeling accept the linguistic and hermeneutical problems which Heidegger's diagnosis lays down. Ebeling believes that language has become loosed from its anchorage in reality, to disintegrate into "atoms of speech ... Everything seemed to me to fall into fragments."[104] This has precipitated "a profound crisis of language ... a complete collapse of language".[105] Today "we threaten to die of language poisoning". "With the dawn of the modern age ... the path was clear for an unrestricted development of the mere sign-function of language ... Words are reduced to ciphers ... and syntax to a question of calculus".[106] Language has wrongly become a mere "technical instrument".[107] Yet, Fuchs argues, language and reality are bound so closely together that there can be no "reality" *for us* outside this language.[108]

The solution, if it is a solution, offered by Heidegger, and indirectly by Fuchs, is to put oneself in the place at which language may, once again, give voice not to a fragmented set of human concepts, but to undivided "Being". First, this "Being" is not the substantial "beingness" (*Seiendheit*) of human thought; but the verbal, eventful, temporal Being-which-happens (*Sein* or better, *Anwesen*). Echoing Heidegger, Fuchs declares, "Language ... makes Being into an event".[109] Second, when language is once again pure and creative, Heidegger believes, "the essence of language is found in the act of gathering".[110] Before the advent of Plato's dualism, the word (*logos*) was "the primal gathering principle".[111] Where modern Western culture and its idle talk merely divides and fragments, the pure language of Being integrates and brings together. Thus Fuchs writes, "The proclamation gathers (i.e. into a community) ... and this community has its being, its 'togetherness', in the possibility of its being able to speak the kind of language in which the vent of its community is fulfilled ... *The language of faith brings into language the gathering of faith.*"[112]

Once again this notion of "gathering" approaches the idea of sharing a common "world", or achieving *Einverständnis*. But Heidegger, followed by Fuchs, insists that language can achieve this "gathering" only when humankind accepts the role of *listener*, rather than that of an epistemological subject scrutinizing "objects". For Heidegger, this means a silent, receptive waiting upon Being. Language is the "house" or "custodian" of

[102] M. Heidegger, *Vom Wesen der Wahrheit* (Frankfurt: Klosterman, 1961⁴), pp.6–13; also rp. in *Wegmarken* (Frankfurt: Klosterman, 1967), pp.74–82.

[103] M. Heidegger, *An Introduction to Metaphysics*, p.132.

[104] G. Ebeling, *Introduction to a Theological Theory of Language* (London: SCM, 1973), p.71.

[105] *Introduction*, p.76.

[106] G. Ebeling, *God and Word*, pp.2 and 17.

[107] G. Ebeling, *Introduction to a Theological Theory of Language*, p.127.

[108] E. Fuchs, *Hermeneutik*, pp. 126-34, and *Marburger Hermeneutik*, pp.228–32.

[109] E. Fuchs, *Studies of the Historical Jesus*, p.207.

[110] M. Heidegger, *An Introduction to Metaphysics*, p.145.

[111] *An Introduction*, p.108.

[112] E. Fuchs, *Studies of the Historical Jesus*, pp.208–9 (his italics).

being (*das Haus des Seins … des Anwesens*).[113] Man's task is to find the "place" (*Ort*) at which Being may come to speech.[114] As listeners, whose task is to cultivate a wakeful and receptive openness to Being, Heidegger urges that "we should *do* nothing, but rather wait".[115] The listener must not impose his or her own concepts of reality onto "Being", but should "know how to wait, even for a whole life-time".[116]

Although in principle he is concerned with the Word of God rather than the voice of Being, Fuchs does at times seem to come close to identifying the two. The word of God relates to "the 'meaning' of Being" (*der "Sinn" des Seins*) and comes as the "call of Being" (*der Ruf zum Sein*).[117] Above all humankind "listens" in receptive silence and openness to the text of the New Testament. To be sure, critical analysis, as in Wink's and Gadamer's "distancing", is first necessary as a preliminary. In this way, by active critical scrutiny, the interpreter "must in the *first instance* strike the text dead".[118] But *after* this he must wait for God, or Being, to speak "in the tranquillity of faith, where noise is reduced to silence, a *voice* is heard … It sings out in Phil. 2:6–11 …".[119]

III.2 A Creative Application of this Hermeneutic: The Parables of Jesus

All these principles about language and "world" apply in particular to Fuchs's handling of the parables of Jesus. By means of the image part or picture-half (*Bildhälfte*) of the parable, Jesus creates and enters a "world" which, in the first place, is shared by the hearer. He stands within the hearer's horizons. But everyday conventions and everyday assumptions are then challenged and shattered by the actual message or content-half (*Sachhälfte*). The hearer is challenged at a deep and pre-conceptual level. It is not simply a matter of his assessing certain "ideas" presented to him by Jesus. Rather, "he is drawn over on to God's side and learns to see everything with God's eyes".[120] The parable is both a creative work of *art* and also a *calling* of love, in contrast to flat cognitive discourse. Thus "Jesus draws the hearer over to his side by means of the artistic medium, so that the hearer may think together with Jesus. Is this not the way of true love? Love does not just blurt out. Instead, it provides in advance the sphere in which meeting takes place."[121]

The difference between entering a "world" and merely assessing ideas receives further clarified from Gadamer in his comments on the nature of games and of art. A game creates a special "world" of experience. The player participates in this world, rather than simply observing it, by accepting its rules, its values and its presuppositions. He or she yields himself to them, and *acts* on them. It is not a matter of their consciously carrying them in their mind. Hence the *reality* of a game is something shared by the players in the

---

[113] M. Heidegger, *Unterwegs zur Sprache*, p.267.
[114] *Unterwegs*, p.19.
[115] M. Heidegger, *Gelassenheit* (Pfullingen: Neske, 1959), p.37.
[116] M. Heidegger, *An Introduction to Metaphysics*, p.172.
[117] E. Fuchs, *Hermeneutik*, p.71.
[118] E. Fuchs, *Studies of the Historical Jesus*, p.194 (his italics).
[119] *Studies*, p.192 (his italics); cf. *Hermeneutik*, pp.103–7.
[120] E. Fuchs, *Studies of the Historical Jesus*, p.155.
[121] *Studies*, p.129.

play itself.[122] Such "real-life" experience (*Wirklichkeitserfahrung*) is also involved when one is grasped by a true work of art.[123] It is not a mere set of concepts to be manipulated by a spectator, but a "world" which takes hold of a person as someone who *enters into it*. It is not something presented as a mere object of scrutiny, or source of theoretical concepts.[124]

In his treatment of specific parables, therefore, Fuchs insists that the main point is not simply to convey a conscious "idea". In this sense, he steps away from Jülicher's "one-point" approach. For the "point" or verdict of a parable may come differently to different people. Thus in his work on the Parable of the Unmerciful Servant, Fuchs declares, first, "the parable is not intended to exemplify general ethics".[125] Second, the verdict for Israel is "God is harder than you are"; while the verdict for the Church is "God insists upon his indulgence."[126] If these verdicts, however, are turned into merely conceptual generalizations, the result is only a self-contradiction: God is hard and indulgent.

Three principles are especially important for understanding Fuchs's approach to the parables:

(1) The image-part or picture-half of the parable is not merely an illustrative or homiletical device to make a lesson more vivid or memorable. It is a means of creating a common world in which Jesus and the hearer stand together. When Jesus speaks "of provisional and family life as it takes place in normal times", of the farmer, of the housewife, of the rich and poor or the happy and sad, he is not simply establishing a "point of contact" but standing with the hearer in *his* "world".[127] "We find *existentialia* wherever an understanding between men is disclosed through their having a common world."[128]

(2) Conventional everyday presuppositions about life and "reality" may then be challenged and shattered. This is where Fuchs's approach relates closely to Heidegger's verdict about the circularity and "fallenness" of man's everyday concepts and everyday talk. Something new and creative must break in to rescue him; in this case, the creative word and person of Jesus. Thus in the parable of the Labourers in the Vineyard (Matt. 20:1–16) at first "we too share the inevitable reaction of the first. The first see that the last receive a whole day's wage, and naturally they hope for a higher rate for themselves."[129] But then comes the shock: "in fact they receive the same ... It seems to them that the lord's action is unjust." Finally comes the verdict on the assumption that has been brought to light: "Is your eye evil because I am kind?" The word of Jesus thus "singles out the individual and grasps him deep down". For the hearer, by entering the world of the parable, has been drawn into an *engagement* with the verdict of Jesus: "The parable effects

---

[122] H.-G. Gadamer, op. cit., p.100; cf. pp.97–115 (E.T., pp.94, 91–108).
[123] Ibid., pp.66–96 (E.T., pp.63–90).
[124] Ibid., p.98 (E.T., p.92); cf. A.C. Thiselton, "The Parables as Language-Event", loc. cit., pp.442–5.
[125] E. Fuchs, "The Parable of the Unmerciful Servant", *Studia Evangelica* (Berlin: Berlin Academy, 1959), p.487.
[126] "The Parable", p.493; cf. pp.487–94, and *Studies of the Historical Jesus*, pp.152–3.
[127] E. Fuchs, "The New Testament and the Hermeneutical Problem", loc. cit., p.126.
[128] E. Fuchs, *Studies of the Historical Jesus*, p.97; cf. *Marburger Hermeneutik*, pp.171–81.
[129] E. Fuchs, *Studies of the Historical Jesus*, p.33; cf. pp.32–8 and 154–6.

and demands our decision." It is *not* simply "the pallid requirement that sinful man should believe in God's kindness. Instead it contains, in a concrete way ... Jesus' *pledge*". Jesus pledges himself to "those who, in face of a cry of 'guilty', nevertheless found their hope on an act of God's kindness".[130]

The creative language-event, therefore, shatters the mould imposed by man's "linguisticality". Even ordinary life, Fuchs suggests, can provide a model of this occurrence: "A new observation can throw all our previous mental images into confusion ... What has already been observed and preserved in mental images comes into conflict with what is newly observed."[131] This conflict, this clash, demands a decision and reorientation. Robert Funk illustrates this principle with reference to the parable of the Prodigal Son (Luke 15:11–32). The "righteous" people find themselves in the "world" of the elder brother, endorsing his conventional ideas of justice and obligation. "Sinners" participate in the "world" experienced by the prodigal son. Funk writes, "The word of grace and the deed of grace divide the audience into younger sons and elder sons – into sinners and Pharisees. This is what Ernst Fuchs means when he says that one does not interpret the parables; the parables interpret him. *The Pharisees are those who insist on interpreting the word of grace, rather than letting themselves be interpreted by it.*"[132] The judges find themselves judged. Sinners find themselves welcomed: "It is man and not God who is on trial."[133] The same principle operates in the parable of the Great Supper (Matt. 22:2–10; cf. Luke 14:16–24). One group is excluded; the other, embraced: "Each hearer is drawn into the tale as he wills."[134]

Walter Wink applies this approach to the interpretation of the parable of the Pharisee and the Publican (Luke 18:9–14). Most of Jesus' own hearers would at first identify themselves with the Pharisee as the hearer of religious and social status; but "then suffer shock and consternation at the wholly unexpected justification of the publican".[135] This of course raises a major hermeneutical problem, to which both Fuchs and Wink are eager to call attention. The *modern* reader already knows that it is the *Pharisee* who will be condemned. Hence nowadays "a simple descriptive approach wrecks the parable".[136] It must come to speech anew, and not merely be "repeated". For the ending of the parable has now in turn become embedded in the conventional judgements of "religious" man, from which the language-event is meant to free us!

(3) There is not sufficient space to comment adequately on the importance of Christology for Fuchs's understanding of the parables. We must note, however, that he stresses this aspect with special reference to the oneness of word and deed in the ministry of Jesus, and also to the status and role of Jesus as one who pronounces God's words in God's stead. God is present in the word of Jesus. Moreover, since Jesus enters the common world of understanding experienced by the hearer, the hearer makes his response to

---

130   Ibid., pp.33–7.
131   E. Fuchs, "Proclamation and Speech Event", loc. cit., p.349.
132   R.W. Funk, *Language, Hermeneutic and Word of God* (New York, 1966), pp.16–17 (his italics).
133   *Language*, p.17.
134   *Language*, p.192; cf. pp.124–222.
135   W. Wink, *Bible*, p.42.
136   *Bible*, p.43.

God's word "together with" Jesus. Thus in the parable of the Labourers in the Vineyard, Fuchs declares, "Jesus acted in a very real way as God's representative" especially in "his conduct ... and proclamation". Jesus gives us "to understand his conduct as God's conduct ... Jesus' proclamation ... went along with his conduct". Finally, if I respond in faith, "I am not only near to Jesus; in faith I await the occurrence of God's kindness together with Jesus."[137] Similarly, in the Parable of the Unmerciful Servant, "God accepted the conduct of Jesus as a valid expression of his will." The hearer "lets Jesus guide him to the mercy of God"; "Jesus does not give a new law, but substitutes himself for the law."[138]

This means that as Jesus stands "together with" the hearer, he becomes in some sense, a model for faith. For as the hearer, through the language-event, enters the "world" of Jesus, he finds a new vision of God and of the world which he shares with Jesus. For Fuchs this means especially the abandonment of self-assertion, even to the point of death, which is the repetition of Jesus' own decision to go the way of the cross and way of love:[139] "To have faith in Jesus now means essentially to repeat Jesus' decision."[140] This is why the new hermeneutic has definite connections with the new quest of the historical Jesus. Fuchs writes, "In the proclamation of the resurrection the historical Jesus himself *has* come to us. The so-called Christ of faith is none other than the historical Jesus ... God himself, *wants to be encountered* by us in the historical Jesus."[141] If the message of Jesus is to come-to-speech creatively and as a liberating language-event, this presupposes some kind of continuity between his words and his life. Ebeling similarly concludes, "The kerygma ... is not merely speech about man's existence. It is also a testimony to that which has happened."[142]

IV
Some Creative Contributions and Cautious Caveats

(1) The new hermeneutic constructively addresses the problem of how the interpreter may understand the text of the New Testament more *deeply* and more *creatively*. This should not be underestimated. However, Fuchs and Ebeling are *less concerned about how we may understand it "correctly"*. Admittedly they insist on the need for historical-critical study, but rightly or wrongly we receive the impression that this is mainly a preliminary to the real task of hermeneutics, which is left behind. Fuchs and Ebeling are looking at *one* side, albeit an unduly neglected and important side, of a two-sided problem. Rather than simply "first" using critical methods, is it not possible *both* to "listen" to the text as subject, and also *alongside this* critically to test one's understanding of it? May not both attitudes be called into play successively and repeatedly as if in dialogue?

---

[137] E. Fuchs, *Studies of the Historical Jesus*, pp.46–8 (his italics).
[138] E. Fuchs, "The Parable of the Unmerciful Servant", loc. cit., pp.491–2.
[139] E. Fuchs, *Studies of the Historical Jesus*, pp.80–82.
[140] *Studies*, p.28.
[141] *Studies*, pp.30–31 (Fuchs's italics).
[142] G. Ebeling, *Theology and Proclamation*, p.38; cf. pp.32–81, which provide a response to Bultmann.

Some may suggest, by way of reply, that this would necessarily surrender the vision of wholeness in exchange for a split "conceptualizing" perspective in which the text becomes once again, a mere "object" of scrutiny. But whilst we may accept the warnings of Heidegger and Gadamer that the subject–object "method" of Descartes is not always adequate, nevertheless conceptualizing thinking must be given *some* place in hermeneutics. Commenting on Heidegger's notion of openness to the call of Being, Hans Jonas points out that *thinking* "is precisely an effort not to be at the mercy of fate".[143] To surrender one's own initiative in thinking in exchange for a mere "listening" is precisely *not* to escape from one's own conditionedness by history and language, but is to make everything "a matter of the chance factor of the historical generation I was born into".[144] Theologians, Jonas concludes, have been too easily seduced by the pseudo-humility of Heidegger's orientation. The Christian has been delivered from the power of fate, and must use his mind to distinguish the true from the false.

We have already seen that Heidegger, and presumably Fuchs, would regard this as a misunderstanding and short-circuiting of the whole problem of human "linguisticality". Subject–object thinking, they believe, as well as distancing us from reality also sets in motion a vicious circularity by evaluating one set of human concepts in terms of another. But the New Testament itself, especially Paul, seems to be less pessimistic than Heidegger about the use of reason or "mind" (*nous*). In this respect Heidegger stands nearer to the sheer non-rationality of Zen Buddhism. After reading a work of Suzuki's, Heidegger declared, "This is what I have been trying to say in all my writings."[145] Moreover the actual practical difficulties of trying to distinguish between the true and the false in "non-objectifying" language are insuperable. Paul van Buren, for example, has exposed these problems in his discussion of Heinrich Ott.[146]

Further, in spite of its over-emphatic character, there is some justice in the verdict of J.C. Weber when he insists that in Fuchs's thought, "There can be no basis for distinguishing the language of the word of God and the language of Being ... In what way can we know that language does not bring to expression illusion, falsehood, or even chaos? If the criterion of truth is only in the language-event itself, how can the language-event be safeguarded against delusion, mockery, or utter triviality? Why cannot the language-event be a disguised event of nothingness? ... Fuchs's ontology is in danger of dissolving into a psychological illusionism."[147]

(2) *The new hermeneutic is also one-sided in its use of the New Testament and in its relation to the New Testament message.* To begin with, large areas of the New Testament are explicitly concerned with rational argumentation and with the elucidation of theological concepts. Bornkamm, among others, has drawn attention to the role of reasoned argument in Paul,

---

[143] J. Jonas in *The Review of Metaphysics* 18 (1964), p.216; cf. pp.207–33.

[144] Ibid.

[145] Quoted by W. Barrett, "Zen for the West", in N.W. Ross (ed.), *The World of Zen. An East-West Anthology* (London, 1962), p.344; cf. p.284 and D.T. Suzuki, "Satori, or Acquiring a New Viewpoint", ibid., pp.41–7.

[146] P. van Buren, *Theological Explorations* (London: SCM, 1968), pp.81–105.

[147] J.C. Weber, "Language-Event and Christian Faith", in *Theology Today* 21 (1965), p.455; cf. pp.448–57.

and Hebrews also invites consideration in this respect.[148] However, the approach of Fuchs and Ebeling better fits such language-categories as hymns, poems, metaphors and parables. It is no accident that Fuchs tends to concentrate his attention on the parables, and also on such passages as 1 Cor. 13 and Phil. 2:5–11. This seems to confirm our claim that the new hermeneutic is one-sided. It is tempting to wonder whether if Fuchs were still pastor to a congregation, they would find themselves confronted regularly by the same kinds of passages. This is partly, too, because Fuchs tends to see the "translated" message of the New Testament itself in over-selective terms. In the end, almost everything in the New Testament can be translated into a call to love, or into a call to abandon self-assertion.

The problem for the new hermeneutic, however, is not only that certain parts of the New Testament take the form of cognitive discourse; it is also that it is frequently addressed to those who *already believe*, and often spoken out of an already existing theological *tradition* in the context of the historical community of the church. But tradition, even *within* the New Testament, is for Fuchs a factor that tends to obscure, rather than clarify, the original proclamation of Jesus, which he directed to *unbelievers*. Just as Heidegger wishes to step back "behind" the conceptualizing tradition of Western philosophy, so Fuchs wishes to step back "behind" the tradition of the primitive church.

The consequences of such a move can be seen most clearly in Fuchs's handling of the resurrection of Christ. This may never be seen as a past historical event known on the basis of apostolic testimony. Like Bultmann, Fuchs sees it simply as expressing the positive value of the cross; as expressing, exhaustively and without historical remainder, Jesus' abandonment of self-assertion in the death of the cross. In his attempt to support such a view, Fuchs even claims (in parallel with Bultmann) that Paul made a mistake in 1 Cor. 15:5–8, being driven to ground the resurrection in history only by the exigency of a polemic against the Corinthians.[149] Fuchs can find no room in his hermeneutic for tradition, the church, or history after the event of the cross. The issue is put sharply by P. J. Achtemeier: "The church itself could, and did, become a historical 'security' for faith, thus robbing faith of its announcement of the danger of all such security … In this way … the new hermeneutic attempts to defend a view of faith based on some portions of the New Testament from a view of faith based on other portions".[150]

Once again, however, these difficulties should not blind us to the positive insights of the new hermeneutic where they occur. Fuchs does make some valid comments on the hermeneutics of the epistles; and from this kind of viewpoint Robert Funk offers some very valuable insights on 1 Cor. 2:2–16 and especially on "Second Corinthians as Hermeneutic". He sees this epistle as "a re-presentation of the Kerygma in language that speaks to the controversy in which (Paul) is engaged".[151] The main contribution of the new hermeneutic, however, concerns the parables of Jesus, and here, although many

---

[148] Cf. G. Bornkamm, "Faith and Reason in Paul", in *Early Christian Experience* (London: SCM, 1969), pp.29–46.

[149] Cf. E. Fuchs, *Marburger Hermeneutik*, pp.123–34 and *Glauben und Erfahrung*, p.216.

[150] P.J. Achtemeier, *Introduction*, pp.156–7 and 162.

[151] R.W. Funk in J.M. Robinson and J.B. Cobb (eds), *New Frontiers II, The New Hermeneutic*, p.168; cf. pp.164–97; cf. also *Language Hermeneutic and Word of God*, pp.275–305.

criticisms about exegetical details could be made, the suggestiveness and value of the general approach is clear.

(3) Just as it represents a one-sided approach to the hermeneutical task and also a one-sided use of the New Testament, *the new hermeneutic further embodies a one-sided view of the nature of language*. This shows itself in two ways.

First, like Heidegger whom they follow here, Fuchs and Ebeling fail to grasp that language functions on the basis of convention, and is not in fact "reality" or Being itself. Whilst language admittedly determines, or at least shapes, the way in which reality is perceived and organized in relation to a language-community, effective language-activity presupposes "rules" or conventions accepted by that community. It is an established principle not only of Korzybski's "general semantics", but also of general linguistics since Saussure, that the word is not the thing. Saussure himself described *"l'arbitraire du signe"* as the first principle of language study, and the point is discussed in the chapter on semantics.[152] Opaqueness in vocabulary, polysemy or multiple meaning, change in language, and the use of different words for the same object in different languages, all underline the conventionality of language. By contrast the attitude of Fuchs and Ebeling comes too close to that which has been described as the belief in "word-magic". Their view is sometimes found especially among primitive peoples. Malinowski comments, "The word ... has a power of its own; it is a means of bringing things about; it is a handle to acts and objects, not a definition of them ... The word gives power."[153] Heidegger, of course, would not be embarrassed that such an outlook is primitive; he is concerned with "primal" language.[154] But this does not avoid the problem when Ebeling writes that a language-event is not "mere speech" but "an event in which *God himself is communicated*".[155]

This is *not* to say that we should reject Ebeling's contrast between a word that speaks *about* reconciliation and a word which actually *reconciles*; between speaking *about* a call and actually *calling*. But in two articles I have tried to show that the sense in which "saying makes it so", is best explained in terms of performative language, and not in terms of word-magic.[156] Furthermore, it should be stressed that, in spite of any appearances to the contrary, Fuchs and Ebeling base their approach on a particular view of language, not on some affirmation of faith about the "power" of God's word.

Second, the new hermeneutic has a one-sided concern with imperatival, conative, directive language, as over against the language of description or information. Ebeling

---

[152] Ferdinand de Saussure, *Cours de linguistique générale* (edn. Critique par R. Engler, Wiesbaden: Harrasowitz, 1967), pp.146–57. Cf. J. Lyons, *Introduction to Theoretical Linguistics* (Cambridge: CUP, 1968), pp.4–8, 38, 59–70, 74–5, 272 and 403; S. Ullmann, *Semantics: An Introduction to the Science of Meaning* (Oxford: Blackwell, 1958[2]), pp.80–115; and A.C. Thiselton, "The Supposed Power of Words in the Biblical Writings", in *JTS* 25 (1974), pp.283–99.

[153] B. Malinowski, "The Problem of Meaning in Primitive Languages", in C.K. Ogden and I.A. Richards (eds), *The Meaning of Meaning* (London: Routledge, 1964[8]), pp.489–90.

[154] Cf. M. Heidegger, *Existence and Being* (London: Vision Press, 1968[3]), pp.291–315, *Wegmarken*, pp.74–82; and *Unterwegs zur Sprache*, thoughout.

[155] G. Ebeling, *The Nature of Faith*, pp.87 and 813 (my italics).

[156] A.C. Thiselton, "The Supposed Power of Words" (1974) and "The Parables as Language-Event" (1970).

writes, "We do not get at the nature of words by asking what they contain, but by asking what they effect, what they set going."[157] "The basic structure of word is therefore not statement ... but appraisal, certainly not in the colourless sense of information, but in the pregnant sense of participation and communication".[158] Here it is important to see exactly what we are criticizing. We are *not* criticizing his concern with function, with communication, with self-involvement. We welcome this. But it is false to make two exclusive *alternatives* out of this, as if description somehow undermined other functions of language. Indeed in my article on the parables as language-event, I have argued in detail, first, that not all descriptive propositions function in the same way (some may be open-ended); and second, that, in Austin's words, "for a certain performative utterance to be happy, certain statements have to be *true* ".[159] Amos Wilder presses this kind of point in a different way. He writes, "Fuchs refuses to define the content of faith ... He is afraid of the word as convention or as a means of conveying information ... Fuchs carries this so far that revelation, as it were, reveals nothing ... Jesus calls, indeed, for decision ... But surely his words, deed, presence, person, and message rested ... upon dogma, eschatological and theocratic".[160]

(4) There is some force in the criticism that the new hermeneutic lets "what is true *for me*" become the criterion of "what is true", and that *its orientation towards the interpreter's subjectivity transposes theology too often into a doctrine of humankind.* We have noted Fuchs's comment that he proposes "a more radical existential interpretation" than even Bultmann. The hermeneutical task, he writes, is "the interpretation of *our own existence ...* We should accept as *true* only that which we acknowledge *as valid for our own person.*"[161] At the same time, we should also note that there is another qualifying emphasis in Fuchs. He insists, "Christian faith means to speak of God's act, not of ... acts of man".[162]

Some conservative theologians believe that we are drawn into a human-centred relativism if we accept either the notion of the hermeneutical circle, or Fuchs's idea of "self-understanding" (*Selbstverständnis*). Thus J.W. Montgomery calls for "the rejection of contemporary theology's so-called hermeneutical circle".[163] He writes "The preacher must not make the appalling mistake of thinking, as do followers of Bultmann and post-Bultmann new hermeneutic, that the text and one's own experience enter into a relationship of mutuality ... To bind text and exegete into a circle is not only to put all theology and preaching into the orbit of anthropocentric sinfulness, but also to remove the very possibility of a 'more sure word of prophecy' than the vagueness of men."[164]

---

[157]   G. Ebeling, *The Nature of Faith*, p.187.

[158]   G. Ebeling, *Word and Faith*, p.326.

[159]   J.L. Austin, *How to Do Things with Words* (Oxford: Clarendon Press, 1962), p.45 (his italics); cf. A.C. Thiselton, "The Parables as Language-Event", loc. cit., p.438.

[160]   A.N. Wilder, "The Word as Address and Meaning", in J.M. Robinson and J.B. Cobb Jr (eds), *The New Hermeneutic*, p.213.

[161]   E. Fuchs, "The New Testament and the Hermeneutical Problem", in *The New Hermeneutic*, p.117 (my italics).

[162]   "The Hermeneutical Problem", p.114.

[163]   J.W. Montgomery, "An Exhortation to Exhorters", in *Christianity Today* 17 (1973), p.606; cf. also his essay in C.F.H. Henry (ed.), *Jesus of Nazareth Saviour and Lord* (London: Tyndale Press, 1966), pp.231–6.

[164]   Ibid.

The problem formulated by Montgomery, however, turns on epistemology, or the theory of understanding, and not upon theological considerations alone. To begin with, there are some areas of discussion in which it is possible to distinguish between "Scripture" and "interpretation of Scripture", and others in which it is not. We can and must distinguish between the two, for example, when we are discussing questions about theological method *in principle* and at a formal level. As Ebeling points out, this was important in the Reformation and for Luther. But as soon as we begin to consider a *particular text*, every way of understanding it constitutes an act of interpretation that is related to the experience of the interpreter. This is clear, for example, when we look back on Luther's handling of specific texts. On this level, it is simply philosophically naïve to imply that some interpreters can have access to a self-evidently "true" meaning as over against their interpretation of it. Moreover, the interpreter's understanding, as Gadamer rightly insists, is a *progressive* one. In the words of Heinrich Ott, "There is no final black-and-white distinction between 'having understood' and 'not having understood' ... Understanding by its very nature takes place at different levels."[165]

The interpreter is partly in the position of students confronted with a new textbook on a new subject. At first their preliminary understanding of the subject-matter is disjointed and fragmentary, not least because they do not yet know how to question the text appropriately. Gradually, however, the text itself suggests appropriate questions, and their more mature approach to it brings greater understanding. At the same time, the parts and the whole begin to illuminate one another. But in all this interpreters are not merely active subjects scrutinizing a passive object. The text "speaks" to them as its object, moulding their own questions. The notion of the hermeneutical circle is not, then, a sell-out to human-centred relativism, but a way of describing the *process of understanding* in the interpretation of a text.

The problem of "self-understanding" is often misunderstood. It does not simply mean a person's conscious understanding of oneself, but his or her grasp of the possibilities of being, in the context of their "world". It concerns, therefore, their *way of reacting* to life or to reality or to God, and not merely their opinions about themselves.[166] In one sense, therefore, it is less human-centred than is often supposed. As Ebeling's writes, "When God speaks, *the whole of reality as it concerns us* enters language anew."[167] In another sense, however, it is true that a preoccupation with self-understanding may narrow and restrict the attention of the interpreter away from a wider theological and cosmic perspective. Indeed this underlines precisely the problem of one-sidedness that we have noted in connection with the task of hermeneutics, with the use of the New Testament, and with language. We noted, for example, that Fuchs fails to do full justice to the resurrection of Christ.

(5) *The new hermeneutic is concerned above all with the "rights" of the text*, as over against concepts which the interpreters may try to bring with them and impose upon it. A

---

[165] H. Ott, "What is Systematic Theology?", in J.M. Robinson and J. Cobb (eds), *New Frontiers in Theology I, The Later Heidegger and Theology*, p.80.

[166] Cf. E. Fuchs, *Marburger Hermeneutik*, pp.20 and 41–7.

[167] G. Ebeling, *The Nature of Faith*, p.190.

"subject–object" scrutiny of the text which takes no account of man's linguisticality *tends to tame and to domesticate the word of God*, so that it merely echoes back the interpreter's own perspectives. By contrast, the text should challenge readers, judge them, and "speak" to them in its otherness. But in order that this word may be understood and "strike home", there must also be a common "world", an *Einverständnis*, in which the horizons of the text become fused with those of the interpreter.

Further strengths and weaknesses appear when we set the new hermeneutic in the wider context of literary interpretation, of art, and even of educational theory. In the world of literature, for example, Susan Sontag argues that "interpretation" as a self-conscious cognitive activity impoverishes, tames and distorts, a literary creation, when "Interpretation makes it manageable, comfortable." Instead of interpreting literature we ought simply "to show *how* it is what it is".[168] In the same vein, R.E. Palmer observes a positive attempt "to transcend the subject–object schema" in the French phenomenological literary criticism of Blanchot, Richard and Bachelard, and in the phenomenological philosophy of Ricoeur or Merleau-Ponty.[169] In the realm of art one could cite the work of Adolph Gottlieb. In education theory it is possible to see both gains and losses in the move away from concerns about "knowledge" and "information", in exchange for an emphasis on participation, engagement and "experience". Pupils will gain from attempts to help them to understand in terms of their own life-experiences; but they may well lose out, as less emphasis comes to be laid on the "content" part of instruction.

We claim that *both* aspects remain important for New Testament interpretation, but that at present there may be more danger of neglecting the new hermeneutic than of pressing its claims too far. Although it would be wrong to reduce its lessons simply to a few maxims for preachers, nevertheless it has something to say about preaching and basic Bible study. For example, it calls attention to the difference between talking about the *concept* of reconciliation or the *concept* of joy, and on the other hand so proclaiming the word of Christ that someone *experiences* joy or reconciliation, even if these concepts are never mentioned. The preacher must concern himself with what his words effect and bring about, rather than simply with what concepts they convey. The Gospel must not merely be spoken and repeated; it must also be *communicated*. Similarly in Bible study students are not only concerned with "facts" and information, but with verdicts on themselves. Moreover as they "listen" to the text they will not be content only to use stereotyped sets of questions composed by others, but will engage in a *continuous* dialogue of question and answer, until their own original horizons become creatively enlarged.

The "otherness" of the New Testament must not be tamed and domesticated in such a way that its message becomes merely a set of predictable religious "truths". Through the text of the New Testament, the word of God is to be encountered as an attack, a judgement, on any way of seeing the world that, in Fuchs's phrase, is not "seeing with

---

[168] S. Sontag, "Against Interpretation", reprinted in D. Lodge (ed.), *Twentieth Century Literary Criticism* (London, 1972), pp.656 and 660; cf. pp.652–9.

[169] R.E. Palmer, *Hermeneutics*, p.246.

God's eyes". The hermeneutical task is a genuine and valid one. Two sets of horizons must be brought together, those of the text and those of the modern interpreter; and this must be done at a more than merely conceptual level. Few questions can be more important than that asked by Fuchs, namely how the text of the New Testament, written in the ancient world, can come alive in such a way as to *strike home* in the present.

CHAPTER TWENTY-SEVEN

Reader-Response Theory is Not One Thing: "Types of Reader-Response Theory" (1992)

I discuss reader-response theory in more than one place, and first in The Responsibility of Hermeneutics *(1985), where I could call upon the literary expertise of my two American collaborators, Roger Lundin and Clare Walhout. Yet I remained discontent with this first survey, in which I was uncertain about how reader-response related to more traditional methods of historical reconstruction. Almost ten years later it had become increasingly clear to me that no single uniform assessment of this approach could be made. First, whether this approach is appropriate depends on the genre of texts in question. Second, differences of approach within reader-response theory seem greater than those between more traditional approaches and more moderate reader-response theories. Third, whether "readers" denote a local community, a broad multiform tradition, or a narrowly individualist "autobiographical criticism" splits apart even further what reader-response theory entails. Thus "Reader Response Theory is Not One Thing".*

In the event I urge that where appropriate settings and genre apply, the theories represented by Iser and Eco assist us to focus on the active role of the reader, as Jesus does through his parables. By contrast, the radical stance of Stanley Fish ends up with a postmodern neo-pragmatism akin to that of Rorty. This approach robs texts of the power to confront a community with a critique that is external, and also rests on some misperceptions about the nature of language, including some that Wittgenstein had addressed. This material is drawn from New Horizons in Hermeneutics *(1992), but with several omissions from the earlier text to avoid undue length for an extract of this kind.*

Reader-response theories call attention to *the active role of communities of readers* in constructing what counts for them as "what the text means". From the point of view of biblical interpretation a potentially positive contribution is offered by any theoretical hermeneutical model that places an emphasis on *the role of readers as participatory and active.* Some reader-response theorists, most notably Wolfgang Iser, draw on a theory of perception to establish the role of readers in *filling in or completing* a textual meaning which would otherwise remain only potential rather than actual. In theological terms, such a theory seems to cohere with expectations that reading the biblical text should constitute not an exercise for passive spectators, but *an eventful, active and creative process.*

Nevertheless reader-response theories also embrace a wide variety of theoretical assumptions. Some raise acute philosophical difficulties about the role of the communication of *knowledge* in transmissive or communicative texts, and the capacity of texts to shape or to transform the expectations of readers *from outside* their community. They invite the possible collapse of critical or socio-critical interpretation into *social-pragmatic* reading which serves only to affirm *prior community norms.* The most polemical and radical statement of a socio-pragmatic context-relative reader-response theory comes from the pen of Stanley Fish.

Fish is unsuccessful in his attempt to ground his context-relative literary theory in an adequate or convincing philosophy of language. I shall argue that if "meaning" is subsumed within the prior horizons of the reading community, we no longer stand where, with Gadamer, we construe engagements between readers and texts as interaction *between two horizons, each of which is first to be respected* before a move toward a fusion of these two horizons can take place.

Moreover, Fish's recent counter-arguments against standard criticisms of his work depend on *an undue polarization between formalist and anti-formalist philosophies of language.* The thrust of his essay "Going Down the Anti-Formalist Road" (1989) entirely misses the points made by Wittgenstein about concepts with blurred edges, family resemblances and the common behaviour of humankind.[1] Wittgenstein in effect *rejects* Fish's artificial alternative that *either* we have a formal system (like the *Tractatus*) *or* there are no interpenetrating or overlapping regularities of a stable nature which transcend the boundaries of a single language-game or context-relative social community. The supposed alternative of *either* formal system *or* social relativism without trans-contextual critique is a false one.

Before we turn to Fish's philosophy of language and its negative consequences for biblical interpretation, we may first survey theories of reader-response that are less sweeping and more modest in their claims. We commence with the moderate theory of Wolfgang Iser. Stanley Fish attacks Iser on grounds of inconsistency; but Iser's angle of approach has stimulated some creative reflection in biblical studies. Fish's provocative onslaught on Iser appears in his essay "Why No One's Afraid of Wolfgang Iser", reprinted in his volume *Doing What Comes Naturally.*[2]

I
Wolfgang Iser's Theory of Reader-Interaction, and its Uses in Biblical Studies

The philosophical background to Wolfgang Iser's literary theory is drawn partly from Roman Ingarden, who was a disciple of Husserl. Susan Wittig, Jouette Bassler, James Resseguie and Robert Fowler, among others, have explored its significance for biblical interpretation. Following Ingarden, Iser pointed out that objects of perception are not perceived by the consciousness of the human subject exhaustively, but *in terms of those aspects which are presented.* A measure of *incompleteness* is involved in all perception. The perceiving subject "fills in" what is missing by *construing* what is not "given" in Husserl's phenomenological consciousness.

Ingarden expanded this model of "filling out a schema". The clearest example in theories of aspective perception is that of perceiving in a three-dimensional object. We do not "see" the back or all the sides of the object; but we *construe* what lies beyond

---

[1] Stanley Fish, "Going Down the Anti-Formalist Road", in *Doing What Comes Naturally.*
[2] Stanley Fish, "Why No One's Afraid of Wolfgang Iser", in ibid., pp.68–86.

immediate perception. Iser pointed out that this principle applies and can even be extended in literary narrative. The text often does not specify whether an object has certain properties (for example, whether a table is wooden or plastic, or has three or four legs) but we regularly "fill in" what we *presuppose* and *construe*. The notion of the reader's activity in "filling in *blanks*" in the text becomes a central theme in Iser's theory.

Iser draws from Ingarden the notion that the reader "*actualizes*" and "*concretizes*" dimensions of meaning that are otherwise only *potential* rather than actual. Iser writes, "Effects and responses are properties neither of the text nor of the reader; the text represents a potential effect that is realized in the reading process."[3] While reading-processes entail the *reorganization* or "grouping" of "thought-systems" invoked by the text, the literary work remains for Iser a potentially communicative act. It impinges on the extra-linguistic world. To describe the reading process is to bring to light "operations which the text activates within the reader".[4] These utilize the reader's imagination, perceptions and capacity both to "assemble" and to "adjust and even differentiate his own focus".[5]

Even more fundamentally, Iser distinguishes explicitly between a theory of reader-response, which "has its roots in the text", and a "theory of reception" which arises from a history of readers' judgements. Thus, unlike the later Fish, he does not question the "givenness" of stable constraints in textual meaning, but underlines their potential and indeterminate status independent of actualization by the reading process. Iser first formulated his notion of indeterminacy and potentiality in 1970 (English edn, 1971).[6] "*Actualization*" is the result of "interaction" between the text and the reader.[7]

Iser concedes that interpretative codes will inevitably reflect something of a reader's own culture: this historically conditioned reader is the "real" reader. By contrast, the technical category of "the ideal reader" would need "to have an identical code to that of the author ... The ideal reader would also have to share the intentions underlying this process."[8] Such a reader, however, remains *hypothetically* "ideal" rather than empirically actual, because this person would thus in principle grasp the textual meaning *exhaustively and without remainder*. He or she is therefore a fictional being. The best that we can seek is literary or reading "competence", which will allow the reader's role to be performed, but in different ways. Iser calls the construct of this typified "competent" reader "the implied reader".[9]

On matter of detail Iser distinguishes his position from that of Ingarden, but stipulates that his own concept of "the *blank*" designates "a vacancy in the overall system of the text, the filling of which brings about an interaction of textual patterns". Part of the

---

[3] Wolfgang Iser, *The Act of Reading: A Theory of Aesthetic Response* (Baltimore, MD and London: Johns Hopkins University Press, 1978 and 1980), p.ix.

[4] Ibid.

[5] Ibid., p.x.

[6] Wolfgang Iser, "Indeterminacy and the Reader's Response in Prose Fiction", in J. Hillis Miller (ed.), *Aspects of Narrative: Selected Papers from the English Institute* (New York: Columbia University Press, 1971), pp.1–45.

[7] Wolfgang Iser, *The Act of Reading*, p.21.

[8] Ibid., p.29.

[9] Ibid., p.38.

"completion", for Iser, involves the building up and establishing of "connections" between different segments of the text. Throughout his long chapter on "How Acts of Constitution Are Stimulated" Iser explores two axes of interaction: the possibility of infinite polyvalence is to be "narrowed down" by an appropriate reading competence which is aware of textual features such as interconnections and code; on the other hand, his theory sees the text–reader interaction as "the productive matrix which enables the text to be meaningful in a variety of different contexts".[10] Helpfully, Iser stresses the "narrowing down" aspect with reference especially to "*expository* texts", and the "productive matrix" aspect especially in relation to "*literary*" texts.[11]

Attempts have been made by several writers to apply this model of the actualization of what is potential to specific biblical texts. In *Semeia* 9 (1977), devoted to "polyvalent narration", Susan Wittig explores the semiotic perspectives offered by C.S. Peirce and by Charles Morris, noting the role of Morris's pragmatic or "rhetorical" axis between sender and receiver.[12] Polyvalence, she argues, is generated first by different perspectives on the part of successive receivers; second, by multiple codes which produce multiple significations, and third, by interactive relations between more than one semiotic system. A parable draws together in polyvalent tension the referential or "literal" semiotic system of the everyday world and the system contributed by the reader who becomes co-author with the text of a "duplex connotative system".[13]

The first and longer part of Susan Wittig's argument draws on semiotic theory. But then she turns to the phenomenology of the act of reading, and at this point takes up the approach of Wolfgang Iser. She observes, "The lack of syntactic or semiotic connections and the omission of detail ... invite the reader to establish his own connections... when the text does not offer it".[14] She considers as an example the opening of the parable of the Prodigal Son (Luke 15:11). The dimensions of "application" or metaphorical extension are "unstated". But this coheres, she argues, with the *purpose* of such a parable. This purpose is "not to create one particular meaning, but *to create the conditions under which the creation of meaning can be defined and examined by each perceiver*" (her italics).[15] In other words, the parable exposes self-knowledge, because *how* the reader completes the meaning constitutes part of the parable's self-involving disclosure-function.

A parallel emerges with Robert Funk's earlier comments on the hermeneutics of parables. Funk took the same parabolic examples (Luke 15:11–32) and argued that the text itself *transforms the audience* into one of two reactive categories: by their *response* the audience identifies *themselves* either as pharisaic "righteous" elder-son critics, or as repentant younger sons who return.[16]

A second exemplification of Iser's models in biblical interpretation is offered by James L. Resseguie in his article "Reader-Response Criticism and the Synoptic Gospels"

---

[10]   Ibid., p.231; cf. pp.180–230.
[11]   Ibid., pp.183–5.
[12]   Susan Wittig, "A Theory of Multiple Meanings", *Semeia* 9 (1977), pp.75–105.
[13]   Ibid., p.84.
[14]   Ibid., p.95.
[15]   Ibid., pp.95–6.
[16]   Robert W. Funk, *Language, Hermeneutic and Word of God. The Problem of Language in the New Testament and Contemporary Theology* (New York: Harper & Row, 1966), p.17.

(1984).[17] Like Susan Wittig, Resseguie underlines the role of reader involvement, and the reader's part in "filling gaps" in the text in his or her own way.[18] He seeks to find a place for *both* the possibility of "infinite" variations of actualization, *and* a measure of constraint on the part of the text. He explores the narrative of the rich man who came eagerly to Jesus but after hearing his words "went away sorrowful; for he had great possessions" (Mark 10:22; cf. 10:17–22). In line with the constraints of the text, Resseguie attends to the Markan context; but in line with an emphasis on the role of the reader, he calls attention to the part played by wealth for the reader and by his or her own axioms about wealth.

This corresponds precisely to the dual aspect or alleged ambivalence of Iser's theoretical model which draws down the wrath of Stanley Fish. Which is the master: the text or the reading-community? Fish's crushing review of Wolfgang Iser's work in his essay, "Why No One's Afraid of Iser", forcefully elaborates the argument that Iser tries to have his cake and eat it too. Iser admits that meaning (to the satisfaction of pluralists) is "there" only when it is "read", actualized and interpreted; but Iser also imagines (to the satisfaction of objectivists or traditionalists) that meaning is a concretization of what was potentially "there" in the text. So neither traditionalists nor pluralists need "fear" Iser, because he has the "ability to embrace contradiction cheerfully".[19]

In his suggestive book *Loaves and Fishes*, Robert Fowler questions the assumption that within the linear and temporal reading process, readers of Mark were expected to project *back* onto Mark 6 and Mark 8 *later* material about the Last Supper. Fowler comments, "*As the author has structured his work, Jesus' last meal with his disciples in Mark 14 presupposes the earlier feeding stories and not vice versa.*"[20] Fowler reflects: "Often the verbal similarities between 6:41, 8:6, and 14:22 are noted and used to justify the discovery of 'eucharistic' overtones in the two feeding stories." But if we follow *reading processes* generated and designed by Mark, such an approach "is to stand the gospel on its head".[21]

Fowler reaches the conclusion that the traditional feeding story of Mark 8, subsequently reflected in Mark 6:30–44, originally contained no reference to fish as well as to loaves. This aspect of his arguments remains open to question.[22] But Fowler's approach achieves success in pinpointing potential differences of expectation about Jesus on the part of the reader from those of the disciples in the narrative. However we account for the two narratives of Mark 6:30–44 and Mark 8:1–10, we can hardly doubt that the disciples' question in 8:4: "How can one feed these people with bread here in the desert?" has an impact *which invites incredulity on the part of the reader who has just read Mark 6.*[23] How can those who have recently witnessed a feeding miracle entertain doubts about what Jesus could do in a closely parallel situation? Can readers still share such obtuse underestimations of Christology? In Fowler's view, Mark himself has inserted Mark 6

---

[17] James L. Resseguie, "Reader Response Criticism and the Synoptic Gospels", *Journal of the American Academy of Religion* 52 (1984), pp.307–24.

[18] Ibid., p.308.

[19] Stanley Fish, *Doing What Comes Naturally*, pp.69–70; cf. pp.68–86.

[20] Robert Fowler, *Loaves and Fishes: the Function of the Feeding Stories in the Gospel of Mark* (Chico, CA: Scholars Press, 1981), pp.134–5.

[21] Ibid., p.134.

[22] Ibid., p.83.

[23] Ibid., pp.93–6.

prior to the traditional story of Mark 8, *in order to heighten the reader's responses to Jesus against the contrasting background and clear inadequacy of the disciples' expectations.*

Iser's theoretical model provides the tools for such an approach, and Fowler acknowledges the value of Iser's work on anticipation and retrospection in reading processes. Iser, Fowler observes, shows that "during the process of reading there is an active interweaving of anticipation and retrospection".[24] The reading process entails both guesses about what is to come, and reflection over what is past.

II
Further Applications of Iser's Approach, and Some Critical Responses

Jouette Bassler also traces the twists and turns by which the Markan text seems to provoke the reader to struggle with apparently insoluble puzzles. To keep the reader in some measure of suspense and in the dark allows the reader initially to share the disciples' sense of puzzlement about Jesus. Narrative "gaps" generate and heighten reader involvement and reader activity, as the reader wrestles with a text which, until the end, constitutes an incomplete jigsaw-puzzle.[25] The release of information, the putting-together of the pieces of the puzzle, comes to be achieved by the text and the reader gradually, until the eucharist and the cross in Mark 14 bring about a *retrospective* understanding of the significance of the long struggle with the text. In a metaphorical sense, Iser's claim in his earlier book *The Implied Reader* (1974) is thereby vindicated, that the *work* is "more" than the *text*. Iser writes, "The text only takes on life when it is realized ... The convergence of text and reader bring the literary work into existence."[26]

R. Alan Culpepper's book *Anatomy of the Fourth Gospel* (1983) combines elements of Iser's conceptual tools with other methodological elements drawn from the narrative theories of Gérard Genette and Seymour Chatman.[27] It also utilizes standard apparatus from the new criticism, such as "point of view", plot development, irony, and so forth. Culpepper's focus of interest is not on John as a "window" onto the Johannine community but as a "mirror" in which to see the world. The Johannine text calls the reader to make *moves*: "through the 'narrator' the 'author' sends signals which establish expectations, distance, and intimacy, and powerfully affect the reader's sense of identification and involvement ... The implicit purpose of the gospel narrative is to alter irrevocably the reader's perceptions of the ideal world ... to 'see' the world as the evangelist sees it".[28]

Culpepper introduces the working distinctions of Seymour Chatman which we have noted: distinctions between narrative time and natural sequence, between story and discourse, and between narrator and narrative, together with Wayne Booth's distinction

---

[24] Ibid., p.171.

[25] Jouette M. Bassler, "The Parable of the Loaves", *Journal of Religion* 66 (1986), p.167; cf. pp.157–72.

[26] Wolfgang Iser, *The Implied Reader: Patterns of Communication in Prose Fiction from Bunyan to Beckett* (Baltimore, MD: Johns Hopkins University Press, 1974), pp.274–5.

[27] R. Alan Culpepper, *Anatomy of the Fourth Gospel: A Study in Literary Design* (Philadelphia, PA: Fortress Press, 1983), pp.6–9, 20–27, 54–70 *et passim*.

[28] Ibid., p.4.

between an author and the "implied author". The implied author is the literary construct that determines how or what we read. The narrator communicates directly with the reader; the implied author must be inferred from the narrative. In this terminology our "author" of the Epistle to the Hebrews in chapter VII [of *New Horizons in Hermeneutics*] above would in certain respects be the "implied" author, although in other respects it remains difficult to distinguish such an entity from the voice that directly addresses us as preacher or writer. Culpepper concedes that only from time to time is such a distinction clear in John. In John 21:24 the "implied author" is identified as the beloved disciple. Since the beloved disciple is a witness, the Gospel "daring in its perspective" establishes an authority and "point of view" for the narrator.[29]

Culpepper expounds the relevance of such literary categories as narrative time, plot development and characterization in John. He turns more specifically to reader-response aspects in his examination of Johannine "implicit commentary" as a rhetorical device. Here John regularly employs "misunderstandings" by narrative characters. The standard examples include John 2:19–21, "this temple"; 3:3–5, "born anew"; 4:10–15, "living water"; 4:31, "food"; 6:32–35, "bread from heaven"; 6:51, "my flesh"; 7:33, "where I am"; 8:31–35, "make you free"; and ten other instances (including the well-known "sleep" in 11:11–15 and "lifted up" in 12:32–34).[30]

These aspects also entail the "silent" communication of the implied author's smile, wink, or raising of eyebrows in instances of Johannine irony over such subjects as the origins of Jesus (1:46; 7:52 "Are you from Galilee?"), or the *double entendre* of the "good wine saved to the end", or the Pharisees' bland question about whether they are to be presumed "blind", like the blind man (9:39). Culpepper expounds the role of dramatic irony, of symbolism, and of misunderstanding, for stimulating the reader into making his or her own response. In language which in a different context would remind us of Dilthey's hermeneutics, Culpepper concludes that the modern reader must enter imaginatively, if need be even by "pretence", into what the evangelist assumed his first-century readers knew or thought. In Iser's words the "implied reader" (that is, the construct-reader for whom the text operates) "embodies all those predispositions necessary for a literary work to exercize its effect", and finds in the text "invitations to shared perceptions".[31]

Although it is arguable that Iser's reader-response theory contributes only one component within a wider range of literary tools including formalism and narrative theory, Culpepper's work demonstrates, like that of Fowler and others, the value of placing an emphasis on *reading processes* not only in terms of temporal, sequential and rhetorical features, but *also more broadly as a focus for hermeneutical questions about reader engagement, interaction and self-involvement.*

Stanley Fish, we have noted, attacked Iser for attempting to satisfy both "objectivists" who still believe in textual "givens", and pluralists who view meaning as constructs determined by the agenda and expectations of *readers*. In his work on Mark 10:17–22 Resseguie has attempted a similar dialectical balance between constraint and

---

[29] Ibid., p.48.
[30] Ibid., pp.161–2.
[31] Ibid., pp.209 and 233.

construction. But here Stephen Moore and Stanley Porter firmly take sides with Fish against Resseguie. Moore insists that Resseguie "follows Iser the critic into deep contradiction".[32] On this same basis Stanley Porter dismisses Iser as "notoriously ambiguous", views the related work of Norman Petersen (discussed below) as "particularly disappointing", and remains highly critical of the approach of Resseguie as well as the work of Jeffrey Lloyd Staley (1988) who has "taken his cue from Resseguie".[33]

Three major factors separate Fish's category of reader-response theory from that of Iser. First, the reason why Fish opposes the supposedly self-contradictory nature of Iser's approach so vehemently is doubtless because with the zeal of the convert Fish perceives it as a position which he himself formerly held, but has now "seen through". This helps to explain the aggressive missionary tone of his writing that is so noticeable as to attract attention in a special paper, namely Susan R. Horton's article "The Experience of Stanley Fish's Prose".[34] He traces his own pilgrimage from the end of *Surprised by Sin* (1967) and *Self-Consuming Artefacts* (1972) when he believed that given texts may draw readers along certain paths, to 1980, when his book *Is There a Text in this Class?* appeared. By now Fish had come to "cease worrying" about how much respectively the text or the reader contributed to interpretation: there was *nothing "in" the text to interpret, because everything is interpretation*.[35] Fish complains that Iser still sees the interpretative relationship as "one of script to performer", whereas Fish himself urges that we cannot "speak meaningfully of a text that is simply there, waiting for a reader who is, at least potentially, wholly free".[36]

A second major difference arises from the contrast between Iser's focus on the *individual reader* and Fish's notion of *communities of readers*. Fish insists that "there is no subjective element of reading because the observer is never individual in the sense of unique or private, but is always the product of categories of understanding that are his *by virtue of his membership in a community of interpretation*" (my italics).[37]

A third point of contrast emerges in a radical difference of attitude and evaluation towards both a philosophy of perception and a philosophy of language. Iser seeks to ground and build a theory of reading on the basis not only of pragmatic assumptions about how reading seems to work, but on *philosophical* issues about the *nature of human perceptions*, the processes of *construal* and *projection*, and relations between perception and *language*. But it is difficult to perceive the same level of rigorous *philosophical* argument in the claims of Stanley Fish. Indeed, as Patrick Grant and others have observed, certain theories of "literary" meaning sometimes rest on the illusion that *philosophy*, after Rorty and Derrida, can be *subsumed under literary theory itself*. But this assumption is a disastrous mistake, and leads to consequences that we shall explicate shortly.

---

[32] Stephen D. Moore, op. cit., p.103.

[33] Stanley E. Porter, "Why Hasn't Reader-Response Criticism Caught On in New Testament Studies?", *Literature and Theology* 4 (1990), pp.280, 281 and 282; cf. pp.278–92.

[34] Susan R. Horton, "The Experience of Stanley Fish's Prose on The Critic as Self-Creating, Self-Consuming, Artifices", *Genre* 10 (1977), pp.449 and 452; cf. pp.443–53.

[35] See Fish's introductory autobiographical essay in *Is There a Text in This Class?*, pp.1–17.

[36] Stanley Fish, *Doing What Comes Naturally*, pp.69–70 and 83.

[37] Ibid., p.83.

III
Umberto Eco's Semiotic and Text-Related Reader-Response Theory, and Some Implications for Biblical Texts

Whereas Iser drew on a *philosophy of perception*, and Fish (as Culler rightly observes) draws on contextual *pragmatism*, Umberto Eco lays a careful foundation for his own reader-response theory by a *rigorous examination of principles of semiotics*. Thus Eco's book *The Role of the Reader: Explorations on the Semiotics of Texts* (1981) draws on theoretical foundations that he laid in his earlier work, *A Theory of Semiotics* (1976). Some aspects are then developed further in his *Semiotics and the Philosophy of Language* (1984).[38] A major step forward arises from Eco's recognition at the beginning of his *A Theory of Semiotics* that semiotic theory needs to include *both* a theory of *codes*, which comes under the heading of *signification*, *and* a semiotics of *sign-production*, which comes under the heading of *communication*. This contrast is *not* to be identified, he insists, simply with the distinction between syntactics and pragmatics; and it does not correspond precisely to the difference between *langue* and *parole*. Eco writes, "One of the claims of the present book is to overcome these distinctions, and to outline a theory of codes which takes into account even rules of discursive competence, text formation, contextual and circumstantial (or situational) disambiguation therefore proposing a semantics which solves within its own framework many problems of the so-called pragmatics."[39]

The *signification system* arises on the basis of codes of social convention, but the *communication process* "exploits" the sign system physically to produce expressions for a variety of practical purposes. Signification has logical primacy in the sense that "every act of communication to or between human beings ... presupposes a signification system as its necessary condition. It is possible ... to establish a semiotics of signification independently of a semiotics of communication: but it is impossible to establish a semiotics of communication without a semiotics of signification."[40]

Wittgenstein made a parallel point by means of an analogy, shared partly with Saussure. To know the rules of chess and to set out the pieces on the board in a certain way (cf. *langue*, system, signification, structure) is not yet to make an actual chess *move* (cf. *parole*, speech-act-in-life-world, language *use*, communication *act*). Wittgenstein observes, "Naming is so far not a move in the language-game – any more than putting a piece in its place on the board is a move in chess ... *Nothing* has so far been done, when a thing is named."[41] Eco's understanding of semantic fields and of semiotic systems has a parallel with Wittgenstein's perceptive observations: these are *conditions of signification* which are activated in what other writers might term "hermeneutical life-worlds" or "speech-acts", in which *interaction occurs* between the *code system* of the writer or sender, and the *code system* of the reader or receiver.

---

[38] Umberto Eco, *A Theory of Semiotics* (Bloomington, IN: Indiana University Press, 1976); *The Role of the Reader: Explorations in the Semiotics of Texts* (London: Hutchinson, 1981); and *Semiotics and the Philosophy of Language* (London: Macmillan, 1984).

[39] Umberto Eco, *A Theory of Semiotics*, p.4.

[40] Ibid., p.9.

[41] L. Wittgenstein, *Philosophical Investigations*, sect. 49; cf. sects 22 and 33.

Eco makes a fundamental advance in his notion of *understanding*: "*The absence of reliable pre-established rules*" *permits readers to make over-generalized assumptions about the code that a given text presupposes.*[42] Still more important, Eco recognizes *the very wide range of models that constitute "texts", ranging from the simplest functional transmissive system in engineering through to complex matrices of productive systems of "literary" meaning.* His introductory example of a semiotic system rightly begins with a very simple model, in this respect like Wittgenstein's simplified model language-game of referential communication between two builders. Eco describes the functional and transmissive "reading" of the pointer of a dial on a control panel which is mechanically linked to a floating buoy in order to indicate water-level or fuel-level. Even in this example, "reading" the dial rests on a social convention; but one which is so widespread today that it is virtually trans-cultural (except in cultures which have no plumbing or traffic vehicles). An ancient culture might not recognize the basis on which the signifying system functions, but almost all modern cultures would presuppose the code that used pointer and dial to communicate data.

Differences between and within codes may entail "*sub-codes*". Eco points out the purely transmissive function of indicating a high water-level as a *fact* differs from communicating some *judgements* about its *significance*, namely what level constitutes a "flood warning" or a "danger level". *Sub-codes may entail a professional training* (just as Wittgenstein also rightly addressed the role of "training" in communicating and on understanding).[43]

Eco takes up a useful methodological distinction embodied in the semiotic theory of Jurij Lotman.[44] Lotman distinguishes between categories of texts which function primarily to *transmit* or to *communicate* meanings, and those that serve to *generate* or to *produce* meanings. He speculates that this contrast represents a difference of *cultural* perspective. The former reflects a "*handbook*" culture, and operates with generally *stable* meanings. In this case, literary texts may embody *multiple coding*. In this case *how texts are read* will depend largely on the *reader's choice of decoding systems*. Thus, following Lotman, Eco concludes that when "re-readings" produce changes of code, this *modifies the very meaning* of the text or work. Petersen, we shall shortly note, makes this kind of observation about the reading of Mark. We have already called attention to Fowler's comments on the difference between "reading" Mark sequentially in a temporal mode for the first time, and second or subsequent rereadings which presuppose a retrospective "timeless" frame.

Lotman's working contrast forms part of the foundation of Eco's work on reader-response theory and reading processes in his book, *The Role of the Reader*. It also features in his book *Semiotics and the Philosophy of Language*, especially in the distinctions in his own sign-theory between "communication signs" (emblems, streetsigns, trademarks) and indirect or "premonitory signs" (metaphors, traces, even ancient ruins). *The former presuppose matching codes; the latter incorporate multiple interpretation.* In principle, the latter can expand into an *outward-moving, growing labyrinth.* In terms of the former category, the *semantic* function of the *encyclopedia* exhibits "*markers*"; in terms of the latter category, *temporal advance* characterizes the "infinity" of chains of signs and language-systems in

---

[42] Umberto Eco, *A Theory of Semiotics*, p.135.
[43] Ibid., p.56.
[44] Ibid., pp.136–9.

the *dictionary*, the function of which is to catch momentary *"transient revaluations" of pragmatic language-uses*.[45] Only "cultural inertia" slows these changes sufficiently to make them adequately stable as "dictionary meanings" or as working definitions.

In *The Role of the Reader*, Eco stresses that in poetry and in literary texts generative strategies aim at "imprecise or undetermined response" on the basis of intertextual competence. Some texts invite *"the co-operation" of their readers by compelling "interpretative choices"*.[46] Arguably many biblical parables, a number of narratives, many parts of the wisdom literature, and biblical apocalyptic precipitate reader-activity of this kind. *But Eco does not categorize all texts in the same way. Every text envisages, or "selects" by its nature, a "model reader". This is the construct-reader who shares the ensemble of codes presupposed by the author.* In comments closely parallel to those of Culler or even Bultmann on "pre-understanding" and "presupposition", Eco suggests by way of example that a text that speaks of "chivalry" presupposes knowledge of the tradition of Romantic chivalry on the part of the *"model reader"*.

Eco observes, "Those texts (which) aim at arousing a precise response on the part of more or less empirical readers ... are in fact open to any possible 'aberrant' de-coding. A text so immoderately 'open' to every possible interpretation will be called a *closed* one."[47] Eco offers examples of "closed texts" which pull the reader along a *predetermined path* in order to arouse specific emotions and effects. These include mass-advertising formats, comic strips and soap-opera romances or Westerns. By contrast, James Joyce's *Finnegans Wake* represents an *open* text, which embodies *generative processes* within its own structure. Some texts are conceived for a general audience. These might include political speeches or scientific instructions. In others, however, the author or reader may be necessarily specific (for example, in the case of a private letter), or the reader may be a construct (an "open" letter), or both author and readers may do no more than perform actantial roles. In such instances, even in such a phrase as "I tell you ...", references to author and reader are no more than textual strategies.[48] The most distinctive advantage of *open* texts, Eco believes, is their greater capacity to resist "aberrant" or mismatching codes.

Eco distinguishes between differing reader processes that relate to language *about states of affairs*, unverifiable hypotheses which would be empirical in principle (that is, *counterfactual conditionals*) and *fiction*. In a series of ten diagrammatic structures or boxes, Eco schematizes a number of combinations of selected responses that a reader might choose to make to different kinds of texts. *In some cases, questions about empirical truth-claims would be invited; in other instances, forecasts and "inferential walks"; in fictional stories, questions about narrative plot and actantial structures.* "Switching" from box to box may be entailed in reading processes.[49] But throughout the processes *code*, and *changes of code*, remain paramount.

Eco demonstrates the role of the reader in filling out or "blowing up" (his term) some textual characterizations or events, and reducing or "narcotising" others. *The reader has to*

---

45 Umberto Eco, *Semiotics and the Philosophy of Language*, pp.68–86.
46 Umberto Eco, *The Role of the Reader*, p.4.
47 Ibid., p.8.
48 Ibid., pp.9–11.
49 Ibid., pp.14–17.

be helped *"to select the right frames, to reduce them to manageable format, to blow up and to narcotise given semantic properties* of the lexemes to be amalgamated, and to establish the isotropy according to which he decides to interpret the linear text manifestation so as to *actualise* the discursive structure of a text" (my italics).[50] In the case of narrative a reader will be invited to wonder about the next step of a given story. This may pose a decision, or disjunction of probabilities, and *different choices may have different values*. Many of the parables of Jesus fall into Eco's category of offering the reader "solutions he does not expect, *challenging every over coded intertextual frame as well as the reader's predictive indolence"*.[51] "Open" narrative-texts allow for the widest possible range of interpretative proposals.

William Ray rightly calls attention to Eco's affinities with Ingarden and Iser. Like Iser, Eco avoids "both pure objectivism and pure subjectivism".[52] Ray comments, "The hermeneutical circle is thus thoroughly embedded in Eco's model of reading."[53] But in Ray's own view, this position is unsatisfactory. He categorizes Eco's supposedly "dubious generic distinction between 'open' and 'closed' texts" as leading to "an impasse".[54] Ray's criticism of Eco runs parallel to Fish's attack on Iser. Eco, he claims, tries to have the best of both worlds. But Eco's careful correlation between *different kinds of texts* and *different reading roles* seems to be more meticulously and convincingly grounded in rigorous semiotic theory that the "literary" approaches of Ray and Fish. As Tremper Longman observes, there is a difference between claiming that there are as many "interpretations" of texts as there are readers, and attempting to establish what active processes readers undertake *"in interaction with the text"* (Longman's italics).[55]

Eco's approach to reader-response theory offers a positive resource for biblical interpretation, and moves beyond the work of Iser, although Iser's work retains its distinctive elements. On the other hand, as against Ray and other advocates of purely "literary" theories of texts and of meaning, Eco's recognition of the *constraints operative on readers in the case of communicative* (less clearly, of "productive") *texts* places him in a different category in relation to biblical studies from Fish.

IV

The Psychoanalytical Approach of Holland, and Bleich's Socio-Political Approach

A number of standard studies and introductions trace the divergent trends within what is commonly called reader-response theory. Well-known introductions to these theories include those of Elizabeth Freund, Jane P. Tompkins, and the volume jointly edited by Susan

---

[50] Ibid., p.27.

[51] Ibid., p.33.

[52] William Ray, *Literary Meaning: From Phenomenology to Deconstruction* (Oxford: Blackwell, 1984), p.134.

[53] Ibid., p.137.

[54] Ibid., p.134.

[55] Tremper Longman III, *Literary Approaches to Biblical Interpretation* (Grand Rapids, MI: Academie and Leicester: Apollos, 1987), p.38.

R. Suleiman and Inge Crosman.[56] Jane Tompkins traces a reader-orientated development from Riffaterre, Iser and Poulet, to Fish, Culler, Holland, Bleich and Walter Michaels.[57] Elizabeth Freund compares the "implied reader" of Booth and Iser, the "model reader" of Eco, Riffaterre's "super-reader", Culler's "ideal reader" and Fish's "interpretative community".[58] Among these, whereas Iser's approach draws on a philosophical phenomenology of perception, Eco draws primarily on semiotic theory, Culler draws on post-structuralist and semiotic explorations of reader-competency, and Fish on socio-pragmatic, postmodern, literary thought. In contrast to all of these, David Bleich operates largely with socio-political and educational concerns, while Norman Holland works on the basis of psychoanalytic theory and other broader psychological observations.

Norman Holland's earlier approaches (1968, 1973 and 1975) draw on a psychoanalytical perspective in the tradition of Freud.[59] Interaction between the self and features of a text as *"other"* set in motion certain *strategies on the part of the reader's conscious self*. Patterns of *desire* on the part of the self give rise to strategies of *self-protection and concealment*, and thus to *overdetermination of meaning*. Multiple meaning-effects emerge, in other words, which can be attributed to conflicts, ambiguities, and overlapping causes within the self. Holland describes *the active operation of these defensive strategies as "transactions" between the self and the other*. In processes of reading, readers shape their strategies and perceptions in *ways that serve their patterns of desire, and what they construct reflects and serves their own unique identity*. Holland summarizes the devices which constitute strategies of reading set in motion by the self's defence of its identity under the acronym "DEFT": Defences, Expectations, Fantasies and Transformations.

Holland's approach shares with Iser's theory an emphasis on the role of *the individual reader*, in contrast to community-centred stress on *communities of readers*, which characterizes the theories of Bleich, Culler and Fish. Holland also attempts to support his theories by experimental observational psychological research. In his book entitled *5 Readers Reading* (1975) he compares the *different quasi-empirical responses* made by five different readers to the same texts. He concluded that these different responses could be significantly correlated with the readers' respective differences of identity, including their narrative experiences and personality types.

The contribution to *biblical hermeneutics* on the part of Holland's theoretical model takes both a positive and a negative form. (i) On the positive side, the ways in which readers read biblical texts produce not only understanding of texts, but also often

---

[56]   Elizabeth Freund, *The Return of the Reader: Reader-Response Criticism* (London and New York: Methuen, 1987); cf. Jane P. Tompkins (ed.), *Reader-Response Criticism. From Formalism to Post-Structuralism* (Baltimore, MD and London: Johns Hopkins University Press, 1980); and Susan R. Suleiman and Inge Crosman (eds), *The Reader in the Text: Essays in Audience and Interpretation* (Princeton, NJ: Princeton University Press, 1980).

[57]   Jane P. Tompkins (ed.), op. cit., esp. pp.xiv–xxiv.

[58]   Elizabeth Freund, op. cit., p.7.

[59]   Norman Holland, *Poems in Persons: An Introduction to the Psychoanalysis of Literature* (New York: Norton, 1973); *5 Readers Reading* (New Haven, CT: Yale University Press, 1975); and "Recovering 'The Purloined Letter': Reading as Personal Transaction", in Susan Suleiman and Inge Crosman (eds), op. cit., pp.350–70; cf. further Norman Holland, *The Dynamics of Literary Response* (New York: Oxford, 1968); "Literary Interpretation and Three Phases of Psychoanalysis", *Critical Inquiry* 3 (1976), pp.221–33; and "Transactive Criticism: Re-Creation through Identity", *Criticism* 18 (1976), pp.334–52.

produce an increased awareness, with appropriate hermeneutical sensitivity, of self-perception and self-identity. Further, as existentialist and narrative theories of hermeneutics underline, *a self-awareness and a strengthening of an individual and corporate identity as one who has a stake in the texts and that to which they bear witness constitutes an important reader-effect in the case of biblical texts.*

(ii) If the *implications* of Holland's theory are adequately noted, this approach also underlines, negatively, *the urgent need for a hermeneutic of suspicion in reading biblical texts.* In an important statement Holland observes: *"We use the literary work to symbolize and finally to replicate ourselves"* (my italics).[60] But if this is the case, the reading of biblical texts, as Paul Ricoeur so cogently argues, *can result in idolatry. We can project our own interests, desires, and selfhood onto that which the biblical text proclaims.* We can thereby unwittingly re-create and *"construct" God in our own image through our reading-processes.*

(iii) We should note in passing how Holland's theory, by its very affinity with certain individualist strands within religious or Christian pietism, offers a warning about innocent subjective reading in *traditions of pietism.* Very often in religious groups an individual is encouraged to "frame" the biblical text with reference to the narrative history of personal testimony, and to "read" the text as "what the text *means to me*". If this is undertaken within a frame of corporate evaluation and testing, the life-experience in question may enhance pre-understanding and weave meaning and textual force with emotional warmth and practices in life. But without any principle of *suspicion,* in Gadamer's terminology a *premature* fusion of horizons will take place *before* readers have listened in openness with respect for the tension between the horizons of the text and the horizon of the reader. The textual horizon has collapsed into that of the reader's narrative biography, and is unable to do more than to speak back his or her own values and desires.

(iv) This example exposes the ultimately *socio-pragmatic* status of Holland's theoretical model. In the end, if "we use the literary work ... to replicate ourselves", as in Fish and in Rorty the text can never transform us and correct us "*from outside*". There can be no prophetic address "*from beyond*". This may still leave room for a measure of *creativity and surprise* in *literary* reading. For *in such cases it does not profoundly matter whether it is ultimately the self* who brings about its own creative discoveries. But in the case of many biblical texts, theological truth-claims constitute more than triggers to set self-discovery in motion. If such concepts as "grace" or "revelation" have any currency, texts of this kind speak not *from the self* but *from beyond the self.*

David Bleich approaches reader-response theory from a different angle. His later work is characterized by a *socio-literary and socio-political context of interests.* Like Holland, Bleich's earlier work focuses on "subjective" reading, but in contrast to Holland *within a framework of a specific theory of inter-subjectivity.* His early book *Readings and Feelings* (1975) explores psychological and psychotherapeutic categories, and in his book *Subjective Criticism* (1978) Bleich argues that differences in reading strategies emerge from personal and communal subjectivity. Like Fish, Bleich firmly emphasizes the creative role of community interests in shaping how readers within a community read; but his notion of *what constitutes a genuine community of readers* distances him from Fish.

---

[60]   Norman Holland, "Transactive Criticism: Re-Creation through Identity", loc. cit., p.342.

In *The Double Perspective: Language, Literacy, and Social Relations* (1988) Bleich insists that a double perspective is necessary to embrace the wholeness of male and female, individual and communal, and the academy and the classroom.[61] He attacks Fish for appearing to presuppose that a "community of readers" means an *academic* community rather than one from the classroom. Fish is allegedly *too elitist*, while Culler is supposedly *too immersed in theory* to handle the issues of "reading" in the everyday world. Bleich's emphasis upon a co-jointly male and female community of readers makes a significant contribution to feminist hermeneutics. He also indirectly re-establishes the status of the *"ordinary"* reader in the use of the Bible.

Nevertheless Bleich's theory degenerates from a healthy ethic to an unhealthy pragmatism. After introducing promising aspects for feminist theory, Bleich stereotypes gender differences, and in effect re-designates any serious critical, metacritical, or trans-contextual criteria as "male" concerns. This is the kind of "feminism" that Janet Radcliffe-Richards regards as a betrayal of feminism. Bleich argues that the philosophies of language expounded by Gadamer, Barthes, Derrida, Hegel and Wittgenstein are "governed by individualist and masculinist ideology".[62]

Bleich's *literary* theory is bound up with a *socio-political agenda. Egalitarian social politics dictate the de-privileging of the author, the de-privileging of academic interpreters, and even the de-privileging of a literary or theological canon of "classics", in order to make the whole mixed community co-authors of texts*: everyone constructs, and no construction is "better" than another *because critical theory would already prejudice an answer in favour of the elite.* This pragmatic approach threatens to collapse into an anarchy in which *the most militant pressure group carries the day about what satisfies their own pragmatic criteria of "right" reading.* It undermines its own laudable goal of human "wholeness", because it rejects "theory" as "male", "white" and "elitist".

V
Jonathan Culler: A Non-Pragmatic, Semiotic, Reader-Response Theory?

Initially, like Eco, Culler bases his approach on semiotic theory. But consistent development in the direction of the role of the reader can be traced from *Structuralist Poetics* (1975) through *The Pursuit of Signs* (1981) to *Framing the Sign* (1988). Jane Tompkins offers an initial summarizing observation: "If meaning is no longer a property of the text but a product of the reader's activity the question to answer is not 'what do these poems mean?' or even 'what do poems do?' but 'how do readers make meaning?' Jonathan Culler's *Structuralist Poetics* provides an answer to this question based on the central insights of French structuralism from Saussure to Derrida."[63] Culler's central concern in his work of 1988, *Framing the Sign*, is to enquire how signs are "constituted (framed) by various discursive practices, institutional arrangements, systems of value, semiotic mechanisms".[64]

---

[61] David Bleich, *The Double Perspective. Language, Literacy, and Social Relations* (New York: OUP, 1988).
[62] David Bleich, *The Double Perspective*, p.24; cf. pp.16–25.
[63] Jane Tompkins, op. cit., p.xvii.
[64] Jonathan Culler, *Framing the Sign*, p.ix.

It will not do, Culler argues, simply to claim that the "context" of a text determines its meaning rather than these semiotic or institutional features, because it is these that determine how we "frame" the sign, where "framing is determining, setting off the object or event *as* ..." what we perceive it to be. Far from viewing this as shifting the focus to the psychological subject, as Holland's earlier work had done, Culler applies and extends the *semiotic emphasis on system* rather than a hermeneutics of life-world. This remains the case even although in *The Pursuit of Signs* he is sympathetic with the view that the notion of inter-textuality has close parallels with hermeneutical presupposition or pre-understanding, and may function like Searle's idea of "Background". He asserts, "Words prove to be not tools ... but machines, with complex internal structures that can generate results not always predictable to their users."[65]

Jonathan Culler shows more philosophical sophistication than neo-pragmatic exponents of reader-response theories. In *Framing the Sign* he states that pragmatic literary theory, and in effect socio-pragmatic, self-affirming hermeneutics, reflects a cultural "complacency" which is "altogether appropriate to the age of Reagan".[66] Such a comment indicates Culler's conscious distancing of himself from the kind of positions held by Fish and Rorty. A certain parallel may be suggested between Culler's work and the critical quest for a *transcendental* hermeneutics which began with Schleiermacher and which reaches its climax in Gadamer, Ricoeur, Apel and Habermas. Thus in his earlier book *Structuralist Poetics* Culler makes it clear by *"Poetics"* he means *the conditions for the possibility of processes of reading.*[67] In a partly parallel way Schleiermacher had also sought to offer critical reflection on *conditions for the possibility* of understanding.

In *The Pursuit of Signs*, however, Culler demonstrates that the subject *matter* of his concern is quite different from that of Schleiermacher and his hermeneutical successors. Culler's focus of interest lies less on understanding a supposed textual "content" in its own right, than perceiving the "conventions", "operations" and "procedures" by which a given system may function operatively for a given community of readers.[68] In *On Deconstruction* Culler accepts Roland Barthes's view that a literary work embodies endless interacting layers of semiotic code or system, with the result that it may offer no stable, identifiable centre or meaning-content.[69] Further, in *Framing the Sign* Culler argues that even conceptualization, in the sense of "framing", does *not arrest* "the play of signs", because *how* a text is contextualized or *re*-contextualized remains variable in relation to decisions, conventions and strategies on the part of communities of readers. In his other works Culler concludes, "There are no final meanings" that bring this process to closure.[70] Interpretation, he writes, is not a matter of "recovering" meaning, but of participating as readers in the play of *possible* meanings to which a text gives access.[71]

---

[65] Ibid., p.95.

[66] Jonathan Culler, *Structuralist Poetics: Structuralism, Linguistics, and the Study of Literature* (Ithaca, NY: Cornell University Press, 1975).

[67] Ibid., p.55.

[68] Jonathan Culler, *The Pursuit of Signs*, p.5.

[69] Jonathan Culler, *On Deconstruction: Theory and Criticism After Structuralism* (Ithaca, NY: Cornell University Press, 1982), p.22.

[70] Jonathan Culler, *The Pursuit of Signs*, p.188.

[71] Jonathan Culler, *Structuralist Poetics*, p.247.

One major difficulty with Culler's work arises precisely from this interrelation between *langue* and *parole*, as it does in Barthes. He seems to give priority to the axes of *langue*, *system* and *linguistic competence* or *possible* meaning, as over against *parole*, *actual* language-*use*-in-life-world, and linguistic *performance* (in spite of Ray's claim to the contrary).[72] What "we do" in Culler's judgement is expressed in the title *Framing the Sign*. This may include the artificial manipulation of a "frame-up". This may regularly entail "*naturalizing*" the text, namely, giving it a place "in the world which our culture defines ... to bring it within the modes of order which culture makes available".[73] Here we come near to the hermeneutical insight that we *begin* by contextualizing a text in terms of the familiar as an implicate of "pre-understanding". But in Schleiermacher and in Betti, and in a different way in Gadamer, further interaction with the text enlarges this horizon and may potentially transform it. If all the weight in reader-orientated hermeneutics is placed on prior expectations, codes, conventions, horizons, *out of which meaning is determined and constructed* it is difficult to see how the text can transform or correct the horizons of reading communities "*from outside*".

VI
Neo-Pragmatic Reader-Response Theory in Stanley Fish

This is precisely the issue that comes to a head prominently and explicitly in the work of Stanley Fish. *The major contribution of Fish is his unflinching acceptance of what is entailed, or not entailed, in socio-pragmatic, or neo-pragmatic, hermeneutics*. Especially in the volume of essays published under the title *Doing What Comes Naturally* (1989) Fish anticipates and checks out every possible move that critics of his pragmatic relativism might make. He disarmingly accepts what must be accepted, and relishes his opponents' confusion when some (by no means all) of his counter-arguments take, in effect, the form: "So, what?". Fish is more interested in the "*non-consequences*" of his theory than in its consequences.

The key issue, namely, whether texts can challenge or transform communities of readers "*from outside*", is identified as a watershed in Fish's important essay "Going Down the Anti-Formalist Road" (1989). Fish writes, "Once you start down the anti-formalist road, there is no place to stop ...". As soon as we grasp the contextual pragmatic relativity of criteria of meaning *to social presuppositions and interests*, "the general conclusion that follows from this is that *the model in which a practice is altered or reformed by constraints brought in from the outside ... never in fact operates ... Theory has no consequences*" (my italics).[74]

Fish, we earlier noted, did not begin his literary pilgrimage from this point. In *Surprised by Sin* (1967) he focused on the capacity of texts (especially in this study, of John Milton's *Paradise Lost*) to lead readers along paths that invite revaluation of the reader's own perceptions. They invite reader awareness. In *Self-Consuming Artefacts. The Experience of Seventeenth-Century Literature* (1972) Fish traces alternative reading strategies that may

---

[72] William Ray, op. cit., p.114; but Ray also claims the centrality of "literary competence" in Culler; cf. p.113.

[73] Jonathan Culler, *Structuralist Poetics*, p.137.

[74] Stanley Fish, *Doing What Comes Naturally*, pp.2 and 14.

characterize relations between readers and texts.[75] The supposed "objectivity" of the text as that which *controls* strategy is an illusion; different strategies of reading represent different *things that readers do with* texts. Thus where *readers* may have *cognitive* reading *expectations*, it is likely that this will give rise to a rhetorical strategy of *discursive* reading; *readers'* quests for self-knowledge, or their *expectations* that the text will enhance self-awareness, may dictate a strategy of *"dialectical"* reading-processes. At this stage in his development of theory (1972) Fish experienced a genuine *tension* between the notion that a text "out there" somehow *constrained* interpretation (and therefore invited quasi-objective questions about style, genre, or purpose) and his growing awareness that *readers' own strategies, goals, assumptions, and expectations* seem to determine what *counts for them as* reading or interpretation.

Fish looks back on this period of "worry" from a later vantage point in his introductory essay to *Is There a Text in this Class?* (1980). He entitles his autobiographical reflections "How I Stopped Worrying and Learned to Love Interpretation".[76] By this stage (1980) he has come to "see through" the illusion that any "meaning" resided *in* the text at all. Interpretation as "reading meaning" is *constructed* by what Fish terms "the authority of interpretive communities". This alone determines what *counts as* interpretation. The notion that texts have meanings is illusory, at least in the sense of their lying "innocently" in the text itself. Fish comments on his own earlier mistaken assumptions: "I did what critics always do: I 'saw' what my interpretive principles permitted or directed me to see, and then I turned around and attributed what I had 'seen' to a text and an intention. What my principles direct me to 'see' are readers performing acts."[77]

Textual meanings, Fish therefore declared, "do not lie innocently in the world; rather, they are themselves *constituted* by an interpretive act. The facts one points to are still there (in a sense that would not be consoling to an objectivist) but only as a consequence of the interpretive (man-made) model that has called them into being."[78] It is thus operationally justifiable, and even necessary if confusion is to be avoided, to *replace* the question "What does this *mean*?" by the question "What does this *do*?" In a key sentence Fish writes: "The reader's response is not *to* the meaning; it *is* the meaning."[79]

The later work undertaken by Fish between 1980 and 1989 consolidates and defends this position. Everything hinges on "social and institutional circumstances".[80] Thus in the large volume of twenty-two essays published under the title *Doing What Comes Naturally*, Fish includes his notoriously polemical review of Wolfgang Iser's work (1981) in which he attacks Iser for stopping half-way on the journey to a consistent reader-response theory; Fish also attacks Owen Fiss's essay "Objectivity and Interpretation" (1982) in "Fish v. Fiss"; he argues that Ronald Dworkin "repeatedly falls away from his own best insights into the fallacies (of pure objectivity and pure subjectivity) he so forcefully challenges".[81] He discusses the nature of change in social frameworks of thought partially with reference to Thomas Kuhn and to

---

[75] Stanley Fish, *Self-Consuming Artefacts. The Experience of Seventeenth-Century Literature* (Berkeley, CA: University of California Press, 1972).
[76] Stanley Fish, *Is There a Text in this Class?*, pp.1–17.
[77] Ibid., p.12.
[78] Ibid., p.13.
[79] Ibid., p.3.
[80] Ibid., p.371.
[81] Stanley Fish, *Doing What Comes Naturally*, p.88; cf. pp.68–86; 87–119; 120–40.

Richard Rorty.[82] A unifying theme emerges in the contrast between formalist systems and socio-contingent pragmatic contexts of life. Fish views performative utterances as "contingent ... [they] cannot be formally constrained".[83] But he detects an ambivalence in J.L. Austin which gives rise to the development of speech-act theory either in a formalist direction (Jerrold Katz) or in contingent-pragmatic terms (H.P. Grice and Mary L. Pratt).[84]

These twenty-two essays offer a panoramic view of diverse twists and turns in contemporary debate. The relation between social institutions and institutional, legal, or performative *force* receives a particular focus in Fish's critique of H.L.A. Hart's philosophy of law.[85] I have argued elsewhere that, in the context of J.L. Austin and John Searle, what may count as "institutional" facts offer a foundation on the basis of which certain illocutions and speech-acts can become operative. In these terms there is prima-facie plausibility in Fish's observations concerning the "temporally contingent nature of our 'fundamental' assumptions".[86] In many of these essays, where his concerns are broader than his earlier work on literary "meaning" and literary texts, Fish seems often to be an ally of speech-act approaches in the hermeneutical enterprise, with its emphasis on the historical contingency of the life-world as against a purely formal system.

Nevertheless we have argued repeatedly in this volume that *socio-pragmatic or neo-pragmatic hermeneutics ultimately betrays the very function that hermeneutics arose to perform.* Fish includes in this volume of essays a very brief skirmish with Habermas, and it is clear that he cannot entertain the possibility of a genuinely critical, socio-critical, metacritical, or trans-contextual hermeneutic. He cannot journey with Habermas or with Apel in the quest for any principle that would *relate* the life-world to a broader system, however loose and open such a system might be. For Fish has committed himself: it is *either* formalism *or* radical pragmatic *anti*-formalism. There is no place to stand, according to Fish, between the two extremes. This is Fish's fatal error.

VII
What Fish's Counter-Arguments Overlook about Language: Fish and Wittgenstein

Wittgenstein was as eager as Fish to shake off the illusion of formal or "ideal" language, "as if our logic were, so to speak, a logic for a vacuum".[87] In retrospect Wittgenstein writes that logic of a purely *formal* kind is "*a priori* order: that is, the order of *possibilities* ... It is *prior* to all experience ... a *super*-order ... *super*-concepts ..." (Wittgenstein's italics).[88] This was the formalist view that Wittgenstein had presented in his early systematic work on the philosophy of logic under the title *Tractatus Logico-Philosophicus*.[89] Wittgenstein

82 Ibid., p.143 and 157–9; cf. pp.141–60 and 485–94.
83 Ibid., p.489; cf. pp.471–502.
84 Ibid., pp.61–7; cf. pp.37–60.
85 Ibid., pp.503–24.
86 Ibid., pp.523–4.
87 L. Wittgenstein, *Philosophical Investigations*, sect. 81.
88 Ibid., sect. 97.
89 L. Wittgenstein, *Tractatus Logico-Philosophicus* (Ger. & Eng., London: Routledge & Kegan Paul, 1961). See further his *Notebooks 1914–16* (Eng., Oxford: Blackwell, 1961).

later comments in his *Philosophical Investigations*: "The *pre-conceived idea* of crystalline purity can only be removed by turning our whole examination round ... A *picture* held us captive ... The confusions which occupy us arise when language is like an engine idling, not when it is doing work."[90]

By contrast with formalist theories of language, Wittgenstein insists that the meaning of such terms as "proposition", "language", and even "meaning" itself depends on "the language-game in which they are to be applied".[91] Wittgenstein observes in his book *On Certainty*, "When language-games change, then there is a change in concepts, and with the concepts the meanings of words change."[92] Rush Rhees comments on Wittgenstein's approach: "Speaking is not *one thing*, and 'having meaning' is not *one thing* either."[93] Wittgenstein notes in his *Zettel*: "What determines ... our concepts is ... the whole hurly-burly of human actions, the background against which we see any action."[94] Finally, in his *Remarks on the Foundations of Mathematics* he writes, "The kinds of use we feel to be 'the point' are connected with the role that such-and-such a use has in our whole life."[95]

Wittgenstein's own journey "down the anti-formalist road" seems in the light of primary sources and secondary literature to be altogether more intense and philosophically serious than Fish's account of his journey in "How I Stopped Worrying ...".Through painful and serious intellectual struggle Wittgenstein passed through the so-called middle period of the *Philosophical Bemerkungen* (1929–30; published in 1964) and earlier parts of *Philosophical Grammar* (1929–34; published in 1974) to the later period of *The Blue and Brown Books* (1933–35; published in 1958), his major work *Philosophical Investigations* (Part I, 1936–45, Part II, 1947–49; first edition, 1953), and *On Certainty* (1950–51, published in 1969). Major studies of Wittgenstein's thought shed additional light on how a view of meaning emerged which is neither formalist nor purely contextual-pragmatic. In addition to the first-generation assessments from Norman Malcolm (1958, 1967) and from Rush Rhees (1970), and the early work of George Pitcher (1964), special note may be taken of the critical studies offered by Anthony Kenny (1975), David Pears (1971), A. Janik and S. Toulmin (1973), and Gordon P. Baker and P.M. Hacker (3 vols, 1983, 1988, 1990), among others.[96] In *The Two Horizons* I devoted two detailed chapters and part of a third chapter to Wittgenstein's relation to hermeneutical theory, and in this connection also alluded to the work of Apel.[97]

---

[90] L. Wittgenstein, *Philosophical Investigations*, sects 108, 115 and 132.

[91] Ibid., sect. 96.

[92] L. Wittgenstein, *On Certainty* (Ger. and Eng., Oxford: Blackwell, 1969), sect. 65.

[93] Rush Rhees, *Discussions of Wittgenstein* (London: Routledge & Kegan Paul, 1970), p.75; cf. pp.71–84 (first italics, Rhees's; second, mine).

[94] L. Wittgenstein, *Zettel*, sect. 567.

[95] L. Wittgenstein, *Remarks on the Foundations of Mathematics* (Ger. and Eng., Oxford: Blackwell, 1956), I, 8, sect. 16.

[96] Anthony Kenny, *Wittgenstein* (London: Penguin Books, 1975); David Pears, *Wittgenstein* (London: Collins, 1971); George Pitcher, *The Philosophy of Wittgenstein* (Englewood Cliffs, NJ: Prentice-Hall, 1964); Allan Janik and Stephen Toulmin, *Wittgenstein's Vienna* (London: Wiedenfeld & Nicholson, 1973); Gordon P. Baker and P.M. Hacker, *Analytical Commentary on Wittgenstein's Philosophical Investigations* (3 vols) I; *Understanding and Meaning; II, Rules, Grammar and Necessity; III, Meaning and Mind* (Oxford: Blackwell, 1983, 1988 and 1990).

[97] Anthony C. Thiselton, *The Two Horizons*, chapters XIII and XIV; cf. also chapter II, and the relevant studies of Karl-Otto Apel cited in chapter XI of *New Horizons in Hermeneutics*.

If both Fish and Wittgenstein see the illusions of formalism, however, their respective methods in distancing themselves from it are entirely different. In *Doing What Comes Naturally*, Fish consciously "sets up" Ruth Kempson's formalist approach to language as a foil for his own *either/or*.[98] For Fish it becomes a matter of *necessity* to reject formalism and to espouse its supposed opposite as a way of being doctrinally *consistent* (in contrast to Iser, Fiss and numerous similar targets of attack). But Wittgenstein has had enough of doctrine and personal narrative ("A picture held us captive"). His method of achieving liberation from this formalist "picture" which had "held him captive" is expressed in his *Philosophical Investigations* under the maxim: "Don't say: 'There *must* be ...' but *look* and see whether there is ... Don't think, but look" (Wittgenstein's italics).[99] Further, whereas Fish sees the alternative to formalism as that of socially conditioned norms *internal to given communities*, in the *Zettel* Wittgenstein observes: "The philosopher is not *a citizen of any community of ideas. This is what makes him into a philosopher*" (my italics).[100] This is different from Fish's socio-pragmatic language about convictions which arise from Kempson's "story" and from "my story".

When he *looked at* language, Wittgenstein observed that *some* language-games could be thought of in entirely context-relative terms, but *for the most part* "we see a complicated network of similarities overlapping and criss-crossing".[101] In other words, although social practices of given communities do indeed provide a background which contextually shapes concepts and meanings, *overlapping and interpenetration also offer certain criss-crossings which constitute trans-contextual bridges*. Sufficient bridging can occur for Wittgenstein to suggest that in many cases a trans-contextual frame of reference for meanings can be found in *"the common behaviour of mankind"*.[102]

It is not the case, as Fish suggests it is, that we must choose between the sharply-bounded crystalline purity of formalist concepts and the unstable concepts of contextual pragmatism. Concepts may function with a measure of operational stability, but with "blurred edges". Differences of social context and practice may *push or pull them into relatively different shapes*, but do not necessarily change their stable *identity*. For Wittgenstein, as for F. Waismann, "concepts with blurred edges" are situated on middle ground along the road from formalism to pragmatism.[103]

The fundamental philosophical weakness in Fish's polarizing of his two alternatives lies in the failure to come to terms with the major transcendental questions which stem from Kant, in which very careful and rigorous attention is given to the working distinction between how the knowing human subject or agent *conditions* raw data and what this subject or agent *constructs* independently of raw data. *Do social contexts condition or do they construct social realities, including texts?* Beyond the Kantian philosophical tradition, the tradition of Hegel which passes on through Gadamer to Habermas wrestles with a parallel tension between the contextually-historically finite and the broader continuum or frame which finite historical phenomena presuppose.

---

[98]   Stanley Fish, *Doing What Comes Naturally*, pp.1–6.

[99]   L. Wittgenstein, *Philosophical Investigations*, sect. 66; cf. sects 126–30.

[100] L. Wittgenstein, *Zettel*, sect. 455; cf. sect. 452.

[101] Stanley Fish, loc. cit., p.3.

[102] L. Wittgenstein, *Philosophical Investigations*, sect. 206; cf. sect. 281.

[103] Ibid., sect. 71.

Fish, as a lawyer and literary critic, "sees through" what has long preoccupied the minds of the great philosophers, endeavouring to move quickly, with little or no reference to the deeper philosophical background, to fairly brief skirmishes with Habermas and with Toulmin, and with passing appeals for support to Thomas Kuhn and to Richard Rorty. However, he does not seem to note that Kuhn has substantially *modified his earlier claims* about the socio-contextual nature of knowledge in science in his later book of essays, *The Essential Tension* (1977).[104] In an essay with the promising title "Critical Self-Consciousness, or Can We Know What We're Doing?", Fish dismisses as untenable or as self-contradictory the "universal pragmatics" or socio-critical theory of Habermas. Fish argues that "the insight of historicity – the fashioned or *constructed* nature of *all* forms of thought and organization" (my italics) relativizes Habermas's claim to offer *critical* theory.[105] He insists that the counter-arguments and defences put forward by Habermas merely "re-start" the argument again and again, and that critical theory, rather than solving the problem, simply reinstates it.

Like Rorty, Fish only "listens" to that aspect of post-Hegelian, post-Gadamerian philosophy which recognizes exclusively the *internal, instrumental function of reason* within social traditions on the basis of a doctrine that all rationality operates at this single level, and can never explore outside socially-determined boundaries in order to provide broader or deeper metacritical reflection.

It is precisely here, however, that we return to Wittgenstein, and to his recognition of *overlap* between language-games. *If* our vision is *always internal to our own language-games,* how could Wittgenstein declare "One learns the game by *watching* how others play"?[106] Why does Wittgenstein recognize the *specific* cultural relativity of *some* language-games, while insisting that the contextual conditions for the operability of *other* language-games lie simply in being "a *living human being*"?[107] Why does he see so many conceptual meanings as simply grounded in "ordinary intercourse with others" (like Apel's universal inter-subjectivity) rather than as context-specific (like Rorty's local traditions)?[108] How would it make sense for Wittgenstein to say "The common behaviour of mankind is the system of reference by means of which we interpret an unknown language"?[109]

Fish offers some recognition in his latest counter-arguments designed to forestall criticism, to the notion that the social roles which arise from contextual institutions may overlap or interpenetrate. Practices and communities, he acknowledges, are not "pure". For example, he suggests, "My way of being a parent is all mixed with my way of being a teacher", or we may bring together two community-traditions in the very notion of "black academics".[110] Feminist academics likewise bring to their work and to their

---

[104] Stanley Fish, *Doing What Comes Naturally*, pp.471–502, esp. p.487; cf. also Thomas S. Kuhn, *The Essential Tension. Selected Studies in Scientific Tradition and Change* (Chicago, IL: University of Chicago Press, 1977), esp. pp.293–319.

[105] Stanley Fish, *Doing What Comes Naturally*, p.455; cf. pp.436–70.

[106] L. Wittgenstein, *Philosophical Investigations*, sect. 54 (my italics).

[107] Ibid., sect. 281 (my italics); cf. sect. 360.

[108] Ibid., sect. 420.

[109] Ibid., sect. 206.

[110] Stanley Fish, loc. cit., p.31.

"reading" more than one set of community interests, presuppositions and expectations.[111] But Fish does not develop this fundamental point in the direction adopted by Karl-Otto Apel. He refines the concept of "reading community" but insists that we cannot gain access thereby to norms or criteria "outside" the community.

The key difficulty is that while he recognizes variables in contingencies of social history, Fish holds to a pragmatic *doctrine* whereby *all* texts depend for *all* meaning on what socio-contextual boundaries construct by internal community norms and practices. Wittgenstein, by contrast, observes diversity among different "texts" and among different examples of "meaning". In the well-known language-game of "Wittgenstein's builders" meanings are created by ostensive reference *only because "this narrowly circumscribed region" presupposes a given communicative situation between these two builders.* It is context-specific.[112] But in his *Culture and Value*, Wittgenstein envisages a different example. Two people, this time, share a joke. Wittgenstein writes, "One of them has used certain somewhat unusual words and now they both break out into a sort of bleating. That might appear *very* extraordinary to a visitor coming from quite a different environment. Whereas we find it completely *reasonable*" (his italics).[113] In the case of laughter, the "meaning" of this "institutional" or social behaviour is trans-contextual or trans-cultural.

The principle, however, can be extended. What about language which expresses pain?[114] Its *embeddedness in universal pain-behaviour* makes it artificially forced to say: "Only these reading-communities which experience pain like *this* construct *this* kind of meaning for pain in texts." How are we to evaluate language about remorse, sincerity, or lying? Wittgenstein sees these as having *stable* meanings in the context of *human behaviour as such.* In his *Zettel* he makes this point clearly. Human beings *as human beings* (not *as* academics or *as* women) "reflect on the past"; but "can a dog feel ... remorse?"[115] In the *Investigations* he seems to make the same point about sincerity: "Why can't a dog simulate pain? Is he too honest? ... A dog cannot be a hypocrite, but neither can he be sincere."[116] This is not to deny the role of education and learning. Thus, for example, "lying is a language-game that needs to be learned like any other one."[117] But *this* tradition of learning weaves in and out through a multitude of socio-cultural communities.

Wittgenstein's arguments about "private language" (in the strictly technical sense of the term) can be applied at a corporate level to interaction between communities of interpretation. Wittgenstein's point is that *without an inter-subjective "checking" or testing process,* there would be no way in which language-users could tell the difference between uses or meanings that were "correct", and those that "seemed" correct. There would be no difference between a "mistake" and a *"systematic mistake".* Wittgenstein declares, "It is not possible to obey a rule privately; otherwise *thinking* one was obeying the rule would

---

[111]   Ibid., pp.31–2.
[112]   Ibid., sects 2 and 3.
[113]   L. Wittgenstein, *Culture and Value*, p.78.
[114]   L. Wittgenstein, *Philosophical Investigations*, sects 281–351; cf. *Zettel*, sects 532–42.
[115]   L. Wittgenstein, *Zettel*, sects 518 and 519.
[116]   L. Wittgenstein, *Philosophical Investigations*, sect. 250 and ii, 229.
[117]   Ibid., sect. 249; cf. *Zettel*, sects 89 and 90.

be the same thing as *obeying* it" (my italics).[118] But this principle can be extended to checking or to testing inter-contextual currency-values *between* communities of readers. *"Hard"* currency can be measured and transacted across national or contextual boundaries; *"soft"* currency meets *only internal demands* in accordance with internal norms. Its pragmatic value is culture-bound. Like the currency of some Eastern Bloc countries at the time of writing, *soft* currency depends on internal subsidies which, when removed, makes them uncompetitive and unusable for our international business. But language, too, can acquire an inflated currency in relation to internal norms, where such criteria as "literary productivity" operate without reference to inter-contextual or trans-contextual human practices and communicative currency-rates. Wittgenstein explores the need for some behavioural "backing" for linguistic currency especially in his *Blue Book*.

In the light of all this, we may look again at the standard criticisms of socio-pragmatic hermeneutics and at Fish's disarming disclaimers in his "Going Down the Anti-Formalist Road".

(i) Fish readily concedes Cornel West's criticism that pragmatism can offer no effective socio-critical assessment for social action. He agrees: "The thesis that theory goes nowhere (except in the contingent ways of all rhetorics) is itself a thesis that can go nowhere."[119] Jonathan Culler, as we have noted, understandably views such a position as "complacent", because it would be tolerable only if one had supreme confidence that one's theory was not itself corrigible in the light of further enquiry and research. While Habermas genuinely takes on board the dimension of historical and hermeneutical contingency, Rorty (as West notes) insists that everyone else must share his own evaluation of social narrative as marking out pragmatic anti-metacritical ground, and he seems unable to "see" the possibility of inter-contextual *exploration*. While Wittgenstein *goes on* "looking", exploring and enquiring, Rorty (and Fish) propound a pragmatic *doctrine* that offers only ghetto-like consistency *on its own terms*. In the end Fish argues that philosophical sterility does not really matter because society and social theory is "propped up", in his view, not by critical thought, theory, or philosophy, but by "the material conditions" of everyday life.[120] Social relations, dollars and military security thus provide the nearest to a metacritical principle; hence Culler associates this pragmatic "complacency" with "the age of Reagan". Pragmatic hermeneutics has more than a touch of Hollywood and John Wayne: "A man's gotta do what a man's gotta do" (given the community's conventions); but we cannot *ask* metacritical questions about whether the community's conventions are testable or right (even if they sometimes glorify retaliation or oppress conquered races) because we cannot get *"outside"* the film without perceiving it *as* a film.

(ii) This brings us precisely to the second standard criticism. *Socio-pragmatic or neo-pragmatic philosophy can never be more than narrative philosophy*. This is why Fish's key essay in *Is There a Text in This Class?* remains narrative testimony about shifting convictions.

---

[118]   L. Wittgenstein, *Philosophical Investigations*, sect. 202; cf. Anthony C. Thiselton, *The Two Horizons*, p.385.

[119]   Stanley Fish, *Doing What Comes Naturally*, p.27.

[120]   Ibid., p.28.

Rorty's style in *Philosophy and the Mirror of Nature* reflects this narrative style: it is the retelling of the story of a particular tradition of philosophy, with a retrospective "pointing up" of what supports pragmatic doctrine. Richard Bernstein and Christopher Norris both engage brilliantly, as we have seen, with the self-contradictory nature of this mode of argument as a claim to *philosophize*.[121] Norris acutely observes that Rorty offers, on the basis of his own pragmatic premise, "*just one story among many*"; but that he (and Fish) could still try to have

> ... the last word against anyone who wanted philosophy to be *more* than just a story ... Under cover of its liberal-pluralist credentials, this narrative very neatly closes all exits except the one marked "James and Dewey". The rejection of a meta-narrative standpoint goes along with *a refusal to entertain any serious alternative account of what philosophy ought to be. It is this use of a liberal rhetoric to frame an authoritative message* which marks the real kinship between Rorty's pragmatism and nineteenth-century narrative forms.[122]

(iii) Earlier we drew attention to Georgia Warnke's careful discussion concerning the trans-contextual nature of rationality in relation to assessments of Gadamer and of Rorty. Such an approach coheres with Wittgenstein's observations about overlaps and criss-crossings among contextual language-games, about publicly accessible criteria of meaning, and about *the philosopher's status as a citizen of no particular given community.* Wittgenstein's work unmasks Fish's attempts to "set up" formalism in a way which superficially invites a rebound into social pragmatism. For while Wittgenstein shares Fish's disillusionment with formalism, whether there is any "place to stop" along the anti-formalist road depends not on pragmatic (anti-formalist) *doctrine*, but on *noticing what kinds of language, what kinds of texts and what kinds of meanings are at issue.* In a *large class* of cases (though not in all cases) it is simply doctrinaire to claim that "meaning" can be reduced exhaustively and without remainder to what the internal norms and conventions of given communities simply construct. The meaning-currency of *many* texts (not all texts) draws its cash-value from the backing of the inter-subjective world out of which it is spoken or written, and in many cases (though not all) its system of reference is the common behaviour of humankind.

VIII
Postscript: Problematic Implications for Theology and Theological Hermeneutics

The greatest weakness of neo-pragmatic reader-response theories, especially in the form advocated by Fish, lies in their inadequacy as a philosophy of language. However, the consequences for theology and theological hermeneutics are disastrous. We conclude with a brief tailpiece on some of their problematic entailments for Christian theology. We select five in particular:

---

[121] Christopher Norris, *The Contest of Faculties: Philosophy and Theory after Deconstruction* (London and New York: Methuen, 1985), pp.139–66 *et passim*; Richard Bernstein, *Habermas and Modernity*, pp.3–10 and 19–23.

[122] Christopher Norris, loc. cit., p.159 (my italics).

(i)   If textual meaning is the *product* of a community of readers, as Fish concedes, texts cannot reform these readers "from outside". In this case *the Reformation* appears to have been little more than a dispute over alternative ecclesiological or community life-styles. It *could no longer claim to be retrieving authentic meanings of biblical texts, let alone texts which address communities "from beyond"*.

(ii)   *Prophetic address* is regarded as coming "from beyond", virtually against human will. This is now perceived as either illusory or to be explained in terms of pre-conscious inner conflict. It is really, after all, an address that coheres with the deepest hopes or expectations of a community, even if it might not seem like this. *It is not, in the end, an address*: the community itself has created the word.

(iii) Such notions as *grace* or *revelation must* (by pragmatic doctrine) be illusory, because Rorty tells us that there are no "givens".

(iv)   *The message of the cross* remains a *linguistic construct* of a tradition. Some gnostics already claimed this in the second or third centuries.

(v)   It would be impossible to determine what would *count as a systematic mistake in the development of doctrine*. Pragmatism allows only the view that what gave rise to *our* past and present must somehow have broadly been right. Social pragmatism accepts only social winners as criteria of truth.

The gains and contributions drawn from reader-response theories can be potentially enormous for biblical hermeneutics; on the other side certain exaggerations and mistakes could be disastrous for theology. There are few reader-response theorists who have nothing of genuine importance to tell us. Iser's work on the active role of readers, Eco's work on codes and texts, Holland's theories about self-identity, and David Bleich's reminders about ordinary people in communities of readers, all have something very important to say. Culler's work on reader competency and Fish's warnings about the context-relative status of so-called "natural" meanings, all assist hermeneutical self-awareness. Fish also reminds us that boundaries between texts and interpretative traditions are by no means sharp and clear-cut.

Nevertheless the notion that biblical texts might not have the capacity to transform readers "from beyond", but merely evoke "constructions" drawn from the hitherto undiscovered inner resources of the reading community, does not cohere readily or well with Christian theology. Theology cannot dispense with metacritical reflection. More than this, socio-pragmatic hermeneutics transposes the meaning of texts into projections that may be *potentially idolatrous* as instruments of indulgent self-affirmation. *Such a model transposes a Christian theology of grace and revelation into a phenomenology of religious self-discovery*. Paul Ricoeur calls us "to destroy the idols, and to listen to symbols".[123] This, he suggests, is the goal of hermeneutics.

---

123   Paul Ricoeur, *Freud and Philosophy*, p.54.

CHAPTER TWENTY-EIGHT

A Retrospective Reappraisal:
Reader-Response Hermeneutics
and Parable Worlds (New essay)

While Essays 23 and 27 both concern reader-response theory, the approach in each case starts from a different angle and follows a different agenda. Both, however, stress the positive contribution of reader-response hermeneutics in enticing or provoking readers into adopting an active role. Yet both essays, from a retrospective viewpoint, might also have drawn attention to the positive strategy of "indirect communication" as this occurs in the Old Testament, parables of Jesus, and later in Kierkegaard and in Wittgenstein. This, I argue, may shed fresh light on the purpose of parables in the ministry of Jesus (Mark 4:11–12 and parallels). I affirm the role of entering a projected "world" in parables, and the attention given to pre-understanding (Essays 24, 25 and 26).

A critique of radical reader-response theories comes in Essay 27. There I argue that the philosophy of language assumed by Fish is inadequate. In retrospect, however, I might also have taken up Rorty's critique of language as a mirror of the world to ask whether language is merely a mirror of self, as the self-constructed "texts" of radical reader-response theory might be taken to imply. Sacred texts do more, although not less, than mirror the self. Finally I attack the intrusion of an egalitarian political agenda that masquerades as a theory of literature or language, as well as the excesses of some instances of "autobiographical criticism".

I
Reader Response Theory and Indirect Communication

Part V has grouped together two essays on different aspects of reader response theory (Essays 23 and 27), two that relate "world" and "pre-understanding" (Essays 23 and 24), and two on pre-understanding, "world", and eventful speech, with illustrations from the interpretations of parables (Essays 25 and 26). Clearly the two themes of reader-response hermeneutics and the interpretative dynamics of parables belong together.

This is because, to repeat the classic definition of C.H. Dodd already cited above, a parable functions very often (although not always) by "leaving the mind in sufficient doubt about its precise application to tease it into active thought".[1] This illustrates probably the most fundamental value of reader-response theory as a hermeneutical strategy.

This is more than a matter of what educational theorists call "active learning", although it is not less than this. The educational principle that a teacher "teaches" no

---

[1]   C.H. Dodd, *Parables of the Kingdom* (London: Nisbet, 1935), p.16 (cited in Essay 23, sect. III).

more than what the student or pupil actually "learns" remains valid in general terms. However, in the case of parables and such other examples of "productive" texts in much of the Old Testament Wisdom literature, the strategy in question provokes not only active learning but also active *wrestling*, active *puzzling*, active thinking, and active engagement of the understanding. Often intuitive, emotional, pre-cognitive dimensions of active understanding also come into play. This is one reason why provocation and surprise regularly find a place in texts that lend themselves to this strategy of reading. A manager who is *dishonest* turns out to receive his master's approval because at once the text confronts the reader with a prima facie puzzle: why does Jesus or the employer (Greek ὁ κύριος might denote either) *commend* a dishonest manager? Is it perhaps simply for his shrewdness, dishonest though he may be (Luke 16:1–8)?

This dynamic of provoking active puzzlement and active wrestling relates not simply to reader-response theory in literary studies, but the strategy of *indirect communication* in philosophy. In addition to Jesus, the masters of the genre include Socrates, Kierkegaard and the later Wittgenstein. Kierkegaard observes, "One must not let oneself be deceived by the word 'deception'... To recall old Socrates, one can deceive a person into the truth. Indeed it is only ... by deceiving him that it is possible to bring into the truth one who is in an illusion."[2] This is precisely the strategy adopted by the prophet Nathan in the Old Testament when God called him to confront David, his King, with his guilt for criminal and immoral action. It might have been both dangerous and ineffective for Nathan to confront his King with a head-on accusation. Instead he tells David a parable about villainous conduct, provoking David to seethe with indignant anger. He is deceived and thereby seduced into leaving himself vulnerable. When Nathan exclaims, "You are the man!", David can only acknowledge the truth and abandon a shattered illusion (2 Sam. 12:1–6).

Kierkegaard writes, "Direct communication presupposes that the receiver's ability to receive is undisturbed. But here ... an illusion stands in the way... One must first of all use the caustic fluid."[3] Kierkegaard may well be offering a clue to the meaning of the one of the difficult sayings of Jesus about his use of parables when he writes, "It would help a little if one persuaded millions of men to accept the truth, if precisely by the method of this acceptance they were transferred into error";[4] "Truth becomes untruth in this or that person's mouth."[5] The well-known crux of interpretation about the parables comes in Mark 4:11b–12: "For those outside everything comes in parables in order that they may indeed look but not perceive, and may indeed listen but not understand, so that they may not turn again and be forgiven" (Greek: τοῖς ἔξω ἐν παραβολαῖς ... Ἵνα βλέποντες βλέπωσιν καὶ μὴ συνιῶσιν ...).[6]

---

[2] S. Kierkegaard, *Point of View for my Work as an Author* (Princeton, NJ: Princeton University Press, 1941), pp.39–40. Cf. also Anthony C. Thiselton, "Kierkegaard and the Nature of Truth", *Churchman* 89 (1975), pp.85–107.

[3] Kierkegaard, *Point of View*, p.40.

[4] S. Kierkegaard, *Concluding Unscientific Postscript to the Philosophical Fragments* (Eng., Princeton, NJ: Princeton University Press, 1941), p.221.

[5] Kierkegaard, *Concluding Unscientific Postscript*, p.181.

[6] For a careful exegetical discussion of Mark 4:11–22, see R.T. France, *The Gospel of Mark: A Commentary on the Greek Text* (Grand Rapids, MI: Eerdmans and Carlisle: Paternoster, 2002), pp.196–201.

Matthew chooses to avoid Mark's use of "in order that" (Greek ἵνα) in his parallel. Matt. 13:13 remains simply a descriptive allusion to Isaiah's diagnosis of human blindness and illusion: "seeing they do not perceive; and hearing they do not listen, nor do they understand." Luke's parallel repeats Mark's purposive ἵνα. He abbreviates Mark's material, but through the wider context he portrays blindness and illusion as a law of diminishing returns that brings an inbuilt penalty by adding a further comment to the broader context. He retains "so that (ἵνα) seeing they may not see, and hearing they may not understand" (Luke 8:10b). This context is bounded by the parable of the sower and its explanation, and he adds: "So take care how you listen; for to those who have, more will be given; and from those who do not have, even what they seem to have will be taken away" (8:18, NRSV).

If Jesus shares a communicative goal that relates to "indirect" communication, the purpose of using parables rather than "direct" discourse may well be *to prevent premature understanding without inner change.*[7] For a hearer to imagine that he or she has "seen" the point of a packaged truth in terms of a take-it-or-leave-it attitude is disastrous. Postponement of understanding until the heart is ready may be part of the shared hermeneutical strategy here. To "know" in a way that fails to *engage* because it is too soon is more likely to invite judgement than appropriation. Those who are ready, however, receive the "more" that additional direct communication may provide. Indirect communication is a necessary strategy when illusion blocks the way.

Wittgenstein acknowledges the role of illusion in philosophy: "A *picture* held us captive." He seeks to solve problems "not by giving new information, but by arranging what we have always known", and to unmask "the bewitchment of our intelligence by means of language";[9] "One is unable to notice something – because it is always before one's eyes."[10] This helps to explain why (according to Anthony Kenny) Wittgenstein's *Philosophical Investigations* contains nearly 800 questions, of which only just over 100 are answered, and of these, seventy answers are meant to be "wrong".[11] Wittgenstein's Preface to the *Investigations* sums up his relation to indirect communication and the active role of readers. He writes, "I should not like my writing to spare other people the trouble of thinking. But, if possible, to stimulate someone to thoughts of his own."[12] It is no accident that Kierkegaard deliberately attacked some of his own work through the use of pseudonyms, and that Wittgenstein considered publishing his "old thoughts and the new ones together: that the latter could be seen in the right light only by contrast with, and against the background of, my old way of thinking".[13] The "new thoughts" remain "sketches of landscapes … long and involved journeyings".[14]

---

[7] The phrase "to prevent understanding which is unaccompanied by inner change" occurs in Stanley Cavell, "The Availability of Wittgenstein's Later Philosophy", in G. Pitcher (ed.), *Wittgenstein: the Philosophical Investigations* (London: Macmillan, 1968), p.184; cf. pp.151–85; also *Philosophical Review* 71 (1962), pp.67–93.

[8] L. Wittgenstein, *Philosophical Investigations* (German & English, Oxford: Blackwell, 1967), sect. 115.

[9] Wittgenstein, *Investigations*, sect. 109.

[10] Wittgenstein, *Investigations*, p.129.

[11] A. Kenny, "Aquinas and Wittgenstein", *Downside Review* 77 (1959), p.235.

[12] Wittgenstein, *Investigations*, p.x.

[13] Wittgenstein, loc. cit.

[14] Wittgenstein, loc. cit., p.ix.

In the same vein Kierkegaard writes, "Everyone who has a result merely as such does not possess it; for he has not the way."[15] The "objective accent" may fall on "*WHAT* is said"; but this avails nothing if we neglect "the subjective accent, ... *HOW* it is said".[16] Ernst Fuchs rightly perceives that Jesus places a huge emphasis upon this in his speech. Fuchs declares, "Jesus draws the hearer over to his side by means of this artistic medium, so that the hearer may think together with Jesus. *Is not this the way of true love?* Love does not just blurt out. Instead, it provides in advance the sphere in which meeting takes place."[17] Often this is the "world" of the parable.

II
Do Readers' Responses Mirror Only the Self?

In all these accounts of the sayings about the purpose of parables, the critical verses are preceded by the exclamation "He who has ears to hear, let him hear" (Greek: ὃς ἔχει ὦτα ἀκούειν ἀκουέτω, Mark 4:9; and Luke 8:8; also Matt. 13:9, with the omission ἀκούειν, [ears] to hear). The twofold presupposition of this triple tradition is: (1) the need for active engagement on the part of the hearer; and (2) how and what is heard matters. It does not mean "make whatever you like of all this; it is entirely up to you". In aiming at *appropriation* it steers a middle path between narrow replication of a propositional content and unconstrained freedom to create one's own text. R.T. France comments that this formula echoes such verses as Jer. 5:21 and Ezk. 12:2, and "leaves hearers with the responsibility of discerning and applying its meaning".[18] Marshall believes that Luke refers to taking hold of "the meaning of the parable".[19] Hagner sees the Matthew version as demanding not only response, but for the hearer "to respond appropriately".[20]

This resonates reasonably well with the kinds of reader-response theories that we explored in the work of Wolfgang Iser in Essays 23 and 27, and with Umberto Eco and in part Jonathan Cullen in Essay 27. On the other hand it would not fit the more radical reader-response theories of Norman Holland, David Bleich and, especially, Stanley Fish, whose work we reviewed in Essay 27. In the terminology of Iser and Roman Ingarden, Jesus invites his hearers actively "to fill in the gaps" that lie between the picture-part (*Bildhälfte*) and content-part (*Sachhälfte*) or a deeper level of the parable. Furthermore, they are to "fill in the gaps" of subsequent understanding and living in the sense in which Wittgenstein perceives the exclamation "Now I can go on!" as a sign and criterion of "understanding". He writes, "The application is still a criterion of understanding."[21]

---

15 S. Kierkegaard, *The Concept of Irony* (Eng., London: Collins, 1966), p.340.

16 S. Kierkegaard, *Concluding Unscientific Postscript*, p.181 (his capitals).

17 E. Fuchs, *Studies of the Historical Jesus* (London: SCM, 1964), p.129 (my italics).

18 France, *The Gospel of Mark*, p.193.

19 I.H. Marshall, *The Gospel of Luke: A Commentary on the Greek Text* (Grand Rapids, MI: Eerdmans and Carlisle: Paternoster, 1978), p.320.

20 D.A. Hagner, *Matthew 1–13* (Dallas, TX: Word, 1993), p.369.

21 Wittgenstein, *Investigations*, sect. 145; cf. sects 140–78.

Richard Rorty robustly exposes the fallacy of insisting that *all* language is necessarily referential with the world and serves as a "mirror of nature".[22] Those literary theorists who are not necessarily also theists may be content with construing the "revelatory" dimension of literary texts as providing simply mirrors of the human self. Without doubt *many of the parables of Jesus do expose and make transparent attitudes, interests and beliefs held on the part of the human self who hears and responds to them.* Robert Funk demonstrates incisively how the Parable of the Prodigal Son (Luke 15:11–32) operates in this way. In the drama of the defiant son who later shows remorse, and the hard-working son who later shows indignation at the younger one's welcome, Funk observes, "The word of grace ... divides the audience into younger sons and elder sons – into sinners and Pharisees ... The auditors ... either rejoice because as sinners they are glad to be dependent on grace; or they are offended because they want justice on top of grace".[23]

Even for Funk, with his "literary" approach, however, grace brings an extra-contextual or transcendent dimension alongside human consciousness and human selfhood. As a New Testament specialist also drawing upon literary theory, Funk does not reduce the dimensions of grace and justice exhaustively to a mirror of the self. On the other hand, if we press Stanley Fish (and by implication Richard Rorty) to identify some "content" over and above how given readers may respond, as we have argued in Essay 21, the community of readers, not the author (or speaker), creates the texts. I modify this judgement of Rorty to some small extent in Essay 36 (the retrospective appraisal of my work on postmodernity) but this fundamental critique remains. Texts that serve as mirrors of selfhood may "clear a space" for the transcendent, as some postmodern writers express the matter, but most parable-forms in the biblical writings achieve more than this.

I have argued in other essays that to view texts as no more than mirrors of the human individual self or even of a community presupposes an inadequate philosophy of language and cannot do justice to a theology of the biblical writings. Transformation derives from more than a hypothetical dissatisfaction with the human condition. It is a response to a beckoning *from beyond.* If this "Beyond" is a mere construct of the self, we fall into the very error from which Paul Ricoeur perceives hermeneutics as partial means of deliverance, namely the sin of idolatry. "Listening" is hardly "listening" if we can only hear our own heartbeat. Communication is more than taking one's own pulse.

One further point deserves note. While exponents of reader-response approaches are correct in insisting that an unduly cognitive or didactic approach such as that adopted by Jülicher and to a lesser extent Jeremias often changes the original hermeneutical dynamic of parables, there nevertheless remains a place for *retrospective* readings of parables. After their first telling, parables *do* permit interpretations that seek to discover the contours of the teaching of Jesus. This is especially the case in view of this primary place as authentic utterances of Jesus. This is part of the *multiple* hermeneutical functions of parables. All that is necessary is to distinguish the reader-effects of parables told *as parables,* and their "canonical" meanings within a retrospective context of reading. This level of reading,

---

22 R. Rorty, *Philosophy and the Mirror of Nature* (Princeton, NJ: Princeton University Press, 1979), especially pp.257–379.

23 R.W. Funk, *Language, Hermeneutic and Word of God* (New York: Harper & Row, 1966), p.16.

however, begins to move further away from the reader-response models of interpretation and to come closer to reconstructionist models, as if these were more didactic, more "closed", genre within the canon. This loses this primary hermeneutical function and impact, but they retain a "content" not only in the ministry of Jesus, but also within the theologies of the evangelists. We discussed these differing models and their respective applications in Essay 21 ("The Hermeneutics of Pastoral Theology: Ten Strategies for Reading Texts") and the Retrospective Reappraisal of Part IV (Essay 22).

III

The Intrusion of a Political Agenda and the "New Grammar" of Autobiographical Criticism

It has become increasingly apparent that, especially in the United States, reader-response theory also serves as a political tool to promote egalitarianism in literature. The astonishing factor about American literary scholarship is that here Rorty's "liberal pluralism" and the egalitarian reader-response theory of David Bleich and others appear to gain acceptance as virtually "value-neutral", that is, as an academic rather than politically motivated theory. Readers become co-authors, and the authors have no special privilege either as producers or as "experts" and witnesses. But is this a *literary* theory?

Once again it becomes necessary to distinguish a theistic from a non-theistic approach to sacred texts. This is not precisely the same issue as "the death of the author" in the earlier and middle writings of Derrida. It is not his or her "death", but his or her reduction in status and authority that is the issue here. In terms of Christian theology, the following statement from Hans von Campenhausen would become emptied of force. He writes, "The apostles ... are in truth earlier than the church, which is based on [their] testimony and must continually renew its relationship with it".[24]

Even if we try to disengage from distinctively theological arguments, Hans-Georg Gadamer exposes the shallowness and naïvety of the secular Enlightenment polarity between "authority" and "reason", in spite of Kant's elevation of human "autonomy". Gadamer declares, "Authority is ultimately based not on the subjection and abdication of reason, but on ... an act of reason itself, which, aware of its own limitations, accepts that others have better understanding".[25] "The fundamental prejudice of the Enlightenment", he also asserts, "denies tradition its power."[26]

A supposedly new movement under the heading of "Autobiographical Biblical Criticism" appears to extend the contours adopted by David Bleich and Stanley Fish. This movement is difficult to assess for two reasons. First, it claims as "new" themes that have long been stock-in-trade in hermeneutical theory since at least the era of Heidegger, Gadamer, and Habermas. Second, examples of this movement in a recent volume

---

[24] Hans von Campenhausen, *Ecclesiastical Authority and Spiritual Power* (London: Black, 1969), pp.22–23.

[25] Hans-Georg Gadamer, *Truth and Method* (2nd English edn, London: Sheed & Ward, 1989), p.279; (cf. part English edn, 1975, p.248).

[26] Gadamer, *Truth*, p.270.

published under this title vary hugely in their respective claims and level of sophistication. The editor claims that all this is so novel that it entails "coming to terms with learning anew one's ABCs". She adds, "This new criticism transcends traditional scholarly categories and uses a new language ... a different reading process results from it."[27] This new genre also "changes with each new example".[28]

The movement, Ingrid Rosa Kitzberger asserts, represents "the shift from the objective paradigm to the subjective paradigm", citing Thomas Kuhn's overworked notion of paradigm shifts (but with a very brief explanation of this complex term in the philosophy of science).[29] It offers "the most personal and intimate variant of personal voice biblical criticism".[30] In practice this means a frank admission of how personal backgrounds and experience either illuminate the pre-understandings of certain texts, or, as Daniel Patte expresses it, influence certain "interpretive choices".[31] Yet the theoretical and hermeneutical discussion is disappointing. To insist that we must not ignore "situatedness" and "interests" (as John Staley declares) or "pre-understanding" (as Patte observes) is to repeat well-known axioms of hermeneutics.[32] They feature throughout this present collection in a number of essays, and have been discussed since the 1960s.

In the end whether their so-called new movement has a future may well depend on how its exponents develop the philosophy and theology of human selfhood that is never fully explicit in this book. Some of its contributors claim that the self in question is not that of isolated, Cartesian self-consciousness, but others may need more persuasion of this. We might well call attention to certain caveats from Gadamer and Ricoeur, as well as to the later Wittgenstein's reservations about the grammar of mental states and memory. Gadamer writes, "Self-reflection and autobiography ... are not primary and are therefore not an adequate basis for the hermeneutical problem, because through them history is made private once more."[33]

Paul Ricoeur comments, "Every hermeneutics is thus, explicitly or implicitly, self-understanding *by means of understanding others*."[34] In his brilliant and incisive work *Oneself as Another*, Ricoeur begins by exploring "The Shattered Cogito" and "A Hermeneutics of the Self".[35] Ultimately Ricoeur reinstates human selfhood and responsible agency, but not, in the sense used above, subjective autobiographical reflection. Rather, the frame of reference concerns *intersubjectivity* and ethical responsibility.[36] These criteria seem to relate more closely to issues of value and criteria than, up to this date, appears to be the case with "autobiographical criticism", but we may need to wait to see. I consider related issues further in the retrospective evaluation of Part VI on postmodernity.

---

[27] Ingrid Rosa Kitzberger (ed.), *Autobiographical Biblical Criticism: Between Text and Self* (Leiden: Deo, 2002), p.9.

[28] Kitzberger, *Autobiographical Criticism*, p.10.

[29] Kitzberger, loc. cit., p.3.

[30] Ibid., p.5.

[31] Daniel Patte, "Can One Be Critical Without Being Autobiographical?", loc. cit., p.33.

[32] J. Staley, loc. cit., p.15; D. Patte, loc. cit., p.35.

[33] H.-G. Gadamer, *Truth and Method*, p.276.

[34] Paul Ricoeur, *The Conflict of Interpretations: Essays in Hermeneutics* (Evanston, IL: Northwestern University Press, 1974), p.17 (my italics).

[35] Paul Ricoeur, *Oneself as Another* (Chicago, IL: University of Chicago Press, 1992), pp.11–25.

[36] Ricoeur, *Oneself as Another*, especially pp.180–202 and 240–356.

PART VI

PHILOSOPHY, LANGUAGE, THEOLOGY AND POSTMODERNITY

Some Issues in Historical Perspective: "Language and Meaning in Religion" (1978)

This article first appeared in The New International Dictionary of New Testament Theology, *edited by Colin Brown (3 vols, Exeter: Paternoster and Grand Rapids, MI: Zondervan) vol. 3, 1978, pp.1123–46, although with several omissions for purposes of abbreviating the length of the article. This is not primarily a research contribution, and in this respect it belongs with Essays 1 and 2 of this volume rather than with the other thirty-eight research essays. I include it because philosophy of language and many of the issues discussed remain fundamental to biblical, philosophical, theological and literary hermeneutics. Some modern and postmodern theories are formulated as if this groundwork had never been laid. This article therefore forms a basic introduction to the other essays in this Part VI. As a reflection of my own approach, it will also be apparent how heavily I have drawn on the later Wittgenstein for insights that apply in a number of directions. In my retrospective evaluation I identify one or two points where these also resonate with parallel insights in Gadamer and Ricoeur. Finally, this sets basic issues about the nature of language in the setting of the three main streams of twentieth-century thought prior to the impact of postmodern perspectives, namely analytical philosophy, phenomenology and general linguistics. I reserve my explorations of postmodern approaches to language for the remaining seven essays of this Part VI.*

I
Language and Meaning: Approaches in the History of Thought

I.1 The Referential Theory of Meaning

One of the oldest and most persistent theories is the referential theory of meaning. Often two principles are held together: first, that the meaning of a word is the object to which the word refers; and second, that even within broader stretches of language the word itself still remains the basic unit of meaning. This stems largely from the practice of Charles W. Morris, according to which "semiotics", or the science of meaning, is divided into three areas: syntax (the interrelationship between linguistic signs); semantics (according to Morris, the relationship between words and their referents), and pragmatics (the use of language in life). Alfred Tarski and Rudolf Carnap also tend to adopt this view of semantics, and it persists even in recent works.[1] The plausibility of this theory of meaning lies partly in the fact that we assume all too readily that meanings are learned on the basis of ostensive definition (that is, pointing to an object and stating its name).

---

[1] For example in A. Grabner-Haider, *Semiotic und Theologie. Religiöse Rede zwischen analytischer und hermeneutischer Philosophie* (Munich: Kösel, 1973).

The theory of reference, as a matter of principle, however, has grave difficulties, at least if it is offered as a comprehensive theory of meaning.[2] A child understands the procedure of ostensive definition only when he has received a certain measure of linguistic training. L. Wittgenstein demonstrates this decisively in his *Blue and Brown Books* and *Philosophical Investigations*. The key difficulty, he explains, is that ostensive definition can be interpreted in all sorts of ways, unless the one who is learning already understands the nature of the language in question. If I hold up a pencil and say, "This is *tove*", it may mean *either* "this is pencil", or "this is wood", or "this is round", or "this is to-be-used", and so on. Wittgenstein writes, "Point to a piece of paper. – And now point to its shape – now to its colour – now to its number (that sounds queer). How did you do it?"[3]

Many years earlier Gottlob Frege underlined a further problem about the theory of reference. In practice, he argued, we sometimes use words that have different meanings to refer to the same object. Thus the meaning of "the morning star" is not the same as that of "the evening star", even though both terms may refer to the planet Venus. This led Frege to distinguish between sense (*Sinn*) and reference. Frege's objection is not fatal to referential theories, since they can be reformulated, as he saw, to take account of this difficulty. Nevertheless it does rob the theory of its common-sense appeal. Wittgenstein concluded that the referential theory of meaning could hold its spell over us only if we restrict our attention to certain kinds of words. He writes, "If you describe the learning of language in this way, you are, I believe, thinking primarily of nouns like 'table', 'chair', 'bread', and of people's names, and only secondarily of the names of certain actions and properties; and of the remaining kinds of words as something that will take care of itself ... Think of exclamations alone, with their completely different functions ...".[4]

I.2 The Fallacy of "One Word, One Meaning": Field Semantics

The second related principle that we often associate with the referential theory of meaning also stands open to question: is *the word* the "basic unit" of meaning? In linguistics the chief criticism of this assumption comes from exponents of field semantics. Thus J. Trier insists that a word has meaning "only as part of a whole" and only "within a field".[5] The semantic scope of the word "red", for example, cannot be assessed in merely abstract terms. Its scope will vary in accordance with whether it stands in contrast to "orange", or only to "yellow", within a field of colour-terms. Admittedly it is legitimate and indeed often necessary to study the meanings of words as such, provided that it is not forgotten that conclusions reached on this basis remain only generalizations arrived at on the assumption that the word in question occurs in a characteristic setting. [I discussed this particular issue at greater length in "Semantics and New Testament Interpretation" included as Essay 13 of this volume, above.]

---

[2] See A.C. Thiselton, *Language, Liturgy and Meaning* (Nottingham: Grove Liturgical Studies, 1975), pp.10–13.

[3] L.Wittgenstein, *Philosophical Investigations* (Oxford: Blackwell, German and English, 1958 and 1967), § 33; cf. Wittgenstein, *Blue and Brown Books* (Oxford: Blackwell, 1969[2]), pp.2–4.

[4] *Philosophical Investigations*, §§ 1 and 27.

[5] J. Trier, *Der Deutsche Wortschatz im Sinnbezirk des Verstandes* (Heidelberg: Winter, 1931), p.6.

Stephen Ullmann writes, "There is usually in each word a hard core of meaning which is relatively stable and can only be modified by the context within certain limits."[6] G. Stern makes a similar point.[7] At the same time, however, it is important to heed the warning of R.H. Robins, that this method of approaching meanings in terms of words is acceptable only "provided it is borne in mind that words have meanings by virtue of their employment in sentences ... and that the meaning of a sentence is not to be thought of as a sort of summation of the meanings of its component words taken individually".[8] Words are more than mere "names".

From a philosophical point of view, too, the equation of the word with the name has caused persistent problems from Plato to Russell and the earlier work of L. Wittgenstein. In his earlier writings Wittgenstein states, "One name stands for one thing, another for another thing, and they are combined with one another. In this way the whole group – like a *tableau vivant* – presents a state of affairs."[9] Wittgenstein came to see, however, that the notion of "simple" elements of language that correspond to "simple" objects is a mere abstraction demanded by the mind of the logician. He had earlier argued that simple objects stand in a determinate relation to one another, thereby constituting a state of affairs (*Sachverhalt*). Similarly, elements of language stand in a determinate relation to one another, in such a way that a statement constitutes a picture (*Bild*), or a model, of reality. On this view, every statement can in principle be wholly and completely analysed with its smallest determinate elements, or "simples". In his later writings, however, Wittgenstein powerfully and convincingly demonstrates that *in practice* language does not operate in this way. If we actually *look* at language, rather than try to force some theory on to it, he urges, we see that even terms like "simple" and "exact" have no self-evident meaning that can be arrived at prior to their actual settings in human life. All language is relative to its "surroundings". The referential theory of meaning, therefore, of which Wittgenstein's early picture theory formed one example, fails to do justice to the ways in which language is actually used, at least if it is offered as a comprehensive theory of meaning.

I.3 Ideational Theories of Meaning: John Locke

The so-called ideational theory of meaning suffers from all of the difficulties of the referential theory. In the Graeco-Roman era the Stoics drew a threefold distinction between (1) "that which signifies" (*to sēmainon*), namely the linguistic sign; (2) "that which is signified" by the sign (*to sēmainomenon*), and (3) the actual object or event in the physical world to which these correspond (*to tynchanon*).

This is the origin of the famous "semantic triangle" which C.K. Ogden and I.A. Richards still offered in the twentieth century as a basic model of the relation between language and meaning. According to these two writers, (1) there is a causal relation of

---

[6] S. Ullmann, *Semantics. An Introduction to the Science of Meaning* (Oxford: Blackwell, 1962), p.49.

[7] G. Stern, *Meaning and Change of Meaning* (Gothenburg: Göteborgs Högskolas Arsskrift, 1931), p.85.

[8] R.H. Robins, *General Linguistics* (London: Longmans, 1964), p.22.

[9] L. Wittgenstein, *Tractatus Logico-Philosophicus* (London: Routledge, German and English, 1961), 4.0311.

reference between an object in the physical world and a concept, thought, or image in the mind (the first side of the triangle). (2) The concept or thought then stands in causal relation to its symbolic expression in language. Here the operative relation is that of symbolizing (the second side of the triangle). (3) Ogden and Richards claim that they have now explained the relation between linguistic symbol and its object of reference. On the basis of the other two *causal* relations, we now have an *imputed* relation between the symbol and its referent (the third side of the triangle).[10] In effect, this is little more than an attempt to add a mentalist dimension to a theory of reference.

In the seventeenth century John Locke argued that words are "external sensible signs ... whereof invisible ideas might be made known to others ... The ideas they stand for are their proper and immediate signification."[11] In the twentieth century this emphasis has affinities not only with Ogden and Richards, but also with the work of Susanne K. Langer.

Rather than easing the difficulties of the referential theory, however, this approach makes matters even worse. It is often associated with the idea that language is a rather shabby vehicle of expression for otherwise clear ideas. Linguistic expression derives its meaning from the image, idea, or mental picture, which the speaker is trying to communicate, "as if it were a kind of internal motion picture accompanying these performances".[12] Once again, however, in his later writings Wittgenstein convincingly attacked the notion that language and thinking can be detached from each other in this way. Meaning is not a kind of mental process that somehow exists alongside actual speaking. In practice we do not usually experience a stream of images accompanying our speaking; nor is it easy to say in what a "thought" consists which we cannot express in language.[13]

We have already suggested that to think of language as that which merely articulates *thoughts already present to the mind* is an inadequate and seriously misleading view of language.[14] Whatever may be said about images or concepts, however, the problem still remains that the ideational theory of meaning escapes none of the difficulties of theories of reference. J. Pelc argues that all theories of meaning are severely limited which simply try to extend what remains basically a theory of words as names. This theory can never progress beyond the assumption "that the meaning of a sentence is a function of the meaning of its components".[15]

---

[10]   C.K. Ogden and I.A. Richards, *The Meaning of Meaning* (London: Routledge, 1923), p.14.
[11]   John Locke, *An Essay Concerning Human Understanding* (Oxford: Clarendon, 1975 [1798]), III, § 21.
[12]   D.M. High, *Language, Persons, and Belief* (New York: OUP, 1967), p.37.
[13]   Cf. L. Wittgenstein, *Philosophical Investigations*, §§ 338–42.
[14]   Cf. also F. Waismann, *Principles of Linguistic Philosophy* (London: Macmillan, 1965), pp.153–93.
[15]   J. Pelc, *Studies in Functional Logical Semiotics of Natural Language* (The Hague, 1971), p.58.

II
Language as a Dimension of Human Activity and Action

II.1 Wittgenstein and Heidegger: Initial Observations

The problem of meaning is best approached when language is viewed as part of a human activity, or of a form of life.[16] We begin neither with words, nor with ideas, nor even with propositions, but with the human being speaking language in a particular situation. Looking back on his earlier writings, Wittgenstein spoke of "turning our whole examination round":[17] "Only in the stream of thought and life (*Leben*) do words have meaning."[18] Both Martin Heidegger in *Being and Time* (though less in his later writings) and Wittgenstein in his later period stress that language and understanding constitute (for Heidegger) an *a priori existentiale* of *Dasein*, or (for Wittgenstein) an inseparable dimension of human life. Meaning, Heidegger urges, is not something that we attach to some otherwise naked object that is present-at-hand (*vorhanden*). Meaning is bound up with the horizon of the human subject (*Dasein*) according to which he understands something *as* what it is to him.[19] In a parallel way Wittgenstein urges: "every sign *by itself* seems dead ... In use it is alive" (*Philosophical Investigations* § 432).

II.2 General Linguistics

We must now ask: if thinkers from two of the three areas of thought outlined above [that is, analytical philosophy, phenomenology and linguistics] adopt this approach, can the same be said of the third area, namely, general linguistics? It must be admitted that in linguistics, language has been more readily (to all appearances) regarded as an "objective" scientific phenomenon in itself. But this is not the whole story. We have said that Ferdinand de Saussure stressed the social character of language. He distinguished carefully between *langue*, the linguistic reservoir of the community, and *parole*, the actual concrete speech-*acts*. Thus in Saussure, hardly less than in Wittgenstein, we have the seminal roots of the modern perspective according to which the basic elements of language are neither words nor sentences as such, but, rather "speech-acts".[20] Saussure's contrast between *langue* and *parole* was taken up and developed in twentieth-century linguistics in terms of the distinction between linguistic *competence* and *linguistic performance*. Chomsky rejects the charge that his own "generative grammar" stresses competence at the expense of performance. Indeed he argues that in practice "the only studies of performance, outside of phonetics, are those carried out as a by-product of work in generative grammar".[21]

---

16 L. Wittgenstein, *Philosophical Investigations*, § 23.
17 *Philosophical Investigations*, § 108.
18 L. Wittgenstein, *Zettel*, 1967, § 173.
19 Martin Heidegger, *Being and Time* (Eng., Oxford: Blaxckwell, 1962), § 32.
20 F. de Saussure, *Course in General Linguistics*, pp.9 and 13–14.
21 Noam Chomsky, *Aspects of the Theory of Syntax* (1965), pp.5–15; quote from p.15.

II.3 Wittgenstein: "An Activity or a Form of Life"

Wittgenstein's approach to the problem of meaning finds expression in his use of the term "language-game". He uses it in order to make two points. First, language is grounded in human life. Wittgenstein writes, "The term *'language-game'* is meant to bring into prominence the fact that the *speaking* of a language is part of an activity, or of a form of life."[22] Thus the term describes not only language itself but also "the actions into which it is woven".[23] Second, language-uses are grounded in *particular* surroundings in human life. What language actually is depends on the nature of the particular language-game under discussion. In a certain particular situation, language may indeed serve to "refer" to an object, and meaning may here be viewed in terms of reference. But language does not operate in a single uniform way. Certainly it does not always "describe". We must make "a radical break with the idea that language always functions in one way ... to convey thoughts".[24] In more positive terms, "For a *large* class of cases – though not for all ... the meaning of a word is its use (*sein Gebrauch*) in the language".[25] Wittgenstein describes such uses of words or sentences as "countless". This is because "this multiplicity is not something fixed, given once for all".[26]

In common with exponents of hermeneutical philosophy, Wittgenstein recognizes *that language is open-ended towards future experience*. New language-uses may emerge as human life develops. Wittgenstein writes, "Think of the tools in a tool-box: there is a hammer, pliers, a saw, a screw-driver ... The functions of words are as diverse as the functions of these objects ... What confuses us is the uniform appearance of words ... Their *application* (*Verwendung*) is not presented to us so clearly."[27] It is, he suggests, like looking into the cabin of a locomotive. We see handles that look more or less alike (since they are all meant to be handled). But they all do different things, and may operate in different ways. To attempt to formulate some comprehensive theory of meaning is to imply that the relation between language and meaning is always the same. It is to be misled by the shape of the handles, or by the surface-grammar of language. By contrast, "we talk about it (language) as we do about the pieces in chess when we are stating the rules of the game, not describing their physical properties."[28]

This approach does not lead to scepticism, however, concerning questions about meaning. On the contrary, it suggests *only that such questions cannot be asked or answered in the abstract, independently of the task of looking at actual particular cases.* We should even resist the temptation to ask: how does "religious language" acquire its meaning? We need to look at particular utterances *in the actual life* of the worshipping community, in order to determine what role these utterances play, and only then can we determine what may be said about their meaning. One of Wittgenstein's further insights was to see that concrete questions about meaning might also be answered with reference to observable

---

[22] L. Wittgenstein, *Philosophical Investigations*, § 23.
[23] *Philosophical Investigations*, § 7.
[24] *Ph. Inv.*, § 304.
[25] *Ph. Inv.*, § 43.
[26] *Ph. Inv.*, § 23.
[27] *Ph. Inv.*, § 11.
[28] *Ph. Inv.*, § 108.

life and conduct within the language-using community (discussed further below). When we ask a question about meaning, "the kinds of use we feel to be 'the point' are connected with the role that such-and-such a use has in our whole life".[29] Wittgenstein himself offers many concrete illustrations of this principle, especially with reference to the meanings of such words or phrases as "think", "expect", "believe", "have pain" and "understand".

III
Uses of Language in Religion

III.1 Ordinary Language in a Religious Setting

The language of religion is not primarily a special kind of language, but is ordinary language put to a special kind of use. For example, when we talk about "hearing" the voice of God, we do not use a special word for "hearing", but we do use the word "hearing" in a special way. Wittgenstein describes this kind of peculiarity as a difference of logical "grammar". He considers the statement: "You can't hear God speak to someone else; you can hear him only if you are being addressed"; and he observes, "That is a grammatical remark."[30] In other words, this statement describes one of the logical peculiarities that marks the word "hear" when it applies, not to sound waves striking the ear, but to hearing the voice of God. If someone finds it difficult to hear, he might be advised to buy a deaf-aid. But we should recommend a different course of action for someone who found it difficult to hear God. This indicates that "hear" has a peculiar grammar in this setting.

Long before Wittgenstein, this feature of language was noted in the Fourth Gospel. Nicodemus is told, in effect, that "birth" into the kingdom of God has a different logical grammar from "birth" into the world (John 3:3–7). The "living water" (that is, running water) offered by Jesus to the woman of Samaria has a different grammatical status from that of "running water" as she imagines it (John 4:10: "Sir, you have nothing to draw with ..."). The disciples misunderstand the grammar of the "food" of which Jesus speaks (John 4:31–34). The Jews misunderstand the peculiar meaning of "bread" (John 6:31–35). In Wittgenstein's terms, John shows that the problem of understanding the language of Jesus is bound up with the fact that its claims that Jesus makes for himself give much of his otherwise ordinary language a distinctive meaning or grammar. Hence understanding his words and acknowledging his Person are bound up with each other.

III.2 The Illusion of "Incommensurability"? Analogy, Models and Qualifiers

At the same time, the peculiarity of the logical grammar of Christian discourse should not be exaggerated. There are at least two viable bridges between "religious" language and that of the ordinary everyday world. The first of these concerns uses of *analogy*. In

---

29 L. Wittgenstein, *Remarks on the Foundations of Mathematics* (Oxford: Blackwell, 1956) I, § 16, 8.
30 Wittgenstein, *Zettel*, § 717.

analogy there is a parallelism, perhaps even an overlapping, between the ordinary everyday grammar of a word and its distinctive logical grammar in the setting of religion. When we say that Jesus is the "Son" of God the "Father", an unwanted area of the everyday grammar of "father" and "son" must be cancelled out. We do not wish to imply that the son was born to the father at a particular moment in time, or that his existence is more recent than that of his Father. In this sense, the Arians were misled by failing to notice a feature of the logical grammar of "son" in this setting. On the other hand, the words "father" and "son" are used precisely because the relationship between God and Christ remains analogous to that of a human father and son. From an ontological rather than a linguistic point of view, Paul states that the fatherhood of God is a prototype of all human fatherhood (Eph. 3:15). Although he is not making a linguistic point here, Paul's statement nevertheless presupposes some degree of continuity between "Father" as applied to God, and "father" as applied to men.

The philosophical theologian Ian T. Ramsey articulated this double phenomenon of similarity and difference by explaining concepts of "model" and "qualifier".[31] Ramsey uses the word "model", where many theologians from Thomas Aquinas onwards might have used the term "analogy". On the basis of linguistic models, God is said to be the "cause" of the universe; to be "wise" and "good"; and to have brought forth "creation" according to his "purpose". But Christians wish to stress not only the continuities of these terms with their everyday meanings, but also their *differences* from them. Hence they add *qualifiers* to the models. God is not only "cause"; he is "First Cause". He is "infinitely" wise and good. Creation is "creation *ex nihilo*", and is in accordance with his eternal purpose.[32]

Ramsey prefers to speak of "models and qualifiers" rather than in the traditional terms of "analogy" because he also wishes to argue that when language functions in this way it provides the basis for what he calls a *disclosure situation*. The "logical oddity" that results from coupling together a model and a qualifier is not merely, negatively, a sign that language is being stretched beyond its usual limits. More positively, it also provokes a situation in which, as the hearer seeks to understand the language, "light dawns", or "the penny drops". A disclosure occurs which operates at a level that is not purely cognitive and informative, but entails the response of the whole human person. In contrast to the merely intellectual, it may carry with it, for example, an expression of awe, of wonder, or of encounter.

III.3 Public Criteria of Meaning: The Public Domain, Community and Tradition

There is also a second major point of contact between the language of religion and the everyday empirical world. This comes to light in the modern philosophical debate about private language and *public criteria of meaning*. Wittgenstein, once again, is the thinker who has done most to set this debate in motion. Wittgenstein's starting-point is to consider the place of regularities, customs and training, in the use of language. This

---

[31] I.T. Ramsey, *Religious Language: An Empirical Placing of Theological Phrases* (London: SCM, 1957), pp.48–89.

[32] Ibid., pp.61–79.

aspect of language is also underlined in general linguistics, where Chomsky, Fodor and Katz talk about mechanisms that are recursive.[33] Wittgenstein is cautious about speaking of rules in any rigid or prescriptive sense. But he does speak of them in the sense of signposts or customs.[34] He writes, "Obeying a rule is a practice. And to *think* one is obeying a rule is not to obey a rule. Hence it is not possible to obey a rule 'privately'."[35] If the distinction between "correct" and "seems correct" disappears, then so has the concept "correct". It is easy to see what can count as a check or whether our use of the word "chair" or "table" is correct. If we were to use the word "chair" consistently in an incorrect way, someone else in the language-using community would soon tell us. But what kind of thing counts as a check on the correct use of words that relate to inner experiences or states of mind?

Wittgenstein insists that if I know what it is to feel joy, grief, pain (and so on), *only from my own case*, I could not be aware of any regularity or custom about the application of these concepts in language. For what would it be to make a *mistake* in their application? In practice, however, such language *is* teachable, and not wholly "private" (in Wittgenstein's technical sense of the term). For we learn what joy, grief, pain, etc., *is*, because they play an observable part in life. Wittgenstein writes, "What would it be like if human beings showed no outward signs of pain (did not groan, grimace, etc.)? Then it would be impossible to teach a child the use of the word 'toothache'."[36]

Although Wittgenstein's arguments about private language are made partly in the form of an attack on a Cartesian view of mind, we may apply this principle to the language of religion. If "being redeemed", "experiencing the Holy Spirit" (and so on), were *purely* (in Wittgenstein's sense of the term) "private" experiences, how could their meaning ever be conveyed to others? To be sure, there is a dimension to these experiences which may be termed, in one sense, "private". But it is also part of their very grammar that they should relate to human life in a public and observable way.

In the same way, we should say that pain is a genuinely "inner" sensation, but it is also necessarily compatible with some forms of overt behaviour and incompatible with others. What makes language teachable is its connection with observable regularities in human behaviour. Hence what makes such a concept as "redemption" intelligible is not only (as we have seen) its analogy with parallel concepts in secular life, but also the cash-value of the concepts in the observable life and ongoing tradition of the Hebrew-Christian community from the Old Testament to the present day.

The Old Testament in particular provides a public, accessible tradition of patterns of events and behaviour that give currency to its language. The events of the Exodus, for example, provide a paradigm case, or a model language-game, of what "redemption" might mean. The notion of "salvation" begins to emerge as Israel passes through experiences of deliverance and prosperity in the period of the Judges. Piece by piece a tradition is built up, providing a continuity or regularity against which the application of

---

[33]   J.A. Fodor and J.J. Katz, *The Structure of Language* (Englewood Cliffs, NJ: Prentice-Hall, 1964), p.11; cf. 1–18 and 479–518.

[34]   *Philosophical Investigations*, §§ 198–9.

[35]   *Ph. Inv.*, § 202.

[36]   *Ph. Inv.*, § 257.

certain concepts may be checked as correct or incorrect. *These concepts do not of course remain static, but are purified and enriched as the biblical tradition grows. One reason why the biblical tradition is indispensable to Christian faith is that it provides paradigm cases of meaning,* without which modern claims to "Christian" experience would face a *problem of identity.* The God who is worshipped in the Hebrew-Christian tradition is not merely the supreme being of speculative thought, but the God of Abraham, of Isaac and of Jacob; and the God and Father of the Christ of the New Testament.

This principle contributes decisively, alongside analogy, to the solution of the problem of meaning in religion. It does not merely result, however, in a backward-looking biblicism. In the modern era, the secular man may *begin* to grasp the meaning of religious language as he is in a position to see its cash-value in terms of observable acts and attitudes on the part of the Christian community, or the religious man. Wittgenstein writes, "One learns the game by watching how others play."[37] Correspondence between word and deed in the Christian community provides a more radical and effective solution to the problem of meaning in religion than attempts to relabel the Christian vocabulary.

III.4 Symbol

Symbols, like metaphor, play an important role in religious language. Part of their power lies in the fact, that, according to Jung, symbols are vital for the necessary interplay between conscious and unconscious. Paul Tillich takes up Jung's approach, but in Tillich's theology the special place that he accords to symbol is bound up with a particular theological evaluation whereby the unconscious is thought to point to God. Tillich also tends towards a naturalistic view of language, arguing that, unlike the sign, the symbol itself "participates in that to which it points".[38] These two assumptions may be questioned. But Tillich is correct in his emphasis on the *power* of symbols. He writes, "Every symbol is two-edged. It opens up reality, and it opens up the soul."[39] "It opens up hidden depths of our own being."[40] Symbols such as the sun, the closed door, inaccessible Eden, or the eschatological feast, reach right down into memories of childhood, or even perhaps through to racial memories. They call forth the response of the imagination and the heart. But pictures, as Wittgenstein reminds us, can be variously applied.

To be sure, symbols (like parables and metaphor) are powerful in reaching through to the heart. But their application must be checked and tested against a broader linguistic content. For this reason, Christian sacraments alone are incomplete without the interpretation of the word.[41] [I note in my retrospective comment that today it would be unthinkable to discuss symbol without a serious engagement with Paul Ricoeur, who is an even more significant writer on the subject than perhaps Tillich or even Jung.]

---

[37] *Ph. Inv.,* § 54.
[38] Paul Tillich, *Theology of Culture* (New York: Galaxy Books, 1964), pp.54–5.
[39] *Theology of Culture,* p.57.
[40] Paul Tillich, *Dynamics of Faith* (London: Nisbet, 1957), p.43.
[41] I have discussed these points at greater length in *Language, Liturgy, and Meaning* (1975), pp.22–32; and "The Theology of Paul Tillich", *The Churchman* 88 (1974), pp.86–107.

IV
Responsibility in Using Language

The biblical writers speak equally of the power of language and of the need for caution, even reticence, in its use: "Death and life are in the power of the tongue" (Prov. 18:21). "The tongue of the wise brings healing" (12:18), and a good word may bring gladness (v. 25). Words may be edifying (10:21) and may bring forth solid and productive results (12:14): "A gentle tongue is a tree of life" (15:4). In the New Testament the speaking of words is bound up with the experience of salvation. Salvation entails verbal confession (Rom. 10:9); and men cannot believe in him "of whom they have never heard" (10:14).

At the same time, people will be called to account for their idle words (Matt. 12:36). Cruel or clumsy words can be like the piercing of a sword (Prov. 12:18). Flattery may ruinously inflate a person's self-esteem (19:5); and the speech of a wicked man spreads strife (16:27, 28). Hasty and thoughtless words are counter-productive: "The mind of the righteous ponders how to answer; but the mouth of the wicked pours out evil things" (15:28). Christians are urged to be slow to speak (James 1:19): for the tongue can be like a fire that sets a whole forest ablaze, and can spread deadly poison (James 3:5, 6, 8).

Wittgenstein's observations about public criteria of meaning raise an even more fundamental issue. We have noted that the publicly observable attitudes and conduct of the Christian community form the necessary "backing" that gives currency to its language: "One learns the game by watching how others play"; "Only in the stream of thought and life do words have meaning." The warning against "idle words" (Matt. 12:36) refers not to the uttering of social pleasantries (these indeed may have social value), but to words that are ineffective because they have no backing in practical conduct. *Empty promises, vain intentions, or smooth blandishments fall into this category.*

Words that merely chase other words give rise to circularity and a relativism that have no anchorage in reality. To cite one of Kierkegaard's similes, it is as if a shop sign which promises: "Trousers Pressed Here", turns out, after all, to be displayed not by a cleaner's, but only by a shop that sells shop signs. Wittgenstein uses a different simile. It is as if someone says, "I know how tall I am", and puts their hand on top of their head to prove it. *Responsible* language is more than "signs chasing signs".

Even the language the Christian communities use for praise must be grounded in attitudes and acts that give them a valid linguistic currency. By contrast with the fallibility of the church, Jesus of Nazareth embodied the word as "the word made flesh". Jesus did not simply *talk about* humility; he took a towel and washed the disciples' feet. He did not only talk about sacrifice; he gave his life for others. He did not merely speak words *about* forgiveness and new life; he *actually gave promised* forgiveness and made new life possible and actual. The language of Jesus derives much of its intelligibility and effectiveness from its being grounded in life and in *action*. The community that Jesus founded in his name is called to accept that same responsibility for what it speaks. Here the biblical witness and the witness of mid-twentieth-century philosophy of language appear to point in the same direction.

CHAPTER THIRTY

The Peril of Uncritical Appropriation: "God as Self-Affirming Illusion? Manipulation, Truth and Language" (1995)

This essay is an extract from Part I of Interpreting God and the Postmodern Self: On Meaning, Manipulation and Promise *(Edinburgh: T. & T. Clark, 1995), pp.3–26, which is an expanded version of the first of four public lectures delivered at the University of Aberdeen and sponsored by the* Scottish Journal of Theology. *One positive aspect of post-modern thought arises from its radical suspicion of the surface-grammar of language. As Nietzsche, among others, demonstrated, language that purports to convey truth may function at a deeper level to gain power. Religions are especially prone to such uses of language, and we need to call on the critical resources of European postmodernism, notably on Nietzsche and Foucault, to assist in unmasking such manipulative uses of language through a hermeneutic of suspicion. Nevertheless we must also question whether* all *uses of language in authentic faith are necessarily guilty of such manipulative strategies.*

I
Suspicion of Language: From Hobbes to Nietzsche

The English political philosopher Thomas Hobbes (1588–1679) well knew that we could play tricks with truth by using language in particular ways. In his *Leviathan* (1651) he discusses the status of claims to receive private revelations of God's will. A person might claim, for example, 'God spoke to me in a dream', and expect others to act on such a claim. Hobbes observes, however, 'to say that God hath spoken to him in a dream is no more than to say that he dreamed that God spoke to him'.[1] The first form of the proposition appears to claim the status of a solemn oracle, perhaps to legitimate some belief or action. The second, we might speculate, could amount to no more than a regretful reflection on how much cheese may wisely be eaten immediately before retiring to bed.

Hobbes writes a short section on dreams towards the beginning of his *Leviathan*. Dreams, he argues, can hardly constitute serious communications, since within a dream nothing whatever seems 'absurd'. Dreams arise as 'phantoms' of past sensations that remain incoherent, because no 'end' or specific purpose seems to guide them coherently.[2] Hence to appeal to dreams as vehicles of truth may deceive both the self and others. Hobbes therefore attacks such appeals as entirely unsupported grounds for belief. Although he accepts that

---

[1] Thomas Hobbes, *Leviathan* (Oxford: Blackwell, 1960, ed. M. Oakeshott), Pt III, ch. 32, p.243.
[2] *Leviathan*, I, ch. 2, pp.10–11.

we cannot exclude the possibility that God may speak through dreams, as a matter of principle, Hobbes concludes that in everyday life this kind of claim 'has not force'.[3]

In other discussions of language, Hobbes extends his analysis of deceptive uses of language that may hide truth. Disguise may occur, for example, when speakers use 'inconstant signification'. Here they slide from one meaning to another. Speakers may also employ 'names that signify nothing'. We assert nothing whatever if we assert some quality, for example, about a 'round quadrilateral'.[4] Deception, however, can too easily lead to the possibility of manipulation. Sometimes clergy, Hobbes observes, speak with 'fraudulent intent'.[5]

Hobbes lived during a period when English Royalists and Parliamentarians sought to legitimate their respective political philosophies by seeking to validate their claims with reference to the will of God. Those who appealed to a theological doctrine of 'the right of kings' argued on different grounds from those of Hobbes's own Royalist sympathies. He himself expressed these in terms of a philosophy of social contract, not by an appeal to God's will. On the other side, Parliamentarians sought to legitimate a more egalitarian view by appealing to the doctrine of the priesthood of all believers.

In this respect, parallels emerge with John Locke (1632–1704). It is easy to overlook the context of Locke's well-known maxim of 1690 that 'reason must be our last judge and guide in everything'.[6] Locke opposed equally the manipulatory use of the Bible by authoritarian Anglican bishops and the deceptive and often manipulatory claims of 'enthusiasts' to know God's will privately. Those whom he calls 'enthusiasts' try, Locke argues, to legitimate as 'truths' what amount to the 'ungrounded fancies of a man's own brain, and assume[s] them for a foundation both of opinion and conduct'.[7] Peter Nidditch and especially Henning Graf Reventlow demonstrate that Locke was a scrupulous exegete of the Bible. His purpose was to recover the 'plain meaning' of the text from otherwise manipulative uses.[8]

It is a mistake merely to ascribe to Hobbes the seeds of 'atheism' in England, as David Berman carefully points out.[9] Likewise, even if he overestimates the role of reason within an empiricist frame, Locke's appeals to 'reasonableness' as Reventlow stresses, reflect a serious religious concern that Christian truth should be neither manipulated nor counterfeited by institutional or 'private' interests.

We cannot claim the same concerns for the German philosopher Friedrich Nietzsche (1844–1900). He shares with Hobbes a serious distrust of 'empty' language, which pretends to convey 'universal' truths. But Nietzsche attacks all religious belief, and in particular its universal misuses of language about truth as a disguise for its interests.

---

3   *Leviathan*, III, ch. 32, p.243.

4   *Leviathan*, I, ch. 4, pp.19–25.

5   *Leviathan*, I, ch. 2, p.12; I, ch. 6, p.35; I, ch. 12 (on religion); and IV, ch. 43–44 and 46–47, pp.435–59.

6   John Locke, *An Essay Concerning Human Understanding* (London: Collins, 1964), Bk. IV ch. 19 'On Enthusiasm', sect. 14, p.432.

7   Locke, *Essay*, IV, 19:3, p.429.

8   Henning Graf Reventlow, *The Authority of the Bible and the Rise of the Modern World* (Eng., London: SCM, 1984), p.259; cf. pp.243–85, Cf. further P.H. Nidditch, *The Locke Newsletter* 9 (1978), pp.15–19.

9   David Berman, *A History of Atheism in Britain from Hobbes to Russell* (London and New York: Routledge, 1988 and 1990), p.57. Cf. further F.S. McNeilly, *The Anatomy of Leviathan* (London: Macmillan, 1968).

In the *Notebooks* of 1873, Nietzsche writes: 'What is truth? A mobile army of metaphors, metonyms, and anthropomorphisms.'[10] Especially in religion, Nietzsche urges, people use 'errors' for their own advantage, self-interest, or power. Some promote erroneous 'lies' merely from sheer personal need. In this sense, Nietzsche exclaims: '*Truth is that kind of error* without which a certain species of living cannot exist. The value of Life is ultimately decisive.'[11] Nietzsche goes further. He includes even 'facts' here. He writes 'All that exists consists of *interpretations*.'[12] 'Truths are illusions we have forgotten are illusions.'[13]

Nietzsche continues to attack the truth-status of both philosophy and theology as resting on metaphor and manipulation. They deal with 'fundamental errors' but as if these were 'fundamental truths'. The theme becomes more developed in his *Human, All-Too-Human* of 1878, and in *The Twilight of the Idols* and *The Antichrist* (published later in 1895).[14] Theology can offer only a manipulative tool by means of which the weak, the insecure and the vulnerable may try to cope with life. It offers them anodyne illusions.

At worst, illusions of legitimacy as supposed 'truth' serve a power-hungry ecclesial priesthood or religious leadership. By claiming that they promote 'truths', they seduce the gullible and credulous into following where they lead.

How can such deception and manipulation be sustained? In Nietzsche's view three major factors give weight to the illusions. Together they serve to convey a seductive credibility to claims about God and about truth.

First, language, especially metaphor, provides the raw material for disguise. Nietzsche addresses the problem of language as that which constructs false 'idols', as 'universal truths'. A key work here is *The Twilight of the Idols*. No doubt, as Walter Kaufmann suggests, Nietzsche's identification of 'four great errors' in this work reflect 'the four idols' exposed by Francis Bacon.[15] Nietzsche declares, 'I fear we shall never be rid of God, so long as we still believe in grammar.'[16] Language appears to imply that theistic belief depends on 'reason'. But this invites the response which Nietzsche describes in the words of his subtitle '*How to Philosophize with the Hammer*'. Hammers are needed to destroy 'idols'.

Elsewhere Nietzsche comments, 'We are still constantly led astray by words ... Language contains a hidden philosophical mythology, which, how ever careful we may be, breaks out afresh at every moment.'[17] He speaks of 'the spell of certain grammatical functions'.[18] Indeed in *The Twilight of the Idols* he exclaims, '"Reason" in language! – oh

---

[10]   Friedrich Nietzsche, 'On Truth and Lie in a Extra-Moral Sense', traditional translation (as above) in Walter Kaufmann (ed.), *The Portable Nietzsche* (New York: Viking Press, 1968 (1954)), p.46; translated as 'movable host' in Daniel Breazeale (ed.), *Philosophy and Truth. Selections from Nietzsche's Notebooks of the Early 1870s* (New Jersey: Humanities Press and Sussex: Harvester Press, 1979), p.84.

[11]   Friedrich Nietzsche, *The Complete Works of Friedrich Nietzsche* (18 vols, ed. O. Levy, Eng., London: Allen & Unwin, 1909–13 [*Works*]), vol. 15, *The Will to Power*, vol. 2, p.20 (aphorism 493, his italics).

[12]   Nietzsche, *Works, 15: The Will to Power*, vol. 2, p.12 (aphorism 481, his italics).

[13]   Nietzsche, 'On Truth and Lie', loc. cit.

[14]   Nietzsche, *Works 6 & 7: Human, All-Too-Human* (2 vols), vol. 1, esp. aphorisms 1–9 and vol. 2, aphorisms 20, 28, 32, et al. (References to the other works appear below.)

[15]   W. Kaufmann 'Editor's Preface', to the work, op. cit., pp.463–4.

[16]   Nietzsche, *Works, 12: The Twilight of the Idols*, p.22 (aphorism 5).

[17]   Nietzsche, *Works, 17: Human, All-Too-Human*, vol. 2, pt ii, 'The Wanderer', p.192, aphorism 11.

[18]   Nietzsche, *Works, 12: Beyond Good and Evil*, 'Prejudices of Philosophers', p.29, aphorism 20.

what a deceptive old witch it has been!'[19] Ludwig Wittgenstein (1889–1951) would speak in due course of philosophy as 'a battle against the bewitchment of our intelligence by means of language', and of being 'held captive' by a linguistic 'picture'.[20] Even in his earlier work, *The Tractatus*, Wittgenstein observed that 'language disguises thought'.[21] Prior to Wittgenstein, Fritz Mauthner (1849–1923) stressed with equal force the capacity of language to generate illusions.

Second, Nietzsche aims to unmask supposed issues of truth as issues of value and issues of power. In *The Will to Power* he writes, 'Knowledge works as an *instrument* of power.'[22] Explicitly dissenting from Darwin's notions of 'survival' as mere perpetuation, Nietzsche observes, 'Where there is a struggle, it is a struggle for power.'[23] Even a value-system, namely 'morality' serves primarily as 'a means of preserving the community', not as any universal imperative or truth-claim.[24]

In *The Antichrist* Nietzsche attacks the motivations that underlie the truth-claims of Christian theology. Among ordinary theistic believers, these often take the form of desire for comfort, security, self-importance, or self-affirmation. Nietzsche writes, 'The "salvation of the soul" – in plain English "the world revolves around me".'[25] But among priests, theologians, and church leaders the motivation is more sinister: 'A theologian, a priest, or a pope, not only errs but actually lies with every word that he utters.'[26] Nietzsche believes with Marx that Christian faith becomes 'repressive', and with Feuerbach that it diminishes humanness. It propagates 'vicious frauds ... systems of cruelty on the strength of which the priest became and remained master'.[27]

Where a falsehood 'serves a purpose', the priest may appeal to the 'Will of God' or to 'Revelation of God'.[28] The priest is 'the *professional* denier ... Truth has already been turned topsy-turvy.'[29] Even among ordinary Christians '"beautiful feelings" ... "the heaving breast" [become] the bellows of divinity'.[30] Nietzsche insists, 'Supreme axiom: "God forgiveth him that repenteth" – in plain English: him that submitteth himself to the priest.'[31] He concludes, 'Transvaluation of all values!'[32]

Third, Nietzsche declared, 'All that exists consists of *interpretations*.'[33] There are no 'givens', not even as raw data awaiting categorization or ordering by the human mind. He has radicalized Kant and Fichte.

[19] Nietzsche, *Works, 16: The Twilight of the Idols*, p.22, aphorism 5.
[20] Ludwig Wittgenstein, *Philosophical Investigations* (Germ. & Eng., Oxford: Blackwell, 1967 (2nd edn 1958)), sects 109 and 115.
[21] L. Wittgenstein, *Tractatus Logico-Philosophicus* (Germ. & Eng., London: Routledge & Kegan Paul, 1961), 4.002.
[22] Nietzsche, *Works, 15: The Will to Power*, vol. 2, p.11, aphorism 480 (his italics).
[23] Nietzsche, *Works, 16: The Twilight of the Idols*, p.71, aphorism 14.
[24] Nietzsche, *Works, 7: Human, All-Too-Human ii*, p.221, aphorism 44.
[25] Nietzsche, *Works, 7: The Antichrist. An Attempted Criticism of Christianity*, p.186, aphorism 43.
[26] Ibid., p.177, aphorism 38.
[27] Ibid., p.213, aphorism 54.
[28] Ibid., aphorism 55.
[29] Ibid., p.134, aphorism 8 (his italics).
[30] Ibid., p.138, aphorism 12.
[31] Ibid., p.161, aphorism 26 (his italics).
[32] Ibid., p.231, aphorism 62.
[33] Nietzsche, *Works, 15: The Will to Power*, vol. 2, p.12, aphorism 481.

Interpretations of interpretations, however, readily lend themselves as tools of self-interest, deception and manipulation. We confine ourselves to one example from Nietzsche, namely his attack on Paul. We have access now to very different approaches to Paul by J. Munck (1954), K. Stendahl (1963), E.P. Sanders (1977), J.D.G. Dunn (1990) and N.T. Wright (1991) than the one-sided portrait of Paul found in radical nineteenth-century Lutheranism on which Nietzsche based his attack.[34] Nietzsche interprets Paul as tormented by his inability to keep the Jewish Law. Hence a theology that abrogated the law appeared to serve his own deepest personal interests. Nietzsche interprets Paul as 'a man with a mind full of superstition and cunning'.[35] Paul, he wishes to argue, 'could not fulfill the Law... But in coming to terms with Jesus of Nazareth his mind was suddenly enlightened ... "Here is my means of escape ... I have the destroyer of the Law in my hands!"... Morality itself was blown away, annihilated ... "I am above the Law", thinks Paul.'[36] Thus it came about, Nietzsche concludes, that Paul 'was the first Christian'.[37]

Nietzsche insists, therefore, that Paul's claims about 'truth', like those of later generations of Christians, rest at least partly on *manipulative interpretations of texts.* He writes, 'He who has interpreted a passage in an author "more profoundly" than was intended, has not interpreted the author but obscured him ... They [Christian interpreters] often alter the text to suit their purpose.'[38] Pilate's question 'What is truth?' Nietzsche concludes, 'is now gleefully brought on the scene as an advocate of Christ'.[39] He offers a parody of the opening of the Gospel of John: 'In the beginning was the nonsense, and the nonsense was with God, and the nonsense was God.'[40]

How relevant are Nietzsche's criticisms to the world of today? First, the notion that religion has more to do with value and power than with truth arises with regularity in English parish life, and perhaps no less in Scotland and North America. When he spoke of 'truth' as '*that kind of error* without which a particular kind of being cannot exist', Nietzsche anticipated a view, widespread among a certain type of self-confident male today that religion serves primarily to comfort vulnerable people.[41]

In the view of a certain type of man characteristically such people include women. We may imagine such a macho figure watching football on television on a Saturday afternoon. The doorbell rings and to his barely suppressed irritation he finds a parish minister on the doorstep. By instant reflex he mutters, 'I'll fetch the wife.' This does not spring from his desire to return to football, for this was forgotten in the surprise of the moment. It reflects the *underlying assumption* that anything to do with religion serves

[34] Cf. J. Munck, *Paul and the Salvation of Mankind* (Eng., London: SCM, 1959), pp.11–35; K. Stendahl, 'Paul and the Introspective Conscience of the West', rp. from *Harvard Theological Review* (1963) in *Paul among Jews and Gentiles and Other Essays* (London, SCM, 1977 and Philadelphia, PA: Fortress Press, 1976); E.P. Sanders, *Paul and Palestinian Judaism* (London: SCM, 1977); J.D.G. Dunn, *Jesus, Paul and the Law: Studies in Mark and Galatians* (London: SPCK, 1990); and N.T. Wright, *The Climax of the Covenant: Christ and the Law in Pauline Theology* (Philadelphia, PA: Fortress Press, 1991).
[35] Nietzsche, *Works, 9: The Dawn of Day*, p.67, aphorism 68; 66–71.
[36] Ibid., pp.68–70 (68).
[37] Ibid., p.71 (68).
[38] Nietzsche, *Works, 7: Human, All-Too-Human*, vol. 2, ii, 'The Wanderer', p.197, aphorism 17.
[39] Ibid., i, p.16, aphorism 8.
[40] Ibid., i, p.20, aphorism 22.
[41] Nietzsche, *Works, 15: The Will to Power*, vol. 2, p.20 (493), his italics.

merely to provide comfort and affirmation to lesser mortals. On this basis he views it as part of his wife's domain, not his.

Even requests for infant baptism sometimes entail a presupposition that truth remains subordinate to issues of value or power. An educated intellectual couple may explicitly seek to distance themselves from 'believing the creeds' or from 'all that'. But at a barely conscious pre-intellectual level they may feel that baptism offers some unspecified value or power, which their child may (just possibly) need. Whether certain claims are true does not seem to enter the picture.

The relevance of Nietzsche's critiques for today appears even more clearly in the academic and intellectual climate that surrounds contemporary theology. One of the major intellectual debates of today concerns an alleged shift from the attitudes of 'modernity' to those of postmodernism. If the challenge of postmodernism invites the transposition of issues of truth and argument into questions of power and rhetoric this becomes a fundamental issue for theology. Hence we must look more closely at postmodernism.

II
Postmodernism, Modernity and the Postmodern Self

The term 'the postmodern self' denotes the predicament of the human self and society that has been caught up in the attitudes and suspicions of postmodernism. But to speak of 'the postmodern self' also leaves open the fundamental intellectual question, which is much debated, about whether postmodernism has *overtaken and eclipsed 'modernity'*, or whether it merely reflects a *specific phase*, perhaps even a degenerate phase, *of modernity*. On the other hand, it also implies a serious engagement with the attitudes, assumptions and perceptions that permeate outlooks which are included within a postmodern stance towards truth, rationality, manipulation and selfhood.

A working distinction between 'postmodernism' and 'the postmodern self' emerges in Norman K. Denzin's *Images of Postmodern Society* (1991).[42] Postmodernism implies a *shattering of innocent confidence in the capacity of the self to control its own destiny*. It signals a loss of trust in global strategies of social planning, and in universal criteria of rationality. It often carries with it emotional by-products of 'anger, alienation, anxiety ... racism and sexism'.[43] In the wake of the collapse of traditional values or universal criteria, the 'postmodern self' becomes 'the self who embodies the multiple contradictions of postmodernism, while experiencing itself through the everyday performances of gender, class, and racially-linked social identities'.[44]

Whether or not we agree with J. Habermas in doubting whether postmodernity brings 'the end of modernity', we cannot recover the lost innocence that characterized the self of

---

[42]   Norman K. Denzin, *Images of Postmodern Society. Social Theory and Contemporary Cinema* (London: Sage Publications, 1991), p.vii. See further David Harvey, *The Condition of Postmodernity. An Enquiry into the Origins of Cultural Change* (Oxford: Blackwell, 2nd edn, 1989), especially pp.3–118.

[43]   N.K. Denzin, *Images*, loc. cit.

[44]   Ibid.

modernity, let alone that of the pre-modern.[45] The postmodern self faces life and society with suspicion rather than trust. The modern self retained a basic optimism about the capacities of human reason, governmental or social strategies and scientific achievement, to shape the world for the general advancement of human society. But such optimism omits too many factors to provide hope for the postmodern self.

The postmodern self follows Nietzsche and Freud in viewing claims to truth largely as devices that serve to legitimate power-interests. *Disguise covers everything. Hence a culture of distrust and suspicion emerges.* Even allegedly 'factual' reports of achievements may be suspected of embodying manipulative editing to protect the interests of some person or group. Hence bureaucracy initiates vast monitoring systems. But here even the monitors are suspected of having interests, which, in turn, invite further processes of monitoring. In Part IV [of *Interpreting God*] we explore these issues further with reference to Foucault.

Yet bureaucracy also brings into focus the self-contradictory character of the postmodern self. On one side it arises because of suspicions about competing manipulative interests. Yet on the other side it claims to retain a supposedly impartial role as arbitrator for the common good, remaining 'above' the competing interests. To the ordinary worker, however, the bureaucrats themselves may appear also to be engaged in empire-building and even in seeking to control or dominate the enterprises or institutions for whose benefit and service they originated. Hence the sense of anger and conflict that they were designed to mitigate and to retrain now escalates and proliferates. The postmodern self perceives itself as having lost control as active agent, and as having been transformed into a passive victim of competing groups. Everyone seems to be at the mercy of someone else's vested interests for power.

Mass advertising has contributed much to the collapse of confidence in claims to truth, along with power-seeking in party-politics. People suspect that here 'truth' disguises only the desire for success and domination. So thin has become the disguise that some advertisements achieve their success by witty self-mockery, conceding that their 'truth-claims' are not truth-claims at all. We know that a beer which 'reaches the parts which other beers cannot reach' gently mocks the whole process of asserting claims at face value. We *know* that the 'claim' has nothing whatever to do with physiology.

In matters of race, class, gender and professional guilds, however, the gloves are off. For what *counts as true* for one group is often disparaged as a *manipulative disguise to legitimate power-claims* by another group. If different groups choose to adopt different *criteria of truth* to determine what *counts* as true, or even *what counts as a meaningful truth-claim*, rational argument and dialogue become undermined by recurring appeals to what one group counts as axioms, but seem far from axiomatic for another. At this point argument becomes transposed into rhetoric. Rhetoric then comes to rely on force, seduction, or manipulation.

---

45 Classic studies on this issue include J. Habermas, *The Philosophical Discourse of Modernity* (Eng., New York: Political Press, 1988); Richard J. Bernstein (ed.), *Habermas and Modernity* (Cambridge: Polity Press, 1985), esp. pp.1–34, 125–39 and 161–216; J.-F. Lyotard, *The Postmodern Explained to Children. Correspondence 1982–1985* (Eng., London: Turnaround, 1992), pp.9–26 and 87–100. A further useful source is R.J. Bernstein (ed.), *The New Constellation. The Ethical-Political Horizons of Modernity/Postmodernity* (Cambridge: Polity Press, 1991).

Two consequences emerge for theology. Both are explored throughout this book. First, some religious people not only use manipulation in place of truth, but may eventually come to believe sincerely in the truth of their own inherited religious rhetoric, even if it may have served initially to further some power-interest. Second, to be manipulated is to be treated as less than a personal self. As Vincent Brümmer stresses in his writings, we do not seek to manipulate someone whom we genuinely respect and love as an Other in their own right.[46] Yet respect for the other as 'Other', as a unique agent or active personal subject, stands at the heart of the Christian gospel.

Equally, this also constitutes the heart of concerns about interpretation or, more strictly, hermeneutics, from Schleiermacher and Dilthey to Gadamer and Ricoeur. We trace these concerns and their implications especially in Part II of this study. For Schleiermacher and for Dilthey, we shall see, genuine 'understanding' of a text or of another human person arises only when we seek to *step out of our own frame*.[47] We need to *renounce those prior categorizations and stereotypifications with which we begin*. In Gadamer's language, we renounce the manipulative 'control' epitomized by 'scientific method', and allow ourselves to enter unpredicted avenues into which mutual listening and genuine conversation leads.[48] In Ricoeur's terminology, we explore new worlds of possibility.[49]

Later [in this book] we shall look more closely at the work of Roland Barthes, Michel Foucault, Jacques Derrida, and others. At an intellectual level such thinkers provide much of the force behind postmodernism, especially in literary and critical theory. We shall also note that a Christian account of human nature accepts the capacity of the self for self-deception and its readiness to use strategies of manipulation.

The term 'heart' (*kardia*) closely approaches in the Pauline letters Freudian notions of the hidden depths that lie below the threshold of conscious awareness. The things of the heart, Bultmann rightly comments, 'need not penetrate into the field of consciousness at all, but may designate the hidden tendency of the self'.[50] Bultmann, J.A.T. Robinson, and Robert Jewett confirm that Paul often uses 'flesh' (*sarx*) to describe the human self in pursuit of its self-interests.[51] Thus Gal. 6:12, Bultmann writes, may allude to a 'secret motive hidden even from themselves'.[52] Motivations of the heart may remain 'darkened' (Rom. 1:21).

At the same time, the New Testament writers perceive self-deception and manipulation as incompatible in principle with the new creation, and subject to change

---

[46] Vincent Brümmer, *What are we Doing When We Pray? A Philosophical Inquiry* (London: SCM, 1984), pp.1–15 and 74–113; *Speaking of a Personal God* (Cambridge: CUP, 1992), pp.83–9 and 115–27; and *The Model of Love: A Study in Philosophical Theology* (Cambridge: CUP, 1993).

[47] F.D.E. Schleiermacher, *Hermeneutics. The Handwritten Manuscripts* (ed. H. Kimmerle) (Eng., Missoula, MT: Scholars Press, 1977), pp.42 and 109.

[48] Hans-Georg Gadamer, *Truth and Method* (2nd Eng. edn, from 5th Germ. edn) (London: Sheed and Ward, 1993), esp. pp.362–79 (1st Eng. edn, 1975), pp.325–41 *et passim*.

[49] For a succinct retrospective account and prospective questioning, cf. Paul Ricoeur, *Time and Narrative* (3 vols) (Eng., Chicago, IL: Chicago University Press, 1984–88), vol. 3, pp.253–61; cf. vol. 2, pp.100–160.

[50] Rudolf Bultmann, *Theology of the New Testament* (2 vols) (Eng., London: SCM, 1952 and 1955), vol. I, p.225; cf. pp.220–27.

[51] Robert Jewett, *Paul's Anthropological Terms. A Study of their Use in Conflict Settings* (Leiden: Brill, 1971), pp.95–104; cf. A.C. Thiselton, 'The Meaning of *Sarx* in I Cor. 5:5', *SJT* 26 (1973), pp.204–28.

[52] R. Bultmann, op. cit., vol. I, p.224.

and transformation. 'Maturity to the measure of the full stature of Christ' (Eph. 4:13) entails an abandonment of 'immature' strategies of 'trickery ... craftiness in deceitful scheming'; rather, believers are 'to speak the truth in love' (4:14, 15). Loving respect for the personhood of 'the other' by truthful speech is part of 'growing up' (4:15). 'Darkened' understanding is self-defeating, for it ends in 'futility' (4:17). When at the advent the 'sleeper awakes' (Eph. 5:14), the tattered remnants of all the former deceits and illusions will fall away, like forgotten dreams in the solid day (5:8–14; 1 Thess. 5:4–8; Rom. 13:11–12).

Christian theology, then, cannot be said to be compatible with the transvaluation of questions about truth into questions about value or power as an ultimate principle. But it entirely coheres with Christian theology to accept that this transvaluation *frequently takes place* where self-interest still holds sway even among otherwise sincere believers. There remains much to learn in this respect from Barthes, Foucault and Derrida.

Roland Barthes (1915–80) exposes the manipulative power-interests with often underlie the 'mythologies' of the second half of the late twentieth century. In his *Mythologies* (French, 1957; English, 1972), he unmasks what we too often perceive as 'natural' or 'given' as socially contrived. Many manipulative devices appear to be natural 'truths'.[53] Photographs in popular magazines, for example, do more than portray the object that appears to be depicted. By the use of perspective, light and shadow, proportion, angle, and so forth, the 'signs' (in the sense used in sign-theory) may be multidimensional. At one level they seem simply to portray a commercial product, but at another level they commend it by associating it with success, sex, or prestige.

Barthes's 'de-naturalizing' of what might otherwise be taken for granted goes deeper. He exposes to view coded signals about middle-class values, about imperialism, about power-interests, as part of a sign-system that generates far more than the 'obvious' meaning. His goal is to unmask hidden power-interests, whether political, social, or commercial. The 'objectivity' of the sign as an innocent truth-claim about a single state of affairs proves to be illusory. Postmodernity means, above all, loss of innocence, especially any innocence that perceives the contrived as 'natural'. Barthes observes, 'I resented seeing Nature and History confused at every turn.'[54] He develops these principles as an explicit theory of signs in the *Elements of Semiology* (French, 1964; English, 1967).[55] Here 'signs' includes the meaning-systems of clothes, furniture, food and other 'messages' from seemingly innocent matrices.

Jacques Derrida (b. 1930) explicitly acknowledges his indebtedness to the principle of suspicion in Nietzsche, as well as to 'forces' in Freud, the work of Husserl, and 'situatedness' and '*Destruktion*' in Heidegger.[56] Indeed in his well-known long essay 'White Mythology' (1971) resonances with Nietzsche are unmistakable: 'Metaphysics – the white mythology ... reflects the culture of the West: the white man takes his own

---

[53] Roland Barthes, *Mythologies* (Eng., London: Cape, 1972), e.g. pp.91–3.
[54] Ibid., II.
[55] R. Barthes, *Elements of Semiology* (Eng., London: Cape, 1967).
[56] Jacques Derrida, *Of Grammatology* (Eng., Baltimore, MD: Johns Hopkins University Press, 1976), p.xxi (translator's preface by G.C. Spivak); cf. his *Writing and Difference* (Eng., London: Routledge & Kegan Paul, 1978), pp.278–93.

mythology ... for the universal form of that he must still wish to call Reason.'[57] The history of Western philosophy, Derrida concludes, largely rests on confusion between 'so-called philosophical metaphors' and the presupposition that these represent truths which constitute 'the solution of important problems'.[58]

Like Barthes, Derrida attempts to underpin this, at least in his earlier work, with a theory of signs drawn initially from Saussure's notion of the dependence of meaning on 'difference'.[59] Neither language nor truth is 'item-centred', but is generated by a shifting flux of variables. Hence meaning (and thereby truth-claims) never reaches 'closure': 'difference' becomes 'deferral'.[60] Meaning is always postponed, in the sense that new meanings constantly overtake it as new interests and new cultural frames repeatedly change its multi-level currencies. Caputo rightly observes, 'Derrida does not overthrow hermeneutics but makes it more radical.'[61] For this follows Nietzsche's view that there are only *interpretations* and nothing else.[62]

In a later section of this book [included as the next extract in this volume] we shall trace further 'unmaskings' of the 'natural' as social habit or disguised power-interests in Michel Foucault (1926–84). His work on 'madness', for example, demonstrates that what 'madness' seemed to *consist in* has largely depended on shifts in social assumptions between the ancient world, the nineteenth century and today. His later work explores relations between knowledge and power, especially institutional power in the penal system or in medicine.[63]

In his introduction to G. Vattimo, *The End of Modernity* (Italian, 1985; English, 1988), J.R. Snyder observes that the writings of Nietzsche lie not only behind Barthes, Derrida and Foucault, but also behind Lacan, Deleuze, Baudrillard and Lyotard.[64] He explains, 'The project of nihilism is to unmask all systems of reason as systems of persuasion.'[65] In other words, issues of truth become issues of rhetoric. Snyder continues, 'All Thought that pretends to discern truth is but an expression of the will-to-power – even to domination – of those making the truth-claims over those who are being addressed by them.'[66]

Jean-François Lyotard rejects not only the possibility of 'universal' truth, but also even the very notion of 'theory' as a construct of 'modernity' (other than in a purely local, ad hoc, functional sense). In his book ironically entitled *The Postmodern Explained to Children* (French, 1986; English, 1992), he not only declares 'war on totality', but, like Derrida,

---

57 J. Derrida, 'White Metaphor: Metaphor in the Text of Philosophy', in his *Margins of Philosophy* (Eng., New York and London: Harvester Wheatsheaf, 1982), p.213; cf. pp.207–72.

58 Ibid., p.228.

59 I use 'supposedly' in the light of my critique in *New Horizons in Hermeneutics. The Theory and Practice of Transforming Biblical Reading* (London: HarperCollins and Grand Rapids, MI: Zondervan, 1992), pp.82–132.

60 J. Derrida, *Speech and Phenomena and Other Essays on Husserl's Theory of Signs* (Eng., Evanston, IL: Northwestern University Press 1973), pp.135–41; cf. also pp.129–60, esp. p.130.

61 John D. Caputo, *Radical Hermeneutics* (Bloomington, IN: Indiana University Press, 1989), p.4.

62 F. Nietzsche, *Works* vol. 15. *The Will to Power* II, 12 (481).

63 Michel Foucault, *Discipline and Punish* (Eng., New York: Pantheon, 1977), p.190.

64 G. Vattimo, *The End of Modernity. Nihilism and Hermeneutics in Post-modern Culture* (Eng., Cambridge: Polity Press, 1988 and 1991), pp.xii–xiii.

65 Ibid., p.xii.

66 Ibid.; cf. pp.1–13, 134–8 and 176–80, where Vattimo discusses Gadamer and Nietzsche.

insists that we cannot grasp reality, because it slips by before we can catch hold of it. Don Cupitt, we shall note in Part III [of *Interpreting God*], makes wide use of this principle. In this sense, truth is not even 'presentable'.[67]

These perspectives constitute the most serious and urgent challenge to theology, in comparison with which the old-style attacks from 'common-sense positivism' appear relatively naïve. Theology has more at stake than perhaps any other discipline because, although philosophy and some other disciplines share the same loss of truth, theology serves to establish critically informed trust, whereas the postmodern perspective rests on suspicion. Theology seeks to recover elements of the authentic and the genuine from among the chaff of self-interest, manipulation and power-claims. It would also become problematic to claim that at the heart of Christian theology stands the paradigm-case of non-manipulative love, namely the theology of the cross and the free gift of resurrection, if all that exists is manipulative interpretation.

We cannot reply to these claims, however, simply by appealing to the 'weakness' of the cross. For Nietzsche such a response would merely confirm his suspicions about the nature of Christianity. He writes, 'Christianity has sided with everything weak, low, and botched; it made an ideal out of *antagonism* towards all the preservation instincts of strong life.'[68] In Nietzsche's view, the God of Christianity degenerated into the *contradiction of life*: 'instead of being its ... eternal Yes! In God a declaration of hostility towards life ... the will to nothingness sanctified ...'.[69]

III
Do All Controlling Models in Religion Serve Manipulative Interests?

Nietzsche has brought a double charge. Christian claims to truth, he asserts, disguise power-bids, and religious faith breeds insipid mediocrity. Both claims find a powerful response in the writings of Dietrich Bonhoeffer (1906–45). Bonhoeffer attacked notions of Christian belief that appeared to offer comfort and self-affirmation while the believer simply lets the world go by as it is. He equally challenged an interpretation of God and of Christian discipleship that settles merely for passive resignation and mediocrity, or entails manipulative interests.

This is no accident. His close friend Eberhard Bethge tells us that Bonhoeffer read very carefully the entire corpus of Nietzsche's writings and was influenced by them.[70] Bonhoeffer's work, however, in these two respects simply reflects the New Testament writings. We may note first of all how these anticipate what Bonhoeffer translates into twentieth-century terms.

---

[67]   J.-F. Lyotard, *The Postmodern Explained to Children*, p.24.

[68]   F. Nietzsche, *Works. Vol. 16, The Antichrist*, p.130 (5 and 6) and p.131 (7).

[69]   Ibid., p.146 (18).

[70]   Eberhard Bethge's Preface to vol. 3 of Dietrich Bonhoeffer, *Gesammelte Schriften* (5 vols) (Munich: Kaiser, 1958–66); cf. E. Bethge, *Dietrich Bonhoeffer: Theologian, Christian, Contemporary* (Eng., London: Collins, 1970), pp.84–5 and 773 and 'The Challenge of Dietrich Bonhoeffer's Life and Theology', *The Chicago Theological Register*, Feb. 1961, p.4.

The Gospel of John explicitly identifies the desire for personal status and power as a fundamental obstacle to believing in Jesus as the Christ. Jesus exclaims, 'How can you believe when you accept glory (Greek *doxa*) from another?' (John 5:44). *Doxa* carries with it notions of 'reputation', 'opinion', or in this context, social and religious prestige and influence.

The Matthean denunciation of pharisaic leadership, which some interpret as a thinly veiled warning to Christian leaders more generally, includes an explicit rejection of the use of 'religion' to gain 'places of honour ... the best seats ... being seen by others' (Matt. 23:5, 6).[71] The Jesus of Matthew does not mince his words. Those religious leaders who revel in titles of respect and power (23:7) are 'snakes' (23:33). Like whitewashed tombs, they seek to disguise their own degenerate rottenness, while simultaneously warning people away from 'religion' (23:27). Authentic religious leadership and faith finds expression in self-giving service of others (23:11).

The Pauline writings expound these themes in detail. Recently much attention has been given to Paul's '*Narrenrede*' ('I am speaking as a fool') in 2 Corinthians 11:21–12:10. At the end, as at the beginning, he says, 'I have been a fool! You forced me to it' (12:10).[72] It is generally agreed that the issue behind these twenty-three verses arises from the manipulative strategies of rival leaders or 'false apostles' at Corinth. Should Paul exert his own leadership by following the same methods? He had already made it clear in earlier correspondence that self-assertion and reliance on the purely causal force of rhetoric stood at odds with the message of the cross (1 Cor. 1:18–2:5). Paul recalls, 'I came to you in weakness ... My speech and my proclamation were not with plausible words of "wisdom"' (2:3, 4). Yet the Christians in Corinth still seem to expect that genuine leaders will show qualities that impress, whether by 'signs', by rhetorical power, by some institutional pedigree or credentials, or by some trait of character that commands submissive response.

For Paul himself, as E. Käsemann, C.K. Barrett, R.P. Martin and many others rightly argue, such principles or appeals remain incompatible with authentic or 'legitimate' apostleship.[73] Yet for the sake of Corinthian expectations, partly tongue-in-cheek Paul adopts a rhetorical form or style of 'boasting' of credentials to establish and legitimate his 'power', while in practice he deconstructs or undermines the game of power-play. As he declares in 2 Cor. 11:30: 'If I must boast, I will boast of the things that show my weakness.' E.A. Judge, followed by S.H. Travis, shows delightfully that Paul reverses the claim to

---

[71] Cf. David Garland, *The Intention of Matthew 23* (Leiden: Brill, 1979), esp. pp.62–3, 116 and 214. For more recent approaches cf. further Richard A. Edwards, *Matthew's Story of Jesus* (Philadelphia, PA: Fortress, 1985), and F.W. Burnett, 'Exposing the Anti-Jewish Ideology of Matthew's Implied Author: Its Characterization of God as Father', *Semeia 59: Ideological Criticism of Biblical Texts* (1992), pp.155–91.

[72] For example, J. Zmijewski, *Der Stil der paulinischen 'Narrenrede'* (Cologne and Bonn: Hanstein, 1978); C.K. Barrett, 'Boasting (*kauchasthai* k.t.l.) in the Pauline Epistles' in A. Vanhoye (ed.), *L'Apôtre Paul – Personalité, style et conception du ministère* (Leuven: Leuven University, 1986), pp.363–8; J.P. Sampley, 'Paul, his Opponents in 2 Corinthians 10–13 and the Rhetorical *Handbooks*' in J. Neusner et al. (eds), *The Social World of Formative Christianity* (Philadelphia, PA: Fortress, 1988), pp.162–77.

[73] E. Käsemann, 'Die Legitimät des Apostels: eine Untersuchung zu II Korinther 10–13', *Zeitschrift für die neutestamentliche Wissenschaft* 41 (1942), pp.33–71; C.K. Barrett, *The Signs of an Apostle* (London: Epworth Press, 1970); R.P. Martin, *2 Corinthians* (Dallas, TX: Word, 1986 and Milton Keynes: Word, 1991), pp.326–424.

fame and honour accorded to a Roman soldier who has the courage and daring to be 'first over the wall' in the storming of a besieged city.[74] Paul 'boasts' that he, too, was 'first over the wall' – but unceremoniously in the reverse direction to escape in a fish basket to secure a quick exit from arrest: 'I was let down in a basket through a window in the wall, and escaped' (11:33); what bravery! Even if we accept that some opponents already cited this incident as disqualifying Paul for leadership, this does not undermine the broader principle that he recites his 'humiliations' as his 'qualifications'.[75] Apostleship depends on identification with the message of the cross, not with religious triumphalism.

By contrast, the 'false' apostles (11:13) use deceit and seduction (11:3, 13, 15), demand 'submission' and exercise domination: they 'make slaves of you, prey on you, put on airs' (11:20) and 'you submit to it readily enough' (11:4). The 'false apostles' are precisely true to type in the context of Nietzsche's analysis. But Paul does not fit this type. Even the 'weakness' and list of 'sufferings' that, against his will, he enumerates, are not qualities of passive mediocrity or unhealthy masochism. He escapes when he can, but endures without complaint those afflictions which become inevitable if he is to share in the self-giving that reflects the principle of the cross. This is venturesome and courageous service for the sake of others: 'I will most gladly spend and be spent for you' (12:15).

The two principles of non-manipulative service and a boldness that is far from servile come together vigorously in Martin Luther (1483–1546). Especially in The Heidelberg Disputation of 1518 he places in contrast a triumphalist, manipulative 'theology of glory', and a self-giving, truthful 'theology of the cross'. He comments, 'The theologian of glory says bad is good, and good is bad. The theologian of the cross calls them by their proper name.'[76] The one deserves the title 'theologian' who comprehends God not through power-seeking or a search for self-affirmation, but in receiving judgement and grace through the cross. The seeker after self and power 'prefers works to sufferings; and glory, to a cross'.[77]

We should not interpret what it is to 'prefer sufferings', however, in the way proposed by Nietzsche as servility or the 'slave morality' of Christians. Indeed Luther quite explicitly opposes those 'fanatics' or 'enthusiasts' who 'select their own cross ... making their suffering meritorious'.[78] This would transpose it into a bid (even if an illusory bid) for power. There is nothing of a servile, lie-down-to-die, insipid, or bland character in Christian faith for Luther. In his Preface to Romans he declares: 'Faith is a living, daring, confidence in God's grace, so sure ... that a man would stake his life upon it ... [It] makes men glad and bold ... ready and glad, without compulsion, to do good to everyone... in love and praise to God who has shown him this grace.'[79]

---

[74] E.A. Judge, 'The Conflict of Educational Aims in New Testament Thought', *Journal of Christian Education* 9 (1966), pp.32–45, and further in 'Paul's Boasting in Relation to Contemporary Professional Practice', *Australian Biblical Review* 16 (1968), pp.37–50; S.H. Travis, 'Paul's Boasting in 2 Corinthians 10–12', *Studia Evangelica* 6 (1973), pp.527–32. Cf. Livy 23:18.

[75] R.P. Martin, loc. cit., p.384.

[76] Martin Luther, 'The Heidelberg Disputation', in *Luther: Early Theological Works* (ed. James Atkinson) (London: SCM, 1962), p.291, Thesis 21.

[77] Luther, loc. cit., Proof 21.

[78] Martin Luther, 'Sermon at Coberg on the Cross and Suffering', (1530) in *Luther's Works*, vol. 51 (Philadelphia, PA: Fortress, 1959), p.199.

[79] Martin Luther, 'Preface to the Epistle of St. Paul to the Romans', in *Luther's Works*, vol. 35 (Philadelphia, PA: Fortress, 1960), pp.370–71.

Dietrich Bonhoeffer takes up these profound interpretations of God as known through the cross and applies them to the confusions of our own century. For Bonhoeffer, belief in God is no hallucinatory anodyne, which merely helps people to cope with discomforts, insecurities, or difficulties. Christian theology has nothing to do with the consumers' wishes to purchase power or comfort.

Bonhoeffer writes, 'If it is I who say where God will be, I will always find there a [false] God who in some way corresponds to me, is agreeable to me, fits in with my nature. But if it is God who says where He will be ... that place is the cross of Christ'.[80] This, he urges, is why the beatitudes in the Sermon on the Mount do not declare 'blessed are the powerful', but 'blessed are those who mourn', 'blessed are the poor'. That this has nothing to do with manipulative interests is demonstrated by the parallel 'Blessed are the pure in heart.'[81]

Bonhoeffer elucidates this principle further in *The Cost of Discipleship*. Here he attacks those who transpose a gospel which demands glad but costly discipleship into a commerce of 'cheap grace ... sold on the market like a cheapjack's wares'.[82] Cheap grace is precisely what Nietzsche characterizes as a self-affirming illusion. Bonhoeffer writes, 'Cheap grace means the justification of sin without the justification of the sinner ... the world goes on in the same old way ... Cheap grace is the preaching of forgiveness without requiring repentance, baptism without church discipline, Communion without confession ... grace without the cross, grace without Jesus Christ'.[83] For the first disciples grace was bound up with obedience to the call of Jesus to follow him in the everyday world.

This theme lies behind Bonhoeffer's equally well-known passage in his *Letters and Papers from Prison* written from Tegel about ten months before his execution. Christians, he writes, must live for others without resort to the notion of God as some 'useful' crutch to soften reality, or to reduce the cost of service. On 16 July 1944 he wrote, 'Before God and with God we live without God. God lets himself be pushed out of the world on to the cross ... Christ helps us, not by virtue of his omnipotence, but by virtue of his weakness and suffering.'[84]

E. Bethge, to whom this letter was personally written, explains in his theological biography of Bonhoeffer: 'The Christian listens to Feuerbach and Nietzsche – with a good conscience ... They, for example, warn the Church against becoming a chemist's shop to minister to heavenly needs, leaving the world to its own desires.'[85] It is as if Bonhoeffer said to Nietzsche from his Nazi prison: 'But not all Christians are as you suggest. For even if you are right about "religion" as a human construct, authentic Christian faith lies in identification with the Christ who neither sought power by manipulation, nor was

---

[80] Dietrich Bonhoeffer, *Meditating on the Word* (Eng., Cambridge, MA: Cowley Publications, 1986), p.45.

[81] Ibid., Cf. D. Bonhoeffer, *The Cost of Discipleship* (Eng. (unabridged edn), London: SCM, 1959), pp.93–176.

[82] D. Bonhoeffer, *The Cost of Discipleship*, p.35.

[83] Ibid., pp.35–6; cf. pp.37–47.

[84] D. Bonhoeffer, *Letters and Papers from Prison* (Eng. (enlarged edn), London: SCM, 1971), pp.360–61 (also 3rd edn, Eng. 1967, p.196; 1953 edn, p.121).

[85] E. Bethge, *Dietrich Bonhoeffer*, p.773.

"weak" in the sense of being bland, conformist, or world-denying. He was "the man for others".'[86]

Thus Bonhoeffer writes further to Bethge: that *metanoia* (Greek, repentance; Hebrew, turning) is 'not in the first place thinking about one's needs, problems, sins, and fears, but allowing oneself to be caught up into the way of Jesus'.[87] Faith does not '*use*' God, either as a pretext for legitimating one's wishes, or to 'explain' gaps in certain intellectual problems.[88] Biblical faith is controlled by the model not of 'religiosity' but of the Christ who goes to the cross 'for the other'.[89]

Bonhoeffer drives another nail into the coffin of Nietzsche's critique of all Christian faith when he turns to attack mistaken strategies on the part of clergy and leaders. Here he attacks, equally, liberalism on one side and pietist strands of Lutheranism and Methodism on the other.

The evangelistic strategy of liberalism remains flawed, he asserts, because 'it conceded to the world the right to determine Christ's place in the world'.[90] But no less the strategy of outreach proposed by pietists, namely 'despair or Jesus' rests on a mistake.[91] Bonhoeffer views this as a manipulative strategy which depends for its success in projecting the world into an infantile regression into an immature dependency-state. Almost echoing Nietzsche, he complains, 'They set themselves to drive people to inward despair and then the game is in their hands ... And whom does it touch? A small number of people who regard themselves as the most important thing in the world, and who therefore like to bury themselves with themselves.'[92]

It is important to sift the wheat from the chaff at this point. On one side, on the basis of such proclamation it becomes scarcely surprising if many churches become havens for self-centred, self-preoccupied religious lives. In Bonhoeffer's eyes this is 'like an attempt to put a grown-up man back into adolescence'.[93] On the other side, however, Gerhard Ebeling wishes to distinguish between his right expression of concern (with Luther) that believing faith is centred on Christ, rather than on some 'inner state' of the self, from a less judicious, over-hasty dismissal of experiences of human plight. Ebeling does not undervalue Bonhoeffer's approach, but wonders whether his importance is recognized 'in spite of' rather than 'because of' some of these reflections from his Tegel prison.[94]

If we heed Ebeling's careful warning, however, Bonhoeffer's main argument stands. Moreover Bonhoeffer attacks all manipulative strategies, even if they have good intentions behind them. For, Bonhoeffer reflects, this 'attack by Christian apologetic on the adulthood of the world' becomes 'ignoble, because it amounts to an attempt to exploit man's weakness' and thereby 'unchristian'.[95] Bonhoeffer's positive alternative comes to

---

86 D. Bonhoeffer, *Letters and Papers* (enlarged 1971 edn), pp.381–2 (my italics).
87 Ibid., p.361 (18 July 1944).
88 Ibid., p.360 (16 July).
89 Ibid., p.361 (16 July).
90 Ibid., p.327 (8 June).
91 Ibid.
92 Ibid., pp.326–7.
93 Ibid., p.327.
94 Gerhard Ebeling, *Word and Faith* (Eng., London: SCM, 1963), p.101 (his italics); cf. pp.98–161.
95 D. Bonhoeffer, *Letters and Papers*, p.327.

the fore in earlier writings, including his *Ethics*. Everything hinges on the demonstration in the public domain of everyday life of 'this really lived love of God in Jesus Christ'.[96] The strategy depends not on 'ideals or programmes' but on '*Ecce homo*'.[97] It is 'to be caught up into the way of Jesus Christ'.[98]

The very notion of defining the 'identity' of Christian discipleship in 'the way of Jesus Christ', anticipates the even more powerful writings by Jürgen Moltmann (b. 1926). We shall postpone our main discussion of Moltmann until Part IV [of *Interpreting God*]. For the present we may note that Moltmann distinguishes authentic Christian hope equally from 'presumption' and from 'the sin of despair'.[99] As our argument progresses, we shall see that while the former reflects tendencies in over-optimistic 'modernity', the latter threatens to damage the more pessimistic postmodern self.

Moltmann, like Bonhoeffer, emphatically rejects any Christian withdrawal from the world. Faith is not genuine that 'can wear the face of smiling resignation' or can become merely 'bourgeois Christianity'.[100] Further, the close conjunction of the cross and the resurrection addresses both Nietzsche's assertion that 'God is dead', and Bonhoeffer's language about 'God-forsakenness'.[101] Far from becoming a manipulative tool to gain security, the truth proclaimed in the cross calls the people of God to leave the security of 'the camp', and to go forth as the 'exodus church', bearing 'the reproach of Christ' as defenceless pilgrims (Heb. 13:13, 14).[102]

In *The Crucified God* Moltmann rejects the notion of the church as 'a social ghetto' that provides artificial affirmation and power by withdrawing from anything alien or threatening. Self-justification and self-deification must be abandoned.[103] Like Bonhoeffer he insists that 'Christian identity can be understood only as an act of identification with the crucified Christ'.[104] In *The Way of Jesus Christ*, Moltmann sees the rejection of power as characterizing those 'who have borne "the abuse of Christ"' (Heb. 11:26).[105]

Might this now fall victim to Nietzsche's opposite criticism concerning 'a slave mentality'? Far from it; for we have already noted that in Moltmann's theology passivity, mediocrity, or 'the face of smiling resignation' finds no place. He explicitly includes examples of Christians whose suffering for others could never be described as 'passive' rather than as brave. Bonhoeffer, for example, 'was not overwhelmed passively by

---

[96]   D. Bonhoeffer, *Ethics* (London: SCM, 1955 (1965 edn)), p.70.

[97]   Ibid.

[98]   D. Bonhoeffer, *Letters and Papers*, p.361. In addition to Bethge's works, see also John A. Phillips, *Christ for Us in the Theology of Dietrich Bonhoeffer* (New York: Harper and Row, 1967), especially pp.71–106, 183–99 and 222–48; John D. Godsey, *The Theology of Dietrich Bonhoeffer* (London: SCM, 1960), esp. pp.248–82; A. Dumas, *Dietrich Bonhoeffer Theologian of Reality* (London: SCM, 1971), esp. pp.163–280; and the introductory anthology of selected extracts, John de Grouchy (ed.), *Dietrich Bonhoeffer. Witness to Jesus Christ* (London: Collins, 1988).

[99]   J. Moltmann, *Theology of Hope* (Eng., London: SCM, 1967), pp.22–5.

[100]   Ibid., p.24.

[101]   Ibid., pp.166, 167 and 197–216.

[102]   Ibid., pp.304–38.

[103]   J. Moltmann, *The Crucified God. The Cross of Christ as the Foundation and Criticism of Christian Theology* (Eng., London: SCM, 1974), pp.27 and 28.

[104]   Ibid., p.19.

[105]   J. Moltmann, *The Way of Jesus Christ. Christology in Messianic Dimensions* (Eng., London: SCM, 1990), p.210.

persecution, suffering, and death. He returned voluntarily to Germany in 1939. He became involved in political resistance knowing exactly what he was doing, and it was a deliberate act of choice when he became a "traitor" to a regime that had shown its contempt for human beings'.[106]

Moltmann's recent work *The Spirit of Life* carries a sub-title which, in effect, meets Nietzsche head on: *A Universal Affirmation* (German, 1991; English, 1992). Here Moltmann explicitly rejects the two-storey dualism that Nietzsche and Heidegger ascribe to Christianity as 'Platonism for the people'.[107] He cuts the ground from under the feet of those who interpret the God of the resurrection as 'world-denying'. For he rejects the Kantian premise that leads some theologians to interpret God as 'within the self', and others to interpret God as 'outside' the world as 'other'.[108] Relationality and otherness constitute a two-sided dialectic. Here the wholeness of life is affirmed not by some autonomous self, but in the reciprocity of mutual self-giving and mutual 'inter-penetration' of love. The early Fathers expressed this mutual regard for the other through the language of '*perichoresis*' and we explore this in Part IV [of *Interpreting God*].[109] Contrary to Nietzsche's notions of 'love', Moltmann asserts, 'Love makes life worth living.'[110] The Christian says 'yes' to life.

---

106   Ibid., p.201.
107   J. Moltmann, *The Spirit of Life. A Universal Affirmation* (Eng., London: SCM, 1992), pp.8–10.
108   Ibid., pp.5–8 and 31–8.
109   Ibid., pp.10–14, 47–51, 58–77 and 114–22.
110   Ibid., p.259.

CHAPTER THIRTY-ONE

The Postmodern Self and Society: Loss of Hope and the Possibility of Refocused Hope (Extracts, 1995)

The following essay consists of extracts from Interpreting God and the Postmodern Self: On Meaning, Manipulation and Promise (*Edinburgh: T. & T. Clark, 1995, here, pp.121–63*), *which is an expanded version of four public lectures delivered at the University of Aberdeen as the first* Scottish Journal of Theology *series of lectures. This work engages with societal aspects of the postmodern condition, and reflects on how a Christian theology of hope might address some of the issues that emerge. Some critics have argued that my picture of postmodern selfhood is more negative and selective than it might have been. As I concede in my retrospective evaluation (below), I do not deny that other aspects of postmodern perspectives may merit a more positive appraisal. But I choose here to focus on those specific aspects that stand in sharp contrast to the equally misguided illusory optimism of secular modernity.*

I
The Collapse of the Hope of the 'Modern' Self: From Active Agency to Passive Situatedness

The most prolific theological writer on hope, Jürgen Moltmann, has compared theologies of hope with theologies of faith and of love. Generally speaking, he writes, 'theologies of the Middle Ages were all theologies of love' while 'theologies of the Reformers ... were decidedly theologies of faith'. But the fundamental issue of modern times 'is the question of the future' which invites theologies of hope.[1] For Moltmann this entails a critique of the present that brings about its transformation.

'Modernity', in contrast to the self-perceptions of the postmodern self, tends to be optimistic. It draws confidence from the mood of the Enlightenment when scientific method appeared to open up new possibilities for the self as active agent to carve out and to control its own destiny. Leaving behind the constraints of authority and medieval hierarchy, the self of modernity becomes, with Descartes, the starting-point for knowledge. With Kant it becomes the locus of autonomy and free decision. This mood of optimism in which the human self seems to be situated at the centre continues from the Enlightenment until perhaps around the end of the 1960s or the early 1970s.

By contrast the self of postmodernity has become *de-centred*. It no longer regards itself as active agent carving out any possibility with the aid of natural and social sciences, but as an opaque product of variable roles and performances which have been

---

[1] J. Moltmann, *Theology Today* (Eng., London: SCM, 1988), p.23.

imposed upon it by the constraints of society and by its own inner drives or conflicts. Even if the sciences hypothetically make almost anything possible, no global strategy can ensure that appropriate scientific activity receives either adequate funding or more especially adequate moral or strategic guidance concerning its constructive and beneficial application. The sciences unleash vast forces, but how these are ordered now appears to depend on scientific guilds and their capacity to invite necessary economic funding.

Ranking orders of societal needs or agenda for the human self are now also more likely to be set by localized guilds, management theorists, economists, or 'quasi-non-governmental organizations' than by the more conscious choices of the human self as agent of decision concerning its own destiny. It has become caught up in a prior agenda as a performer of pre-determined roles. The subjectivity of the self as agent in Descartes, Kant and Kierkegaard has collapsed into an imposed functionalism within a social system and a sign system. The social situation appears to reflect the literary theory implied in the post-structuralism of Derrida. The self appears to be constituted not by consciousness and moral agency but by Heidegger's 'situatedness' (*Befindlichkeit*), 'historicality', (*Geschichtlichkeit*), or 'being-there' (*Dasein*).[2]

Can a theology of hope, or more precisely a Christian theology of promise, address the postmodern condition? The collapse of the selfhood of modernity, I propose to argue, opens the way for, and invites, such a theology. For the argument of Feuerbach that theism positively reduces the humanness of humanity remains arguably credible only as long as the self is perceived as a primary source of moral worth, which controls its destiny. Practical atheism may remain cheerful, provided that the self is free to make its own choices, and influence its future.

In ancient Greece Epicurus could base his materialist philosophy of life on the supposed ultimacy of present experiences of pleasure or pain on the ground that the intelligence (*phronēsis*) directs choice. Practical wisdom measures pleasure against pain, choosing pains only if they lead to greater pleasures. The virtues of courage, justice and moderation ensure that while the body lives in and for the present moment, the mind projects forward possibilities as hopes, which then constitute a basis for stable patterns of meaning and action. But what happens when the self of 'the virtues' has become de-centred as a product of social and psycho-linguistic forces? Alasdair MacIntyre's well-chosen titles of his influential works from 1981 to 1990 make the point. His *After Virtue* (1981, 1985) leads on to *Whose Justice? Which Rationality?* (1988), and to *Three Rival Versions of Moral Enquiry*.[3] In technical philosophical terms we face the problem of *incommensurability*, and the disastrous consequences of contextual pragmatism. What rational criteria or norms, if any, can command agreement as common measurements (*commensurable* ones) which can arbitrate between the competing truth-claims of rival social groups, or are the respective claims of each simply 'untranslatable' as what *counts* as rational or 'normal' within a competing group?

---

[2] M. Heidegger, *Being and Time* (Eng., Oxford: Blackwell, 1962 (1973)), esp. sects 29–31, pp.179–88.

[3] Alasdair MacIntyre, *After Virtue. A Study in Moral Theory* (London: Duckworth, 1981, 2nd edn, 1985); *Whose Justice? Which Rationality?* (London: Duckworth and Notre Dame, IN: University of Notre Dame Press, 1988); and *Three Rival Versions of Moral Enquiry* (London: Duckworth, 1990).

Atheism, in such a situation, can no longer offer the apparent cheerfulness which marked the 'practical' or 'virtual' atheism of pre-moderns such as Epicurus, or the 'avowed atheism' (as David Berman calls it, by contrast) of Feuerbach, Marx and other thinkers from after around the 1770s.[4] Berman follows Schopenhauer in perceiving the influence of Kant's third Critique as decisively providing a basis for 'avowed' atheism.[5] For Kant's *Critique of Judgment* ascribed order, purpose and evidence of design not to nature or to the world as it is, but to patterns read into it by the mind. Hence it no longer seemed necessary to presuppose some intelligent ground for this sense of intelligible order beyond the 'modern' self. Whereas previously it seemed irrational to ascribe order to mere chance, Kant now diagnosed 'the formal purposiveness of nature as a transcendental principle of judgment'.[6]

Within the context of Enlightenment modernity, it followed that, if this supposition were valid, an atheistic philosophy such as several 'left-wing' Hegelians proposed could be more effectively 'emancipatory' or liberating for the self than even Hegel's attempt to offer an 'emancipatory' philosophy. Hegel's historical and logical dialectic presupposed that 'order' was compatible with freedom; indeed that it was necessary for freedom. His philosophy of historical reason served to underpin an explicit politics of order and structure in society, and his political philosophy carried weight in defending constitutional monarchy.[7] By contrast, many of the 'left-wing' Hegelians offered very different 'emancipating' philosophies. Ludwig Feuerbach (1804–72) wished explicitly to liberate the self of modernity from its double bondage '*to heavenly and earthly monarchy ...* into *free, self-confident* citizens of the world' (my italics).[8]

Feuerbach anticipated Nietzsche in regarding the notion of 'God', other than in the form of a recognized human construct, as diminishing humanity, and as repressing the creativity of the self. In his Epigrams he equates Christianity with servile obedience to authority and convention. He writes, 'Christianity is now the pass into the land of the Philistines, where one can securely eat one's bread in obedience to authority.' 'What distinguishes the Christian from other honourable people? At most a pious face and parted hair.'[9] But the self of modernity need not be constrained in this fashion: 'God ... is only smoke left when these gentleman (theologians) have exploded all their powder'.[10]

Can Feuerbach's optimistic atheism survive, however, in a postmodern era in which many (rightly or wrongly) perceive *all* instantiations of postmodern self-hood as victim of imposed role-performances and social norms constructed by a variety of social groups, whether theist or anti-theist, male or female, professional or artisan, black or white?

---

[4] David Berman, *A History of Atheism in Britain from Hobbes to Russell* (London & New York: Routledge, 1988 and 1990), pp.1–43 and 153–89.

[5] Ibid., pp.27–8; cf. Schopenhauer's Appendix to his *World as Will* (1819).

[6] Immanuel Kant, *Critique of Judgment* (Eng., New York: Haffner Press, 1951), p.17; cf. also I:10, pp.54–72.

[7] G.W.F. Hegel, *The Philosophy of Right* (German 1821, 2nd edn, 1833) (Eng., Oxford: OUP, 1942); on 'lordship and bondage' cf. further his *Phenomenology of Mind* (German 1807) (Eng., London: Allen & Unwin, 1931).

[8] L. Feuerbach, *Gesammelte Werke*, vol. 6 (Berlin: Akademie Verlag, 1967), p.31.

[9] L. Feuerbach, 'Epigrams' in *Thoughts on Death and Immortality* (Eng., Berkeley, CA and London: University of California Press, 1980), pp.214 and 205.

[10] Ibid., p.198.

Every counter-culture of protest takes on its own internal norms of truth, value, acceptability, and selfhood. It has become fully evident that Feuerbach was mistaken in imagining that simply to jettison belief in a personal God would guarantee the new 'Bethlehem' of freedom which he imagined that Hegel had made possible, once his system had been purged of 'absolute spirit' or 'God'. Even Kant's 'autonomy' has a hollow ring in the light of the immense gap which has opened between Kant's self of the categorical moral imperative and the postmodern self.

Karl Marx (1818–83) and (as we have seen) Friedrich Nietzsche (1844–1900) shared Feuerbach's view concerning the damaging effects of theism, as well as its illusory basis. In one respect, however, Marx anticipated a perspective of postmodern selfhood. He diagnosed its powerlessness as due to structural forces which dominate and oppress the self in the interests of the powerful. Vested interests depersonalize the self into a mere unit of production, valued only as a unit of exchange-value in the market of labour. Here indeed emerges the postmodern self.

Nevertheless Marxism remains 'modern', not postmodern, because it also adopts a global universalized philosophy or 'meta-narrative' in accordance with which history-as-a-whole moves towards a universal goal. The conflict in which the isolated self would be a powerless victim becomes transposed into a collective, structural, class struggle. As a collectivity it has an active part in a grand design. Just as capitalism subsumed and overcame feudalism and property became diversified into the hands of a middle-class bourgeoisie, even so capitalism will *inevitably* become subsumed within, and overcome by, the rise of the proletariat and the *parousia* of universal public ownership. Eventually even state socialism will wither away, and the need for coercion be replaced by the eschaton of voluntary communism. Even if Engels retained reservations about historical inevitability, Marx proclaimed in principle an unstoppable gospel of the final emancipation of the self.[11]

In such a context, theism merely appeared to slow down the process. It did so by pacifying the proletariat with language about order, providence and authority. But whereas Christian faith appeared merely to slow down the process, the collapse of Marxism as an efficient socio-economic system has more fundamentally undermined it over the last few years than any theory about religion. Even if the Republic of China, at the time of writing, still clings to a 'modern', centrally structured, monolithic system, elsewhere in formerly Marxist societies, for the most part, even nation-states threaten to break up into diverse, more 'tribal', entities, while economic productivity has entered a potentially chaotic period of transition into fragmented interest-groups which struggle for economic power. It is arguable that Marxist theory transparently failed to take account of human nature with the realism of Christian theology. Feuerbach's epigram 'If you wish to be delivered from sin ... become a pagan; sin came into the world with Christianity' appears, in the light of current civil wars at the time of writing, to be naïve, if not infantile.[12]

---

[11] Karl Marx, *Capital* (Eng., 3 vols, New York: International Publishers, 1967), cf. *The Writings of the Young Marx on Philosophy and Society* (Garden City, NY: Doubleday, 1967).

[12] L. Feuerbach, 'Epigrams', p.224.

Moreover, the warnings of non-theist postmodern writers, especially those of Michel Foucault, confirm that the Marxist faith in bureaucrats to hold the ring against potentially competing power-groups was also naïve. Foucault has little difficulty in showing that the power of bureaucrats to define 'norms' and 'acceptable' procedures, together with the escalating of power which they gain through 'surveillance' and the possession of files and databanks, makes it impossible for them to fail to exercise power-play.[13] At the very least they build their own empires. At worst they load norms and agendas to try to ensure that their position of control becomes unassailable. They have become the new elite. The history of the Eastern Bloc has amply vindicated this analysis, while the West flounders in its attempts to balance centripetal and centrifugal forces.

Nietzsche's self-confidence, we have already noted, was as great as Feuerbach's in his misplaced trust in the 'freedom' and 'affirmation of life' that would result from heeding the message that 'God is dead'. Nietzsche's 'madman' proclaims the death of God in *The Gay Science* of 1882.[14] In his later work, *The Anti-Christ*, he speaks of 'God', especially in Christianity, as a 'contradiction of life', which denies 'the eternal *Yes*' of humanity. Belief in God, he says, is 'a declaration of hostility towards life, nature, the will to life … [It is] the will to nothingness sanctified'.[15]

In the late nineteenth century, before the First World War, 'Yes' seemed to affirm progress, science, autonomy, human dignity. Moreover, while secular culture appeared to offer grounds for optimism, much Christian theology was at the same time trapped with an idealist philosophical frame which lent support to a dualist or 'Hellenized' version of the Christian gospel. Nietzsche and Heidegger perceived it as 'Platonism for the people'. The physical realm appeared to reflect something inferior to the supposed realm of 'the soul'.

Moltmann rightly protests against such a distortion of biblical faith. He comments, 'In this gnostic form the Christian hope no longer gazes forward to a future when everything will be created anew. It looks upwards, to the soul's escape from the body and from this earth, into the heaven of blessed spirits.'[16] Moltmann rightly laments the effects of this 'dualism of body and soul', and will have none of it. Hence, almost as if he were explicitly addressing Nietzsche, Moltmann affirms, 'True spirituality will be the restoration of the love for life … The full and unreserved "yes" to life … the "well of life"'.[17] With this theme Moltmann links 'vitality' and 'liberty'. But Moltmann's liberty is not the 'autonomy' of Cupitt or Feuerbach, or of the lone Kantian thinker. It is grounded in social bonds that it shares with *the Other* and with *Others* in love. It is *social in its very nature*.

---

[13] Michel Foucault, *Discipline and Punish* (French, *Surveiller et punir*, 1975) (Eng., New York: Pantheon, 1977) (and other works cited below).

[14] F. Nietzsche, *Complete Works vol. 10: The Joyful Wisdom/The Gay Science*, aphorisms 108 and 343 (also in W. Kaufman, op. cit., p.447).

[15] F. Nietzsche, *Complete Works vol. 16; The Anti-Christ*, p.146, aphorism 18; cf. pp.142–50, aphorisms 16–21.

[16] J. Moltmann, *The Spirit of Life: A Universal Affirmation* (Eng., London: SCM, 1992), p.90.

[17] Ibid., p.97.

II

More Social Consequences of Postmodern Selfhood: Despair, Conflict and Manipulation

The work of Sigmund Freud (1856–1940), like that of Nietzsche, contributes to perceptions of the self that characterize the self of postmodernism. In contrast to the notion of the modern self in control of its own choices, values and goals, Freud portrays the self, first, as an amalgam of neurological, quasi-physical, or psychic 'forces' which serve to define and to shape it; second, as victim of its manipulative deceptions.

Freud explicitly stated that psychoanalysis derives 'all mental processes ... from *the interplay of forces* which assist or inhibit one another'.[18] Whereas Hume, as a sceptic but also a sceptic of modernity, spoke of the self as a bundle of 'perceptions', Freud interprets selfhood in terms of force-flows of psychic energies. His models are physical, neurological, mechanical, or even drawn from economics. Thus, for example, *cathexis* and *countercathexis* represent inputs and outputs of energy-forces which become 'invested' in another person or in some object. Ricoeur and Küng, two of the most astute commentators on Freud who write from within a non-reductionist, anti-positivist frame, expose the far-reaching consequences of Freud's reliance on largely mechanistic models. Küng observes, 'A method of investigation was turned into a world view; people "believed" in it.'[19]

Freud offers a perceptive analysis of the capacity of the self to fall victim to its own deceptive, self-protective and manipulative devices. The interpreter, on this basis, seeks to understand 'another text ... beneath the text of consciousness'.[20] Deception disguises one or more sets of opposing interests. For example, the self may mask battles between the pressures of social, moral, or moralistic constraints (cf. the *superego*) and drives towards self-satisfaction or self-gratification (cf. Freud's *id*).

We need not dispute that *in some or in many cases* a neurosis that emerges from the pressures of inner conflicts may give rise to religious projections. This may lie behind certain religious myths, or trigger infantile regressions into a strong need for religious affirmation or religious dependency. It cannot be demonstrated that this applies, however, to all cases, and no doubt even within the selfhood of those who may hold valid religious beliefs, elements of religious manipulation and self-deception may co-exist with other motivations and responses.

This coheres entirely with the perspective in Paul, in Hebrews and in the Johannine writings that believers remain fallible and fully capable of continuing self-deception (1 John 1:8; cf. 1 Cor. 3:18; Heb. 3:13). As Cullman memorably asserts, Christians still sin and still die, since the transforming processes of the work of the Holy Spirit constitute the 'first-fruits' of a future yet to be actualized fully.[21] Nevertheless, if we follow Freud in

---

[18] S. Freud, *Standard Edition* (cited above in Pt II), vol. 20 (1959), p.265.

[19] Hans Küng, *Freud and the Problem of God*, p.15; cf. P Ricoeur, *Freud and Philosophy* (both cited above).

[20] S. Freud, *Standard Edition*, op. cit., vols 4–5: *The Interpretation of Dreams*, 1953, and P. Ricoeur, *Freud and Philosophy*, p.392. For a further exposition and critique, cf. A.C. Thiselton, *New Horizons in Hermeneutics*, pp.344–50.

[21] O. Cullman, *Christ and Time* (Eng., London: SCM, 1951), p.155.

speaking either metaphorically or literally of 'forces', in the context of Christian theology other 'forces' which elude a positivist approach also become operative, as part of a wider picture. In the theology of Paul, for example, the renewed self does not remain entirely victim to the social, moral, or cause-and-effect forces that determined its historical situatedness. In theological terms, bondage to a cause-effect of process of sin, law, and death does not have the final word (Romans 6–8). Although forces from the past still operate, the Holy Spirit also brings about a process of transformation 'from ahead', which loosens and eventually breaks the ties which bind the self to its pre-given situatedness. The goal of promise now becomes transformation from a failed or distorted 'image' of humanness into the 'image' of Jesus Christ (1 Cor. 15:49; 2 Cor. 3:18). In Cullman's words 'the Holy Spirit is nothing else than that anticipation of the end in the present'.[22]

Karl Rahner rightly related this 'openness to the future' to 'interior truthfulness'. Those who become open in this way have 'the courage to accept themselves as they are ... because one whom God has accepted ... can accept himself'.[23] The need no longer remains to hide behind devices of deceit and manipulation. There is no need for interior deceitfulness with one's self, dishonesty, '"putting up a façade" ... affectation and other forms in which a man tries to avoid facing up to his own nature'.[24] The biblical writings allude to this dimension of self-deception and concealed depths within the self under the terminology of 'the heart'. The 'heart', thus becomes the sphere for the 'pouring out' of the Holy Spirit. The heart may be 'slippery' or 'deceitful' (Jer. 17:9); and the 'depths' of the heart may conceal hidden things (1 Cor. 4:5). But, Paul declares, 'God's love has been poured into our hearts through the Holy Spirit' (Rom. 5:5). Where conflict within the self has hitherto been provoked by a series of forces which Paul describes in Romans 6–8 as corporate or individual self-interests (sin, Rom. 6), as inescapable cause-effect processes (law, Rom. 7), and as self-defeating, stultifying projects (death, Rom. 8), these chapters hold out the corresponding promises of liberation from self-interest, the future-orientated work of the Spirit rather than past entanglements with the law, and creative transformation rather than the collapse of present projects into decay.

Three theologians corroborate these themes in different ways. As against the illusory optimism of 'modernity', which lacks any adequate notion of the self's vulnerability and bondage in the grip of stronger forces, Emil Brunner declares 'Belief in progress as hope resting upon self-confidence is the opposite of Christian hope, which is founded upon trust in God.'[25] In the same vein, Anders Nygren sees the experience of self-worth in the creative, transforming, power of divine love. The self, he comments, 'acquires worth just by becoming the object of God's love ... *Agapē is a value-creating principle ... a creative work of divine power*' (his italics).[26] Moltmann sees in these processes the restoration of a genuinely reciprocal openness to others and to the Other which defines the very nature of personhood as it is intended to be: 'Personhood is always being-in-relationship.'[27] Only

---

[22] Ibid., p.72.

[23] Karl Rahner, 'On Truthfulness', in *Theological Investigations*, vol. 7 (Eng., London: Darton, Longman, & Todd, 1971), p.239; cf. pp.229–59.

[24] Ibid., p.235.

[25] Emil Brunner, *Eternal Hope* (Eng., London: Lutterworth Press, 1954), p.10.

[26] Anders Nygren, *Agapē and Eros* (Eng., London: SPCK, 1953), pp.78 and 80.

[27] J. Moltmann, *The Spirit of Life*, p.11.

within a content of love can the self eventually come to discard its self-deceptions (for in this context it has no need for self-protection or to disguise 'interests'): 'Love never ends … the partial will come to an end … Now we see in a mirror dimly, but then we shall see face to face. Now I know only in past; then I will know fully, even as I have been fully known' (1 Cor. 13:8, 10, 12). Liberation becomes a possibility, and the promise of redemption in due course becomes substantiated (Rom. 5:5).

Freud's emphasis on self-deception, then, entirely coheres with Christian theology. As Ricoeur comments, this necessitates a hermeneutics of the self as 'text' for the human subject, which, contrary to Descartes and to secular modernity, 'is never the subject one thinks it is'.[28] Christian theology also coheres with Freud's analysis of the self as falling victim to forces which it does not fully understand and which certainly it cannot fully control. The postmodern self at this point stands closer to biblical realism than to the innocent confidence of modernity. Yet even if, to reapply J.L. Austin's phrase, this is indeed the first word, it is nevertheless not the last word. For where experiences of bondage, constraint, or domination at the hands of external forces or groups nourish despair, conflict and anger, the Christian *kerygma* holds out the possibility or even promise of 'God's love … poured into our hearts through the Holy Spirit' (Rom. 5:5), against the background axiom that 'love builds' (1 Cor. 8:1).

[Part of the text of this book is omitted here for purposes of abbreviation.]

Paul speaks of 'supra-personal forces which enslave people, destroy their world, and make the whole creation … "groan"'.[29] But the renewed self of God's promised future involves 'the personal experience of sociality … To call God Lord, promises freedom.'[30] But, as we have recently noted, such freedom, in Moltmann's view, has little or nothing to do with the illusory 'autonomy' of Kant; rather 'the hitherto unexplored creative powers of God are thrown open in men and women … which [are] life-giving through *love*'.[31]

However, without this promise, the transition from the selfhood of optimistic modernity to the postmodern self has deeply destructive social consequences. First, a loss of stability, loss of stable identity and loss of confidence in global norms or goals breeds deep uncertainty, insecurity and anxiety. To recall the incisive analysis offered by David Harvey, the postmodern self lives daily with fragmentation, indeterminacy and intense distrust of all universal or 'totalizing' discourses. Insecurity, in turn, invites a defensiveness, a letting-down of shutters and an increasing preoccupation with self-protection, self-interest, desire for power and the recovery of control. *The postmodern self is thus predisposed to assume a stance of readiness for conflict.*

Second, in the case of the self of modernity, misfortune or loss of privilege may be construed at best as a challenge to courageous action, in the belief that such action can make a difference; or at worst, as bad luck arising from random forces or from some

---

28 Paul Ricoeur, *Freud and Philosophy*, p.420.
29 J. Moltmann, *The Spirit of Life*, p.88.
30 Ibid., pp.94 and 101.
31 Ibid., p.115.

inevitable by-product of an otherwise stable strategy for society as a whole. But if the modern self is content to say, *'That's life'*, the postmodern self assumes the discourse of *accusation and conflict: 'It's Them'*. For the loss of power, loss of privilege, or loss of well-being is now ascribed *to the manipulative power-interests of competing persons or competing groups*. Misfortune seems to be neither random nor unavoidable, but a by-product of the success of some other group. This group may take the form of some professional guild, especially lawyers, doctors, clergy, or managers, or of some different social class, gender, or ethnic profile. At all events, *blame, accusation* and *hostility* come to absorb the concerns of the postmodern self. A breakdown of trust in virtually all governments, whether democratically elected or not, has become a hallmark of the mid-1990s.

It is not difficult to identify the initial emergence of this trend with the rise of postmodern perspectives towards the end of the 1960s. In Britain it became noticeable that whereas in the 1950s it was broadly conventional to speak of 'the' British Government, by the late 1960s the phrase had widely become 'this' government, implicitly subordinating 'national' to 'party' hopes, fears, or interests. But this phenomenon did not arise from purely social or political factors. More deeply, the impact of *literary and political postmodern philosophies* lay behind everyday events and attitudes, especially in the main writers to whom we have already called attention, namely Jacques Lacan (1901–81), Roland Barthes (1915–80), Michel Foucault (1926–84) and Jacques Derrida (1930–2004). We might readily extend these to Jean Baudrillard, Jean-François Lyotard and Gianni Vattino, as well as perhaps Julia Kristeva and a number of others.[32]

In his work *Postmodernity* (1994), David Lyon has shown clearly how the social and philosophical, as well as the literary and political, became inextricably woven together.[33] He observes, 'Here is one way of seeing the postmodern: it is a debate about reality. Is the world of solid scientific facts and purposive history, bequeathed to us by the European Enlightenment, mere wishful thinking? Or worse, [is it] the product of some scheming manipulation by the powerful? ... What are we left with? A quicksand of ambiguity ... artificial images, flickering from the TV screen, or joyful liberation from imposed definitions of reality?'[34] What would count as a 'real' thing? Is a self-constructed photo-fit an identity or a self? Is anything still 'solid'? In *The Archaeology of Knowledge*, Foucault rejects any notion of 'objects prior to discourse'.[35]

We alluded to Roland Barthes's fundamental distinction between the contrived and the supposedly 'natural' or allegedly value-neutral, which emerges powerfully in his *Mythologies* and more technically in his attempt to utilize Saussure in his *Elements of Semiology*. We noted, similarly, that especially in his 'White Mythology' Derrida followed Nietzsche in viewing metaphor largely as concealing values and power-bids under the guise of promoting truth-claims. The meanings of texts never achieve a stable 'closure',

---

[32] Kevin Hart, *The Trespass of the Sign* (Cambridge: CUP, 1989); S. Benhabib, *Situating the Self* (Cambridge: Polity Press, 1992); L.J. Nicholson (ed.), *Feminism/Postmodernism* (New York and London: Routledge, 1990), cf. from another angle, R.J. Bernstein, *The New Constellation* (Cambridge: Polity Press, 1991); and P. Berry and A. Wernick (eds), *Shadow of Spirit. Postmodernism and Religion* (New York and London: Routledge, 1992).

[33] David Lyon, *Postmodernity* (Buckingham: Open University Press, 1994).

[34] Ibid., p.2.

[35] M. Foucault, *The Archaeology of Knowledge* (Eng., New York: Pantheon Books, 1972), p.47.

for successive shifts of 'codes' generate successive shifts of 'performances' of meaning.[36] We alluded finally to Foucault's work on the social construction of norms and criteria of meaning in his earlier works *A History of Madness* (French, 1961) translated as *Madness and Civilization* (1965).

Norms or criteria shift as history moves on. In the classical period, Foucault observes, 'madness' is perceived primarily as *unreason*. Hence in a minority of instances, mad people may have been revered as 'inspired'; but more often they assumed the virtual status of animals without reason: to be fed and watered, but confined. By the nineteenth century a concept of madness as *mental illness* had emerged. 'Asylums' became, at least in theory, places of sanctuary, where the illness could be treated away from the stresses of everyday life.[37] Since 'illness', for most people today has become what madness *is*, perhaps here we may speak with Peter Berger and Thomas Luckmann of the *Social Construction of Reality*.[38]

A moment's reflection on issues about 'madness' in the Eastern Bloc of the Cold War years, will remind us of how closely socio-political views of what counts as 'normal' are related to issues of power and control. How often is mere deviation of outlook characterized as madness? A deviant or idiosyncratic university teacher in the West may be described as 'eccentric' with tolerance or even affection. Among ordinary working people or, among schoolchildren, however, such deviancy is more likely to invite suspicion or even ostracism. 'Eccentricity' becomes 'oddity'. In some political regimes, the consequences may be severe, sometimes leading to deprivation or confinement.

Foucault turns his attention more explicitly to institutions and to language in his book translated under the title *The Order of Things* (English, 1970; French *Les mots et les choses*, 1966). As against the 'modern' innocence of Descartes, 'I think' already operates from a pre-given social situatedness within an order, namely in the system of all its own possibilities.[39] Whatever 'thought' touches, it 'causes to move'; thus self and society cannot be perceived as 'given', but 'shimmer' as ever-changing norms, structures and language move on.[40] Language cannot 'represent'.[41]

In the middle period of *The Archaeology of Knowledge* (French, 1969, English, 1972) and *Discipline and Punish* (French, *Surveiller et punir*, 1975; English, 1977) Foucault turns in more detail to *social power*, especially in relation to the penal service. 'Surveillance' provides the tools for correction and control. Data are organized into files, databanks and documented sources. In such institutions as prisons, hospitals, the armed services and schools these effectively become mechanisms for control and manipulation.[42] Further,

---

[36] The detailed theories of Barthes and Derrida are expounded and criticized in my *New Horizons in Hermeneutics*, pp.80–141; cf. also pp.393–405, 495–507 and 534–50.

[37] M. Foucault, *Madness and Civilization. A History of Insanity in the Age of Reason* (Eng., New York: Pantheon, 1965).

[38] Peter Berger and Thomas Luckmann, *The Social Construction of Reality* (London: Penguin edn, 1971 (1966)).

[39] M. Foucault, *The Order of Things* (Eng., New York: Random House, 1970), p.324; cf. p.357.

[40] Ibid., pp.325, 327 and 339.

[41] Ibid., p.354; cf. p.324.

[42] M. Foucault, *Discipline and Punish* (Eng., New York: Pantheon, 1977), pp.190 (on 'medical discipline') and 143 (on 'knowing, mastering, using').

'accepted' knowledge which is documented in the 'right' sources can become a vehicle through which 'education' can now serve power interests. Bureaucrats build empires on the basis of 'privileged' information. Even if feudal and high-modern structures were paternalistic, at least kings, leaders, heads, or fathers could in many cases invite and repay trust. But in the bureaucratic world of the late twentieth century the database has now become the depersonalized instrument of power for those anonymous bureaucrats or managers who have gained access to these resources.[43]

Structures that depend on 'accepted' knowledge maintain their power by 'regimes'. Independently of regimes, Foucault argues, 'truth' cannot *amount to* anything. Knowledge is not the same as power. But 'epistemic fields' or recognized areas of what 'counts' as knowledge provide for what Foucault calls 'strategic alignments' of power. The self, as an individual, falls victim to a regime. Not only cannot the self evade its control, but little or no room has now been left for negotiation *through rational dialogue and argument*. Where truth has largely become absorbed into structures and spheres of power, argument and reason *collapses into a rhetoric of force*, using persuasion or pressure.

The devaluation of the currency of rational dialogue into that of rhetoric, I suggest, brings about *one of the most socially sinister and destructive consequences for the postmodern self*. For let us return to my earlier point about the contrast between a courageous or accepting 'That's life', and an accusatory 'It's them'. How can the human self respond to the power-interests of 'them'? There is nothing new about the problem of competing power-interests. From the politics of the city-states of ancient Greece to the democratic parliaments or congress of early twentieth-century Britain and America, rational debate in the public domain supposedly held the ring between these competing interests. As Alasdair MacIntyre, among others, reminds us, as long as there remains a sufficient consensus concerning *what counts as reasoned, rational, or moral*, reasoned debate in the public domain remains an effective arbiter within that frame or common tradition. But if each competing group, class, ethnic tradition, gender, guild, or party produces its own *internal* criteria of supposed rationality in order to serve its own power-interests, rational debate collapses *not only into mere rhetoric*, but soon also into *accusation, blame, corporate self-righteousness and conflict*.

The social consequences now become severely damaging. For where reasoning and appeal to decency fails, resort to *pressure* takes its place. In place of reasoned letters to the press, people try to force the hand of elected governments by 'demonstrations', by 'pressure groups', and by a rhetoric of force. This inevitably invites a response in kind from the competing group. What can the 'weaker' party do when they believe that their cause is rational or just, against opposing power-interests? Inevitably, *the pressure of rhetoric escalates into the pressure of violence*. Violence, in turn, may further escalate from the limited physical aggression of an angry demonstration to the violence of weapons and armed forces in a full-scale civil war. Similarly, where confidence in reason or justice has been lost, and deprivation is ascribed to opposing power-interests, what begins in petty vandalism against the owners of houses or vehicles readily escalates into the violence of assault on persons, and in turn, into major, organized crime. At the time of

---

[43] Ibid., pp.176–7, on 'anonymous' power.

writing many economically and socially secure people speak of this 'loss of the feel-good factor'. But for underprivileged others, the prospect of the postmodern self seems to be simply hopeless.

On one side, the postmodern condition has de-centred the self, de-centred ethics and de-centred society; on the other side it claims simply to leave everything as it is. But how can it be 'emancipatory' if it leaves everything as it is? It rightly unmasks instances of manipulative power that disguise themselves or claims to truth. But *does this lost innocence entail the universal doctrinal cynicism* that *all* truth-claims are bids for power? Does it invite contextual pragmatism which views *all* truth-claims as relative only to the internal norms of given communities?

III
Corporate Power and Corporate Self-Deception

Reinhold Niebuhr (1892–1971) has been described by Richard Harries, currently Bishop of Oxford, as 'in the realm of public affairs ... the most influential theologian of our century'.[44] Although he became most widely known for his two-volume work *The Nature and Destiny of Man* (1941 and 1943), he regarded his book *Moral Man and Immoral Society* (1932, but first published in Britain only in 1963) as his 'first major work'.[45] In this work he offered an incisive and at times brilliant analysis of the connection between social power-interests and the capacity of the human self to deceive itself and to manipulate values and actions in the name of supposed 'morality' or 'truth'. His social analysis is masterly; yet he draws on authentic traditions about grace, sin and the human predicament, from Paul through Luther to the present. The author of his standard biography, Richard Fox, observes that 'he saw society as a realm of power blocs to be adjusted ... America was culturally pluralistic, devoid ... of moral consensus ... Society is in a perpetual state of war.'[46] Fox suggests that the major importance of *Moral Man and Immoral Society* is to subvert the liberal optimism that dominated American thought from 1880 to 1930. Clearly there are affinities with postmodern perceptions of selfhood, but these find their place within a firmly theological frame.

Niebuhr argues that human persons allow themselves to be seduced into operating manipulative power-interests by deceiving themselves into interpreting their own acts as altruistic concerns for the sake of the corporate structures to which they belong. In the name of some corporate or social entity they devise programmes and implement policies of which, on a purely individual level, they would be ashamed. 'National interest' as concern for the nation offers a key example. Niebuhr writes, 'The selfishness of nations is proverbial ... There is an alloy of projected self-interest in patriotic altruism.'[47] Individuals will support the structural, corporate, aggressive self-interest of their own nation in trade,

---

[44] Richard Harries (ed.), *Reinhold Niebuhr and the Issues of our Time* (London and Oxford: Mowbray, 1986), p.1.

[45] Kenneth Durkin, *Reinhold Niebuhr* (London: Chapman, 1989), p.41.

[46] Richard W. Fox, *Reinhold Niebuhr. A Biography* (New York: Pantheon, 1985), p.140.

[47] Reinhold Niebuhr, *Moral Man and Immoral Society* (London: SCM, 1963 (1932)), pp.84 and 93.

economics, treaty, in war, on the grounds of loyalty to their fellows, and the desire for the well-being of their neighbours.

The presentation of essential national cultural values offers a subtler pretext for corporate self-interest. German soldiers fought British and American troops in the name of the heritage of Beethoven and Goethe; British trade agreements were made in the name of stability of the British Empire. Western nations still give 'aid' which entails trade agreements that may then widen the gap between rich and poor nations.[48] In situations which call for 'patriotism', Niebuhr writes, often 'the rational understanding of political issues remains such a minimum force that national unity for action can be achieved only ... by popular emotions and hysterias which from time to time run through a nation'.[49] 'Loyalty to the nation' appears in the dress of 'a high form of altruism when compared with lesser loyalties ... Altruistic passion is sluiced into the reservoir of nationalism with great ease.'[50]

The welfare of the group therefore invites what Niebuhr calls 'that self-deception and hypocrisy (which) is an unvarying element in the moral life of all human beings'.[51] Political speeches are often addressed to a different audience from the one in the presence of the politician, and may even decisively determine the agenda and claims of the speaker: 'The dishonesty of nations "becomes" a political necessity.'[52]

Class-interests, Niebuhr continues, invite the same element of corporate self-deception and manipulation. Professional guilds may 'load' procedures and performance criteria in their own favour. Anticipating a postmodern analysis, Niebuhr identifies a tendency to elevate a social power-interest into 'general interests and universal values'.[53] A dominant group may succeed in defining norms for the whole of society, but only to ensure its own continued dominance. Yet, although his main criticisms fall in the socially privileged, Niebuhr equally exposes the 'cynicism' of a Marxism that reduces *all human value* to the power interests of labour, production or class struggle.[54] He comments, 'The exaltation of class loyalty as the highest form of altruism is a national concomitant of the destruction of national loyalty.'[55] A fighting proletariat absolutizes class-interests as an ultimate, but Marxist theorists seem to be too involved in moral cynicism to notice this.[56]

Religious group-interests undergo the same incisive critique. Churches and theological traditions may become manipulative and self-serving. Individuals may even be deceived into doing something otherwise shameful 'for the sake of the family', or to sustain a religious tradition. Nevertheless, in principle, Niebuhr insists, Christian theology has made persons *'conscious of the sinfulness of their pre-occupation with the self. There is nothing that modern psychologists have discovered about the persistence of egocentricity in man that has not first been anticipated in the insights of the great mysteries of the classical periods of religion.'*[57]

---

[48] Ibid., pp.89–90.
[49] Ibid., p.88.
[50] Ibid., p.91.
[51] Ibid., p.95.
[52] Ibid.
[53] Ibid., p.117.
[54] Ibid., pp.142–51.
[55] Ibid., p.152.
[56] Ibid., p.161.
[57] Ibid., p.54 (my italics).

At the heart of the Christian gospel lies the words of Jesus, 'Whoso seeketh to find his life shall lose it, and he that loseth his life for my sake shall find it' (Matt. 10:39).[58] *Love* binds together into one and remains the highest virtue. Yet theological realism 'would *distinguish between what we expect of individuals and of groups*'.[59] In the case of the latter, the drive to self-interest is deeply hidden and disguised, but none the less powerful.

In two respects Niebuhr's analysis of society and of hope owed much to Luther. First, Niebuhr shared Luther's view that 'order' must be preserved in defence of justice for the weak and of peace for the work of the kingdom, by the civil law supported by duly appointed powers of state. He endorses Luther's injunction 'to place the gospel in heaven and the law on the earth ... In civil policy obedience to law must be severely required.'[60] He shares with Luther too much realism about human nature to propose that the Christian believer should guard the lambs of the flock by laying down his or her weapons and inviting in the oppressor. In Luther's words, 'If anyone attempted to rule the world by the gospel, and to abolish all temporal law and the secular sword ... he would be loosing the ropes and chains of the savage wild beasts and letting them bite and mangle everyone'.[61] Second, like Luther, Niebuhr accepted that much of the promised transformation of the Church and society lay in the future, not in the present. He endorsed Luther's belief that 'the pretension of finality and perfection in the Church was the root of spiritual pride and self-righteousness'.[62] Against what he termed 'ecclesiasticism', Niebuhr stressed divine promise and divine agency.

Although similarities may be perceived between the respective approaches to 'power' by Niebuhr and by Foucault, this first point about a kingdom of 'order' stands in tension with attitudes towards the state and 'authorities' in Foucault. For Foucault, power-structures and institutions are in principle 'arbitrary' products of particular areas in social history: the tribal chief, the king, the feudal lord, the modern manager, and, Foucault's most focused target, 'those in which power wears a white coat and a professional smile'.[63] Foucault's approach stands in tension, for example, with Emil Brunner's view in theology that, together with commitments of marriage, the restraining and stabilizing authority of the state constitutes one of two 'natural' ordinances of God. The state, Brunner insists, has an ordained 'order' to restrain evil and to conserve justice. Indeed, Brunner perceives five beneficial 'orders' which are not shifting because they stem from the structures of divine creation: male–female relations and family, achievement in work and exchange structures, state and law, cultures, and communities of worship.[64] The German title behind the less happy English *The Divine Imperative* (1934) alludes explicitly to Brunner's positive evaluation of orders *Das Gebot und die Ordnungen* (1932).

---

[58] Ibid., p.56.

[59] Ibid., p.271 (my italics).

[60] R. Niebuhr, *The Nature and Destiny of Man* (2 vols), (London: Nisbet, 1941 and 1943), vol. 2, p.199.

[61] Martin Luther, 'Temporal Authority', (1523) in *Luther's Works XLV: The Christian Society II* (Philadelphia, PA and Cambridge: Concordia Publishing, 1962), p.91.

[62] R. Niebuhr, *Nature and Destiny*, vol. 2, p.192.

[63] The memorable phrase occurs in Stephen D. Moore, *Poststructuralism and the New Testament. Derrida and Foucault at the Foot of the Cross* (Minneapolis, MN: Fortress, 1994), p.112.

[64] Emil Brunner, *The Divine Imperative* (Philadelphia, PA: Westminster, 1947). Cf further *Natural Theology* (Eng., London: Bles, 1946) for his debate with Barth on the issue.

Admittedly this issue remains controversial in Christian theology. Recently Elizabeth Castelli and Stephen Moore have both appealed to the approach of Foucault to provide a critique not only of institutional power within the New Testament writings and especially in Paul, but also of the 'pastoral power' instantiated in such Pauline injunctions as that of 'imitating' his own style of discipleship and obedience.[65] 'Imitation' (*mimesis*), E.A. Castelli argues, becomes part of Paul's strategy of power and social control. She writes, 'By promoting the value of sameness he [Paul] is also shaping relations of power', although she adds, 'Whether Paul *meant* or *intended* that his discourse be understood in the way I have argued is not a question that I have answered ... My reading is not the only possible or plausible one.'[66] Nevertheless, in effect Paul, she claims, utilizes for his purpose the approach that we have just noted in Brunner: 'orders' or a 'regime' promotes stability and unity as if it were 'natural' and pre-ordained. Castelli appeals in particular to a specific interpretation of such passages as 'be imitators of me, as I am of Christ' (1 Cor. 11:1) and 'become imitators of us and of the Lord' (1 Thess. 1:6) as moving 'only in one direction ... the hierarchical view of imitation ... power relations; an issue of "group identity" ... exclusively ... sameness'.[67] She also discusses 1 Thess. 2:14; Phil. 3:17; 1 Cor. 4:16; and Gal. 4:12.

Following Foucault's particular interest in such areas as medicine, penal correction and gender, Castelli argues that Paul shows a special concern to impose power and to eliminate deviancy in matters relating to the physical dimensions of life, such as food practices and sexual conduct (1 Cor. 5:1–5; 7:10–11; 10:14–22; 11:3; 11:27–32). Paul 'punishes' his own body (9:27). She suggests that to appeal to one's own submission in order to obtain the submission of others constitutes a manipulative device, which serves purposes of power and social control in the interests of predetermined norms which exclude 'deviancy' (1 Cor. 5:5).

Stephen Moore expounds this approach more broadly, with reference of Foucault's works. He writes, 'Christian discipline is also bound up with power: "The kingdom of God does not consist in talk but in power" (1 Cor. 4:20) ... Discipline has only one purpose, according to Foucault: the production of "docile bodies".'[68] Hence Paul initiates the practice of using the threat of divine judgement (Rom. 2:16, 29; 1 Cor. 4:5) to extract admissions, acknowledgements, agreements and 'confessions'.

Following Foucault, Moore sees 'confession' as a fundamental tool in the process of manipulative power play. He quotes Foucault with approval: 'One confesses – or is forced to confess. When it is not spontaneous or dictated by some internal imperative, the confession is wrung from a person by violence or threat.'[69] Whether we think of the medieval church or in very many instances the modern state, power-techniques, whether open or 'pastoral', regulate 'the individual's inner existence'.[70] As a former monk who

---

[65] Elizabeth A. Castelli, *Imitating Paul: A Discourse of Power* (Louisville, KY: Westminster and John Knox, 1991), pp.21–58, and S.D. Moore, op. cit., pp.83–112.

[66] E.A. Castelli, op. cit., pp.119, 120 and 121; cf. esp. pp.35–58.

[67] Ibid., pp.113 and 114; cf. pp.89–117.

[68] S.D. Moore, op. cit., p.109.

[69] Ibid., III; M. Foucault, *The History of Sexuality* (Eng., 3 vols, New York: Pantheon, 1978–86), vol. 1, pp.58–9.

[70] Ibid.

finally experienced emancipation from the 'regime' of the monastery with 'great exhilaration and deep sadness', Moore recalls that the image of the tortured Jesus on the cross was repeatedly used in his earlier years to enact what Foucault calls 'the quiet game of the well behaved'.[71]

Castelli and Moore interpret Paul's motivations very differently from most main-line New Testament scholars. Robert Jewett's book *Christian Tolerance* presents the very opposite claim about Paul, namely that he showed a strong concern for tolerance and for the acceptance of a measure of diversity and pluralism within the church.[72] Andrew D. Clark's work *Secular and Christian Leadership in Corinth* offers a social and historical analysis which demonstrates precisely the difference between three models of power: between Graeco-Roman modes of leadership based on power, Corinthian attitudes towards leadership based largely on expediency or on borrowed notions about claims to 'wisdom', and Paul's own redefinition of leadership in relation to Christ and the cross.[73] But this appeal to 'Christ crucified' has nothing to do with Moore's notion of pointing to an image of a tortured man to promote moral blackmail. Quite the reverse: it springs from the freedom of love to which we alluded in our discussion of Bonhoeffer's understanding of discipleship in the previous essay, and in our comments here on Moltmann's theology of love and freedom.

We may cite also S.M. Pogoloff's *Logos and Sophia. The Rhetorical Situation of I Corinthians* (1992), P. Marshall, *Enmity at Corinth: Social Conventions in Paul's Relations with the Corinthians* (1987), Margaret M. Mitchell's *Paul and the Rhetoric of Reconciliation* (1991) and W.L. Willis's *Idol Meat in Corinth* (1985).[74] Pogoloff does not question that issues of social status and of rhetoric come to the fore. But Paul's call to the community to imitate a pattern of humility and servanthood is not for the purpose of 'conformity' or 'control'. It is precisely to protect those who might otherwise be despised or socially inferior; in other words, precisely to *protect* the 'social deviants' for whom Foucault shows concern. Marshall also agrees that the rejection and humiliation of Jesus 'provides the intellectual and practical basis for Paul's expression of apostleship', but not as a device of manipulation; rather, to attack 'discrimination of social standing' on behalf of those whom the privileged regarded as 'weak' or of low esteem at Corinth.[75]

Paul's social analysis of the plight of the social world of Gentile 'pluralism' in Rom. 1:18–31 substantiates precisely the kind of analysis proposed by Niebuhr, while his stress on 'duly appointed authorities' in Rom. 13:1–8 as providing an 'order' necessary for peace, relative justice, and a measure of stability corroborates the aspect of Niebuhr's approach which also finds expression in Brunner. They are to protect the weak, not to

---

[71] S.D. Moore, op. cit., p.114.

[72] Robert Jewett, *Christian Tolerance. Paul: Message to the Modern Church* (Philadelphia, PA: Westminster, 1982).

[73] Andrew D. Clarke, *Secular Christian Leadership in Corinth: A Socio-Historical and Exegetical Study of I Corinthians 1–6* (Leiden: Brill, 1993).

[74] S.M. Pogoloff, *Logos and Sophia. The Rhetorical Situation of I Corinthians* (Atlanta, GA: Scholars Press, 1992); P. Marshall, *Enmity at Corinth: Social Conventions in Paul's Relations with the Corinthians* (Tübingen: Mohr, 1987); M.M. Mitchell, *Paul and the Rhetoric of Reconciliation. An Exegetical Investigation of the Language and Composition of I Corinthians* (Tübingen, Mohr, 1991); and Wendell L. Willis, *Idol Meat at Corinth. The Pauline Argument in I Corinthians 8 and 10* (Chico, CA: Scholars Press, 1985).

[75] P. Marshall, op. cit., pp.402 and 403.

impose uniformity within a pluralist Empire. 'Living at peace' (Rom. 12:18) stems not from the notion of 'docility' (as Nietzsche and Foucault imply) but from a oneness of relationality grounded in 'what Christ does ... to span the chasm between Jew and Gentile'.[76] It is implausible to suggest that manipulation on behalf of apostolic power could be at issue here. Paul does not appeal to 'order' in the state to impose 'order' in the church. He is not trying to impose 'agreement' or 'docility'. Rather, in recognition that the weak need the protection of civil authorities, even with all the blemishes of Roman imperial administration, he endorses 'the sword' (Rom. 13:4) 'legitimately possessed ... to coerce recalcitrant citizens ... for the common good'.[77]

This example calls into question a postmodern tendency to doubt the integrity of *all* 'order' or irredeemably linked with individual or corporate power-interests on behalf of some specific group. As Gadamer stresses, the basis of Roman law lay in a strong sense of the *sensus communis*. Sweeping generalizations that attack all 'order' merely instantiate the difficulty of a formed rhetoric among those postmodern writers who wish simultaneously to reject all 'isms' or 'metanarratives' while making *general* claims about power and order. Baudrillard and Lyotard perhaps more consciously seek consistency here than Foucault and some of his theological imitators. Wherever there is civil war, virtual anarchy and 'might is right', the oppressed long for 'order'.

IV
Hope and the God of Promise: the Self Re-centred in Love

Hope and promise come to occupy a central place in theology when the present situation is perceived to 'stand in contradiction' with what God has promised.[78] In these circumstances, Moltmann observes, 'the language of promise will then be an essential key to the unlocking of Christian truth'.[79] There is even a convincingly and appropriate postmodern ring to Moltmann's approach to promise. Theological concepts 'do not limp after reality ... but they illuminate reality by displaying its future. Their knowledge is *grounded not in the will to dominate, but in love* to the future of things ... engaged in a process of movement [they] *call forth practical movement and change*' (my italics).[80]

Whereas flat propositions in theology often simply describe what is the case, the logic of promise (like that of directives) is to bring about some transformation. If an agent who is both faithful and capable of implementing the promise makes a promise, some *change* in the situation of the present will occur. The Bible and Marx offer in different ways not simply 'interpretations' of the world, but also that which will 'change' it.[81] Further, the transcendent is often more appropriately expressed in temporal terms as 'ahead' of us,

---

[76] Ibid., p.664.

[77] Ibid., p.668.

[78] J. Moltmann, *Theology of Hope*, p.103.

[79] Ibid., p.41.

[80] Ibid.

[81] Marx's eleventh thesis in his *Theses on Feuerbach* reads 'The philosophers have only *interpreted* the world ... the point is, to *change* it' (*Writings of the Young Marx on Philosophy and Society*, New York: Doubleday, 1967, p.402).

rather than in exclusively spatial imagery as 'above' us. This opens up the possibility of incorporating the present moment within a larger narrative or temporal plot, which establishes its significance without resort to more problematic notions of a so-called two-storey world-view.[82] Without this temporal dimension, Christian theology plays into the hands of the criticisms of Nietzsche and Heidegger that Christianity becomes a world-denying 'Platonism for the people'.

Moltmann takes up the powerful temporal imagery of the experience of the transcendent in the New Testament as dawn or daybreak. The 'beyond' enters our present horizons, he writes, as 'the divine quickening power of the new creation ... It places the whole earthly and bodily person in the daybreak colours of the new earth ... the raising from death to eternal life.'[83]

This temporal contrast between present and future entails promise. The 'formerly' of predicament and bondage and the 'now' or 'then' of promised freedom for a new future finds paradigmatic expression in the Old Testament especially in Exodus. Thus J. Severino Croatto sees the exodus events as a model of renewed selfhood for liberation theology.[84] The importance of this theological twentieth-century context and example is that it firmly gives the lie to any suggestion on the part of Nietzsche, Foucault, or others, that Christian theology *causes 'docility'*. Liberation theology encourages *the throwing off of 'docility'*. Deliverance from a servile life-style in Egypt to a life of risk and venture in a pilgrim journey renders claims about Christianity and 'docility' implausible.

[*A section of this book is omitted here for the purpose of abbreviation.*]

Divine action and presence through 'weakness', humiliation and renunciation of 'power' in the incarnation and the cross reflect the dimension of immanence. It is a model of the rejection of manipulative power. But divine transcendence is disclosed more openly in a promised series of future events which culminate in the public disclosure of the end-time. Language about the kingdom attains its most effective currency when we perceive that divine transcendence finds expression in temporal imagery, alongside other modes of language. Thereby it places promise at the forefront of the agenda.

In Acts the theme of an ever-onward call ahead appears strongly in Stephen's speech (Acts 7:2–53). Fixed institutions, such as the temple, remain ambivalent, for they lose the ever-onward symbolism of the mobile tabernacle. David's request to build a temple was refused, since, 'the Most High does not dwell in houses made with hands' (Acts 7:46–48). The call of Abraham carried with it no advance information about his eventual destination (7:3). Moreover, 'possession' of the Promised Land lay beyond his own temporal horizon, except *as promised* (7:5).

Acts 7 has close affinities with the theology of the Epistle to the Hebrews, as most agree. We have already noted Cullmann's proposal that when faith is defined as 'the assurance of things hoped for' and the substance of 'things not seen' (Heb. 11:1), the parallelism may most convincingly be explained as 'not seen' because they have not yet taken place. This

---

[82] J. Moltmann, *The Spirit of Life*, p.90.
[83] Ibid., p.95.
[84] J Severino Croatto, *Exodus. A Hermeneutics of Freedom* (Eng., New York: Orbis, 1981).

coheres with the series of examples of faith throughout this chapter.[85] Noah, for instance, built an ark to save his family from drowning when as yet any evidence of an impending flood was simply 'not seen' (Heb. 11:7). The exodus and the entry into Canaan proceeded on the basis of promise alone, and thereby are described as taking place 'by faith' (11:29–31). Again, this has nothing to do with 'docility' or passive conformism. It invites venture and courage. It entails neither the 'presumption' of modernity that everything can be known and controlled, nor the 'despair' of postmodernity that no strategy, no purpose, no order, no future, can beckon from 'beyond' the horizons of the self in its present situatedness, to borrow Moltmann's terms. He comments, 'Both forms of hopelessness ... cancel the wayfaring character of hope'.[86] Divine promise 'points beyond'.[87]

We have noted already the promissory orientation of the Pauline writings in passages about the Holy Spirit as the 'first fruits' of a yet fuller harvest still to come (Rom. 8:23; 2 Cor. 1:22). Paul resonates with a specific postmodern theme, however, in his emphasis on the *pluriform grammar of hope*. Hope can be born out of diverse situations. Sometimes, as in Rom. 4:18 it consists in 'hoping against hope' when the sheer emptiness of the present shifts our focus to the word of promise. As Moltmann declares in *The Crucified God*, '*unless it apprehends the pain of the negative, Christian hope cannot be realistic and liberating as hope*'.[88] In Paul's words, who 'hopes' for what they see? (Rom. 8:24). On the other hand, hope also functions with a different grammar. In other situations it is the prior experience of the faithfulness of God to perform his promise that engenders and nurtures a hope that is founded on more that a sheer act of venture: 'The One who calls you is faithful, and he will do this' (1 Thess. 5:24). There is nothing monolithic or globally 'fixed' about the grammar of hope in Paul and in other biblical writings.

We do not have space to trace this pluriform grammar of hope elsewhere. But this is hardly necessary, since most can recall such Psalms as that which begins 'Out of the depths have I cried to Thee' (Psalm 130:1) and can compare such examples with expressions of confident hope based on successive experiences (whether corporately or individually) of promises already faithfully performed.

If we consider briefly one or two specific examples from the history of Christian thought, it emerges that a theology of the word of God in Luther and in Tyndale remains closely related to a theology of promise. Luther attacks 'presumption' (to use Moltmann's phrase) in the 'realized eschatology' of Carlstadt, Müntzer and the radical 'enthusiasts' or 'spiritual fanatics'. They act as if all promise had already been performed and transposed into triumphalist statement. They abandon a *theologia crucis* for an illusory and manipulative *theologia gloriae*. But, Luther writes, God 'rules through the Word, and not in a visible and public manner. It is like beholding the sun through a cloud ... But after the clouds have passed, both light and sun rule ... It is dark and hidden at present, or concealed and covered, comprehended entirely in faith and in the Word.'[89]

---

[85] On Hebrews 11, cf. especially Paul Ellingworth, *Commentary on Hebrews* (New International Greek Testament) (Grand Rapids, MI: Eerdmans and Carlisle: Paternoster, 1993), pp.558–633.

[86] J, Moltmann, *Theology of Hope*, p.23.

[87] Ibid., p.201.

[88] J. Moltmann, *The Crucified God* (Eng., London: SCM, 1974), p.5 (my italics).

[89] Martin Luther, *Luther's Works, vol. 28* (St Louis, MO: Concordia, 1973), p.124.

This theme of 'hiddenness' appears especially in the *Heidelberg Disputation* of 1518, where Luther speaks of 'the hinder parts of God'. God is not to be found 'except in sufferings and in the cross'.[90] But it would contradict all that Luther says elsewhere about faith or joyful boldness based on promise if we were to interpret this, with Nietzsche, as 'world-denying'. The issue is quite different and more profound. Faith is not some psychological 'inner state', but a bold appropriation of divine promise, upon which a person acts.

Among the English Reformers, William Tyndale stands closest to Luther in his recognition of the close relation between the biblical writings and promise. Again, space prohibits a detailed comment. But 'promise' becomes Tyndale's most favoured term for the effective 'performance' of reading biblical tests. In his *A Pathway into the Holy Scripture* he defines the New Testament as 'a book wherein are contained the promises of God; and the deeds of them which believe them, or believe them not'.[91] 'Gospel' is the 'joyful tidings' which enact a series of what we nowadays call speech-acts: naming, appointing, declaring, condemning, forgiving, justifying, but most repeatedly in these pages, promising.[92]

In the twentieth century Karl Barth has most characteristically related word and promise in the context of a contrast between the present and the future. God's word, he asserts, is God's very act and his very presence. Yet because of the temporal situation 'I understand myself as confronted with promise ... I see myself in the specific light that falls upon my existence from this.'[93] God's promise, however, is not 'empty', but 'is the transposing of man into a wholly new state of one who has accepted and appropriated the promise'.[94] A series of liberating and empowering speech-acts, namely 'election, revelation ... calling ... all denote a promise'.[95] These are not simply timeless statements about states of affairs as they now exist: 'the Word of God is itself the act of God'.[96]

For Barth, all this is fundamental for any possibility of interpreting or understanding God *as God*. God discloses his identity in acts of promise by which he 'gives himself', in that he freely chooses to bind himself to perform what he has pledged. Here we encounter two features that hardly appear in the perceptions of the postmodern self. First, *gift*, which *depends on nothing in return*, constitutes the *rejection of manipulative power or self-interest*. Second, gift comes *from beyond the horizons of the situatedness of the self*. That is why an 'expected' gift may lose something of its character of 'gift'. Gift ideally includes the delight of surprise. Part of Barth's peculiar stature lies in his interpreting God as self-imparting

---

[90] Martin Luther in *Luther: Early Theological Works* (ed. J. Atkinson) (London: SCM, 1962), p.291. The theme is developed in A.C. Thiselton, 'Luther and Barth on 1 Corinthians 15', in W.P. Stephens (ed.), *The Bible, the Church and the Reformation: Studies in Honour of James Atkinson on his Eightieth Birthday* (Sheffield: Sheffield Academic Press, 1995), pp.258–89.

[91] William Tyndale, 'A Pathway into the Holy Scripture', in *Doctrinal Treatises and Introductions to Different Portions of the Holy Scriptures* (Cambridge: CUP (Parker Society edn) 1848), pp.1–29. See further P. Satterthwaite and D.F. Wright (eds), *Pathway into the Holy Scripture* (Grand Rapids, MI: Eerdmans, 1994), (especially essays by Carl R. Trueman and A.C. Thiselton).

[92] W. Tyndale, loc. cit., pp.8–14.

[93] Karl Barth, *Church Dogmatics* I:1, sect. 6, p.218.

[94] Ibid., sect. 5, p.152.

[95] Ibid., pp.149–50.

[96] Ibid., p.143.

Trinity whose nature is to give in sovereign, unconstrained love. His gift of himself includes his pledge to give 'His time' in that his commitment of himself to act in love is bound up with a created sequence of 'a time of promise' and a contrast between 'what is and what is not yet'.[97] As we shall see, this decisively fits 'a logic of promise', in which God pledges himself to act. In this time of 'not yet', what the non-theist may construe as the *absence* of God in practice represents only a pregnant period of *hiddenness* in readiness to act.

Wolfhart Pannenberg (b. 1928) unfolds a pluriform grammar of hope and promise with impressive weight. At one level trust in God's promise arises on the basis of an ongoing tradition of experiences of hope and fulfilment in the public history of Israel and the New Testament communities. As successive hopes find fulfilment, a tradition of effective-history, or history of effects (*Wirkungsgeschichte*) emerges in which horizons of promise become enlarged and filled with new content.[98] The new coheres with emerging, stable patterns, but genuine newness leaves room for surprise. The content of hope becomes ever richer, fuller, and more capable of provisional definition.

Yet at a different level, the unsatisfactory absences or limitations of the present remain without meaning *until these receive meaning in the light of a promised future. Only within a larger temporal frame do the possibilities and constraints of the present moment given meaning and significance.*[99] Hence, primarily through biblical and systematic theology, but also partly through Hegel, Pannenberg arrives at a fundamental insight about an enlarged temporal context of meaning. We noted close parallels in Ricoeur's hermeneutics of the self as finding meaning within the enlarged horizon of temporal narrative and temporal plot. In Part II [of *Interpreting God*] we considered the value of this approach, in contrast to the problematic claims in Part III from Cupitt about 'instaneousness' as a privileged vantage point. Such a narrow account, we observed, leaves insoluble problems about meaning, identity, self and God.

Pannenberg expounds with great rigour and sophistication a perspective that entirely matches the everyday experiences of ordinary people. In a play or in a story (and similarly in life) 'who a person is' emerges in that person's interaction with others within an unfolding temporal sequence. But our interpretation remains provisional until the last scene or the last chapter. Even so, in the case of Christian people *'who we are' emerges in terms of God's larger purposes and promises for the world, for society, for the Church and for us.* This purposive anticipation of the future finds expression in our sense of *being called by God to a task within that frame.* We find our identity and meaning when we discover our *vocation.* This does not exclude a multiplicity of compatible vocations. For example, one may be called to work at a certain job, to be a good husband or wife, to give support to some community or person, and so forth. But this 'purposive "beyond"' makes the matter quite different from the imposed role-performances of the postmodern self which form *part of* his or her pre-given situatedness in life.

On the same basis we may discover what it means to interpret God *as God*. Pannenberg begins with Israel's experience of promise. He writes, 'On the basis of promise and

---

97   K. Barth, *Church Dogmatics* II:2, sects 14 and 15.
98   W. Pannenberg, *Basic Questions in Theology* (3 vols), (Eng., London, SCM, 1970–73), vol. 1, pp.15–80 and 96–136 and in other writings.
99   Ibid., vol. 3, pp.192–210.

beyond all historically experienced fulfilments, Israel expected further fulfilment.'[100] 'Effective history' provides a continuity within which Israel discovered a stability of meaning in the acts of the faithful God, while this also allowed for an 'open' future which points to an unfulfilled hitherto 'not yet'. Horizons of hope begin to assume stable directions or reference points, but these do not foreclose new surprising events or experiences that nevertheless cohere with God's self-imparting 'character' hitherto disclosed. Regularities approximate to what Wittgenstein (in another context) called 'rules' of sufficient stability to provide markers for meaning, but also of sufficient flexibility to allow for the new creation in unpredicted ways. Continuity and stable markers, in Pannenberg's terms, arise from 'the one history which binds together the eschatological community of Jesus Christ and ancient Israel ... Jesus Christ is the revelation of God only in the light of the Old Testament promises ... Jesus ... is understood in the framework of the history of God with Israel ...'.[101] Even the events of the ministry of Jesus point beyond themselves to the resurrection; his resurrection and the event of Pentecost point, in turn, to yet future modes of promise and fulfilment. As Pannenberg (following Gadamer) expresses it, 'A new horizon is formed.'[102]

[*A further omission from the book occurs here, again to abbreviate the text.*]

This process of creative transformation through the Holy Spirit, however, begins in the present, even if as partial 'first fruits' only. Again, Moltmann gives profound expression to the main point:

> Through faith the *hitherto unexplored creative powers of God are thrown open* in men and women. So faith means *becoming creative with God and his Spirit*. Faith leads to a creative life which is life-giving *through love*, in places where death rules and people resign themselves and surrender to it. Faith *awakens trust* in the still unrealised possibilities in human beings – in oneself and in other people.[103]

Moltmann has earlier made it clear that such 'possibilities' depend not on *human* 'spirituality' in the sense of cultivating the so-called 'inner' human spirit; but in the biblical sense of 'that which pertains to the Holy Spirit of God'.[104] (This also decisively determines our understanding of 'spiritual body' [RSV] in 1 Cor. 15:44.)

Yet this 'creativity', which transforms and reverses the passive situatedness of the postmodern self, becomes possible through the Holy Spirit because the Spirit transposes self-interest, conflict and bids-for-power into *love for others* (for individuals and groups) *and for the Other* (for God and for whatever is not-self). Hence the cooperative effects of the Holy Spirit and the cross of Christ together actualize God's self-giving *as God*. Thus E. Jüngel writes, '*The crucified is, as it were, the material definition of what is meant by*

---

[100] Ibid., vol. 1, p.23.

[101] Ibid., pp.25 and 26.

[102] Ibid., p.117.

[103] J. Moltmann, *The Spirit of Life*, p.115 (my italics).

[104] Ibid., pp.8–10.

[105] E. Jüngel, *God as the Mystery of the World* (Eng., Edinburgh: T. & T. Clark, and Grand Rapids, MI: Eerdmans, 1983), p.13 (my italics).

"*God*".[105] If God is interpreted *as God* because we understand him as self-imparting *love*, then the paradigmatic expression of his identity is his *cruciform acts and being*. Here Jüngel broadly follows Luther and Barth. But more remains to be considered. If the cross constitutes the paradigm of God's gift of himself *to others*, not only suffering, pain and cost come to view, but also its *interpersonal, interactive relation to others*.

The postmodern self knows what it is to be trapped by its own past decisions and placed in bondage to a situatedness that is not of its choice. It knows the need to be released from external forces beyond its control, and to be delivered from tyranny of corporate self-interests and competing power-interests. Hence the biblical language about 'redemption' may be heard in a more objective sense (Rom. 3:24; 1 Cor. 1:30, 6:20; Col. 1:14; Heb. 9:15). Redemption 'from the curse of the law' (Gal. 3:13) may plausibly be interpreted as more than freedom from legalism or moralism. It promises deliverance from all the cause-and-effect chains of forces which hold the self to its past, through the work of Christ and the agency of the Holy Spirit who opens new possibilities of futurity 'from beyond' the situatedness of the self.

The Holy Spirit, however, acts as more than a 'new force'. Woven into the logic of the work of Christ and the Spirit is the *interpersonal, interactive character of love*. Love is given and received by two or more persons *in relationship*. The cross *restores* this. Vincent Brümmer among others expounds the interpersonal and creative character of this love, drawing on Nygren as well as his own conceptual analysis of personal language.[106] Brümmer points out that whereas Nygren saw *agapē* as creative, and *eros* as self-centred, Nietzsche regarded *agapē* as promoting a 'slave morality' which keeps humanity 'weak and inferior' as over against a 'superior' God, while *eros* reflected a will-to-power.[107] Brümmer himself offers a different conceptual analysis: 'In a relation of fellowship or love I identify with you by *serving your interests as being my own*. This devotion to your good is unconditional ... I do not serve your interests on condition that you serve mine in return.'[108]

This at once invites a discussion of the *basis* of this self-giving, interactive, interpersonal love *as characterizing the very nature of God himself as Trinity. A solitary being cannot 'give' or 'love'* unless 'another' enters the scene *to receive and to be loved*. Yet if God's nature *as love* cannot find expression unless or until he creates a created order, must we not conclude that his identity *as God* depends on his creation?

[*Another, fourth, omission occurs here to avoid an over-long textual extract.*]

We may now gather together strands from other parts of this study. David Harvey, we noted, perceives the postmodern self as characterized by fragmentation, indeterminacy and an intense distrust of all claims to universal truth, or of claims to offer universal strategies for arbitration or for progress. The postmodern self lives within a labyrinth of diversified networks, and suspects 'order' and ordered structures as disguising power-

[106] Vincent Brümmer, *The Model of Love. A Study in Philosophical Theology* (Cambridge: CUP, 1993), esp. pp.127–245.
[107] Ibid., pp.139–40.
[108] Ibid., p.239 (my italics).

interests on behalf of the privileged. Its multi-media linguistic world bombards the postmodern self with images, myths and signs; but these carry subtexts and multi-layered meanings that never reach 'closure'. Signs point only to other signs, *ad infinitum*.

The postmodern self, as Lyon reminded us, has a 'constructed' identity. With Norman Denzin we noted the anger, alienation and conflict that marks the situatedness of the postmodern self. Loss of hope, we saw, sprang at least in part from the collapse of any norm or truth that might otherwise be independent of someone else's power-interest, into sexism, racism, or socio-economic competition. Even the bureaucrats and politicians whose reason for existence was to arbitrate between competing groups have become drawn into the same empire-building power-interests as, at a more modest level, the postmodern self seeks for own security and self-protection.

Worst of all, if, with Lyotard, no meta-narrative or 'larger picture' can be trusted as constituting more than the disguised power-interests of some tradition or sub-culture, what is the 'point' of trying ceaselessly to become or to remain a 'winner'? In pragmatic power play there are only winners and losers; we cannot ask about 'the point' of seeking to win, other than to secure the self-protection that keeps us from losing. But is this all that human life consists in? Is every utterance to be 'erased' before its sound has died away, every written word 'to move on' before the ink is dry? Is every act of sacrifice for the company, for the family, for the profession, for the nation, merely a competitive power-bid at the expense of other families, other businesses, other nations, or the public?

Is everything only instantaneous and ethnocentric? Dilthey, Ricoeur and Pannenberg from quite different viewpoints have urged that 'the point' can emerge only within some larger frame or 'temporal narrative'. But how can the postmodern self, which has become habituated to suspect and to distrust, know whether such an extended narrative is anything but a wish-fulfilment deceptively projected by the self, or, still worse, a manipulative construct which serves the power-interests of those who suggest it?

We can only entertain a hypothesis to question this distrust. Let us suppose that all that Christian traditions claim about love, and about God as self-imparting Trinity, may be true. If love, to refer again to Brümmer, 'serves your interests as being my own' (not my own as yours), what reason could there be for one who loves like that to use manipulation, or for the other to suspect it? A love in which a self genuinely *gives* itself to the other *in the interests of the other* dissolves the acids of suspicion and deception. For, as Rahner so powerfully argues, why should there be any need for the deception that serves to protect the self if the self is loved, welcomed, accepted and reconciled-as-one with the Other?

If this hypothesis is considered with sufficient seriousness to constitute a *working hypothesis*, then, as the author of the Epistle to the Hebrews and Luther, among others, point out, acting in the present on the basis of that which is yet to be proven or 'seen' constitutes a faith that has world-transforming and self-transforming effects. It transforms the self because, like the experience of resurrection, it *'re-constitutes' self-identity* as no longer the passive victim of forces of the past which 'situated' it within a network of pre-given roles and performances, but opens out a new future in which new purpose brings a 'point' to its life. The self perceives its call and its value as one-who-is-loved within the larger narrative plot of God's loving purposes for the world, for society and for the self. *Perhaps the self of modernity had been right to hope, but wrong about the basis on which it built its hope. Perhaps the postmodern self had been right to despair* if will-to-power exhausted the content of all reality, *but wrong in its assumption that this exhausted all that might be called 'real'.*

Indeed, it becomes arguable that a life based wholly on a hermeneutic of suspicion and iconoclasm has about it more than an element of self-contradiction. Granted that *many* bureaucrats live only to build empires, that *many* professional people put the interests of their guild before those of the public, or that *many* religious people treat religion and 'God' as a means of self-affirmation or for purposes of power, by what *doctrine* (when the postmodern self rejects doctrine) can we say that *all* bureaucrats, professionals, or religious people live in this way?

A theology of the cross underlines that the strategy of seeking *to gain goals by power or for power* is a *self-defeating strategy.* The will-to-power merely provokes conflict which escalates and can never be finally resolved in that those who gain it are trapped into ever more complex manipulative strategies to retain it. By contrast, *giving the self to the other in love and serving the other's interests as one's own remains ever fresh and creative, in that it builds.* It does not have to struggle ceaselessly with some other external force. It builds its own self-identity as lover-in-relation-to-the-loved, or as loved-in-relation-to-lover. In theological terms the transformation of will-to-power into will-to-love means being transformed into the image of Christ. To be sure, the Holy Spirit comes to be experienced in the present only as the 'first fruits' or first sample sheaf, of a fuller harvest yet to come. No human person may yet be innocent of all manipulation or self-interest. Yet just as in the present the active agency of the Holy Spirit begins to reshape the self and to reshape the world, so the divine promise of love to complete this transformation constitutes a pledge to reshape every horizon and interest. Divine promise is the 'sure and steadfast anchor' (Heb. 6:19) that recentres the self. It bestows upon the self an identity of worth within a stable frame of purpose. One of my former doctoral candidates, Mark Chan, writes that in contrast to 'the kingdom of Mammon' where people are commodities or objects to be manipulated, 'Self does not exist except in relation to others ... though not in a way that gobbles up a person's individuality'.[109]

---

[109] Mark Chan, "Corporate Spirituality", in Mark Chan (ed.), *Mercy, Community, and Ministry* (Singapore: Catalyst Books/Eagle Communications, 1993), pp.108–9.

CHAPTER THIRTY-TWO

Two Types of Postmodernity: "Signs of the Times: Towards a Theology for the Year 2000 as a Grammar of Grace, Truth and Eschatology in Contexts of So-Called Postmodernity" (2000)

This essay was my Presidential Paper for the Society for the Study of Theology in 1999, edited for publication in David Fergusson and Marcel Sarot, The Future as God's Gift: Explorations in Christian Eschatology *(Edinburgh: T. & T. Clark, 2000), pp. 9–39. Although, as I observe, I did not warm to the suggested part of the title "Signs of the Times", I now agree with Graham Ward that it serves very well as shorthand for "asking about where we stand", which coheres well, in turn, with postmodern concerns about what we might call "human situatedness" (Ward, "Where we Stand", in Ward (ed.),* Blackwell Companion to Postmodern Theology, *Oxford: Blackwell, 2001, pp.xii–xiii).*

In my retrospective evaluation I recognize that my emphasis here falls perhaps too readily more upon critique than on exploring potential insight, but the central purpose of this essay at the time was to warn against a fashionable flirtation in some quarters with the work of Rorty and Fish, as well as with the undervaluing of ontology in so-called post-liberal theologies. I argue that whereas the European postmodern thought of Nietzsche, Foucault, Barthes and Derrida provide valuable critical tools for theology, the postmodern approaches of Rorty and Fish too readily become complacent vehicles for self-affirmation, and may transpose theology and hermeneutics into mere affirmation of "people like us". American postmodernism is also entangled with pragmatism and progressivism, which stand in tension with Christian eschatology.

The first part of the title was suggested to me, not chosen by me.[1] For me, it raises at least three concerns. First, it invites a danger of pontificating about generalities. It risks replacing specific concrete questions by abstract formulations. Second, it risks a serious mismatch between a hopeful and portentous title and becoming mired into the well-worn grooves of playing black chess pieces on behalf of theology in reactive mode while initiatives have been surrendered to socio-economic, political, or intellectual trends outside theology. Although, as Tillich urged there is a place for "answering theology", all theology cannot be subsumed under this model. Third, it invites the kind of extrapolation from trends in the present that David Tracy, Jürgen Moltmann and Karl Rahner distinguish firmly from *Christian eschatology* with its different dimension of new creation

---

[1] I accepted the Committee's request in appreciation of the honour of being elected President for the two years 1999 and 2000.

and surprise. Thus Tracy observes, "To propose that what we can most expect is *the unexpected* is not utopian but cold reality."[2]

Jürgen Moltmann points out that "under pressure of 'progress' ... 'What next?' is a typical modern question – generally an American one".[3] In another volume also he draws a distinction between *futurum* which "develops out of the past ... [and] is already implicit" and the logic of eschatology in which *adventus* may combine divine promise with unexpected novelty.[4] Eschatology "transcends all remembered, experienced, and still-to-be-experienced presents".[5] Karl Rahner distinguishes between "the future which does not evolve ... [but] springs out upon us, rips up the nets of all our plans" and "the false 'future' that we ourselves have constructed".[6] This *contrast between futurology and eschatology* will be fundamental to the argument of this paper.

I
Is the Notion of a "Theology for the Year 2000" Viable? Futurology and Progressivism or Transformative Eschatology?

This question forms the first of six that we shall formulate and address. Each of these six questions will introduce, in turn, six specific theses. These will, like the first, contain two distinct components.

Thesis 1a: *To attempt to formulate a "Theology for the Year 2000" and beyond becomes viable if this task is construed as taking moral responsibility for the shaping of a transformative discipline in which much is at stake. It loses viability if it is conceived only or primarily as a merely reactive agenda to futurological extrapolations from present trends.*

Thesis 1b: *In terms of content, such an agenda will entail a creative and critical engagement with a so-called postmodern context or mind-set, but also avoids compromising a genuinely theological grammar of grace, truth and eschatology.*

Our observations about the logical distinctions between futurology and eschatology underlined by Tracy and by Moltmann, among others, might seem to suggest that we cannot attempt to formulate an agenda for theology ahead of our own times. However, their warnings concern the fallibility and seductions of extrapolating from the past and present as being of a different order from the more solid realities that depend on eschatological promise and the gift of new creation. They pave the way for what we wish

---

[2] David Tracy, 'Some Concluding Reflections on the Conference', in Hans Küng and David Tracy (eds), *Paradigm Change in Theology: A Symposium for the Future* (Edinburgh, 1989), p.470 (my italics).

[3] Jürgen Moltmann, 'Can Christian Eschatology become Post-Modern? Response to Miroslav Volf', in Richard Bauckham (ed.), *God Will Be All in All: The Eschatology of Jürgen Moltmann* (Edinburgh, 1999), p.259.

[4] J. Moltmann, *The Coming of God: Christian Eschatology* (London, 1996), p.25; cf. pp.25–9. Moltmann observes that '*Zukunft* is not a translation of the Latin *Futurum*. It is a translation of *adventus*. But *adventus*, in its turn, is a rendering of the Greek word *Parousia* ...' (p.25).

[5] Moltmann, 'The Interlaced Times of History', in Küng and Tracy (eds), *Paradigm Change*, p.326; cf. pp.320–39.

[6] Karl Rahner, *Theological Investigations*, vol. 10 (London, 1973), p.237.

to explore about the logical grammar of grace or gift. Our Conference title speaks of the future as "God's gift" in contrast to the progressivist pragmatism of human achievement and social construction. On the very same page as that on which he excludes mere prediction on the ground of "the unexpected", David Tracy also asserts, "The signs of the times are once again upon us. These signs are signs of the priority of the future; of possibilities we have not yet dared to imagine; of promises and threats like nuclear holocaust, massive global suffering and oppression, endemic sexism, racism, and ecological disaster we have not yet fully faced; of the full actuality of the always-already-not-yet-event of Jesus Christ in our midst."[7]

The Synoptic Gospels discourage placing too much weight on "signs of the times", and warn us against seeking them (Mark 8:11–13; par Matt. 16:1–4; Luke 11:16, 12:54–56; also cf. John 6:30).[8] On the other hand, certain signs may be identified from time to time which point beyond themselves and require responsible understanding and interpretation (Mark 13:28–29; par Matt. 24:32, 33; Luke 21:29, 30). To be blind to what may be discerned for constructive action is sheer irresponsibility. Daniel Hardy holds together these two sides with explicit reference to the future of theology. In his essay "The Future of Theology in a Complex World", he concedes that to attempt to address this subject may be perceived as "presumptuous". Nevertheless, he continues, "We are morally responsible for the future of theology. Not only in what we say, but in the manner in which we deal with the questions and disagreements with which we shall be concerned, we are exemplifying theology and fashioning it for the future."[9]

David Ford underlines the point that even if some onlookers, or even some theologians, construe theological projects which address issues of truth merely as disguised bids for power, even this should not deter us from taking full moral responsibility for our subject in the context of the university.[10] Too much is at stake in the transformative potential of theology to allow us to retreat from including within its agenda questions of truth, meaning and value. The very accountability raised by the financial and public sources needed to sustain theological exploration make retreat into mere supposedly value-neutral phenomenological description more like a betrayal of public responsibility than an outworking of it. Ford insists: *"Theological and religious studies deals with questions of meaning, truth, beauty, and practice raised in relation to religions and pursued through a range of academic disciplines"* (his italics).[11]

It is imperative as a matter of ethical responsibility and accountability to society, Ford continues, to sustain "an ethical coherence ... for this field" as it moves into the future.[12] He allows for a duality of responsibilities that relate respectively to the academy and to religious

---

[7]   D. Tracy, 'Some Concluding Reflections', in Küng and Tracy (eds), *Paradigm Change*, p.470.

[8]   Paul discourages 'seeking' a sign (1 Cor. 1:22) but he also speaks more positively of 'signs of a true apostle' (2 Cor. 12:12). Cf. also Mark 13:24–25; Luke 21:25.

[9]   Daniel W. Hardy, *God's Ways with the World: Thinking and Practising Christian Faith* (Edinburgh, 1996), p.31; cf. pp.31–50.

[10]   David F. Ford, 'Theology and Religious Studies at the Turn of the Millennium', *Teaching Theology and Religion* 1 (1998), 5; cf. 4–12.

[11]   Ford, 'Theology and Religious Studies', p.6.

[12]   Ford, 'Theology and Religious Studies', p.6.

communities.[13] In 1982 I published an essay specifically on these dual responsibilities under the title "Academic Freedom, Religious Tradition and the Morality of Christian Scholarship" [Essay 37 in this volume]. This drew on Max Black's philosophical explorations of the morality of scholarship, Donald MacKinnon's conception of the theological task as one of a necessarily painful tension, and a range of political philosophers, social theorists and theologians from Charles Taylor, Stuart Hampshire, Alan Montefiore and Alfred Schutz to Bernard Lonergan, Gerd Theissen and Wolfhart Pannenberg.

The very term "ethical coherence", however, begins to enter an area where questions are raised by the controversial notion of "postmodernity". Certainly, as Richard Roberts rightly insists, it simply runs counter to any analysis of our social and cultural situation to conceive of the pre-modern, modern, and postmodern as three neatly sequential stages of development rather than three sources of conflicting cross-currents which seek to draw us in different directions simultaneously through choppy waters.[14] In his response to Richard Robert's essay, Daniel Hardy firmly agrees that the three phenomena of pre-modernity, modernity and postmodernity "coexist", but interprets this as indicating that linkages and a sense of social cohesion or provisional wholeness need not and should not be entirely lost.[15] The moral responsibility for shaping theological methods and agenda arises precisely because theology "enhances or destroys relationship to God, others, and the world" and may promote some kind of vision of "deep unity between peoples ... based on their service of a common good".[16]

Miroslav Volf identifies similar issues, focusing in particular on the phenomenon of consumerism, which Roberts has described in terms of "an ever expanding market society ... driven forward by the rhetoric of 'choice'".[17] With Roberts, Volf observes "a plurality of often contradictory social worlds" which generates centrifugal force. However, he also notes a centripetal counter-movement of "the process of globalization". Just as Dan Hardy responds to Richard Roberts not to surrender a vision of unity too hastily, so Jürgen Moltmann responds to Miroslav Volf that present-day society is not simply or even primarily marked by "diversity, complexity and plurality".[18] Moltmann asserts:

> The trend towards the globalization of the free market society is reducing the world to uniformity. First, China is Coca Cola-ized, then Moscow is Macdonald-ized, and in the end the world everywhere looks just the same as it does in Chicago, London, and New York: the same clothes, the same high-rise blocks, the same brand names on what we buy. The cultural multiplicity and diversity of the different peoples which once existed is now processed into folklore, and is then marketed by the tourist industry.[19]

---

[13] Ford, 'Theology and Religious Studies', p.8. In 1992 I published an essay specifically on these dual responsibilities under the title 'Academic Freedom, Religious Tradition and the Morality of Christian Scholarship'. In Mark Santer (ed.), *Their Lord and Ours: Approaches to Authority, Community and the Unity of the Church* (London, 1992), pp.20–45.

[14] R.H. Roberts, 'A Postmodern Church?', in D.S. Ford and D.L. Stamps (eds), *Essentials of Christian Community* (Edinburgh, 1996), pp.179–95.

[15] D.W. Hardy, in Ford and Stamps (eds), *Essentials*, pp.336–7.

[16] D.W. Hardy, 'The Future of Theology', in *God's Ways with the World*, pp.31, 33.

[17] Miroslav Volf, 'Introduction', in M. Volf, C. Krieg and T. Kucharz (eds), *The Future of Theology* (Grand Rapids, MI: 1996), esp. p.x; and R.H. Roberts, 'Postmodern Church?', p.182.

[18] Moltmann, 'Can Christian Eschatology become Post-Modern?', pp.259–64.

[19] Moltmann, 'Can Christian Eschatology become Post-Modern?', p.263.

We may sum up some of our arguments under this first question and first thesis in terms of some cross-references to other essays or papers within this volume [*The Future*]. First, the use of "post" in the term "postmodernity" should not seduce us into imagining that this complexity of attitudes, assumptions and mind-set is either sequentially subsequent to "modernity" nor necessarily an "improved" progressivist "advance" on modernity in every aspect. Further, Kim Yong Bok's paper challenges both an over-optimistic progressivism and secular futurology, and any unduly simplistic diagnosis of so-called radical pluralism, as if centripetal and globalizing forces were not equally active alongside those in fragmentation and pluralism. A healthy reminder of the ambivalence and negative aspects of postmodernity is well identified in Jürgen Moltmann's preference for the term "sub-modernity".[20]

Second, several papers draw attention to the *transformative* potential of theology, especially of Christian theology, in ways that raise the stakes for our taking moral responsibility for how it is shaped. Thus Garrett Green underlines what he calls "the imaginative character of the Christian vision of another world ... an alternative vision of the world in which the world is ... transformed imaginatively".[21] Richard Bauckham and Trevor Hart head one of their sections "The Shape of Living and the Shape of Time" and speak subsequently of "expanding our perceived horizons of possibility ... If there is no ultimate meaning, no final truth, then it is possible to ignore with impunity the piercing eyes of the starving child or the bewildered refugee ...".[22]

Third, this last statement brings us back to the need for a theological grammar of grace, truth and eschatology that has not been compromised by a need to engage with a postmodern climate. Theology makes truth-claims that transcend the merely local or pragmatic. Truth is more than seeking "justification" (to use Richard Rorty's language) in the eyes of some specific local community who determines what counts as "true". If the future is "God's gift" of grace, social constructivism cannot tell the whole story, and other essays in this volume confirm our distinction between eschatology and futurology. Thus Bauckham and Hart warn us against "substituting immanent for transcendent eschatology" which appears to under-gird the illusory progressivism of the Enlightenment myth of the eighteenth and nineteenth centuries and beyond. Here hope rests not in divine promise but on "the mastery of the future by human rationality and freedom, education and technology" [their p.6].[23] Their later allusion to Jüngel on the ontology of possibility presses this further [their p.25].[24] Progressivism of this kind finds no place at all in Kim Yong-Bok's approach to eschatology. All this invites us to explore a second question and thesis.

---

[20] Jürgen Moltmann, *God for a Secular Society: The Public Relevance of Theology* (London, 1999), pp.11–17; cf. pp.3–45.

[21] In this volume [i.e. *The Future as God's Gift*], p.70.

[22] In this volume [*The Future*], pp.48, 53, 57.

[23] In this volume [*The Future*], p.39.

[24] In this volume [*The Future*], pp.60–61.

II

What Kind of Postmodernity? Ideological Suspicion in Continental Europe, or Ethnocentric, Consumerist Neo-Pragmatism in America?

Thesis 2a: *The postmodern condition in Continental Europe draws on critical suspicions that some truth-claims may all too often represent disguised bids for power. The postmodern condition in America more optimistically tests truth-claims by what can be justified as furthering "progress" for ethnocentric or "local" communities who buy into them as consumers.*

Thesis 2b: *Whereas many see the latter mind-set as less threatening to theology than the former, we argue the reverse. The critical, pessimistic suspicion of European postmodernity can serve to filter authentic truth-claims from those that seek to legitimate power and interests through idols of "religion". The optimistic progressivism of American ethnocentric neo-pragmatism reduces theology and ethics to the status of a commodity shaped by consumer choice.*

Pauline M. Rosenau also distinguishes firmly between these two types of postmodernity. However, she regards the mood of the phenomenon in Continental Europe as "sceptical" and potentially more seriously destructive, than "affirmative" elements within what she perceives as the more optimistic Anglo-American tradition.[25] This is not to forget that in the end she regards both mind-sets as inconsistent and self-defeating.

I have argued elsewhere that the ideological suspicion of Roland Barthes, Michel Foucault, Jacques Derrida and even Friedrich Nietzsche before them, embody elements of prophetic value for truth-claims in theology.[26] Because of its more self-aware, self-critical philosophical tradition, a balance sheet which both informs and distorts a theological grammar of truth may be derived from the ideological suspicion of Barthes, Foucault and Derrida. By contrast the American pragmatic tradition has assumed the status of a "scaffolding" (in the sense in which Wittgenstein uses this term) which redefines truth in consumerist terms. When this is imported into theology, the result is the systematic distortion of the task of theology for the new millennium. "Truth" becomes a pragmatic social construct. This leaves no room for the contribution of grace and Christian eschatology to the logical grammar of truth. In much American theology this emerges as a focus on *narrative* as against *history*, on *practices* as against *epistemology*, and on the supposedly *incommensurable* truth-claims of *local communities* as against the global community (vertically through history and promise; horizontally by including Jew and Gentile, male and female, slave and free) of the *"one Body"* of Christ.

In his *Truth and Progress* Richard Rorty would have us believe that if we follow the path indicated by William James, John Dewey, W.V.O. Quine, Hilary Putnam and (by implication) Stanley Fish, we shall come to see that the grammar of truth consists in nothing more or less than what can be justified (that is, is accepted as a justification) as of

---

[25] P.M. Rosenau, *Post Modernism and the Social Sciences* (Princeton, NJ, 1992).

[26] A.C. Thiselton, *Interpreting God and the Postmodern Self: On Meaning, Manipulation and Promise* (Edinburgh, 1995); cf. also *New Horizons in Hermeneutics* (London, 1992), pp.80–141, 379–409 and 495–508 in contrast to the mistaken verdict of Linda Woodhead on my work in 'Theology and the Fragmentation of the Self', *International Journal of Systematic Theology* 1 (1999), pp.68–9; cf. pp.53–72.

use or utility within a liberal democratic society, or more particularly justified as useful to specific local ("ethnocentric") communities within it. Other grammars of truth which may entail ontology, metaphysics, trans-contextual or trans-pragmatic criteria define themselves as prime candidates for the great "rubbish-disposal projects" of pragmatic American philosophy.[27]

What A.J. Ayer called exposing "non-sense" from an empiricist-positivist viewpoint, and Richard Rorty calls "rubbish-disposal" from a pragmatist angle, Gayatri Spivak and Jacques Derrida call "cutting away", "erasing", or deconstructing. Spivak, Derrida's close collaborator and translator, points out that Derrida singled out Nietzsche, Freud, Husserl and Heidegger as his "acknowledged 'pre-cursors' ... Nietzsche cut away the grounds of knowing; Freud ... put the psyche in question; Heidegger ... put Being under erasure".[28] Where Nietzsche comes closest to Rorty is in his claim that "what is believed to be true" has the "highest importance", while "what is true" remains "a matter of absolute indifference".[29]

Barthes has an entirely valid "feeling of impatience at the 'naturalness' with which newspapers, art, and common sense constantly dress up reality".[30] The use of a semiotic code relating to dress-style or furniture-styles, for example, may serve to make claims to belong to a social "management" or "professional" group.[31] On the other hand, Barthes does not exclude the possibility that what is chosen may depend on judgements about the weather or comfort in one's home. This self-critical and socio-critical awareness of issues of language and truth serves theology positively. The regular occurrence of social construction, which Barthes unmasks, assists in disentangling counterfeit religion or idolatry from genuine responses to divine grace. This differs, however, from Rorty's view that *all* "truth-claims" are exhaustively and without remainder to be counted as true-or-false on the basis of a consensus of consumer choices within a series of local communities in a liberal democracy.

It is a necessary stock-in-trade of any serious course in the philosophy of religion to take account of the need to explore controlling models and metaphors in religious language, and to disentangle those which may embody cognitive truth-claims from those which may appear to do so while merely expressing recommendations, attitudes, or emotive slogans. Derrida merely raises the stakes, but hardly invents the problem when he calls our attention to metaphors that "derive from a theory of *value* and not only from a theory of *signification*" (his italics).[32] In the same way, while most theologians would find it difficult to follow Foucault in the extent and range of his social constructivism, no "theology for the year 2000" should fail to gain sensitivity and critical resources from his

---

[27] Richard Rorty, *Truth and Progress: Philosophical papers*, vol. 3 (Cambridge, 1998), p.10; cf. pp.1–15. Cf. also esp. 19–42, 153–65 and 433–62. See also his *Objectivism, Relativism and Truth: Philosophical papers*, vol. 1 (Cambridge, 1991).

[28] G. Spivak, 'Translator's Preface', in J. Derrida, *Of Grammatology* (Baltimore, MD, 1976), p.xxi.

[29] F. Nietzsche, *Complete Works* (18 vols, London, 1909–13), vol. 16, *The Antichrist*, aphorisms 13 & 23 (in improved translation by R.J. Hollingdale, London, 1990).

[30] R. Barthes, *Mythologies* (London, 1972), p.11.

[31] R. Barthes, *Elements of Semiology* (London, 1967), pp.58–88.

[32] J. Derrida, 'White Mythology: Metaphor in the Text of Philosophy', in Derrida, *Margins of Philosophy* (New York, 1982), pp.217–18 (his italics); cf. pp.207–71.

work on discourses of power. *Knowledge* in the shape of bureaucracy, professionalism, records, and medical and social data can indeed be absorbed into the processes of regimentation and domination which often characterize "the smiling face in the white coat" in prisons, hospitals and other "regime-focused" institutions.[33] The proof (if any were needed) that all this is fundamental for theology at the turn of the millennium as part of its critical resources can be seen in theological publications that explore relations between truth-claims, knowledge and power in social and ecclesial institutions.[34] However, this need not lead, and should not lead, to the denigration of epistemology, which we find in much "postmodern" or "non-foundationalist" American theology.

Rorty claims that the task of "getting reality right" dissolves into nothing, or is mere rubbish to be removed: "There is no such task, because there is no Way the World is."[35] Rorty "finds persuasive" the controversial aphorism of William James that "'The true' ... is *only the expedient* in the way of our thinking, just as 'the right' is *only the expedient* in the way of our behaving (my italics).[36] The true is the name of whatever proves itself to be good in the way of belief ...".[37] "*What proves itself to be good*" resonates with two contexts in American society at large: what proves itself to be deemed good *in the eyes of consumers*, and what proves itself to be good within the trajectory of a *progress-orientated futurology*. For Putnam any notion of the world "as it is in itself" remains *identical to a "world" considered wholly by human needs, choices and interests, that is, the world of consumers in the marketplace.*[38]

Rorty provides his most transparent and explicit bonding between pragmatism and consumerism when he proposes that the grammar of truth has no residue of content beyond what may be offered as a justification for holding a belief or for pursuing a course of action. He adds, "But ... if we say 'justified' rather than 'true'" (as he advocates) then "justification is always relative to an audience".[39] *The audience*, not the speaker, *the consumer*, not the producer, defines the criteria for what counts as "true".

We can now see more clearly how different the European and American moods become. If European movement generates in John Caputo's phrase "the great project of hermeneutical trouble-making" which causes "worries" that are "only for the hardy", this serves as an area with which theology must engage and to which it must listen. By contrast, the very opposite to "worrying" emerges from the American pragmatic agenda. Stanley Fish learns here how to "*stop worrying*"; Richard Rorty "*dissolves*" (re-applying the term from Wittgenstein) the supposed pseudo-problems of the grammar of truth. The upshot is to provide a brash, self-affirming philosophy of futurological progress that

---

[33] M. Foucault, *Discipline and Punish* (New York, 1977), e.g. pp.138, 176–7.

[34] E.g., Christine Firer Hinze, *Comprehending Power in Christian Social Ethics* (Atlanta, GA, 1995), pp.85–97; 108–26; 146–63; E.A. Castelli, *Imitating Paul: A Discourse of Power* (Louisville, KY, 1991), pp.35–58, 119–24; S.D. Moore, *Poststructuralism and the New Testament: Derrida and Foucault at the Foot of the Cross* (Minneapolis, MN, 1994).

[35] R. Rorty, *Truth and Progress: Philosophical Papers*, vol. 3 (Cambridge, 1998), p.25.

[36] Cited Rorty, *Truth and Progress*, p.21, from W. James, *Pragmatism and the Meaning of Truth* (Cambridge, MA, 1975), p.106 (my italics).

[37] Rorty, *Truth and Progress*, and James, *Pragmatism*, p.42.

[38] See H. Putnam, *Renewing Philosophy* (Cambridge, MA, 1992), ch. 5.

[39] Rorty, *Truth and Progress*, p.4.

waves away any cause for heart-searching and discomfort as the part of the "rubbish-disposal projects" which American philosophers are called upon to undertake.[40]

In his volume *Doing What Comes Naturally*, Stanley Fish adopts the standard strategy of American neo-pragmatism. If opponents produce "problems", Fish and Rorty need only (in their eyes) reply "So what?" As we shall see, for them, "serious man" is *passé*; only "rhetorical man" remains. Hence, by giving undue privilege to a version of the *early* paradigm-theory of Thomas Kuhn, and by giving Richard Rorty "the last word" in his essay on rhetoric, Fish not only endorses the view that *"there is no standard higher than the assent of the relevant community"* but also concludes, "There are 'two ways of thinking about various things' ... It is the *difference between serious and rhetorical man*."[41] "Serious" man is dogged by self-imposed burdens of moral responsibility. "Rhetorical" man "sees through" philosophy and theology to the "pragmatist" assumption that *only socio-political forces of persuasion* instrumentally determine who are *"winners"* in the marketplace of life and thought.

It might be thought that such a world-view is so patently secular that theology would hardly offer it hospitality within its internal communities. Especially but not exclusively in America, however, this is far from being the case. A loss of confidence by many theologians in the very possibility, need, or relevance of epistemology and ontology for theology is a symptom of the seduction, while history and effective traditions (*Wirkungsgeschichte*) are too readily lost from view as the focus shifts to local or "narrative" communities whose truth-claims are often said to be incommensurable. Some conservatives see this as an alibi for rejecting "historical-critical" scholarship as "rationalist", and *history* and *knowledge* comes to be replaced by *role-performance* (linguistic or social), regardless of the presuppositions or foundations that are necessary to give currency to truth and language beyond the socially constructed worlds of consumers.

III
Why Should a Pragmatic-Progressivist Grammar of Truth Prove to be so Seductive to Theology, especially in America?

Thesis 3a: *The American pragmatic tradition has its origins in the secularization of New England Puritan theology and achieves the status in some quarters of the "scaffolding of our thought".*

Thesis 3b: *A neo-pragmatic grammar of truth distorts theology if or when it is filtered through such writers as Fish and Rorty.*

---

[40] Rorty, *Truth and Progress*, p.10; J.D. Caputo, *Radical Hermeneutics* (Bloomington, IN, 1987), p.2; S. Fish, *Is There a Text in This Class?* (Baltimore, MD, 1980), pp.1–17.

[41] S. Fish, *Doing What Comes Naturally: Change, Rhetoric and the Practice of Theory in Literary and Legal Studies* (Oxford, 1989), pp.487 (from Kuhn, but note the predictable and unfortunate appeal still to the 1962 edition without reference to Kuhn's later quasi-retractions or modification) and 501–2 (alluding to Rorty); from 'Rhetoric', pp.471–502.

I am largely indebted to my American collaborator and friend Roger Lundin, whose specialist fields include literary theory, American literature, and the history of ideas, for Thesis 3a.[42] In his discussion of the background surrounding Emily Dickinson, Lundin points out that "experiential acquaintance with the grace of God" replaced any notion of being born into a Christian tradition. Together with "experience" went "testimony" and "community", but the *local* community, not a universal community: "In the seventeenth century, Puritan leaders had required lengthy narrative accounts of the soul's struggles and the Spirit's blessings as evidence of the applicant's 'acquaintance with the grace of God'. These narratives often scaled the bright peaks of spiritual bliss and traversed the darkened valleys of sin and despair. They were elaborate dramatic tales of the special providences of God" and as well as concerning "the individual soul" they projected also "the future of God's covenanted people in the New World".[43] The building blocks begin to emerge in the form of narrative, experience, struggle issuing in "winning", and a futurology. The context is a local community of the present, not a historic global community born within traditions. Lundin speaks of "one of the paradoxes at the heart of American experience ... a tradition of disclaiming tradition".[44]

As communities sought to be faithful to God and prospered, a robust optimistic correlation between well-being and the right, or between the successful and the true, became a habit of mind. Liberation from earlier traditions left behind in the Old World revealed itself in the shape of "Progress", that is, futurology. Rorty, it seems, fails to note self-critically how, in Wittgenstein's language, this mind-set of predictable extrapolated optimism becomes "the scaffolding of [our] thoughts"; "hinges" on which enquiries turn, which precisely because they are never doubted come to "lie apart from the route travelled by enquiry" and eventually become "fossilized".[45] Ironically in view of American "non-foundationalism" (which often mistakenly appeals to Wittgenstein), Wittgenstein observes that such ways of seeing things function "as a *foundation* for research and action" often "isolated from doubt" (his italics).[46]

Confidence in the unstoppable progress of the mastery of nature by natural sciences hastens a movement away from earlier Puritan interpretations of providence and nurtures the rule of human self-reliance. Lundin endorses the verdict of Sacvan Bercovitch that "they substituted a regional for a biblical past, consecrated the American present as a movement from promises to fulfillment, and translated fulfillment, from its meaning within ... sacred history into a metaphor for limitless secular improvement".[47]

---

[42] R. Lundin, 'Reading America, Hermeneutics in the City Upon a Hill', Conference paper *Crossing the Boundaries: Interpretive Theory and the Christian Faith* (Gloucester, MA, April 16–19, 1998); also R. Lundin, *The Culture of Interpretation: Christian Faith and the Postmodern World* (Grand Rapids, MI, 1993); R. Lundin (ed.), *Disciplining Hermeneutics* (Leicester, 1997), R. Lundin, *Emily Dickinson and the Art of Belief* (Grand Rapids, MI, 1998) and (with Thiselton and Walhout) *The Promise of Hermeneutics* (Grand Rapids, MI, 1999).

[43] Lundin, *Emily Dickinson*, p.49.

[44] Lundin, *The Culture of Interpretation*, pp.140–41; cf. also Robert Bellah, *Habits of the Heart: Individualism and Commitment in American Life* (Berkeley, CA, 1985), pp.56–62.

[45] Ludwig Wittgenstein, *On Certainty* (Oxford, 1969), sects 211, 343 and 655, 88, 657, respectively.

[46] Wittgenstein, *On Certainty*, sect. 87 (his italics); discussed further in A.C. Thiselton, *The Two Horizons* (Grand Rapids, MI, 1980), pp.392–401.

[47] S. Bercovitch, *The Rites of Assent: Transformations in the Symbolic Construction of America* (New York, 1993), p.147; cited by R. Lundin, 'Reading America', p.10.

Thus Benjamin Franklin (1706–90) comes to set up an implicit contrast between criteria of the true or good based on the will of God and criteria dependent on "the benefits of humanity". Acts are good, or opinions "true" when these are "beneficial to us".[48] In Ralph Waldo Emerson (1803–82) we encounter a political philosophy that clearly embodied pragmatic progressivism: in the 1830s he compared his own political movement as "the party of the Future" while labelling his opponents "the party of the Past". William James and John Dewey saw him as a liberating and inspiring mentor who saw "boundless possibilities" for a self-achieved future.[49]

Rorty transposes this into a postmodern key. On *Rorty's* definition of "truth", "nobody should even to try to specify the nature of truth ... Truth is not a goal of inquiry. If 'truth' is the name of such a goal then, indeed, there is no truth ... There is nothing to the notion of objectivity save that of intersubjective agreement."[50] Rorty disarmingly concedes the circularity of his own arguments, but this does not matter: "There is no central faculty, no central self, called 'reason'."[51] We cannot go beyond epistemological behaviourism, not only conditioned by, but also constructed by, the "contingencies" of language, selfhood and community.[52] "Irony" comes down to futurology: our accounts of present or future achievements remain irredeemably "Whiggish".[53] "Solidarity" with a community of enquiries within which consensus emerges defines what we *call* "truth" in a democratic society.[54] Ethics becomes a matter of raw consequentialism in social practices, concerning which we may ask "what?" or "how?" but not "why?"[55]

A parallel may be suggested with the seductions that held in thrall a large segment of British intellectuals in the 1930s and 1940s who had not noticed the "scaffolding" of *empiricist assumptions in British traditions*. Precisely with the kind of self-assured self-confidence with which Fish and Rorty write, A.J. Ayer thought that he had shown that all language that was not either verifiable with reference to empirical observation or logically analytic was "non-sense" (cf. "rubbish" in Rorty, or "without consequences" in Fish).[56] It took less than twenty years for philosophers and theologians to unmask Ayer's work as merely a positivist world-view dressed up in the disguise of a theory of language. Once its sheer secularity and reductionism as a world-view had been exposed, logical positivism lost its spell, and *the positivist "scaffolding" came to view*. Just as half a century ago, a British public wondered why they had ever accepted the initial assumption laid down by Ayer, how long will it be before what Rorty concedes amounts

---

[48] Benjamin Franklin, *Autobiography*, conveniently available in N. Baym et al., *The Norton Anthology of American Literature* 1 (New York, ⁴1994), p.524.

[49] On the further development of the American pragmatic tradition, see R.S. Corrington, *The Community of Interpreters: On the Hermeneutics of Nature and the Bible in the American Philosophical Tradition* (Macon, GA, 1987).

[50] Rorty, *Truth and Progress*, 3, pp.6–8.

[51] R. Rorty, *Contingency, Irony and Solidarity* (Cambridge, 1989), pp.33. (Might this fall under the same criticism by Linda Woodhead as above?)

[52] Rorty, *Contingency*, pp.3–69.

[53] Rorty, *Contingency*, pp.73–137.

[54] Rorty, *Truth and Progress*, pp.1–163; Rorty, *Objectivity, Relativism and Truth*, pp.35–77; Rorty, *Contingency*, pp.141–98.

[55] Rorty, *Contingency*, pp.141–98.

[56] A.J. Ayer, *Language, Truth and Logic* (1936; New York, ²1946).

to a circular argument grounded simply in "what a democratic society does" also loses its spell?

There can be no doubt that in American theology a so-called post-critical or post-liberal emphasis upon "what communities do", in contrast to Cartesian questions about epistemological foundations, finds various levels and forms of expression among numerous writers. Notably Peter Ochs includes in his anthology of "Post-critical" writers George Lindbeck, Stanley Hauerwas and (for example) John E. Smith's essay "Jonathan Edwards: Piety and its Fruits".[57] In his larger work of 1998, Peter Ochs associates the legacy of C.S. Peirce and pragmatism explicitly with Frei, Lindbeck, Hauerwas and Gregory Jones, and with such Jewish interpreters as Moshe Greenberg and Michael Fishbane.[58] We alluded above to Robert Corrington's convincing arguments about a distinctively American hermeneutic of "effects", as against "givens".[59] Christopher Norris identifies a distinctively American "pragmatist cultural politics", while Jonathan Culler speaks of the "complacency" of a neo-pragmatism characteristic of "the Age of Reagan".[60]

All the same, it does not remain entirely accurate to lump together the more sophisticated pragmatism of the later Peirce, with the neo-pragmatism of Rorty, Fish and others who transform epistemology into no more than an instrumental device to promote "rhetorical" truth-claims. This leads to a fourth thesis.

IV

How May a Theology for the Year 2000 Best Clarify the Difference between a Fruitful, Critical Pragmatism of Proven Wisdom and a Postmodern Pragmatism of Consumerism and Ethnocentric Pluralism?

Thesis 4a: *Peirce's attempt to "supplement" epistemological determinacy by life-related pragmatic criteria may cohere with theological grammars of truth without thereby reducing theology to consumerism or rhetoric.*

Thesis 4b: *Rorty's attempt to "replace" epistemological determinacy by ethnocentric pragmatic criteria distorts and destroys theological grammars of truth, and thereby necessarily reduces theology to consumerism and rhetoric.*

The "re-reading" of C.S. Peirce by Peter Ochs clearly serves to distinguish the pragmatism of Peirce from the more reductionist claims of Rorty. Nevertheless, even Ochs notes "two conflicting models" in Peirce's early work.[61] Since Peirce believes that there is no "given" apart from signs, sign-relations and human behaviour, the emphasis

---

[57] Peter Ochs (ed.), *The Return to Scripture in Judaism and Christianity: Essays in Postcritical Scriptural Interpretation* (New York, 1993), pp.83–103, (cf. also G. Lindbeck, *The Nature of Doctrine* [London, 1984], pp.308–26; also S. Hauerwas in Volf et al. [eds], *Future*, pp.26–34, esp. p.27); and pp.277–91.

[58] Peter Ochs, *Peirce, Pragmatism and the Logic of Scripture* (Cambridge, 1998), pp.290–325.

[59] R.S. Corrington, *The Community of Interpreters: On the Hermeneutics of Nature and the Bible in the American Philosophical Tradition* (Macon, GA, 1997), pp.1–29, 43–6.

[60] C. Norris, *Contest of Faculties* (London, 1985), p.162; J. Culler, *Framing the Sign* (Oxford, 1988), p.55.

[61] Ochs, *Peirce*, pp.58–9.

in questions about *meaning* falls largely on "cash-currency". At the same time in his *later* work Peirce avoids reducing truth exhaustively to this level. Thus, in "What Pragmatism Is" (1905), Peirce explicitly includes within his "pragmatic maxim" of "practical consequences" an "intellectual conception" of conditional propositions of the form "if *p*, then *q*".[62] In other words, Peirce's *broad* appeal to the words of Jesus "by their fruits ye shall know them" *supplements but does not replace* enquiry about logical relations between concepts.[63]

Even if Peirce anticipates some aspects of what later becomes a local contextualism in Rorty, as Apel argues, it is possible to interpret Peirce as offering an "enlargement" of epistemology, not its reduction or replacement by raw consequentialism.[64] Indeed even Dewey, to whom Rorty appeals as his own inspiration, gives due warning that raw pragmatism will too readily breed a scepticism which paralyses moral effort and the notion that "might is right". These approaches, Cornel West notes, differ from Rorty's ethical complacency.[65] In the analysis presented by Ochs, Peirce came to see in his later work that his earlier writings had uncritically "sought to *replace rather than help correct*" (my italics) an over-reliance on human reason alone. Ochs writes with a respect for traditions, which finds no parallel in Rorty.[66]

This brings us to a fundamental question for our main task of exploring "Theology for the Year 2000". Do the so-called post-liberal, post-critical, or self-styled "non-foundationalist" theologians of American thought who stand in the Peirce-Dewey frame of reference remain entirely free from the epistemological reductionism and community-centredness of the earlier Peirce and Rorty's neo-pragmatism?

On one side, Ochs stands alongside Frei, Lindbeck, Hauerwas and theologians often associated with "narrative theology". Later Peirce saw that these cognitive dimensions needed to be subsumed into a more comprehensive paradigm, and not simply rejected. Where Rorty would speak of "rubbish-disposal" in this context, Peirce conceived of his own later work as one of "repair".[67] Practical "wisdom" embraces both elements.[68]

George Lindbeck, however, argues that "the ultimate test" of post-liberal theology "is performance". Even allowing for the ecumenical aims of his work, we find it problematic that he groups together "an experiential-expressive model" which focuses on "experience" as an "*alternative*" (his word) to a so-called cultural-linguistic model.[69] Lindbeck's unduly pragmatic classificatory method fails to integrate the cognitive and pragmatic with the degree of subtle interaction that characterizes both human language and more complex grammars of truth.[70] Indeed he views these models as "fundamentally

---

[62] C.S. Peirce, 'What Pragmatism Is', *Monist* 15 (1905), pp.161–81 rpt. In his *Collected Papers* (Cambridge, 1935/1958), vol. 5.

[63] Ochs, *Peirce*, p.187; cf. pp.185–91. On the primary sources in Peirce, also p.347, notes 13–15.

[64] Karl-Otto Apel, *Towards a Transformation of Philosophy* (London, 1980), p.46; cf. pp.58–60, 80–92, 101–35.

[65] Cornel West, 'The Politics of American Neo-Pragmatism', in J. Rajchman and C. West (eds), *Post-Analytic Philosophy* (New York, 1985), p.267.

[66] Ochs, *Peirce*, pp.3–19, 23–6, 36–50 (cf. the critique of the earlier work in 55–103).

[67] Ochs, *Peirce*, pp.59, 61, 62.

[68] Ochs, *Peirce*, pp.58–64.

[69] Lindbeck, *Nature of Doctrine*, pp.31–40.

[70] Lindbeck, *Nature of Doctrine*, pp.41–2; cf. pp.47–52.

different notions of what religion is".[71] Further, his borrowing from the philosophy of science the term "incommensurable" without a rigorously critical exposition of its range of meanings brings us too easily to Rorty's "local" or "ethnocentric" stance. There is insufficient argument to lead us back to a more judicious and rounded understanding of how this term becomes transposed into different keys in the respective repertoire of philosophy of science, postmodern philosophy, and what he far too simply lumps together as "propositionalism".[72]

Rorty uses the term "ethnocentrism" to replace the more obvious word "relativism" which he rejects. This new preferred term identifies the distinctive practices of particular communities, which depend, in effect, on consumer choice. To claim that "truth" may be reduced to what beliefs can be justified to a specific audience-community is not, Rorty claims, to dissolve "truth" into relativism. It is to acknowledge *the pluralism and diversity of contingent ethnocentric communities* in a continent-wide democracy. "Truth" is relative to "our" practices. Tellingly, Rorty declares:

> I have tried to sketch the connections between anti-representationalism, *ethnocentrism,* and the virtues of the socio-political culture of the liberal democracies. *As I have repeatedly suggested, I view the position developed in these essays as continuous with Dewey's* – the figure who, in the decade since I wrote *Philosophy and the Mirror of Nature* [1979] has, in my imagination, *gradually eclipsed Wittgenstein and Heidegger.*[73]

There we have it: a distinctively *American* progressivist pragmatism tied into futurology, and the ethnocentrism of a series of communities whose truth-claims are incommensurable *because we can only ask what is justifiable to each them,* never to all of them.

The influence of Rorty and Fish in American theology comes through a one-sided misappropriation of the later Wittgenstein, partly through an unaccountably "postmodern" reading of Gadamer, and partly through an uncritical transposition of "incommensurability" from the earlier (not the later) Kuhn and philosophy of science. Many have offered criticisms of Fish and Rorty's reading of Wittgenstein. This *Tendenz* began with Rorty's re-reading of philosophers through neo-pragmatic spectacles in *Philosophy of the Mirror of Nature* (1979). Jane Heal and Richard Bernstein are among those who question this reading by Rorty, just as I have questioned Fish's use of Wittgenstein.[74] To be sure Rorty discusses various interpretations of Wittgenstein in secondary literature.[75] However, in his later works this is mainly in relation to "anti-realism" and to issues of "theory". Rorty never fully takes account of Wittgenstein's observation that for someone attempting to understand *human beings,* "the common behaviour of mankind (*die gemeinsame menschliche Handlungsweise*) is the system of reference by which we interpret an unknown language".[76] Understanding pain-behaviour does not depend on

---

71 Lindbeck, *Nature of Doctrine,* p.41.
72 Lindbeck, *Nature of Doctrine,* pp.48–51.
73 Rorty, *Objectivity, Relativity and Truth,* p.16 (my italics); cf. pp.1–17.
74 Jane Heal, 'Pragmatism and Choosing to Believe', in A.R. Malachowski (ed.), *Reading Rorty: Critical Responses to 'Philosophy and the Mirror of Nature' and Beyond* (Oxford, 1990), pp.101–14; R.J. Bernstein, *Beyond Objectivism and Relativism* (Philadelphia, PA, 1991), pp.197–207 and *The New Constellation* (Cambridge, 1991), pp.15–30, 230–92. Cf. Thiselton, *New Horizons,* pp.540–50.
75 Rorty, *Truth and Progress,* pp.33–40, 103–7, 331–3; and *Objectivity, Relativism and Truth,* pp.2–7, 144–8.
76 Ludwig Wittgenstein, *Philosophical Investigations,* sect. 206.

observing the practices of a community whose truth-claims are incommensurable with others, but on observing "the pain-behaviour ... of a living human being".[77] If an alien from space witnesses someone shaking and up and down and uttering "bleating noises", it is in relation to understanding *what it is to be human* that this will be perceived as laughter. It is *not* simply context-relative to some given community. Wittgenstein insists that such concepts as "repentance", "pain", or "love" depend on experiencing or engaging with the *human as human*, or "the whole hurly-burly of human actions".[78] In the same way, Georgia Warnke and Karl-Otto Apel expose the inadequacy of the misplaced appeals by Rorty and Fish to Gadamer's supposed denigration of rationality and epistemology.[79]

It is not as if Rorty and Fish manage entirely to avoid any appeal to "foundations". The new "foundation" has become in effect, even if not in intention, simply "This is what *we* (or 'our people') *do*." This even produces a self-conscious style in some American theology that seems to many uncongenial, even pretentious, if it were not a symptom of the new "foundation" of peer-group practices. Thus Rorty often uses such phrases as "we pragmatists think ..." as if he were duly appointed spokesperson of a "local" community of neo-pragmatists.[80] Margaret Thatcher hinted at such a "foundation" when she asked the widely reported question about a candidate considered for promotion: "but is he really *one of us*?" Here indeed is Rorty's "ethnocentrism". Similarly, while he cannot be accused of consumerism (which he explicitly recognizes as a looming danger for theology), Hauerwas finds it "puzzling" that theologians in universities "come to the defence of the human, the rational ..." when a community of faith should adhere to the distinctive "story" that binds it together.[81] By contrast, the British theologian Nicholas Lash seeks an interaction "between narrative and metaphysics" which avoids Rorty's pragmatism while addressing the *both ... and ...* which the *later* Peirce also addressed.[82]

One unwelcome symptom of pragmatic consumerism in theology is the tendency to pursue the method of cartography, most especially by mapping the "positions" of writers without regard to their ongoing development or the complexity of differing networks of beliefs within a diversity of dynamic traditions. From the turn of the last century onwards too much American theology has operated *by this method*: a mapping of theological terrain in which market-competitors, with their *goods and services*, take up *categorized "positions" on the display shelf.* Such an imposition of "categories" or pre-shaped pigeonholes *in advance of* understanding remains *profoundly unhermeneutical*. This is precisely what Hans-Georg Gadamer means by "method" when he rejects the notion of providing a network or grid of prior questions, concepts, or spaces *into which that which we seek to understand must fit*. Such a "method" cannot fail to *prevent* understanding, and cannot therefore be commended even as a didactic exercise. As Gadamer notes, it has to do with "preserving

---

[77] Wittgenstein, *Philosophical Investigations*, sect. 281.
[78] Ludwig Wittgenstein, *Zettel*, sect. 567.
[79] G. Warnke, *Gadamer: Hermeneutics, Tradition and Reason* (Cambridge, 1987) and K.-O. Apel, 'Regulative Ideas or Truth Happenings?', in L.E. Hahn (ed.), *The Philosophy of Hans-Georg Gadamer*, pp.67–94.
[80] Rorty, *Truth and Progress*, p.39.
[81] S. Hauerwas, 'No Enemy, No Christianity', in Volf et al. (eds), *Future*, p.27; cf. pp.26–34.
[82] N. Lash, *Theology on the Way to Emmaus* (London, 1986), p.119.

one's own 'position'" in the market, and fails to "break into my egocentredness".[83] This places premature "explanation" (*Erklärung*) *before understanding* (*Verstehen*).

"Positions" in systematic theology are no more than provisional cross-sections of developing traditions and growth in thought. One hermeneutical corrective to consumerist categorization is to place historical theology and theologians *before* systematics in a teaching course, and to be wary of teaching theology by de-contextualized "mapping". Too often, "positions" are set out like packages lumped together in packaging designed to influence consumer choice in a free market. This sacrifices truth and integrity for a pragmatic rhetoric of persuasion. Such a rhetoric may be enhanced by connecting it with progressivism. Thus a writer might utilize the prefix "post-" to designate the preferred view, implying a rhetoric of the *passé* for other less favoured "positions". Such terms as post-liberal, and postmodern or "post-dualist", "post-noeticentric" seems sometimes to be used to this effect.[84] Yet Bauckham and Hart unmask this as seductive illusion: "progress itself has turned threatening".[85] Theology looks to eschatology, not to futurology.

V
Epistemology and Argument, or "Rhetoric"? Does the New Testament have a Voice?

Thesis 5a: *The church of ancient Corinth offers a model of postmodern "rhetorical man".*
Thesis 5b: *Paul identifies this as a subversion of Christian grace, truth and eschatology that must be subverted, in turn, by the proclamation of the cross.*

For Stanley Fish and Richard Lanham, nothing distinguishes two major world-views more sharply than the vast divide between *"homo seriosus* or Serious Man" and *"homo rhetoricus"*:[86] "The contrast ... can hardly be exaggerated ... The ground is itself *foundational*" (my italics).[87] "Serious Man possesses a central self, an irreducible identity" and he/she can be characterized by "sincerity, faithfulness to the self".[88] On the other hand *"Rhetorical man ... is an actor ... centred in ... local events ... Rhetorical man is trained not to discover reality but to manipulate it. Reality is ... what is useful"* (my italics).[89] This is the so-called postmodern sea change. It enjoys hospitality not only in secular world-views, but also in theology and in biblical studies.[90]

---

[83]   H.-G. Gadamer, 'Reflections on my Philosophical Journey', in Lewis E. Hahn (ed.), *The Philosophy of Hans-Georg Gadamer* (Chicago, IL, 1997), pp.36, 46; cf. pp.3–63, and *Truth and Method* (2nd Eng. edn, London, 1989), pp.3–30 and 265–370.

[84]   Cf. S.J. Grenz's use of such terms in *A Primer of Postmodernism* (Grand Rapids, MI, 1996), p.161.

[85]   In this volume [*The Future*], p.44.

[86]   Fish, *Doing What Comes Naturally*, p.482.

[87]   Fish, *Doing What Comes Naturally* (my italics).

[88]   Fish, *Doing What Comes Naturally*. Fish cites R. Lanham, *The Motives of Eloquence* (New Haven, CT, 1976), p.1.

[89]   Cited from Lanham, *Motives*, p.4, in Fish, *Doing What Comes Naturally*, p.483 (my italics).

[90]   On the turn to 'rhetoric' in biblical studies, cf. Duane F. Watson and Alan J. Hauser, *Rhetorical Criticism of the Bible: A Comprehensive Bibliography with Notes on History and Method* (Leiden, 1994), Stanley E. Porter and Thomas H. Olbricht (eds), *Rhetoric and the New Testament* (Sheffield, 1993); D.F. Watson, *Persuasive Artistry* (Sheffield, 1991).

A flood of research on the Corinthian epistles since around 1990 offers a consensus on "rhetoric", "audience", "performance" and social status at Corinth. Stephen Pogoloff even notes how the current interest in rhetoric in biblical scholarship "is tied to a major shift in world-view. This ... anti-foundational world view can lead us to reformulate interpretation itself as a rhetorical enterprise".[91] This, however, he argues is the *sophia logou* beloved at Corinth, which Paul repudiates (1 Cor. 1:17; cf. 2:1–5).[92] Pogoloff compares the rhetorical competitions (*agōna logōn*) held at Rome with the approval of the rhetorical giants Cicero, Quintillian and Seneca, with the quite different, manipulative, applause-seeking, audience-orientated rhetorical contests held in many provincial centres such as Corinth.[93] Seneca and Quintillian note that in good, solid, classical Roman rhetoric the issues turn upon the well-articulated, clear communication of *the truth of an argument.* But the kind of rhetoric which captured Corinthian minds around AD 51–55 was whatever "won approval for yourself [the rhetorician] rather than the case ... Every effusion is greeted with a storm of ready-made applause ... The result is vanity and empty self-sufficiency ... intoxicated by the wild enthusiasm of their fellow-pupils" (that is, "truth" becomes *what "wins" in peer-group consensus and performance*).[94] Rhetoricians were not communicators of truth, but "performers" whose aim was to *"win" the approval of the audience* whether they thought their case was *true or not.*

Aristotle, Quintillian, Cicero and Seneca were *"homo seriosus"* (Fish) who valued truth and sincerity, while the expectations of Corinth were directed towards *homo rhetoricus*, more like a late twentieth-century chat-show host or "actor" (Fish). Pogoloff discusses the divisive and competitive tendencies that replaced questions of *truth* by "performance" in which "winners" were judged by the consumer (cf. 1 Cor. 4:7–13). Endorsements of, and parallels with, Pogoloff's portrayal abound in recent literature.[95] Witherington admirably captures the mood. Like a modern/postmodern pragmatic-consumerist culture, "in Paul's time many in Corinth were 'status-hungry people'".[96] *The new religion, with its "spiritual gifts" and "rights"* (cf. *exesti/exousia* 1 Cor. 6:12; 10:23) and its supposed autonomy had affinities with a Sophistic rhetoric of "manipulation":[97] "The Corinthians felt that they had the right to judge Paul and his message, and were evaluating him by the same criteria by which popular orators ... were judged. Paul disputed this right."[98] For *"truth" based on pragmatic success and consumer choice generated a different spirituality, theology and life-style from truth based on the criterion of the cross.*

---

[91] S.M. Pogoloff, *Logos and Sophia: The Rhetorical Situation of 1 Corinthians* (Atlanta, GA, 1992), p.8.

[92] Pogoloff, *Logos and Sophia*, p.10.

[93] Pogoloff, *Logos and Sophia*, pp.173–96; also pp.129–72.

[94] Seneca (Elder), *Controversiae* 9:1; Quintillian, *Institutio Oratoria* II:2:9, 12; further, Pogoloff, *Logos and Sophia*, pp.175–8.

[95] E.g., A.D. Clarke, *Secular and Christian Leadership in Corinth* (Leiden, 1993), pp.23–58; D. Litfin, *St Paul's Theology of Proclamations: 1 Corinthians 1–4 and Greco-Roman Rhetoric* (Cambridge, 1994); B. Witherington, *Conflict and Community in Corinth: A Socio-Rhetorical Commentary* (Grand Rapids, MI, 1995), pp.20–48; B.W. Winter, *Philo and Paul among the Sophists* (Cambridge, 1997), pp.113–201.

[96] Witherington, *Conflict*, pp.20, 24.

[97] Witherington, *Conflict*, p.42.

[98] Witherington, *Conflict*, p.47.

Wolfgang Schrage, on the other side, sees that for Paul the proclamation of the cross constitutes the "ground and criterion of community and apostle" alike.[99] If this *kerygma* is the criterion of the entire Christian community globally (not a series of incommensurably-justified communities), any emphasis on "community" gains a proper "foundational" epistemological footing. Alexandra Brown constructively and decisively breaks the Rortian and postmodernist polarization between "performance" and epistemology.[100] The cross addresses Corinth transformatively and eventfully in such a way as to transpose the boundaries and content of their epistemology from one of self-affirming, local group-centredness to a knowing-in-love by grace of global proportions. If it is *"given"* through *grace*, this logically excludes, we may infer, a *knowledge born of social construction*. If *"grace"* however, is also socially constructed, *grace is no longer grace, and Christian faith collapses into a secular world-view*. In Paul's language, it becomes sheer "folly" (1 Cor. 1:24).

Raymond Pickett also speaks of Paul's proclaiming the cross as "performing an act of projecting ... a meaning".[101] This event brings about a transvaluation of the social identities or corporate identity of the Corinthian church.[102] The "world" of knowledge and behaviour that the cross "founds" or "re-founds" is that which is "congruous with the gospel of 'Jesus Christ and him crucified'".[103] In contrast to a pragmatism in which consumer and audience call the tune and determine what counts as "true", the argument in 1:10–4:21 "is dependent on their recognition that the event of Christ's death is, so to speak, the very ground of their being".[104] It addresses their "identity crisis".

It would be naive to argue that neither Paul nor Corinth fully understood "pluralism". Corinth was refounded as a *Roman* city on *Greek* soil in 44 BC, and settled with freedpersons and veterans by Julius Caesar. Freedpersons had almost always proved their worth either by initiative, ambition and entrepreneurial skills, or by skills of literacy or competency in various areas of life. Corinth soon became a Mecca for those who sought business opportunities from Asia, from Italy, or from North or South, including Jews. It stood on the narrow isthmus with the harbour of Laecheum facing west, and the harbour of Cenchreae facing east – an unavoidable cross-roads for trade, commerce, business and social intercourse between east and west, and north and south. Various sub-systems of influence by patrons, accumulation of wealth through the right networks, and means of gaining favour, honour, or prestige, saturated the whole of society from slave to city benefactor. The extant Latin inscriptions that lie open to public view at the site of ancient Corinth today readily bring all this to life.[105]

---

[99] W. Schrage, *Der erste Brief an die Korinther*, vol. 2 (Zürich, 1995), p.165.

[100] A.R. Brown, *The Cross and Human Transformation: Paul's Apocalyptic Word in 1 Corinthians* (Minneapolis, MN, 1995), pp.3–12, 34–64 on apocalyptic and epistemology, 65–96 on speech-acts; and 97–169 on epistemological appropriation of the cross.

[101] R. Pickett, *The Cross in Corinth: The Social Significance of the Death of Jesus* (Sheffield, 1997), pp.24, 25.

[102] Pickett, *Cross*, pp.58–84.

[103] Pickett, *Cross*, p.59.

[104] Pickett, *Cross*, p.59.

[105] The literature is too vast to cite here. However, cf. J.K. Chow, *Patronage and Power: A Study of Social Networks in Corinth* (Sheffield, 1992).

Paul did not infer from these social phenomena that all that Christians can do is to exhibit performances, and that an "ugly ditch" of epistemological incommensurability divides off practices on the basis of what is perceived as "true" within each sub-system or peer group. Indeed he insisted on the trans-local, trans-contextual significance of creation, apostolicity, the church and the cross, that sustained an "ordered" commonality of confession and allegiance.[106] "We the Paul group ...", "We the Apollos group ..." (1:12) was not good enough. *Part of the offence of the gospel was its transformation of "rhetorical man" into "serious man"*, that is, one who on the basis of the truth of Christian theology took responsibility for the weak, the despised and those who were not "winners" in the Corinthian congregation. Ahead of his time, Karl Barth diagnosed the problem as the Corinthians' bold confidence not in the "given" of the gift of grace but in "the enthusiasm with which they believe ... in their own belief in God".[107]

Sometimes the claim that only Christianity can provide a viable alternative to such social constructionism is described as "triumphalist". Antoinette Wire fully accepts the portrait of Corinthian theology as one of rhetorical self-affirmation in the Spirit but casts Paul in the role of a manipulator who is no less "rhetorical".[108] However, such an analysis fails to explain adequately Paul's consistent concern for "the weak", "the other" and the disempowered, primarily on the basis of grace (4:7). Is identification with "the man for others", as Paul urges "triumphalist"? While the Corinthians claim to "reign as kings", the apostolic witnesses are perceived at Corinth "as it were, as the world's scum, the scrapings from everybody's shoes" (1 Cor. 4:8, 13; my translation).

The work of John D. Moores on "rationality" in Paul well illustrates and instantiates how modern/postmodern theories of language, truth and signs may be tested in relation to Pauline texts without hermeneutical anachronism. Moores is fully conversant with the theories of Umberto Eco, Luis Prieto and Jacques Derrida, and explores Paul's use of enthymemes rather than a bald deductive and inductive logic, without sacrifice of rationality.[109] Moores insists:

> Paul ... does *not* think (as some modern upholders of the importance of the reception factor do) *that the identity of the message* in a piece of communication is in any sense determined by what it means for those *at the receiving end*. For him it is rather *their* identity than that of the message that is determined by their response. To subject him to the criteria of present-day reception or reader-response theory would be to turn *his* ideas on the subject *upside down*.[110]

---

[106] Cf. W. Schrage, *Der erste Brief an die Korinther*, vol. 1 (Zürich, 1991), pp.99–101; J.H. Schültz, *Paul and the Anatomy of Apostolic Authority* (Cambridge, 1975), pp.187–203; J.A. Crafton, *The Agency of the Apostle* (Sheffield, 1991), pp.62–3.

[107] Karl Barth, *The Resurrection of the Dead* (London, 1933), p.17.

[108] A.C. Wire, *The Corinthian Women Prophets: A Reconstruction through Paul's Rhetoric* (Minneapolis, MN, 1990), pp.9–38.

[109] J.D. Moores, *Wrestling with Rationality in Paul: Romans 1–8 in a New Perspective* (Cambridge, 1995), pp.21–32 and throughout.

[110] Moores, *Wrestling*, pp.133–4 (first and last italics mine; middle italics, Moores's).

VI
Towards a Grammar of Grace, Truth and Christian Eschatology

Thesis 6a: *Theology for the Year 2000 requires a multiform grammar of truth that, while recognizing the limits of reason, does not thereby reduce it to the merely local or instrumental or rhetorical. It will also respect history, traditions and wisdom.*

Thesis 6b: *Theology for the Year 2000 will locate its grammar of truth within a decisive framework of grace and eschatology and will permit the grammar of each to interpret transformatively.*

To suggest that truth is manifold and multiform does not entail the proposition that each context in which *truth* occurs has no logical or semantic relationship to others in which it also occurs. If Rorty and Fish had been true to their contextual insights, it would have been apparent that each "theory of truth" may be what Wittgenstein observes concerning notions of referential meaning; they may be "appropriate but only for this ... circumscribed region".[111] No doubt Fish may be swayed by legal contexts in which "truth" often seems to be defined by what a judge or jury *counts* as true. But we are not claiming that all life or all of theology depends on what Lindbeck terms a cognitive-propositional model.

Many philosophers of logic distinguish between the logical grammar of "correspondence-as-correlation" and a more atomistic, isomorphic theory that may well fall victim more readily to Rorty's criticisms of "representationalism" in his *Philosophy and the Mirror of Nature*. Correspondence-as-correlation leaves room for Wittgenstein's valid recognition that often "what I hold to is not *one* proposition but a nest of propositions".[112] Each twig of the nest remains interlaced with "what lies round it".[113] The very fact that "what counts as a test" for a truth-claim depends on what is being asserted in varied situations in life underlines the axiom that no *single* grammar of truth can do justice to the complexities and particularities of human life.

One version of a "weak" correspondence-as-correlation theory can be found in J.L. Austin. In his essay "Truth", Austin entertains his readers with a series of truth-claims that are *"broadly"* true. We cannot do without them in everyday life. Further, since Christian eschatology still reflects a dialectic of fulfilment and non-fulfilment, the notion of a "loose" (provisional, proximate) fit in theological statements also has a place, in spite of Rorty's rejection of the whole grammar of any "fit" with reality. Austin observes, "Statements fit the facts more or less loosely, in different ways on different occasions."[114] Thus whether we judge such examples of propositions as "Belfast is north of London" or "the galaxy is shaped like a fried egg" as "fitting" reality (that is, true) will depend on whether the contexts concern cartography and astronomy or explaining about Belfast or galaxies to a child over the breakfast table. Some British theologians have appealed to the

---

[111] L. Wittgenstein, *Philosophical Investigations*, sect. 3.
[112] L. Wittgenstein, *On Certainty*, sect. 225.
[113] Wittgenstein, *On Certainty*, sect. 144.
[114] J.L. Austin, 'Truth', in *Philosophical Papers* (Oxford, 1961), rpt. in G. Pitcher (ed.), *Truth* (Englewood Cliffs, NJ, 1964), p.28; cf. pp.18–31.

notion of "a loose fit" in the context of Christology. The debate between Maurice Wiles, Peter Baelz, John Robinson and others in the early 1970s about how "two stories" might replace a Chalcedonian metaphysic of "two storeys" raised questions about whether New Testament Christology projected a "loose fit" between the career of Jesus of Nazareth and the public world of empirical or historical observation.[115]

The turn from historical enquiry to literary theory in many areas of biblical studies has provided some more promising and constructive explanations of the artistry of biblical narratives than many hypotheses about clumsy editing and the failure of biblical redactors to note when their supposed scissors-and-paste editing produced mismatching duplicate sources or gross errors in historical reconstruction. Thus Robert Alter argues that the differences between the accounts of David's rise to kingship in 1 Sam. 16:12, 13 and in 1 Sam. 17 to 2 Sam. 5:5 rest on a need to present a stereoscopic dialectic; between divine election and the hurly-burly of human life, rather than an uncritical use of incompatible historical sources.[116] Numerous writers have expounded different patterns and tempos of narrative time in the Synoptic Gospels to account for apparently insoluble "historical" problems. Nevertheless this should not lead to a "postmodern" retreat from history, rationality and epistemology, in favour of a study of "rhetorical strategies" that are only rhetoric. None of this gives us leave to translate all historical knowledge into mere strategies of rhetoric or of "successful" impacts on a community of readers. It may, on the other hand, allow us *the additional resource* of tracing the witness of *successive communities of interpretation* in exploring and comparing multiple textual interactions with a stable *history of reception*. Hans Robert Jauss's utilization of H.-G. Gadamer's exposition of *Wirkungsgeschichte* in terms of the historical interpretations of texts against the background of *successive horizons of expectation*, each explored in the light of continuities or changes which preceded it, can assist in restoring what Kevin Vanhoozer calls "literary knowledge".[117]

Here the logical grammar of truth shifts again. This is truth that, in W. Pannenberg's phrase, "must prove itself anew".[118] Contrary to what might be inferred from Rorty's discussion of his work, Gadamer insists that temporal processes, with their mixture of continuities and changes, allow a "provocation" that impinges upon our prior horizons in such a way as to challenge and to transform "our prejudices".[119] Gadamer virtually repudiates the notion of "rhetorical man" when he writes, "To reach an understanding ... is not merely a matter of putting oneself forward and successfully asserting one's own point of view, but of being transformed ... We do not remain what we were."[120] In Jauss's reception theory we encounter reactualizations of texts not in community contexts

---

[115] S.W. Sykes and J.P. Clayton (eds), *Christ, Faith and History: Cambridge Studies in Christology* (Cambridge, 1972), esp. pp.1–38 (M.F. Wiles and P. Baelz).

[116] R. Alter, *The Art of Biblical Narrative* (New York, 1981), pp.147–54. Cf. W.A. Kort, *Story, Text and Scripture* (University Park, PA, 1988).

[117] H.R. Jauss, *Towards an Aesthetic of Reception* (Minneapolis, MN, 1982), esp. pp.3–45, 110–38; and *Aesthetic Experience and Literary Hermeneutics* (Minneapolis, MN, 1982).

[118] W. Pannenberg, 'What is Truth?', in *Basic Questions in Theology*, vol. 2 (London, 1971), p.8; cf. pp.1–27.

[119] Gadamer, *Truth and Method*, p.299.

[120] Gadamer, *Truth and Method*, p.379.

abstracted from traditions and deemed to be incommensurable but within a history of *continuities and discontinuities:* the transformative effects of texts operate in communities which share a *stable core of tradition while also embodying different social and theological contexts.* To illustrate: part of the "meaning" of 1 Cor. 2:6–16 may be explicated not solely or exclusively in the reconstruction of the worlds of Paul and of Corinth, but also in the shifts of hermeneutical agenda which led Basil the Great and Athanasius to address questions about the personhood and deity of the Holy Spirit, while Luther and Calvin let the text address epistemological questions concerning truth revealed by the Holy Spirit. In Jauss's reception history, the sequence of each agenda remains significant.

For our part, one particular value of paying attention to the post-history or reception-history of the text is to break the spell of the pragmatic futurology which treats present and potentially future communities as determinants of truth, while ignoring the larger horizon of truth disclosed through the continuities and discontinuities of a history and tradition of effects. But, as Lundin's analysis showed so clearly, this recognition does not fit well with the "new frontier" mentality of much American progressive theology that often gives less attention to tradition than to novelty. Gadamer's linkages between truth and *Wirkungsgeschichte, Bildung* and *phronēsis* may become lost in the concern for *technology* and how the present generation utilizes it to construct a future.[121]

Karl Rahner shares Gadamer's conviction that surrender to self-affirming, seductively assertive rhetoric will come to destroy reverence for truth, and to devalue its currency until it is perceived to be merely instrumental.[122] Rahner and Gadamer have the same profound concerns about the impact of propaganda and mass advertising in consumer-dominated societies: "What one has to exercise above all is the ear."[123] *A fortiori* the worlds of virtual reality and the social constructions of the Web and Internet provide models that may well generate even more pragmatic, instrumentalist scepticism. In this context David Ford insists that to refuse to surrender epistemology remains part of the public responsibility of theology. He quotes the axiom formulated by Samuel Taylor Coleridge: "He who begins by loving Christianity better than truth will proceed by loving his own sect or church better than Christianity, and end in loving himself better than all."[124]

At this point our distinction between the grammar of futurology and the grammar of Christian eschatology returns to re-enter the picture, together with the second part of our sixth thesis. For, against most trends in postmodernity/submodernity, Wolfhart Pannenberg insists that "the unity of truth is constituted only by the proleptic revelation of God in Jesus Christ".[125] He agrees that in history truth does not exist "as a finished product" in the abstract.[126] Nevertheless, eschatology combines the themes of the final judgement (the definitive verdict on a completed process); the new creation of resurrection (which displays both continuity and discontinuity with the old), and a link

---

[121] Gadamer, *Truth and Method*, pp.9–19, 277–306 and 340–79.
[122] Rahner, *Theological Investigations*, vol. 7 (London, 1971), pp.230–33.
[123] Gadamer, 'Philosophical Journey', p.17; cf. pp.3–63.
[124] David F. Ford, 'Epilogue', in Ford (ed.), *The Modern Theologians*, pp.721–2.
[125] Pannenberg, 'What is Truth?', p.27.
[126] Pannenberg, 'What is Truth?', p.21.

with the present not in terms of extrapolation but in terms of *adventus* and newness within a frame of divine faithfulness to promise.

On the subject of promise, many writers, in which I include myself, have argued that speech-acts of *promise* would collapse if we face only an unqualified textual indeterminacy. *If there is no specificity to a promise, it is not a promise.*[127] Further, if there is no temporal interval in which faithfulness to the promise can be maintained and finally effected, faithfulness *to promise* becomes logically empty. Pannenberg also clarifies a further logical distinction that limits the determinative role of *human wishes and needs.* He notes the different linguistic currencies of eschatological *promise* and eschatological *threat* or *warning.*[128] As if against Rorty, he argues that "we can understand the present precisely as fragmentary only in the light of our knowledge of its ultimate wholeness".[129] "The promise links our present ... to God's future, but at the same time keeps them apart".[130]

John Macquarrie argues that we should not simply sweep aside F.H. Bradley's insight that only the whole *as a whole* can be *wholly* true. Once we lose the unified vision of an eschatological final judgement and the goal of a completed new creation when this "whole" will become publicly transparent, the grammar of truth fragments into instrumental components locked into different (some say incommensurable) communities of contextual-pragmatic justification. Yet such a unifying vision of truth lies ahead as a theological entailment of divine new criterion. Macquarrie urges, "They do not freeze the question, but open up the possibility of new insights."[131] However, these "new" insights are more than merely "useful" insights. If the *truth* of Christian theology *draws its currency as an anticipation of God's final judgement and glory* in as far as these may be appropriated in the present (even if in fragmentary and provisional forms), then, as Jürgen Moltmann expresses it, *the functional, the utilitarian, the drive to achieve has no place*: "To glorify God means to love God *for his own sake,* and to enjoy God as he is in himself ... All moral purposes are excluded. *The praise of God has ... no utility ... The glorification of God has this in common with the child's self-forgetting delight in its game ... an echo of the Creator's good pleasure in the creations of his love*" (my italics).[132]

The grammar of truth and of divine promise brings us inevitably to the grammar of divine grace. Just as *truth* in theology has overarching unity of future vision, but is also instantiated in many everyday contexts in many contextual grammars, so grace, *charis*, is *"given" both* as "countless *charismata*" *and as "charis ...* life drawn from the fullness of God".[133] Where Moltmann speaks of the self-giving of the "fullness" of God, David Ford speaks of the subject-matter of theology as "the many-faceted richness" which comes ultimately from "the abundance of God".[134] Yet, if the logical grammar of grace entails the

[127] See Lundin, Thiselton and Walhout, *Promise of Hermeneutics,* esp. pp.209–39 (Thiselton); Pannenberg, *Systematic Theology,* vol. 2, p.202; vol. 3, pp.527–55; and Moltmann, *Coming of God,* pp.282–95.
[128] Pannenberg, *Systematic Theology,* vol. 3, p.541.
[129] Pannenberg, *Systematic Theology,* vol. 3, p.543.
[130] Pannenberg, *Systematic Theology,* vol. 3, p.545.
[131] J. Macquarrie, *Thinking about God* (London, 1975), p.25. Cf. F.H. Bradley, *Essays on Truth and Reality* (Oxford, 1914).
[132] Moltmann, *The Coming of God,* p.323 (my italics); cf. also pp.257–72, 308–39.
[133] Moltmann, *The Coming of God,* p.337.
[134] Ford, 'Epilogue', pp.720–21.

notion that, as our Conference title expresses it, the future is *"God's gift"*, it is difficult to see how this can fail to exclude any grammar of social pragmatism in which reality and truth become *wholly* human constructs and achievements.

To be sure, one alternative might be to abolish a theology of grace. However, what would then remain of Christian theology and Christian identity? Is not grace irreducible also in Judaism and other theistic religions? In Wittgenstein's simile that describes such an alternative, it would be to "saw off the branch on which I am sitting". *Giving,* Wittgenstein further observes, carries a *logical grammar of consequences*: "Why can't my right hand give my left hand money? My right hand can put it into my left hand. My right hand can write a deed of gift and my left hand a receipt. But the further practical consequences would not be those of a gift."[135] So what are the "consequences" of grace-gift in theology?

If we view positively the role of tradition, reception-history and *Wirkungsgeschichte* in theology, it may be logically possible to argue that corporate or structural grace to humankind filters through legacies of teaching, wisdom and practices of goodness and thereby may be inherited *through* others *from* God. Yet if Lundin's analysis of the antipathy towards tradition that may be found in American pragmatism carries conviction, this is not the kind of grammar that coheres with a progressivist account of human achievement.

By contrast, Karl Barth brings together coherently an understanding of *grace as God's self-imparting, (his gift of himself rather than of "religion"); his understanding of truth* in terms of God's readiness to be known where or when he wills, and covenantal promise as the guarantee *eschatological* consummation.[136] This should not be interpreted, with Robert Jenson, as "postmodern", except in the most simplistic sense.[137] For this perpetuates the mere equation of "postmodernity" with a rejection of the epistemology of Enlightenment rationalism or of the specific "basic beliefs" of so-called *classical* foundationalism (that is, that of Descartes, centred in the self). However, this does not demand that all truth-questions are disengaged from epistemological issues of any kind in all traditions of epistemology in, for example, Hebrew, Greek, Christian, Patristic, mediaeval and post-Hegelian thought.

Eschatology provides a paradigm case for Barth's emphasis on the distinction between divine grace and the capacities of the human self as such. The immortality of the soul, which is not part of biblical or Christian eschatology, presupposes some innate capacity of the self to survive death by virtue of who or what it is. The resurrection of the dead, by contrast, rests on a grammar of gracious new creation whereby God chooses to enact "a primal miracle, like the creation of the world" entailed in sharing in the dying-and-having-been-raised of Christ.[138] Barth's portrait of the issues at Corinth entirely captures this perspective in ways that cohere with our arguments about Paul and Corinth above. The Corinthians believe "in their own beliefs"; however, for Paul the source of truth is not

---

135 Wittgenstein, *Philosophical Investigations*, sect. 268.

136 Karl Barth, *Church Dogmatics* (14 vols, Edinburgh, 1957–75), I/1 sects 1, 4, 6, 7; II/2 sects 27, 32–9.

137 R.W. Jenson, 'Karl Barth', in Ford (ed.), *Modern Theologians*, p.22; cf. pp.21–36.

138 W. Künneth, *The Theology of the Resurrection* (London, 1965), p.39; cf. O. Cullmann, *Immortality of the Soul or Resurrection of the Dead* (London, 1958), p.55 and throughout.

the bringing of success and self-affirmation to a community. It is whether truth-claims will be shown to correspond to the definitive verdict of the last judgement (1 Cor. 4:5).[139]

Explicit connections in the New Testament between epistemology and eschatology are identified in the context of the grace of the cross by J. Louis Martyn. Martyn declares, "Paul's statements establish an inextricable connexion between eschatology and epistemology."[140] *Those who called themselves "spiritual people"* at Corinth had already pre-empted and utilized the contrast between "ordinary human knowledge" (knowing *kata sarka*) *and revealed "spiritual" knowledge* (knowing *kata pneuma*). However, for Paul, Martyn writes:

> The implied opposite of knowing *kata sarka* is not knowing *kata pneuma*, but rather knowing *kata stauron*. He who recognizes his life to be God's *gift* at the *juncture of the ages* recognizes also that until he is completely and exclusively in the new age, his knowing *kata pneuma* can occur only in the form of knowing *kata stauron*. For until the *parousia*, the cross is *and* remains *the* eschatological crisis.[141]

While Rorty's claim that truth is "not a goal of enquiry" has validity in one sense, such a view is profoundly mistaken and a distraction for theology in a more important sense. In as far as an eschatology of the last judgement identifies *truth* with a future verdict of God, the notion that truth is determined by what consumerist preferences dictate both remains incompatible with theism and especially with Christian eschatology, and carries self-defeating entailments which we have tried to identify above. On the other hand, "goal" should not be taken to imply a final resting-place. The God of the future remains living and active, and if we may venture to exercise imagination about whatever "Heaven" may denote, the heavenly life can hardly fail to be characterized by the creativity and livingness of God's own presence which makes "glory" an open-ended crescendo, not a full stop.

The grammar of resurrection as God's creative act also rests on grace. Our limited imaginations need not limit the open-ended glory. Luther writes of the resurrection mode of existence: "Be content to hear what *God will do. Then leave it to him what will become of it*" (my italics).[142] A theology for the year 2000 will explore further the dimensions of eschatological promise, but keeping the *grammar of grace and the nature and activity of God fully in view as that which grounds and shapes Christian eschatology*. It is no accident that Paul chooses to expound the inexhaustible versatility of God as the creator of richness and diversity in creation as the key to what the resurrection of somatic existence in all its fullness might entail (1 Cor. 15:35–44). This understanding of God as the ground of the resurrection fullness of life is not disengaged from epistemology: many Corinthians have missed the point *agnōsian gar theou tines echousin*: they lack *knowledge* (1 Cor. 15:34).

This coheres entirely with Martyn's juxtaposition of knowledge, eschatology and the cross. "*Knowledge" is inextricably bound up with respect, care and love for the other as "other"* as

---

139 K. Barth, *Resurrection*, p.18.

140 J.L. Martyn, 'Epistemology at the Turn of the Ages: 2 Cor. 5:16', in W.R. Farmer, C.F.D. Moule and R.R. Niebuhr (eds), *Christian History and Interpretation: Studies Presented to John Knox* (Cambridge, 1967), p.272; cf. pp.269–87.

141 Martyn, 'Epistemology', p.285.

142 Martin Luther, *Luther's Works*, vol. 28 (St Louis, MO, 1973), p.180 (my italics); also Luther, *WA* 36, p.647.

epitomized in the paradigm case of Jesus Christ as "the Man for others" (Bonhoeffer) and *"the Man for God"* (Barth). This qualifies Paul's ambivalence towards *gnōsis* throughout 1 Corinthians. If *gnōsis* facilitates concern on the part of "the strong" for "the weak", *knowledge* becomes a gift (within the grammar of grace) for which Paul can give genuine thanks to God (1 Cor. 1:5b). It does not follow that simply because Cartesian and Enlightenment rationalism had promoted certain theories of knowledge more appropriate for the natural sciences, theology should appeal to postmodern devaluations of *all* epistemologies as a constructive strategy. In conservative circles this is often seen as the quickest and easiest way of relegating all uses of historical-critical methods in Rorty's rubbish-disposal bin, to clear the decks for an agenda of uncritical community confessionalism. Yet, as Pannenberg urges, this disengages theology from any seriously critical capacity both to test its own truth-claims and to engage with other academic disciplines.

It is essential that a theology for the year 2000 should engage and interact with social sciences, philosophy, literary theory, linguistics, semiotics, cultural studies, art, critical theory and a host of other disciplines. I have gained immeasurably from collaborative work with colleagues in philosophy, linguistics, semantics, politics, literary theory and critical theory. Although the devaluing of epistemology allegedly comes from writers in certain other disciplines, especially literary and political deconstructionism, *the surrender of epistemological truth-claims disastrously hinders necessary interaction with the resources of other academic disciplines.* Why should any other discipline bother to spend time and energy with a community which can say little more than "this is our story: this is *what we do*"? At best, religious activities and texts become phenomena to be understood wholly within the terms of the methods used in other disciplines rather than capable of being understood on the basis of their own truth-claims, and such communities of faith could offer little in interactive return.

While some writers argue that such categories as "canon" or "story" are more faithful to theology than epistemology (as if these were alternatives), W. Jay Wood (1998) more constructively and convincingly argues that for theologians and others *epistemology takes its place as an intellectual virtue* of positive ethical as well as noetic currency.[143] For Jay Wood, however, epistemology entails tradition and wisdom as habits of mind; not simply "knowledge" construed in accordance with paradigms drawn from certain sciences or technologies. For Paul, to live out Christian identity, that is, that which instantiates the work of Christ, requires reflection on Christian tradition as part of a theological and moral responsibility. These considerations must also feature in a theology for the year 2000.

Above all, however, *theology concerns the God whose grace, presence, promise and new creation is itself inexhaustible.*[144] Theology for the year 2000 is stamped with this quality when we reflect that eschatological promise identifies grace, truth and promise with God himself. This promise points to the openness of a future that is boundless because "God will be all in all". Meanwhile the eschatology of both "now" and "then" permits the writer of the Fourth Gospel to declare that grace and truth may already be "seen" in Jesus Christ as the instantiation and embodiment of the Divine *logos* (John 1:14b).

---

[143] W.J. Wood, *Epistemology: Becoming Intellectually Virtuous* (Leicester, 1998), as against e.g. (also recently) W.J. Abraham, *Canon and Criterion in Christian Theology* (Oxford, 1998).

[144] Cf. Ford, 'Epilogue', pp.720–21.

CHAPTER THIRTY-THREE

"Postmodern" Challenges to Hermeneutics: "'Behind' and 'In Front Of' the Text – Language, Reference and Indeterminacy" (2001)

This essay was originally delivered as a Conference Paper for the Third International Symposium in the Scripture and Hermeneutics Seminar Series held in Ancaster, Canada, in June 2000. It was subsequently published in the Scripture and Hermeneutics Series, *volume 2,* After Pentecost: Language and Biblical Interpretation, *edited by Craig Bartholomew, Colin Greene and Karl Möller, and dedicated "for Professor Canon Anthony Thiselton on his retirement, in recognition of his work in biblical hermeneutics" (Carlisle: Paternoster and Grand Rapids, MI: Zondervan, 2001), pp.97–120.*

This essay rejects such polarized alternatives as referential versus non-referential, intra-linguistic versus extra-linguistic, and single, determinate, meaning versus indeterminate multiple meaning, at least in advance of exploring specific cases. Different genres function in varied ways, not least within the biblical writings. In many (but not all) instances of textual communicative action three integrated dimensions of meaning and understanding are operative, two of which are indicated in the title of this essay. Postmodern approaches rightly suspect that much language is non-representational, but traditional biblical scholarship rightly looks "behind" texts and resists a "docetic" reduction of meaning.

I
The Metaphorical Force of "Behind" and "In Front Of" in Hermeneutics

Most of us are familiar with the metaphor of "reading between the lines". It might well be taken as a description for the trained critical faculty of reading texts with a measure of both intuitive insight and political or theological suspicion that looks for a subtext concerning what the text or its author was genuinely "after". Such hermeneutical training characterizes a major goal or outcome in most professional or academic courses in biblical studies in universities or seminaries. To take a text at its face value can be misleading, certainly in such genre as mass advertising or in texts of political rhetoric.

The metaphor of "what lies behind it" identifies the critical approach that characterizes the suspicious stance of the detective who seeks to "understand" a situation that involves interpersonal or communicative inter-subjective events where one or more of the participants may have hidden motives or goals. These may be either consciously or unconsciously concealed. The historian and philosopher of history, R.G. Collingwood, identifies the difference between the less productive question "Did you murder the victim?" and the more fruitful one "What happened to the third button which seems to be torn from your jacket?" Both Gadamer in his philosophical hermeneutics and Bultmann in his theological hermeneutics write approvingly of Collingwood's attention to the "logic of question and answer". Gadamer insists, "Thus a person who wants to understand must question what lies behind what is said. He must understand it as an answer to a question. If we go back behind what is said, then we inevitably ask questions beyond what it said ... Almost the only person I find a link with here is R.G. Collingwood".[1]

The notion of reaching back "behind" the text arose, however, in a broader context and in close connection with a specific world-view in the era of the dawn of modern hermeneutical theory, in part in the eighteenth century but more especially in the early nineteenth century as the era of rationalism gave way to the era of Romanticism. In his search for "Correct Interpretation" (1742) Johann Martin Chladenius (1710–59) recognized that different people describe or write from different perspectives or view-points (*Sehe-Punkt*). A monarchist and a revolutionary may describe the same political event in different terms; even three spectators of a battle may report the event from different angles of view. Hence "behind" our understanding of the event must lie a recognition of the part played by perspective (*Sehe-Punkt*).[2] Only thus can we reach a "right" (*richtigen*) interpretation.

Chladenius is still writing, however, within a largely rationalist frame. With Friedrich Schleiermacher (1768–1834) and Philip August Boeckh (1785–1867) came an insight associated with the Romanticist movement and with Herder that not only "correct" understanding but also more personal "divinatory" or intuitive understanding of authors and text entailed the attempt to recapture the vision that prompted the author to write or to express the vision through some medium. "Understanding" (*Verstehen*) is not simply scrutinizing a text as an "object" of enquiry: it is more akin to listening to, and thereby coming to understand, a friend. The interpreter must step out of his or her own frame of reference and try to place himself or herself "in the position of the author".[3] I have urged elsewhere that to reduce Schleiermacher's hermeneutics to a system of mere genetic historical reconstruction does violence to the subtlety and complexity of Schleiermacher's carefully nuanced and dialectical work.[4] On the other hand Schleiermacher did define the role of "New Testament Introduction" as a necessary way

---

[1] H.-G. Gadamer, *Truth and Method* (2nd Eng. edn, London: Sheed & Ward, 1989), p.370. Cf. R. Bultmann, *History and Eschatology* (Edinburgh: Edinburgh University Press, 1957), p.130; and R.G. Collingwood, *An Autobiography* (Oxford: OUP, 1939), and *The Idea of History* (Oxford: Clarendon Press, 2nd edn, 1946).

[2] J.M. Chladenius, *Einleitung zur richtigen Auslegung vernünftiger Reden und Schriften* (1742; rp. Düsseldorf: Stern, 1969, sects 308 and 312.

[3] F.D.E. Schleiermacher, *Hermeneutics. The Handwritten Manuscripts* (ed. by H Kimmerle, Eng., Missoula, MT: Scholars Press, 1977), pp.112–13. See also the new revised edition, F. Schleiermacher, *Hermeneutics and Criticism, and Other Writings* (ed. by Andrew Bowie, New York: CUP, 1999).

[4] A.C. Thiselton, *New Horizons in Hermeneutics. The Theory and Practice of Transforming Biblical Reading* (Carlisle: Paternoster and Grand Rapids, MI: Zondervan, 1992 [First printing also London: HarperCollins]), pp.204–55, 474–6 and 558–64.

of reaching behind the text to "understand" similarities, differences, genre, motivations and goals that the text presupposed.[5]

Schleiermacher's younger contemporary, Philip August Boeckh, whom Schleiermacher also taught in Berlin, emphasized still more strongly that to reach through "behind" the text provided clues to reach an understanding of the subject-matter which might even surpass the conscious awareness and explicit formulations of the author.[6] Both writers had in view not antiquarian research for its own sake, but the deployment of historical research precisely for the sake of reaching the fullest possible understanding on the part of the present generation. Many considered, and some still consider, that Boeckh's *Encyclopedia and Methodology of the Philological Sciences* represents a paradigm of the classical-humanist model of hermeneutics.

Nevertheless a reaction against this approach took place with the rise of literary and linguistic formalism that captured attention especially in the United States and Russia from the 1930s to the 1950s. Some of its origins sprang from the Russian formalism of the Moscow Linguistic Circle of the 1920s, especially from Roman Jakobson's approach to language as a virtually self-contained linguistic system. In turn, the notion of "meaning" as a product generated by "differences" within the linguistic or semiotic system, which took the form of semiotic "forces", drew on the work of Ferdinand de Saussure's *Course in General Linguistics*, published in 1913. Under the pressures of Stalinism Jakobson moved to Prague, where the Prague School approached "meaning" as the interplay of linguistic forces within the text itself. Questions about origins and authors appeared to import intrusive questions about human emotions, agencies and actions that allegedly distorted the pure world of linguistic "science", even if Schleiermacher had insisted that understanding and hermeneutics was an "art".

In the West this formalist, systemic emphasis set in motion what became known in the early 1940s as "the new criticism". This term appears to have originated in John C. Ransom's work *The New Criticism* (1941). The "literariness" of linguistic and poetic forces took the centre of the stage. By the end of this decade René Wellek and Austin Warren wrote *Theory of Literature* (1949), which became hugely dominant as a textbook for literary theory in America for the next twenty years. In particular these authors dismissed the emphasis associated with Boeckh on the author and the author's intention "quite mistaken ... The total meaning ... cannot be defined merely in terms of its meaning for the author and his contemporaries".[7] In the same vein, William Wimsatt and Monroe Beardsley specifically attacked what they termed "The Intentional Fallacy" (1954).[8] Two slogans which emerged from such an attack took the form of "The Text and Nothing But the Text" and "The Autonomy of the Text". The text was seen as an autonomous world of literary, poetic, linguistic, semantic, stylistic and semiotic forces.

---

⁵ Schleiermacher, *Hermeneutics*, p.38; cf. further, pp.107 and 113.

⁶ P.A. Boeckh, *On Interpretation and Criticism* (Eng., Norman, OK: University of Oklahoma Press, 1968; longer German *Enzyklopädie und Methodologie der philologischen Wissenschaften*, 2nd edn, Leipzig: Teubner, 1886).

⁷ R. Welleck and A. Warren, *Theory of Literature* (London: Penguin, 1973 [1949]), p.42.

⁸ W.K. Wimsatt and M. Beardsley, "The Intentional Fallacy", in W.K. Wimsatt, *The Verbal Icon: Studies in the Meaning of Poetry* (New York: Noonday Press, 1966 [1954]), also in D.D. Molina (ed.), *On Literary Intention* (Edinburgh: Edinburgh University Press, 1976), pp.1–13.

The metaphor of reaching "behind" the text now seemed to have become overtaken by a preoccupation with the world "within" the text. Biblical studies inevitably continued for a time with its traditional classical-humanist model, although in due course the dividends of an approach which could prove its worth specifically for some narrative and poetic texts began to make an impact, especially in Old Testament studies of these genres. The problems which arose from a move away from the more traditional model did not fully emerge until some biblical specialists who had been trained in literary studies adopted the view that formalism, the new criticism and the genetic "fallacy" began to accord to a phrase or fashion the status of a hermeneutical dogma. A number of otherwise respected biblical scholars began to suggest that we now needed a so-called "paradigm shift" from history to literature. Little attention was given to the fact that Ransom, Wellek and Warren, and most of the "new" critics were concerned with those specific literary and poetic devices and forces which genuinely shed light on texts of a particular genre. We may suggest, by way of example, that to view the Book of Jonah as a virtually self-contained satire on incoherent self-centred theoretical theistic belief is more "to the point" than speculating about its possible authorship and origins. However, to fail to look "behind" the text of 1 Corinthians, or "behind" as well as "within" the world of the Gospels would fatally detach text from the extra-textual world of reality as well as missing nuances about Corinth and Paul, or about Jerusalem and Galilee, which are fundamental for understanding.

In due course of time, even literary theorists came to recognize that the notion of an "autonomous" text is an illusion. Its supposed "scientific objectivity" is deceptive and false. At one level, it cannot be detached from the world of human life and reality; at another level, as Chladenius had urged in 1742, the perspective (*Sehe-Punkt*) of readers plays a serious role in determining what counts as significant in viewing a supposedly autonomous text. Hence linguistic and semiotic structuralism collapsed into post-structuralism and formalism collapsed, in effect, into reader-response theory. Thus Wolfgang Iser drew upon Roman Ingarden (and ultimately Husserl) for the view that readers "complete" what counts as "the text" by "filling in" presuppositions and assumptions that are not explicitly "given". Iser regarded the text (in practice more faithfully to Saussure than many who claimed his patronage) as merely potentially meaningful until readers appropriated, completed and "actualized" it. Iser writes, "The text represents a potential effect that is realized in the reading process."[9] "Actualization" results from "interaction" between the text and the reader.[10]

In biblical studies it was eventually recognized that such an emphasis accorded well with the hermeneutical strategy that Jesus employed in the telling of those parables which projected a narrative-world in which the listener or reader was either gently seduced or abruptly provoked into an active response. Only provocation into a sense of outrage at "injustice" on the part of a listener to the Parable of the Labourers in the Vineyard (Matt. 20:1–15) could convey the full meaning of the privilege and affront of

---

[9] W. Iser, *The Act of Reading: A Theory of Aesthetic Response* (Baltimore, MD: Johns Hopkins University Press, 1978), p.ix.

[10] Iser, *Act of Reading*, p.21.

sheer grace: "Do you begrudge my generosity?" (v. 15). Indeed it became apparent that the evangelists sometimes arranged their sequence of narrative material to provoke their readers into active response. Only the sense of puzzlement about the disciples' dullness of understanding and expectation in the feeding miracle of Mark 8:1–10 when it follows the parallel miracle of Mark 6:30–44 could provoke readers to see (along with the Gospel narrator) the limitations of the kind of Christology reached by the disciples.[11]

We need not pursue the subsequent history of reader-response theory. In Umberto Eco it is applied constructively to "open", "productive", or "literary" texts, with a judicious recognition that other texts may be of different kinds, and may perform communicative functions of a more "closed" or determinate nature.[12] In Stanley Fish this approach is taken to an untenable extreme, which leaves very serious communicative and epistemological difficulties, and has affinities with the neo-pragmatic postmodernist world-view of Richard Rorty.[13]

The positive point that has emerged in broad terms is that the relation between the text and the present reader(s) has rightly become an increasing focus of attention. This has consistently constituted a concern for Paul Ricoeur, among others. His early aphorism "The symbol gives rise to thought" at once focuses upon the issue of effects.[14] In his masterly three-volume *Time and Narrative* he retains his life-long concern about "meaning-effects".[15] In contrast to the classical-humanist focus (Boeckh, Schleiermacher, Collingwood) of reading "behind" the text and equally in contrast to any formalist world (Ransom, Wellek and Warren) "within" the text, writers on hermeneutics have come to describe this concern with what the act of reading sets going or effects (Iser, Eco, Ricoeur) as that which is "in front of" the text. (In practice, Schleiermacher also showed some concern for this, as we have argued in the study already cited above.)

In a textbook on this subject W. Randolph Tate explicitly organizes his discussion around these three metaphors. He calls these prepositions terms that denote respectively the three "worlds" of textual interpretation, and argues rightly and convincingly that what is needed is an "integrated" approach which takes all three fully into account, in their distinct but complementary roles. Only this "integrated" interpretation can be fully adequate, fully responsible, and in the end, valid.[16] Yet this leads on to further questions about the relation

---

[11] Expounded in Robert Fowler, *Loaves and Fishes: the Function of the Feeding Stories on the Gospel of Mark* (Chicago, IL: Scholars Press, 1981), esp. pp.83–96. (This issue of strategy is not dependent on Fowler's form-critical theories.)

[12] Discussed in Thiselton, *New Horizons*, pp.524–9.

[13] The anti-theistic implications of this neo-pragmatism are well identified in Kevin Vanhoozer, *Is There a Meaning in This Text? The Bible, the Reader, and the Morality of Literary Knowledge* (Grand Rapids, MI: Zondervan, 1998), pp.55–62, 168–74; cf. Thiselton, *New Horizons*, pp.540–50, and also "Signs of the Times: Towards a Theology for the Year 2000 as a Grammar of Grace, Truth and Eschatology in Contexts of So-Called Postmodernity" (Presidential Paper of the Society for the Study of Theology) in D. Fergusson and M. Sarot (eds), *The Future as God's Gift: Explorations in Christian Eschatology* (Edinburgh: T. & T. Clark, 2000), pp.9–39.

[14] Paul Ricoeur, *The Conflict of Interpretations* (Evanston, IL: Northwestern University Press, 1974), p.288.

[15] P. Ricoeur, *Time and Narrative* (Eng., 3 vols, Chicago, IL: University of Chicago Press, 1984–88), vol. 1, p.ix.

[16] W. Randolph Tate, *Biblical Interpretation: an Integrated Approach* (Peabody, MA: Hendrickson, 1991), pp.xv–xxi, 173–212, and throughout.

between texts and the extra-linguistic world or extra-textual reality which lies beyond the text and to which the text may point, or which the text may presuppose. This confronts us with a fourth approach to textuality, namely with claims nurtured by a postmodern climate that texts are not "representational" at all. Indeed "determinacy" of meaning, it may be claimed, remains tenable only if the classical-humanist model is retained, which would become problematic within many strands of postmodernity.

II
Why is There Dissatisfaction with Representational or Referential Accounts of Texts and Language?

The present issue is beset with confusions. A first confusion arises because while it is right to recognize that some poems or complex literary works of art do not primarily draw their meaning from how they refer to persons, events, or objects in the external world, it does not thereby follow that any referential account of language and meaning has therefore become untenable. Yet many see the latter as a linguistic doctrine, demanded by the former observation. It would be a mistake to invoke the Saussaurean notion of "difference" within a linguistic system as an alternative to theories of reference and representation. In general linguistics the phenomenon of deixis reveals that in certain contexts extensive definition cannot be avoided. Deictic words include such instances as you, me, here, that one there, and next Tuesday, and the attention given by linguisticians to deixis suggests that these mechanisms are by no means trivial.

Ironically, in view of the contrast in Heidegger and Wittgenstein between *saying* (that is, stating) and *showing*, historically referential deixis derives from the Greek *deiknumi*, I show, although the cognate noun *deigma* means both a thing shown and a specimen or instantiation.[17] In short, the claim that referential and representational theories of meaning are flawed does not follow logically from the proposition that such theories of meaning fail to provide a comprehensive account of the relation between language and meaning.

The postmodern tendencies to undervalue any referential or representational account of language are often derived from the Kantian principle that all knowledge of all truth-claims is decisively conditional by prior categories of the mind which shape perception and construe cognition. A second stage emerges largely from the legacy of Fichte that ends in social constructionism. A third step arises from Nietzsche's contention that there are no "givens", but only interpretations.[18] The fourth and final part of the journey comes with Rorty's attempt to give a supposedly positive spin to "relativism" by substituting the terms "local" or "ethnocentric" in order to disguise this fourth step as a modest disengagement from larger truth-claims in favour of allegedly humbler claims about "my"

---

[17] Heidegger argues that *Zeigen*, showing "subverts" (*umwerfen*) referential and representational language (*sage*), *On the Way to Language* (Eng., New York: Harper & Row, 1971), pp.47, 107; cf. "The Nature of Language", ibid., pp.57–108; see also L. Wittgenstein, *Tractatus Logico-Philorophicus* (Eng. and Germ., London: Routledge, 1961), 5.6, 6.522 and 5.4–7.

[18] F. Nietzsche, *Complete Works* (Eng., 18 vols, London: Allen & Unwin, 1909–13), *vol 15. The Will to Power ii*, aphorism 481, "All that exists consists of *interpretations*" (his italics).

world, even if this has the effect in following Protagoras in rendering "my world" as the neo-pragmatic criterion of all other claims to truth. Yet to turn this supposed promotion of the relative or (as Rorty prefers it) "the local" into a universalizing "rubbish-disposal" exercise (Rorty's language again) constitutes a seduction of promoting a sweeping-aside of all referential or representational theory under the pretence of arguing on the basis of local contextual criteria from community to community.[19] In truth, a carefully "local" understanding would at once accommodate the referential theory, as Wittgenstein did, as applicable to "the circumscribed region" of Wittgenstein's builders.[20]

Yet the attack on anti-representationalism can reflect an equally misguided mirror image when a proponent of the opposite view seeks to reinstate reference and representation, as well as single determinate meanings, to contexts in language that they simply fail to fit. In spite of my immense admiration for Kevin Vanhoozer's *Is There a Meaning in This Text?* I find an over-readiness to ask whether rather than when defences and attacks concerning reference and determinate meaning are theologically constructive or destructive.[21] It tends to demote the importance of non-referential, non-representational language if we resort to suggesting that the grossly over-simple, over-general, exhausted distinction between meaning and significance, could serve as a panacea for all hermeneutical headaches by the revered E.D. Hirsch. Hirsch's attempts to revitalize the humanist model of language contained much of value, but unfortunately his conceptual and semiotic tools were too dated and general to address fully the complexities and nuances of the "postmodern" world.

To begin from elementary common-sense examples drawn from the biblical writings, Jesus told parables precisely to draw hearers and audience into the process of working out meaning, force and application. As Wittgenstein, once again, urged, it is the application of a piece of language in which meaning and understanding, as a communicative act or process, reside; not some second-level category distanced and demoted into mere connotation or resonance by the term "significance" in contrast to meaning. The parables of the Old Testament (Nathan to David, 2 Sam. 12:1–10) and of Jesus himself provide a prototype of what Kierkegaard would call indirect communication addressed to the will for decision, and what Wolfgang Iser would term reader-response in the sense of the reader's filling in what was needed to actualize the potential communicative event. The issue of how precisely the communicative "sender" encodes the genetic instructions for the transmission of the encoded message was helpfully described by J. Lotman and by Umberto Eco in terms of the degree to which a text was produced as "open" or "closed".[22] Bible translators are utterly familiar with this

---

[19]   R. Rorty, *Truth and Progress: Philosophical Papers*, vol. 3 (Cambridge: CUP, 1998), p.10; cf. pp.1–10, 19–42 and 153–65.

[20]   L. Wittgenstein, *Philosophical Investigations* (Germ. and Eng., Oxford: Blackwell, 2nd edn, 1967), sects 1–3 and 27.

[21]   K. Vanhoozer, *Is There a Meaning in This Text?* (Grand Rapids, MI: Zondervan, 1998), esp. pp.76–86 and 246–65.

[22]   U. Eco, *A Theory of Semantics* (Bloomington, IN: Indiana University Press, 1976), pp.136–9; also *Semantics and the Philosophy of Language* (London: Macmillan, 1984), pp.68–86; *The Role of the Reader: Explorations in the Semiotics of Texts* (London: Hutchinson, 1981), pp.4–33; and J. Lotman, *The Structure of the Artistic Text* (Eng., Ann Arbor, MC: University of Michigan Press, 1997).

contrast in dealing with metaphor. "The moon shall be turned to blood" (Acts 2:20) has all the power, energy and ambivalence of apocalyptic. The insipid "and the moon blood-red" (*Twentieth-Century New Testament* version) tries to "close" the meaning on behalf of a puzzled reader and thereby emasculates the apocalyptic.

This brings us to our second category. Metaphor, no less than parable, relies on something more than a single determinate meaning and a referential account of language. Paul Ricoeur builds upon the interactive model of Max Black whereby metaphor is more than substitution, more than vivid embellishment, and more than the added sum of two referential propositions. Even if we reduce metaphor to plainer simile, "my love is like a red, red rose", means more than the mathematical sum of the attributes of love and red roses. Nor is it a rose-like love with enhanced but unstated significance. Multiple meaning and inter-textual allusion conspire to produce a semantic richness to which a hermeneutic of understanding must do justice.[23]

A third category is the variation of hermeneutical agenda which even an historical author may envisage as situated within the boundaries of a spectrum of "implied" or "ideal" readers. In spite of the once fashionable but now surely discredited trend of dismissing notions of authorial intention as depending on what some formalists had called "the intentional fallacy", even the language of literary theorists about "the implied reader" or "ideal" reader reintroduced through the back door the notion of an authorial will or decision (rightly underlined by Kevin Vanhoozer and Nicholas Wolterstorff). This has in view a so-called target readership or target audience whose specific values, needs, assumptions and horizons the author held in view in the production of the text. The implied reader, Powell and others observe, is "the reader presupposed by the text".[24] Malbon speaks of an "intended readership".[25] Yet, on the other side, can Scripture address only the immediately implied readers? Has 1 Corinthians 2 nothing to communicate to twenty-first century philosophers seeking to understand the conceptual grammar of revelation, or a university class discussing the personhood and deity of the Holy Spirit?

Here the work of Hans-Robert Jauss, among others, becomes instructive.[26] On one side he accepts the importance of a given tradition of continuity of interpretation that suggests constraints beyond which interpretation becomes idiosyncratic or irresponsible. Meaning is not grossly indeterminate and unbounded. Nevertheless, hermeneutical agenda are not simply replicated from era to era. New questions and new thought-forms arise in relation to which new paradigms exhibit both continuity and discontinuity as traditions of interpretation expand. This is far from the "local" contextual pragmatism of Rorty and

---

23 P. Ricoeur, *The Rule of Metaphor* (Eng., Toronto: University of Toronto Press, 1977), esp pp.6–24; *Time and Narrative* (3 vols, Chicago, IL: University of Chicago Press, 1984–88), eg vol. 3, p.101.

24 M.A. Powell, *What is Narrative Criticism?* (London: SPCK, 1993), p.20.

25 E.S. Malbon, "Narrative Criticism: How Does the Story Mean?", in J.E. Anderson and J.D. Moore (eds), *Mark and Method: New Approaches in Biblical Studies* (Minneapolis: Fortress, 1992), pp.27–8; cf. pp.23–49.

26 H.-R. Jauss, *Literaturgeschichte als Provokation* (Frankfurt: Suhrkamp, 1970); *Toward an Aesthetic of Reception* (Eng., Minneapolis, MN: University of Minnesota Press, 1982); "Paradigmawechsel in der Literaturwissenschaft", *Linguistische Berichte* 3 (1969), pp.44–56; discussed in my chapters in R. Lundin et al., *The Promise of Hermeneutics* (Grand Rapids, MI: Eerdmans, 1999), pp.191–208.

Fish. Nevertheless it challenges the notion that biblical interpretation is nothing but the endlessly wooden replication of "a single determinate meaning". In my view the most constructive recent development in biblical studies has been that of scattered attempts to offer a *Wirkungsgeschichte* of exegetical issues; that is, a critical account of how the reception of biblical texts has in turn shaped the agenda and pre-understanding of the next generation to be addressed by the text. This is not to be reduced to the mere "history of interpretation" which is historical and descriptive rather than hermeneutical and creatively critical. Yet few, to date, have explored this area in more than a very basic way. U. Luz describes the *Wirkungsgeschichte* of the exegesis of Matthew as "history, reception and actualising of a text in media other than commentary, e.g. in sermons, canon law, hymns, art and in the actions ... of the church".[27]

The significant point for our purposes is that the choice between (1) a single determinate meaning based on reference and representation, and (2) a radical indeterminacy that sweeps aside reference and representation provides a contrived, artificial and misleading alternative. In concrete terms, Paul's specific communicative action in 1 Corinthians 2 hinges on redefinition and "code-switching" about what counts as being "a spiritual person" at Corinth. In my commentary I have argued in detail that whereas many at Corinth applied to themselves the designation "spiritual people" in a way which appeared to invite "recognition" and to enhance their status in the eyes of others, Paul himself insists that the nature of authentic "spirituality" is a Christomorphic experience of the transformative work of the Holy Spirit, as evidenced and tested by conformity with the criterion of the proclamation of the cross. There is nothing "status-enhancing" about identification with a crucified Christ (1 Cor. 1:18–25; 2:1–5; 3:1–3; 4:8–13; 12:1–3; 13; and corresponding pages in my commentary, including pp.900–989. "Code-switching" is discussed in *The First Epistle*, pp.43, 325–26, 396, 587, 996, and elsewhere. See further, below.) However, this is not to exclude the possibility of layered meanings when Basil and Athanasius asked about entailments for the personhood and deity of the Holy Spirit, or when Luther and Calvin enquired about the transformative implications of communicative action initiated by the Holy Spirit. This is more than a matter of "significance", but does not invite all and sundry to "complete" whatever meaning arises from any kind of agenda.

This brings us to the title assigned to this essay. What occurs "in front of" the text, that is, what it sets going, its "influence, history, reception, actualisation ..." (Luz) is not a self-generated process, as if the text were reduced to a unit of semiotic or literary production. Here I not only endorse Vanhoozer's concerns about the theological and anti-theological implications of such views, I go further: such views relate too often to an egalitarian politics which reduces the status of the author to that of another co-reader; further, it

---

[27] One of the very few examples is Ulrich Luz, *Das Evangelium nach Matthäus* (3 of 4 vols, Zurich: Benziger [Evangelisch-Katholischer Kommentar zum NT], 1989, 1990, 1997); see Introduction, sect. 6; W. Schrage, *Der erste Brief an die Korinther* (3 vols of 4 to date, same publisher and series, 1992, 1996, 1999) is more "historical". I have attempted to treat selected passages in my *The First Epistle to the Corinthians: A Commentary on the Greek Text* (Grand Rapids, MI: Eerdmans [NIGTC] and Carlisle: Paternoster, 2000). Esp. pp.196–204, 276–86, 330–44, 479–82, 531–40, 658–61, 998–1026, 1306–14. Changes of agenda within the Patristic, mediaeval and Reformation eras provide the most telling material.

borders upon a mechanistic account of a theory of literary texts which attempts to eradicate such irreducibly personal features as will, purpose, aim, goal, intent, exchange for such mechanistic and market categories as production, effect and criteria of what-is within a prior socially constructed world. In a world where everything has become socially constructed as media-shaped virtual reality, it no longer makes sense to return to the language that assumes that the agency of a personal voice any longer "makes a difference". It is precisely at this point that Vanhoozer's 1998 work comes into its own (if we may hesitate over its neat polarities, over-exclusive alternatives, and uniformly triadic patterns to be correlated with Trinitarian modes of action).

III

Does Drawing Distinctions between Worlds *Behind* the Text and *In Front Of* the Text Still Retain Some Value?

Like most creative metaphors these terms served to open up a new understanding of valid hermeneutical distinctions when they were first employed by Ricoeur and others, but like "paradigm", "postmodernity", "incommensurability" and "non-foundationalist", these become thinned, flattened and discoloured by overuse, and we may hope for their replacement by a less sullied currency in due course. The world "behind" the text does not merely relate to its genetic origin or even to the historical world and value-system inhabited by the author. It is a gross over-simplification of F. Schleiermacher's hermeneutics to attribute to him, as is regularly done, the view that interpretation is simply and exclusive the converse of composition, in which the goal is to trace the originating circumstances. I have pointed out elsewhere that Schleiermacher was sufficiently sophisticated to note that an emphasis on cause, effect, genre, vision, or goal depends largely on strategic decisions about what specific questions are being addressed within hermeneutical agenda. As Vanhoozer implies, the "world" behind the text has links with whether or how a "control" or "directedness" may be said to characterize a text apart from its perception and reception by successive audiences.[28]

As long ago as 1946 Wimsatt and Beardsley speak of a world "beyond [the author's] power to intend ... or control ..."; even the "dramatic speaker" who sets the textual effects in motion at the moment of its recital articulates the text's "autonomy" with greater privilege than the forgotten author.[29] This reflects not simply a literary overreaction against origination in Romanticism, but also a liberal political overreaction against control on the part of authority-figures of status or learning. The liberal pseudo-rationalism against which Gadamer protests together with the individual's "autonomy" and a doctrine of progressivist social construction leads to the levelling-down of all tradition and authority to "one of us". Hence Gadamer argues for "the rehabilitation of authority and tradition" in the light of the fallibility and finitude of individual subjective consciousness.[30]

---

[28] Vanhoozer, *Is There a Meaning in This Text?*, pp.48–90 and 229–59.

[29] W.K. Wimsatt and M.C. Beardsley, "The Intentional Fallacy", (1946) rp. in Wimsatt and Beardsley, *The Verbal Icon* (Lexington, KY: University of Kentucky Press, 1954 and London: Methuen, 1970), pp.4–18.

[30] H.-G. Gadamer, *Truth and Method* (2nd Eng. edn, London: Sheed & Ward, 1989), pp.270–300.

Undeniably, these overreactions rest on half-truths. The "sender" alone does not complete the whole communicative act. Textual actualization entails author or personal sources, code, content, contact, context, and reception, appropriation, application, or understanding on the part of implied readers, addressees, or actual readers. In Christian theology the definitive givenness of Scripture remains both authoritative and potential in meaning on the ground that the same Holy Spirit who inspired the agents who wrote will also inspire the prophets, teachers, congregations and seekers who read. In this sense the creativity of the Holy Spirit who gives organic birth and life rather than mechanistic replication confirms Schleiermacher's insistence that hermeneutics and understanding constitutes a creative art, not a science.[31] Like the gift of manna, it is received anew day-by-day, not stored and siphoned off in mechanistic packages.

Many theorists who have not become obsessed with the "postmodern turn" now emphasize an "integrated" hermeneutics. In spite of its "text-book" level of writing, W. Randolph Tate's *Biblical Interpretation* provides a useful unintimidating, modest example. His three main parts are headed *"author-centred* (with attention directed to the world behind the text); *text-centred* (with the focus on the world within the text, or the textual world); and *reader-centred* (where the spotlight is trained upon the world in front of the text, or the reader's world)" (Tate's italics).[32] "This model of communication sets the agenda."[33] Nevertheless a survey of the contents demonstrates that these three "worlds" remain inseparable. Is such textual phenomena as the distinction between, for example, narrative, poetry and prophecy simply a textual "property", or does it not equally reflect an act of decision, direction and purpose on the part of the writer?[34]

In the context of Christian theology this principle becomes transparent. In the case of catechetical instruction concerning the Two Ways, or doctrinal affirmation concerning the *kerygma* of the crucifixion of Jesus of Nazareth, such formula as γνωρίζω δὲ ὑμῖν ... τὸ εὐαγγέλιον ὃ εὐηγγελισάμην ὑμῖν, ὃ καὶ παρελάβετε, ἐν ᾧ καὶ ἑστήκατε, δι᾽ οὗ καὶ σώζεσθε (1 Cor. 15:1–2) cannot make sense unless they are referential and representational, even if they also generate deeply affective and volitional implicates and resonances. This is confirmed by 15:3: παρέδωκα γὰρ ὑμῖν ἐν πρώτοις ὃ καὶ παρέλαβον ὅτι χριστὸς ἀπέθανεν ... . As Anders Eriksson convincingly and incisively argues, Paul uses shared pre-Pauline traditions as "rhetorical proofs": "Traditions constitute agreed upon premises which are the starting-point for argumentation."[35] Eriksson acknowledges, with literary theorists and postmodern interpreters that even argument can have diverse, multiple rhetorical effects upon an audience (that is, the argument behind and in text generates a pluralism "in front" of it). However, this raises the issue of redefinition and code-switching.

---

[31] F.D.E. Schleiermacher, *Hermeneutics. The Handwritten Manuscripts* (Eng., Missoula, MT: Scholars Press 1977 [ed. H Kimmerle]), pp.100–105; discussed in A.C. Thiselton, *New Horizons in Hermeneutics*, pp.218–21, 558–62. Gadamer goes further here, although Ricoeur emphasizes both creative art and constraining criticism.

[32] W. Randolph Tate, *Biblical Interpretation: An Integrated Approach* (Peabody, MA: Hendrickson, 1991), p.xvi.

[33] Ibid., p.xx; respectively pp.1–58; 59–142; 143–212.

[34] Ibid., pp.74–106.

[35] A. Eriksson, *Traditions as Rhetorical Proof. Pauline Argumentation in 1 Corinthians* (Stockholm: Almqvist & Wiksell, 1998), p.3.

Most up-to-date interpreters of 1 Corinthians acknowledge that the Corinthians (or many of them) have a different view from that of Paul about what constitutes, or counts as, being "a 'spiritual' person". Paul does not at this point shrug his shoulders and say, "Well, 'spiritual' for your peer-group of addressees is how you define it." He insists on employing allusive or referential criteria which ground the definition (meaning) of "spiritual persons", "people led by the Holy Spirit" in terms of the crucified Christ and the cross. He insists that only a cruciform definition or meaning of "spiritual" is valid. A.C. Wire's argument (in her view in criticism of Paul) that Corinth understands with freedom while Paul seeks to speak with authority carries some force.[36] Thus "redefinition" or "code-switching" applies to the contrast between wisdom and folly in 1:18: Paul transposes the wisdom–folly contrast as it is understood by many at Corinth by "reversal" and by correlating the former (as they understand it) with self-destruction, and the latter (as they understand it) as effective, operative, saving power.[37]

The same principle of redefinition and code-switching occurs in 1:26, where claims to "high status" become redefined and reversed in the light of the cross. Honour–shame and grounds for "glory" are redefined in terms of sharing the status of a humiliated Messiah, not triumphalism of a social or religious nature.[38] Such redefinition is an "affront" to many. In 2:5–16 Paul borrows the Corinthian sloganizing about *pneuma* and *pneumatikos* to redefine and subvert it in accordance with Christ and the cross as the source of "spiritual" transformation. "Spirituality" means more than "religious experience".[39] Twenty-seven years ago I called attention to "persuasive definition" in the contrasts between the meaning of "flesh" and "spiritual" between Paul and his addressees in 3:1–5 and 5:1–5.[40]

How can so much hang upon a rhetoric of redefinition and a strategy of code-switching if in the world behind the text a single meaning is not at issue, and also deemed to be communicated as textual effect to the audience? We cannot impose the "doctrine" of a literary theory upon the particularities of exegesis and also logical analysis. Recently Garrett Green distinguished between postmodernity as a cultural description of society and "normative" or "doctrinaire" postmodernity which is actually "a philosophical doctrine".[41]

Nevertheless other biblical texts reflect a "world behind the text" where double meaning or multiple meaning or even indeterminate meaning plays a role. In Hebrew the introduction of poetic meter sometimes (not always) gives a cue for such "play" of language. If God is more than an existent object within the world, such poetic creative

---

36 A.C. Wire, *The Corinthian Women Prophets* (Minneapolis, MN: Fortress, 1990).

37 Ulrich Wilckens, *Weisheit und Torheit* (Tübingen: Mohr, 1959), pp.5–41 and 205–24; W. Schrage, *Der erste Brief an die Korinther* I, pp.165–92; J.D. Moores, *Wrestling with Rationality in Paul* (Cambridge: CUP, 1995), pp.5–32, esp. pp.24–8 (on code-switching) and 132–8.

38 S.M. Pogoloff, *Logos and Sophia. The Rhetorical Situation of 1 Corinthians* (Atlanta, GA: Scholars Press, 1992), pp.113–27; 153–72; 197–216.

39 R.A. Horsley, "Pneumatikos vs Psychikos: Distinctions of Spiritual Status among the Corinthians", *HTR* 69 (1976), pp.269–88. B.A. Pearson, *The Pneumatikos-Psychikos Terminology in 1 Corinthians* (Missoula, MT: Scholars Press, 1973); P. Lampe, "Theological Wisdom and the 'Word about the Cross': The Rhetorical Scheme in 1 Cor 1-4", *Int* 44 (1990), pp.17–31.

40 A.C. Thiselton, "The Meaning of σάρξ in 1 Cor. 5:5: A Fresh Approach in the Light of Logical and Semantic Factors", *SJT* 26 (1973), pp.204–28 [Essay 11 above].

41 Garrett Green, *Theology, Hermeneutics and Imagination* (Cambridge: CUP, 2000), p.9.

hymnic form as "Holy, holy, holy is the Lord of hosts; the whole earth is fully of his glory" (Isa. 6:3) transcends representational, referential "single" meaning. In Tillich's use of the term, we enter the realm of double-edged symbol, which opens up both reality and our own selfhood. It is not for nothing that Ricoeur and Derrida focus largely on Job and on apocalyptic. A referential understanding of the Book of Revelation becomes, in George Caird's phrase, an attempt to unweave the glory of the rainbow. As I have argued elsewhere, like Bakhtin and Dostoevsky's *The Brothers Karamazov* the Book of Job offers polyphonic dialogue, which conveys the divine word only through the plurality of its voices.[42] In the case of the Psalms, when the speaker is both author and reader sharing address to God, how could meaning be single, determinate and "plain" for all? Paul Ricoeur is utterly right to complain that too often we give privilege to the prophetic model of communication that is, after all, only one of five or more which he identifies.[43] This is almost as bad as the misguided attempt of many literary theorists to assimilate all modes of biblical discourse into parables, poetry, or fictive narrative.

My point is that the will and purpose of the author (to take up terms used by Vanhoozer) utilize code as well as message to indicate the degree of constraint or freedom appropriate to this or that text. Even then, the issue remains one of degree. If the degree becomes boundless, so that "anything goes", such a view, as Vanhoozer urges, is anti-theological.[44] "God" becomes the human projection shaped by human wishes and social construction. Craig Bartholemew identifies the point at issue when he links a radically postmodern approach to biblical interpretation with the post-industrial social phenomenon of consumerism. David Clines disarmingly concedes and indeed claims that he proposes a "pluralist" model of biblical interpretation which constitutes

> ... an end-user theory of interpretation, a market philosophy of interpretation ... First comes the recognition that texts do not have determinate meanings ... The social axis for my framework is provided by the idea of interpretative communities ... There is no ... standard by which we can know whether one interpretation or other is right; we can only tell whether it has been accepted. There are no determinate meanings ...[45]

As in Rorty's neopragmatism, the words "true" and "right" have been sold out in favour of a pluralism of undecidability elevated to the status of "ethics" in place of "God", to be defined by the consumer. Such an approach is often promoted as one based on "ethics", that is, an ethics of pluralism. However, there remains an exclusivist aspect that is disguised as a tolerant pluralism. Few Muslims, for example, could endorse such treatment of Islamic texts as "ethical"; rather to them it would more probably be judged as simply idolatrous, that is, as equating the sacred with social constructions of "interest" and instrumental reason on the part of a world-view based on secular liberal political democracy.

---

42 Thiselton, "Communicative Action and Promise in Interdisciplinary, Biblical and Theological Hermeneutics" in Lundin, Thiselton and Walhout, *The Promise of Hermeneutics*, pp.172–83.

43 P. Ricoeur, *Essays on Biblical Interpretation,* (Eng., London: SPCK, 1981), pp.73–118.

44 Vanhoozer, *Is There a Meaning in this Text?*, pp.49–59, 105–6, 427–9.

45 D.J.A. Clines, "Possibilities and Priorities of Biblical Interpretation in an International Perspective", *Bib Int* 1 (1993), pp.78–80; cf. pp.67–87; and also cited in Craig Bartholemew, "Consuming God's Word: Biblical Interpretation and Consumerism", in C. Bartholemew and T. Moritz (eds), *Christ and Consumerism. A Critical Analysis of the Spirit of the Age* (Carlisle: Paternoster, 2000), p.83; cf. pp.81–99.

IV

Conflict between Consumerist Hermeneutics and "Reasonable" Theism?

It may not be accidental that this "consumerist" hermeneutic is advocated from within what is probably the only Department of Biblical Studies in the UK that does not explore biblical studies *within* a Department of *Theology* (where its entailments for theism are explored) or *Religious Studies* (where its entailments for the sacred scriptures of other religions, especially Judaism and Islam, are usually explored) or *Philosophy of Religion* (where the philosophical and ethical world-views in which it is grounded are made explicit and assessed). Even dialogue with a robustly "secular" School of *Critical Theory* may more readily demonstrate just how illusory are the pretensions of consumerist approaches to claim to offer a "descriptive", "comparative", or value-free approach. For consumerism at the beginning of the twenty-first century relies on a manipulative strategy of devising and promoting virtual reality generated by the interests of market-forces in which money, not even goods nor persons, has become the controlling commodity.

For example, teenage "desire" for designer clothes, or for products connected with films or sports teams are usually the fruit of careful market manipulation. They have nothing to do with genuine "democratic choice" as most parents well know. Ironically the very globalization of market-forces in terms of powerful international conglomerates demonstrates the partial validity of the very concerns of the early Marx in his Paris manuscripts about the dehumanization of persons and agents into mere units of production or into "commodities". Craig Bartholemew has noted the significance of "the capitulation of the eastern bloc to consumer culture", and the manipulative portrayal of such "innocent" images as children and the family for value-laden commercial purposes.[46] Peter Selby explores the consequence of regarding money itself as a market commodity.[47]

In his 1998 volume of essays *Truth and Progress*, Richard Rorty repeats his endorsement of the pragmatic tradition of James, Dewey and Davidson, including Donald Davidson's rejection of those aspects of truth-claims that relate to "correspondence, coherence [or] warranted assertibility".[48] Just as A.J. Ayer with the brash confidence of a positivist who had disguised himself as a philosopher of language swept aside all religious propositions about God as "non-sense" on the ground of unverifiability, so Rorty sees "the task of getting reality right" as a task to be consigned to rubbish-disposal because "there is no Way the World Is".[49] Like Clines, Rorty sees the issue of truth as derivative from prior "social practices"; these are shaped by the responses of those who judge what is justified in relation to these practices:[50] "Decisions about truth and falsity are always a matter of rendering practices more coherent or of developing new practices." Truth, Rorty urges, is what people accept as a justification, usually within the context of a liberal democratic

---

[46] Bartholemew, "Christ and Consumerism. An Introduction", loc. cit., pp.5 and 7.

[47] Peter Selby, *Grace and Mortgage. The Language of Faith and the Debt of the World* (London: Darton, Longman & Todd, 1997). There is no level playing field generated by "liberal democracy" for value-laden strings-attached loans to the two-thirds world: it is a time bomb, based on power.

[48] R. Rorty, *Truth and Progress. Philosophical Papers vol. 3* (Cambridge: CUP, 1998), p.11.

[49] Rorty, "Is Truth a Goal of Inquiry?", *Truth and Progress*, p.25 (cf. also p.131).

[50] Rorty, *Truth and Progress*, p.129.

society. Needless to say, "what people accept" as such varies within different local groups. Hence Rorty prefers the term "ethnocentric" (in a positive, "progressive" sense) as against "relativist" (even if he concedes that the two terms convey virtually the same content with different associations).[51] Even "what proves itself to be good" is deemed to be such in the eyes of consumers: "Justification is always relative to an audience."[52]

In my Presidential Paper to the Society for the Study of Theology (Edinburgh, 1999) I set this consumer-orientated progressivism in contrast to a grace-orientated eschatology.[53] As Bonhoeffer, Moltmann, Pannenberg and many others perceive, whereas pragmatism is linked with an illusory confidence in human self-generated progress, eschatology allows for discontinuity, critique, transcendent reversal and not least for reversals of the cross which negate or at least question what is "conformable" (Bonhoeffer's word) to human consumer-choice. Most especially in first-century Roman Corinth the major issue for Christians was whether "the audience" defined truth in terms of the competitive rhetoric which impressed them most and won most applause, or whether the "affront" of the cross proclaimed by those regarded as dirt to be scraped off the shoes held a prior claim over those who sought to redefine themselves as "spiritual people" (1 Cor. 1:18–25; 2:1–5; 4:8–13).

I have argued this case recently not only in the paper identified above but also in my detailed commentary on the Greek text of 1 Corinthians.[54] Paul in no way appeals to an ethnocentric or "local" perception of truth, as if "reasonableness" had nothing to do with issues of epistemological and interpretative judgement. Anders Eriksson and John Moores, among others, have shown that Paul seeks to convey not a rhetoric of mere causal persuasion (bare rhetorical force or perlocution) but a reasonable chain of inferences from shared promises, that is, shared pre-Pauline traditions which define Christian identity in the basis of God's grace, the cross and eschatological resurrection.[55]

Moores asserts:

> [Paul] does not think (as some modern upholders of the importance of the reception factor do) that the identity of the message in a piece of communication is determined by what it means for those at the receiving end. For him it is rather *their* identity than that of the message that is determined by their response. To subject him to the criteria of present day ... reader-response theory would be to turn *his* ideas on the subject upside down.[56]

Moores is far from being unaware of theories of sign-production especially in Umberto Eco, Luis Prieto and Pierre Guiraud, and is familiar with the so-called new rhetoric of C.

---

[51] Ibid., p.10; cf. pp.1–15, 19–42 and 433–62. See also R. Rorty, *Objectivism, Relativism and Truth. Philosophical Papers vol. 1* (Cambridge: CUP, 1991).

[52] Rorty, *Truth and Progress*, p.4.

[53] A.C. Thiselton, "Signs of the Times: Toward a Grammar of Grace, Truth and Eschatology in Contexts of So-Called Postmodernity", in David Fergusson and Marcel Sarot (eds), *The Future as God's Gift. Explorations in Christian Eschatology* (Edinburgh: T. & T. Clark, 2000), pp.9–39 [Essay 32 above].

[54] A.C. Thiselton, *1 Corinthians: A Commentary on the Greek Text* (Grand Rapids, MI: Eerdmans [NIGTC] and Carlisle: Paternoster, 2000).

[55] A. Eriksson, *Traditions as Rhetorical Proof. Pauline Argumentation in 1 Corinthians* (Stockholm: Almqvist & Wiksell, 1998), throughout.

[56] J.D. Moores, *Wrestling with Rationality in Paul. Romans 1–8 in a New Perspective* (Cambridge: CUP, [SNTS Mon Ser 82], 1995), pp.133–4, Moores' italics.

Perelman. It is precisely his recognition of the importance of semiotic code, however, (with its spectrum from closed and tightly matching codes to open codes and code-switching) that determines Moores' emphasis not only upon authorial agency but also upon a "rationality" that finds expression not merely in deductive and inductive logic but more especially in the "enthymeme".[57] This is a shared basis for advocating a reasoned and reasonable case, which in Paul's view embraces (1) appeals to Scripture, and (2) appeals to reason.

Where hearers or addressees already possess precisely the same mind-set, belief-system and stance as the authorial agent, the code presupposed by each in the communicative act may be not only matching but also identical. But in this case the speech-act is not transformative; persuasion need not be involved. Replication, not creative shaping, takes place. This is the perception that lies behind much postmodern dissatisfaction with merely representational or referential accounts of language. Scripture does not merely report or replicate: it also shapes, persuades and transforms. Biblical reading (in the ancient world usually a corporate and oral temporal recital, not a private "inner" experience) occurs in a context of expectancy of a creative, transformative, impact-making event. Hence, as Moores (taking up and applying Eco) insists, usually "the superimposition of one code upon another ... is a pervasive feature of sign-production ... To designate such supplementation and superimposition the term 'over-coding' is often used."[58] As Paul Ricoeur also emphasizes, the double-meaning effect of symbol or of metaphor "gives rise to thought" creatively at a supra-cognitive level as "surplus of meaning".[59]

Where a source-signal (for example, the sound of a musical texture which cannot easily be put into words) cannot readily be interpreted into encoded and decoded texts within the hearer's world, "under-coding" may have occurred. Interplay in Scripture occurs between exploratory polyphonic multivalent Wisdom literature (Job, Ecclesiastes); heart-laments; paeans of hymnic praise or expressions of longing for God beyond words (Rom. 8:26, 27; 1 Cor. 14:2, Psalm 42:1–3, 5–7, 9); parables, riddles and jokes (Matt. 5:29; 7:3–5 (the log and speck in the eye); 13:10–15; Jonah 1:3, 9; 2:2, 4, 10; 4:11–5, 8–11 (satire on a self-centred, self-important, "godly" prophet!); parallel sequential accounts of events (Mark 14:1–15:39; par Matt. 26:1–27:54; Luke 22:1–23:48, the Passion Narrative); shared pre-Pauline creeds and confessions (both with cognitive declarative content and with commissive self-involvement) 1 Cor. 12:3; Rom. 10:9; 1 Cor. 11:23b–26; 15:3b–5 (6, 7?); 1 Cor. 8:4b, c (Jesus is Lord; Jesus died for our sins ...; there is One God ...); illlocutionary acts of promise (for example, Heb. 6:11b–20; 4:16) based on the stability of covenant security (Heb. 8:6–10:23), and multi-functional speech-acts (Heb. 1:1–13).[60] Perhaps our

---

[57] Ibid., pp.21–32.

[58] Ibid., pp.26–7.

[59] Paul Ricoeur, *Freud and Philosophy. An Essay on Interpretation* (Eng., New Haven, CT: Yale, 1970), p.19; cf. pp.5–33; *The Conflict of Interpretations. Essays in Hermeneutics* (Evanston, IL: Northwestern University Press, 1974), p.288; cf. pp.287–334; *The Rule of Metaphor. Multidisciplinary Studies of the Creation of Meaning in Language* (Eng., London: Routledge, 1978), p.6.

[60] To avoid overlap with the essay on speech-act theory, I have relegated these examples to a footnote: (i) a homily which (ii) confesses faith; (iii) cites Scripture; (iv) provides exegesis; (v) recites salvation-history; (vi) expresses acclamation and praise; (vii) teaches; and (viii) promotes assurance by stressing the completeness of the finished work of Christ (eg 1:3b).

traditional emphasis upon "a single determinate plain meaning" has impoverished the creative potential of our preaching, even violating the biblical example of "homily" in Hebrews 1.[61]

On one side of the argument, a consumer-philosophy or consumer-hermeneutic of indeterminate meaning open to the shaping of ethnocentric communities may be regarded as compatible with Christian theism only with great difficulty. For theism asserts certain universal truth-claims about "how things are" (against Rorty). Nevertheless, on the other side we must also concede that any approach which limits textual meaning to either a *single* meaning or a *tightly determinate* meaning *in all genres of Scripture in every case* will reduce and emasculate the capacity of Scripture to act *transformatively and creatively.*

The proof of this is that even when we accord to authorial agency the indispensable role which Vanhoozer (rightly) gives to it, authors *choose* sometimes to communicate in terms of a goal of *matching* codes through *closed* texts, for example, in cases where information or description is more important and more primary than creative shaping or transformation. On the other hand, they sometimes *choose* "open" texts or a "switching" of codes, when creative transformation or iconoclasm becomes their aim. *Promise* also presupposes a degree (although not an absolute degree) of specificity concerning conditions, stance and appropriation, or the identity of addressees. Promises to individuals, however, differ from those made to the world. We have noted many communicative modes in which the emphasis lies on projecting a world into which the reader or hearer enters to perform self-involving action for which a rigid protocol has *not* been laid out in advance. Here Gadamer is right: always to insist that some "method" is laid out in advance is to risk transposing creative understanding into mere response to propaganda. It is to substitute *technē* for *phronēsis.*[62]

David Lyon attempts (as we note elsewhere) to distinguish between *postmodernism* as a polemic against the "universal" claims of Enlightenment *rationalism* and epistemology in favour of the local and ethnocentric, and *postmodernity* as a *social* polemic against the solidity of the "real" in favour of the *virtual reality* of media-construction, sign-construction and local community-construction.[63] *The latter, he urges, replaces means of production by a consumerist culture. Virtual reality* is a construct dependent on the tastes, inclinations and distorted perceptions of consumers. Scripture, we may urge by contrast, proclaims a *kerygma* that liberates humankind from this illusory "reality". Moreover, Scripture is less ready to be associated with the first type of "postmodernism" in dismissing too readily "reasonableness" and responsible argument as a God-given weapon against the anxiety of "anything goes". That kind of postmodernism is only for "winners", its "ethics" remain illusory. In Paul's view it is precisely this that the cross has

---

[61]   It is unnecessary to cite the mass of literature on Heb. 1–12 as homily. See eg W.L. Lane, *Hebrews* (Dallas, TX: Word, 1991), vol. 1, pp.ixx–ixxx; and W.G. Übelacker, *Der Hebräerbrief als Appell* (Stockholm: Almqvist & Wiksell, 1989). I endorse this in A.C. Thiselton, "Hebrews", in J.W. Rogerson and J.D.G. Dunn (eds), *Eerdmans Commentary on the Bible* (Grand Rapids, MI: Eerdmans, 2003), pp.1453–7.

[62]   H.-G. Gadamer, "Reflections on my Philosophical Journey", in Lewis E. Hahn (ed.), *The Philosophy of Hans-Georg Gadamer* (Chicago, IL: Open Court, 1997), pp.3–63, esp. pp.17, 36, 43–6, 53.

[63]   David Lyon, *Postmodernity* (Buckingham: Open University, 1994), pp.6–7.

exposed as "foolish" and "weakness" in contrast to the transformative power of the gospel (1 Cor. 1:18–25). It is ironic that Rorty links hermeneutics with "edification" in contrast to epistemology. As Vielhauer argues, "to edify (*oikodomē*) oneself" (1 Cor. 14:4) is a self-indulgent contentless activity.[64] By contrast, Stanley Stowers demonstrates conclusively the importance of reason and reasonableness for Paul, while Alexandra Brown shows the link between transformation, the cross and epistemology.[65]

V
A Tentative Postscript

I have argued that with the proviso that we take full account of textual genre, interpreters need to explore processes behind, within and in front of the text, more often as complementary than as alternative tasks. Moreover, the interpreter diminishes rather than enhances understanding by setting aside as irrelevant all questions about how the text may relate to the external world in this or that case.

As a speculative but, I hope, suggestive analogy it may be constructive to compare Aristotle's pre-modern but sophisticated account of causality. When a sculptor creates a marble statue, he suggests, we may distinguish between four kinds of cause that explain its coming into being. The "efficient" cause lies in the blows of the chisel upon the marble block. This lies "behind" what comes to constitute the statue. The "material" and "formal" causes are the marble and the structure that we may compare with the actual world of the text itself, as it structured "within" this world. Yet crucially, Aristotle observes, there is a "final" cause at work: the reason why the sculptor makes the statue and what effects upon those who view it are envisaged. In part this retraces what lies "behind" it; but it also brings into focus the effects that it sets in motion "in front of" it.

All aspects together combine to make the statue what it is. Yet, as Gadamer and Ricoeur insist, hermeneutics moves beyond mere "explanation" (*Erklärung*) to understanding (*Verstehen*). A higher level and fuller horizon is at issue than knowledge, even if, as Vanhoozer urges against a doctrine of postmodernity, we should not assume that in every case it is less than knowledge. One thinker whom we perhaps too readily ignore here is Bernard Lonergan, who should be ranked with those who contribute to this subject. Involved in the processes of experiential understanding, he urges, is "experiencing, understanding, judging, and deciding" including "understanding the unity and relations ... and relatedness" of these.[66] Hermeneutics embraces more than this, but it does not embrace less.

---

[64]   P. Vielhauer, *Oikodomē: Das Bild vom Bau in der christlichen Lituratur vom NT bis Clemens Alexandrinus* (Karlsruhe: Harrassowitz, 1940), esp. pp.91–8.

[65]   S.K. Stowers, "Paul on the Use and Abuse of Reason", in D.L. Balch et al. (eds), *Greeks, Romans and Christians. Essays in Honor of AJ Malherbe* (Minneapolis, MN: Fortress, 1990), pp.253–86; and A.R. Brown, *The Cross and Human Transformation* (Minneapolis, MN: Fortress, 1995).

[66]   B. Lonergan, *Method in Theology* (London: Darton, Longman & Todd, 1972), pp.14–15.

CHAPTER THIRTY-FOUR

Can "Authority" Remain Viable in a Postmodern Climate? "Biblical Authority in the Light of Contemporary Philosophical Hermeneutics" (Paper delivered 2002, new essay)

This lecture was first delivered on 7 March 2002 in Union University, Jackson, Tennessee, during my appointment there as Visiting Scholar in Residence for that month, at the invitation of the Carl Henry Centre. Since my lectures in the university were on philosophical, literary and biblical hermeneutics, the request was to reassess in this public lecture how these contemporary approaches in philosophical hermeneutics might relate to more traditional questions about biblical authority. I have edited out some parts of the material in order to avoid undue overlap with other essays in this volume. The approach to "biblical authority" adopted in this essay touches only those aspects that emerge strictly in relation to contemporary hermeneutical theory. I adopt a different approach and emphasis, for example, in my essay "Authority and Hermeneutics: Some Proposals for a More Creative Agenda" in P.E. Satterthwaite and David F. Wright (eds), A Pathway into the Holy Scripture *(Grand Rapids, MI: Eerdmans, 1994), pp.107–41. There I relate corrigibility of interpretation to the "not yet" of eschatology, and the locus of authority not only in the past and present, but also as derived from the future: from the definitive verdictive utterances of God brought forward from the last judgement. However, recognition of the role of speech-action and its illocutionary force derivatively on the basis of ontology plays a role in both essays. Such an approach might have prevented a distraction into fruitless debates about "propositional revelation", since its exponents surely use the wrong term, and probably mean "ontology". In the present essay the concern is to explore how currents of thought in contemporary philosophical hermeneutics and in postmodern perspectives serve to offer positive resources and negative challenges for reformulating an approach to the question on biblical authority.*

The task assigned to me is to enquire into what impact contemporary philosophical hermeneutics may be said to make upon traditional and other approaches of the authority of the Bible. Contemporary philosophical hermeneutics has diversified into a wide range of approaches, explorations and crosscurrents. Some streams of thought serve in positive ways either to undermine more naïve attacks on biblical authority or to broaden earlier arguments on behalf of the authority of the Bible. Other streams of thought, by contrast, place new question marks against earlier assumptions or approaches, and cohere less readily with theological defences of scriptural authority. The main part of the essay will trace four points of potential resonance with more positive views of biblical authority, but I shall conclude by identifying three points of potential tension or conflict with traditional arguments for the authority of the biblical writings.

I
Authority, Tradition, Community and "the Other"

Three-quarters of a century ago, the Cambridge New Testament scholar Charles H. Dodd drew a contrast between the pretensions of supposedly self-sufficient individual reason and experience, and the corporate, communal, historical testimony of the Bible as revelation. In "horizontal" terms, the witness of Scripture spreads far beyond the narrow horizons of a single individual human mind, which in "vertical" terms the continuities and novelties of the revelation of God over centuries and the historical experience of God on the part of Israel and the Christian Church dwarfs the span of a single lifetime into a tiny fragment of historical thought, experience and responses to God.

Thus C.H. Dodd declares:

> We may well turn away from the narrow scene of individual experience at the moment, to the spacious prospect we command in the Bible. Here we meet with men whom we must acknowledge as experts in life ... Here also we trace the long history of a community which through good fortune and ill tested their belief in God ... The impressive witness ... has not indeed overborne our individual judgement, but it has delivered us from the tyranny of private impressions ... and helped us to a true objectivity of judgement.[1]

If we were to translate the mood of Dodd's concern into the language of contemporary philosophical hermeneutics, we might say that his recognition of the continuities of traditions together with the role of a range of communities rooted in their life histories provides one starting-point on the road toward a formulation of issues about the nature and role of "authority".

This approach resonates closely with aspects of the hermeneutical theory of Hans-Georg Gadamer (1900–2002). Gadamer is concerned to challenge and to correct the individualism and brash over-confidence that seeks understanding (*Verstehen*) on the basis of *individual self-reflection and consciousness alone*, especially "consciousness" only of a single point in time.[2] Even W. Dilthey's emphasis on autobiographical narrative is insufficient.[3] The tradition of individual "inner-ness" and rationalism that runs from Descartes through Kant lays claim to the power of "method" (*Méthode*) which is created by subjectivity and constitutes "a distorting mirror ... The self-awareness of the individual is only a flickering in the closed circuits of historical life."[4]

"Method", Gadamer insists, cannot be imposed upon the understanding of texts or of life in advance of a genuine engagement with "the other". In one of his most recent

---

[1] C.H. Dodd, *The Authority of the Bible* (London: Nisbet, 1928), pp.298–9.
[2] H.-G. Gadamer, *Truth and Method* (London: Sheed & Ward, 2nd revised English edn, 1989), pp.277–85 and throughout.
[3] Gadamer, *Truth and Method*, p.276.
[4] Gadamer, *Truth and Method*, loc. cit.

surveys of his own philosophical journey Gadamer declares: "*It is the other who breaks into my ego-centredness and gives me something to understand. This* ... motif ... guided me from the beginning ..." (my italics).[5] The problem with "method", especially as it is conceived of in rationalism or in the natural sciences, is that it imposes upon what is to be understood a *prior conceptual grid* which presupposes a given rethink of assumptions, questions and belief, *in advance of* encounter with that which in the event may shatter and transform this prior grid. Hence this *cannot* constitute a path to understanding anything beyond where "I" stand already at present. Such illusory "understanding" will merely confirm prior assumptions, which may be false.

However, it is of the essence of biblical authority that Scripture challenges, transforms, corrects and reshapes the prior horizons or network of assumptions that humankind brings to the text on the basis of natural reason, individual consciousness and prior experience. The Holy Spirit communicates a life-changing word from "Beyond". The word of Scripture is *creative*; it is no merely passive "mirror" of prior or private prejudices.

Thus, in broader terms that apply more generally than to scriptural authority alone, Gadamer speaks in positive terms of "the rehabilitation of authority and tradition".[6] He rejects the view of the Enlightenment that "methodologically disciplined use of reason can safeguard us from all error. This was Descartes' idea of "method".[7] Descartes, he concludes, did exclude morality from this sweeping assumption. However, this principle must be expanded. For the notion of "authority" does not entail any "abdication of reason", since to acknowledge that another or others may be "superior to oneself in judgement and insight" is an eminently reasonable view to adopt, and it implies that this superior "other" has "priority over one's own" judgments.[8] It is based "on an act of reason itself which, aware of its own limitations, trusts to the better insight of others".[9]

Not only does the shallow complacency of an egocentric rationalism begin to emerge: an ethical dimension relating to *hubris*, humility, community, and wisdom (*phronēsis*) also plays a part. Indeed in Part I of *Truth and Method* Gadamer paves the way for his philosophical hermeneutics by explicating the positive roles of "wisdom" and "community" in relation to historical human life. Central to the guiding concepts of humanism and the hermeneutics is *Bildung*, "formation", or more broadly "culture" in the sense of what shapes or forms human life. Wilhelm von Humboldt, Gadamer notes with approval, speaks of *Bildung* as "higher" than *Kultur*, namely as a "disposition of mind" that is "formed" or "fashioned": the Latin equivalent is *formatio*.[10] "The general characteristic of *Bildung*, Gadamer declares, is "keeping oneself open to what is other ...".[11]

---

[5] Gadamer, "Reflections on My Philosophical Journey", in Lewis E. Hahn (ed.), *The Philosophy of Hans-Georg Gadamer* (Chicago and La Salle, IL: Open Court, 1997), p.46; cf. pp.3–63, and also H.-G. Gadamer, "Mit der Sprache denken", in his *Gesammelte Werke, band 10: Hermeneutik und Rückblick* (Tübingen: Mohr, 1995), pp.346–53.

[6] Gadamer, *Truth and Method*, pp.277–85.

[7] Ibid., p.277.

[8] Ibid., p.279.

[9] Ibid.

[10] Ibid., pp.10, 11.

[11] Ibid., p.17.

Again, this brings us near to what resonates in Christian theology with how the Bible or the Word of God exercises its authority in practice. It shapes; it fashions; it forms life and thought. Too often this authority becomes reduced to "acts of knowing" in abstraction from such creative formation.

Gadamer develops this theme in terms of a contrast between the respective epistemological traditions of René Descartes (1596–1650) and Giambattista Vico (1668–1744). Vico was not satisfied with "the new science", or with the over-cerebral rationalism of Descartes. Even with "the new science", Gadamer observes in Vico's view "we still cannot do without the wisdom of the ancients and their cultivation of *prudentia* ... The most important thing ... is ... the training in the *sensus communis* ... not the abstract universality of reason, but the concrete universality represented by the community of a group, a people ... or the whole human race ... Developing this communal sense is of decisive importance for living."[12] "*Historia* is a source of truth totally different from theoretical reason."[13]

This tradition found partial expression in England through Shaftesbury (Anthony Ashley Cooper, Third Earl of Shaftesbury, 1671–1713). His work on virtue, humour, wit and moral sense related, in Gadamer's phrase, to "the heart more than the head". In Scotland, Gadamer adds, the positive role of "common sense" found further expression in Thomas Reid (1710–96).[14] Gadamer also cites the reactions of German pietism against a sterile rationalism. Oetinger is no less concerned about "the heart" as a focus of understanding and formation. For Oetinger, Gadamer concludes, "The important thing is the understanding of scripture ... mathematical demonstration method fails here ...".[15]

This relates not only to the testimony of communities, in contrast to individual reflection alone; not only to the heart and "formation", in contrast to the head alone; but also to the historical particularly of apostolic witness (although this is not part of Gadamer's agenda) in contrast to an individual starting with a supposed blank sheet. The originating focus of a tradition plays a key role. Hence, in Hans von Campenhausens's words, "The apostles ... are not simply preachers and teachers, but also founders of Christian communities ... With this testimony, therefore, they are in truth earlier than the Church, which is based on that testimony and must constantly review its relationship with it." He adds that this apostolic authority can in this respect "be neither continued nor renewed" once the apostolic age has come to an end.[16]

While he does not address this issue explicitly, Gadamer's attack on the rationalist or Kantian notion of "problems" as detached from history, as if they exist "like stars in the sky" having an independent existence, has something further to say here.[17] Gadamer insists: "Problems are not real questions that arise of themselves."[18] He explains:

---

[12] Ibid., p.21.

[13] Ibid., p.23.

[14] Ibid., pp.24–5.

[15] Ibid., p.28.

[16] Hans von Campenhausen, *Ecclesiastical Authority and Spiritual Power* (London: Black, 1969), pp.22, 23.

[17] Gadamer, *Truth and Method*, p.377.

[18] Ibid., p.376. On the relation of Gadamer's section here to dialectic and biblical interpretation, see further Brook W.R. Pearson, *Corresponding Sense: Paul, Dialectic and Gadamer* (London, Boston, MA and Cologne: Brill, 2001 [Biblical Interpretation Series Vol. 58]), pp.93–7 and throughout.

"reflection on the *hermeneutical* experience transforms problems back to *questions that arise and that derive their sense from their motivations*" (my italics). In other words, in the context of the authority of the Bible, part of that authority lies in directing and formulating the kind of questions that stand within the framework of biblical and apostolic tradition and speak to a listening heart rather than to an over-confident head.

It would be simplistic to suggest that "contemporary philosophical hermeneutics" demands such an approach to biblical authority. Gadamer does not represent all strands of thought in philosophical hermeneutics, and in any case these are inferences drawn from Gadamer's angle of approach rather than explicitly from his own thoughts. Yet these perspectives are consonant with Gadamer's philosophical hermeneutics and, with Ricoeur, he remains the most important and influential exponent of philosophical hermeneutics over the last hundred years.

Gadamer's emphasis on hermeneutical "openness", his logic of question and answer, and his recognition of the power of "formation" (*Bildung*) and of "pre-judgements" (*Vorurteile*) reminds us of T.F. Torrance's observation about the recovery of scriptural authority at the Reformation. Here, Torrance writes, we encounter "a repentant readiness to rethink all preconceptions and presuppositions ... a readiness to submit to radical testing ...".[19] In terms of a theological doctrine of revelation, Torrance adds, "If God really is God", we cannot know him or become "formed" into the image of Christ "except out of Himself and in a way appropriate to his transcendent nature"; to think otherwise would be "a form of irrationality".[20] This coheres philosophically with Gadamer's observations both about authority and reason, "the other", and the motivations of question and answer. It coheres theologically with one of Karl Barth's well-known principles: "The possibility of the knowledge of God springs from God."[21] "God's Word is itself God's act."[22]

II
The Multi-Functional, Multi-Layered Nature of Language

A number of the more traditional discussions of the authority of the Bible have suffered impoverishment through inadequate and simplistic understandings of the nature and function of language. Ludwig Wittgenstein, whose philosophical thought has influenced both Anglo-American philosophy and Continental European hermeneutics, constituted a watershed on the subject. As a starting-point we may cite his remark that we can see language for what it is "only if we make a radical break with the idea that language always functions in one way, always serves the same purpose: to convey thoughts – which may be about houses, pains, good and evil, or anything else you please".[23]

[19] T.F. Torrance, *Theological Science* (London: Oxford University Press, 1969), p.75.

[20] Ibid., p.54.

[21] K. Barth, *Church Dogmatics II: 1: The Doctrine of God* (Edinburgh: T. & T. Clark, 1957), §26, sect. 1, p.63.

[22] K. Barth, *Church Dogmatics I: 1, The Doctrine of the Word of God* (Edinburgh: T. & T. Clark, 1975), §5, sect. 3, p.147.

[23] L. Wittgenstein, *Philosophical Investigations* (Oxford: Blackwell, German and English, 2nd edn, 1967), sect. 304.

Some biblical interpreters have appealed to the overused typology of Karl Bühler, to the effect that language serves one of three distinct functions: to communicate ideas informatively, to give expression to inner states, or to urge action volitionally. This over-neat apportionment between intellect, emotions and will imposes artificial categorizations onto language. Functions of language repeatedly overlap, and they occur frequently in more than one mode simultaneously. Further they are by no means restricted to three. Surprisingly thinkers as relatively sophisticated as Rudolf Bultmann and more recently perhaps even George Lindbeck distort their work by too readily leaning upon these misleading simple categorizations.[24] Wittgenstein observes: "But how many kinds are there? ... There are countless kinds ... Singing catches, guessing riddles, making a joke; telling it – solving a problem ... translating ... Asking, thanking, cursing, greeting, praying ...".[25]

We need not replicate here what I have claimed about William Tyndale's approach in the section of this volume on speech-act theory. Tyndale, in part following Luther, explicitly anticipated Wittgenstein's point in his *Treatise* of 1531 on ways in which Scripture effected its authority. Neither law nor promise is primarily "informational", although they do indeed presuppose "information" in performing their function. Law *directs*, promise *appoints*, *gives*, *conveys*, *permits*, *liberates*, *pledges*, or *performs* other covenantal *actions*. Given appropriate conditions and contexts, promise represents that special category of *first-person* utterances (as in Wittgenstein) or *"performatives"* (as in J.L. Austin). Within a dozen pages, Tyndale specifies no less than eighteen distinct speech-acts as linguistic activities which Scripture performs: it promises, names, appoints, declares, gives, condemns, curses, binds, kills, drives to despair, delivers, forbids, ministers to life, wounds, blesses, heals, cures and wakes.[26] Scripture "maketh a man's heart glad"; it proclaims "joyful tidings".[27] I have included more on promise in this present volume (especially in Essay 8), and have enlarged upon Tyndale's approach elsewhere.[28]

Two streams within philosophical hermeneutics come into play at this point. The first is that of *speech-act theory*. There is no need to trace the development of this approach, as I had done in the original form of this essay, since I have already outlined this in Part II on speech-act theory above. In *New Horizons in Hermeneutics*, as I have noted above, I explored Searle's suggestion that a broad distinction may be drawn between speech-acts that seek to transform the world in accordance with what is spoken ("to get the world to match the words"), and the opposite "direction of fit" ("to get the word to match the world").[29] Examples of the former "direction of fit" would include such speech-acts as

---

[24] See my critique of Bultmann in Anthony C. Thiselton, *The Two Horizons* (Grand Rapids, MI: Eerdmans and Carlisle: Paternoster, 1980), pp.205–92, esp. pp.252–92. On Wittgenstein, cf. also pp.357–438. Cf. also G. Lindbeck, *The Nature of Doctrine: Religion and Doctrine in a Postliberal Age* (London: SPCK, 1984).

[25] Wittgenstein, *Investigations*, sect. 23. We need not over-press the word "countless": P.F. Strawson has questioned whether this multiplicity is really "infinite".

[26] William Tyndale, "A Pathway into the Holy Scripture" [1531], in *Doctrinal Treatises and Introductions to Different Portions of Holy Scripture* (Cambridge: CUP [Parker Society], 1848), esp. pp.1–11.

[27] Ibid.

[28] A.C. Thiselton, "Authority and Hermeneutics", in P.E. Satterthwaite and David F. Wright (eds), *A Pathway into the Holy Scripture* (Grand Rapids, MI: Eerdmans, 1994), pp.107–41.

[29] Thiselton, *New Horizons*, p.294; also pp.291–307.

bequeathing property through a legal will after decease and probate; commissioning or empowering an agent with executive or deputizing authority naming someone as one's adopted son and heir; or pledging assistance in the event of certain circumstances. Biblical texts abound in such examples of promising, commissioning, appointing, naming and pledging, and they "change the 'world'" not least for those whom they address. In my essay on speech-acts in Christology (1994) I argued that when Jesus Christ performed speech acts that rest upon *the authority of God* (for example, forgiveness of sins) such acts *presuppose* an implicit Christology beyond what Jesus has *explicitly stated*.[30]

This capacity of language "to shape" the world provides one example of how the authority of the biblical writings may be cashed out in terms of the currency of life and belief. Yet it also operates as "words" that describe what is. These convey authoritative truth, and possess what might best be viewed as an *ontological* dimension. However, this is too often clumsily and not entirely accurately called "propositional" in some theological circles.

The terminology "propositional" and "non-propositional" sets the discussion off in unhelpful directions, but what those who *use* this term generally seek to express is that some genres within the Bible authoritatively declare *the truth* of certain *states of affairs*. If such terms are useful, distinctions of *genre* must also be borne in mind. For it would be patently absurd to claim that poetry or parables are "propositional" in the same sense as historical assertions within the Passion narrative that record the facts of the crucifixion. This unfortunate terminological misunderstanding may well have been set off by the reaction of the conservative Charles Hodge of Princeton (1797–1878) against the liberal Horace Bushnell of Yale (1802–76). Bushnell earned the name "father of American Liberalism", and his theology of the atonement fell short in ways that provoked Hodge. But Bushnell appealed to the role of metaphor in the Bible in ways that in principle would seem almost axiomatic to most biblical specialists and to virtually all literary theorists today. The problem was not *that* Bushnell appealed to metaphor, but *how* and *when* he did this. To call Jesus a "sacrifice", he urged, is the same level of metaphor as to call him a "lamb". Rather than debating the *scope* and *function* of metaphor, Hodge reacted by claiming the whole of the Bible was "propositional" and "cognitive". The Bible "is a storehouse of facts". He had no interest in the creative power of metaphor. In 1870 after fifty years of teaching he declared as praise for Princeton: "I am not afraid to say that a new idea never originated in this seminary."[31] The consequences of this dreadful polarization have devastated American theology and hermeneutics for about a century, and the damage remains in terms of extremism here and there on both sides.

The philosophical hermeneutics of Paul Ricoeur (b. 1913) assists us here. Ricoeur insists throughout his writings that *creative* language of "figuration" characteristically functions *at more than one level*. In certain cases (not in every case) "the showing-hiding of double meaning ... can ... sometimes be a manifestation, a revelation, of the sacred".[32]

---

[30] Essay 7 in this volume: "Christology in Luke, Speech-Act Theory, and the Problem of Dualism in Christology".

[31] A.A. Hodge, *Life of Charles Hodge* (New York: Arno, 1969), p.521. A fuller account is provided in W. Baird, *History of New Testament Research*, vol. 2 (Minneapolis, MN: Fortress, 2003), pp.31–42.

[32] Paul Ricoeur, *Freud and Philosophy: An Essay on Interpretation* (New Haven, CT: Yale University Press, 1970), pp.7–8.

When Scripture speaks of sin as missing the mark, or as distortion, stain, deviation, bondage, or burden, "symbols are not a non-language; the split between univocal and plurivocal language extends across the empire of language".[33] The Bible is "inexhaustible" in its symbolic resonances, for example, of "the double meaning of the words 'earth', 'heaven', 'water', 'life', etc".[34] Sometimes this multi-level meaning results from multiple uses within the canon. Thus Christopher Seitz speaks of "figural reading, under the rule of faith", which is of a kind that ensures that "the Holy Spirit could speak to the Church from the witness of prophets and apostles ...".[35]

Ricoeur explores the *creative, shaping, formative* and *transformative* power of language at a variety of levels. He correlates with word, sentence and narrative-discourse the creative roles respectively of symbol, of metaphor and of narrative plot or temporal refiguration: *"The symbol gives rise to thought"* (my italics).[36] Metaphor operates interactively, by bringing together two different semantic domains and operating with "split-level" meaning.[37] Narrative-plot operates with a dialectic of "concordance", or drawing together, in the logic of plot; and "discordance", or separating sequentially in narrative-time.[38] Ricoeur insists rightly that "double-meaning" invites, rather than bypasses, critical or explanatory controls. He observes (as we have noted elsewhere), "Hermeneutics seems to me to be animated by this double motivation: willingness to suspect, willingness to listen; vow of rigor, vow of obedience. In our time we have not finished doing away with *idols* and we have barely begun to listen to *symbols*" (Ricoeur's italics).[39]

Arguably then biblical authority remains an *ontological given*, because its basis resides in the sovereignty and grace of God, but also its derivative *currency* resides in its appropriation as an *effective communicative event or act* whereby believing readers live out their response to this authority. "Authority" is no merely theoretical concept. As Calvin insisted, it relates directly to acknowledgement of Christ's Lordship in life and thought. The very close parallel with confessing Christ's Lordship that emerges also in our section on speech-act is clear. What it is to confess Christ as my (or our) Lord is seen *in practice* by whether I regard myself (and live) as Christ's *doulos* or "slave", in trust and obedience. As Bultmann (here, rightly) observes, such a one can let go care for the self, since the "Lord" (*ho kyrios*) has the care of them: "He lets this care go ... (Rom. 14:7, 8) ... He knows only one care: how he may please the Lord (1 Cor. 7:32)".[40] Notions of slavery that derive from practices in the eighteenth and early nineteenth centuries should not mislead us.

---

[33] Ibid., p.19; cf. pp.38–40.

[34] Ibid., p.15.

[35] Christopher R. Seitz, *Figured Out: Typology and Providence in Christian Scripture* (Louisville, KY: Westminster John Knox, 2001), p.10.

[36] Paul Ricoeur, *The Conflict of Interpretations* (Evanston, IL: Northwestern University Press, 1974), p.288.

[37] Paul Ricoeur, *The Rule of Metaphor* (Toronto: University of Toronto Press, 1977).

[38] Paul Ricoeur, *Time and Narrative* (3 vols, Chicago, IL: University of Chicago Press, 1984–88), esp. vol. 1, chapters 1–3. On "narrative-time" see Thiselton, *Promise of Hermeneutics*, pp.183–91; and *New Horizons*, pp.354–68 and 478–81.

[39] Ricoeur, *Freud and Philosophy*, p.27.

[40] R. Bultmann, *Theology of the New Testament*, vol. 1 (London: SCM, 1952), pp.331 and 351. See further, Thiselton, *New Horizons*, pp.282–91.

What being a slave might mean in the Roman world depended on multiple factors, especially on *who* is "Lord".[41] To call Christ "Lord" involves placing oneself under his authority and obeying his "word".

This currency (as explained above) depends on certain states of affairs being the case. Nevertheless, as Ricoeur insists, *exclusive preoccupation with the prophetic and didactic material* within the biblical writings gives us an unduly *reduced*, simplistic, and often "impenetrable concept of 'revealed truth' [or] ... 'revealed truths'".[42] Ricoeur is partly right when he insists, "Wisdom ... recognizes a hidden God".[43] That is to say, the God of the wisdom literature transcends easily packaged "answers" (especially in Job and Ecclesiastes), and regularly deploys exploration, dialogue and "polyphonic" discourse. "Polyphonic" discourse, as we have set out in this volume, denotes a dialogue between several "voices", as we find for example in the Book of Job, where it is the *process of the whole dialogue* rather than any *single* voice, that addresses the heart of the issue. In Job, neither the narrator, nor even the speeches of God, nor Job himself, nor any of Job's "friends" offers a single, pre-packaged "answer"; for each adds to a multiform picture the *whole* of which is set before us as interactive revelation. In modern literature, Fyodor Dostoevsky (1821–81) adopts this method in *The Brothers Karamazov*, as Mikhail Bakhtin demonstrates. I have discussed this way of approaching the problem of suffering and evil in the extract from the *Promise of Hermeneutics* included in this volume.[44] Here "biblical authority" demands not simply the "reading off" of a proposition, system, or instruction handed to us on a plate, but genuine wrestling, search and struggle, in expectancy of a divine event of "speaking" to a ready heart.

Jesus frequently used the genre of *mashâl*, that is, parable, riddle, joke, aphorism, or narrative-world: "How can you say to your neighbour, 'Let me take the speck out of your eye', while the log is in your own eye?" (Matt. 7:4). "If your right eye causes you to sin, tear it out and throw it away; it is better to lose one of your members than ... to be thrown into hell" (Matt. 6:29). Ever since Adolf Jülicher tried to transpose the parables of Jesus into what became virtually broad prudential platitudes that reflected "ethical truths", interpreters of the parable-genre have rightly insisted that their revelatory power is not to be diluted into flat propositional abstractions. I have expounded this point too many times for it to require further explication here.[45] Once again, the hermeneutics demanded by "indirect" genre within the Bible, unfold dimensions of "the authority of the Bible" beyond narrower understandings of the concept. It extends beyond the head, to heart and to life. Like biblical laments and biblical praise, it demands a heart "in tune" with Scripture.

---

[41] See esp. Dale Martin, *Slavery as Salvation: The Metaphor of Slavery in Pauline Christianity* (New Haven, CT: Yale University Press, 1990); see also Thiselton, *First Epistle to the Corinthians*, pp.459–60, 476–9, 553–65 amd 700–703.

[42] Paul Ricoeur, *Essays on Biblical Interpretation* (London: SPCK, 1981 and Philadelphia, PA: Fortress, 1980), p.74.

[43] Ibid., p.89.

[44] Essay 40 of this volume, "Polyphonic Voices and Theological Fiction".

[45] See, for example, Thiselton, *Two Horizons*, pp.342–56; and *New Horizons*, pp.115–21.

III
Exposure of "Interest", Self-Deception and Manipulative Interpretation

The turn to postmodernity has brought both gains and losses in relation to Christian theology and hermeneutics. A general distrust of rationality, traditions and universal truth-claims, together with an over-ready hospitality to radical pluralism, pragmatism and the giving of privilege to the "local" criteria of "my" group stand on the negative side. However, on the positive side, recognition of the illusory nature of value-neutral perception and value-neutral horizons coheres precisely with biblical insights into the deceitfulness of the human heart and the realities of human bondage to sin as self-centred criteria of value.

In Essay 30 of this volume, taken from part of *Interpreting God and the Postmodern Self*, we traced the work of Friedrich Nietzsche in exposing the scope of self-deception in this area. Nietzsche, in spite of his scepticism and frequent misperceptions, accurately exposes the role of self-deception in inauthentic "religion", even if he appears to attribute it to all "religion". Among his many incisive aphorisms in *The Antichrist*, he notes the desire for comfort, security, safety and even importance that too often accompanies religious conversion. He writes, "The 'salvation of the soul' – in plain English, 'the world revolves around me'."[46] Nietzsche especially reserves his bitterest reproach for religious leaders or priests: "Supreme axiom: 'God forgiveth him that repenteth' – in plain English: him that submitteth himself to the priest."[47]

Nietzsche identified a major critical principle, which still informs most contemporary philosophical hermeneutics. In Jürgen Habermas the critical principle is formulated in terms of the "interest" or interests that may predispose readers or interpreters to approach texts with questions and agenda that are far from value-neutral. These often reflect social and political motivations and concerns.[48] In his later work this extends to a discussion and critique of "instrumental" or functional reason.

The work of Roland Barthes and Jacques Derrida takes up this critical principle and thereby assists us in seeking to explore inauthentic appeals to "biblical authority" in order to serve human interests or desire for power and control. On the other hand it brings about damaging effects by deconstructing the very notion of a stable "text". Hence Vanhoozer characterized Barthes and Derrida as "un-doers": "Derrida is an unbeliever in the reliability [and] decidability ... of the sign".[49] He adds: "Derrida's deconstruction of the author is a more or less direct consequence of Nietzsche's announcement of the death of God."[50] Once the text is cut loose from its author, Vanhoozer insists, "It is pointless to 'decipher' a text."[51]

---

[46] Nietzsche, *The Complete Works* (18 vols, London: Allen & Unwin, 1909–13), vol. 16, *The Antichrist*, p.186, aphorism 43.

[47] Ibid., p.231, aphorism 62.

[48] J. Habermas, *Knowledge and Human Interests* (Eng., London: Heinemann, 2nd edn, 1978); and *The Theory of Communicative Action* (2 vols, Eng., Cambridge: Polity Press, 1984 and 1987).

[49] K.J. Vanhoozer, *Is There a Meaning in This Text?* (Grand Rapids, MI: Zondervan, 1998), pp.38 and 39.

[50] Ibid.

[51] Ibid, p.69.

If Vanhoozer is right [we discuss this further in Essays 32–36]), "the authority of the Bible" becomes on one side a problematic concept in the light of Derrida's claims. However, on the other side, Barthes and Derrida also unmask how thoroughly "sub-texts" come into play into our everyday reading of texts. Roland Barthes, as we have noted, expounded a semiotics of clothes and furniture that reveals how much perceptions of social class or desires about how we wish others to perceive us influence our choices or arrangements of clothes and furniture rather than simply the weather or practical convenience alone.[52] Derrida's "White Mythology" seeks to unmask the espousal of certain metaphysical beliefs in order to justify or legitimize doctrines that amount to no more than metaphor pressed to support a world-view.[53]

These considerations reveal and re-enforce an aspect of the authority of the Bible to which especially Martin Luther, Dietrich Bonhoeffer and Gerhard Ebeling repeatedly appeal. Ebeling declares, "According to Luther, the word of God always comes as *adversarius noster*, our adversary. It does not simply confirm and strengthen us in what we think ... It negates [that] ... which has fallen prey to illusion ... This is the way the word of God affirms our being and makes it true."[54] The Bible is not merely a manipulative device to confirm the wishes of the reader, as if "God" were a mere projection of the reader's will.

Dietrich Bonhoeffer makes precisely this point explicitly. Bonhoeffer writes:

> If it is I who say where God will be, I will always find there a [false] God who in some way corresponds to me, is agreeable to me, fits in with my nature. But if it is God who says where He will be ... that place is the cross of Christ. This, he urges, is why the beatitudes in the Sermon on the Mount do not declare "blessed are the powerful" but "blessed are those who mourn", "blessed are the poor".[55]

In his study of the inspiration and authority of the Bible, Bruce Vawter applies this principle especially to the inner awareness of the prophets. "Often enough", he writes, "they gave words not of their own devising that at times they would even have preferred to leave unsaid ...".[56]

IV
The Three-Dimensional Integrity of Biblical Authority

Prior to the period of the 1930s, the model of *historical reconstruction* remained the key to understanding the meaning of the biblical text. The dominance of this approach reached a high-water mark in the nineteenth and early twentieth centuries, under the combined impact of the rise of modern biblical criticism and the influence at that time of Romanticist and Humanist models of hermeneutics.

---

[52] Roland Barthes, *Elements of Semiology* (Eng., London: Cape, 1967); cf. also his *Mythologies* (Eng., London: Cape, 1972).

[53] J. Derrida, "White Mythology: Metaphor in the Text of Philosophy", in his *Margins of Philosophy*, (Eng., New York: Harvester, 1982), pp.207–72.

[54] G. Ebeling, *Introduction to a Theological Theory of Language* (London: Collins, 1973), p.17.

[55] D. Bonhoeffer, *Meditating on the Word* (Eng., Cambridge, MA: Cowley Publications, 1986), p.45; and further cf. *The Cost of Discipleship* (Eng., London: SCM, 1959), pp.93–176 (unabridged edn).

[56] B. Vawter, *Biblical Inspiration* (Louisville, KY: Westminster John Knox, 1971), p.17.

This approach led to what I described in the previous essay (Essay 33) as an emphasis upon processes *"behind"* the text. I also argued that it constituted an essential part of meaning and interpretation (at least in many contexts) in Essay 3, "Resituating Hermeneutics". However, it also tends to orientate discussions about the authority of the Bible towards issues of *source*, that is, to related but different issues about the nature if the *inspiration* of the Bible and the apostolic or prophetic origins of biblical writings. The question, "How did the text originate?" was asked not only as a way of entering into the situation and world behind the text in *historical* terms but also as a way of asking about sources of the text in *theological* terms. If the Epistle to the Hebrews, for example, is non-Pauline, does this diminish its authority, especially if the author is unknown to us?

From the 1930s onwards however, the movement in literary theory known as "the New Criticism", or sometimes as "literary formalism", came upon the stage as a major tool in American and in part also English lecture rooms. John C. Ransom's *The New Criticism* (1941) and René Wellek and Austin Warren's *Theory of Literature* (1949) both assumed the role of dominant textbooks in American literature classes. With a critical eye on the hermeneutics of Boeckh, these writers claimed that to begin with the author and the author's intention is "quite mistaken" as an approach to the meaning of the text.[57] Wimsatt and Beardsley attacked what they called "The Intentional Fallacy".[58]

By the 1970s a mood of disenchantment with purely "historical" interpretation had emerged, coupled with an impatience over a failure of "the assured results of biblical criticism" ever to appear, and this paved the way for a new hospitality towards such slogans as "the text and nothing but the text". During the 1970s a temporary flirtation with structuralism dominated the "experimental" biblical journal *Semeia*, while by the end of the 1970s the two different movements of "canonical" approaches and "literary" approaches often complemented more traditional approaches. In 1988 Robert Morgan criticized an over-preoccupation with what he called "the historical paradigm" in biblical studies, and argued that many problems could be "eased by a switch to a literary paradigm for biblical interpretation".[59] The issue of biblical "authority" now became refocused in some quarters into an attribute of a given text without reference to its origins. Sometimes this was formulated in terms of inter-textuality: does a text resonate with the witness of the biblical canon or with other texts? Might it be said that the text of the Epistle to the Hebrews operates with an authority of its own?

A concern for "the text itself", *rather than* "historical" approaches, receives advocacy from several writers, of whom Christopher Seitz is one of the most significant. Seitz sees the providential hand of God "within" rather than merely "behind" the text of Scripture. More explicitly, historical and especially "developmental" approaches, Seitz argues, too readily become descriptive accounts of a past "religion". "Scripture becomes religion or religions", and this constitutes "a disfigurement of scripture in the name of relating the

57 R. Welleck and A. Warren, *Theory of Literature* (London: Penguin [1949] 1973), p.42.
58 W.K. Wimsatt and M.C. Beardsley, "The Intentional Fallacy", in *The Verbal Icon* (Lexington: University of Kentucky Press, 1954), pp.1–18.
59 Robert Morgan (with John Barton), *Biblical Interpretations* (Oxford: OUP, 1988), p.25; repeated on p.198.

testaments developmentally".[60] We should read, as a church, "the final forms of Christian scripture as canon, the parts informing the whole, the whole informing the parts, according to the rule of faith".[61]

In the previous essay (Essay 33), account was taken of the effects of texts "in front of" the texts, that is, their transformative power upon readers. Several more recent movements bring this aspect into clearer focus. First, Paul Ricoeur asks as of primary hermeneutical significance, "What does the word or the text set going?"[62] Second, reader-response theory, which we discuss in Part V, and especially in Essay 27 of this volume, adds another angle of approach to this dimension. Third, the "History of Reception", or the *Wirkungsgeschichte* of texts, has placed renewed emphasis upon this third dimension in a less subjective way. This traces what effects the biblical text actually set going in various contexts in history. Ricoeur declares: "A proposed world ... is not *behind* the text, as hidden intention would be, but *in front* of it, as that which the work unfolds, discovers, reveals" (Ricoeur's italics).[63] This includes the experience of readers of being addressed: "To understand is *to understand oneself in front of the text*" (also Ricoeur's italics).[64] Again in Essay 33 I allude to the integration of all dimensions as a goal rightly adopted in a class-level textbook on hermeneutics written by W. Randolph Tate.[65]

On the subject of the authority of the Bible, then, might it not be argued that, in addition to questions of interpretation, that such "authority" also belongs to all three of these dimensions, understood as an integrated whole?

(1) The *agents "behind"* the text (divine and human) remain an ontological *source* of authority: for the "word" of God, as Barth insists, is nothing other than God himself speaking and acting, especially if we accept Nicholas Wolterstorff's notion of "deputized" discourse.[66]

(2) The *text* itself embodies a word written *"within"* it, just as the incarnate Christ embodies the word "lived" and enfleshed, and preaching and teaching representing the word proclaimed. This is not to place all manifestations of this word on the same level: Jesus Christ is to be worshipped; while preaching or prophetic utterance is to be tested.

(3) The word of God is "living and active, sharper than any two-edged sword" (Heb. 4:12). What it sets going, as part of its *formative and transformative power* takes place *"in front of"* the text, as life-changing and thought-shaping in its effects.

This brings us back full circle to the first of our four points. The authority of Scripture operates at many levels and in many ways, but not least as *Bildung*, as "formation",

[60] Seitz, *Figured Out* (2001), cited above, p.15.

[61] Ibid., p.81.

[62] Ricoeur, *The Conflict of Interpretations*, p.28.

[63] Paul Ricoeur, "The Hermeneutical Function of Distanciation", in his *Hermeneutics and the Human Sciences* (Cambridge: CUP, 1981), p.143.

[64] Ibid.

[65] W. Randolph Tate, *Biblical Interpretation: An Integrated Approach* (Peabody, MA: Hendrickson, 1991).

[66] N. Wolterstorff, *Divine Discourse* (Cambridge: CUP, 1995), pp.37–57 and 114–23.

among individuals and communities. Contemporary philosophical hermeneutics does not explicitly embody these arguments about the authority of the Bible. However, without the rise of contemporary philosophical hermeneutics this importance might more easily be lost from view, and their claims may have appeared less readily credible. Their relevance and force can no longer be ignored, and they take their place alongside more traditional understandings of the authority of the Bible.

V

Issues of Conflict with Concepts of Biblical Authority: Textual Indeterminacy, The Death of the Author, and a "Local" Neo-Pragmatism

(a) The Problem of Textual Indeterminacy

In my original lecture I gave more detailed attention to the three issues cited under this fifth heading. But if they were included here, some details would overlap with other essays in this volume. Hence I offer only a short summary of key points. The problem of indeterminacy of meaning has long been recognized in philosophical hermeneutics, and in the last twenty-five years has been closely associated with Derrida's notion of "deferred" meaning. Yet there is a difference between claiming on one side that a text or a word bears a *single*, determinate, meaning and claiming that even where specific contextual influences generate multiple meaning, this meaning remains *stable* rather than infinitely open to radical instability. The *second* is essential if we are to retain currency for the authority of the Biblical text. The *former* is difficult to sustain in the light of studies of language on the part of linguisticians, philosophers of language, lexicographers, exegetes, and exponents of hermeneutics, and it is *not* a necessary presupposition or axiom for expounding a working understanding of the authority of Scripture.

Even the most conservative writer accepts that, for example, a full canonical context may expand the strictly semantic boundaries of a passage in the Old Testament. Is the meaning (not just the significance) of the Servant Songs determined exhaustively by a single specific historical situation and context? Moreover, while historical genre may well depend on a determinate meaning for such a statement as "Jesus was crucified under Pontius Pilate", or "Gallio was Proconsul in AD 51", poetic genre would be tortured and "disfigured" (to use Seitz's word) by the reductive assumptions about language on the part of what J. Lotman and H.-G. Gadamer refer to as "an engineering culture". George Caird observes that in the Book of Revelation to insist upon a determinate meaning for every single atom of a composite picture or image is to "unweave the rainbow". Jüri Lotman and Umberto Eco rightly enquire about the *degree* of determinacy exhibited within a wide spectrum of language, and show how this relates to whether we are reading "open" texts (that is, poetic, creative, parabolic, image-laden, language) or "closed" texts (that is, texts that are more tightly bounded for transmissive communication, such as creeds, teaching, or history).

There needs to be a *measure* of stability in language, which calls a *relative degree* of determinacy. Otherwise the concern of James Smart would be given substance that "the remembered Christ becomes an imagined Christ, shaped by the religiosity and the unconscious desires of his worshippers".[67] "Boundaries" cannot be *entirely* fluid if the word, the sentence, the discourse, or the canon, is to speak with authority. James Dunn observes in the context, "The canon ... served to mark out the circumference of acceptable diversity".[68]

Interpretation, I have argued in a number of places (including especially in Essay 33), needs to find and to follow a middle path. The authority of the Bible does not depend upon a supposed wooden literalism, which assigns a single, sharply bounded meaning to every word and to every sentence. Biblical poetry would thereby be reduced to the pragmatic, unimaginative prose of an engineering handbook. Conservative theologians who veer towards this view have actually *absorbed* the very Enlightenment rationalism that they often attack, even if they imagine that they protest against it. On the other hand, those postmodern exponents of philosophical hermeneutics who collapse all stable meaning into a vanishing cloud of "traces" (to use Derrida's term), fail to do justice to the nature of language, as well as to the force of biblical authority. Those biblical scholars who wrestle daily with Greek and Hebrew lexicography will take some persuading that biblical texts are as "open" as (for example) the writings of James Joyce or, within biblical examples, the Song of Songs.

(b) "The Death of the Author"

Roland Barthes and Jacques Derrida do not hesitate to agree that their claims about the death of the author would have destructive consequences for theology, even if they call it "onto-theology". Their approach "liberates an activity we may call counter-theological ... for to refuse to halt meaning is finally to refuse God".[69] Derrida adds that deconstruction is the death of God put into writing.

Two distinct dimensions or functions of language suffer when the author's role, a role that Julia Kristeva often calls that of "the speaking subject" (especially in dialogue with Derrida) becomes too readily lost from view. For Derrida, meaning is primarily a matter of *signification*, of a chain of words pointing to other words, sentences to other sentences, *within language*. However, as soon as the concept of responsible agents and knowing subjects enter back into the picture, a *noetic* dimension arises. Has language nothing to do with *epistemology* or cognition? Nicholas Wolterstorff, among others, makes this point incisively in relation to Derrida.[70] He rightly links the problem (with Kristeva) with Derrida's rejection of metaphysics. Derrida's *world-view* conditions his approach to language, and causes him to read and to interpret Ferdinand de Saussure in ways, we may infer, that would not have been congenial to Saussure himself.

Once again, some fine, necessary distinctions have become obscured. As I have argued in my commentary on 1 Corinthians, the essence of apostolic witness is *pointing away from*

---

[67] James Smart, *The Strange Silence of the Bible in the Church* (London: SCM, 1970), p.25.
[68] J.D.G. Dunn, *Unity and Divinity in the New Testament* (London: SCM, 1977), p.376.
[69] R. Barthes, *The Rustle of Language* (New York: Hill, 1986), p.54.
[70] N. Wolterstorff, "In Defence of Authorial Discourse Interpretation: Contra Derrida", in *Divine Discourse*.

self to Christ.[71] "Authority" does not, for Paul, imply a personality cult of apostles or "authors". On the other hand apostolicity does constitute a unique foundation-testimony, just as prophetic speech reflects the mediation of the divine word through active and reflective agents. Since, however, apostolic and prophetic witness points away from self to *God* or *Christ*, and is of such a nature that the apostle does not seek honour or applause for himself (cf. 1 Cor. 3:5, 6; 4:1–5, 9–13; 9:1–12; 15:8–10; 2 Cor. 4:7–12), in *some* genres, the "author" recedes to almost nothing. The narrative of Jonah projects a "narrative world" of satire, in which the reader is caught up in a world of irony and "deconstruction" which does its own formative work. The dialogue of Job presents an interplay of polyphonic "voices", in which it is the conversation and wrestling that "speaks". Contemporary philosophical hermeneutics helps to alert us to these issues.

Nevertheless if "the death of the author" is *absolutized*, this becomes, as Barthes concedes, "counter-theological"; it is "to refuse God". It would erode away biblical authority as amounting to little more than that of a classic text. This claim is not over-dramatic or exaggerated. For if we move from the noetic to the realm of speech-acts, in the event of the death of the author, who is behind the act of *promising*? In whose name is the promise? Who is *forgiving*? Who has the *authority* to forgive? Who is *commissioning* and *naming*? Who has the right to commission or to name? Derrida's appeal to the radical cutting-loose of texts from their stable moorings through "iteration" cannot operate in the cases cited above. If, as we suggest, the Bible is a love-letter from the heart of God, to read "I love you" as the words of a dead or anonymous lover would destroy this act of love and transpose it into a tragedy.

(c) A Neo-Pragmatism of the Merely "Local"?

According to Richard Rorty, "Hermeneutics ... is what we get when we are no longer epistemological".[72] Rorty transfers the notion of "incommensurability" from the philosophy of science (where it properly belongs, and carries a more rigorous and technical meaning), and perceives "hermeneutics" as "not 'another way of knowing' ... [but] as another way of coping".[73]

Yet if we were to accept Rorty's view of what constitutes "hermeneutics", any notion of biblical authority would rapidly evaporate. First, he asserts, "Truth is not the goal of inquiry. If 'truth' is the name of such a goal then, indeed, there is no truth."[74] The correspondence theory of truth and coherence theory of truth cannot be sustained; there is merely the possibility of having conversations with "the right people" in the hope of some kind of pragmatic "progress".[75] But where are we to find criteria of what counts as progress? Only in terms of what seems "justified" to this or that "local" community. There is no talk of "getting reality right" because "there is no Way the World Is".[76] I refer

---

[71] A.C. Thiselton, *The First Epistle to the Corinthians* (Grand Rapids, MI: Eerdmans and Carlisle: Paternoster, 2000), pp.64–9, 663–76 and 846–8.

[72] R. Rorty, *Philosophy and the Mirror of Nature* (Princeton, NJ: Princeton University Press, 1979), p.325.

[73] Ibid., p.356; cf. pp.357–65.

[74] Rorty, *Truth and Progress: Philosophical Papers*, vol. 3 (Cambridge: CUP, 1998), p.3.

[75] Ibid., pp.11–12.

[76] Ibid., p.25.

readers to other essays in this volume for a development of this account and critique of Rorty.[77]

Rorty's "hermeneutics", I believe, owes far more to a world-view based on non-theistic pragmatism than to a genuine hermeneutical theory of language and truth. Like A.J. Ayer's "Logical Positivism", which came to be unmasked as mere positivism in linguistic dress, Rorty's sophisticated appeals to "philosophical hermeneutics" barely disguises a world-view in which in the end only dollars and tanks can provide pragmatic quasi-ultimates, in spite of later claims to reflect a philosophy of social value or critique. In his later work Rorty shows sincerity (is he tending towards Fish's despised "Serious Man"?) in his concern for "progress" and well-being in liberal democracies. But this is still a version of American "progressivism", in which "well-being" may be defined in terms comfortably derived from technological progress, or from almost any value compatible with "The American Dream".[78] But can a philosophy with no ultimates beyond the welfare of "people like us" sustain justice and hope in a world as complex as that of the twenty-first century?

The biblical writings exercise their formative authority partly by beckoning from *beyond* such horizons as those of communities "like us". They concern a wider community in space and time, and a reality which speaks from a "Beyond" that transcends everyday life. Rorty uses the term "local" in preference to the terms "relative" and "relativist", but he concedes that there may not be a vast difference between them. This may perhaps bring us back full circle to the comments of C.H. Dodd about communities of communities through space and time, with which this paper began.

The early chapters of 1 Corinthians, I have argued, embody a re-proclamation of the Gospel of the cross to a consumerist, competitive society that valued and esteemed the "winners" of competitive rhetoric more than the "truth" of apostolic witness or of patient, unspectacular argument. It valued the local above the universal, and self-promotion above respect for "the other". The "authority" of Paul's apostolic proclamation is not that of another consumer product designed to bring "progress".[79] Its authority becomes evident in its power to overturn the drive for self-promotion and "success" in favour of respect for "the other", just as the work of Christ in the incarnation, the cross and the resurrection, likewise serves "the other". The authority of the Gospel *to subvert and to transform* (1 Cor. 1:18–25), derives its status from the person, ministry and work of Christ, and derives its power from the Holy Spirit and the "Word". This brings about a new "formation" of thought, life and character.

"Philosophical hermeneutics" reflects a broad spectrum. On one side, a "local" pragmatism would evaporate the Bible of any authority to speak "from Beyond". On the other side the hermeneutical tradition from Schleiermacher to Gadamer, Betti and Ricoeur may be seen to nurture and to facilitate "listening" and understanding what is initially "other" and strange to the self, and to learn respect for the "otherness" of the

---

[77] Especially Essay 32, "Two Types of Postmodernity".
[78] See R. Rorty, *Philosophy and Social Hope* (London: Penguin Books, 1999).
[79] Thiselton, *The First Epistle to the Corinthians*, pp.2–33 and 134–223, and Essay 33 [this volume].

other. Gadamer observes that hermeneutics has little or nothing to do with "preserving one's own 'position'": "Hermeneutics is above all ... the art of understanding ... In it what one has to exercize above all is *the ear* ...".[80] This is a proper starting-point for questions about biblical authority.

---

[80] Gadamer, "Reflections on My Philosophical Journey", loc. cit., p.17.

CHAPTER THIRTY-FIVE

The Bible and Postmodernity: "Can a Pre-Modern Bible Address a Postmodern World?" (2003)

This essay originated in the form of a public lecture delivered in the University of St Andrews as part of a series to mark the bi-millennial year. Other lecturers in this series included Jürgen Moltmann, Paul Ricoeur and René Girard. The eight lectures were published (with an additional chapter) as 2000 Years and Beyond: Faith, Identity and the "Common Era", *edited by Paul Gifford with David Archard, Trevor A. Hart and Nigel Rapport (London and New York: Routledge, 2003). The essay below is from pp.127–46.*

There are numerous reasons why the Bible, written in the pre-modern era, might prima facie *appear to be incapable of addressing a postmodern world. It embodies what some would call "a grand narrative" of God's dealings with the world; it might seem to lack the degree of critical self-awareness that more readily suggests "innocence"; it appears unaware of when its claims to truth serve as claims to power, and its anchorages in history and utterances of promise seem to presuppose a degree of linguistic determinacy that some would dismiss as illusory. These issues set an agenda for this essay, and I argue that Paul's dialogue with Christians in Corinth provides a model for apostolic engagement with attitudes that overlap with what we might well call "postmodern".*

I

Some Reasonable Grounds for Scepticism about the Question

I shall try to set out a positive answer to what may seem *prima facie* to demand a necessarily negative response in five sections of arguments. First, postmodern writers are deeply suspicious of truth-claims that relate to universals, or to trans-contextual criteria of truth that claim to operate outside the prior interests of fragmented peer-groups, or (in Rorty's terms) "local" or ethnocentric interests. Yet biblical writers speak not only of a creation and end that concern "universal" world history, but also of a gospel that explicitly transcends the ethnocentric interests and truth-claims of Jew and Gentile, male and female, slave and free. Can such an ambitious agenda rest on anything more than pre-Kantian, pre-Nietzschean innocence?

Second, clearly the very term "postmodern" seems to presuppose a sequential following of a period of "modernity", in relation to which it is variously construed as a reaction, critique, modification, or degeneration. Jürgen Moltmann has expressed a preference for the use of the term "sub-modernity" for what many describe as postmodernity.[1] Richard Bernstein calls postmodernity "a rage against humanism and

---

[1] J. Moltmann, *God for a Secular Society: The Public Relevance of Theology* (London: SCM, 1999), pp.11–17.

the Enlightenment legacy".[2] In my second section I shall argue that postmodernity does not primarily or only represent a sequential advance or decline in relation to modernity, but what some have already described as a "mood", attitude, or ethos. In more specific terms I shall argue that it describes a mood widespread in ancient Roman Corinth which leads Paul the Apostle to draw a conscious, critical contrast between a socially constructed value-system based on "recognition" and virtual realities created by rhetoric, consumerism, peer-group competition and self-promotion, and broader non-instrumental, non-pragmatic truth-claims conveyed by the givenness of grace from beyond local communities. Indeed "local" construals of truth go back to pre-Socratic philosophy concerning which Nietzsche and the later Heidegger propose some rehabilitation for more recent times.

Third, I recognize and accept the need to focus more sharply on the level of critical self-awareness which might have been possible for pre-modern biblical writers in appearing to participate in such sophisticated debate. Those who hold a progressivist and broadly developmental view of the history of human thought may more readily identify themselves with Hegel's claim that until his own times "religions" tended to use uncritical imagery or representation (*Vorstellung*) rather than the critical concept (*Begriff*) made possible with the advent of historical reason in Hegel's philosophy. Such an assumption lies behind the work of Strauss, Feuerbach and (in effect more recently in the mid-twentieth century) the proposals of Rudolf Bultmann about myth in the New Testament. In my third section I shall argue (i) that if this assumption is valid, Bultmann cannot claim that demythologizing begins within the New Testament, or that he is merely following the path already begun by Paul and John; and (ii) that the subtle and complex use of such rhetorical and logical phenomena as code-switching, persuasive definition, an awareness of logical grammar, and use of sophisticated devices of Graeco-Roman rhetoric would hardly have been open to Paul and to the writer of the Epistle to the Hebrews, not to mention subtle uses of narrative time, flashbacks, strategies of reader-response and so forth regularly attributed today to the "simple" Gospel of Mark, with its colloquial Greek which invited "improvements" from Matthew-Luke, serve in any case to make such a sweeping assumption entirely problematic.

Fourth, postmodern writers often have an overtly political agenda that is regularly aimed at deconstructing the norms and boundaries presupposed as "truths" by an Establishment into instrumental constructs of social power-interests. The incisive demolitions and reformulations of Barthes and especially Foucault relate closely to issues of power and marginality within the pages of the Bible. Jesus of Nazareth exposed some of the supposed boundaries imposed by pharisaic or scribal piety as social constructions that embodied inconsistencies generated by interests of privilege rather than by authentic truth, even in terms of Old Testament traditions (cf. for example Mark 7:11 on *corban*). Nevertheless neither Jesus nor the writers of the Epistles see all differentiation as social construction. Indeed accounts of creation (Gen. 1:1–2:4), of gender (1 Cor. 11:2–16), and of "order" even in the eschatological consummation (1 Cor. 15:20–58), presuppose that distinctions of role or nature may in many cases depend on the givenness of divine

---

[2]   R.J. Bernstein (ed.), *Habermas and Modernity* (Cambridge: Polity Press, 1985).

decree, not on the power-interests of social construction. To be sure, debate is needed concerning whether the very notion of divine decree is itself a device of social control and construction, but here we are beginning to raise the very contrast between theistic and anti-theistic world-views. What is at stake is now no longer postmodernity but the validity of theism.

A fifth cluster of issues, addressed in our final section, concerns claims about linguistic indeterminacy and the correlative problem of the role of human and perhaps also divine agency in communicative linguistic acts. I shall argue that to subsume theories of linguistic indeterminacy and an anti-representational view of language into a comprehensive theory of language is as untenable and as one-sided as the opposite error of regarding all language as deriving its meaning from a single determinate referential relation to states of affairs within the extra-linguistic world. Both of these views fail to take account of the multi-functional and multi-dimensional nature of language and meaning. The biblical writings function consciously to perform a variety of linguistic functions. Paul Ricoeur, for example, convincingly underlines the diverse hermeneutical and linguistic or semiotic dimensions which are called into play when specific biblical genres function explicitly as *narrative* discourse (fictive or fictional), *prophetic* verdict (declarative or inter-subjective), *prescriptive* law (contextually constrained or potentially trans-contextual), *hymnic* expression (psalms of praise, lament, accusation, or other modes of address), *didactic* communication (relating to states of affairs, conduct, in persons), and *wisdom* modes (undertaking exploration in the face of what is largely but not wholly hidden).[3] To try to impose on all these modes of discourse a postmodern doctrine of indeterminacy and radical plurality or "erasure" on one side, or the early-modern notion of a single determinate meaning derived from simple extra-linguistic reference and representation on the other, becomes exposed as an absurdity in the face of the particularities and contingencies of diverse biblical language-functions and varied textual performances.

II
Some Characteristics of a Postmodern Mind-Set

We return to our contention that postmodernity does not depend for its currency or its appeal primarily or solely as a reaction against, or modification of, "modernity" in the Western tradition of philosophical, scientific and social thought. This is not to deny Bernstein's point (cited above) that it is very often fired and inspired by a "rage" against the presumptuous illusions of high modernity as expressed in secular Enlightenment thought. Its optimistic progressivism, its individualism and its claim to universality often based on abstract rationalism and on a disregard for historical reason and historical situatedness do indeed invite and provoke many of the most characteristic negations and reactions of postmodernity. In practice the Christian gospel also and equally rejects these

---

[3]   Paul Ricoeur, "The Hermeneutics of Revelation", in *Essays on Biblical Interpretation* (ed. L.S. Mudge, London: SPCK, 1981), esp. pp.85–93.

claims of high modernity as presumptuous and as based on illusion, as well as on over-extending the legitimate scope of scientific method to include, in effect, a world-view or comprehensive account of all that is. Nevertheless within the New Testament the "postmodern mood" of social construction has more in common with the culture of first-century Roman Corinth, which Paul opposes, than with apostolic faith and apostolic preaching.

Paul has a respect for rational argument which presupposes a shared notion of reasonable entitlement for this or that belief-system that refuses to collapse belief into the product of mere causal persuasion or rhetoric, or into socially habituated patterns of assumptions or into the power-interests of socially-defined peer groups. The whole of 1 Corinthians constitutes a plea for coherent, "centred" belief and conduct as over against the fragmented interests of specific socio-religious groups whose main self-justification was the construction of a "reality" within which they perceived themselves as "spiritual people".[4]

In universities of our times, Christian theology at its best seeks to hold together two poles: on one side the particularities and social contingencies which mark serious hermeneutical and historical awareness, and on the other side a retention of epistemological courage and nerve to consider, to put forward and to test truth-claims which transcend the limits of specific local contexts. As Pannenberg convincingly observes, whereas Nietzsche and Freud locate the grounding of faith in "God" in such limited contexts as that of the experience of a guilty conscience, "God" confronts us with "the one totality of reality"; it is "a key word for awareness of the totality of the world in human life".[5] Pannenberg also alludes to Karl Rahner's formulation of this point, and earlier speaks of the intellectual obligation entailed in speech about God to address the problem of universals, since God is creator of all.[6] Because Christian theists perceive the action of God in and through "the non-exchangeable individuality and contingency" of events in history, above all in the historically conditioned event of the incarnate life and work of Jesus Christ, and yet also in transcendent patterns of action and meaning such as eschatological promise, newness and the resurrection, a dialectic of the particular or contingent and the universal or trans-contextual is set up.[7]

In my own University of Nottingham this dialectic finds expression in the possibility of genuine dialogue between the Department of Theology and Critical Theory on one side, and Philosophy on the other. With one it shares a sense of the importance of ideological suspicion and at times for deconstruction (surely a method reflected here and there perhaps in Ecclesiastes and most certainly in Job), and with the other it shares a deep concern for the validity of rational truth-claims made on behalf of given logical

---

4   I have argued this case, in effect, over a sustained exegesis and theological exposition of some 1,450 pages in Anthony C. Thiselton, *The First Epistle to the Corinthians: A Commentary on the Greek Text* (The New International Greek Testament Commentary, Grand Rapids, MI: Eerdmans and Carlisle: Paternoster, 2000), esp. pp.12–17, 120–75, 204–39, 669–76, 900–1214.

5   Wolfhart Pannenberg, *Systematic Theology* (3 vols, Eng., Edinburgh: T. & T. Clark and Grand Rapids, MI: Eerdmans, 1991, 1994, and 1998), vol. 1, pp.65 and 71.

6   Cf. Karl Rahner, *Foundations of Christian Faith* (New York: Seabury, 1968), p.48; and W. Pannenberg, *Basic Questions in Theology* (3 vols, Eng., London: SCM, 1970, 1971 and 1973), esp. vol. 1, pp.39–50 and 164–74 and vol. 2, p.25.

7   See W. Pannenberg, *Basic Questions*, vol. 1, pp.46–8, and vol. 3, pp.14–68.

arguments and systems of thought, within the constraints of constructive questions about human rationality, responsibility and active agency. While my doctoral candidates have engaged in debate with their peers in both of these other departments or schools, I should be surprised if the same kind of dialogue proved to be possible between Critical Theory and Philosophy. The former tends to accuse the latter of failure to take historicality and historical situatedness seriously; while the latter tends to view the former as reducing ideas and rational thought to mere socio-historical forces. A leaning towards one side or the other can be detected within the Faculty of Arts. The Inaugural Lecture of a Professor of Hispanic Studies, for example, explicitly promoted deconstruction as a political, rather than literary, tool, to expose an ideology of North American domination over the economies and cultures of Latin Americans. By contrast, humanist accounts of historical causality tend to find more ready hospitality in the School of History and Art History.

Our university also has lively inter-faculty debates on the ethical, social and legal implications of genetic research. Here, on one side, those from Theology, Law, and Social Sciences tend to focus on issues of personhood in contrast to more mechanistic approaches to this area. On the other hand, some geneticists welcomed social scientists into their laboratories with delight, to underline that genetic "givens" could not be reduced to the mere constructs of social constructionism: delight shared by those from Theology.

In these contexts a balance sheet emerges with sympathies on both sides. Positively, David Harvey sees postmodernity as a reaction against "positivist technocratic and rationalistic universal modernism" and against "the standardization of knowledge" which characterizes a naïve privileging of science and technology as a world-view in high modernity.[8] From the standpoint of Christian theology, the negative corollary is what Harvey identifies as "fragmentation, indeterminacy, and intense destruct of all universal or 'totalizing' discourses": characteristics that constitute "the hallmark of postmodernist thought".[9] If we place the two sides of the balance sheet in closer contrast, the spirit of (secular) modernity gives priority and privilege to the development of "objective science", and gives privilege also to "autonomy" (as exemplified in Kant); but on the other side modernity retains a respect for universal moral law. On one side (with Christian theology), postmodernity challenges the progressive optimism of modernity with its illusory faith in the natural sciences to solve almost all human problems, and underlines the limits and illusions of autonomous individualism. On the other side (in contrast to Christian theology), postmodernity feeds on a culture of suspicion rather than trust, replaces truth-claims and argument by pragmatism and rhetoric, disengages meaning from human agency to reduce it to an unstable product of changing textual forces, and, in the context of Derrida's thought, perceives "signatures" as having "more to do with absence than presence", as against the promissory function of named discourse in much biblical material.[10]

---

[8] David Harvey, *The Condition of Postmodernity* (Oxford: Blackwell, 1989), p.9.

[9] Ibid.

[10] The phrase and argument is amplified by Kevin Vanhoozer, *Is There a Meaning in This Text? The Bible, The Reader, and the Morality of Literary Knowledge* (Grand Rapids, MI: Zondervan, 1998), pp.65–97; cf. J. Derrida, *Writing and Difference* (Eng., London: Routledge, 1978) and *Of Grammatology* (Eng., Baltimore, MD and London: Johns Hopkins University Press, 1976).

Even the postmodern critique of the privileging of the natural sciences as offering world-views rather than "local" methods of discovery reveals a deep ambivalence in relation to values and attitudes which Christian theology derives ultimately from the Bible. David Harvey rightly attributes this disillusion with progressivism and universal science to "the re-discovery of pragmatism in philosophy (e.g. Rorty, 1979), the shift of ideas around 1975, Foucault's emphasis upon discontinuity and difference in history ... new developments in mathematics emphasising indeterminacy (catastrophe and chaos theory, fractal geometry ...)".[11] These movements or moods remain ambivalent in relation to the Bible and to theology because on one side they underline the radical historical finitude of human agents and their discoveries and "advances" as heavily conditioned by their location or situatedness in the contingencies of space (local geographical resources) and time (what has gone before); nevertheless on the other side they over-extend the borrowed metaphor of "incommensurable" paradigms (on which Kahn modifies his earlier work of 1962), and, worse, with Lyotard they undermine and reject the very notion of a "grand narrative", a providential design or purpose in tradition and history, or "meta-narrative". In a very widely quoted comment Jean-François Lyotard offers what is probably the most frequently used definition of postmodernity when he observes: "Simplifying to the extreme, I define *postmodern* as incredulity towards metanarratives."[12]

One of Lyotard's interpreters, Bill Readings, defines "Grand Narrative" as a story that "claims the status of universal metanarrative, capable of accounting for all other stories in order to reveal their true meaning".[13] Traditionally Christian theologians, however, have claimed to perceive the Bible as a wide and contextualizing narrative of God's purposive and covenantal dealings with the world, with nations, with communities and with individuals in ways which bring to light the meanings of these smaller stories within this overarching frame. Yet, with the challenge of postmodernity, many theologians have generated the irony of seeking to escape an ontological "foundationalism" precisely by elevating the status of narrative. Unless, however, we remain at the level of individual, congregational, or local story, such a manoeuvre can suggest little more than a misunderstanding of what is at stake in a three-cornered encounter between modernity, postmodernity and biblical Christian theology. If we return from Lyotard's meta-narrative to Derrida's erasure of meaning and Barthes's radical plurality of meaning, Kevin Vanhoozer's suggestion that these are "counter-theological" also remains convincing: "To refuse to halt meaning is finally to refuse God", as Barthes explicitly concedes.[14] Vanhoozer concludes, "Derrida's deconstruction of the author is a more or less direct consequence of Nietzsche's announcement of the death of God."[15]

We are not yet ready to anticipate our fuller discussion of biblical material and the issue of the level of its self-awareness and critical consciousness. Nevertheless it is worth

---

[11] Harvey, *Condition*, p.9.
[12] J.-F. Lyotard, *The Postmodern Condition: A Report on Knowledge* (Eng., Minneapolis, MN: University of Minnesota Press, and Manchester: Manchester University Press, 1984), p.xxiv.
[13] Bill Readings, *Introducing Lyotard: Art and Politics* (London and New York: Routledge, 1991), p.xxxiii.
[14] Roland Barthes, "Death of Author", in *The Rustle of Language* (New York: Hill and Wang, 1986), p.54; Vanhoozer, *Is There a Meaning?*, p.30.
[15] Vanhoozer, *Is There a Meaning?*, p.48.

drawing attention to Paul's conscious rejection of hidden meanings, manipulative strategies of persuasion, and transparency in matters of truth (for example, 1 Cor. 2:1–5; 2 Cor. 3:12–4:6). He alludes to the practice of Moses (2 Cor. 3:13; cf. Exod. 34:29–35) in hiding the fading nature of the glory which shone from his face after his encounter with God, by the strategy of hiding his face behind a veil. Paul draws a contrast between such a strategy and that of "boldness", "openness" and transparent statements of truth-claims which he himself consciously chooses to adopt with an integrity in which word and deed are matched. Covenant promise presupposes a substantial degree of continuity and stability that Paul expounds and adopts. David Harvey underlines, by contrast, the "virtual reality" of postmodern construction; that which in due course we shall identify with the obsessive desire for a self-perception and status defined by how peer groups "recognize" themselves or others. In contrast to "representation", Harvey observes, the postmodern condition confronts us with "illusion, myth, aspiration", projection and "signs chasing signs".[16] It projects "diverse networks" which, I argue, reflect the "status inconsistency" generated by competing "multidimensional" recognition-systems, status-systems and value-systems in the Roman Corinth of AD 50–55, in the period of Paul's visit and writing.[17]

All of this resonates with party politics and with popular Western culture today. "Reality" becomes the plaything of the media, of political spin, of chatshow hosts, of manipulative journalists and politicians, and the atheistic aphorisms of Nietzsche appear as duly fulfilled prophecy: "Truth is that kind of error without which a certain kind of person cannot live."[18] "All that exists consists of interpretations."[19] "Knowledge works as an instrument of power."[20] "The salvation of the soul" means "The world revolves round me."[21] Paul and other New Testament writers, however, profoundly and emphatically reject the notion of "religion" or "salvation" as a vehicle of self-affirmation, peer-group self-promotion, or triumphalism, together with a notion of "God" that amounts to a projection of human desires and interests. This claim constitutes the central thesis of my published lectures sponsored by the *Scottish Journal of Theology*, delivered in the University of Aberdeen and revised as a coherent book.[22] Paul continues his exposition of integrity and transparency in 2 Cor. 3:12–4:6 with the comment that far from offering a self-affirming human construct Paul proclaims what has been "given" at huge personal cost for the sake of the flourishing of others (2 Cor. 4:7–15). I shall argue in due course that a critical self-awareness of the role of self-deception concerning these issues was virtually forced upon Paul by the transparently instrumental use of religious slogans for

---

[16] Harvey, *Condition*, pp.5 and 6.

[17] See Wayne A. Meeks, *The First Urban Christians. The Social World of the Apostle Paul* (New Haven, CT: Yale, 1983), p.34; and Thiselton, *First Epistle*, pp.12–17 and throughout (see Index, Postmodernity).

[18] F. Nietzsche, *Complete Works* (18 vols, Eng., London: Allen & Unwin, 1909–13), vol. 15, *The Will to Power*, ii, II, Aphorism 481.

[19] Ibid., p.12, Aphorism 481.

[20] Ibid., p.11, Aphorism 480.

[21] Nietzsche, *Works*, vol. 16, *The Antichrist* 186, Aphorism 43.

[22] Anthony C. Thiselton, *Interpreting God and the Postmodern Self: On Meaning, Manipulation and Promise* (Edinburgh: T. & T. Clark and Grand Rapids, MI: Eerdmans, 1995), throughout.

self-promotion and "recognition" in Corinth. Margaret Mitchell, L.L. Welborn and many other specialists have argued convincingly and in great detail that the "splits" (*schismata*) in the church of Corinth instantiated notably in 1 Cor. 1:10–12 utilized the language of politics (Mitchell); indeed, the language of power-play (Welborn).[23]

The biblical writers, especially Paul, not only reject the reduction of truth-claims about acts of God or salvation to instrumental power-play, but also more especially reject what have now become postmodern assumptions that truth-claims have no "hard" currency beyond the "soft" currency of local groups and interests largely determined by social class, race, gender, cultural conditioning, peer-group interests and correlative "recognition" within a guild. Thus Richard Rorty accepts that "relativism" has become an exhausted term, but substitutes in its place "ethnocentric" or "local" for the soft currencies of neo-pragmatism which he views with approval.[24] Truth is little more than inter-subjective agreement among given persons at given times. He endorses the claims of Foucault that, for example, "human rights" and "homosexuality" are concepts that resist such questions as "whether there really are human rights"; these are "recent social constructions".[25]

From the standpoint of Christian theism and biblical faith, this looks very like a re-run of A.J. Ayer's doctrinaire dismissal of religious and ethical language as expressing no more than non-cognitive, emotive expressions of approval or preference which, in the absence of universal scientific empirical verifiability, were to be regarded as "non-sense". Ayer's category of "non-sense" runs closely parallel with Rorty's project of "rubbish disposal".[26] In Rorty's view "the true" is simply what proves itself to be useful and acceptable in relation to the projects of particular persons or groups. He approves the maxim of William James that "'The true' ... is only the expedient in the way of our thinking ...".[27] "Truth" is no more than "justification", and "justification is always relative to an audience".[28] For the theist, however, consigning to the "rubbish" bin everything except pragmatic preference (backed in some cases by tanks, nuclear weapons and dollars) is as irrational and as downright narrow and blind as Ayer's attempt to label as "non-sense" everything except a quantifiable world of empirical observation. Ayer's view took about ten years to collapse under its internal self-contradictions which exposed it as sheer positivism disguised as a theory of language. The self-contradiction in Rorty is the pretence of offering a "local", modest, unassuming pragmatism, while elevating it at the same time into a sweeping reductionism of all serious epistemology and ontology, and dubbing these as "rubbish". As Kierkegaard might have observed, how can such a finite, situated human being assume such a quasi-omniscient trans-local view? Rorty

---

23 M.M. Mitchell, *Paul and the Language of Reconciliation: An Exegetical Investigation into the Language and Composition of 1 Corinthians* (Louisville, KY: Knox/Westminster, 1992), esp. pp.1–99 and 198–201; L.L. Welborn, *Politics and Rhetoric in the Corinthian Epistles* (Macon, GA: Mercer University Press, 1997), pp.1–42; cf. Thiselton, *First Epistle*, pp.107–33, which includes a detailed bibliography of sources.

24 Richard Rorty, *Truth and Progress: Philosophical Papers, vol. 3* (Cambridge: CUP, 1998), p.7.

25 Ibid., p.8.

26 A.J. Ayer, *Language, Truth and Logic* (London: Gollancz, 2nd edn, 1946 [also Penguin edn, 1971]), and Rorty, *Truth*, pp.8–12 and 19–42.

27 Rorty, *Truth*, p.21.

28 Ibid., p.4.

insists: "There is no Way the World is."[29] Clearly, by contrast, the biblical writings include assertions and confessions about the way the world is, as well as laws about how the world should be, and promises about how the world will be. In my Presidential Paper to the Society for the Study of Theology (University of Edinburgh, 1999) I have argued that American pragmatic postmodernity constitutes a more insidious influence upon Christian theology than the more pessimistic iconoclastic postmodernity of France, Germany and Italy, which at least serves to deconstruct idolatrous religion.[30]

III

The Apostolic Gospel and Roman Corinth: Must Postmodernity Always be Seen in a Sequential Relation to "Modernity"?

Does "postmodernity" presuppose a sequential relation to modernity, whether it is described as a reaction against it, modification to it, or degeneration from it? Enough has been said already to indicate that postmodernity reflects a mind-set, attitude, ethos, or *mood*, which does not depend on a conscious comparison with, or sequential relation to, modernity to discuss its main features. Admittedly, to use comparisons with high modernity may help both to explain its historical origins and to trace its contours. Thus Rex Ambler perceives as its major theme a sense of disillusion that "the typically modern relation to the self can no longer be sustained".[31] Jameson insists that postmodern aesthetics and politics are "necessarily linked" with issues of classical or high modernism.[32] Seyla Benhabib speaks of "skepticism ... towards continuing the 'project of modernity' based on disillusionment".[33] Elizabeth Ermarth argues that since postmodernity may be seen as a kind of sequel to modernity, the term and its mood depends on how we understand "modernity" for its currency of meaning.[34]

Most of these writers, however, set postmodernity in relation to modernity in order to focus on some particular philosophical or political feature. Although these claims are not false, it remains no less true that, with Thomas Docherty, we may also characterize postmodernity as "*a mood, and not a period*" (my italics).[35] A number of theological writers rightly also disengage postmodernity from a sequential stage in the supposed advancement or development of human thought. Richard Roberts insists that the pre-

---

[29] Ibid., p.25.

[30] A.C. Thiselton, "Signs of the Times: Towards a Theology for the Year 2000 ...", in David Fergusson and Marcel Sarot (eds), *The Future as God's Gift: Explorations in Christian Eschatology* (Edinburgh: T. & T. Clark, 2000), pp.9–40, and Essay 32 above.

[31] R. Ambler, "The Self and Postmodernity", in K. Flanagan and P.C. Jupp (eds), *Postmodernity, Sociology and Religion* (New York and London: Macmillan, 1996), p.134; cf. pp.134–51.

[32] F. Jameson, *Postmodernism: Or, the Cultural Logic of Late Capitalism* (London: Verso, 1991), p.55.

[33] S. Benhabib, *Situating the Self: Gender, Community and Postmodernism in Contemporary Ethics* (Cambridge: Polity, 1992), p.2.

[34] E.D. Ermarth, *Sequel to History: Postmodern and the Crisis of Representational Time* (Princeton, NJ: Princeton University Press, 1992).

[35] T. Doherty, "Postmodernist Theory: Lyotard, Baudrillard and Others", in Richard Kearney (ed.), *Twentieth-Century Continental Philosophy* (Routledge History of Philosophy, vol. 8, London: Routledge, 1994), p.475; cf. pp.474–505.

modern, the modern and the postmodern respectively do not represent three neatly sequential stages rather than three sources of co-existent cross-currents often in conflict, drawing us in different directions.[36] Thus in the same essay Roberts proposes that the church today should include among its combined resources "residual tradition" (in part, the pre-modern), processes of education (in part, the modern), and an awareness of consumerist market-forces (largely the neo-pragmatic or postmodern). Dan Hardy endorses the view that pre-modern, modern and postmodern forces "co-exist" (that is, are not sequential), but advocates a stronger emphasis upon unity and coherence than is fully compatible with most postmodern thought.[37]

I have argued in my commentary on 1 Corinthians that a historical, archaeological and socio-cultural reconstruction of mid-first-century Roman Corinth identifies precisely this *postmodern mood* with the Corinth of Paul's day.[38] We have already noted above the research of Wayne Meeks to the effect that in their obsessive sense of insecurity and search for "status" and "recognition", the Corinthians operated with a radically pluralist diversity of scales and types of recognition. Status was viewed not in terms of any "single thing", but in terms of a "multidimensional phenomenon [in which] ... one must attempt to measure their rank along *each* of the relevant dimensions" (Meeks's italics).[39] "Status-indicators" included at different levels "occupational prestige, income or wealth, education and knowledge, religious and moral purity, family and ethnic-group position, and local community status (evaluation within some sub-group independent of the larger society ...".[40] The second important point is not merely the radical plurality of this "local" diversity but still more fundamentally that "the weight of each dimension [of evaluation or recognition] depends upon who is doing the weighing".[41] Both of these two aspects resonate entirely with the approach of Rorty: radical pluralism of the local or ethnocentric, and the transposition of truth about states of affairs into "recognition" by some persons or group as the criterion of evaluation (see above).

The emphasis placed upon evaluation and recognition by the audience in rhetoric runs parallel with the mind-set in which consumers determine the value and importance of production by market-forces. Archaeological research on ancient Corinth confirms the claims of Donald Engels that Corinth was a commercial centre in which competitive market-forces determined huge variations in the amassing of business wealth and international trade.[42] Its very geographical position on the Isthmus between its eastern harbour of Cenchraea, which faced across the Saronic Gulf to Asia and Ephesus, and its western harbour of Lechaeum, which faced across the Corinthian Gulf to Italy and Rome,

---

[36] R.H. Roberts, "A Postmodern Church? Some Preliminary Reflections on Ecclesiology and Social Theory", in D.F. Ford and D.L. Stamps (eds), *Essentials of Christian Community* (Edinburgh: T. & T. Clark, 1996), pp.179–95, esp. pp.182–3.

[37] D.W. Hardy, "The Future of Theology", in Hardy, *God's Ways with the World* (Edinburgh: T. & T. Clark, 1996), p.31; cf. pp.31–50; and esp. "Magnificent Complexity", in Ford and Stamps, *Essentials*, pp.336–7.

[38] Thiselton, *First Epistle*, pp.12–17, 40–43, 50–51, 75, 548, 1002, 1054–9, 1255 and throughout.

[39] Meeks, *First Urban Christians*, p.54.

[40] Ibid.

[41] Ibid.; cf. also pp.72–3, and Thiselton, *First Epistle*, pp.12–17.

[42] Donald Engels, *Roman Corinth: An Alternative Model for the Classical City* (Chicago, IL and London: University of Chicago Press, 1990), throughout.

joined by a paved roadway, the *diolkos* of only some six kilometres, placed it at the intersection of trade between east and west, and north and south. Light ships and cargo could be transported over the *diolkos* and sailors were eager to avoid the often treacherous voyage around the southern Cape of Malea.[43] Archaeological discoveries of coinage witness to abundant trade of a cosmopolitan nature, published in successive volumes of *Hesperia*, the official journal of the American School of Classical Studies at Athens.[44]

Most striking for today's visitor to the site of ancient Corinth are the remains of the monument erected by Gnaeus Babbius Philinus, which records twice that as "aedile and pontifex he had this monument erected at his own expense" and adds that in his office as *duovir* he also approved its construction. This typifies the way in which a *nouveau riche* man of influence could not only rise to high office, but employ the construction of monuments and no doubt also rhetoricians to ensure "media recognition" of his new-found status as an admired city benefactor. This illustrates "the ideas of self-promotion, publicity and recommendations written in stone".[45] It is important to recall that the Greek city of Corinth was largely destroyed when it rebelled against Rome in 146 BC and was refounded as a Roman colony in 44 BC by Julius Caesar, when its core population was made of Roman veterans, Roman freedpersons, and probably also slaves and those seeking to succeed in manufacture and trade.[46] Ben Witherington admirably sums up the cultural mood of simultaneous insecurity and ambition within competing value-systems when he observes: "for Paul's time many in Corinth were already suffering from a self-made-person-escaper-humble-origins syndrome".[47]

The Apostle Paul was *critically aware* of the huge gulf that separated the givenness of divine grace and the givenness of the *kerygma* of a crucified Christ on one side and the socio-rhetorical expectations of a message designed to match the specified self-affirmations of a variety of groups. Bruce Winter convincingly demonstrates that in contrast to the truth-seeking rhetoric of rational argument advocated by Cicero and by Quintillian, "in Alexandria and Corinth there was a high-profile sophistic movement in the first century ... the 'Second Sophistic'".[48] "Truth" was generated not by rationality and coherence, but by pragmatic rhetorical effect and audience applause. The Sophists anticipate entirely Richard Rorty's "Postmodernity". There is no such task as "getting reality right ... because there is no Way the World is".[49] "Justification is always relative to an audience."[50] Yet this is what *Paul consciously and critically rejects*. To the Second Sophistic, to first-century Corinth and to Rorty's pragmatism, the cross cannot be other

---

[43] Strabo, *Geography*, 8:6:20; Pausanias, *Description of Grace*, 2:1:5–7; in modern literature James Wiseman, "Corinth and Rome, I, 228 BC–AD 267", in *Aufstieg und Niedergang der römischen Welt* 2:7:1 (Berlin: deGruyter, 1979), esp. pp.439–47; and Engels, *Roman Corinth*, pp.8–21.

[44] Listed in Thiselton, *First Epistle*, pp.6–12, esp. *Hesperia* 6 (1937), pp.261–56; 10 (1941), pp.143–62; 41 (1972), pp.143–84; 44 (1975), pp.1–59; 51 (1982), pp.115–63; 58 (1989), pp.1–50; 59 (1990), pp.325–56.

[45] J. Murphy-O'Connor, *St Paul's Corinth: Texts and Archaeology* (Wilmington, DE: Glazier, 1983), p.171.

[46] See e.g. W. Schrage, *Der erste Brief an die Korinther* (Zürich: Benziger and Neukirchen-Vluyn: Neukirchener, 3 vols to date, 1991, 1995, 1999 [Ev-Kath Kom z NT VII, 1–3]), vol. 1, pp.25–9.

[47] B. Witherington, *Conflict and Community in Corinth* (Carlisle: Paternoster and Grand Rapids, MI: Eerdmans, 1995), p.20.

[48] B.W. Winter, *Philo and Paul among the Sophists* (Cambridge: CUP [SNTS Mon Ser 96], 1997), p.238.

[49] Rorty, *Truth and Progress*, p.25.

[50] Ibid., p.4.

than an *affront* (1 Cor. 1:18–25). For Paul the issue is whether the Christian proclamation has to accord with the pre-given criterion of the cross, or whether "the cross", "Christ" and "being people of the Spirit" become constructs shaped by what affirms and pleases consumer-audiences. Hence Schrage perceptively entitles 1 Cor. 1:18–2:5 *"Das 'Wort vom Kreuz' als Grund und Kriterium von Gemeinde und Apostel"*.[51]

Together with Winter, Stephen Pogoloff, Andrew Clarke and John Moores have contributed greatly to our appreciation of Paul's necessary awareness of this gulf. Pogoloff cites the rhetorical competitions concerning which Cicero, Quintillian and Seneca lament the applause-seeking, audience-orientated criteria presupposed in such provincial centres as Corinth and Alexandria as against the traditional truth-seeking arguments of classical rhetoric in Rome. Truth (with Richard Rorty and the later Stanley Fish) becomes the property of "winners". The rhetorician, Seneca the Elder, Cicero and Quintillian complain, thinks more of himself and of audience approval than of the case and its merits: "Every effusion is greeted with a storm of ready-made applause ... The result is variety and empty self-sufficiency."[52] The genius of Pogoloff's research on Corinth is his recognition of how closely Corinthian attitudes anticipate the mind-set of so-called anti-foundationalism, and of the collapse of epistemology into causally, psychologically, or politically persuasive pragmatic rhetoric.[53] This is precisely why Paul makes a firm decision (1 Cor. 2:2) to reject methods of pleasing speech shaped by audience approval-ratings and manipulative "cleverness", but to declare the *kerygma* of a Christ crucified, "so that your faith might rest not on human 'wisdom', but on the power [what is solid and effective] of God" (1 Cor. 2:5; cf. 2:1–5). The "criterion of the cross" (Schrage) brings *all people* under judgement and grace. As Pogoloff shows, audience-constituted rhetoric is bound to divide wider communities into local or ethnocentric groups.[54]

Andrew Clarke explicates this contrast in terms of differences between secular and Christian patterns of leadership in Corinth. In contrast to the secular style of leadership that seeks "recognition" and the high status accorded by rhetoric, social standing, professional expertise, or the influence of patrons and reciprocal favours, Paul is content with "weakness": to pin everything on the Gospel which entails identification with a crucified Christ who is regarded by many as a shameful affront. He therefore dissociates himself from the path of those "who sought personal advancement ... the pursuit of esteem and praise".[55] He does not seek to use such manipulative power-tools as patronage or benefaction.[56] Apostolicity meant the very opposite of "leadership ... on show", but points to the "given" of the grace of Christ crucified and raised.[57] Paul rejects

---

[51] Schrage, *Der erste Brief*, vol. 1, p.165.

[52] Seneca, *Controversiae*, 9:1; Quintillian, *Institutio Oratoria*, 2:2:9, 12; further references in S. Pogoloff, *Logos and Sophia. The Rhetorical Situation of 1 Corinthians* (Atlanta, GA: Scholars Press [SBL Diss Ser 134], 1992), pp.175–8.

[53] Pogoloff, "Rhetoric and Antifoundationalism", in *Logos and Sophia*, pp.26–35; see further, pp.71–172.

[54] Pogoloff, *Logos and Sophia*, pp.173–235.

[55] A.D. Clark, *Secular and Christian Leadership in Corinth. A Socio-Historical and Exegetical Study of 1 Corinthians 1–6* (Leiden and New York: Brill [Arb z Gesch. des Ant Jud und des Urchr 18], 1993), p.25.

[56] Ibid., p.32.

[57] Ibid., p.39.

the manipulative strategy that seems to have functioned in the church of civil litigation where financial and social influences could prove decisive.

Finally John Moores vigorously relates Paul's strategy to issues today. He writes that Paul does not think "the identity of a message ... is in any sense determined by what it means for those at the receiving end. For him it is rather *their* identity than that of the message which is determined by their response. To subject him to the criteria of present-day ... reader-response theory would be to turn *his* ideas on the subject upside down" (his italics).[58] This is all the more convincing because Moores writes as one fully familiar with the work of Umberto Eco and C. Perelman, and enthymemic logic and semiotic theory. The Corinthians' postmodern *mood* well resonates with Stanley Fish's "Rhetorical Man", in contrast with the transformative, transcontextual power of the proclamation of the cross, which Fish's "Serious Man" could perceive as transformative. When he advocates the stance of rhetorical man, Fish describes precisely what much Corinthian culture admired and what Paul rejected: "Rhetorical man is trained not to discover reality but to manipulate it ... Serious man ... can be characterized by sincerity, faithfulness to the self", while rhetorical man necessarily remains "an actor".[59]

IV
Do Biblical Writers Reflect Self-Aware, Critical Thinking?

If Paul sees the cross as, in Schrage's words, "the ground and criterion" of what is at issue here, would it be anachronistic to speak of his awareness of all that is at stake as less than one of "critical consciousness"? After all, even if the writer uses a touch of irony in his choice of words, Fish is right to say that this "contrast ... can hardly be exaggerated ... The ground is itself foundational."[60]

The word "critical" may well set us off track by three historical contexts that influence its application. First, it need not imply any opposition between doubt and tradition that many associate with Descartes. Gadamer, among others, has exposed the shallow inadequacy of this supposed opposition. Second, it need not imply endorsement of the critical or transcendental philosophy of Kant. Kant's attempts to define the limits of reason and the role of mental construction in the perception of order remain at very least controversial, and those who question Kant are not thereby "uncritical" thinkers. Third, Hegel's comparison between the uncritical use of *Vorstellung*, representation, in religion, as against *Begriff* [*critical*] *concept* in philosophy addresses the issue more closely, but did critical thought await Hegel's formulation of historical reason, and is the contrast as clear-cut as Hegel and D.F. Strauss maintained?

It is noteworthy that the later Heidegger, for all his earlier emphasis in radical historical situatedness and finitude, returned not to Hegel, who (Heidegger maintained) still elevated *Geist* or Spirit in quasi-dualist terms, but to the pre-Socratic philosophers of pre-modernity.

---

[58]   J.D. Moores, *Wrestling with Rationality in Paul* (Cambridge: CUP [SNTS Mon Ser 82], 1995), pp.133–4.
[59]   S. Fish, *Doing What Comes Naturally. Change, Rhetoric and the Practice of Theory in Literary and Legal Studies* (Oxford: Clarendon, 1989), pp.482 and 483.
[60]   Ibid.

The Milesian School of the sixth century BC acknowledged the instability of change, but nevertheless allowed for a continuity in terms of that which underwent change. Heracleitus, by contrast, tended to undermine the notion of continuity "behind" change ("You cannot step twice into the same river, for fresh waters are ever flowing in upon you"). Yet even Heracleitus allowed for a stability of the constitutive principles that govern change. Zeno of Elea formulated his paradoxes to seek to undermine Heracleitus and the Pythagoreans, but it was left to Gilbert Ryle to show the logical consequences of differences between the logic of an observer and the logic of participants. Ironically, the arch-ontologist Parmenides in effect promoted scepticism by arguing that change itself was illusory, while Protagoras (c. 490–420 BC) came nearest to the mind-set of postmodernity by urging notions of truth and of virtue rested in general on sheer norms of convention in human behaviour. Even if Aristophanes overdraws the picture in *The Clouds* to provide fun at his expense, the dictum of Protagoras – "Man is the measure of all things" – means *either* (1) that "true" means only what certain people *believe* to be true; or (2) that whatever a person believes is "true" *for that person*. Either interpretation, but especially the first, paves the way for Foucault's scepticism about "norms" and for social constructivism.

Is all of this pre-modern thinking, then, entirely "uncritical"? To be sure, as J.B. Skemp urges, most first-century Christian writers were not Greek philosophers.[61] Nevertheless Skemp's work (1964) on the "Ordinary Greek" still tends to presuppose the agenda of Adolf Deissmann, which sought to underplay the level of education and conceptual sophistication that marked the earliest Christian communities and the New Testament writers.[62] The debates since set up by E.A. Judge, Wayne Meeks, Gerd Theissen and Bruce Winter serve to redress the balance, even if Meggitt still emphasizes the economic poverty of many.[63] We noted Winter's convincing arguments above, coupled with those of Pogoloff, Clarke and Moores, that a replay of all the issues about the collapse of "truth" as given, into "recognition" as constructed by rhetoric and social power-interests, took place in mid-first-century Corinth.

It is not the case that Paul could have held an "uncritical" conceptual awareness of these high stakes on both sides. It was the case, however, that a transformative proclamation of a Christ crucified presented a *theological critique*, not a philosophical one. The Gospel could not be marketed as a package shaped and defined by the interests of consumers or by market-forces. This is why Paul explicitly describes it as an *affront* (Greek *skandalon*) to those who have this horizon of expectation (1 Cor. 1:18–25), and why he insists on proclaiming what is "given" (1 Cor. 2:1–5; cf. 11:17–23, 15:3–6). Indeed this very point brings us to note the level of *critical rigour and sophistication* with which Paul uses the patterns and devices of classical Graeco-Roman rhetoric to put forward *rational argument on the basis of shared premises*.

---

[61] J.B. Skemp, *The Greeks and the Gospel* (London: Carey Kingsgate, 1964), esp. pp.1–45 and 90–120.

[62] A. Deissmann, *Light from the Ancient East* (Eng., London: Hodder & Stoughton, 1927). Deissmann made no secret of his own "egalitarian" political agenda.

[63] E.A. Judge, *The Social Pattern of Early Christian Groups in the First Century* (London: Tyndale Press, 1960); Meeks, *First Urban Christians*; G. Theissen, *The Social Setting of Pauline Christianity* (Eng., Philadelphia, PA: Fortress, 1982); Winter: *Philo and Paul*; *Seek the Welfare of the City* (Grand Rapids, MI: Eerdmans, 1994); and *After Paul Left Corinth* (Grand Rapids, MI: Eerdmans, 2001). Cf. however also J.J. Meggitt, *Paul, Poverty and Survival* (Edinburgh: T. & T. Clark, 1998).

Anders Eriksson provides a masterly study of Paul's rigorous methods of argumentation in 1 Corinthians, usually on the basis of shared premises. Paul consciously uses rhetorical strategies with a high level of sophistication. The treatise on the resurrection, for example, which is the most carefully polished rhetorical argument, embodies shared tradition in the *exordium* (15:1–2), in the *narratio* (15:3–11), the first *refutatio* (15:12–19), the first *confirmatio* (15:20–34), a second *refutatio* (15:35–49) and *confirmatio* (15:50–57) and the *peroratio* (15:58).[64] But this strategy is not confined to chapter 15. Traditions constitute premises in 8:6, 11; 10:16; 11:17–34; 12:3; 16:22 and elsewhere. Throughout several of his epistles Paul uses assonance, chiasmus, *insinuato*, irony, *narratio*, *propositio* and antithesis.[65] M. Bünker demonstrates Paul's knowledge of contemporary rhetorical theories in 1 Cor. 1:10–4:21 as well as in 15:1–58.[66] We have already noted the significant contributions of Margaret Mitchell and John Moores (above). In particular, Moores examines the phenomenon of "code-switching", in which the logical currency of a term such as "spiritual persons" is drawn from a communicative code presupposed by the readers and "switched" into a decisively different conceptual currency by the writer.[67] This assumes a high degree of critical conceptual awareness and rigour, but I have traced numerous examples of such code-switching and redefinition in 1 Corinthians.[68]

Even Paul, however, does not embody the most sophisticated rhetorical style in the New Testament. The Epistle to the Hebrews, which is agreed by specialists to be non-Pauline, opens as a brilliant homily which employs alliteration, rhythm, elegance, force and careful, conscious artistry, with many intra-textual allusions and resonances.[69] At what was once regarded as the other end of the spectrum in terms of lack of linguistic polish, the Gospel of Mark is nowadays widely credited with a highly sophisticated narrative strategy, including a conscious differentiation between "clock-time" and narrative-time. Thus Mark begins the narrative of Jesus at a rapid pace, slows down the tempo following Peter's confession of the Messiahship of Jesus at Caesarea Philippi, and finally projects the events of the passion in slow motion.[70] This focuses attention on the dominance of the cross as the purposive goal of the life of Jesus. More controversially, Frank Kermode attributes to Mark a conscious strategy of puzzlement which invites readers to look to "church" or apostolic interpretation for the clue to the meaning of the story.[71] If Kermode's account of Mark were convincing (and I do not find it so), Mark

---

[64] A. Eriksson, *Traditions as Rhetorical Proof. Pauline Argumentation in 1 Corinthians* (Stockholm: Almqvist & Wiksell [Con Bib NT Ser 29], 1998), pp.251–78. See also Thiselton, *First Epistle*, pp.1169–314.

[65] N. Schneider, *Die rhetorische Eigenart der paulinischen Antithese* (Tübingen: Mohr [HUT, 11], 1970).

[66] M. Bünker, *Briefformular und rhetorische Disposition im 1 Korintherbrief* (Göttingen: Vandenhoeck & Ruprecht, 1983).

[67] Moores, *Wrestling*, pp.6–10, 25–8, 132–8.

[68] Thiselton, *First Epistle*, pp.43, 154, 173–5, 240, 325–6, 469, 499–500, 560–61, 602, 627, 930, 996 and 1024.

[69] See W.L. Lane, *Hebrews* (2 vols, Dallas, TX: Word, 1991), pp.lxix–lxxxviii; A. Vanhoye, *Homilie für halbbedürftige Christen* (Regensburg: Pustet, 1981); W.G. Überlacker, *Der Hebräebrief als Appell* (Stockholm: Almqvist & Wiksell [Con Bib NT Ser 21], 1989).

[70] See Wesley A. Kort, *Story, Text and Scripture. Literary Interests in Biblical Narratives* (University Park, Pa: Pennsylvania State University Press, 1988), p.44.

[71] F. Kermode, *The Genesis of Secrecy. On the Interpretation of Narrative* (Cambridge, MA: Harvard University Press, 1979).

would not only be critically aware of the strategies of postmodernity, but also seen to be employing them.

A further argument about the degree of critical self-consciousness shown by the New Testament writers arises, probably surprisingly, from the debate that followed Rudolf Bultmann's proposals about demythologizing the New Testament. His definitions of myth have been widely recognized to be inconsistent and even contradictory.[72] Although he attributes to "myth" an uncritical pre-modern view of the world as a "three-decker" universe, Bultmann more emphatically insists that the programme of demythologizing, especially in its second and third senses relating to analogy and to de-objectification both exposes metaphor or analogy *as* metaphor or analogy, and perceives objectification as a process **begun** *within the New Testament itself*. Both, he insists, constitute demands of the New Testament itself rather than of "modern man".[73] He writes, "Very soon the process of demythologizing began, partly with Paul, and radically with John."[74] However, if the difference between pre-critical embodiments of myth and critical awareness of when analogy is analogy and of when de-objectification relates to attitudes, participation and self-involvement (as well as presupposing often also states of affairs), this *"waking out of a pre-critical sleep"* is fundamental to Bultmann's understanding of the level of conceptual awareness that he attributes to biblical writers. For again and again he claims that his proposals follow their example, and are not imposed either by a liberal theology or by a modern philosophy.[75]

In addition to these *conceptual* considerations, we may return finally to *theological* factors that enhance this critical self-awareness. Paul not only struggles with a "postmodern mood" at Corinth; he is also fully aware of *the capacity of the human heart for self-deception*. This biblical theme goes back to Jeremiah and to the Psalms, and is internally entailed in the notion of "hidden depths" below the surface of the human heart (Hebrew, *lēbh*; Greek, *kardia*). The fullest modern exposition of the importance of this motif for Paul is found in Theissen's *Psychological Aspects of Pauline Theology*. Paul concedes that such are the hidden depths of the heart that he cannot, and should not, pronounce verdicts on himself (1 Cor. 4:1–5): "Paul does allow for unconscious intentions that could stand in tension with his consciousness."[76] Paul speaks elsewhere of human secrets hidden from the conscious mind (Rom. 2:29), and of secret motivations which prophetic preaching may expose to consciousness (1 Cor. 14:20–25). Only the realities of the last judgement can reveal the true nature of human motivations and achievement (1 Cor. 3:5–17). Self-perception grows from the work of the Holy Spirit (Rom. 8:26–27) who "searches the heart", and the Johannine sphere of "darkness" underlines the

---

[72] R.W. Hepburn, "Demythologizing and the Problem of Validity", in A. Flew and A. MacIntyre (eds), *New Essays in Philosophical Theology* (London: SCM, 1955), pp.227–42; A.C. Thiselton, *The Two Horizons* (Grand Rapids, MI: Eerdmans and Exeter: Paternoster, 1980), pp.252–63; and the varied discussions in H.-W. Bartsch (ed.), *Kerygma und Mythos: ein theologisches Gespräch* (6 vols, Hamburg: Reich & Heidrich, from 1948).

[73] R. Bultmann, *Jesus Christ and Mythology* (London: SCM, 1960), pp.322–34.

[74] Ibid., p.32.

[75] R. Bultmann, "The Case for Demythologizing: A Reply", in H.-W. Bartsch (ed.), *Kerygma and Myth*, vol. 2 (London: SCM, 1964), pp.182–3.

[76] G. Theissen, *Psychological Aspects of Pauline Theology* (Eng., Edinburgh: T. & T. Clark, 1987), p.63.

deceptiveness of what only God's Spirit can bring to light (John 16:8–13; cf. 14:17). We cannot claim with any degree of credibility that biblical writers were unaware of the problem so sharply focused on later by Nietzsche and by Foucault that truth-claims about the self, about others, or about God, could be put forward as disguised ways of promoting power, self-interest, or strategies of manipulation.

V
Points of Resonance between the Bible and the Postmodern Mind-Set

We may conclude by summarizing, by way of contrast, some points at which the biblical writings address postmodernity by way of support and endorsement, even if also with a critique. First, we may take up the issue of self-deception. Nietzsche, Barthes, Foucault and Derrida have exposed the "mythologies" which serve as mechanisms of disguise to promote truth-claims on behalf of the power-interests of persons or groups. On one side, Theissen and other biblical scholars have identified a self-awareness of the seductions of self-deception within the pages of the Bible, especially in Paul, but not exclusively so. Elsewhere I have argued in detail that in the Pastoral Epistles and other biblical writings there is a subtle awareness that "true" and "false" is not only a matter of the correspondence of propositions to what is the case, or coherence between them, but a relation of integrity and disengagement of self-interest in matters of life and conduct.[77] The logic of "All Cretans are liars" put onto the lips of a Cretan serves to bring out the self-contradictory notion of first-person utterances in which their truth-value is undermined by the character and conduct of the speaker.[78] On the other side, the theological understanding of the consequences of *corporate* self-deception is brilliantly exposed long before it was thought to be a distinctively "postmodern" insight by Reinhold Niebuhr in his *Moral Man and Immoral Society*, published as long ago as 1932. People will commit the most unethical acts, he argued, if they can deceive themselves into claiming that these are "for my family", "for my country", or even "for my social class or my race". Already a *theological* critique, at least in embryo, is anticipated in advance of Rorty's neo-pragmatic ethnocentrism. However, Niebuhr is simply explicating in his own context a critical principle that is also reflected in the biblical writings.

We also noted in our Introduction some common ground between Jesus and the New Testament on one side, and Foucault and postmodern deconstructionism on the other, concerning "marginality" and "boundaries". Jesus, we earlier noted, rejected the arbitrary fencing-off of degrees of religious and ethical purity in such a way that some were branded as "outsiders" whatever their attitude of heart. Such scribal or pharisaic

---

[77] A.C. Thiselton, "The Logical Role of the Liar Paradox in Titus 1:12, 13: A Dissent from the Commentaries in the Light of Philosophical and Logical Analysis", *Biblical Interpretation* 2 (1994), pp.207–23; cf. Thiselton, "Truth", in C. Brown (ed.), *The New International Dictionary of NT Theology* (Exeter: Paternoster and Grand Rapids, MI: Zondervan, vol. 3 (1978), pp.1123–46, see Essays 14 and 17.

[78] A somewhat simplified but nevertheless useful exploration of these logical issues in the framework of the later Wittgenstein is offered by D.M. High, *Language, Persons and Belief* (New York: OUP, 1967).

traditions placed obstacles in the path, and burdens on the backs, of those very outsiders whom the host of the wedding feast in Luke insists are welcome at what clearly represents the divine and Messianic banquet (Luke 14:15–24, where the emphasis falls upon urging outsiders to come and be welcome; cf. the more allegorical version of the royal wedding in Matt. 22:1–14, where the emphasis falls upon judgement for "insiders" who remain content with their self-sufficiency).

Nevertheless, Jesus and the biblical writers do not deconstruct all differentiation as mere social construction in defence of interests. Creation is diverse because God decreed "differences" of order which give rise to what Thomas Aquinas associates with the principle of plenitude. He cites Gen. 1:4: "And God divided the light from the darkness", and comments, "Distinction and variety in the world is intended by the first cause ... He makes creatures many and diverse ... Divine wisdom is the cause why things are distinct; also why they are unequal. It would be an unfinished world were it all on one level of goodness."[79] Similarly, even the events of the end-times are characterized by differentiated order (1 Cor. 15:23–28), while boundary-distinctions in service and ministry, while neither absolute nor inflexible, are related to divine decree which reflects the "ordered differentiation" within the Godhead (1 Cor. 12:4–11, 27–30).

To be sure, the metaphor of the body, with its unity and diversity of members, is drawn from Roman and Greek literature; but whereas in Livy it is applied on behalf of the elite to dissuade slaves from revolt, in Paul it is turned upside down. The supposedly "less honourable" are to be honoured as indispensable to the welfare of the whole (1 Cor. 12:21–25).[80] Distinctions of roles and boundaries of identity are not merely social constructions to be deconstructed in the interests of the weak; Paul defends the weak and the marginalized by a more subtle and lasting route. Respect for the otherness of the other, mutuality and reciprocity provide a more constructive strategy than an egalitarian politics of "sameness" or "interchangeability", whether we are speaking of parents and children, church polity and gender, the gift of diverse "somatic" modes of being at the resurrection, or of God as Father, Son and Spirit.

The controversial issue of indeterminacy in language also reveals similarities and dissimilarities with the varied genres employed within the biblical texts, and once again demonstrates the genuineness of address and engagement between the Bible and postmodernity. The wisdom literature and the parables of Jesus (in contrast to similitudes, similes and allegories) reflect the open-endedness of exploration in which hearers or readers are invited to "complete" a meaning, but with ever-new reappraisals and discoveries. On the other hand, shared kerygmatic traditions, embryonic creeds and confessional formulae, and above all promissory language demand a stability and degree of specificity that gives them operative currency. The biblical canon includes both traditions and iconoclasm. Sacred texts that offer only iconoclasm would be as self-defeating as the so-called paradox of scepticism. Most significantly, as Vanhoozer and Wolterstorff among others urge with passion, a Bible that addresses humankind with

---

[79] Thomas Aquinas, *Summa Theologiae* (60 vols, Latin and English, Oxford: Blackfriars, 1963), Part Ia: qu 47: art. 1 and art. 2.

[80] See D.B. Martin, *The Corinthian Body* (New Haven, CT and London: Yale University Press, 1995), pp.3–61 and 94–103; and Thiselton, *First Epistle*, pp.990–1011.

words of renewal, promise, hope and love, is a text that presupposes agency.[81] It is not the mere product of textual forces, even if it draws on language-systems that remain potential until they are actualized by speakers, writers and specific texts.

In the end, the question of "givens" may ultimately turn on the contrast between a theistic and non-theistic world-view. At the heart of the Bible and of Christian faith stands the divine sovereign initiative of giving the gift of Godself in sheer grace. As I noted in 1980, in Romans 11:6 Paul expounds a piece of logical or conceptual grammar: if "grace" is a consumer product even in part constructed by the recipient or by the church, "grace is not grace".[82] If this is not a conscious address to challenge the scope of human or social construction, it is difficult to see what might count as such.

---

[81] Vanhoozer, *Is There a Meaning?*, pp.37–280; N. Wolterstorff, *Divine Discourse* (Cambridge: CUP, 1995), pp.37–170 and throughout.
[82] Thiselton, *The Two Horizons*, p.389; cf. pp.386–407.

CHAPTER THIRTY-SIX

A Retrospective Reappraisal: Postmodernity, Language and Hermeneutics (New essay)

Of the seven retrospective reappraisals of the seven parts in this work, this is perhaps the most substantial and the most significant in terms of indicating advances on, and partial modifications of, earlier views. I stand by my earlier identification of themes and my criticisms of these themes, but I recognize that the earlier essays were all written out of specific contexts that now invite a broader appraisal. I modify my earlier comparisons between American neo-pragmatic postmodern philosophy and European postmodern thought in two ways.

First, while I stand by, and even develop further, my critiques of Rorty's pragmatic progressivism and "internalism", I recognize that he promotes a two-sided attempt to market "liberal pluralism" as a backup for an otherwise empty and bankrupt socio-ethical approach. Nevertheless I retain the view that no logical, coherent link between the two sides can be found. Second, a more intensive reading of Lyotard since the earlier essays has convinced me that Lyotard escapes none of the difficulties found in Rorty and Fish. Indeed Lyotard's claims about "difference" and "differend" cut the ground from beneath the hermeneutical enterprise as such.

I also examine Lyotard's notion of grand narrative in relation to roles performed by biblical texts. In the closing sections I compare postmodern views of language with explorations of conceptual grammar, finding initial parallels, but then greater divergences. I ask once again about Derrida's views of language as semiotic systems in effect without agency, and consider agency and embodiment as the backcloth to what Jüngel calls the "conceivability" or "thinkability" of God.

I

Context-Specific Essays Invite a Broader Approach to Postmodernity than the Themes of Fragmentation, Suspicion of Language and Loss of Hope

Six of the seven essays in Part VI address some aspect or aspects of postmodernity. Yet taken together, even as a whole this collection does not fully convey a rounded, systematic, or comprehensive exposition and critique of postmodernism or postmodernity.[1] This is because each of these essays arose out of a specific context of

---

[1]   I have alluded above to David Lyon's useful distinction between *postmodernism* and *postmodernity*. He defines *postmodernism* as a *philosophical* and intellectual rejection of Enlightenment rationalism and the privileging of a scientific world-view as the paradigm for human knowledge, and *postmodernity* as a *social* phenomenon in which "truth" becomes absorbed into a sense of virtual-reality worlds constructed by consumer profiles, information technology and *social contributionism* (David Lyon, *Postmodernity*, Buckingham: Open University Press, 1994, pp.6–7). More recently Graham Ward seeks to revive this broad distinction (Graham Ward, ed., *The Blackwell Companion to Postmodern Theology*, Oxford: Blackwell, 2001, pp.xiv–xv). But most writers use the two terms indiscriminately.

purpose and readership, and each context generated, in turn, a particular agenda. Hence any critical suggestion that more needs to be said in order to offer a more rounded exposition and critique would be valid. To address this "more" is part of the purpose of this retrospective reappraisal.

The six essays above focus on a series of themes within postmodernity that I still firmly believe characterize the mood of this mind-set. If this reappraisal appears to shift ground, this is not because I retract this diagnosis, but because I acknowledge that these themes are far from comprehensive. Further, by asking specifically how postmodern perspectives impinge on language-theories and hermeneutics, these essays may have given more prominence to negative critiques than to recognizing significant potential contributions, albeit within limits. The essay on language and meaning in religion (Essay 29), which precedes the six on postmodernity, offers a backcloth by laying down certain markers within the framework of more traditional approaches to language. It is not clear from the writings of exponents of postmodern approaches why so many of these more traditional markers are simply to be discarded. Too many writers "talk past" them, rather than address them with sympathetic understanding as well as critique.

Essays 30 and 31 formed part of the lectures delivered in the University of Aberdeen that were subsequently revised, expanded and published as *Interpreting God and the Postmodern Self: On Meaning, Manipulation and Promise* (1995). The first of these on "God as Self-Affirming Illusion? Manipulation, Truth and Language" places two characteristics of postmodern perspectives at the centre of the stage: (1) *the capacity of language to promote disguises and deception*, in particular disguising bids for power and self-affirmation as propositions that convey disinterested truth. This led to (2) the *fragmentation* of value-systems and truth-claims, and less directly its fragmentation of human selfhood, in the condition of postmodernity. The second of the two essays, Essay 31, traced a third theme, namely (3) *the loss of hope* generated by postmodern perspectives.

I supported the identification of these three themes or characteristics as "postmodern" by first-hand engagement with the primary works of postmodern writers. Moreover, they feature equally in the work of recognized critical exponents of postmodern thought. Thus David Harvey and David Lyon emphasize the phenomenon of *fragmentation*.[2] John O'Neill presents a memorable aphorism about postmodern *loss of hope*. He writes, "In the postmodern scene, power is knowledge of our voluntary servitude. In the Enlightenment scene, our knowledge is the power to end servitude." We are (in postmodernity) "surrounded by so many corpses: Reason, Desire, Woman, God".[3] The claim about *language* is too widely acknowledged to require further support. The essay quotes extensively from Nietzsche.

In response to any suggestion that my assessment of the postmodern is too negative, I have consistently expressed the view that this last-mentioned characteristic or feature may be both valid and constructive for hermeneutics and for theology. It provides a major resource for what Paul Ricoeur calls a hermeneutics of suspicion, based upon

---

[2] David Lyon, *Postmodernity*, pp.37–99; David Harvey, *The Condition of Postmodernity* (Oxford: Blackwell, 1989), pp.11–12, 42–9, 82–3, 103–7 and 302–3.

[3] John O'Neill, *The Poverty of Postmodernism* (London and New York: Routledge, 1995), pp.5 and 23.

"willingness to suspect".[4] Moreover, if *fragmentation* were to be the only alternative to promoting *closed, abstract, timeless systems*, it is not self-evident which alternative would impose the worse plight. *Closed system* would signal the death of hermeneutics and set the stage for potentially oppressive philosophies or political regimes. On the other hand, we should resist the blandishments of Stanley Fish to the effect that we must choose between absolute formalism or closed systems and radical pluralism.[5] Postmodernity may facilitate liberation from closed systems, but radical pluralism is not the only alternative.

Precisely the same principle applies to issues concerning *hope and loss of hope*, especially in terms of the aphorism coined by John O'Neill. For exponents of Christian theology, the disillusion expressed among most postmodern writers concerning the myth of the inevitable progress brought about by science and technology coheres well with Christian theologies of hope. But the deconstruction of this illusion neither condemns humanity to loss of hope nor submerges persons into the bondage imposed by assimilation into "local" groups who cannot look beyond their self-generated norms and boundaries. In three of his works Jürgen Moltmann contrasts "going out" from self associated with life and the Holy Spirit of life as an affirmation of intersubjective engagement and vulnerability against a narcistic closure inwards upon the self that marks absence of openness to the life and to "the other".[6]

Many writers have also drawn attention to the sense of *exhaustion* conveyed by the prefix "post-". Terrence Tilley expresses this well in his introduction "The 'Post-Age' Stamp". Ours is a *"post*-age": "Manifestos appear with disheartening regularity, announcing that our era is postmodern, postchristian ... postcolonial, postindustrial ... postanalytic ... poststructuralist, postliberal, etc. ... Each distances our present from our past", but also "shows the present power of the transcended past".[7] A "post" age "is ... an unstable era". Where an era is called "reconstructionist" rather than "post-war", the term indicates some *shaping power*. "Post-age" vocabulary suggests things that are "rotted". It suggests a future that is "indeterminable and invisible" rather than life purposively moving toward a goal with energy and confidence. Yet there remains a positive side: "clearing space" may leave an opportunity for the discovery of what lies "beyond". Each of the three themes identified here invite further, more positive, comment, which we offer below.

II

The Problem of "Internal" Neo-Pragmatic Criteria: A Partial Reappraisal of Earlier Assessments of American Postmodernity

In Essay 32, "Two Types of Postmodernity", while I offer a partly positive but carefully qualified appraisal of certain features within European versions of postmodernism, I

---

[4] Paul Ricoeur, *Freud and Philosophy: An Essay on Interpretation* (New Haven, CT: Yale University Press, 1970), p.27.

[5] Stanley Fish, "The Anti-Formalist Road", in *Doing What Comes Naturally* (Oxford: Clarendon, 1989), pp.1–33.

[6] J. Moltmann, *The Trinity and the Kingdom of God* (Eng., London: SCM, 1981); *God in Creation* (Eng., London: SCM, 1985); and *The Spirit of Life: A Universal Affirmation* (Eng., London: SCM, 1992).

[7] Terrence W. Tilley, *Postmodern Theologies* (Maryknoll, NY: Orbis, 1995), p.vi; cf. pp.vi–vii.

nevertheless remain critical of the disastrous effects of an *alliance between neo-pragmatism, secular progressivism and postmodernism* among some influential American thinkers. Peter Ochs, I concede, has called attention to positive aspects of the work of C.S. Peirce, who retained sufficient respect for logic and semiotics to guarantee a degree of restraint over more clearly pragmatic aspects of his philosophy. But such restraint is relatively absent from the work of William James and John Dewey, while Rorty and Fish go to extremes, and assimilate hermeneutics and linguistic theory into a radical neo-pragmatism that undermines, rather than promotes, what hermeneutics has emerged to achieve.

In one respect, however, I do offer a genuine modification and *re*appraisal of my earlier argument in Essay 32. I argued in 1998 that Rorty left *no* viable criteria for *any* serious critique of social, economic and political values other than those embedded already within a "local" community of "people like us". *I now modify this critique in two ways.*

(1) While the above evaluation remains a reasonable criticism, I also perceive *a duality in Rorty's pragmatism that permits two answers to questions about critiques of a community from sources external to that community.* Rorty's writings from *Contingency, Irony and Solidarity* (1989) through to *Philosophy and Social Progress* (1999) allow a certain privilege to "liberal democracy" or more specifically to the "local" community of "we liberals" *provided that* we accept the self-contradiction that such privilege has *no grounds* in Rorty's philosophy as an axiom of his approach to philosophy. His pragmatism can be held together with some social critique only *at the price of inconsistency*.[8] Among numerous critics of Rorty who make valid points, I find especially persuasive Honi Fern Haber's formulation of this point as part of her comparative assessments of Lyotard, Rorty and Foucault.[9]

(2) I also recognize more clearly now that this critique of an absence of "external" criteria applies no less to some strands within European postmodernity. Most radically it applies to Lyotard's even more violent and uncompromising rejection of any criteria, whether internal or external. Lyotard, as I argue in the next section, undermines hermeneutics even more drastically than Rorty or Fish. Lyotard sees negotiation over "difference" and the very search for consensus or commonality as oppressive. He escapes none of the difficulties that apply to Rorty, and compounds them.

Rorty, to return to the American neo-pragmatic tradition, cannot see any "use" for the notion "that finite, mortal, contingently existing human beings might derive the meanings of their lives from anything except other finite, mortal, contingently existing human beings".[10] Any notion of "objective moral values" is "merely quaint", and his work "de-divinizes" the contingent world of humankind. Yet for all his talk about plurality, solidarity and community, Rorty, as Haber urges, remains entrenched in "the Anglo-Saxon tradition, which is staunchly individualist".[11] "Values" can be retained only "by subordinating the demands of the ironist to the demands of the liberal".[12] *His* (sub-)

---

[8]   Richard Rorty, *Contingency, Irony and Solidarity* (Cambridge: CUP, 1989), and the essays in *Philosophy and Social Hope* (London: Penguin, 1999).

[9]   Honi Fern Haber, *Beyond Postmodern Politics: Lyotard, Rorty, Foucault* (New York and London: Routledge, 1994).

[10]   Rorty, *Contingency*, p.45.

[11]   Haber, *Beyond Postmodern Politics*, p.61.

[12]   Haber, *Beyond Postmodern Politics*, p.65.

community is that of "we liberals".[13] This community tends to be that of "the leisured, white, bourgeois, male liberal [who is] immune to critique from discordant voices".[14] To accord privilege to the internal norms of "local" communities may destroy the illusion that language serves as "a mirror of nature", but it substitutes a new and different "mirror", namely that of language as the narcissistic mirror of the "local" community and its practices.

Some may even reflect, without necessarily presuming to criticize the *actions* of American foreign policy during these early years of the twenty-first century, that this elevation of the *internal* norms of a community may not be entirely unrelated to *the rhetoric* of American governmental language addressed often with an eye to internal voters concerning foreign nations and global issues. *Internal criteria* govern first and foremost "people like us". The problems of *"internal" and "local" criteria* take their place alongside other themes identified in Essay 34 as not least promoting further fragmentation. Middle Eastern nations may receive support if they are "like us".

This *"internalism"* promotes fragmentation in two further specific ways. First, Rorty and Fish appeal to the work of Thomas Kuhn on paradigms in the philosophy of science, and to a pluralist interpretation of the later Wittgenstein.[15] Although they do allude to the later modifications of "paradigm" theory presented in Kuhn's earlier *The Structure of Scientific Revolutions*, in practice they work with the theory that Kuhn promotes in his earlier work. This tended (1) to stress discontinuities between competing paradigms; (2) to view scientific discovery as a product of social history with insufficient qualification, and (3) to overstate the problems of "incommensurability". The more pluralist assumptions of the earlier work find expression in such slogans as "There is no standard higher than the assent of the relevant community"; and "There is no principled (i.e. non-rhetorical) way to adjudicate the dispute."[16]

It would merely go over old ground to cite the arguments of Karl Popper in his classic 1965 debate with Kuhn, although Popper's work *The Logic of Scientific Discovery* retains force at various points. A recent reappraisal of this debate comes from Steve Fuller, who trained as a philosopher of science and is currently Professor of Sociology at Warwick University; he might be said to share in part Rorty's universes of discourse, even if he does not share his views.[17] Fuller acknowledges that paradigm-shifts occur when a set of shared beliefs or values faces a crisis, and may be replaced by a kind of new orthodoxy. New *"a priori's"* may become established, and in this new mood certain external criticisms tend to be bounced back too readily as untenable. Nevertheless Fuller places

---

[13]   The phrase recurs too frequently to invite documentation, just as *Truth and Progress* does to death the phrase "we pragmatists". But see *Contingency*, pp.64–5.

[14]   Haber, *Beyond Postmodern Politics*, p.70.

[15]   Fish and Rorty do refer to the second edition of T.S. Kuhn, *The Structure of Scientific Revolutions* (Chicago, IL: University of Chicago Press, 2nd edn, 1970), e.g., in Richard Rorty, *Philosophy and the Mirror of Nature* (Princeton, NJ: Princeton University Press, 1979), pp.322–35 and 343–47 and *Objectivity, Relativism and Truth: Philosophical Papers volume 1* (Cambridge: CUP, 1991), pp.35–62; and S. Fish, *Doing What Comes Naturally*, pp.125–6 and 486–8.

[16]   Fish, *Doing What Comes Naturally*, p.487.

[17]   Steve Fuller, *Kuhn Vs. Popper: Prophets of the End of Science* (Cambridge: Icon, 2003), and Fuller, *Thomas Kuhn: A Philosophical History of Our Times* (Chicago, IL: University of Chicago Press, 2000).

more weight upon the gradual, nuanced, self-correcting processes that are more akin to Popper's emphasis upon the patient and steady growth of knowledge and the critique of knowledge. He respects inter-disciplinary and trans-contextual dialogue and tradition of a kind that we might readily associate with the hermeneutics of Gadamer. In his *Philosophy, Rhetoric and the End of Knowledge* Fuller explicitly attacks the grounds of pragmatic relativism put forward by Fish.[18]

Popper's approach veers too closely towards a kind of positivism to offer a satisfactory alternative as such. A more acceptable "middle way" finds expression in the work of David N. Livingstone, among others. Livingstone considers examples of "local" factors in scientific enquiry, notably local geography. Local factors *condition* what is possible by way of "discovery" in the physical sciences.[19] Livingstone addresses "some of the ways in which scientific knowledge and its circulation have been shaped by spatial factors".[20] He attacks the notion that the physical sciences operate at the level of a universal abstracted from place, from history, from national cultures, from physical resources, or even from conditions of climate.[21] Livingstone accepts neither positivism nor a radical relativism of the local, but explicitly states his sympathy with Gadamer's belief that "the meaning of any text is bound up with the history of the interpretation – the post-history of the text".[22] Geographers and scientists belong to "a tradition of enquiry", but these are not closed off from inter-contextual understanding. Indeed Livingstone uses a term that regularly occurs in these essays in the context of theology: they belong to "an *incarnated* tradition of enquiry" (my italics).[23] Hermeneutics, I have argued, emerge as a dialectic between a "Beyond" that transcends "my" immediate context, and the "embodied", contingent, particular, "here and now".

Second, Rorty follows another path that also leads to fragmentation and "local" pluralism. This stems from a questionably pluralist interpretation of the later Wittgenstein. Jane Heal expresses the heart of the matter: "Rorty believes that Wittgenstein, among others, had an outlook similar to his own ... This is not an entirely accurate reading of Wittgenstein."[24] Wittgenstein's metaphor of philosophical thinking as a "therapy" that unties knots in our thinking and "dissolves" mental cramp may appear superficially to offer parallels with Rorty's "rubbish-disposal" exercises.[25] Rorty claims that for Wittgenstein the great metaphorical issues about truth were in effect "never there".[26] To be sure, Wittgenstein states, "If I have exhausted the justifications I have reached bedrock, and my spade is turned. Then I am inclined to say, 'This is simply what

---

[18] Steve Fuller, *Philosophy, Rhetoric, and the End of Knowledge: The Coming of Science and Technology* (Madison, WI: University of Wisconsin Press, 1993).

[19] David N. Livingstone, *Science, Space and Hermeneutics* (Heidelberg: University of Heidelberg [Department of Geography: Hettner lectures], 2002).

[20] Livingstone, *Science, Space and Hermeneutics*, p.12.

[21] Livingstone, "Tropical Hermeneutics and the Climatic Imagination", loc. cit., pp.43–73.

[22] Livingstone, "Tropical Hermeneutics", p.73.

[23] Livingstone, *Science, Space and Hermeneutics*, p.78; cf. also his *The Geographical Tradition: Episodes in the History of a Contested Enterprise* (Oxford and Cambridge, MA: Blackwell, 1992).

[24] Jane Heal, "Pragmatism and Choosing to Believe", in Alan Malachowski (ed.), *Reading Rorty* (Oxford: Blackwell, 1990), p.101; cf. pp.101–14.

[25] Richard Rorty, *Truth and Progress: Philosophical Papers, Volume 3* (Cambridge: CUP, 1998), p.8.

[26] Rorty, *Truth and Progress*, p.35.

I do'."[27] Rorty might well imagine that his dismissal of "getting reality right" together with any language about "the nature of truth" merely reflects Wittgenstein's rejection of questions about "essence" independent of context.[28] Philosophical methods offer "different therapies".[29] But three responses must be made.

(1) The self-assurance, even ironic complacency that marks the style of Rorty and Fish sits ill with the seriousness of Wittgenstein. Wittgenstein observed to Malcolm: "You can't think decently if you don't want to hurt yourself."[30] Malcolm recalls "his passionate love of truth … ruthless integrity" and "extreme seriousness".[31] Stanley Fish pits "Serious Man" against "Rhetorical Man" as reflecting respectively the different world-views of modernity and postmodernity.[32] The turning-point for Fish in "seeing through" the illusory difficulties of interpretation was when "I stopped worrying".[33] Wittgenstein does not have the postmodern outlook of "rhetorical man".

(2) The relation between "language-games" in Wittgenstein is nothing like how Rorty and Fish seem to understand "incommensurability". We may leave aside the problem that when they export the term from the domain of philosophy of science they and some other writers appear to fail to see how this change of frame changes the application and precise meaning of the metaphor. Rorty and Fish tend to use the notion to devalue the possibility of transcontextual communication, understanding, and *criteria* of understanding and value. Admittedly Rorty at one point modifies his metaphor with that of an "archipelago" rather than a collection of self-contained, independent islands. Nevertheless Wittgenstein regards "being human" as a trans-contextual frame and condition for understanding in the case of many communicative actions. Expressions of laughter, pain, love and belief regularly display such close family-resemblances among different communities as to suggest a wider basis for understanding than "local" communities alone.

(3) Wittgenstein's very emphasis upon particularity saves him from offering any *general* declarations of the kind found in Rorty, for example, about truth as justification to a given community, and about the dismissal of a substantial area of philosophy as resting upon un-askable questions. As we have observed elsewhere, A.J. Ayer also proposed a huge imperialist linguistic veto, now recognized as sheer positivism disguised as linguistic theory. Even the celebrated slogan "meaning is use" applies only "to a large class of cases".[34] Wittgenstein's injunctions that we find out what questions remain meaningful "by watching" rather than by presupposing requires more humility and patience than seem readily to fit the more self-confident pronouncements of Rorty and Fish.[35]

---

27   L. Wittgenstein, *Philosophical Investigations* (German and English, Oxford: Blackwell, 1967), sect. 217.

28   R. Rorty, *Truth and Progress*, pp.3–4 and 25; Wittgenstein, *Investigations*, sects 38–47, 65, 92, 96–8, 109, 115 and 119.

29   Wittgenstein, *Investigations*, sect. 133.

30   Norman Malcolm (with G. von Wright) *Wittgenstein: A Memoir* (London: OUP, 1958), p.40.

31   Malcolm, *Wittgenstein*, pp.26–7.

32   Fish, "Rhetoric", in *Doing What Comes Naturally*, p.482; cf. pp.482–4.

33   Stanley Fish, *Is There a Text in This Class?* (Baltimore, MD: Johns Hopkins University Press, 1980), pp.1–17.

34   Wittgenstein, *Philosophical Investigations*, sect. 43.

35   Wittgenstein, *Investigations*, sect. 31.

Any insistence that only norms and criteria *internal* to particular communities have currency *cannot* serve a hermeneutic that can fulfil its tasks. However, it is not the case that all postmodern thought necessarily carries with it these assumptions, and in the rest of this reappraisal we turn to other features, including some more constructive ones.

III

Further Reappraisals, and Lyotard's Rejection of Grand Narrative and of Criteria as Ways of Repressing "Difference"

Essays 33 and 34 also pursue agenda shaped by contextual factors. The essay on "Language, Reference and Indeterminacy" addresses theories of texts that are found especially in European postmodern writers. The positive contribution of these theories to hermeneutics lies in their recognition that not *all* language is directly referential and representational. I supported this approach by including the first of the seven essays that, together with the present essay, make up the eight of Part VI. We do not need to subscribe to a postmodern world-view to recognize the limits of representational and *directly* referential language, although many postmodernist writers also seek to account for *all* language as non-representational and non-referential. It is here that differences arise.

This brings us onto new ground, as well as involving the arguments set out in Essay 33. For with hindsight, I should have discussed Derrida's "modification" to his earlier and "middle" view in his "afterward" to his work *Limited Inc.* (1988).[36] We consider this briefly in the last section of this essay. The remaining two essays also invite discussion of other aspects of postmodernity. Essay 34 discusses the relation between authority, traditions and communities along lines suggested by Gadamer's hermeneutics. Essay 35 discusses whether postmodernity nurtures a "mood", especially a mood of consumerism and at times possible manipulation, which might be compared with that of first-century Corinth. If so, this stands in tension with an apostolic theology of the cross in Christian theology. All of these issues invite some expansion in this reappraisal. However, the more important starting-point for fresh discussion is Lyotard's deliberated definition of postmodernity as rejection of "grand narratives", or "metanarratives".

If the above essays had not emerged from specific contexts of arguments, it might have proved helpful to take as a starting-point what is probably the only one-sentence definition of the postmodern that a major postmodernist thinker has written. Jean-François Lyotard explicitly defines the postmodern as consisting in "incredulity toward metanarratives".[37] By contrast "modernity" drew its major systems of truth and value from such "grand narratives" as those of Darwinianism, Freudianism, or Marxism. We might explicate these in terms of the myth of the inevitable progress of natural science in Enlightenment rationalism, the grand narrative of evolution as a comprehensive world-view in Darwinianism, the narrative of historical determinism through nodal points of

---

[36] J. Derrida, *Limited Inc.* (Evanston, IL: Northwestern University Press, 1998); also *Limited Inc.* (Paris: Éditions Galilée, 1990).

[37] J.-F. Lyotard, *The Postmodern Condition: A Report on Knowledge* (Manchester: Manchester University Press, 1984), p.xxiv.

revolution in Marxism, or the narrative of the externalization and repression of human desire and conflict in Freud. These are all-embracing and conditioning structures into which specific questions about truth and value become inserted in order to "discover" what the system and its grand narrative would yield as "answers".

These, especially the rationalism that held sway from Descartes to its more mechanistic form in the secular Enlightenment, provided the so-called foundations of knowledge, that gives rise to the questionable and ambiguous term "foundationalism" in theories of knowledge. Against this, and in reaction to it, so-called non-foundational and anti-foundational theories have more recently emerged, with new understandings of what might count as "rationality" and "knowledge".[38]

It may be tempting to assume that if the biblical writings provide a "grand narrative" of God's dealings with the world, and if they also offer a metanarrative that provides meaning and norms to history, to communities, and to individuals who allow themselves to become "inserted" into a biblical frame of reference, Lyotard would wish to reject the power of this narrative. However, Richard Bauckham suggests that while postmodernism, as defined by Lyotard and others, rejects all metanarrative, nevertheless "when Lyotard rejected grand narrative he was not thinking of the Christian story".[39]

Lyotard rejects those metanarratives that impose "totalizing" systems of meaning upon humankind, in order to homogenize the heterogeneity of history and human situations. The Illusory systems imposed, for example, by the Enlightenment myth of the invisible progress for humankind of science and technology, or the systems of exchange, labour, and revolution imposed by Marxism, have *oppressive* affects, and are often founded upon "tacit violence" to conform. They are offshoots of the political philosophy of imperial power. The idioms of one party are imposed upon another.

It is this concern to throw off the dead weight of conformity to "majority" world-view (the secular Enlightenment; exclusive trust in science; Marxist and Freudian understandings of human nature) that have led many Christian theists to welcome postmodernism as a counter-force to the values and assumptions drawn from the secular Enlightenment that have dominated biblical studies in the modern West. "Postfoundationalists" welcome the release from oppressive assumptions that were bound up with the high modernity of the nineteenth and early twentieth centuries. In biblical hermeneutics they regularly turn to narrative theologies that rehearse the histories of smaller, particular, groups and peoples, and even welcome a pluralism of hermeneutical norms in the belief that this brings deliverance from slavery to "received" news.

Nevertheless, Richard Bauckham rightly discourages a simple reaction away from the tyranny of the universal into the arms of a tyranny of the relative and local. Bringing together an exceptional expertise as a biblical scholar who earlier worked in the history of ideas and Christian doctrine, he perceives *both* the biblical narratives *and* biblical and

---

[38] Cf. Stanley J. Grenz and J.R. Franke, *Beyond Foundationalism: Shaping Theology in a Postmodern Context* (Louisville, KY: Westminster-Knox, 2001) and J. Wentzel von Huyssteen, *Essays in Postfoundationalist Theology* (Grand Rapids, MI: Eerdmans, 1997).

[39] Richard Bauckham, *Bible and Mission: Christian Witnesses in a Postmodern World* (Grand Rapids, MI: Baker Academic and Carlisle: Paternoster, 2003), pp.88 and 90.

philosophical hermeneutics as *embodying a dialectic between the particular and the universal*. We encounter "special characteristics of the biblical metanarrative which distinguish it crucially from the metanarratives of modernity".[40] These metanarratives are "imperialism, Marxism, Nazism ... global capitalism and the Americanization of the world".[41]

In one sense "Christianity and Islam are among the world religions that tell a story about the meaning of the whole of reality. The Bible in some sense encompasses all other human stories, draws them into the meaning that God's story within the world gives them."[42] All the same, if this constitutes a "grand narrative" because it embraces all reality, or a "metanarrative" because it provides norms and criteria for the meaning of lesser narratives, the biblical writings present neither the monolithic "myth of universal history" that constitutes the scientific progressivism of the Enlightenment nor the deterministic Marxist myth of socio-economic progress. The biblical material does not fall under the "universal or 'totalizing' discourses" distrust of which is "the hallmark of postmodernist thought".[43] To quote Bauckham again, "postmodern is ... a rejection of all metanarratives because as attempts to universalize one's own values or culture they are necessarily authoritarian or oppressive. Postmodernism exposes metanarratives as projects of power and domination. In place of such pretensions postmodernism opts for particularity, diversity, localism, and relativism."[44]

Of three main elements of metanarrative, the biblical writings fully embody only one: they only partially embody the second; and they fail to embody the third at all.

First, the biblical writings *do* function to provide metacritical legitimization, legitimacy, or validation, for certain value-systems and for multiple life-stresses, communal histories, or ethical models that they project or portray. They *do* offer criteria for what is valid, true, advantageous, or health giving.

Second, however, only in part are they continuous narratives of a universal history. Such narratives not only embody twists and turns, surprises, reversals and novelties; they also break down into "local" narratives of specific persons and specific communities, and above all they are *not monolithic*. The largely (but certainly not exclusively) *narrative* mode of the biblical writings, together with the four other modes or genres identified by Ricoeur as *hymnic, prophetic, prescriptive "wisdom"* (as well as *dialectic*) is *far from the discourse genre of systematic theology*.[45] Divine transcendence resists a monolithic system from one side, for as Ricoeur observes, "The God who reveals himself is a hidden God and hidden things belong to him."[46] The Mode of Wisdom discourse is exploratory, not "closed", while hymnic discourse turns on communication "from a first person to a first person".[47] None of these modes of discourse alone exhaustively conveys

---

[40] Bauckham, *Bible*, p.89.
[41] Bauckham, *Bible*, p.89.
[42] Bauckham, *Bible*, p.5.
[43] David Harvey, *The Condition of Postmodernity*, p.9.
[44] Bauckham, *Bible*, pp.6–7.
[45] Paul Ricoeur, "Toward a Hermeneutic of the Idea of Revelation", in his *Essays on Biblical Interpretation* (London: SPCK, 1981), pp.73-95.
[46] Ricoeur, *Essays*, p.93.
[47] Ricoeur, *Essays*, p.92.

the whole. Moreover from the other side, namely of human situations, Bauckham writes, "The Bible does *not* have a carefully plotted story-line ... This plurality of angles on the same subject matter [for example in Kings and Chronicles] disrupts any expectation of a single perspective ... We are encouraged to view the same events from varying perspectives."[48]

Bauckham expands this point: "There is the profusion and sheer untidiness of the narrative materials: the proliferation of little stories within the longer ones, the narrative directions left unfinished ... All this makes any sort of *finality* in summarizing the biblical story inconceivable."[49] "The particular has its own integrity that should not be suppressed for the sake of a too readily comprehensible universal."[50]

Finally, in addition to all this, the biblical writings, responsibly interpreted, bring *liberation* rather than *oppression*. Admittedly some have used them, as Nietzsche and others have readily pointed out, to enslave persons and nations by force. However, in Essay 35, "Can a Pre-Modern Bible Address a Postmodern World?" I have expounded the argument that the apostle Paul confronts the competitive, self-affirming consumerism of mid-first-century Corinth with the liberating power of the proclamation of the cross. Far from serving to effect the "docility" of the Christians in Corinth, as Michael Foucault might claim, the heart of this gospel consists in a liberating respect for "the other" that *builds* and promotes *life*. I have argued this in my commentary over some fourteen hundred pages.[51]

Indeed Paul's appeal to traditions that presuppose dialogue and certain commonality between the "local" community of Corinth and communities of other cultures and histories enable them to look *beyond* the narrow confines of criteria *internal* to their own community. The gospel offers them liberation from the narrowness of a cultural and religious narcissism. Many of the Christians in Corinth had sought to transpose the gospel into a mirror of the culture of self-promotion (of religious pragmatism?), that is, into an instrumental vehicle of self-affirmation that made transformation and new growth appear unnecessary. The gospel of the cross beckons them from *beyond* into broader, liberating, horizons.

In one respect, then, Lyotard's rejections of "Grand Narrative" may serve to turn over attention to the *lack* of monolithic abstraction or closed system in the Bible, just as he also breaks the spell of regarding "science" as a single, unified narrative.[52] Nevertheless, as Zygmunt Bauman points out, to deconstruct the *systemic* exhaustively into the *social* may brings chaos.[53] Systems *need* not be *closed*. In systems theory, the input and output of data depends upon *some* kind of systemic channelling, however loose and open-textual, to guarantee some element of continuity in what is transmitted. In the case of Christian doctrine, for example, creeds and catechisms perform this function. In language-theory

---

[48] Bauckham, *Bible*, p.92.
[49] Bauckham, *Bible*, pp.92–3 (his italics).
[50] Bauckham, *Bible*, p.93.
[51] Anthony C. Thiselton, *The First Epistle to the Corinthians: A Commentary on the Greek Text* (Grand Rapids, MI: Eerdmans and Carlisle: Paternoster, 2000).
[52] Northrop Frye, *The Great Code: The Bible and Literature* (New York: Harcourt Brace Jovanovich, 1982) tends to regard the biblical writings as a whole as a single over-arching grand narrative.
[53] Zygmunt Bauman, *Intimations of Postmodernity* (London: Routledge, 1992), p.38.

we return to the point regularly made in the essays of this volume: *some* language and literature is *"productive"*, open and "literary", *other* language may be "transmissive". I have argued this point with particular reference to Jurij Lotman and especially Umberto Eco.[54]

It would be misleading, however, to isolate Lyotard's concerns about "metanarrative" and "legitimization" from the rest of his more complex thought. These considerations belong to a radical context. We select, because of the limits of space, three sets of considerations to sketch out some of this wider context.

First, Lyotard is radically "postmodern" in his rejection of *all unifying structures*. One example concerns his assessment of social planning. Any systematic governmental planning that produces system is "terror". Honi Fern Haber explains: "'Lyotard's equation' of consensus, commensurability, unity, homology, and efficiency with terror ... is at least understandable, if not necessarily defensible, once we recognize that his understanding of language and the self ... commits him to defend what he calls 'the pagan ideal' ... which amounts to radical pluralism".[55]

Lyotard expresses this polemically: "Let us wage a war on totality."[56] Bill Readings offers a glossary of terms used by Lyotard, and defines "pagan" as "a mode of action characterized by the impiety of proceeding without criteria, making a series a site-specific *little narratives* that work as ruses rather than the embodiment of overarching rules".[57] This explains why homogeneity and consensus suggests "terror": it arises from some kind unreasoned force, under the pretext of assuming a criterion of value. In view of the biblical emphasis in unity, "order" and coherence, it is possible that Richard Bauckham is a little too optimistic about Lyotard than the evidence might lead us to assume, although he is right to insist that the Bible is no monolithic "open narrative" without a dialectical balance of "little narratives" also. This outlook does, however, also betray Lyotard's view of human selfhood as "de-centred" and fragmented.[58]

Second, Lyotard approaches the *"differend"* (his term), *or the problem of opposed views, initially* with a premise that appears profoundly *hermeneutical*. He considers the situations of two parties who face each other in confrontation. Too often, he observes, the opposed views find expression in the idiom of one side only, to the exclusion of genuine understanding of the other. The party who sues his or her own idiom and "controls" the discourse cannot accommodate what the other perceives as a wrong or as an injustice. Up to this point, this approach seems to reflect the kind of hermeneutical concern that we have described in Emilio Betti, or more broadly in Gadamer.

However, Lyotard takes a *"postmodern" turn that will not serve hermeneutics*. He doubts the very possibility of common ground. "Consensus" betrays the exercise of oppressive power by one party against the other. Lyotard coins the tern *"differend"* to denote a point, in effect, of *incommensurability between two language-games*, where neither language-game

---

54   Anthony C. Thiselton, *New Horizons in Hermeneutics* (London: HarperCollins [rp. Carlisle: Paternoster] and Grand Rapids, MI: Zondervan, 1992), pp.525–7.

55   Honi Fern Haber, *Beyond Postmodern Politics*, p.15.

56   Lyotard, *The Postmodern Condition*, p.82.

57   Bill Readings, *Introducing Lyotard: Art and Politics* (London: Routledge, 1991), p.xxxiii.

58   Honi Fern Haber makes this point convincingly, loc. cit., pp.9–13.

can express the point of difference without reducing it, repressing it, or distorting it.[59] Hence, in spite of a positive beginning, Lyotard moves from affirming the particularities of a hermeneutical dialectic to dissipating hermeneutics through a belief in the kind of "incommensurability " that we have criticized in Rorty and Fish.

Third, in contrast to the previous two points that raise difficulties for hermeneutics and theories of language, Lyotard offers a more positive contribution in exposing a distinctive dimension of *"relativism"* from the point of view of his postmodern philosophy. He perceives the fallacy of relativism to lie in a covert appeal to *its disguised status as metanarrative*. Relativists face the dilemma that one view of truth or value may be as good as another on their own premises, yet usually they opt for one as preferable over the other. How can they evade the paradox? Lyotard acutely notes that "subjective consciousness" or "experience" usually emerges as a metanarrative to justify the preference. Yet its role is not exactly that of a narrative. It disguises "non-narrative" as "narrative": the narrative of subjective consciousness.

This may seem to be valid. However, in his later work Lyotard concedes that in *The Postmodern Condition* and in *The Differend* "I exaggerated the importance to be given to narrative genre."[60] Perhaps in the end, the greatest difficulty of Lyotard's contribution lies in an in-built *instability* that results precisely from his dislike of the systemic.

Hermeneutics, and indeed the biblical writings, as Richard Bauckham also argues, reflect a dialectic of the particular and the universal, the dialectic of understanding and explanation. Lyotard may offer some positive observations on one side of the dialectic, but he offers little or no resource for appreciating the necessary role of the other.

IV

Postmodern Suspicion of Language: An Extension of the Exploration of Conceptual Grammar?

Fritz Mauthner, Bertrand Russell and Ludwig Wittgenstein all recognized that "distrust of grammar" provides the starting-point for critical philosophy. In the *Tractatus* Wittgenstein wrote, "All philosophy is a 'critique of language' (though not in Mauthner's sense). It was Russell who performed the service of showing that the apparent logical form of a proposition need not be its real one."[61] Russell formulated the device of logical quantifier as part of his Theory of Descriptions to distinguish the precision of "logical form" from the ambiguities of natural language. For example, the innocent word "is" in natural language may not perform its more everyday function in such a proposition as "The present King of France is ...". The use of an existential quantifier generates some such logical form as "For at least one x, there is an x such that x is f (King of France)." This disengages the logical form from questions about whether France currently has a king.

[59] Jean-François Lyotard, *The Differend. Phrases in Dispute* (Minneapolis, MN: University of Minnesota Press, 1983), esp. pp.65–85. For a detailed exposition, see Bill Readings, *Introducing Lyotard*, pp.113–25.

[60] Jean-François Lyotard, *The Postmodern Explained to Children: Correspondence 1982–1985* (London: Turnaround, 1992 [French, 1986]), p.31.

[61] L. Wittgenstein, *Tractatus Logico-Philosophicus* (London: Routledge, 1961), 4.0031.

Similarly, "a round square does not exist" may be understood as a *negation* if the proposition "there is at least one x such that x is f (round) and x is g (square)". The anomalies imposed by natural language disappear, by "bracketing out" the issue of "existence" from the central proposition.[62]

In *Interpreting God and the Postmodern Self* I traced this suspicion of language from Thomas Hobbes to Friedrich Nietzsche.[63] Nietzsche writes, "I feel we shall never be rid of God, so long as we still believe in grammar."[64] "Language contains a hidden philosophical mythology."[65] This accords in outline with the aphorisms of the later Wittgenstein: "Philosophy is a battle against the bewitchment of our intelligence by means of language ... A picture held us captive."[66] Philosophy entails "the uncovering of one or another piece of plain nonsense and of bumps that the understanding has got by running its head up against the limit of language. These bumps make us see the value of discovery."[67]

It would be replicating what we have written elsewhere to trace Wittgenstein's exploration of conceptual grammar through his use of many varied examples.[68] Among the most striking we cited above Wittgenstein's observations on the grammar of love, pain, belief, understanding and expecting. In particular this opened an enquiry about public criteria of meaning and "private" language.

The postmodern legacy from Nietzsche to Derrida may be seen as following an initially parallel route of enquiry before branching off in other directions. Nietzsche diagnosed three distinct factors that serve to separate surface-functions of language from disguised, hidden depth-functions. First, *metaphor* becomes reified into metaphysical doctrine. Nietzsche evaluates these reifications as "idols". Second, *motivations* involving *will-to-power* clothe bids for self-importance and control as claims to truth expressed often as descriptive propositions: "A theologian, a priest, or a pope ... lies with every word that he utters".[69] "'God forgives him who repents' – in plain language: him who submits himself to the priest."[70] Third, there are no "givens": "All that exists consists of interpretations."[71]

Derrida and Foucault radicalize and extend these three starting-points. Metaphors begin as transparent figures, but displacement occurs: "the metaphor is no longer noticed ... Philosophy would be this process of metaphorization which gets carried away in and of itself."[72] "Metaphysical metaphor has turned everything upside down ... 'God', 'soul',

---

[62]   Much of this phase of Russell's work, including "On Denoting", *Mind* (1905), pp.479–93, has been represented in R.C. March (ed.), *Logic and Language* (London: Allen & Unwin, 1956).

[63]   Anthony C. Thiselton, *Interpreting God and the Postmodern Self* (Edinburgh: T. & T. Clark and Grand Rapids, MI: Eerdmans 1995), pp.3–9.

[64]   F. Nietzsche, *The Complete Works* (London: Allen & Unwin, 18 vols, 1909–13), vol. 12, *The Sunlight of the Idols*, p.22, aphorism 5.

[65]   Nietzsche, *Works. Vol. 7 Human, All-Too-Human*, vol. 2 part ii, p.192, aphorism 11.

[66]   L. Wittgenstein, *Philosophical Investigations*, sects 109 and 115.

[67]   Wittgenstein, *Investigations*, sect. 119.

[68]   See Essay 15, "A Retrospective Reappraisal: Conceptual Grammar and Inter-Disciplinary Research".

[69]   Nietzsche, *Complete Works, 7: The Antichrist*, p.177 aphorism 38.

[70]   Nietzsche, *The Antichrist*, p.161, aphorism 26.

[71]   Nietzsche, *Works 15: The Will to Power*, vol. 11, p.12, aphorism 481.

[72]   J. Derrida, "White Mythology", in *Margins of Philosophy* (New York and London: Harvester Wheatsheaf, 1982), p.211.

'absolute' ... are *symbols* and not signs" (Derrida's italics).[73] *Metaphysics is "the white mythology" that reflects the culture of the West.*[74] Exploring attitudes towards metaphor in Plato, Hegel, Nietzsche, Husserl and Bergson, Derrida observes: "Bergson is far from alone in being wary of spatial metaphors", alongside metaphors that relate to time.[75]

This last observation has affinities with Wittgenstein's explorations of logical grammar in the earliest phase of his later work in *The Blue Book.* An expression, he notes, "misleads us by calling up pictures and analogies ... It is extremely difficult to discard these pictures unless we are constantly watchful ... We shall try to construct new notations in order to break the spell of those we are accustomed to."[76] "We may be irresistibly attracted or repelled by a notation."[77] We cannot rid ourselves of what "our symbolism" seems to imply: hence we ask such questions as "Where does the flame of a candle go to when it's blown out?" "Where does the past go to?" "We have become obsessed with our symbolism."[78] Our metaphors, symbolism, or surface-grammar lends us to have extraordinary notions of the "existence" of the past and the future.

Yet, although they appear to travel initially together, Wittgenstein and Derrida soon part company. For Derrida's view of the depth-grammar behind our metaphors is shaped decisively by his world-view of this self as a semiotic construct in which Saussure's notion of the arbitrariness of the sign is displaced from the Saussurian context, where it refers primarily to the language-system (*la langue*), to embrace the whole variety of language-uses (*la parole*) that are treated merely as raw-material for the production of shifting meanings for a changing sign-system. A *generality* and a *doctrine* characterizes Derrida's view of language and of the self, of a kind that finds no place in the more patient explorations of Wittgenstein. Wittgenstein exercises the self-denying vow of rigour and restraint: "Don't cry: 'there *must* be ... – but *look and see* whether there is' ..." (his italics).[79]

Michel Foucault sees linguistic disguise as operating on a massive communal scale. He has moved far beyond "conceptual grammar" in many respects, but the principle of suspicion of language shares the same starting-point. In particular, his exposure of the dynamics of power in regimes and in wider society does constitute a diagnostic hermeneutic. In pre-modern times, he argues, the power of kings and sometimes parliament was relatively transparent and open. The problem with "modern" power is that it is without a transparent centre. It has become diffused through "the smiling face in the white coat": through social scientists, social workers, doctors, teachers, psychiatrists and bureaucratic officials. In both *Discipline and Punish* and in *The History of Sexuality*, he declares, "Power is everywhere, not because it embraces everything, but because it comes from everywhere."[80] Among its effects is the power to define both what counts as "normal" and what is acceptable. Thereby it shapes aspirations and desires. It

[73] Derrida, *Margins*, p.212.
[74] Derrida, *Margins*, p.213.
[75] Derrida, Margins, p.227; cf. pp.221–9.
[76] L. Wittgenstein, *The Blue and Brown Books* (Oxford: Blackwell, 1958), p.23.
[77] Wittgenstein, *The Blue and Brown Books*, p.57.
[78] Wittgenstein, *The Blue and Brown Books*, p.108.
[79] Wittgenstein, *Investigations*, sect. 66.
[80] M. Foucault, *History of Sexuality*, vol. 1 (New York: Random House, 1980), p.93.

is no longer power "from the top down", but power "from the bottom up", and thereby all the more insidious.[81]

It would take us too far from our subject to pursue the thought of Foucault further here. Our single concern at this point is his exposure of linguistic disguise. With regard especially to Derrida, to explore conceptual grammar might be regarded as *beginning along the same path*, but *without imposing* a specific world-view upon our linguistic enquiries. In this respect, Wittgenstein's philosophy "leaves everything as it is ... Philosophy simply puts everything before us."[82] In retrospect we can see clearly that what A.J. Ayer promoted as a theory of *language* in his Logical Positivism was merely positivism dressed up as a linguistic theory. Lyotard, Derrida, Rorty and Fish all hold views of the world that they purport to offer to readers as theories of *texts*, of *language*, of *signs*, or of literary *reading*. Nevertheless, as Ricoeur shows in his own works, hermeneutical theory and theories of reading texts are difficult to separate from accounts of human selfhood. These postmodern writers use the very sleight of hand that they accuse more traditional philosophers, theologians and metaphysicians of using.

V

Agency and Embodiment: Modernity and the Postmodern Imagination

The deepest differences between Wittgenstein's exploration of conceptual grammar and exposure of linguistic disguise and many postmodern writers lie not only in the postmodern imposition of a world-view, but also in the postmodern rejection of Wittgenstein's axiom based upon observation that logical grammar rests upon "the natural history of human beings"; not in a *sign* that "by itself seems dead", while "in use it is *alive*".[83] Meaning arises "only in the application that a living being makes of it".[84] A language-game is "the whole, consisting of language and the actions into which it is woven".[85]

I do not suggest that Wittgenstein must be our criterion for the validity of any linguistic theory; simply that his work is to be reckoned with. My arguments that Derrida confuses the language-system (signs without a "speaking subject") and language-*uses* (how agents *deploy* what they select from the system) are set out in *New Horizons in Hermeneutics*, and need not be replicated here.[86] I argue that Derrida presents an "intermixture of semiotics and world-view".[87]

Nevertheless in his later works Derrida does appear to offer a certain minimal modification of his earlier views. In *The Ear of the Other*, which is based upon an earlier colloquium, he does not retract his basic thesis of *différance* and erasure, nor the view that there is no "self" in abstraction from language, but he does attempt to hold this together

[81] Foucault, *Sexuality*, vol. 1, p.94.
[82] Wittgenstein, *Investigations*, sects 124 and 126.
[83] Wittgenstein, *Investigations*, sects 415 and 432 (his italics).
[84] Wittgenstein, *Investigations*, sect. 454.
[85] Wittgenstein, *Investigations*, sect. 7.
[86] Thiselton, *New Horizons in Hermeneutics*, pp.80–141.
[87] Thiselton, *New Horizons*, pp.99–113; the title of a sub-section of chapter III.

with some recognition of the role of personal responsibility in using or interpreting language.[88] His afterword to *Limited Inc.*, which includes some discussion with J.L. Austin and John Searle, attempts to allow for some limited stability of meaning in texts, although texts are never "finished" structures, and generate a fluidity that moves as successive horizons of textual meaning evolve and change.[89]

Yet the agency of "the speaking subject" remains ambivalent, and the dianoetic content of communication remains marginalized. Nicholas Wolterstorff convincingly argues that Derrida's world-view is deeply self-contradictory. *He rejects metaphysics on the basis of a metaphysical assumption.* He retains the thesis, Wolterstorff comments, "that nothing expressible in a 'that' clause antedates and transcends the use of language signifying that so-and-so – no fact that so-and-so – no thought that so-and-so".[90] Derrida rejects the notion that "truth and falsehood are metaphysical concepts" while arguing that metaphysics has to go because it is "false".[91]

Wolterstorff comments further, "Self-referentially incoherent arguments are bad arguments. But Derrida is there before us. He concedes the incoherences."[92] But like so much in postmodern thought this ends as declarative rhetoric rather than argument. Wolterstorff concludes that while he does not reject everything on Derrida, "I have only rejected the imperialism of Derrida's rejection of authorial-discourse interpretation ... rejected his violence against authors".[93]

In his subtle reflections in "Hegel and the gods of postmodernity", Archbishop Rowan Williams observes, "In spite of Derrida's disclaimers it has proved very hard for religious writers *not* to read the language of trace and *différance* as a negative theology. For Derrida himself it is reasonably clear that 'God' is 'an effect of the trace': to speak of God is to try to put a face upon ... what is by stipulation not capable of being confronted, of being *faced*. Thus to speak of God is to try to erase the genuine trace."[94] But does this mean that grace is assimilated to absence? "There are no *words* of grace."[95] In the exchange of language there is "an extinguishing of true or final otherness":[96] "It 'reminds' speech ... of the illusoriness of presence, transparency, authorship/authority ... My anxiety has to do with the relegation of profanity of the temporal, the communicative, the implied devaluation of 'exchange'."[97]

All this imparts to the discourse of theology and religion a tragic quality that relates to a speechless void. What is "thinkable" is so because it moves on from mutual exclusivities, and "struggles to conceive of a structural wholeness nuanced enough to

[88] J. Derrida, *The Ear of the Other: Otobiography, Transference, Translation* (Lincoln: University of Nebraska Press, 1988).

[89] J. Derrida, *Limited Inc.* (Evanston, IL: Northwesternn University Press, 1988).

[90] Nicholas Wolterstorff, *Divine Discourse* (Cambridge: CUP, 1995), p.164.

[91] Wolterstorff, *Divine Discourse*, loc. cit.

[92] Wolterstorff, *Divine Discourse*, loc. cit.

[93] Wolterstorff, *Divine Discourse*, p.169.

[94] Rowan Williams, "Hegel and the gods of postmodernity", in Philippa Berry and Andrew Wernick (eds), *Shadow of Spirit: Postmodernism and Religion* (London and New York: Routledge, 1992), p.72 (his italics); cf. pp.72–80.

[95] Williams, "Hegel", p.73 (his italics).

[96] Williams, "Hegel", p.74.

[97] Williams, "Hegel", loc. cit.

contain what appeared to be contradictories".[98] Hegel was aware that thinking entailed the balance of discovering what kind of understanding might be adequate to a conflictual and mobile reality without reducing it to a fixed state of affairs.

Eberhard Jüngel is also concerned, like Wolterstorff and Williams, with what is "thinkable". To this end he reflects on the incarnate "embodiment" of God in Christ. Jüngel engages with the nature of language and "linguisticality" at length, especially with the distinctive significance of the language of *address*, and performative language.[99] In a particular sense "the word" is "the place of the conceivability of God", but more specifically since "the word of the cross is the self-definition of God in human language" the event of the cross *as both a linguistic and extra-linguistic event* provides the ground for God's being *"speakable" and "thinkable"*:[100] "This hermeneutical thesis does presuppose the *event* in which the analogy of faith ... was carried out ... the incarnation of the word of God in Christ ... Through this Christological event of identification a nearness between God and man is expressed ... as the ending of distance".[101] Hence "God is thinkable as one who speaks ...".[102]

Without embodied agents, or "speaking subjects", we set in motion a docetic reduction whereby we transpose "the Word made flesh" back into un-embodied word again. Sign-systems without their *use* by agents imply a docetic theology without the incarnation or without prophets and apostles who bear witness and communicate through life and embodied word. As we have observed, the conceptual grammar of "believe", "expect", "think", "understand" and "love", collapses in upon itself as empty and silent without the "backing" of human behaviour that gives it its currency.

It is no accident that in Christian theology everything derives from "grace", which denotes "gift" without strings; while radical postmodern thought apparently rejects any notion of "givens", in contrast to social construction. Kevin Vanhoozer rightly observes, "Postmodernity is a breakdown in the 'givens' of modernity"; but it is not only a breakdown in the givens "of modernity".[103] Vanhoozer adds, "For Derrida, the gift is as 'impossible' as justice ... The gift disappears in a web of calculation, interest, and measure."[104] He observes in his earlier volume on hermeneutics, "The death of God is linked to disappearance of the authority of the human author", and citing words from Roland Barthes: *"to refuse to halt meaning is finally to refuse God"*.[105] All of these intensely negative considerations leave us with serious problems for hermeneutics, language-theories and theology. Moreover another factor compounds the problem: with all these negative factors that pile up, why do so many theological writers and biblical interpreters

[98]   Williams, "Hegel", p.76.
[99]   E. Jüngel, *God as the Mystery of the World* (Edinburgh: T. & T. Clark, 1983), pp.9–14 and throughout. Jüngel engages with Aquinas, Wittgenstein, Freye, Fuchs, Heidegger and Austin among others.
[100] Jüngel, *God as the Mystery of the World*, pp.11, 152 and 229.
[101] Jüngel, *God*, p.288.
[102] Jüngel, *God*, p.289.
[103] Kevin Vanhoozer, "Theology and the Condition of Postmodernity", in Kevin J. Vanhoozer (ed.), *The Cambridge Companion to Postmodern Theology* (Cambridge: CUP, 2003), p.14.
[104] Vanhoozer, "Theology", p.17.
[105] Kevin J. Vanhoozer, *Is There Meaning in This Text?* (Grand Rapids, MI: Zondervan, 1998), p.30, his italics. He cites R. Barthes, "Death of Author", in *The Rustle of Language* (New York: Hill & Wang, 1986), p.56.

appear to welcome the new mood that postmodernity brings into these disciplines, while others reject these perspectives as ill-founded?

One finds the same split in many universities, especially in Faculties of Arts and Social Sciences. Schools of Critical Theory often welcome postmodern perspectives. Departments that include gender studies are often divided. There is usually more hospitality toward postmodernism in Departments of German, French and Hispanic Studies than broadly among historians, classicists, archaeologists and philosophers. Part of the reason for this is that scholars sometimes readily fasten upon *particular aspects* of postmodern thought without asking whether they can responsibly buy into the whole.

In biblical interpretation those who welcome postmodern perspectives usually tend to regard this phenomenon as above all a powerful tool for deconstructing and disempowering the mythologies and metanarratives of *secular Enlightenment* modernity and biblical criticism as offering "assured results" on the basis of descriptive science. They welcome the attack on undue privilege accorded in high modernity to the methods and world-view of the natural sciences and technology. Typically Walter Brueggemann argues, "Our context for ministry is *the failure of the imagination of modernity.*"[106] By contrast he urges that we need to "fund" *postmodern imagination.* "Modern" imagination presupposes hegemony, systems, hierarchies and the trappings of a mechanistic world. For example, imagination focused in the creation of the world has been "bewitched ... with scientific categories".[107] Postmodern imagination may break through these old boundaries in ways that are "therapeutic". We need to focus on a "zone of imagination" between the inputs of the text and the outcome of belief and behaviour that will entreat a new processing and "a wondrous liberating moment" of "listening".[108]

The question that this raises is how "postmodern" all this call for change really is. Does not the new hermeneutic of Fuchs and Ebeling and especially the hermeneutics of Gadamer and Ricoeur already affirm all this without any need to travel down the postmodern road? If "postmodern" merely denotes liberation from the model of the secular Enlightenment and scientific methods that elevate "*mastery*", this is all for the good, but is it not *philosophical hermeneutics* rather than postmodernity?

To a limited extent the same might be said of the over-rhetorically self-advertised work entitled *The Postmodern Bible.*[109] Neither collaborative team writing, nor reader-response theory as such, nor "defamiliarization", nor structuralism, nor feminist hermeneutics are *necessarily* postmodern, although poststructuralist readings take on a closer relation to postmodernity. Ideological criticism can also readily merge into radical deconstruction. The seven "collective" essays reflect a postmodern *mood* and postmodern attitude towards "modernity", but their assimilation of postmodern perspective remains eclectic.

If "the politics of reading is ... an obvious focus for our book", this hardly *demands* a

---

[106] Walter Brueggemann, *The Bible and Postmodern Imagination: Text under Negotiation* (London: SCM, 1993), p.19.

[107] Brueggemann, *Imagination*, p.33.

[108] Brueggemann, *Imagination*, p.62.

[109] G. Aichele and others ("the Collective") (eds), *The Postmodern Bible* (New Haven, CT: Yale University Press, 1995).

postmodern view of selfhood or texts.[110] The chapter on reader-response criticism rightly begins with American literary theory and with writers such as Jane Tompkins and Wayne Booth; it moves on to Roman Ingarden and Wolfgang Iser, and only later to Stanley Fish, David Bleich and Jonathan Culler.[111] Indeed it covers almost the very same ground as my chapter on reader-response theory in *New Horizons in Hermeneutics*, except that it hardly touches upon the deeply theoretical issues that separate Fish's postmodern pragmatism from Iser's more responsible concern for reader-activity.[112]

Works on biblical interpretation that claim affinity with postmodern perspectives cover a very wide range and spectrum of views. Stephen D. Moore reflects a thoroughgoing engagement with postmodern perspectives in his poststructuralist approach to Mark and Luke.[113] On the other hand Garret Green in his *Theology, Hermeneutics and Imagination* may be more akin to Brueggemann's attempt to forge new paths in the wake of a decline in the privileging of "scientific" models drawn from "modernity".[114] Hermeneutical studies at the beginning of the twenty-first century reflect a keen awareness of the sterility of the quasi-scientific model of "mastery". However, postmodernity is a more complex phenomenon than many may seem to appreciate. Its varied elements will invite a diversity of judgements and evaluations, and varied effects upon hermeneutics. Some aspects may serve positively to sharpen and to refine certain hermeneutical critiques; other more radical approaches end by undermining the very purposes and goals that define constructive hermeneutical endeavour.

---

[110] *Postmodern Bible*, p.3.

[111] *Postmodern Bible*, pp.20–67.

[112] Thiselton, *New Horizons in Hermeneutics*, pp.516–557; cf. also pp.393–410 and 430–515.

[113] Stephen D. Moore, *Mark and Luke in Poststructuralist Perspectives* (New Haven, CT: Yale University Press, 1992).

[114] Garratt Green, *Theology, Hermeneutics and Imagination: The Crisis of Interpretation at the End of Modernity* (Cambridge: CUP, 2000).

PART VII

HERMENEUTICS, HISTORY AND THEOLOGY

Scholarship and the Church: "Academic Freedom, Religious Tradition and the Morality of Christian Scholarship" (1982)

This comes from a book of eight essays commissioned by Archbishop Robert Runcie to mark the occasion of the Papal visit to England and to engage further with issues raised by the Anglican–Roman Catholic International Commission. Bishop Mark Santer edited the volume under the title Their Lord and Ours: Approaches to Authority, Community, and the Unity of the Church *(London: SPCK, 1982). I argue that a Christian scholar, especially one who holds a formal church office, should seek to conduct his or her theological and interpretative enterprise in awareness of a double set of loyalties or commitments: to the professional standards and criteria of the academic community, and to the life and witness of the Gospel and the Christian Church. In particular I cite parallels with dualities of commitment and openness in other academic disciplines; here theology is not unique. I also draw on a philosophical and ethical distinction between neutrality and impartiality. A Christian scholar needs to remain impartial in handling evidence and arguments, but this is not to demand neutrality from a person of faith. Amid the complexity multiple roles demand multiple virtues. I argue that problems arise when a Christian scholar becomes obsessed with upholding some single role or virtue, for example* exclusively *as a guardian of a doctrinal system or as a lone explorer following new paths.*

I
Issues that Transcend Debates about Religion and Theology Only

The phrase 'the morality of scholarship' denotes an area of ethical problems that are by no means peculiar to the academic study of Christian theology. In 1967 a philosopher of language published a collection of essays under this title that made little or no mention of problems of theology or of Christian thought.[1] These essays discussed the moral constraints experienced by sociologists, philosophers and political theorists, who were simultaneously committed to teach their subject with appropriate rigour and objectivity, and yet also committed as human beings or as citizens to certain practical, social, or political programmes.

An examination of the growing body of literature on the morality of scholarship outside the distinctive context of Christian theology brings several fundamental principles to light. First, it is a mistake to construe the long and bitter debates about the academic study of theology simply as a struggle to wrest academic freedom from the clutches of a defensive religious dogmatism. The debate is not simply a matter of

---

[1] Max Black (ed.), *The Morality of Scholarship* (New York: Cornell University Press, 1967).

personal integrity *versus* church doctrine. Moral issues and moral constraints emerge on *both* sides of the debate. The Christian scholar belongs to more than one community, and membership of each community carries with it certain moral obligations towards the community in question.

Second, we can no longer take for granted what is meant by 'objective' academic scholarship. Admittedly, appeals to redefine this concept have sometimes been little more than a shallow propagandist device to give subjectivism or dogmatic prejudice some pretended veneer of academic respectability. It may offer a supposedly rational argument for an irrational position. But at a deeper level, the debates in the social sciences and in hermeneutical theory about the limitations of value-free knowledge constitute a proper and urgently necessary dimension of the discussion.

Third, an over-simplistic view of the debate about academic freedom and the morality of scholarship has sometimes seemed plausible on the basis of an unduly individualistic understanding of the nature of scholarly enquiry. The simplistic model of the scholar is that of the lone individual pioneer cutting through the errors of tradition and arriving on his own at some startling novelty. But creative scholarship in actual practice takes place *within* the framework of a tradition and of the knowledge of the community, and scholarly creativity involves something far more profound than mere novelty.

This chapter is an attempt to bring these three factors to bear on the otherwise well-worn debate about academic freedom in theology, in the hope that we may then be in a better position to see what *both* sides in the debate are trying to say. The really interesting and urgent debates in theology are not usually those in which all of the best arguments seem to be on the same side. It is when we wish somehow to say 'Yes' to *both* sides of an argument which seems, at least in popular thought, to offer incompatible alternatives, that we are encouraged to continue to wrestle with a familiar problem. This is certainly the case with the present subject. If theology is removed from the realm of genuinely objective, rigorous and critical academic study, Christians lose their claim to intellectual integrity and honesty. Theology would then have retreated into a ghetto world of mere propaganda. On the other hand, the Christian scholar remains a Christian and a human being whose faith is nourished, and whose actions are directed, by the tradition to which he belongs and the God whom he worships. An 'ivory tower' scholar is one who forgets that as a human being he experiences constraints and recognizes concerns which make claims upon him above and beyond those of the academic community. No one would condone, for example, a scholar's spending so long at his desk as to become an irresponsible and unloving parent on the ground that his commitment to the pursuit of truth was all that mattered to him as a scholar.

II
The Variety of Standpoints Represented in the Debate

Do all Christian scholars experience the problems and tensions that are implied by the history of the present subject? Certainly some find no tension at all between the demands of Christian discipleship and the expectations of the academic community. One well-known and eminent British biblical scholar makes this point explicitly and strikingly: in a recently published autobiography F.F. Bruce writes

> I am sometimes asked if I am aware of the tension between my academic study of the Bible and my approach to the Bible in personal or church life. I am bound to say that I am aware of no such tension ... There is no conflict between my critical or exegetical activity in a university context and my Bible exposition in church ... The Christian acceptance of the Bible as God's word written does not in the least inhibit the unfettered study of its contents and setting.[2]

Bruce underlined the importance of academic freedom in 'this subject of all subjects' in his inaugural lecture as Professor of Biblical History and Literature in the University of Sheffield, noting that in the context of the university his commitment in teaching Biblical Studies was the same as what it had been when in earlier years he had lectured in classics: 'one's only commitment is to truth ... to follow the evidence wherever it leads, in an atmosphere of free enquiry'.[3] Even though his own theology is conservative rather than radical, he expresses a strong preference for the environment of the university as over against that of the theological seminary.

By contrast, however, another British theologian, Donald MacKinnon, offers a diametrically opposite verdict concerning the presence or absence of tension between academic freedom and Christian commitment. Like F.F. Bruce, he insists that 'it is of course essential for the health of theology as a subject that it should be carried on in the setting of a university, and not be in the restricted, specially orientated atmosphere of a denominational seminary'.[4] But part of the reason for this is that the cross-fertilization with ideas flowing from other fields of study should serve to stimulate a sense of *restlessness* and *discontent* with theology as a task completed and adequately done.

This stands in the Reformation tradition of *ecclesia reformata semper reformanda*. The sense of pressure and tension which are made by the simultaneous demands of Christian faith and academic openness make the academic theologian 'a rootless man, restless and awkward, ill at ease with himself ... It should not be easy to be a theologian in a modern university; indeed it should never have been easy ... Theology lives through interrogation.'[5] MacKinnon concludes by comparing the pain and tension that is inescapable for the academic theologian with the inescapable signs of costly and authentic apostleship experienced by Paul in the struggles reflected in 2 Corinthians.

The history of the debate witnesses to a degree of controversy and passion which underlines the genuineness of the problems posed by our subject. Since at least the time of Clement and Origen, on the one hand, and of Tertullian, on the other, Christians have debated the extent to which theology should be done within the distinctive context of the church alone or also within the wider context of man's universal quest for truth wherever it is to be found. G.R. Evans and others have traced the history of the debate about the

---

[2] F.F. Bruce, *In Retrospect: Remembrance of Things Past* (London: Pickering and Inglis, 1980), pp.143–4.

[3] Ibid., p.143.

[4] Donald MacKinnon, 'Theology as a Discipline of a Modern University', in T. Shanin (ed.), *The Rules of the Game: Cross-Disciplinary Essays on Models in Scholarly Thought* (London: Tavistock Publications, 1972), p.170.

[5] Ibid., p.172; cf. pp.164–78.

status of theology as an academic discipline to the era of the foundation of the universities in twelfth-century Europe. Evans cites the notorious public conflicts between the 'academic' approach of Peter Abelard and Gilbert of Poitiers and the church's 'defender of the faith' in the person of Bernard of Clairvaux.[6] Wolfhart Pannenberg also dates the beginnings of theology as an academic discipline from the twelfth and thirteenth centuries, arguing that its scientific status as a university subject is part and parcel of a wholly proper and necessary concern that the truth of Christianity should be seen publicly to stand the test of 'generally accepted criteria'.[7]

A number of writers, including from a Lutheran perspective Gerhard Ebeling and J. Pelikan, and from a more Calvinist or Barthian standpoint T.F. Torrance, have rightly urged that the academic context of theology as a scientific discipline was of fundamental importance to the Reformers. We shall look more closely at this argument in due course. When we move, however, into the post-Enlightenment era, and especially into the controversies of the nineteenth century, it is clear that the debate has become transposed into a new key which sadly allows and even invites polarization into two bitterly opposed camps. As a sample of the issues that came to the surface most characteristically in this nineteenth-century era, we may briefly allude to four well-known episodes.

First, the foundation of the University of Berlin in 1810 was preceded by a sharp debate in 1807 between Friedrich Schleiermacher and the philosopher J.G. Fichte about the status of theology in the university. Standing in the tradition of philosophical idealism, Fichte saw theology as the handling of ideas that should be taught in the university as a purely academic subject, without reference to any ecclesiastical or dogmatic context. Schleiermacher, on the other hand, stood in the tradition of Romanticism with its emphasis on 'life' and 'experience'. He refused to reduce religion, as a phenomenon of human life, to 'theology', as the abstract, objectivist study of ideas or concepts. Hence he urged that theology or religious studies should take its place within the university as a vocational or applied subject, oriented towards ministerial training. To train competent clergy, he argued, lay no more outside the province of a state university than any other course of study that equipped the professional leaders of the nation to perform their role in the national community. He believed that this principle in no way compromised the necessary distinctiveness of the church over against the state or society in general.

If Berlin brought into focus one aspect of the nineteenth-century debate, the University of Halle served as a focus for another. In 1810 Wilhelm Gesenius became Professor at Halle. But the devout and orthodox of the German church saw his teaching and writing as an intolerable example of the excesses and destructive effects of the application of Enlightenment rationalism to biblical studies. In 1830, which was the Jubilee year of the Augsburg Confession, E.W. Henstenberg published a bitter attack on Gesenius on behalf of church orthodoxy. A long and biting public debate took place, in which one major theological issue became that of whether the questioning of church tradition was entailed

---

[6]   G.R. Evans, *Old Arts and New Technology. The Beginnings of Theology as an Academic Discipline* (Oxford: Clarendon Press, 1980), p.57 and *passim*.

[7]   Wolfhart Pannenberg, *Theology and the Philosophy of Science* (Philadelphia, PA: Westminster Press, and London: Darton, Longman and Todd, 1976), p.13.

as a fundamental of the theology of the Reformation. So widespread was public concern over the debate that a report was submitted to the Prussian king, even though in the event no actual legal proceeding was taken against Gesenius.

A third facet of the nineteenth-century debate appears in the careful enquiries that took place among scholars more moderate than Gesenius but less cautious than Hengstenberg, about the scientific status of biblical studies. Wellhausen's teacher, Heinrich Ewald, provides a notable example of a scholar who at one and the same time rejected the radical extremes of F.C. Baur and D.F. Strauss, but also insisted on the necessity of using scientific method in biblical studies.

Finally, in England and the English-speaking world, these issues came most strikingly before the public eye with the publication in 1860 of the volume entitled *Essays and Reviews* and through the work of Bishop J.W. Colenso of Natal. The English bishops censured Bishop Colenso, and many leading figures were drawn into a widespread and often harsh debate about subscription and assent to the Articles of Religion of the Church of England. Up to this period, assent to the Articles was required from members of the older universities proceeding to degrees. In the ensuing debate Benjamin Jowett, one of the contributors to *Essays and Reviews*, argued for the abolition of the university tests on the ground that those who were genuinely free to speak what they believed without constraint from the church could do so with greater authority and effectiveness than if matters were otherwise.

Although university tests as such were indeed abolished, the Church of England has always retained the requirement for assent to its doctrine on the part of its clergy. The lay theological scholar stands in a different position from the scholar who is also the holder of a teaching office within the Church of England. Arguments for and against subscription on the part of the clergy feature in Reports of the Church of England Doctrine Commission in 1938 and most recently in 1981.[8] Indeed, the 1981 Report reaffirms the traditional Anglican standpoint that while the integrity of the individual theological explorers must be respected, there are definite limits to the freedom that can be enjoyed by those who are authorized to teach and to minister 'in the Church's name'.[9]

Today the debate is as wide-ranging as ever, and embraces still the widest possible divergence of views. Perhaps the most startling contrast can be achieved by comparing the passionately held convictions of Eric Mascall, on the one hand, and Gerd Theissen, on the other. Each believes that the kind of approach represented by the other constitutes a kind of moral *betrayal* of authentic theological scholarship. Mascall writes, 'We have been so anxious to be accepted as intellectually respectable in our modern secularised universities ... that we have taken for granted the desupernaturalization of Jesus and have substituted the study of early Christian psychology for the study of divine revelation'.[10] Theissen comments, 'There can be no recourse to privileged knowledge or

---

[8]   *Doctrine in the Church of England. The Report of the Commission on Christian Doctrine Appointed by the Archbishops of Canterbury and York in 1922* (London: SPCK, 1938), pp.36–9; and *Believing in the Church. The Corporate Nature of Faith,* A Report by the Doctrine Commission of the Church of England (London: SPCK, 1981), especially pp.129–34.

[9]   *Believing in the Church,* p.296.

[10]   E.L. Mascall, *Theology and the Gospel of Christ. An Essay in Reorientation* (London: SPCK, 1977), p.1.

authorities ... I shall ignore the view that it is possible to have privileged access to the truth. Instead of this I shall look for technical competence ... There can be no question of defending religion in its traditional form.'[11]

III

Some Causes of the Problem and a Way Forward: a Need for Academic Virtues and for Multiple Roles on the Part of an Integrated Human Agent

Why is such a divergent range of standpoints represented in the debate, and why has the debate so often led to bitterness and misunderstanding? We have already suggested that too often it is forgotten, or has never been understood, that there are *moral* constraints and pressures from *both* sides of the traditional arguments. Too often the debate has been misconstrued as a *moral* issue of honesty or academic integrity on one side, and as a *religious* matter of faithfulness to authoritative doctrine on the other. But such a way of construing the issue leaves much out of account. Even worse, it invites one side to see themselves as martyrs in the cause of theological faithfulness.

Membership of the academic community does indeed carry with it certain moral obligations. Each academic discipline evolves certain 'rules of the game', and a scholar has a moral obligation either to play by these rules or at least to offer rigorous rational justification for calling the rules in question. Knowledge of 'the rules' on the part of the teacher and student is part of what we think of as 'professional' competence in the area. Like a good referee, while a scholar may have a strong personal preference about which side wins in a particular game, the moral rules of scholarship dictate that the scholar gives each side their maximum opportunity to win, within the rules. Scholarly integrity, according to the philosopher Alan Montefiore, involves helping or hindering either side

> ... in completely equal measure with respect to his application of the rules of the game ... It is a matter of complete indifference to him *qua* referee whether it is one side or the other that has incurred a penalty. It is true that in imposing a penalty he is hindering the offending side and helping its opponents, but *he would have behaved in exactly the same way had their positions been reversed.*[12]

Whatever his *personal* desires, he has a professional *role* that imposes the moral constraint of fairness in handling evidence and arguments, akin to that of a judge in the courtroom or a referee in the field. To confuse *neutrality*, or lack of it, with *impartiality*, or lack of it, would be to betray the moral trust placed in him by the university, his academic peers and his students.

Nevertheless, this very disjunction, or at least distinction, between person and role has implications for the other side of the debate. For very often, the Christian scholar performs not only the role of a member of the academic community, but also the role of a teacher or minister of the church. This role, too, is one that carries with it the privilege

---

[11] Gerd Theissen, *On Having a Critical Faith* (London: SCM, 1979), pp.10–11.
[12] Alan Montefiore (ed.), *Neutrality and Impartiality. The University and Political Commitment* (Cambridge: Cambridge University Press, 1975), p.9 (my italics).

of trust on the part of others, and this, too, carries with it its own *moral* obligations. Those who look to their Christian pastors and teachers for spiritual nourishment and for edification of faith cannot but feel a sense of moral betrayal if or when these very teachers seem to undermine aspects of the corporate witness of the believing community. The church no less than the academic community, has 'rules' by which it lives and hands on its spiritual resources.

The more closely we look at the problems and issues, the more clearly we see the moral complexity of constraints that are experienced on all sides. The scholar who works in the best tradition of academic objectivity and respect for evidence and argument may be called upon to find the moral quality of *courage* as he finds himself irresistibly drawn along towards conclusions which he may have wished to avoid. He may need the moral quality of *honesty* as he discovers a fatal flaw in a case that he has laboriously and painstakingly built up over a number of years. He may need the moral quality of *humility* to recognize when a suspense of judgement or admission of ignorance is more appropriate than asserting his own view, or what others would like him to say. Conversely, an over-prolonged appeal to ignorance, an endless suspense of judgement, may represent moral cowardice or a lack of love for others who are left in a state of perplexity or indecision. At the same time, moral integrity is not the exclusive monopoly of the liberal scholar who believes that he or she is driven to cast doubt on tradition. It may be no less a matter of moral integrity to stand by a truth which is held in common with the whole community in whose life and testimony the Christian scholar shares, than to discard that truth in the light of recent arguments which have not yet had the chance to pass or to fail the test of time and the verdict of the wider community. Honesty, courage, patience, humility, integrity and loyalty, are demanded of the Christian scholar not only by his membership of the academic community, but also by his membership of the church.

Once this point has been recognized, it should not surprise us that such divergences of opinion exist in the present debate. For *moral* decisions are notoriously difficult and closely related to the scale of value-judgements which a given individual or community may hold. Indeed part of the problem is that many insist on trying to simplify a complex network of moral claims by constructing a simple and straightforward hierarchy of priorities that apply in advance of any specific question. For example, sometimes in the interests of orthodoxy it is suggested that the scholar's problems would be solved if he put 'God' first, when the very thing that is at issue is whether the church's formulations adequately articulate what *God* has revealed or is revealing. Conversely, sometimes in the interests of the liberal scholar 'truth' is said to claim priority over all other commitments, when the very thing that is at issue is whether the lone explorer is more likely to have grasped the *truth* than the whole Christian community throughout the world and down the centuries.

It is far more instructive to return to our earlier distinction between the different *roles* played by the Christian scholar in the respective communities to which he belongs. Problems emerge when a Christian scholar is identified (either by himself or by others) *exclusively with some single overarching role.* He may see his basic overarching role in life, for example, as guardian of the faith, as defender of orthodox theology, or as pioneer, explorer, or original researcher. Clearly each of these models dictates a quite different scale of moral priorities in his understanding of what Christian scholarship entails. A scholar who is historically sensitive, however, will see that all of these roles arise in given religious or intellectual traditions, and that his own adoption of one or more such roles is a matter, first of all, of institutional appointment or personal choice. Both the church and the academic world need equally the transmission and the testing of the knowledge that they mediated through *the community and the tradition of which the individual scholar is part.* The church needs its guardians of the faith, but it also needs its researchers. It needs its teachers, but it also needs it pioneers. In practice, the overwhelming majority of Christian scholars quite rightly and properly see themselves as performing *multiple* roles. This is precisely why no predetermined hierarchy of priorities can be established in the abstract in advance of each theological task.

The scholar who suffers from psychological or intellectual imbalance (either produced by himself or imposed on him by the demands of a community) may allow himself to work exclusively within the dictates imposed by a single model, regardless of the demands of the particular theological task in hand. If he sees himself as wearing the mantle of the Enlightenment critic, he will be inclined to adopt an attitude of suspicion and scepticism towards religious tradition. If, on the other hand, he sees himself only as shepherd and guardian of the flock, he may become almost obsessively paranoid about 'dangers' and 'threats' in theological teaching and research. The Christian scholar who is historically sensitive to the functions and limitations of all these adopted roles, however, will refrain from assigning some overarching model to his own scholarly activity in advance of knowing the nature of the specific theological task in hand. There are times when the urgent task is to move discussion forward beyond tired arguments and well-worn grooves, and there are times when it is more appropriate to issue a prophetic summons to renewed faithfulness.

It is instructive to note, however, that once again this principle is not exclusive to Christian theology. A considerable amount of research has been carried out in the area of educational psychology on the nature of creativity in the school and in the university. What emerges most clearly is that creative thinking is not to be equated simply with sheer novelty. It is true that creative scholarship entails individual insight, individual critical judgement and, above all, a dimension of willingness to engage in risk. This is why, to return to D.M. MacKinnon's essay, 'the university teacher of theology must be a man at once committed and uncommitted ... He must be prepared to find the outcome of his work totally other than his hopes and anticipations.'[13] Nevertheless individualist criticism and novelty is creative rather than merely eccentric and destructive only when it performs a productive and constructive function in relation to the wider tradition *within* which the novelty or criticism means anything significant. In terms of the psychology of education, creativity depends on *interaction between* the convergent-type thinking which characterizes the tradition of the community and the divergent-type thinking of the individual. A number of writers urge that 'creativity arises out of

---

[13] Alan Montefiore (ed.), *Neutrality and Impartiality. The University and Political Commitment* (Cambridge: Cambridge University Press, 1975), p.9 (my italics).

conventional intelligence ... Creative thinking occurs when the boundaries of the known are first mastered through convergent processes, and then extended, by the application of divergent processes.'[14]

In a less obvious and less direct way this principle may be said to operate even in some schools of modern art, where the 'common-sense' plain man may be tempted to feel that the distinction between creativity and arbitrary novelty is no longer possible. Creativity in some schools of art depends on what Merleau-Ponty calls the principle of 'coherent deformation'. The familiar is skewed and presented from a strikingly unusual physical or imaginative angle, in such a way that it is seen in an entirely fresh light. But if it is not the *familiar* that is re-presented in this way, the whole exercise loses its point as a creative presentation, and becomes mere fantasy or self-indulgence on the part of the artist.

In the event, then, the Christian scholar who is entirely dominated by the model of himself as pioneer, explorer, or Enlightenment critic, is less likely to contribute genuinely creative work than the Christian scholar who adopts a plurality of models which allow room for the constraints of tradition, or for what is 'familiar' from the standpoint of the whole Christian community. The particular complexity and delicacy of the debate about academic freedom arises, however, from the fact that the post-Enlightenment scholar stands in a multiplicity of traditions. The 'familiar' in the tradition of the Church is no longer the same as the 'familiar' in the history of the academic discipline within which he works. What constitutes convergent thinking within the context of the academic community is not the same as what constitutes convergent thinking in the context of the Church. Here we reach the heart of the matter. Any genuinely creative thinker works from within a given context. And the constraints and tensions experienced by the Christian scholar arise from the duality, or more correctly, multiplicity of contexts or traditions, within which he works.

IV
The Force of Some of the Standard Arguments on Both Sides of the Debate

We have space only to select some of the standard arguments that are put forward from both sides of the debate. First, (a) we look at those that are offered in defence of the importance of academic freedom as a necessary context for theological teaching and research.

(1) The customary starting-point concerns the importance of intellectual honesty and integrity. Bultmann cites this quality as the most important positive feature of theological liberalism, although he allows that it also seduced liberal scholars into a naïvely optimistic and objectivist view of the task of historical research, especially in relation to the figure of Jesus. He speaks of 'the development of *the critical sense* ... freedom and veracity ... the earnest search for radical truth'. He recalls his sense of gratitude as a

---

[14] A.J. Cropley, *Creativity* (London: Longmans, 1967), p.29. Cf. H.E. Gruber and G. Terrell (eds), *Contemporary Approaches to Creative Thinking* (New York: Atherton Press, 1962), especially J.S. Bruner's essay, 'The Creative Surprise'; and C.W. Taylor (ed.), *Creativity: Progress and Potential* (New York: McGraw-Hill, 1964).

student to G. Krüger's insistence that theology was 'unchurchly': 'He saw the task of theology to be to imperil souls, to lead man into doubt, to shatter all credulity. Here, we felt, was the atmosphere of truth in which alone we could breathe.'[15] Bultmann contrasts this with the atmosphere of intellectual compromise that as a student he believed characterized the orthodox university theology of the day. That Bultmann overpresses his point is clear from the fact that he feels obliged to offer a peculiar kind of theological defence of this approach. The Pauline doctrine of justification by grace alone is applied as a theory of knowledge, as if to suggest that intellectual defence of the Christian faith constitutes a kind of self-justification by intellectual 'works'. By this means Bultmann can solve the problem of academic freedom and the morality of Christian scholarship in a highly distinctive way, making a virtue out of the post-Enlightenment necessity of scepticism and doubt. But intellectual honesty and integrity is not the exclusive preserve of liberalism or radicalism. The fundamental importance of intellectual honesty is wholly correct; but the liberalism which Bultmann describes merely oversimplifies a complex moral problem by placing the doubts of the individual scholar at the top of a descending hierarchy, regardless of what the actual issue under discussion happens to be.

(2) Even though Bultmann's particular use of the doctrine of justification by grace is open to question, it nevertheless remains true that to argue for the place of theology in the setting of academic freedom within the university reflects certain basic insights of the Reformation. Indeed this point was raised in the controversy surrounding Gesenius and the University of Halle to which we have already referred. Gerhard Ebeling and Jaroslav Pelikan are among those who insist that Martin Luther saw himself first and foremost as a university professor of Old Testament, standing in the tradition of humanistic scholarship. Scripture must be allowed to speak in such a way that it may correct and reform the life of the church; but if it is taught and studied only by those who already see everything through the eyes of that life, how can the Bible speak freely and powerfully to the church's condition, confronting even 'churchman' as a word of both grace and judgement? For this reason, Pelikan observes, the Bible and theology are 'too important a part of scholarly enquiry to be left only to churchly theologians'.[16] In other words, it is to the good of the *church* that the Bible is not studied and taught exclusively by the official spokesmen of the church of the day. Otherwise there is the danger that the church will hear only what it wishes to hear. Thus Ebeling asserts that Luther received his certainty of vocation 'from the sober fact of his academic calling, which gave him the right and the duty to speak, even against his monastic vows and his duty of obedience to the hierarchy and the Church: "I have often said, and say again, I will not exchange my professorship for anything in the world"'.[17] T.F. Torrance considers that in this respect the Reformers raised the question of objectivity in theological method. The Reformation, he argues, sprang from 'a repentant readiness to rethink all preconceptions and presuppositions, to put all traditional ideas to the test face to face with the object'.[18]

---

[15]   R. Bultmann, *Faith and Understanding. Collected Essays* (Eng. tr., London: SCM, 1969), pp.29–30.
[16]   J. Pelikan, *The Christian Intellectual* (London: Collins, 1966), p.103.
[17]   G. Ebeling, *Luther, An Introduction to his Thought* (Eng. tr., London: Collins, 1972), p.17.
[18]   T.F. Torrance, *Theological Science* (Oxford: Oxford University Press, 1969), p.75.

(3) It follows from all this that theology can never be confined to the ghetto of one particular tradition or segment of life. Perhaps no one makes this point more cogently than Wolfhart Pannenberg, who is also thoroughly aware of the subjective dimension of human understanding. Pannenberg points out that the concern about the scientific status of theology in the university has been bound up since the twelfth or thirteenth century with the desire 'to defend Christianity by generally accepted criteria ... If theology were now forced to disappear from universities on the grounds maintained by many people, that it is essentially tied to authority and therefore unscientific, this would be a severe setback for the Christian understanding of truth.'[19] In one of his earlier essays Pannenberg speaks of 'the intellectual obligation that goes along with the use of the word "God" ... Because God is the creator of all things, it belongs to the task of theology to understand all being in relation to God.'[20] The target of Pannenberg's criticisms is especially those Protestant theologians, who, following the disintegration of the naïve historical objectivism of liberalism, sought to locate Christian truth wholly in the realm of the subjective or existential. W.W. Bartley has traced the course of this trend under the suggestive title *The Retreat to Commitment*, published in 1962. Paul Tillich, with his notion of ultimate concern, comes under attack no less sharply than theologians in the Barthian tradition. In particular, the argument that we cannot escape a ghetto theology since 'everything depends on one's presuppositions' is dismissed as a *rational* excuse for *irrational* commitment.

(4) A number of pragmatic arguments have been put forward for the importance of academic freedom in theology. A genuine openness to revise conclusions, for example, may seem less defensive, self-centred, or even arrogant, than a dogmatism which cannot tolerate any challenge. More to the point, defensive dogmatism has almost always had unproductive historical consequences. It is also worth noting the warning offered by Ebeling in his recent essay on the place of the Bible in the university. He points out that if Christian theologians withdraw, or are forced to withdraw, from the university, those from non-theological disciplines will be left to fend for themselves in their own study of the Bible. Many disciplines, he observes, have continuous encounters with the Bible, whether we think of classical studies, English literature, social history, or the history of ideas: 'The loss would not be that the Bible would no longer be available, but that the university would be left alone with it.'[21] It would be possible to cite other arguments that have been put forward in the debate, but we have selected, by way of example, those which seem to be most important.

(b) The other side of the debate, however, also offers its standard arguments, and some of these also invite a measure of reappraisal in the light of the earlier part of our discussion. They can perhaps be stated rather more briefly:

---

[19] W. Pannenberg, *Theology and the Philosophy of Science*, p.13.
[20] W. Pannenberg, *Basic Questions in Theology*, vol. 1 (Eng. tr., London: SCM, 1970), p.1.
[21] Gerhard Ebeling, 'The Bible as a Document of the University', in Hans Dieter Betz (ed.), *The Bible as a Document of the University* (Chico, CA: Scholars Press, 1981), p.14. Cf. also G. Ebeling, *The Study of Theology* (Eng. tr., London: Collins, 1979), pp.81–94.

(1) The major cause of unhappiness about theology in the context of the university is that it loses its character as proclamation, confession, witness and worship. Instead it seems to become reduced to the level of a merely empirical or phenomenological study. This problem is also bound up with the different methodological approaches of biblical studies and systematic or doctrinal theology. The rise and development of biblical criticism rightly called attention to the importance of using methods of linguistic, literary and historical research which are not peculiar to Christian theology, and the effectiveness or validity of which have been proved or tested in other disciplines. But from the point of view of the believing Christian community, the study of the Bible also involves more than this, even if it does not involve less than this. So dominant have the empirical aspects become that Eric Mascall complains, 'The study of God and of his revelation of himself to man in Jesus Christ has been overshadowed, and indeed effectively superseded, by the various disciplines which in the past were held to be ancillary to it ... Theology, having lost its unifying factor ... has fallen apart into a number of disparate activities ...'.[22] Mascall lays the blame for this largely on attempts to make theology 'respectable in the context of a virtually secularised university'.

(2) The trans-empirical dimension of theology is further underlined by the part played by understanding, judgement and decision in theological argument, especially in the context of the transmission and criticism of tradition. The work of Bernard Lonergan, among others, serves to call attention to this point. Indeed, Lonergan forcefully reminds us that the grave limitations of empirical or merely descriptive methods are seen in the human sciences in general no less than in theology.[23] The philosopher Stuart Hampshire puts his finger on the point when he observes, 'The really difficult issue of commitment and of the morality of scholarship, is this: how are we to decide what questions are worth asking, what problems are worth raising, or, more strongly, what problems must be raised?'[24] A university course in Biblical Studies, for example, would certainly raise questions about the Exile. It would ask why *Israel* saw the Exile as an act of God, but would be much less likely to ask whether the Exile *was* an act of God, since the answer could not be given in terms of generally accepted criteria. Thus, from a confessional or church viewpoint, a university syllabus in Biblical Studies often chooses to omit some quite fundamental questions in the name of objectivity. The church might even claim that the university course was unduly *narrow*.

(3) The third major argument of those who are anxious about unrestrained freedom for the Christian scholar concerns his moral and theological obligations to the Christian community of which he is part. His Christian confession carries obligations with it, and these are still more pronounced if the scholar in question is also the holder of some

---

[22] Gerhard Ebeling, 'The Bible as a Document of the University', in Hans Dieter Betz (ed.), *The Bible as a Document of the University* (Chico, CA: Scholars Press, 1981), p.14. Cf. also G. Ebeling, *The Study of Theology* (Eng. tr., London: Collins, 1979), pp.81–94.

[23] E.L. Mascall, *Theology and the Gospel of Christ*, p.22.

[24] Bernard J.F. Lonergan, *Method in Theology* (London: Darton, Longman, and Todd, 1972), pp.248–9 and *passim*.

Christian office, to whom others look with trust for guidance. We have already said that part of the tension experienced by many Christian scholars is due to their recognition of two quite distinct sets of obligations to the academic community and to the Christian community, both of which have given them privileges that also lay responsibilities upon them. If a scholar who belongs to both communities acts or thinks in unscholarly or in unchristian ways, he risks perplexing outsiders who begin to doubt the credibility of the community, and he risks betraying the trust of the community.

(4) The whole notion of 'guarding the faith' has become unfashionable today, especially since Western society, partly in reaction against Marxism and all forms of totalitarianism, prizes tolerance, good humour, freedom and a pluralism of 'viewpoints' almost above every other virtue. Certainly when we compare the attitude of the early Church Fathers and the later parts of the New Testament towards the rule of faith and tradition, we move into a different world of values. One unfortunate result of this is that many Protestants have retreated so far from the notion of a succession of faith or doctrine that the entire weight of the idea of succession is left to rest on more Catholic ideas concerning ecclesiastical institution. One small movement in Anglicanism that attempts slightly to redress the balance, however, is the very recent report of the Church of England Doctrine Commission, *Believing in the Church*. There, John Bowker points out, for example, that the Church performs the necessary function of a 'system' in systems-theory, of preserving the continuity and identity of the community's spiritual resource. He shows further, that certain boundary markers must be operative if this continuity is to be maintained in an effective and recognizable way. In my own essay in the report I have tried to argue for these principles in the area of theory of knowledge, showing that the growth and criticism of knowledge rest on the corporate memory of the community and its tradition, no less than on individual enquiry. I include this essay as the next in the present volume. When he spoke of freedom of conscience, Luther spoke as one whose conscience was captive to the word of God, and not as the individual of Enlightenment rationalism.[25]

V
Tradition, Community and the Debate about Fact and Value

It is clear that the standard arguments on both sides of the debate carry weight, and that either side can be ignored only at the price of gross oversimplification. The Christian scholar is subject to at least two distinct sets of moral constraints, deriving on the one hand from the standards demanded by the academic community, and on the other hand from those which belong to the Christian community and the Gospel that it represents.

In the light of what we have already said about the diversity of *roles* adopted by the Christian scholars, it is tempting to think that the answer to our problem is for him to follow the imperatives dictated by the given roles assigned by each community in given situations. But the scholar is not simply a collection of separate role-performances; he or

---

[25] *Believing in the Church*, pp.45–78 and 159–89.

she is a single, responsible, thinking human being. He cannot, as F.F. Bruce's reflections remind us, be one person in the pulpit and an entirely different person in the lecture-room. At least, he or she cannot be two different people with moral integrity, even though in actual practice a sensitive Christian scholar will assess what it is appropriate to say or not to say, in the light of the needs and conventions that belong to each particular situation.

If we compare the constraints experienced by the theological scholar with those felt by his counterpart in political theory or the social sciences, we may see that further light is shed on his problem by the debate about value-free knowledge and the role of 'tradition', or the communal foundations of enquiry, action and criticism. It is a mistake to assume that if only he could free himself from the constraints of 'church' theology the Christian scholar would be liberated simply to follow 'the facts'. In none of the humanities (whatever might be claimed for the physical sciences) is it possible to achieve a totally clear-cut disjunction between 'facts' and values. Several writers in political theory underline this lesson. For example, in an essay entitled 'Neutrality in Political Science', Charles Taylor discusses the status of such facts as the number of French workers who vote Communist, or the number of Americans who vote Republican. No one disputes that such statistics constitute genuine facts. However, it is a matter of scholarly *judgement* what particular facts and statistics are selected from an almost infinite number of situations or events, and within what frame of reference they are placed in order to formulate explanatory hypotheses concerning their significance.

After examining several examples of facts and their evaluation, Taylor concludes, 'The non-neutrality of the theoretical findings of political science need not surprise us. In setting out a given framework, a theorist is also setting out the gamut of possible polities and policies.'[26] Any coherent attempt to arrive at explanation or significance entails an interaction between factual findings and some value position.

In the debate about the morality of Christian scholarship, each of the two opposite sides has been tempted to overstress fact or value, whereas a more balanced approach would take account of the interaction between the two. Sometimes academic theologians in the tradition of liberal Protestantism have stressed the work of the lone individual scholar dealing with 'the facts', as if the key to his success was simply to emancipate him from the chains of a dogmatic tradition. On the other side, theology is withdrawn into the protective ghetto of the Christian community on the grounds that only the framework of the tradition can determine what counts as a fact and what constitutes its meaning, as if a fact such as that of the rise of Easter faith could never stand on its own feet and speak for itself at the bar of general enquiry.

In practice, the debate among such thinkers as Schutz, Kuhn and Popper has shown that *both* poles of this dialectic must be taken fully into account. Alfred Schutz, among others, has rightly shown that all meaning results from interpretation; that meaning is constructed, not simply discovered, and that the typifications through which a community perceives reality have their place in shaping how that meaning is constructed.[27] For this reason, hermeneutics has become increasingly important in the

---

[26] Charles Taylor, 'Neutrality in Political Science', in Peter Laslett and W.G. Runciman (eds), *Philosophy, Politics, and Society*, Third Series (Oxford: Blackwell, 1967), p.55; pp.25–57.
[27] Ibid.

social sciences, no less than in theology and in biblical studies.[28] Thomas Kuhn has convincingly shown us the important part played by controlling models, or paradigms, within the scholarly community. Until they are modified, or until others take their place, they make certain ways of setting out problems easier to arrive at than others, and they tend to suggest the kind of solution that will most readily count as an answer.[29] Nevertheless, the standard counter-arguments of Karl Popper and others remain equally valid. The paradigms do no more than suggest, rather than dictate, the course of subsequent debate and their adequacy can be tested alongside that of other paradigms by a rational process of trial and error.[30]

A balanced account of the morality of Christian scholarship will try to hold all these insights together. On one side, Popper's insistence on the universality of rational criteria must be respected. Theological arguments and conclusions must be submitted to testing outside the protective confines of some Christian intellectual ghetto. Theology must take its place alongside other disciplines, and be studied in an atmosphere of academic freedom. But the insistence of Kuhn and Schutz on the importance of the community must also be given due weight. *If it fails to submit its formulations to testing outside its own tradition, the Christian community risks the loss of its claims to rationality and universality. But equally, if it shows inadequate concern for the preservation of its tradition, it risks the loss of its continuity and recognizable identity.* The Christian scholar takes up his position between the two sets of constraints imposed by these considerations.

Traditionally it might have been said that Roman Catholic theology was more concerned with the maintenance of tradition and Protestant theology was more concerned with its criticism. But the situation is no longer so straightforward, even if it ever was so. On one side, Barthian theology stands as a witness to the inadequacy of the liberal tradition in Protestant theology, and it is especially Barthian theologians such as Hermann Diem and others who most strongly stress the status of Christian theology as that which is done within the Christian community. As confession, as testimony and as doxology, it belongs to the realm of value and not merely fact. Such an outlook might be said to stand in contrast to the traditional Thomist emphasis on natural theology. On the other side, the Second Vatican Council has shown a striking concern for freedom of enquiry. One of its documents urges, for example, that all higher education should be undertaken 'with a true liberty of scientific enquiry'.[31] Indeed while many official Catholic pronouncements urge the importance of tradition, an increasingly wide range of attitudes seems to be emerging towards the questions that have been under discussion among individual Catholic scholars, especially in biblical studies.

We conclude, then, that the Christian scholar has to live with the tensions and pressures that arise from a plurality of moral constraints and obligations. Perhaps, as D.M. MacKinnon has argued, for many Christian scholars (although by their own

---

[28] Cf. Zygmunt Bauman, *Hermeneutics and Social Science* (London: Hutchinson, 1978); and A.C. Thiselton, *The Two Horizons* (Exeter: Paternoster, 1980).

[29] Thomas S. Kuhn, *The Structure of Scientific Revolutions*, 2nd edn (Chicago, IL: University of Chicago Press, 1970).

[30] Karl Popper, 'Normal Science and its Dangers', in I. Lakatos and A. Musgrave (eds), *Criticism and the Growth of Knowledge* (Cambridge: Cambridge University Press, 1970), pp.51–8.

[31] Vatican II, *Gravissimum educationis* (28 October 1965), sect. 10.

testimony not for all), an experience of pressure and painful struggle is a sign of authentic vocation and discipleship. Certainly there is no abstract, generalizing, sweeping solution to the problem. In his discussion of the morality of scholarship in philosophy and the social sciences, Stuart Hampshire offers the scholar one consolation for this. He points out that the experience of being drawn in more than one direction, the experience of wanting to say 'Yes' to more than one path of argument, is precisely what gives *vitality* to scholarship.[32] The task of wrestling with resisting *complex* material is what gives the scholarly mind its edge and stimulates the scholar's imagination. If this is so, a recognition of the complexities of our subject and of the need to say 'Yes' to both sides of its main arguments will serve the Christian scholar better than some simplistic but one-sided attempt to offer any over-easy solution.

---

[32] S. Hampshire, 'Commitment and Imagination', in Max Black (ed.), *The Morality of Scholarship*, pp.42–3.

CHAPTER THIRTY-EIGHT

Theology and Credal Traditions: "Knowledge, Myth and Corporate Memory" (1981)

This material comes from the Church of England Doctrine Commission Report of 1981, published under the title Believing in the Church: The Corporate Nature of Faith *(London: SPCK, 1981), pp.45–78. The Chairman of that period of the Commission was Rt Revd John V. Taylor, then Bishop of Winchester. Although in subsequent Reports we wrote essays corporately without named contributors, these essays were individually written subject to consultation with the other thirteen members of the Commission. Much of the argument presented below is congruent with the emphasis on corporate foundations of knowledge found in Gadamer and philosophical hermeneutics, but here it relates closely to the role of tradition in Christian theology and Christian interpretation. Creeds, sacred texts and sacraments, for example, constitute mechanisms for the transmission of corporate memory and communal truth. However, I express extreme caution over describing this process in terms of myth, which is too ambiguous and open to abuse to remain a constructive tool in this context. As in other essays in this collection, I argue that belief cannot be abstracted from its self-involving and practical consequences in life. That in which belief is grounded relates more closely to wisdom* (phronēsis) *than to technical knowledge or skill* (technē).

I
The Problem and the Task

I.1 The Problem: Knowledge versus Belief; Individual versus Community and Tradition

The modern Western intellectual tradition is largely founded on our capacity to distinguish *knowledge* from mere belief or opinion. From Socrates and Plato onwards, it has become customary to regard knowledge as that which can be apprehended and tested by the individual for himself, while opinion or belief is thought of as that which the individual has merely 'taken over' from the community, or has learned from others at second hand.

Plato illustrated this principle by means of some everyday examples. If someone asks for, and receives from others, travel directions for the way to Laurissa, we may say that he acquires *beliefs* (correct or incorrect) about the way to Laurissa. But only the individual who has actually made the journey for himself may be said to have *knowledge* of the way to Laurissa. Similarly, Plato urged, in understanding the principles of geometry or even the principles of moral conduct, what is learned passively from others, or taken over from the community, may be said to constitute correct or incorrect belief. But the individual who actively engages with the problems of geometry or moral conduct, and works out the issues for himself, may be said to have genuine knowledge of them.

The encouragement and growth of this kind of approach, with its emphasis on individual critical thought, has been the legacy not only of Greek philosophy, but also of the Renaissance and more especially of the Enlightenment of the seventeenth and eighteenth centuries. Critical thought begins when the individual no longer takes for granted as true what he has merely taken over from parents, teachers or the general assumptions of the community into which he is born. To doubt the opinions of others and to question the traditions of society is the starting-point on the road to knowledge.

So deeply is this outlook embedded in the foundations of our thought that we may fail to notice a problem to which it all too readily gives rise. The respective parts played by the individual and by the community in the growth and criticism of knowledge tend to become opposed to each other and polarized. Worse, the part played by the community comes increasingly under suspicion and relegated to a secondary category, while the role of the individual is accorded a privileged position and comes to occupy the centre of the stage. From this angle, the very idea of corporate knowledge, or a knowledge grasped, transmitted and tested by the community, seems to be almost self-contradictory. Communities are thought to hand down opinions, beliefs, myths, or codes of conduct, but only the individual, it seems, can grasp and test knowledge.

The problem receives sharp focus in the history of philosophy both in the rationalism of Descartes and in the empiricism of Hume. The well-known dictum of Descartes, "I think, therefore I am", expresses the principle that true knowledge begins when the isolated ego shuts itself off from all other resources of knowledge except its own thoughts, and subjects everything else to doubt. It was not without reason that Archbishop William Temple described the moment when Descartes shut himself away with his own thoughts as "perhaps the most disastrous moment in the history of Europe".[1] The empiricist tradition, however, is no less individualistic in its approach to the problem of knowledge. Receiving knowledge is still a matter of the individual's receiving ideas or impressions from the outside world, as if his mind were a sheet of blank paper. Indeed, so firmly is this approach rooted in individualism that Hume saw grounds for scepticism about evidence for the very existence of the external world. Berkeley was saved from the doctrine that all I can know is my own states of mind only by invoking, theologically, the idea of God as a guarantor of some further reality.

It is this dominant tradition in the history of Western thought that poses the problem to which we refer in this essay. For this account of the nature of knowledge has far-reaching implications for our attitude towards parallel issues in Christian faith and practice. Once again, the shape of the problem emerges all too clearly in the attitude of the thinkers of the Enlightenment. In the legitimate and proper quest for critical thought and tested knowledge, the value of religious traditions, or the deposit of faith handed down by the community, tended to be underrated. Individual critical reflection took the centre of the stage at the expense of the wisdom cumulatively gathered over the centuries

---

[1]   William Temple, *Nature, Man, and God* (London: Macmillan, 1940), p.57.

by successive generations in interpersonal experience. Little or no attention was given to the public or inter-subjective world, which pre-existed individual reflection, and was of special significance for Christian faith and practice.

I.2 The Task: Reinstating and Respecting Corporate Foundations of Knowledge

The thinkers of the Enlightenment saw only one side of the picture, and it is still the side that receives most attention today. We are not making some kind of special appeal to theology or religion when we assert that the individual does not in fact begin his quest for knowledge *de novo*, as if he were an isolated individual abstracted from history and society. A shared public world pre-exists both him and his own thinking. This public world shapes his thought in such a way that it not only provides and transmits shared resources of knowledge, but also shapes the terms on which he examines and tests that knowledge. It conditions what he regards as appropriate criteria for evaluating it. If an individual were cut off from birth from the shared resources of language and knowledge of human society, he could scarcely achieve much beyond a semi-instinctual quasi-animal awareness of a tiny world of private individual experience. In particular, without the resources of language he or she would lack the conceptual tools necessary for critical evaluation and even access to the resources of a community's corporate memory.

The task of this essay is first to redress the imbalance which leads all too often to a devaluing of the corporate foundations of knowledge, and then to apply what we have said about corporate knowledge to questions about Christian believing. Our argument, in practice, is set out in three overall stages. In the first half of this essay we introduce some of the more theoretical and philosophical considerations that lead us towards an appreciation of the corporate foundations of human knowledge. Every effort is made to avoid unduly technical discussion, but it would weaken our argument if we failed to allude to the work of one or two important thinkers in the history of ideas, including those who have worked in the area of the sociology of knowledge. One of our aims is not only to elucidate the part played by public or interpersonal knowledge, but also to show that appeals to the knowledge transmitted through tradition on the basis of the corporate memory of the Christian community in no way rests on a kind of special pleading for religion which would have no place in a more general account of human knowledge.

In the second main stage of the argument we then apply these arguments and concepts to issues of Christian belief and practice. Philosophical and sociological concepts of knowledge, training, custom and habituation come to a fresh focus in Christian theology when we reassess the significance of tradition, authority, orthodoxy, creeds, the reading of the Bible and the use of the sacraments. Some aspects of the discussion look back to what Anthony Harvey has said about the need to understand the authority of the Bible in terms of its function or role rather than in terms of some quality, which it is said to possess. But our arguments in this section find their closest affinity and parallel in the claims made by John Bowker in his chapter "Religions as Systems" about what he calls mechanisms of transmissions and control.[2] Creeds, sacraments, the use of the Bible, and

---

[2] John Bowker, in *Believing in the Church* (London: SPCK, 1981), chapter 6, pp.159–89.

other mechanisms, ensure the preservation and transmission of corporate memory, with the result that the community (cf. Bower's "system") remains *this* community, with its ongoing resources of corporate knowledge and identity.

In the third main stage of discussion we look more closely at the actual interrelation of roles performed by the community and by the individual in the growth and criticism of knowledge within the context of Christian faith. First we ask whether any light is shed on this part of the discussion by invoking the term "myth". Myths embody stories which have (or at least had in the past) the status of believed truth within a given community. Yet they lend themselves to reinterpretation by the individual in accordance with revised and more critical knowledge. Does the idea of myth, then, serve to carry the discussion forward constructively? Or might we perhaps find a more fruitful and less distracting model elsewhere?

Our major purpose in this final section, however, is to expand the following argument: to understand most clearly the corporate or interpersonal dimension of Christian belief, and to see why it *necessarily* rests on corporate knowledge, we must appreciate that the grammar of faith involves not only an inner or vertical dimension of response to God, but also a social or horizontal dimension of public behaviour. The Christian lives out his faith, or shows what it amounts to, in a public interpersonal world. He cannot, as it were, "believe privately", in the sense that faith towards God necessarily involves attitudes towards other people.

These practical or "self-involving" aspects of faith imply a measure of freedom and tolerance for the individual. However, the complementary point is no less to heed the corporate memory and testimony of the community, and this invites some degree of modesty in assessing the scope and basis of private judgement. The repression of individual conscience ignores one side of the dialectic; the notion of Christian belief as a merely individual or private affair ignores the other. Any theology that simply *opposes* the individual and the community, as if to invite us to choose one or the other, is inadequate. Our task is to try to elucidate the positive roles of both sides of the dialectic, but more especially to call attention to the corporate foundations of knowledge and to the necessary role played by corporate memory in making faith possible for the individual.

II
The Corporate Foundations of Knowledge

II.1 *'Common Sense' and Human Language*

Knowing, believing and, especially, understanding depend on some kind of sharing and on some kind of experience of continuity. We have already noted that the traditional 'theories of knowledge' in rationalism and empiricism failed to take adequate account of this. The individual who from birth was totally isolated from society would not be the 'knowing subject' of Kantian philosophy. The recognition of this very important fact may be said to represent the fundamental starting-point of a movement in the history of ideas that has come to be known as the 'sociology of knowledge'. Thus, from this viewpoint, one writer observes, 'There is no such thing as an isolated man ... Kant was operating with a construct rather than a reality ... What he [that is, a human person in the concrete world] becomes conscious of, must, or at any rate may, depend on the shape which his [or her] mind has acquired in the process of social living.'[3]

We are not obliged, however, to appeal to the sociology of knowledge for this basic insight. Behind his or her appeal to 'common sense' lies the ordinary person's tacit and perhaps barely conscious recognition of the importance of the experience and judgments of the community in the growth and transmission of knowledge. 'Common sense' represents what 'everyone' already knows. It draws on the community's cumulative wisdom and shared experience. As *sensus communis*, it stands in contrast to some merely individual or idiosyncratic interpretation of the world, offering the corporate judgement of the wider community in the course of whose experience something has become accepted as self-evident. On the basis of what is common sense, an individual does not have to begin reflecting on a problem *de novo*.

From this point of view, it is no accident that Vico, as an opponent of Descartes and the whole Cartesian method, appeals to the *sensus communis* as something always present in the tradition of the humanities going back to the classical concept of practical wisdom. Wisdom represents the accumulated body of experience and skills that the community (or a specific sub-community) may bring to bear on a question. As such it is usually practical rather than purely theoretical. Vico contrasts this 'wisdom' with the mere 'reason' of the Stoics, urging that the sense of what is right and true is acquired not simply by theoretical reflection, but by *living out one's life within the community*; what is fundamental is the historical context of its ongoing life and experience.

Over the last fifty or so years, several writers have shown that the positive role of 'common sense' (in the broadest meaning of the term) as an aspect of knowledge was never really lost sight of in the history of ideas. It was merely temporarily swamped out by Enlightenment rationalism, with its obsessive suspicion of tradition. This is most noteworthy in the tradition of German philosophy that approaches problems of knowledge under the heading of 'understanding' or 'hermeneutics', and in sociological work that stresses the importance of typifications and social interaction as points of departure for exploring questions about relevance and meaning.[4] Even in accordance with the narrower meaning of the term 'common sense' as 'knowledge of everyday life', from a sociological viewpoint, communities encourage common-sense knowledge. Their elders often remind the younger generations of 'common sense', even though amidst the conditions of rapid change prevalent in modern industrial societies, each generation also works out its own corporate common-sense knowledge in the light of its own corporate experience.[5]

---

[3] W. Stark, *The Sociology of Knowledge: An Essay in Aid of a Deeper Understanding of the History of Ideas* (London: Routledge & Kegan Paul, 1958), pp.13–14.

[4] H.-G. Gadamer, *Truth and Method* (Eng. tr., London: Sheed & Ward, 1975 [cf. 2nd edn, 1989]), pp.19–29 *et passim*, and Alfred Schutz, *Collected Papers* (The Hague: Nijhoff, 1962–66). Cf. also Ronald R. Cox, *Schutz's Theory of Relevance: A Phenomenological Critique* (The Hague: Nijhoff, 1978), pp.1–32, for a useful summary.

[5] Georges Gurvitch, *The Social Frameworks of Knowledge* (Oxford: Blackwell, 1971), pp.27–8 and 53–4.

The corporate foundations of knowledge are exposed more clearly when we consider, next, the relation between knowledge and language. Because of the heritage of oral or written language, a human being is never dependent merely on his own experience for information or knowledge. If he were left entirely to the limitations of his own individual experience, he would be relatively helpless and ignorant, even in a very primitive society. Language makes it possible to pool, to store and to transmit the common stock of knowledge shared by the community not only geographically but, more important, from generation to generation. False trails may be set aside and the repetition of errors avoided. The method of trying to begin *de novo*, either for the growth or the criticism of knowledge, may seem attractive as a theory amidst the security of one's own bookshelves or library; but it strikes out the life-line through which the individual gains access to the intellectual resource and cumulative experience of past generations, and which is stored in language. Seen in these terms, the belittlement of tradition as an object of suspicion and doubt seems to stem not from 'criticism' but from arrogance.

Once this basic point about language has been accepted, we are free to consider more complex issues that arise on the basis of the relation between language and thought. It is unfortunate that this relation has sometimes been formulated in mistaken ways that claim too much, or from another viewpoint, too little. Sometimes a crude account is suggested according to which language is said to determine the scope and limits of thought on the basis of vocabulary-stock or even surface-grammar. Such a view has been shown to rest on a mistaken view of language, including the mistaken assumption of a one-to-one correlation between words and concepts. However, even if the influence of language on thought (and thought on language) does not operate significantly at the level of mere linguistic morphology, language-habits become important at the level of language-*use*, or the 'grammar' of concepts. I have explored these issues in some detail elsewhere, concluding that language 'hands on an inherited tradition which then makes it easier or more difficult for a later generation to raise certain questions, or to notice certain aspects of life'.[6] Language shapes the frame of reference through which knowledge is *grasped*, and within which it is *criticized*. It does not exclude certain ways of seeing the world, but it does encourage certain ways of seeing the world, and of deciding what counts as a test or as a solution in the examination of the problems which have been posed. In the kind of terminology used in the sociology of knowledge, language is the storehouse of the day-to-day typifications of experience that we share with others, and on the basis of which the growth and criticism of knowledge proceeds. 'Language', it may be added, may also be understood (in the context of the present discussion) to include a very wide range of potentially symbolic material, such as non-verbal artefacts which may nevertheless 'speak' in such a way as to transmit attitudes, values and knowledge, from the past.

---

[6] Anthony C. Thiselton, *The Two Horizons: New Testament Hermeneutics and Philosophical Description* (Grand Rapids, MI: Eerdmans and Exeter: Paternoster, 1980), p.137; cf. pp.115–39.

II.2 The Transmission of Corporate Memory

Our considerations about language suggest that the corporate foundations of knowledge may be viewed not only in terms of a society spreading outwards from the individual in space, but also spreading backwards and forwards in time. From this angle, the individual biography of a single thinking individual represents only a single passing episode in the cumulative development and testing of human knowledge. Although we should be on our guard against the kind of relativism which comes from views of historical or sociological necessity sometimes implied by certain thinkers in the sociology of knowledge, there is much truth in Karl Mannheim's dictum that all human thought represents a 'thinking further' of what others have thought before us. Even the way that people raise questions and the terms in which they examine and *test* knowledge, builds on the thought and experience of others. Corporate memory is preserved and transmitted in the form of what we could happily call 'tradition', were it not for the widespread disparagement of the word 'tradition' and the failure to appreciate its positive role. Tradition transcends the scope of immediate individual knowledge and experience, and provides the framework within which one's own thought develops and becomes critically sharpened.

If the corporate memory of a community constitutes an important source of its knowledge, and if the biography of the individual thinker represents no more than an episode in its transmission and critical control, it follows that the community which wishes to preserve its knowledge, experience and cultural identity will employ *instruments for the transmission and institutionalization* of its corporate knowledge. What is recollected in corporate memory will be transmitted in proverb, story, sermon, myth or, equally, in (for the scientific sub-community) the pages of a modern technical journal. What is believed to be of value for the community, or on which its cultural identity is thought to depend, will be *reiterated in formulae* such as laws, ethical maxims, creeds, rites, songs and so on. In the context of religious or specifically Christian belief, the *reiteration of shared knowledge* on the basis of corporate memory finds expression in creeds, sacraments, sermons and the reading of narratives of the foundation-events out of which the community was born. That this is something which is *essential* to, but not *distinctive* to, the Christian community is confirmed in John Bowker's chapter 6 of *Believing in the Church*, 'Religions as Systems', in which he discusses mechanisms employed for the maintenance of 'systems' in such a way as to preserve their continuity and identity.

We shall examine these last claims further in the next section when we consider the significance of all this for questions about Christian belief. Meanwhile, however, we note that corporate memory represents much more (for almost any community, including that of scientists) than a mere access-point to knowledge of the past. As John Ziman forcefully argues in his book on the corporate foundations of knowledge in science, even the scientist does not simply consult his journals and books for knowledge of the past. In science (and we may note in passing, in matters of Christian faith), corporate memory provides a frame of reference in the light of which the scientist (and the Christian) assesses or interprets knowledge and determines procedure in the *present*.[7]

---

[7] John Ziman, *Public Knowledge: The Social Dimension of Science* (Cambridge: Cambridge University Press, 1968), p.103, *et passim*.

To see the force of these points, it is not necessary to appeal to those who are acknowledged authorities in the academic world. However, it would be a mistake to imagine that these arguments could not be underpinned if necessary, with reference to a recent and more rigorous argument on the part of those who have undertaken lengthy and thorough research into the issues involved. A host of writers have shown in some detail how, from a sociological point of view, the corporate memory of the community hands down ways of classifying people, places, things and events, which determine, or at least condition, the terms on which knowledge grows and undergoes criticism by a present generation and its individual thinkers.[8] This does not of course mean that this frame of reference may not itself undergo conscious criticism and a measure of revision. If this were not possible, we should be imprisoned in historical relativism, and the very notion of human rationality would be evaporated of content in the inevitability of being determined solely by contingence. It does mean, however, that, as we have already claimed, the growth and criticism of knowledge takes place as part of a process of *dialectic* between corporate and individual knowledge.

II.3 Inherited Knowledge as the Indispensable Context for Individual Understanding: A Philosophical Example

Those who may still have reservations about the present arguments may find themselves wondering how much depends on considerations now fashionable in the sociology of knowledge rather than arguments that are grounded more broadly in philosophy. After all, there are schools of thought in sociology which seem to lay such heavy emphasis on the role of class-interest, educational expectation and so on, in determining our view of what counts as 'reality or objectivity' that some may hesitate to accept an account of human knowledge which seems to owe much to the insights of sociology.

Such misgivings would be understandable, but they are misplaced. For in relatively recent years, a recovery of the realization of the importance of corporate knowledge has emerged in certain areas of philosophy, as well as in the sociology of knowledge. We select for attention the contribution to the debate by two very different philosophers, namely, Gadamer and Wittgenstein.

The tradition of philosophy that is represented by Gadamer approaches questions about 'reality' or Being from the standpoint of the problem of *understanding*. For this reason, this tradition of philosophy is sometimes given the name (in Gadamer's phrase) 'philosophical hermeneutics'. Understanding, it is argued, can *never* be the product of the individual's autobiographical reflection alone. Inherited knowledge constitutes the framework or context into which, so to speak, the individual slots his own perceptions and experiences in such a way that they acquire *significance* or meaning, to be understood

---

[8] A mass of literature could be cited, but see especially Peter Berger and Thomas Luckmann, *The Social Construction of Reality: A Treatise in the Sociology of Knowledge* (London: Penguin Books, 1966 and 1971). Cf. also Barry Barnes, *Interests and the Growth of Knowledge* (London: Routledge & Kegan Paul, 1977); Keith Dixon, *The Sociology of Belief: Fallacy and Foundation* (London: Routledge & Kegan Paul, 1980); Nicholas Abercrombie, *Class, Structure and Knowledge: Problems in the Sociology of Knowledge* (Oxford: Blackwell, 1980); and Georges Gurvitch, op. cit.

as what they *are*. Gadamer calls this inherited knowledge and the way in which it operates 'effective history', or (in a specialized and entirely positive sense of the term) 'tradition'.

This ongoing process of effective history is *prior* to actual self-conscious critical reflection on the part of the individual because it is mediated through family, society, the national culture and so on, constituting the basis on which individual awareness and critical judgement become *possible*. It provides the background against which it makes sense for the individual even to think about what is in his mind. Hence Gadamer observes, 'The self-awareness of the individual is only a flickering in the closed circuits of historical life ... the pre-judgments of the individual, far more than his judgments, constitute the historical reality of his being'.[9]

Gadamer rejects the antithesis between *authority* and reason, or between corporately based knowledge and individual reflection, which he associates with Enlightenment rationalism. Rationalism and individualism, he urges, give rise to 'a mutually exclusive antithesis between authority and reason'. However, in actual practice the notion of authority gives recognition to the fact that knowledge is grounded in the experience of others in the community: 'It rests on recognition and hence on an act of reason itself which, *aware of its own limitations, accepts that others have better understanding* ... There is no such unconditional antithesis between tradition and reason.'[10]

All education, in fact, depends on this principle. Schools give the pupil access to resources of knowledge that are wider than those of individual experience or even that of the family. Through transmission of specialist knowledge that has been acquired even beyond the local or national community, universities draw still more widely on resources of corporate knowledge. The use of these corporate resources and of the cumulative understanding of successive generations in no way contradicts the use of individual 'reason' or the student's thinking for himself. The student who attempted to ignore the lessons embodied in the understanding and tradition of the academic community would be regarded, with either pity or contempt, as falling victim to his private intellectual arrogance. He could hardly plead that he had to choose *between* 'reason' and 'tradition'. Indeed, only on the basis of exercising his rational judgement *within* the context of effective history, could he claim to achieve a proper *understanding* of the subject matter before him. I have discussed Gadamer's approach to these issues more fully elsewhere.[11]

II.4 The Contribution of Ludwig Wittgenstein

It may be hoped that each stage of the present discussion will spell out more clearly the nature and importance of the corporate foundations of knowledge and the inadequacy of any account of knowledge that is centred only on the individual. However, the English-speaking reader who hesitates to place any confidence on the sociology of knowledge may be only marginally reassured by the work of Gadamer. In the later writings of the

---

[9] Gadamer, *Truth and Method*, p.245.
[10] Ibid., p.248.
[11] Thiselton, *The Two Horizons*, pp.293–326, *et passim*.

philosopher Ludwig Wittgenstein we encounter a thinker whose stature and influence is beyond question, and whom no one could ever accuse of yielding to mere fashion or intellectual gamesmanship. Wittgenstein's earlier writings show beyond all doubt his total commitment to wrestling with the problems of logic, and indeed much of his earlier work concerned the nature of logical necessity.

Yet Wittgenstein himself saw that abstract reflection in isolation from the context of human life related only to part of the whole picture. In his later writings he consistently called attention to the corporate or social foundations of language, and its grounding in the institutions or practices of human life. In his last notes, entitled *On Certainty*, he turned his attention to the corporate foundations of knowledge. Because (it is generally agreed) Wittgenstein cannot easily be summarized without reduction and loss of what he wished to say, we shall include one or two direct quotations in our brief account of his work in these last notes.

Wittgenstein argues that propositions that appear to represent truths of 'common sense' (see our discussion under II.1) do so because they presuppose a certain inherited frame of reference. This frame of reference constitutes a 'foundation' on the basis of which normal day-to-day research and action can take place. This foundation of inherited thought belongs to, or has emerged from what was once, 'the *scaffolding* of our thoughts', for, Wittgenstein adds, 'Every human being has parents.'[12] He writes, 'The *truth* of certain empirical propositions belongs to our frame of reference ... All testing, all confirmation and disconfirmation of a hypothesis takes place already within a system.' What actually *'counts* as its [a proposition's] test' depends on the system to which it belongs.[13] Contrary to the individualism of the rationalist tradition, Wittgenstein observes, 'The child learns by believing the adult. Doubt comes *after* belief'; and even then, 'my doubts form a system ... From the child up, I learned to judge like this.' 'If you tried to doubt everything, you would not get as far as doubting anything. The game of doubting itself presupposes certainty.'[14]

It would be a mistake to regard Wittgenstein's approach in *On Certainty* as somehow radically different from his observations on language in the main writings of the later period. These last notes represent a logical development of the central place occupied in the *Philosophical Investigations* by 'training', 'custom', 'rules' and especially 'forms of life'. What gives point to Wittgenstein's masterly explorations of concepts, or 'logical grammar', is precisely his recognition of the crucial importance of what he calls 'the surroundings' of words and language in the ongoing stream of life. But 'life', or 'practice', is grounded in the shared conduct and attitudes of the language-using communities. Only in the ongoing stream of life and thought do words have meaning, Wittgenstein's whole discussion of 'private' language forms the background to his claims about corporate knowledge. An individual trying to manipulate concepts in total isolation from how others have used them is like someone saying '"But I know how tall I am!" and laying his hand on top of his head to prove it.'[15] It is 'as if someone were to buy several

---

[12] Ludwig Wittgenstein, *On Certainty* (Eng. and German, Oxford: Blackwell, 1969), sect. 211 (his italics).

[13] Wittgenstein, *On Certainty*, sects 83, 105 and 110 (his italics).

[14] *On Certainty*, sects 115, 128 and 160; cf. especially sects 106–70.

[15] Wittgenstein, *Philosophical Investigations* (3rd edn, Oxford: Blackwell, 1967), sect. 279.

copies of the morning paper to assure himself that what it said was true'.[16] Even checking and testing is a more-than-individual affair: 'Only in the stream of thought and life do words have meaning.'[17]

II.5 Examples from the History of Science

Because of the pressures of space, we must limit this part of the discussion to only one more type of example of work on the corporate foundations of knowledge, even though many different writers and approaches might have been mentioned. One of the best known, although he is also widely criticized, is Thomas A. Kuhn. Although, as far as I know, he does not seem to make more than a relatively minor acknowledgment to Wittgenstein, Kuhn is remarkably close to some of the themes that we have noted in *On Certainty*, except that Kuhn's special interest is in the foundations of knowledge in science. Like Wittgenstein and Gadamer, Kuhn urges that the advancement and criticism of knowledge takes place within the context of the growing framework of experience and knowledge handed down by the community. This frame of reference takes the form of a system, 'paradigm', or a way of seeing the world, which conditions the terms in which certain questions are posed, or problems solved. Indeed Kuhn argues that the paradigm influences what problems are put on the agenda, and what may be said to count as their solution.

Kuhn defines paradigms as 'models from which spring coherent traditions of scientific research'. He comments, 'Men whose research is based on shared paradigms are committed to the same rules and standards for scientific practice.'[18] Each generation of scientists operates with a kind of 'network of theory through which it deals with the world'.[19] This network is the legacy of the scientific community. From time to time in the history of science, paradigms are found to be inadequate, and at such moments a 'revolution' occurs in the models and methods adopted by the scientific community. However, this in turn gives rise to a new era of 'normal' procedure, during which current paradigms are once again taken for granted as a basis for research and inquiry.

Scientists, Kuhn urges, view the world 'through their own research training and practice', and use 'conceptual categories prepared by prior experience' on the part of the scientific community.[20] Thus, 'What a man sees depends both upon what he looks at and also upon what his previous visual-conceptual experience has taught him to see.'[21] What he has been 'taught' to see owes as much, if not more, to the community or even 'tradition' as to his own individual inquiries. For these individual inquiries have normally been carried out within a framework received from the community.

A number of writers have put forward criticisms of Kuhn's arguments, and those which are most widely known come from Karl Popper. Popper gives special emphasis to two points. First, he insists that there has never been any *one* particular paradigm that has

---

[16]   Wittgenstein, op. cit., sect. 265. Cf. further Thiselton, *The Two Horizons*, pp.379–85.
[17]   Wittgenstein, *Zettel* (Oxford: Blackwell, 1967), sect. 173.
[18]   Thomas S. Kuhn, *The Structure of Scientific Revolutions* (2nd edn, Chicago, IL: University of Chicago Press 1970), pp.10–11.
[19]   Kuhn, op. cit., p.7.
[20]   Kuhn, op. cit., pp.51 and 62.
[21]   Kuhn, op. cit., p.113.

dominated scientific inquiry in such a way as to set its entire agenda. Second, even if scientists do accept and use some corporate framework of knowledge, such a framework certainly does not *dictate* what knowledge is possible. He concludes, 'A critical discussion and a comparison of the various frameworks is always possible.'[22]

If we had argued in this essay that the growth and criticism of knowledge was wholly and entirely a corporate process, Popper's comments would cause pause for thought. However, as they stand, his criticisms serve only to underline what we have already said about the dialectic between the corporate and individual aspects. Indeed, the debate which has followed the statement of Kuhn's claims serves to show that even when a new paradigm in the history of science seems to suggest a divergent conclusion about 'what is the case', individual exponents of the new paradigm nevertheless may be seen often to *rely* on what was taken to be 'the case' under the old paradigm, or at least in the work of predecessors. Kepler continued to rely on the astronomical observations of Tycho Brahe; Einstein made use of observations undertaken by Leverrier in accordance with a mechanistic pre-Einsteinian paradigm. In the transition from Newton to Einstein it is simply not the case that all work carried out within the framework of the earlier paradigm was dismissed as 'wrong'.

The lesson to be learned from all this is that Kuhn's approach cannot be understood in a simplistic way, and that to accept its implications for our argument about corporate knowledge reinforces the claim that neither side of the dialectic can be ignored. The inescapable conclusion which emerges from the whole discussion up to this point is that arguments about corporate knowledge require no special pleading on behalf of religion or the Christian community. The same fundamental considerations appear whether we look at the history of science, at Wittgenstein, at 'hermeneutical' philosophy, or at basic facts about language and even the role of common sense. It is also clear that corporate knowledge in no way stands in contrast to critical thought, but, rather, constitutes a precondition for it. We may now turn, in the second half of our essay, to examine the bearing of all this discussion on questions about corporate believing, with special reference to criteria for 'authentic' Christian faith and the theological problem of tradition and 'orthodoxy'.

III
The Transmission of Corporate Knowledge and Corporate Memory in the Community of Christian Faith

III.1 The Roles of the Individual and the Community in the Quest for Authentic Faith

Just as both sides of our dialectic are fundamental for the growth and criticism of knowledge in general, so also in questions about Christian faith neither the role of the community nor that of the individual should be underestimated. There is what we may term (for want of a better shorthand word) a 'vertical' dimension to faith, in the light of

---

22   Karl Popper, 'Normal Science and its Dangers', in I. Lakatos and A. Musgrave (eds), *Criticism and the Growth of Knowledge* (Cambridge: Cambridge University Press, 1970), p.56.

which faith can never be reduced to a mere acceptance of 'orthodoxy', or of the tradition passed on by the community.

In his letter to the Galatians, for example, Paul insists that there is nothing second-hand about his call or his gospel: 'For I did not receive it from man ... it came through a revelation of Jesus Christ' (Gal. 1:12). Nearer to our own times, the prophetic protest against any merely second-hand faith has been voiced with special force by Søren Kierkegaard. Kierkegaard writes, 'The most ruinous evasion of all is to be hidden in the crowd ... to get away from hearing God's voice as an individual'.[23] Christianity, he comments in his *Attack upon 'Christendom'*, 'has been abolished by expansion, by these millions of name-Christians the number of which is surely meant to conceal the fact that there is not one Christian'.[24] The very notion of a 'Christian state' or of a 'Christian world', he continues, is 'shrewdly calculated to make God so confused in His head by all these millions that He cannot discover that He has been hoaxed; that there is not one single Christian'.[25]

Becoming a Christian, Kierkegaard urged, is not merely a matter of taking over the orthodox Christian beliefs of the day. It involves inner transformation and personal commitment. Hence: 'It would help very little if one persuaded millions of men to accept the truth, if precisely by this acceptance they were transferred into error ... Truth becomes untruth in this or that person's mouth.'[26] A faith that merely takes up the routines prescribed by a tradition is for Kierkegaard (and for Paul and for Jesus) not 'true' faith. Nevertheless, it would be a mistake to assume that this contradicts the notion of a *corporate framework* of knowledge *within* which the individual may reach authentic faith. Jesus, Paul, Luther and Kierkegaard were all conscious of the limitations and seductions of tradition; but all lay down their calls to faith within a framework of knowledge and experience which transcended individual autobiography. When they spoke of God, Jesus and Paul spoke of the God of Abraham, of Isaac and of Jacob. When Luther spoke of God, this was the God of Israel, the God of Jesus, and even for Luther, the God of the Church Fathers. When Kierkegaard insisted that the 'jovial mediocrity' of Danish-state Christianity did not represent authentic, obedient faith, his standard of comparison was not simply his own experience or reflection; his complaint was that 'being a Christian becomes something different from what it is in the New Testament'. 'Official Christianity ... is in no sense the Christianity of the New Testament'.[27]

The example of Paul is parallel in this respect to that of Kierkegaard. Paul does not abstract his first-hand knowledge of the risen Christ from the frame of reference of what was believed about Jesus Christ in the primitive church, or from beliefs about God embodied in the Old Testament. These elements contribute to the overall framework within which he was able to reflect on, interpret and understand his encounter with Jesus

---

[23] S. Kierkegaard, *Purity of Heart is to Will One Thing* (London: Collins Fontana), p.163.

[24] S. Kierkegaard, *Attack upon 'Christendom' 1854–5* (Eng. tr., Oxford: Oxford University Press, 1946), p.127.

[25] Ibid.

[26] S. Kierkegaard, *Concluding Unscientific Postscript to the 'Philosophical Fragments'* (Eng. tr., Princeton, NJ: Princeton University Press, 1941), pp.181 and 221.

[27] S. Kierkegaard, *Attack upon 'Christendom'*, pp.24 and 34.

Christ. Indeed, the examples of Paul and Kierkegaard help us to see more clearly the interplay of each side of the dialectic. For both are concerned about the authenticity of Christian faith; that it should be, in this sense a critical faith. But what is at issue in any prophetic summons to authenticity is a relation to the referent of faith in which both the *identity of the referent* and the *basis of the relationship* is not merely a product of the individual's own religious aspirations. We have already seen, however, from our examination of corporate knowledge in the previous section that *questions about identity and continuity can be answered only within the larger framework of shared experience and public knowledge. Conceptual or linguistic reference, we saw, depends on a pre-existing framework of conceptual or linguistic regularity,* which may be described in terms of *rule, custom, training, or a succession of interrelated forms of life flowing on through history.*

Once again, it is a matter of holding together the two poles of a dialectic, rather than opposing the parts played by the individual and the community. Sometimes the life and thought of the community drifts into implausibility and even, at times, into glaring self-contradiction. At such times the prophetic summons of a Luther or a Kierkegaard is vital to the rediscovery of the community's true identity and of the authenticity of Christian faith. There is force and truth in the well-known dictum of Calvinist theology that the church that has been reformed always stands in the need of reformation: *ecclesia reformata semper reformanda.* Sometimes it is the prophetic insight of an individual thinker and man of faith that spearheads the necessary corrective. The classic example is Luther's ringing declaration at the Diet of Worms: 'Here I stand. I can do no other.' Nevertheless, Luther saw that challenge not as a summons to innovative departure from the corporate memory and knowledge of the community, but as a call to return to it and to heed its testimony more seriously. He could boldly assert the importance of reason and the integrity of conscience not because he saw himself in the way that Descartes conceived of the isolated 'I' of individual reflection, but because, in his own words, his conscience was 'captive to the word of God'; because it gave expression to a more authentic focus, as he saw it, of the corporate knowledge of the community. Contrary to widespread popular misunderstanding, Luther not only appealed to the faith and testimony of the biblical writers, but also quite consciously invoked the corporate witness of the Church Fathers. Augustine, Ambrose, Cyprian and Chrysostom all feature in his thought. In this sense, Luther's great affirmation of 'Here I stand' is entirely compatible with the equally patristic dictum that 'there is no salvation outside the church'. Certainly any 'theory of knowledge' which Luther's faith might be said to presuppose would have more in common with Irenaeus and Augustine than with the kind of individualism represented by Enlightenment rationalism or by Descartes.

The conclusion that we draw from these allusions to Luther and Kierkegaard is that the kind of 'individualism' which is usually ascribed to them (and to many other examples of prophetic or reforming figures) is not the kind of individualism that it is often imagined to be, at least from the standpoint of questions about corporate knowledge. The appearance of an *opposition* or *polarization* of the individual and corporate knowledge is merely an *appearance* that is behind their criticisms or protest. They did not see themselves as innovators, not least because their understanding, testing and criticism of 'tradition' depended, in turn, on appeals to continuity of its 'effective history'. What is true from a philosophical point of view applies also in Christian theology: 'I must not saw off the branch on which I am sitting.'[28] The point requires no special theological pleading. Individual criticism rests on corporate foundations of knowledge.

III.2 The Transmission of Corporate Memory in Inherited Patterns of Belief and Practice

Over the centuries the Christian community has had its own ways of maintaining and preserving the stable background against which the faith could spread, and also could undergo critical examination and testing. *Creeds, liturgy, pastoral oversight* and perhaps most notably *the use of the Bible and of the sacraments* represent such instruments. They effectively anchor the community's present both in the founding events of its past and within the overall framework of its ongoing life in a way which transcends individual experience and provides a control against undue novelty or individual innovation.

It is significant, therefore, that our earliest accounts of the Eucharist and of Baptism place these observances within a tradition that even by the time of Paul is already described explicitly as a 'tradition' (*paradosis*).[29] Paul recalls, 'For I received ... what I also delivered to you' (1 Cor. 11:23). Participation in the Lord's supper is seen as a 'proclamation' of the founding events of the death and resurrection of Christ which give the community its life, its existence and its identity (11:26). It constitutes a 'remembrance' (*anamnesis*) in which the present community, through its corporate memory, both reflects on the founding events and pledges itself anew to their present significance and practical effectiveness. All this is far more, but certainly not less, than what sociologists describe as the *legitimating formulae* whereby the shape of a society's institutional order and values are passed on from generation to generation. Baptism, in the same way, from the earliest pre-Pauline theology, grounds the experience of the individual believer in the once-and-for-all saving events which found the community: 'Do you not know that all of us who have been baptized into Christ Jesus were baptized into his death? ... the death he died, he died to sin, once for all' (Rom. 6:3 and 10; cf. vv. 4–11).

Every Christian who rightly and duly participates in the sacraments sees himself as, in a sense, 'there' at the founding events of the community ('You proclaim the Lord's death'; 'Do this in "remembrance" of me'). At this level individual biography is transcended, and corporate memory *makes possible* a common biography. The creeds, sacraments, Bible readings and liturgy all amount to a *reiteration of shared experience*. Whether this should be described as a mythological way of grasping reality will be discussed shortly. Our primary concern at this point is to assert the significance of all this for continuity and identity, and hence for knowledge. Corporate memory provides access to an understanding and knowledge of realities that transcend individual experience.

These considerations shed a new light on the concern for *orthodoxy* that has been a persistent feature of much Christian thought from the era of the New Testament onwards. As long as this concern is seen merely as an attempt to impose on a minority the view of

---

[28] Wittgenstein, *Philosophical Investigations*, sect. 55.
[29] R.P.C. Hanson, *Tradition in the Early Church* (London: SCM, 1962).

some controlling party or dominant interest, a concern for orthodoxy necessarily appears in a negative and restrictive light. Thus it is often said, for example, that the Pastoral Epistles and other 'secondary' literature of the New Testament reflect a self-preserving defensive posture which is at odds with the self-denying faith and creative fervour of the great Pauline writings or the teaching of Jesus. But even the earlier writings speak of the need to hold fast to a tradition, and it is clear that the concern expressed in these writings is not a matter of mere authoritarianism or a defensive judgementalism. What is at stake is whether the Christian way is turned into 'another gospel' (Gal. 1:8). The concern which is expressed appears quite other than negative and restrictive when it is seen that what is at issue is the maintenance of that degree of continuity which is necessary for Christian *identity* and more especially for participation in the *patterns of behaviour which have been instituted and prescribed* by those events on which the community itself has been founded.

At this point it would have been helpful to draw on what has been said about 'roles' in sociology and in the sociology of knowledge. The difficulty is that in everyday speech the word 'role' tends to have a negative meaning as that which is somehow artificial or insincere. Existentialist philosophers have rightly criticized and attacked the whole notion of an individual having to assume 'roles' imposed by the social conventions and expectations of society. Such expectations put pressures on the individual to live in a way which is second-hand, superficial, or 'inauthentic' for him. This mood of suspicion has (also rightly) found its way into the area of Christian faith, where (following Kierkegaard whose approach we have just discussed) many are on their guard against the danger of reducing authentic Christian faith to the mere 'taking over' of second-hand attitudes and routines. To assume the *role* of one who merely 'goes to church' is not necessarily the same thing as having authentic Christian faith.

Nevertheless, when all this has been said and accepted, it remains the case that Christian believing involves taking up certain *patterns* of attitudes and behaviour, which can be said to be recognizably 'Christian' precisely because they are patterns. They can be identified because they embody an element of regularity and repetition. Certain attitudes and behaviour may rightly be 'expected' of the Christian if he is genuinely a Christian. In this *sociological* sense, Christian belief does entail adopting a 'role', although some may still prefer to think of them simply as 'patterns of response'.

The central point which now emerges is that, in accordance with sociological inquiry, roles presuppose a process of repetition of habituation, and usually also carry with them some explicit or implicit status. This status, in turn, often (although not always) depends on some authoritative act or event such as that of appointing, employing, directing, allowing and so on. A person assumes the role of waiter, managing director, husband, or secretary, because he or she has been given, and has accepted, that 'understood' status and role. Usually, a given status carries with it certain rights and privileges on one side, and certain obligations on the other. A secretary is obliged to type letters, but has the right to a salary, and so on. 'Belonging' to the firm with its pensions, its holidays and its rules also provides rights and obligations.

Christian believing also is founded on an event or events which make possible the offer and acceptance of a given status and the ascription of appropriate roles. Because of God's saving acts in Christ, the status of 'son', or 'one of the redeemed' (and so on) may now be offered and accepted, and the role of worshipper, obedient servant (and so on) 'taken over' or appropriated. For all this to be meaningful, however, there *must* be a relatively stable background of repetition, habituation or 'expected' belief and conduct. Language which identifies appropriate roles (forgiven sinner, obedient son) now functions as a firm semantic marker for identifying what we mean when we talk about being a Christian or having Christian faith. From a sociological viewpoint these are 'institutional" responses.

The early church gave expression to its sense of the need to preserve such a framework by the place which it accorded to creeds, catechism and what was then (in an entirely positive way) called 'tradition'. The early Christian confession of Christ as Lord brought into focus the Christian's expected pattern of behaviour as servant and worshipper. The creeds, confessions and 'traditions' thus mediated to later generations the corporate knowledge and memory on which the authenticity of faith depended. Habitualized action depends on shared experience and corporate knowledge. The individual, cut off from the community, could never discover and test (entirely on his own) what is 'expected', 'appropriate', or 'relevant'. But it is 'built into' Christian faith, through its very grammar, that Christians adopt the role of servant to their Lord, of obedient subject to their King, of adopted sons to their Father. Moreover, these roles constitute stable elements in the Christian understanding of *God*. On the basis of corporate knowledge and experience *God is* Lord, King, Redeemer and Father, because in these roles (habituated patterns of action) he has been experienced in Israel and in the Christian Church.

It now becomes clear why *corporate memory* (especially as this is articulated and preserved in the biblical writings) represents much more than a mere 'source' for knowledge of the past. Corporate memory is the frame of reference which gives meaning to the present, and even guides present action. There is nothing necessarily 'pious' about using ancient writings in this way; still less does this represent antiquarianism. In modern society, for example, ancient legal documents may sometimes be used as 'sources' from which to study the past, but more often laws, even from earlier times, serve to guide present judgments and procedures, especially when the community wishes to retain what it regards as a cultural *identity* reading back into the past. The possession and 'effective history' of corporate memory is what makes a society (or a nation, or a church) *this* society, and not some other.

We must return, however, to the relation between corporate memory and *roles*. At this point the sociological descriptions of Peter Berger and Thomas Luckmann prove to be helpful. They argue that roles can be adopted and made operative only on the basis of 'an objectified stock of knowledge common to a collectivity of actors'. They then comment, 'In the common stock of knowledge, there are *standards of role-performance* that are accessible to all members of a society, or at least to those who are potential performers of the roles in question.'[30] In these terms, a Christian concern about the place of the Bible, or about tradition or orthodoxy, has little or nothing to do with intellectual conformity as such. What is at stake is the maintenance of conditions under which it still makes sense to speak of 'standards of role-performance'.

---

[30] Berger and Luckmann, op. cit., p.91.

When we apply these considerations to what have traditionally been described as the problems of heresy and orthodoxy, it is important to make one point clear. In order to be able to speak of standard role-performance, it is certainly not necessary that *every individual* who claims to be part of the Christian community should *actually perform* every role prescribed as standard to Christian belief. What matters from this standpoint, is whether, when deviation or eccentricities occur, they are identified as permitted *deviations or eccentricities*. If the community itself were to revise what it has hitherto regarded as standard role-performance *across the board*, then in the case of the Christian community, the two consequences would follow what we have already described: first, what it would now mean to stand in *this* tradition or to use *these* concepts would become problematic; second, language about *God* would also lose its groundings and its stability. If these concepts were cut loose from what the community had regarded as paradigm cases of their use, we should be left with the kind of individualism which Lewis Carroll gently mocked through the lips of Humpty-Dumpty: 'When *I* use the word, it means just what I choose it to mean – neither more nor less' (*Through the Looking Glass*, Chapter 6).

IV
The Problem of 'Myth' and the Relation between Belief and Behaviour

IV.1 The Use and Abuse of "Myth" to Denote the Transmission of Corporate Memory

Theology and other related disciplines often employ the concept or category of *myth* in order to bring together many of the considerations which we have set out above. Myth hands down corporate memory not in the form of abstract theory or systematic ideas, but in the form of story (although not strictly of factual report). In particular, myths have the status of *believed truth within a given community*. David Strauss regarded them as ideas presented as narratives.

The popular notion of myth as that which is false emerged precisely because the truth of myth is relative to the beliefs of a specific community. When myths are viewed from a standpoint which is different from that of the myth-making community, their content may be regarded as false. Thus, in popular thought, myth is generally associated with falsehood because the standard paradigm of the myth in modern Western culture is the stories of the gods and goddesses of ancient Greece.

As well as being grounded in the thought and experience of a community, myths also lay claim to truth that is believed to be significant for *present* thought and conduct. In accordance with our earlier observations, they function characteristically as 'legitimating formulae' for attitudes handed down through corporate memory, which the community wishes to preserve and validate for the present generation. Myths thereby draw the individual into the frame of reference bequeathed by corporate experience. Yet an individual, or even a whole generation in later times, may wish to reformulate or revise the beliefs and practices which are being legitimated, in accordance with truth perceived outside the community or in the light of recent experience and knowledge. Hence myths may undergo *reinterpretation* in the course of the dialectic between corporate memory and critical reflection.

It may seem, in the light of these basic characteristics, that myth represents the category best fitted to express and describe the nature of the dialectic that is at present under discussion. Have we not already given an account of how corporate memory and critical faith interact and condition each other within the Christian tradition?

We shall argue that the term 'myth' in fact *raises more problems than it solves*. Nevertheless it would be cavalier not to examine more closely some of the advantages that might be claimed for its use, especially since such an examination carries our discussion of corporate memory further. We shall focus on each, in turn, of the three major characteristics of myth to which we have already drawn attention.

First, myths, we observed, take the form of stories or narratives, not that of abstract systematic doctrine. Thereby they have the power to draw the hearer into the 'world' of the story. The individual and the present generation are enabled to be '*there*' at the great founding events of the community, as these have been held and transmitted by corporate memory. They operate, therefore, at a far deeper level than mere concepts or intellectual 'information'. Stories also do justice to the uniqueness of persons as persons. They are not concerned with mere generalities, but with what *this* person did on *that* occasion. A person comes alive as a person not when we describe his general characteristics or attributes, but when we tell stories about what he did on particular occasions. We see his unique personhood through personal traits of behaviour. In myth, this applies especially to stories about gods or about God. Indeed, many have argued that this anthropomorphic way of describing God brings us to the very heart of what may be said to constitute myth. At all events the highly personal God of the story or narrative belongs no less equally to myth and to the biblical and Christian tradition.

A second characteristic shared by myth and the biblical material is that truth about God is presented from a number of different angles in which language utilizes analogy, model, metaphor, or symbol. The reality to which the material itself stands witness somehow (at least in the judgement of a community) transcends the language that is used. Christians often speak of the truth of the Bible as 'inexhaustible', seeing attempts to speak to God as like the attempt to cup hands around the ocean. This gives rise to attempts in biblical interpretation to move beyond the conscious horizons of the author of the text. There is often, it is urged, 'something more' than that of which the author himself was aware. Similarly, the reinterpretation of myth depends on the belief of a later generation or individual that it is possible to reach 'behind' the myth to understand it 'better' than the original community, at least in relation to later problems and questions.

Third, and perhaps most important of all, both myth and the biblical writings embody language which may appear to be merely descriptive, but which in fact serves also to summon the reader to appropriate attitudes and conduct. It invites the latest generation to share in the attitudes and conduct that were demanded by the founding events of the community. There is thus a *reiteration of shared memory, shared reality and shared experience, but also a reiteration and reappropriation of shared attitudes, shared imperatives and shared practices.* What may appear to be only a statement (Christ was raised; Christ is Lord) is seen *also* to function as a self-involving commitment (We are raised; we are Christ's servants who belong to him).

If this were all that need be said (or more significantly *had* been said) about myth, we might have been free to draw what positive insights we could from the use of category to describe corporate memory in the Christian tradition. But the history of modern research into the nature of myth reveals pitfalls and difficulties which far outweigh any advantages in such use. Moreover, even the three characteristics so far discussed all too often in modern discussion carry with them unwanted implications which prove to be seriously misleading when applied to the Christian story.

First, we spoke of myth as a story. But partly because it takes this relatively unreflective, unselfconscious and unsophisticated form, and avoids more precise abstract critical reflection, many modern writers have associated it with a world-view which is *necessarily* uncritical, primitive and pre-scientific. This view of myth owes much, once again, to the period of the Enlightenment, and betrays the influence of Fontenelle, Eichorn and Strauss, as well as that of Hegel. But although recent research has shown the inadequacy of such an account of myth, it persists in many quarters and has been popularized in the theological world through Bultmann (even if other understandings of myth also coexist uneasily in Bultmann's writings). It is argued, for example, that precisely because of its pre-scientific nature, myth ascribes the occurrence of certain events in the world to supernatural causes. Hence the advent of a more sophisticated world-view is said to demand the reinterpretation of all such references to supernatural causality, which is assumed to represent a viewpoint owing more to cultural factors than to religious convictions. The complex mass of literature which has emerged on this subject, however, shows that these issues cannot be foreclosed in this oversimplistic fashion.[31] Hegel draws a contrast between the *uncritical* "representations" used in religions (*Vorstellungen*) and the use of the *critical concept* (*Begriff*) in philosophy.

Second, while it is true that neither myth nor the Christian story articulates the reality to which it points in such a way that there is nothing more to be said, we must guard against the mistaken view that language is simply some kind of opaque wrapping which can be detached from the pure thought which it expresses but also obscures. How do we gain access to the reality said to lie 'behind' the myth or story, other than through the myth or story itself? It is very easy to speak disparagingly or patronizingly of what the community in earlier generations was 'trying' to say, as if to imply that its original formulations may now be set aside. But there are two quite different senses in which something may be said to need 'reinterpretation'.[32] There is, on the one hand, the analogy of the code that needs to be translated. Once we have the key to the code, we may translate the code into our own everyday languages, and then dispense with the original, which is now obsolete. The Enlightenment view of myth encourages this approach to the New Testament.

---

[31] I have set out a few of the issues involved, in *The Two Horizons*, pp.53–63, 69–84, 205–92, 392–401 and 439–45.

[32] This distinction is suggested by Ian Henderson, *Myth in the New Testament* (London: SCM, 1952), p.31.

However, we may also take up a very different analogy. A masterpiece may need to be interpreted to a later generation. The modern 'commentary' may shed a flood of light on it, and be necessary for full understanding in the changed culture of a later time. But in this case, the original will not be thrown away. The whole purpose of the interpretation is to help the hearer to return to the original masterpiece, this time with eyes to see. The second analogy describes the task of biblical interpretation; the first does not. But the term 'myth', with all its slipperiness and accumulation of mistaken theories, allows the second kind of interpretation to be confused with the first. The Christian story indeed needs fresh *interpretation* from generation to generation; but in terms of the theory of knowledge presented above, it also contains irreducible paradigms that cannot be dispensed with without 'sawing off the branch on which I am sitting'. It embodies the corporate memory of the Christian community.

Third, in stressing the practical or self-involving function of myth, many writers adopt an unduly negative attitude towards the descriptive function of story or narrative. Bultmann, for example, believes that this 'objectifying' or descriptive aspect simply impedes the practical impact of its language, even to the point of misleading the modern reader about the content of its message. But self-involving language cannot be effective if it is *wholly* instrumental or 'practical', without being anchored in some understanding of reality. The self-involving or practical aspect becomes operative precisely because it is grounded in an understanding of 'what is the case', or in the founding events of the community. This is one of several reasons why a number of modern writers insist that 'myth', as a category, cannot do justice to the particularity, uniqueness, or once-for-allness (however this is expressed) which marks the Christian story. We are not obliged to depend for this point on waning remnants of the once-fashionable 'biblical theology' movement. No sane account of the faith of the New Testament communities can brush over this aspect, and it is noteworthy that correctives have emerged in New Testament studies to the older idea that early Christian preaching was wholly 'confessional', as if descriptions of events were of no interest at all to the primitive communities.[33]

It seems, then, that the category 'myth', in spite of the promise that it seems initially to hold out, does not in the end take us very far along the path of trying to clarify the nature of the relation between corporate knowledge and individual criticism. At very least it leaves too many loose ends that lend themselves easily to misunderstanding.

IV.2 Two Further Perspectives: The Problem of Interpretation and the Self-involving Nature of Christian Belief

If the idea of 'myth' fails, in the end, to carry the discussion forward constructively, we may perhaps suggest two other alternative perspectives in the light of which we may more easily avoid the temptation to polarize corporate knowledge and individual criticism as opposites, and may see the complementary and positive ways in which the two poles interact and interrelate as contributions to the one ongoing dialectic.

---

[33] Cf., for example, Graham N. Stanton, *Jesus of Nazareth in New Testament Preaching* (Cambridge: Cambridge University Press, 1974); SNTS Monograph 27.

First, light is shed on the nature of this interaction by the history of biblical interpretation. There has always been an emphasis in Christian theology on the 'givenness' of the biblical writings. The 1938 Doctrine Commission Report entitled *Doctrine in the Church of England* saw the Bible as the 'classical literature' of God's self-revelation, and viewed its authority as lying at least partly in its function of carrying us 'back to the concrete richness of the facts in which our religion is grounded'.[34] In the present Doctrine Commission Report (1981) we emphasize the givenness of the Bible, and discuss its authority partly in terms of its function. In current biblical studies, however, two further emphases can be found. In the first place, to the older recognition of the variety of literary forms which can be found in the Bible (noted in the 1938 Doctrine Report) is now added a further emphasis on the multiformity of its actual content or theological subject-matter. But this simply underlines the fundamental fact that the Bible embodies the corporate memories and corporate knowledge of *a community*, or (perhaps more accurately) of *a community of communities*. In the second place, increasing emphasis is laid today on the problem of biblical interpretation. How can an ancient text speak to our own times? The importance of both issues, the multiformity of the biblical writings and the problem of interpretation, was underlined in the Doctrine Commission Report of 1976, *Christian Believing*.[35] Both are of positive importance for the present discussion.

C.H. Dodd noted the connection between the authority of the Bible and the corporate foundations of Christian knowledge, memory and belief, many years ago. It is worth quoting some of his sentences. There may be times, he wrote, 'when doubts are stronger than faith'. It would not be honest at such times simply to silence our questionings with a text. Nevertheless,

> We may well turn away from the narrow scene of individual experience at the moment, to the spacious prospect we command in the Bible ... Here we trace the long history of a community which, through good fortune and ill, tested their belief in God, and experimented too in varieties of belief, with the result that the 'logic of facts' drove deeper and deeper the conviction that while some ways of thinking of God are definitely closed *this* way lies open and leads on and on.[36]

Dodd went on to stress the corporate dimension of faith by describing individual belief as being primarily a matter of 'living oneself into' the corporate experience and corporate memory of community. The very nature of the biblical literature draws attention to this aspect of Christian believing.

However, if one pole in the use of the Bible is that of the corporate knowledge of the community, the other pole concerns the Christian's understanding and interpretations of that knowledge in the present. We have already argued in the first half of this essay that 'understanding' depends on a context of 'effective history' or corporate knowledge. The two poles of the past 'givenness' of the Bible and its present interpretation do not (or at least should not) stand in opposition to each other. In this respect the history of biblical

---

[34]   Church of England Doctrine Commission, *Doctrine in the Church of England* (London: SPCK, 1938), pp.31 and 34.

[35]   Church of England Doctrine Commission, *Christian Believing* (London: SPCK, 1976), pp.6–14, 21–31 and 43–51.

[36]   C.H. Dodd, *The Authority of the Bible* (2nd edn, London: Nisbet, 1938), p.298.

interpretation is the history both of false trails to be avoided and of insights to be developed further. Over the course of the history of the church, different interpreters, and different eras of interpretation, have stressed the importance of each pole in turn. The Reformers urged that the Bible should not be made to wear 'a nose of wax', with the result that it could be made to say anything that the current generation wanted to hear, under the pretext of 'interpretation'. Others have stressed that meaning transcends the conscious intention of the original writer, and that meaning *cannot* remain unchanged when it is understood in a changed situation.

In an attempt to give some place to both the past and present aspects, an analogy may be suggested. The Bible may be compared to a musical score. What 'controls', or sets limits to the scope of, the present performance is the notation of the composition as it was composed at some time in the past. If it is not based on the score, the present performance is not a performance of *this* composition. Nevertheless, what the current audience experiences in the present is the actual *performance*, and no two performances will be quite the same. Wooden repetition may turn out to be less faithful to the score than the use of creative imagination. Yet the creativity of the performer still takes place within clear limits. For without faithfulness to the score, the performance would not be a *faithful* interpretation of *that* work. Indeed, to return to our earlier observations about the nature of the Bible, to offer an 'interpretation' which did violence to the text would be to substitute some narrower individual viewpoint for the breadth and range of successive layers of corporate memory, belief and knowledge, gained by a community, or by a community of communities.

We turn now to our second suggestion about the way of looking at the problem of corporate knowledge that allows us to see how the corporate and individual poles of knowledge interact positively together, rather than standing in a relation of opposition or contradiction. If we are tempted to view Christian belief as being primarily a 'mental state', or a matter of thinking certain thoughts, it may seem as if creeds, confessions or the corporate testimony of the community represent a threat to make the individual think what everyone else thinks. But this way of understanding belief is inadequate, mistaken and, in the context of the present discussion, also misleading. Christian believing by its very nature carries with it the appropriation of certain attitudes and patterns of behaviour that are called into play only on the basis of the shared public world of interpersonal relations. Belief involves, or commits, the self who claims to be a believer not merely (if at all) to the acceptance of certain theoretical statements, but to ways of understanding and acting towards God and others that transcend the limits of a strictly 'private' or individual world. In this sense, Christian belief has been described as 'self-involving'. It has practical as well as theoretical dimensions, and these practical dimensions make themselves apparent, and indeed make sense, only on the basis of a setting or context in the public world of *shared* attitudes and *shared* patterns of behaviour. Christian beliefs are thus, by definition, we shall argue, *shared* beliefs.

We have already seen that Christian belief entails more than thinking certain thoughts in our earlier discussions about expected patterns of behaviour and the significance of status and (in the sociological sense) role. Christian belief entails not so much *theoretical* assent to the possible existence or relevance of such roles, as their actual acceptance, adoption and appropriation. Here we enter the realm of 'performative' utterances, or first-person expressions of commitments, or pledges of belief. As the assays on 'promising' in the present collection indicate, to say 'I promise to do *x*', is not simply to give *information* about myself; the utterance *commits* me to certain subsequent actions. The utterance itself, therefore, is an act that is *performed in* the saying of the words. I *make* a promise, for the promise itself constitutes a pledge or commitment. But in the context of the present argument, this means that making a promise cannot, *by definition*, be a merely *private* or *individual* matter. It would not make sense (apart from the very odd and derivative notion of giving oneself a promise) to speak of 'promising', except on the basis of *public*, shared, interpersonal relations.

The same principle applies to Christian believing. One cannot believe 'privately', for belief involves commitment to shared attitudes and patterns of behaviour. It is not simply a matter of an individual having certain ideas in his head. To say 'I believe' is to make a pledge, to make a commitment. It is like nailing one's colours to the mast. Even in a situation of political oppression where 'secret' discipleship might be thought necessary in certain exceptional circumstances, the secrecy of belief would not be 'private' in the full philosophical sense.

All these kinds of considerations have been carefully examined in a number of philosophical discussions of these issues.[37] Each discussion seems further to underline the importance of the 'performative' character of confessions of belief, even though it is also rightly asserted that belief is *more* than a pledge or first-person commitment. It has been pointed out, for example, that if I claim to believe, this cannot mean that I have a certain mental state continuously; for I hardly stop being a believer when I fall asleep or lose consciousness. It means that I am committed (at least in principle) to those actions and attitudes which are appropriate in circumstances which would call belief into play. If I 'believe' that Christ is Lord, what gives content to that belief is my acceptance and appropriation of the role of Christ's servant. Whether I show fear, joy, shame, courage, or hope in certain situations is part of what my belief may be said to amount to. This is not to deny the possibility of insincerity or hypocrisy. For I can *claim* to believe in such a way as to deceive even myself; just as I may promise to do something and then fail to carry the promise through. What is being said is that a statement of belief that does not affect action or attitude is (like a promise which is later broken) without substance. The Epistle of James is of course at pains to make this particular point. This does not invalidate the Pauline insight that faith is a *response*. For it entails the *acceptance* or *appropriation* of attitudes or patterns of behaviour that are 'given' prior to individual thought, and which are lived out in the shared world of interpersonal relations. It would make no more sense to speak of 'private' Christian belief than it would to speak of being a doctor, teacher, or servant 'privately'.

To be aware, then, of the practical or self-involving aspects of belief is to move some way towards seeing how the dialectic between the corporate and individual aspects of knowledge and experience comes to operate in practice. Christian believing is possible

---

[37] See especially H.H. Price, *Belief* (London: Allen & Unwin, 1969) and D.M. High, *Language, Persons and Belief* (New York: Oxford University Press, 1967).

only on the foundations of corporate knowledge and experience. It operates within the framework of corporate memory. But it does not demand a merely second-hand or uncritical acceptance of 'what others have said'. For *critical* faith, far from being a 'private' or individual affair, depends on the capacity to employ concepts which are themselves embedded in a process of corporate experience and knowledge. Luther's 'Here I stand' is not in the end incompatible with the patristic dictum (understood in its broadest sense): 'There is no salvation outside the Church.' Indeed, Luther explicitly endorsed Cyprian's maxim: 'He cannot have God for his father who has not the Church for his mother.'[38]

---

[38]   Martin Luther, *Commentary on the Psalms, Weimarer Ausgabe*, IV, 239. 21.

CHAPTER THIRTY-NINE

Time and Grand Narrative?
"Human Being, Relationality and Time
in Hebrews, 1 Corinthians and
Western Traditions" (1997–98)

The following article first appeared under the title, "Human Being, Relationality and Time in Hebrews, 1 Corinthians and Western Traditions" in Ex Auditu *volume 13 (1997), pp. 76–95. This essay might equally well be placed in Part VI on Postmodernity, since it traces the theological necessity for "Grand Narrative" of the kind that Lyotard and many other postmodern thinkers explicitly reject. However, it also places the theological doctrine of "being human" (what we formerly called "the doctrine of man") within a temporal rather than dualistic conceptual frame, thereby providing a more appropriate hermeneutical agenda for exploring the human within the historical created order in "human" time. Part of what it is to be human emerges in relation to the correlate of God's faithfulness. This article, then, is multi-disciplinary, involving Christian theology, the Bible, philosophical thought, and hermeneutics.*

I
Western Traditions and the New Testament: Some Similarities and Contrasts

Among a series of answers to the question "What is a Human?" many Christian and secular thinkers in the Western tradition have isolated reason and *rationality* as a key distinguishing mark of the human. Plato perceived reason or mind (*nous*) as that which made human beings capable of responsible action, and perceived "the soul" as an immortal entity imprisoned within the body and awaiting liberation from it.[1] While the New Testament writers lay a positive emphasis on mind and reason in appropriate contexts, the distinctiveness of the human does not find its primary expression here, and physical and bodily life remains of the utmost possible importance. Life in the body is affirmed: it is no prison-house, and liberation is defined entirely differently.

Aristotle also perceives the human mind (*nous*) as that which activates human capacities (*dynameis*) for action.[2] However, alongside certain biblical perspectives, he also believes that the genuinely human is *relational*: the humanity of humans emerges in collaborative groups, especially that of the family and the city-state. Whereas non-human animals may relate socially to one another in packs, hives, or flocks, only humankind as a rational and political animal can construct a dialectic of cooperation and conflict in

---

1   Plato, *Phaedrus*, 247c; *Republic*, VI: 508d; cf. *Phaedrus*, 64e; *Gorgias*, 524b.
2   Aristotle, *On the Soul*, II: 3:432b.

which political structures for human welfare and moderation can flourish: "A human is by nature a political animal."[3] This anticipates the problem raised by Reinhold Niebuhr. Although he rejects the Hegelian rationalism "which glorifies rational man as essential man", Niebuhr also observes "Man ... shares his social character with some animals who live in herds and with insects in hives ... His rational character is uniquely human."[4]

A sharp dualism between body and mind, or between body and soul, however, so pervasively permeated Western traditions from Plato to Kant that from the very first some Christian writers defended "our psychosomatic unity as a basic principle of Christian anthropology", while others allowed their thought to be dominated by the Platonic tradition.[5] Thus the second-century Christian writer Athenagoras underlined the importance of the resurrection of the *sōma* in 1 Cor. 15 on the ground that a resurrection of the "soul" would not constitute a resurrection of the whole person.[6] This entirely coheres with the Old Testament tradition of conceiving of *She`ol* as a mode of "thinned down", reduced, isolated, life (Ps. 6:5; 31:17; 49:14, 15; Prov. 30:15; Eccles. 9:10; Isa. 38:18), in contrast to the "somatic" mode of being which, as we shall note from Käsemann's work, includes communication, identity and visibility in the public domain. *Sōma*, we shall argue, denotes human *relationality*, not a "component" in contrast to "soul". On the other hand Tertullian, writing over the turn of the second and third centuries, declares, "All that we are, is soul (*anima*) ... Without the soul we are nothing ... only a carcase".[7] On Gen. 1:26, Tertullian writes, God took mere dust, and by breathing into it a soul, "gave humankind dominion over all things".[8] Indeed, Tertullian returns to a dualism that gives privilege to *reason* in defining the human: to be made in God's image and likeness (Gen. 1:26) is "to possess reason in yourself, who are a rational creature, made by a rational Creator".[9]

Augustine's writings effectively ensured that for the next thousand years, at least, Christian writers in the West would identify the distinguishing characteristic of being made "in the image of God" (Gen. 1:26) as the human possession of reason and rationality. Augustine writes, "The soul is not the whole of man, but the better part of man ... for what sense man is said to be in the image of God ... is spoken of as the soul, which is rational".[10] Origen anticipates Thomas Aquinas as perceiving the rational in human beings as demonstrable from the order of concepts and ability to abstract and to generalize that defines characteristic humanness.[11] Thomas Aquinas then expounds the role of *reason* and *dominion*, among other qualities, as characterizing a human being made in God's image: to possess "intellectual soul" is what "raises man above the beasts of the

---

3   Aristotle, *Politics*, I: 2:1253a; cf I: 5: 1254b.
4   Reinhold Niebuhr, *Man's Nature and his Communities* (London: Bles, 1966), p.21; and on Hegel's rationalism, *The Nature and Destiny of Man* (2 vols, London: Nisbet, 1941), vol. I, 37.
5   The phrase "psychosomatic unity" here comes from W. Pannenberg, *Systematic Theology* II (Eng., Edinburgh: T. & T. Clark, 1994), p.182.
6   Athenagoras, *On the Resurrection of the Dead*, p.15.
7   Tertullian, *On the Flesh of Christ*, p.12.
8   Tertullian, *Against Marcion*, II:4; cf. also V:8.
9   Tertullian, *Against Praxeas*, p.5.
10   Augustine, *City of God*, XIII:24:2.
11   Origen, *De Principiis*, I:1:7.

field", and exhibits God's image: "All animals are naturally subject to man."[12] Thomas declares, "Mind (*mens*) is the soul's essence (*animae ... essentia*) ... Understanding (*intellectus*) is the soul's very essence (*ipsa essentia animae*)."[13] This whole section is carried forward as a discussion with Aristotle and Augustine.

Reason and "dominion" cannot be left out of account in discussing humanness as defined in terms of being made in God's image.[14] But we have not yet reached the heart of the matter for the New Testament writers, especially Paul and the author of Hebrews. Migliore notes that in addition to a more anthropomorphic understanding of "*image of God*", four interpretations of image of God in Gen. 1:26 have dominated Western traditions: (i) human "capacity to reason"; (ii) humanity's being accorded "*dominion over the earth*"; (iii) "*human freedom*", and (iv) "*human life in relationships* with God and with other creatures" (his italics).[15] Migliore rightly places most emphasis on the fourth: "*Being created in the image of God means that humans find this true identity in Co-existence with each other and with all other creatures*" (his italics).[16] It also entails being "*addressed* by God", being placed within finite historical boundaries in "historical embeddedness", being drawn beyond the self in "self-transcendence", and especially moving towards "*a goal: human beings are restless for a fulfilment of life not yet realized*" (his italics).[17]

In practice, Augustine and Thomas Aquinas do leave room for an emphasis on relationality. As Thomas concedes, Augustine associates "*love* with the essence of the power of the soul (*amor ... in anima ... essentialiter*)".[18] Although Aquinas finds *relationality* in Aristotle, the problem of time poses greater difficulties for a "soul" which supposedly belongs to a non-temporal realm. Nevertheless, he accepts Augustine's argument that embedded in human selfhood is *memory* alongside *attention* and hope: "activity belongs to the compound whole of the human self".[19] Paul Ricoeur has shown how in combination *Augustine* underlines the *temporal* nature of the human self, while Aristotle emphasizes its structural, organizational capacity for *purpose*. Hence Ricoeur draws out the importance of an ordered "narrative plot" for understanding human relationality.[20]

Only with the loosening of the grip of Enlightenment rationalism and Kantian "autonomy", which places the human self at the centre did Barth initially, then Moltmann, Jüngel and especially Pannenberg bring together relationality and temporality as being characteristic of the human. All four writers argue that what a *human* is cannot be fully understood without reference to human destiny and to God. Pannenberg asserts, "The emphasis is not on intellectual ability but on the destiny of

---

[12]   Thomas Aquinas, *Summa Theologiae* (London: Blackfriars, Latin & English, 1969–70), I a, Qu 93:2; and Qu 96:1.

[13]   Aquinas, *Summa*, I a Qu 79:1:ii (London: Blackfriars, XI, 145; Latin, 144).

[14]   For Aquinas's detailed views, cf. *Summa*, I a, Qu 90–102 (vol. XIII, London: Blackfriars edn).

[15]   D.L. Migliore, *Faith Seeking Understanding: An Introduction to Christian Theology* (Grand Rapids, MI: Eerdmans, 1991), pp.121–2.

[16]   Migliore, *Faith*, p.125.

[17]   Ibid., pp.124–8.

[18]   Aquinas, *Summa*, I a Qu 77:1, i (vol. XI, 89, English; 88, Latin).

[19]   *Summa*, ibid., 1, i and 1, ii (XI, 93).

[20]   Paul Ricoeur, *Time and Narrative* (Eng., 3 vols, Chicago, IL: University of Chicago Press, 1984–88) I, pp.5–87; and *Oneself as Another* (Eng., Chicago, IL: University of Chicago Press, 1992), pp.1–39, 140–68 and 203–39.

fellowship with God and the position of rule associated with closeness to God."[21] Everything that is creaturely is "ec-centric", that is, not to be centred on the self. The human characteristic of bearing the image of God lies in "Being with others as others."[22] Moreover, human identity presupposes a pattern of action or continuity that reveals character in such activities as responsibility in the keeping of a promise, and this entails both *relationality* and *time*: "Those who make a promise that they can keep only many years later ... have to retain their identity if they are to meet the promise. *Actions owe their unity to* **the** *time-bridging identity of their subjects*" (my italics).[23]

Three points should be made about contrasts between this approach and the Enlightenment tradition. First, to borrow Migliore's language, if knowledge of God and understanding of the human are intertwined, "we cannot know God without being shocked into new self-recognition, and we cannot know our true humanity without new awareness of who God is".[24] Indeed, far from beginning with the human self and postulating a projection of the human as God (with Feuerbach), Barth insists that we first attend to what relationality consists in with reference to God, before we attempt to determine in what sense, if any, we can speak of relationality as characterizing the human.[25]

Second, Niebuhr, Jüngel, Moltmann and Pannenberg insist on a reappraisal of what "being accorded dominion over the earth" means in the context of God's own rule or reign in Christ. Moltmann writes of the solidarity that bonds human beings with the created order of the earth. The way in which humankind exercises a "dominion" in stewardship must reflect, mirror and radiate God's living, loving presence and care. Reinhold Niebuhr traces how fallen humanity transposes "dominion" into "exploitation" which is motivated by will-to-power and greed "beyond natural requirements".[26] Moltmann urges that the Old Testament prohibition of images reminds us that humankind is to be God's image. As against Feuerbach and Nietzsche, Moltmann declares, "Man becomes more human if he is put in the position of being able to abandon his self-deification and his idolatry with all its gains and achievements. But what *can* put him in this position?" (Moltmann's italics).[27] Pannenberg likewise comments, "If the divine likeness is a standard for our ordination to rule over creation, ... what is this likeness? "[It is] not exploitation".[28] Jüngel insists that humans must not abdicate "rule" if the earth is not to be destroyed, but in a form which exercised responsible self-control.[29]

In the wake of Enlightenment rationalism and its obsession with science and technology, however, dominion is perceived in secular terms as "mastering": the new

---

[21] Pannenberg, *Systematic Theology*, II, p.190.

[22] Ibid., p.193.

[23] Ibid., p.202.

[24] Migliore, *Faith Seeking Understanding*, p.120.

[25] A recent exposition can be found in A.J. Torrance, *Persons in Communion. Trinitarian Description and Human Participation* (Edinburgh: T. & T. Clark, 1996), pp.120–212.

[26] Reinhold Niebuhr, *The Nature and Destiny of Man* I, p.203.

[27] J. Moltmann, *Man, Christian Anthropology in the Conflicts of the Present* (Eng., London: SPCK, 1971 and Philadelphia, PA: Fortress, 1974), pp.107, 108 and 109; cf. p.106.

[28] Pannenberg, *Systematic Theology*, II, p.205. Cf. Niebuhr's use of this word, above.

[29] E. Jüngel, in J. Moltmann (ed.), *How I Have Changed: Thirty Years of Theology* (London: SCM, 1997), p.11.

autonomous self bends to its own will not only the powers of rivers and mountains, wood and stone, domestic animals and fossil fuels; it also seeks to tame nuclear energy, the genetic transmission of human traits, *in vitro* fertilization from sperm stored from anonymous donors, animal cloning, the electronic construction of "virtual reality" simulated worlds, and social control through instant global media. Yet the so-called computer errors which are usually due to fallible human programming, the transportation of nuclear waste through population centres, the dumping of nuclear waste with thousands of years of "half-life radiation", and the mutations of new diseases in crops, animals and humans in response to new compounds of biochemical experiments: all these may serve to question the optimism of the Enlightenment era which transposed the Christian tradition of responsible, caring "dominion" in solidarity with the created order into exploitation for short-term, easy commercial "success" on the part of the autonomous self. It is scarcely surprising that "modernity" is being overtaken by a postmodern awareness of the vulnerability of a humanity too greatly at the mercy of social construction and exploitation by commercial profit or power interests. How much credibility attaches to Kant's "autonomy" when commercial interests already determine the "expected" choices of young people, for example, about even clothes and recreation? Such a human self belongs neither to Enlightenment optimism nor to biblical understandings of human being as God purposed it to display him as his image.

Third, any account of the human which takes seriously questions of human identity must also address issues of *time* and *temporality*. The significance of time and narrative for issues of identity (as against systems which concern "essences" rather than personal identity) has gained wide familiarity through the work of Ricoeur in Europe, and of Hans Frei, Lindbeck, Niebuhr and others in America. However, even within the limits of a barely modified Cartesian dualism, John Locke recognized that we cannot address issues of personal identity without reference to time. Identity, Locke believed, entailed the rational capacity to extend consciousness backwards and forwards in the context of memory, witness and accountability. To be accountable I must recognize actions as "mine" even if they occurred at another time.[30] Even though, as his well-known parable of the prince and the cobbler illustrates, Locke still faced the problems of a mind–body dualism, his approach nevertheless moves in the direction of an account of humanness which in this specific respect reflects biblical concerns and paves the way for Dilthey and Ricoeur.

One huge gap still remains, however, in our introductory exploration of Western traditions. Paul and the Epistle to the Hebrews expound humanness in terms of relationality and time, especially of destiny and relationship with God. But above all, each portrays Christ, and Christ alone, as the only authentic paradigm-case of what is to manifest the image and likeness of God in perfect, unhindered radiance. It is no accident that many theological treatments of the human begin with an explicit quotation "What is a Human Being?" which renders the Hebrew *mah—enosh* in Psalm 8:4, translated as a plural, "What are human beings?" in NRSV and NJB, and in traditional versions (KJV / AV, RSV, JB) as "What is Man?".[31] But the Epistle to the Hebrews contains the fullest

---

[30]   John Locke, *Essay Concerning Human Understanding* (Oxford: OUP, 1894), II:27.
[31]   Cf. E. Mascall, *The Importance of Being Human* (London: OUP, 1959).

exposition of Psalm 8:4–6 that can be found within the biblical writings. The author to the Hebrews argues that the impressive scope of human "dominion" and most especially humankind's being "crowned with glory and honor" (NRSV) remains God's purpose but has come to pass, to date, only in one case, namely that of Jesus Christ (Heb. 2:6–8): "As it is, we do not yet see everything in subjection ... But we do see Jesus, who for a little while was made lower than the angels, now crowned with glory and honor because of the suffering of death ... [to] taste death for everyone" (Heb. 2:7–9, NRSV).

The many specialists who discuss the use of Psalm 8:4–6 in Hebrews concur in their exegesis with the general theological assertion put forward by Karl Barth: "Jesus is man as God willed and created him ... *The nature of the man Jesus is the key to the problem of the human* (my italics). This man is *man*" (Barth's italics).[32] Pannenberg's allusion to time and promise becomes closely relevant to identity here: Barth speaks, as the Epistle to the Hebrews does, of the importance of divine appointment, promise, covenant, vocation and honour, and of the relationality of the recipient to these acts.[33] The dimension of time is ever at the forefront: patience, lack of weariness in enduring, and "learning" through suffering how to reach the *telos* (*teleiotheis*, Heb. 5:2, 8, 9).[34]

Yet Hebrews has been curiously overlooked as a response to the question "What is a Human?". Even Uno Schnelle's book *The Human Condition* examines the teaching of Jesus, Paul and John, but never mentions Hebrews.[35] Yet this is surprising if Jesus Christ is our paradigm-case of humanness. Cullmann claims that "Hebrews understands the humanity of Jesus in a more comprehensive way than the Gospels or any other early Christian writing"; just as Murphy O'Connor observes about Paul that "in order to find the true and essential nature of humanity he did not look to his contemporaries but to Christ, for he [Christ] alone embodied the authenticity of humanity".[36]

II
Humanness, Relationality and Time in Hebrews: Accepting Constraints and Suffering

The Epistle to the Hebrews perceives the paradigm of humanness as exhibited and fulfilled in Jesus Christ as part of an *ongoing temporal narrative* which concerns the interrelatedness or *relationality* of human beings. The very use of the relational terms *Son* and *God* in 1:1–4 stands in contrast to the isolated "parentless" self of the Cartesian *cogito*. Descartes, as one of the founders of Western modernity, aimed "to rid myself of all the

---

[32] Karl Barth, *Church Dogmatics*, III:2 (Eng., Edinburgh: T. & T. Clark, 1960), [sect. 43], p.50; cf. also S. Kistemaker, *The Psalm Citations in the Epistle to the Hebrews* (Amsterdam: van Soest, 1961), pp.102–8.

[33] Barth, *Church Dogmatics*, III:4, sect. 56, pp.565–685.

[34] Barth, *Church Dogmatics*, III:2, sects 43–47; and III:4 (Eng., Edinburgh: T. & T. Clark, 1961), sects 54–56.

[35] Uno Schnelle, *The Human Condition: Anthropology in the Teachings of Jesus, Paul and John* (Eng., Edinburgh: T. & T. Clark, and Minneapolis, MN: Augsburg, 1996).

[36] Oscar Cullmann, *The Christology of the New Testament* (Eng., London: SCM, 2nd edn, 1963), p.94; and Jerome Murphy-O'Connor, *Becoming Human Together. The Pastoral Anthropology of St Paul* (Wilmington, DE: Glazier, 1982 and 1984), p.45.

opinions I had adopted, ... commencing anew ... Thinking ... alone is inseparable from me".[37] The traditions of earlier generations cannot be trusted (except for certain concessions in the moral realm). By contrast, the opening of the powerful sermon that constitutes the text of Hebrews draws both a contrast and a narrative continuity between *the prophets* (1:1) who mediated revelation *in various ways* NRSV; Greek *polumeros* (cf. *bit by bit*, C.B. Williams' version) and the decisive, definitive climax of this same revelation in *these last days* (1:2).[38] Hughes declares, "There is certainly a conception of a longitudinal 'revelation history' in which the earlier and more fragmentary forms of God's Address have been overtaken ... by a perfected form of the same thing ... a recognizable continuity ... in spite of their discontinuity ... parts of a single process".[39]

The very presuppositions of *promise* and *covenant*, which stand at the centre of Hebrews, entail notions of past, present and future as a frame within which responsibility, accountability, and identity acquire currency. The human dimensions of vulnerability, constraint and instability find a counterbalance in a *sense and steadfast anchor* (6:19) which is shown to be one of *hope* for the *future* (v. 19) resting on *a guarantee by an oath* (6:17) which God decreed in the past to give present encouragement and future actualization. We already begin to glimpse a very distinctive conceptual model in Hebrews by means of which the author sets in contrast the fragility of human beings and their propensity to "drift" (2:1–4) with the sovereign otherness of the covenant God who moves ahead of them in their pilgrimage. There could be no greater contrast between this conceptual scheme and that which has too often dominated Western traditions about the human. In *Christ and Time*, Cullmann writes, "Primitive Christian faith and thinking do not start from the spatial contrast between the Here and the Beyond, but from the time distinction between Formerly and Now and Then."[40] Hence when the author to the Hebrews defines faith as "the assurance of things hoped for", the parallel allusion to "things not seen" refers primarily not to the invisible, timeless, noumenal world of the Absolute in Plato or in Kant, but to that which cannot be seen because God has not yet brought it about (11:1). As we noted above from Pannenberg, *promise* and its appropriation presuppose *time*.

The eleventh chapter on faith and its successive instantiations in a biblical tradition that leads up to the coming of Christ presents three features: first, it portrays human life and human identity not as an isolated Cartesian ego, but in the context of temporal succession and inherited *promise*. Second, it movingly portrays the unseen *as a future* on which believers under the old covenant staked their lives even though death supervened before the corporate promise was actualized ("these ... did not receive what was promised", 11:39). Third, "spirituality" was not located in some "upper" supersensory realm in which the mental and spiritual were sealed off from a "lower" life, but defined

---

[37] René Descartes, *The Meditations* (Eng., La Salle, IL: Open Court, 1901, rp. 1988), pp.21 and 33.

[38] On the sermon form, see among many others William Lane, *Hebrews 1–8, 9–13* (Dallas, TX: Word Books [Word Bib Com 47A, 47B], 1991), pp.lxix–lxxxviii; and Albert Vanhoye, *Homilie für halfbedürftige Christen: Struktur und Botschaft des Hebräerbriefes* (Regensburg: Pustet, 1981).

[39] Graham Hughes, *Hebrews and Hermeneutics. The Epistle to the Hebrews as a New Testament Example of Biblical Interpretation* (Cambridge: CUP [SNTS Mon Ser 36], 1979), p.6.

[40] Oscar Cullmann, *Christ and Time: The Primitive Conception of Time and History* (Eng., London: SCM, 1951), p.37.

as a *future stance towards the promises of God lived out in the hurly-burly of the relationalities of everyday life*. Both self-transcendence and divine transcendence are formulated in *temporal* terms rather than as a "two-level" spatial system. As Barth, Hans Frei and numerous other writers have urged, issues of human and divine identity take on a different nature in the context of narrative from their more problematic role within a supposedly timeless system. Systems raise questions about "essences"; narratives raise questions about identity, purpose and character.

Abstract categorizations of human beings in terms of classes and stereotypes never reach the heart of what it is to be human. A human being does not fall in love with another human who can be exhaustively categorized as (i) gender: female; (ii) hair: blonde; (iii) eyes: blue; (iv) weight: below average; (v) height: 5' 4"; (vi) complexion: pale; (vii) face: oval; (viii) academic qualifications: BA English; (ix) occupation: librarian; (x) hobbies: squash, chess. A person falls in love with "Mary" or "John": a fellow-human whose character has been interactively shaped by a unique variety of events and experiences through time, and whose unique identity can be revealed primarily by recounting stories about their past experiences, present attitudes and the shaping of their hopes for the future. It is axiomatic that a good medical consultant will take account of the unique interaction between physiological, anatomic and biochemical conditions which relate to ("M") categorizations found in medical textbooks; but also of more *personal* ("P") factors which treat a patient *as a human person* also. The psychosomatic unity of human selfhood invites simultaneous understanding of "personal" predicates and "material" predicates together. P.F. Strawson made a major contribution to issues of human identity by going beyond Locke in exploring the "primitive" concept of *person*, in which "P" predicates and "M" predicates overlap. "M" predicates include, for example, "goes for a walk"; "P" predicates may include, for example, "believes in God".[41]

The Epistle to the Hebrews unfolds the humanness of Jesus with reference to these overlapping predicates within a frame of temporality. M-predicates and P-predicates overlap in the public domain in Jesus' standing in such complete solidarity with humanness that he finds the need for *trust in God* (2:13) when the path is dark and difficult; shares the sensitivity and openness to weakness and pain in sharing *likewise flesh and blood ... the same things* (2:14); experiencing *death* (v. 14) and becoming *like his brothers and sisters in every respect* (2:17), including *suffering* (v. 18). The overlapping of predicates in the public domain reaches a climax in the clear allusion to Gethsemane: "in the days of his flesh Jesus offered up prayers and supplications with loud cries and tears ... he learned obedience through what he suffered ..." (5:7–8); cf. Mark 14:32–42; Matt. 26:36–46. Yet the narrative progression of this "learning of obedience" *pinpoints the fundamental phenomenon that true humanness entails the acceptance of constraints*.

The Garden of Gethsemane lies to the right (east) at the foot of the age-old track which leads up the hill out of Jerusalem to Bethany, where Jesus would have been safe. But he delays his departure, aware of the virtual inevitability of arrest. According to the Markan tradition of the Gethsemane event, Jesus prays *with deep distress* (Heb. 5:7, with loud cries

---

[41] P.F. Strawson, *Individuals: An Essay in Descriptive Metaphysics* (London: Methuen, 1959), p.104; cf. esp. pp.87–116.

and tears; Greek *dakruon*) and at the arrest Jesus experienced the loneliness of abandonment: "they all forsook him and fled" (Mark 14:50). In the Matthean tradition Jesus' voluntary *acceptance of constraints* entailed in being *human* is underlined: "Do you think that I cannot appeal to my Father, and he will at once send me more than twelve legions of angels?" (Matt. 26:53). The torment of preference for the easier way ("remove this cup from me", Mark 14:36; cf. Matt. 26:27, with "if it be possible"; Luke 22:42, with "if you are willing") as against the acceptance of "yet not what I want, but your will ..." (Mark 14:36 and parallels) offers a poignant commentary on the human condition. In what sense did God "*hear*" (Greek, *eisakoustheis*) the agony of Jesus' prayer (Heb. 5:7c)? Jesus was "heard" not in the sense of *removing* the cup but in the hearing of Jesus' acceptance of God's way.[42]

As we shall note more explicitly below, the whole notion of "cutting corners" by pleas for miraculous interventions to short-circuit difficulties and hardships may turn out to be not an enhancement of redeemed humanness, but an attempt, in many contexts of life, to deny it. It may at times entail a search to "escape from the body" more akin to Plato, to Cartesian dualism of mind and body, and to the Enlightenment obsession with autonomy and "control", than to the paradigm case of an answer to the question "What is Human?" as this is lived out in temporal experience and relationality to God, to others, and to all creation by Jesus as the Adam of the new order.

The emphasis of this epistle or sermon on the temptations of Jesus underlines this. In Matthew and Luke, the three temptations that immediately follow the baptism of Jesus and his anointing by the Holy Spirit represent distinctively Messianic temptations, in the sense of tests of his Messianic vocation. Even these, however, constitute temptation to avoid constraints and to opt for short cuts. To outdo the feeding miracles of Moses in the wilderness wanderings, and to transpose stones of the desert into bread for the multitude; to perform the miraculous feat of remaining alive after a suicidal leap from the temple rock into the valley of Kidron far below; to use the devil's means to achieve supposedly good ends; all these could guarantee instant success of a kind. But the denial of the way of patient obedience, patient suffering and patient acceptance of the constraints of humanness would not constitute the kind of kingdom or "kingly reign" which Jesus came to proclaim and to inaugurate. Hence the Synoptic Gospels recount the rejection by Jesus of these less costly, more supposedly instant, ways (Matt. 4:1–11; Luke 4:1–13; cf. Mark 1:12, 13). In the Epistle to the Hebrews Jesus experienced the phenomenon of temptation not primarily in the context of Messiahship but in the context of what it is to be human. Ellingworth comments "The meaning here [4:15] as in 2:16–18 and 5:2, is ... that Christ's earthly life gives him inner understanding of human experience".[43]

---

[42] The exegesis is controversial. We follow e.g. W. Lane, *Hebrews* (cited above), pp.119–20 and T. Boman, "Das Gebetskampf Jesu", *NTS* 10 (1964), pp.261–73; But cf. H.W. Attridge, *The Epistle to the Hebrews* ((Philadelphia, PA: Fortress, 1989), pp.148–52; E. Käsemann, "Hebräer 4:14–16", in *Exegetische Versuche und Besinnungen* (Göttingen, Vandenhoeck & Ruprecht, 1970), I, pp.303–7 and C. Spicq, *L'Épître aux Hébreux* (2 vols, Paris: Gabalda, 1953), II, pp.112–17 and 119–39.

[43] Paul Ellingworth, *The Epistle to the Hebrews: A Commentary on the Greek Text* (Grand Rapids, MI: Eerdmans and Carlisle: Paternoster [New Int Greek Test Com], 1993), p.268.

Part of being like other humans "in every respect" entails experiencing the anguish of the genuine pull of temptation: a conflict, in psychological terms, between immediate wishes generated by objects of desire and the constraint of character which diverts the will to long-term faithfulness to established purposes. The reality of this experience in the narrative of the experience of Jesus is underlined, for example, in Heb. 2:17, 18; 4:15, and 5:2, but most especially in 4:15. Bruce endorses an illuminating comment from Westcott: "Sympathy with the sinner in his trial does not depend on the experience of sin but in the experience of the strength of the temptation to sin which only the sinless can know in its full intensity. He who falls yields before the last strain."[44]

III
Humanness in Hebrews: A Way of Approach to Pilgrimage and Covenant Faithfulness

The portrayal of Jesus as the paradigm-case of what it is to be human explains much about the remaining themes and arguments of the Epistle to the Hebrews: "The stress on Jesus' full humanity makes it necessary to prove that he is superior to Moses, since Moses was admitted to be superior to all other men."[45] This view was clearly held by Philo and by Josephus, among others (for example, Philo, *Vita Mos* II:2:3, 187: Josephus, *Ant* IV:8:49). The central issue, however, concerns the status and role of Jesus Christ as *representative high priest and mediator*. This carries numerous entailments for our notion of the human.

In Western traditions, especially in those which combine secular value-systems with vestiges of religions, it is often assumed that human beings have a natural right to approach God. Indeed, in the context of the problem of evil, if God appears to be remote, God is "blamed" for a supposed lack of active presence. Yet in the Epistle to the Hebrews, humankind is portrayed as persons for whom an invitation *to approach* the holy God *with frank boldness* (4:16, Greek, *proserchometha meta parrēsias*) depends on the perfect, once-for-all (Greek, *ephapax*) completed work of a fully qualified high-priestly mediator. Such is the holiness of God and the creaturely, finite fallenness of humankind, that *to approach* requires one who will "stand between in the middle" (Greek, *mesitēs* 8:6; 9:15) to open the way of approach into the "sanctuary" of the holy divine presence. To be sure, God in grace has "appointed" this means of access. Indeed for Christ, or for any mediator, to achieve valid mediation, *appointment* is essential (5:5, 6: 6:13–20; 7:17–25; 8:3–6; 9:11–14; 10:4–10). This is one of several reasons why the irrevocable priestly commission of the Melchizedek figure drawn from Ps. 110:4 (cf. Gen. 14:17–21) and probably also from first-century Judaism features with prominence (5:6; 7:1–19).

Furthermore, in contrast to human instability and human tendencies to "drift" without anchorage (2:1–4; cf. 6:19), Jesus is the mediator of the new covenant promised in Jer. 31 (8:6–13; 10:16–18). Jesus ratifies and actualizes the covenant by his own self-offering in fulfilment of a final, complete, finished work of atonement (9:6–28), offered *once-for-all*

---

[44] B.F. Westcott, *Epistle to the Hebrews* (London: Macmillan, 1892); endorsed by F.F. Bruce, *The Epistle to the Hebrews* (London: Marshall, Morgan & Scott, 1964), p.86.

[45] H.W. Montefiore, *The Epistle to the Hebrews* (London: Black, 1964), p.71.

(*hapax*, 9:26, cf. 10:1–14). To act effectively as mediator of salvation, however, Jesus Christ represents God to humankind and humankind to God. On one side, as "descending" mediator Christ is the *exact imprint of God's very being* (1:3) and God's *mirror* or *radiance* (Greek, *apaugasma* 1:3). In Jüngel's suggestive phrase, through Christ God becomes "thinkable" or "conceivable" for humans.[46] On the other side, only as humankind, as God intended humankind to be (to which Ps. 8:4 and other Old Testament passages serve as pointers), does Jesus represent human beings "as faithful high priest to make sacrifice and atonement for the sins of the people" (2:12).

This Christological paradigm of humanness, now gives an unexpected turn to the language of Ps. 8:6: "Thou hast given him dominion over the works of thy hands", and Ps. 110:1, 6: "Sit at my right hand until I make your enemies your footstool ... He will execute judgment ...". As Moltmann observes, the "dominion" of the Son of Man in Daniel 7 is not like that of oppressive empires, monsters, "usurpers in animal form". The Son of Man, unlike the brute force of the monsters, does not rise from chaos but [like Jesus in Hebrews] comes from God. The Son of Man reveals "humanity ... not then an ideal superman who makes an end of misery with violence which creates a new misery ... He receives the lost and accepts the untouchable ... It is the suffering figure of the crucified Jesus ... In the Christian faith man discovers his humanity ... life means being able to love ...".[47] Indeed in Hebrews *dominion* over every obstacle to "*entry into*" the inner presence of God is achieved through *the acceptance of constraints*: covenant, which limits autonomy by faithfulness; the way of love. Here we see both Barth's "Man for God" and Bonhoeffer's "Man for Others": if "others" are so loved as to be "gift" not "claim" then, Bonhoeffer observes "this tension between being *isolated* and being *bound* to others is abolished" in Christ's paradigm of human being.[48]

The imagery of *entering into* or *approaching* is pilgrimage image, as Robert Jewett, among others, has forcefully argued. Hence humanness in Hebrews entails not only *relationality with God and with brothers and sisters* (2:11, 17), but also the emergence of human identity and character within the setting and framework of time and temporality. Awaiting God's promise may demand patience on an individual and corporate scale (11:1–39). It requires "*running with perseverance* (or with *patience*) *the race that is set before us*" (12:2). Jesus is two or three times portrayed as *pioneer* (*archegos*) or *trailblazer* of humankind (2:10; 12:2) who goes ahead into the holy of holies of God's most intimate presence. But even Jesus, as the paradigm or supreme model, journeys through constraints to the ultimate sanctified "perfection" of his high-priestly role.

Robert Jewett's study *Letter to Pilgrims* implicitly recognizes that a temporal construal of the contrast and continuity between God and humankind excludes a two-storey dualism of "above" and "below", and locates renewed humanness within the everyday hurly-burly of life. Jewett alludes to Käsemann's interpretation of Hebrews as conceiving "of the Christian life as a journey to the heavenly homeland".[49] But Käsemann diminishes

---

46   E. Jüngel, *God as the Mystery of the World* (Eng., Edinburgh: T. & T. Clark, 1983), pp.152–68.

47   Moltmann, *Man* (cited above), pp.111, 113, 114 and 117.

48   D. Bonhoeffer, *Sanctorum Communio* (London: SCM, 1963), p.106; cf. Barth, *CD* III:2:44.

49   Robert Jewett. *Letter to Pilgrims: A Commentary on the Epistle to the Hebrews* (New York: Pilgrim Press, 1981), p.12. Cf. E. Käsemann, *The Wandering People of God* (Minneapolis, MN: Augsburg, 1984).

this otherwise valid insight by postulating the readers' belief in gnostic theologies of evil cosmic powers which threaten this wilderness pilgrimage, and an alternative emphasis on the immediate presence of God. Pilgrimage is a fundamental dimension of temporal narrative experience, within which human identity, character and maturity (*teleiosis*) emerge. The addressees were immature to the point of remaining unfit for adult nourishment (6:11–14). Jewett observes, "The Christ of Hebrews is daringly re-interpreted as the one who redeems his pilgrim community by sharing the conditions of pilgrimage and insecurity."[50] All the more, therefore, human *relationality* must be "anchored" by covenant faithfulness, whether it is in loyalty to one's church (10:23–5); loyalty in marriage (13:4); loyalty to leaders (13:12), or loyalty in the faith (6:4–8, 19; 10:16–38; 12:1, 2: 13:13–16). Christian character and *identity* entail coherent patterns over *time*.

The unfolding of a purposive history of the prophets (1:1–4), Moses and Joshua (3:1–4:10), the Psalmists (Ps. 8:4–6; 40:6–8; 95:7–11, and 104:4; cf. Heb. 2:3–9; 2:17, 18; 3:12, 13, 18; 4:9; 5:1–10; 7:13–25; 8:6; 10:5); the heroes of faith (11:1–39); the temporal life of Jesus (2:5–18; 4:15; 5:7–10; 10:5–10; 12:2–4), and the pilgrimage of God's people (also 13:4) provides a frame of reference within which we may speak, in the terminology of Hans Frei, of the "unsubstitutable individuality of Jesus with the presence of God" and of "public history" as an "intention-action pattern" within which humanness displays temporality and relationality with others.[51] This perspective differs radically from that of Philo, whose conceptual influence many seek to find in this epistle. Ronald Williamson rejects the force of this argument in his detailed critique, mainly on the basis of their respectively different views of time and eschatology.[52] Hebrews knows nothing of a timeless realm of archetypes or Ideal Forms, unrelated to temporal life. C.K. Barrett insists that in Hebrews the difference between humanity and God is "not the difference between the phenomena of sense-perception and pure being, but the difference between holiness and sin ... Jesus is ... an actor in the eschatological drama of redemption rather than ... standing between the real and phenomenal worlds".[53]

Yet Hebrews has too often been wrongly regarded as an idiosyncratic strand of liturgical theology within the New Testament. We need now to test the respective perceptions of what it is to be human that we find in Western traditions and in other strands of the New Testament. We select a major Pauline epistle that also makes much of time and temporality, namely 1 Corinthians.

---

[50] Jewett, *Letter*, p.13.
[51] Hans W. Frei, *The Identity of Jesus Christ* (Philadelphia, PA: Fortress, 1995), pp.154 and 161.
[52] R. Williamson, *Philo and the Epistle to the Hebrews* (Leiden: Brill, 1970), pp.95–103 and 142–59.
[53] C.K. Barrett, "The Eschatology of the Epistle to the Hebrews", in W.D. Davies and D. Daube (eds), *The Background of the NT and its Eschatology: in Honour of C.H. Dodd* (Cambridge: CUP, 1956), pp.388 and 389; cf. pp.363–93.

IV

Humanness, Relationality and Time: Some Anthropological Terms in 1 Corinthians

Two of the principles under discussion remain decisive for our understanding of 1 Corinthians. First, Christ and the cross constitute what Schrage terms "the basis and criterion" for both the Corinthian community and for the apostle.[54] An exploration of passages reveals that, as in Hebrews, Christ is perceived as the paradigm-case of what it is to be authentically human. Second, a temporal dynamic runs throughout this epistle. Paul writes to the addressees as those who still eagerly *await* (Greek, *apekdechomenous*) the *apokalypsis* of Christ (1:7), and whose salvation be complete at the end *(heōs telous), at the day of the Lord* (1:8).[55] The gospel is God's power to us who are *on the way to salvation* (present ptc. *sōzomenois*, 1:19). The Corinthian Christians are *still unspiritual (eti gar sarkikoi este,* 3:3). Life is perceived as a steady process of *building* and *growing,* as against the manipulation of supposedly instant stature by *self-inflation* (3:4–15; 5:2; 8:1: *oikodomō,* 3:10, 8:1; *physiō,* 8:1).[56] It is false for the addressees to imply that they are *already glutted, enriched* and *"reigning"*; Paul wishes, in a way, that this were so (4:8).[57] We shall note further examples.

The first and the second of these principles come together transparently in the resurrection chapter. Christ is the "first fruits" *(aparche),* the first sample sheaf of the harvest to come which will constitute restored humanity (15: 20, 23). Thus "just as we have borne the image *(eikōn)* of the one created from 'dust', so *we shall bear* (see textual note) *the image of the [man] from heaven" (ten eikona tou epouraniou,* 15:49).[58]

The destiny of restored humanness is expressed through the concept of a *sōma* (or "somatic" mode of existence) which has exchanged *decay* or declining capacities *(phthora), dishonour* associated with self-centred action, ineffectiveness or *weakness,* and *ordinary life-force (sōma psychikon),* for the reversal of laws of decline *(aphtharsia),* restored *glory,* operational effectiveness *(dynamis),* and a mode of being entirely characterized by the presence and operation of the Holy Spirit *(sōma pneumatikon;* 1 Cor. 15:42–44). However, as in 2:6–16; 6:11; 11:23–31; 12:3; 12:12–27 and elsewhere, Paul defines being "of the Spirit" or "spirituality" in terms of Christ and Christlikeness. He is *ho eschatos Adam* (15:45).

It is an axiom of Pauline studies, however, that notions or definitions of the human in Paul cannot be interpreted on the basis of any single anthropological term in abstraction from others. Robert Jewett once again (see above on Hebrews) has contributed a masterly study which not only traces the vicissitudes of histories of research on Paul's anthropological terms, but also proves the importance of close attention to varied contexts for exegesis.[59] Jewett's study concentrates on a semantic spread of seven terms

---

[54] Wolfgang Schrage, *Der erste Brief an die Korinther* (4 vols, Zürich: Benziger and Neukirchen-Vluyn: Neukirchener [EKK, vii], 1991–2005), I, p.165; cf. pp.165–203.

[55] P. von der Osten-Sacken, "Gottes Treue bis zur Parusie ... 1 Kor 1:7b–9", *ZNW* 68 (1977), pp.176–99.

[56] Ingrid Kitzberger, *Bau der Gemeinde: Das paulinische Wortfeld Oikodomè/(ep)oikodomein* (Würzberg: Echter, 1986), esp. pp.64–72.

[57] A.C. Thiselton, "Realized Eschatology at Corinth", *NTS* 24 (1978), pp.510–26.

[58] "B" reads the future indicative that is followed by UBS Greek 4th edn. This is defended by B.M. Metzger, *A Textual Commentary on the Greek New Testament* (2nd edn, Stuttgart: UBS, 1994), p.502, who emphasizes the didactic rather than hortatory character of these versions. This may be right, but p[46], A, Sinaiticus and D read the aorist subjunctive.

[59] Robert Jewett, *Paul's Anthropological Terms. A Study of their Use in Conflict Settings* (Leiden: Brill, 1971).

and their history of interpretation: the human *pneuma*, *sōma*, *kardia*, *psychē*, *nous*, *exo/eso anthropos* and *syneidēsis*. We shall argue several points about these various terms, in as far as this assists us to address the question "What is a Human?" primarily in 1 Corinthians but also with wider reference to Paul and similarities with, and differences from, major Western traditions concerning the human.

(i) Paul does not primarily set *pneuma* (spirit) and *sōma* (body) or even *pneuma* and *sarx* (often rendered *flesh*) in the kind of contrast that closely resembles the mind–body dualism of eternal mind and sensuous matter found in Plato or in the "ghost in the machine" of Cartesian thought. Whether Paul speaks of the human spirit or the Spirit of God, Bultmann rightly asserts, "*Pneuma* does not mean 'spirit' in the Greek-Platonic and the idealist sense, i.e. it does not mean mind in contrast to body (regarded as the vehicle of sensuous life)."[60] We may concede that Robert Gundry is also correct in identifying passages where such a contrast does exist to make a specific point within a given context.[61] It would be false to claim that Paul consistently avoids any hint of anthropological dualism at every single point. Nevertheless, as J.N. Sevenster insists, to try to argue from such a passage as 1 Thess. 5:23 (where Paul speaks of *body*, *soul* and *spirit*), whether his view of human persons is "dichotomous or trichotomous" is entirely to miss Paul's point.[62] I am not making a statement about human nature when I tell an underperforming student to put their heart and soul into their dissertation.

In 1 Corinthians the use of adjectival forms, *sarkikos*, *sarkinos*, *psychikos* and *pneumatikos* especially in 1 Cor. 3:1–4 make it abundantly clear that Paul uses these forms to denote *modes of being* or a variety of *disposition* or *stances* that human beings may adopt. A *sarkikos* person is characterized by self-concern and self-centredness; a *psychikos* human is one who does not seem to show concern for the things of the Holy Spirit, but simply lives life (*psychē*) as it comes; a *pneumatikos* person is motivated and characterized by the presence and shaping of the Holy Spirit of God (2:14–3:4). Since *psychē* is the animating life of creation, a *psychikos* person is one who has merely human aspirations and values, as against those prompted by the Holy Spirit.[63] Further, *psychē* in the NT often reflects Semitic poetic parallelism, just as in many liturgies today "The Lord be with you" invites the parallel "And with your spirit", that is, "and with you".

(ii) Whereas *sarx* (and often *psychē*) regularly denotes a human person in his or her individuality or even (in the case of *sarx*) self-absorbed self-centredness, *sōma* regularly denotes human beings in the context of their *relationality* to others, both in terms of *reciprocity* and *time*. Although I cannot recover the precise reference, I believe that it was Paul Feine who most widely propagated the pernicious notion that since neither Hebrew

---

[60] Rudolf Bultmann, *Theology of the NT* (Eng., 2 vols, London: SCM, 1952 and 1955), I, p.153; cf. pp.204–10.

[61] R.H. Gundry, *Soma in Biblical Theology with Emphasis on Pauline Anthropology* (Cambridge: CUP [SNTS Mon Ser 29], 1976).

[62] J.N. Sevenster, *Paul and Seneca* (Leiden: Brill [Nov T Suppl 4], 1961), p.64.

[63] Cf. B.A. Pearson, *The Pneumatikos-Psychikos Terminology in 1 Corinthians* (Missoula, MT: Scholars Press [SBL Diss Ser 12], 1973), and R.A. Horsley, "Pneumatikos vs. Psychikos: Distinctions of Spiritual Status among the Corinthians", *HTR* 69 (1976), pp.269–88.

nor Greek possesses a term that fully corresponds with the more modern concept of *a person*, the Greeks and Hebrews could not conceive of human beings as *persons* in "our" sense of the word. As long ago as 1961 James Barr put an end to such nonsense by demonstrating that the capacity to understand or to use a given *concept* did not depend on the existence of a corresponding *word* in a given vocabulary stock.[64] Writing nearly ten years before Barr's book, J.A.T. Robinson observes, "*Sōma* is the nearest equivalent to our word 'personality'."[65]

By contrast, however, human beings viewed as *sarx* are those who *de-personalize* themselves by regarding the self as a mere tool or instrument for self-gratification. We may readily grant that Paul uses the noun *sarx* to denote a wide range of nuances. Thus in 1 Cor. 1:26 Paul asks how many Christians at Corinth had status or influence *kata sarka*, that is, in accordance with the generally accepted criteria of Graeco-Roman society. Sometimes he borrows the Septuagintal phrase *pasa sarx* to denote a mass of all kinds of people (1:29). On occasion, also notably when he borrows from the OT *sarx mia*, one flesh, may denote the intimate relationality of a sexual relationship (6:16). But in its adjectival form (3:1; 3:3) the word denotes the individual self-seeking which reveals not concern for the other, but jealousy, strife and status-seeking for the individual self at the expense of others. This coheres well with passages in which *sarx* denotes "human self-sufficiency (2 Cor. 3:5, 6)".[66] Bultmann describes its most distinctively theological use in Paul as denoting "the self-reliant attitude of the man who puts his trust in his own strength and in that which is *controllable* by him" (my italics) while Robinson links *sarx* in Paul with the notion of "distance" from God, to which we might add, in a social and ethical sense, also distance from others.[67]

By contrast, *sōma* heightens the personal dignity and agency of human beings by viewing them under the aspect of their *relationality* to other persons and also to others in time. This entails far more than what Robinson implies when he discusses human "solidarity", or Bultmann's view of *sōma* as "man's relation to himself", which misses Paul's main point.[68] In this respect Gundry is wholly justified in attacking Bultmann's view as inadequate. However, where Gundry tends to stress the physical dimension as such, Käsemann more acutely perceives that through his use of *sōma* Paul denotes *human beings in terms of their actions, especially communicative actions in the public domain and in relation to others*. This interaction in the spatial and temporal dimensions of the everyday world would *define a human being as having temporally significant responsibility for the disposition, public stance and action for which he or she is accountable in the future*, as having a *history within a community* of other human persons which allows for *address and response in reciprocity*, and also a *destiny* in which love for others does not become obsolete (cf. 1 Cor. 13:9–13).

Käsemann therefore defines *sōma* as "that piece of the world which we ourselves are and for which we have responsibility".[69] We must not interpret *sōma* from the standpoint

---

64 J. Barr, *The Semantics of Biblical Language* (London: OUP, 1961), pp.226–46.
65 J.A.T. Robinson, *The Body: A Study in Pauline Theology* (London: SCM, 1952), p.28.
66 Robinson, *The Body*, p.25.
67 Bultmann, *Theology of the NT*, I, p.240; cf. pp.232–46; and Robinson, *The Body*, p.19.
68 Robinson, *The Body*, p.8; and Bultmann, *Theology of the NT*, I, pp.195–66.
69 E. Käsemann, *New Testament Questions of Today* (Eng., London: SCM, 1969), p.135.

of the individual, but as a human person in the everyday world of relationships "in his ability to communicate", and in the public domain. He continues, "In the bodily obedience of the Christian, carried out in the world of everyday, the lordship of Christ finds visible expression."[70] Thereby, Käsemann concludes, the Gospel acquires credibility.

V
Anthropological Terms in the Light of Claims for "My Rights" at Corinth

All this stands in the sharpest possible contrast to demands for "autonomy" and "status" at Corinth. A flood of recent research literature since 1990 has underlined the competitive individualism that beset the church at Corinth as "status-hungry people".[71] Many at Corinth perceived human lives as instruments for the achievement of status, self-fulfilment and self-gratification. The tragedy of Corinth was that these secular de-personalizing values entered the church as part of a supposedly "religious" right to freedom. The Corinthian slogan, often translated "all things are lawful" (1 Cor. 6:12; 10:23) turned on the relation between the verbal form of the Greek *exesti* (it is permitted) and the cognate noun *exousia* (*authority* or *right*). Hence the slogan is about the *individual right to choose*, regardless of consequences for others. It is best translated: *I have the right to anything; or, I have the right to do what I like.*[72] It thus represents the de-personalized reversal of what characterizes human beings as *sōma*, let alone as *to sōma tou Christou*. Indeed this individualism causes *splits* (*schismata*) in the one body of the community (1:10–12). Individualist believers perceived "leaders" as individuals around whom to gather.[73]

A list of specific case studies demonstrates some of the issues. *The right to choose* a person's own "private" sexual boundaries (1 Cor. 5–6) results in tearing apart members or *limbs* which form part of Christ's own body (1 Cor. 6:15–20). *The right to choose* whether to eat things sacrificed to idols actually inflicts pain and damage on the self-awareness (*syneidēsis*) of certain fellow-believers (1 Cor. 8:8–13; 10:23–29a) turns others into secondary objects in relation to the self. Claims to go it alone in hosting the Lord's Supper (11:17–32), to reject a reciprocity and differentiated complementarity of gender (11:1–16), or to lavish praise upon the most self-advertising spiritual gifts (12:4–14:40), all serve to bring about a reversal of the *relationality of soma*, entails especially when Christ and the cross constitutes "the basis and criterion" of humans as individuals and as community.

---

[70] Ibid.

[71] This excellent descriptive phrase comes from Ben Witherington III, *Conflict and Community at Corinth. A Socio-Rhetorical Commentary on 1 & 2 Corinthians* (Grand Rapids, MI: Eerdmans and Carlisle: Paternoster, 1995), p.24 (see pp.19–48 *et passim*), cf. further e.g. S.M. Pogoloff, *Logos and Sophia. The Rhetorical Situation of 1 Corinthians* (Atlanta, GA: Scholars Press [SBL Diss 134], 1992), pp.97–236; A.D. Clarke, *Secular and Christian Leadership in Corinth* (Leiden: Brill, 1993), pp.23–134; and T.B. Savage, *Power through Weakness* (Cambridge: CUP [SNTS Mon 86], 1996), pp.19–53 and 130–63; among others.

[72] A.C. Wire, *The Corinthian Women Prophets: A Reconstruction of Paul's Rhetoric* (Minneapolis, MN: Fortress, 1990), p.13 supports this approach, but her sympathies are with the (women) prophets' demand for freedom, not with Paul's "authoritarian patriarchy".

[73] On this aspect cf M.M. Mitchell, *Paul and the Rhetoric of Reconciliation: An Exegetical Investigation of the Language and Composition of 1 Corinthians* (Louisville, KY: Westminster/Knox, 1992), esp. pp.66–9.

In any case, Paul adds, "autonomy", in the sense claimed at Corinth (and subsequently also in the individualism of Enlightenment rationalism) is illusory. For underlying every human stance and every human attempt at self-evaluation, lie *the secrets of the heart* (4:3–5), so that Paul refrains from assessing even his own progress (4:3). *Self-awareness* or "conscience" (*syneidēsis*) can be damaged (8:12) and operates only in context-relative ways (8:7–13; 10:23–30).[74] Whereas *knowledge (gnosis)* may seem to enhance humanness by appearing to accord *instrumental control and status to the individual self*, in Paul's view *inter-subjective concern for the other in relational terms*, that is, *love*, constitutes the one stable and abiding dimension of human life which never becomes obsolete in any context (8:1–13; 13:1–13, esp. 13:4–13). This principle controls his pastoral concern over the view of spiritual gifts (12:4; 14:40): "Those who speak in a tongue 'build up' themselves, but those who prophesy (that is, speak an address from God) 'build up' the church" (14:4). *Relationality* concerns reciprocity between a human being and others; *time* concerns the unwillingness to take short-cuts to supposedly instant "success", rather than a thoughtful, patient progress to adulthood (14:20; cf. 13:4).

(iii) The point made above in terms of a contrast between the adjectives *sarkikos-sarkinos* and *sōma* is brilliantly pressed by Paul Gardner in his account of the relation between *syneidēsis* and *gnosis* in 8:1–11:1. The quasi "gnostic" emphasis on "knowledge" fostered a "self-centred theology" at Corinth.[75] Being "puffed up" (8:1) "involves a flaunting of something for one's own benefit ... Paul contrasted love ...".[76] Moreover the issue in these chapters is not "moral" conscience, but on how the behaviour of the self-centred generates a feeling of low self-esteem in the "self-awareness" of the "weak": a *lack of relational concern* by the "strong" damaged the self-perceptions (not primarily sense of guilt) of *the vulnerable and insecure*.[77] The vulnerable were manipulated, and therefore de-humanized, by "the strong". In seeking to promote their own claims to be "mature and knowledgeable human beings", the influential or (socially) "strong" thereby diminished the humanness of all.[78]

Although in a number of contexts in Paul *syneidēsis* may denote pain consequent upon a stance or action which stands in conflict with a human person's "better judgement", two points should be emphasized. First, the findings of "conscience" or "self-awareness" always remain relative to the standards or norms that the self has assimilated: second, *syneidēsis*, especially in 1 Corinthians, means both more and also less than "moral conscience". It has to do with *self-awareness* or *self-perceptions that can either hinder or nurture human relationality with other persons and with God*. A "good conscience" will encourage an outgoing concern for others; a bad or damaged self-awareness brings

---

[74] P.W. Gooch, "'Conscience' in 1 Corinthians 8 and 10", *NTS* 33 (1987), pp.244–54; Khiok-khing Yeo, *Rhetorical Interaction in 1 Cor 8 and 10* (Leiden: Brill [Bib Int Ser 9], 1995), pp.76–211; H.-J. Eckstein, *Der Begriff Syneidèsis bei Paulus* (Tübingen: Mohr, 1983).

[75] P.D. Gardner, *The Gifts of God and the Authentication of a Christian: An Exegetical Study of 1 Cor 8–11:1* (Lanham, MD: University Press of America, 1994), p.5.

[76] Ibid., p.31.

[77] Ibid., pp.45–8: a considerable measure of support can be found in Gooch and Yeo, cited above.

[78] On "the strong" see also G. Theissen, *The Social Setting of Pauline Christianity* (Eng., Philadelphia, PA: Fortress, 1982), pp.121–44; cf. T. Söding, "Starke ... in 1 Kor 8–10 ...", *ZNW* 85 (1994), pp.69–142.

inhibition, timidity, withdrawal and thereby defensiveness and perhaps eventually neurotic aggression. Paul is aware of the part played by *syneidēsis* in understanding what it is to be human, and he firmly addresses the issues.

(iv) The ease with which self-perception can be distorted by self-deception emerges forcefully from another important anthropological term in 1 Corinthians. The word *kardia*, heart, occurs only five times in this epistle (2:9; 4:5; 7:37 [twice]; 14:25). Typically 4:5 alludes to the hidden *motivation (tas boulas)* of the human heart, while 14:25 speaks of *secrets (ta krypta)* of the heart. These passages emphasize not only that *fallibility* is part of humanness, but also that *self-deception* plays its part. Only when the Lord comes will these hidden things beneath the surface be exposed and explained as what they are. Hence Paul quite explicitly underlines the role of *time* as part of the human process: "Do not pronounce judgements on anything before the proper time, until the Lord comes, who will shed light upon the hidden things of darkness and will disclose the hidden motivations of our lives" (*kardia*, 4:5).

Gerd Theissen's incisive *Psychological Aspects of Pauline Theology* demands our attention here. Although many years earlier Bultmann had compared the Greek *kardia* in Paul (like *lēb* in Hebrew) to the human unconscious, in Theissen this becomes a detailed and major theme.[79] It well matches the parallelism in 2:9 with "the depths": a human being cannot fully know his or her own innermost motivations; even so the penetrating, sifting work of the Holy Spirit alone penetrates the divine "depths" (*ta bathe tou Theou*, 2:10). In 7:37 a carefully sifted decision remains "firm" because it involves the *kardia* as well as emotion, whim, idea, constraint, or any merely superficial aspect of human consciousness alone. 4:1–5 provides the most decisive passage. Theissen observes, "Even this claim of innocence contains the acceptance of possible unconscious guilt ... But he [Paul] is convinced that these unconscious intentions can no longer existentially endanger him in the judgement ... *Paul no longer experienced the relationship of consciousness and the unconscious as a contradiction* ... the unconscious is that which no human court – not even one's own conscience – can bring to light but which is revealed only in the divine judgement" (my italics).[80] Theissen's judicious discussion of glossolalia as the welling-up of unconscious longings would take us beyond the boundaries of our present study.[81]

(v) The remaining anthropological term which sheds light on the human in 1 Corinthians is *nous*, mind (1 Cor. 1:10; 2:16; 14:14, 15, 19). 1:10 simply conveys the idea of *stance, attitude*, or *outlook*, and this is probably also the main thrust of *the mind of Christ* in 2:16. Robert Jewett shows in his masterly review of the history of research on this subject that, depending on the context in Paul, *nous* varies the emphasis across a spectrum from *outlook* or constellation of belief to a more rational or intellectual focus. Here 1 Cor. 14:14–19 provides an admirable model for Jewett's claims about the role of "conflict settings". He observes, "The anti-enthusiastic intention of 'mind' in this context is

---

[79] Bultmann, *Theology of the NT*, I, pp.223–4 and G. Theissen, *Psychological Aspects of Pauline Theology* (Eng., Edinburgh: T. & T. Clark, 1987), esp. pp.59–80 and 179–341.

[80] Ibid., pp.61, 63.

[81] Ibid., esp. pp.303 and 41.

unmistakable."[82] The ultra-enthusiasts verged on the belief that the blotting out of the intellectual or rational could constitute a sign of the "spiritual". As Jewett demonstrates, this was a common assumption in certain first-century Hellenistic religious circles (cf. Philo, *Quis rerum heres* 263 ff.): in contrast, Paul insists that the mind must play its part if "spirituality" is to serve the relational dimension of building up others, rather than as individualist self-centred experience (14:15–17 in relation to 14:4, "those who speak in a tongue build up themselves"). Elsewhere I have argued that in 14:13 Paul urges that the one who prays in tongues should pray for the ability to express these pre-conscious yearnings in articulate speech when the context is a public one.[83]

Nous does call attention to human rationality and reason in Paul, but only in specific contexts. Jewett readily shows, for example, that fanatical or "enthusiastic" claims about the arrival of the Parousia in 2 Thess. 2:2 are countered by plain appeal to rational common-sense reflection.[84] However, Paul nowhere associates mind or reason with a "higher" element or aspect of humanness. As Bornkamm and Stacey long ago argued, reason is an important human capacity which of itself can be used to promote good or evil, but with a renewed orientation constitutes a fundamental resource for human good and responsible living.[85] As Bornkamm and Pannenberg note, Paul frequently uses *argument* that addresses *the mind*; his style is "not that of revelation-speech".[86] All the claims that we considered in the first section from Augustine, Thomas Aquinas and others about "reason" and the image of God prove to depend on human relationality to God in Christ.

VI
Concluding Remarks: 1 Cor. 12–15 and the Human in Modernity/Postmodernity

The patterns which we have traced in Hebrews and in 1 Corinthians portray humanness as reaching its divinely-purposed form only in relation to God and to others, and as a personal identity that acquires character and maturity as it accepts the constraints of life and its opportunities for renewal and growth through a narrative history of relations with God and with others through time. These patterns know nothing of any sharp dualism between body and soul, although the psychosomatic unity of human beings is revealed and takes shape through bodily interaction in the public domain. Although a dialectic emerges between freedom and constraint, this has nothing in common with a Kantian and Corinthian deification of human autonomy, which in the case of the addressees in Hebrews led merely to drifting and to the danger of sitting loose to covenant faithfulness and to promise in various areas of life.

Yet a rejection of the autonomous individualism of Kant and the Enlightenment should not push us in the opposite direction, where the optimism of individualistic modernity,

---

[82] Jewett, *Paul's Anthropological Terms*, p.378; cf. pp.358–67 and 375–84.

[83] A.C. Thiselton, "The 'Interpretation' of Tongues? A New Suggestion in the Light of Greek Usage in Philo and Josephus", *JTS* 30 (1979), pp.15–36, and Essay 16 above.

[84] Jewett, *Paul's Anthropological Terms*, pp.367–9.

[85] G. Bornkamm, "Faith and Reason in Paul", in *Early Christian Experience* (Eng., London: SCM, 1969), pp.29–46; W.D. Stacey, *The Pauline View of Man* (London: Macmillan, 1956), pp.198–206.

[86] Bornkamm, loc. cit., p.36.

with its obsession about "my rights to choose", becomes transposed into the pessimism of secular postmodernity where the self is perceived as little more than a social construct, a victim whose capacities and expectations are determined by the power and politics of gender, race, guild and every competing peer-group in a pluralist society. In postmodernity there is little danger of over-stressing human rationality as distinctively human. Reason is dissolved into rhetoric, and dialogue becomes manipulative power-play. In the face of this, those resources of the biblical and Christian traditions which do call attention to the importance of mind, reason and the power of the self to shape its environment in active trust rather than passive cynicism may be called for once again.

1 Cor. 12–15 offers an especially prophetic word to this interplay in the battle between secular modernity, with its deification of individual autonomy, and secular postmodernity, with its deification of social construction and pluralism. 1 Cor. 12–14 represents a subtle dialectic between the individual and the community as "members" of Christ's own body (*sōma*). Paul portrays this relationality as one in which the weak and vulnerable are respected and valued, not exploited as mere objects to serve the status and power-play of the strong. Indeed no group or individual can say of those whom it deems to be "weak", "I have no need of you ..." (12:20, 21). Nor, on the other hand, should the supposedly less gifted ever be permitted to feel that they do not "belong" to the body. Moltmann writes of the mentally or physically handicapped as having a "charisma" to offer to others, by revealing God's strength in weakness, which we cannot do without.[87] In opposition to Sartre's famous phrase ("hell is other people"), "hell" is to be isolated: from God and from others. This indeed is loss of humanness. So no one should say, "Because I am not the hand, I do not belong to the body" (12:15, 16). Here Christian love opposes both the elitism of the individual-centred self of modernity, and the obsession with race, gender, class and guild, which builds self-protective barriers for peer-groups amidst the pluralism and social constructivism of postmodernity.

In the end, as 1 Cor. 15 reminds us, it is God alone who determines "what kind of body" (*sōma*) he chooses to give (15:38). God raises a corporate "body" of which Christ is the first fruits or sample (15:23), but also places dignity and value on the differentiation that characterizes the creation of species and individuals within the created order: "There is one glory of the sun, and another glory of the moon, and another glory of the stars, and star differs from star in glory" (15:41). Meanwhile, prior to this end-time, human judgements about what is most "glorious" about specific individuals or groups remain fallible and open to revision in the light of the last judgement (4:1–5). Although humanness will reach its Christ-like goal at the end-time, even the supposedly "weak", the deprived, despised, or handicapped still belong to the *sōma* of humanity as Paul, and recently Moltmann, remind us. However, neither Hebrews nor 1 Corinthians places the human in a static frame without reference to time and to change: "We shall bear *the image of the man from heaven* ... We shall all be *changed* ..." (15:49, 51). The disposition which will for ever nurture *continuing relationality* is *love* (13:8–13).[88]

---

[87]   J. Moltmann, The *Source of Life: The Holy Spirit and the Theology of Life* (Eng., London: SCM, 1997), p.67.

[88]   The themes of this last section are developed in A.C. Thiselton, *Interpreting God and the Postmodern Self. On Meaning, Manipulation and Promise* (Grand Rapids, MI: Eerdmans and Edinburgh: T. & T. Clark, 1995).

CHAPTER FORTY

Dialogue, Dialectic and Temporal Horizons: "Polyphonic Voices and Theological Fiction" and "Temporal Horizons in Hermeneutics" (1999)

This extract brings together two closely related sections from The Promise of Hermeneutics *(Grand Rapids, MI: Eerdmans and Carlisle: Paternoster, 1999), pp.171–82 (sections I and II below), and 183–99 (sections III and IV, with some omissions). After noting the formative value of fiction for human transformation, this essay explores three examples of the role of "polyphonic voices": the* Book of Job, *George Eliot's* Adam Bede, *and Dostoevsky's novel* The Brothers Karamazov. *When biblical or theological reflection concerns such a complex theme as the problem of evil, language may need to burst though the confines of a single voice, to offer the process of a dialogue among multiple voices as the way to lead readers to wrestle with issues too deep for an easy or "packaged" response.*

The complexities of narrative time provide a parallel in the temporal domain. In many cases a simple, linear, chronological presentation of events in accordance with "natural" time reduces the impact and truth of a narrative as against restructuring it in accordance with narrative time to reveal its truth more clearly. This applies to texts as different from one another as detective stories and the Gospel of Mark. Finally, we revisit the reception theory of Jauss, but from a different angle and with a different agenda from our earlier discussions of Jauss in Essays 3 and 18. In order to explain these differences, I have included a paragraph written in 2004 at the beginning of section IV. Scarcely any overlap remains after some substantial editing.

I
Fictional Texts as "Productive" Texts

"Transmissive" texts reflect the interests of an information-driven culture, of which "engineering" is regarded as a paradigm. *To reread a "handbook" text* is simply to seek greater *clarity* concerning a *single, fully determinate meaning.* "Productive" texts, by contrast, reflect the interests of literary cultures. *To reread a "literary" text* is not always to seek clarity, but *resonances, inter-textual allusions, new perspectives, transformed horizons.* Here a solid contribution of biblical criticism, frequently too readily dismissed by some as destructive, is to force us to appreciate the *diversity of biblical texts and genres.* When the Reformers insisted on a meaning that was "single" or "plain", the context most regularly concerned issues of *transmission.* When mediaeval mystics contemplated distinctions between locutionary acts performed by biblical writers and further acts (of which these texts were instruments) that pertained to modes of living or to God's larger eschatological purposes, the focus of meditative contemplation was often *generative, productive, or poetic texts* such as those of the wisdom literature or apocalyptic. Yet even the four canonical Gospels are not all of a piece. Very often texts operate in multi-functional mixed modes.

Biblical *fiction* deserves special consideration because beyond question it has explicitly entered a domain foreign to the culture of the "engineer" *qua* engineer. Conservative writers are now far more open than was the case twenty years ago to recognize this distinction and even to identify as "literary" or "productive" texts those which an earlier generation insisted on reading as historical report. Thus Tremper Longman III writes in the Westminster Theological Seminary Symposium of 1988 entitled *Inerrancy and Hermeneutic* that the Book of Job contains "literary artifice", and that the Scriptures are "multi-functional". Standard conventions of literary production (for example, that "human" time may not correspond to astronomical or "natural" time, and that multiple "points of view" may underline different aspects of a narrative) are accepted as part and parcel of biblical narrative.[1] Sidney Greidanus rightly urges that in Job and in Jonah "the historical referent is *hermeneutically* inconsequential" (his italics), but that the historical referent of the Exodus narrative remains "indispensable".[2] These distinctions are not, as Frei might claim, mere social constructs of the eighteenth and nineteenth centuries; they are integral to issues of "authorial discourse" (Wolterstorff) or to what I call the "directedness" of the text.

The most striking examples of a "directed" textual generation of multiple reader-responses can be found in those texts that embody several "voices". In biblical hermeneutics we suggest the example of the Book of Job, while in the context of "theological" fictional texts we turn to Dostoevsky's *The Brothers Karamazov*, and then to George Eliot's *Adam Bede*. It is no accident that all three texts address the problem of intense human suffering, and the nature of evil, even if in very different ways.

II
Polyphonic Voices in Theological Fiction: Job, Eliot and Dostoevsky on the Problem of Evil

An important hermeneutical resource has been provided in more general terms by Terrence Tilley, who argues that the problem of evil cannot be addressed adequately or appropriately by any neatly packaged system of propositions designed merely to argue or to inform. Hence he entitles his book *The Evils of Theodicy*.[3] Tilley devotes the first part of his book (more than 80 pages) to an exposition of speech-act theory, including illocutionary acts of declaring, preaching, swearing, praying and confessing. He concludes that the great Christian literature that addresses the issues of evil and suffering does not function primarily as "assertives"; this is "read back" in the light of

---

[1] Tremper Longman in H.M. Conn (ed.), *Inerrancy and Hermeneutics* (Grand Rapids, MI: Baker, 1988), pp.137–49, esp. pp.140, 148, 149.

[2] S. Greidanus, *The Modern Preacher and the Ancient Text* (Leicester: IVP and Grand Rapids, MI: Eerdmans, 1988), pp.194 and 195.

[3] T.W. Tilley, *The Evils of Theodicy* (Washington, DC: Georgetown University Press, 1991).

"Enlightenment theism".[4] Indeed such reading *obscures* the writings: "Job ... cannot be taken as an assertive which conveys doctrines".[5]

Tilley further maintains, "Augustine did not write a theodicy. He wrote numerous works to various audiences, for various purposes, and with various illocutionary forces which touch on God and evils ... in various ways".[6] Typically, his *Confessions* perform confessional acts; while his early *On Free Will* and his later *The City of God* and anti-Pelagian writings perform a variety of defensive and polemical communicative acts. Against the Manichees, he defended the freedom of the will; against the Donatists, he called attention to habituated patterns in constraining human will and choice; against the Pelagians he urged that only grace could liberate a will under bondage.[7] But our concern at present is with fictional discourse. Tilley applies his speech-act theory not only to Job and to Augustine, but also to George Eliot's *Adam Bede*. I agree with Tilley that *Adam Bede* performs multiple communicative actions and it speaks with polyphonic voices. The same is to be said, following especially Malcolm Jones, about *The Brothers Karamazov*.

Amos Wilder notably urges that biblical speech performs a variety of linguistic acts. These include dialogue, narration, fictional parable, poetic discourse, exhortation, instruction, testimony, hymnic praise, confession, promise, letter writing and many others.[8] However, where *dialogue* is involved, this need not be the artificial dialogue between question and "answer". Gadamer repeatedly insists that in true dialogue something emerges which transcends the sum of the two individual standpoints initially represented, as the horizons of each expand to take respectful and listening account of the other.[9] Gadamer declares, "Conversation does not advance the view of one interlocutor against the view of another. Nor does conversation simply add the view of one to the view of another. The conversation alters both."[10] This Gadamerian theme is discussed and illuminated in detail by Hans Kögler.[11] If this is so, then it suggests that it may be a mistake to ask whether the Book of Job speaks through the "omniscient" narrator, or through one of the "friends", or through Job, or with or without a "happy-ending" postscript. As typical wisdom literature, the Book of Job, like Kierkegaard's interplay with his own pseudonymous texts, constitutes a *productive* text, which "speaks" *not through any one character or even narrator but in and through reading processes of wrestling with its plurality of voices.*

---

[4] Ibid., p.86.

[5] Ibid.

[6] Ibid., p.115.

[7] Tilley convincingly points out that the *Enchiridion* comes nearest to an open "assertive" or didactic mode of communicative action. Nevertheless many of the standard textbooks on the problem of evil abstract "doctrines" of freedom and of the nature of evil from situations in Augustine's works, and not surprisingly identify inconsistencies, cf. J. Hick, *Evil and the God of Love* (New York: Harper & Row, revd edn, 1978).

[8] A.N. Wilder, *Early Christian Rhetoric* (London: SCM, 1964); also as *The Language of the Gospel* (New York: Harper & Row, 1964), pp.26–62.

[9] H.-G. Gadamer, *Truth and Method* (2nd Eng. edn, London: Sheed & Ward, 1989), pp.362–80, and "Reflections on my Philosophical Journey", in Lewis Hahn (ed.), *The Philosophy of Hans-Georg Gadamer* (Chicago, IL: Open Court, 1997), pp.50–55.

[10] H.-G. Gadamer, *Gesammelte Werke II* (Tübingen: Mohr, 1986), p.188.

[11] H.H. Kögler, *The Power of Dialogue: Critical Hermeneutics after Gadamer and Foucault* (Cambridge, MA and London: MIT Press, 1996), esp. pp.1–56 and 113–58.

Admittedly, as David Clines argues, this text, probably above all other biblical texts, lends itself to deconstruction. The "doctrine" that God rewards those who do righteously is undermined by Job's experience. But, as Clines expresses it, here it does not help to "cure the problem of a dogma with another dogma".[12] Ricoeur, too, observes that the questions that Job asks in Job 42:1–6 are never "answered". The themes of wisdom literature emerge in "the limit-situations spoken of by Karl Jaspers ... solitude ... suffering and death".[13] But by definition a limit-situation unveils truth only to the person who experiences it. Thus any perspective which is more than individual can be produced only by many voices in dialogue, whether in harmony or dissonance. Deconstruction suggests a *serial* undermining of each voice by another. Hence, deconstruction would end not by multiple voices but in silence. But, as we shall see from *The Brothers Karamazov* and from *Adam Bede*, those who suffer need at very least *a voice*. Deconstruction may serve to knock away the corners of any otherwise complacent, over-confident, dogmatic voice; but in the end the Book of Job invites readers' active, agonized responses to multiple voices that refuse to package the problem into neat concepts. *Conversation with the voices (plural) of Job* carries us forward, even if inch-by-inch; it does not leave us in silence, even if wrestling with the voices is hard.

Tilley's contribution to the hermeneutics of Job is mainly of a negative nature: no single perspective or speech-action, whether of Job, or of the "framework" perspective, will be adequate for the performance of the book: "closure of the meanings of [the] texts ... may not be possible".[14] His exposition of a reading of George Eliot's *Adam Bede* offers a more distinctive example of how not only do "multiple voices" address suffering and evil, but "giving a voice to the victim" also stands at the heart of Eliot's book.[15] Tilley engages with major interpreters and critics of George Eliot's novels.[16]

One of the two central characters is Hetty Sorrel, a farm-girl, or dairymaid, who daydreams of marrying to become "a lady", kept in luxury and style. She sets her cap at the heir to the estate, Arthur Donnithorne, and later the reader learns that she bears his child. The second main character is the devout Dinah Morris, a sincere, believing "Methody" whose goodness and piety is beyond question. The fourth major character is Adam Bede, the master carpenter, who discovers that Arthur is toying with Hetty, beats him and secures his exile from the estate. The centrepiece emerges when we discover Hetty, having left home to search for Arthur, in prison, convicted of murdering her own baby. Dinah visits her, and seeks to pray with her and to speak with her, but Hetty cannot speak: she cannot find a voice to express her grief, shame and anger at

[12]   D.J.A. Clines, "Deconstructing the Book of Job", in M. Warner (ed.), *The Bible as Rhetoric* (London and New York: Routledge, 1990), p.79; cf. pp.65–80; also in Clines, *What Does Eve Do to Help?* (Sheffield: JSOT Suppl 94, 1990).

[13]   P. Ricoeur, " Toward a Hermeneutic of the Idea of Revelation", in *Essays on Biblical Interpretation* (ed. L.S. Mudge, London: SPCK, 1981), p.89.

[14]   Tilley, op. cit., p.109.

[15]   Ibid., pp.189–216.

[16]   E.g. R. Liddell, *The Novels of George Eliot* (New York: St Martin's, 1977); J. Carlisle, *The Sense of an Audience: Dickens, Thackeray and George Eliot at Mid-Century* (Athens, GA: University of Georgia Press, 1981); M.W. Carpenter, *George Eliot and the Landscape of Time* (Chapel Hill: University of North Carolina Press, 1986).

Adam and Arthur. Eventually Hetty inches a little way forward: "Help me", she implores Dinah, "I can't feel anything ... My heart is hard", and Dinah performs the speech-act of prayer when "all her soul went forth in her voice".[17] At last the speech-acts of prayer and expressed co-suffering enable Hetty to acknowledge, accept and confess the reality of her acts. But George Eliot is too much a realist to imply that this "resolves" it all. Through the voice of Adam, "the blackness of it" is that, whatever is said, "it cannot be undone".[18] Evil is irrevocably evil, even if it can also generate certain redemptive effects. Moreover, in a final twist typical of Eliot's critique of institutional religion, ironically Dinah, who has "given Hetty a voice" loses her own voice within the church when the Methodist Conference forbids women to preach. Yet this was Dinah's vocation.

Multiple voices, again, *together* address the evil and part-redemption. No single character expresses any "answer"; but in the inter-subjective interplay of three or four distinct voices, the dynamic of the "possible world" which enlarges our imagination takes place. The tortured price of confession and acknowledgement can be paid only in co-suffering dialogue in a plurality of speech-acts. Adam's declarative assertion, "it cannot be undone", resists a "solution" which transforms evil simply into an instrument for good. Even the act of speaking cannot be taken for granted: the Methodist Conference, within the narrative world, withdraws it from Dinah. No single packaged statement by any single voice can adequately address the existential anguish and complexities of suffering and evil in human life. Both the Book of Job and *Adam Bede* address the issues through multiple voices, and through conversations that the reader may take up and continue, albeit with struggle and wrestling. As Kierkegaard and Gadamer would urge within their own contexts of thought, this continuing *process* of *conversation* with a *plurality* of voices permits further discovery and decisions on the part of readers, as they wrestle with possibilities in *possible* worlds.

Fyodor Dostoevsky (1821–81) pursues the same kind of imaginative strategy in his magisterial work *The Brothers Karamazov*. As we observe at the end of this example, it is Mikhail Bakhtin who first identified his polyphonic voices in 1929.[19] We cannot doubt the theological nature of much of Dostoevsky's fiction. Even his first novel *Poor Folk* (1846) constitutes a social critique on behalf of the oppressed. From the period of "Notes from the Underground" (1864) and *Crime and Punishment* (1866), he produced a series of writings which reflect disenchantment with the influential positivism of Feuerbach and with the merely utilitarian ethics of J.S. Mill. In *The Idiot* (1868) he portrays a "saintly fool", Prince Myshkin, the embodiment of childlike compassion and beauty of soul who combines Russian traditions of the saintly fool with quasi-allegorical resonances drawn from the narratives of the Gospels.[20] Like Jesus, Prince Myshkin's "goodness" entails a "powerlessness" in the world's sense of power. The reader must find his or her way through the paradox, the ambivalence, or the "voices" that are presented.

---

17 George Eliot, *Adam Bede* (1859; New American Library edn, 1981), pp.422–31.
18 Ibid., p.434.
19 Bakhtin, *Problems of Dostoevsky's Poetics* (Eng., Ann Arbor, MI: Ardis, 1973).
20 See H. Murav, *Holy Foolishness: Dostoevsky's Novels and the Poetics of Cultural Critique* (Stanford, CA: Stanford University Press, 1992).

Nevertheless *The Brothers Karamazov* (1880) represents the novel of greatest power, at least if this is to be judged in terms of its "effective-history" or history of effects on varied readers. Albert Camus identifies its central "voice" as that of Ivan Karamazov who takes the part of the metaphysical rebel. He identifies Ivan with Dostoevsky. However, the novel also speaks through the Christian brother Alesha (or Alyosha) and the Orthodox church elder Zosima. Here N. Berdyaev identifies the major "voice" which articulates Berdyaev's own Christian philosophy of freedom. Yet neither of these interpretations does justice to the subtlety and multivalency of the work. It is worth noting, in passing, that Dostoevsky's own life was complex and stamped by suffering. His father was murdered by serfs when he was a child, and his mother died when he was fifteen. In 1849 he was imprisoned for supposed subversion, condemned to death and reprieved only moments before his scheduled death. He endured solitary confinement, forced labour in Siberia and compulsory military service. The experiences of a sensitive man of letters forced to live in close physical contact with brutal prisoners are reflected in *The House of the Dead* (1861), even if the hero of *Crime and Punishment* (1865–66) finds rebirth and renewal.

Two chapters in *The Brothers Karamazov* leave an indelible mark on the history of the effects of fictional texts, or literary history, namely "Rebellion" and "The Legend of the Grand Inquisitor". In "Rebellion", Ivan tells a series of tales about cruelty inflicted upon innocent children. A person rarely, if ever, grasps and understands the suffering of another: not the real suffering which degrades, humiliates and takes away the spirit of the other. Ivan compares the ways in which different cultural conditionings can obscure what counts as cruelty. The very "defencelessness" of a victim can tempt the tormentor. The high point of the tales is that of the little girl, brutally beaten and locked away in an outhouse who prays to "Dear, kind God ..." in her misery. Why is this permitted? Ivan is aware of the "answers" of his pious brother Alesha (Alyosha) and other orthodox Christians about a "higher harmony" for which freedom and suffering is a necessary condition. But Ivan is a rebel against orthodox theism and against metaphysical argument: "I renounce the higher harmony. It's not worth the tears of that one tortured child who beat itself on the breast with its little fist and prayed in its stinking outhouse with an unexpiated tear to 'dear kind God'. It's not worth it." Ivan would not give his consent if it is possible "to make men happy in the end, giving peace and rest" at the price of needing "to torture one tiny creature".

Yet this is not a denial of God's existence. Ivan wishes to opt out of a debate which, he believes, transcends any *logical* solution: "It isn't God I don't accept, Alesha, only I most respectfully given him back his ticket" [that is, ticket of admission to the metaphysical enterprise]. Moreover, the narrative (the polyphonic voices of the novel) has not yet reached closure. There are hints from the devout Alesha and from the mystic Zosima that whether or not Ivan "keeps his ticket", the suffering of the child has at least had the effect of inviting from this "hard" man the deepest compassion. How could such compassion arise if all is forever well with the world? Further, the next chapter narrates the long poem by Ivan of the Legend of the Grand Inquisitor. The elderly Grand Inquisitor has presided over the burning of nearly a hundred "heretics" in the Spanish Inquisition, set here in Seville. Suddenly Jesus appears in Seville and mingles with the crowd, healing the sick, until he encounters the Grand Inquisitor who has him arrested and places him under sentence of death.

The Inquisitor's charge is that Jesus gave to his disciples a freedom that is too great a burden for ordinary people to bear. The Inquisitor's accusations resonate with the Messianic temptations of Jesus as the Christ: the masses need to be fed with bread, confronted by an unambiguous object of worship, and persuaded by openly miraculous power (cf. Matt. 4:1–11; Luke 4:1–13). The Grand Inquisitor turns out to be the atheist, rejecting the responsibility of faith and freedom in favour of "religion". It is the seductions of the devil that define the Grand Inquisitor's religion, while in the Legend the figure of Jesus silently kisses him. Yet it would be too simple to reduce this to a narrative "message" of a critique of institutional religion. For paradox of paradoxes, it is Ivan the rebel through whose "voice" the Grand Inquisitor is unmasked, while Ivan's voice hardly represents "the message" of the novel, whether this is construed, with Camus, as a "message" of metaphysical rebellion, or with Berdyaev, as a "message" or "gospel" of freedom.

As my University colleague and Dostoevsky specialist Malcolm V. Jones convincingly argues, the clue lies neither with the reading of Camus nor with that of Berdyaev, but with the polyphony of voices in which, alongside the two chapters I have been discussing, "he [Dostoevsky] placed the Testament of the Elder Zosima which set forth the Elder's deviant but basically Orthodox religious credo, based upon the ideal of a life of active love which facilitates our sense of links with other worlds in which everyone accepts responsibility (i.e. guilt) for everything".[21] Through no *single* voice is Dostoevsky "seeking to present Christianity in all its fullness in fictional form ... but its fragmentary expression in the lives of individuals".[22] The Eastern Orthodox conception of *sobornost*, in which each remains co-jointly responsible for the mutuality and reciprocity of the whole while retaining an individual freedom within the constraints of this frame constitutes a distinctive Russian theme in Christian interpretation to which Dostoevsky gives expression through possible worlds of fiction. This stands in contrast both to the Cartesian individualism of partially secularized Protestantism and to the authoritarianism of partially secularized Roman Catholicism.

Just as the *process* of hearing multiple voices in the Book of Job and perhaps in *Adam Bede* projects worlds of possibility which invite a variety of transformations and refigurations in the processes of reading, so *The Brothers Karamazov* present not a "closed" message but a polyphonic chorus which presents variations on a theme, and invites active participation in the choral conversation.[23] As Kierkegaard and the later

---

[21] Quotation from Malcolm V. Jones, "Dostoevsky: Re-thinking Christianity", Research Seminar Paper, Dept of Theology, June 1997, p.3; more fully and in further detail in Malcolm V. Jones, *Dostoyevsky after Bakhtin* (Cambridge: CUP, 1990). For much of this section (but none of its faults) I am indebted to his specialist insights. He is Emeritus Professor of Slavonic Studies in the University of Nottingham.

[22] Ibid.

[23] On *The Brothers Karamazov*, see esp. Malcolm V. Jones, "The Brothers Karamazov: The Whisper of God", in his *Dostoyevsky after Bakhtin*; S. Hackel, "The Religious Dimension: Vision or Evasion", in M.J. Jones and G.M. Terry (eds), *New Essays on Dostoyevsky* (Cambridge: CUP, 1983), pp.139–68; S. Sutherland, *Atheism and the Rejection of God* (Oxford: Blackwell, 1977); and A.B. Gibson, *The Religion of Dostoevsky* (London: SCM, 1973).

Wittgenstein would agree, without such multivalency it would be difficult to maintain, as Dostoevsky wishes to maintain, that the process of unravelling mysteries remains inseparable from action and from how readers live their lives. That in which "freedom" and responsibility for the Other consists can appear only in the context of living out active love. If love entails interaction, the "voices" also interact. We have travelled a thousand miles from the abstract individual *cogito* of Descartes; but we have already entered the hermeneutical world of communicative action and of active respect for the otherness of the Other, not least through the "possible worlds" of narrative fiction.

Ultimately, however, the recovery of understanding of Dostoevsky as "the creator of the polyphonic novel" goes back to Mikhail Bakhtin in his work of 1929. Bakhtin asserts, *"The plurality of independent and unmerged voices and consciousnesses, and the genuine polyphony of full-valued voices, are in fact characteristics of Dostoevsky's novels"* (Bakhtin's italics).[24] In Walhout's terminology, the textual worlds projected by Dostoevsky's main characters are more than merely *objects* of textual action; each becomes a co-joined quasi-independent *instrument* of textual action. In Bakhtin's language they are "not only objects of the author's word, but subjects of their own directly significant word as well ... Dostoevsky is the creator of *the polyphonic novel*. He originated an essentially new novelistic genre" (his italics).[25] Does this imply, then, that our "polyphonic" reading of the Book of Job was anachronistic? Walter E. Reed's work *Dialogue of the Word* explicitly reads Job "according to Bakhtin", and finds such multiple voices there.[26] Indeed, once philosophers of language and literary and hermeneutical theorists have identified the importance of understanding texts as communicative acts which perform diverse functions and which leave a "history of effects" in Jauss's sense of Reception Theory as literary "history", the perspective which we have identified in the context of Job, Dostoevsky, Bakhtin and perhaps also George Eliot becomes all the more convincing as a means of provoking responsible, thoughtful reader-response and reader-transformation.

Nevertheless we must beware of understanding Bakhtin in the way in which many Marxist critics assimilated him into Marxist literary theory. Bakhtin is not interested in "de-privileging" an elite author under the principle of the reader's egalitarian co-authorship or in detaching the text as a system of self-generating forces. It may well be that the combination of Dostoevsky's social critique of oppression in conjunction with this polyphonic strategy allowed him to remain a "permitted" text in the era of Soviet Marxism, in spite of his own Christian faith. But neither Bakhtin's polyphony nor that of Dostoevsky should be equated with the radical pluralism and indeterminacy that arises from Barthes' multiple codes or Derrida's deconstruction.[27] To permit Dostoevsky's text to speak through his "voices" is to allow us to hear the voice of "the other" on whom Dostoevsky bestows his own ethical and Christian concern. Hence, as K. Vanhoozer declares in Lundin's essays *Disciplining Hermeneutics* (1997), "Deconstruction, far from protecting ... an 'other', licences interpretive violence ... Deconstruction claims to be ethically responsible for the 'other' ... I do not agree. Deconstruction does not serve the

---

[24] M. Bakhtin, *Problems of Dostoevsky's Poetics* (cited above), p.4.
[25] Ibid.
[26] W.E. Reed, *Dialogue of the Word. The Bible as Literature according to Bakhtin* (Oxford: OUP, 1993).
[27] On Barthes and Derrida, cf. Thiselton, *New Horizons in Hermeneutics*, pp.80–141.

other."[28] This coheres with Lundin's suggestion that since interpretations are interpretations *of* the texts, there can be "wrong" interpretation, but since no single interpretation merely replicates another we can hardly claim that there is only one "right" interpretation.[29] Lundin is explicating the observations of Joel Weinsheimer, who is also an expositor and translator of Gadamer.[30]

In this respect it would be injudicious to try to claim that the readings of *The Brothers Karamazov* by Camus (in terms of protest) or by Berdyaev (as gospel of freedom) are as "good" or "right" as those of Bakhtin, Sutherland, or Malcolm Jones. Thus polyphony does not imply indeterminacy. We continue to steer between our Scylla and Charybdis: between the shallows of a Cartesian paradigm and the quicksand of radical postmodern relativism, which admits to no stable marker.

Fiction may convey truth, as well as stimulating imagination. We may recall that Gadamer drew a contrast between the abstract rationalism of Descartes and the more historical, full-blooded "human" approach of Giambattista Vico (1668–1744). Vico simultaneously notes the creative importance of "imagination" and its seductive potential noted by Tacitus: people no sooner imagine than they believe (*fingunt simul creduntque*).[31] Samuel Taylor Coleridge (1772–1834) likewise perceives the limitations of "lifeless technical rules" and abstract rational reflection. In spite of the constraints of his Romanticist expressivism he begins to anticipate Gadamer and Ricoeur in urging the temporal dimension of imagination as that which relates to memory and hope, and like them he perceives how imagination transcends mere replication: "If the artist copies the mere nature, the *natura naturata*, what idle rivalry!"[32] The artist "abandons" what he or she interprets and presents "for a time", but also returns to it, presenting not just replications but genuine *possibilities*. Claims about imagination and "possible worlds" do not mean abandoning "the Discipline of Hermeneutics", but steering between the Scylla of lifeless replication and the Charybdis of making what the reader wishes to make of the text. This principle remains true to life in the lecture-room in biblical studies. A student who is requested "to interpret" a biblical text invites a zero grade if he or she offers *either* mere replication in the form of close paraphrase, *or* a speculative construct which bears no relation to the "directedness" of the text or to the history of the effects of the text in successive traditions of interpretation.

All this serves to throw into relief the gains and losses of so-called reader-response theory. Gain occurs in the active engagement of readers with texts, their entry into the text's projected world, and the participatory and potentially transforming effects especially of hearing more than one possible voice, or comparing more than one possible

---

[28] K. Vanhoozer, "The Spirit of Understanding: Special Revelation and General Hermeneutics". in R. Lundin (ed.), *Disciplining Hermeneutics* (cited above), pp.158 and 161; cf, pp.131–65.

[29] R. Lundin, "Introduction", in *Disciplining Hermeneutics*, p.13.

[30] Cf. J. Weinsheimer, *Philosophical Hermeneutics and Literary Theory* (New Haven, CT: Yale University Press, 1991), p.87.

[31] G. Vico, *The New Science* (Eng., Ithaca, NY: Cornell University Press, 1968).

[32] The citation is from S.T. Coleridge, "On Poesy or Art" (1818). Cf. also his observation in *The Statesman's Manual* that "Faith is either buried in the dead letter or its name ... usurped by a counterfeit product of the mechanical understanding which ... confounds symbols with allegories. Allegory is but a translation of abstract notions in picture language."

world. But reader-response theory, especially that of the American literary criticism of the late 1970s up to the 1980s shares a certain abstraction from time and history with Cartesian traditions. "History" entails not only looking to the past, but also exploring the effects of processes of reading between the past and the present. Hence we need now to examine further issues of temporality and time, and in this context the contribution of reception theory.

III
Hermeneutics within the Horizon of Time: Clock Time, Human Time and Narrative Time

Paul Ricoeur's magisterial *Time and Narrative* draws on Aristotle, Augustine, Heidegger and narrative theory to explore the indispensable status of the temporal dimension for understanding in hermeneutics, for issues of narrative identity and for projecting worlds of "possibility", in Heidegger's sense of the term.[33] Five years later his crowning work *Oneself as Another* firmly and convincingly situates personal identity, humanness, personal agency and action within a frame of temporal narrative history.[34]

In his fifty-page Introduction to *Being and Time*, Heidegger observes that Descartes attempted to enquire about Being without reference to temporality, while in spite of attempts to the contrary "Kant could never achieve an insight into the problematic of Temporality ... Instead of this, Kant took over Descartes' position quite dogmatically", even if he goes well beyond him in many other respects.[35] Descartes provided a "seemingly new beginning" which entailed "the implantation of a baleful prejudice" detrimental to "later generations", namely in abstracting "the Present" in less historical, dynamic and concrete terms than even Parmenides or Aristotle.[36] Descartes not only isolates the individual self in lone subjective reflection and consciousness, but also as Lundin forcefully argues, in effect "orphaned" the self from the temporality which lends it identity, meaning and the narrative history of the community to which the self concretely belongs. The turning-point which reunites timeless "mind" and historical contingency comes with Hegel's exploration of historical reason. Lundin has argued that Hegel perceived the problem and attempted a new direction, but also that his work provided no more than a start in this more fruitful direction.

It is not difficult to understand why hermeneutics, even in Schleiermacher, still awaited proper attention to the temporal dimension that began to emerge in Hegel, Droysen and Dilthey, and then as "life" and "life-worlds" assumed more prominence implicitly in Husserl and Yorck, and explicitly in Heidegger, Gadamer and Ricoeur. For

---

[33] P. Ricoeur, *Time and Narrative* (3 vols, Eng., Chicago, IL: University of Chicago Press, 1984–88; French, *Temps et Récit*, Paris: Editions du Seuil, 1983–85, esp. I, pp.5–30 (Augustine); pp.31–51 (Aristotle); III, pp.60–98 (Heidegger) and I, pp.95–230; III, pp.104–274 and throughout (on narrative theory).

[34] P. Ricoeur, *Oneself as Another* (Eng., Chicago, IL: University of Chicago Press, 1992; French *Soi-même comme un autre*, Paris: Editions du Seuil, 1990).

[35] M. Heidegger, *Being and Time* (Eng., Oxford: Blackwell, 1962), p.45 (7th Germ. edn, cf. *Sein und Zeit*, p.24).

[36] Ibid., Eng., pp.46, 48; Germ., pp.25, 26.

many centuries hermeneutics was bound up with the interpretation of sacred texts. The dynamic, temporal nature of the biblical writings first became submerged in the need to formulate Christian theology in the Hellenistic world, especially in the context of Alexandrian and Graeco-Roman thought, and then in the context of the legacy bequeathed by Augustine. Augustine wrestles with issues of temporality. Nevertheless by insisting that God created the world *cum tempore* rather than *in tempore*, Augustine may seem unwittingly to deprive temporality, in Heidegger's sense of the term, of ontological seriousness.[37] The very context of reflection on time in *The Confessions* seems to presuppose the very "private subjectivity" that Gadamer perceives as excluded for the first time since Aristotle in Hegel's *Logic* and temporal dialectic.[38]

All the same Augustine achieved at very least one lasting gain in his reflections on time. Time, for Augustine, constitutes a fundamentally *"human"* phenomenon. Metaphysical speculation about time, he reflects, is difficult to formulate, but memory and hope are fundamentally *human* modes of being: *"Quid est ergo tempus? si nemo ex me quaerat scio; si quaerenti explicare velim, nescio."*[39] To be *human* is to live among day-to-day experiences of "before" or "after" even if Augustine cannot answer the question "What is time?" in purely abstract terms. His insistence that there is no "before" and "after" with God, since nothing can be "before" him or "after" him (that is, past and future seem to become an eternal present) does not locate God in some "timeless" Platonic realm of Ideas. Rather, it cancels out the applicability of *human* time to God. He lays a foundation, in effect, for Heidegger's distinction between *time* (*Zeit*) and *temporality* (*Zeitlichkeit*), which provides *the ground for the possibility of modes of time*.[40] Since in the biblical writings God is the living God (Hebrew *el chay*; Greek, *theos zōn*), God as embodying "temporality" (but not astronomical time, clock time, or human time which all belong to the creaturely) remains capable of the experience of succession and can act purposively and in active faithfulness. But astronomical time depends on the stars and solar system; clock time depends on technical reason, and "human" time on every experience of human allocation, organization, periodicity, tempo, planning and subjective perception. All these belong to the created order, and form irreducible dimensions in the processes of human understanding, and in the reactualizations of texts, art, wisdom, traditions, and varieties of communicative acts.

Sociologists have explored "human time" in contrast to "natural" time in terms of the allocation of time for purposes of human organization and social planning. Literary theorists have demonstrated that narrative embodies a working distinction between "natural" and "human" time in terms of flashbacks, tempo and so forth. Physicists have indirectly endorsed the notion of time (that is, natural and human time) as "creaturely" by exploring equations that correlate time with space in theories of relativity. Thus time

---

[37] Augustine, *Confessions*, XII: 12:13.

[38] H.-G. Gadamer, *Hegel's Dialectic: Five Hermeneutical Studies* (Eng., New Haven, CT: Yale University Press, 1976), p.85; cf. pp.54–74 (dialectic) and 75–99 (logic).

[39] Augustine, *Confessions*, XI: 14:17. Further, *ibid* XI:14–28; and on his view of time cf. L. Wittgenstein, *The Blue and Brown Books* (Oxford: Blackwell, 1958), p.26; and more allusively in *Philosophical Investigations*, sect. 89.

[40] It is no accident that *Zeitlichkeit*, temporality, is closely linked in Heidegger with *Möglichkeit*, or "possibility", which in turn invites authentic decision (*"existentiell eigentliche Ganzseinkönnen ... als ... Entschlossenheit"*, *Being and Time*, pp.351–2; German, pp.304–5).

is perceived to pass *more slowly in the direction of spatial motion*. In accordance with dominant relativity theory, the pilot of a space capsule would spend one year of his life travelling at 260,000 kilometres per second, while two years of earth-time, or Newtonian clock-time, would have elapsed during the same period.[41] To separate the divine creation of space and "creaturely" time would be as arbitrary as to abstract time or location from processes of contingent hermeneutical understanding.

Several theologians endorse this explicitly. Barth writes, "Time ... is the form of existence of the creature ... God is temporal, precisely in so far as he is eternal ... But time as such, i.e. our time, relative time, itself created, is the form of existence of the creature ... in that one-way sequence".[42] "Human" time in contrast to natural time or clock time is seen in the model of "man as isolated from God" when time becomes "a flight" and in God's eyes is "lost time" or time with "no real past and future, no centre ... As the time of lost man it can only be lost time."[43] In contrast to cyclical or timeless myth, which does not do justice to the biblical material, redeemed time moves towards what is symbolized in "the event of God's Sabbath freedom, Sabbath rest, Sabbath joy, in which man has been summoned to participate".[44] Human time for the self-sufficient individual remains "'our' time [that is, human time], distorted and caricatured".[45]

The contrast between natural time and human time in literary theory has been explored by Seymour Chatman, Gérard Genette and Paul Ricoeur, and will already be familiar to many readers. The distinction is correlative with that between narrative and story, or between story and plot, or (in Russian Formalism) between fable (*fabula*) and plot (*siuzhet*). Where Chatman distinguishes *Story and Discourse*, Emile Benveniste contrasts *histoire* and *discours*, while Gennette uses the distinction between *historie* and *récit*.[46] As I observed in *New Horizons in Hermeneutics* the plot of a detective story almost invariably holds back reports of earlier happenings which gradually come to light through flashbacks, conversations, or various editorial devices. How could Charles Dickens write *Great Expectations* as a narrative plot if he chronologically placed the event of Pip's benefactor's making financial arrangements for Pip in the sequence of "natural time" as it unfolded through the story?[47] As Ricoeur insists, and as Walhout argues concerning fiction, mere replication of the events of natural time in the form of a report would have different effects from "the effects of fiction, revelation and transformation [which] are essentially the effects of reading".[48]

Wesley Kort is one of many who note that the Gospel of Mark uses this temporal device, especially in terms of speed or tempo. The first eight chapters proceed with a very

---

[41] L.D. Landau and G.B. Rumer, *What is Relativity?* (New York: Bantam, 1960), pp.47–55.

[42] K. Barth, *Church Dogmatics*, III:1 (Eng., Edinburgh: T. & T. Clark, 1958), sects 41, 67, 68.

[43] Ibid., p.72.

[44] Ibid., p.98; by contrast cf. "myth", ibid., pp.84–94.

[45] Ibid., p.73.

[46] G. Gennette, *Narrative Discourse* (Eng., Ithaca, NY: Cornell University Press, 1980) and *Narrative Discourse Re-visited* (Eng., Ithaca, NY: Cornell University Press, 1988), pp.13–16; S. Chatman, *Story and Discourse: Narrative Structure in Fiction and Film* (Ithaca, NY: Cornell University Press, 1978), pp.19–21; and P. Ricoeur, *Time and Narrative*. On further details cf. also M. Toolan, *Narrative* (London: Routledge, 1988), pp.12–14; and Thiselton, *New Horizons in Hermeneutics*, pp.354–58 and 479–85.

[47] Thiselton, *New Horizons*, p.355, also p.479.

[48] Ricoeur, *Time and Narrative*, III, p.101.

fast pace, rushing through a diversity of actions, situations and events.[49] The pace clearly slows, however, when serious questions begin to be raised about the identity of Jesus and the nature of his mission. Arguably the transition occurs in Mark 8:27–38, where Peter makes his confession of the Messiahship of Jesus, but only to receive a rebuke that he does not perceive this as standing under the shadow of the cross. The middle, slower, section concludes with warnings to be on the watch (13:33–37), and this leads to the final section which from 14:1 onwards portrays the Passion in detailed slow motion. Slow motion is a widely used device to highlight "this is what it is all about". Since the ancient world was aware of utilizations of the contrast between natural (chronological) time and human (narrative) time for the purposes of suspense or emphasis in emplotment, some of the supposed "discrepancies" in sequence or timing between parallel narratives in the Gospels need not cause disquiet about historical accuracy, unless "the point" of a specific episode in question has more to do with replicated report than proclamation. It would be a different matter, for example, if the crucifixion were depicted as occurring at different incompatible times. A "narrative" reading should not become a "docetic" reading, since this would contradict the directionality (cf. Wolterstorff's "authorial discourse") of the Gospels themselves.

We are concerned, however, with more than literary theory and its contribution to hermeneutics. These issues have *ethical, social and political import*. In this context the work of such sociologists as Robert Lauer and Alvin Toffler assume a special importance. Lauer shows that human concern, some might say obsessional human concern, with clock time constitutes the hallmark of the organizational technological efficiency of the post-Enlightenment Industrial Revolution. Clock time assures not only punctuality, but also periodicity: the strategic division of natural time into operational units for maximal efficiency.[50] A mid-morning coffee break and a mid-day lunch break enhance concentration and allocate measurable periods for jobs of work. However, executive management may have greater flexibility to refigure or reshape a timetable around designated or necessary tasks than a work force. Moreover, a measure of social control is exercised in day-to-day social or professional politics about who sets the timetable for whom, who waits for whose prior claims of timing, and who sets the pace of timing.

In practice, as Lauer argues, five markers differentiate "human" socio-political time from natural time through clock time. These turn on: (i) the allocation of units of time, that is, *periodicity*, for tasks, leisure, or rest; (ii) the control of the speed with which tasks are to be completed, or the rapidity with which we handle a series of tasks, that is, *tempo*; (iii) the setting or "take up" of so-called windows of opportunity, that is, *opportune timing* or *kairos*-determination; (iv) the determination of appropriate lengths of time which define the units of time which are allocated for different tasks, that is, *duration*, and finally (v) the specific ordering of tasks by a scale of temporal priority, that is, *sequence*.[51] Clearly

[49] W.A. Kort, *Story, Text and Scripture. Literary Interests in Biblical Narrative* (University Park, PA and London: Pennsylvania State University Press, 1988), p.44; cf. pp.14–42; On Mark, see further P. Grant, *Reading the New Testament* (London: Macmillan, 1989).

[50] R.F. Lauer, *Temporal Man: The Meaning and Uses of Social Time* (New York: Praeger, 1981), pp.1–28 and throughout.

[51] Ibid., pp.28–51. See further W.E. Moore, *Scarce Resource: Man, Time and Society* (New York: Wiley, 1963).

a hermeneutic of selfhood and the hermeneutics of the understanding of human institutions and the texts produced in the context of management interests or consumerist interests cannot pretend indifference towards these aspects of "human" time. It is to be noted, for example, that stability, rationality and humanness come under threat when an unacceptable acceleration of tempo coincides with a clash of competing value-systems.[52] Those versions of postmodernity that reflect irrational excess are symptoms of human breakdown. Stress disorders today derive not only from the acceleration of tempo imposed by "performance-related pay" but also from its being coupled with huge bureaucratic monitoring systems that simultaneously bring disempowerment.

In few areas can the difference between Christian and secular values be discerned more clearly than in the deployment of these five axes of social time. They can be used to exercize control for self-interest, regardless of de-humanizing effects. The stress of the overworked and the unemployed stands in contrast to the common ground shared by hermeneutics and Christian theology where patience, respect for the other, and responsibility in relation to periodicity, tempo, timing, duration and sequence suggests that "results" can be "forced" only at the expense of serious risk, and that time is more than a commodity or an unlimited space for autonomous "play". Only Cartesian individualism could permit us to imagine that how one person spends his or her time has no repercussions on the "human time" of others. What is known as inter-subjectivity of understanding in hermeneutics, that is, respect for the subjectivity of the other as agent, becomes a matter of cooperative "teamwork" in the marketplace or factory. But just as in hermeneutics or theology we can given undue privilege to "our" community, so teamwork in the allocation of time can become tribalism or company loyalty at any cost when it is transformed to the public domain of conduct.

This profoundly illustrates a major principle expounded by Kevin Vanhoozer in Lundin's collection *Disciplining Hermeneutics*. Using italics, Vanhoozer states, "the following thesis: *All hermeneutics, not simply the special hermeneutics of Scripture, is 'theological'* ... I am arguing that general hermeneutics is inescapably theological ... Interpretation ultimately depends upon the theological virtues of faith, hope and love ... a mutual relation of self-giving ...".[53] He expounds this theme in more detail in his book *Is There a Meaning in This Text?*.[54]

The theologies of Barth, Jüngel, Moltmann and Pannenberg confirm that, in Pannenberg's phrase, true humanness that bears the image of God entails "being with others as others".[55] It does not reside in "autonomous ... life", but in an "openness" to the other, in contrast to a Cartesian or psychological "fixation on the self".[56] "Absolute self-

[52]   See A. Toffler, *Future Shock* (New York: Random, 1970) on the disruption of "the human" in psycho-social breakdown.

[53]   K.J. Vanhoozer, "The Spirit of Understanding: Special Revelation and General Hermeneutics", in R. Lundin (ed.), *Disciplining Hermeneutics*, pp.160–61.

[54]   K.J. Vanhoozer, *Is There a Meaning in This Text?* (Grand Rapids, MI: Zondervan, 1998), pp.407–41 and elsewhere.

[55]   W. Pannenberg, *Systematic Theology* (3 vols, Eng., Edinburgh: T. & T. Clark and Grand Rapids, MI: Eerdmans, 1991–97), II, p.193; cf. J. Moltmann, *The Spirit of Life* (Eng., London: SCM, 1992), pp.83–143; and E. Jüngel, *God as the Mystery of the World* (Eng., Edinburgh: T. & T. Clark, 1983), pp.299–396.

[56]   Pannenberg, loc. cit., pp.193, 204, 229, 250.

willing ... alienates us from God by putting the self in the place that is God's alone".[57] In contrast to Cartesian isolation and Kantian autonomy, both of which give privilege to the self, "it is of the nature of our human form of life to be 'eccentric' relative to other ... beings".[58] Barth and Pannenberg both follow the New Testament witnesses in arguing that Jesus Christ, in his relation to others, to God and to time, constitutes the paradigm of what it is to be truly human. Barth observes, "Jesus is man as God willed and created him ... The nature of the man Jesus is the key to the problem of the human. This man is *man*" (Barth's italics).[59] Jesus, unlike fallen humanity, lived within the framework of what Barth terms "given time" and "allotted time".[60] In contrast to Lundin's orphan imagery, Jesus's "own time extends backwards and embraces all prior time ... and extends forwards ...".[61] He bases his trust on the pre-given promises of God and the history of God's saving acts, accepts the constraints of allotted time in the present, and understands the meaning of his life and work within the frame of past promise and future purpose and goal.

Hence humanity in relation to God is not "in time in such a way that it continually slips away into infinity and is therefore lost ... Human life means to have been, to be, and to be about to be", as is also my fellow human being, "the thou without whom I could not be a human".[62] Even human finitude which provides the boundary of death thereby defines the allotted time which God bestows as a gift for the determination of periodicity, duration, tempo. Opportunity comes as a gift of grace under his lordship as the one who assigns time and task, and thereby the meaning of the present.[63] In Pannenberg's view this provides the very stuff that makes promising an act of *promise*. A hermeneutic of promise brings together issues of personal identity, personal agency, action and time. Pannenberg writes, "All action presupposes the identity of those who act, at least to the extent that this identity is needed to bridge the difference in time between the planning and execution of an act ... *Those who make a promise that they can keep only many years later, or over a whole life, have to retain their identity if they are to meet the promise*" (my italics). Actions owe their unity to the time-bridging identity of their subjects."[64] Pannenberg adds that identity becomes what it will be "during our whole life-history". *Human and divine faithfulness in the acceptance of constraint for the performance of promise presupposes a temporal horizon of understanding and action.*

The Epistle to the Hebrews insists that the only instance of a visible display of humankind "crowned with glory and honour" as bearer of the image of God is Jesus Christ (Heb. 2:7–9; cf. Ps. 8:4–6). Yet this Epistle speaks more movingly than any other passage in the New Testament of Jesus as the One who showed patience, endurance and even "learning through suffering" in his determination to reach the *telos* appointed by God (Heb. 5:2, 8, 9 and throughout).[65] A hermeneutics of promise then, presupposes a

---

57 Ibid., p.261.
58 Ibid., p.229.
59 Barth, *Church Dogmatics*, III:2, sects 43, 50.
60 Ibid., sect. 47, pp.511–72.
61 Ibid., pp.511–12.
62 Ibid., pp.521, 522, 523.
63 Ibid., sect. 47, pp.587–640.
64 Pannenberg, *Systematic Theology*, II, p.202.
65 I have expounded this theme elsewhere: partly in "Human Being, Relationality and Time", forthcoming in *Ex Auditu* 13 (1997); and more fully in Thiselton, "The Epistle to the Hebrews", in J.D.G. Dunn and J.W. Rogerson (eds), *Commentary 2000* (Grand Rapids, MI: Eerdmans, 2001).

hermeneutic within the horizon of time. Here, as Vanhoozer insists, hermeneutics and Christian theology converge, for respect for "the other" embraces the Other of past, present and future, not merely the Other of spatial differentiation. This is the missing dimension of *otherness* which has emasculated and to some degree sidelined reader-response theory. To place reader-effects within a temporal horizon it is more constructive to explore the reception theory of H.R. Jauss. To this we now turn.

IV

The Temporal Horizon of Hermeneutics: Further Explorations of Jauss's Aesthetics of Reception

We have already explored several aspects of the work of Jauss in Essay 3 (the retrospective reappraisal of Part I) and in Essay 18 (in which we investigate the post-history and reception of texts about the Holy Spirit in 1 Corinthians in the Patristic period). This third excursion into reception theory does not merely replicate these other essays. Here we consider Jauss's poetics, compare the work of Tracy, look at provocation and history, and note the phenomenon of de-familiarization. In the other two essays we focused on different issues, including horizons of expectation, successive textual readings (with examples), reception history as a response to Räisänen's claims, and the respective pedigrees of different versions of this broad approach.

Hans Robert Jauss acknowledges Gadamer, who was his teacher at Heidelberg, as his determining influence.[66] However, from 1963 onwards he worked in collaboration with a circle of literary theorists based at the University of Constance in Southern Germany, whose approach is widely described as that of "aesthetics of Reception" (*Rezeptionsästhetik*), or more loosely and less precisely as "Reception Theory". Those aspects which find common ground with certain American literary theorists may be compared with reader-response theory; but the Constance Group, and especially Jauss, deliberately and self-consciously describe their work as combining *both literary poetics and hermeneutical theory*. If one stream of influence comes from Gadamer and hermeneutics, the other comes from Lotman, Iser and literary theory. Thus, hermeneutics are "historical" in the sense of tracing a successive and dynamic history of the transmission of traditions, including both continuities and twists and turns of discontinuity, normally around a stable core.

As in reader-response theory, the emphasis lies on the impact of the text on readers. David Tracy urges in the context of religious texts as "classics" that hermeneutical enquiry entails attention, with varying degrees of emphasis, "upon any one of the four elements basic to the total situation of any work of art: the artist who creates the work (expressive theories ...); the work itself (objective theories ... often formalist); the world the work creates or reveals (mimetic theories ...); and the audience the work affects (pragmatic theories from Philip Sidney to ... Lukacs)".[67] Without appearing to mention Jauss, Tracy

---

[66] H.R. Jauss, *Toward an Aesthetic of Reception* (Eng., Minneapolis, MN: University of Minnesota Press, 1982, German essays from 1970–80). The comment is from Paul de Man, "Introduction", p.xi.

[67] D Tracy, *The Analogical Imagination. Christian Theology and the Culture of Pluralism* (London: SCM, 1981), p.113.

then declares, "The position defended here emphasizes, above all, the *reception* by the reader of the classic text" (Tracy's italics).[68] Attention is given to the "personal questions, opinions, responses, expectations, even desires, fears and hopes" which readers already bring with them as the text addresses them.[69] These make up their "pre-understanding" (from Schleiermacher, Heidegger and Bultmann), "Background" (from Searle), or "competency" (from Culler).

Although he does not appear to locate the theoretical dialogue in the explicit contrast between Gadamer on one side and reader-response theory on the other, Tracy adopts a thoroughly Gadamerian perspective. He writes, "Every present moment is, in fact, formed by both the memories of the tradition and the hopes, desires, and critical demands for transformation for the future. The notion of the present moment as pure instant, an ever-receding image, is as mistaken as the allied notion of a pure-isolated, purely autonomous, subject."[70]

Into this Gadamerian context of thought Jauss transposes the notion of the *directedness* of texts as "address" or "appeal" to audiences or readers (*Appellstruktur*). This at once *modifies any version of literary formalism* into a speech-event that *addresses an extra-linguistic readership*. Jauss opposes any theory of hermeneutics or of literary reception that is either merely intra-linguistic or "timeless".[71] Following Gadamer, he traces the legacy of "historical" hermeneutics through Droysen and Heidegger. His key programmatic statement appeared in his Inaugural Lecture of 1967 in the University of Constance entitled "Literaturgeschichte also Provokation der Literaturwissenschaft" (translated into English under the title "Literary History as a Challenge to Literary Theory").[72] Before formulating seven major theses Jauss urges that the past of history is not a "closed" past; it remains open to renewed understanding as it remains open to fresh perceptions which are generated by subsequent events and experiences. Similarly, every literary or artistic work is not "timeless" in the sense of being abstracted from processes of history and tradition, but *reactualized as eventful* in each changing context of successive processes of understanding. In Walhout's terminology, texts which were once objects of action become also instruments of action in this process of reactualization.

Like Gadamer, Jauss perceives literary *history* as a *story* of the literary work and its effects *in process* (*Literaturgeschichte*). This in turn constitutes an essential component of literary theory (*Literaturwissenshaft*), in which successive impacts or impressions (*stossen*) present discontinuities, differences, disturbances, or challenges (*Provokation*) which "hit" readerships in such a way that the history of effects of texts (*Wirkungsgeschichte*) moves beyond any bland descriptive collection of cumulative continuities of reading. Like Gadamer, Jauss perceives differences and tensions between past and present, or between successive reactualizations, as essential for the process of understanding.

In his essay of 1969 Jauss draws a contrast between a bland, innocent assumption of developmental continuity in the appropriation of the meaning of texts, and

---

68 Ibid., p.118.
69 Ibid.
70 Ibid, p.119.
71 H.R. Jauss, *Literaturgeschichte also Provokation* (Frankfurt: Suhrkamp, 1970), p.231.
72 Printed as Chapter 1 in Jauss, *Toward an Aesthetic of Reception*, pp.3–45.

discontinuities and points of departure of the kind that we may describe as creativity within the constraints of tradition, as over against the Cartesian choice between barren replication and novelty for the sake of novelty.[73] As Paul de Man notes, Jauss rejects literary approaches which makes too much of "play" in the Barthesian sense.[74] Each new event of understanding and interpretation within the context of the history-of-effects (*Wirkungsgeschichte*) of a text produce, in turn, new effects (*Wirkungen*).[75] These are not, however, the merely "causal" effects of a positivist view of history, or of a "causal" or Marxist sociology of literature, but a matter of more subtle "influences" which operate at an aesthetic level and may even lead to paradigm-shifts (*Paradigmawechsel*) in the sense explored by Thomas Kuhn in his philosophy of science.[76] This criticism lies behind Jauss's critique of so-called "genetic" models of hermeneutics. Even the emphasis in audience-reception in much Marxist literary theory suffers, in Jauss's view, from such a quasi-positivist reduction of more complex human agencies to mere socio-economic "forces". Metaphors of "production" and "consumption" of works of art take us only partly along the way. An inter-subjective reciprocal mutuality is entailed (as Gadamer's language about conversation implies).[77]

We earlier noted that Jauss brings together two streams of influence: that of literary theory, which includes Russian formalism and the work of J.M. Lotman and W. Iser, and the hermeneutical and historical concerns of Droysen, Heidegger and Gadamer. His emphasis on the discontinuities or disruptions within traditions of reading brings together "tension" or "distance" in Gadamer (and subsequently Ricoeur) and "defamiliarization" (*ostraneniye*) or "estrangement" in V. Shklovsky and Russian formalism.[78] "The gradual course of tradition (*Überlieferung*) [is] a procession with fracturing changes, the revolts of new schools, and the conflicts of competing genres".[79] It is only through the critical recognition of these changes in the "paradigms" of historical eras (as in the sense used by Thomas Kuhn noted above with reference to the history of the natural sciences) "that the work enters into the changing horizon-of-experiences of a continuity in which the perpetual inversion occurs from simple reception to critical understanding, from passive to active reception, from recognized aesthetic norms to a new production that surpasses them".[80] The goal of "reappropriation" of a text occurs only in the interaction of temporal processes of past and present.[81]

For the appropriation of the sacred text of the biblical writings this brings us into a different world from that of a more "timeless" reader-response theory, which may allow the kind of "free play" which Jauss rejects. Jauss allows for the creativity of fresh

---

[73] H.R. Jauss, "Paradigmawechsel in der Literaturwissenschaft", *Linguistische Berichte* 3 (1969), pp.44–56.

[74] "Introduction" to Jauss, *Toward an Aesthetic of Reception*, p.xix.

[75] Jauss, "Paradigmawechsel", pp.55–6.

[76] Jauss, *Toward an Aesthetic of Reception*, p.8. Note the changes, however, in the second edition of T. Kuhn, *The Structure of Scientific Revolutions* (Chicago, IL: University of Chicago Press, 2nd edn, 1970) and *The Essential Tension* (Chicago, IL: University of Chicago Press, 1977).

[77] Ibid., p.15.

[78] Ibid., pp.16–17.

[79] Ibid., p.17.

[80] Ibid., p.19.

[81] Ibid., p.20.

appropriation, but within the witness of a tradition. Different eras neither merely replicate earlier understandings, but neither do they merely make what they like of the text. Our exegesis, understanding, and appropriation of justification by grace in the Epistle to the Romans can never be the same again after the work of Luther, Calvin, Kierkegaard, Barth, Stendahl and Sanders, but that does not thereby necessarily lead to a radical pluralism in interpretation. It means that present interpretation takes place on ground which has both been made more fertile and yet also yields certain boundary-markers. The post-history of the text has become an indispensable but unduly neglected area of biblical studies. We need to recover the hermeneutical insight of G. Ebeling and K. Froehlich when they plead for an understanding of "Church History as the History of the Exposition of Holy Scripture".[82] Froehlich urges, "Understanding must take into account the text's post-history as the paradigm of the texts' own historicity, i.e. as the way in which the text itself can function ... in a variety of contexts ... in the shaping of life".[83]

Jauss takes up a stance that does justice to the emphasis upon the active role of the reader in reader-response theories, but also locates changing horizons of readers within formative processes of historically constituted tradition. Thereby he places greater emphasis on the constraints and boundaries of a public inter-subjective world, and softens the problems of supposed potential incommensurability which the more subjective or pragmatic stances of Fish or Rorty may be thought to suggest. Like Ricoeur, Jauss envisages a surplus of meaning that may "surpass" previous interpretations in a "new production": but this need not imply distortion or subjectivism. If it were otherwise, the marketing, let alone the writing, of new biblical commentaries would be only for homiletical rather than exegetical and interpretative purposes. It would be a mistake, Jauss argues, to over-simplify the process as if to imply that each new interpretation merely takes an earlier one as its point of departure. The "first" effect combines with the text or with the work itself in "co-producing" a "second" effect interactively.[84]

If he places as a first thesis a warning against an unduly positivist, causal, or objective view of historical processes of understanding, Jauss balances this by a second thesis which excludes reducing changing horizons of expectation to the merely psychological or subjective. Processes in which horizons of expectation are "varied, corrected, altered, or even just reproduced" enter the public domain as open to public and historical scrutiny.[85] The ways in which *texts perform actions* in the multiple effects of *both* projecting a meaning-content *and* satisfying, disappointing, frustrating, confirming, or refuting the expectations, or horizons of expectation, of readers, therefore perform the third action of effecting, disrupting, or transforming social formation.[86] This represents Jauss's third main thesis.

---

[82] The title of Ebeling's "Habilitation Lecture" 1947, Eng., in G. Ebeling, *The Word of God and Tradition* (Philadelphia, PA: Fortress, 1968), pp.11–31; and developed and endorsed by K. Froehlich, "Church History and the Bible", in M.S. Burrows and P. Rorem (eds), *Biblical Hermeneutics in Historical Perspective: Studies in Honor of Karlfried Froehlich* (Grand Rapids, MI: Eerdmans, 1991), pp.1–18, esp. p.7.

[83] Froehlich, loc. cit., pp.8, 9.

[84] Jauss, *Toward an Aesthetic of Reception*, esp. pp.15–20.

[85] Ibid., pp.22–4.

[86] Ibid., pp.25–8.

This process and approach yields a fourth thesis. It brings "to view the hermeneutic difference between the former and the current understanding of a work; it raises to consciousness ... the potential for meaning that is embedded in a work and actualized in the stages of its historical reception".[87] This reminds us at once of Gadamer's comment that if "horizon" denotes the range of vision that includes everything that can be seen from a particular vantage point", it becomes possible to speak of narrowness or "expansion" of horizons, "of the opening up of new horizons", but conversely of "tensions" between horizons of differing historical epochs when "the hermeneutic task consists in not covering up this tension by attempting a naïve assimilation of the two but in consciously bringing it out".[88] However, Jauss construes the stable marker of a "classic" text itself in different terms from Gadamer's more Hegelian account. Certain texts or works retain a status as decisive markers for interpretative vision in the history of effects. In Jauss's view the differential tension facilitates the unfolding of the text itself, rather than placing most or all of the emphasis on the multiple reactualizations.[89] Paul Ricoeur finds himself in broad agreement with Jauss's greater readiness to combine both explanation and understanding, suspicion and surplus, in the effects which texts produce on acts of reception.[90]

Jauss's fifth main thesis amplifies the fourth. It expounds the historical unfolding of understanding. As Lundin, once again, urged at the beginning of this volume, once we have gained the kind of historical perspective which is here advocated, the "new", Jauss notes, "is not [merely] absorbed into factors of innovation, surprise ... re-arrangement, to which Formalist theory assigned exclusive importance. The new also becomes a *historical category*" (his italics).[91]

In this programmatic essay Jauss concludes with a sixth and a seventh thesis which co-jointly affirm the interrelation of synchronic and diachronic dimensions. Together these present a succession of engagements of reading and display "the creative capability" of literary or classic texts, most especially revealing their "socially formative function".[92] We should note, however, that it is precisely because he agrees with Marxist literary critics that "social formation" arises from the historicity of literary texts in *life* (not simply in thought) that Jauss is so careful to distance himself at the same time from the Marxist-positivist view that these effects are *causal* or linked in any way with historical determinism. Neither socio-economic causality nor any supposed quasi-mechanical causality linked with cruder versions of structuralism is acceptable to Jauss. Literary theory for him remains grounded in hermeneutics as against a mere sociology or psychology of literature.

Ricoeur helpfully distinguishes between Wolfgang Iser's reader-response theory as "a phenomenology of the individual act of reading" and Jauss's aesthetic of reception as "a hermeneutic of the public reception of a work".[93] Thus, after stating the seven

---

[87] Ibid., pp.28 and 30; see further loc. cit., pp.146–7.
[88] H.-G. Gadamer, *Truth and Method*, pp.302 and 306.
[89] Cf. H.H. Kögler, *The Power of Dialogue: Critical Hermeneutics after Gadamer and Foucault* (Cambridge, MA: MIT, 1996), p.137; and Ricoeur, *Time and Narrative*, III, pp.172–3.
[90] E.g. Ricoeur, *Time and Narrative* I, p.77, and III, pp.171–9.
[91] Jauss, *Toward and Aesthetic of Reception*, p.35.
[92] Ibid., pp.36, 39, 41 and 45.
[93] Ricoeur, *Time and Narrative*, III, p.171; see also p.318 n. 44.

programmatic major theses in his Inaugural Lecture which are designed to distance his programme from mistaken forms (including Marxist forms) of assimilating aesthetic theory into literary history, Jauss proceeds to explore in more positive detail the key theme that "the meaning of a literary work rests upon the dialogical (*dialogisch*) relation established between the work and its public in each age".[94] Behind this approach lies a logic of question and answer explored previously by R.G. Collingwood and by Gadamer, except that, as we have observed, Jauss sees "recognition" and "innovation" as complementary, and uses the now-familiar model of the reader as one "who performs the 'score' of the text in the course of the reception ...".[95]

This coheres with our argument on temporality and time. Jauss refuses to abstract a "classic text" from temporal processes: *part of what the text is consists in its performance of the temporal action of opening up a new horizon.* A text makes an impact (*Stossen*): it invites new questions and sets a new agenda. Creativity and integration constitute positive features; but a text may also challenge, provoke and provide change of direction. Jauss's argument runs very close to Walhout's work (above) on fiction and "possible worlds". In tracing a variety of ways in which different kinds of texts may make an impact on different kinds of readers Jauss writes, "Through the opposition between fiction and reality, between the poetic and the practical function of the language", readers may find horizons of expectation reshaped, sometimes "within the wider horizon of the experience of life", sometimes within a more narrowly-focused horizon of "literary expectations".[96] "The horizon of expectation peculiar to literature does not coincide with that of everyday life."[97]

Issues of purpose and ethics cannot be excluded from hermeneutics; questions of understanding necessitate a historical and relational (as against Cartesian) frame; interrogation of the questions and answers to which the text provides an address demands exegetical rigour and critical reflection. Jauss's concern for aesthetic impact allows room for the acceptance and indeed positive evaluation of "pleasure" or "enjoyment" (*Genuss*). This can creatively open a space for fresh perception. Nevertheless against the "free" play of postmodern deconstruction, Jauss believes that "play" is bounded by the constraints of what it is to perform the "score" of *this* text, as against another. In his introduction to one of Jauss' key works Paul de Man dryly observes, "He has always treated such Parisian extravagances with a measure of suspicion."[98]

---

[94] Ibid.
[95] Jauss, *Toward an Aesthetic of Reception*, p.145; cf. p.143.
[96] Ibid., p.24.
[97] This is Ricoeur's summary of Jauss's point: Ricoeur, *Time and Narrative*, III, p.173.
[98] Paul de Man, "Introduction" in Jauss, *Toward an Aesthetic of Reception*, p.xix.

CHAPTER FORTY-ONE

God will be All in All: "Luther and Barth on 1 Corinthians 15: Six Theses for Theology in Relation to Recent Interpretation" (1995)

The choice of this subject owes much to the role of this essay as part of a tribute to Professor James Atkinson on his 80th birthday. James Atkinson was my Head of Department for the greater part of my fifteen years as Lecturer and Senior Lecturer in Biblical Studies in the University of Sheffield (1970–85). He conveyed a burning passion for Luther, for 1 Corinthians, for the Bible and for the Gospel, but always within the context of careful scholarship as Professor of Biblical Studies and also as a loyal churchman. The title of the volume, The Bible, the Reformation, and the Church: Essays in Honour of James Atkinson, *admirably makes this point (editor, W.P. Stephens, Sheffield: Sheffield Academic Press [JSNT Supplement Series 105] 1995). This essay is reprinted from pp.258–89.*

1 Corinthians has remained a passion of mine from the early 1960s when I prepared a dissertation for the MTh in King's College, University of London, on the subject "Eschatology and the Holy Spirit in Paul with Special Reference to 1 Corinthians". In these early days Karl Barth's small but prophetic book The Resurrection of the Dead *also deeply impressed me. Luther and Barth capture Paul's stress on the resurrection as a sheer gift of God's sovereign grace. It is a gift no less from God alone than justification by grace through faith. Luther and Barth demonstrate the pastoral role that this emphasis plays in relation to the rest of the epistle. The study below combines exegesis, hermeneutics, history of interpretation and especially Christian theology.*

I
The Bible, The Reformation and the Church

This study consciously draws together the three elements that form the title of this volume. First, attention to *the Bible* finds expression in an exegetical discussion of 1 Corinthians 15. Further, this work explores the hermeneutical claim made explicitly by the early Barth that 1 Corinthians 15 provides the most appropriate vantage-point from which to understand the argument and theology of the first fourteen chapters of the epistle. This claim might also be said to be implicit, though not openly stated, in the approaches of Luther and Calvin to the resurrection chapter.

Second, this discussion focuses also on issues fundamental to *the Reformation*. In the first place, and most obviously, from among the many interpretations of this chapter in 1 Corinthians which have been offered I have chosen to enter into dialogue primarily with that of Luther. I have also selected for special consideration Karl Barth's exposition of this chapter, since Barth represents a voice, if not the voice, of Reformation theology in modern times. The whole of Barth's exposition centres in the proposal that throughout 1 Corinthians, when Paul makes such a declaration as 'Everyone shall receive praise of God' (1 Cor. 4:5), then, in Barth's words: 'This "of God" is clearly the secret nerve of this whole (and perhaps not only this) section.'[1]

This becomes evident most clearly in the resurrection chapter. Life after death is *not an innate capacity of human nature* or of 'the soul' but a *sovereign, gracious, transforming act of God*. Hence Gaston Deluz observes, 'Like many modern Christians, they confused this pagan doctrine of immortality with Christian teaching on the resurrection.'[2] But this contrast between the initiative and all-sufficiency of God's grace in Christ as pure *gift* and the notion of some *human capacity* as a contribution which 'the dead' who have been brought to nothing can supposedly provide, constitutes a recurring theme which coheres with Reformation theology.

The third theme of the title, namely *the Church*, stands as an inescapable theme in 1 Corinthians. The epistle raises issues about unity and groups or factions; about ministry and charismatic enthusiasm; about order, freedom and ethics, and about gifts and worship. But the very prominence of ecclesiology in the agenda serves only to reveal the unqualified contrast between the ecclesial self-importance and obtrusiveness which shapes the agenda at Corinth and Paul's own counter-agenda: 'What do you have that you have not received? If, then, you have received it, why do you boast as if it were not a gift?' (4:6). The church, or certain groups within the church, might lay claim to possess *gnosis*, but 'our knowledge is imperfect ... now we see in the mirror dimly' (13:9, 12). Prior to the resurrection of the dead, Corinthian triumphalism and their enthusiasm of the Spirit is to be held in check by *theologia crucis* – in Luther's sense of the term. Paul proclaims the implications of the cross (1:18–3.4). If the Corinthians think that they are 'already filled', why do the apostles suffer as 'offscourings' (περίψημα) and are treated like 'dirt' (περικαθάρματα 4:13)?

The resurrection chapter offers an answer. Only when the whole person (σῶμα) comes fully under the unhindered transforming agency of the Holy Spirit at the last day (ἐγείρεται σῶμα πνευματικόν 15:44) do claims made by the Corinthians to be 'people of the Spirit' at last become properly timely. For what was 'sown in weakness' (15:43) will at last be raised by God to be transformed fully into the image of the likeness of Christ, the last Adam, the Man from Heaven (15:48, 49). Although in the present it has already begun, transformation into the image of Christ reaches full completion only in the post-resurrection mode of existence to which Paul points the Corinthian community in ch. 15. The future orientation of 1 Corinthians 15, then, says much about the nature of the church in the present, including its fallibility, its need of correction and continuous reform, and the impropriety of any unqualified spiritual 'enthusiasm', which despises order.

---

[1] K. Barth, *The Resurrection of the Dead* (ET; London: Hodder & Stoughton, 1933), p.18; German: *Die Auferstehung der Toten* (Munich: Kaiser Verlag, 1924), p.4.
[2] G. Deluz, *A Companion to 1 Corinthians* (London: Darton, Longman and Todd, 1963), p.225.

II

Resurrection as a Sovereign, Creative, Gracious Act of God: Six Theses, Including a Comparison with Justification by Grace

The interweaving of these three themes of the Bible, the Reformation and the Church constitutes a pre-understanding that informs the exegesis of 1 Corinthians 15. This, in turn, leads us to propose six specific theses that we table for discussion. After we state the theses we shall compare them with modern exegesis and with recent reconstructions of theologies in Corinth. The following represents a preliminary formulation of these six theses.

(1) 1 Corinthians 15, in the view of Karl Barth, 'forms not only the close and crown of the whole Epistle, but also provides the clue to its meaning, from which place light is shed onto the whole, and it becomes intelligible ... as a unity'.[3] Luther's exposition of this chapter also presupposes that its argument takes up threads already apparent in various other chapters. For example, he recognizes, anticipating certain modern arguments, that a variety of grounds for denials of the resurrection may reflect outlooks of different groups or factions at Corinth, to which Paul alludes from the first chapter onwards (1:10–13). If a person does not believe in the resurrection, Luther declares, 'he must deny in a lump the Gospel and everything that is proclaimed of Christ and of God. For all of this is linked together like a chain ... Whoever denies this article must simultaneously deny far more ... in brief, that God is God'.[4] If these approaches are valid, it may be necessary to re-evaluate the partition theories of J. Weiss, W. Schmithals, R. Jewett and others, as an analysis of 1 Corinthians, or at least to consider their possible implications.

(2) The resurrection chapter places the central weight of its argument on the 'of God' which Barth identifies as the 'secret nerve' behind most of the epistle. H.A.A. Kennedy rightly argues that if there is any 'organic link' between the 'bare grain' (γυμνός) of the corpse which rots away (15:37) and the future 'whole person' (σῶμα 15:38), Paul answers with 'the only one we can expect him to give... "the sovereign power of God". "He giveth it a body according as he willed" (v. 38) (ἠθέλησεν) "the aorist denotes the final act of God's will, determining the constitution of the nature" ... illustrated by Gen. 1:11, "And God said ... and it was so"'.[5] Karl Barth rightly singles out as the key to whether resurrection belief is intelligible, or whether its denial renders the effects of the gospel

---

[3] Barth, *Resurrection*, p.11.

[4] M. Luther, *Luther's Works. XXVIII. Commentaries on 1 Corinthians 7, 1 Corinthians 15, Lectures on 1 Timothy* (ed. H.C. Oswald, Saint Louis, MO: Concordia Publishing House, 1973), pp.94 and 95; on denials of the resurrection and their multiple reasons see p.59. In *Martin Luthers Werke*, Weimar edn (hereafter abbreviated as WA), the *Commentary on 1 Corinthians 15* appears in vol. 36, pp.482–696; cf. here pp.525 and 526, and p.482. In a very recent study no less than five possible reasons are traced for the denial of the resurrection, out of which the author selects one as the most probable: G. Barth, 'Zur Frage nach der 1 Korinther 15 bekämpften Auferstehungsleugnung', *ZNW* 83 (1992), pp.187–201. For a historical survey see B. Spörlein, *Die Leugnung der Auferstehung: Eine historisch-kritische Untersuchung zu 1 Kor 15* (Regensburg: F. Pustet, 1971).

[5] H.A.A. Kennedy, *St Paul's Conceptions of the Last Things* (London: Hodder & Stoughton, 1904), p.243.

'void' or 'empty' (15:14–17) the central problem: 'Some have no knowledge *of God*' (15:34).[6]

Martin Luther expresses this principle with the words: 'Be content to hear what God will do. Then *leave it to Him* what will become of it.'[7] Everything rests, not on a doctrine of human capacities, but on a recognition of the inexhaustible and infinitely resourceful creative power of God already evidenced in creation, to bring about that mode of existence which is appropriate and glorious for its *new role*. Luther makes precisely this point. He writes, 'Since He once before *created us from nothing*, He can also again give us life from the grave and *give the body a new form* ... Each will have its *own peculiar glory*.'[8]

(3) A dead person cannot contribute anything to a new process of life, at least in the sense of initiating life or rendering it possible as an 'achievement'. A creative and transforming act of God brings this new life into being. As Jeremias rightly pointed out in a well-known research article, there is more to Paul's words 'flesh and blood cannot inherit the kingdom of God' (15:50) than the dualistic problem of how a physical mode of existence can enter into a trans-physical realm.[9] Luther, in fact, anticipates Jeremias' line of approach by citing this very verse with the explanatory gloss: 'Christ also says (John 3:3, 6) "Unless one is born anew, he cannot see the kingdom of God", for "that which is born of the flesh is flesh".'[10] This is why resurrection, as Deluz asserts, invites a different focus and a different logic of belief from that of notions of immortality.

Luther therefore insists that belief in the resurrection 'is surely not man's competence and power ... When reason approaches this article of faith and reflects on it, it is entirely at a loss.'[11] In a 500-page study of resurrection published in 1984 Pheme Perkins makes this same point. Philosophically it may be possible, she argues, to conceive a personal identity in ways that do not limit it to a physical body. Thus the *Vedanta Sutra* presupposes continuing threads of consciousness, and Socrates and Plato argue that the human soul belongs to the indestructible realm of forms or of trans-empirical reality. But, Pheme Perkins concludes, 'Resurrection cannot be made philosophically coherent without distorting some of its fundamental commitments ... In the end the two [notions of immortality and resurrection] must part company.'[12]

(4) If resurrection entails an act of new creation which lies entirely beyond the capacities of the human self to achieve, there emerges a clear and a close parallel between the grace of God which bestows new life out of nothing, and the grace of God which bestows a new relationship or 'putting to rights in righteousness' which transcends all human capacity or competency to achieve. Paul alludes to this parallel explicitly in Romans 4, where he

---

6   Barth, *Resurrection*, p.139; see equally pp.17–18, 189–91, and elsewhere.

7   LW 28.180 (my italics; WA 36.647).

8   LW 28.182 and 183 (my italics; WA 36.649, 651).

9   J. Jeremias, ' "Flesh and Blood Cannot Inherit the Kingdom of God" (1 Cor. XV.50)', *NTS* 2 (1955), pp.151–9.

10   LW 28.198 (WA 36.672).

11   LW 28.59 (WA 36.492–93).

12   P. Perkins, *Resurrection: New Testament Witness and Contemporary Reflection* (London: Chapman, 1984), p.438.

expounds the nature of Abraham's faith as trust in the God 'who *gives life to the* dead and calls into existence the things *that do not exist'* (Rom. 4:17).

This 'believing against hope' (v. 18) entails Abraham's self-perception that it did not lie within his own capacities or competence to actualize God's promise, since he 'was as good as *dead'* (v. 19). But 'fully convinced that *God was able* to do what he had promised ... his faith was "reckoned to him as *righteousness*" ... It will be reckoned to us who believe in him that *raised from the dead* Jesus our Lord' (Rom. 4:21, 22, 24). Luther sums up the point in his *Lectures on Romans*: 'Let him cease to believe *in himself* and believe in God.'[13] This is closely parallel, however, to Barth's comment on the issue that shaped the entire argument of 1 Corinthians: 'They believe not in *God* but in *their own belief* in God and in particular leaders ... They confuse belief with specific human experiences, conviction ...'.[14]

To accept that one is justified by grace is part of the same logic as trust in the promise of the God of resurrection. Resurrection transforms the believer into the image and likeness of Christ as the last Adam, from whose character and righteousness the nature of the resurrection mode of existence is drawn. Hence Luther urges that the event of resurrection entails 'divesting' the nature of the prototype who was the first Adam to 'become like the celestial Man, Christ ... We shall divest ourselves of that image and essence and receive another's, namely the celestial Christ's.'[15] But language about clothing draws together the discourse of justification and the discourse of resurrection. Without such 'reclothing', Luther observes, Paul declares that 'you are still in your sins' (15:17). On this turns whether, in Luther's words, the reader is 'justified by His resurrection'.[16] Christ's resurrection completes what Luther perceives to be a substitutionary work of Christ: 'Christ brought it about that the venom ... [was] deadened and completely swallowed up by Him ... "Death, where is your sting?"'.[17] Among twentieth-century writers Oscar Cullman most notably calls attention to this Christological basis of a 'stingless' death. Paul's joyous exclamation: 'Death, where is your sting?' (15:55) belongs together with his trustful assurance: 'Whether we live or die, we are the Lord's' (Rom. 14:8).[18]

(5) If this close relation between resurrection and justification, each on the basis of divine grace alone, genuinely reflects the arguments of Romans and of 1 Corinthians, this now invites a radical reappraisal of the particular line of argument associated with A. Schweitzer and others to the effect that justification occurs in Romans and Galatians only as a polemic imposed by force of the circumstances of controversy. Schweitzer rejects the Reformation principle which ascribes to justification by grace the status of a central hermeneutical principle in Pauline theology. This conceptual scheme, Schweitzer argues, arises only when Paul is confronted with Jewish–Gentile controversy in Galatians and Romans.

---

[13] M. Luther, *Luther's Works*. XXV. *Lectures on Romans* (Saint Louis, MO: Concordia, 1972), p.284 (=LW 28.284, my italics; WA 56.296).

[14] Barth, *Resurrection*, p.17 (my italics).

[15] LW 28.196 (WA 36.670 and 671).

[16] LW 28.102 (WA 36.536).

[17] LW 28.204 (WA 36.681).

[18] O. Cullmann, *Immortality of the Soul or Resurrection of the Dead* (London: Epworth Press, 1958), p.55.

Schweitzer's heavy metaphor about justification as a mere 'subsidiary crater which is formed within the rim of the main crater' in Pauline thought is known to all students of Pauline theology.[19] If, however, the concept remains implicit in, or very closely related to, Paul's theology of grace in 1 Corinthians, and is focused especially in the event of resurrection, Schweitzer's arguments become seriously problematic. The theme becomes more than the product of circumstantial factors; it lies at the heart of Pauline theology. 1 Corinthians, no less than Romans and Galatians, stresses the priority and exclusivity of grace, and the event of the resurrection of the dead provides a paradigm case.

This principle receives added confirmation in the light of Schweitzer's own ready admission that justification by grace through faith 'belongs strictly speaking' to the future in Paul's thought. For it belongs to the conceptual scheme in which 'believers possess in advance the state of existence proper to the Messianic kingdom'.[20] This calls into question the claim which Schweitzer inherits from Lipsius and from Lüdemann that justification belongs to a conceptual frame which is incompatible with, or at least radically different from, a participatory notion of Christ-union. Both conceptual schemes, if they differ, derive this currency from eschatological promise. Thus J. Weiss, who stands close to Schweitzer in this context, views justification in Pauline thought as a 'pre-dating of what is really an eschatological act'.[21] P. Stuhlmacher develops further the apocalyptic context presupposed by Ernst Käsemann, in which justification operates as both gift and power. For Stuhlmacher it is equally a creative and a forensic act of God, in which God actualizes an eschatological promise of freedom and righteousness. In the present there remains an 'eschatological reservation', a 'now-and-not-yet', a 'hiddenness', prior to the apocalyptic manifestation of judgement and resurrection as declarative and promissory speech-acts by the Creator.[22]

Karl Barth likewise associates justification by grace in his *Church Dogmatics* with 'the right of God' as vested in the eschatological judgement of God and the resurrection. He observes, 'The event of the resurrection is the revelation of the sentence of God which is executed in this judgement; of the free resolve of his love ... the righteousness which has come to man ...'.[23] He rightly criticizes Schweitzer and Wrede at this point for allowing themselves to be misled by subordinating Christology to an eschatological programme. In 1 Corinthians, no less than in Galatians or in Romans, '"Christ Jesus is made unto us wisdom, righteousness, sanctification and redemption" (1 Cor. 1:30).'[24] Strikingly, R. Bultmann entirely endorses Barth's view here, in his essay of 1926. Bultmann agrees, 'The contending parties in Corinth rob God of what is his, of his right of judgement ... his freedom'.[25] He accepts Barth's 'masterly exegesis' which identifies this 'of God' as 'the

---

[19]   A. Schweitzer, *The Mysticism of Paul the Apostle* (London: A. & C. Black, 1931), p.225; cf. pp.219–26 and also pp.294–7.

[20]   Schweitzer, *Mysticism,* p.205.

[21]   J. Weiss, *Earliest Christianity* (New York: Harper & Row, 1959), II, p.502.

[22]   P. Stuhlmacher, *Gerechtigkeit Gottes bei Paulus* (Göttingen: Vandenhoeck & Ruprecht, 1965), pp.217–36.

[23]   K. Barth, *Church Dogmatics* (15 vols, Edinburgh: T. & T. Clark, 1965–77), IV.1, p.514 (hereafter cited as *CD*).

[24]   Barth, *CD*, IV.1, p.524.

[25]   R. Bultmann, 'Karl Barth, *The Resurrection of the Dead in Faith'*, in *Faith and Understanding*, I (London: SCM Press, 1969), p.68; cf. pp.66–94.

secret nerve' of 1 Corinthians: '"Let no man glory in men" (iii.21), or expressed in positive form: "He that glorieth, let him glory in the Lord" (i.31).'[26] Bultmann endorses Barth's view of the importance of the resurrection chapter for the rest of the epistle. Paul attacks 'a spiritualistic belief in immortality'. But this belongs to the logic of grace and divine promise: 'Death is not overcome by us by means of a pious frame of mind'; faith is 'a waiting for … what is promised'.[27] In Galatians this is how Paul formulates the nature of justification by grace: 'By faith we wait for the hope of righteousness' (Gal. 5:5).

Luther, as we may expect, perceives this dimension in 1 Corinthians 15. God, he writes, 'will create a new and eternal life … We must judge contrary to our feeling and in accordance with what God says, as convinced as though this had already come to pass … trusting in it … I on my part contribute nothing … I merely accept this, or receive it by faith.'[28]

(6) Our sixth thesis concerns the relation between the future promissory focus of the fifteenth chapter and claims among groups in the church at Corinth to have direct possession already of a fullness of experience of the Holy Spirit which, in Paul's judgement, will become a reality only when the entire person (σῶμα) will be transformed into a σῶμα πνευματικόν at the last resurrection (15:44). The term 'spiritual body' denotes the openness of the whole person to the unhindered transforming agency of the Holy Spirit, who will change the hitherto flawed character into the image of Christ (15:49).

If Luther and Barth are correct in seeing the epistle as a unity which receives light from the fifteenth chapter, here is the climax of a sustained argument in earlier chapters to redefine the Corinthians' notions of 'spiritual' and 'spirituality' in accordance with what it is to be like Christ, to 'bear the image of the Man from heaven'. The first explicit appearance of this theme comes in 3:1: 'I could not address you as "spiritual" people' (οὐκ … ὡς πνευματικοῖς αλλ᾿ ὡς σαρκίνοις). The reason for this that Paul offers lies in their being characterized by the un-Christlike qualities of jealousy and quarrelsomeness (3:3). However, even the passage from 1:18 to 2:5 contains an allusive or implicit overture for those with eyes to see. For if the message is, in Luther's sense, a *theologia crucis*, not a *theologia gloriae*, it is telling that Paul recalls his own 'weakness, fear and trembling' when he preached the cross. God's choice of the socially and intellectually lowly stands in contrast to the church's preoccupation with wisdom and the Spirit. As we shall note, some argue that 'weakness' includes a social dimension in 1 Corinthians.

Spiritual 'enthusiasm' leaves little room for a sense of need: the eye says to the hand, 'I have no need of you' (1 Cor. 12:21). It seems that all wish to be apostles, prophets, teachers, or miracle-workers (12:29). The charismatic 'spiritual people' have become like kings (ἐβασιλεύσατε 4:8); the apostles are treated like dirt (περικαθάρματα 4:13). To be so far above the law that they can welcome a believer whose life-style is incestuous is a cause of inflated self-congratulation (πεφυσιωμένοι 5:2). Every single one has

---

[26] Barth, *Resurrection*, p.17, cited with approval by Bultmann.
[27] Bultmann, 'Karl Barth', p.85.
[28] LW 28.99 and 121 (WA 36.530 and 564).

'knowledge' (γνῶσις 8:1). Unlike Paul, they claim certain 'rights' (ἐξουσία 9:13 as against 9:15). As long as they can make their presence felt at worship as 'spiritual' people (14:27) it does not matter if 'lesser' believers feel like strangers in their own home community (βάρβαρος 14:11; ἐν ἑτερογλώσσοις 14:21; μαίνεσθε 14:23).

In contrast to all this, the resurrection chapter reminds the reader the *whole* person is not yet fully under the unhindered control of the Holy Spirit. The test of this, moreover, turns on whether transformation has yet reshaped them fully into the image of Christ, 'the Man from heaven'. Luther makes this clear. The one who will receive the σῶμα πνευματικόν will be like 'the spiritual Adam ... completely new and spiritual and lives solely of and by the Spirit'.[29] Luther anticipates the supposedly 'modern' view (which in fact can be traced to Chrysostom and which I have advocated elsewhere) that there were some at Corinth 'who tried to be clever and subtle and alleged that the resurrection had taken place a long time ago'.[30] This provides one reason among others for their denial of the resurrection.

Karl Barth points out in this connection that chapters 13 on love and 15 on the resurrection radically relativize chapters 12 and 14 on spiritual gifts. Love and resurrection constitute permanent eschatological realities that cannot become obsolete. 'Spiritual gifts' will pass on and will pass away because they are circumstantial. Thus chapter 13 indicates 'a great passing away of all those things that are not love'.[31] Thus whether the *phenomenon* of spiritual gifts can offer parallels in pagan religion remains for Barth neither here nor there. He writes, 'What we are really concerned with is not *phenomena* in themselves, but with their *whence*? and *whither*? to what do they point?'[32] If they are reduced to instrumental tools for mere self-affirmation or for self-fulfilment, they do not correspond with the eschatological and Christological realities to which the chapters on love and on the resurrection bear witness. It becomes a different matter if their basis is authentically 'of God' and their use and purpose genuinely for 'mutual edification'.[33] But 1 Corinthians 11 and 1 Corinthians 15 speak of 'order': God, Christ and Spirit relate to one another in ordered, purposive, structured ways, in which even the Son hands back ultimate dominion to God (15:26–28; cf. 11:3). The resurrection of Christ and of believers proceeds 'each in his own order' (15:21). Barth comments that if someone is a 'real' prophet or pneumatic, such a person 'will understand that'.[34] The result will not be 'the troubled sea of spiritualistic and theosophical illumination ... the bliss and terror of hysterical hallucination and intuition which should be more the concern of the nerve specialist than of us theologians'.[35]

Luther was compelled to address such claims in some of the effects of the work of Carlstadt and of Thomas Müntzer. Luther urged by contrast that a 'full' experience of the Spirit would be perfected only at the resurrection. In his Sermon on *The Creed* of 1528 he

---

[29] LW 28.192 (WA 36.665).
[30] LW 28.59, and A.C. Thiselton, 'Realised Eschatology at Corinth', *NTS* 24 (1978), pp.510–26.
[31] Barth, *Resurrection*, p.76.
[32] Barth, *Resurrection*, p.80 (my italics).
[33] Barth, *Resurrection*, p.94; cf. p.96.
[34] Barth, *Resurrection*, p.99.
[35] Barth, *Resurrection*, p.75.

declares: 'The Holy Spirit ... begins to sanctify now; when we have died, he will complete this sanctification through both "the resurrection of the body" and "the life everlasting" ... Then we will be ... raised "in glory"'.[36] Luther and Barth both stress, however, that the issue of 'spiritual phenomena' does not turn only on such manifestation as the contrast between triumphalism and suffering. Even 'the fanatics' (as Luther calls the followers of Müntzer) may 'select their own cross ... make their suffering meritorious' as if it were a kind of 'achievement'. All 'spirituality', for Paul, for Luther and for Barth, depends for its validity on whether it reflects the character of Christ. In such circumstances, Luther continues, 'you suffer willingly ... because Christ and his suffering is being bestowed upon you and made your own'.[37] This is the kind of experience to which Paul alludes in 1 Cor. 4:9–13, and especially in several passages of 2 Corinthians also.

III
What Did Some Doubt in Corinth?

Luther's exegesis of 1 Corinthians 15 has a far more 'modern' ring about it, in the sense that it seriously engages with historical questions about the Corinthian community than might be suggested by those who often view him as the last medieval exegete prior to the 'modern' era of Calvin. To be sure, the vast range of Luther's commentaries written over a long period of development allows for a variation of assessments of his different exegetical material. But here Luther writes sometimes ahead of his times. Our next task is to compare the exegetical work of Luther and of Barth on this chapter which has contributed to the formulation of our six specific theses with issues discussed in recent specialist biblical scholarship. This will both clarify the significance of our theses and assist in evaluating certain exegetical conclusions. We begin with the extensive modern literature which has been produced on reasons for the denial of the resurrection at Corinth.

Luther rightly perceived that denials of the resurrection may well have emerged on a different basis within different groups at Corinth.[38] The recent discussion by Gerhard Barth (1992) together with the historical exegetical surveys of Bernhard Spörlein (1971) and Christian Wolff (1982) seem to bear this out.[39] A.J.M. Wedderburn insists that whatever the fine-print details concerning Paul's understanding of the theologies of the groups at Corinth, there is a general scholarly consensus that 'he quotes them accurately' when Paul observes, 'Some' (τινες) say 'there is no resurrection of the dead'.[40] But within this general recognition about 'some', five explanatory hypotheses have been offered in detail.

---

[36] LW 51.168.

[37] M. Luther, 'Sermon at Coburg on Cross and Suffering' (1530), in LW 51.99 (WA 32.30).

[38] LW 18.59 (WA 36.482).

[39] G. Barth, 'Zur Frage nach der in 1 Corinther 15 bekämpften Auferstehungsleugnung', ZNW 83 (1992), pp.187–201; cf. B. Spörlein, *Die Leugnung der Auferstehung;* and C. Wolff, *Der erste Brief des Paulus an die Korinther (Zweiter Teil)* (THKNT; Berlin: Evangelische Verlagsanstalt, 2nd edn, 1982).

[40] A.J.M. Wedderburn, The Problem of the Denial of the Resurrection in 1 Corinthians XV', *NovT* 23 (1981), p.229; cf. pp.229–41.

(1) Some writers have held that the church at Corinth in general denied the possibility of life after death as such. W.M.L. de Wette argued that these believers had been over-influenced by Epicurean philosophy; hence Paul seems to cite an Epicurean slogan 'let us eat and drink, for tomorrow we die' (15:32) in order to reject it.[41] Conzelmann (1969, Eng. 1979) and others reject this view, but Gerhard Barth (1992) urges that we should not underestimate the importance of pagan influences. Paul's allusion to his willingness to sacrifice his life (1 Cor 15:19, 30–32), G. Barth argues, utilizes a recognized *topos* in these circles for hope beyond the grave. H.A.W. Meyer follows Michaelis in construing the denial of the resurrection also as a denial of survival after death as such; but now he does this not on the basis of *pagan* influence, but through the effect of *Sadducean Jewish* influence.[42] Wedderburn (1981) attacks the plausibility of such a diagnosis on the ground that if they did not believe in life after death in any form, why should the Corinthians practise 'baptism for the dead' (15:29)? But quite apart from the multiple interpretations of this verse, Wedderburn concedes that the group identified by de Wette or by Meyer may not be the same group as that to which Paul alludes in 15:29. This, in turn, contributes to the plausibility of Luther's claim that because of factions or differences in outlook at Corinth, more than one basis for the denial of the resurrection may be involved.

(2) Luther also cites the possibility that denials of the resurrection might come from those who 'alleged that the resurrection had taken place a long time ago'.[43] A number of modern scholars express sympathy with this view, including J. Schniewind (1952), J. Munck (1954, Eng. 1959), U. Wilckens (1959), R.M. Grant (1963), E. Käsemann (1965), H.M. Shires (1966), J.H. Wilson (1968), C.K. Barrett (1968), F.F. Bruce (1971), my own analysis (1978) and that of C.H. Talbert (1992).[44] Although in my study I suggested certain counter-replies, this view has also been attacked and rejected (at least as a major or comprehensive explanation) by H. Conzelmann (1969), W. Schmithals (1971), E. Earle Ellis (1974), R.A. Horsley (1978), in part A.J.M. Wedderburn (1981) and G. Barth (1992).[45]

---

[41] Spörlein, *Die Leugnung*, p.7.

[42] H.A.W. Meyer, *Critical and Exegetical Handbook to the Epistles to the Corinthians*, II (Edinburgh: T. & T. Clark, 1884), p.36.

[43] LW 28.59; WA 36.482.

[44] J. Munck, *Paul and the Salvation of Mankind* (London: SCM Press, 1959), p.165; U. Wilckens, *Weisheit und Torheit: Eine exegetische-religionsgeschichtliche Untersuchung zu 1 Kor. 1 und 2* (Tübingen: Mohr, 1959), p.11; R.M. Grant, *An Historical Introduction to the NT* (London: Collins, 1963), p.204; H.M. Shires, *The Eschatology of Paul in the Light of Modern Scholarship* (Philadelphia, PA: Westminster Press, 1966), pp.53–4; J.H. Wilson, 'The Corinthians Who Say There is No Resurrection of the Dead', *ZNW* 59 (1968), pp.90–107; C.K. Barrett, *A Commentary on the First Epistle to the Corinthians* (London: A. & C. Black, 1968), p.109; F.F. Bruce, *1 and 2 Corinthians* (London: Oliphants, 1971), pp.49–50; E. Käsemann, *New Testament Questions of Today* (London: SCM Press, 1968), pp.125–6; Thiselton, 'Realised Eschatology at Corinth'; C.H. Talbert, *Reading Corinthians: A Literary and Theological Commentary on 1 and 2 Corinthians* (New York: Crossroad, 1987 and 1992), p.98.

[45] E. Earle Ellis, 'Christ Crucified', in R. Banks (ed.), *Reconciliation and Hope* (Exeter: Paternoster Press, 1974), pp.73–4; H. Conzelmann, *A Commentary on the First Epistle to the Corinthians* (Philadelphia, PA: Fortress Press, 1975), p.262; R.A. Horsley, '"How Can some of you Say that there is no Resurrection of the Dead?" Spiritual Elitism at Corinth', *Nov.T.* 20 (1978), pp.203–31, esp. pp.203–5; Wedderburn, 'Problem of the Denial', pp.231–3; and W. Schmithals, *Gnosticism in Corinth* (Nashville, TN: Abingdon, 1971), pp.157–9.

In the end, however, all that these critiques appear to establish is that hints of different problems may apply to different groups, as Luther rightly implied.

This situation of confusion was perceived as long ago as in Chrysostom's Homily 38 on this chapter, where he considers the hypothesis that some of the Corinthians anticipated the problem that 'the resurrection is past already' (citing Hymenaeus and Philetus in 2 Tim. 2:17, 18). However, he then adds, 'At one time they said thus, but at another that the body rises not again but the purification of the soul is the resurrection.'[46] This entirely coheres with the most appropriate translation of εἰκῆ in 15:2. Paul would be less likely to suggest that as a whole the church has 'believed in vain' (15:2 RSV) even as a hypothesis in a *reductio ad absurdum*; more probably they believed 'in a *confused, haphazard* way'. This offers a perfectly acceptable lexicographical meaning.

(3) Chrysostom's alternative suggestion that the readers also confused the resurrection of the body with the immortality of the soul finds sympathy among many modern scholars. However, this view may be held in two distinct versions. Both cohere with our six theses. The first version strengthens our second, third and fourth theses; the second version coheres especially with our sixth thesis. We have already noted the comments of G. Deluz (1963) and P. Perkins (1984) that whereas the notion of the survival of the self as threads of continuing consciousness beyond the boundaries of the body may find a home within philosophical exploration of pagan religion, the notion of resurrection as a sovereign act of divine gift belongs to a distinctively Christian theology.[47] In this sense, confusion between immortality of the soul and resurrection of the whole person distinguishes faith in God's sovereign power to create from nothing, and faith in innate human capacities to survive. This represents the first of the two versions under discussion and is central to my argument.

Hans Leitzmann (1949), Paul Hoffmann (1966), R.J. Sider (1977), Jerome Murphy O'Conner (1979), G. Sellin (1986) and A. Strobel (1989) follow W. Bousset (1907) and J. Weiss (1910) in seeing behind the denial of the resurrection a confusion with a notion of a state of immortality which was achieved when the soul was released from the physical body.[48] Such a view not only rests on a dualistic anthropology, but also presupposes in the strongest form that life after death continues as a natural human capacity. If such a view was current among a group at Corinth, this alone is sufficient to explain Paul's appeal to an apocalyptic framework of thought (whatever the current criticism about the 'loose fit' of this term), since all apocalyptic looks for a divine sovereign act of providing, or of setting to rights, that which human persons cannot provide or set to rights through their own natural capacities and resources. Martinus de Boer (1988) is correct to conclude

---

[46] J. Chrysostom, *Homilies on the Epistles of Paul to the Corinthians* (Nicene and Post-Nicene Fathers; Edinburgh: T. & T. Clark; rpr. Grand Rapids, MI: Eerdmans, 1989), Homily 38, p.226.

[47] G. Deluz, *Companion to 1 Corinthians*, p.226; P. Perkins, *Resurrection*, pp.293–308 and 431–40.

[48] J. Weiss, *Der erste Korintherbrief* (Göttingen Vandenhoeck & Ruprecht, 1910), p.344; H. Leitzmann, *An die Korinther 1/11* (Tübingen: Mohr, 1949), p.79; P. Hoffmann, *Die Toten in Christus: Eine religionsgeschichtliche Untersuchung zur paulinischen Eschatologie* (Münster: Aschendorff, 1966), pp.241–3; R.J. Sider, 'St Paul's Understanding of the Nature and Significance of the Resurrection in 1 Cor. 15.1–19', *NovT* 19 (1977), p.137; J. Murphy O'Connor, *1 Corinthians* (Wilmington, DE: Michael Glazier, 1979), p.137; and G. Sellin, *Der Streit um die Auferstehung der Toten* (Göttingen: Vandenhoeck & Ruprecht, 1986), p.290.

that 'what he [Paul] says about death in 1 Corinthians 15 ... is to be understood in the light of Paul's christological apocalyptic eschatology.'[49] Indeed his valid coupling of 1 Corinthians with Romans 5 in this context strengthens our third and fourth theses, about the relation between resurrection and justification by grace, as well as our second thesis about resurrection as a sovereign act and gift of God.

(4) A second specific version of this more general explanatory hypothesis relates to the phenomenon of spiritual enthusiasm at Corinth. Since at least 1908, with the proposals of Wilhelm Lütgert, a steady stream of modern writers have identified Paul's main opponents at Corinth as 'spiritualistic enthusiasts' of libertine or triumphalist outlook. R. Reitzenstein attempted to argue that this was compounded by influences from Hellenistic mystery religions; while U. Wickens (1959) and most especially W. Schmithals (1956, Eng. 1971) argue for a gnostic or proto-gnostic influence. Certainly, as *De resurrectione epistula ad Rheginum* demonstrates, gnostic sources later than Paul recontextualized and thus reconceptualized 'resurrection' in a sense other than that used by Paul.[50] Birger A. Pearson correctly asserts:

> We can see at work a conflict of dualisms. The opponents were operating on a non-eschatological plane in dividing man's present existence into a duality of heavenly-earthly, spiritual-psychic, incorruptible-corruptible immortal-mortal, levels. Paul can use the *same* terminology, but employs it in a completely eschatological fashion, in which a dualism of 'the present age' and 'the age to come' are the principle factors.[51]

A consensus has emerged to the effect that Schmithals overstated his case concerning a developed and explicit 'gnosticism' at Corinth. R.McL. Wilson launched a convincing attack, and by 1980 R.A. Horsley is able to comment, 'Scholars are gradually relinquishing the belief that the Corinthians were Gnostics.'[52] But this does not invalidate the claims of Pearson and Cullmann that a temporal or eschatological conceptual contrast was in danger of being replaced by a spatial 'elitist' or quasi-ecclesial one. Further, it does not call into question Horsley's contention about a 'hellenistic Jewish religiosity focused on *sophia* and *gnosis*'.[53] John Painter makes this point explicitly. He comments, 'There is no evidence of a Corinthian gnostic redeemer myth. Paul was opposed to their understanding of man and "spirituality".'[54] In particular Paul attacks their notion of 'those who boasted in their "natural abilities" ... the privileged elite ... Theirs is not true wisdom.'[55]

---

[49]   M.C. de Boer, *The Defeat of Death: Apocalyptic Eschatology in 1 Corinthians 15 and Romans 5* (JSNT Sup, 22; Sheffield: JSOT Press, 1988), p.181.

[50]   M.L. Peel (ed.), *The Epistle to Rheginos* (London: SCM Press, 1969), pp.143–9 on 'spiritual resurrection' in *De resurrectione ep. ad. Rheg* 45.32–30, and more broadly S. Laeuchli, *The Language of Faith: An Introduction to the Semantic Dilemma of the Early Church* (London: Epworth Press, 1965).

[51]   B.A. Pearson, *The Pneumatikos-Psychikos Terminology in 1 Corinthians: A Study in the Theology of the Corinthians Opponents of Paul and its Relation to Gnosticism* (SBLDS, 12; Missoula: University of Montana Press, 1973), p.26.

[52]   R.A. Horsley. 'Gnosis in Corinth: 1 Corinthians 8.1-6', *NTS* 27 (1980), p.32; cf. pp.32–51, and R.McL. Wilson, 'How Gnostic were the Corinthians?', *NTS* 19 (1972), pp.65–74.

[53]   Horsley, 'Gnosis', p.32.

[54]   J. Painter, 'Paul and the Pneumatikoi at Corinth', in M.D. Hooker and S.G. Wilson (eds), *Paul and Paulinism: Essays in Honour of C.K. Barrett* (London: SPCK, 1982), p.245; cf. pp.237–50.

[55]   Painter, 'The Pneumatikoi', pp.240 and 241.

James A. Davis in *Wisdom and Spirit* (1984, based on a Nottingham PhD thesis supervised by J.D.G. Dunn) presses further the role of this influence of Jewish wisdom traditions on notions of 'spirituality' at Corinth.[56] These encouraged an achievement-orientated enthusiasm, he argues, which stood in sharp contrast to Paul's 'spirituality' of the cross. 1 Corinthians 1–3 revealed distorted attitudes towards the cross, towards 'wisdom' and towards the ministry. Davis concedes, however, that this may characterize a segment rather than the whole, of the Corinthian community. C.K. Barrett's essay 'Christianity and Corinth' also relates the Corinthian claims about 'wisdom' and 'knowledge' to a 'spiritualistic' background, just as R.A. Horsley also associates 'the language of exalted religious status and spiritual perfection provided by Sophia' with 'spiritual elitism in Corinth'.[57] This 'spiritual elitism', Horsley concludes, manifests itself in such varied forms as ecstatic prophecy, including glossolalia, a sense of being 'ethically pure and incapable of sin (implications of viii 7ff.; x 1–13, 14–22)'. He adds

> In so far as they possessed the divine Sophia they possessed all things ... they belonged to the type of heavenly 'anthropos', as opposed to that of the 'anthropos' who is still too much attached to earthly and bodily matters ... expressed in terms of *perfect vs. children* ... The true self (soul or mind) is secure in its incorruptible spiritual nature ... Accordingly the Corinthian *teleioi* denied 'the resurrection of the dead' (the body) ... a threat to their immortality.[58]

Even if Horsley's complex and wide-ranging explanation may perhaps over-paint the picture, there remain key elements of validity that cohere well with the six theses proposed above.

(5) Finally, two sub-categories of explanation may be grouped together. Both propose that the problem rested on misunderstanding between the Corinthians and Paul. Both are too implausible, however, to invite equal consideration with the other four, each of which contains some element of truth with respect of some specific group at Corinth. A. Schweitzer speculated that an 'ultra-conservative eschatology' of imminent expectation overtook the hope of the resurrection, because it rendered it unnecessary except for the few who, surprisingly, had died before the Parousia (11:30). W. Schmithals attempts to argue that Paul misread the problem 'in his ignorance of the actual situation'.[59] But both of these writers are swept along by the logic of the very distinctive approach that each wishes to advocate, and neither now commands a wide following. The other four explanations, however, especially the second, third and fourth, add weight to the six theses formulated above to which the approaches of Luther and of Barth gave firm encouragement.

---

[56] J.A. Davis, *Wisdom and Spirit: An Investigation of 1 Corinthians 1.18–3.20 against the Background of Jewish Sapiential Traditions of the Graeco-Roman Period* (Lanham, MD: University Press of America, 1984).

[57] C.K. Barrett, 'Christianity at Corinth', rpr. in his *Essays on Paul* (London: SPCK, 1982), pp.1–27, esp. pp.8–10; and Horsley, 'Spiritual Elitism', pp.215 and 229–31.

[58] Horsley, 'Spiritual Elitism', p.231.

[59] Schmithals, *Gnosticism*, p.157.

IV
The Integrity and Unity of 1 Corinthians

Before I offer some concluding comments about the theology of the resurrection chapter with particular reference to Luther and to Barth, I need first to note the state of recent discussions about the unity of 1 Corinthians. Barth concedes that superficially the variety of topics raised in 1 Corinthians 1–14 may seem 'haphazard' since Paul responds to a series of different controversies. Nevertheless, deeper reflection reveals 'a thread ... which binds them internally into a whole'.[60] Further, the disclosure of this single thread occurs primarily in the light of 1 Corinthians 15.[61] In my study of 1978, I argued that in this epistle 'Paul builds up a systematic and coherent set of replies to a varied range of issues, all of which have arisen from the same two basic causes.'[62] These two causes concerned distorted views of eschatology and of the Holy Spirit, for which Paul achieves a positive and proper focus in 1 Corinthians 15.

Luther's exposition of ch. 15 regularly picks up allusions to issues in chapters 1–14 which receive in this resurrection chapter a due focus. These include, for example, in Luther's words, the issue of 'factions' (1:10–17; 3:3; 10:23–30; 11:21–22; 12:25; 15:12); of claims to be 'excellent teachers' (3:18; 8:1; 12:29); of over-confidence that 'spiritual' people 'cannot fall' (10:12); of irresponsible pastors (3:17) who 'spoil and undo' what Paul 'planted' (3:6); of the scope of 'reason and human competence' (1:18–2.5).[63] This is to cite only allusions which occur in the first ten pages of 155 pages of Luther's exposition. Calvin likewise insists that 1 Corinthians 15 constitutes the crown of the whole epistle, since without the resurrection 'the whole Gospel collapses', and this subject 'takes precedence over everything else'.[64]

Hans Conzelmann adopts an utterly different view of the relation between this chapter and the rest of the epistle. He asserts, 'Chapter 15 is a self-contained treatise on the resurrection of the dead.'[65] But in his commentary his comment is brief and virtually assumed rather than argued, and in his introduction to his commentary he contents himself with observing that 'differences of situation' at Corinth cause 'breaks' in the material which suggests the kinds of partitions advocated by Weiss and by Schmithals.[66] The most serious difficulty of these partition theories, however, is identified by Gordon Fee (1987). Although he gives surprisingly little space to a discussion of this major issue in a commentary of over 800 pages, Fee puts his finger on the central point when he observes, 'The very fact that there is so little agreement in the theories suggest that the various reconstructions are not as viable as their proponents would lead us to believe.'[67]

---

[60] Barth, *Resurrection*, p.12.
[61] Barth, *Resurrection*, p.13.
[62] Thiselton, 'Realized Eschatology', p.256.
[63] LW 28.59–60, 61, 65–66 and 69 (WA 36.482–93).
[64] J. Calvin, *The First Epistle of Paul to the Corinthians* (Edinburgh: St Andrew Press, 1960), pp.14 and 312.
[65] Conzelmann, *1 Corinthians*, p.249.
[66] Conzelmann, *1 Corinthians*, p.3.
[67] G.D. Fee, *The First Epistle to the Corinthians* (Grand Rapids, MI: Eerdmans, 1987), p.15.

We need not delay on these theories in detail, except to substantiate this point about their diversity. J. Weiss (1910) posits a first letter (letter A), 10:1–23; 6:12–20; 11:2–24, with 2 Cor. 6:14–7:1; a second (letter B) 7–9; 10:24–11:1; and 12–15; and a third letter (letter C) 1:1–6:11.[68] Maurice Goguel (1926) also postulates three letters, but assigns different blocks to each. Although he follows Weiss broadly in his view of letter A, his 'letter B' contains 5:1–6:11; 7:1–8:13; 10:23–14:40; 15; and 16:1–9, 12; and 'letter C' includes 1:10–4:21; 9:1–27; and 16:10, 11.[69] J. Héring (1948) carefully assesses these proposals, as entailing contradictions, but concludes that two separate letters exist within 1 Corinthians: 'letter A' contains 1–8, 10:23–11:1, and 16:1–4 and 10–14; 'letter B' contains the rest, including ch. 15.[70] W. Schmithals (1973) proposes that Paul wrote *nine* letters to Corinth, the first four of which contain no less than *thirteen or fourteen fragments from our 1 Corinthians.*[71] Robert Jewett (1978) distinguishes six letters, five of which contain sections from 1 Corinthians. 1 Corinthians 15 comes in letter B, together with 6:12–20; 9:24–10:22; 16:13–22 and 2 Cor. 6:14–7:1; while letter C, 'the main frame' contains eight separate blocks; letter D, various fragments; and letter E, 1 Cor. 9:1–18 and 2 Cor. 10–13.[72] W.O. Walker and Gerhard Sellin both write in 1987. Their schemes are simpler, but Sellin still proposes a complex series of blocks for more than one letter, which derive from 1 Corinthians.[73] J.C. Hurd and W.G. Kümmel catalogue allusions to other approaches.[74]

Three distinct responses may be offered. The first is to note the insuperable difficulty identified by Gordon Fee, mentioned above, concerning the very striking lack of consensus in such theories. The second is to recall that writers such as Schmithals are easily carried along by the logic of the distinctive thesis they make. The third point is that, even if partition theories could be established, all of the material at issue remains part of a sustained and extended dialogue between Paul and the groups at Corinth. Hence it does not become incoherent to argue that 1 Corinthians 15 remains a key hermeneutical vantage-point in the light of which these other specific issues can best be understood, even if they are articulated on more than one occasion.

Moreover, Karl Barth believes that the theological significance and the role of 1 Corinthians 15 *crosses the boundaries of this epistle to shed light on the whole Pauline corpus,* or even beyond, into *other parts of the New Testament.* Barth declares, 'What is disclosed here is *Paul's key position.* The resurrection of the dead *is the point from which Paul is speaking* and to which he points. From this standpoint, not only the death of those now living, but above all their life *this side* [Barth's italics] of the threshold of death is ... seen,

---

[68] Weiss, *Der erste Korintherbrief,* pp.xxxix–xliii; also *Earliest Christianity,* I, pp.323–41.

[69] M. Goguel, *Introduction au Nouveau Testament,* IV.2 (Paris: Leroux, 1926), p.86.

[70] J. Héring, *The First Epistle of St Paul to the Corinthians* (London: Epworth Press, 1962), pp.xii–xiv.

[71] W. Schmithals, 'Die Korintherbriefe als Briefsammlung', *ZNW* 64 (1973), pp.263–88; cf. his *Gnosticism,* pp.87–113.

[72] R. Jewett, 'The Redaction of 1 Corinthians and the Trajectory of the Pauline School', *JAAR, suppl.* 46 (1987), pp.398–444.

[73] G. Sellin, 'Hauptprobleme des ersten Korintherbriefes', *Aufstieg und Niedergang der römischischen Welt* II.25.4 (1987), pp.2964–86. cf. W.O. Walker, 'The Burden of Proof in Identifying Interpretations in the Pauline Letters', *NTS* 33 (1987), pp.610–18.

[74] W.G. Kümmel, *Introduction to the New Testament* (London: SCM Press, 1966), pp.203–5, and J.C. Hurd, Jr, *The Origin of 1 Corinthians* (London: SPCK, 1965), pp.43–7.

understood.'[75] Barth adds, 'The ideas developed in 1 Corinthians 15 could better be described as the *methodology of the apostle's preaching* [Barth's italics] ... It is really concerned *not with this or that special thing, but with the meaning and nerve of its whole*'.[76]

In positive terms a number of writers have consciously argued for the integrity of the epistle in full awareness of the analyses offered by those who dispute it. I entirely endorse the view of E.-B. Allo, who, having carefully examined the theories of Weiss and Goguel, concludes, 'We do not hesitate to endorse the judgment of Godet, who sees an intellectual edifice admirably conceived and executed, in spite of the diversity of the material.'[77] Allo offers some tart comments about the methods and aims, and limited perspectives of Weiss, Goguel and others. Lest it might be thought that Allo has become outdated (imprimatur apparently 1934; publication 1956), we may note that recent study by Margaret M. Mitchell (1991) equally stresses the logical (or, to use her term, 'rhetorical') coherence of the epistle as rhetorical unity. She traces a 'rhetoric of reconciliation' through, from a focus on the issue in 1.10 to ch. 15.[78] Although from a different angle, her work nevertheless coheres with Barth's firm and valid assertion: 'the discourse of the whole epistle proceeds from a single point and harks back again to this same point'.[79]

V
Some Exegetical, Hermeneutical and Theological Conclusions

We may now return to review the six theses formulated in section II. For the sake of brevity I shall consider them in three pairs, although sequential attention will be given to theses 5 and 6.

(1) and (2) The key, the 'secret nerve', of the epistle remains the '*of God*' which Barth has identified in such passages as 'everyone shall have praise [or whatever verdict] of God' (4:5); 'Sober up! Some have no knowledge of God' (15:34); '*God* gives it a body as *he has chosen*' (15:38). Barth rightly observes that in 15:34–44 one might well speak of the issue of the 'conceivability' of the resurrection. But, he urges, Paul is not conceptualizing, as if he were a philosopher, the nature of the new σῶμα as such; rather, its 'conceivability' depends on how and whether we can *conceive of God* who as inexhaustibly resourceful and versatile creator has the power to create the kind of σῶμα which he decrees as appropriate for its mode of existence in his presence. This surpasses 'the limitations of human knowledge'.[80]

Luther urges a parallel point. We may need to judge 'contrary to our feelings' and 'contrary to our experience', because the focus of confidence lies not in the boundaries of

---

[75] Barth, *Resurrection*, p.107 (first two italics mine; last italics, Barth's as indicated).

[76] Barth, *Resurrection*, p.115. (first italics, Barth's; second italics mine).

[77] E.-B. Allo, *Saint Paul: Première Epître aux Corinthiens* (Paris: Gabalda, 1956), p.lxxxv.

[78] M. Mitchell, *Paul and the Rhetoric of Reconciliation: An Exegetical Interpretation of the Language and Composition of 1 Corinthians* (Tübingen: Mohr, 1991).

[79] Barth, *Resurrection*, p.113.

[80] Barth, *Resurrection*, pp.194 and 195; cf. A. Robertson and A. Plummer, *A Critical and Exegetical Commentary on the First Epistle of St Paul to the Corinthians* (Edinburgh: T. & T. Clark, 1914), p.368.

human thought, but in the promise of God concerning that which transcends what 'can be believed humanly' because it derives purely from 'God's own power and might'.[81] This invites four comments by way of elaboration.

(a) This theme becomes so transparent when it applies the resurrection that it substantiates Barth's claim to view ch. 15 as the hermeneutical key to all the precious chapters. In 1:18 the 'folly' and the word of the cross reflects the limitations of working within a previously determined frame of reference in contrast to which 'the power of God' opens new horizons. Hence in 1:19 'I will destroy the wisdom of the wise'; for this sets us on the wrong track: 'God chose what is foolish ... that no human being might boast in the presence of God' (1:27, 29). This is because the only ground on which to boast is 'to glory in the Lord' (1:31). Thus, as we saw in section III, wisdom traditions may minister, even if unwittingly, to notions of spiritual or pietistic 'achievement', which misses the point which emerges transparently from ch. 15 that everything depends on the creative power and gift of God.

(b) This invites attention to what M. de Boer calls 'the pneumatic triumphalism' of certain groups at Corinth.[82] As Luther notes, Paul's allusion in 1 Corinthians 15 to the apostolic experience of struggle and conflict ('Why am I in peril every hour?' 15:30) looks back theologically to the principle which is also expressed in 4:8–13: 'you have become kings ... we hunger and thirst ... we have become, and are now, the refuse of the world' (4.8, 10, 13). By contrast, Luther writes, only in the post-resurrection mode of existence for which all believers still wait 'we shall have all spiritual gifts'.[83]

(c) This represents precisely the broad significance of resurrection that has been exemplified in theological terms by such writers as W. Künneth, who declares, 'The resurrection witness itself produces a crisis for every philosophical optimism which imagines it can command life and immortality'; it speaks of 'a life which does not lie within the power of men'.[84] This latter concept of life, he insists, would distort the uniqueness of the resurrection of Christ as the basis of resurrection for believers. But resurrection, he continues, *'is a primal miracle, like the creation of the world ... the assault of life upon the spatio-temporal reality of death'*.[85] As such, it delivers those from bondage to decay and chaos into the glorious liberty of new life in Christ. This theme reverberates throughout 1 Corinthians as a hope of glory which underlines the *theologia crucis* of the present period and reflects part of the doctrine of sovereign grace and new creation which may also be formulated as a theology of justification by grace.

(d) These observations also will match the concept of faith shared by Paul and Luther, which many at Corinth had misinterpreted. To quote the sentences of the writer in whose

---

81   LW 28.99 (WA 36.530).
82   De Boer, *The Defeat of Death*, p.103.
83   LW 28.142; cf. pp.105–6 (WA 36.594, 540–41).
84   W. Künneth, *The Theology of the Resurrection* (London: SCM Press, 1965), p.39.
85   Künneth, *Theology*, pp.75 and 76.

honour this volume has been prepared, James Atkinson declares, 'Luther emphasises faith as *the work of God* and not man's own ... He removes it *out of the realm of psychological subjectivizing altogether* and sets it in its happy, healthful, sphere, of *divine* activity and *initiation*'.[86] M.E. Dahl stresses the important point that in the Pauline writings 'God' always remains the *active, initiating subject* or agent, even when Paul refers to the resurrection of Christ. The heart of Paul's logic is: 'He who raised Christ Jesus from the dead will give life to your mortal bodies also through his Spirit who dwells in you' (Rom. 8:11). Dahl comments, 'For the whole eschatological plan of creation demands that all Powers hostile to God shall be forced into his service ... Death is such a power ... God does not suffer his Holy One to "see corruption".'[87] Resurrection is the sovereign act of God which, like creation, calls being into existence out of the Void, out of chaotic non-being. Through solidarity with Christ, the New Creation can never slip back into the Void again, for 'The last Adam became a life-giving Spirit ... Death is swallowed up in victory' (1 Cor. 15:45, 54). This contrast between God's creative life in Christ and 'subjective' notions of faith runs through the whole of 1 Corinthians, but can be fully grasped in all its implications only in the light of the resurrection as creative act and gift.

(3) and (4). I have begun already, in effect, to expound my third and fourth theses. Each of the four observations that I have just made also constitutes an exposition of the theological ground on which justification by grace through faith alone depends. Luther writes concerning the resurrection: 'Be content to hear what God will do. Then leave it to Him what will become of it.'[88] But is this not equally an invitation to accept the grace of acceptance through promise, which is justification? The resurrection shares with any concept of justification that it is, in Luther's words, 'really the work of God'.[89] If faith is a glad confidence, then Luther writes, 'Our confidence is built entirely on the fact that He [Christ] has arisen and that we have life with Him already and are no longer under the power of death.'[90]

Even the introductory passage on witnessing to the resurrection, confessing and preaching, far from suggesting a 'break' in the logic, as Conzelmann proposes, promotes this theme. J.H. Johansen notes, 'Luther's emphasis on the saving quality of faith led directly to his high evaluation of preaching, one of the chief means by which faith is engendered.'[91] Moreover, preaching, like the sacraments, remains necessary because, as Johansen remarks in the same article, Luther could speak of the church simultaneously as 'the bride of Christ and the mother of all Christians' and 'as a wretched assemblage (*coetus miserrimus, armes heuffin*) plagued by the devil and the world'.[92] Similarly Paul's dual description of the church at Corinth as, on one side, 'God's temple' (3:16), and on the

---

[86] J. Atkinson (ed.), *Luther: Early Theological Works* (London: SCM Press, 1962), p.25 (my italics).

[87] M.E. Dahl, *The Resurrection of the Body* (London: SCM Press, 1962), pp.76 and 77, cf. pp.78–84 and 98–9.

[88] LW 28.180 (WA 36.647).

[89] LW 28.187 (WA 36.657).

[90] LW 28.111 (WA 36.349).

[91] J.H. Johansen, 'Martin Luther on Scripture and Authority and the Church, Ministry and Sacraments', *SJT* 15 (1962), p.363; cf. pp.350–68.

[92] Johansen, 'Luther on Scripture', pp.357–8. He cites Luther's 'Sermons on Romans' in WA 49.684.

other as 'not spiritual but fleshly' (3:1–3), and as 'arrogant' (4:18; 5:2) reflects this double frame of reference. The two sides in turn correspond to the dual logic of *simul iustus simul peccator* in justification by grace. I have attempted in two studies to shed some light on the dual logic which is entailed.[93]

VI
More on the Fifth and Sixth Theses: Grace, Gift and Justification

(5) Although the fifth and sixth theses may also belong together as a pair, more space is needed for comment on each, and we may therefore address them in two stages. Our discussion up to this point has, I hope, rendered increasingly precarious Schweitzer's claim that justification by grace constitutes no more than a 'subsidiary crater' within Paul's theology. J. Jeremias rightly rejects the claims of Schweitzer and Wrede, but none the less accepts the contention that 'the doctrine occurs exclusively where Paul is engaged in debate with Judaism'.[94] In 1 and 2 Corinthians, he argues, 'righteousness' usually means 'salvation', and the sense of 'justified' occurs only in 1 Cor. 6:11. Jeremias is right to urge that much of the issue depends on how broadly or how narrowly we define 'justification', and on the importance of the principle that 'the doctrine of justification should not be isolated'.[95] But this makes it all the more surprising that he appears to overlook that what Paul says *explicitly* about justification by grace in Galatians and Romans, he also says *implicitly* in 1 Corinthians.

There is also an important relationship between the emphasis on gift and grace in 1 Cor. 15 and the move by Stendahl, Sanders and others to interpret Romans in a more 'objective', 'historical', or 'social' way than that of 'existential inwardness' concerning guilt which many (rightly or wrongly) associate with a so-called 'Lutheran' approach to Romans.[96] Luther himself is less obsessed with 'inwardness' than many seem to suppose. Indeed such a claim is seriously weakened by Luther's very insistence that *God, not the human condition*, stands at the centre of the picture. This becomes transparent in his exposition of 1 Corinthians 15. We may go further. Luther sees the final, public, vindication and victory displayed in the cosmic event of the resurrection of the dead as the very paradigm of the notions of salvation, in the light of which the present is to be understood.

Luther and Barth stand together here. In the present, the church is on one side the temple of God, and on the other side utterly fallible and flawed; but an objective end lies ahead to which it is drawn. Luther writes, 'We will not only be enraptured and carried heavenward ... We will be changed ... The time will come when that which is *now always*

---

93   A.C. Thiselton, *The Two Horizons: New Testament Hermeneutics and Philosophical Description* (Grand Rapids, MI: Eerdmans and Exeter: Paternoster Press, 1980, rpr. 1993), pp.415–22; cf. further my *New Horizons in Hermeneutics* (London: HarperCollins, 1992), pp.300–304.

94   J. Jeremias, *The Central Message of the New Testament* (London: SCM Press, 1965), p.58.

95   Jeremias, *Central Message*, p.60.

96   K. Stendahl, *Paul among Jews and Gentiles* (London: SCM Press, 1977), pp.23–52 and 78–96; E.P. Sanders, *Paul and Palestinian Judaism* (London: SCM Press, 1977), esp. pp.442–7 and 544–6.

preached and spoken about *will actually happen and be carried out* ... He has transferred the victory to us.'[97] The Reformers do not, as Sanders seems to claim, miss this 'transference' aspect; they see that what in the *present* is *hidden* and appropriated by faith *becomes a public* event in the *public domain* at the future resurrection. These comments acquire still added point when we turn again to Barth. We noted that he sees 1 Cor. 15 not only as a hermeneutical key to 1 Cor. 1–14, but also as a key to other Pauline letters. Barth roundly asserts, 'The Epistles to the Romans, the Philippians and the Colossians cannot even be understood unless we keep in mind the sharp accentuation which their contents receive in the light of 1 Cor. XV, where Paul develops what elsewhere he only indicates and outlines.'[98]

Perhaps, however, we should ask whether Barth is here only carried along by his own study of this theme in 1924, or whether it maintains a firm place in the development of his theology. Further, how does this theme relate to that of justification in his other writings?

The early second edition of *Romans* (1922) stresses, as is well known, the limits of human self-achievement and knowledge not only in dialogue with Paul but also in dialogue with Kierkegaard. It has been urged that in the early Barth, the present hardly allows room for divine *deed*, only for *word*. F.W. Camfield, a sympathetic early interpreter, observes, 'The final *deed* as it reaches the actual world can only reach it as final *word*; a message, an address ... a promise ... That which is new arises in faith, but strictly speaking *only in faith: not in actuality*, not in experience.'[99] This reflects part of Paul's own concern in addressing the problem of spiritual 'enthusiasm' and 'religious achievement' at Corinth, and it coheres with the background of earlier Barthian polemic against the 'religion' of liberal theology. Nevertheless, neither in Paul nor in Barth is a positive emphasis on new creation lost from view and this allows for an *interaction between word and deed*. In *Church Dogmatics* I.2 (1939, Eng. 1956) Barth speaks of the event of Christ's resurrection as 'the Archimedean point of the story and message of Easter', in which creative divine word is *grounded in creative divine deed*.[100] Still more strikingly, he repeats here his earlier theme: '*Not a line of the New Testament can be properly understood unless* it is read as a witness to *a finally achieved divine revelation and grace*, and therefore as the *witness to hope*.'[101]

As the thought of *Church Dogmatics* proceeds, these themes never disappear. In volume II, part 1 (1940) in which he stresses that 'God is known by God, and by God alone', he speaks at length of 'the hiddenness of God' in the present.[102] God expresses his love freely, independently of 'any conditioning from without', retaining his sovereign initiative as creator.[103] In volume II, part 2 (1942) he expounds the theme found in Luther that only 'the *crucified* Jesus is the "image of the invisible God"'.[104] In this sense, in the period of the

---

[97] LW 28.196, 201, 213 (my italics); cf. WA 36.670–96.
[98] Barth, *Resurrection*, p.11.
[99] F.W. Camfield, *Revelation and the Holy Spirit: An Essay in Barthian Theology* (London: Elliot Stock, 1933), pp.50 and 51 (my italics).
[100] Barth, *CD*, I.2, p.117.
[101] Barth, *CD*, I.2, p.117 (my italics).
[102] Barth, *CD*, II.1, p.179.
[103] Barth, *CD*, II.1, p.307; cf. pp.256 and 321.
[104] Barth, *CD*, II.2, p.123 (Barth's italics).

present, the identity of God himself remains cruciform, and is *not* disclosed as a *theologia gloriae*. Justification by grace and futurity of the resurrection promise bear this out. All of this coheres with 1 Cor. 2:11 (only the Spirit of God knows God); with 3:5 (God's 'choice' of his ministerial agents), and 15:38–56 (God *gives* it a body as he *chooses*). It is therefore entirely in keeping with the argument when, in volume III, part 2 (1945), he repeats his theme that resurrection promise holds 'the key to the whole'.[105] Because God remains sovereign and gracious, even someone under the illusion of strength and wisdom 'may let go of God, but God does not let go of him'.[106] The divine decree of creation and new creation remains the bulwark against the 'chaos' of non-existence, purpose, promise and futurity.[107]

In volume IV, part 1 (1953) this pattern interacts with the doctrine of justification by grace as an issue of 'the right of God'. Barth asks, 'What kind of a right is this?' He replies: 'We cannot see it except in the judgement of God.'[108] But judgment constitutes an End event together with the resurrection, which, as a decisive act of God, also throws its light on the present. Weiss, we noted, described justification in Paul as a 'pre-dating' of the verdict of the last day. Thus for Luther resurrection shares with justification in showing 'in brief, that God is God'.[109] Barth concludes in *Church Dogmatics* IV that in 1 Corinthians 15 'God has ratified and proclaimed ... the alteration of the whole human situation, as it will finally be directly and everywhere revealed ... That it has happened is our justification ... It is itself the verdict of God ...'.[110] All this serves to add further weight to our fifth thesis. It may suggest that it is a pity that some biblical specialists who have recently called into question 'Lutheran' interpretations of Paul should have confined their attention, in effect, mainly to issues in Romans and Galatians. Too often they address this question on the assumption that 1 Corinthians concerns a quite different set of issues.

(6) I have left little space to address my sixth thesis. But its validity has already been implied by much of the discussion up to this point. If the emphasis of Paul in 1 Corinthians lies on divine act, divine grace and divine gift, the logic remains unassailable: 'What have you that you did not receive? If then you received it, why do you boast as if it were not a gift?' (1 Cor. 4:7). What room is there for spiritual triumphalism, or for religious self-importance? In practical terms such self-importance leads only to obsessions about status within the church, and therefore naturally enough, to potentially sectarian groups.

This may also distort a theology of ministerial function or office. As R.E. Davies remarks in his more popular study of this epistle, Paul wishes to save his reader 'from too high a doctrine of the Ministry – from supposing that the Minister is the person who makes the Church', but equally 'from too low a doctrine of the Ministry ... Ministers are God's agents ...' (3:5–15).[111] Yet all this faulty ecclesiology arises ultimately from a religious enthusiasm which has misconstrued the futurity emphasized in 1 Corinthians 15.

---

105 Barth, *CD*, III.2, p.443.
106 Barth, *CD*, II.2, p.317.
107 Barth, *CD*, III.3, pp.302–49.
108 Barth, *CD*, IV.1, p.529.
109 LW 28.95 (WA 36.526).
110 Barth, *CD*, IV.1, p.334.
111 R.E. Davies, *Studies in 1 Corinthians* (London: Epworth Press, 1962), p.42.

As Moltmann rightly notes, whereas a *premature* anticipation of a divine 'no' generates *despair*, a *premature* anticipation of the divine 'yes' generates *presumption*. By contrast, Christian believers live on the basis of trustful hope in the promise of God.[112]

Luther had been forced to struggle with Carlstadt, with Müntzer, and the radical 'spiritual fanatics' over issues of ministerial office, of claims on the part of the self to speak with the voice of the Holy Spirit, and of a *theologia gloriae* which saw self-assertion and spiritual manipulation as a supposed way of promoting the gospel. It comes as no surprise, against such a background, to see how well the hermeneutical situation matches his exposition of Paul's eschatology of futurity in 1 Corinthians 15. He comments strikingly on 15:24: 'Then comes the end, when He [Christ] delivers the kingdom of God the Father'. Is Christ's kingdom, he asks, not present already now? He replies: 'He rules through the Word, and not in a visible and public manner. It is like beholding the sun through a cloud. To be sure, one sees light, but not the sun itself. But after the clouds have passed, both light and the sun rule simultaneously ... It is dark and hidden at present, or concealed and covered, comprehended entirely in faith and in the Word.'[113]

In this present period 'God has hidden himself in Christ, so that we must seek God and acknowledge God only in Him.'[114] Luther anticipates Barth in seeing the very identity and character of God, as disclosed before the resurrection of the dead, as bound up with the humiliation of the cross of Christ. Here lies the death of 'spiritualistic enthusiasm'.

We do not have space to pursue this theme in other parts of Luther's writings. It is worth noting, however, that if Luther's commentary of 1534 on 1 Corinthians 15 received added poignancy from the events between 1521 and 1525, the theme nevertheless occupied a central and explicit place in Luther's theology before any of these events took place, most especially in the *Heidelberg Disputation* of 1518. The *Heidelberg Disputation* is most readily accessible in *Luther: Early Theological Works*, edited by James Atkinson. Allusions to 1 Corinthians lie behind a number of Luther's statements. He speaks of the 'hinder parts of God' as his 'supposed weakness and foolishness (1 Cor. 1:25)'.[115] God is not to be found 'except in sufferings and in the cross' (cf. 1 Cor. 1:18; 4:9–13).[116] Christ is the believer's 'wisdom and righteousness ... (1 Cor. 1:30)'. Love does not seek its own interests (1 Cor. 13:15).[117] It is worth noting here that *in recent social-historical readings of 1 Corinthians*, Ronald F. Hock and others have made much of Paul's deliberate decision to accept the term 'weak' as a (voluntary) designation of *low social status* on the basis of his decision to work as a tentmaker or artisan.[118]

In the more troubled waters of the Peasants' War we can see parallels between the radical enthusiasts at Corinth and in Germany: 'All things are lawful' (1 Cor. 6:12a); Paul

---

[112] J. Moltmann, *Theology of Hope* (London: SCM Press, 1967), pp.22–6.

[113] LW 28.124; WA 36.569.

[114] LW 28.126; WA 36.571.

[115] 'Heidelberg Disputation', xx, in Atkinson (ed.), *Luther: Early Theological Works*, p.290.

[116] 'Heidelberg Disputation', xxi, p.291.

[117] 'Heidelberg Disputation', xxv, p.294; and 'Further Proofs', p.302.

[118] R.F. Hock, *The Social Contexts of Paul's Ministry, Tentmaking and Apostleship* (Philadelphia, PA: Fortress Press, 1990); cf. also E. Schüssler Fiorenza, 'Rhetorical Situation and Historical Reconstruction in 1 Corinthians', *NTS* 33 (1987), pp.386–403; cf. further M. Carrez, 'With What Body do the Dead Rise Again?', in *Concilium* 10.6 (*Immortality and Resurrection*) (1970), pp.92–102.

and Luther reply, 'But not all things are helpful' (6:12b). In each case the opponents lay claims to γνῶσις, and to have gifts of prophetic insight. Yet neither Paul nor Luther could deny that effective proclamation depended on the Holy Spirit, without contradicting their own theologies. Both adopt the same strategy. The test of the Holy Spirit's agency is Christological, and the fullness of the Spirit's power remains eschatological. These two streams of thought merge in Paul's resurrection chapter and in Luther's exposition of it.

Nothing can adequately translate the phrase 'spiritual body' (15.44), for neither term offers a one-to-one match with any English word. Modern biblical specialists agree that σῶμα, body, conveys human existence in its totality, regardless of the specific form which this 'totally' uses for self-expression. Bultmann calls it 'the most comprehensive term which Paul uses to characterise man's existence ... A man does not *have* a *sōma*; he is *sōma*.'[119] M.E. Dahl plays safe, and adheres to the term, as the nearest English possible, 'somatic identity'.[120] We have moved away from the implausible suggestions of such writers as Weiss and Pfleiderer nearly a century ago who erroneously spoke of 'spiritual body' here as 'fine, imperishable, heavenly fabric'(!).[121] C.K. Barrett convincingly sums up the issue: '*Spiritual* does not describe a higher aspect of man's life; the noun spirit ... refers to the Spirit of God, and the *spiritual body* is the new body, animated by the Spirit of God, with which the same man will be clothed and equipped in the age to come ... by way of resurrection'.[122]

Luther anticipates this exegesis that became partly lost from view in the nineteenth century. Rather than restate any of our six theses, it is appropriate in this volume, of all volumes, to give to Luther himself the last word. Those who claim already to be wholly 'spiritual' are invited to recall, in Luther's own words, that only at the resurrection the raised entity 'becomes completely new and spiritual and lives solely of and by the Spirit'.[123] This raised mode of existence will be 'strong and vigorous, healthy and happy ... more beautiful than the sun and moon ... we shall all have spiritual gifts'.[124]

We cannot doubt a double allusion to those who claimed in 1 Corinthians 12–14 and in Luther's own time to possess 'all spiritual gifts' before the resurrection. But the resurrection creation will entail both transformation and continuity of identity. It will be 'endowed with a more beautiful and better form than the present one'.[125] Yet 'each body will have its own peculiar glory'.[126] This transformation, above all, is achieved by the power of God through the agency of the Holy Spirit in accordance with the image of Christ. For the ground on which the new creation now comes to be 'endowed with beauty', whereas in its earthly existence it shared in the cross, is, in Luther's words, that the raised new creation bears the image of the last Adam (15:47–49) and thus of 'another Man who can ... bring it about, a Man who is called Christ'.[127]

---

[119] R. Bultmann, *Theology of the New Testament* (London: SCM Press, 1952), pp.193–4.
[120] Dahl, *Resurrection*, p.94.
[121] Weiss, *Earliest Christianity*, II, p.535.
[122] Barrett, *First Corinthians*, pp.372–3.
[123] LW 28.192.
[124] LW 28.142.
[125] LW 28.181.
[126] LW 28.183.
[127] LW 28.113.

CHAPTER FORTY-TWO

A Retrospective Reappraisal of Part VII: The Contributions of the Five Essays to Hermeneutics, and the Possibility of Theological Hermeneutics (New essay)

This final retrospective assessment covers the last five essays of Part VII rather than the volume as a whole. It might appear that some essays of Part VII stray away from hermeneutics, but this is not the case. Essay 37, on the morality of scholarship, redresses an imbalance to which writers on hermeneutics are too prone, namely to invoke a proper concern about the role of pre-understanding as an improper alibi to pursue personal or corporate interests under that flag of convenience. "Neutrality" may be an illusion, but to strive for "impartiality" is a necessary scholarly virtue. The next essay defends a corporate epistemology that allows room for the transmission of traditions, and demonstrates the kind of theories of knowledge and understanding with which hermeneutics operates. We reject the claim that hermeneutics "replaces" epistemology as "a way of coping".

Essay 39 uses the term "Grand Narrative", but this invites a careful qualification. As we argue elsewhere (Essay 36) "little narratives" also have a place, and caution is invited about the scope of grand narrative as applied to biblical material and in relation to Lyotard and postmodernity. Essay 40 explores further the implications of polyphonic narrative for hermeneutics. Essay 41 invites further reflection about "theological hermeneutics". Do Luther and Barth demonstrate that this can be done without undermining either of the two disciplines involved, or is there more to be said? Proposals introduced in Essay 3 are explored a little further, in part with Essay 41 in mind.

I
The Contributions of the Five Essays to Hermeneutics: Essay 37

At first sight the five essays above (Essays 37–41) may appear to constitute a miscellany of publications that could not properly be fitted into any other of the other main Parts of this collection. Is the relation between academic freedom and the morality of Christian scholarship (Essay 37), or "Knowledge, Myth and Corporate Memory" (38) genuinely about hermeneutics? Does the fifth essay about Luther and Barth on 1 Corinthians 15 represent any more than a study in the history of biblical interpretation?

In practice all of these five essays genuinely raise questions about the nature of hermeneutical enquiry, or make contributions to hermeneutical reflection, although some in relation to Christian theology.

Essay 37, on academic scholarship and the Christian church, addresses, first, a widespread assumption about *hermeneutical pre-understanding*. My arguments in Essay

25, "The Bible and Today's Readers" as well as chapters in *The Two Horizons* and *New Horizons in Hermeneutics* will demonstrate that I fully accept the principle of pre-understanding and its entailment of the hermeneutical circle. Nevertheless I have strong reservations about how some writers over-press and abuse this principle, as if to suggest that a professional scholar who brings his or her beliefs, interests, backgrounds and commitments to a text cannot even *try to aim at* a modicum of "objectivity", in the sense of fair-mindedness or fair play, but must and will inevitably succumb to the pressures and constraints of pre-understanding in such a way as to destroy *all possibility of openness*. If this were true, Gadamer, Betti and Ricoeur have wasted a lot of ink.

The attack on "objective" scholarship entails one or other of two quite different strategies and beliefs, both of which have given rise to common appeals based on "hermeneutics". The search for sheer "objectivism" in biblical scholarship takes various forms. First, a naïve, misguided, or deceitful attempt to present "descriptive" empiricism or positivism in the guise of a value-neutral world-view is not value-neutral. Francis Watson, among others has demonstrated that this is an illusion.[1] Such pretence would not be tolerated as good professional practice in the philosophy of religion, where thinkers rightly perceive theism, agnosticism, anti-theism and atheism as representing four competing belief-systems.[2]

Second, some attack an "objective" approach to biblical interpretation in a relatively legitimate way, but in a sense that distorts and devalues positive aspects of the term "objective". They suggest that objective scholarship approaches the Bible as if the interpreter *had no personal stake* in it. This is akin to Kierkegaard's attack on reducing everything to third-person theoretical statements about abstractions.

However, in contrast to *both* of these inadequate approaches, some writers appear to hold the view that all human beings are trapped into being such slaves to their interests and belief-systems that even if they could see the force of an argument that conflicted with these, they could not bring themselves to give it the respect or weight that it deserves.

To counter such confusions in Essay 37 we drew upon Alan Montefiore's work *Neutrality and Impartiality*, on the philosophy of political beliefs in the university.[3] Montefiore insists that to debate whether a scholar should be "*neutral*" is an entirely different matter from debating whether he or she should be "*impartial*". Like a good referee in a football match (or even, we might add, like a good referee for job-applicants) a scholar may legitimately have strong personal wishes and desires. He or she need not be neutral. However, to be impartial remains a professional obligation to a wider community. It involves "helping or hindering either side in completely equal measure with respect to his [or her] application of the rules of the game ... He [or she] would have

---

[1] Francis Watson, *Text, Church and World: Biblical Interpretation in Theological Perspective* (Edinburgh: T. & T. Clark, 1994), pp.3–14, especially pp.7–9.

[2] On the radically differing senses of "objective", see Anthony C. Thiselton, *A Concise Encyclopaedia of the Philosophy of Religion* (Oxford: Oneworld, 2002), pp.204–5; and under "Subject, Subjectivity, Subjectivism", pp.294–5.

[3] Alan Montefiore, ed., *Neutrality and Impartiality: The University and Political Commitment* (Cambridge: CUP, 1975).

behaved in exactly the same way had their positions [that is, of the two sides] been reversed."[4]

It would be mistaken and far-fetched to describe my approach, after teaching hermeneutics for nearly 40 years, as that of an old-fashioned liberal. To be sure, every scholar has blind spots and these sometimes allow desire to get the better of reason. Sometimes reason functions merely as instrumental reason, or, as Hume might express it, as "the slave of the passions". But three more things must be said. (1) In Essay 37 we trace differing traditions on these issues within academic scholarship, each of them professionally acceptable. In theology, for example, we compared the respective stances of F.F. Bruce and Donald MacKinnon, both of whom express concerns for the moral health of theology within the university. (2) We argued that attitudes and procedures in scholarship have to draw upon *moral virtues* as well as professional codes of conduct. These include courage, patience, integrity, honesty and a willingness to adopt multiple roles in a diversity of situations and contexts. (3) To be aware of the difficulties and constraints of "objective" scholarship is different from relishing a flight of sheer self-indulgence into unconstrained subjectivism or subjectivity.

However painful it may be to cite specific examples, some writers appear to confuse these distinctions, and even to relish such confusion. In an earlier retrospective reappraisal (Essay 28) I alluded to the volume edited by Ingrid Rosa Kitzberger under the title *Autobiographical Biblical Criticism* (2002). Some essays in that volume seem to confuse the positive value of what she calls "the personal voice" with "the shift from the objective paradigm to the subjective paradigm", for which a very brief appeal is made to Thomas Kuhn's notion of the social conditioning of "paradigms" in science.[5] This "conversion to a subjective paradigm" becomes merged in this collection of essays with appeals to Heisenberg (in the case of Kitzberger), human "situatedness" versus "third-person voice" and "scientific objectivity" (in the case of Staley) and the inevitable influences of "pre-understanding", "the hermeneutical circle", and being "freed from the subject/object dichotomy" (to a more modest extent in Daniel Patte).[6]

In the early 1980s certain claims in feminist hermeneutics tended to make parallel appeals to "subjective" approaches (although Kitzberger seems to imply a greater novelty for this so-called paradigm switch). In 1983 Mary Ann Tolbert wrote, "The most common objection to a feminist reading of a text ... is that it is subjective". She replies, that on the contrary "*all* interpretations are 'subjective' ... Interpretation is always a subjective activity."[7] It might have been a more compelling strategy to urge, with Janet Radcliffe Richards (in the same year) that feminist approaches, far from being necessarily subjective or less rationally based find their ground in universal ethical concerns for justice and human transformation.[8] Fifty years ago professors used to ridicule the

----

[4] Montefiore, *Neutrality*, p.9; cited on p.35 of the original essay (1982).

[5] Ingrid Rosa Kitzberger (ed.), *Autobiographical Biblical Criticism: Between Text and Self* (Leiden: Deo, 2002) p.3.

[6] *Autobiographical Biblical Criticism*, pp.4 and 5 (Kitzberger); 15 (Staley); 35 and 37 (Patte).

[7] Mary Ann Tolbert, "Defining the Problem", *Semeia* 28 (1983), p.117; cf. 113–26.

[8] Janet Radcliffe Richards, *The Sceptical Feminist: A Philosophical Enquiry* (London: Penguin edn, 1983), throughout.

defensive device of certain conservative theological students when they might respond to complex arguments with the formula, "It all depends on your presuppositions."

In ways that are too obvious to need further explication the "conservative" formula makes a genuine point in purely general terms. But the *use* of the formula, like the appeal to "pre-understanding" that we are considering, often serves merely *to block negotiation as a patient, ongoing re-adjustment, of working assumptions through argument.* Yet patient listening and dialogue is the very stuff of hermeneutics. Thus Schleiermacher speaks of stepping *"out of one's own frame of mind".*[9] Betti speaks of the need for *patience, tolerance and humility* and *"open mindedness"* (*Aufgeschlossenheit*).[10] Gadamer pleads for the use of *the ear* rather than always the voice, even if it is a "personal" voice.[11]

In addition to these points, Essay 37 explicates a model of scholarship that suggests a strategy for coping with the claims of such radically postmodern writers as Lyotard. Lyotard claims, as we noted in Essay 36, that when two parties disagree or hold different beliefs, there is no way of negotiating any common criteria for dialogue or negotiation without one party's assimilating the other under its control.[12] This goes further than even Rorty to ending dialogue. On one side of an abyss stand Betti, Gadamer and Ricoeur, who believe in a dialogue characterized by openness and by respect for "the other"; on the other side stand Lyotard and also in effect, if not in intention, the radically contextual neo-pragmatists. The models of academic practice expounded in Essay 37 serve the genuine hermeneutics of the first group in contrast to the "radical" hermeneutics of the second. The second approach actually undermines genuine *hermeneutical* enquiry.

II
Hermeneutics and the Transmission of Traditions: Essay 38

Essay 38 attacks unduly individualistic accounts of belief and knowledge. The move from individual-centred epistemologies to the corporate foundations or communal framework of belief, knowledge and understanding brings us to the heart of the hermeneutical tradition. There are hints of this shift in Schleiermacher, a clear shift in Dilthey, and a full-blooded, uncompromising radical change in Gadamer. Gadamer looks back to Vico rather than to Descartes, and to Greek *phronēsis* and Roman *sensus communis* rather than instrumental reason and *technē*. The latter belong to the tradition of Enlightenment rationalism, which Gadamer disowns.[13] The former also coheres with the later Wittgenstein's account of "training", human life, and his aphorisms about the respective

---

[9] F. Schleiermacher, *Hermeneutics: the Handwritten Manuscripts* (Eng., Missoula, MT: Scholars Press, 1977), pp.42 and 109.

[10] E. Betti, *Allgemeine Auslegungs Lehre als Methodik der Geisteswissenschaften* (Tübingen: Mohr, 1967), p.11.

[11] H.-G. Gadamer, "My Philosophical Journey", in Lewis Hahn (ed.), *The Philosophy of Hans-Georg Gadamer* (Chicago, IL: Open Court, 1997), p.17.

[12] See the discussion of Lyotard in the Retrospective Reappraisal of Essay 36, on postmodernity.

[13] H.-G. Gadamer, *Truth and Method* (2nd Eng. edn, London: Sheed & Ward, 1988), pp.9–14, 17–30 and 268–77.

roles of doubt and belief.[14] "Vico", Gadamer writes, stands "in a humanistic tradition that stems from antiquity".[15] Even natural sciences cannot do without "the wisdom of the ancients ... But the most important thing in education is still something else – the training in the sensus communis."[16] "Developing this communal sense is of decisive importance for living."[17] This tradition approaches the problem of understanding (hermeneutics) by taking account of "social virtues, a virtue of the heart more than of the head".[18] Gadamer cites the insights of Shaftesbury here, including the seminal point that to "see" or to understand a joke presupposes a commonality of social intercourse among a group of persons.[19]

In a recent introductory textbook on hermeneutics, David Jasper puts these issues in historical perspective. He rightly begins by observing, "Hermeneutics is about the most fundamental ways in which we perceive the world, think and understand."[20] He devotes about half of his book to pre-Kantian hermeneutics (pp.25–77), pointing out that a huge shift in attitudes took place first with the advent of printing and then with "the age of reason" in the eighteenth century. Prior to that, Jasper notes, "reading" sacred texts remained more communal.[21] The reading of the Jewish Midrash, engagement with the Qur'an in Islam, and reflection upon the Bhagavad Gita in Hinduism still more powerfully question the model of a lone individual applying scientific "reason" only in order to engage with these sacred texts.[22]

Three specific points emerge as contributions from Essay 38 to hermeneutics. First, "epistemology" is not to be limited to the individualist model of Descartes and rationalism. Hence, if we broaden the scope of what comes under the heading of epistemology and understand its corporate nature, Richard Rorty no longer has grounds for claiming that "hermeneutics" replaces epistemology simply in the form of "a way of coping".[23] On what basis does Rorty's explicit emphasis upon communities, habituation, traditions and everyday life lead supposedly to the dissolution of "epistemology", unless he restricts the term to an individualistic content? Like A.J. Ayer's sleight of hand when he disguised positivism as a theory of language, Rorty dresses up raw pragmatism as a theory of hermeneutics.

Second, as against Gadamer's huge emphasis on the transmission of traditions through texts and language, Ricoeur rightly stresses the equal importance of critical scrutiny, or a hermeneutic of suspicion. However, too often in other writers the critical dimension has over-tilted the balance in such a way that many over-stress the role of

---

[14]   Cf. L.Wittgenstein, *On Certainty* (Oxford: Blackwell, 1969), sect. 160: "The child learns by believing the adult. Doubt comes *after* belief" (his italics).

[15]   Gadamer, *Truth*, p.19.

[16]   Ibid., p.20.

[17]   Ibid., p.21.

[18]   Ibid., p.24.

[19]   Ibid., p.25.

[20]   David Jasper, *A Short Introduction to Hermeneutics* (Louisville, KY and London: Westminster John Knox, 2004), p.3.

[21]   Ibid., pp.8–28 and 45–65.

[22]   Ibid., pp.19–20 and 25–8.

[23]   R. Rorty, *Philosophy and the Mirror of Nature*, Princeton, NJ: Princeton University Press, 1979), p.356; cf. pp.315–56.

sacred texts to *subvert* and to *deconstruct* tradition and doctrines. We have already questioned J.D. Crossan's claim that parables *in general* subvert, even if *many* parables do subvert. Essay 38 calls attention to the role of sacred texts, alongside creeds and liturgical speech and action, in serving as vehicles for the restoration and conservation of shared traditions and practices. In particular, they renew, re-enact and actualize corporate memories of the founding events of sacred communities.

Third, Gadamer's emphasis on the transmission of traditions through *language* as an ontological medium does not go far enough in one specific direction. Wolfhart Pannenberg points out that the successive horizons of expectation and understanding that characterize traditions are *anchored in history, as well as* mediated through language. Event and interpretation are intertwined. Hence, on the central but sensitive issue of Christology he observes in *Jesus – God and Man*, "The historical process of the development and transmission of traditions" provides the hermeneutical conditions "in the course of which the unity of the man Jesus with God became recognized".[24] Pannenberg discusses these Christological issues in more detail in his later work.[25]

Much of Essay 38 suggests an epistemology and an implicit hermeneutics that coheres with this. Further, my reservations about the use of the term "myth" as an over-extended and over-worked resource in hermeneutics also find resonances with Pannenberg's conclusions on this subject.[26]

III
Grand Narrative and "Little" Narratives: Essay 39

Essay 39 explores what it is to be human with special reference to the Epistle to the Hebrews, 1 Corinthians and Western traditions. In particular it sees Hebrews in terms of a "grand narrative" of God's dealings with God's people as a model of pilgrimage, discipleship, worship and human life shaped by Divine promise.

In our retrospective reappraisal of the earlier essays on postmodernity, we modified our earlier comments about "grand narrative" within the Bible in the light of Richard Bauckham's more recent observations about "little narratives" (Essay 36). Bauckham concedes that at one level the Bible does offer an interpretative framework for understanding the divine will for all people. On the other hand, the Bible is not a "totalising" system of the kind that J.-F. Lyotard rejects as oppressive when he attacks "grand narrative".[27] Bauckham identifies such totalising systems as Marxist economics, global capitalism, the myth of inevitable scientific progress and "the Americanisation of the world".[28] The Bible "narrative" is not of this kind, and is liberating rather than oppressive.

---

[24] W. Pannenberg, *Jesus – God and Man* (Eng., London: SCM, 1968), p.33.

[25] W. Pannenberg, *Systematic Theology* (3 vols, Eng., Edinburgh: T. & T. Clark, 1991, 1994 and 1998), vol. 2, pp.325–63; cf. also pp.363–96.

[26] W. Pannenberg, *Basic Questions in Theology*, vol. 3 (Eng., London: SCM, 1973), pp.1–79; cf. also pp.192–210.

[27] Richard J. Bauckham, *The Bible and Mission: Christian Witness in a Postmodern World* (Carlisle: Paternoster, 2003), pp.87–8.

[28] Bauckham, *The Bible and Mission*, p.89.

Further, Bauckham points out that far from offering a single monolithic "grand narrative" of all history, the biblical material bubbles with numerous "little" narratives: tales about particular persons in particular places at particular times through whom God performs particular acts. He rightly observes that in positive terms Lyotard's hostility to universals can remind us that the Bible and biblical interpretation take place within a dialectic between unity and diversity, between coherence and particularity, between grand narrative and little narrative. The Bible does speak of God's universal purposes for the world, and of creation and human destiny, but it also addresses me in my situation, and everyday people in everyday life. A constructive "untidiness", he argues, characterizes the Bible and its meanings. This last observation on loose ends and constructive untidiness, however, brings us neatly to Essay 40 on polyphonic voices and temporal horizons.

IV
Contingency and Coherence: The Contribution of Essay 40 to Hermeneutical Reflection

Essay 40 draws together four distinct strands that contribute to hermeneutical reflection. First, we comment on the importance of fiction, including theological fiction, as a formative, creative and transforming influence on human thought and life. Our earlier discussions of parables made this point in terms of drawing readers into "worlds" within which formative texts may make a life-changing impact. Some biblical narratives take on the status virtually of symbols that invite action. The sheer power of biblical texts to inspire and direct human life then becomes evident.

Some uses of narrative in this way are powerful, but open to question. The narrative of the conquest of the Promised Land in Joshua has been used to validate conquest of land that some readers believe has been "promised" to them. The Afrikaner draft constitution of 1942 saw the acquisition of South African land by the white Voortrekkers as a national calling "in obedience to God and his holy Word". Takatso Mofokeng, an expositor of Black Hermeneutics, coined (or if not, cited) the aphorism: "When the white man came to our country he had the Bible, and we had the land ... After prayer, the white man had the land, and we had the Bible."[29]

Second, the examples of polyphonic voices from Job, *Adam Bede* and *The Brothers Karamazov* are not intended to suggest that *all* biblical texts speak with polyphonic voices. On the other hand the early Church Fathers, most especially Irenaeus, understood the four gospels of the New Testament as plural but harmonic witnesses to Christ, in contrast to which the Ebionites, according to Irenaeus, selected only Matthew; Marcion preferred Mark and mutilated Luke, and the Valentinians restricted their attention to John:[30] "It is not possible that the Gospels can be either more or fewer in number than ... four".[31] God

---

[29] Takatso Mofokeng, "Black Christians, the Bible, and Liberation" in *Journal of Black Theology* 2 (1988), p.34.

[30] Irenaeus, *Against Heresies*, IV:11:7.

[31] Irenaeus, *Against Heresies*, IV:11:8.

"has given the Gospel under four aspects, but bound together by one Spirit".[32] In the history of biblical hermeneutics Johann Martin Chladenius (1210–59) urged that meaning, interpretation and understanding entail "perceiving" from a given viewpoint or perspective (*Sehe-Punkt*). If many people witness an event, each would pay particular attention to a particular aspect.[33]

In approaching a phenomenon as complex and sensitive as the problem of evil no single perspective or "solution" seems adequate without reducing what eludes over-easy answers. Hence the Book of Job and much theological literature adopt a variety of strategies and perspectives to wrestle with it. David Jasper considers the dictum of the Jewish interpreter and literary critic Geoffrey H. Hartman to the effect that reading is often "a struggle for the text", reminiscent of Jacob's wrestling with the angel in Genesis 32:22–32: "The reader encounters the mystery of the Torah, demanding, like Jacob, to know the mystery of 'the name' ... Jacob is even wounded in the fight, but he persists ... saying, 'I will not let you go unless you bless me'. What we seek from the text is ... a blessing on us, and we should be prepared to struggle with it, even if wounded by its mystery".[34] In this light polyphonic narratives or four gospels may seem less surprising as part of a sacred text.

Third, in Essay 3 I argued that "polyphonic voices" do not suggest that biblical texts embody a radical pluralism of a kind that would prohibit the Bible as Christian Scripture from providing a foundation for Christian theology. I state this in full awareness that Heikki Räisänen makes the opposite claim.[35] We need not repeat the argument. Essay 40 complements these arguments. Christian theology that is sensitive to hermeneutics will embrace a dialect between coherence and contingency, of the kind that J. Christian Beker rightly attributes to Pauline theology. Paul's "hermeneutic consists in the constant interaction between the coherent centre of the gospel and its contingent interpretation".[36]

Fourth, reception history provides an inverted mirror image of this. The particularities of "actualisation" (or in Wittgenstein's sense of the term, "application") trace threads of continuity and discontinuity through changing horizons of history that take up our earlier comments in this essay on the transmission of traditions through history, but also allow for twists and turns through the medium of horizons of expectations, language, and developing corporate understanding or critique.

V

The Possibility of Theological Hermeneutics

This brings us to the final essay, which is more than a study of the history of exegesis (Essay 41). Luther and Barth share an exceptional insight in understanding the unity of

---

[32] Ibid.

[33] J.M. Chladenius, *Einleitung zur richtigen Auslegung Vernünftiger Reden und Schriften* ([1742] rp. Dusseldorf: Stern, 1969), sect. 308.

[34] Jasper, *Introduction*, p.27.

[35] H. Räisänen, *Challenge to Biblical Interpretation* (Leiden: Brill, 2001), especially "The New Testament in Theology", pp.227–49.

[36] J.C. Beker, *Paul the Apostle* (Edinburgh: T. & T. Clark, 1980), p.11.

Paul's thought in 1 Corinthians, especially in the way in which chapter 15 on the resurrection contributes to Paul's main argument in the epistle as a whole. We have noted in these reappraisals of 2004 that David R. Hall has recently defended and underlined the unity of the whole Corinthian correspondence not only against partition theories, but also against an undue fragmentation of Pauline thought in 1 and 2 Corinthians.[37] Nevertheless it is as *theologians* who seek to express Paul's *theology* of resurrection that Luther and Barth make their most exceptional contribution to our understanding of chapter 15. Resurrection, like justification by grace through faith, is entirely a sovereign gift of free and unmerited grace. Resurrection, together with other gifts of sheer grace, is the ultimate answer to those who still fail to appropriate the truth that the gifts of God, or the gifts of the Spirit, are *gifts*: they preclude "boasting", or what David Hall calls "puffed-upness".[38]

To what extent is the work of Luther and Barth here an example of theological *hermeneutics*? Many claim, for example, that Barth's great commentary on the Epistle to the Romans tells us more about Barth than about Romans, and, to be fair, I would not normally put it with the commentaries of C.K. Barrett, Charles Cranfield, Ernst Käsemann and James D.G. Dunn, as obligatory set reading for a New Testament course on the exegesis of Romans. Nevertheless on 1 Cor. 15, both Luther and Barth genuinely interpret the text both as exegetes and as theologians.

On one side Luther anticipates much modern exegesis, but explicitly put to the service of Christian theology. Thus he anticipates the sane view that the problem that Paul addresses in Corinth was neither simply lack of belief in post-mortal existence, nor problems about "bodily" (somatic) existence, nor belief that the resurrection had occurred already, but that all of these problems could be found among different groups in Corinth to a greater or lesser extent. Further he attends to the somatic nature of the resurrection body, but avoids being more specific about it than Paul. He writes, "Be content to hear what God will do. Then leave it to Him what will become of it."[39] Finally he urges that the exegesis of "spiritual body" is a raised mode of existence wholly open to the Holy Spirit. Because resurrection is exclusively a gracious act and sheer gift of the sovereign God to which humankind does not "contribute", Barth also can offer textual "interpretation". He can rightly assert that chapter 15 "forms not only the ... crown of the whole epistle, but also provides the clue to its meaning, from which place light is shed onto the whole ... as a unity".[40] This resonates with Luther's comment on Romans, "Let him cease to believe in himself and believe in God."[41]

On the other side, Karl Barth stakes out his theological battle cry concerning the contrast between "God" and "religion". In other contexts this may seem to be imposed on a biblical text if or when this is not the point at issue. But through a diligent

[37] David R. Hall, *The Unity of the Corinthian Correspondence* (London and New York: T. & T. Clark and Continuum, 2002), pp.30–51, 86–106 and throughout.

[38] Hall, *Unity*, p.32.

[39] Martin Luther, *Luther's Works vol. XXVIII: Commentaries on 1 Cor. 7 and 15; Lectures on 1 Timothy* (St Louis, MO: Concordia, 1973), p.180; German, Weimar edn, *Luthers Werke*, 36, p.647.

[40] Karl Barth, *The Resurrection of the Dead* (Eng., London: Hodder & Stoughton, 1933), p.11.

[41] Martin Luther, *Luther's Works, vol. XXV: Lectures on Romans* (St Louis, MO: Concordia, 1972), p.284; *Luthers Werke*, 56, p.296.

application of the hermeneutical circle Barth perceives that *in this epistle* it is *precisely the central issue at stake*. Here the relation between theology, interpretation, and the diversity of the canon assumes importance. Barth writes about Corinth, "They believe not in God but in their own belief in God and in particular leaders ... they confuse belief with specific human experiences".[42] For Barth's passion for this issue allows him to interpret the text of 1 Corinthians with a prophetic fervour and incisiveness that could hardly emerge in quite the same way in an exposition of many other texts where this may not form part of the main the argument.

These comments may seem to pre-empt the question that we raised briefly in Essay 3, namely: is "*theological* hermeneutics" *possible*? Have we not shown that Luther and Barth practise this? Much rested, however, on my hermeneutical judgement that the theme and role of 1 Corinthians 15 cohered with their theological understanding of it. In Essay 3 I argued that hermeneutics must resist becoming assimilated into a prior system of theology, and that theology must avoid compromise by being shaped by an independent discipline of hermeneutics. I argued that we need to find a way forward by facilitating a genuine process of dialectic between the two disciplines.

A hermeneutic that has been imperialized by theology to serve a prior system will be unable to exercise necessary *critique and creativity for the benefit of theology*. It will already have become captive to serve prior interests. On the other hand, even a relation of dialectic cannot take the form of a mere "principle of correlation" as this is understood and practised, for example, by Paul Tillich, for Tillich admits that his *agenda of philosophical questions shapes theology*. We offer the following signposts as marking a possible way forward, although as no more than rough signposts.

(1) As our starting-point we need simply to repeat the distinction that we made in Essay 3. This is Gadamer's distinction between de-contextualized "problems" and a dialectical process of motivated, directed, contingent question and answer. Because of its importance we repeat a few lines broadly set out above in Essay 3. "Problems" often seem to feature within a network of freestanding "ideas". These often serve as the fabric of a philosophical system or a systematic theology. However, in their origination these often *arise from a dialectical process of question and answer,* from which they later become detached and, in effect, abstracted and *reified*. Gadamer explains, "The concept of the problem is clearly an abstraction."[43] It has become detached and abstracted "from the questions that in fact first reveal it".[44] In a key sentence of diagnosis he adds, "Such a 'problem' has fallen out of *the motivated context of questioning, from which it receives the clarity of its sense. Hence it is insoluble* ... 'Problems' have lost their original character as 'real questions'" (my italics).[45]

Dialectic, rather than "ideas" and abstract propositions, might open the way for a theological hermeneutic. Whereas Aristotle focused on the logic of demonstration and non-contradiction, the dialectic of Socrates and Plato tended to expose false opinion through conversation and questions. Even Hegel, in spite of his ending with an abstract

---

[42] Karl Barth, *The Resurrection of the Dead* (Eng., London: Hodder & Stoughton, 1933), p.17.
[43] H.-G. Gadamer, *Truth and Method*, p.376.
[44] Ibid.
[45] Ibid.

system that may fail to convince us, attempted to unfold a process of dialectic beginning with the contingent and particular, and only then seeking to raise (*erheben*) this level of contingency by "sublating" it (*aufheben*) into a higher order of enquiry. By contrast, a system of more static "problems" addressed or defined as sets or subsets of one another or of a single overarching problem, may lose the "Why?", "Whence?" and "Whither?" that motivate a journey of questioning. Due respect for particularity and contingency remains the hallmark of hermeneutics, and if respect for particularity and history operates interactively with a search for theological coherence, we might hope for a hermeneutic that leaves room for an "open" system within which cross-currents of diverse motivations and conflicting voices contribute to ongoing understanding.

(2) Such a process will constantly stand under criteria derived from the biblical writings as decisive for the basis of Christian identity. This is not necessarily a controversial claim among most mainline Christian or theist biblical scholars. John Bright, for example, writes, "The Bible provides us with the primary, and thus normative, documents of the Christian faith ... To ask, as we continually do, is this teaching Christian? ... is to be driven ... back to the Bible ...".[46] James Smart observes, "Let the Scriptures cease to be heard, and soon the remembered Christ becomes the imagined Christ, shaped by the religiosity and the unconscious desires of his worshippers."[47] More recent writers tend to construe the role of the Bible more dynamically. Telford Work declares, "A Trinitarian doctrine of Scripture ... appreciates the Bible as reaching into the very plan of God and the very heart of the Christian life".[48] It is "more than simply foundational for the rest of Christian doctrine".[49]

This places a necessary distance between our proposal and formulations of "the principle of correlation" of the kind practised by Paul Tillich. *This would compromise the integrity of Christian theology.* Paul Tillich writes of his method, "In using the method of correlation, systematic theology proceeds in the following way: it makes an analysis of the human situation out of which existential questions arise, and it demonstrates that the symbols used in the Christian message are the answers to these questions."[50] Throughout his *Systematic Theology,* he formulates five such principles of correlation: that between reason as question and revelation as answer; between Being and God; between concrete human existence and Christ; between life in its ambiguities and the Spirit, and between the meaning of history and the Kingdom of God. *But the questions themselves are large and generalized ones.* Although Tillich describes them as "existential", they are *more akin to Gadamer's "problems"* than to Gadamer's ongoing dialectic. The "questions" are *not historical, contingent particularities,* but a way of framing traditional philosophical problems outside a series of specific historical contexts. Tillich's hypothesis about the non-necessity of a "historical" Jesus for the truth of Christianity tells us of his view of history and particularity.

---

[46] J. Bright, *The Authority of the Old Testament* (London: SCM, 1967), p.30.

[47] J. Smart, *The Strange Silence of the Bible in Church* (London: SCM, 1970), p.25.

[48] Telford Work, *Living and Active: Scripture in the Economy of Salvation* (Grand Rapids, MI: Eerdmans, 2002), p.9.

[49] Work, *Living and Active,* loc. cit.

[50] Paul Tillich, *Systematic Theology* (3 vols, London: Nisbet, 1953–64), vol. 1, p.70.

Although he states that his answers "cannot be derived from the questions", Tillich also writes, "Every theologian is committed *and* alienated; he is always in faith *and* in doubt; he is inside *and* outside his theological circle."[51] This kind of approach has little in common with what we propose here.

(3) Our proposal will inevitably encounter doubts about whether we take sufficient account of human fallenness and sin and its effects upon the limited capacities of human reason. Responses emerge at several different levels. First, in this essay, and throughout this collection, we have urged that hermeneutics encourages and nurtures above all an attitude of *listening* (with Gadamer), of *humility and patience* (with Betti), of *openness* and watchfulness *against idolatry* (with Ricoeur). It is diametrically opposed to the *hubris* of Enlightenment rationalism that the individual human subject "knows better" than others or the wisdom of traditions.

Further, the biblical writings urge a more positive view of human reason than many appear to perceive. We addressed this issue briefly in Essay 3, and must avoid repeating the same arguments. Here, therefore, we may simply add that Stanley K. Stowers rightly traces much misunderstanding to the tendencies of thinkers of the Enlightenment to pit "reason" against faith, revelation, grace, authority and tradition, aided by elements within the Augustinian tradition and the mediaeval West.[52] Stowers blames misinterpretations of 1 Corinthians chapters 1–4, and Romans 1:18–2:5. Against these he asserts, "Worldly and fleshly wisdom is certainly not reason."[53] The arrogant person is one who will not recognize his need to listen and learn: "Far from opposing faith and tradition to reason, 1 Cor. 1:18–4:21 criticizes a lack of openness to that which is new and different."[54] Paul urges "responsible deliberation".[55] He does not demand blind obedience to his authority.

Jewett and Bornkamm adopt a similar view, which we considered in Essay 3. Paul sees reason as "the agent of self-control and rational communication".[56] Bornkamm observes that even in relation to human fallenness "Paul speaks of reason ... to convict the hearer of his guilt before God".[57] "Paul allots to reason and to the rationality of men an exceedingly important role ... for all areas of life".[58] Paul's method of preaching and writing is not "revelation-speech", but appeals to rational judgement and argument: "The motif of reason plays a not insignificant role in the ethical directive of the apostle."[59] W. Pannenberg sees this emphasis on rational understanding as in no way in competition with claims about the work of the Holy Spirit or revelation. He dryly observes, "In trusting to the Spirit Paul in no way spared himself thinking and arguing."[60]

[51] Tillich, *Systematic Theology*, vol. 1, pp.13–72.

[52] S.K. Stowers, "Paul on the Use and Abuse of Reason", in D.L. Balch, E. Ferguson and Wayne Meeks (eds), *Greeks, Romans and Christians: Essays in Honor of Abraham J. Malherbe* (Minneapolis, MN: Fortress, 1991), p.253; cf. pp.253–86.

[53] Stowers, loc. cit., p.258.

[54] Ibid., p.261.

[55] Ibid., pp.262–6.

[56] R. Jewett, *Paul's Anthropological Terms* (Leiden: Brill, 1970), p.380.

[57] G. Bornkamm, "Faith and Reason in Paul", in *Early Christian Experience* (London: SCM, 1969), p.35; cf. pp.29–44.

[58] Ibid.

[59] Ibid., p.40.

[60] W. Pannenberg, *Basic Questions in Theology*, vol. 2 (Eng., London: SCM, 1971), p.35.

Even if, in itself, reason and rationality are conditioned by fallenness and sin, this does not exclude the use of rational reflection as part of the Spirit-led path to spiritual understanding. Even in the mediaeval Western church, while "disinterested" reason was perceived to be illusory, this in no way exempted readers of Scripture from disciplined contemplation. Jeremy Worthen observes concerning Hugh of St Victor: "It is Hugh's doctrine of the fall that makes ... disinterested investigation ... appear worse than trivial ... The eye of reason and the eye of contemplation have become darkened outside of Eden ... Disciplined, intelligent, reading of scripture marks the road to salvation, and it would be unpardonable frivolity, from Hugh's point of view, to engage in it from any other motivation or lesser end."[61]

(4) The dialectic of the contingent and the coherent finds ready expression in what many philosophers call the dispositional character of *belief*. We have explored this notion already in this collection of articles and essays, including Essay 3. We have alluded to the role of Wittgenstein in initiating this approach. He writes, "I believe" is not "describing my own state of mind ... It is a kind of disposition of the believing person."[62] We see what belief (or doctrine) amounts to when we see "what are the consequences of this belief, where it takes us".[63] If hermeneutics seeks above all *to understand*, and to understand *meanings*, it is appropriate for a hermeneutic of Christian theology or doctrine to ask (in Wittgenstein's words): what are the consequences of this belief? *Where* does *it take us?* Elsewhere in his later work Wittgenstein compares the grammar of "understanding" with the experience of being able to exclaim: "Now I can go on."[64]

Belief is more than a "mental state": do we become unbelievers when we fall asleep? On the other hand it is also more than a behaviourist disposition to respond, as if belief were merely like the program of a computer. Nevertheless "this 'spreading' of belief from a proposition to its consequences is one of the most important ways in which such a disposition is concurrently manifested ... Our beliefs are like posts which we plant in the shifting sands of doubt and ignorance. They are ... stable landmarks ... That is why loss of belief can be such a serious matter for us."[65] A belief is "a multiform disposition, which is manifested or *actualised* in many different ways" (my italics).[66] Belief is "actualised" in actions and in restraint from actions, in hope and fear, in feeling of doubt, in confidence or surprise, and finally in inferences, *both inferences of the kind that "spread" to consequences in life, and also those that lead to self-conscious critical reflection.*[67]

We have already compared the philosophical analyses of H.H. Price and others with New Testament language about "the body". Here the Greek term *sōma* denotes the *public* face of Christian living, that is, what it is to live as a Christian *in the public domain*. The word denotes the interpersonal, social, public mode of living out what it is to be a Christian. Christian belief is not a private, individualistic, purely "inner" mental state. We

---

[61] J. Worthen, "Interpreting Scripture for the Love of God", in John Court (ed.) *Biblical Interpretation: The Meanings of Scripture – Past and Present* (London: T. & T. Clark International, 2003), p.61; cf. pp.54–70.

[62] L. Wittgenstein, *Philosophical Investigations*, Part II, x, p.190.

[63] Wittgenstein, *Investigations*, sect. 578.

[64] Wittgenstein, *Investigations*, sect. 151; cf. also sects 183 and 321–23.

[65] H.H. Price, *Belief* (London: Allen & Unwin, 1969), p.293.

[66] Price, *Belief*, p.294.

[67] Ibid.

have noted Käsemann's definition of *sōma* in Paul as "that piece of the world that we are", and urges that belief is never a matter of "interior piety". He declares, "In the bodily obedience of the Christian, carried out as the service of God in the world of everyday, the lordship of Christ finds visible expression, and only when this visible expression takes personal shape in us does the whole thing become credible as Gospel message."[68] In my exegetical work on 1 Corinthians I have argued that this approach is true to Pauline thought at numerous points, especially in 1 Cor. 6.[69]

VI

The Coherence of Hermeneutics with Christian Theology: The Corrigibility of Interpretation and the Horizon of Eschatology

In the end, many of the complaints made about the discipline of hermeneutics turn on its unavoidable open-endedness, which Schleiermacher identified as a never fully completed, never-ending task, with corrigible conclusions. If they affirm the fallibility of the church, which is the traditional belief, Protestants might find it difficult to expect "infallible" interpretation on the part of the church, at least this side of the last judgment. Otherwise the church would hardly be fallible. Luther believed in the clarity of Scripture in the sense that Scripture provides firm ground for action in taking the next step in Christian believing and living, as I have argued elsewhere.[70] I have also argued that while the *decisive* verdict of Divine grace and judgement came in the coming of Christ, the *definitive* verdict will be revealed in all its *public* dimensions at the last judgement.[71]

Meanwhile, Daniel Migliore describes the nature of a theology that respects hermeneutics. He writes, "Theology grows out of this dynamism of Christian faith that incites reflection, inquiry, and the pursuit of truth not yet possessed, or only partially possessed."[72] Yet this is not the *ground* or *root* of theology. Theology, he observes, has two roots. The first is *God*; the living God revealed as sovereign love. Migliore continues, "The second root of the quest of faith for understanding is the *situation* of faith. Believers ... do not live in a vacuum. Like all people, they live in particular historical situations that have their own distinctive problems and possibilities. The changing, ambiguous, and often precarious world poses ever-new questions of faith ... Questions arise at the edges of what we can know and what we can do as human beings. They thrust themselves on us with special force in times and situations of crises such as sickness, suffering, guilt, injustice, personal or social upheaval, and death."[73]

---

68 E. Käsemann, *New Testament Questions of Today* (Eng., London: SCM, 1969), p.135.

69 Anthony C. Thiselton, *The First Epistle to the Corinthians*, esp. 458–79; cf. also pp.491–2, 505–6, 801–9, 989–1013 and 1273–81.

70 Thiselton, *New Horizons in Hermeneutics*, pp.179–90.

71 Thiselton, "Authority and Hermeneutics: Some Proposals for a More Creative Agenda", in Philip E. Satterthwaite and David Wright (eds), *A Pathway into the Holy Scripture* (Grand Rapids, MI: Eerdmans, 1994), pp.107–42.

72 D.L. Migliore, *Faith Seeking Understanding* (Grand Rapids, MI: Eerdmans, 1991), p.2.

73 Ibid., p.3.

Index of Names and Subjects